HANDBOOK OF
INTERPERSONAL
COMMUNICATION

THIRD EDITION

HANDBOOK OF INTERPERSONAL COMMUNICATION

THIRD EDITION

EDITORS

MARK L. KNAPP
University of Texas at Austin

JOHN A. DALY
University of Texas at Austin

SAGE Publications
International Educational and Professional Publisher
Thousand Oaks ▪ London ▪ New Delhi

For information:

 Sage Publications, Inc.
2455 Teller Road
Thousand Oaks, California 91320
E-mail: order@sagepub.com

Sage Publications Ltd.
6 Bonhill Street
London EC2A 4PU
United Kingdom

Sage Publications India Pvt. Ltd.
M-32 Market
Greater Kailash I
New Delhi 110 048 India

Printed in the United States of America

Library of Congress Cataloging-in-Publication Data

Handbook of interpersonal communication / Mark L. Knapp and John A. Daly, editors.—3rd ed.
    p. cm.
Includes bibliographical references and index.
ISBN 0-7619-2160-5 (cloth)
1. Interpersonal communication. I. Knapp, Mark L. II. Daly, John A. (John Augustine), 1952-
BF637.C45 H287 2003
302.2—dc21

                              2002007908

02 03 04 05 10 9 8 7 6 5 4 3 2 1

Acquiring Editor:	Margaret H. Seawell
Editorial Assistant:	Alicia Carter
Copy Editor:	Judy Selhorst
Production Editor:	Claudia A. Hoffman
Typesetter:	C&M Digitals (P) Ltd
Indexer:	Molly Hall
Cover Designer:	Michelle Lee

Contents

PART I

Basic Issues and Approaches

1

Background and Current Trends in the Study of Interpersonal Communication

MARK L. KNAPP
JOHN A. DALY
KELLY FUDGE ALBADA
GERALD R. MILLER

This is the third edition of the *Handbook of Interpersonal Communication*. As in the first two editions, we have brought together a number of experts in the multifaceted field of interpersonal communication. Each author has assessed within his or her own area of the field where we have been, what we know, what we don't know, what we need to know, and where we should be going. We hope that, like previous editions, this will be an important reference work for graduate students and faculty interested in the study of interpersonal communication.

In addition to major updates and changes to some of the chapters from the previous edition, five new chapters are included here: Chapter 4, "Discourse Analysis"; Chapter 5, "Personality and Interpersonal Communication"; Chapter 13, "Interpersonal Conflict: A Review"; Chapter 14, "Cues Filtered Out, Cues Filtered In: Computer-Mediated Communication and Relationships"; and Chapter 17, "Interpersonal Processes in Romantic Relationships." We believe these chapters represent areas of central concern for understanding interpersonal processes and areas that have experienced growth during the years since the second edition appeared.

The organization of this *Handbook* is similar to that of the previous editions. The first four chapters open up some of the key theoretical and methodological issues facing those who study interpersonal communication. The next five chapters focus on component parts of the process—verbal and nonverbal behavior, cognitions, cultural influences, and the characteristics each communicator brings to the encounter. The next six chapters focus on various processes and functions of interpersonal communication, such as social support, affect, influence, conflict, and mediated interaction. These chapters conclude by asking the question, What is interpersonal competence? Chapter 15 tackles that difficult issue. The final chapters examine interpersonal processes in four important and familiar relational contexts: relationships among coworkers, relationships between physicians and their patients, relationships among family members, and romantic relationships.

In the rest of this introductory chapter, we set the stage for what follows by (a) giving a brief historical perspective on the current study of interpersonal communication, (b) speculating on the trends that may have strong influence on future studies of interpersonal communication, (c) looking at the term *interpersonal communication* itself, and (d) setting forth in capsule form the conceptual themes we see represented throughout the book.

HISTORICAL HIGHLIGHTS

In far more extensive historical accounts, other communication scholars have situated the study of interpersonal communication within the larger field of communication (Delia, 1987) and as a focus of study within speech communication (Rawlins, 1985). We make no pretense of documenting, in the

brief history we sketch here, all the important authors and streams of thought that are in some way tied to current approaches to interpersonal communication. Instead, we have selected what we think are important contributions from the wide variety of disciplines and interdisciplinary thinkers in this area. As we will note later, it was not until the 1960s that the study of interpersonal communication per se began to bloom profusely in the United States. As the following shows, a great deal of pioneering work preceded that period.

Early 20th century. In the early 1900s, Georg Simmel (1908/1950) was making astute observations about interpersonal communication that are still debated today—these included such concepts as "reciprocal knowledge," "characteristics of the dyad," interaction "rituals," "secrecy," "lies and truth," and "types of social relationships."

The 1920s and 1930s. Many intellectual seeds for the study of interpersonal communication were sown during the 1920s and 1930s. Elton Mayo and his colleagues at the Harvard Business School were uncovering the potential power of social interaction and social relationships in work settings. Their studies conducted at the Western Electric Hawthorne plant raised important questions about supervisor-employee interaction as well as the influence of peer interactions on productivity. This "human relations" movement set in motion subsequent thinking about the nature of supportive communication, openness, and the effects of showing concern for another's needs during interaction (Roethlisberger & Dickson, 1939).

The origins of group dynamics are recounted elsewhere (Cartwright & Zander, 1960; Hare, Borgatta, & Bales, 1955), but the field of interpersonal studies owes much to this line of work that was in its infancy in the 1930s. Topics such as cooperation/competition, feedback, conflict, interaction sequences, methods for coding responses, sociometric choices, and social networks are all areas of shared interest for group and interpersonal scholars. The study of children's interaction during the 1930s also provided insights into systematic observation methods as well as identified patterns of interaction, such as cooperation and dominance (Murphy, Murphy, & Newcomb, 1937). It was the analysis of children's interaction during this period that also revealed the crucial process of role taking (Piaget, 1926).

The belief that the self emerges out of the individual's interaction with significant others provided the foundation for the intellectual movement known as *symbolic interactionism* (Blumer, 1969; Mead, 1934). With the recognition that the way we respond to symbols affects the development of our selves and the nature of the society we live in, the 1930s also spawned the general semantics movement, which asked us to scrutinize closely our responses to symbols. Korzybski's *Science and Sanity* (1933) put forth the principles of general semantics, but books like Hayakawa's *Language in Action* (1941) were responsible for disseminating such ideas to the general public. Through examples of everyday experiences, the principles of general semantics continue to play an important role in textbooks devoted to the improvement of individuals' interpersonal communication skills.

The 1940s and 1950s. Eliot Chapple (1953, 1970) believed that the matching of interaction rhythms leads to an impression of harmony, whereas mismatching of rhythms signals discord—regardless of the content. Intensity, timing, and patterns of temporal organization were all elements elicited through the use of Chapple's "standardized interview" (meaning one interviewer's behavior was predictable) and recorded by his "interaction chronograph." According to Chapple, interaction rhythm is central to an understanding of everyday competence in interpersonal communication as well as psychopathology.

In the field of psychiatry, the shift from an intrapersonal orientation to an interpersonal one was largely due to the lectures and writings of psychiatrist Harry Stack Sullivan (see Chapman, 1976). Sullivan believed that adult schizophrenia is rooted in problematic interpersonal relations during childhood and adolescence. Another psychiatrist, Jurgen Ruesch, teamed up with anthropologist Gregory Bateson on a book that also explicated the role of communication in mental illness as well as issues of cultural organization (Ruesch & Bateson, 1951). Ruesch later cowrote the first book to use the term *nonverbal communication* in its title (Ruesch & Kees, 1956). Bateson's work was later to be the foundation for one of the most influential works in interpersonal communication scholarship of the 1960s, *Pragmatics of Human Communication* (Watzlawick, Beavin, & Jackson, 1967).

Anthropologists Ray Birdwhistell (1952) and Edward T. Hall (1959) were interested in the total process of communication, but their pioneering efforts and observations of body movement, gestures, postures, and the use of space laid the groundwork for the area of study called *nonverbal communication*—predominantly examined as interpersonal behavior.

In the late 1950s, psychologist Fritz Heider's book *The Psychology of Interpersonal Relations* (1958) helped launch a line of research on attribution theory that is integral to the study of interpersonal communication today. The 1950s concluded with the first of many influential books by sociologist Erving Goffman (1959, 1963), whose influence on the study of interpersonal communication has been enormous. Goffman's in-depth and provocative insights about the organization of social behavior and the important role played by seemingly mundane behaviors stimulated an interest in inter-personal life across the social sciences.

The 1960s, 1970s, and 1980s. Despite the wealth of ideas and writings produced during the decades preceding the 1960s, the blos-soming of interpersonal communication as an academically identifiable area of study was primarily the result of societal forces. The social turmoil accompanying the civil rights movement and the subsequent involve-ment of the U.S. military in Vietnam trig-gered in many citizens, particularly the young and idealistic, a deep-seated aversion to the manipulative and deceitful aspects of many mass-media messages. An emerging concern for self-development and personal aware-ness gave rise to such face-to-face communica-tive activities as sensitivity training and consciousness-raising groups. Attacks on the traditional public and mass communication orientations of most communication scholars at that time emphasized the importance of interpersonal communication to personal authentication. The critics proclaimed that the daily quality of individuals' lives is shaped by the integrity of their personal relation-ships, rather than by the persuasive wiles of media messages crafted by Madison Avenue hucksters and political consultants. Referring to the field of speech communication, Delia (1987) contends that the events that tran-spired in the 1960s made interpersonal com-munication "the field's core research area" (p. 84) and that this has significantly influ-enced the field since. Buley, Petronio, Hecht, and Alberts (1993) underscored and extended this observation by stating, "Today, inter-personal communication is one of the largest areas within the field of communication" (p. 3).

Given the prevailing climate in the 1960s, it is hardly surprising that a book such as *Pragmatics of Human Communication* (Watzlawick et al., 1967), which had a profound effect on the subsequent study of interpersonal communication, had nothing to say about the ways individuals can use com-munication to extract money or concessions from others but offered considerable advice about the ways people can think about and perform their communicative activities so as to improve their personal relationships with mar-ital partners and close friends. In a similar vein, Barnlund's (1968) anthology of theoretical and empirical papers, which stimulated interest in interpersonal communication among persons in university speech communication and com-munication departments, focused on factors influencing the origination, development, and maintenance of interpersonal relationships. Argyle's (1969) review of research on "social interaction" and his resulting "social skills model" maintained a similar orientation.

Other manifestations of this heightened interest in interpersonal communication are readily identifiable. The burgeoning number of college and university courses covering aspects of interpersonal communication and interpersonal relations was accompanied by a spate of textbooks dealing with these topics, such as those authored by Giffin and Patton (1971), Keltner (1970), and McCroskey, Larson, and Knapp (1971). The formal estab-lishment of areas of emphasis in scholarly and professional associations of the commu-nication disciplines, such as the Interpersonal and Small Group Interaction Interest Group of the Speech Communication Association (now the National Communication Associa-tion) and the Interpersonal Communication Division of the International Communication Association, signaled accelerating interest in the teaching and study of interpersonal com-munication processes. Convention programs dealing with aspects of interpersonal commu-nication became the rule rather than the exception. One of these programs, held at the 1976 meeting of the International Communi-cation Association in West Berlin, spawned two state-of-the-art papers that were later published in the association's journal,

Human Communication Research (Bochner, 1978; Miller, 1978). Evidence that interpersonal communication had become an important dimension of graduate education was provided by the convening of two national doctoral honors seminars sponsored by the National Communication Association, one at Michigan State University and the other at Northwestern University. Since then, several addition doctoral honors seminars have included interpersonal communication as one of the core areas of study in communication.

Thus by the late 1970s the study of interpersonal communication had been established as a major area of study along with mass communication in the United States. This was not the case in Europe, Asia, and South America, however. Even today, outside the United States the study of interpersonal communication is likely to be housed within psychology, sociology, or anthropology and to have a different identifying label.

During the 1980s, the study of interpersonal communication was characterized by a number of fresh theoretical perspectives. Some of the concepts and theories that exerted important influence at that time were the coordinated management of meaning (Cronen, Pearce, & Harris, 1982; Pearce, 1976), uncertainty reduction (Berger & Bradac, 1982), contructivism (Delia, O'Keefe, & O'Keefe, 1982), dialectical theory (Baxter, 1988; Rawlins, 1983), and expectancy violations (Burgoon, 1983).

The bywords of the 1980s were *relationships* and *messages*. For some, the term *relationship* was a synonym for the *process* designated by the phrase *interpersonal communication;* for others, a relationship was one context (usually a personal relationship) for studying interpersonal communication. The focus on messages (which included the cognitive processes *and* the spoken or written products) assumed a special importance for those who believed this was where communication scholars could make a special

contribution to an understanding of interpersonal transactions.

The 1990s. The late 1980s and early 1990s seemed to be characterized by a tendency for interpersonal communication scholars to embrace a variety of approaches to their investigations (e.g., quantitative and qualitative, micro and macro) and to face difficult questions about what we know and how we know it. Throughout the 1990s, the field of interpersonal communication became both broader and narrower. New issues emerged in various contexts, such as health, the workplace, cultures, and mediated environments. Organizationally, what were once single divisions within both the National Communication Association and the International Communication Association devoted to the study of interpersonal and small group behavior divided into numerous organizational entities that employed in their names such terms as *intrapersonal communication, family communication, social interaction, communication avoidance and apprehension,* and *small group communication.*

The 1990s was also a time when edited volumes expanded the knowledge bases for various areas of interpersonal communication. This, in turn, helped to increase the recognition that scholarship in this area received within the field of communication and across other disciplines. At the same time, increasing specialization began to differentiate what was included in the term *interpersonal communication.* New journals and new professional associations emerged that focused solely on personal relationships. Some scholars today believe that the study of interpersonal communication is limited to the study of relationships. This volume clearly shows that the boundaries of the field go well beyond that narrow definition. The 1990s continued the discussion of the importance of theoretical thinking in the field of interpersonal communication. Debates arose about whether or not the discipline had any theories as well as about what theories were worthy (Berger, 1991, 1992; Burleson, 1992). At the same time, new theories about, and approaches to the study of, interpersonal communication were emerging in such areas as nonverbal behavior (Burgoon, Stern, & Dillman, 1995), privacy (Petronio, 2000), cognition (Berger, 1997; Greene, 1997), and the potentially harmful (or "dark") side of interpersonal communication (Cupach & Spitzberg, 1994; Spitzberg & Cupach, 1998).

THE FUTURE

There are at least four well-established social and/or academic trends that are likely to have distinct impacts on future studies of interpersonal communication. These are the increasing attention being paid to technology, culture, and biology as well as the continuing concern for an "applied" perspective.

The widespread availability of technology for communicating is bound to play an important role in the way interpersonal transactions are thought of and manifested. Interactive video, virtual reality, computer bulletin boards, and portable and video phones (among other technological changes) forecast an interpersonal world that is potentially very different from the current one. Interpersonal studies also have a history of being by and large culture and socio-economic-class specific. In the future, it is reasonable to expect that more interpersonal research questions will cut across cultural, class, and international boundaries. Interpersonal studies have only begun to explore the biological foundations of behavior. The central and guiding premise in interpersonal communication research until recently has been the assumption that virtually all of our interpersonal behavior is "learned." This assumption, we believe, will be increasingly challenged (Beatty, Marshall, & Rudd, 2001;

Beatty & McCroskey, 2001). Although we are not likely to see the study of interpersonal communication handed over to the geneticists in the near future, we do believe that social scientists and humanists will pay increasing attention to questions concerning possible genetic influences on interpersonal behavior.

Applied scholarship in interpersonal communication has a long tradition, but the resurgence of interest that took place in the 1980s and 1990s remains strong enough to suggest that this trend will continue. The central question seems to be this: What do we/can we/should we take from our knowledge of interpersonal communication for application to the problems of everyday life? Assessment, accountability, and policy—long the practical provinces of larger and more formal systems—may become of increasing concern for those who study interpersonal communication as well. For many years, students of public communication have taken their knowledge and helped people become better practitioners of communication. Scholars in interpersonal communication may increasingly see the value of using their knowledge to enhance the interpersonal effectiveness of people in their everyday lives.

THE HANDBOOK OF WHAT?

What is interpersonal communication? Obviously, a large number of scholars collectively identify with and use the term *interpersonal communication* to describe their own work. These scholars also recognize, however, that there is considerable variety in how they and their colleagues conceptually and operationally define this area of study. In some respects, the construct of interpersonal communication is like the phenomenon it represents—that is, dynamic and changing. Thus attempts at specifying exactly what interpersonal communication *is* and *is not* are often frustrating and fall short of consensus. Bochner (1989) is probably correct when he suggests that the most we can expect interpersonal scholars to agree to is that they are studying "at least two communicators; intentionally orienting toward each other; as both subject and object; whose actions embody each other's perspectives both toward self and toward other" (p. 336). Cappella (1987), employing what he calls "definitional minimalism," states: "If interpersonal communication has any essential feature, it is that persons influence one another's behavior over and above that attributed to normal baselines of action" (p. 228).

Some of the key definitional issues that garner less consensus include the number of communicators involved, the physical proximity of the communicators, the nature of the interaction units used to explain an encounter, and the degree of formality and structure attending the interactants' relationship. In an effort to distinguish interpersonal communication studies from research in group, organizational, or mass communication, researchers have commonly designated the number of communicators in interpersonal exchanges as two. However, two-person interactions may be extensions of larger networks; the parties may have membership in a larger group, and their conversation thus may be subject to the structures and norms of that group. In short, the assumption that the influence taking place in two-person transactions is entirely due to the behavior of those two persons is open to question. Another common research practice, also open to question, is that of gathering data about a particular two-person interaction or two-person interactions in general by asking *individuals* to provide the data. Another assumption made by some researchers is that interpersonal communication involves "face-to-face" interaction in which the communicators are in close physical proximity. Nevertheless,

interactions mediated by telephone, computer, and other technologies are also a part of the literature on interpersonal communication. There are interpersonal scholars, for example, whose research focuses on "long-distance relationships."

The nature of the interaction units used as a basis for describing and explaining interpersonal transactions varies considerably among those who study interpersonal communication. Miller and Steinberg (1975) have argued that the degree of "interpersonalness" in a relationship is determined by the kind of information participants use to make predictions about message exchanges. The more idiosyncratic, personal, and psychological information is considered "more interpersonal," and sociological or cultural information is considered "less interpersonal" or even "impersonal." Interactions in which communicator roles are key and sociological and cultural information is central are, however, very much a part of the literature of interpersonal communication. Furthermore, some researchers limit themselves to observable units, whereas others do not; single message units satisfy some, whereas others require sequences of messages; naturally occurring talk is crucial to some, whereas others are satisfied with analyzing anticipated behavior or imagined interactions. Using published research as an indicator, we can see that interpersonal communication scholars still do not agree on whether it is important to examine nonverbal as well as verbal behavior or whether both parties to the interaction have to speak. Finally, it has been customary for interpersonal communication studies to focus on informal and unstructured interactions. But physician-patient interactions (see Chapter 18) and supervisor-employee interactions (Chapter 16), job interviews, and other role-oriented exchanges are clearly a part of this literature.

In the remaining pages of this chapter, we address the conceptual perspectives and themes that seem to crop up repeatedly in the contributions to this *Handbook*. Each of these perspectives and themes is characterized by multiple conceptualizations, thereby creating a corpus of issues that are likely to be of constant concern to those who study interpersonal communication.

CONCEPTUAL PERSPECTIVES AND THEMES

The Interaction Process

Most students of interpersonal communication believe that it is accurately thought of as a process—an ongoing, ever-changing event. Understanding the communication process, then, is largely a matter of understanding what happens over a given period of time.

Despite the widespread belief that interpersonal communication is best studied as a process, this is not a consistent perspective manifested in the research. Philosophically, one might argue that process, by definition, is not something we can ever "capture" in our studies. Once we have identified a unit of interaction for study, the argument goes, we no longer "have" process. A less extreme position assumes that we can learn about process by making multiple observations at multiple points in time over a given time span. According to this view, an understanding of mutual adaptation in interpersonal communication can be achieved through the observation of moment-to-moment changes during interactive events. Kendon (1970), for example, using a filmed record, described moment-to-moment changes in movement, eye gaze, and speech during the flow of interaction; Gottman (1979) made some important discoveries about marital interaction from analyses of sequential exchanges between husbands and wives in happy and unhappy couples; Cappella and Planalp

(1981) analyzed a continuous audio record of informal conversation for moment-to-moment changes in vocalizations and pauses produced by both interactants; and Jacobs (Chapter 7, this volume) describes the work of several scholars who have examined the sequential nature and effects of dialogue in conversation.

Studies of the process of interpersonal communication must account for a variety of temporal characteristics. From both speaker and listener perspectives, it is important to know how often a behavior occurs during a given period of time, what order or sequence characterizes the behavior under study, how long the behavior lasts when it occurs, and the rhythm, pacing, or "timing" of the behavior relative to co-occurring behaviors. Each of these temporal qualities occurs and can be analyzed at four levels: during a specific utterance, during a specific conversation (see Chapter 7), during the course of a relationship (see Chapter 17), and during the course of a lifetime. The study of time and timing in interpersonal transactions should also provide us with a much better understanding of how to distinguish behaviorally the developmental phases common to many experiences, such as accomplishing a goal for the first time, reestablishing the goal state, maintaining the goal state in the absence of threat, and maintaining the goal state in the presence of threat.

Persistent and guiding questions for any efforts directed at the study of interaction as a process include the following: (a) If change is a constant, how should we conceptualize and operationalize periods of stability and periods of transition? (b) How much change is change, and from whose perspective? (c) If we can't examine all aspects of the interaction process, how do we explain the potential changes in the system brought about by the units we choose not to examine?

A Focus on Behavior

A strong and persistent theme throughout this volume concerns the value of describing and analyzing naturally occurring overt verbal and nonverbal behavior. Our current focus represents a return to the rich tradition of systematic observations of behavior represented by scholars such as Birdwhistell, Goffman, Scheflen, Ruesch, and Bateson. This is in contrast to the once predominant method of gathering data about interpersonal communication, which was through the use of self-report questionnaires and/or scales. These inventories were easily administered to large numbers of respondents, and the data they generated were expected to provide a foundation for broad-based generalizations about interpersonal communication.

Although some research programs continue to rely heavily on self-report data, more and more researchers are questioning the adequacy of knowledge about communication behavior based solely on such data. Can people accurately recall or predict some aspects of their interpersonal communication behavior—for example, their touching behavior? Have we developed a body of knowledge that is limited to what people *think* they would do? Isn't there a need to supplement or seek validation of self-reports with observations of actual interaction behavior? Is it enough to know the attitudes, opinions, and perceptions of *one* interaction partner, often removed from any interaction context? How will the preferences expressed on a questionnaire manifest themselves in the presence of another person or persons governed by various situational constraints?

To address such questions, the members of an expanding cadre of communication scholars have chosen to focus on manifest behavior. These efforts have provided an important supplement to our understanding of interpersonal communication and have pointed out some of the inadequacies of focusing *exclusively* on overt behavior. Even though we still have much to learn from the study of overt behavior, it is already clear that, first, what transpires during interpersonal transactions is more than mere responses to manifest signals. Communicator expectations, fantasies, plans, and the like may provide the bases for responses; behaviors *not* shown by the interaction partner may provide the bases for responses; behaviors shown in previous interactions (with and not with the current partner) may guide and direct subsequent reactions. Ironically, then, our examination of overt behavior has shown us the necessity of obtaining self-report data. Unlike those gathered in many past efforts, however, these self-descriptions are much more likely to be anchored by specific contexts. In like manner, the study of behavior within the confines of a two-person transaction has made it clear that if we are to understand dyadic behavior, we need to extend our analyses beyond the dyad. We will more fully understand interpersonal behavior as we extend the boundaries of analysis to include the social networks impinging on the two communicators, rules and constraints imposed by social and institutional cultures, interaction history, and so forth. Second, what transpires behaviorally during interpersonal transactions is often extremely subtle and complex—involving behavioral configurations amenable to multiple interpretations, multiple intensities, and multiple degrees of consistency.

Another perspective associated with the focus on behavior is the gradual merging of verbal and nonverbal observations. Interpersonal communication scholars have probably always recognized the vital contributions of proxemic, kinesic, olfactory, vocal, and verbal signals to the understanding of interpersonal communication, but the early emphasis was clearly on verbal behavior.

As the number of scholars studying nonverbal behavior increased, it gradually became a separate area of study. The study of verbal behavior and the study of nonverbal behavior appeared, for practical purposes, to be independent of one another. Researchers who studied facial expressions, eye gaze, and proxemics commonly did not spend much time analyzing co-occurring verbal behavior, and researchers who described themselves as discourse or conversation analysts did not commonly claim expertise in nonverbal phenomena. We can learn much by tapping the depths of verbal and nonverbal behaviors separately, but we will learn more about interpersonal communication when the interaction of both systems forms the basis for analysis, as is the case with some analyses of turn-taking and lying behavior.

As we learn more about analyzing verbal and nonverbal signals, there will probably be fewer studies that simply sum the frequency of several behaviors and more that address the interdependence and coordination of behaviors. When we have reached that point, our current preoccupation with the question of whether verbal or nonverbal behavior is more important should be moot. Studying the interrelationships of verbal and nonverbal behavior in social interaction will also demand more attention to how these signals are perceived. We do not observe all those signals made available to us, nor do we process all that we do perceive in the same way. Some of these questions about the perception of signals require an understanding of the perceiver and the signal interpretation process, but describing the nature of the signals themselves is also an integral part of understanding the process. We have much to learn about the impacts of signals and combinations of signals that is related to their intensity, relevance, and location.

Our focus on behavior has also shifted from laboratory settings for observation to naturally occurring contexts. Once more popular than today, the study of communicative behavior in controlled laboratory settings attempted to discover the bases for predicting interpersonal behavior. Although behavior was the focus in the early experimental studies, the validity of the findings for naturally occurring interactive events was often challenged. For instance, some charged that interpersonal communication scholars did not have enough descriptive information about how normal interaction proceeds to draw conclusions about how one might manipulate it realistically. As a result, they argued, research participants were asked to react to unusual and sometimes extreme stimuli. Further, critics believed that the employment in studies of interaction partners who were unable to respond (partners presented in slides or on audiotape), who were unwilling to respond ("neutral" confederates), or who responded inflexibly (partners programmed to respond only in certain ways) did not elicit typical interaction behaviors from research participants. Even the fundamental tenet of experimental research that requires some components of the interaction situation to be "kept constant" while others are manipulated seemed to run counter to the prevailing theoretical belief that constancy is not characteristic of ongoing interaction. As a result of these and other challenges, it became increasingly apparent that we needed to find out more about the structure and operation of interpersonal behavior in naturally occurring situations. Researchers could use the data from these observations to construct laboratory conditions that would more closely approximate naturally occurring interactions.

The observation of behavior outside the laboratory context seems to have underlined the impact of context on behavior and to have given us a renewed appreciation for the difficulty of predicting behavior across different contexts. We also seem more aware of the need to measure the sequencing and quality of responses as well as the quantity.

Context

Bateson (1978) states, "Without context, words and actions have no meaning at all" (p. 15). This assertion about the critical dependence of communication on context for the generation of meanings is likely to garner substantial agreement among interpersonal communication scholars and practitioners. Contextual information is considered crucial for "thick description" (Geertz, 1973) of communication events. An examination of retrospective contexts (all actions that precede a particular behavior that might help one to interpret that behavior) and emergent contexts (all events that follow the behavior that might help one to interpret the behavior) adds further depth of understanding to the interpersonal episodes.

Communication contexts have been considered in many diverse ways: (a) as broad areas defining the field of communication (interpersonal communication and so on), (b) as social settings (e.g., cocktail parties) and institutional settings (e.g., schools, prisons), (c) as types of relationships and roles (e.g., task, social, and family), (d) as objects or characteristics of the environment, and (e) as message variables (e.g., language style, affect displays preceding and subsequent to text). Therefore, context may encompass psychological, behavioral, and environmental perspectives.

Given the diversity of perspectives on the nature of context, the multiplicity of methods for studying context is not surprising. For contemporary schema theorists, general contextual information leads the investigator to examine patterns in linguistic organization, and linguistic and other contextual cues mobilize the search for particular schematic patterns. Ethnomethodologists describe context in terms of the reflexivity of language understanding (Leiter, 1980). Linguistic utterances are taken as prompts to the overall pattern of meaning, and that pattern operates as a context within which the utterances make sense (see Chapter 7). For uncertainty reduction theorists, in contrast, context is a source of information (Berger, 1987) and an object of uncertainty. Likewise, attribution theorists and expectancy violation theorists consider context to be a source of information for evaluating the other's behavior (see Chapter 8). A key source of difference in these perspectives is the interrelationship of context and communication. Is context so much a part of the communication process that it is distorted when considered apart from the process? Or is it one of the many external and isolated sources of influence on message selection and interpretation? Chapters 15, 16, and 18 are just a few of the contributions to this *Handbook* that highlight how communication is embedded in context.

Minimally, we need to consider the extent to which our research contexts (however conceptualized) match the contexts to which we apply our findings and the extent to which we can learn more about contexts (however conceptualized) by studying them directly. Furthermore, interpersonal communication researchers need to specify how and why context affects communication, for, as Rawlins (1987) states, people and messages both transform and are transformed by context.

Social Cognition

In one way or another, each chapter in this book addresses the role of human thought processes as they interface with interpersonal transactions. The study of interpersonal communication has, from the beginning, recognized the important reciprocal relationship between thought and overt behavior, but in recent years we have greatly advanced our understanding of this area—largely because some scholars in communication and social psychology have made this their sole focus of investigation. The work in this area can be subdivided into two nonexclusive categories: understanding the interrelationships of social cognition and social behavior, and understanding the formation and organization of social cognition.

Virtually any thought about any aspect of our experience has the potential to affect behavior in any given encounter. However, the thoughts that are likely to have the most relevance for communicative events are thoughts about the nature of human interaction itself. Usually the thoughts about self, other, and situation are the designated units for investigation. Information representing thought is usually gathered before and/or after encounters, rarely during them. In the past, some researchers ignored perceptual information from actual interactants, relying instead on the reactions of large groups of uninvolved observers as a basis for understanding the overt and covert behavior of interactants.

Thoughts that influence behavior may be relatively abstract ("Friends are people who stick by you when the going gets tough") or concrete ("Mary is a person who would probably turn me in for taking a pencil home from the office"). Similarly, more abstract thoughts of what kind of person one is and more concrete thoughts about what kind of person one is as a communicator, or as a communicator with *this* person in *this* situation, may influence the manifested behavior. Individuals think of situations, too, in general ways and as specific communication contexts. Researchers often focus on a single unit of analysis; for example, studies of others include impression formation, attribution theory, or perspective taking; studies of communicator cognition include work on self-consciousness, self-awareness, self-monitoring, and communicative apprehension. We are just beginning to undertake the more complex job of studying

the influence of combined self/other/situation thoughts on behavior. If it were merely a matter of determining how thoughts influence behavior, the task would be easier but less representative of what actually seems to happen. Thoughts affect behavior, and behavior, in turn, reshapes the memory of the original thought(s) as well as ensuing thoughts. If the process of gathering information for research purposes is thought of as a communicative process, our understanding of social cognition will continue to affect our methods of research, too—as it already has (see Chapters 2, 3, and 4).

As researchers worked to understand how social thoughts and social behavior are interrelated, it became clear that we needed to know more about how people form, organize, and interpret information germane to human interaction. These processes are discussed throughout this volume as attitudes, expectations, inferences, scripts, schemata, fantasies, rules, and wishful thinking. The study of how we form and organize our social thoughts has reemphasized the multilevel process involved in interpreting and/or assigning meaning to behavioral signals. Any given signal or sequence of signals may be taken at any one or a combination of at least five levels: (a) the literal message content, (b) a response to how the partner's preceding response was interpreted, (c) an indicator of how the partner should respond to a message, (d) an indicator of how one partner feels about him- or herself or the other partner as a person, and (e) whether further interaction (now or later) is desired.

Consciousness and Intent

Throughout this book, readers will be confronted repeatedly with issues bearing on consciousness and intent. Communication scholars periodically acknowledge the importance of these issues, but a variety of perspectives continue to permeate the literature. For many, intentionality is essential for defining communication (Bowers & Bradac, 1984).

From one perspective, the central question is the extent to which communicators "know what they're doing" or, in the case of recalled experiences, the extent to which they "know what they did." Consciousness is prerequisite to communicating. Much of the research on persuasion and compliance gaining, for example, rests on the belief that communicators identify their goals, analyze their targets and situations, and select strategies that are calculated to maximize their desired outcomes. Research programs reported in a number of the chapters in this book highlight this focus on control and planned social influence, with the treatments in Chapters 6 and 12 being lengthy and explicit. In contrast, ritualistic communication acts, spontaneous displays of emotion, various actions related to the management and structure of conversation, and habitual patterns of interaction occurring in long-term relationships suggest a very low (or absent) level of awareness and planning. Again, this perspective is implicitly or explicitly manifested in a number of different chapters.

Theoretically, there seems to be agreement on some fundamental issues concerning consciousness and intent, such as that (a) there are multiple levels and degrees of consciousness involved in communicating, (b) more than one intention can occur during a communicative act, (c) consciousness and intent can change during the act of communicating, and (d) communicators may be aware of a general goal and unaware of some specific intentions for reaching that goal (Stamp & Knapp, 1990). Nevertheless, our research often seems to assume a far less complex process. For example, the truism that we don't always "say what we mean or mean what we say" has not been much of a driving force for research in interpersonal communication to date.

The question of what is going on in the mind of a communicator is of little relevance to those who believe attributions of intent are what really matter in human transactions. In this view, observable behavior is what counts. Planning and consciousness are assessed behaviorally, and perceptions of effort, persistence, emphasis, and situational expectations are used as representative criteria for assessing intent. Despite the long-standing interest in the subject of intentions and the widespread belief that interaction is best conceived of as a process, relatively little work has been directed at how communicators negotiate intentions. From this perspective, neither the nature of the cognitive activity nor the perception of a person's behavior gives us the information necessary for understanding intentions in everyday communicative life. Intent from this perspective is a jointly constructed product.

Meaning

How do we conceptualize meaning in interpersonal transactions? How is meaning created? Is meaning something that can be "located" in a particular place? Answers to these questions permeate our research—usually as undiscussed but guiding assumptions. In theory development, however, the centrality and importance of meaning require that it receive more explicit treatment. Symbolic interactionists, among others, believe things have no meaning apart from our interaction with others. In this sense, then, the way we think about meaning in interaction is inseparable from the way we view human understanding and action.

The meanings of meaning among scholars concerned with human interaction, while diverse, are not wholly incompatible. Grossberg (1982) has uncovered three predominant perspectives among communication scholars: (a) those who view meanings as entities that can be exchanged, (b) those who view meanings as emergent products shared by the interactants, and (c) those who view meanings as the environment through which life is experienced. Littlejohn (1989) concludes his review of various theoretical contributions to communication study by identifying three major approaches to meaning: structural, interactional, and cognitive. The attempt to "locate" meaning in space and time and the attempt to specify how meaning emerges seem to be the goals shared among these different approaches.

To those who think of meaning as infused in the totality of the environment through which life is experienced, the idea of "locating" the site of meaning must seem like a strange task indeed. Nevertheless, there are those who locate meaning in the text or message itself, those who subscribe to "finding" meaning in the process of interaction, and those who pinpoint meaning in the confines of the brain. Beliefs about how meaning emerges are, not surprisingly, dependent on beliefs about the site of meaning. For some, it is important to focus on the supposed inherent properties associated with signs and their referents; for others, it is the structure and sequencing of messages that trumpet meaning. Some combine various textual aspects with interpreter decisions, whereas for others, cultural and interactional rules pave the way to meaning. Some believe that the key to unlocking meaning is found in the negotiated process involved in the development of shared interpretations, whereas it is the way information is mentally processed that brings meaning to life for others. Littlejohn (1989) offers the following as a way of bridging some of these divergent perspectives. Meaning, he says, is probably best thought of as "an outcome of the interplay between the structure of the message, the use of the message in actual situated interaction, and the mental process necessary to manage information and make interpretation" (p. 381).

As the interpersonal communication literature is not shy about praising the value of shared experiences and shared understandings, we would like to underline what others have said: The concept of "sharing" itself is a construct that is subject to considerable variation. Daily discourse is replete with incongruent, ambiguous, and incomplete messages, and it is quite likely that interactants are able to coordinate their behavior effectively without much shared meaning (Cronen et al., 1982; Pearce, 1976). Bochner (1989) hints that when sharing does occur, it may not be so much a sharing of meanings associated with a specific interaction as it is a sharing of beliefs about interactions in general and our mutual contributions thereto: "The 'real' world of interpersonal communication is only partially a shared one in which a sense of sharing is the product of mechanisms of control over meanings as well as the mutual faith in a shared social world" (p. 338).

A Perspective on Perspectives

Interpersonal communication scholarship contains both the manifest content of its research findings and a latent content of ideological assumptions (Lannamann, 1991). While we have spent considerable time in this chapter performing self-critiques of our methodology and our research findings, we have focused far less attention on an examination of our ideological assumptions. Some have argued that interpersonal scholars have been slower to engage in this process of questioning our ideological assumptions than have scholars in other subareas of communication (Leeds-Hurwitz, 1992). In fact, Bochner (1994) asserts that interpersonal communication scholars have generally ignored the moral, ideological, and narrative knowledge attendant to their subject matter.

Lannamann (1991) believes that we need an understanding of the role of ideology in interpersonal communication if we are to avoid the perils of reifying cultural practices and legitimating current social orders through our research findings. "Ideology," says Lannamann, "is effective; it frames the struggle over which meanings are naturalized as common sense" (p. 182). Fitzpatrick (1993) concurs that an examination of our ideologies is called for and that we can gain much insight into personal and social relationships by incorporating interpretive and cultural perspectives. Further, an examination of our ideological assumptions will help to protect interpersonal communication studies from a single, orthodox position that constrains or stifles new ideas and innovative approaches.

Parks (1982) addresses this issue directly and demonstrates how the ideology of intimacy (i.e., individuals are on an unending quest for closeness) has defined the research agenda for many interpersonal communication scholars, thus resulting in the devaluation of other phenomena for study. Other ideologies, many of which are only implicit in the research, also frame our research endeavors. For instance, the ideology of control (i.e., persons desire and are driven to regulate others and their environment) steers researchers to search for and label communicative behaviors as manipulative, influencing, compliance gaining, or persuading (Miller & Knapp, 1985). Perhaps less common historically, but no less influenced by ideological assumptions, feminist studies are directed by the beliefs that gender is a pervasive category for understanding human experience in general and interpersonal communication in particular and that the prevailing gender assumptions of society should be challenged.

Ultimately, questions directed at our ideological assumptions will also prompt us to reflect on our assumptions about how we go about determining what we know and don't know and how we search for answers to puzzling aspects of interpersonal communication.

Poststructuralists and postmodernists have challenged the core ideological assumptions of social science. These critics maintain that the dominance of facts over meanings and values is a practical issue rather than an ontological one; research need not be restricted to prediction and control. Accordingly, a meaning-centered approach to interpersonal studies calls for a breaking of the norms that have equated distance and disengagement with objectivity, that have favored universals over particulars, that have made standardized criteria for making judgments the sole province of rationality, and that have relegated history and context to the status of factors that need to be "controlled." Fitzpatrick (1993) believes in a discovery process that maintains a social dimension and, simultaneously, a "scientific" foundation. By rejecting a scientific approach completely, she argues, scholars are unable to specify how to judge among competing claims; however, by rejecting a more interpretive approach, they may miss the broader social issues of theory and thus perpetuate social structures. Bochner (1994) suggests that other research practices—whether they aim to predict, interpret, criticize, change, or create—represent different discursive strategies that are useful modes of description for certain purposes. Thus a singularly "correct" perspective, he argues, does not exist, because natural events and processes lend themselves to a multiplicity of descriptions, depending on the individual's point of view.

REFERENCES

Argyle, M. (1969). *Social interaction.* New York: Lieber-Atherton.

Barnlund, D. C. (1968). *Interpersonal communication: Survey and studies.* Boston: Houghton Mifflin.

Bateson, G. (1978). *Mind and nature: A necessary unity.* New York: E. P. Dutton.

Baxter, L. A. (1988). A dialectic perspective on communication strategies in relationship development. In S. Duck (Ed.), *Handbook of personal relationships: Theory, research and interventions* (pp. 257-273). New York: John Wiley.

Beatty, M. J., Marshall, L. A., & Rudd, J. E. (2001). A twins study of communicative adaptability: Heritability of individual differences. *Quarterly Journal of Speech, 87,* 366-377.

Beatty, M. J., & McCroskey, J. C. (2001). *The biology of communication: A communibiological perspective.* Cresskill, NJ: Hampton.

Berger, C. R. (1991). Communication theories and other curios. *Communication Monographs, 58,* 101-113.

Berger, C. R. (1992). Curiouser and curiouser curios. *Communication Monographs, 59,* 101-107.

Berger, C. R. (1987). Communicating under uncertainty. In M. E. Roloff & C. R. Berger (Eds.), *Interpersonal processes: New directions in communication research* (pp. 39-62). Newbury Park, CA: Sage.

Berger, C. R. (1997). *Planning strategic interaction: Attaining goals through communicative action.* Mahwah, NJ: Lawrence Erlbaum.

Berger, C. R., & Bradac, J. J. (1982). *Language and social knowledge: Uncertainty in interpersonal relations.* London: Edward Arnold.

Birdwhistell, R. L. (1952). *Introduction to kinesics: An annotation system for analysis of body motion and gesture.* Washington, DC/Ann Arbor, MI: U.S. Department of State, Foreign Service Institute/University Microfilms.

Blumer, H. (1969). *Symbolic interactionism: Perspective and method.* Englewood Cliffs, NJ: Prentice Hall.

Bochner, A. P. (1978). On taking ourselves seriously: An analysis of some persistent problems and promising directions in interpersonal research. *Human Communication Research, 4,* 179-191.

Bochner, A. P. (1989). Interpersonal communication. In E. Barnouw, G. Gerbner, W. Schramm, T. L. Worth, & L. Gross (Eds.), *International encyclopedia of communications* (pp. 336-340). New York: Oxford University Press.

Bochner, A. P. (1994). Perspectives on inquiry II: Theories and stories. In M. L. Knapp & G. R. Miller (Eds.), *Handbook of interpersonal communication* (2nd ed., pp. 21-41).

Bowers, I. W., & Bradac, J. J. (1984). Contemporary problems in human communication theory. In C. C. Arnold & I. W. Bowers (Eds.), *Handbook of rhetorical and communication theory* (pp. 871-893). Boston: Allyn & Bacon.

Buley, J., Petronio, S., Hecht, M. L., & Alberts, J. K. (1993). Interpersonal communication theory. In S. Petronio, J. K. Alberts, M. L. Hecht, & J. Buley (Eds.), *Contemporary perspectives on interpersonal communication* (pp. 3-17). Dubuque, IA: William C. Brown/Benchmark.

Burgoon, J. K. (1983). Nonverbal violations of expectations. In J. M. Wiemann & R. P. Harrison (Eds.), *Nonverbal interaction* (pp. 77-111). Beverly Hills, CA: Sage.

Burgoon, J. K., Stern, L. A., & Dillman, L. (1995). *Interpersonal adaptation: Dyadic interaction patterns.* New York: Cambridge University Press.

Burleson, B. R. (1992). Taking communication seriously. *Communication Monographs, 59,* 79-86.

Cappella, J. N. (1987). Interpersonal communication: Definitions and fundamental questions. In C. R. Berger & S. H. Chaffee (Eds.), *Handbook of communication science* (pp. 184-238). Newbury Park, CA: Sage.

Cappella, J. N., & Planalp, S. (1981). Talk and silence sequences in informal conversations III: Interspeaker influence. *Human Communication Research, 7,* 117-132.

Cartwright, D., & Zander, A. (Eds.). (1960). *Group dynamics: Research and theory.* Evanston, IL: Row, Peterson.

Chapman, A. H. (1976). *Harry Stack Sullivan: His life and his work.* New York: Putnam.

Chapple, E. D. (1953). The standard experimental (stress) interview as used in interaction chronograph investigations. *Human Organizations, 12,* 23-32.

Chapple, E. D. (1970). *Culture and biological man: Explorations in behavioral anthropology.* New York: Holt, Rinehart & Winston.

Cronen, V., Pearce, W. B., & Harris, L. (1982). The coordinated management of meaning. In F. E. X. Dance (Ed.), *Human communication theory: Comparative essays* (pp. 61-89). New York: Harper & Row.

Cupach, W. R., & Spitzberg, B. H. (Eds.). (1994). *The dark side of interpersonal communication.* Hillsdale, NJ: Lawrence Erlbaum.

Delia, J. G. (1987). Communication research: A history. In C. R. Berger & S. H. Chaffee (Eds.), *Handbook of communication science* (pp. 20-98). Newbury Park, CA: Sage.

Delia, J. G., O'Keefe, B. J., & O'Keefe, D. J. (1982). The constructivist approach to communication. In F. E. X. Dance (Ed.), *Human communication theory: Comparative essays* (pp. 147-191). New York: Harper & Row.

Fitzpatrick, M. A. (1993). Communication in the new world of relationships. *Journal of Communication, 43*(3), 119-126.

Geertz, C. (1973). *The interpretation of cultures: Selected essays.* New York: Basic Books.

Giffin, K., & Patton, B. R. (1971). *Fundamentals of interpersonal communication.* New York: Harper & Row.

Goffman, E. (1959). *The presentation of self in everyday life.* Garden City, NY: Anchor.

Goffman, E. (1963). *Behavior in public places: Notes on the social organization of gatherings.* New York: Free Press.

Gottman, J. M. (1979). *Marital interaction: Experimental investigations.* New York: Academic Press.

Greene, J. O. (Ed.). (1997). *Message production: Advances in communication theory.* Hillsdale, NJ: Lawrence Erlbaum.

Grossberg, L. (1982). Does communication theory need intersubjectivity? Toward an immanent philosophy of interpersonal relations. In M. Burgoon (Ed.), *Communication yearbook 6* (pp. 171-205). Beverly Hills, CA: Sage.

Hall, E. T. (1959). *The silent language.* Garden City, NY: Doubleday.

Hare, A. P., Borgatta, E. F., & Bales, R. F. (Eds.). (1955). *Small groups: Studies in social interaction.* New York: Alfred A. Knopf.

Hayakawa, S. I. (1941). *Language in action.* New York: Harcourt Brace Jovanovich.

Heider, F. (1958). *The psychology of interpersonal relations.* New York: John Wiley.

Keltner, J. W. (1970). *Interpersonal speech-communication: Elements and structures.* Belmont, CA: Wadsworth.

Kendon, A. (1970). Movement coordination in social interaction: Some examples described. *Acta Psychologica, 32,* 100-125.

Korzybski, A. (1933). *Science and sanity: An introduction to non-Aristotelian systems and general semantics.* Lancaster, PA: Science Press.

Lannamann, J. W. (1991). Interpersonal communication research as ideological practice. *Communication Theory, 1*(3), 179-203.

Leeds-Hurwitz, W. (1992). Forum introduction: Social approaches to interpersonal communication. *Communication Theory, 2*(3), 131-139.

Leiter, K. (1980). *A primer on ethnomethodology.* New York: Oxford University Press.

Littlejohn, S. (1989). *Theories of human communication* (3rd ed.). Belmont, CA: Wadsworth.

McCroskey, J. C., Larson, C., & Knapp, M. L. (1971). *An introduction to interpersonal communication.* Englewood Cliffs, NJ: Prentice Hall.

Mead, G. H. (1934). *Mind, self, and society.* Chicago: University of Chicago Press.

Miller, G. R. (1978). The current status of theory and research in interpersonal communication. *Human Communication Research, 4,* 164-178.

Miller, G. R., & Knapp, M. L. (1985). Introduction: Background and current trends in the study of interpersonal communication. In M. L. Knapp & G. R. Miller (Eds.), *Handbook of interpersonal communication.* Beverly Hills, CA: Sage.

Miller, G. R., & Steinberg, M. (1975). *Between people: A new analysis of interpersonal communication.* Chicago: Science Research Associates.

Murphy, G., Murphy, L. B., & Newcomb, T. M. (1937). *Experimental social psychology.* New York: Harper & Row.

Parks, M. (1982). Ideology in interpersonal communication: Off the couch and into the world. In M. Burgoon (Ed.), *Communication yearbook 5* (pp. 78-108). New Brunswick, NJ: Transaction.

Pearce, W. B. (1976). The coordinated management of meaning: A rules-based theory of interpersonal communication. In G. R. Miller (Ed.), *Explorations in interpersonal communication* (pp. 17-35). Beverly Hills, CA: Sage.

Petronio, S. (Ed.). (2000). *Balancing the secrets of private disclosures.* Mahwah, NJ: Lawrence Erlbaum

Piaget, J. (1926). *Language and thought of the child* (M. Gabain, Trans.). London: Routledge & Kegan Paul.

Rawlins, W. K. (1983). Negotiating close friendships: The dialectic of conjunctive freedoms. *Human Communication Research, 9,* 255-266.

Rawlins, W. K. (1985). Stalking interpersonal communication effectiveness: Social, individual, or situational integration? In T. W. Benson (Ed.), *Speech communication in the 20th century* (pp. 109-129). Carbondale: Southern Illinois University Press.

Rawlins, W. K. (1987). Gregory Bateson and the composition of human communication. *Research in Language and Social Interaction, 20,* 53-77.

Roethlisberger, F. J., & Dickson, W. J. (1939). *Management and the worker.* Cambridge, MA: Harvard University Press.

Ruesch, J., & Bateson, G. (1951). *Communication: The social matrix of psychiatry.* New York: W. W. Norton.

Ruesch, J., & Kees, W. (1956). *Nonverbal communication: Notes on the visual perception of human relations.* Los Angeles: University of California Press.

Simmel, G. (1950). *The sociology of Georg Simmel* (K. H. Wolff, Ed. and Trans.). New York: Free Press. (Original work published 1908)

Spitzberg, B. H., & Cupach, W. R. (Eds.). (1998). *The dark side of close relationships.* Mahwah, NJ: Lawrence Erlbaum.

Stamp, G. H., & Knapp, M. L. (1990). The construct of intent in interpersonal communication. *Quarterly Journal of Speech, 76,* 282-299.

Watzlawick, P., Beavin, J. H., & Jackson, D. D. (1967). *Pragmatics of human communication: A study of interaction patterns, pathologies, and paradoxes.* New York: W. W. Norton.

PART II

Perspectives on Inquiry

2

Hypothesis Testing and Modeling Perspectives on Inquiry

MARSHALL SCOTT POOLE
ROBERT D. MCPHEE
DANIEL J. CANARY

with Mary Claire Morr

A social scientist is much like a detective in a murder mystery. The researcher confronts a confusing pattern of clues that is meaningful in both an immediate and a deeper, sometimes hidden, sense. To unravel the mystery, the detective must probe and order this deeper "reality," relying on improvisation, inspiration, and luck. Once things fall into place, there is the possibility of true understanding and insight, but there is also the danger of misinterpreting the multitude of available signs. As the detective deduces the how and why of the crime, so must the researcher constitute and cast up the object of research. This requires a capacity to ask the right questions as well as a sense of what form the answer should take. Detective novels are replete with devices and strategies for attacking a mystery, and this is no less true of social scientific writing. Foremost among these is theory.

Theory, as Cappella (1977) has noted, is a "god-term" of social science, guiding and ordering observations and imposing patterns on an overwhelmingly complex world. Theory should guide method; it should indicate what data are appropriate and suggest the types of evidence best suited to test ideas. On this view, an emphasis on method apart from theory is misguided and may be downright misleading.

In other words, an emphasis on methodology might imply mindless technicianship, the resort of tinkerers steeped in "dust-bowl empiricist" philosophy. History gives some credence to this position. Cappella (1977) argues that researchers tend to obey the "law of the hammer" with respect to methods; the methodologies that are in vogue tend to be used over and over, even if they are ill suited for addressing the questions being asked.

The sharp distinction between theory and method implied by many discussions oversimplifies the nature of research. Although all observation is theory laden, what we can conceive is determined by the available methods for knowing. The social detective must have an effective method, because method is the individual's point of contact with the world. The types of constructs and propositions in our theories, as well as the degree of credibility attached to them, are dependent on our methodological repertoires. Accordingly, we should think of *theory-method* complexes as the driving force in the research enterprise.

Consider the example of strategic interaction. Those research programs employing laboratory methods, such as Wilson's (e.g., Wilson, Aleman, & Leatham, 1998), tend to focus on variables conducive to experimental control—for example, importance of goal, time pressure, plan complexity, and type of request. Other programs, such as that described by Cody, Canary, and Smith (1994), are inductively derived from surveys of actors' goals and diary studies, which in turn support their models based on participant experience. Theoretical choices and methodological choices determine each other in a bidirectional manner.

The key intersection of theory-method codetermination occurs where method ties into the process of scientific reasoning. To understand this tie, we find it useful to distinguish four elements: substantive theoretical assumptions, modes of explanation, modes of inquiry, and methodological technique. *Substantive theoretical assumptions* are those aspects of a theory's content that are particular to the phenomena the theory covers. Substantive assumptions may be quite specific (for example, a definition of *goals*) or general, expressing some assumption about the way a phenomenon "is" (for example, the assumption that goal-directed behavior is largely mindless). In addition to substantive assumptions, all theories take a characteristic approach to explaining or understanding phenomena, a characteristic *mode of explanation*. Some theories attempt to delineate causal forces determining a phenomenon; others explain them as a product of rule-governed action; still others employ a complex of the two modes. *Mode of inquiry* refers to the strategy the researcher employs in studying a phenomenon. In particular, it indexes the relationship between theory and observational practices: Does theory precede or follow from observation, or do the two develop simultaneously? Finally, *methodological technique* represents what have traditionally been referred to as "methods," procedures of design, data collection, and analysis used to investigate interpersonal phenomena.

Substantive assumptions clearly belong to the realm of "theory," and techniques clearly belong to "methods." Modes of explanation and modes of inquiry are sometimes treated as part of theory and sometimes as part of methodology; they constitute the linchpin of the theory-method complex. Together, substantive assumptions, modes of explanation, and modes of inquiry should dictate the range of appropriate techniques. In practice, researcher preferences usually determine

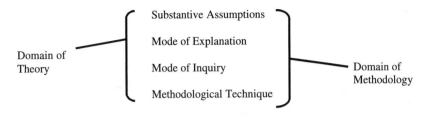

Figure 2.1   Four Elements of the Theory-Method Complex

techniques in one of the three areas—for example, a commitment to laboratory experimentation—but ideally all three elements should be considered. The relationships among substantive assumptions, modes of explanation, and modes of inquiry are complex. In combination, a mode of inquiry and a mode of explanation form a *template* that determines the form substantive theory can take, as in the example about grounded theory presented below. At the same time, characteristics of the phenomenon under study make some templates more suitable or more attractive than others. Clearly, the researcher must strike a balance among substantive assumptions, mode of inquiry, and mode of explanation, trading off one against the others to find a fruitful combination.

In this chapter we define methodology in the broadest sense, referring to relationships among modes of explanation, modes of inquiry, and techniques. In the first section we consider the modes of explanation and modes of inquiry applicable to the study of interpersonal communication. We exemplify various templates implied by combinations of modes of inquiry and explanation, and consider some techniques that these templates emphasize. We are concerned here with quantitative methods, so we do not cover qualitative techniques relevant to the templates (or templates primarily focused on qualitative inquiry). In the second and third sections, we address various quantitative techniques utilized in interpersonal communication research and how they relate to

the theoretical templates. In the second section we cover data collection and measurement techniques, and in the third we discuss a broad spectrum of techniques for data analysis. In our conclusion, we consider new directions in quantitative methodology for interpersonal communication research.

Our primary concern in this chapter is not to provide detailed description of how to employ the techniques in question; detailed discussions are available in primary sources. Rather, we focus on (a) what a given technique can do, (b) the crucial assumptions required to employ the technique properly, (c) the kinds of claims that can be made by researchers using the technique and to which templates these apply, and (d) common abuses of the technique and how they might be avoided. We attempt to specify guidelines for technical choices that permit the most effective possible match between theory and technique. We intend for this chapter to equip the social sleuth with a "method" for detecting the patterns and relationships in interpersonal communication.

MODES OF EXPLANATION, MODES OF INQUIRY, AND THEORETICAL TEMPLATES

In this section we explicate four basic modes of explanation and three modes of inquiry. In combination, the modes of explanation and inquiry form 12 theoretical templates. These templates, portrayed in Figure 2.2, define

Mode of Inquiry

Hypothetico-Deductive	Modeling	Grounded	
1	2	3	Causal
4	5	6	Conventional
7	8	9	Process
10	11	12	Dialectical

Mode
Of
Explanation

Figure 2.2   Twelve Research Templates

the form a research study can take. They constitute an array of possibilities for interpersonal communication research. The templates should be regarded as ideal types for research; they constitute standards for selecting and planning research strategies and for making technical choices. In order to understand them, one must first consider the two sets of modes.

Modes of Explanation

Explanation and understanding are the primary goals of social science. However, there are different points of view on the meanings of these two terms. We believe explanation and understanding can best be understood through a consideration of the nature of the reasoning and thinking they involve. We can distinguish four types of theoretical explanation and understanding (generally called *explanation* here), each involving different operations and assumptions and a different sense of what scientific inquiry entails: causal explanation, conventional

explanation, narrative explanation, and dialectical explanation. These explanations can be distinguished in terms of (a) the assumptions they make about the researcher's relation to the object of study, (b) the forms of explanation they advance and the criteria by which these forms are evaluated, and (c) their assumptions about the proper reference point for inquiry.

Causal explanations assume that the researcher is an independent observer of the phenomenon under study. The object of research is taken to exist in a real, objectifiable world that serves as the starting point of inquiry (even social phenomena are assumed to be objectifiable). Causal explanations consist of integrated networks of propositions of the form "X causes Y, under conditions $C_1, \ldots C_n$," where X and Y are variables or constructs identified by the researcher and $C_1 \ldots C_n$ are statements of scope or qualifying conditions for the causal relation to hold. For example, Leary's (1957) "interpersonal reflex" can be explained by a law of the following form: Hostile (affiliative) behavior from one party causes the other to respond in like manner when (a) the two parties have nearly equal power, and (b) the parties belong to the same culture. The list of scope conditions would become unmanageably long if every possible qualifier were included, so most causal propositions include an "other things being equal" clause. The nature of causality is the subject of considerable debate, but general agreement exists that a valid causal law must (a) be general and (b) describe a necessary relationship between cause and effect (Achinstein, 1971). The causal linkage in the law may be strictly deterministic, or it may state that effect follows cause only with a certain probability. In perhaps the most useful analysis of causality for social scientists, Harré and Madden (1975) argue that an adequate causal explanation specifies a generative mechanism that can account for the phenomenon and its effects. Such a *generative mechanism* consists of a "causal agent" that provides the driving force behind the cause and a mechanism that governs the action of that agent.

Causal explanation presumes that the researcher occupies the best position from which to define constructs, discern causal linkages, and test or verify causal hypotheses. There is no need for cross-checking or verification from the participants of study. Evaluation of causal explanations thus turns on tests of the adequacy of the researcher's reasoning and procedures: The researcher's explication of constructs is checked for internal logic and richness, measures are checked for construct validity with reference to the researcher's theoretical network (Cronbach, 1990), and causal linkages are tested using designs and statistical procedures that permit control of intrusive factors and errors not allowed for in the researcher's formulation (Cook & Campbell, 1979). In short, causal explanation privileges the researcher's perspective as an objective, legitimate viewpoint from which to conduct scientific inquiry.

Like causal explanations, *conventional explanations* presume the independence of the researcher and the participant in the research. However, rather than assuming an objectifiable, natural world, conventional explanation assumes that the world is a social product and takes the perspectives of people in that world as its starting point. Accordingly, conventional explanations consist in demonstrating how people—who could have done otherwise—acted or reacted in a fashion that is meaningful, understandable, or efficacious in the context of pertinent conventions. An adequate conventional explanation does not have to be necessary or general, nor does it have to show temporal ordering of cause to effect. A conventional explanation seeks to fit phenomena into a pattern meaningful to the active participant, and this pattern entails the possibility of events and the capability of actors rather than a necessary connection. For example, a conventional explanation of Leary's interpersonal reflex might explore what behaviors count as hostile or affiliative to participants and account for matching behavior in light of participants' adherence to the norm of reciprocity. This explanation would not rest its claim to validity on its generality or on showing a necessary linkage between behavior and norm, but rather on its ability to show how the norm makes matching behavior meaningful and sensible to participants.

In form, conventional explanations range from the rather loose interpretive account implied above to deductive models such as the practical syllogism (Cushman & Pearce, 1977). Regardless of their level of formality, conventional explanations are grounded in the individual's point of view. The researcher discovers conventions by probing the actor's culture, and conventional explanations attempt to account for action in a manner that reflects people's experience. The researcher's formulation of conventions and his or her explanations may differ from the actor's own statements, but even these second-order formulations are presumed to be grounded in the actor's rules and meanings. The researcher may test conventional schemes by assessing whether the behaviors or cognitions they entail correspond to the actor's behaviors or cognitions (as is done with systems of linguistic rules), usually by asking participants directly whether the rules or schemes hold. Conventional explanation subordinates the researcher's point of view to the participant's, but it leaves the researcher independent, as knower and cataloger of the participant's schemes.

Causal and conventional explanations represent the two "simple" modes of explanation. The other two, narrative explanation and dialectical explanation, are complex modes that incorporate causal and conventional generative mechanisms. By *narrative explanation* we refer to a general type of explanation, and not to the content of the specific narrative theory, as advanced by Fisher (1984). And we mean *dialectical explanation* also to refer to a general *type* of theory and its features, and not to the content of the theoretical approach known as *dialectical theory*, as reflected in the work of Baxter and Montgomery (1996.)

A *narrative explanation* accounts for interpersonal communication phenomena in terms of developing and dynamic processes that create and sustain them. Narrative explanation is part of a larger research model, the process approach (for a general account of process research and narrative explanation, see Poole, Van de Ven, Dooley, & Holmes, 2000). The process approach conceptualizes development and change processes as sequences of events that have unity and coherence over time. It explains outcomes as the result of the order in which the events unfold and of particular conjunctions of events and contextual conditions. Hence it takes the form of a theoretical narrative that

explains change and development in terms of a formulation such as, "First a, then there is a transition to b, then to c, ..."

In contrast to causal or conventional types, narrative explanations (and dialectical explanations, described below) do not presume the independence of the researcher and the subject of research. Because of this, narrative (and dialectical) explanations combine aspects of causal and conventional explanations. The generative mechanism for narrative explanations is an array of prototypical events, with either causal or conventional force, in a sequence or cycle that traces the developing entity's path through space and time in a manner shaped by a final or formal cause. Any observed sequence is due to the action of the final and formal cause within a particular context that includes other causal and conventional influences that may add particular turns to the process or even interfere with realization of the form or purpose of development. These other influences are presumed to exert immediate influence on the sequence, in contrast to the formal and final causes, which recursively guide the process both locally and globally and have their full effect only when the form is realized at the end of the sequence.

A narrative explanation of Leary's interpersonal reflex would conceptualize it as an interaction cycle between the partners whereby one partner initiates a hostile or affiliative act and the second responds with a like act based on his or her interpretation of the first act, triggering a like response by the first partner in a positive feedback loop. This conceptualization is based on a narrative that posits that "vicious cycles" develop due to actors' immediate, short-term interpretations of and reactions to others. The narrative identifies a positive cycle that will result in escalation or closer relationships, depending on whether the first act is hostile or affiliative. How the cycle plays out in a specific case depends not only on this narrative, but also on immediate causal or conventional factors; for example, if one party watched *The War of the Roses* the previous night, she might recognize the vicious cycle and act to break it by taking a "time out" and talking to the first party about the futility of matching hostility levels. The process theory explains development through a narrative plus other factors that may change the course of development at a single point in the sequence.

Narrative explanations operate on a level different from that of causal or conventional explanations. A process theory can incorporate the other explanations as part of the generative mechanism that advances the process through phases or cycles. It also incorporates them as immediate shocks that may reroute the change and development process. Because the nature of the phenomenon and its context changes as the process unfolds over time, the same cause or convention may have different effects or implications, depending on when it occurs and its particular conjunction with other factors. The insightful actor's metastatement on the futility of matching will have a different meaning and impact if it occurs right after the first hostile act than if it occurs after 10 hostile exchanges.

Like causal theories, process theories are judged by their generality. The generality of a narrative explanation, however, stems not from its uniformity and consistency, but from its *versatility,* the degree to which it can encompass a broad domain of developmental patterns without modification of its essential character. The broader its domain—the greater the variety of cases, contexts, events, and patterns to which the theory can adapt—the more general the explanation. Ideally, a narrative explanation provides an account of how and why a sequence of events typically unfolds that is sufficiently flexible to encompass a range of observed cases, yet sufficiently powerful to help the researcher discern the operation of the generative mechanism in a multitude of particularized sequences.

To evaluate a narrative explanation, the researcher must (a) test whether the pattern of events over time corresponds to that hypothesized by the model and (b) test the causal or conventional model that explains movement through successive events or phases. The stance of the researcher developing a process theory is akin to that of the historian or biologist: The researcher is presumed to be outside of the phenomenon, but she or he seeks to understand its meaning in terms of a narrative that portrays how it comes about.

Like narrative explanation, *dialectical explanation* assumes that the objects of study are both causally and socially constituted. Dialectical explanations emphasize the interplay of causal forces that condition action while actors influence the operation of these same forces. Causality plays an important role in dialectical explanation, but it moves along a complex path. People act, but not in circumstances of their own choosing. Forces beyond actors' control determine the available rules, schemes, and structures, and how they can be applied. Within this determination, actors' conventions form the grounds for the operation of causal forces and shape the impact of those forces in the situation. Moreover, systems of action are themselves involved in the generation and movement of causal forces. So action is conditioned by causal forces, which are themselves shaped by action, which is conditioned by causal forces, which are shaped by action, and so forth.

A dialectical explanation of Leary's interpersonal reflex might emphasize a norm such as reciprocity, but it would also take into account the larger conventional and causal context that shapes how that norm operates in any specific instance. For instance, A's friendly gesture might be systematically misinterpreted (or strategically interpreted) as submissiveness in a situation where B thinks (or wants) status differences to be important and has (or wants) high status. If A anticipated this situation, A would have to be careful to design his or her gesture of simple friendliness to appear "friendly but not weak" (e.g., as enthusiastic and energetic, as well as friendly; see Burgoon, Johnson, & Koch, 1999). The appropriateness of this strategy would depend on the larger conventional and causal context, and other conditions might render it ineffective. Such a gesture might be inappropriate in a more egalitarian situation; it might be impossible to avoid B's status consciousness; or showing friendliness might be possible only if causal factors such as A's cultural experience and communicative competence permit.

Unlike conventional explanations, the only requirement of which is the explanation of action in terms of rules or schemes, dialectical explanations must also specify causal forces that determine the types of conventions available and how actors can use these conventions. Hence the dialectical explanation must probe the nature of domination in our society and how this carries over into interpersonal relationships. The researcher cannot take rules as given (as a conventional explanation does) but must explore what gives the rules pattern and force. Historical evidence frequently plays an important role in this process, because causes are embedded in previous, often long-established action systems. However, discovering causal forces does not complete a dialectical explanation. Causes operate through shaping the action system, and because of this, the mediation of causal forces by action must be explored. In this case, the impact of causal forces on matching behavior must be understood as actively "filtered" through schemes and structures associated with interpersonal relationships. This filtering does not represent "slippage" or "error" (as a purely causal explanation would assume); rather, filtering provides the mechanism through which the cause operates and represents an integral aspect of any explanation. Causality does not entail a direct "X → Y" relationship, but rather something

like "X influences conventions $Z_1, \ldots Z_n$, which lead to Y, in the context of the action system W." Causes and conventions interact in this type of explanation, and the ratio of determinism to action varies considerably.

From this perspective, the researcher occupies a better position from which to identify causal forces, but can understand how these forces operate and how significant they are only by taking the active role of the individual and the channeling influence of society into account. Hence evaluation of dialectical explanations uses two sets of criteria, those for causal explanations and those for conventions. Once the operation of causal forces has been established through the use of statistical techniques, their impact on the action system must be spelled out. A successful dialectical explanation articulates causal forces and their impacts on social actors.

Causal explanations emphasize objectifiable forces, conventional explanations focus on subjectivity (or intersubjectivity), narrative explanations center on patterns informed by final or formal causes, and dialectical explanations emphasize conditioned subjectivity (or intersubjectivity). In drawing these distinctions, it is not necessary to argue that one mode of explanation is better than any other. Each mode has its advocates, and each possesses strengths and weaknesses relative to the others.

Modes of Inquiry

Even when a researcher is clear on his or her substantive assumptions and mode of explanation, the question remains as to how theory and data are related during the process of inquiry. Three modes of inquiry can be distinguished: hypothetico-deductive, modeling, and grounded theory.

In the *hypothetico-deductive* mode of inquiry, the researcher generates hypotheses from theory, develops operational definitions of theoretical constructs, and executes a study (experimental, field, or survey) to test the hypotheses. Theory is prior to data collection and hypothesis testing, and these steps are strictly separated. By far, the majority of interpersonal communication studies operate in this mode.

A second mode of inquiry is *modeling*, in which theory, operationalization, and data patterns are treated simultaneously (see Levine & Fitzgerald, 1991; McPhee & Poole, 1982). A model is a representation of a situated theory. It gives a direct depiction of how the theory generates the observed data in a specific context. For example, Newton's mechanics presents a general theory of motion; a model of the solar system would consist of equations consistent with Newtonian principles, but would represent the forces exerted on each specific planet by others and by the sun. The behavior of the data (in this case, the observed planetary movements) is directly described by the equations of the model, which represent a situated case of the general theory. Models often use mathematical representations (e.g., Hunter, Danes, & Cohen, 1984) but may also be cast in logical verbal or pictorial formalisms (e.g., Pearce & Cronen's, 1980, model of rule following). Comparing model predictions with observed data enables the researcher not only to test the model, but also to pinpoint problematic aspects of the model. Treating theory, operationalization, and data simultaneously is obviously more demanding and difficult than the traditional mode of inquiry, but it has the advantages of greater precision and of clarifying assumptions behind the theory (Cappella, 1977; McPhee & Poole, 1982).

The third mode of inquiry is the development of *grounded theory* (Charmaz, 2000; Glaser & Strauss, 1967). The researcher goes directly to the phenomenon itself and develops concepts, hypotheses, and theoretical propositions from direct experience with the data. Grounded theory takes a "bottom-up" approach, as opposed to the "top-down"

move of the traditional mode; theory emerges from observation, rather than being prior to it. Once hypotheses or generalizations have been developed, they may be "tested" in the situation or in another context, but this is by no means equivalent to hypothesis testing in the traditional mode. Advocates of grounded theory argue that it makes the researcher more sensitive to particular nuances of the phenomenon and removes "blinders" imposed on the researcher by a priori theory. Critics argue that the situated nature of grounded theory does not allow for generalization or for rigorous testing of its propositions.

Over the years, there has been considerable controversy concerning which mode of inquiry is best. We would submit that, rather than any of these modes being correct or incorrect, the three are comparatively advantageous or disadvantageous, depending on the subject of study. We would encourage researchers to be flexible in choosing a mode of inquiry.

Templates and Tools

When modes of explanation and modes of inquiry are crossed, 12 templates result, each of which represents a different methodological strategy. These templates form the grounds for methodological choice and function on at least two levels.

First, the templates represent *descriptions* of the range of options open to interpersonal communication research. In addition to the many efforts that fall clearly in a single template, numerous "borderline" or mixed studies appear to combine aspects of several templates. Some are misconceived projects that should be organized by a single template. Others are hybrids that employ different templates in different phases of research (e.g., grounded inquiry at first, then modeling in later stages) or different templates side by side in parallel research efforts (for example, research into rules that poses some hypotheses but also uses grounded inquiry to look for other rules).

The templates also serve a *normative* function. Each template embodies different assumptions and characteristic forms of inference and proof. Within these limits, some techniques are more appropriate than others. In this vein, the scheme can be used to guide selection of techniques and evaluation of previous technical choices. Further, the templates also suggest how the results of applying techniques should be interpreted. Most techniques can be used in several different templates. Because the various templates involve different types of claims and makes different assumptions about the nature of the phenomenon under study, the same technique can yield quite different evidence and conclusions under different templates.

A complete discussion of the 12 templates is beyond the scope of this chapter (see previous editions of this *Handbook* for more detail on some of them), but we will cover a few of the most common ones in terms of their strengths, weaknesses, and technical affinities.

Cell 1: Causal explanation, hypothetico-deductive inquiry. Traditionally, this template has been the norm for empirical research in interpersonal communication. As its name implies, the researcher first specifies causal hypotheses, then sets up a research design to test the hypotheses and rejects or fails to reject the hypotheses based on the data. Theory development precedes and is independent of data collection and analysis. This is by far the most frequently employed strategy in interpersonal communication research; most attraction, nonverbal, and self-disclosure research, for example, falls within Cell 1 (e.g., Dindia, Fitzpatrick, & Kenny, 1997; Guerrero, 1996). At present, the techniques most commonly employed in this template include experimental designs, statistical model-testing methods (such as path analysis), and those developmental techniques designed to establish causality.

Causal, hypothetico-deductive research has several advantages: (a) It yields general, necessary explanations; (b) cast correctly, its hypotheses are clearly falsifiable; and (c) it can result in extremely powerful theories that permit precise prediction and control. Along with these strengths come weaknesses and biases as well. Cell 1 research tends to gloss over unique particular aspects of the phenomenon under study. It favors precise, tightly controlled conceptualization and measurement of constructs that may lead to a reification of variables and dismissal of the participant's meanings. Moreover, causal, hypothetico-deductive explanation is not adequate for cases with recursive effects and those in which phenomena are continually renegotiated and redefined by actors. Overemphasis on causal understanding can lead to distortion and oversimplification of cases in which narrative explanations are more appropriate.

Cell 2: Causal explanation, modeling inquiry. Cappella (1977) advocates this approach to communication research, which has been used increasingly in recent years. In this template, a causal theory is represented as a model directly depicting the pattern or "behavior" of data. Cappella (1979, 1980; Cappella & Planalp, 1981) has used this approach to study talk-silence sequences in conversations, Hunter et al. (1984) have used it to study attitude change, and Caplan and Greene (1999) have used it to study message acquisition. In many cases, this template involves the development of nonlinear dynamic models that can account for a number of complex phenomena, such as sudden shifts in behavior, self-sustaining periodic patterns, and apparently random change (Buder, 1991; Levine & Fitzgerald, 1991). The causal, modeling template should not be confused with path analysis and structural equation modeling techniques, which are often termed *causal modeling*.

These two are statistical rather than research techniques.

Modeling enables the researcher to develop simulations of the interaction of a complex network of variables; from such simulations, the researcher can determine which variables or parameter values are central to the causal process, as well as the general qualitative behavior of dependent variables. The researcher can then translate the results of these simulations into testable predictions. As Pavitt and Cappella (1979) note, simulation modeling enables the researcher to identify "discriminable features" of the process being modeled, features whose presence or absence can enable falsification of the model. Modeling also forces the researcher to specify precisely and completely the theoretical assumptions, constructs, and connections among variables (see Cappella, 1977). One particularly interesting feature of this and the other modeling cells is that the researcher often learns more when the model fails than when it succeeds, because the failure highlights previously unnoticed aspects of the phenomenon or faulty assumptions (McPhee & Poole, 1982). The methods used to test causally based models include statistical model-testing methods, techniques for evaluating descriptive models, time-series techniques, and developmental techniques (for an excellent introduction, see Levine & Fitzgerald, 1991).

In terms of shortcomings, theories based on models are often less generalizable than Cell 1 theories because models are tied to particular cases and particular instantiations of variables. Then, too, some theoretical statements cannot be represented in a model (especially a mathematical model) without becoming distorted or impoverished (for examples, see McPhee & Poole, 1982). Finally, data are often so unreliable and "fuzzy" that they do not permit the researcher to select among competing models.

Cell 5: Conventional explanation, modeling inquiry. In Cell 5, the researcher is explicit about the process by which conventions enter into behavior and the relationships among conventions. Unlike models in Cell 2, Cell 5 models are usually verbal or logical in form. Once a model is developed, it is tested against actual behavior. Further, the test should involve checking to see whether participants actually hold the conventions in question. Examples of Cell 5 research include Sacks, Schegloff, and Jefferson's (1974) model of turn taking in conversation, the rule models described by Pearce and Cronen (1980), and Donohue's (1981) model of negotiation rules. Vroom and Jago's (1974) model of leadership behavior presents a paradigmatic example of rule modeling and testing.

The advantages of Cell 5 include those of conventionalist inquiry in general: It is sensitive to the active role of subjects and does not impose strict causality. It also enjoys the benefits of modeling over hypothetico-deductive inquiry discussed in relation to Cell 2. Like other modeling templates, this one may require more precision than the phenomenon allows. Moreover, a large number of models involving different conventions may fit a single phenomenon, and it may be impossible to determine which model works best. The techniques commonly used in this cell include experimental designs, statistical model testing, and quantitative descriptive techniques such as Markov modeling. Both Cells 4 and 5 are too seldom used. They provide the critical step of falsification or verification needed to supplement the discovery stage, which represents the extent of most conventionalist research (see Tudor, 1976).

Cell 7: Narrative explanation, hypothetico-deductive inquiry. In this template the researcher posits hypotheses about the properties of a process based on the narrative generative mechanism. These hypotheses test (a) that observed events occur in an order consistent with the narrative and (b) that the forces driving development and change are those in the narrative. For instance, Walton (1968) posits a model of interpersonal conflict with two moments, differentiation and integration. The differentiation period emerges from a period of equilibrium due to a triggering incident that results in a period of escalation. In an effective conflict management process during this period, parties come to understand their differences and accept the fact that they must work things out. The transition to integration occurs when the parties (or some third party) come to these understandings and also manage to synchronize their behavior so that they are both motivated to try to work out their differences rather than compete. During effective integration, parties test options and ensure that their needs are met.

To test whether this model is consistent with observed interpersonal conflicts, the researcher would need to measure behaviors and attitudes to be expected in differentiation (e.g., intense language, competitive conflict style, statements of positions and differences) and integration (e.g., commitments to cooperate, statements of needs, questions about possible compromise). If the narrative explanation holds, the researcher would expect to find more differentiation behavior at the outset of a discussion and then a transition to integrative behavior. This transition may be marked by one or more "false starts" indicating that the parties have not synchronized their motivation. These would be marked by cycles of integrative overtures and differentiating replies. In order to test whether the understandings help to drive the transition, a researcher using a multiple-condition design might stop some dyads right after the transition point and have them respond to items tapping their degree of respect for the other and understanding of the differences between their positions.

In terms of strengths, Cell 7 focuses on the unfolding of a process in terms of the narrative that explains it, rather than a static causal model that generates it piecewise. Cell 7 represents a flexible approach in that it

acknowledges that not all dyads will pass through the stages in lockstep fashion; some may not reach integration and others may have trouble synchronizing and take some time to get into integration. This template also can incorporate both causal and conventional forces, although it does not necessarily place them in the type of recursive relationship that the dialectical mode posits. Cell 7 also has disadvantages. Processes are complex, and it is often difficult and time-consuming to code valid indicators. Also, the very flexibility of narrative explanations may make it difficult to ascertain when they are not supported.

Cell 10: Dialectical explanation, hypothetico-deductive inquiry. This cell constitutes the most common of the three dialectical templates. The researcher generates hypotheses about how conventions and the causal factors that influence them and give them force will function in action systems. The researcher must test hypotheses about how the participant behaves in the given action system as well as several hypotheses about the action system itself. These system tests include (a) whether the hypothesized conventions are held and used by participants, (b) whether causal factors hold and operate as hypothesized, and (c) whether participants are conscious of the causal factors and, if so, how this consciousness influences the system. Generation of the insights needed to produce a dialectical theory suggests the need for powerful discovery techniques, which are then complemented by hypothesis-testing techniques. A study of group decision making by Poole and DeSanctis (1992) provides one example of Cell 7. These researchers analyzed the use of rules in decision-making interaction and determined the influence of two types of procedural agendas on the structuration of rules. They also explored the relationships of various types of rule use to decision outcomes. Another example concerns the perceptions and responses that people in close involvements make in light of dialectical tensions (e.g., Baxter & Erbert, 2000).

Cell 10 studies combine many of the advantages of Cells 1 and 4. They have a degree of sensitivity to the phenomenon characteristic of conventional studies, but also incorporate strong tests in the tradition of causal, hypothetico-deductive studies. Moreover, dialectical studies are more powerful than conventional research because they also focus on the forces that shape conventions and condition their operation. However, the same features that give Cell 10 studies their unique advantages can also generate problems. For one thing, Cell 10 studies are quite complex and require considerable time and resources; for many projects, the payoff in terms of insight may not justify the investment. Compared with the straightforward, powerful accounts provided by the causal cells, dialectical theories may sometimes seem overly complex and convoluted. One is tempted to apply Occam's razor. Second, because dialectical theories posit a recursive spiral of dependencies among causal and conventional features, their constructs may sometimes lack integrity. Unless the researcher carefully specifies and traces out these interweaving influences, the resulting account may be too fluid to be useful.

Summary. Researchers have tended to confine themselves to only a few of the 12 templates. Social science is ideological, and arguments about the "right" way to conduct inquiry tend to create the assumption that only certain templates are valid. For example, causal explanation is generally associated with the traditional hypothetico-deductive mode of inquiry and conventional explanation with development of grounded theory. There is no reason either causal or conventional explanations cannot be associated with another mode of inquiry, but their uses with the other templates are not widely advertised. Arguments in favor of particular templates are often cast as critiques of other positions, and, unfortunately, defending a particular mode of inquiry or explanation sometimes assumes more importance than addressing substantive questions. We would suggest that although debate is valuable, generalized attacks often hide other possibilities and blind us to the fact that all research involves making choices from a range of potential approaches, each of which should be considered on its own merits for the question at hand. Advocacy of one "correct" template flies in the face of effective, creative research. But beyond innovation, effective research is grounded in the capacity to match investigative strategies to the object of research. The matching process not only creates a happy marriage of theory and technique, but also serves as an important means of exploring the nature of the phenomenon by finding out how it can be conceptualized, measured, and analyzed.

In the following two sections, we report on our reading of the "state of the art" in quantitative methodology in interpersonal communication research. In updating this chapter from our contribution to the second edition of the *Handbook of Interpersonal Communication* (Poole & McPhee, 1994), we reviewed the major communication journals that published interpersonal communication research from 1995 to the present, as well as books and yearbooks.[1] We attempted to ascertain the direction of the field based on methods employed as well as on the recent methodologically oriented articles published.

DATA-GATHERING AND MEASUREMENT TECHNIQUES

Interpersonal communication researchers have always been eclectic in their choices of data-gathering techniques. These techniques span a wide range, including questionnaires, interviews, behavioral observation, interaction and content analysis, and indirect, unobtrusive measures. Without trying to catalog all the measures that researchers' ingenuity has concocted, we consider in this section key common denominators of measurement and data gathering, the issues of validity and reliability. Reliability, the consistency of measurement, is a necessary condition for validity of measurement. It is fairly easy to assess directly, and it is here that many reports start. However, validity is the ultimate question in any consideration of data collection procedures. Research is fruitless without valid data, and it is not sufficient simply to assume that the data are good. In the case of quantitative instruments and unobtrusive measures, researchers must ask whether their measures do indeed tap the variables or constructs they are designed to assess. For methods involving coding or content analysis, researchers must ask what types of information their systems yield and how meaningful this information is to their subjects. Validity is much less straightforward than reliability and, for this reason, may be given short shrift. However, doing so impairs researchers' ability to build on prior studies with confidence.

This section is made up of three parts. First, we consider the construction and validation of tests and questionnaire instruments (the most commonly employed quantitative tools in interpersonal communication research) as well as techniques for observation. We then focus on interaction analysis, and, finally, we consider some additional measurement issues.

Tests and Questionnaire Instruments

Much interpersonal communication research utilizes questionnaires, interviews, and other instruments to elicit participant reports of attitudes, behavior, attributes, communication, recall of cognitive processes, and so forth (for a collection of communication measures, see Rubin, Palmgreen, & Sypher, 1994). Researchers sometimes construct these instruments in ad hoc fashion, giving a nod to

the gods of psychometrics by calculating reliability coefficients and perhaps running factor analyses. It is true that many statistical methods are fairly robust to violations of scale assumptions. It is also true that face validity of an instrument often signals other forms of validity. However, researchers can never be sure their instruments are good unless they follow systematic and careful procedures in constructing and evaluating them.

Comprehensive treatments of the development and design of instruments can be found in the psychometric and survey research literature (e.g., Crocker & Algina, 1986; Cronbach, 1990; Fink & Kosecoff, 1985; Rossi, Wright, & Anderson, 1983). Here we focus on issues useful for communication researchers and on some problems in current interpersonal communication research.

Conceptualization and design is the first step in the development of instruments. Ideally, instrument design should start with a construct definition rooted in theory before any items are written or questions tested. However, construct definition and revision continues as item generation and evaluation force the researcher to consider whether a construct is a state or a trait, subjective or objective, a uni- or multidimensional construct.

One useful way to use construct definitions to guide item construction is to specify *facets,* a set of independent item properties that stake out the universe of possible items that could be included in the measure (Bell, 1986; Borg, 1979). For instance, a network-related question about amount of communication might be, "How often per week do you talk with your best friend [name previously supplied]?" Facets characterizing such an item might include (a) focus (own communication behavior), (b) object (own best friend), (c) behavior specification ("talk with"), and (d) time period (week). Some of those facets might be varied to generate items (for example, "talk with" might be changed to "influence" to generate another item), whereas others would remain stable. Ideally, the facet list enables the researcher to specify precisely the universe of possible items by stating which facets are important. It can also ground statistical methods such as generalizability analysis, described below.

Instrument design requires that the researcher sample from the universe of possible items in order to meet theoretical, methodological, and practical (e.g. test length) specifications. A good source of guidance in writing items and constructing tests is the rapidly growing empirical base of knowledge about instrumentation effects. Some representative reviews include those conducted by Dillman (1978), Fink and Kosecoff, (1985), and Rossi et al. (1983).

At the conceptual level, all tests should explicitly refer to some model of the relationship between responses and the underlying construct. The most common and most robust model is classical true-score theory (Crocker & Algina, 1986; Lord & Novick, 1968). This model assumes that responses are distributed normally about the value of the measured trait or construct. The use of factor analysis and confirmatory factor analysis to construct and evaluate tests assumes the classical true-score model. A second test theory, known as item response theory or latent trait theory, has developed in recent years (Jones & Appelbaum, 1989; Lord & Novick, 1968; van der Linden & Hambleton, 1997). It assumes that different nonlinear curves (normal ogive, logistic, Poisson) relate item responses to levels of underlying traits or constructs. Although item response models require more restrictive assumptions than classical test theory, tests that include these assumptions have certain advantages, including the following: (a) An item response model enables precise estimation of the examinee's latent trait value from any subset of items that fits the model, thus reducing testing time and permitting easy development of alternative questionnaire forms; (b) items or subtests can differ in difficulty and discriminative power, corresponding to estimable model parameters; and (c) the measured trait can be adjusted to deliver invariance across groups, provided the test is unidimensional.

Once the instrument has been defined and constructed, the second step is empirical evaluation. The researcher should address at least two questions in this evaluation: (a) Does the instrument meet the assumptions of its measurement model and scale type? and (b) Is the instrument reliable and valid?

Methods to assess whether an instrument satisfies the assumptions of its measurement model and scale type are described in most psychometric texts. The best way to ensure that an instrument meets measurement model assumptions is through the careful application of empirical test construction methods. Good examples of the application of classical test theory to interpersonal communication constructs are the evaluation of rival measurement models for communication apprehension (Levine & McCroskey, 1990) and the measurement of interpersonal dominance (Burgoon et al., 1998) as well as relational features of communication more generally (Burgoon & Hale, 1987). The classical model of test theory underlies nearly every communication scale we reviewed. Researchers in the field have not yet taken advantage of item response theory, even for constructs that seem to fit it well, such as communication competence.

Little interpersonal communication research has evaluated scaling assumptions. However, this is an important issue. If what a researcher thinks is an interval or ratio scale can satisfy only the assumptions of an ordinal scale, then he or she may inadvertently use the wrong statistical methods. The debate over which question and response format should be used to assess compliance-gaining strategies illustrates the importance of scale development (see Burleson et al., 1988, and the responses to this article in *Human Communication Research,* volume 15, issue 1, 1988; see also

Dillard, 1988). Another interesting study is Rothenbuhler's (1991) use of a log-linear latent class model to test a Guttman scale of community involvement. Woelfel and Fink (1980) present an interesting and unique approach to scaling that does not fit any current test theory (for a critique of this approach, see Craig, 1983).

The second empirical question concerns reliability and validity assessment (Crocker & Algina, 1986). The assessment of reliability depends on the underlying measurement model and the type of scale utilized. For instance, use of coefficient alpha is appropriate for measures composed of multiple-item Likert scales, but it is not appropriate for assessing reliability of a Guttman scale, because items low and high in difficulty on a Guttman scale are not expected to have very high correlations.

The most widely used methods of assessing reliability (test-retest, split-half, coefficient alpha) are designed for the assessment of reliability between two sets of measures—such as a test and a retest, or ratings by two different judges—or internal consistency of a single test. But these approaches do not handle more complex cases as easily, such as when three or more judges rate the same behaviors, when two or more different (but nonparallel) forms of the same test are used, or when two or more raters score events on more than one occasion. Generalizability theory (Crocker & Algina, 1986) is a general approach to reliability assessment that covers most cases.

The theory of generalizability posits that a measure is useful insofar as its findings generalize to a broader set of measurements. For instance, from a given observation we might wish to generalize to observations made using other tests constructed in an identical way (the idea behind internal-consistency reliability), observations made at a later time (Time 1-Time 2 reliability or stability), observations by other raters (interrater reliability), or observations using different but valid measures of the same construct.

A generalizability analysis estimates variance components corresponding to each of these facets or sources of difference (and their combinations), plus generalizability coefficients that, like reliability coefficients, quantify how well our initial measure represents a "universe score" applying to the whole range of options. Computation of generalizability statistics is easy using standard computer packages (Shavelson & Webb, 1991). One other recently developed approach to the measurement of reliability is reliability generalization (Vacha-Haase, 1998; but see Sawilowsky, 2000), a meta-analytic technique for evaluating and explaining differences in reliability across studies.

Validity assessment has been described by numerous authors (e.g., Crocker & Algina, 1986; Cronbach, 1990). The classic types of validity are *content* validity (measuring the intended content, evaluated in varied ways), *criterion* or predictive validity (correlated with some important consequence of the variable being measured), and *construct* validity (including *convergent* and *discriminant* validity as subtypes, which refer to behaving similarly to and differently from the ways other measures in the pattern theory would predict). One of the most common methods used for construct validation in interpersonal communication research has been the multitrait, multimethod (MTMM) approach described originally by Campbell and Fiske (see Crocker & Algina, 1986). Simple methods formulated by Campbell and Fisk have been found invalid and rejected, and formal methods of interpreting MTMM matrices using analysis of variance (ANOVA), nonparametric methods, and confirmatory factor analysis have been developed. Schmitt and Stults (1986) reviewed studies that compared the various methods for analysis of MTMM matrices just mentioned and concluded that, frustratingly, different methods led to different conclusions. Schmitt and Stults make a strong argument that confirmatory factor analysis is the most comprehensive method for validity analysis. Tomas, Hontangas, and Oliver (2000) identify two different confirmatory factor analysis approaches that deal with method factors in different ways and note that the commonly used approach is usually inferior to one emphasizing unique item variance. Structural equation modeling, the general methodology that includes confirmatory factor analysis, also has great potential for validity studies (Bollen, 1989; see the discussion below). It enables researchers to separate reliability from validity, to isolate validity components from other error components that cloud the interpretation of traditional validity coefficients, and to locate specific items causing reliability/validity problems.

Ideally, the researcher should not stop once a test has been empirically evaluated; evaluation of a measurement instrument should continue during its use in research. In particular, it is often wise for the researcher to dry-run several subjects through the whole study procedure, then interview them about their understanding of and reasons for responses to the measurement instrument to make sure the research context does not invalidate it. Furthermore, accumulation of validity evidence is an ongoing process, and it is often a good idea to reassess measures in light of emerging results (e.g., Burleson et al., 1988).

We believe that two practices common in instrument development by interpersonal communication researchers should be reconsidered. First, communication researchers still rely too much on exploratory factor analysis as a basis for understanding and evaluating questionnaire instruments. Exploratory factor analysis is very broad and flexible, but the information it gives about a test is also complex, incomplete, and often not what is needed to show content and construct validity. Moreover, the results of exploratory factor analysis may not replicate because of error due

to the particular sample and situation utilized. Cronkhite (1976) reports some very interesting findings on the interaction effects of rater, concept rated, and scale identity on the factor structure of multi-item evaluative semantic differential scales. Confirmatory factor analysis, which tests hypotheses about factor structures, is a more powerful and comprehensive method (see also the discussion of factor analysis below).

A second problem in some communication test development procedures is that important properties of the measure or underlying construct are not adequately articulated and evaluated. Hewes and Haight (1979) examined the "cross-situational consistency" of several supposed communication "traits" that were thought to characterize participants. The relatively low correlations they found seem to indicate that the measured behaviors displayed much less consistency than the term *trait* suggests. They traced these failings in part to inadequate conceptualization of constructs.

As described here, the instrument development process seems to be associated most strongly with the causal templates. However, it is also appropriate for the conventional or dialectical templates, if item generation and test design and validation take into account participant understandings and concepts. A measurement model for these templates must be discovered, not imposed a priori, probably through an initial phase of grounded research, and the final test should possess representational validity (see the following subsection).

Interaction Analysis

The term *interaction analysis* refers to any systematic method of *classifying* verbal and nonverbal behavior, including conflict behaviors (Sillars, 1986), marital interaction (Weiss, 1993), and levels of supportiveness (e.g., Kunkel & Burleson, 1999). These methods have in common the interpretation of utterances according to a standard set of rules developed by the researcher. Four key issues facing interaction analysis are category construction, reliability, validity, and the adaptation of coding systems to different contexts.

Several authors have discussed how to construct content and interaction analysis systems (Folger, Hewes, & Poole, 1984; Hewes, 1979; Neuendorf, 2001; Poole, Folger, & Hewes, 1987; Trujillo, 1986). Construction of systems can follow two routes. In one, a logically complete system is developed that yields an exhaustive classification, usually according to a logical choice tree that rigidly specifies coding choices (see, for example, Anderson, 1983). Such an approach makes classification straightforward, but the logical demands of constructing the decision tree may distort the meaning of the discourse to its speakers. It is easy to replace a speaker's sense of the language with the classifier's "neater" and "more logical" interpretations. The second, more common approach involves compiling categories that index relevant functions in the discourse being studied. These functions are often specified by the researcher's theory, as in the case of Rogers and Farace's (1975) relational coding system, and they may also have considerable internal structure, as does Weiss's (1993) Marital Interaction Coding System (MICS). Alternatively, the system may be developed with a grounded approach to reflect the functions the observer sees in the situation. As opposed to the logically complete approach, this second strategy relies more on the coder's natural interpretive abilities to determine classifications. It is advantageous because it is more responsive to the particular nature of the discourse than the first, but it is correspondingly less "clean," and its rules are harder to apply consistently.

Coding reliability, a necessary condition for classificatory validity, can be separated into two components: (a) *unitizing reliability*, which involves the coder's ability to agree on how the discourse should be parsed into units, and (b) *classificatory reliability*, which involves the level of agreement on how units should be classified. Folger et al. (1984) provide an extensive discussion of different means of assessing reliability and of special cases in which reliability is particularly critical. It is important that the researcher assess reliability at the level of the overall coding system as well as at the level of the individual categories. As Hewes (1985; Folger et al., 1984) has noted, even for coding systems with high overall reliability, there may be particular categories with low reliability, and this can seriously disrupt certain types of data analysis methods.

In abstract terms, the validity of interaction analysis systems is the degree to which they actually yield the types of information they are designed to obtain. Exactly what constitutes validity and how validity is assessed depends on what types of claims the researcher is attempting to make about interaction (Folger et al., 1984; Poole et al., 1987). At least three types of claims might be made about codings of interaction. First, a researcher may want to identify only those acts that are theoretically interesting to him or her, regardless of how the actors themselves interpret the acts. In this mode of observation, which Poole et al. (1987) term *observer-privileged*, the researcher aspires to explain interaction from the outside, without reference to participants' perspectives. Much research with interaction analysis, particularly in the causal templates, works under this assumption. For example, to identify how people develop their ideas in conversation, Canary's (1992) *Manual for Coding Conversational Argument* relies on theoretical terms (e.g., "convergent arguables") that defy lay understanding. But a researcher may also want to use a coding system to identify how participants interpret interaction. The researcher may seek to develop categories that identify the shared meanings utterances have for members of a culture. This observational mode, which Poole et al. (1987) call the *generalized subject-privileged* mode, is the aspiration of many coding systems, including those based on the identification of speech acts. Sillars, Roberts, Leonard, and Dun (2000), for example, had individuals recall their thoughts as they watched videotapes of themselves in conflict interactions with their spouses. Sillars et al. then correlated these recollections with their coded conflict behaviors. But a researcher may try to go even further and use a coding system to identify the idiosyncratic meanings of utterances for people in a particular relationship, in *restricted subject-privileged* mode. Labov and Fanshel use this mode of observation in their book *Therapeutic Discourse* (1977).

Whichever of the three modes of observation the researcher aspires to, claims about the meaning of classifications must be backed up by evidence for their validity. Each mode of observation requires different types of evidence. For observer-privileged systems, which code according to the researcher's point of view, the classic techniques of assessing construct validity are sufficient. However, for subject-privileged systems, which attempt to get at participants' meanings, the researcher also must provide evidence that they actually represent participants' interpretations. Several methods for assessing the *representational validity* of coding systems have been developed (for a review of these methods, see Folger et al., 1984). The importance of formally establishing the validity of coding systems is illustrated by O'Donnell-Trujillo's (1982) comparison of two relational coding systems that purported to code the same constructs. He found a very low degree of overlap in codings, suggesting that one or both were "off base." But which one? Without validity assessment, it is impossible to establish.

Finally, even coding systems designed for general use must be adapted to specific cases; for example, Weiss's (1993) MICS is often adapted to meet particular research needs,

with codes being combined in various ways. Such adaptation generally involves the researcher's making special assumptions about what rules mean and how they are applied. Cicourel (1980) has argued that researchers should report these adaptations in methodological appendixes to their published studies, along with more detail on coder background and training than is normally supplied.

Other Issues

An increasingly common method of measuring communication involves the use of participants' *reports or recollections* of their interactions. Researchers collect these through several methods, including the following: (a) having participants or observers make retrospective global ratings of interaction episodes (Metts, Sprecher, & Cupach, 1991; Poole et al., 1987), (b) having participants provide retrospective accounts or narratives of interaction (Burnett, 1991; see also Bochner, Chapter 3, this volume), (c) having participants keep interaction diaries or logs (Duck, 1991), and (d) having participants comment on videotapes of their own interactions (i.e., stimulated recall; Frankel & Beckman, 1982; Sillars et al., 2000). Advantages of these methods include the ability to capture participants' interpretations of their interactions (often in their own words), the generation of meaningful summary data for complex events, and access to otherwise inaccessible interactions, such as intimate encounters. These approaches seem quite promising, and guidelines for utilizing them are growing more sophisticated.

However, these methods, too, must shoulder the burden of proving their validity and reliability in the face of several possible problems. As Poole et al. (1987) note, global ratings of interaction often do not correlate highly with direct coding on similar dimensions and may be subject to bias due to raters' implicit theories of interaction. In addition, global ratings do not provide representations of patterns of interaction (Markman & Notarius, 1987). All four methods are vulnerable to various cognitive biases (Metts et al., 1991, pp. 168-169) and limitations on what can be recalled (Duck, 1991; Ericsson & Simon, 1980; Nisbett & Wilson, 1977). Accounts and stimulated recall data may also be problematic due to participants' language deficiencies and lack of insight. In addition, recollections of behavior do not allow for precise assessments of how interaction unfolds. The various authors cited here discuss other limitations, as well as means for mitigating the various problems.

Another important issue is the measurement of *change*. It has become more pressing with the development of increasingly sophisticated methods for analysis of communication processes and longitudinal data. At first, calculating change scores seems to be simply a matter of subtraction; however, change scores suffer from several problems, including low reliability, "regression toward the mean," and a tendency for measures to change in meaning to participants over time (Collins & Horn, 1991; Cronbach & Furby, 1970). The upshot of this argument is that researchers should use simple change scores very carefully, or they should use alternative methods, such as analysis of covariance with pretest scores as covariates (Cook & Campbell, 1979). However, some authors have argued more recently that change scores are valuable in many cases and have advanced methods for analyzing them (Burr & Nesselroade, 1990). Several of the contributors to an excellent book edited by Collins and Horn (1991) discuss the measurement of change.

A final measurement issue centers on the degree to which quantitative variables are *meaningful*. Several scholars, including Blumer (1956), Churchill (1963), and Cicourel (1964), have raised objections to quantitative measurement as traditionally practiced. One

stems from the fact that once a variable or construct is defined, it often becomes a taken-for-granted feature of the observer's or theorist's world, regardless of whether it has meaning or impact in the participants' world. Constructs such as attitude, norm, and attraction become second nature for the researcher, and it is easy to confuse the construct measured by a set of technical rules with the phenomenon itself. One problem with this interpretation of variables is that it may "freeze" or present too static a picture of a construct that is negotiated or "in process" (Cicourel, 1972). Also, it may hide cases where a concept is forced into a measurement scale that oversimplifies or distorts it (Churchill, 1963). These arguments can be taken as indictments of quantitative research, but we believe it is more profitable to consider them as topoi for critiquing and gaining insight into our constructs and measures. Studies such as Rawlins's (1983) research on openness clearly illustrate the power of scrutinizing traditional concepts.

ANALYTIC TECHNIQUES

In this section we group analytic techniques into five genres: experimental design; statistical model testing; factoring, scaling, and clustering; time-series techniques; and change and development methods. For each genre, we discuss its core assumptions and range of applications, predominant techniques, affinities to the templates, strengths and weaknesses, and new methodological opportunities. At the conclusion of this section we discuss several other techniques, including network analysis and meta-analysis.

Experimental Design

When social scientists discuss methods, their most general concerns are with matters of measurement, design, and analysis. We will devote little attention to the second area, design, because it has seen little fundamental change in recent years (for extensive treatments of experimental design, see, e.g., Kirk, 1982; Winer, Brown, & Michels, 1991).

The design of studies is concerned with three goals: testing for the effects of interest, avoiding or controlling threats to inferential validity, and generalizing the conclusions. It takes a great deal of ingenuity to control distracting or deceptive elements in order to isolate and analyze the effects of interest. Most research in interpersonal communication tests for effects through simple, traditional designs such as two- and three-way completely crossed ANOVAs or analysis of covariance. More complex and "exotic" designs, such as Latin square or blocked designs, have advantages over the simple designs in terms of efficiency, power, and control. A study of second-guessing by Hewes, Graham, Doelger, and Pavitt (1985) provides a good example of this, as does the within-subjects ANOVA design discussed in the subsection below on interdependence.

The second goal, that of dealing with validity threats, has been articulated by Campbell and Stanley (1966). In their extension, Cook and Campbell (1979) note four major types of validity: the construct validity of causes and effects, statistical conclusion validity, internal validity, and external validity. These refer to our confidence in our ability to answer four questions about a study: (a) Do the manipulations and measurements correspond to the variables we intend to study? (b) Do the data indicate a relationship between these variables? (c) Given the relationship, is it causal in this study? (d) Can we generalize the presence of causation to a wider context than this sample? Cook and Campbell emphasize internal validity, although they note debate on whether it should be accorded this primacy (pp. 83-91).

Randomization and controlled manipulation help to guard against validity threats. The classic experimental design, with random assignment to treatments and controlled manipulation, provides the most rigorous protection. It enables unambiguous identification of causal effects and partitioning of variance among effects. Neither nonexperimental designs, which do not control manipulations, nor quasi-experimental designs, which do not have random assignment, permit this degree of protection or inferential rigor. However, analytic adjustments are available for improving the rigor of these designs (Cook & Campbell, 1979). Path analysis and structural equation modeling (see below) permit causal analysis in nonexperimental designs. There are also methods for achieving approximate variance partitions for factors in nonexperimental designs (McPhee & Seibold, 1979).

The third goal, generalization, is the one on which most controversy in interpersonal communication research has centered. Jackson and Jacobs (1983) have raised concerns regarding how messages are experimentally represented, and Brashers and Jackson (1999) have recently addressed this issue. These authors note that studies often use a single message to represent a communication variable category or level. For example, Brashers and Jackson argue that of the experiments reported in *Human Communication Research* in the 15 years preceding 1999, only one-third of those that should have used replications of messages or situations actually did so. And when multiple messages are employed, an incorrect statistical tool (fixed-effects rather than random-effects ANOVA) is almost always employed. Neither procedure supports conclusions that generalize to messages in general, and Jackson and Jacobs show that general conclusions drawn in the past are subject to error. They recommend that researchers develop multiple messages, despite the difficulty of that enterprise, and that they use random-effects ANOVA procedures that treat message variations as nonsystematic representations of the broader class of messages.

Jackson and Jacobs's (1983) essay has generated considerable controversy and reflection, and several qualifications and counterarguments have been raised (Burgoon, Hall, & Pfau, 1991; Hunter, Hamilton, & Allen, 1989; Jackson, O'Keefe, Jacobs, & Brashers, 1989; Morley, 1988). Morley (1988) and others have noted that the use of fixed-effects designs is appropriate when the levels chosen exhaust all possible levels of the message phenomenon (e.g., the speaker is male or female) or when generalizing only to the fixed levels is conceptually important. Morley also notes some problems with the quasi-F statistic typically used to analyze random-effects designs, including low power and lack of a reference distribution. Hunter et al. (1989) argue that individual studies using single messages have definite advantages, because they allow researchers to examine a variety of rigorously controlled studies for differential message impacts using meta-analysis. For instance, Greene and Ravizza (1995) used four experiments, each one building on the one before it, in examining how thought complexity affects people's ability to articulate messages fluently.

The controversy has not yet been resolved. Over the long run, both strategies enable researchers to detect general treatment effects and treatment-by-replication interactions that indicate variations in treatment effects across different message contexts. And meta-analysis (see below) of multiple studies does permit the attainment of large sample sizes and diversity of experimental contexts, which will enhance the generalizability of conclusions. Nonetheless, we think the multiple-message, random-effects strategy that Jackson and Jacobs (1983) advocate is preferable. First, single-message studies are unable to detect treatment-by-message interactions or to distinguish their effects from those of a main treatment effect of theoretical interest. They are thus liable to have an inflated Type I error rate, and even if multiple messages are used, fixed-effect statistics incur this inflated error rate (Brashers & Jackson, 1999).

Second, the random-effects approach seems to possess the advantages of "face validity" and caution. Most researchers do, in practice, seek to generalize ideas about message variables to an infinite population of messages characterized by those variables, and the random-effects strategy registers that intent. And if the message context in which a treatment is embedded does make a difference, the random-effects strategy has protected us.

The cornerstone of experimental statistics, analysis of variance, continues to be preeminent in interpersonal communication research. ANOVA examines how differences in group membership lead to variation in a dependent variable. Its multivariate companion, MANOVA, explores group differences in the linear combination of dependent variables (allowing for their intercorrelation). Critically, the violation of certain assumptions can dramatically change outcomes of ANOVA and MANOVA. In particular, ANOVA and MANOVA are susceptible to violations of the independence assumption (i.e., that every observation refers to a unique case; Bray & Maxwell, 1985). When conducting research involving dyads or groups, researchers need to be careful to avoid the violation of independence or somehow to build interdependence into the analyses, a topic we address below. Moreover, MANOVA and ANOVA are susceptible to violations of the assumption of homogeneity of variance across groups, especially when group sizes are unequal (Bray & Maxwell, 1985; Wilcox, 1987). Wilcox (1987), for example, marshals convincing evidence that heterogeneous variance can be much more damaging than is commonly assumed, inflating Type I error rates as much as fourfold and seriously reducing statistical power. He suggests several alternatives to the traditional F test that may be more appropriate when one finds significant heterogeneity. On a different note, Rosenthal and Rosnow (1985) have argued that when the researcher has definite expectations regarding the pattern of results across cells, omnibus *F* tests may be inappropriate and may actually miss real differences. Instead, they recommend the use of planned contrasts that test the predicted pattern of means.

MANOVA and ANOVA provide very different results and are based on different terms in examining the relative amount of systematic variance due to group membership versus error. Current thinking on the topic indicates that researchers should first determine whether their hypotheses point to the use of a multivariate test. For example, if a researcher wants to examine the manner in which equity group membership affects the overall use of five proactive and constructive relational maintenance behaviors, then MANOVA would be the appropriate statistic. But if the researcher hypothesizes that equity groups affect only two maintenance behaviors (e.g., positivity and assurances), then ANOVA would be the more appropriate statistic.

Conventional wisdom and textbooks have long held that MANOVA should be used before ANOVA, to reduce the likelihood of Type I error due to undetected experiment-wise error. Recently, however, scholars have noted that MANOVA does little to prevent against Type I errors in subsequent univariate tests using ANOVA (e.g., Huberty & Morris, 1989; Keselman et al., 1998; Sheehan-Holt, 1998). In addition, one might find significant multivariate effects using MANOVA but no significant univariate effects using ANOVA, or one might find significant univariate effects but no multivariate effects (Bray & Maxwell, 1985). Huberty and Morris (1989) identify conditions that warrant the use of ANOVA rather than MANOVA (e.g., when the research is exploratory, when outcome variables are conceptually independent) and conditions when MANOVA is appropriate, but not ANOVA (e.g., identification of an underlying construct that explains the set of dependent variables). If the researcher opts for ANOVA, he or she must anticipate how many ANOVAs

a given hypothesis requires. If more than one, then the researcher should correct the alpha level by dividing alpha by the number of comparisons (the Bonferroni procedure) or by adjusting alpha using a multiplicative inequality (Huberty & Morris, 1989). If the hypothesis can be tested with a single ANOVA, then the alpha level associated with the omnibus *F* test does not require adjustment. Ultimately, selection of MANOVA or ANOVA depends on the assumptions behind the hypotheses to be tested, not on any presumption that MANOVA somehow warrants the use of follow-up ANOVAs.

Statistical Model-Testing Techniques

Many statistical approaches have been advanced for testing correlational or causal relationships among variables. The mainstream of statistical analysis in social science involves (a) developing a hypothesis that one or more (independent) variables are unidirectionally related to another (dependent) variable, (b) working out a statistical model that reflects this hypothesis, and (c) testing the model. This approach is clearly consistent with the hypothetico-deductive mode of inquiry. A statistical model is clearly subordinate and subsequent to the conceptual hypothesis and thus is not related to the modeling mode of inquiry.

The decision about whether a statistical model fits a particular data set can be highly complex, but usually it simply consists of rejecting a general null hypothesis of no relationship between dependent and independent variables in favor of the hypothesis of relationship. Often the statistical models are special versions of the "general linear model," a relatively simple and flexible functional form that is very well understood by statisticians and is easy to use in most cases of interest to social scientists (Searle, 1971).

The array of techniques for statistical hypothesis testing include correlation,

ANOVA, regression, MANOVA, canonical correlation, path analysis, structural equation modeling, and multivariate categorical analysis (log-linear analysis, logit analysis, and their relatives). This literature is so large that it is impractical for us to attempt a summary here. Particularly good sources include Gujarati (1995), Pedhazur (1982), and Weisberg (1985) for regression and its variants; Keppel (1991) and Bray and Maxwell (1985) for MANOVA; Morrison (1990) and Tatsuoka (1988) for multivariate techniques in general; Maruyama (1998) for structural equation modeling and path analysis; and Bishop, Feinberg, and Holland (1975), Christensen (1990), and Feinberg (1989) for multivariate categorical analysis. Instead of reviewing how researchers can use all of these statistical tools, we first briefly illustrate model building using multiple regression (MR). Then we focus on four statistical tools that have gained momentum since the previous edition of this *Handbook:* structural equation modeling (SEM), meta-analysis, interdependence modeling, and multivariate categorical analysis.

The researcher's goal in using multiple regression is to identify the set of independent variables (IVs) that best predicts variation in the dependent variable (DV). Assuming that assumptions of MR have been met (e.g., the IVs are not highly correlated with each other), the researcher must decide how to enter the IVs to compose the regression model. Several methods for inclusion are standard, including stepwise, forced entry, and hierarchical. *Stepwise* regression involves the consideration of all the independent variables simultaneously in order to identify which IV is the most predictive, which then constitutes Model 1. Once variance accounted for by the most important variable is explained, then the second most powerful variable is identified using partial regression, which yields Model 2. This procedure continues until no new variance in the DV can be explained. The problem with stepwise regression is that it says little theoretically

about the relative influence of the models. Moreover, it is sample dependent, meaning that the pattern of correlations and partial correlations might change in subtle but theoretically significant ways across samples. Stepwise regression is best used when the researcher has a general research question (e.g., Which maintenance strategies are most predictive of commitment?). Using *forced entry,* the researcher enters the variables in a predetermined manner, sometimes individually and sometimes in groups (blocks). In this way, the researcher can assess in a planned manner whether the increases in variance explained by the addition of new IVs are significant. Using *hierarchical* regression, the researcher creates alternative sets of models, entering one IV first in one model and entering it last in an alternative model. In this manner, the researcher can assess which model is most powerful and parsimonious. Forced entry and hierarchical approaches are better suited for testing specified hypotheses or models than stepwise regression, because they rely on the researcher's thinking to set up their models.

Structural Equation Modeling

The use of structural equation modeling, which subsumes causal modeling and path analysis, has grown rapidly in interpersonal research. SEM is a technique for stipulating models and assessing their fit to data, where the models can involve relationships among empirical variates and specified latent constructs, and "fit to data" involves both overall match to a covariance matrix and estimation and testing of specific model parameters. Regression and factor analysis can be treated as special cases of SEM, but SEM's main attraction is its power to express varied theoretical structures of relations as testable models.

In Table 2.1, we list research using SEM published in national and regional journals between 1994 and 2000; this list displays the

Table 2.1   Causal Modeling Articles in Communication: 1994-2000

Article	Procedure	Measurement Model Fit?	Theoretical Model Fit?	Fit Measurement Model First?	Used Modification Indices to Change Model?	Statistical Package Used
Caughlin & Vangelisti, 2000	Path analysis		X			EQS
Goldsmith et al., 2000	CFA	X			Yes	EQS 5.6
Emmers-Sommer & Allen, 1999	OLS causal modeling		X			Path
Gilbertson et al., 1998	CFA	X			Yes; dropped one item	
Solomon & Samp, 1998	CFA	X				LIMSTAT
Burleson et al., 1996	CFA (ML)	X				
Mitchell, 2000	Path analysis		X			
Le Poire et al., 1999	CFA	X				LIMSTAT
Boster et al., 1999	OLS causal modeling	(Used CFA separately for one variable)	X			
Dillard et al., 1999	CFA	X			Yes	LIMSTAT
Caughlin & Vangelisti, 1999	Path analysis		X			
Burgoon et al., 1999	CFA (least squares, oblique multiple-group analysis)	X			Yes; dropped one item	PACKAGE
Goldsmith & MacGeorge, 2000	CFA	X			Yes; dropped one item	
Jordan, 1998	SEM		X			LISREL 8.1
Dillard et al., 1995	SEM (ML)	X (all were single-item measures)	X	X	Yes	EQS/ Windows

(Continued)

Table 2.1 (continued)

Article	Procedure	Measurement Model Fit?	Theoretical Model Fit?	Fit Measurement Model First?	Used Modification Indices to Change Model?	Statistical Package Used
Scheer & Cline, 1994	SEM (weighted least-squares estimation)	X (3 variables measured by single items)	X	X (used exploratory FA on scales)		LISREL 7 (PRELIS used)
Witte & Morrison, 2000	CFA, path analysis	X	X	(CFA and path models completely separate)		PATH for path analysis
Guerrero et al., 1995	CFA	X				LISREL 7
MacIntyre et al., 1999	SEM	X	X	Unclear		AMOS 3.5
Floyd & Morman, 1998	CFA (least squares, oblique, multiple groups)	X				PACKAGE
Keaten et al., 1997	CFA	X				
Roberto & Finucane, 1997	CFA	X				PACKAGE
Hample & Dallinger, 1995	CFA	X			Yes; modified subscales	
Martin & Anderson, 1995	Path analysis		X			
Sassi & Greene, 1998	Path analysis (ML)		X		Deleted one path non-significant due to multi-collinearity	LISREL
Samp & Solomon, 1998	CFA	X				LIMSTAT
Thomas & Levine, 1994	Path analysis		X			

NOTE: CFA = confirmatory factor analysis; SEM = structural equation modeling; OLS = ordinary least squares; ML = maximum likelihood. An empty cell indicates a "no" answer or no information in the article.

growth in SEM use to the point where it is now a standard data-analytic option. Its growth is due to developments such as user-friendly programs, more powerful and flexible software (reviewed below), and useful teaching/learning tools and research models. SEM can be used to test traditional path models, causal models with unobserved latent variables with multiple indicators, causal models with feedback loops, models of experiments, multilevel models, and longitudinal/developmental models, any of which can incorporate correlated errors and unreliability of measurement, and it can also be used to conduct confirmatory factor analysis. Methods to analyze nonlinear and interaction models (see Li et al., 1998) and models involving categorical or nonnormal data exist, but they are currently being developed toward greater flexibility.

The first step in SEM is theory-based stipulation of relations among constructs. Often, this can be separated into stipulation of a "measurement model" linking specific indices to the latent or theoretical constructs they measure and stipulation of a "theoretical model" capturing the theoretical relations among the latent constructs (Anderson & Gerbing, 1988). However, this division of models assumes that measurement concerns are independent of theory and thus is controversial (Hayduk, 1996). The second step requires the researcher to convert stipulated relations into software instructions, an operation that is often challenging but has been eased recently by the development of user-friendly software such as AMOS (Arbuckle, 1995). The next step is actual estimation, possibly in two stages and often in contrast to a number of predetermined comparison models (Maruyama, 1998, p. 248). The third step is model assessment based on output, which includes parameter estimates, deviations of real from estimated covariances, and a variety of indices of model performance relative to both data and other models, plus, in some cases, cross-validation results.

West (2000) provides a list of SEM software; however, this list does not include Mplus, a recent, well-received software package adapted to categorical and other ill-behaved data forms (see the on-line list of recent papers using special Mplus features at http://www.statmodel.com/index2.html). Many packages have supplemented maximum likelihood analysis with generalized least squares and other robust routines that are less dependent on the multivariate normality of the data.

Although maximum likelihood (ML) analyses have undergone critiques that have spawned varied alternatives, the ML approach seems to have considerable robustness (see Fan, Thompson, & Wang, 1999; Olsson, Troye, & Howell, 1999). We should mention one quite different alternative, partial least squares (PLS), developed by Wold (e.g., 1985) and implemented in LVPLS (Lohmöller, 1984). PLS uses iterative estimation among sets of variable indicators to create linear composites of indicators that stand in place of latent variables and allow estimation of inter-variable parameters. PLS has several advantages: It is quite robust to distributional variety, it avoids indeterminate solutions and other problems plaguing systems estimation procedures, and it gives direct factor scores for the latent variables. On the other hand, the PLS process creates inconsistent estimators that may be biased, especially for small sample sizes and unbalanced sets of indicators. According to Jöreskog and Wold (1982), "ML is theory-oriented, and emphasizes the transition from exploratory to confirmatory analysis. PLS is primarily intended for causal-predictive analysis in situations of high complexity but low theoretical information" (p. 270).

Developments are so rapid and complex in SEM that Hayduk (1996) advises ignoring the literature for a few years, until things settle.

Nonetheless, two issues require attention. First is the issue of fit indices, which are summarized in Maruyama (1998). To be sure, assessing the fit of a model is vital for practically all analytic purposes. Yet fit indices involve a number of problems. Almost all authorities now are skeptical about the traditional and most popular indices—chi-square, chi square/ df, GFI, and AGFI. Some sources present cut-off values for good fit (e.g., Schumacker & Lomax, 1996), but the indices themselves have been shown to perform badly or lead to alarmingly high combinations of Type I and Type II error (Hu & Bentler, 1999). Some indices attempt to take model parsimony into account, yet there is no good formula for weighing parsimony against raw fit, and different indices do that differently (Hayduk, 1996). Indices also perform differently for different estimation procedures (Fan et al., 1999). Some studies have supported the value of McDonald's (1989) noncentrality index and the AIC (e.g., Bandalos, 1997; Williams & Holahan, 1994), yet Raykov (2000) finds the former highly errant and Hayduk (1996) attacks the latter for multiple formulas misused in software, lack of norm, and oversensitivity. Hayduk seems to provide the best advice: that researchers should provide information about chi-square, degrees of freedom, sample size, and an index such as the AGFI, as well as information about any patterning of residuals. We would add to that Hu and Bentler's (1999) mandate to depend on a combination of the RMSEA (see also Fan et al., 1999), with the cutoff shifted to >.06, and the SRMR, with cutoff >.09. Their Monte Carlo study showed this combination of criteria resulted in very low Type I and Type II error rates.

A second issue is model modification. Any statistical routine providing parameter estimates also provides information that allows the analyst to modify the model so that it conforms to the data. However, existing arguments suggest that this is not a prudent course of action. Researchers who perform such modifications fly in the face of arguments and simulation results showing that empirically motivated model modification is rarely successful. MacCallum (1986) found success in strikingly low percentages of cases in a simulation study: for sample size of 300, modification procedures led to a correct model 40% (counting liberally) or 4% (counting stringently) of the time; for samples of 100, the modification procedures *never* led to the correct model. There seem to be three reasons for this. First, SEM procedures are so flexible that they can fit a set of parameters even for an incorrectly specified model. Second, modification capitalizes on chance by fitting data features that are the result of sampling error. Third, modification is likely to move toward not the true causal model but a statistically equivalent, theoretically invalid one. "For essentially any model there exist potentially many equivalent models representing equally plausible, distinct means of description and explanation of the analyzed data" (Raykov & Penev, 1999, p. 199). This problem is especially insidious because cross-validation and replications cannot correct such errors. A study that includes some new variables and a different causal network but can still test the original theory is one way of avoiding the equivalence trap. We are happy to note that of the studies listed in Table 2.1, almost none of the researchers made significant model modifications. Having said this, we must note an interesting routine called TETRAD (Scheines, Spirtes, Glymour, & Meek, 1994), which searches for covariance patterns that signal an absence of direct causal path between two variables, pruning down to a minimal empirically adequate model, in a way that can be constrained by theoretical assumptions.

Interdependence Models

Interpersonal research often involves the observation of dyads or groups. However, most statistics are predicated on the assumption that units of analysis are independent of each other, and violation of the independence assumption leads to inflated levels of alpha or beta error that can go undetected. If scores within dyads are correlated, which they often are, then interpersonal researchers are faced with a quandary regarding how to analyze their dyadic or group data. One can *divide* the data into two sets and analyze them separately (or throw out the data from one person); one can *control* for the influence of nonindependence by building the partner's score into the actor's analysis (e.g., insert husband commitment measure as an independent variable that predicts wife commitment); or one can examine the nature of interdependence, which explicitly indicates separate effects—those due to the individual actor and those due to types of interdependence. The first two approaches reflect a loss of information, whereas the last best promotes an understanding of the dyad as an interdependent system (Gonzalez & Griffin, 1997).

Kenny (1996b) specifies three types of interdependence that are common in relationship research. Figure 2.3 illustrates these three types as models, using relational maintenance behaviors as the independent variable and commitment as the dependent variable. *M* refers to maintenance behaviors and *C* refers to commitment; *H* denotes husband and *W* denotes wife. In the first model, the partner effect refers to how much husband maintenance affects wife commitment, and vice versa. In the second model, mutual influence occurs when husband and wife commitment affect each other. In the third model, both husband and wife maintenance constitute an overall measure of maintenance and, similarly, husband and wife commitment compose an overall measure of maintenance.

In assessing the actor-partner interdependence model, two sources of variance in commitment are examined: The first source is the influence of the actor's independent variable on the actor's dependent variable; the second

is the influence of the partner's independent variable on the actor's dependent variable. To assess the relative influence of each source of variance, one measures the actor effect by summing the between and within dyadic variation, whereas one measures the partner effect by using difference scores (for a full explanation of procedures, see Kashy & Kenny, 1999; Kenny, 1996b). Unstandardized pooled regression coefficients are then used to indicate, for both members of the dyad, actor and partner effects. One could answer the question of whether the actor's maintenance behaviors or the partner's maintenance behaviors more powerfully predict relational satisfaction, and whether there are any differences for husbands and wives. For example, Cole (2001) was able to distinguish the relative influence of self and partner deception on relational satisfaction. Of many findings, Cole found that self-reported deception was significantly and negatively related to the actor's own relational satisfaction, whereas the partner's self-reported deception was unrelated to the actor's relational satisfaction.

The second model in Figure 2.3 represents how the partner's dependent variable affects the actor's dependent variable, in addition to the influence due to the actor's independent variable. Researchers using this model theorize that only actor effects on the independent variable exist; that is, no statistical procedures are used to assess partner effects given a priori theoretical hypotheses about the causal links among the variables. Moreover, the mutual influence on the dependent variable is assumed to be equal, such that one can use the intraclass correlation in a formula to assess mutual influence (Kenny, 1996b, p. 289). The intraclass correlation is used when partners cannot be consistently identified (e.g., gay or lesbian partners) versus when partners can be identified (e.g., husbands and wives). When partners can be identified, then the Pearson correlation coefficient is used to assess mutual dependence.

Actor-Partner Interdependence

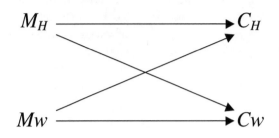

Mutual Influence

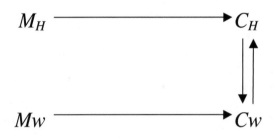

Common Fate

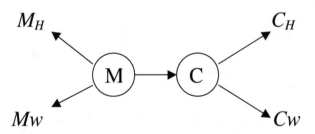

Figure 2.3   Models of Interdependence

SOURCE: Adapted from Kenny (1996b, p. 281).

NOTE: M = maintenance behavior, C = commitment, H = husband, W = wife.

Finally, the common fate model examines the extent to which the association between variables is influenced by an unmeasured external force (Kenny, 1996b). To obtain measures of common fate, one computes and correlates the means for the dyad for each variable (Kenny, 1996b). One then adjusts these correlations by the within-dyad correlation (for a thorough description, see Kenny & La Voie, 1984). This adjustment is warranted to control for individual variation in the measures. For example, husband and wife relational maintenance measures are averaged and correlated with the couple satisfaction average. These correlations are then adjusted by the within-dyad correlations for both maintenance and satisfaction. The resulting correlation reveals the extent to which an external factor impinges on both husband and wife assessments.

These interdependence models represent variations on the "social relations" model, which we have discussed in our chapter in the previous edition of this volume (Poole & McPhee, 1994). More generally, the social relations model is a *multilevel model*, designed to distinguish effects due to individuals from effects due to relations between those individuals or to larger social units of which the individuals are members (family, school, organization) (Kenny, 1996a; Snijders & Kenny, 1999). Multilevel models enable researchers to sort out effects due to individual characteristics or psychological processes from those due to social processes and interaction. The "social relations model" (Kenny & La Voie, 1984) uses data from cases in which each person in a group interacts with everyone else to isolate effects on each person's behavior due to (a) the person's own general tendencies, (b) the general tendencies of the other with whom the person is interacting, (c) the specific relationship of the two, and (d) occasion-specific error variance. For example, Dindia et al. (1997) found that different types of self-disclosure were affected by the relationship, actor, and partner effects. They concluded that strangers engaged in more low intimate evaluations than spouses, that certain people exhibited stable disclosure behaviors, and that the partner effect accounted for about 10% of the variance in cross-sex descriptive disclosures, meaning that some people were able to elicit descriptive disclosures across actors. Other approaches to multilevel analyses exist (Bryk & Raudenbush, 1992; Collins & Horn, 1991).

Categorical Data Modeling

For some time, interpersonal communication researchers have utilized categorical data analysis methods, most notably *log-linear analysis* of multiway contingency tables (e.g.,

Burggraf & Sillars, 1987; Honeycutt, Cantrill, Kelly, & Lambkin, 1998). Goodman (e.g., 1978) and Bishop et al. (1975; Feinberg, 1989) have developed different approaches to log-linear analysis. For the analysis of binary data, these methods are both logically and empirically superior to ordinary least squares regression analysis of dummy variables (Knoke, 1975). For the prediction of binary dependent variables by continuous and categorical variables, logistic regression is the method of choice (Hosmer & Lemeshow, 1989; for applications, see Bell, Abrams, Clark, & Schlatter, 1996; Katz, 1994). Methods have been developed for the analysis of causal relationships among categorical variables (Goodman, 1978) and for the analysis of social interaction (Bakeman & Gottman, 1997).

Our review of the use of categorical data analysis in interpersonal communication found nine articles published since 1995. Six of these used categorical modeling, five fitting log-linear models, and two fitting logistic regressions. In view of the fact that many interpersonal constructs are categorical in nature, the relative scarcity of this type of analysis is surprising.

Factoring, Scaling, and Clustering

Researchers have developed a number of techniques for describing or dimensionalizing data. Techniques that do this for items or persons include factor analysis, multidimensional scaling (MDS), and cluster analysis. The three techniques are similar in some respects, but there are critical differences. All three methods permit the researcher to identify clusters of items or persons. However, factor analysis and MDS are more complex than cluster analysis because they also identify dimensions along which items or persons vary. In turn, factor analysis is more complex than MDS procedures because it assumes that the dimensions reflect variables or constructs underlying the items or persons, whereas MDS makes no such assumption.

Factor Analysis

This is still the most common clustering technique in interpersonal communication research. As noted above, the factor-analytic model posits one or more factors underlying a set of items (for good treatments of factor analysis, see Cureton & D'Agostino, 1983; McDonald, 1985). The factors may be a personality variable, such as communication apprehension, or variables that allow discrimination among or ordering of a number of stimuli, such as the compliance-gaining situations studied by Cody, Woelfel, and Jordan (1983). In each case, participants respond to a number of items designed to be representative of the underlying constructs and the analysis derives the factors basic to the items. Compared with the other two clustering methods, factor analysis is advantageous because it attempts to allow for measurement error through the use of commonalities. It also permits a clear determination of the amount of variance in the items accounted for by the factor solution.

Among the problems in using factor analysis is that the solution is not unique, hence interpretation of factors has a large subjective component and is influenced by the researcher's theories or preconceptions. This can be problematic because researchers often label factors with names drawn from previous factor analyses, even though different items may load on them (Cronkhite & Liska, 1976). Second, as Cronkhite and Liska (1976) note, a factor analysis is only as good as the item pool. They recommend having participants generate items to replace the common practice of using researcher-generated items, which may artificially restrict the scope of the analysis. Cronkhite (1976) also found instability in evaluative-factor solutions based on rater-concept-scale

interactions, suggesting that much more care must be taken with factor-analytic designs than is often recognized.

There are at least two problems with current uses of factor analysis in interpersonal communication research. First, interpersonal communication research has placed too much emphasis on orthogonal factor rotations. Although orthogonality guarantees that dimensions are independent, it is unclear why this is always a desirable property. Often participants' judgmental criteria are correlated, and forcing a solution into orthogonality may distort the representation. Using an oblique rotation may result in a better representation of underlying dimensions and certainly facilitates identification of clusters of variables.

Second, exploratory factor-analytic procedures are sometimes used to assess hypotheses about factor structures. However, factor indeterminacy makes assessments suspect. A better approach is to use confirmatory factor analysis (Bollen, 1989; McDonald, 1985). With this technique, a hypothesized factor structure is tested against the data (see, e.g., Burgoon & Hale, 1987).

Multidimensional Scaling

MDS derives a multidimensional representation of a set of items (persons) based on a measure of distance between each pair of items (see Borg & Groenen, 1997; Davison, 1983; Lingoes, Roskam, & Borg, 1979; Young, 1987). The nature of this measure can vary widely, from correlations (smaller correlations signaling greater distances) to participants' judgments of similarity of each pair of items. Varieties of MDS can be distinguished along two dimensions. First, we can distinguish metric procedures, which assume distance measures are continuous, from nonmetric procedures, which assume only that distance measures reflect a rank order of distances among points (for examples of nonmetric MDS, see Bell, 1986, and Kellermann, Reynolds, & Chen, 1991; for metric MDS applications, see Woelfel & Fink, 1980; for a critique of metric methods, see Craig, 1983). Nonmetric MDS techniques can work with ordinal or interval data not suitable for metric methods, but they do not yield unique solutions, whereas most metric techniques do. This latter property represents a clear advantage of metric techniques over factor analysis. A disadvantage of nonmetric techniques lies in the difficulty of determining the correct dimensionality of the solutions, which is normally done through comparison of a stress (or alienation) coefficient for various solutions. Distributions of stress values derived via Monte Carlo techniques make this judgment somewhat easier (Spence & Ogilvie, 1973). Weeks and Bentler (1979) compared metric and nonmetric techniques and found that metric methods gave better results than nonmetric techniques, even with rank distance data.

Second, MDS procedures that take averages or weighted averages of distances across participants as their distance measures can be distinguished from those that do not. If MDS uses social or averaged distances, it raises two questions: Does an averaged distance represent a cohesive social perception? and How does an individual solution (i.e., set of output) relate to the averaged social solution? One way to answer the first question is to answer the second, which one can do using individual-difference MDS programs such as INDSCAL (Carroll & Chang, 1970) and PINDIS (Lingoes & Borg, 1978; see also Young, 1987). The latter fits a common solution and then represents individual differences in several ways, including (a) individual weights for dimensions, like INDSCAL; (b) unique perspectives (origins) for each participant; and (c) shifts in certain items for subsets of participants. Each of these solutions has a unique psychological interpretation, and PINDIS

estimates the amount of variance accounted for by each, permitting determination of which solution, if any, is better than a common solution for all participants.

Cluster Analysis

Cluster analysis groups items on the basis of some measure of association (Arabie & Hubert, 1992; Cormak, 1971; Milligan & Cooper, 1987). These techniques operate through iteratively combining (or dividing) items and clusters, one pair at a time. Milligan and Cooper (1987) identify four major types of clustering methods: (a) hierarchical methods, which start by combining entities and successively generating larger clusters (these include the most common methods used in interpersonal communication research, including single link, complete link, and group average methods); (b) partitioning methods, which start with the entire group and partition it into subsets; (c) overlapping methods, which create overlapping clusters (these include clique identification or clumping methods); and (d) ordination methods (including MDS and other scaling methods). Of the hierarchical methods, Ward's and other group-average methods generally turn out to provide the best results in Monte Carlo and other validation studies (Milligan & Cooper, 1987; Morey, Blashfield, & Skinner, 1983). For the partitioning methods, convergent K-means procedures tend to provide the best results (Milligan & Cooper, 1987). Milligan and Cooper (1987) found that no definite comparisons could be drawn between overlapping methods or seriation methods. Several tests have been developed to aid researchers in determining the numbers of clusters and in testing hypotheses about clusters (Arabie & Hubert, 1992; Milligan & Cooper, 1987).

In general, the techniques discussed in this section have been employed by researchers using hypothetico-deductive templates. Confirmatory clustering techniques have also been used by those working in the modeling templates. Factor-analytic and MDS methods can also be employed to map participants' interpretive schemes (for example, see Poole & Folger, 1981). This is useful for conventional and dialectical approaches.

Time-Series Analysis

There has been some interest in time-series analysis in interpersonal communication research (Cappella, 1980; Cappella & Planalp, 1981; Gottman, 1981; Van Lear, 1991). A number of texts are available that outline time-series procedures for social scientists (Gottman, 1981; Gujarati, 1995; on experiment-related time-series analysis, see Cook & Campbell, 1979). Time-series analysis usually involves one or more continuous variables, measured for one or more "participants" (which may be individuals, families or other groups, and so on) at several regularly spaced points in time (40 observations is often mentioned as the minimum number of observations for a time-series analysis). Arundale (1980) provides detailed information on the importance of the length of the intervals between data points. Methods are also available for the analysis of nominal-level time series, although Markov or other stochastic models are usually utilized instead (see below).

Time-series analysis involves filtering out the random error associated with a series of data and then identifying two types of temporal dependence in observations: *autoregression* (dependence of each observation on past observations) and *moving average processes* (dependence of each observation on some of the "shocks" that caused change in past observations). Based on time-series analysis, one can answer several questions, including the following: (a) Is there order in the longitudinal process or is it random? (b) Is there a general trend in development?

and (c) Are there cycles in the data that suggest regular social processes? It is also possible to study the impacts of causal factors on time series using time-series regression and vector autoregression, and to identify relationships between time series.

Time-series methods have great potential for interpersonal communication research. They provide rigorous descriptions of the nature and constitution of temporal processes, along with clear accounts of the complexities of temporal data. Time-series methods enable us to disentangle relationships and causal effects from correlated errors common in longitudinal data (Catalano, Dooley, & Jackson, 1983, list a hierarchy of strategies). Also, knowledge of time-series methods aids one in recognizing, describing, and analyzing nonlinear models in data (Poole et al., 2000, chap. 9).

A problem with time-series techniques is that it is hard to specify the model of temporal dependence a priori. The inductive process involved in the identification of the time-series model should not extend to substantive relationships among variables. The best protection against this is to have a clear theory. Second, when temporal dependencies are more complex than the two types of dependencies identified by normal time-series analysis, these methods are liable to fail or mislead (McCleary & Hays, 1980).

The importance of theory in time-series analysis suggests that it is most often used in the hypothetico-deductive, causal template. However, it is also possible to develop models of longitudinal data that are more complex than typical time-series models. Nonlinear models such as those discussed by McPhee and Poole (1982) and Buder (1991) and by the contributors to Levine and Fitzgerald's (1991) edited volume are one class of models that could be used for this purpose. They can capture very complex, even chaotic, temporal patterns (Poole et al., 2000, chap. 9). Another alternative is event history analysis, which enables researchers to trace when critical events or turning points occur (Snyder, 1991).

Techniques for the Analysis of Change and Development Processes

Our discussion of process research and narrative explanation in the first section of this chapter highlights the unique theory and methods required for the study of change and development. Studies on development in interpersonal communication include research on interpersonal communication among children (for example, Delia, Kline, & Burleson, 1979) and relationship development (for example, Huston, Surra, Fitzgerald, & Cate, 1981; Van Lear, 1991).

At the outset it is useful to distinguish among development, change, and growth. Development is a specialized form of change that is continuous and patterned, with a clear sense of directionality, either progress or decay. Development can be distinguished from growth because it involves the interrelationship of several variables over time, whereas growth can involve simply an increase in a single variable. The study of change and development is most naturally suited for longitudinal designs that track the same participants. However, cross-sectional designs have also been used (for example, a cross-sectional study of relational development might sample couples who have been together for 1, 3, and 6 months in a single administration, as opposed to a longitudinal study tracking the couples through 6 months).

Schaie (1965) developed a comprehensive analysis of the components underlying developmental change. According to Schaie, three classes of independent variables can account for developmental changes:

1. *Age:* Variables associated with the aging process in the participant at the time of measurement. This component indexes effects tied to "purely" developmental processes.

2. *Cohort:* Variables that influence all participants born or initiated at the same time. This class includes general environmental and historical effects that the set of participants of a given age or length of participation may have experienced in common. For example, in a study conducted in 1984, middle-class couples who had been together 2 years would have gone through a recession together, whereas couples together 3 months would likely have relationships that had not been touched by serious economic fears.

3. *Time of measurement:* Variables affecting participants at the time they are measured but that are noncumulative. These have only immediate or transient effects, although their effects may be important.

Schaie and his colleagues describe several designs for sorting out which of the three effects is responsible for observed developmental changes. Clearly, only *age* effects index developmental influences in the "pure," internally driven sense. *Cohort* effects index influences of exogenous forces on development and are therefore also important. *Time of measurement* effects are accidental and do not index developmental processes. Greater attention to Schaie's components and their interrelations would pay off in enhanced understanding of interpersonal processes and greater confidence in the reliability of research results.

Poole et al. (2000) present a theoretical framework for the study of change and development processes and four classes of methods for conducting process research: sequential analysis, phasic analysis, event time-series analysis, and nonlinear process analysis. Their framework was developed for group and organizational studies, but its application to interpersonal phenomena is straightforward. Within this theoretical frame, two classes of techniques for studying development can be distinguished: techniques for describing and testing whether a given developmental pattern occurs and techniques for assessing correlational or causal relationships among developmental variables. Both of these classes enable researchers to identify and evaluate hypotheses regarding the final or formal causes shaping change and development.

Establishing Developmental Patterns and Testing Models of Change and Development

Several research tasks are involved in the study of development and change. Among these are (a) identification of the events that make up the change and development, (b) characterization of event sequences and their properties, (c) identification of temporal dependencies in event sequences, (d) testing of hypotheses of formal and final causality, (e) identification of coherent patterns that integrate narratives, and (f) evaluation of developmental models (Poole et al., 2000). Both nominal and continuous data may be used to study development and change. Nominal data generally consist of series of longitudinal observations and codings of events that describe the unfolding process, whereas continuous data are variable properties of the events (such as intensity or immediacy).

Sequential Analysis

Markov models and their relatives can be used to model event-to-event relations for nominal data (Hewes, 1975; Poole et al., 2000). These models map event patterns at the micro level, facilitating both descriptive and causal analysis. They help researchers uncover recurrent event sequences that describe larger dynamics; as these dynamics change, so too do the patterns, and Markov models can divulge significant changes. The description of event patterns can also be used to test hypotheses about narratives or other causal forces that drive them. A particularly interesting method takes the values in the Markov transition matrix as dependent variables in a causal model specifying factors that determine transition probabilities. This approach, employed by Cappella (1979, 1980), permits direct inclusion of theoretical factors in the model. We discuss lag sequential analysis, another sequential technique, in our chapter in the previous edition of this *Handbook* (Poole & McPhee, 1994).

Phasic Analysis

Phases are molar patterns of events constituted by individual events or interacts, and generally describe developmental progressions, such as the stages of development of a relationship. Holmes and Poole (1991; Poole et al., 2000) describe a flexible phase mapping method that can derive a phase sequence from categorical indicators of phases. The method does not require researchers to posit a set number of phases prior to analysis; it can adapt to the number of phases in the case at hand, and it can identify phases of varying lengths. Phase mapping makes it possible for the researcher to identify multiple sequences of development that differ qualitatively, rather than simply assessing whether, on average, observed sequences conform to a model. Phase analysis allows description of developmental patterns and comparison of these patterns to those displayed by developmental motors or more complex theories. Once a set of sequences has been identified, the researcher can identify typologies of developmental paths by using sequence comparison methods such as optimal matching and clustering (Holmes & Poole, 1991). Poole et al. (2000, chap. 7) also describe a number of other tests for specific patterns of phase development, such as Guttman scales.

Event Time-Series Models

Event time-series models enable researchers to describe and test hypotheses about whole event sequences or major segments of them. They require the event time series to be converted into continuous data, such as number of acts per month, or a rating of a property of events, such as intimacy. Time-series analysis can be used to describe long-term developmental patterns, to uncover causal and other types of relationships among developmental constructs, and to test the plausibility of individual generative mechanisms or motors (Poole et al., 2000, chap. 8). An extension of this method can be used to study nonlinear dynamic systems in development and change. Tests can be conducted to determine whether an observed pattern in an event time series reflects (a) an orderly periodic progression of stages or phases, (b) a random sequence of chance "blind" events, or (c) a seemingly random process of chaotic or colored noise events. Knowing what pattern exists in an event time series enables the researcher to construct time-series models to explain the observed dynamics.

Characterizing Developmental Curves

Methods are also available for describing and testing hypotheses about developmental curves based on continuous measures. The best known is trend analysis, which permits tests for nonlinear components of curves (quadratic, cubic, quartic, and so forth). Van Lear (1991) used Fourier analysis of time series to study relationship development. There is also a procedure that takes a set of curves for a sample of participants and groups the participants together based on similarity in development (Huston et al., 1981).

Relationships Among Variables

Two types of relationships among variables can be considered in developmental studies. First, researchers may be interested in whether two or more ordered variables are linked together in developmental processes—that is, whether they codevelop or one leads to another. For example, this issue is very important in studies of the development of communicative skills. Are certain skills correlated and, therefore, related to an underlying developmental

process, or does one skill presuppose (or prefigure) another? It is also important for phenomena that involve parallel development on two or more variables. For example, relational development might involve parallel evolution of intimacy and life aspirations, and it would be useful to know if these progress through the same stages. Poole et al. (2000, chap. 8) discuss methods of studying codeveloping relationships with time-series analysis. It is also possible to use factor analysis to determine whether a single dimension underlies diverse developmental phenomena (Bentler, 1973). For example, Rubin (1973) found a single factor for measures of four types of egocentrism—communicative, cognitive, spatial, and role-taking—for children ages 2 to 8. Factor analysis can also be used to find changes in the factor structure through the course of development (Tisak & Meredith, 1990).

Researchers may also be interested in causal relationships among developmental variables. Most often, this refers to linear causality, which can be assessed through panel designs and structural equation modeling, discussed above. However, as Overton and Reese (1973) note, linear causality may hold unambiguously only for mechanistic developmental models. Another class of models, organismic models, posit reciprocal and dialectical causation, governed by a teleological relationship implicit in the evolving whole (Werner's theory of development is one example of an organismic model). Because it is difficult to sort out reciprocal causation (particularly in cases with uneven development), codevelopment may be the only relationship researchers can establish for many organismic models.

Miscellaneous Issues

Statistical Power

The important concern of statistical power applies to all procedures employing statistical tests. Power analysis is important because it permits researchers to calculate sample sizes and alpha levels needed to avoid Type II errors. It is generally recommended that estimates of power of statistical tests be reported along with tests of assumptions. In a review of communication studies, Chase and Tucker (1975) found that actual power was low for small or medium effect sizes and interaction effects, making Type II errors extremely likely. Reporting of power in communication journals has improved since Chase and Tucker's analysis, but it still seems to be a secondary concern at best. In particular, it seems rare for researchers to report power for statistical techniques that differ from the traditional F, t, and x^2 tests for which power tables are provided in Cohen's (1988) well-known book or statistical texts (see Kraemer & Thiemann, 1987). The power of tests for methods such as SEM or log-linear analysis is often omitted, despite the fact that methods for power analysis have been developed for these techniques (e.g., Kaplan, 1995; Maruyama, 1998).

Meta-Analysis

Meta-analysis has become more common in interpersonal communication research since 1990. It provides an efficient and powerful way to summarize a vast amount of data to answer a research issue, question, or hypothesis (Glass, 1977). Instead of relying on traditional narrative reviews, which are naturally prone to researchers' personal biases, the goal of conducting a meta-analysis is to find a maximally simple statistical model that can integrate and explain the results of multiple data sets. As Rosenthal (1991) notes, "Meta-analytic reviews go beyond the traditional reviews in the degree to which they are more systematic, more explicit, more exhaustive, and more quantitative" (p. 11).

In the context of interpersonal communication, meta-analysis has been applied to many research issues, including social skills, sexual coercion, and sex differences, among many other topics (for an excellent and representative anthology, see Allen, Preiss, Gayle, & Burrell, 2002). The only limitation on the topics one can address using meta-analysis is the availability of previous quantitative research on the topic of interest.

More precisely, and using various criteria for inclusion (Canary & Mattrey, 2002; Hunter & Schmidt, 1990; Rosenthal, 1991; Wolf, 1986), the researcher conducts an extensive literature review to obtain the most representative and inclusive set of findings. Of the several decisions to be made, one concerns whether unpublished studies, such as conference papers and dissertations, should be included in the sample. This decision is critical, because many such papers are difficult to obtain, have not passed peer scrutiny, and often contain more null findings than do published articles.

Next, the researcher records effect sizes, or the extent to which variables covary. In comparing groups, Cohen's (1988) d is often used, where d is the difference between two groups in terms of standard deviation units. A d of .20, for example, is equal to one-fifth of a standard deviation difference between groups that accounts for about 1% of the variance in the behavior under question. In examining associations between variables, a standardized correlation coefficient, such as r (or the multivariate correlation coefficient, R), is used; the square of the correlation term (r^2 or R^2) reflects the percentage of variance accounted for by the systematic link between or among the variables. If effect sizes are not reported, which is too often the case, the researcher can compute them (adjusting them for sample size and error; for procedures, see Rosenthal, 1991; Wolf, 1986).

Once the effect sizes are computed, the researcher can explore the manner in which these effect sizes vary due to moderating factors. For example, Dindia and Allen (1992) found that men and women varied in their self-disclosure behavior; women were slightly more likely than men to disclose. In addition,

Dindia and Allen were interested in whether the general tendency was affected by the composition of the dyad—that is, whether it was all male, all female, or mixed. They found that women were more likely than men to disclose to women and to members of the opposite sex, but men were just as likely as women to disclose to men. In addition, the researcher can explore potential connections between methods, for example, whether effects vary according to survey versus observational measures, whether the sex of the researcher affects the results, or whether year of study alters the findings.

The interpretations of meta-analyses can be controversial. For example, researchers who have conducted recent meta-analyses have reported that children are slightly *more* adjusted when living with homosexual (versus heterosexual) parents (Allen & Burrell, 1996) and that children's adjustment is not affected by divorce as much as it is by parents who engage in competitive conflict (Amato & Keith, 1991). It is possible that one could use these and other results from meta-analyses to make extraordinary conclusions and proposals (e.g., for the sake of our children, dissolve the traditional family whenever conflict arises).

The interpretation of effect sizes can also be debated. We believe that this controversy is tied to researchers' expectations about how much variance in behavior should be accounted for in various domains. Consider, for example, that people often believe that men and women behave in radically different ways. However, in two separate summaries, researchers have reported that meta-analytic studies of sex differences yield an average *d* of .23, indicating that only 1% of variation in behavior is due to sex differences (Canary & Hause, 1993; Dindia, 1998). People who assume large differences between men and women are disturbed by these findings, whereas people who do not presume large sex differences across the board have little trouble

accepting the small effect sizes due to sex (for a more complete debate on the topic, see Eagly, 1995; Hyde & Plant, 1995). Statistical criteria exist for assessing the magnitude and importance of effect sizes (e.g., Cohen, 1988). In terms of overall *d* scores, .20 is a small effect accounting for 1% of the variance, .50 is a moderate effect accounting for about 5% of the variance, and .80 constitutes a large effect accounting for about 13% of the variance (Cohen, 1988; Wolf, 1986). Over time and cases, even small effects can be quite meaningful in some contexts. In most cases, however, when one wants to make generalizations about general tendencies or associations, small effect sizes should be interpreted conservatively (i.e., small remains small unless the substantive issue calls for broader interpretation). In brief, effect sizes need to be interpreted in terms of researcher expectations, statistical properties, and practical significance.

Network Analysis

In our contribution to the previous edition of this *Handbook* (Poole & McPhee, 1994), we noted the growth and promise of interpersonal applications of network analysis (Borgatti, Everett, & Freeman, 1999). Since then, a good deal of such research has been published, but relatively little of it by communication researchers. The studies fall into two clusters: those focused on network phenomena per se and those focused on network effects on relationships. In the first group, one especially interesting study focused on changes in personal networks following the fall of communism in East Germany and found personal networks becoming smaller and more homogeneous, with high-intimacy networks that are less dense, as people rely less on personal ties to procure essential goods and less on very high trust as a basis for choosing intimates (Volker & Flap, 1995). Another researcher used logistic regression to study transitivity in personal networks (whether two of a subject's close friends know each other) and separated important effects of relational strength, relational context (shared role or group membership), and ethnic/gender homophily of the friends on the probability of their acquaintanceship (Louch, 2000). In the second group, for instance, Burger and Milardo (1995) found that wives' listing of their brothers-in-law as network members correlated with the wives' own, and their husbands', reports of relational conflict and ambivalence (perhaps as a result of withdrawal from spouse toward kin group orientation).

We should note that, unfortunately, in these studies and in the vast majority of interpersonal network studies, the "network" is the personally reported net elicited from a single subject or a couple, not the result of network data collection from all members in the personal net, let alone a larger group. Also, there may be some problems with elicitation procedures; most studies use terms such as *close friend,* but Milardo (1983) raises the concern that definitions of "closeness" vary widely, introducing important bias into personal network definition procedures. Burger and Milardo instead used a 12-question procedure crystallized by Milardo (1987). Parks and Floyd (1996) did find considerable variety in subjects' definitions of "closeness," but found considerable stability in meanings across demographic categories (which does not constitute univocality, of course). Similarly, Straits (2000) found little difference in personal nets elicited using very different terms across demographic categories. Milardo (1992) places this controversy in context by estimating the actual size (1,700) of the average personal network and noting respondents' inability to guess at its extent.

CONCLUSION

In our contributions to previous editions of this *Handbook,* we were guided by our conviction that interpersonal communication research

should pay attention to the theory-technique linkage. The present review reinforces that conviction. That researchers should justify the adequacy of their methods for answering research questions is one of the great imperatives of social science. But it is also important that we work out how templates and techniques shape theory, because this makes us aware of unspoken underlying assumptions.

The 12 templates defined by the intersections of modes of explanation and modes of inquiry are meant to define possible stances researchers might take in approaching research projects. Although some techniques simply do not fit some of the templates, generally the templates will not clearly indicate specific techniques. Rather, they suggest how techniques should be applied and how researchers should interpret the outputs. For example, experiments have been used to test hypotheses in causal, hypothetico-deductive research and to ascertain the fit of systems of rules to behavioral choices in the conventional modeling template. The differences between the templates are not in the choice of technique, but in how the experiment is set up and in how the results are interpreted.

It is important to break the tyranny of certain theory-technique links, in particular the marriage of causal explanation to hypothetico-deductive inquiry and conventional explanation to grounded inquiry. These templates represent valuable approaches, but they often discourage researchers from trying other approaches. Greater use of the other 10 templates could greatly enhance the power and sensitivity of communication research. Truly important and robust discoveries should hold across investigative domains, and exploring them with several distinct approaches should make their implications much clearer than a one-sided strategy.

It is also important to bridge the greatly overestimated gap between "qualitative" and "quantitative" approaches. Close examination of the patterns of reasoning underlying the various techniques clearly reveals affinities between the "camps." Canons of causal analysis such as the necessity to assess or control for competing causes, to establish necessary connections, to control for factors introducing errors, and to employ systematic sampling are also exhibited in qualitative reasoning. Conversely, premises of interpretive research— for example, going below surface phenomena to uncover underlying meanings, focusing on the significance or meanings of phenomena rather than objectifying them, and strategies for avoiding reification of the researcher's constructs—can be important correctives for quantitative investigations.

Much more attention needs to be directed to nonindependence of observations. The statistical methods used in the majority of studies of interpersonal communication—ANOVA, correlation, regression, SEM—presume that subject responses are independent. However, many of the most interesting contexts for interpersonal communication research, including friendships, families, peer groups, and classrooms, foster interdependencies among subject responses due to their history of previous interaction. Nonindependent data require special methods of analysis, and this review has covered several appropriate methods, including special ANOVA techniques, the interpersonal relations model, network analysis, and Markov analysis. Taking interdependence seriously implies that researchers must (a) theorize how the various forms of interdependence relate to interpersonal constructs and processes and (b) build measures to assess and deal with interdependence into their study designs. The advantage of doing so is that this positions our research as truly relational and interpersonal rather than simply the study of individual reactions.

Interpersonal communication research should also pay more attention to development and change processes. Our field has been one of the leaders in the development of methods for the study of processes. However,

most interpersonal communication research tests causal models that are not really dynamic or focuses on change over very short periods of time, on the order of hours. Long-term development and change is a fundamental part of the human condition. It is an interesting phenomenon in its own right, and it moderates the operation of many short-term phenomena in interpersonal communication. As part of a field dedicated to the study of process, interpersonal communication research should rise to the occasion.

In concluding, let us call for interpersonal communication researchers to resist the narcissism of technique. Communication research, and social science generally, continues to witness increasing emphasis on the importance of method. This is a healthy development in many respects because it contributes to more deliberate and discriminating technical choices. However, problems lurk beneath the shimmering surface. Researchers without extensive backgrounds in statistics and mathematics must take the operations of complex procedures on faith. Techniques such as MANOVA, multiple regression, time-series analysis, structural equation modeling, and complex factor-analytic or clustering procedures involve sophisticated algorithms and restrictive assumptions that can easily be misunderstood and misapplied by even the wariest investigator. The statistical properties of many procedures are not well understood, and experts acknowledge ambiguous areas. These considerations lead us to recommend that researchers take great care in interpreting the results of these procedures; the path from raw data to output is often tortuous and unclear. The only correctives are careful assessment of the assumptions underlying the methods and attention to features that might qualify results, such as standard errors of estimates, as well as a healthy dose of skepticism.

The narcissism of technique also supports another dangerous tendency—the substitution of method for quality of thought. In the end, insight and creativity are the wellsprings of good research. Without good, solid ideas, the most sophisticated and careful research strategy is fruitless. The complexities of analytic reasoning encourage greater attention to method than to ideas, and this can result in sophisticated studies that do little to advance the field. Significant progress depends on both substance and method; neither can be slighted without harm to the whole.

NOTE

1. The journals surveyed were *Communication Monographs, Communication Research, Communication Quarterly, Communication Studies, Human Communication Research, Journal of Social and Personal Relationships, Personal Relationships, Southern Communication Journal,* and *Western Communication Journal.*

REFERENCES

Achinstein, P. (1971). *Laws and explanation.* Oxford: Oxford University Press.

Allen, M., & Burrell, N. (1996). Comparing the impact of homosexual and heterosexual parents on children: Meta-analysis of existing research. *Journal of Homosexuality, 32*(2), 19-35.

Allen, M., Preiss, R. W., Gayle, B. M., & Burrell, N. (Eds.). (2002). *Interpersonal communication research: Advances through meta-analysis.* Mahwah, NJ: Lawrence Erlbaum.

Amato, P. R., & Keith, B. (1991). Parental divorce and the well-being of children: A meta-analysis. *Psychological Bulletin, 110,* 26-46.

Anderson, J. C., & Gerbing, D. W. (1988). Structural equation modeling in practice: A review and recommended two-step approach. *Psychological Bulletin, 103,* 411-423.

Anderson, P. A. (1983). Decision making by objective and the Cuban missile crisis. *Administrative Science Quarterly, 28,* 201-222.

Arabie, P., & Hubert, L. J. (1992). Combinatorial data analysis. *Annual Review of Psychology, 43,* 169-203.

Arbuckle, J. L. (1995). *Amos for Windows: Analysis of moment structures (Version 3.5).* Chicago: SmallWaters.

Arundale, R. B. (1980). Studying change over time: Criteria for sampling from continuous variables. *Communication Research, 7,* 227-263.

Bakeman, R., & Gottman, J. M. (1997). *Observing interaction: An introduction to sequential analysis.* Cambridge: Cambridge University Press.

Bandalos, D. L. (1997). Assessing sources of error in structural equation models: The effect of sample size, reliability, and model misspecification. *Structural Equation Modeling, 4,* 177-192.

Baxter, L. A., & Erbert, L. A. (2000). Perceptions of dialectical contradictions in turning points of development in heterosexual romantic relationships. *Journal of Social and Personal Relationships, 16,* 547-569.

Baxter, L. A., & Montgomery, B. M. (1996). *Relating: Dialogues and dialectics.* New York: Guilford.

Bell, R. A. (1986). The multivariate structure of communication avoidance. *Communication Monographs, 53,* 265-275.

Bell, R. A., Abrams, M. F., Clark, C. L., & Schlatter, C. (1996). The door-in-the-face compliance strategy: An individual differences analysis of two models of an AIDS fundraising context. *Communication Quarterly, 44,* 107-124.

Bentler, P. M. (1973). Assessment of developmental factor change at the individual and group level. In J. R. Nesselroade & H. W. Reese (Eds.), *Life-span developmental psychology: Methodological issues.* New York: Academic Press.

Bishop, Y. M., Feinberg, S., & Holland, P. W. (1975). *Discrete multivariate analysis: Theory and practice.* Cambridge: MIT Press.

Blumer, H. (1956). Sociological analysis and the "variable." *American Sociological Review, 21,* 683-690.

Bollen, K. A. (1989). *Structural equation models with latent variables.* New York: John Wiley.

Borg, I. (1979). Some basic concepts of facet theory. In J. C. Lingoes, E. E. Roskam, & I. Borg (Eds.), *Geometric representations of relational data: Readings in multidimensional scaling* (pp. 65-102). Ann Arbor, MI: Mathesis.

Borg, I., & Groenen, P. (1997). *Modern multidimensional scaling: Theory and applications.* New York: Springer.

Borgatti, S. P., Everett, M. G., & Freeman, L. C. (1999). *UCINET IV version 1.0 reference manual.* Natick, MA: Analytic Technologies.

Boster, F. J., Mitchell, M. M., Lapinski, M. K., Cooper, H., Orrego, V. O., & Reinke, R. (1999). The impact of guilt and type of compliance-gaining message on compliance. *Communication Monographs, 66,* 168-177.

Brashers, D. E., & Jackson, S. (1999). Changing conceptions of "message effects": A 24-year overview. *Human Communication Research, 25,* 457-477.

Bray, J. H., & Maxwell, S. E. (1985). *Multivariate analysis of variance.* Beverly Hills, CA: Sage.

Bryk, A. S., & Raudenbush, S. W. (1992). *Hierarchical linear models.* Newbury Park, CA: Sage.

Buder, E. H. (1991). A nonlinear dynamic model of social interaction. *Communication Research, 18,* 174-198.

Burger, E., & Milardo, R. M. (1995). Marital interdependence and social networks. *Journal of Social and Personal Relationships, 12,* 403-415.

Burggraf, C. S., & Sillars, A. L. (1987). A critical examination of sex differences in marital communication. *Communication Monographs, 54,* 276-294.

Burgoon, J. K., & Hale, J. C. (1987). Validation and measurement of fundamental themes of relational communication. *Communication Monographs, 54,* 19-41.

Burgoon, J. K., Johnson, M. L., & Koch, P. T. (1999). The nature and measurement of interpersonal dominance. *Communication Monographs, 65,* 308-335.

Burgoon, M., Hall, J., & Pfau, M. (1991). A test of the "messages-as-fixed-effect fallacy" argument: Empirical and theoretical implications of design choices. *Communication Quarterly, 39,* 18-34.

Burleson, B. R., Kunkel, A. W., Samter, W., & Werking, K. J. (1996). Men's and women's evaluations of communication skills in personal relationships: When sex differences make a difference—and when they don't. *Journal of Social and Personal Relationships, 13,* 201-224.

Burleson, B. R., Wilson, S. R., Waltman, M. S., Goering, E. M., Ely, T. K., & Whaley, B. B. (1988). Item desirability effects in compliance-gaining research: Seven studies documenting artifacts in the strategy selection procedure. *Human Communication Research, 14,* 429-486.

Burnett, R. (1991). Accounts and narratives. In B. M. Montgomery & S. Duck (Eds.), *Studying interpersonal interaction* (pp. 121-140). New York: Guilford.

Burr, J. A., & Nesselroade, J. R. (1990). Change measurement. In A. von Eye (Ed.), *Statistical methods in longitudinal research: Vol. 1. Principles and structuring change* (pp. 3-34). London: Academic Press.

Campbell, D. T., & Stanley, J. C. (1966). *Experimental and quasi-experimental designs for research.* Skokie, IL: Rand McNally.

Canary, D. J. (1992). *Manual for coding conversational argument* (rev.). Unpublished manuscript, Arizona State University, Hugh Downs School of Human Communication.

Canary, D. J., & Hause, K. S. (1993). Is there any reason to research sex differences in communication? *Communication Quarterly, 41,* 129-144.

Canary, D. J., & Mattrey, M. J. (2002). How does meta-analysis represent our knowledge of interpersonal communication? In M. Allen, R. W. Preiss, B. M. Gayle, & N. Burrell (Eds.), *Interpersonal communication research: Advances through meta-analysis* (pp. 389-406). Mahwah, NJ: Lawrence Erlbaum.

Caplan, S. E., & Greene, J. O. (1999). Acquisition of message-production skill by younger and older adults: Effects of age, task complexity, and practice. *Communication Monographs, 66,* 31-48.

Cappella, J. N. (1977). Research methodology in communication: Review and commentary. In B. D. Ruben (Ed.), *Communication yearbook 1* (pp. 37-53). New Brunswick, NJ: Transaction.

Cappella, J. N. (1979). Talk-silence sequences in informal conversations I. *Human Communication Research, 6,* 3-17.

Cappella, J. N. (1980). Talk and silence sequences in informal conversations II. *Human Communication Research, 6,* 130-145.

Cappella, J. N., & Planalp, S. (1981). Talk and silence sequences in informal conversations III: Interspeaker influence. *Human Communication Research, 7,* 117-132.

Carroll, J. D., & Chang, J. J. (1970). Analysis of individual differences in multidimensional scaling via an N-way generalization of Eckart-Young decomposition. *Psychometrika, 35,* 283-320.

Catalano, R. A., Dooley, D., & Jackson, R. (1983). Selecting a time-series strategy. *Psychological Bulletin, 94,* 506-523.

Caughlin, J. P., & Vangelisti, A. L. (1999). Desire for change in one's partner as a predictor of the demand/withdraw pattern of marital communication. *Communication Monographs, 66,* 66-89.

Caughlin, J. P., & Vangelisti, A. L. (2000). An individual difference explanation of why married couples engage in the demand/withdraw pattern of conflict. *Journal of Social and Personal Relationships, 17,* 523-551.

Charmaz, K. (2000). Grounded theory: Objectivist and constructivist methods. In N. K. Denzin & Y. S. Lincoln (Eds.), *Handbook of qualitative research* (2nd ed., pp. 509-535). Thousand Oaks, CA: Sage.

Chase, L. J., & Tucker, R. K. (1975). A power-analytic examination of contemporary communication research. *Communication Monographs, 42,* 29-41.

Christensen, R. (1990). *Log-linear models.* New York: Springer-Verlag.

Churchill, L. (1963). Types of formalization in small group research. *Sociometry, 26,* 373-390.

Cicourel, A. V. (1964). *Method and measurement in sociology.* New York: Free Press.

Cicourel, A. V. (1972). Basic and normative rules in the negotiation of status and role. In D. Sudnow (Ed.), *Studies in social interaction* (pp. 229-258). New York: Free Press.

Cicourel, A. V. (1980). Three models of discourse analysis: The role of social structure. *Discourse Processes, 3,* 101-132.

Cody, M. J., Canary, D. J., & Smith, S. W. (1994). Compliance-gaining goals: An inductive analysis of actors' goal types, strategies, and successes. In J. A. Daly & J. M. Wiemann (Eds.), *Strategic interpersonal communication* (pp. 33-90). Hillsdale, NJ: Lawrence Erlbaum.

Cody, M. J., Woelfel, M. L., & Jordan, W. J. (1983). Dimensions of compliance-gaining situations. *Human Communication Research, 9,* 99-113.

Cohen, J. (1988). *Statistical power analysis for the behavioral sciences* (2nd ed.). Hillsdale, NJ: Lawrence Erlbaum.

Cole, T. (2001). Lying to the one you love: The use of deception in romantic relationships. *Journal of Social and Personal Relationships, 18,* 107-129.

Collins, L. M., & Horn, J. L. (1991). *Best methods for the study of change.* Washington, DC: American Psychological Association.

Cook, T. D., & Campbell, D. T. (1979). *Quasi-experimentation: Design and analysis issues for field settings.* Chicago: Rand McNally.

Cormak, R. M. (1971). A review of classification. *Journal of the Royal Statistical Society, 143,* 321-367.

Craig, R. T. (1983). Galilean rhetoric and practical theory. *Communication Monographs, 50,* 395-412.

Crocker, L., & Algina, J. (1986). *Introduction to classical and modern test theory.* New York: Holt, Rinehart & Winston.

Cronbach, L. (1990). *Essentials of psychological testing* (5th ed.). New York: HarperCollins.

Cronbach, L., & Furby, L. (1970). How should we measure "change"—or should we? *Psychological Bulletin, 74,* 68-80.

Cronkhite, G. (1976). Effects of rater-concept-scale interactions and use of different factoring procedures upon evaluative factor structure. *Human Communication Research, 2,* 316-329.

Cronkhite, G., & Liska, J. (1976). Critique of factor analytic approaches to the study of credibility. *Communication Monographs, 43,* 91-107.

Cureton, E. E., & D'Agostino, R. B. (1983). *Factor analysis: An applied approach.* Hillsdale, NJ: Lawrence Erlbaum.

Cushman, D. P., & Pearce, W. B. (1977). Generality and necessity in three types of human communication theory with special attention to rules theory. *Human Communication Research, 3,* 344-353.

Davison, M. L. (1983). *Multidimensional scaling.* New York: John Wiley.

Delia, J. G., Kline, S. L., & Burleson, B. R. (1979). The development of persuasive communication strategies in kindergartners through twelfth-graders. *Communication Monographs, 46,* 241-256.

Dillard, J. P. (1988). Compliance-gaining message selection: What is our dependent variable? *Communication Monographs, 55,* 162-183.

Dillard, J. P., Palmer, M. T., & Kinney, T. A. (1995). Relational judgments in an influence context. *Human Communication Research, 21,* 331-353.

Dillard, J. P., Solomon, D. H., & Palmer, M. T. (1999). Structuring the concept of relational communication. *Communication Monographs, 66,* 49-65.

Dillman, D. A. (1978). *Mail and telephone surveys: The total design method.* New York: John Wiley.

Dindia, K. (1998, June). *Men are from South Dakota, women are from North Dakota.* Paper presented at the conference of the International Network on Personal Relationships, Norman, OK.

Dindia, K., & Allen, M. (1992). Sex differences in self-disclosure: A meta-analysis. *Psychological Bulletin, 112,* 106-124.

Dindia, K., Fitzpatrick, M. A., & Kenny, D. A. (1997). Self-disclosure in spouse and stranger interaction: A social relations analysis. *Human Communication Research, 23,* 388-412.

Donohue, W. A. (1981). Development of a model of rule use in negotiation interaction. *Communication Monographs, 48,* 106-120.

Duck, S. (1991). Diaries and logs. In B. M. Montgomery & S. Duck (Eds.), *Studying interpersonal interaction* (pp. 141-161). New York: Guilford.

Eagly, A. H. (1995). The science and politics of comparing women and men. *American Psychologist, 50,* 145-158.

Emmers-Sommer, T. M., & Allen, M. (1999). Variables related to sexual coercion: A path model. *Journal of Social and Personal Relationships, 16,* 659-678.

Ericsson, K. A., & Simon, H. A. (1980). Verbal reports as data. *Psychological Review, 87,* 215-251.

Fan, X., Thompson, B., & Wang, L. (1999). Effects of sample size, estimation methods, and model specification on structural equation modeling fit indexes. *Structural Equation Modeling, 6,* 56-83.

Feinberg, S. (1989). *The analysis of cross-classified categorical data* (2nd ed.). Cambridge: MIT Press.

Fink, A., & Kosecoff, J. (1985). *How to conduct surveys: A step-by-step guide.* Beverly Hills, CA: Sage.

Fisher, W. (1984). Narration as a human communication paradigm. *Communication Monographs, 51,* 1-22.

Floyd, K., & Morman, M. T. (1998). The measurement of affectionate communication. *Communication Quarterly, 46,* 144-162.

Folger, J. P., Hewes, D., & Poole, M. S. (1984). Coding social interaction. In B. Dervin & M. J. Voigt (Eds.), *Progress in communication sciences* (Vol. 5, pp. 115-161). Norwood, NJ: Ablex.

Frankel, R. M., & Beckman, H. B. (1982). Impact: An interaction-based method for preserving and analyzing clinical interactions. In L. S. Pettegrew, P. Arnston, D. Bush, & K. Zoppi (Eds.), *Explorations in provider and patient interaction* (pp. 71-86). Nashville, TN: Humana.

Gilbertson, J., Dindia, K., & Allen, M. (1998). Relational continuity, constructional units, and the maintenance of relationships. *Journal of Social and Personal Relationships, 15,* 774-790.

Glaser, B. G., & Strauss, A. L. (1967). *The discovery of grounded theory: Strategies for qualitative research.* Chicago: Aldine.

Glass, G. (1977). Integrating findings: The meta-analysis of research. *Review of Research in Education, 5,* 351-379.

Goldsmith, D. J., & MacGeorge, E. L. (2000). The impact of politeness and relationship on perceived quality of advice about a problem. *Human Communication Research, 26,* 234-263.

Goldsmith, D. J., McDermott, V. M., & Alexander, S. C. (2000). Helpful, supportive, and sensitive: Measuring the evaluation of enacted social support in personal relationships. *Journal of Social and Personal Relationships, 17,* 369-391.

Gonzalez, R., & Griffin, D. (1997). On the statistics of interdependence: Treating dyadic data with respect. In S. Duck (Ed.), *Handbook of personal relationships: Theory, research and interventions* (2nd ed., pp. 271-302). New York: John Wiley.

Goodman, L. A. (1978). *Analyzing qualitative/categorical data: Log-linear models and latent structure analysis.* Cambridge, MA: Abt.

Gottman, J. M. (1981). *Time-series analysis: A comprehensive introduction for social scientists.* New York: Cambridge University Press.

Greene, J. O., & Ravizza, S. M. (1995). Complexity effects on temporal characteristics of speech. *Human Communication Research, 21,* 390-421.

Guerrero, L. K. (1996). Attachment-style differences in intimacy and involvement: A test of the four-category model. *Communication Monographs, 63,* 269-292.

Guerrero, L. K., Andersen, P. A., Jorgensen, P. F., Spitzberg, B. H., & Eloy, S. V. (1995). Coping with the green-eyed monster: Conceptualizing and measuring communicative responses to romantic jealousy. *Western Journal of Communication, 59,* 270-304.

Gujarati, D. N. (1995). *Basic econometrics* (3rd ed.). New York: McGraw-Hill.

Hample, D., & Dallinger, J. M. (1995). A Lewinian perspective on taking conflict personally: Revision, refinement and validation of the instrument. *Communication Quarterly, 43,* 297-319.

Harré, R., & Madden, E. H. (1975). *Causal powers: A theory of natural necessity.* Oxford: Basil Blackwell.

Hayduk, L. (1996). *LISREL: Issues, debates, and strategies.* Baltimore: Johns Hopkins University Press.

Hewes, D. E. (1975). Finite stochastic modeling of communication processes. *Human Communication Research, 1,* 217-283.

Hewes, D. E. (1979). The sequential analysis of social interaction. *Quarterly Journal of Speech, 65,* 56-73.

Hewes, D. E. (1985). Systematic biases in coded social interaction data. *Human Communication Research, 11,* 554-574.

Hewes, D. E., Graham, M. L., Doelger, J., & Pavitt, C. (1985). "Second guessing": Message interpretation in social networks. *Human Communication Research, 11,* 299-335.

Hewes, D. E., & Haight, L. R. (1979). The cross-situational consistency of communication behaviors: A preliminary investigation. *Communication Research, 6,* 243-270.

Holmes, M. E., & Poole, M. S. (1991). The longitudinal analysis of interaction. In B. M. Montgomery & S. Duck (Eds.), *Studying interpersonal interaction* (pp. 286-302). New York: Guilford.

Honeycutt, J. M., Cantrill, J. G., Kelly, P., & Lambkin, D. (1998). How do I love thee? Let me consider my options: Cognition, verbal strategies, and the escalation of intimacy. *Human Communication Research, 25,* 39-63.

Hosmer, D. W., & Lemeshow, S. (1989). *Applied logistic regression.* New York: John Wiley.

Hu, L., & Bentler, P. M. (1999). Cutoff criteria for fit indexes in covariance structure analysis: Conventional criteria versus new alternatives. *Structural Equation Modeling, 6,* 1-55.

Huberty, C. J., & Morris, J. D. (1989). Multivariate analysis versus multiple univariate analysis. *Psychological Bulletin, 105,* 302-308.

Hunter, J. E., Danes, J. E., & Cohen, S. H. (1984). *Mathematical models of attitude change.* New York: Academic Press.

Hunter, J. E., Hamilton, M. A., & Allen, M. (1989). The design and analysis of language experiments in communication. *Communication Monographs, 56,* 341-363.

Hunter, J. E., & Schmidt, F. L. (1990). *Meta-analysis: Cumulating research findings across studies* (2nd ed.). Newbury Park, CA: Sage.

Huston, T. L., Surra, C., Fitzgerald, N., & Cate, R. (1981). From courtship to marriage: Mate selection as an interpersonal process. In S. Duck & R. Gilmour (Eds.), *Personal relationships 2: Developing personal relationships* (pp. 53-90). New York: Academic Press.

Hyde, J. S., & Plant, E. A. (1995). Magnitude of psychological gender differences: Another side to the story. *American Psychologist, 50,* 159-161.

Jackson, S., & Jacobs, S. (1983). Generalizing about messages: Suggestions for the design and analysis of experiments. *Human Communication Research, 9,* 169-191.

Jackson, S., O'Keefe, D. J., Jacobs, S., & Brashers, D. E. (1989). Messages as replications: Toward a message-centered design strategy. *Communication Monographs, 56,* 364-384.

Jones, L. V., & Appelbaum, M. I. (1989). Psychometric methods. *Annual Review of Psychology, 40,* 23-43.

Jordan, J. M. (1998). Executive cognitive control in communication: Extending plan-based theory. *Human Communication Research, 25,* 5-38.

Jöreskog, K.G., & Wold, H. (1982). The ML and PLS techniques for modeling with latent variables: Historical and comparative aspects. In H. Wold & K. G. Jöreskog (Eds.), *Systems under indirect observation: Causality, structure, prediction* (Vol. 1, pp. 263-270). Amsterdam: North-Holland.

Kaplan, D. (1995). Statistical power in structural equation modeling. In R. H. Hoyle (Ed.), *Structural equation modeling: Concepts, issues, and applications* (pp. 100-117). Thousand Oaks, CA: Sage.

Kashy, D. A., & Kenny, D. A. (1999). The analysis of data from dyads and groups. In H. T. Reis & C. M. Judd (Eds.), *Handbook of research methods in social psychology* (pp. 451-477). London: Cambridge University Press.

Katz, J. E. (1994). Empirical and theoretical dimensions of obscene phone calls to women in the United States. *Human Communication Research, 21,* 155-182.

Keaten, J., Kelly, L., & Finch, C. (1997). Development of an instrument to measure reticence. *Communication Quarterly, 45,* 37-54.

Kellermann, K., Reynolds, R., & Chen, J. B. (1991). Strategies of conversational retreat: When parting is not sweet sorrow. *Communication Monographs, 58,* 362-383.

Kenny, D. A. (1996a). The design and analysis of social-interaction research. *Annual Review of Psychology, 47,* 59-86.

Kenny, D. A. (1996b). Non-independence. *Journal of Social and Personal Relationships, 13,* 279-294.

Kenny, D. A., & La Voie, L. (1984). The social relations model. In L. Berkowitz (Ed.), *Advances in experimental social psychology* (Vol. 18, pp. 141-182). New York: Academic Press.

Keppel, G. (1991). *Design and analysis: A researcher's handbook* (3rd ed.). Englewood Cliffs, NJ: Prentice Hall.

Keselman, H. J., Huberty, C. J., Lix, L. M., Olejnik, S., Cribbie, R. A., Donohue, B., et al. (1998). Statistical practices of educational researchers: An analysis of ANOVA, MANOVA, and ANCOVA analyses. *Review of Educational Research, 68,* 350-386.

Kirk, R. E. (1982). *Experimental design: Procedures for the behavioral sciences* (2nd ed.). Belmont, CA: Brooks/Cole.

Knoke, D. (1975). A comparison of log-linear and regression models for systems of dichotomous variables. *Sociological Methods and Research, 3,* 416-434.

Kraemer, H. C., & Thiemann, S. (1987). *How many subjects? Statistical power analysis in research.* Newbury Park, CA: Sage.

Kunkel, A. W., & Burleson, B. R. (1999). Assessing explanations for sex differences in emotional support: A test of the different cultures and skill specialization accounts. *Human Communication Research, 25,* 307-340.

Labov, W., & Fanshel, D. (1977). *Therapeutic discourse: Psychotherapy as conversation.* New York: Academic Press.

Leary, T. (1957). *Interpersonal diagnosis of personality.* New York: Ronald.

Le Poire, B. A., Shepard, C. A., & Duggan, A. (1999). Nonverbal involvement, expressiveness, and pleasantness as predicted by parental and partner attachment style. *Communication Monographs, 66,* 293-311.

Levine, R. L., & Fitzgerald, H. E. (Eds.). (1991). *Analysis of dynamic psychological systems.* New York: Plenum.

Levine, T. R., & McCroskey, J. C. (1990). Measuring trait communication apprehension: A test of rival measurement models of the PRCA-24. *Communication Monographs, 57,* 62-72.

Li, F., Harmer, P., Duncan, T. E., Duncan, S. C., Acock, A., & Boles, S. (1998). Approaches to testing interaction effects using structural equation modeling methodology. *Multivariate Behavioral Research, 33,* 1-39.

Lingoes, J. C., & Borg, I. (1978). A direct approach to individual differences scaling using increasingly complex transformations. *Psychometrika, 43,* 491-519.

Lingoes, J. C., Roskam, E. E., & Borg, I. (Eds.). (1979). *Geometric representations of relational data: Readings in multidimensional scaling.* Ann Arbor, MI: Mathesis.

Lohmöller, J.-B. (1984). *LVPLS program manual: Latent variables path analysis with partial least-squares estimation.* Cologne, Germany: Zentralarchiv für empirische Sozialforschung.

Lord, F. M., & Novick, M. R. (1968). *Statistical theory of mental test scores.* Reading, MA: Addison-Wesley.

Louch, H. (2000). Personal network integration: Transitivity and homophily in strong tie relations. *Social Networks, 22,* 45-64.

MacCallum, R. C. (1986). Specification searches in covariance structure modeling. *Psychological Bulletin, 100,* 107-120.

MacIntyre, P. D., Babin, P. A., & Clement, R. (1999). Willingness to communicate: Antecedents and consequences. *Communication Quarterly, 47,* 215-229.

Markman, H. J., & Notarius, C. I. (1987). Coding marital and family interaction: Current status. In T. Jacob (Ed.), *Family interaction and psychopathology: Theories, methods, and findings* (pp. 329-390). New York: Plenum.

Martin, M. M., & Anderson, C. M. (1995). The father-young adult relationship: Interpersonal motives, self-disclosure, and satisfaction. *Communication Quarterly, 43,* 119-130.

Maruyama, G. M. (1998). *Basics of structural equation modeling.* London: Sage.

McCleary, R., & Hays, R. L. (1980). *Applied time series analysis for the social sciences.* Beverly Hills, CA: Sage.

McDonald, R. P. (1985). *Factor analysis and related methods.* Hillsdale, NJ: Lawrence Erlbaum.

McDonald, R. P. (1989). An index of goodness-of-fit based on noncentrality. *Journal of Classification, 6,* 97-103.

McPhee, R. D., & Poole, M. S. (1982). Mathematical modeling in communication research: An overview. In M. Burgoon (Ed.), *Communication yearbook 5* (pp. 159-161). New Brunswick, NJ: Transaction.

McPhee, R. D., & Seibold, D. R. (1979). Rationale, procedures, and applications for decomposition of explained variance in multiple regression analysis. *Communication Research, 6,* 345-384.

Metts, S. R., Sprecher, S., & Cupach, W. R. (1991). Retrospective self-reports. In B. M. Montgomery & S. Duck (Eds.), *Studying interpersonal interaction* (pp. 162-178). New York: Guilford.

Milardo, R. M. (1983). Social networks and pair relationships: A review of substantive and measurement issues. *Sociology and Social Research, 68,* 1-18.

Milardo, R. M. (1987). Changes in social networks of males and females following divorce: A review. *Journal of Family Issues, 8,* 78-96.

Milardo, R. M. (1992). Comparative methods for delineating social networks. *Journal of Social and Personal Relationships, 9,* 447-461.

Milligan, G. W., & Cooper, M. C. (1987). Methodology review: Clustering methods. *Applied Psychological Measurement, 11,* 329-354.

Mitchell, M. M. (2000). Able but not motivated? The relative effects of happy and sad mood on persuasive message processing. *Communication Monographs, 67,* 215-226.

Morey, L. C., Blashfield, R. K., & Skinner, H. A. (1983). A comparison of cluster analysis techniques within a sequential validation framework. *Multivariate Behavioral Research, 18,* 309-329.

Morley, D. D. (1988). Meta-analytic techniques: When generalizing to message populations is not possible. *Human Communication Research, 15,* 112-126.

Morrison, D. F. (1990). *Multivariate statistical methods* (3rd ed.). New York: McGraw-Hill.

Nisbett, R. E., & Wilson, T. D. (1977). Telling more than we can know: Verbal reports on mental processes. *Psychological Review, 84,* 231-259.

Neuendorf, K. (2001). *The content analysis guidebook.* Thousand Oaks, CA: Sage.

O'Donnell-Trujillo, N. (1982). Relational communication: A comparison of coding systems. *Communication Monographs, 48,* 91-105.

Olsson, U. H., Troye, S. V., & Howell, R. D. (1999). Theoretic fit and empirical fit: The performance of maximum likelihood versus generalized least squares estimation in structural equation models. *Multivariate Behavioral Research, 34,* 31-58.

Overton, W. F., & Reese, H. W. (1973). Models of development: Methodological implications. In J. R. Nesselroade & H. W. Reese (Eds.), *Life-span developmental psychology: Methodological issues* (pp. 65-86). New York: Academic Press.

Parks, M. R., & Floyd, K. (1996). Meanings for closeness and intimacy in friendship. *Journal of Social and Personal Relationships, 13,* 85-107.

Pavitt, C., & Cappella, J. N. (1979). Coorientational accuracy in interpersonal and small group discussions: A literature review, model, and simulation. In D. Nimmo (Ed.), *Communication yearbook 3* (pp. 123-156). New Brunswick, NJ: Transaction.

Pearce, W. B., & Cronen, V. E. (1980). *Communication, action and meaning.* New York: Praeger.

Pedhazur, E. J. (1982). *Multiple regression in behavioral research: Explanation and prediction.* New York: Holt, Rinehart & Winston.

Poole, M. S., & DeSanctis, G. (1992). Microlevel structuration in computer-supported group decision-making. *Human Communication Research, 19,* 5-49.

Poole, M. S., & Folger, J. P. (1981). A method for establishing the representational validity of interaction coding systems: Do we see what they see? *Human Communication Research, 8,* 26-42.

Poole, M. S., Folger, J. P., & Hewes, D. E. (1987). Analyzing interpersonal interaction. In M. E. Roloff & G. R. Miller (Eds.), *Interpersonal processes: New directions in communication research* (pp. 220-256). Newbury Park, CA: Sage.

Poole, M. S., & McPhee, R. D. (1994). Methodology in interpersonal communication research. In M. L. Knapp & G. R. Miller (Eds.), *Handbook of interpersonal communication* (2nd ed., pp. 42-100). Thousand Oaks, CA: Sage.

Poole, M. S., Van de Ven, A. V., Dooley, K., & Holmes, M. (2000). *Organizational change and innovation processes: Theory and methods for research.* New York: Oxford University Press.

Rawlins, W. K. (1983). Openness as problematic in ongoing friendships: Two conversational dilemmas. *Communication Monographs, 50,* 1-13.

Raykov, T. (2000). On the bias, variance, and mean squared error of the conventional noncentrality parameter estimator of covariance structure models. *Structural Equation Modeling, 7,* 431-441.

Raykov, T., & Penev, S. (1999). On structural equation model equivalence. *Multivariate Behavioral Research, 34,* 199-244.

Roberto, A. J., & Finucane, M. E. (1997). The assessment of argumentativeness and verbal aggressiveness in adolescent populations. *Communication Quarterly, 45,* 21-36.

Rogers, E., & Farace, R. (1975). Analysis of relational communication in dyads: New measurement procedures. *Human Communication Research, 1,* 222-239.

Rosenthal, R. (1991). *Meta-analytic procedures for social research* (2nd ed.). Newbury Park, CA: Sage.

Rosenthal, R., & Rosnow, R. L. (1985). *Contrast analysis: Focused comparisons in the analysis of variance.* Cambridge: Cambridge University Press.

Rossi, P. H., Wright, J. D., & Anderson, A. B. (Eds.). (1983). *Handbook of survey research.* New York: Academic Press.

Rothenbuhler, E. W. (1991). The process of community involvement. *Communication Monographs, 58,* 63-78.

Rubin, K. H. (1973). Egocentrism in childhood: A unitary construct? *Child Development, 14,* 102-110.

Rubin, R. B., Palmgreen, D., & Sypher, H. E. (Eds.). (1994). *Communication research measures: A sourcebook.* New York: Guilford.

Sacks, H., Schegloff, E. A., & Jefferson, G. (1974). A simplest systematics for the organization of turn-taking in conversation. *Language, 50,* 696-735.

Samp, J. A., & Solomon, D. H. (1998). Communicative responses to problematic events in close relationships I: The variety and facets of goals. *Communication Research, 25,* 66-95.

Sassi, M. S., & Greene, J. O. (1998). The impact of individual differences on message-production skill acquisition. *Communication Research, 25,* 306-326.

Sawilowsky, S. S. (2000). Psychometrics versus datametrics: Comment on Vacha-Haase's "reliability generalization" method and some EPM editorial policies. *Educational and Psychological Measurement, 60,* 157-173.

Schaie, K. W. (1965). A general model for the study of developmental problems. *Psychological Bulletin, 64,* 92-107.

Scheer, V. C., & Cline, R. J. (1994). The development and validation of a model explaining sexual behavior among college students: Implications for AIDS communication campaigns. *Human Communication Research, 21,* 280-304.

Scheines, R., Spirtes, P., Glymour, C., & Meek, C. (1994). *TETRAD II: Tools for discovery.* Hillsdale, NJ: Lawrence Erlbaum.

Schmitt, N., & Stults, D. M. (1986). Methodology review: Analysis of multitrait-multimethod matrices. *Applied Psychological Measurement, 10,* 1-22.

Schumacker, R. E., & Lomax, R. G. (1996). *A beginner's guide to structural equation modeling.* Mahwah, NJ: Lawrence Erlbaum.

Searle, S. R. (1971). *Linear models.* New York: John Wiley.

Shavelson, R. J., & Webb, N. M. (1991). *Generalizability theory: A primer.* Newbury Park, CA: Sage.

Sheehan-Holt, J. K. (1998). MANOVA simultaneous test procedures: The power and robustness of restricted multivariate contrasts. *Educational and Psychological Measurement, 58,* 861-881.

Sillars, A. L. (1986). *Procedures for coding interpersonal conflict* (rev.). Unpublished manuscript, University of Montana–Missoula, Department of Communication Studies.

Sillars, A. L., Roberts, L. J., Leonard, K. E., & Dun, T. (2000). Cognition during marital conflict: The relationship of thought and talk. *Journal of Social and Personal Relationships, 17,* 479-502.

Snijders, T. A. B., & Kenny, D. A. (1999). The social relations model for family data: A multilevel approach. *Personal Relationships, 6,* 471-486.

Snyder, L. B. (1991). Modeling dynamic communication processes with event history analysis. *Communication Research, 18,* 464-486.

Solomon, D. H., & Samp, J. A. (1998). Power and problem appraisal: Perceptual foundations of the chilling effect in dating relationships. *Journal of Social and Personal Relationships, 15,* 191-209.

Spence, I., & Ogilvie, J. (1973). A table of expected stress values for random nonmetric multidimensional scaling. *Multivariate Behavioral Research, 9,* 511-517.

Straits, B. C. (2000). Ego's important discussants or significant people: An experiment in varying the wording of personal network name generators. *Social Networks, 22,* 123-140.

Tatsuoka, M. (1988). *Multivariate analysis: Techniques for educational and psychological research* (2nd ed.). New York: Macmillan.

Thomas, L. T., & Levine, T. R. (1994). Disentangling listening and verbal recall: Related but separate constructs? *Human Communication Research, 21,* 103-127.

Tisak, J., & Meredith, W. (1990). Longitudinal factor analysis. In A. von Eye (Ed.), *Statistical methods in longitudinal research: Vol. 1. Principles and structuring change* (pp. 125-150). London: Academic Press.

Tomas, J. M., Hontangas, P. M., & Oliver A. (2000). Linear confirmatory factor models to evaluate multitrait-multimethod matrices: The effects of number of indicators and correlation among methods. *Multivariate Behavioral Research, 35,* 469-499.

Trujillo, N. (1986). Toward a taxonomy of small group interaction coding systems. *Small Group Behavior, 17,* 371-394.

Tudor, A. (1976). Misunderstanding everyday life. *Sociological Review, 24,* 479-503.

Vacha-Haase, T. (1998). Reliability generalization: Exploring variance in measurement error affecting score reliability across studies. *Educational and Psychological Measurement, 58,* 6-20.

van der Linden, W. J., & Hambleton, R. K. (1997). *Handbook of modern item response theory.* New York: Springer-Verlag.

Van Lear, C. A. (1991). Testing a cyclical model of communicative openness in relationship development: Two longitudinal studies. *Communication Monographs, 58,* 337-361.

Volker, B., & Flap, H. (1995). The effects of institutional transformation on personal networks: East Germany, four years later. *Netherlands Journal of Social Sciences, 31,* 87-107.

Vroom, V. H., & Jago, A. G. (1974). Decision making as a social process: Normative and descriptive models of leader behavior. *Decision Sciences, 5,* 743-769.

Walton, R. E. (1968). *Interpersonal peacemaking: Confrontations and third party consultation.* Reading, MA: Addison-Wesley.

Weeks, D. B., & Bentler, P. M. (1979). A comparison of linear and monotone multidimensional scaling models. *Psychological Bulletin, 8,* 349-354.

Weisberg, S. (1985). *Applied linear regression* (2nd ed.). New York: John Wiley.

Weiss, R. L. (1993). *Marital Interaction Coding System-IV (MICS-IV).* Unpublished manuscript, University of Oregon.

West, J. (2000). *Structural equation software.* Retrieved from http://www.gsm.uci.edu/%7ejoelwest/sem/software.html

Wilcox, R. R. (1987). New designs in analysis of variance. *Annual Review of Psychology, 38,* 29-60.

Williams L. J., & Holahan P. J. (1994). Parsimony-based fit indices for multiple indicator models: Do they work? *Structural Equation Modeling, 1,* 161-189.

Wilson, S. R., Aleman, C., & Leatham, G. B. (1998). Identity implications of influence goals: A revised analysis of face-threatening acts and application to seeking compliance with same-sex friends. *Human Communication Research, 25,* 64-96.

Winer, B. J., Brown, D. R., & Michels, K. M. (1991). *Statistical principles in experimental design* (3rd ed.). New York: McGraw-Hill.

Witte, K., & Morrison, K. (2000). Examining the influence of trait anxiety/repression-sensitization on individuals' reactions to fear appeals. *Western Journal of Communication, 64,* 1-27.

Woelfel, J., & Fink, E. L. (1980). *The measurement of communication processes: Galileo theory and method.* New York: Academic Press.

Wold, H. (1985). Partial least squares. In S. Kotz & N. L. Johnson (Eds.), *Encyclopedia of statistical sciences* (Vol. 6, pp. 581-591). New York: John Wiley.

Wolf, F. M. (1986). *Meta-analysis: Quantitative methods for research synthesis.* Beverly Hills, CA: Sage.

Young, F. W. (1987). *Multidimensional scaling: History, theory, and applications.* Hillsdale, NJ: Lawrence Erlbaum.

3

Perspectives on Inquiry III

The Moral of Stories

ARTHUR P. BOCHNER

Human life is storied life. From bedtime stories to life reviews—across the span of our lives—we tell stories and listen to the stories other people tell. Sometimes we find ourselves in stories we would rather not be living; sometimes we construct new story lines for ourselves that help us exert control over life's possibilities and limitations. In some of our stories we claim ourselves as heroes; in others we are dreamers; in still others we are sufferers or victims or survivors. The people in our lives exist as characters in our stories, and we are characters in theirs. Indeed, one of the main functions of interpersonal communication is to negotiate and mediate the plots we collaboratively enact with other people and in groups. As Arthur Frank (1997) says, "Stories are the ongoing work of turning mere existence into a life that is social, and moral, and affirms the existence of the teller as a human being" (p. 43).

Stories are the narrative frames within which we make our experiences meaningful. In the study of interpersonal communication, we must heed the call of stories in order to understand how people make sense of their experiences, how they wrestle with the difficulties of attaching meanings to events under the press of human contingency and uncertainty, and how they struggle to do the right

AUTHOR'S NOTE: I would like to express my appreciation to Carolyn Ellis, who provided helpful comments and editing on various versions of this chapter.

thing(s). As Brody (1987) observes, "The primary mechanism for attaching meaning to human experience is to tell stories about them" (p. 5). To have a self is to have a story and, usually, to want to tell your story to somebody. Richardson (1990) refers to narrative as "the best way to understand the human experience because it is the way humans understand their own lives" (p. 133). When we narrate our lives, we engage in what Jerome Bruner (1990) calls "acts of meaning." The success with which we cope with the contingencies of our interpersonal lives depends largely on how effectively we respond to the contradictions and conflicts that social life necessarily poses. The narratives we create, discover, and apply help us maintain a sense of coherence and continuity over the course of our lives.

In this chapter, I focus on the burgeoning development of narrative inquiry as a paradigm for the study of interpersonal communication. This is the third in a series of essays that I have called "Perspectives on Inquiry" (Bochner, 1985, 1994). I use the word *perspectives* in the pragmatist sense to indicate that more than one legitimate view exists of what we should be doing when we study interpersonal communication. In each perspective, what we select as important is relative to the point of view we take. Thus the standards for judging the merits of a particular point of view are relative, not absolute; usually they are deeply embedded in the taken-for-granted vocabulary of the particular perspective. People who take different perspectives on events or actions, such as inquiry on interpersonal communication, may be thought of as living in different worlds or at least in different language communities. Often, they occupy what Thomas Kuhn (1962) once called "incommensurable viewpoints" (p. 200). They may be looking at the same world, Kuhn observed, but what they see will be quite different. When we become aware of these differences we have the urge to convince others to

change their views and convert to ours. Usually, it is difficult to talk across the divides of these differences, let alone to be persuasive. I have suggested, after Rorty (1982), that we treat these differences not as issues to be resolved but as differences to be lived with (Bochner, 1985, 2001).

In the first of this series of essays, written more than 16 years ago, I argued that no single methodology or perspective is uniquely appropriate to the study of interpersonal communication. Although conflicts between empiricists and interpretivists usually center on which methods should be used to study human beings, the dissension actually boils down to preferences for different vocabularies— that is, different ways of describing and doing things with human beings. To quarrel over method is to have a goal in common but to disagree about how best to achieve the goal. But empiricists and interpretivists do not agree on a goal. Empiricists usually want to predict and control human behavior, whereas interpretivists want to understand human beings and help them decide what to do. These different goals belong to different universes of discourse. Empiricists use a vocabulary that expresses the values of objectivity, moral neutrality, the search for facts, and the kind of understanding given by explanatory theories and covering laws. Interpretivists speak in a vastly different tongue. Their work is couched in a vocabulary that emphasizes horizons of human meaning, moral reflection, subjectivity, embodiment, and empathy.

Researchers who seek better predictions do not speak the same language as those who want to understand how different people make sense of the world in which they live and can better cope with the contingencies of human experience. Neither vocabulary is the one and only suitable vocabulary for studying and/or understanding human beings and their communicative activities. Each mode of description may be more or less useful, depending on the purposes for which it is being applied. By acknowledging that there is more than one legitimate goal to which inquiry on interpersonal communication can be addressed, we free ourselves from the chains of a monolithic model of research practices that would sabotage the unique opportunities provided by recognizing and validating the multiple goals and perspectives that exist in the study of interpersonal communication. Research on interpersonal communication should be oriented not only toward facts but also toward meanings; not only under the rules of rigor, but also under the inspiration of the imagination; not only to achieve better predictions and more control, but also to achieve peace of mind and to alleviate human suffering; not only from the position of neutrality and distance, but also from the position of caring and vulnerability; not only toward the production of conventional, received research texts, but also toward the performance of creative, artistic, and dialogic modes of representing lived experience.

In the second essay in the series, "Theories and Stories" (Bochner, 1994), I argued that interpersonal communication is an activity imbued with moral, ideological, and ethical concerns. The tacit goal of many researchers who share an interest in interpersonal communication is the moral one of enlarging and deepening the sense of human community; building better, more satisfying relationships; and learning how to converse with people who are different from us. One of the strongest inspirations for studying interpersonal communication is a desire to act well—that is, to do the right thing(s). In this sense, what we want from research is moral and ethical guidance. Normally, we have not thought of the social sciences as a source of moral guidance, but instead have turned to poetry, drama, and literature for that kind of value-centered direction. But, as Rorty (1982) points out, when our research focuses on achieving the kinds of descriptions that would help us decide what to do, we step outside the vocabulary of

prediction and control and must poke around for a different terminology, one that is continuous with literature and the arts. In "Theories and Stories," I drew fuzzy borders between science and literature, suggesting that distinctions between researchers and subjects, reason and emotion, and social sciences and literature could be usefully dissolved, at least insofar as one of our goals in the study of interpersonal communication is to show and understand people caught up in the process of grappling with meanings and seeking to do the right thing(s).

I also argued that the legitimation of meaning-centered, narrative inquiry is contingent on our breaking free of the tight grip of certain disciplinary norms that idealize the significance of abstractions over details, stability over change, graphs over stories. The problem is not with science per se, but with a reverent and idealized view of science that positions science above the contingencies of language and outside the circle of historical and cultural interests (Bochner & Waugh, 1995). In my view, the "crisis of representation" (Clifford, 1988; Clifford & Marcus, 1986; Geertz, 1988; Marcus & Fischer, 1986; Turner & Bruner, 1986) raised serious doubts about the validity and efficacy of the theory of language on which most orthodox approaches to scientific knowledge are based. The "correspondence theory of knowledge" to which I refer hinges on the assumption that language can achieve the denotative and referential function of describing objects in a world *out there,* apart from and independent of language users (Bochner & Waugh, 1995; Rorty, 1967, 1982, 1989). To hold to this assumption is to grant that the words used in "scientific" descriptions do not specify *a* world, but rather represent *the* world, and that words can denote what is *out there* in the world apart from, or prior to, the interpretations of the researchers who use them. But the history and philosophy of science since Kuhn (1962) shows that we should understand language not as simply a tool for mirroring what is describable about reality, but rather as an ongoing and constitutive part of reality (Bochner & Waugh, 1995). What it is possible to say about the world involves the indistinguishable provocations of the world *and* the interventions of language by which we make claims about it. In short, the world we seek to describe as social scientists does not exist in the form of the sentences we write when we theorize about it (Rorty, 1989).

If language is not simply a tool for mirroring reality, but rather an ongoing and constitutive part of reality, then our research agenda needs to take into account how, as social scientists, we are part of the world we investigate and the ways we use language to make and change it. Accordingly, our focus becomes showing how meaning is performed and negotiated by speakers and interpreters (Bochner & Waugh, 1995), including ourselves as researchers. Although academic disciplines that have been deeply entrenched in the correspondence theory of knowledge, such as mainstream psychology, sociology, and communication studies, have been slow to respond to the challenges posed by the crisis in representation, a new generation of social scientists who understand and appreciate language as a way of dealing with the world have responded by opening new vistas of inquiry, experimenting with new research practices, and turning increasingly toward narrative, interpretive, and qualitative approaches to inquiry that emphasize the ways in which research is a relational, political, and moral process (Bochner & Ellis, 2002; Denzin & Lincoln, 2000a; Ellis & Bochner, 1996a, 2000; Gergen & Gergen, 2000).

I concluded "Theories and Stories" by introducing five central concerns that characterize a narrative perspective on interpersonal communication. The first focuses on the connection between the self who is writing/observing/researching and the other(s) who are written about, observed, and/or studied. Appealing to the idea of reflexivity promoted by Jackson's (1989) observation that "our understanding of others can *only* proceed from within our own experience" (p. 17), I urged that we think of ourselves as researchers not as *apart from* but as *a part of* the "data" to be analyzed in our research.

The second concern emphasized the desire to achieve an authentic researcher's voice. If, as a researcher, I am part of the data, then I cannot ignore and I should not hide the ways in which my observations and conclusions may follow from my own experiences, my own feelings and values, and my own self-interests. Thus my presence as an author in the text should be seen, felt, and respected. Instead of producing research reports that represent authorship as if it were a voice of nobody (in particular) from nowhere (in particular), we should encourage and legitimate the first-person voice.

The third concern centered on narrative conventions and the cultural transmission of narrative practices. Here I drew attention to the narrative "scripts" that are transmitted by popular forms of culture such as cinema, television, and popular music, shaping the meanings and values we attach to romance, love, intimacy, and sexuality (Denzin, 1992). Functioning as socializing frameworks of intelligibility, these narrative scripts are woven into the fabric of our cognitive and emotional experience, and, as we come to take them for granted, we may lose sight of the ways in which they are chosen not so much by us as for us.

The fourth concern revolved around the need to develop new and alternative modes for representing interpersonal experiences. I suggested that we needed to consider alternatives to the "received" conventions of social science writing and reporting. I emphasized forms of representation that would be "reader"- or "viewer"-friendly, encouraging interactive and evocative participation, such as poetic representation (Austin, 1996; Kiesinger, 1995; Richardson, 1992), photographic narrative

(Harper, 1982, 2000; Quinney, 1996), art-based ethnography (Church, 2002; Picart, 2002; Scott-Hoy, 2002), ethnographic theater (Gray, Ivonoffski, & Sinding, 2002; Mienczakowski, 1996), documentary film (Siegel & Conquergood, 1985, 1990), co-constructed narrative (Ellis & Bochner, 1992), autoethnographic short stories (Ellis, 1993, 1995c, 1995d, 2001; Zola, 1982), and layered accounts (Ronai, 1992, 1995, 1996).

⑤ The fifth and final concern emphasized the relational connections between writers and readers of social science texts. Narrative inquiry aspires to an ideal of participation and involvement, promoting the inclusion of multiple voices, encouraging dialogue, and attempting to keep a conversation going. Recognizing the competing demands of communication and representation that can close down conversation and multiple interpretation (Tyler, 1986), narrative inquiry drops the presumption of language as representation in order to forge a dialogue between writers and readers that emphasizes the collaborative dimensions of composing a life and its meanings (Ellis, 1997; Tyler, 1986).

Thus narrative inquiry dissolves traditional boundaries between researchers and subjects, between theories and stories, and between authors and readers. As researchers, our own lives and experiences significantly influence what we project onto the people and events we study, and the people and events we study act back reflexively on who we become and what we do. As social scientists, we may adopt professional personae and call the stories we tell "theories," but we also recognize that the tales we tell must be placed into an intelligible frame of reference that is contingent on accepted conventions for transforming "knowing" into "telling" (White, 1980). When we have to turn research into a text, we become narrators, and to this extent all social science research is narrative and all researchers are storytellers. In the kind of narrative inquiry on which I focus in this chapter, the relationship

between writers and readers is transformed into a dialogic engagement that presumes an active and reflexive reader. In contrast to the "received model" that grew out of a paradigm that characterized the researcher as a distant spectator, the dialogic model of narrative inquiry promotes a framework of co-constructed meaning—that is, a reader who wants to enter into dialogue with the writer and the story. This aspect of narrative research can be easily misunderstood if one looks at and judges narratives exclusively on epistemological grounds. While some narrative research may make traditional knowledge claims, most narrative research functions ontologically, practically, and existentially. As Jackson (1995) suggests, the question becomes not so much how we know as how we should live. This is the moral of stories—its ethical domain. When it comes to communicating ethical consciousness, as Fasching and deChant advise (2001), it is much more effective to tell a story than to give an abstract explanation.

In this chapter, I extend the discussion of narrative that I began in "Theories and Stories." Specifically, I emphasize epistemological, existential, methodological, and ethical issues related to the development of narrative inquiry on interpersonal communication. I begin by discussing the epistemological and existential conditions that inspired the rapid development of narrative inquiry as a major perspective on social science research. Then I focus on the assumptions on which evocative narrative inquiry is based and the goals to which it is directed. I turn next to the question of narrative truth, where I try to show the kind of truth to which personal narratives aspire. This leads me into a consideration of the ways in which stories may be viewed as theoretical and how readers of personal narratives ideally should hear and interact with them. I emphasize Arthur Frank's (1995) distinction between thinking about stories and thinking with them. In the final two sections, I address methodological and ethical concerns related to narrative inquiry, emphasizing the democratization of the connections between researchers and participants and the obligations we have to the people and communities we write about as well as to the societies we seek to understand and/or change.

WHY NARRATIVE? WHY NOW?

In 1986, Theodore Sarbin published *Narrative Psychology,* an edited collection of essays and research monographs that focused on "the storied nature of human conduct." Reacting to "the epistemological crisis in social psychology," Sarbin offered narrative psychology as "a viable alternative to the positivist paradigm" of psychological research (p. vii). Prior to Sarbin's book, "narrative" had no recognizable status in psychology either as a methodological orientation or as a topic of research in the study of lives and/or interpersonal relationships. By 1992, however, Kreiswirth (1992) felt it necessary to account for what he called "the narrative turn" in the human sciences. Not only was psychology turning toward narrative, but so were economics, law, education, psychiatry, psychotherapy, sociology, and ethnography. Between 1986 and 1992, Bruner (1986, 1987, 1990) published his essay on "life as narrative" and his books on "possible worlds" and "acts of meaning"; Rosenwald and Ochberg (1992) introduced a critical-cultural perspective for investigating the stories people tell about their lives; Mair (1989) made the case for a narratively grounded "poetics of experience"; Parry (1991), Schafer (1992), and White and Epston (1990) created a framework for narrative-based therapies; Shotter and Gergen (1989) edited a collection of essays that examined the narrative textuality of the self; Richardson (1990) argued for a sociology that narrated lives instead of abstracting forces; Ellis and Bochner (1992) developed the methodology of co-constructed personal narratives and

promoted the idea of performed autobiographical research stories that would give audiences the kind of experiential, emotional immediacy lacking in traditional forms of research (Bochner & Ellis, 1992); Tedlock (1991) and Edward Bruner (1986) described the emergence of narrative ethnography; Langellier (1989) gave credibility to the study of personal narratives as a means of validating the voices of marginal and silenced individuals and groups; and Coles (1989) called for more stories and less theory in order to open up the moral imagination of teachers and researchers. Kreiswirth (1992) pointed out what had by then become obvious: "As anyone aware of the current intellectual scene has probably noticed, there has recently been a virtual explosion of interest in narrative and in theorizing about narrative" (p. 629).

The narrative turn accelerated during the 1990s. In particular, personal narratives (Clandinin & Connelly, 1994; Ellis & Bochner, 2000), life histories (Freeman, 1993; Tierney, 2000), testimonios (Beverley, 2000), and memoirs (Couser, 1997; Freeman, 1993; Miller, 1996) became widely viewed as significant methods for conducting inquiry as well as major topics of research across the human sciences (see, e.g., Church, 1995; Denzin, 1997; Denzin & Lincoln, 1994; Ellis & Bochner, 1996a; Gubrium & Holstein, 1997; Plummer, 2001). As Denzin and Lincoln (2000b) conclude, "Now, at the beginning of the 21st century, the narrative turn has been taken" (p. 3). In some circles, narrative has become a rallying point among those who believe strongly that the human sciences need to become more human. To a large extent, the burst of enthusiasm for personal narrative and the study of lives (Josselson & Lieblich, 1995) is a response to the questionable ethics and doubtful appropriateness of standard methodological practices in the social sciences (Apter, 1996). We are supposed to be studying people, looking at and trying to understand their lives, and narratives may come closer to representing the contexts and integrity of those lives than do questionnaires and graphs (Freeman, 1998b). But it is more likely that the enthusiasm for narrative inquiry was sparked as much by existential and moral concerns as by any scholarly change of heart. Narrative is as much about the *possible* as it is about the actual. Many of those drawn to narrative inquiry want to imagine, discover, or create new and better ways of living. As Freeman (1998b) says, "We need to understand lives and indeed to *live* lives differently if we are to avoid further fragmentation, isolation, and disconnection from each other" (p. 46).

The turn toward narrative is not a passing fancy, nor is it merely a reflection of a small group of cynical, renegade, eccentric, self-indulgent, and/or alienated individuals (Atkinson, 1997; Bochner, 2001; Bochner & Ellis, 1999; Sparkes, 2002). On the contrary, the inspiration for the narrative turn penetrates deep into the consciences of those who embrace it. To comprehend the sources of this inspiration, one must understand the demographic, social, and cultural conditions under which the most recent generation of researchers and graduate students in the social sciences have been educated. They have been exposed to a conception of how knowledge is produced, and for what purposes, that is far different from that experienced by those of us who entered the social sciences and built our research programs in the 1960s, 1970s, and 1980s. Consider just a few of the now standard sources in postmodernism and poststructuralism that have challenged and deconstructed our most venerable notions about scientific knowledge and truth. Kuhn (1962) used the history of science to show that the building-block model of science lacked foundations, that scientific revolutions were more akin to conversions than to discoveries. Rorty (1979, 1982), Toulmin (1969), Feyerabend (1975), and Sellars (1963) illustrated how the "facts" that scientists see are inextricably connected to the vocabularies they use to express or represent them. Lyotard (1984) debunked the belief in a unified totality of knowledge, questioning whether master narratives (or general theories) were either possible or desirable. The work of Barthes (1977), Derrida (1978, 1981), and Foucault (1970) effectively obliterated the modernist conception of the author, altering how we might understand the connections among authors, texts, and readers/audiences. Bakhtin (1981) broadened the interpretive space available to the readers of social science texts further by encouraging the recognition of multiple perspectives, unsettled meanings, plural voices, and local knowledge that transgresses claims to a unitary body of theory. Feminist critical theorists such as Harding (1991), Clough (1994), Hartsock (1983), and Smith (1990, 1992) promoted the unique and marginalized standpoints and particularities of women, and multicultural textualists such as Trinh (1989, 1992), Anzaldúa (1987), and Behar (1993, 1996) exposed how the complexities of race, class, sexuality, disability, and ethnicity are woven into the fabric of concrete, personal lived experiences.

Students entering graduate schools in the 1990s thus began their lives as researchers and scholars under a cloud of considerable epistemological doubt. During this period, a dramatic shift took place in the demographic composition of the graduate student population. There was a rapid increase in the enrollment of women, middle- and lower-class people, blacks and Hispanics, and students from Third and Fourth World countries. Gradually, these demographic changes led to a globalization of the curriculum and courses that stressed a greater appreciation for divergent rationalities grounded in cultural, racial, ethnic, gender, and class diversity (Shweder, 1986). Prepared by their lived histories to understand how a vocabulary of neutrality, objectivity, and scientific detachment could very easily function as a tool of oppression and domination, the newcomers hungered for a research agenda that resonated with their lives and self-interests. In the aftermath of postmodernism, they were reluctant to view the task of producing knowledge and representing reality as unproblematic. They understood research as a social process, as much a product of interaction as of observation, and inextricably bound to the embodied experiences and participation of the investigating self. Already inspired to question conventionality, power, and a monolithic view of research practices, and now reinforced by sustained critiques of orthodox writing practices, institutionalized knowledge production, and the crisis of representation, they were eager to locate engaging, creative, and useful alternatives to the existing models of research. Inevitably, they were drawn toward a radical democratization of the research process— an intention to minimize the power differential between researchers and participants (subjects)— and a greater emphasis on activism and applied research (Tedlock, 1991). Ultimately a new research vocabulary evolved that emphasized terms such as *social practices, interactive interviewing, co-constructed knowledge, action, agency, praxis, performance,* and *lived experience.*

In retrospect, the turn toward narrative inquiry and qualitative research appears to be a consequence of intellectual, social, and cultural changes, most notably the crisis in representation, greater access to previously marginalized minority populations, and a growing commitment to use research to make a difference, personally, emotionally, politically, and culturally. Initially reactive, the turn toward narrative became proactive. Social scientists drawn to narrative now are pursuing constructive responses to the agitating critiques of realism, modernism, and the correspondence theory of language. On the whole, they view these critiques not as an end but as a beginning, not as a reason for despair but as a cause for hope, not as a curtain closing on the excesses and illusions of the past but as a door opening to a future that is ripe with possibilities and promise. As Gergen (1999) has recently advised, we should be careful not to undermine the critical impulse, but at the same time we should be inspired by what we have learned from these critiques to emphasize the creation of alternatives. If we have learned that language is the medium of expression we use to create our reality, then we need to investigate what we can do with language to create the kinds of realities in which we want to live.

NARRATIVE INQUIRY: ASSUMPTIONS AND GOALS

A narrative approach to interpersonal communication focuses on the stories people tell about their lives. Our interest is in how lives and relationships develop communicatively; our access to lives and relationships is through the stories people tell about them. These stories may be told within the contexts of particular relationships, such as friendships or marriages, or outside relationships, in the contexts of research interviews, conversations, or dialogues. Stories should be thought of as social performances, at least insofar as they involve a teller and an audience—the husband or wife, the friend, the researcher, and so on. Normally, the stories people tell follow certain conventions of storytelling; that is, most stories contain similar elements and follow similar patterns of development. These include (a) people depicted as characters in the story; (b) an epiphany or crisis of some sort that provides dramatic tension, around which the emplotted events depicted in the story revolve and toward which a resolution and/or explanation is pointed; (c) a temporal ordering of events; and (d) a point or moral to the story that provides an explanation and gives meaning and value to the crisis.

Storytellers portray the people in their stories, including themselves, as characters: protagonists, antagonists, heroes, victims, and so on. A story usually revolves around an epiphany or dramatic event in an individual's life. The point or goal of the story is to help the teller to come to terms with, explain, or understand the event. Why did this happen to me? How can I understand what it means? What lesson have I learned? The events that are depicted occur over time. Most personal stories are told in an order that follows linear, chronological time. Each story has a beginning, a middle, and an end. The end point is particularly important, not only because it represents the goal toward which events or actions are pointed, and thus gives the story its capacity for drama and closure, but also because it is imbued with value. As MacIntyre (1981) observes, "Narrative requires an evaluative framework in which good or bad character helps to produce unfortunate or happy outcomes" (p. 456).

When people tell stories, they interpret and give meaning to the experiences depicted in their stories. The act of telling is a process of interpretation in which the teller and listener collaborate in sense making. It is assumed that meaning does not exist independent of or prior to the interpretation of experience. Storytelling connects experiences to meanings. In the process of interpreting experiences through storytelling, people activate subjectivity, emotionality, and available frames of narrative intelligibility. Once told, the storied experiences become constitutive of the storyteller's life. The story not only depicts life, it also shapes life reflexively. Stories are in a continual process of production, open to editing, revision, and transformation. Narratives lived, told, and anticipated occur in cultural contexts and are influenced by canonical stories circulating in everyday life. Often, but not always, the frames of intelligibility that function as narrative resources are canonical and cultural stories. But people are not condemned to live out the stories passed on through cultural productions and institutional traditions. If our stories never thwarted or contested received and canonical ones, we would have no expectation of change, no account of conflict, no

real demand to account for our actions, no sense of agency. Evidently, humans have a dazzling capacity to reform or reframe the meanings of their actions through stories. As Rosenwald (1992) points out, there is always an uncomfortable tension between restless desire and stabilizing conventions.

The stories people tell should not be understood as "maps," "mirrors," or "reflections" of the experiences they depict. They are fluid, co-constructed, meaning-centered reproductions of experience achieved in the context of relationships and subject to negotiable frames of intelligibility and the desire for continuity and coherence over time. Thus we always have options and alternatives (Carr, 1986). We reframe, revise, remake, retell, and relive our stories over the course of our lives.

Narrative inquiry is a mode of research that invites readers to think *with* stories (Frank, 1995). Readers are invited to enter into dialogue with narratives that depict the difficult choices about how to act that we all face in our lives, and to contemplate the possibilities and limitations we encounter when we attempt to become authors of our own stories. Baxter (1992) refers to narrative inquiry as an alternative to the dominant psychological approaches to the study of interpersonal communication. Looking toward the future almost a decade ago, she predicted that "personal narratives are likely to emerge as the distinguishing method of social approaches to personal relationships" (p. 333).

Polkinghorne (1995) has developed a taxonomy of different kinds of narrative inquiry that corresponds to Jerome Bruner's (1986) distinction between paradigmatic and narrative reasoning. In Polkinghorne's schema, *analysis of narratives* refers to projects that are grounded on paradigmatic reasoning. These projects treat stories as "data" and use "analysis" to arrive at *themes* that hold across stories or delineate types of stories and/or story lines. Often the method of analysis is akin to grounded theory (Charmaz, 1995, 2000;

Glaser and Strauss, 1967), in which the investigator works inductively, presumably from the ground of the story upward, and the text in which the analysis is presented assumes the form of a traditional social science report. Polkinghorne's second form of narrative inquiry, *narrative analysis,* denotes a class of inquiry in which the product is a story—a case, a biography, a life history—that the researcher configures to represent the events, characters, and issues that he or she has studied. Polkinghorne emphasizes the difference in the research products of analysis of narrative and narrative analysis; whereas the former ends in abstractions, the latter results in a story. This distinction is important and useful, but the vocabulary in which it is articulated can be confusing. For example, Riessman (1993) has written a methodological primer called *Narrative Analysis,* but, in Polkinghorne's typology, the kinds of narrative inquiry on which Riessman focuses would fall under the genre of analysis of narrative, not narrative analysis.

My colleagues and I have introduced a less confusing typology that distinguishes *evocative narratives* from two other types of narrative studies, *accounts* and *storied lives* (Bochner, Ellis, & Tillmann-Healy, 1997). Whereas research on accounts and storied lives normally conforms to the paradigmatic form of social science reporting, evocative narratives are stories that break with this traditional form. The word *evocative* contrasts the expressive and dialogic goals of this type of narrative inquiry with the more traditional orientations of mainstream, representational social science. Denzin (1997) refers to evocative narratives as a form of "ethnographic poetics" and emphasizes the crucial need to set off this form of research storytelling from traditional empiricist approaches to the analysis of narratives. Following Trinh (1989, p. 141), Denzin opposes the inclination to turn a story told into a story analyzed because, in effect, the meaning of the story is sacrificed at the alter of methodological rigor, and we lose what makes the story a story. "They only hear and read the story from within a set of predetermined structural categories. They do not hear the story as it was told" (Denzin, 1997, p. 249).

Depictions of interpersonal communication that fall under the rubric of evocative narratives show how people cope with exceptional, difficult, and transforming crises in their interpersonal lives, how they invent new ways of speaking when old ways fail them, how they make the absurd sensible and the disastrous manageable, how they turn calamities into gifts. What is special and important about evocative narratives, and what makes them so appallingly difficult to digest for more orthodox researchers, are the alternatives they offer to traditional perspectives on social science research. Stories activate subjectivity and compel emotional response; stories long to be used rather than analyzed, to be told and retold rather than theorized and settled, to offer lessons for further conversation rather than truths without any rivals; and stories promise the companionship of intimate detail as a substitute for the loneliness of abstracted facts. Thus evocative stories not only breach ordinary and canonical inscriptions about living, they challenge traditional norms of writing and research, forcing us to reconsider the goals of our research, the forms we use for expressing relationship experience, and the divisions we accept and enforce that separate literature from social science.

Personal writing akin to evocative narrative has recently proliferated in the mainstream press, in new journalism, in creative nonfiction, and in the genres of literary memoir, autobiography, and autopathography (Buford, 1996; Harrington, 1997; Hawkins, 1993; Parini, 1998; "True Confessions," 1996). All of the genres of "life writing" (see, e.g., Tierney, 2000) seem to have turned toward more intimate, personal, and self-conscious writing. Similarly, social science researchers have turned increasingly toward less anonymous, more personal styles of writing that parallel the focus on personal writing genres in literature, nonfiction, and journalism. Among the abundant examples of this movement within the social sciences are the recent special issues of such journals as the *Journal of Contemporary Ethnography* (Ellis & Bochner, 1996b), *Qualitative Sociology* (Glassner, 1997; Hertz, 1996; Zussman, 2000), and *Communication Theory* (Geist, 1999-2000); the book series Ethnographic Alternatives (for which Carolyn Ellis and I serve as series editors; see Angrosino, 1998; Banks & Banks, 1998; Bochner & Ellis, 2002; Drew, 2001; Ellis & Bochner, 1996a; Goodall, 2000; Jones, 1998; Lagerway, 1998; Markham, 1998); the collections edited by anthropologists (Benson, 1993; Brady, 1991; Okely & Callaway, 1992), sociologists (Ellis & Flaherty, 1992; Hertz, 1997; Zola, 1982), communication researchers (Banks & Banks, 1998; Ellis & Bochner, 1996a; Perry & Geist, 1997), psychologists (Josselson & Lieblich, 1995), and educators (Hertz, 1997; Tierney & Lincoln, 1997); and the numerous articles and monographs (e.g., McLaughlin & Tierney, 1993) featured in academic journals and annuals such as *American Anthropologist, Anthropology and Humanism Quarterly, Auto/Biography, Feminist Studies, Journal of Loss and Trauma, Narrative Inquiry, The Narrative Study of Lives, Qualitative Inquiry, Sociology of Sport Journal, Sociological Quarterly, Studies in Symbolic Interaction, Symbolic Interaction, Text and Performance Quarterly,* and *Women's International Quarterly.*

A good example of evocative narrative and life writing is Linda Gray Sexton's (1994) memoir *Searching for Mercy Street*, in which she tells the riveting story of her troubled relationship with her mother, the poet Anne Sexton, who committed suicide in 1974 at the age of 45. Linda begins with the event that defined both her childhood and Anne's motherhood—her being sent away to live for 2 years in the home of relatives while her mother recuperated from a psychotic episode. Expressing complex feelings of abandonment and confusion, isolation and yearning, and disgust and admiration, Linda describes her lifelong struggle to free herself from the grip of her powerful, dependent mother without relinquishing the love and empathy she felt for her. She recounts details of her mother's extramarital affairs with women and with men, her sexual abuse of her children, her cruelty toward her husband, and her disturbed reversal of the mother-child bond. She accounts for her mother's destructive behavior as "the price and reward of madness . . . and . . . genius" (p. 276). Linda refuses to demonize her mother as a monster or exempt her as a victim, and she is unwilling to oversimplify her complicated feelings of love and rage:

> I loved my mother when she was alive; I love her still—despite anger, despite her mental illness and the things it allowed her to do. I never wanted her to seem like "a monster" to anyone. She was loving and kind, but she was also sick and destructive. She tried to be "a good mother," but in truth, she was not. Mother was simply human, subject to all sorts of frailties and problems. (p. 281)

Linda Sexton challenges her readers to question the usefulness of applying simplistic labels such as "abused child" or "vengeful daughter" to summarize terribly complicated family relationships. Her narrative is a graceful exposition of the concrete lived circumstances within which a person struggles to deal with the dialectics of attachment/loss, separation/integration, vulnerability/cruelty, and expression/protection. Moreover, *Searching for Mercy Street* is uniquely self-reflexive. The text bends back on itself and its author as Linda puts words to her memories in order to mourn her losses and better understand the meaning of a rich and agitated bond between daughter and mother. As her mother once said, "I write to master experience," so Linda writes to "take control of the demons inside and let them know who was boss"—to earn "the reward of a mind clearer for the effort, a soul cleansed and released" (p. 296). Inevitably her insistence on telling the whole painful truth as she remembers it leads her to confront not only the demons of a disturbed relationship but also the taboos that silence writing from the heart:

> Though I am no longer a child, to write of these things feels forbidden, to give voice to memories such as these, taboo. Family matters: dark and secret. I remember the snake who comes in the dark, the taste of fear sour in my mouth, the blackness of a bedroom not my own, and worst of all the voice whispering: *If you tell they will not love you anymore. If you tell they will send you away again.* (p. 21)

Searching for Mercy Street is an exemplar of the kind of narrative inquiry that fuses social science and literature by creating texts in which the language of science merges with the aesthetics of art (Benson, 1993, p. xi). The products of what Ivan Brady (1991) calls "artful science" are narratives that simulate reality, applying the imaginative power of literary, dramatic, and poetic forms to create the effect of reality, a convincing likeness to life as it is sensed, felt, and lived.

I want to emphasize five distinguishing features of this type of narrative inquiry. First, the author usually writes in the first person, making herself or himself the object of research (Tedlock, 1991), thus transgressing the conventional separation of researcher and subject (Jackson, 1989). Second, the narrative breaches the traditional focus on generalization across cases by focusing on generalization within a single case extended over time (Geertz, 1973). Third, the text is presented as a story replete with a narrator, characterization, and plotline, akin to forms of writing associated with the novel or biography, and thus fractures the boundaries that traditionally

separate social science from literature. Fourth, the story often discloses hidden details of private life and highlights emotional experience, and thus challenges the rational actor model of social performance that dominates social science. And fifth, the ebb and flow of relationship experience are depicted in an episodic form that dramatizes the motion of connected lives across the curve of time (Weinstein, 1988), and thus resists the standard practice of portraying a relationship as a snapshot (Ellis, 1993).

Each of these features is present in *Searching for Mercy Street*. Sexton writes her story as a first-person account in which she is both the narrator and the main character. She observes and interprets the meanings of her own actions as well as those of her mother and other family members. Thus she acts as both a researcher and a subject.

Second, Linda's story covers events that took place in her family over a period of nearly 40 years. She does not try to extend the meanings and conclusions she draws about her family to other families, although readers certainly can locate some of their own experience within that of the Sextons. Rather, she focuses on the patterns of interaction that recurred over time within the case of her particular family (across the span of three generations). In the process, she shows how reality was constituted in this family culture, within this time frame, and at this place.

Third, Linda presents her family history as a story. She uses many of the storytelling techniques associated with fiction to animate the drama of her experience and to heighten interest in the story. But she relies on a core of empirical "facts" that give her story credibility as a "true" account. As a reader, you are aware that Linda Sexton is negotiating the meaning of these events as she goes along, using what Bruner (1990) calls the "shadowy epistemology of the story" (p. 54) to try on different interpretations. She keeps you open to the multiple and uncertain meanings of a good story. Thus her narrative falls *between* fiction and fact, *between* the imaginary and the real. As John Berger (1983) observes that "life outstrips our vocabulary" (p. 77), so Linda Sexton (1994) recognizes the complex connection between words and reality: "Words can capture truth or promulgate lies. Words can clarify or disguise. . . . what I seek is only the truth of how I *felt,* a truth far more revelatory *about me* than any exact history" (p. 39).

Fourth, by articulating her feelings within the intelligible frame of family relationships, one that centers on painful, hidden family secrets, Linda openly confronts the moral predicament of what constitutes a good life *for her.* She has to come to grips with what really matters—her children, her husband, her career as a writer—and what she gives to and takes from other people. Thus, by making sense of her past, she clears a path for her future.

Finally, the story of life in the Sexton family is revealed in concrete episodes of interaction. Linda re-creates scenes from her history in which the members of her family enact the patterns that bind them. Readers witness family members interacting with each other, feel their moods, and sense their entrapment. These scenes include both the commonplaces of everyday life (cooking, cleaning, transporting, and celebrating holidays) and the exceptional events that characterized the family's particularity (sexual abuse, family violence, corruption of normal family roles). We learn that the Sextons are like most families much of the time, but they also endure episodes of extreme deviance and disturbance. If we witnessed only one or two of these episodes, our capacity to grasp the larger configuration of imbalance between ordinary and extraordinary events would be greatly inhibited.

NARRATIVE TRUTH

To what kind of truth do stories such as Linda Sexton's aspire? The precise connection between experience and story is hotly debated among narrative theorists (Bochner et al., 1997; Freeman, 1998a, 1998b; MacIntyre, 1981; Mink, 1969-1970). Is life narratively structured, or is human narration an ad hoc grafting of story onto experience? Some writers allege that humans impose narratives on their experiences. For example, Louis Mink (1969-1970) argues that life is not lived as a story. Instead, stories are projected onto experience after the fact. Accordingly, the meanings of experience are not given by or inherent in the experience itself. As Hayden White (1980) observes, "It is because real events do not offer themselves as stories that their narrativization is so difficult" (p. 8). When we form stories out of the rawness of lived experience, we give them a structure and meaning that, as Shotter (1987) suggests, "they did not in themselves possess but which nonetheless they will afford or allow" (p. 235).

Other theorists, however, dispute the idea that stories arbitrarily impose a narrative structure on memories. They argue that experience seems to call forth narration, not only because humans feel a need to tell stories about their lives, but also because "consciousness is itself an insipient story" (Crites, 1971, p. 297). Storytelling is a direct and obvious form of recollecting memories because the modalities of experience are temporal, and the images preserved in memory are cinematic, transient episodes that gain significance and continuity by being situated in stories (Crites, 1971). Alasdair MacIntyre (1981) opposes the idea that experience can be severed from narrative because "we all live out narratives in our lives and . . . we understand our lives in terms of the narratives we live out" (p. 197). MacIntyre's sentiments are echoed by Kerby (1991), who argues that "our unexamined life is already a quasi-narrative, and that lived time is already a drama of sorts" (p. 42), and by Carr (1986), who contends that "narrative form is not a dress which covers something else but the structure inherent in human experience and action" (p. 65). Accordingly, the prenarrative level or narrative "nature" of experience constitutes what Ricoeur (1983) calls "a demand for narrative." *Life anticipates narrative.*

The dispute over the connection between lives and stories about them revolves mainly around the question of whether stories falsify experience. What is the truth value of a story that depicts meanings attached to one's lived experiences? To say that stories are imposed on experience is to suggest that narrative gives experience a structure it does not have, that stories fictionalize life. Shotter (1987) expresses this point of view when he laments the distortions introduced by the plot structures of stories. Stories have the effect of giving a determinate ordering to indeterminate and incomplete experiences. Because stories about communicative relationships are based on details that may be vague and uncertain—that is, open to many interpretations—Shotter seeks an alternative to narratives that would be more grounded in facts and less prone to distortion.

Shotter's concern about the distortions of narrative, however, runs the risk of limiting the ground claimed by narrative to that of a mirrored retrieval of the past. He is correct to say that narratives cannot depict the way things are or were, and this is precisely the point. Narrative truth seeks to keep the past alive in the present. Through narrative we learn to understand the meanings and significance of the past as incomplete, tentative, and revisable according to contingencies of our present life circumstances. The factual "distortions" that may arise from contingencies of narrative emplotment are worrisome, however, only if one sees narrative interpretation as a neutral attempt to mirror the facts of one's life, to recover already constituted meanings. But it is not the "facts" themselves that one tries to redeem through narrative tellings, but rather an articulation of the significance and meaning of one's experiences. Indeed, it is within the frame of a story that "facts" gain

their importance. Life stories are thus based on facts but not determined by them. The "facts" achieve significance and intelligibility contextually by being articulated within a temporal frame that considers what came before and what came after. Stories that address the meanings of a life (experience) always seek a way of extending them into the future (Rosenwald, 1992).

If self-narration is a "distortion," then what is the Truth? How can we know it? By consigning narratives to the realm of fictions, Shotter implies that stories do not measure up to the experiences, the selves, or the lives they seek to represent. In effect, experiences become something more tangible than the stories that depict them. Otherwise, how can we know that narratives are fictions? By what grounds could we judge them as "falsifying"? The question is, Against what are narratives to be judged? The events they depict? The self they represent? Lived experiences? As Freeman (1998a) observes, the whole argument about the distortions of narrative usually turns out to be parasitic on an empiricist account of reality. The charge of distortion is inextricably tied to the possibility of undistortion, a getting to the true or ultimate bottom of things that writers such as Shotter usually deem impossible or unlikely.

The kind of truth we seek with narrative, then, is not akin to correspondence with prior meanings assumed to be constituted in prenarrative experience. We need not assume that narratives seek to represent lives correctly, only that narrators believe they are doing so. We can judge one narrative interpretation of events against another, but we cannot measure any narrative against the meaning of events themselves because the meaning of prenarrative experience is constituted in its narrative expression. Life and narrative are inextricably and dialectically connected. *Life both anticipates telling and draws meaning from it. Narrative is both about living and part of it.*

To eschew human storytelling because of its possible distortions is to miss or ignore the interpretive importance of narrative for understanding, showing, and accepting life's contingencies. Personal narratives are not so much academic as they are existential, reflecting as they do our desire to grasp or seize the possibilities of meaning, which is what gives life its imaginative and poetic qualities (Freeman, 1998a). As human beings living in the world, we are not scientists seeking laws that govern our behavior; we are storytellers seeking meanings that help us cope with our circumstances. Our stories must be adequate for the situations with which we must deal. Even if we wanted to, we could not turn off our narrative sensibilities. As adults we have lost any semblance of narrative innocence by being socialized into a narrative realm of consciousness. We use language; we have seen, heard, read, and interpreted stories; we are already embedded in a story and committed to a life imbued with meaning (Kerby, 1991). We tell our stories in particular styles, for particular purposes, at particular times. Often our purpose is to foster a story of the past that helps us function effectively in the present. Our tellings rework, refigure, and remake our past in accordance with a future onto which we project our possibilities. Thus narrative truth is pragmatic truth (Spence, 1982). The question is not whether narratives convey the way things actually were, but rather what narratives do, what consequences they have, to what uses they can be put. Narrative is our means of recollecting the meanings of past experiences, turning life into language, and disclosing to us the truth in our experiences (Bochner, 2001).

STORIES AS THEORIES

To achieve the goals of a meaning-centered, narratively oriented perspective on interpersonal communication, we need to be able to talk and think differently about what we mean by the term *theory*. Ideally, we ought to be able to understand that there is nothing as theoretical as a good story, at least insofar as we can move directly from a story to our own lives. The line that often is drawn between theory and story is false—and not false. The split is not false when theory is viewed in the vocabulary of traditional empiricism, as objective, scientific, detached, value-free, and beyond human consciousness. Described in these terms, theory becomes an end in itself, divorced from its consequences, politics, and uses. This is the sense of theory promoted by those who see the purpose of communication research, to take one representative example, as the development of middle-range (Burleson, 1992) or general theories of communication (Berger, 1991), but who do not consider the ways in which describing or explaining "reality" is different from dealing with it. As Rorty (1979) queries: "What is the point? What moral is to be drawn from our knowledge of how we and the rest of nature work?" Or "What do we do with ourselves now that we know the laws of our own behavior?" (p. 38). When we don't ask questions like these we run the risk of forgetting that theorizing is not an activity devoid of context or consequences. Sometimes the consequences turn out to be wretched, as suggested by the tragic story of the kin of Europeans killed in the July 1996 crash of TWA Flight 800. Stuck for seven days and nights in uncomfortable hotel rooms in an unfamiliar city, frustrated by the cross-purposes of theory and experience, and bewildered by the insensitivity of officials to their emotional trauma, the kin of victims had reached the limits of their tolerance. At a hastily called news conference, a spokesman for the French contingent expressed the feelings shared by many in the group, saying, in essence: "We don't care about your theories or your examination of the causes of the crash. We want our bodies and we want to go home."

But there is no split between theory and story when theorizing is conceived as a social and communicative activity. The use of the term *social theory* is an effective way of expressing the communicative functions of theorizing that I have in mind. Social theory is less concerned with representation and more concerned with communication. By seeing the work of our theorizing as social, we move away from the pretensions of transcendental observation and emphasize, instead, the possibilities that are opened for dialogue and collaboration. Social theory works the spaces between history and destiny. The social and interpersonal world is understood as a world of connection, contact, and relationship. It is also a world where consequences, values, politics, and moral dilemmas are abundant and central.

As social beings, we live storied lives (Rosenwald & Ochberg, 1992). Our identities—who we are and what we do—originate in the tales passed down to us and the stories we take on as our own. In this sense, stories constitute our mode of being (Schafer, 1980). Storytelling is both a *method* of knowing—a social practice—and a way of telling about our lives (Richardson, 1990). As an academic practice, the approach to narrative inquiry that centers on sense making and acts of meaning changes the activity of theorizing from a process of thinking *about* to one of thinking *with* (Frank, 1995). Theory meets story when we think with a story rather than about it. As Frank (1995) points out, "To think with a story is to reduce it to content and then analyze the content. . . . To think with a story is to experience its affecting one's own life and to find in that effect a certain truth of one's own life" (p. 23).

Thus we do not turn stories into data to *test* theoretical propositions. Rather, we *link* theory to story by thinking *with* a story, trying to stay with the story, letting ourselves resonate with the moral dilemmas it may pose, recognizing its ambiguities, examining its contradictions, feeling its nuances, letting ourselves become part of the story (Ellis,

1995b). We think with a story from the framework of our own lives. We ask what kind of a person we are becoming when we take the story in and how we can use it for our own purposes, what ethical directions it points us toward, and what moral commitments it calls out in us (Coles, 1989).

NARRATIVE INQUIRY AS A WRITING PROJECT

Plummer (2001) refers to the issue of writing as "the dark secret of social science" (p. 168). Until recently, writing has not been a topic of discussion even in social science methods courses (Richardson, 2000). Of course, when we take the point of view that data speak for themselves, then we are unlikely to view a researcher as a writer who makes choices about how to express and communicate with readers. Then the social scientist becomes only a translator who reports or presents "findings" as if he or she were not there. Beginning with Gusfield's (1976) provocative analysis of scientific papers on "drinking-driving," however, scholars interested in the rhetoric of science (e.g., Simons, 1989) have shown the many ways in which scientific writing is permeated by rhetorical choices and conventions and how it has become dull, dry, saturated with jargon, and largely inaccessible to all but a few select readers (Richardson, 2000).

As a genre of writing, narrative inquiry resists the presumption that data speak for themselves. Taking its inspiration from the deconstruction of the picture theory of language, narrative inquiry considers the practices of interactive communication and dialogue as the appropriate model for telling about the empirical world (Bochner & Waugh, 1995). If we can no longer cling to the presumption that the world decides which descriptions of it are true or false, then we must warrant that all attempts to represent reality involve transforming a speechless world into a discursive form that makes sense (has meaning for or to someone). Traditional science is one discourse that does this, but not the only one. Narrative inquiry gained its momentum and inspiration largely from the doubt that was cast on the special or unique truth-bearing status of scientific discourse. Thus narrative inquiry begins by shifting the function of social science representation from description to communication (Bochner & Waugh, 1995). In narrative inquiry, the presumption of a detached observer using neutral language to produce an unmediated mirroring of reality is replaced by the premise that all attempts to speak for, write about, or represent other people's lives necessarily are partial, situated, and mediated ways of creating value and inscribing meanings. The texts we craft as social scientists thus become sites of moral responsibility (Richardson, 1992). The lesson to be learned is that we should promote the ideal of multiplicity. As Rorty (1982) says, "Narratives as well as laws, redescriptions as well as predictions serve a useful purpose in helping us deal with the problems of society" (p. 198).

Writing is a process of turning life into language. Written reality is always a second-order reality (Jackson, 1995). Whether we use qualitative or quantitative methods, or we call our work empiricist, interpretivist, or critical, makes little difference. All of us rework and reshape the events we are representing or expressing when we render them as language. As Rorty (1989) states, "Where there are no sentences there is no truth" (p. 5). When we fit language to the world, all of us are mucking around looking for truth (Bochner, Ellis, & Tillmann-Healy, 1998).

Nevertheless, I do not want to understate the differences between traditional social science writing and the stories associated with narrative inquiry. Traditional social science writing privileges the types of events and data that can be subjected to conceptual analysis and theoretical explanation. Ambiguous, vague, and contingent experiences that cannot easily be covered by concepts or organized into a coherent system of thought are bypassed in favor of experiences that can be controlled and explained. Immediate experience becomes grist for the theoretical mill. Moreover, distancing oneself from the subject matter (like a spectator at a sporting event) is taken as an appropriate and normative model of research and writing practices. Thus the text is written in a neutral, authoritative, and scientific voice.

Jerome Bruner (1986) regards narrative and traditional scientific (logico-scientific) "ways of knowing" as two distinctively different but complementary ways of organizing experience and constructing reality. According to Bruner, the logico-scientific or "paradigmatic" mode emphasizes general causes and uses standardized procedures to assure public verifiability and to reach empirical truths. The paradigmatic mode tests logically derived possibilities (hypotheses) against observables to reach formal conclusions about general causes, however tentative, that are warranted by empirical observations. Truthfulness is established through the marshaling of empirical evidence.

Like paradigmatic arguments, narratives also function as a means of persuasion. But, as Bruner (1986) observes, they are "fundamentally different: arguments convince one of their truth, stories of their lifelikeness" (p. 11). The storyteller is preoccupied with showing how lived experience is endowed with meaning. The result is not so much conclusive as it is believable. Stories invite readers to enter horizons of the human condition where lived life is shown as comic, tragic, and absurd, and where opportunities exist to mold a reality and live in it. "How to encompass in our minds the complexity of some lived moments in life?" asks Robert Coles (1989). "You don't do that with theories. You don't do that with a system of ideas. You do it with a story" (p. 128).

The written and performed texts associated with narrative inquiry fracture the boundaries of conventional textuality in the social sciences. Denzin (1997) identifies several ways in which the poetic and storied texts that he classifies as narrative push against and extend conventional boundaries. First, they adopt literary devices that erase distinctions between fact and fiction (Banks & Banks, 1998; Ellis, 1995b; Krieger, 1983). Second, they move outward from personal experience to a story of the experience designed to create for the reader or listener an experience of the experience (Ellis & Bochner, 1992). Third, they privilege emotion and emotionality, not only the feelings of the writer, but also those of the reader (Ellis, 1995b). Fourth, the validity of the narrated text rests on this evoked emotion (Ellis, 1995b; Richardson, 1994); the capacity to evoke emotional response becomes a measure of the narrative's authority (Ellis, 1995b). Fifth, the narratives show concrete, detailed actions and events embedded in the contexts from which experiences derive their meanings; snippets that strip actions and utterances from their contexts are avoided. Sixth, stories encourage identification and empathy between writer and reader, breaching the traditional hierarchy between an all-knowing writer and a passive receiver. Seventh, the evocative form encourages a therapeutic experience for the reader and the writer and thus transgresses the boundary between research and therapy. As Denzin (1997) concludes, these narrative texts "reject the search for absolute truth and pursue a form of narrative truth that is suspicious of totalizing theory, breaking down, in the process, the moral and intellectual distance between reader and writer" (p. 215).

How do writers working within the narrative inquiry paradigm move from experience to narrative text (Kiesinger, 1998)? Space limitations preclude my attempting a comprehensive treatment of narrative method here, but I do want to review briefly four promising methodological innovations: autoethnographic stories, co-constructed narratives, interactive interviewing, and layered accounts.

Autoethnographic stories include narratives variously classified as first-person accounts, personal narratives, self-narratives, native ethnographies, impressionist tales, and feminist ethnographies (Ellis & Bochner, 2000; Ellis, Kiesinger, & Tillmann-Healy, 1997). They often start with experiences of the researchers; however, they also may come from personal experiences of participants encouraged by researchers to tell their stories. Sometimes researchers' stories are integrated with or told alongside participants' stories (e.g., Behar, 1993; Brown, 1991). The personal story is told within and moves through the layers of the social, from relationships to family outward to culture. Back and forth autoethnographers gaze, first through an ethnographic wide-angle lens, focusing outward on social and cultural aspects of their personal experience; then they look inward, exposing a vulnerable self that is moved by and may move through, refract, and resist cultural interpretations (Deck, 1990; Ellis & Bochner, 2000; Neumann, 1996; Reed-Danahay, 1997). In autoethnographies, the inner workings of the self are investigated, presented, and/or performed in concrete actions, thoughts, and feelings; developed and problematized through dialogue; shown processually in vivid scenes and dramatic plot; and shown contextually through history, social structure, and culture, which themselves often operate as unstated subtexts that are dialectically revealed through action, thought, and language. Various methodological strategies have been developed in connection with autoethnographic projects. These include systematic sociological introspection (Ellis, 1991), biographic method (Denzin, 1989), personal experience methods (Clandinin & Connelly, 1994), feminist methods (Reinharz, 1992), consciousness-raising (Hollway, 1989), interactive interviewing (Ellis et al., 1997) and co-constructed narrative (Bochner & Ellis, 1992).

Ellis emphasizes that she works from field notes about the relationships on which her autoethnographies (see, e.g., Ellis, 1993, 1995a, 1995b, 1995c, 1998a, 1998b) are based, and she also keeps notes on the writing process as it moves along. For *Final Negotiations,* a book that concentrates on the interplay between Ellis's partner's deteriorating health and their relationship, her notes on the writing process "became the basis for telling how I transformed ethnographic fieldwork into a story that I hoped would speak therapeutically to a mass audience and sociologically to an academic one" (Ellis, 1995b, pt. V).

Co-constructed narratives are stories jointly constructed by relational partners that focus on an epiphany or crisis in the relationship. These stories show partners engaged in the specific, concrete details of daily living (Ellis & Bochner, 1992). This type of research focuses on the interactional sequences by which interpretations of relationship life are constructed, coordinated, and solidified into stories. The local narratives that are jointly produced thus display couples in the process of "doing" their relationships, trying to turn fragmented, vague, or disjointed events into intelligible, coherent accounts. Ideally, participants would be two researchers who have a relationship outside the research process, a researcher and a partner, or a researcher who serves as a coordinator and moderator for the joint construction by another relational pair. Carolyn Ellis and I have described the methods of co-constructed narrative in detail (Bochner & Ellis, 1992; Ellis & Bochner, 1992).

Interactive interviews, not unlike co-constructed narratives, are produced through collaborative communicative processes (Ellis et al., 1997). They take place in small group settings in which both participants and researchers are accorded space to share their stories in the context of their developing relationships. The feelings, insights, and stories that researchers bring to these interactive sessions are as important as those of the other participants; the understandings that emerge among all parties during interaction—what they learn together—is as compelling as the stories each brings to the research sessions. Ideally, all participants should have some history together or be willing to develop a

deeper connection. It is also helpful for researchers as well as coparticipants to have personal experience with the topic that is the focus of the group research sessions. If that is not the case, the researcher should be willing to engage in new experiences that can provide a basis of personal connection to the topic, to make him or her a more equal coparticipant. In Ellis et al.'s (1997) narrative, which is based on interactive interviewing sessions that focused on women's eating disorders, the authors express what happened in the collaborative sessions as a multivoiced and multilayered account. The story shows how they managed discussions on the difficult topic of bulimia and how they moved back and forth between expression and protection and between disclosure and restraint, making each other's personal feelings the highest priority in the research. Their project raises provocative questions about orthodox interviewing practices and the boundaries typically erected between therapy and research.

A *layered account* is told in a writing style intended to convey the blurred, conflicting, and intertwined voices that speak within the consciousness of the writer of a narrative inquiry as he or she undertakes the task of communicating lived experiences (Ronai, 1992, 1995, 1996). Layered accounts often rotate between more conventional forms of social science reporting and more experimental forms that communicate subjectivity and emotionality. Whereas the former may make reference to citations, bibliography, and research procedures, the latter emphasizes biographical details, introspective thoughts, and emotional and subjective responses. Sometimes these voices are separated clearly, but often they merge or become indistinct. Often, the goal of layered accounts is to unite the academic and experiential voices in an unobtrusive way that makes the narrative seamless (Bochner, 1997; Jago, 1996; Tillmann-Healy, 1996, 1999, 2001). Ronai (1992) speaks eloquently about the dilemma to which layered accounts respond:

My identity is fracturing as I spill my guts while trying to produce in my audience an emotional knowing of my experience as dancer/researcher. I cannot smoothly switch hats and write, "Here is how the dancer in me feels, and here is how the researcher feels, and here is how the wife feels, and so on." It is dishonest and contrived to sort out separate influences, and label them, though occasionally one voice will speak loudly and clearly. (pp. 104-105)

Richardson (2000) subsumes all of these forms of narrative representation under the broad class of new writing in the social sciences that she refers to as creative analytic practices (CAP). She uses this term to make the point that these research practices are both creative and analytic, and that imagination and rigor not be perceived as contradictory or incompatible. Other species of CAP that I have not considered in detail here include poetry (Austin, 1996, 1998), drama (Gray et al., 2002; Paget, 1990, 1993), and visual (Picart, 2002), art-based (Scott-Hoy, 2002), conversational (Richardson & Lockridge, 1998, 2002), and polyvocal texts (Butler & Rosenblum, 1991).

RESEARCH ETHICS

Narrative inquiry poses important questions that each researcher ideally should confront. The questions include the following:

1. What kind of relationship should exist between the researcher and the research participants (subjects)?

2. What are the researcher's ethical obligations to the participants?

3. How should the experiences and/or voices of the participants be represented in the research story (report, article, chapter, monograph, or whatever)?

4. How should the experiences and voice(s) of the researcher(s) be represented in the research story?

5. For whom—what audience(s)—is the research being conducted, written, and/or performed?

6. Whose interests are served by the presentation and/or performance of the research?

7. How should the research be written, presented, and/or performed?

I do not claim to have definitive answers for these questions, but I do wish to consider why they need to be asked and what is at stake in the answers one gives. The questions boil down to issues of authorship, voice, authority, relationship, audience, reflexivity, function, and ethics. Taken together, they go to the heart of why we do research, how we expect our research to be used and by whom, who we become in the process of doing research, and how we conceive of our ethical obligations and responsibilities. Who gets to speak and who gets to respond? When and where does research begin, and when and where does it end? Who benefits from research and who may suffer? Who should have access to what gets spoken and what opportunities should they have to speak back (Ellis & Flemons, 2002)?

What is at stake in our answers to these questions is much more than whether a new group of social scientists who want to do research differently will be allowed to speak. Rather, at issue are the material and ethical practices of the entire discipline (Denzin, 1997). The profusion of new alternatives—such as action research; appreciative inquiry; community-engaged, collaborative scholarship; and polyvocal pedagogy—suggests a growing and widespread concern about the moral center of our work, the connections between research and practice, and the link between the university and society. We can no longer shelter ourselves in the ivory tower and put off questions about how useful the work we do is and for whom.

From the perspective of narrative inquiry, research is a reflexive, relational, dialogic, and collaborative process grounded in the following seven assumptions:

1. The researcher is part of the research data.

2. A social science text always is composed by a particular somebody someplace.

3. Research involves the emotionality and subjectivity of both researchers and participants.

4. The relationship between researchers and research participants should be democratic; at the very least, researchers should always be concerned about their obligations to the people they study and write about.

5. What researchers write should be written for participants as much as about them; researchers and participants should be accountable to each other; researchers' voices should not dominate the voices of participants.

6. Research should be about what could be (not just about what has been).

7. Researchers should conceive of their readers or audiences as coparticipants, not as spectators, and should give them opportunities to think with (not just about).

Thus the goals of narrative inquiry are to keep conversation going, to activate subjectivity and feeling, to raise consciousness, to promote empathy, and to encourage activism.

If the human sciences are to become more human, then as researchers we have to come to terms with our ethical practices honestly, vulnerably, and with a willingness to change standard practices wherever we find them abusive and/or exploitative. Robert Coles (1997) asks what gives us the right as researchers to elicit other people's stories, leave the scene, and tell their stories to others (see also Plummer, 2001). From the perspective of the sort of narrative inquiry that I have embraced in this chapter, we should no longer treat this as a question raised by constituencies who don't understand the purity and purposes of academic research. We have to give something back to the people we study. We have to be ethically

cognizant of what we take into research contexts and what we take away from them. What we write needs to speak to more than a handful of experts or authorities sitting comfortably in protected and polished offices while the people we write about continue to suffer in silence and gain little or no access to the knowledge we claim to produce. Whether we embrace narrative inquiry or not, those of us who do interpersonal research undoubtedly will have to answer to the larger society beyond the university who want to know how useful our research is and want to be told in a jargon-free fashion that makes the logic and practicality of what we do understandable.

CODA

When I was writing the first "Perspectives on Inquiry" essay in 1984 (Bochner, 1985), I was concerned about the marginality of interpretive and critical perspectives on interpersonal communication. My main goal was to open a conversation between those who worked on the margins and those who occupied the center and to find a way to keep the conversation going. I did not anticipate the reformist academic movement referred to as "the qualitative revolution" (Gergen, 1999; Gergen & Gergen, 2000; Schwandt, 2000), which has so dramatically expanded the choices and alternatives to which research on interpersonal communication can be directed. Fueled initially by the dual crises of representation and legitimation, the qualitative movement developed an astonishing array of new research orientations that reflect radically different ethical commitments, methodological and writing practices, and conceptions of representation, validity, and objectivity (Bochner, 2000; Denzin & Lincoln, 2000a; Ellis & Berger, 2001). Under the banner of qualitative inquiry, this new generation of activist, interpretivist, constructivist researchers is transforming the intellectual, emotional, and ethical commitments of the social sciences.

Although controversies continue to brew over which research perspective(s) should govern our scholarly journals and which methodological requirements should be imposed on our graduate students, no doubt remains about the necessity for multiple research perspectives. No single research paradigm exists to which all social scientists must be committed. As Lincoln and Guba (2000) put it: "There can be no question that the legitimacy of postmodern paradigms is well established and at least equal to the legitimacy of received and conventional paradigms" (p. 164). Lincoln and Denzin (2000) conclude, in fact, that the paradigm wars have ended. While we were fighting over where to draw the boundaries, the territory itself was reconfigured. As a conservative organization resistant to change, the university continues to hold on to modernist formations and methods, but the ideals and commitments of a new generation of social researchers are reshaping the field and gradually taking hold (Lincoln & Denzin, 2000).

The mind-set of this new era is reflected by the changes embodied in the ethical commitments, methodological practices, and research goals of narrative inquiry. Where once we saw subjects, now we see participants and co-collaborators; where once we sought to predict and control, now we want to learn to talk with, to empower, to transform, and to empathize; where once we were concerned with the accuracy of descriptions, now we ask how useful they are and what we can do with them; where once we thought ethics meant debriefing before leaving, now we see ethics as an obligation to return and to give something back; where once we conceived of our readers as passive receivers of our knowledge, now we construe them as active co-constructors of meaning; where once we focused on what they can learn about themselves from us, now we also stress what we can learn about ourselves from them; where once we thought it was enough to show that our voice had authority, now we insist that the voices of the people we study be put on a plane equal to our own; where once we thought we were talking about *them,* now we sense that we are talking about ourselves; where once we elevated ourselves to the position of confident theorists in command of knowledge, now we can more humbly understand ourselves as vulnerable storytellers with moral imagination; and where once we saw ourselves as apart from, now we see ourselves as a part of those we study.

As I look toward a promising future for the study of interpersonal communication, what I see is the increasing influence of a new generation of researchers, under the influence of narrative inquiry and the reforms of the qualitative movement, who do work that calls people to action; connects to history and culture; expresses many diverse voices; encourages pluralism; invites dialogue; erases distinctions between art and science; merges the personal and political; shows that everything is enmeshed in values and emotions; becomes a stage for critical conversations about difference, race, gender, ethnicity, and community; eschews inaccessible prose; and reaches out to a broader audience of readers and listeners who can engage with the work in a collaborative and democratic fashion. This work will produce an intermediate zone between science and art, self and others, theories and stories, one that will be understood and appreciated as a meeting ground that promotes multiplicity, where head and heart go hand in hand, a rigorous *and* creative body of scholarship that is passionate, political, personal, critical, open-ended, enlightening, pleasurable, meaningful, useful, and sufficiently evocative to keep us talking.

REFERENCES

Angrosino, M. V. (1998). *Opportunity House: Ethnographic stories of mental retardation.* Walnut Creek, CA: AltaMira.

Anzaldúa, G. (1987). *Borderlands/la frontera: The new mestiza*. San Francisco: Aunt Lute.

Apter, T. (1996). Expert witness: Who controls the psychologist's narrative? In R. Josselson (Ed.), *Ethics and process in the narrative study of lives* (pp. 22-44). Thousand Oaks, CA: Sage.

Atkinson, P. (1997). Narrative turn or a blind alley? *Qualitative Health Research, 7,* 325-344.

Austin, D. (1996). The same and different. In C. Ellis & A. P. Bochner (Eds.), *Composing ethnography: Alternative forms of qualitative writing* (pp. 206-230). Walnut Creek, CA: AltaMira.

Austin, D. (1998). *Understanding close relationships among African Americans in the context of the Million Man March.* Unpublished doctoral dissertation, University of South Florida.

Bakhtin, M. M. (1981). *The dialogic imagination: Four essays* (M. Holquist, Ed.; M. Holquist & C. Emerson, Trans.). Austin: University of Texas Press.

Banks, A., & Banks, S. P. (Eds.). (1998). *Fiction and social research: By ice or fire.* Walnut Creek, CA: AltaMira.

Barthes, R. (1977). *Image, music, text* (S. Heath, Trans.). New York: Hill & Wang.

Baxter, L. A. (1992). Interpersonal communication as dialogue: A response to the "Social Approaches" forum. *Communication Theory, 2,* 330-337.

Behar, R. (1993). *Translated woman: Crossing the border with Esperanza's story.* Boston: Beacon.

Behar, R. (1996). *The vulnerable observer: Anthropology that breaks your heart.* Boston: Beacon.

Benson, P. (Ed.). (1993). *Anthropology and literature.* Urbana: University of Illinois Press.

Berger, C. R. (1991). Communication theories and other curios. *Communication Monographs, 58,* 101-113.

Berger, J. (1983). *Once in Europa.* New York: Pantheon.

Beverley, J. (2000). Testimonio, subalternity, and narrative authority. In N. K. Denzin & Y. S. Lincoln (Eds.), *Handbook of qualitative research* (2nd ed., pp. 555-565). Thousand Oaks, CA: Sage.

Bochner, A. P. (1985). Perspectives on inquiry: Representation, conversation, and reflection. In M. L. Knapp & G. R. Miller (Eds.), *Handbook of interpersonal communication* (pp. 27-58). Beverly Hills, CA: Sage.

Bochner, A. P. (1994). Perspectives on inquiry II: Theories and stories. In M. L. Knapp & G. R. Miller (Eds.), *Handbook of interpersonal communication* (2nd ed., pp. 21-41). Thousand Oaks, CA: Sage.

Bochner, A. P. (1997). It's about time: Narrative and the divided self. *Qualitative Inquiry, 3,* 418-438.

Bochner, A. P. (2000). Criteria against ourselves. *Qualitative Inquiry, 6,* 266-272.

Bochner, A. P. (2001). Narrative's virtues. *Qualitative Inquiry, 7,* 131-157.

Bochner, A. P., & Ellis, C. (1992). Personal narrative as a social approach to interpersonal communication. *Communication Theory, 2,* 165-172.

Bochner, A. P., & Ellis, C. (1999). Which way to turn? *Journal of Contemporary Ethnography, 28,* 485-499.

Bochner, A. P., & Ellis, C. (Eds.). (2002). *Ethnographically speaking: Autoethnography, literature, and aesthetics.* Walnut Creek, CA: AltaMira.

Bochner, A. P., Ellis, C., & Tillmann-Healy, L. M. (1997). Relationships as stories. In S. Duck (Ed.), *Handbook of personal relationships: Theory, research and interventions* (2nd ed., pp. 307-324). New York: John Wiley.

Bochner, A. P., Ellis, C., & Tillmann-Healy, L. M. (1998). Mucking around looking for truth. In B. M. Montgomery & L. A. Baxter (Eds.), *Dialectical approaches to studying personal relationships* (pp. 41-62). Mahwah, NJ: Lawrence Erlbaum.

Bochner, A. P., & Waugh, J. B. (1995). Talking-with as a model for writing-about: Implications of Rortyean pragmatism. In L. Langsdorf & A. R. Smith (Eds.), *Recovering pragmatism's voice: The classical tradition, Rorty, and the philosophy of communication* (pp. 211-233). Albany: State University of New York Press.

Brady, I. (Ed.). (1991). *Anthropological poetics.* Savage, MD: Rowman & Littlefield.

Brody, H. (1987). *Stories of sickness.* New Haven, CT: Yale University Press.

Brown, K. (1991). *Mama Lola: A Voodoo priestess in Brooklyn.* Berkeley: University of California Press.

Bruner, E. M. (1986). Ethnography as narrative. In V. W. Turner & E. M. Bruner (Eds.), *The anthropology of experience* (pp. 139-155). Urbana: University of Illinois Press.

Bruner, J. (1986). *Actual minds, possible worlds.* Cambridge, MA: Harvard University Press.

Bruner, J. (1987). Life as narrative. *Social Research, 54,* 11-32.

Bruner, J. (1990). *Acts of meaning.* Cambridge, MA: Harvard University Press.

Buford, B. (1996, June 24). The seductions of storytelling. *New Yorker,* pp. 11-12.

Burleson, B. R. (1992). Taking communication seriously. *Communication Monographs, 59,* 79-86.

Butler, S., & Rosenblum, B. (1991). *Cancer in two voices.* San Francisco: Spinster.

Carr, D. (1986). *Time, narrative, and history.* Bloomington: Indiana University Press.

Charmaz, K. (1995). Grounded theory. In J. A. Smith, R. Harré, & L. van Langenhove (Eds.), *Rethinking methods in psychology* (pp. 27-49). Thousand Oaks, CA: Sage.

Charmaz, K. (2000). Grounded theory: Objectivist and constructivist methods. In N. K. Denzin & Y. S. Lincoln (Eds.), *Handbook of qualitative research* (2nd ed., pp. 509-535). Thousand Oaks, CA: Sage.

Church, K. (1995). *Forbidden narratives: Critical autobiography as social science.* Newark, NJ: Gordon & Breach.

Church, K. (2002). The hard road home: Towards a polyphonic narrative of the mother/daughter relationship. In A. P. Bochner & C. Ellis (Eds.), *Ethnographically speaking: Autoethnography, literature, and aesthetics* (pp. 234-257). Walnut Creek, CA: AltaMira.

Clandinin, D. J., & Connelly, F. M. (1994). Personal experience methods. In N. K. Denzin & Y. S. Lincoln (Eds.), *Handbook of qualitative research* (pp. 413-427). Thousand Oaks, CA: Sage.

Clifford, J. (1988). *The predicament of culture: Twentieth-century ethnography, literature, and art.* Cambridge: MA: Harvard University Press.

Clifford, J., & Marcus, G. E. (Eds.). (1986). *Writing culture: The poetics and politics of ethnography.* Berkeley: University of California Press.

Clough, P. T. (1994). *Feminist thought: Desire, power and academic discourse.* Cambridge, MA: Blackwell.

Coles, R. (1989). *The call of stories: Teaching and the moral imagination.* Boston: Houghton Mifflin.

Coles, R. (1997). *Doing documentary work.* New York: Oxford University Press.

Couser, G. T. (1997). *Recovering bodies: Illness, disability, and life writing.* Madison: University of Wisconsin Press.

Crites, S. (1971). The narrative quality of experience. *Journal of the American Academy of Religion, 39,* 291-311.

Deck, A. (1990). Autoethnography: Zora Neale Hurston, Noni Jabavu, and cross-disciplinary discourse. *Black American Literature Forum, 24,* 237-256.

Denzin, N. K. (1989). *Interpretive biography.* Newbury Park, CA: Sage.

Denzin, N. K. (1992). *Symbolic interactionism and cultural studies: The politics of interpretation.* Oxford: Basil Blackwell.

Denzin, N. K. (1997). *Interpretive ethnography: Ethnographic practices for the 21st century.* Thousand Oaks, CA: Sage.

Denzin, N. K., & Lincoln, Y. S. (Eds.). (1994). *Handbook of qualitative research.* Thousand Oaks, CA: Sage.

Denzin, N. K., & Lincoln, Y. S. (Eds.). (2000a). *Handbook of qualitative research* (2nd ed.). Thousand Oaks, CA: Sage.

Denzin, N. K., & Lincoln, Y. S. (2000b). Introduction: The discipline and practice of qualitative research. In N. K. Denzin & Y. S. Lincoln (Eds.), *Handbook of qualitative research* (2nd ed., pp. 1-28). Thousand Oaks, CA: Sage.

Derrida, J. (1978). *Writing and difference* (A. Bass, Trans.). Chicago: University of Chicago Press

Derrida, J. (1981). *Positions* (A. Bass, Trans.). Chicago: University of Chicago Press.

Drew, R. (2001). *Karaoke nights: An ethnographic rhapsody.* Walnut Creek, CA: AltaMira.

Ellis, C. (1991). Sociological introspection and emotional experience. *Symbolic Interaction, 14,* 23-50.

Ellis, C. (1993). "There are survivors": Telling a story of sudden death. *Sociological Quarterly, 34,* 711-730.

Ellis, C. (1995a). Emotional and ethical quagmires in returning to the field. *Journal of Contemporary Ethnography, 24,* 711-713.

Ellis, C. (1995b). *Final negotiations: A story of love, loss, and chronic illness.* Philadelphia: Temple University Press.

Ellis, C. (1995c). The other side of the fence: Seeing black and white in a small, southern town. *Qualitative Inquiry, 1,* 147-167.

Ellis, C. (1995d). Speaking of dying: An ethnographic short story. *Symbolic Interaction, 18,* 73-81.

Ellis, C. (1997). Evocative autoethnography: Writing emotionally about our lives. In

W. G. Tierney & Y. S. Lincoln (Eds.), *Representation and the text: Re-framing the narrative voice* (pp. 115-140). Albany: State University of New York Press.

Ellis, C. (1998a). Exploring loss through autoethnographic inquiry: Autoethnographic stories, co-constructed narratives, and interactive interviews. In J. H. Harvey (Ed.), *Perspectives on loss: A sourcebook* (pp. 49-62). Philadelphia: Taylor & Francis.

Ellis, C. (1998b). "I hate my voice": Coming to terms with minor bodily stigmas. *Sociological Quarterly, 39,* 517-537.

Ellis, C. (2001). With mother/with child: A true story. *Qualitative Inquiry, 7,* 598-616.

Ellis, C., & Berger, L. (2001). Their story/my story/our story: Including the researcher's experience in interview research. In J. F. Gubrium & J. A. Holstein (Eds.), *Handbook of interview research: Context and method* (pp. 849-875). Thousand Oaks, CA: Sage.

Ellis, C., & Bochner, A. P. (1992). Telling and performing personal stories: The constraints of choice in abortion. In C. Ellis & M. G. Flaherty (Eds.), *Investigating subjectivity: Research on lived experience* (pp. 79-101). Newbury Park, CA: Sage.

Ellis, C., & Bochner, A. P. (Eds.). (1996a). *Composing ethnography: Alternative forms of qualitative writing.* Walnut Creek, CA: AltaMira.

Ellis, C., & Bochner, A. P. (Eds.). (1996b). Taking ethnography into the twenty-first century [Special issue]. *Journal of Contemporary Ethnography, 25*(1).

Ellis, C., & Bochner, A. P. (2000). Autoethnography, personal narrative, reflexivity: Researcher as subject. In N. K. Denzin & Y. S. Lincoln (Eds.), *Handbook of qualitative research* (2nd ed., pp. 733-768). Thousand Oaks, CA: Sage.

Ellis, C., & Flaherty, M. G. (Eds.). (1992). *Investigating subjectivity: Research on lived experience.* Newbury Park, CA: Sage.

Ellis, C., & Flemons, D. (2002). High noon: A "fictional" dialogue. In A. P. Bochner & C. Ellis (Eds.), *Ethnographically speaking: Autoethnography, literature, and aesthetics* (pp. 344-356). Walnut Creek, CA: AltaMira.

Ellis, C., Kiesinger, C. E., & Tillmann-Healy, L. M. (1997). Interactive interviewing: Talking about emotional experience. In R. Hertz (Ed.), *Reflexivity and voice* (pp. 119-149). Thousand Oaks, CA: Sage.

Fasching, D. J., & deChant, D. (2001). *Comparative religious ethics: A narrative approach.* Oxford: Blackwell.

Feyerabend, P. (1975). *Against method.* New York: Schocken.

Foucault, M. (1970). *The order of things: An archaeology of the human sciences.* New York: Random House.

Frank, A. (1995). *The wounded storyteller: Body, illness, and ethics.* Chicago: University of Chicago Press.

Frank, A. (1997). Enacting illness stories: When, what, and why. In H. Nelson (Ed.), *Stories and their limits: Narrative approaches to bioethics* (pp. 31-49). New York: Routledge.

Freeman, M. (1993). *Rewriting the self: History, memory, narrative.* London: Routledge.

Freeman, M. (1998a). Experience, narrative, and the relation between them. *Narrative Inquiry, 8,* 455-466.

Freeman, M. (1998b). Mythical time, historical time, and the narrative fabric of self. *Narrative Inquiry, 8,* 27-50.

Geertz, C. (1973). *The interpretation of cultures: Selected essays.* New York: Basic Books.

Geertz, C. (1988). *Works and lives: The anthropologist as author.* Cambridge: Polity.

Geist, P. (Ed.). (1999-2000). Surreal illusions, genuine realities: Disenchantment and renewal in the academy [Special issue]. *Communication Theory, 9*(4)-*10*(1).

Gergen, K. J. (1999). *An invitation to social construction.* London: Sage.

Gergen, M. M., & Gergen, K. J. (2000). Qualitative inquiry: Tensions and transformations. In N. K. Denzin & Y. S. Lincoln (Eds.), *Handbook of qualitative research* (2nd ed., pp. 1025-1046). Thousand Oaks, CA: Sage.

Glaser, B. G., & Strauss, A. L. (1967). *The discovery of grounded theory: Strategies for qualitative research.* Chicago: Aldine.

Glassner, B. (Ed.). (1997). Qualitative sociology as everyday life [Special issue]. *Qualitative Sociology, 20*(4).

Goodall, H. L. (2000). *Writing the new ethnography.* Walnut Creek, CA: AltaMira.

Gray, R., Ivonoffski, V., & Sinding, C. (2002). Making a mess and spreading it around: Articulation of an approach to research-based theater. In A. P. Bochner & C. Ellis (Eds.), *Ethnographically speaking: Autoethnography, literature, and aesthetics* (pp. 57-75). Walnut Creek, CA: AltaMira.

Gubrium, J. F., & Holstein, J. A. (1997). *The new language of qualitative method*. New York: Oxford University Press.

Gusfield, J. (1976). The literary rhetoric of science. *American Sociological Review, 41*, 16-34.

Harding, S. (1991). *Whose science? Whose knowledge? Thinking from women's lives*. Ithaca, NY: Cornell University Press.

Harper, D. (1982). *Good company*. Chicago: University of Chicago Press.

Harper, D. (2000). Reimagining visual methods: Galileo to *Neuromancer*. In N. K. Denzin & Y. S. Lincoln (Eds.), *The handbook of qualitative research* (2nd ed., pp. 717-732). Thousand Oaks, CA: Sage.

Harrington, W. (Ed.). (1997). *Intimate journalism: The art and craft of reporting everyday life*. Thousand Oaks, CA: Sage.

Hartsock, N. (1983). The feminist standpoint: Developing the ground for a specifically feminist historical materialism. In S. Harding & M. B. Hintikka (Eds.), *Discovering reality: Feminist perspectives on epistemology, metaphysics, methodology, and philosophy of science* (pp. 283-310). Boston: Reidel.

Hawkins, A. H. (1993). *Reconstructing illness: Studies in pathography*. West Lafayette, IN: Purdue University Press.

Hertz, R. (Ed.). (1996). Ethics, reflexivity and voice [Special issue]. *Qualitative Sociology, 19*(1).

Hertz, R. (Ed.). (1997). *Reflexivity and voice*. Thousand Oaks, CA: Sage.

Hollway, W. (1989). *Subjectivity and method in psychology: Gender, meaning and science*. London: Sage.

Jackson, M. (1989). *Paths toward a clearing: Radical empiricism and ethnographic inquiry*. Bloomington: Indiana University Press.

Jackson, M. (1995). *At home in the world*. Durham, NC: Duke University Press.

Jago, B. (1996). Postcards, ghosts, and fathers: Revising family stories. *Qualitative Inquiry, 2*, 495-516.

Jones, S. H. (1998). *Kaleidoscope notes: Writing women's music and organizational culture*. Walnut Creek, CA: AltaMira.

Josselson, R., & Lieblich, A. (Eds.). (1995). *Interpreting experience: The narrative study of lives*. Thousand Oaks, CA: Sage.

Kerby, A. (1991). *Narrative and the self*. Bloomington: Indiana University Press.

Kiesinger, C. E. (1995). *Anorexic and bulimic lives: Making sense of food and eating*. Unpublished doctoral dissertation, University of South Florida.

Kiesinger, C. E. (1998). From interview to story: Writing Abbie's life. *Qualitative Inquiry, 4*, 71-95.

Kreiswirth, M. (1992). Trusting the tale: The narrativist turn in the human sciences. *New Literary History, 23*, 629-657.

Krieger, S. (1983). *The mirror dance: Identity in a women's community*. Philadelphia: Temple University Press.

Kuhn, T. S. (1962). *The structure of scientific revolutions*. Chicago: University of Chicago Press.

Lagerway, M. (1998). *Reading Auschwitz*. Walnut Creek, CA: AltaMira.

Langellier, K. (1989). Personal narratives: Perspectives on theory and research. *Text and Performance Quarterly, 9*, 243-276.

Lincoln, Y. S., & Denzin, N. K. (2000). The seventh moment: Out of the past. In N. K. Denzin & Y. S. Lincoln (Eds.), *Handbook of qualitative research* (2nd ed., pp. 1047-1065). Thousand Oaks, CA: Sage.

Lincoln, Y. S., & Guba, E. G. (2000). Paradigmatic controversies, contradictions, and emerging confluences. In N. K. Denzin & Y. S. Lincoln (Eds.), *Handbook of qualitative research* (2nd ed., pp. 163-188). Thousand Oaks, CA: Sage.

Lyotard, J. F. (1984). *The postmodern condition: A report on knowledge* (G. Bennington & B. Massumi, Trans.). Minneapolis: University of Minnesota Press.

MacIntyre, A. (1981). *After virtue: A study in moral theory*. Notre Dame, IN: University of Notre Dame Press.

Mair, M. (1989). *Beyond psychology and psychotherapy: A poetics of experience*. London: Routledge.

Marcus, G. E., & Fischer, M. M. J. (1986). *Anthropology as cultural critique: An experimental moment in the human sciences*. Chicago: University of Chicago Press.

Markham, A. N. (1998). *Life online: Researching real experience in virtual space*. Walnut Creek, CA: AltaMira.

McLaughlin, D., & Tierney, W. G. (Eds.). (1993). *Naming silenced lives: Personal narratives and the process of educational change*. New York: Routledge.

Mienczakowski, J. E. (1996). The ethnographic act: The construction of consensual theatre. In C. Ellis & A. P. Bochner (Eds.), *Composing ethnography: Alternative forms of qualitative writing* (pp. 244-263). Walnut Creek, CA: AltaMira.

Miller, N. K. (1996). *Bequest and betrayal: Memoirs of a parent's death*. New York: Oxford University Press.

Mink, L. (1969-1970). History and fiction as modes of comprehension. *New Literary History, 1,* 541-558.

Neumann, M. (1996). Collecting ourselves at the end of the century. In C. Ellis & A. P. Bochner (Eds.), *Composing ethnography: Alternative forms of qualitative writing* (pp. 172-198). Walnut Creek, CA: AltaMira.

Okely, J., & Callaway, H. (Eds.). (1992). *Anthropology and autobiography*. London: Routledge.

Paget, M. (1990). Life mirrors work mirrors text mirrors life. *Social Problems, 37,* 137-148.

Paget, M. (1993). *A complex sorrow: Reflections on cancer and an abbreviated life*. Philadelphia: Temple University Press.

Parini, J. (1998, July 10). The memoir versus the novel in a time of transition. *Chronicle of Higher Education,* p. A40.

Parry, A. (1991). A universe of stories. *Family Process, 30,* 37-54.

Perry, L. A. M., & Geist, P. (Eds.). (1997). *Courage of conviction: Women's words, women's wisdom*. Mountain View, CA: Mayfield.

Picart, C. J. S. (2002). Living the hyphenated edge: Autoethnography, hybridity, and aesthetics. In A. P. Bochner & C. Ellis (Eds.), *Ethnographically speaking: Autoethnography, literature, and aesthetics* (pp. 258-273). Walnut Creek, CA: AltaMira.

Plummer, K. (2001). *Documents of life: An invitation to a critical humanism*. London: Sage.

Polkinghorne, D. E. (1995). Narrative configuration in qualitative analysis. In J. A. Hatch & R. Wisniewski (Eds.), *Life history and narrative* (pp. 5-23). Washington, DC: Falmer.

Quinney, R. (1996). Once my father traveled west to California. In C. Ellis & A. P. Bochner (Eds.), *Composing ethnography: Alternative forms of qualitative writing* (pp. 357-382). Walnut Creek, CA: AltaMira.

Reed-Danahay, D. (1997). *Auto/ethnography: Rewriting the self and the social*. Oxford: Berg.

Reinharz, S. (1992). *Feminist methods in social research*. New York: Oxford University Press.

Richardson, L. (1990). Narrative and sociology. *Journal of Contemporary Ethnography, 19,* 116-135.

Richardson, L. (1992). The consequences of poetic representation: Writing the other, rewriting the self. In C. Ellis & M. G. Flaherty (Eds.), *Investigating subjectivity: Research on lived experience* (pp. 125-137). Newbury Park, CA: Sage.

Richardson, L. (1994). Nine poems: Marriage and the family. *Journal of Contemporary Ethnography, 23,* 3-14.

Richardson, L. (2000). Writing: A method of inquiry. In N. K. Denzin & Y. S. Lincoln (Eds.), *Handbook of qualitative research* (2nd ed., pp. 923-948). Thousand Oaks, CA: Sage.

Richardson, L., & Lockridge, E. (1998). Fiction and ethnography: A conversation. *Qualitative Inquiry, 4,* 328-336.

Richardson, L., & Lockridge, E. (2002). Beirut letters. In A. P. Bochner & C. Ellis (Eds.), *Ethnographically speaking: Autoethnography, literature, and aesthetics* (pp. 308-326). Walnut Creek, CA: AltaMira.

Ricoeur, P. (1983). *Hermeneutics and the human sciences: Essays on language, action and interpretation* (J. B. Thompson, Ed. and Trans.). New York: Cambridge University Press.

Riessman, C. K. (1993). *Narrative analysis*. Newbury Park, CA: Sage.

Ronai, C. R. (1992). The reflexive self through narrative: A night in the life of an erotic dancer/researcher. In C. Ellis & M. G. Flaherty (Eds.), *Investigating subjectivity: Research on lived experience* (pp. 102-124). Newbury Park, CA: Sage.

Ronai, C. R. (1995). Multiple reflections of child sex abuse: An argument for a layered account. *Journal of Contemporary Ethnography, 23,* 395-426.

Ronai, C. R. (1996). My mother is mentally retarded. In C. Ellis & A. P. Bochner (Eds.), *Composing ethnography: Alternative forms of qualitative writing* (pp. 109-131). Walnut Creek, CA: AltaMira.

Rorty, R. (Ed.). (1967). *The linguistic turn*. Chicago: University of Chicago Press.

Rorty, R. (1979). *Philosophy and the mirror of nature*. Princeton, NJ: Princeton University Press.

Rorty, R. (1982). *Consequences of pragmatism (Essays 1972-1980)*. Minneapolis: University of Minnesota Press.

Rorty, R. (1989). *Contingency, irony, and solidarity*. New York: Cambridge University Press.

Rosenwald, G. C. (1992). Conclusion: Reflections on narrative self-understanding. In G. C. Rosenwald & R. L. Ochberg (Eds.), *Storied lives: The cultural politics of self-understanding* (pp. 265-289). New Haven, CT: Yale University Press.

Rosenwald, G. C., & Ochberg, R. L. (Eds.). (1992). *Storied lives: The cultural politics of self-understanding.* New Haven, CT: Yale University Press.

Sarbin, T. R. (Ed.). (1986). *Narrative psychology: The storied nature of human conduct.* New York: Praeger.

Schafer, R. (1980). Narrative in the psychoanalytic dialogue. *Critical Inquiry, 7,* 29-34.

Schafer, R. (1992). *Retelling a life: Narration and dialogue in psychoanalysis.* New York: Basic Books.

Schwandt, T. A. (2000). Three epistemological stances for qualitative inquiry: Interpretivism, hermeneutics, and social constructionism. In N. K. Denzin & Y. S. Lincoln (Eds.), *Handbook of qualitative research* (2nd ed., pp. 189-213). Thousand Oaks, CA: Sage.

Scott-Hoy, K. (2002). The visitor: Juggling life in the grip of the text. In A. P. Bochner & C. Ellis (Eds.), *Ethnographically speaking: Autoethnography, literature, and aesthetics* (pp. 274-294).Walnut Creek, CA: AltaMira.

Sellars, W. (1963). *Science, perception and reality.* New York: Routledge.

Sexton, L. G. (1994). *Searching for Mercy Street: My journey back to my mother, Anne Sexton.* Boston: Little, Brown.

Shotter, J. (1987). The social construction of an "us": Problems of accountability and narratology. In R. Burnett, P. McGee, & D. Clarke (Eds.), *Accounting for relationships: Explanation, representation, and knowledge* (pp. 225-247). London: Methuen.

Shotter, J., & Gergen, K. J. (Eds.). (1989). *Texts of identity.* London: Sage.

Shweder, R. A. (1986). Divergent rationalities. In D. W. Fiske & R. A. Shweder (Eds.), *Metatheory in social science: Pluralisms and subjectivities* (pp. 163-196). Chicago: University of Chicago Press.

Siegel, T., & Conquergood, D. (Producers & Directors). (1985). *Between two worlds: The Hmong shaman in America* [Video documentary]. Chicago: Siegel Productions.

Siegel, T., & Conquergood, D. (Producers & Directors). (1990). *The heart broken in half* [Video documentary]. Chicago: Siegel Productions.

Simons, H. W. (Ed.). (1989). *The rhetorical turn: Invention and persuasion in the conduct of inquiry.* Chicago: University of Chicago Press.

Smith, D. E. (1990). *The conceptual practices of power: A feminist sociology of knowledge.* Boston: Northeastern University Press.

Smith, D. E. (1992). Sociology from women's experience: A reaffirmation. *Sociological Theory, 10,* 88-97.

Sparkes, A. C. (2002). Autoethnography: Self-indulgence or something more? In A. P. Bochner & C. Ellis (Eds.), *Ethnographically speaking: Autoethnography, literature, and aesthetics* (pp. 209-232). Walnut Creek, CA: AltaMira.

Spence, D. (1982). *Narrative truth and historical truth: Meaning and interpretation in psychoanalysis.* New York: W. W. Norton.

Tedlock, B. (1991). From participant observation to the observation of participation: The emergence of narrative ethnography. *Journal of Anthropological Research, 41,* 69-94.

Tierney, W. G. (2000). Undaunted courage: Life history and the postmodern challenge. In N. K. Denzin & Y. S. Lincoln (Eds.), *Handbook of qualitative research* (2nd ed., pp. 537-553). Thousand Oaks, CA: Sage.

Tierney, W. G., & Lincoln, Y. S. (Eds.). (1997). *Representation and the text: Re-framing the narrative voice.* Albany: State University of New York Press.

Tillmann-Healy, L. M. (1996). A secret life in a culture of thinness: Reflections on body, food, and bulimia. In C. Ellis & A. P. Bochner (Eds.), *Composing ethnography: Alternative forms of qualitative writing* (pp. 77-109). Walnut Creek, CA: AltaMira.

Tillmann-Healy, L. M. (1999). *Life projects: A narrative ethnography of gay-straight friendship.* Unpublished Ph.D. dissertation, University of South Florida.

Tillmann-Healy, L. M. (2001). *Between gay and straight: Understanding friendship across sexual orientation.* Walnut Creek, CA: AltaMira.

Toulmin, S. (1969). Concepts and the explanation of human behavior. In T. Mischel (Ed.), *Human action* (pp. 71-104). New York: Academic Press.

Trinh T. M. (1989). *Woman, native, other: Writing postcoloniality and feminism.* Bloomington: Indiana University Press.

Trinh T. M. (1992). *Framer framed.* New York: Routledge.

True confessions: The age of the literary memoir [Special issue]. (1996, May 12). *New York Times Magazine.*

Turner, V. W., & Bruner, E. M. (Eds.). (1986). *The anthropology of experience.* Urbana: University of Illinois Press.

Tyler, S. A. (1986). Post-modern ethnography: From document of the occult to occult document. In J. Clifford & G. E. Marcus (Eds.), *Writing culture: The poetics and politics of ethnography* (pp. 122-140). Berkeley: University of California Press.

Weinstein, A. (1988). *The fiction of relationship.* Princeton, NJ: Princeton University Press.

White, H. (1980). The value of narrativity in the representation of reality. *Critical Inquiry, 7,* 5-27.

White, M., & Epston, D. (1990). *Narrative means to therapeutic ends.* New York: W. W. Norton.

Zola, I. K. (Ed.). (1982). *Ordinary lives: Voices of disability and disease.* Cambridge, MA: Applewood.

Zussman, R. (Ed.). (2000). Autobiographical occasions [Special issue]. *Qualitative Sociology, 23*(1).

4

Discourse Analysis

JANET BEAVIN BAVELAS
CHRISTINE KENWOOD
BRUCE PHILLIPS

In this chapter, we first define discourse analysis and illustrate the breadth of its usefulness as a research method. We also emphasize how choosing to use this method can be part of a larger change of theoretical perspective. We devote the rest of the chapter to one of the main purposes of a handbook such as this one, which is to assist readers in the use of the method; thus we include many hands-on issues, such as choices about data, recording, transcription, and reliability. In reviewing these issues, we focus on principles that might be useful for helping readers to develop new and original methods of discourse analysis that suit their particular interests and goals, guided by explicit theoretical assumptions.

WHAT IS DISCOURSE ANALYSIS?

Discourse analysis is the systematic study of naturally occurring (not hypothetical) communication in the broadest sense, at the level of meaning (rather than as physical acts or features). However, a survey of the literature on discourse analysis would quickly reveal that, although some researchers employ the

AUTHORS' NOTE: We acknowledge the contributions of Dr. Linda Coates to the planning of this chapter, the Social Sciences and Humanities Research Council of Canada for research grants to the first author, and our continuing research team for sharing our daily immersion in these issues.

term to describe a particular kind of analysis, it is also a label that has widespread usage across several disciplines with diverse goals. Consequently, it is more accurate to think of discourse analysis as a cluster of methods and approaches with some substantial common interests rather than as a single, unitary technique.

As Wood and Kroger (2000, p. 18) explain, the existence of several kinds of discourse analysis is undoubtedly due to the developing nature of the field as well as to its diverse disciplinary origins. Discourse analysis began in branches of philosophy, sociology, linguistics, and literary theory, and it is continuing to develop in additional disciplines such as anthropology, communication, education, and psychology. We find this newness and diversity a positive feature of the field. It is not bound by any single discipline, which means that there is a rich infusion of ideas and methods across disciplines. Nor is it committed to traditions of the past; indeed, many discourse analysts are rebels and innovators within their own home disciplines who have moved out to join other like-minded researchers.

It is intriguing that one of the original meanings of the verb *discourse* was "to travel across a course or terrain." We like to think of discourse analysis as still doing that, traveling across many disciplines, often into new territory, rather than staying in one place. In that spirit, in this chapter we travel through (but by no means claim hegemony over) the many domains of discourse analysis and a wide variety of other territories where researchers study naturally occurring language, including conversation analysis, microanalysis, ethnography, some areas of nonverbal communication, and mediated communication. As is appropriate to this kind of intellectual internationalism, the stimulus for our survey of definitions and approaches is a traveler's curiosity about how people do things differently rather than any goal of standardization.

Defining Discourse

In new disciplines, familiar terms often take on new specialized or professional meanings that differ from their commonly used informal or everyday definitions. Discourse analysis is no different. Van Dijk (1997c) points out that the term *discourse* is commonly used to refer to a particular form of language use (e.g., public speeches) or more generally to spoken language or ways of speaking, such as the "the discourse of former President Ronald Reagan." Another informal usage refers to the ideas or philosophies propagated by particular people or groups of people (van Dijk, 1997c, pp. 1-2). In this usage, van Dijk notes, the actual language used by a person or persons is ignored in favor of a focus on the ideas or philosophies expressed. According to van Dijk, the more specialized or professional definition of discourse includes a particular focus on the actual language used in a communicative event. A discourse analyst is essentially interested in "*who* uses language, *how*, *why* and *when*" (van Dijk, 1997c, p. 3). So, for example, a discourse analyst might examine talk occurring during encounters with friends, phone calls, job interviews, doctor's visits, and so forth.

Van Dijk (1997c) also touches on another important distinction when he points out that language can be spoken, written, or printed. Each kind of language use, he notes, has distinct properties; for example, the communication may be passive (as in when an individual reads a newspaper), more active (as in e-mail communication), or fully active (as in face-to-face dialogue). It is important that researchers consider these characteristics when conducting analyses. Van Dijk's inclusion of both spoken and written forms of language use is a fairly common view (e.g., Gilbert & Mulkay, 1984; Potter & Wetherell, 1987, p. 7; Wood & Kroger, 2000, p. 19). It is not the case, however, that all discourse analysts agree. Some would reserve the term *discourse* for spoken language and use the term *text* to describe written or printed language; others use the two terms interchangeably. Most researchers define discourse as the activities of speaking or writing, but there are some researchers who include other aspects of communication in their definitions as well. Brown (1995) studied the role of *listeners* as they participate in dialogues, and Kroger and Wood (2000) point out that some theorists, such as Fairclough (1993) and Harré (1995), have extended the definition of discourse to include "semiotic practice in other semiotic modalities" (p. 19). That is, these researchers have a broader definition of discourse that includes not only words (spoken or written) but also other kinds of meaningful communication, such as visual images and nonverbal movements (e.g., gestures). Our research group can be counted among those who accept all of these broader definitions.

Finally, there are some implicit agreements among discourse analysts that become significant in contrast to other approaches to language and communication. Discourse analysts would always look closely at the actual language itself rather than at secondary sources such as reports or descriptions of what was said, meant, or understood. That is, virtually all discourse analysts would agree with the conversation analysts, such as Atkinson and Heritage (1984), who use only data from behaviors generated in their own context. The observers' and participants' descriptions, interpretations, and comments on conversations are necessarily gathered in different contexts, for different purposes, and these inevitably affect the descriptions. These reports might be analyzed as "accounts" (Scott & Lyman, 1990) or as "remembering" (as opposed to "memory"; Bartlett, 1932; Edwards & Middleton, 1987), but they are not substitutes for the discourse they describe.

Kinds of Discourse Data

Another way to define discourse is to illustrate some of the many possible sources of data for discourse analysis. Face-to-face dialogue occurs in families, in most workplaces and public places, in psychotherapy, in courtroom settings (e.g., examination and cross-examination), in police interviews, in medical examinations and interviews, on social occasions, in classrooms, in meetings, and some in psychology experiments, to name just a few settings.[1]

Individuals communicate in writing through memos and letters, when they post notices, when they publish books and articles, when professors write comments on students' exams or papers, and in many other settings.

Mediated communication includes telephone conversations and communication via answering machines or voice mail, radio call-in shows, and computer-mediated forms such as e-mail, Internet chat rooms, and bulletin boards. In the mass media, mediated communication occurs through newspapers, comic strips, TV talk shows, and political interviews. We provide more examples throughout this chapter, especially in the sections on recording and transcription. Undoubtedly, readers can immediately think of many other examples we have not mentioned here.

Levels of Analysis

Nunan (1993), who comes from a more linguistic background, takes an even different cut at the definition of discourse. He uses *text* to refer to the written or taped record of a communication event and *discourse* to refer to the interpretation of that event in the context in which it occurs. For Nunan, the difference between text analysis and discourse analysis is that the former is the study of formal linguistic devices that distinguish a text from random sentences, whereas the latter is also the study of such devices but is conducted by the researcher with the intention of coming to understand the purpose and function of the discourse as well as the context in which it developed (p. 20). What he calls discourse analysis involves language *as it is being used,* whereas text analysis is concerned with patterns and regularities that occur in written language, such as phonemic or grammatical analyses. That is, discourse analysis is concerned with patterns and regularities in language but also with the people using language (what they mean and the purpose to which language is put) and the context in which it is used. Nunan (1993) says of discourse analysts, "Their ultimate aim is to show how the linguistic elements [found in language] enable language users to communicate in context" (p. 20). Thus Nunan's interest in linguistic elements leads him to study, among other things, linguistic devices such as pronoun usage and conjunctions that enable people to build explicit relationships between entities and events in their discourse with each other in different contexts (p. 57). He is also interested in analyzing how smaller components of language contribute to broader social meanings. Thus his research spans two levels in that he breaks discourse down into its component parts and also looks at how the parts contribute to the formation of meaning in social contexts.

Although they often use different terms, other researchers often make the same kind of distinction (between analyzing parts of language versus broader issues of meaning) when outlining their positions. Stubbs (1983) distinguishes between language analysis below the level of the sentence and "language above the sentence or above the clause" (p. 1; quoted in Schiffrin, 1994, p. 23). Schiffrin (1994) proposes that the distinction is between *formalist* (or *structuralist*) and *functionalist* views of language. Linell (1998) makes a similar point:

> Language can be conceptualized in basically two ways, as *system* or *structure,* or as *discourse, practice* (praxis) or *communication.* If one gives priority to the former, we can talk about a formalist(ic) framework; here, linguistic expressions can be treated in abstracto. Priorities to the latter yield a more functionalist(ic) paradigm; its focus on communicative meanings and functions makes it necessary to take contexts into account. (p. 3)

We have already encountered a functionalist view in van Dijk's (1997c) stated interest in *"who* uses language, *how, why* and *when"* (p. 3). With respect to our own research group's approach to discourse analysis, we take a strongly functional approach, focusing mainly on how dialogue works and what a particular phenomenon is doing (or how it works) in its immediate communicative context.

So far, we have looked at discourse analysts who are concerned primarily with language use, that is, at researchers whose main interest is in what is said or written. However, some analysts focus on the kind of discourse that involves ideas or philosophies propagated by particular people or groups of people (van Dijk, 1997c, pp. 1-2). Analysts such as Caldas-Coulthard and Coulthard (1996b) call themselves critical linguists and, along with researchers such as Fairclough (1992), Fowler (1996), and Hodge and Kress (1993), call their research *critical discourse analysis* (CDA), which they define as "an analysis of public discourse, an analysis designed to get at the ideology coded implicitly behind the overt propositions, to examine it particularly in the context of social formations" (Fowler, 1996, p. 3).

In CDA, the focus is not entirely on the actual words written or spoken but also on the representations implicit in the words. This kind of analysis, one might observe, can be far above the level of the sentence, because it may be less concerned with what is spoken or written and more concerned with the broader message, philosophy, ideology, or idea conveyed. CDA might, for example, reveal that particular views of gender or race misrepresent or distort characteristics of the people represented. The goal of critical discourse analysts is to expose the misrepresentation or distortion in order to "defamiliarize" the public at large with the negative representation:

> Discourse is a major instrument of power and control and Critical Discourse Analysts . . . feel that it is indeed part of their professional role to investigate, reveal and clarify how power and discriminatory value are inscribed in and mediated through the linguistic system: Critical Discourse Analysis is essentially political in intent with its practitioners acting upon the world in order to transform it and thereby create a world where people are not discriminated against because of sex, colour, creed, age or social class. (Caldas-Coulthard & Coulthard, 1996a, p. xi)

Parker (1992), a social psychologist, advocates a similar kind of critical analysis. His particular interest is on the role of discourse in the reproduction and transformation of meaning. Discourses "both facilitate and limit, enable and constrain what can be said (by whom, where, when)" (p. xiii). Parker defines discourse as "sets of statements which constitute an object" (p. 3; see also p. 5). His goal, like that of Caldas-Coulthard and Coulthard, is unequivocally emancipatory. That is, he endeavors to reveal problematic views as such. He states the case quite strongly, maintaining that an "amoral/apolitical psychology is worse than useless" (p. 2).

Within the writings of critical discourse analysts, the term *text* has a different (and more complex) meaning from the ones discussed above, which usually define it as written records of discourse. As Parker (1992) explains:

> I want to open up the field of meanings to which discourse analysis could be applied beyond spoken interaction and written forms by saying that we find discourses at work in *texts*. Texts are delimited tissues of meaning reproduced in any form that can be given an interpretative gloss. (p. 6)

He provides an example that is useful in clarifying his meaning. He describes an electronic game that displays a small moving male figure waving a crucifix at ghosts descending from the top of the screen to their graves. Each ghost that is prevented from landing by the crucifix-waving man is consumed in flames, and the player is awarded 10 points. This, in Parker's view, is a text that conveys Christian discourse. (Interestingly, we can also see by Parker's example that he is another researcher who extends the meaning of discourse to include means of communication in addition to written and spoken language use.)

Language and Reality

One further important difference must be mentioned. Discourse analysts clearly differ on how they conceive the relation between language and reality. We use the terms *realist* and *antirealist* to refer to two contrasting positions with respect to their subject matter. In stating the distinction so briefly, we identify the crucial issue; however, as is often the case with brevity, we risk oversimplifying at the cost of the loss of finer distinctions. Here we attempt only to introduce some of the issues involved.

Some analysts, such as critical discourse analysts among many others, are realists in that they maintain that certain descriptions or constructions of reality are more accurate than and preferable to others, even if not perfectly accurate and universally valid. Important in this view is the idea that it is possible to replace unfair, inaccurate constructions or representations with fairer and more accurate representations. Note that only if there is a real reality can any representation of it be seen as accurate or inaccurate.

The point at which this topic becomes complex and sometimes very confusing is when we attempt to answer the question, What is real? Most theorists (but not all) would agree that the physical world exists. However, theorists vary on whether the *social* practices and institutions created by humans—which are therefore social constructions and would not exist without human participation—should be considered real in the objective sense. Further, theorists also differ on how language is related to reality, whether physical or social.

Analysts such as Potter (1996) and Willig (1999) are antirealists, who maintain that reality in the commonly understood meaning of the term does not exist. What exist are descriptions, constructions, and representations that cannot be judged to be either true or false. In explaining her position, Willig (1999) proposes:

> [These] discourse analysts conceptualize language as constitutive of experience rather than representational or reflective [of experience]. They argue that the linguistic categories we use in order to "describe" reality are not in fact reflections of intrinsic and defining features of entities. Instead, *they bring into being the objects they describe.* Furthermore, there is always more than one way of describing something and our choice of how to use words to package perceptions and experiences gives rise to particular versions of events and of reality. It is in this sense that *language can be said to construct reality.* (p. 2; emphasis added)

In this view, reality is itself a construction made in language. Crucially lacking, antirealists claim, are any universal standards by which to judge the veracity of any particular representation or construction. For example:

> The [conventional] assumption is that meaning resides in movements—we just need to

identify the meaning correctly. But movements have no inherent, essential meaning; rather, they can be given multiple meanings by different interpreters (and by the same interpreter on different occasions), meanings that can vary across situations. (Wood & Kroger, 2000, p. 12)

Having briefly described the range of realist and antirealist positions, we would like to clarify our own position here. First, it is important to distinguish between physical events or objects in the world and the *meanings* of those events or objects. Suppose someone opens a door in the presence of another person. It is possible to say that this event is real in the sense that a movement occurred and the door is now open. However, this movement can take on almost any meaning, depending on context and interpretation: It could mean that the person who opens the door is declaring an intention to carry out a requested errand or an intention to leave the relationship; that he or she is just letting in fresh air or implicitly complaining about smoking; that he or she is advertising that the ensuing conversation is to be public rather than "behind closed doors"; and so forth. In a great deal of social life, such interpretations are elastic, as the antirealists propose. The two individuals in the room can disagree about what the act means, and either of them can change (or lie about) what he or she says it means. However, we would point out two significant qualifications on this elasticity. First, there are occasions when certain meanings of events are not negotiable. If the door is a hatch on a deeply submerged submarine, then opening it means, among many other things, that unprotected occupants are (really) going to die. Second, for a great deal of what we do in everyday life, there is substantial social consensus about meaning. Opening a door ahead of another person who is walking toward it usually means holding the door open for that person, and the other is very likely to go through the doorway first. The possibility that the act could sometimes be a trap or a joke does not obviate the higher likelihood that it was an act of courtesy; indeed, that very consensus makes the trap or joke possible. We are able to navigate social life because there is a great deal of consensus about meaning; if this were not so, almost no social action would be possible. Perhaps one of our tasks should be to explore such consensus as a topic in itself.

We can extend the same reasoning to a discursive example: When a witness takes an oath in a courtroom, this discursive act changes the status of subsequent testimony. If the witness lies, he or she can then be prosecuted and imprisoned for perjury, a penalty that does not exist in other settings. Therefore the oath, its meaning, and its consequences are, we could argue, effectively real although clearly a social construction.

Summary

The reader can see by now that the terrain of discourse analysis is varied but has some common features. First, there are differences between what different analysts treat as discourse. These range from just written (or just spoken) language to other modes of communication, such as nonverbal gestures. As well, *discourse* can be used to describe a particular ideology or philosophy that is implicit in different forms of language use.

It is not surprising that approaches to analysis also differ. Some researchers look at language from a more structural or formal point of view in order to analyze, for instance, the linguistic devices that can be seen to constitute language. Other researchers take a more functional approach, looking at language use in its social context—for example, examining questions about who uses language, when, how, and for what purposes.

Finally, an important issue in the field is the relation between language and reality. Some discourse analysts maintain that language describes or constructs different versions of something real that exists independent of language. The meanings given can be more (or less) accurate. Others maintain that there are only versions of reality; it is language itself that creates and constitutes reality.

NEW PERSPECTIVES

Discourse analysis can be a method that complements existing communication research tools (questionnaires, interviews, ratings, and so on), to be used within traditional theoretical frameworks. Or it can be part of a substantially different approach with several new theoretical and methodological premises. We describe these alternative premises in this section, noting that, although our research group has eventually adopted all of them, readers may wish to consider some but not others.

The Primacy of Discourse

A significant theoretical choice can be to focus on the discourse itself rather than on inferred intrapsychic (mental) processes, such as cognition, emotion, motivation, abilities, goals, intentions, attitudes, and personality characteristics. Communication is often treated as secondary to mental processes, in one of two ways. First and most obviously, communicative acts may be of interest simply because they provide a means of revealing or studying mental processes. For example, answers on questionnaires and responses on rating scales are typically seen as direct indications of attitudes and preferences, not as discourse. Similarly, interviews are usually seen as a way of finding out what is on interviewees' minds rather than as dyadic communication between interviewer and interviewee. And many if not most studies of facial expression derive from a primary interest in emotion (e.g., Ekman, 1993; but see also Bavelas & Chovil, 1997; Kraut & Johnston, 1979). Emotions are not directly observable, so the study of facial expression is a preferred behavioral method for inferring them. Used in these ways, discourse is a behavioral means to intrapsychic ends. The alternative is to become attracted to the discourse itself, treating it as intrinsically interesting and worth analyzing in detail.

The second way in which researchers can treat discourse as secondary is to explain it by mental models. That is, even when the discourse is the initial focus of interest, the focus quickly shifts to mental processes that might explain it. The question of "why" individuals or groups communicate in particular ways is most often answered by hypothesized mental processes, such as their cognitions or personality. If the cause is intrapsychic, the discourse becomes merely an effect or by-product and may not even be examined closely. (For a fuller discussion of the problems with and alternatives to this approach, see Bavelas, 1991.)

We can illustrate these issues with the example of language production, which is usually seen as the outcome of the speaker's cognitive processes. There are many elaborate cognitive models that explain how an individual finds a word or produces sentences, and of course sophisticated mental processes must be involved in this most skilled of human activities. However, Bavelas and Coates (1992) have questioned whether existing mental models of language production and comprehension can account for the observed precision and complexity of dialogue. At the very least, a thorough appreciation of the nature of the discourse itself (versus hypothetical examples) must be the criterion by which such models are generated or judged.

An even greater shift is to examine the discourse of language production without reference to mental models. Clark and Wilkes-Gibbs (1986) proposed that the speaker and addressee work together to choose a word or term to describe something. For example:

A. That tree has, uh, uh

B. Tentworms.

A. Yeah.

B. Yeah. (p. 6)

Sacks (quoted in Jefferson, 1973, p. 59) provides another example:

A. I heard you were at the beach yesterday. What's her name, oh you know, the tall redhead that lives across the street from Larry? The one who drove him to work the day his car was

B. Oh *Gina!*

A. Yeah Gina. She said she saw you at the beach yesterday.

Clark and Wilkes-Gibbs (1986) point out that such excerpts are highly social and collaborative. Clark and his collaborators have conducted experiments showing how, even when one person is the official speaker, both individuals contribute possible terms, modify them, and work out mutually meaningful references (which are not necessarily intelligible to outsiders) (Clark & Wilkes-Gibbs, 1986; Schober & Clark, 1989). Our main point here is that their research focus is on the dialogue that produces references, not on the mental processes of the speaker.

Thus one can choose to study the discourse itself without using or invoking mental processes at all. This proposal is not the same as a radical behaviorism that denies the existence of mental phenomena—which clearly exist and are important—but rather a shift of interest to the other, equally interesting phenomena to be found in discourse. There is no a priori reason why inferred mental phenomena should be given primacy over discourse.

One might fairly ask, however, if researchers turn away from mental models, are they not also abandoning theory and becoming merely descriptive? If individual or intrapsychic explanations were the only way theory could be built, then eschewing them to focus on discourse would indeed be atheoretical. However, it is also possible to answer the question of "why" by examining *how* and *what for* (Watzlawick, Beavin Bavelas, & Jackson, 1967, p. 45), that is, by looking at interpersonal processes and at the social effects of communicative acts. As theorists, we can look outward rather than inward. For example, in our studies of equivocal communication, we focused on goals, not as mental intentions or plans, but as properties of the social world: the options available and their consequences (Bavelas, 1991; Bavelas, Black, Chovil, & Mullett, 1990). Specifically, we have shown that equivocation occurs when all of the direct options (e.g., lying or telling a hurtful truth) are negative and to be avoided. In this view, equivocation is a way of traversing a social minefield rather than the product of inferred intrapsychic processes.

So far, we have suggested a primacy of discourse as both the focus of interest and the source of explanation. It is possible to go a step further and adopt the even stronger premise that discourse creates our social world. Unseen mental processes are not social. Only observable actions or their consequences can have social effects, and language use is arguably the predominant social action out of which our social lives are created. Thus it is possible to see interpersonal communication not merely as reflecting individuals' views of the social world, but as creating and sustaining the social world, as the fabric of social life itself. A discursive theoretical approach focuses on how the participants *do* social actions.

An Inductive Approach: Learning from the Discourse

Another new perspective one can adopt is an inductive stance. Most researchers, especially students, have learned that one starts a research project by (a) going to the literature to find previous theory and research, (b) forming a hypothesis, and then (c) going to the data (e.g., discourse) to test the hypothesis. An alternative approach that is consistent with discourse analysis is to go "backward," that is, to start inductively by studying the discourse first, generating hypotheses or explanations from what one observes, and only then going to the literature.[2] (For further discussion and examples, see Bavelas, 1987, 1995.)

An inductive approach to discourse analysis involves at least two new premises. The first is a different assumption about the role of the literature in research. Traditionally, research extends an existing literature, building on it study by study to ensure the accumulation of knowledge. However, entirely new insights and approaches cannot come from the literature. If the idea is already in the literature, it is by definition not new. Moreover, the lenses imposed by the literature will inevitably constrain the way in which one can see the discourse. Often, these constraints are unrecognized because they are implicit in a particular paradigm and therefore difficult even to be aware of, much less to question. Without disparaging the obvious importance of previous research, we propose a balance between continuity and innovation that values working both within and outside of existing topics and frameworks. As Yngve (1970) observes, "There is nothing like viewing video tapes of actual communicative activity to dispel any preconceptions one may have" (p. 573).

The most likely source of new ideas in many natural sciences is direct observation, the results of which often violate our preconceived notions:

> A good way to tell how the work is going is to listen in the corridors. If you hear the word, "Impossible!" spoken as an expletive, followed by laughter, you will know that someone's orderly research project is coming along nicely. (Thomas, 1974, p. 140)

For example, Coates (1991) took an inductive approach to irony in dialogue and discovered that it is a collaborative, not an individual, phenomenon. Microanalysis of actual discourse has been a fruitful source of entirely new ideas, from the original Natural History of an Interview project in the 1950s (Leeds-Hurwitz, 1987) to conversation analysis. Indeed, given the relative paucity of data about the nature and workings of actual discourse, there is a great deal of observational work to be done. Researchers in our field may be like the 19th-century naturalists (of whom Darwin was only one) who faced an exciting new world of animals and plants to carefully describe and understand.

If we begin to question the traditional role of the literature, we can also question the role of theory and hypothesis testing, which are usually seen as necessary to guide research. In the traditional view, one moves from general to specific; theory and hypothesis come first, then observation: *theory and deduction → hypothesis → confirmatory observation*. In contrast, observation can lead to theory by moving from the specific to the general. An initial inductive phase may lead to exciting new hypotheses and even theories: *observation and induction → hypothesis and theory*. Some inductive researchers, including our group, add a third step by returning to the data to test the new hypothesis, in a cycle of induction and deduction: *observation and induction → hypothesis and theory → confirmatory observation*. We return to these two alternative approaches later in this chapter.

There are two common and reasonable criticisms of an inductive approach. The first is that one cannot approach data free of preconceptions; no researcher's mind is a blank slate, to be written on by data without any prior ideas influencing what he or she sees. Therefore, some conclude, researchers will see only what they are prepared or guided by their theories to see. The first statement is

unassailably true; the conclusion is not. All veteran researchers have enough experience of failed projects or of cherished but consistently unsupported hypotheses to know that thinking and wishing do not make it so. A great deal of the methodological logic and machinery of scientific inquiry has been devised to guard against this unwanted possibility. Put more positively, the researcher will certainly choose to observe data that fit his or her interests (e.g., dyadic or group interaction, the media) and will also approach these data with a set of assumptions, preconceptions, and even hunches. Curiosity, which is the driving force of research, is rarely neutral, but this need not shut out new or unexpected possibilities. If one is truly curious, then theoretical preferences will not dictate one's observation. Virtually all inductive researchers require a number of instances of a phenomenon before they conclude that it is more than one of a kind.

The second concern about conclusions derived from inductive research is the danger of a particular kind of circularity. If the researcher is creative enough, so the argument goes, he or she will always be able to find some pattern that fits this particular set of data, but that pattern may fit only these data because it was created from and for them. Again, new data are the answer. That is, although it is true that humans are very good at finding patterns and can even find them in random numbers (or the stock market!), new observations will not confirm a pattern that fits only the limited set of data that generated it.

For both of these concerns, there are also procedures that provide technical safeguards, namely, interanalyst reliability and cross-validation, to be described below. Some researchers characterize these techniques as positivist and quantitative, and will not adopt them. In the next section we try to show how they can be a natural extension of a logic shared by all researchers, of whatever stripe.

GETTING DOWN TO DETAILS: TECHNICAL ISSUES

All research is about details; the big picture of theory exists only insofar as the details of data create and support it. Discourse analysis differs somewhat in the kinds of technical issues that are important; these are quite different from, for example, the details of experimental research using questionnaires. Technical issues such as recording and transcription replace more familiar ones, such as the psychometric aspects of rating scales or the intricacies of factorial designs. In this section we consider choices of research design, reliability, recording, transcription, and some ethical issues. We continue to emphasize the broader theoretical assumptions that underlie particular methodological choices.

Research Design

A research design is simply an orderly plan for gathering and analyzing data, one that serves the particular goals of the researcher for a particular study. It is not necessarily or even usually an experimental design. What is crucial is that researchers give considerable forethought to the plans and goals embodied in their design decisions before acting on them, so that the time and effort to be invested in carrying them out are likely to serve their purpose. In our view, researchers should make decisions that fit their own goals and interests, not any particular ideology; questioning methodological dogma and divisions can lead to creative new options (see Bavelas, 1995). An examination of our group's research, for example, reveals a considerable heterogeneity of choices.

Inductive Versus Hypothesis-Testing Designs

As described above, one major choice to be made at the outset is between inductive and hypothesis-testing designs; here we describe some of the more specific aspects of that choice. Anyone exposed to typical methods courses is likely to be more familiar with hypothesis-testing ("theory-driven") research, which is often described as the pinnacle of research design. Because of the status afforded it in some quarters, hypothesis testing is often the design that researchers choose first, for any topic. We do not subscribe to this "evolutionary scale" view of research design, especially when it relies on the natural sciences as a role model. A careful reading of the history of (and contemporary research in) life sciences such as biology reveals a strong foundation of painstaking inductive observation. However, design prejudice runs in both directions. Just as some experimentalists mistrust inductive research, some inductive researchers reject experimental or hypothesis-testing designs out of hand, primarily because of historical positivist associations. Our eclectic view is going to offend extremists on both sides, so we address our remarks to those who want to make up their own minds.

If we put preconceptions and received wisdom aside, what are the differences between hypothesis-testing research and inductive research? In hypothesis-testing research, the theory drives the design for gathering the data. Ideally, the researcher has a clearly formulated hypothesis, that is, a serious bet about what is going on and why. Multivariate statistical data dredging is not the same as hypothesis testing. The researcher has to develop a design that clearly anticipates all possible outcomes, including one that would support his or her hypothesis and others that would not. Only if the outcome can either advance *or diminish* the plausibility of the researcher's theory is there true hypothesis testing. A hypothesis-testing design demands an up-front commitment, and a great deal of experimental, quantitative, statistical research does not meet this standard. On the other hand, contrary to a common antirealist criticism, experiments never attempt to (and cannot) "prove" that a hypothesis is "true." Rather, experiments are one way of finding out which explanation of the data is more probable or which hypothesis is the best fit—at least until a better one comes along.

In inductive research, the data lead to the theory. Inductive research serves the goal of a researcher who, at a particular point, has a strong intuition that something new and interesting may be going on, which he or she needs to learn about. This approach may be an early stage in the research, or it may be the continuing preference of the researcher at any stage. The inductive researcher's primary motivations is curiosity about the data. As noted earlier, no inductive researcher is free of a general framework of assumptions, but the ideal is to learn from the data and be prepared to have one's preconceptions changed by the data. New ideas or entirely new frameworks are not going to come from the library; they will come from carefully observed data. There are some guidelines for embarking on this open-ended process (e.g., Bavelas, 1987; Wood & Kroger, 2000), which requires a good deal of faith in oneself and one's ability to observe closely and to be fair.

The major objection to inductive research is a concern that the researcher will invent a pattern in the data whether one is there or not. That is, the valuable creative possibilities of this method must be weighed against the more mundane possibility of the researcher's simply fooling him- or herself. However, logic provides an answer that many inductive researchers follow, formally or informally. Having observed and made inductive propositions based on observed data, most inductive researchers go on to seek confirmation of their conclusions in new sets of data. One design for formalizing this process is analogous to the statistical procedure of *cross-validation* in multiple regression. When approaching a new

set of data inductively, the researcher limits the analysis to a subsample of the whole (ideally, a randomly chosen subsample). Based on this initial inductive analysis, the researcher makes a commitment to what has been found and then is prepared to test it in the remainder of the sample. If the original pattern was random, it will disappear in the new data set. Depending on the outcome, a cross-validation strategy provides either a useful safeguard against the potential weakness of inductive research or a powerful demonstration of its validity.

Returning to the choice between inductive and hypothesis-testing designs, one possibility is to use both, at different times. In our own research, we often follow a cycle of, first, going to the data to learn, then cross-validating on a larger data set, and then experimentally testing the hypotheses developed in the inductive phase. The challenge for all researchers is to practice tolerance toward others who make different choices. In the end, all of us must be able to provide precise answers to these questions: What are you claiming? How do you know?

Agreement Among Analysts (Reliability)

It is hard to believe that the ordinarily boring topic of interanalyst (also called interrater, interjudge, and interobserver) reliability is as controversial as it is in the field of discourse analysis. Some researchers reject all discourse analysis on the grounds that it is not reliable or "objective," whereas others reject reliability procedures as futile efforts to establish "truth." We discuss both of these positions here.

Experimental researchers, especially those in psychology, place a high value on objectivity, in the sense that the researcher must not influence the measurement of events. (Readers will recognize that this is a strong realist stance, as described earlier.) To the extent that discourse analysis focuses on meaning and not on physical actions, it must rely on interpretation by the analyst. In the view of some critics, all interpretation is intrinsically biased and subjective. Because the researcher is making interpretations, he or she is influencing the measurement, which therefore cannot yield objective data.

The answer to this criticism is that *all* sensory data are interpretive, including readings on a dial or thermometer and counts of physical movements. Certain measures are conventionally called *objective* simply because it is obvious that independent observers are very likely to agree: If each of us looks at the same thermometer at the same time, presumably we would have 100% agreement about the temperature. However, there could be disagreements due to different viewing angles, differences in eyesight, or just plain error. Early astronomers learned that their own reaction times affected the measurements they made and had to be compensated for; this did not stop astronomy from becoming accepted as an objective science. If one accepts the interpretive role of the researcher in all measurement, then the dichotomy between objective and nonobjective measurement becomes, instead, *a continuum of demonstrated agreement between independent observers,* ranging from 100% to much lower or even nonexistent agreement. When independent analysts agree highly, then the fear of interpretive bias is unfounded, and any such measure must be accepted on equal footing with other, more conventionally objective measures.

However, a different group of researchers rejects the pursuit of interanalyst agreement for other reasons. Some simply feel that the original analyst must be correct, by definition, or that the skilled intuition of an experienced analyst is not replicable. Others, especially antirealists, see any attempt to establish interanalyst reliability as an effort to establish the "truth," and they reject the entire realist

epistemology—the belief that there is a reality independent of the observer. This is not an unreasonable reaction to the strong pro-objectivity stance outlined above; the two positions are mirror images of each other. And if, as argued above, all measurement involves at least some interpretation, then the pursuit of an objective truth free of interpretation is indeed a misleading, even useless, exercise.

We would like to articulate an alternative reason for and use of interanalyst agreement, one that does not claim that it establishes the truth of a measure or an interpretation. One simple way of debunking that criticism is to point out that there is no standard of truth in the calculation of interanalyst reliability. The usual calculation for qualitative data is simply the number of agreements between analysts divided by the number of their agreements plus disagreements. For the rarer quantitative measures, agreement is calculated by correlation, or r, between analysts' decisions, but the same point holds: The analysts are being compared only to each other, not to some independent "correct" standard. The question that a reliability figure answers is simply, How well do analysts agree? There is no claim to the truth or correctness of what they agree on (which is conventionally called *validity*).

Stripped of the claim of truth, there is quite a different benefit to this kind of reliability. Establishing agreement among independent analysts requires the careful explication of what is being examined and how it is being interpreted. That is, achieving high agreement on complex interpretations of discourse requires careful and explicit description of the interpretive and reasoning processes. This requirement is as valuable as the goal of demonstrating agreement itself. In our experience, we always understand the phenomenon more clearly and deeply after we have done the hard and iterative work of describing (and debating!) it sufficiently to achieve agreement.

The extended definitions that are necessary for high agreement require clear statements of what the phenomenon is and is not; many, many examples; and a guided decision process. (It is often helpful to put the latter in the form of a decision tree, which articulates the interpretive reasoning as a series of nested decisions.) When new analysts can follow the process and agree, we know we are clear about the phenomenon we are studying, and this increased clarity also helps us in our responsibility to describe it fully in research articles.

There is a final, technical point we want to make about interanalyst agreement, for readers who decide to pursue it. In discourse analysis, unlike other occasions for interrater reliability, there are often two levels of decision: (a) *locating* instances where the phenomenon is occurring and then (b) a more specific decision about *what kind* of instance this one is. The first level is not necessary in, for example, questionnaire research, because the answer will be located where the question was asked. However, in naturally occurring language, the individuals structure their own discourse, usually for reasons that are very different from the researcher's interest, and much of what they say and do is not relevant to what the researcher is focusing on at the moment. So the researcher needs, first, to locate sites where relevant discourse is occurring. A concrete example will illustrate this process. Coates (1997) was interested in the kinds of attributions that trial judges make about what causes offenders to commit crimes—that is, in how judges discursively construct responsibility. The legal texts that Coates analyzed were the full judgments delivered at the ends of trials, so they contained a great deal of information unrelated to attributions. Therefore her first step was to locate, reliably, places in the texts where the judges were making attributions about the causes of the crimes (e.g., "due to his alcoholism"). In

the second step, she analyzed each of these located instances for the kind of attribution being made; a separate reliability was required for this analysis. (A detailed summary of the process our group uses for developing and assessing the reliability of new methods of analysis is available in Coates, 1998.)

Choosing and Recording the Data

We have two purposes in this subsection. First, we want to provide readers with several ideas about where to locate discursive data that will suit their interests—not an exhaustive list, but one intended to fuel readers' imaginations. Second, we discuss the options for recording the data for later analysis, which necessarily differ depending on whether the original discourse occurred in writing, in spoken form, or face-to-face.

Recording and Transcription as Theoretical Decisions

In a classic article, Ochs (1979) proposes that transcription itself is theory; we would add that recording embodies theory as well. That is, knowingly or unknowingly, researchers make important theoretical decisions when they decide how to record and transcribe their data. We review some of these theoretical decisions below, as well as some practical considerations.

Choices regarding how and what to record and transcribe are inevitably guided by assumptions and presuppositions about the phenomenon or process being studied. These assumptions may not constitute a fully articulated theory; they may not even be recognized as assumptions. However, the act of choosing to record or transcribe in a particular way inevitably makes some aspects of the discourse more salient while other aspects are unrecorded or left on the cutting room floor, so to speak. It is therefore essential that the researcher be explicit about these decisions, making deliberate choices about what is to be included and excluded and ensuring that these choices are guided by and consistent with the goals of the research.

It will become obvious in the following that our research group's theoretical position is always that we should record in the same mode in which the participants are interacting, on the assumption that they will use all of the features available to them in any given mode. That is, if one is prepared to analyze only words, then one should study messages that were originally written (Bavelas, 1984; Bavelas et al., 1990, chap. 5). This reveals our assumption that participants select or omit certain behaviors because their receivers will or will not see or hear them; for example, they will use voice quality when they know it will be heard, but will use other alternatives in writing. Many other researchers have different views of communicators and communication and would therefore disagree with our position and make other decisions; their assumptions and rationales should be equally explicit.

We want to emphasize here the advantages as well as the limitations of any recording or transcribing decision. It would be possible to misread what follows as our suggesting that, because all data are limited and fallible, no data are satisfactory, but this is very far from our position. In our view, all discourse is context specific. There is no easy source of "naturalistic" data in the sense of their being unaffected by the contexts in which they occur and the ways in which researchers choose to analyze them (Bavelas, 1984, 1995).[3] The challenge is to understand these contextual and technical factors and to incorporate them in a creative manner into one's research. Understanding the contextual factors that affect the participants' communication can be a substantive gain as well as a methodological necessity. An understanding of how technical decisions such as those regarding recording

and transcription can affect the data and their interpretation is essential to the researcher's reaching either goal.

Textual Material

If the researcher has chosen to work with written or visual material (e.g., newspaper articles, e-mail messages or chat room exchanges, memos or letters, written legal judgments, media ads depicting nonverbal communication), it is fairly easy for him or her to obtain a printed copy of the entire text. Another potential advantage to this choice is that written data can often be rendered anonymous, so ethical issues such as the protection of the participants' identities are simpler, and participants may be much more likely to give their permission for use of the data. Also, some written data are in the public domain and require no permission at all for their use.

In approaching a printed record of written dialogues, it is important that the researcher remember that the *timing* of the participants' contributions has been lost. For example, between the times when they are writing e-mail or other correspondence, the participants are out in the world doing other things, and each returns anew to the previous message and his or her own reply. So, although the researcher can read the participants' messages in close sequence, he or she must remember (and preferably encode into the data) that the messages were in fact separated by time and many other events.

As Linell (1982) has pointed out, written language differs from spoken language (and especially from face-to-face dialogue) in timing and many other important respects; a summary of these differences is presented in Table 4.1. When individuals communicate in writing, it is important to remember that, even though the printed record of their exchanges may sometimes look like a record of face-to-face dialogue, there are crucial differences: For

Table 4.1   Differences Between Written and Spoken Language

Written Text	*Face-to-Face Dialogue*
Is a persistent, static "object"	**Is ephemeral, "dynamic"**
It can be reread any time.	It cannot ordinarily be reviewed.
It seldom requires a rapid response.	The participants must respond immediately, "on-line."
Consists of discrete, separate symbols	**Is virtually continuous**
Words are easily separated.	Words and other acts merge.
Text is organized spatially.	Dialogue is organized temporally.
Is relatively context-free	**Is highly dependent on context**
It uses only words and punctuation	It uses face and hand gestures as well as prosodic features.
The words are highly explicit.	The words can be less explicit.
Text is monologue and solitary.	Dialogue is a "social interplay."
There is no immediate reader.	There is an addressee present.
The writer and reader are in different places.	The participants are in the same setting.
Text must often be addressed to a general audience.	Dialogue can draw on the setting and the ongoing conversation.
Is acquired as secondary socialization	**Is acquired as primary socialization**
Literacy is learned institutionally (in schools).	Dialogue is learned interpersonally (at home).
It is taught with explicit, conscious norms.	It is practiced rather than explicitly taught.
The norms are more standardized, with less variation.	The norms are freer, with more variation.

SOURCE: Adapted from Linell (1982, pp. 5-10); reprinted from Bavelas and Chovil (2000). Copyright 2000 by Sage Publications.

NOTE: Some of the features of written text noted here do not apply to computer-mediated communication, especially if both parties are on-line at the same time.

example, the participants were usually not in the same social context or physical setting, and they may not have been responding only to each other (e.g., memos go to other recipients as well; newspaper editorials and letters to editors have larger audiences). Even the immediate participants may have been drawing on different memories or versions of what they previously corresponded about (or even of the messages they were currently responding to). They may have given more or less time to thinking about and writing or editing their replies. The way the recipient (or researcher) reads a reply may not be the way the writer "said" it; that is, the writer may have intended an emphasis on one word whereas, lacking any auditory cues, the reader may assume an emphasis on a different word. Although the written version that the researcher possesses may be exactly what the participants wrote and read, it is important that he or she be alert to unwarranted assumptions about *how* they wrote and read their messages. Ideally, the record of their exchange should be annotated to remind the analyst constantly of these factors.

Real-time electronic exchanges (e.g., ICQ, chat rooms) overcome some of the above limitations, but only if they are videotaped (e.g., Garcia & Jacobs, 1999; Phillips & Bavelas, 2000). A printout alone cannot capture the precise timing of the exchanges and in fact may even misrepresent the sequence in which responses were actually made.

Spoken (Voice-Only) Communication

There are many important settings where interpersonal communication occurs in voice-only dialogues. The best example is a telephone conversation; conversation analysis began with Harvey Sacks's analyses of recorded telephone conversations, and this format continues to be a fascinating source of data (e.g., Hopper, 1992). Other examples include answering-machine or voice-mail exchanges and radio call-in programs. We have used telephone exchanges in the lab when we wanted to deal only with audible features of communication rather than with both audible and visible features (Bavelas et al., 1990, chap. 6). Participants in spoken records are more identifiable than those in written records (although less identifiable than those in video-taped records), so the researcher should obtain permission to use the data. In our experience, it is a good idea to use a multipart permission form that allows participants to consent to the researcher's analysis of their tapes and still withhold permission, for example, for the researcher to play the tapes in public presentations where someone might recognize the participants' voices.

Many of the same cautions given above for written communication still apply, especially if the exchanges examined are not real-time dialogues. Even for a telephone conversation, it is crucial that the researcher hear the exchange as itself and not as if it were a face-to-face dialogue, staying constantly aware of contextual factors that affect the participants (they are not in the same physical or social context, they cannot see each other's actions, and so on). With this awareness, and if the recording of a real-time telephone conversation is of the same quality as the participants heard, the researcher can come very close to "being there." Indeed, one significant advantage of the telephone format is that in making the recording, the researcher has potentially captured the conversation as it originally occurred. In contrast, for example, speakers who leave messages on answering machines are responding in part to their own circumstances and even to the outgoing messages they just heard, which the researcher may overlook (e.g., if an outgoing message is humorous, unexpected, unclear, or offers limited choices, it may affect incoming messages in systematic and interesting ways).

Face-to-Face Dialogue

Arguably, most interpersonal communication occurs in real-time face-to-face dialogue, which, as Table 4.1 shows, has several unique features. Of particular relevance for the researcher's decision about recording is the fact that face-to-face dialogue has both audible and visible features, so arguably the best method of recording such dialogue is by videotaping. However, before we discuss this technique, we want to consider other possibilities. Again, the method the researcher chooses to use for the recording of data should follow from and be consistent with the research questions he or she is interested in answering and also with the broader theory that guides the research.

Most social interaction occurs too quickly to be recorded by hand (in writing) as it occurs. It might be possible for a researcher to record the frequency of certain obvious features if they do not happen too rapidly or too often (e.g., the use of particular words or phrases), but there is no possibility of accurately recording their immediate context or sequence, which most discourse analysts would consider essential. Only real-time recording will do.

Audio recording of face-to-face dialogue. The use of audio-only recordings in discourse analysis is common and offers several advantages. The equipment can be relatively inexpensive and small, making it portable and unobtrusive; convenient standard transcription equipment is available that allows repeated playback; and, as noted earlier, audio recordings provide a degree of anonymity for participants. However, one may need relatively sophisticated equipment to ensure that voice qualities are accurately reproduced, that all voices are equally audible, and that overlapping speech can be disentangled.

The central issue (and potential controversy) concerning the use of audio recordings of face-to-face dialogue is whether such recordings are necessarily incomplete—and not just for researchers whose primary interest is in nonverbal communication. Unlike telephone conversants, participants who interact in person are in the same physical and social setting and able to see each other as well as the same objects or events around them. Each can see how the other looks, both can refer to features of the environment that they can see, each knows when the other person is looking at him or her, both can see and interpret any nonverbal actions, and so forth.

There may be instances where the researcher's interest is entirely lexical, that is, focused on verbal or grammatical features. Or the researcher's theory may hold that any visible features (e.g., gaze, body orientation, hand and facial gestures, or the physical objects or events in the setting) are noncommunicative, redundant, or irrelevant. Thus the decision to audiotape a face-to-face dialogue is part of a clear theoretical position and must be recognized as such. If the phenomenon or process under study can occur only audibly and could not be affected by what the researcher cannot see, then the use of audio recording is a good option. We offer several

cautions, however, about accepting this assumption immediately.

First, in face-to-face dialogue, the participants often use deictic expressions, such as "over here," "that one," or "like this." In such cases the words are insufficient, because they were intended by the speaker to be supplemented by a visible action such as looking, pointing, or gesturing.

Second, the meaning of a polysemous word can be specified by a nonverbal demonstration. In Kendon's (1985) example:

> I have a Minolta SLR [still-photo] camera, and whenever I refer to this in my family I always refer to it as "my Minolta." Recently, I acquired a Minolta super-8 movie camera. Consequently the word "Minolta" became ambiguous, for it could refer to either [camera]. In the course of a conversation with my son—soon after this new camera had been acquired—he said to me: "You could do it with yours, your Minolta." As he said "Minolta" he lifted his hands up, thumb and forefinger of each hand extended at right angles to one another and held on either side of his face, thereby modeling the action of holding a [still-photo] camera. . . . By doing this he disambiguated "Minolta," clearly indicating that it was the SLR he was referring to and not the movie camera. (pp. 225-226)

In this case, the hand gestures specified the meaning of the word. In other cases, the speaker may complete a verbal phrase entirely with a gesture or facial display rather than finding the word ("mixed syntax"; Slama-Cazacu, 1976), so that an observer needs both parts to understand the utterance. Kendon (1985) describes a host who said to his guest, whom he needed to drive home,

> "Last night I had more coffee than usual . . . and I didn't sleep well, so maybe we oughta /GESTURE/." In this gesture he placed his two extended index fingers side by side and then extended both arms away from himself

and upwards in the direction of the door. He thereby clearly indicated that he and [his guest] should leave. (p. 224)

Third, some aspects of communication are typically not put into words. In multiparty interactions, whom the speaker is addressing (and who is attending to the speaker) is typically indicated by gaze, rather than verbally (Vertegaal, 1998). Finally, an audio recording will not capture what happens in the ubiquitous (auditory) pauses. A "pause" on audiotape is only a verbal pause. It is not likely that the participants were momentarily frozen in time, doing nothing; they may have been smiling at each other, gesturing, avoiding each other's gaze, or engaging in any number of other communicative acts. Researchers who interpret (auditory) pauses as, for example, hesitation or reluctance might have reached entirely different interpretations if they had worked from video recordings. (As will be seen below, we are by no means suggesting that a video recording misses nothing.)

The reader may appreciate by now why we have proposed that this issue is both theoretical and potentially controversial. Researchers who insist on videotaping face-to-face dialogue (as our research group does) often hold the theoretical position that visible features such as hand and facial gestures or gaze are an integral part of communication (Bavelas & Chovil, 2000). Researchers who prefer audiotapes often hold the theoretical position that these visible features are not so important as to justify the expense and inconvenience of video recording. We obviously cannot seek to resolve this issue here, but we suggest two guiding principles. First, the theoretical choice should be explicit and considered. Researchers who choose audio-only recording should explain in their research reports their underlying theoretical position and rationale as it applies to the particular studies at hand; the same burden falls on proponents of video. Second, many of the issues that guide these theoretical choices could be resolved empirically. Much more research is needed that compares audio-based and video-based analyses of the same data. Those who advocate video recording should support their position by showing empirically that it matters. For example, we found in our own work that speakers often made certain gestures (*interactive gestures*) that elicited responses such as back channels from the listener, yet 80% of these gestures were completely nonredundant with speech (Bavelas, Chovil, Coates, & Roe, 1995; Bavelas Chovil, Lawrie, & Wade, 1992). That is, there was no verbal indication of the speaker's action and meaning, so the speaker's influence on the listener's response would be ignored, inexplicable, or spuriously interpreted from an audio-only recording. A later study demonstrated the interaction between speaker gaze and listener responses (Bavelas, Coates, & Johnson, 2002; this article is accompanied by a video on CD that lets the reader see the effect).

Video recording of face-to-face dialogue. In most of this subsection we discuss issues related to researchers' making their own video recordings. We want to note, however, that researchers who find that this is not possible, or who want to examine wider ranges of contexts than are directly available to them, may want to consider the possibility of analyzing documentary films. For example, the National Film Board of Canada specializes in high-quality documentary films, hundreds of which are available through the board's Web site at www.nfb.ca. We have also used training or demonstration films of psychotherapy because of the ethical problems of filming actual sessions (Bavelas, McGee, Phillips, & Routledge, 2000; Phillips, 1999).

It is important to say at the outset that researchers who study videotapes should have no illusions that viewing such recordings is the same as being there. As we note below, even when a video recording is made with the best equipment, it is a smaller-than-life, selective, two-dimensional image that cannot in any case capture everything the participants could perceive (e.g., temperature, smells, and sights and sounds out of range of the recording equipment).

Video recordings also present researchers with the most challenging ethical issues, because participants are clearly identifiable to anyone who knows them. If the participants' facial features and voice qualities are not of interest, they can be electronically scrambled, but this is usually not the case. In our own research, we use a multipart participant permission form that lets each participant (after having viewed his or her tape) give or withhold permission separately for keeping the tape at all, analysis by the research team, viewing by audiences at other universities or at conferences, viewing in classes at our university, and any other uses we can reasonably anticipate (e.g., on our Web site). Then we transfer the coded permission status to all copies of the tapes.

One potential ethical decision, whether or not to hide the camera in the first place, is becoming a nonissue. With more experience in videotaping interaction, researchers have discovered that filming openly does not produce "artificial" data. For example, Goodwin (1981) films openly in the field, as we do in the lab. Certainly, presenting the camera as a nonthreatening aspect of the study is essential, but we also have popular technology on our side: Most participants are now used to being videotaped in banks, stores, and airports, and many have their own camcorders.

Researchers who choose to record on video must consider many factors prior to collecting the data (Goodwin, 1993). First, they must choose a format to record in. Popular choices are VHS, SuperVHS, 8mm, and digital. Analog cameras and camcorders are relatively cheap. Digital video is more expensive, but it offers improved image quality, does not degrade with repeated viewing, and provides more options for later storage and analysis. In any case, a permanent time signal on the tape is invaluable for later locating and identifying segments.

With whatever equipment, camera placement is an important decision: What you see is what you get. A video recording will include only the view and focus the researcher selects. Studies of social interaction usually require that the behaviors of both participants be captured by both lens and microphone. (Choosing to film only one of the participants would be a major theoretical decision.) The field researcher is usually limited to only one camera, which must capture everyone of interest; this probably means a fixed perspective and no close-ups. If the participants are moving around, the camera must track them or be set for a wide-angle shot. When there is a choice of focus, the researcher must usually choose, for example, between being far enough away to see hand gestures and being close enough to see facial expressions.

In the lab, it is possible to use more than one camera; the shots from two or more cameras can be configured and fed onto one split-screen videotape by a special-effects generator or "splitter." It is also possible to seat the participants in preselected places. We will illustrate some of the possibilities with a two-person interaction. With two cameras, the researcher can capture a front view of both participants as they looked to each other, by seating them almost face-to-face (but not perfectly, so they do not block each other's cameras) and placing the cameras opposite each other, behind each participant. This configuration aims a camera over the shoulder of each person, directly at the face of the other, so the viewer sees both individuals as they looked to each other. Then, choosing a vertical split produces a recorded image that looks as though the participants were side by side, which is something the analyst must adjust to. (It is also possible to produce a two-way split-screen effect with just one camera by placing a mirror behind one of the participants, provided this does not distract the other participant.) If there is a third camera available and a suitable splitter, the third camera can capture both participants from the side with a wide-angle lens. This third image can then be split onto the bottom of the recorded image, where it creates a pseudo-three-dimensional perspective, in that the analyst can see the participants' spatial movements, including hand gestures and their movements toward or away from each other. It can take an analyst a while to get used to this view and be able to reconstruct from it mentally the three-dimensional interaction; it is certainly not a literal recreation of the interaction.

Finally, whether recording by audio or video, researchers must remember the practical wisdom that all of us have learned the hard way. First, set up the equipment and try it out, from a trial recording through analysis of that recording. It is much better to find out that you cannot analyze one trial recording (because the sound is inaudible, the image is too small, you did not include something that had not seemed important at the time, and so on) than to find out after having recorded all of your data. And second, technophiles and technophobes alike can solve the vast majority of equipment problems by asking three questions: Is it turned on? Is it plugged in? Is it connected?

Transcribing

Why transcribe? There are several reasons that researchers need to consider separately before embarking on this time-consuming activity. The first is ease of access. Consider that, with textual materials (such as e-mails or letters), the analyst can work directly with the printed data and can therefore easily study any part of the data in any order and in any time sequence. Because written transcripts of non-textual data (e.g., telephone conversations)

provide similar and familiar ease of access, they are often more convenient to use than audio or video recordings. That is, perusing audio or video recordings and locating particular segments can be awkward and time-consuming, so many researchers prefer to work with transcripts instead. Note, however, that the advent of digitization may be reducing the transcript's advantage of convenience because the linear viewing constraint does not hold. With a digitized video (even of an originally analog recording) and appropriate software,[4] it is possible to go immediately to specified segments and to view them repeatedly with a simple command. Segments that seem to demonstrate the same process or phenomenon can be stacked up together for comparison. (Digitized video is also easier to transcribe, because the video image and word-processing program can be tiled side by side on the computer monitor, rather than using several pieces of equipment.)

The other reasons for transcribing audio or video records are increasingly theoretical, in that they involve assumptions (either implicit or explicit) about the nature of the discourse. The researcher may simply produce a verbal transcript because he or she implicitly assumes that words are the significant feature of communication. Or the researcher may be explicitly organizing the data according to his or her theoretical interests, and a specific kind of transcription is the first step. In either case, the effects of transcription can be made clear by an analogy with formulations in conversation (in which one person summarizes or describes what the other person has just said; Garfinkel & Sacks, 1970). Heritage and Watson (1979) point out that formulations inevitably *preserve* something of the original statement, *delete* part of it, and *transform* other parts. A transcription is like a formulation; it preserves some aspects (e.g., the words), deletes others (e.g., visible features), and transforms others (e.g., prosodic features may be represented in words or symbols). The challenge to the researcher is to be aware of these changes and to be explicit about his or her rationale.

Many established transcription systems exist (e.g., Jefferson, 1985). The method the researcher chooses to use in transcribing the data—whether a method developed by someone else or by the researcher him- or herself—determines what will be preserved, what will be ignored, and how the data are transformed. Choosing a transcription method or creating one is therefore an important theoretical decision and should be treated as such. Several papers have been written on transcription (e.g., Edwards, 1993; Ochs, 1979), so we cover only the main considerations here, organized into content (what to include) and format. As you consider the following, keep in mind that *not* transcribing is also an option.

What to Include?

First, the researcher must consider his or her own research goals. Transcription is an extremely time-consuming process—an hour or more for each minute of dialogue would not be unusual—so it is wasteful to transcribe more (or less) information than one needs. Most researchers transcribe all of the words spoken, but practices vary. If a researcher is interested only in where listeners' responses occur (Bavelas, Coates, & Johnson, 2000), for example, he or she might transcribe all of the listeners' responses from the videotape but transcribe the speaker only around the points where listener responses occur. Such a transcript would be unusable as a version of the speaker's contribution, but that is not its purpose.

Whether one is working with an audio or video recording, the prosodic and other paralinguistic features are available to be included. Many researchers, for example, are interested in phenomena such as intonation, stress, pauses, and timing of exchanges (for a review, see Dressler & Kreuz, 2000). The transcripts these researchers create therefore include precise description and timing of these phenomena (e.g., "u:h" means an elongated sound). Researchers working from a functional perspective, on the other hand, will emphasize the rhetorical or meaningful impacts that behaviors have in a conversation. These researchers will be less interested, for example, in the absolute duration of a pause than in an interpretive evaluation of what that pause means in a conversation (Gumperz & Berenz, 1993), so a pause might be transcribed with an annotation marking it as an indication of uncertainty.

With a video record, the researcher has a great deal more to decide about, including how to transcribe hand gestures, facial displays, gaze direction, and postural and limb positions. If these are included in the transcript, how should they be represented? One important choice is between a purely physical description and a meaning-based description. For example, in Kendon's "Minolta" example above, he first describes the physical actions and then adds information about what those actions were meant to depict ("holding a [still-photo] camera"). Ekman and Friesen's (1978) Facial Action Coding System (FACS) describes facial expression by referring to the muscle groups involved—a purely physical description. In contrast, Chovil (1989, 1991-1992) has developed a meaning-based system in which the analyst describes what the facial display is depicting (sadness, skepticism, and so on). It is worth pointing out that Chovil's data demonstrate higher interanalyst reliability than the FACS. The same can be true for interpretive approaches to gestures (for further description of meaning-based systems for describing nonverbal acts, see Bavelas & Chovil, 2000, pp. 175-183). This agreement is encouraging because such approaches are more suited to the goal of discourse analysis, which is to study communication at the level of meaning.

Format

The format of the transcript will influence the analysis carried out by the reader. Transcripts should be formatted so that they are easy to read and the appropriate information can be extracted quickly. To make transcripts readable, the researcher should consider both the visual prominence and the spatial arrangement of the data (Edwards, 1993). Visual prominence refers to how the data appear, such as the use of italic or boldface type, underlining, and font size. Using any one or a combination of these tools can give prominence to particular elements of the transcript. In addition, data elements can be positioned spatially on a transcript so as to improve both readability and efficiency.

Note that the spatial format of the transcript also reflects often unrecognized theoretical assumptions. For example, because of Western writing conventions, behaviors for which descriptions are placed either to the left or above other descriptions of behaviors in a transcript are seen as occurring before (and potentially as causes of) behaviors transcribed to the right or below them (Ochs, 1979).

Several similar features can be found across different transcription systems. First, *related events* tend to be located near each other. For example, descriptions of gestures are usually located near the speech events with which they co-occur. Similarly, transcriptions systems that include prosodic information (e.g., the London-Lund Corpus; Svartvik & Quirk, 1980), such as prominent syllable stress, will put that information with the relevant syllables. Second, visual prominence is used to *separate* qualitatively different data. Transcribers' comments are usually bracketed or presented in font that is different from that used for the data. Third, as noted above, *temporal relationships* are usually presented in a left-to-right and top-down format, so that earlier events are presented before later events. Similarly, explanatory material is placed at the beginning, where it frames all that follows.

Although there are many similarities among different transcription systems, there are also many differences, reflecting the differing goals, theoretical assumptions, and sometimes unrecognized presuppositions of different researchers. For example, an important formatting choice concerns how to arrange speakers into turns. Notice that this format presupposes that alternating speaking turns are a basic unit of dialogue, which makes simultaneous or overlapping speech problematic and ignores the simultaneous, noninterruptive facial expressions and nods of those who are not speaking. There are at least three different arrangements used in existing transcription systems: vertical, column, and partiture (Edwards, 1993), as shown in the following examples (which come from Tannen, 1989, p. 60). The *vertical* format is perhaps most common. It is similar to the script of a play, but usually with overlapping speech shown in aligned square brackets:

A: Like he says that he says that American[s]

B: [Yeah]

A: or Westerners tend to be u:h think of the
    body and the soul as two different th[ings,]

B: [right]

As Ochs (1979) points out, this format has several effects: It encourages the reader to link adjacent utterances and to see each as successively contingent on those preceding it; it also tends to make the reader see participants as equally involved and influential in the interaction.

When the researcher wants to highlight the influence of one person on the other, a *column* format may be more appropriate:

Speaker A	Speaker B
Like he says that he says that Americans . . .	Yeah.
or Westerners tend to be u:h . . . think of the body and the soul as two different things.	Right.

In this format, the speaker on the left is given prominence over the speaker on the right; thus Speaker A may be implicitly seen as initiating the behaviors of Speaker B. This format does not provide an easy way to indicate precisely when the speakers overlap, as they often do in spontaneous dialogue. However, it might be suitable for capturing asymmetries in dialogue or for depicting parallel speech (e.g., when both are trying to get the floor or are having a shouting match).

Partiture formats (Tannen, 1984) are designed to capture interaction in which there may be many instances of simultaneous behaviors. They are similar to multipart musical scores and preserve both timing (horizontally as opposed to vertically) and the assumption of conversational equality:

A: . . . American[s]

B: [yeah]

A: or Westerners . . .

This format is continued, with line breaks as needed.

Another important choice the researcher must make when creating a transcript is where to put visible elements of the dialogue, such as hand gestures and facial displays, if indeed they are systematically included. Some systems separate the visible elements by placing them in their own column on the right-hand side of the transcript, roughly parallel to the spoken words in the left column. This format has several effects: First, it imposes a theory of verbal and nonverbal (audible and visible) acts as separate channels and gives words priority by placing them on the left. Second, the relationship between the two is lost. For example, the use of a gesture to supplement words is less clear, and the precise verbal context of the gesture may be lost.

Researchers who take an integrated view of audible and visible acts would use a format that integrates the verbal and the visible and also preserves their timing as precisely as possible. For example, one can underline the words that overlap the gesture and describe the gesture in brackets underneath. The following example (adapted from Bavelas, 1994, p. 207) also illustrates meaning-based description of the gestures; the speakers are discussing the Royal Canadian Mounted Police (Mounties, or RCMP):

A: Is—the only RCMP in the area
    is—what? Colwood or?

    [draws jagged circles,

    as if on a map]

B: Well that's, that's a, a
    regular detachment in Colwood,

    [draws tighter circle]

A final, practical warning: The transcription process takes a toll on audio or video records. Repeatedly playing, pausing, and rewinding an analog tape will soon degrade its quality. Therefore, researchers should always work from copies, using the originals only to make new copies. As noted above, one advantage of digital records is that they will not degrade; however, it is still wise to make at least one copy.

New Technologies

Although most of us develop or adapt our own systems for managing our data and coding social interactions, commercial software systems designed specifically for these tasks are available. One of these, Noldus Observer Pro, is a system for collecting, analyzing, and presenting observational data (see the Web site at www.noldus.com). It can be used to record behaviors such as postures, movements, positions, and facial expressions. The analyst uses key presses to log events and the times at which they occur. This system makes it possible for the researcher to work directly from the video record rather than from a written transcript of it. It also allows the analyst to add notes and comments that are then stored with the video data. The system provides facilities for descriptive statistics, lag sequential analysis, and reliability analysis. The data can be exported into spreadsheets, databases, or statistical packages. The Noldus Observer package (which costs several thousand dollars for the software alone) can be purchased either as software only or as part of a complete hardware/software bundle that includes analog or digital cameras, VCRs, video capture cards, and time-code generators. Transana, on the other hand, is a free tool for transcription and qualitative analysis of videotape (see the Web site at www2.wcer.wisc.edu/Transana/index_ html).

Several attempts have been made, such as the Text Encoding Initiative (TEI), to introduce guidelines for electronic text encoding and interchange (see the TEI Web site at www.tei-c.org). The goal of these systems is to create a common encoding scheme for transcripts and other text, that is, to reduce the diversity of existing encoding practices and to encourage the sharing of data, as well as to make it possible for the data to be read by machines. The TEI is one of the only systematized attempts made thus far to develop a fully general text encoding model and encoding conventions. Because these guidelines are meant to be applicable over a wide variety of data, they are necessarily restrictive in terms of what they permit the user to do, as well as being time-consuming to learn. We would expect the same trade-off to apply to any new system—that is, the user must choose between the potential benefits of a common system and its methodological constraints, which, as we have emphasized throughout, also impose implicit theoretical assumptions.

WHERE TO FIND MORE

To return to our introductory metaphor, we have traveled through a lot of territory in the far-flung field of discourse analysis and have stopped to look briefly at many of its features,

from theoretical and philosophical debates to technical considerations. As on any tour, we could have stayed longer in each place, and interested readers may want to know more than we have provided here or in our references. Van Dijk's (1997a, 1997b) two-volume introduction covers the many kinds of discourse analysis in much more detail, and each chapter has a list of further readings on its topic. Finally, many journals (such as *Discourse Processes, Discourse and Society, Research on Language and Social Interaction,* and the *Journal of Language and Social Psychology*) include studies that have used some form of discourse analysis. Interested readers will find that locating such articles in their own areas of interest is an excellent way to continue the tour and to decide where (and if) they want to go on their own.

NOTES

1. Many readers will be startled to see data from a psychology lab included as "naturally occurring." However, we agree with Schegloff (1992, p. 116) that, as long as the participants are not confederates and are interacting spontaneously, even within an assigned task or topic, their discourse cannot be arbitrarily dismissed because of the context in which it occurred.

2. It is undoubtedly because of the inductive preferences of many discourse analysts that they eschew the term *coding,* which has implications of an a priori system that the term *analysis* does not.

3. Ironically, the term *naturalistic* actually means "as if natural" (e.g., a naturalistic painting).

4. We are currently using the software Broadway (www.b-way.com) because of its higher-quality AVI format and because it allows us to create "loops," that is, to isolate and replay selected segments easily.

REFERENCES

Atkinson, J. M., & Heritage, J. (Eds.). (1984). *Structures of social action: Studies in conversation analysis.* Cambridge: Cambridge University Press.

Bartlett, F. C. (1932). *Remembering*. Cambridge: Cambridge University Press.

Bavelas, J. B. (1984). On "naturalistic" family research. *Family Process, 23,* 337-341.

Bavelas, J. B. (1987). Permitting creativity in science. In D. N. Jackson & J. P. Rushton (Eds.), *Scientific excellence: Origins and assessment* (pp. 307-327). Newbury Park, CA: Sage.

Bavelas, J. B. (1991). Some problems with linking goals to discourse. In K. Tracy (Ed.), *Understanding face-to-face interaction: Issues linking goals and discourse* (pp. 119-130). Hillsdale, NJ: Lawrence Erlbaum.

Bavelas, J. B. (1994). Gestures as part of speech: Methodological implications. *Research on Language and Social Interaction, 27,* 201-221.

Bavelas, J. B. (1995). Quantitative versus qualitative? In W. Leeds-Hurwitz (Ed.), *Social approaches to communication* (pp. 49-62). New York: Guilford.

Bavelas, J. B., Black, A., Chovil, N., & Mullett, J. (1990). *Equivocal communication*. Newbury Park, CA: Sage.

Bavelas, J. B., & Chovil, N. (1997). Faces in dialogue. In J. A. Russell & J.-M. Fernandez-Dols (Eds.), *The psychology of facial expression* (pp. 334-346). Cambridge: Cambridge University Press.

Bavelas, J. B., & Chovil, N. (2000). Visible acts of meaning: An integrated message model of language use in face-to-face dialogue. *Journal of Language and Social Psychology, 19,* 163-194.

Bavelas, J. B., Chovil, N., Coates, L. J., & Roe, L. (1995). Gestures specialized for dialogue. *Personality and Social Psychology Bulletin, 21,* 394-405.

Bavelas, J. B., Chovil, N., Lawrie, D. A., & Wade, A. (1992). Interactive gestures. *Discourse Processes, 15,* 469-489.

Bavelas, J. B., & Coates, L. J. (1992). How do we account for the mindfulness of face-to-face dialogue? *Communication Monographs, 59,* 301-305.

Bavelas, J. B., Coates, L. J., & Johnson, T. (2000). Listeners as co-narrators. *Journal of Personality and Social Psychology, 79,* 941-952.

Bavelas, J. B., Coates, L. J., & Johnson, T. (2002). Listener responses as a collaborative activity: The role of gaze. *Journal of Communication, 52.*

Bavelas, J. B., McGee, D., Phillips, B., & Routledge, R. (2000). Microanalysis of communication in psychotherapy. *Human Systems, 11,* 47-66.

Brown, G. (1995). *Speakers, listeners and communication: Explorations in discourse analysis.* Cambridge: Cambridge University Press.

Caldas-Coulthard, C. R., & Coulthard, M. (1996a). Preface. In C. R. Caldas-Coulthard & M. Coulthard (Eds.), *Texts and practices: Readings in critical discourse analysis* (pp. xi-xii). London: Routledge.

Caldas-Coulthard, C. R., & Coulthard, M. (Eds.). (1996b). *Texts and practices: Readings in critical discourse analysis.* London: Routledge.

Chovil, N. (1989). *Communicative functions of facial displays in conversation.* Unpublished doctoral dissertation, University of Victoria, Department of Psychology.

Chovil, N. (1991-1992). Discourse-oriented facial displays in conversation. *Research on Language and Social Interaction, 25,* 163-194.

Clark, H. H., & Wilkes-Gibbs, D. (1986). Referring as a collaborative process. *Cognition, 22,* 1-39.

Coates, L. J. (1991). *A collaborative theory of inversion: Irony in dialogue.* Unpublished master's thesis, University of Victoria, Department of Psychology.

Coates, L. J. (1997). Causal attributions in sexual assault trial judgments. *Journal of Language and Social Psychology, 16,* 278-296.

Coates, L. J. (1998). *Methods for developing scoring systems and calculating reliability in discourse analysis.* Unpublished manuscript, University of Victoria, Department of Psychology.

Dressler, R. A., & Kreuz, R. J. (2000). Transcribing oral discourse: A survey and model system. *Discourse Processes, 29,* 25-36.

Edwards, D., & Middleton, D. (1987). Conversation and remembering: Bartlett revisited. *Applied Cognitive Psychology, 1,* 77-92.

Edwards, J. A. (1993). Principles and contrasting systems of discourse transcription. In J. A. Edwards & M. D. Lampert (Eds.), *Talking data: Transcription and coding in discourse research* (pp. 3-32). Hillsdale, NJ: Lawrence Erlbaum.

Ekman, P. (1993). Facial expression and emotion. *American Psychologist, 48,* 384-392.

Ekman, P., & Friesen, W. V. (1978). *The Facial Action Coding System: A technique for the measurement of facial movement.* Palo Alto, CA: Consulting Psychologists Press.

Fairclough, N. (1992). *Discourse and social change.* Cambridge: Polity.

Fairclough, N. (1993). Critical discourse analysis and the marketization of public discourse:

The universities. *Discourse and Society, 4,* 133-168.

Fowler, R. (1996). On critical linguistics. In C. R. Caldas-Coulthard & M. Coulthard (Eds.), *Texts and practices: Readings in critical discourse analysis* (pp. 3-14). London: Routledge.

Garcia, A. C., & Jacobs, J. B. (1999). The eyes of the beholder: Understanding the turn-taking system in quasi-synchronous computer-mediated communication. *Research on Language and Social Interaction, 32,* 337-367.

Garfinkel, H., & Sacks, H. (1970). On formal structures of practical actions. In J. C. McKinney & E. A. Tiryakian (Eds.), *Theoretical sociology* (pp. 337-366). New York: Appleton-Century-Crofts.

Gilbert, G. N., & Mulkay, M. (1984). *Opening Pandora's box: A sociological analysis of scientists' discourse.* Cambridge: Cambridge University Press.

Goodwin, C. (1981). *Conversational organization: Interaction between speakers and hearers.* New York: Academic Press.

Goodwin, C. (1993). Recording human interaction in natural settings. *Pragmatics, 3,* 181-209.

Gumperz, J. J., & Berenz, N. (1993). Transcribing conversational exchanges. In J. A. Edwards & M. D. Lampert (Eds.), *Talking data: Transcription and coding in discourse research* (pp. 91-122). Hillsdale, NJ: Lawrence Erlbaum.

Harré, R. (1995). Discursive psychology. In J. A. Smith, R. Harré, & L. van Langenhove (Eds.), *Rethinking psychology* (pp. 143-159). Thousand Oaks, CA: Sage.

Heritage, J., & Watson, R. (1979). Formulations as conversational objects. In G. Psathas (Ed.), *Everyday language: Studies in ethnomethodology* (pp. 123-162). New York: Irvington.

Hodge, R., & Kress, G. (1993). *Language as ideology* (Rev. ed.). London: Routledge & Kegan Paul.

Hopper, R. E. (1992). *Telephone conversation.* Bloomington: Indiana University Press.

Jefferson, G. (1973). A case of precision timing in ordinary conversation: Overlapped tag-positioned address terms in closing sequences. *Semiotica, 9,* 47-96.

Jefferson, G. (1985). An exercise in the transcription and analysis of laughter. In T. A. van Dijk (Ed.) *Handbook of discourse analysis: Vol. 3. Discourse and dialogue* (pp. 25-34). London: Academic Press.

Kendon, A. (1985). Some uses of gesture. In D. Tannen & M. Saville-Troike (Eds.), *Perspectives on silence* (pp. 215-234). Norwood, NJ: Ablex.

Kraut, R. E., & Johnston, R. E. (1979). Social and emotional messages of smiling: An ethological approach. *Journal of Personality and Social Psychology, 37,* 1539-1553.

Leeds-Hurwitz, W. (1987). The social history of the Natural History of an Interview: A multidisciplinary investigation of social communication. *Research on Language and Social Interaction, 20,* 1-51.

Linell, P. (1982). *The written language bias in linguistics.* Linkoping, Sweden: University of Linkoping, Department of Communication.

Linell, P. (1998). *Approaching dialogue: Talk, interaction and contexts in dialogical perspectives.* Amsterdam: John Benjamins.

Nunan, D. (1993). *Introducing discourse analysis.* London: Penguin.

Ochs, E. (1979). Transcription as theory. In E. Ochs & B. B. Schieffelin (Eds.), *Developmental pragmatics* (pp. 43-72). New York: Academic Press.

Parker, I. (1992). *Discourse dynamics: Critical analysis for social and individual psychology.* London: Routledge.

Phillips, B. (1999). Reformulating dispute narratives through active listening. *Mediation Quarterly, 17,* 161-180.

Phillips, B., & Bavelas, J. B. (2000, June). *Comparing collaborative versus autonomous models of conversation in computer-mediated communication.* Paper presented at the annual meeting of the International Communication Association, Acapulco.

Potter, J. (1996). *Representing reality: Discourse, rhetoric and social construction.* London: Sage.

Potter, J., & Wetherell, M. (1987). *Discourse and social psychology: Beyond attitudes and behaviour.* London: Sage.

Schegloff, E. A. (1992). On talk and its institutional occasions. In P. Drew & J. Heritage (Eds.), *Talk at work: Interaction in institutional settings* (pp. 101-134). Cambridge: Cambridge University Press.

Schiffrin, D. (1994). *Approaches to discourse.* Cambridge, MA: Blackwell.

Schober, M., & Clark, H. H. (1989). Understanding by addressees and overhearers. *Cognitive Psychology, 21,* 211-232.

Scott, M. B., & Lyman, S. (1990). Accounts. In D. Brissett & C. Edgley (Eds.), *Life as theater:*

A dramaturgical sourcebook (2nd ed., pp. 219-242). New York: Aldine de Gruyter.

Slama-Cazacu, T. (1976). Nonverbal components in message sequence: "Mixed syntax." In W. C. McCormack & S. A. Wurm (Eds.), *Language and man: Anthropological issues* (pp. 217-227). The Hague: Mouton.

Stubbs, M. (1983). *Discourse analysis: The socio-linguistic analysis of natural language.* Chicago: University of Chicago Press.

Svartvik, J., & Quirk, R. (1980). *A corpus of English conversation.* Lund, Sweden: Gleerup.

Tannen, D. (1984). *Conversational style.* Norwood, NJ: Ablex.

Tannen, D. (1989). *Talking voices: Repetition, dialogue and imagery in conversational discourse.* Cambridge: Cambridge University Press.

Thomas, L. (1974). *The lives of the cell.* New York: Bantam.

van Dijk, T. A. (Ed.). (1997a). *Discourse studies: A multidisciplinary introduction: Vol. 1. Discourse as structure and process.* Thousand Oaks, CA: Sage.

van Dijk, T. A. (Ed.). (1997b). *Discourse studies: A multidisciplinary introduction: Vol. 2. Discourse as social interaction.* Thousand Oaks, CA: Sage.

van Dijk, T. A. (1997c). The study of discourse. In T. A. van Dijk (Ed.), *Discourse studies: A multidisciplinary introduction: Vol. 1. Discourse as structure and process* (pp. 1-34). Thousand Oaks, CA: Sage.

Vertegaal, R. (1998). *Look who's talking to whom.* Enschede, Netherlands: University of Twente, Cognitive Ergonomics Department.

Watzlawick, P., Beavin Bavelas, J., & Jackson, D. D. (1967). *Pragmatics of human communication: A study of interactional patterns, pathologies, and paradoxes.* New York: W. W. Norton.

Willig, C. (1999). Introduction: Making a difference. In C. Willig (Ed.), *Applied discourse analysis: Social and psychological interventions* (pp. 1-21). Buckingham: Open University Press.

Wood, L. A., & Kroger, R. O. (2000). *Doing discourse analysis: Methods for studying action in talk and text.* Thousand Oaks, CA: Sage.

Yngve, V. H. (1970). On getting a word in edgewise. In *Papers from the Sixth Regional Meeting of the Chicago Linguistics Society* (pp. 567-578). Chicago: Chicago Linguistics Society.

PART III

Fundamental Units

Personality and
Interpersonal Communication

JOHN A. DALY

The idea that people differ from one another in systematic ways has a long history. Aristotle organized the notion of character in *Nichomachean Ethics;* Galen proposed a theory of humors. Beginning in medieval times, classification schemes for people abounded. Scholars today, in various academic disciplines, continue this tradition. In the field of communication, research on personality dispositions has a long and distinguished history. Indeed, some of the earliest empirical studies of communication revolved around individual differences in people's proclivities to be comfortable speaking in front of others. And if one were to tabulate the focus of academic work in the field of interpersonal communication over the past 50 years, one would discover, unsurprisingly, that the greatest proportion of articles in our journals have explored topics directly or indirectly related to personality.

Given the enormous number of studies on topics related to individual differences in communication, in this chapter I highlight only major trends and limit my summaries to work done on only some of the major dispositional differences associated with communication. Although one could focus on a variety of dispositional characteristics, including abilities (e.g., intelligence), physical characteristics (e.g., stigmas, physical appearance), interests (e.g., vocational preferences), and personality, in this review, with some notable exceptions tied to demographic variables, discussion is limited to psychological dispositions that affect interpersonal communication. I first briefly review recent studies on the development of individual differences, and then examine the controversial issue of the role of individual differences in predicting behavioral tendencies. Finally, I offer a catalog of various individual differences that affect social interaction.

HOW DO INDIVIDUAL DIFFERENCES EMERGE?

In recent years, a good deal of attention has focused on the apparent heritability of certain personality dispositions. Across characteristics, heritability has been estimated to range from 30% to 50% (e.g., Plomin, DeFries, & McClearn, 1990). Clear evidence exists that many communication-related personality constructs have some degree of genetic or biochemical components. For instance, sociability has been found to be strongly influenced by genetic inheritance (Bouchard & McGue, 1990; Loehlin & Nichols, 1976; Tellegen et al., 1988), as has self-monitoring (Snyder & Gangestad, 1986). Some research has even gone further and suggested that there are genetic propensities for behaviors and attitudes related to personality constructs. Jockin, McGue, and Lykken (1996), for example, discovered that the risk of divorce is associated with genetic predispositions. Scarr and Weinberg (1981) found that the genetic transmission of verbal ability is partially responsible for the inheritance of authoritarianism. Olson, Vernon, Harris, and Jang (2001) found that a number of communication-related behaviors (e.g., enjoying big parties, enjoying public speaking, being assertive) have significant heritability. As in previous research, Olson et al. found that sociability has quite strong genetic components. Sociability has also been linked to hormonal differences in testosterone (Dabbs, Strong, & Milun, 1997), and extraversion has been tied to the reactivity of the mesolimbic dopaminergic system (Depue, Luciana, Arbisi, Collins, & Leon, 1994). Only recently have scholars in communication

begun to consider genetic predispositions toward communication-related variables such as communication apprehension (Beatty, McCroskey, & Heisel, 1998) and argumentativeness (Beatty & McCroskey, 1997).

The study of genetics in personality uses a number of different investigative techniques. Most studies compare monozygotic and dizygotic twins' correlations on various personality dimensions. When monozygotic twins have a significantly higher correlation on a trait than do dizygotic twins, the assumption is that genetic influences are present. The challenge with this method is, of course, that monozygotic twins are often treated differently than dizygotic ones. In communication, Beatty, Marshall, and Rudd (2001) found strong evidence using this method for the heritability of social composure and wit, modest heritability for social confirmation, and no heritability for articulation ability and disclosure appropriateness. Beatty, Heisel, Hall, Levine, and LaFrance (2002), in a meta-analysis, determined that interpersonal affiliation, aggressiveness, and social anxiety are substantially heritable.

Other studies have examined the similarity of adult twins who were raised apart from one another beginning at early childhood. Researchers using this approach typically find more than chance resemblance between twins on various personality measures suggesting the role of genetics. More recently, in an area that has been called *adoption studies,* scholars have found strong evidence for the heritability of traits such as sociability (e.g., Daniels & Plomin, 1985; Scarr, Webber, Weinberg, & Wittig, 1981). In these studies, children raised by adoptive parents have been found to resemble more closely their birth parents, with whom they have no relationship, than their adoptive parents who have raised them. And, most recently, scholars have begun to tie specific genes to personality dispositions (e.g., Greenberg et al., 2000; Hamer, Greenberg, Sabol, & Murphy, 1999; Jang et al., 2001).

There have, of course, been important critiques of various biological/evolutionary analyses (e.g., Funder, 2001).

There are other explanations for the development of personality variables such as reinforcement, social norms, and modeling (e.g., Kraut & Price, 1976). Each of these alternative explanations is, to some degree, relevant to the development of various communication-related predispositions (e.g., Rickman & Davidson, 1994). The notion behind these alternative approaches is that genetics may predispose a person to certain traits, but environmental factors exacerbate or ameliorate the development of those traits. For instance, in the case of social-communicative anxiety, evidence exists that people's anxiety may be shaped by the sorts of reinforcements they received for communicating as children, the level of social skills they were taught, and the adequacy of the models of communication to which they were exposed as they moved through childhood (Daly & Friedrich, 1981).

ARE INDIVIDUAL DIFFERENCES IMPORTANT?

For many years, there have been debates about the validity of personality constructs. Are there really individual differences? Moreover, if there are, how important are they in the explanation and prediction of behavior? A thorough review of these issues in the discipline of communication is available in Daly and Bippus (1998). In this section I will highlight only some of the important conclusions about the nature of personality differences as they relate to communicative behavior.

Questions about the validity of individual differences revolve around a very basic concern: Is personality a useful explanatory concept? In seeking an answer to this, scholars have undertaken a plethora of research and theorizing over the past 25 years. Perhaps the major starting point was a critique by Mischel (1968), who pointed out that presumably, for

a trait to have validity, behaviors typically associated with that trait ought to have cross-situational consistency. In looking at a number of traits, Mischel and others found an average correlation across situations of only about .30 (more recently, the cross-situational consistency has been found to be .40; Funder & Colvin, 1991).

Mischel's critique resulted in a bevy of responses arguing for the validity of traits. One of the major ones suggested that personality constructs represent general predispositions, and consequently the correlation between any two very specific individual actions should be small. But the correlation among many behaviors, aggregated over time, context, and behavioral manifestations, ought to be high (Hogan, 1998). Epstein (1979), for instance, using classical notions of reliability, found that an aggregate of several behaviors correlated quite nicely with an aggregate of other behaviors all presumed to represent some disposition. In my own research, I have approached this issue slightly differently, by suggesting that general dispositions ought to predict patterns of behavior substantially but be associated only weakly with individual behaviors (Daly, 1978; Jaccard & Daly, 1980). In examining communication apprehension, I found that the correlation between the anxiety and any self-reported single behavior at one time was, as one would expect, quite small. Alternatively, the correlation between the personality variable and a summation of various behaviors across time was quite large. This notion of matching dispositional generality to behavioral breadth is critical in many formulations. For instance, in trying to predict general behavior patterns (e.g., job performance), Ones and Viswesvaran (1996; but for an important extension, see Paunonen, Rothstein, & Jackson, 1999) suggest that it is logical to use broad dispositional tendencies such as the Big Five (discussed below). Paunonen and Ashton (2001) found that very specific personality facets predicted very specific behaviors as well as or better than the Big Five. The point is that measures of traits must match the specificity of the assessed behavior. Moreover, and importantly, the magnitude of the relationship between behaviors and personality constructs is not that different from the magnitude of situational effects found in traditional experiments (Funder & Ozer, 1983).

Another approach has tied personality to situations. One strand of scholarship, drawn from Lewin's (1935) suggestion of behavior being a function of the person and the situation, suggests that any personality variable is relevant only in some situations. This person-by-situation-interaction approach (Koestner, Bernieri, & Zuckerman, 1989; Magnusson & Endler, 1977; later conceptualized, in a somewhat different way, as conditional, if-then traits by Mischel, 1999; Shoda, Mischel, & Wright, 1994) supposes that traits vary in their relevance to an individual depending upon the situation that person is in. For example, a highly anxious individual might do well in relaxed settings, whereas a less anxious person might do better in situations that raise his or her anxiety. Other research suggests that personality correlates with behavior in meaningful ways only in some contexts. For example, personality characteristics are most strongly related to performance in jobs with high autonomy (Barrick & Mount, 1993) and to behaviors in settings where social norms are less apparent (Buss, 1989).

An alternative strand of scholarship proposes that individual differences shape the situational choices people make (Ickes, Snyder, & Garcia, 1997). This is a long-standing argument (Allport, 1937). Furnham (1981) and Emmons, Diener, and Larson (1986), for example, demonstrated that extraverts gravitate toward situations that involve assertiveness, sociability, and intimacy. Daly and McCroskey (1975) found that highly communicatively apprehensive individuals choose professions that require less social

interaction than do their counterparts low in the apprehension.

Closely related to situational choice models is the observation that traits may be differentially relevant to individuals. For Person A, shyness may be a very relevant construct; for Person B, it may be quite irrelevant. People vary, in other words, in the extent to which dispositions influence them. Scholars contrast the trait relevance approach with the nomothetic approach, which assumes that traits are equally relevant to everyone. Trait relevance has received significant attention for any number of years (Britt & Shepperd, 1999). Allport (1937) suggested that some traits are cardinal (most influential), some central, and others peripheral to any one individual. Since Allport developed his formulation, extensive research has been conducted that suggests that relevance is, or at least should be, an important consideration in studies. Parenthetically, trait relevance is not the same as trait extremity or trait importance (although they may be related; see Britt & Shepperd, 1999). In helping us to understand the relationship between traits and behaviors, trait relevance may play an important role. It clearly moderates the size of the correlation between self-reports and peer ratings (Biesanz, West, & Graziano, 1998; Chaplin, 1991). Bem and Allen (1974; compare Chaplin & Goldberg, 1984) argue that individuals differ on how consistently their behaviors are tied to any particular trait, and Baumeister and Tice (1988) offer a similar argument for the concept of "traitedness." Finally, the nature of the dependent measure used in studies matters. Some traits, for instance, are more observable than others. Not surprisingly, Funder and Colvin (1988) have found that self-peer correlations are higher with traits that are more visible.

Mischel's (1968) critique forced scholars to grapple with the issue of the validity of personality in understanding behavior. Their conclusion, after many years, is that personality clearly reflects and affects behavior. Traits arise from many sources, and they affect behavior. In the sections that follow, I describe various traits relevant to interpersonal communication and provide some examples of research using them. I begin by looking at some integrative models of personality that attempt to organize traits. From there, I review many of the dispositions one would encounter in communication scholarship. They are clustered, for purposes of structure, into five groups: (a) demographic correlates, (b) cognitive dispositions, (c) social-personal dispositions, (d) communicative dispositions, and (e) relational dispositions.

ORGANIZING THE TRAITS

Integrative Models

Scholars in communication, psychology, and related fields have proffered an enormous number of individual differences. Seeking parsimony, many scholars during the past 60 years have suggested major clusters of dispositions (e.g., Fiske, 1949; Norman, 1963). Drawing from lexical analyses of the vocabulary of the English language, researchers have typically identified five orthogonal dimensions (McCrae & John, 1992) that have been labeled "the Big Five" (Goldberg, 1993). The assumption in the research that produced these clusters was that the relative frequency of words related to the various dimensions is proportional to their psychological importance. The five dimensions are (a) neuroticism (anxiety, angry hostility, depression, self-consciousness, impulsiveness, vulnerability), (b) extraversion (warmth, gregariousness, assertiveness, activeness, excitement seeking, positive affect), (c) intellect or openness to experience (experience seeking, education, reading widely, memory), (d) agreeableness (trustingness, straightforwardness, altruism, compliance, modesty, tender-mindedness), and (e) conscientiousness (competence, order, dutifulness, achievement striving, self-discipline, deliberateness).

There have been debates about how inclusive the Big Five are as well as whether the presumed factor structure is reliable. Saucier and Goldberg (1998) argue that the Big Five incorporates virtually all personality constructs. The Big Five are seen as superordinate traits that may be universal (McCrae, Costa, del Pilar, Rolland, & Parker, 1998). On the other hand, Paunonen and Jackson (2000) provide compelling evidence for the exclusion from the Big Five of some important dimensions (e.g., religiosity, manipulativeness, humorousness, honesty; Ashton, Lee, & Son, 2000). Other scholars have argued that differing conceptions of what composes the Big Five have added confusion to a clear understanding of what the Big Five really represent. Depue and Collins (1999) found that almost all models included extraversion, sociability, and affiliation as part of their main components. However, constructs such as sensation seeking, optimism, and agency were only sometimes included. Moreover, there is disagreement about what should be included within each component (for a review of different schemes, see Watson & Clark, 1997). In addition, when researchers have attempted to test the factor structure of the Big Five systematically, they have often been unsuccessful (Dabady, Bell, & Kihlstrom, 1999; Vassend & Skrondal, 1997).

Although the Big Five taxonomy has been used in numerous psychological studies, very little research regarding the Big Five has been published in communication journals. This is disappointing, for communication-related correlates of the Big Five have often been discovered in other disciplines. Consider the extraversion dimension as an example. Compared with introverts, extraverts engage in more social activities (Argyle & Lu, 1990; Watson & Clark, 1997; compare Pavot, Diener, & Fujita, 1990); are more cooperative in groups as well as more likely to raise issues in those groups (LePine & Van Dyne, 2001); are more likely to engage in conversations with a positive focus (Zellars & Perrewe, 2001);

experience higher levels of general positive affect (Cote & Moskowitz, 1998); are more socially skilled (Akert & Panter, 1988); are more likely to spend time in geographic locations that require high interaction (Eddy & Sinnett, 1973); engage in more agreeable behavior (Cote & Moskowitz, 1998); play greater leadership roles (Chan & Drasgow, 2001; Watson & Clark, 1997); engage in sexual activities more often, in more different ways, and with more partners (Gangestad & Simpson, 1990; Wright & Reise, 1997); are more adaptive parents (Belsky, Crnic, & Woodworth, 1995); are more satisfied in their marriages (Watson, Hubbard, & Wiese, 2000) and less likely to experience negative feelings in their marriages (Belsky & Hsieh, 1998); perceive typical social interactions to be more enjoyable (Barrett & Pietromonaco, 1997); have lower speech anxiety (Watson & Clark, 1997); are somewhat happier (DeNeve & Cooper, 1998); have more friends (Watson & Clark, 1997); and have higher status among their peers (Anderson, John, Keltner, & Kring, 2001). Extraverts differ from introverts in their speech behaviors as well. For example, Dewaele and Furnham (2000) found that in informal settings, extraversion was positively associated with speech rate and inversely related to length of utterance. In formal settings, extraversion was positively associated with an implicit speech style, higher speech rates, and more semantic errors and was negatively correlated with lexical richness.

Other dimensions of the Big Five also have communication consequence. For instance, neuroticism is linked to negative marital outcomes (Bouchard, Lussier, & Sabourin, 1999; Karney & Bradbury, 1995; Kelly & Conley, 1987; Robins, Caspi, Moffitt, 2000) such as extramarital affairs (Buss & Shackelford, 1997), less adaptive parenting (Belsky et al., 1995), more complaining (Buss, 1991), and negativity (Caughlin, Huston, & Houts, 2000). Agreeableness is positively correlated with engaging in positive conversations (Zellars & Perrewe, 2001), marital satisfaction (Belsky &

Hsieh, 1998; Botwin, Buss, & Shackelford, 1997), cooperativeness (LePine & Van Dyne, 2001), and an ability to control anger and frustration in conflict settings (Graziano, Jensen-Campbell, & Hair, 1996).

An alternative structural formulation of traits more tied to interpersonal behavior is the interpersonal circumplex model (Leary, 1957). Using two primary dimensions such as (a) affiliation, communion, or love (dominant-submissive) and (b) control, status, dominance, or agency (friendly-hostile), scholars have suggested that certain traits (e.g., gregariousness) are complementary to some other traits (e.g., aloofness) and closely related to still others (e.g., assuredness and warmth) (Kiesler, 1996; Wiggins, 1979; Wiggins & Trobst, 1997).

The presumption of these integrative frameworks is that a panoply of unorganized traits hinders the development of theory. What is necessary is an organizing scheme that offers a heuristic framework for understanding personality. Although neither the Big Five nor the circumplex model can, at this point, adequately meet a sufficiency criterion, both represent interesting and useful starts.

In communication scholarship, little attention has been paid to integrative models of personality. Instead, individual variables have been the focus of attention. In the following subsections, I briefly review, in catalog form, a number of personality variables that communication scholars have studied. The list is not exhaustive; given space limitations, I am forced to ignore many dispositions noted in the communication journals. I start with demographic variables and move from those to more cognitively oriented dispositions. From there, I turn to communication-related personality dispositions that focus more on social and relationship issues.

Demographic Correlates

Surprisingly little research examining demographic correlates of interpersonal communication has been conducted by scholars in communication. The most often explored variables are cross-cultural differences and sex. Other issues, such as race, ethnicity, birth order (e.g., Sulloway, 1996), and social class (e.g., Haslett, 1990), have received far less attention.

Cross-Cultural Differences

One could spend an entire chapter addressing differences in the ways people from varying cultures communicate. Clearly, cultural differences are individual differences that meaningfully affect communication. Research on cultural differences can be organized in a number of ways. Some scholars suggest that people vary in their willingness and ability to interact in different cultures (e.g., van der Zee & van Oudenhoven, 2001). Others contrast the communication styles of individual cultures. For instance, Adair, Okumura, and Brett (2001) found that Japanese negotiators are more indirect in what they say but use more distributive-power-based moves than American negotiators and are also less willing to offer information to their opponents. Asian Americans take longer to develop friendships (Collier & Shimizu, 1993) but maintain them longer than white Americans. Japanese interactants tend to have greater equality of participation in meetings than do their North American counterparts (Yamada, 1990; but see Oetzel, 1998, who finds this is limited to particular sorts of meetings).

Alternatively, many scholars have argued that it is intellectually silly to compare one culture with another: Given the large number of different cultures, there is an almost infinite number of possible comparisons. Instead, these researchers propose that there are some underlying psychological dimensions along which cultures fall. For instance, Hall (1976) suggests that cultures could be classified along a continuum ranging from low to high context. Low-context cultures make use of direct, explicit messages, whereas high-context ones use more implicit and indirect messages.

Hofstede (1980, 2001) suggests that cultures vary on a number of dimensions, such as power distance, uncertainty avoidance, individualism/collectivism, masculinity/femininity, and time orientation. Gudykunst and Ting-Toomey (1988) propose four cultural dimensions tied directly to communication: (a) direct versus indirect style, (b) succinct versus elaborate style, (c) personal versus contextual style, and (d) instrumental versus affective style. Schwartz (1999) proposes seven value types (conservatism, intellectual autonomy, affective autonomy, hierarchy, mastery, egalitarian commitment, and harmony) that are derived from two dimensions: conservatism versus autonomy and hierarchy/mastery versus egalitarian commitment/harmony.

One of the most common distinctions is between individualist cultures (in which people view themselves as unique individuals) and collectivist cultures (in which people view themselves primarily as members of groups) (e.g., Triandis, 1995). The former choose personal goals at the expense of group goals, whereas the latter opt for the opposite. Persons in collectivist cultures are more likely to avoid conflicts, and when they do enter into conflicts, they are more likely to use avoiding or compromising styles (Ting-Toomey et al., 1991). Members of such cultures can be very competitive, however, with out-groups (Triandis, 1995). Collectivist mothers encourage listening and empathy (Choi, 1991). Persons in individualist cultures are more likely to engage in in-group conflict, have dominating and competing styles, and make few distinctions between in-group and out-group members (Ting-Toomey et al., 1991). They also tend to make stronger dispositional attributions and weaker situational attributions about communication events (Knowles, Morris, Chiu, & Hong, 2001). When asked to explain behaviors, persons from individualist cultures make fewer references to contextual factors than do those from collectivist cultures (Miller, 1984).

One challenge raised by any of the dimensional approaches is that within any given cultural group all of these tendencies exist. In the Japanese culture, there are certainly some individualist people and some collectivist people; there are some people who are more high context and others who are low context. It appears to be the case that people's individual levels of these differences mediate the influence of the cultural-level variables (Gudykunst et al., 1996). This observation has led scholars to consider psychological variables akin to cultural differences. For example, the concepts of individualism and collectivism are reflected in Markus and Kitayama's (1991) notion of independent and interdependent self-construals. Independents see themselves as unique individuals whose behaviors are internally driven. They are direct in their communication, emphasize internal abilities, and promote their own ideas. Interdependents reference the importance of fitting in and see contextual features as having a great deal to do with their lives. They are more attuned to status and relationships; they are concerned about relationships and about ensuring that they play appropriate roles in their relationships. Compared with independents, interdependents are more persuaded by messages that come from higher-status sources (Tasaki, Kim, & Miller, 1999). Interdependence correlates positively with leadership consideration, whereas independence is positively correlated with a leadership style that emphasizes structuring (Hackman, Ellis, Johnson, & Staley, 1999). Singelis and Brown (1995) as well as Gudykunst et al. (1996; for items, see Hackman et al., 1999) offer measures of Markus and Kitayama's (1991) construct. Oetzel (1998) nicely links the concepts of individualism/collectivism and self-construals. The presumption underlying attention to self-construals is that within any one culture there are individual differences in construals. Cultures that might be seen as collectivist may have members with interdependent self-construals as well as members with independent construals (although there is evidence to suggest that

individualist cultures have people who are more independent and less interdependent [Kim, Aune, Hunter, Kim, & Kim, 2001] and that, across cultures, there is a tendency for people to report themselves as more independent than interdependent [Park & Levine, 1999]).

A final alternative approach to understanding cultural differences is to consider how skilled individuals are when they are working, living, or communicating in cultures other than their own, a concept that has been labeled *intercultural communication competence* (Bradford, Allen, & Beisser, 2000). People with higher levels of intercultural communication competence interact more effectively with people from different cultures.

Age

Until recently, relatively little scholarship in communication (aside from the work of people interested in children) has focused on age-related differences. In the past few years, communication scholars have started to study communication among and with older adults. For example, there have been studies of perceptions of older people as well as some work on the ways in which younger individuals interact with the aged (e.g., Hummert, Shaner, Garstka, & Henry, 1998; Ryan, Hummert, & Boich, 1995). The results suggest that people have stereotypes of older people and communicate in ways that reflect those stereotypes, although this is less true for people who are themselves older (Hummert et al., 1998). The more familiar younger individuals are with older people, the more comfortable they are communicating with older people in general (Ng, Liu, Weatherall, & Loong, 1997). Other studies have compared older and younger individuals in how they evaluate communicative behaviors (Caplan & Samter, 1999) and in their message production skills (Caplan & Greene, 1999). Coupland and Coupland (2001) provide an excellent review of how language is used with individuals of various ages.

Ethnicity and Racial Differences

Surprisingly, comparatively little research has explored ethnic and racial differences in communication. Typical of the work that has been done are findings that there are differences in the ways Latinos, Asian Americans, African Americans, and white Americans conceive of friendships (Collier, 1996) and handle conflict (Collier, 1991). European Americans are dispositionally higher in forgivingness than Asian Americans and Hispanics (Berry, Worthington, Parrott, O'Connor, & Wade, 2001). Collier (1996) found differences in the ways persons of different ethnicities perceive friendships. Using national survey data, Vangelisti and Daly (1988) found racial differences in communication skills.

Sex and Gender Differences

There are sex-related differences in personality traits. Why women and men might differ in traitlike–behaviors is an interesting and provocative question. One explanation is tied to innate differences that may have evolutionary roots. Some evidence buttresses this explanation, given notable cross-cultural consistencies in patterns of certain sex differences (Costa, Terracciano, & McCrae, 2001). The notion is that men and women have faced different adaptive challenges throughout history. Consequently, for instance, women tend to seek attributes in prospective mates that are different from those sought by men (Stewart, Stinnett, & Rosenfeld, 2000). The strongest proponent of this approach is probably Buss (1998), who has argued from an evolutionary perspective that women have a preference in mates for individuals who can offer such resources as security (e.g., income), whereas males prefer females who offer reproductive value (e.g., attractiveness). Buss's explanation

appears to have received support from studies across a variety of cultures (Buss & Schmitt, 1993) as well as within cultures (e.g., Davis, 1998; Kenrick, Gabrielidis, Keefe, & Cornelius, 1996) using various criteria, ranging from income and attractiveness preferences to feelings about types of infidelity (Buss et al., 1999), jealousy (Buss & Schmitt, 1993), and differential expectations for short and long-term relationships (Regan, 1998; Stewart et al., 2000).

A second explanation focuses on socialization and norms. Women and men are taught from childhood how to behave and react, and this is reflected in the behaviors that are seen as socially desirable for each gender. When it comes to emotions and communication, some communication scholars have suggested that there are two basic accounts for observed differences in men's and women's communication. One, labeled the *different cultures* account, suggests that men and women really live in different emotional cultures; the other, called the *skill specialization* account, suggests that although men and women live in the same emotional culture, men have not learned the social skills that women often have (Kunkel & Burleson, 1999; Vangelisti & Daly, 1997).

There is evidence that men and women differ in their use of language. Mulac, Bradac, and Gibbons (2001) summarize much of research on language differences, noting that men tend to exceed women in (a) references to quantity ("6 feet, 4 inches tall"), (b) judgmental adjectives ("good," "dumb"), (c) elliptical sentences ("Great picture"), (d) directives ("Write that down"), (e) locatives ("in the background"), and (f) "I" references ("I think . . ."). Women, more than men, have been found to use (a) intensive adverbs ("really," "so"), (b) references to emotions ("happy," "hurt"), (c) dependent clauses ("where the shadows are"), (d) sentence initial adverbials ("Actually, it's . . ."), (e) uncertainty verbs ("it seems to be . . ."), (f) oppositions ("it's peaceful, yet full of movement"),

(g) negations ("it's not a ..."), (h) hedges ("kind of"), and (i) questions ("What's that?"). Although findings are mixed, studies have also found that women are more likely than men to use (a) personal pronouns ("we," "she") and (b) tag questions ("That's not right, is it?"). It is important to remember, however, that these differences are quite small (Ng & Bradac, 1993) and that for each type of language difference there are greater complexities. For instance, when it comes to tag questions, women use forms that enhance interaction, whereas men use forms that seek validation (Cameron, McAlinden, & O'Leary, 1988).

There are also sex differences in broader communicative behaviors. For example, compared with men, women are more tentative during disagreements with men (Carli, 1990), are less assertive (Costa et al., 2001; Maccoby & Jacklin, 1974) and less hostile (Scherwitz, Perkins, Chesney, & Hughes, 1991), are more likely to be interrupted by men (Smith-Lovin & Brody, 1989), are less visually dominant in settings where power is ambiguous (Brown, Dovidio, & Ellyson, 1990), are more interpersonally oriented and less task oriented (Eagley & Karau, 1991; Forsyth, Schlenker, Leary, & McCown, 1985; Wood, 1987; Zahn-Waxler, 2000), are more democratic as leaders (Eagley & Johnson, 1990), are more nonverbally involved during social interactions, smile and gaze at their interaction partners more often, and are more expressive (Hall, 1984; Riggio, 1986) and more easily persuaded, at least under some circumstances (Eagley & Carli, 1981). In terms of emotions, women are more sensitive to emotions (Eisenberg, Fabes, Schaller, & Miller, 1989; Fujita, Diener, & Sandvik, 1991; McClure, 2000), better at distinguishing facial expressions (except, perhaps, those indicating anger; McClure, 2000; Wagner, MacDonald, & Manstead, 1986), more emotionally aware and better able to describe emotional experiences (Barrett, Lane, Sechrest, & Schwartz, 2000), and more likely

to express their emotions than men (Kring & Gordon, 1998). Women are almost two times more likely than men to suffer from depression (Nolen-Hoeksema, 1987, 2001); women score lower than men in self-esteem along some dimensions (Kling, Hyde, Showers, & Buswell, 1999) and experience more anxiety (Maccoby & Jacklin, 1974) and neuroticism (Lynn & Martin, 1997). More positively, women are more gregarious, warm (Costa et al., 2001), trusting, and nurturing than men (Feingold, 1994).

Males and females also differ in the ways in which they approach relationships. Women's sense of self is more relationally interdependent than is men's (Acitelli & Young, 1996; Cross & Madson, 1997). Women's friendships are marked by more disclosure than men's (Taylor & Belgave, 1986), and women receive greater disclosure than men from both other women and men (Helgeson, Shaver, & Dyer, 1987). Women are better than men at interpreting their spouses' emotional messages (Noller & Fitzpatrick, 1990) and when distressed can more accurately decode their husbands' negative messages (Notarius, Benson, Sloane, Vanzetti, & Hornyak, 1989). Men and women differ in their preferred love styles (e.g., Morrow, Clark, & Brock, 1995). Women spend more time thinking about their relationships (Ross & Holmberg, 1990), are more upset about arguments with their spouses (Almeida & Kessler, 1998), are more likely to engage in conflict talk (men are more likely to be avoidant and conciliatory; Gottman & Levenson, 1988), and have more vivid and specific recall of marital disagreements (Ross & Holmberg, 1990). They are more likely to enunciate their unhappiness with their marriages (Hagestad & Smyer, 1982) and are more likely to initiate the end of a marriage (Cross & Madson, 1997). Women are more willing to provide emotional support to others than are men (Trobst, Collins, & Embree, 1994) and are more effective at comforting and offering social support

(Burleson, 1994). When offering support, women offer more emotion-focused responses, whereas men provide more problem-solving responses (Barbee, Gulley, & Cunningham, 1990). Women are also less argumentative and less verbally aggressive than men (Infante, 1985; Infante & Wigley, 1986; Nicotera & Rancer, 1994).

At the same time, other research has found that men and women differ little on many communication-related variables. Dindia and Allen's (1992) meta-analysis of sex differences in disclosure found very few differences due to gender. Grob, Meyers, and Schuh (1997) looked at language choices and found no empirical differences due to sex in terms of typical powerless speech variables (e.g., interruptions, hedges, and tag questions) except the use of disclaimers (women more than men). Canary and Hause (1993) looked at the bulk of studies that have included sex differences and communication as part of their focus and found there were minimal differences. Indeed, many of the differences observed in research may change as a function of the times. Twenge (2001) found, for instance, that although historically men have been more assertive than women, that difference has become progressively smaller over recent years. Some scholars have argued that sex differences mask differences in other variables, such as status and roles. For instance, Moskowitz, Suh, and Desaulniers (1994) found that men's and women's dominant-submissive behaviors were tied more to their roles as supervisors or supervisees than to sex.

In the last few decades of the 20th century, scholars began to distinguish between sex (male versus female) and gender (masculine versus feminine). The observation was that people vary not only in terms of biological sex but also in the ways they approach issues psychologically. Bem (1974) suggested two independent dimensions, masculinity and femininity, which were later reconceptualized as instrumentality and expressiveness,

respectively (Spence, 1993). The category that was most intriguing to scholars was the notion of androgyny—the state of being high in both masculinity and femininity. Androgynous individuals are socially more competent (Ickes, 1985; Lamke & Bell, 1982), although high femininity for both partners is the strongest predictor of relational satisfaction (Lamke, 1989). In discussing the literature on sex differences, I would be remiss not to mention emerging research on homosexuality (e.g., Haas & Stafford, 1998; Nardi & Sherrod, 1994).

Cognitive Dispositions

Locus of Control

Rotter's (1966) concept of locus of control concerns an individual's beliefs about his or her control over the environment. At one end of the continuum are individuals with internal locus of control; these "internals" believe they have mastery over what happens to them. They believe that they themselves are the "origins" of their actions. If they want something to happen, they can make it so. At the other end of the continuum are those with external locus of control; "externals" believe that they have little control over their fates, that they are "pawns." Externals believe that their lives are shaped by chance, luck, and other powerful variables over which they have no control. Communicatively, internals are more attuned to information that bears on their lives (Rotter, 1966) and are less likely than externals to experience negative stressors (Thoits, 1995). Internals are more attentive listeners, more socially skilled in conversations, more sensitive to social cues (Lefcourt, Martin, & Fick, 1985), and less likely to withdraw in conflict situations (Canary, Cunningham, & Cody, 1988).

In marital and romantic relationship settings, locus of control may well be a coping response (Miller, Lefcourt, Holmes, Ware, & Saleh, 1986; Myers & Booth, 1999), for internals tend to be more achievement focused and task oriented, especially when it comes to marital problem solving. Not surprisingly, internality is positively related to marital quality (Doherty, 1983; Myers & Booth, 1999; Smolen & Spiegel, 1987) and inversely related to marital commitment (Scanzoni & Arnett, 1987) and verbal aggression (Winkler & Doherty, 1983). Internals find romance and love less mysterious than do externals, and they approach relationships in less idealistic ways (Dion & Dion, 1973). Behaviorally, internals are more likely to use birth control (Lundy, 1972). Closely related to the construct of locus of control is the concept of personal control (Turner & Noh, 1983), which is inversely related to relational distress (Umberson, 1993).

Since Rotter's (1966) initial conceptualization, arguments have been made that locus of control is better understood in various contexts. Consequently, scholars have suggested a number of situation-specific control motivations, such as health (e.g., Wallston & Wallston, 1981), political affairs, and marriage (e.g., Miller, Lefcourt, & Ware, 1983), as well as specific sorts of interactions, such as conflict (Canary et al., 1988).

Cognitive Complexity

In the past 20 years, probably no cognitive disposition has received more attention from scholars in communication than cognitive complexity. In communication scholarship, complexity has been defined in terms of the number of different constructs an individual has to describe others (differentiation), the degree to which those constructs cohere (integration), and the level of abstraction of the constructs (abstractiveness).

The bulk of the research has demonstrated positive consequences for complexity. Cognitively more complex individuals offer more person-centered responses (Applegate, 1980; for a summary, see Burleson, 1998) when it comes to communication, whether it

be in terms of comforting (Burleson, 1994), persuading (O'Keefe & Shepherd, 1989), or the use of regulative messages (Adams & Shepherd, 1996). The reason for this appears to be that cognitively complex individuals are better able to perform a variety of tasks related to successful communication, such as recognizing affect (Burleson, 1994), decoding non-verbal behaviors (Woods, 1996), integrating information (O'Keefe, Delia, & O'Keefe, 1977), and engaging in role taking or perspective taking (Kline, Pelias, & Delia, 1991). The messages that are produced by cognitively complex individuals are, consequently, more impactful or effective than those produced by their less complex counterparts. Relationally, perspective taking has been linked to a variety of positive outcomes (e.g., Long & Andrews, 1990). Recently, scholars have discovered that the capability to think complexly is also linked to more negative communicative behaviors. For instance, Bacue and Samter (2001) found that people high in cognitive complexity were able to create messages that were more effective at making romantic partners feel guilty than were people who were less complex. Burleson (1998) offers a very thorough and integrative review of the entire complexity literature as it relates to interpersonal communication, so I will not spend much space on the topic, as important as it is in communication scholarship.

Authoritarianism and Dogmatism

In the early years of the empirical study of communication, authoritarianism (Adorno, Frenkel-Brunswik, Levinson, & Sanford, 1950) and dogmatism (Rokeach, 1960) were of special importance to researchers. In many ways, the constructs (as well as a third, labeled *tolerance for ambiguity*) tap into the same broad idea: Some people are more rigid than others, and this rigidity affects both how they communicate and how they respond to communication. For instance, authoritarians choose not to accept information that may change their attitudes (Dillehay, 1978) and dogmatic individuals are more responsive to source cues when it comes to persuasion (DeBono & Klein, 1993). Steinfatt (1987) offers an excellent and thorough summary of the research on these variables.

Emotional Intelligence

In recent years, researchers have paid significant attention to a construct labeled *emotional intelligence*. Although many consider this a relatively new construct, Thorndike (1920) presaged the concept early in the 20th century when he discussed social intelligence as one of three sorts of intelligence. In the popular literature, Goleman (1995) has suggested that the construct has five components: self-awareness, managing emotions, motivating oneself, empathy, and handling relationships. In academic work, Salovey and Mayer (1990) have defined emotional intelligence as the ability of people "to monitor their own and others' emotions, discriminate among them, and use the information to guide [their] thinking and actions" (p. 189). Mayer and Salovey (1997) have more recently argued that emotional intelligence is best construed as an ability. The notion underlying the construct (be it Goleman's or Salovey and Mayer's) is that emotional intelligence is very different from intelligence as it is typically narrowly defined, with a focus on academic achievement and capability. In some ways, it reflects newer models of intelligence such as Gardner's (1993).

The research on emotional intelligence has been conceptually mixed. Davies, Stankov, and Roberts (1998) found that the variables typically falling under the rubric of emotional intelligence are well described by existing measures of traits (aside from the ability to perceive emotions). Nonetheless, some sort of emotional intelligence does seem to exist, and it affects interpersonal exchanges. For example, the ability of children to recognize different emotions successfully at the age of 5 is positively correlated with their level of social skills (e.g., assertiveness, cooperativeness) and academic performance at the age of 9 (Izard et al., 2001). In the case of adults, people who are better at recognizing emotions are also higher in empathy (Mayer, DiPaulo, & Salovey, 1990), and individuals who are more socially perceptive are more sociable, less socially anxious (Schroeder & Ketrow, 1997), and seen as more socially skilled by friends (Costanzo & Archer, 1989). Emotional intelligence is positively associated with life satisfaction, empathy, self-esteem, relational quality, and the ability to manage one's moods (Ciarrochi, Chan, & Caputi, 2000), as well as with extraversion, independence, and self-control; it is inversely associated with anxiety (Newsome, Day, & Catano, 2000). It is also positively related to emotional stability, optimism, stress tolerance, and self-regard (Bar-On, 1997). Information about individuals' emotional intelligence has been found to aid in the prediction of their work performance (Mount & Barrick, 1995) as well as academic achievement (Furnham & Medhurst, 1995). Additionally, there is a gender difference: Women score higher on measures of emotional intelligence than do men (Ciarrochi et al., 2000).

Other, more cognitive variables, such as intelligence, private and public self-consciousness, tolerance for ambiguity, and need for achievement, affiliation, and power, are clearly important to scholars in interpersonal communication. Space limits, however, prevent me from discussing them in this chapter.

Social-Personal Dispositions

Loneliness

It is important to understand that the defining characteristic of loneliness is an unpleasant or unacceptable discrepancy between what individuals want in terms of relationships and what they believe they have (Perlman & Peplau, 1981). Thus one person might be lonely and yet report having numerous friends, whereas another may have very few friends and yet describe herself as not at all lonely. The quantity of relationships per se is not necessarily related to loneliness. Weiss (1975) further distinguishes between emotional loneliness (the absence of close emotional attachments leading to feelings of aloneness regardless of the companionship of others, which is often subdivided into family and romantic subtypes; DiTommaso & Spinner, 1997) and social loneliness (absence of an engaging social network, resulting in feelings of boredom and marginality). There is evidence for significant heritability of loneliness (McGuire & Clifford, 2000).

Lonely people report lower self-esteem (Wittenberg & Reis, 1986) and feel less satisfied in their romantic relationships (Flora & Segrin, 2000). Behaviorally, compared with people who are not lonely, they are less self-disclosive (Solano, Batten, & Parish, 1982), less expressive (Segrin, 1996), more socially passive (Vitkus & Horowitz, 1987), more avoidant in terms of social reaction style (Eronen & Nurmi, 1999), particularly sensitive to rejection (Stokes, 1987), more jealous (Rotenberg, Shewchuk, & Kimberly, 2001), less socially skilled (Jones, Hobbs, & Hockenbury, 1982; Solano & Koester, 1989), and less empathic and less responsive to the needs, concerns, and feelings of others (Jones, 1982). Lonely people rate the social situations they are in less positively (Duck, Pond, & Latham, 1994) and are less skilled in planning social encounters (Berger & Bell, 1988). Lonely people attribute their interpersonal failures to internal and stable causes and their successes in interpersonal activities to external and unstable causes (Anderson, Miller, Riger, Dill, & Sedikides, 1994). They believe others have negative feelings toward them (Jones et al., 1982) and they feel less

socially competent than do people who are not lonely (Spitzberg & Canary, 1985). Loneliness is correlated, in expected ways, with a variety of communication-oriented dispositions, such as communication apprehension (Bell & Daly, 1985). Demographically, men tend to report higher loneliness than women (Schultz & Moore, 1986). Lonely men are more aggressive than other men, especially toward women (Check, Perlman, & Malamuth, 1985); they are also shyer (Cheek & Busch, 1981).

Depression

Depression affects and is affected by communication. Theories of depression suggest that people who are depressed will seek out others for personal reassurance. Paradoxically, they will then often reject that reassurance because they doubt the sincerity of the people who offer it and see it, instead, as pity (Coyne, 1976). This pattern creates a depressive spiral. Central to Coyne's (1976) theory is the notion of reassurance seeking. Joiner and Metalsky (2001) offer a measure of people's tendencies to seek reassurance. They found that an individual's proclivity to seek excessive reassurance is associated with a greater likelihood of his or her being depressed, becoming depressed, and experiencing depression after stress events. Depression is moderately heritable (Kendler & Prescott, 1999).

Depression is correlated with less secure attachment and greater fearful avoidant attachment (Carnelley, Pietromonaco, & Jaffe, 1994; Roberts, Gotlib, & Kassel, 1996), greater femininity (Cheng, 1999), greater shyness (Bruch, Rivet, & Laurenti, 2000), lower self-esteem (Tarlow & Haaga, 1996), less optimism (Vikers & Vogeltanz, 2000), and more sensitivity to criticism (Gilbert & Miles, 2000). Depressed people, when making social comparisons, are less likely to make downward comparisons that would make them feel better about themselves (Giordano, Wood, & Michela, 2000). They believe that they, themselves, and their interaction partners are colder (Thompson, Whiffen, & Blain, 1995) and less socially competent than nondepressed individuals (Gable & Shean, 2000; Segrin, 1990; Segrin & Abramson, 1994), although the evidence for actual behavioral differences is limited (Segrin, 1990). They also are seen as less socially competent (Dykman, Horowitz, Abramson, & Usher, 1991), yet are more likely to seek out social information about themselves (Hildebrand-Saints & Weary, 1989). The consequences of these sorts of behaviors and feelings are predictable. Depressed individuals describe their interactions as less satisfying (Nezlek, Imbrie, & Shean, 1994) and feel they are more rejected by others (even though, in reality, they are not; Dobson, 1989). Over time, people around depressed individuals, such as roommates, withdraw and become more negative about those with depression (Hokanson & Butler, 1992). Depressed individuals have a pessimistic attributional style; they make internal, stable, and global attributions about negative events (Day & Maltby, 2000). Interestingly, they are better than nondepressed people at detecting deception (Lane & DePaulo, 1999) even though they are slower (Cooley & Nowicki, 1989) and less accurate at reading many nonverbal cues (Persad & Polivy, 1993) and are not as effective at solving interpersonal problems (Gotlib & Asarnow, 1979).

Relationally, marriages of depressed people are characterized by negativity and conflict (Beach, Whisman, & O'Leary, 1994). The disposition is associated with rejection by members of the opposite sex (Hammen & Peters, 1978), marital problems (Dew & Bromet, 1991), and divorce (Bruce, 1998). In family settings, depression affects the ways parents communicate with their children (Cummings & Davies, 1999). Depressed mothers communicate toward their children in more negative ways than do nondepressed mothers (Beach & Nelson, 1990; Messer & Gross, 1995), and those sorts of messages lead to children's

externalizing problems (Cummings & Davies, 1994), being more irritable (Hops et al., 1987), and even being more depressive themselves (Davies, Dumenci, & Windle, 1999). Those around depressed persons often exhibit more depressed moods (Benazon & Coyne, 2000). When depressed family members communicate, other family members' reactions are typically not positive (this phenomenon is called *positivity suppression*), perhaps reflecting that depression (Jacob & Johnson, 2001; Slesnick & Waldron, 1997).

Self-Esteem

One of the most influential models of the self that is tied directly to communication is Cooley's (1902) theory of the "looking-glass self," which led, over time, to symbolic interaction theory. The premise is that how we see ourselves is determined by how we believe our significant others see us. We construct our self-images from how we internalize what we believe others think of us (compare Kenny & DePaulo, 1993). Consequently, the stability of self-esteem is affected by the interactions people have with valued others, such as family members (Kernis, Brown, & Brody, 2000). There are multiple sorts of self-esteem. Rubin and Hewstone (1998) suggest three continua: (a) global versus specific esteem, (b) trait versus state esteem, and (c) personal versus social esteem. Others have suggested that people have three domains of self—actual, ideal, and ought (Higgins, 1987). Still others have proposed domain-specific sorts of esteem (e.g., Marsh, 1989). McGuire and McGuire (1981) suggest that an individual's self-concept is determined by those things that make him or her distinctive from others. For example, a boy raised with many female siblings will, when asked to describe himself, quickly offer his sex as a descriptor; his sisters, asked for self-descriptions, will not mention their sex, because it fails to distinguish them in their environment.

Self-esteem has clear relationships with a variety of communication-related outcomes. People lower in self-esteem are shyer (McCroskey, Daly, Richmond, & Falcione, 1977), less likely to believe they have a voice in decisions (Brockner et al., 1998), less likely to ask questions in classrooms (Daly, Kreiser, & Roghaar, 1994), more lonely (Brage, Meredith, & Woodward, 1993) and depressed (Brage & Meredith, 1994), more verbally aggressive (Rancer, Kosberg, & Silvestri, 1992), less likely to report marital satisfaction (Larson, Anderson, Holman, & Niemann, 1998), and more likely to experience relational jealousy (White & Mullen, 1989). Self-esteem, parenthetically, also affects the ways in which jealousy is expressed (Buunk, 1995). Research on persuasion suggests that there is a quadratic relationship between esteem and persuasibility (Rhodes & Wood, 1992), although low self-esteem individuals may be more susceptibility to inoculation manipulations (Pfau, Van Bockern, & Kang, 1992).

There is evidence for sex differences in self-esteem. Males generally have slightly more positive self-esteem than do females (Kling et al., 1999; compare Deaux & LaFrance, 1998; Page, Stevens, & Galvin, 1997), although women have stronger self-esteem in areas such as reading and relationships with same-sex friends (men have higher domain-specific self-esteem in areas such as physical abilities, math, and appearance; Marsh, 1989). Women's self-esteem is positively related to their memory for information about people, whereas men's self-esteem is positively associated with individualism (Josephs, Markus, & Tafarodi, 1992).

Narcissism

Extreme self-esteem might reach the point of narcissism. Narcissistic people deny negative feedback (Smalley & Stake, 1996), engage in greater self-enhancement (Campbell, Reeder, Sedikides, & Elliot, 2000), and are more likely to engage in infidelity (Buss &

Shackelford, 1997). Arguing that people vary in the degree they need to be the center of attention in social interactions, Vangelisti, Knapp, and Daly (1990) offer a communication-related version of narcissism under the rubric of "conversational narcissism."

Humor

The notion that people vary systematically in sense of humor has a long history. Empirical research has suggested that there is an inverse relationship between sense of humor and neuroticism (Kohler & Ruch, 1996) and health, although the latter finding is not consistent across studies (Martin, 2001). Bippus (2000) and Booth-Butterfield and Booth-Butterfield (1991) have devised individual-difference measures of an individual's propensity to use humor.

Machiavellianism

Christie and Geis (1970) introduced the notion that people differ in the degree to which they enjoy and are manipulative of others. Highly Machiavellian individuals prefer face-to-face interactions because such settings provide them with the most information they can use in taking advantage of others (Geis, 1978). Machiavellianism is positively related to such variables such communication flexibility (Martin, Anderson, & Thweatt, 1998), interaction planning (Allen, 1990), helping (Wolfson, 1981), self-monitoring (Riggio & Friedman, 1982), persuasiveness (Burgoon, Lombardi, Burch, & Shelby, 1979; Burgoon, Miller, & Tubbs, 1972), group interaction (Bochner & Bochner, 1972) and effectiveness (Jones & White, 1983), and managerial success (Gable & Topol, 1991).

Empathy

Measures of empathy (e.g., Davis, 1983) assess components such as sympathy (other-oriented concern or sorrow), personal distress (self-oriented discomfort), and perspective taking (cognitively orienting oneself to the other). The different components of empathy are associated with people's responses to problematic situations. For example, personal distress is positively correlated with negative emotional intensity and weak behavioral regulation (Okun, Shepard, & Eisenberg, 2000). Overall, empathy is positively related to social intelligence, extraversion, and affective communication (Davies et al., 1998), conversational sensitivity (Daly, Vangelisti, & Daughton, 1987), a communal orientation in relationships (Feeney & Collins, 2001), and willingness to offer social support (Trobst et al., 1994). When it comes to parenting, empathy is inversely associated with child abuse (Rosenstein, 1995) and positively related to more positive parent-child relations (Kochanska, 1997).

Over the past few years, researchers have directed increasing attention toward understanding how, why, and when people forgive others for transgressions. Presumably, forgiveness is tied to empathy (McCullough, 2001). Very recently, scholars have conceptualized forgiveness as a dispositional construct. Berry et al. (2001) and McCullough (2001) found that dispositional forgiveness is positively correlated with agreeableness, extraversion, conscientiousness, emotional stability, and religiosity or spirituality, and inversely related to trait anger, neuroticism, and hostility.

An interesting strand of recent research has examined dispositional tendencies to be interrogatively suggestible (e.g., Baxter & Boon, 2000; Gudjonsson & Clark, 1986). The construct, perhaps most relevant to the validity of eyewitness testimony, suggests that some people are more likely than others to change their accounts of what they have "seen" based upon questioning.

Self-Monitoring

Snyder (1974; Snyder & Gangestad, 1986) introduced the construct of self-monitoring.

He proposed that people vary in the degree to which they are both aware of and willing to adapt to others in social settings. Individuals high in self-monitoring are attentive to what others do and are skilled at controlling the images of themselves that they present to others. In social situations, they assess what the situations require and then adapt themselves to those requirements. Because of their greater sensitivity to social contexts, they are more likely to tailor their images in ways that best serve their goals (Snyder, 1987). Compared with low self-monitors, they are more skilled social interactors: They are more active and talkative in groups (Dabbs, Evans, Hopper, & Purvis, 1980; Ickes & Barnes, 1977) and are more expressively friendly, more outgoing, and less worried, anxious, and nervous when teaching (Lippa, 1978). They are better able to detect others' intentions (Jones & Baumeister, 1976) and remember more information about others (Berscheid, Graziano, Monson, & Dermer, 1976). They are also more conversationally sensitive (Daly et al., 1987). High self-monitors are likely to manipulate information in order to present better images of themselves to others (Fandt & Ferris, 1990) and can easily adapt their styles of working with others (Anderson, 1990). They are better able than low self-monitors to feign interest in people verbally (Leck & Simpson, 1999). In romantic relationships, high self-monitors report experiencing feelings of intimacy sooner, are more likely to date many different people, and feel less committed to their partners than do low self-monitors (Snyder & Simpson, 1984, 1987). They are more likely to emerge as leaders in work groups (Zaccaro, Foti, & Kenny, 1991) when social interaction is critical (Garland & Beard, 1979) and are more likely to be promoted in organizations (Kilduff & Day, 1994). They are more prone than low self-monitors to resolve conflict through collaboration and compromise (Baron, 1989). High self-monitors are more effective at managing impressions in ways that others like. When their low self-monitoring counterparts use similar impression management moves, they are often viewed more negatively—their moves are too obvious (Turnley & Bolino, 2001). Low self-monitors have a desire to be themselves in spite of the requirements of the situation. Low self-monitors keep the same friends regardless of activities, whereas high self-monitors choose different friends for different activities (Snyder, Gangestad, & Simpson, 1983). The picture of the low self-monitor is not necessarily bleak. Gangestad and Snyder (2000) suggest that low self-monitors may develop deeper, more trusting relationships with others than do high self-monitors. These authors offer a thorough and excellent summary of the theory, research, and measurement issues associated with this disposition.

Communicative Dispositions

Argumentativeness and Verbal Aggressiveness

An extensive amount of scholarship has accumulated on argumentativeness and verbal aggressiveness. Argumentativeness is considered to be constructive. It involves an individual's willingness to attack another's arguments while defending his or her own position (Infante & Rancer, 1982). Compared with people low in argumentativeness, highly argumentative individuals are more willing to participate in decision-making tasks (Anderson, Martin & Infante, 1998) and are perceived as more influential in decision making (Schultz, 1982) as well as more interesting, dynamic, competent, and credible (Infante, 1981; Onyekwere, Rubin, & Infante, 1981). They are more willing to dispute others' statements, having a sense that arguing is a good, enjoyable, and useful activity (Rancer, Kosberg, & Baukus, 1992). They are more resistant to persuasive attempts (Kazoleas, 1993); consequently, they are less likely to withdraw from

conflict situations (Caughlin & Vangelisti, 2000). Rancer (1998) provides an excellent review of this construct.

Verbal aggressiveness is different from argumentativeness. Verbally aggressive individuals attack the self-concepts of others, attempting to cause psychological pain (Infante & Wigley, 1986). They attack and tease others regarding their character, competence, and physical appearance as well as make verbal and nonverbal threats. People who are especially aggressive have lower communication skills (Infante, Trebing, Shepherd, & Seeds, 1984), report stronger dislike for others (Infante, Riddle, Horvath, & Tumlin, 1992), are less satisfied with the interaction of the work groups to which they belong (Anderson & Martin, 1999), have lower levels of argumentative skills (Infante, 1995), are higher in psychoticism (Valencic, Beatty, Rudd, Dobos, & Heisel, 1998), engage in more physical aggression (Kassing, Pearce, & Infante, 2000), and are more likely to engage in spousal abuse (Infante, Chandler, & Rudd, 1989; Sabourin, Infante, & Rudd, 1993). In addition, they are less open, more defensive, less willing to acknowledge their mistakes (Rancer, Kosberg, & Baukus, 1992), less flexible (Martin, Anderson, & Thweatt, 1998), less responsive (Myers, 1998), and less likely to offer verbal praise (Wigley, Pohl, & Watt, 1989). Consequently, people prefer not having them as teachers (Myers & Knox, 2000), as managers or subordinates (Infante & Gorden, 1985, 1989), or as roommates (Martin & Anderson, 1995). Verbally aggressive individuals are less likely to be selected to serve on juries (Wigley, 1999). In family settings, verbal aggressiveness is positively related to parental anger, especially when parents are frustrated (Rudd, Vogl-Bauser, Dobos, Beatty, & Valencic, 1998), and inversely correlated with the number of positive affect messages parents offer to children (Bayer & Cegala, 1992). This disposition affects the degree of trust and satisfaction siblings feel for one another (Martin, Anderson, Burant, & Weber, 1997). Wigley (1998) presents a useful summary of the research on verbal aggressiveness.

Related to verbal aggressiveness is the construct of emotional expression, which is conceptually composed of two variables: overinvolvement and critical comments. Emotional expression has been linked to depression (Asarnow, Goldstein, Tompson, & Guthrie, 1993), hostility (Shields, Franks, Harp, Campbell, & McDaniel, 1995), marital satisfaction (Gavazzi, McKenry, Jacobson, Julian, & Lohman, 2000; Hooley & Hahlweg, 1986), and the quality of relational communication (Baucom & Sher, 1987).

Communication Apprehension

Clearly, the most studied individual difference in the field of interpersonal communication has been communication apprehension. The earliest research in the field focused on stage fright, and that work continues to this day (e.g., Daly, Vangelisti, & Weber, 1995). However, the majority of work in recent decades has been more interpersonally oriented. Under a variety of labels—such as *reticence, unwillingness to communicate,* and, more broadly, *social-communicative anxiety* (Daly, Caughlin, & Stafford, 1997), *shyness* (Cheek & Melchior, 1990), and *social anxiety*—the construct taps into the propensity of people to enjoy and seek out opportunities to communicate (approach) or instead to find communication opportunities punishing (avoid). In recent years, a number of conceptual distinctions have started to appear in the literature. For instance, Cheek and Buss (1981) demonstrated that shyness (social discomfort) and sociability (affiliation) are not highly related. McCroskey and Richmond (1998) have suggested an overarching construct called *willingness to communicate* that has, as potential precursors, anomie, alienation, introversion, communication apprehension,

self-esteem, and self-perceived communication competence. Although there are numerous and important conceptual differences among the various constructs, for the purposes of this review we will assume they all tap into the same basic predisposition. Demographically, some scholars suggest that more than 30% of Americans consider themselves shy (Pilkonis, Heape, & Klein, 1980).

Space limitations preclude a full recitation of the profound effects of the disposition here (for a much fuller rendition, see Daly, Caughlin, & Stafford, 1997). Behaviorally, people with high levels of communication apprehension are less likely to talk in social settings (Garcia, Sinson, Ickes, Bissonnette, & Briggs, 1991), and when they do participate, they engage in mostly acknowledgments and confirmations (Leary, Knight, & Johnson, 1987). When shy people are forced to communicate, they often prefer settings where they can self-handicap (Arkin & Baumgardner, 1988, as cited in Bradshaw, 1998), where they can involve others (e.g., bring a friend, let a friend do the talking; Bradshaw, 1998), or where they can plan ahead (Arkin & Grove, 1990). Compared with nonshy people, they engage in less eye contact (Garcia et al., 1991), are more self-protective (Meleshko & Alden, 1993), and are less disclosive (Meleshko & Alden, 1993). There is evidence that shy people are less likely to seek health-related advice (Bruch & Hynes, 1987; Kowalski & Brown, 1994) and are less likely to be successful in positions that require communication, such as sales (Barrick & Mount, 1991). Perceptually, they are seen less positively by others (Daly, McCroskey, & Richmond, 1977) in a variety of settings, such as interviews (Daly, Richmond, & Leth, 1979) and social interactions (e.g., Jones & Carpenter, 1986), and especially in initial exchanges (Alden & Wallace, 1995).

In terms of personality correlates, apprehensive individuals are less assertive (Leary, 1983), less argumentative (Infante & Rancer, 1982), less conversationally sensitive (Daly et al., 1987), and more embarrassable (Maltby & Day, 2000), and have a less independent and more interdependent self-construal (Kim et al., 2001). They have lower self-esteem (McCroskey et al., 1977) and are more likely to have insecure (fearful or dismissive) attachment styles (Duggan & Brennan, 1994), experience greater depression (Alfano, Joiner, & Perry, 1994; Bruch et al., 2000; Ingram, 1989), experience greater sociotropy (Bruch, Rivet, Heimberg, Hunt, & McIntosh, 1999), have feelings that they believe don't match up to what they "ought" to be (Bruch et al., 2000), are less willing to take risks (Addison & Schmidt, 1999), and even see themselves as less physically attractive (Bruch, Giordano, & Pearl, 1986; Bruch et al., 1999). Not surprisingly, shy individuals suffer from more social isolation and more emotional and psychosomatic health problems than do nonshy people (Schmidt & Fox, 1995).

Developmentally, shyness affects identity formation (Hamer & Bruch, 1997). Shy individuals do not participate as much in classroom interactions (Comadena & Prusank, 1988) and do less well in school, perhaps because of their unwillingness to engage in social exchanges (McCroskey, Andersen, Richmond, & Wheeless, 1981). Communication apprehension is inversely related to academic achievement (e.g., McCroskey & Andersen, 1976; Messman & Jones-Corley, 2001) and cognitive performance (Bourhis & Allen, 1992). Occupationally, this disposition affects career development (Hamer & Bruch, 1997) and occupational choices (Capsi, Elder, & Bem, 1988). Apprehensive individuals are more likely to select occupations that do not require communication (Daly & McCroskey, 1975) and are less willing to seek advancement in work situations (McCroskey & Richmond, 1979). Relationally, shyness affects dating (Jones & Carpenter, 1986) and the decision to marry (Kerr, Lambert, & Bem, 1996; Schneier, Johnson, Hornig, Liebowitz, & Weissman, 1992). There are numerous

cross-cultural differences in communication apprehension (e.g., Kim et al., 2001; Klopf, 1984; McCroskey, Fayer, & Richmond, 1985; Watson, Monroe, & Atterstrom, 1989).

There has also been a plethora of research on the treatment of the anxiety. The harmful effects of this disposition can be reduced through the use of a variety of behavioral techniques. The most common of these are systematic desensitization, cognitive restructuring, and visualization. In recent years, pharmacological solutions have also become available. Drugs such as monoamine oxidase inhibitors, high-potency benzodiazepenes, and the selective serotonin reuptake inhibitors have been linked to the reduction of anxiety, as have various beta-blockers. The only medication approved by the U.S. Food and Drug Administration for this purpose is paroxetine (Paxil). A recent volume edited by Daly, McCroskey, Ayres, Hopf, and Ayres (1997) contains extensive summaries of the treatment literature. In examining how shyness might be alleviated, it is important to note that situational variables can affect the impact of shyness. Shy people are less comfortable in formal settings (Russell, Cutrona, & Jones, 1986), in settings where they feel particularly conspicuous (Daly, Vangelisti, & Lawrence, 1989), in novel settings (Watson & Cheek, 1986), and in mixed-sex interactions (Turner, Beidel, & Larkin, 1986).

The construct of communication apprehension has produced a number of close relatives, such as dating anxiety (Hope & Heimberg, 1990; Powers & Love, 2000), receiver apprehension (Wheeless, 1975) or informational reception apprehension (Wheeless, Preiss, & Gale, 1997), singing apprehension (Andersen, Andersen, & Garrison, 1978), and intercultural communication apprehension (Neuliep & Ryan, 1998).

Conflict

For many years, scholars have suggested that people vary in how they approach conflict. The most popular typology is the model developed by Kilman and Thomas (1977), which suggests that underlying the dimensions of assertiveness and cooperativeness are five styles: avoiding, accommodating, confronting, compromising, and collaborating. Research has suggested the empirical validity of these five styles (Rahim & Magner, 1995) and has tied the styles to varying forms of family interactions (e.g., Dumlao & Botta, 2000). Christensen (1988) has proposed six conflict strategies (reason, assertion, partner support, coercion, manipulation, and avoidance) that have been used in relationship research (e.g., Noller, Feeney, Bonnell, & Callan, 1994). Hample and Dallinger (1995) propose that people vary in how they respond to conflict. Some people, they argue, take conflict far more personally than others. Their measure, tapping six dimensions (direct personalization, persecution feelings, stress reactions, positive relational effects, negative relational effects, like/dislike valence) is positively correlated with argument avoidance.

Communication Competence and Social Skills

People may vary in how competently they interact with others. Those who exhibit socially competent skills are preferred in interactions (Flora & Segrin, 1998). Duran and Spitzberg (1995) have devised a measure that assesses one individual difference related to this notion—that of cognitive communication competence, which is composed of five subscales (planning cognitions, modeling cognition, presence cognition, reflection cognition, and consequence cognition). The five factors are significantly and positively related to communication knowledge, self-monitoring, and interaction involvement. Spitzberg (1993; Spitzberg & Hurt, 1987; see also Spitzberg & Cupach, Chapter 14, this volume) has also devised a measure of conversational competence that proposes four subcomponents: altercentrism, composure, expressiveness, and interaction management. Depressed people rate themselves

lower on all of these dimensions than do nondepressed individuals (Gable & Shean, 2000). Buhrmester, Furman, Wittenberg, and Reis (1988) suggest that there are five dimensions of interpersonal competence (initiating conversations, asserting displeasure, self-disclosure, providing support, managing conflict) and that these are related to a variety of variables, such as social self-esteem, shyness, loneliness, and masculinity/femininity. D'Zurilla, Maydeu-Olivares, and Kant (1998) have devised a social problem-solving inventory.

A variety of communication-oriented variables are indirect measures of social-communicative competence. Interaction involvement (Cegala, 1981), for instance, assesses the proclivity of individuals to interact in face-sensitive ways. The Interaction Involvement Scale is composed of three factors: responsiveness, perceptiveness, and attentiveness. The measure successfully discriminates between successful and unsuccessful interactants; it is negatively correlated with variables such as self-consciousness and communication apprehension, and positively correlated with self-reported communication competence. Conversational sensitivity (Daly et al., 1987) is a seven-factor construct that measures an individual's ability to assess and respond to various communicative challenges. The seven factors are: detecting meaning, conversational memory, conversational alternatives, conversational imagination, conversation enjoyment, interpretation, and perceiving affinity. Sensitivity is positively related to the ability to draw high-level inferences when listening to social exchanges, parsing ability, and the tendency to emphasize conversation in memory. O'Keefe (1988; O'Keefe & Lambert, 1995) has argued that there are broad individual differences in the ways in which people produce messages. Her model suggests that at the lowest levels, individuals are direct and often quite insensitive to situational contingencies. At the highest level, people are rhetorically quite sophisticated in understanding that communication actually creates the situation. Suggesting three levels, Hart, Carlson, and Eadie (1980) propose a construct called *rhetorical sensitivity* that taps into a similar idea (although the reliability of the measure has been called into question). Assertiveness, as a communication disposition, has a long history (Richmond & Martin, 1998). In 1978, Wheeless proposed a dispositional tendency to disclose that has received far less attention than it merits (Wigley, 1995). Finally, a construct labeled *communicator style* (Norton, 1978) has a variety of dimensions, such as attentiveness, friendliness, relaxation, dramaticism, impression-leaving, openness, contentiousness, animation, and image conscientiousness.

Relational Dispositions

Attachment

One of the most important relational dispositions studied in the past 10 years has been attachment style. Drawing from work by Bowlby (1982), scholars have argued that there are individual differences in people's beliefs about their senses of self and other. People's early interactions with caregivers shape how they construe themselves and others as well as their expectations about the amount and types of support they might receive from others. Attachment has major impacts on a variety of interpersonal issues in marriage, parenting, and other family relationships (e.g., Eiden, Teti, & Corns, 1995; Klohnen & Bera, 1998; Paley, Cox, Burchinal, & Payne, 1999; Pearson, Cohn, Cowan, & Cowan, 1994).

Models of attachment vary in how they organize individuals. In early models of attachment, three styles of attachment were conceptualized: secure, avoidant, and anxious-ambivalent (Hazen & Shaver, 1987). The latter two styles were considered different variants of insecure attachment. Secure individuals believe that people will be available and supportive. Avoidant individuals see themselves

as independent and self-reliant; in their relationships they feel uncomfortable with dependency, minimize the importance of attachment, and demonstrate low levels of commitment, interdependence, and trust. Anxious individuals fear being abandoned and unloved, are dependent upon others' acceptance of them, and can be distrusting of others. George, Kaplan, and Main (1984, as cited in Paley et al., 1999) suggest three classifications: secure (sometimes divided into continuous secure and earned secure [Pearson et al., 1994]), dismissive (devalue the importance of attachment relationships), and preoccupied (remain overtly involved in past attachment experiences). Bartholomew and Horowitz (1991) suggest that there are four attachment styles derived from two dimensions: individuals with a positive model of self see themselves as worthy of love, attention, and support, and those with negative views of self see themselves in far less positive terms. Individuals with a positive model of others consider others to be trustworthy, caring, and available, whereas those with a negative model of others see other people as unreliable, uncaring, distant, and rejecting. The four specific styles are secure (positive self and positive other), preoccupied (negative self and positive other), dismissive avoidant (positive self and negative other), and fearful avoidant (negative self and negative other).

Although the dimensions that constitute attachment are multifaceted and complex, the research findings that describe differences between secure and insecure individuals are relatively clear. For example, when it comes to comforting, secure individuals are more likely than avoidant ones to seek out aid from others (Simpson, Rholes, & Nelligan, 1992) and to offer comfort and reassurance to people under stress (Fraley & Shaver, 1998; Rholes, Simpson, & Orina, 1999). As children, they are more willing to view their parents as sources of emotional support (Ainsworth, Blehar, Waters, & Wall, 1978). They report greater joy (Magai, Distel, & Liker, 1995) and less depression (Roberts et al., 1996), anxiety (Mikulincer, Florian, & Weller, 1993), and loneliness (Kobak & Sceery, 1988), as well as less arousal during stressful events (Feeney & Kirkpatrick, 1996). In conversations, secure individuals are more trusting and more likely to gaze at partners than are less secure individuals; they also demonstrate greater positive affect, more attentiveness, and less vocal anxiety (Guerrero, 1996). In their romantic relationships, secure individuals report greater satisfaction, commitment, and trust than do insecure people (Keelan, Dion, & Dion, 1994). Secure people also react differently to stimuli related to attachment issues than do those who are insecure (Baldwin, Fehr, Keedian, Seidel, & Thomson, 1993) and are better able to recall positive outcomes (Mikulincer, 1998; Miller & Noirot, 1999). Avoidant people are less likely to seek help from others (Simpson et al., 1992) even in trying times, such as during a transition to parenthood (Rholes, Simpson, Campbell, & Grich, 2001). They have beliefs that others will not help them, feel less satisfied with their support systems, and mistrust potential support providers (Bartholomew, Cobb, & Poole, 1997). They are less responsive to partners and more controlling, especially when partners have great needs; as children, they distance themselves from caregivers when distressed (Ainsworth et al., 1978). When their adult romantic relationships are doing well, ambivalent individuals are likely to idealize their partners (Hazen & Shaver, 1987), yet they view their partners more negatively after major conflicts (Simpson, Rholes, & Phillips, 1996). Anxious-ambivalent individuals are more self-focused; they have less trust in their relationships, yet feel more interdependent upon them (Feeney & Collins, 2001). Such individuals offer less positive support and more negative support (Collins & Feeney, 2000). They are particularly sensitive to rejections from their romantic partners (Downey & Feldman, 1996).

Some research has begun to suggest that attachment styles may have greater plasticity than originally imagined. Keelan et al. (1994) found that over a 4-month period, one-fifth of the individuals in their sample reported having different attachment styles. Hazen and Hutt (1990, as cited by Le Poire et al., 1997) also found a significant tendency for people to change their reports of attachment style, as did Baldwin and Fehr (1995). Davila, Burge, and Hammen (1997) and Le Poire et al. (1997) found that changes in attachment styles are tied, to some degree, to the ways in which people's partners respond to them.

Rejection Sensitivity

Rejection sensitivity is an interpersonal construct that has only recently received attention. This disposition is a tendency to "anxiously expect, readily perceive, and intensely react to rejection" (Ayduk et al., 2000, p. 777). People who are particularly sensitive to rejection are more likely to experience depression after a romantic breakup (Ayduk, Downey, & Kim, 2001), be hostile and nonsupportive toward their partners when they feel rejected (Ayduk, Downey, Testa, Yen, & Shoda, 1999), feel more rejected when they engage in ambiguous conversations, see insensitive behavior on the part of a new partner as having more harmful intent, feel that their partners are more likely to leave the relationship, feel less satisfied in their relationships, and (in the case of men) feel more jealousy and be more controlling (Downey & Feldman, 1996). Given the strong tendency of these individuals to focus on possible rejection, it is not surprising that their romantic relationships are likely to end sooner (Downey, Freitas, Michaelis, & Khouri, 1998). Rejection sensitivity is positively correlated with neuroticism, social avoidance, social distress, interpersonal sensitivity, and insecure attachment. It is inversely related to extraversion, self-esteem, and secure attachment (Downey & Feldman,

1996). At a more focused level, Gilbert and Miles (2000) have introduced an interesting concept of people's sensitivity to "put-downs"; they have found that it correlates in predictable ways with a variety of other personality constructs.

Other Dispositions

Numerous additional individual differences have been tied to communication-related variables, but space constraints require that I do no more than mention them here. Positive and negative affect constitute a very general predisposition. Positive affect is marked by enthusiasm, favorable expectations, and general optimism (Watson, Clark, & Tellegen, 1988). Sensation seeking is inversely correlated with people's willingness to seek information about alternatives to drugs or ways of resisting peer influence about drugs (Dsilva, 1999; Stephenson & Palmgreen, 2001). Social desirability (Crowne & Marlowe, 1964) emphasizes how willing individuals are to act in ways they imagine will be socially correct. Sociotropy (Beck, 1983; Robins et al., 1994) is a construct that references people's excessive concern for obtaining and maintaining the approval and support of others. It is a component of interpersonal dependency and is related to variables such as jealousy and ill health (Bornstein, 1998; Pincus & Gurtman, 1995). Reciprocation wariness—a fear of being exploited in relationships (Cotterell, Eisenberger, & Speicher, 1992)—is another construct, as are emotional regulation (Roger & Najarian, 1989) and agency and communion (Helgeson & Fritz, 1999). Mills and Clark (1994) suggest that people vary in their orientations to relationships. They suggest two primary orientations: communal and exchange. Studies of dispositional embarrassability (e.g., Maltby & Day, 2000) hint at some interesting communication-related outcomes. In addition, there are measures of love ways (Hecht, Marston, & Larkey, 1994) and

love styles (Hendricks & Hendricks, 1986) based on Lee's (1973) conceptualization, as well as envy (Smith, Parrott, Diener, Hoyle, & Kim, 1999) and intimacy motivation (McAdams, 1980, 1992). The concept of intimacy motivation follows from work on social motives such as achievement motivation and power motivation (McClelland, 1986).

SUMMARY

The role that personality plays in communication is clear: Individual differences affect how people communicate in various interpersonal settings. Over and above contexts and experimental manipulations, dispositions add significantly to our understanding of communicative phenomena. In this chapter I have identified, in a very brief way, many of the more important variables studied by communication scholars and related some of the correlates of those variables. Obviously, space limitations preclude encyclopedic coverage of any one of those variables.

This review of the literature makes apparent some useful future directions for communication scholarship. First, the discipline very much needs an integrative model of personality variables tied to communication, something akin to the Big Five and circumplex models found in psychology. Communication scholars need some way of conceptually organizing the variables they find important. More broadly, theorizing about traits is notably weak in the discipline. For example, many researchers define traits and their effects by the traits themselves. "Shy people don't talk as much as nonshy individuals" is a definition claim, not an explanatory claim. Why shy people do not talk, what communicatively competent people do to be competent, and so on, are important and, largely, unanswered questions. In many of the literatures reviewed here, critical constructs are poorly defined. A good example would be how one might operationalize a construct such as "adaptability" or "flexibility" beyond a self-report questionnaire or descriptive definition (e.g., how would you teach a person to be flexible?).

Second, measurement techniques need to be improved. The vast majority of variables studied by communication scholars use self-report methods that are open to numerous challenges, such as their obvious susceptibility to social desirability effects (e.g., Daly & Street, 1980). In a few instances, notably in the area of cognitive complexity (that uses sorting tasks) and work on motives (that uses TAT techniques), measurement techniques have been employed that are more opaque. In other areas of communication-oriented personality work, scholars would be wise to probe new methods.

Third, scholars need to keep in mind that it is always important to be cautious when examining single traits. People are, for lack of a better phrase, composed of a multitude of traits, and these traits certainly interact. For example, people low in communication apprehension may behave very differently from one another, depending on their degree of conscientiousness. Or an argumentative person with high self-esteem may act very differently in arguments than an equally argumentative person with low self-esteem. Looking at how different traits combine to create a behavioral predisposition is an important future approach for scholarship.

Fourth, personality work in communication needs to consider the dyadic nature of most relationships. One person's personality characteristics can, and do, affect the behavior of the other person (e.g., Bouchard et al., 1999). Studies have long looked at how traits of one person affect the behavior of another; more recently, some studies have explored the joint impact of two interactants' traits (e.g., a competent communicator trying to interact with an incompetent one; a very extraverted individual working with a very shy one), but much more remains to be done. Findings have emerged that suggest, for instance, that romantic partners who are similar on some traits are happier than partners who are dissimilar (e.g., Arrindell & Luteijn, 2000). Le Poire, Shepard, and Duggan (1999) have demonstrated the impact of one partner's sort of attachment on the behavior of the other partner who is similar or different in attachment style. Other work indicates that people judge others by the sorts of individuals with whom they are copresent; for example, if your roommate has low positive affect, you are judged more positively in contrast (Joiner, 1996).

Finally, scholars may need to broaden the notion of "trait." Some have suggested that there are traits that go beyond the individual. McLeod and Chaffee (1972), for example, suggest that there are four sorts of family communication patterns based on two dimensions: socio-orientation and concept-orientation. Children of sociocentric parents are more susceptible to persuasion and more responsive to source-related variables such as credibility, whereas children of concept-oriented parents are less open to persuasion and, if swayed, are convinced by variables such as the strength of arguments. Concept-oriented parents produce children who are more politically involved. Ritchie and Fitzpatrick (1990) revised the McLeod and Chaffee measure using, as dimensions, conformity orientation and conversation orientation. Self-reported conversation orientation (i.e., person reports family is conversation oriented) is positively related to self-esteem, self-disclosive tendencies, and sociability, whereas self-reported conformity orientation is inversely associated with self-esteem and positively correlated with shyness and self-monitoring (Huang, 1999). Other family and relationship-oriented personality variables include parenting style, which represents two underlying dimensions (demandingness and warmth or responsiveness) that yield four styles (authoritative, directive, permissive, and uninvolved; Lamborn, Mounts, Steinberg, & Dornbusch, 1991; Maccoby & Martin, 1983).

Authoritative parenting has been found generally to be the best of the four styles (Darling & Steinberg, 1993; Gray & Steinberg, 1999) and all have been connected, in different ways, to parent-child interaction (Gauvain & Huard, 1999). Early research found, for instance, that authoritarian and controlling parents have children who are less socially competent than those whose parents are authoritative (Baumrind, 1967).

Perhaps most important is the "so what" question. Just because we find that certain sorts of people behave differently than others in interpersonal settings, why is that important? To the degree that traits are basic to a person, and to the degree that they are very difficult to change, what is the value of studying them? One answer is that, given enough knowledge, we can aid people varying in dispositions to be more successful. In educational settings, personality differences are often chosen as a way of segmenting student populations. Alternative kinds of instructional methods are used with different sorts of students. Just as important, in some strands of research on personality, scholars have offered more clinically based responses. There are successful therapies for social anxieties such as communication apprehension. Various methods exist to alleviate depression. Communication competence can be improved with training. Indeed, it would be well worth the time of some students of communication to take a more clinical role when it comes to their studies. Finally, individual differences deepen our understanding of the phenomenon of interpersonal communication. Science is about making distinctions that matter. Clearly, the study of personality in communication has demonstrated that differences do matter. The study of personality has long played an important role in scholarship in interpersonal communication. It has survived so long because it offers an intellectually interesting avenue of research that is grounded in the realities of people's lives.

REFERENCES

Acitelli, L. K., & Young, A. M. (1996). Gender and thought in relationships. In G. J. O. Fletcher & J. Fitness (Eds.), *Knowledge structures in close relationships: A social psychological approach* (pp. 147-168). Mahwah, NJ: Lawrence Erlbaum.

Adair, W. L., Okumura, T., & Brett, J. M. (2001). Negotiation behavior when cultures collide: The United States and Japan. *Journal of Applied Psychology, 86,* 371-385.

Adams, C., & Shepherd, G. J. (1996). Managing volunteer performance: Face support and situational features as predictors of volunteers' evaluations of regulative messages. *Management Communication Quarterly, 9,* 363-388.

Addison, T. L., & Schmidt, L. A. (1999). Are women who are shy reluctant to take risks? Behavioral and psychophysiological correlates. *Journal of Research in Personality, 33,* 352-357.

Adorno, T. W., Frenkel-Brunswik, E., Levinson, D. J., & Sanford, R. N. (1950). *The authoritarian personality.* New York: Harper & Row.

Ainsworth, M. D. S., Blehar, M. C., Waters, E., & Wall, S. (1978). *Patterns of attachment: A psychological study of the strange situation.* Hillsdale, NJ: Lawrence Erlbaum.

Akert, R. M., & Panter, A. T. (1988). Extraversion and the ability to decode nonverbal communication. *Personality and Individual Differences, 9,* 965-972.

Alden, L. E., & Wallace, S. T. (1995). Social phobia and social appraisal in successful and unsuccessful social interactions. *Behavior Research and Therapy, 33,* 497-505.

Alfano, M. S., Joiner, T. E., & Perry, M. (1994). Attributional style: A mediator of the shyness-depression relationship. *Journal of Research in Personality, 28,* 287-300.

Allen, T. H. (1990). An investigation of Machiavellianism and imagined interaction. *Communication Research Reports, 7,* 116-120.

Allport, G. W. (1937). *Personality: A psychological interpretation.* New York: Holt.

Almeida, D. M., & Kessler, R. C. (1998). Everyday stressors and gender differences in daily distress. *Journal of Personality and Social Psychology, 75,* 670-680.

Andersen, P. A., Andersen, J. F., & Garrison, J. P. (1978). Singing apprehension and talking apprehension: The development of two constructs. *Sign Language Studies, 19,* 155-186.

Anderson, C., John, O. P., Keltner, D., & Kring, A. M. (2001). Who attains social status? Effects of personality and physical attractiveness in social groups. *Journal of Personality and Social Psychology, 81,* 116-132.

Anderson, C. A., Miller, R. S., Riger, A. L., Dill, J. C., & Sedikides, C. (1994). Behavioral and characterological attributional styles as predictors of depression and loneliness: Review, refinement, and test. *Journal of Personality and Social Psychology, 66,* 549-558.

Anderson, C. M., & Martin, M. M. (1999). The relationship of argumentativeness and verbal aggression to cohesion, consensus, and satisfaction in small groups. *Communication Reports, 12,* 21-31.

Anderson, C. M., Martin, M. M., & Infante, D. A. (1998). Decision-making collaboration scale: Tests of validity. *Communication Research Reports, 15,* 245-255.

Anderson, L. R. (1990). Toward a two-track model of leadership training: Suggestions from self-monitoring theory. *Small Group Research, 21,* 147-167.

Applegate, J. L. (1980). Adaptive communication in educational contexts: A study of teachers' communicative strategies. *Communication Education, 29,* 158-170.

Argyle, M., & Lu, L. (1990). The happiness of extraverts. *Personality and Individual Differences, 11,* 1011-1017.

Arkin, R. M., & Grove, T. (1990). Shyness, sociability, and patterns of everyday affiliation. *Journal of Social and Personal Relationships, 7,* 273-281.

Arrindell, W. A., & Luteijn, F. (2000). Similarity between intimate partners for personality traits as related to individual levels of satisfaction with life. *Personality and Individual Differences, 28,* 629-637.

Asarnow, J. R., Goldstein, M. J., Tompson, M., & Guthrie, D. (1993). One year outcomes of depressive disorders in child psychiatric inpatients: Evaluation of the prognostic power of a brief measure of expressed emotion. *Journal of Child Psychology and Psychiatry, 34,* 129-137.

Ashton, M. C., Lee, K., & Son, C. (2000). Honesty as the sixth factor of personality: Correlations with Machiavellianism, primary psychopathy, and social adroitness. *European Journal of Personality, 14,* 359-368.

Ayduk, O., Downey, G., & Kim, M. (2001). Rejection sensitivity and depressive symptoms in women. *Personality and Social Psychology Bulletin, 27,* 868-877.

Ayduk, O., Downey, G., Testa, A., Yen, Y., & Shoda, Y. (1999). Does rejection elicit hostility in high rejection sensitive women? *Social Cognition, 17,* 245-271.

Ayduk, O., Mendoza-Denton, R., Mischel, W., Downey, G., Peake, P. K., & Rodriguez, M. (2000). Regulating the interpersonal self: Strategic self-regulation in coping with rejection sensitivity. *Journal of Personality and Social Psychology, 79,* 776-792.

Bacue, A. E., & Samter, W. (2001, July). *The dark side of cognitive complexity II: The production of guilt-inducing messages.* Paper presented at the Conference of the International Network on Personal Relationships, Prescott, AZ.

Baldwin, M. W., & Fehr, B. (1995). On the instability of attachment style ratings. *Personal Relationships, 2,* 247-261.

Baldwin, M. W., Fehr, B., Keedian, E., Seidel, M., & Thomson, D. W. (1993). An exploration of the relational schemata underlying attachment styles: Self-reports and lexical decision approaches. *Personality and Social Psychology Bulletin, 19,* 746-754.

Barbee, A. P., Gulley, M. R., & Cunningham, M. R. (1990). Social support seeking in personal relationships. *Journal of Social and Personal Relationships, 7,* 531-540.

Bar-On, R. (1997). *Emotional quotient inventory: Technical manual.* Toronto: Multi-Health Systems.

Baron, R. A. (1989). Personality and organizational conflict: Effects of the type S behavior pattern and self-monitoring. *Organizational Behavior and Human Performance, 44,* 196-281.

Barrett, L. F., Lane, R. D., Sechrest, L., & Schwartz, G. E. (2000). Sex differences in emotional awareness. *Personality and Social Psychology Bulletin, 26,* 1027-1035.

Barrett, L. F., & Pietromonaco, P. R. (1997). Accuracy of the five-factor model in predicting perceptions of daily social interactions. *Personality and Social Psychology Bulletin, 23,* 1173-1187.

Barrick, M. R., & Mount, M. K. (1991). The Big Five personality dimensions and job performance: A meta-analysis. *Personnel Psychology, 44,* 1-26.

Barrick, M. R., & Mount, M. K. (1993). Autonomy as a moderator of the relationship between the Big Five personality dimensions and job performance. *Journal of Applied Psychology, 78,* 111-118.

Bartholomew, K., Cobb, R. J., & Poole, J. A. (1997). Adult attachment patterns and social support processes. In G. R. Pierce, B. Lakey, I. G. Sarason, & B. R. Sarason (Eds.), *Sourcebook of social support and personality* (pp. 359-378). New York: Plenum.

Bartholomew, K., & Horowitz, L. M. (1991). Attachment styles among young adults: A test of a four-category model. *Journal of Personality and Social Psychology, 61,* 226-244.

Baucom, D. H., & Sher, T. G. (1987). Applications of marital research and methodology to the study of the family. In K. Hahlweg & M. J. Goldstein (Eds.), *Understanding major mental disorder: The contribution of family interaction research.* New York: Family Process Press.

Baumeister, R. F., & Tice, D. M. (1988). Metatraits. *Journal of Personality, 56,* 571-598.

Baumrind, D. (1967). Child-care practices anteceding three patterns of preschool behavior. *Genetic Psychology Monographs, 75,* 43-88.

Bayer, C. L., & Cegala, D. J. (1992). Trait verbal aggressiveness and argumentativeness: Relations with parenting style. *Western Journal of Communication, 56,* 301-310.

Baxter, J. S., & Boon, J. C. W. (2000). Interrogative suggestibility: The importance of being earnest. *Personality and Individual Differences, 28,* 753-762.

Beach, S. R. H., & Nelson, G. M. (1990). Pursuing research on major psychopathology from a contextual perspective: The example of depression and marital discord. In G. H. Brody & I. E. Sigel (Eds.), *Methods of family research: Vol. 2. Clinical populations* (pp. 227-259). Hillsdale, NJ: Lawrence Erlbaum.

Beach, S. R. H., Whisman, M. A., & O'Leary, K. D. (1994). Marital therapy for depression: Theoretical foundation, current status, and future directions. *Behavior Therapy, 25,* 345-371.

Beatty, M. J., Heisel, A. D., Hall, A. E., Levine, T. R., & LaFrance, B. H. (2002). What can we learn from the study of twins about genetic and environmental influences on interpersonal affiliation, aggressiveness, and social anxiety? *Communication Monographs, 69,* 1-18.

Beatty, M. J., Marshall, L. A., & Rudd, J. E. (2001). A twin study of communication adaptability: Heritability of individual differences. *Quarterly Journal of Speech, 87,* 366-377.

Beatty, M. J., & McCroskey, J. C. (1997). It's in our nature: Verbal aggressiveness as temperamental expression. *Communication Quarterly, 45,* 446-460.

Beatty, M. J., McCroskey, J. C., & Heisel, A. D. (1998). Communication apprehension as temperamental expression: A communibiological paradigm. *Communication Monographs, 65,* 197-219.

Beck, A. T. (1983). Cognitive therapy of depression: New perspectives. In P. J. Clayton & J. E. Barrett (Eds.), *Treatment of depression: Old controversies and new approaches* (pp. 265-290). New York: Raven.

Bell, R. A., & Daly, J. A. (1985). Some communicator correlates of loneliness. *Southern Speech Communication Journal, 50,* 121-142.

Belsky, J., Crnic, K., & Woodworth, S. (1995). Personality and parenting: Exploring the mediational role of transient mood and daily hassles. *Journal of Personality, 63,* 905-931.

Belsky, J., & Hsieh, K. (1998). Patterns of marital change during early childhood years: Parent personality, co-parenting, and division-of-labor correlates. *Journal of Family Psychology, 12,* 511-528.

Bem, D. J., & Allen, A. (1974). On predicting some of the people some of the time: The search for cross-situational consistencies in behavior. *Psychological Review, 81,* 506-520.

Bem, S. L. (1974). The measurement of psychological androgyny. *Journal of Consulting and Clinical Psychology, 42,* 155-162.

Benazon, N. R., & Coyne, J. C. (2000). Living with a depressed spouse. *Journal of Family Psychology, 14,* 71-79.

Berger, C. R., & Bell, R. A. (1988). Plans and the initiation of social relationships. *Human Communication Research, 15,* 217-235.

Berry, J. W., Worthington, E. L., Parrott, L., O'Connor, L. E., & Wade, N. G. (2001). Dispositional forgivingness: Development and construct validity of the transgression narrative test of forgivingness. *Personality and Social Psychology Bulletin, 27,* 1277-1290.

Berscheid, E., Graziano, W. G., Monson, T., & Dermer, M. (1976). Outcome dependency: Attention, attribution, and attraction. *Journal* of Personality and Social Psychology, 34, 978-989.

Biesanz, J. C., West, S. G., & Graziano, W. G. (1998). Moderators of self-other agreement: Reconsidering temporal stability in personality. *Journal of Personality and Social Psychology, 75,* 467-477.

Bippus, A. M. (2000). Humor usage in comforting episodes: Factors predicting outcomes. *Western Journal of Communication, 64,* 359-384.

Bochner, A. P., & Bochner, B. (1972). A multivariate investigation of Machiavellianism and task structure in four-man groups. *Speech Monographs, 39,* 277-285.

Booth-Butterfield, S., & Booth-Butterfield, M. (1991). Individual differences in the communication of humorous messages. *Southern Journal of Speech Communication, 56,* 205-219.

Bornstein, R. F. (1998). Interpersonal dependency and physical illness: A meta-analytic review of retrospective and prospective studies. *Journal of Research in Personality, 32,* 480-497.

Botwin, M. D., Buss, D. M., & Shackelford, T. K. (1997). Personality and mate preferences: Five factors in mate selection and marital satisfaction. *Journal of Personality, 65,* 107-136.

Bouchard, G., Lussier, Y., & Sabourin, S. (1999). Personality and marital adjustment: Utility of the five-factor model of personality. *Journal of Marriage and the Family, 61,* 651-660.

Bouchard, T. J., Jr., & McGue, M. (1990). Genetic and rearing environmental influences on adult personality: An analysis of adopted twins reared apart. *Journal of Personality, 58,* 263-292.

Bourhis, J., & Allen, M. (1992). Meta-analysis of the relationship between communication apprehension and cognitive performance. *Communication Education, 41,* 68-76.

Bowlby, J. (1982). *Attachment and loss: Vol. 1. Attachment* (2nd ed.). London: Hogarth.

Bradford, L., Allen, M., & Beisser, K. R. (2000). Meta-analysis of intercultural communication competence research. *World Communication, 29,* 28-51.

Bradshaw, S. D. (1998). I'll go if you will: Do shy persons utilize social surrogates? *Journal of Social and Personal Relationships, 15,* 651-669.

Brage, D., & Meredith, W. (1994). A causal model of adolescent depression. *Journal of Psychology, 128,* 455-468.

Brage, D., Meredith, W., & Woodward, J. (1993). Correlates of loneliness among midwestern adolescents. *Adolescence, 28,* 685-693.

Britt, T. W., & Shepperd, J. A. (1999). Trait relevance and trait assessment. *Personality and Social Psychology Review, 3,* 108-122.

Brockner, J., Heuer, L., Siegel, P. A., Wiesenfeld, B., Christopher, M., Grover, S., et al.(1998). The moderating effect of self-esteem in reaction to voice: Converging evidence from five studies. *Journal of Personality and Social Psychology, 75,* 394-407.

Brown, C. E., Dovidio, J. F., & Ellyson, S. L. (1990). Reducing sex differences in visual displays of dominance: Knowledge is power. *Personality and Social Psychology Bulletin, 16,* 358-368.

Bruce, M. L. (1998). Divorce and psychopathology. In B. P. Dohrenwend (Ed.), *Adversity, stress, and psychopathology* (pp. 219-234). New York: Oxford University Press.

Bruch, M. A., Giordano, S., & Pearl, L. (1986). Differences between fearful and self-conscious shy subtypes in background and current adjustment. *Journal of Research in Personality, 20,* 172-186.

Bruch, M. A., & Hynes, M. J. (1987). Heterosexual anxiety and contraceptive behavior. *Journal of Research in Personality, 21,* 343-360.

Bruch, M. A., Rivet, K. M., Heimberg, R. G., Hunt, A., & McIntosh, B. (1999). Shyness and sociotropy: Additive and interactive relations in predicting interpersonal concerns. *Journal of Personality, 67,* 381-406.

Bruch, M. A., Rivet, K. M., & Laurenti, H. J. (2000). Type of self-discrepancy and relationships to components of the tripartite model of emotional distress. *Personality and Individual Differences, 29,* 37-44.

Buhrmester, D., Furman, W., Wittenberg, M. T., & Reis, H. T. (1988). Five domains of interpersonal competence in peer relations. *Journal of Personality and Social Psychology, 55,* 991-1008.

Burgoon, M., Lombardi, D., Burch, S., & Shelby, J. (1979). Machiavellianism and type of persuasive message as predictors of attitude change. *Journal of Psychology, 101,* 123-127.

Burgoon, M., Miller, G. R., & Tubbs, S. L. (1972). Machiavellianism, justification, and attitude change following counter-attitudinal advocacy. *Journal of Personality and Social Psychology, 22,* 366-371.

Burleson, B. R. (1994). Comforting messages: Significance, approaches, and effects. In B. R. Burleson, T. L. Albrecht, & I. G. Sarason (Eds.), *Communication of social support: Messages, interactions, relationships, and community* (pp. 3-28). Thousand Oaks, CA: Sage.

Burleson, B. R. (1998). Cognitive complexity. In J. C. McCroskey, J. A. Daly, M. M. Martin, & M. J. Beatty (Eds.), *Communication and personality: Trait perspectives* (pp. 233-286). Cresskill, NJ: Hampton.

Buss, A. H. (1989). Personality as traits. *American Psychologist, 44,* 1378-1388.

Buss, D. M. (1991). Conflict in married couples: Personality predictors of anger and upset. *Journal of Personality, 59,* 663-688.

Buss, D. M. (1998). The psychology of human mate selection: Exploring the complexity of the strategic repertoire. In C. B. Crawford & D. L. Krebs (Eds.), *Handbook of evolutionary psychology: Ideas, issues, and applications* (pp. 405-429). Mahwah, NJ: Lawrence Erlbaum.

Buss, D. M., & Schmitt, D. P. (1993). Sexual strategies theory: A contextual evolutionary analysis of human mating. *Psychological Review, 100,* 204-232.

Buss, D. M., & Shackelford, T. K. (1997). Susceptibility to infidelity in the first year of marriage. *Journal of Research in Personality, 31,* 193-221.

Buss, D. M., Shackelford, T. K., Kirkpatrick, L. A., Choe, J. C., Lim, H. K., Hasegawa, M., et al. (1999). Jealousy and the nature of beliefs about infidelity: Tests of competing hypotheses about sex differences in the United States, Korea, and Japan. *Personal Relationships, 6,* 125-150.

Buunk, B. P. (1995). Sex, self-esteem, dependency, and extradyadic sexual experience as related to jealousy responses. *Journal of Social and Personal Relationships, 12,* 147-153.

Cameron, D., McAlinden, F., & O'Leary, K. (1988). Lakoff in context: The social and linguistic functions of tag questions. In J. Coates & D. Cameron (Eds.), *Women in their speech communities: New perspectives on language and sex* (pp. 74-93). London: Longman.

Campbell, W. K., Reeder, G. D., Sedikides, C., & Elliot, A. J. (2000). Narcissism and comparative self-enhancement strategies. *Journal of Research in Personality, 34,* 329-347.

Canary, D. J., Cunningham, E. M., & Cody, M. J. (1988). Goal types, gender, and locus of control in managing interpersonal conflict. *Communication Research, 15,* 426-446.

Canary, D. J., & Hause, K. S. (1993). Is there any reason to research sex differences in communication? *Communication Quarterly, 41,* 129-144.

Caplan, S. E., & Greene, J. O. (1999). Acquisition of message-production skill by younger and older adults: Effects of age, task complexity, and practice. *Communication Monographs, 66,* 31-48.

Caplan, S. E., & Samter, W. (1999). The role of facework in younger and older adults' evaluations of social support messages. *Communication Quarterly, 47,* 245-264.

Capsi, A., Elder, G. H., & Bem, D. J. (1988). Moving away from the world: Life-course patterns of shy children. *Developmental Psychology, 24,* 824-831.

Carli, L. L. (1990). Gender, language and influence. *Journal of Personality and Social Psychology, 59,* 941-951.

Carnelley, K. B., Pietromonaco, P. R., & Jaffe, K. (1994). Depression, working models of others, and relationship functioning. *Journal of Personality and Social Psychology, 66,* 127-140.

Caughlin, J. P., Huston, T. L., & Houts, R. M. (2000). How does personality matter in marriage? An examination of trait anxiety, interpersonal negativity, and marital satisfaction. *Journal of Personality and Social Psychology, 78,* 326-336.

Caughlin, J. P., & Vangelisti, A. L. (2000). An individual difference explanation of why married couples engage in the demand/withdraw pattern of conflict. *Journal of Social and Personal Relationships, 17,* 523-551.

Cegala, D. J. (1981). Interaction involvement: A cognitive dimension of communication competence. *Communication Education, 30,* 109-121.

Chan, K., & Drasgow, F. (2001). Toward a theory of individual differences and leadership: Understanding the motivation to lead. *Journal of Applied Psychology, 86,* 481-498.

Chaplin, W. F. (1991). The next generation of moderator research in personality psychology. *Journal of Personality, 59,* 143-179.

Chaplin, W. F., & Goldberg, L. R. (1984). A failure to replicate the Bem and Allen study of individual differences in cross-situational consistency. *Journal of Personality and Social Psychology, 47,* 1074-1090.

Check, J. V. P., Perlman, D., & Malamuth, N. M. (1985). Loneliness and aggressive behavior. *Journal of Social and Personal Relationships, 2,* 243-252.

Cheek, J. M., & Busch, C. K. (1981). The influence of shyness on loneliness in a new situation. *Personality and Social Psychology Bulletin, 7,* 572-577.

Cheek, J. M., & Buss, A. H. (1981). Shyness and sociability. *Journal of Personality and Social Psychology, 41,* 330-339.

Cheek, J. M., & Melchior, L. A. (1990). Shyness, self-esteem, and self-consciousness. In H. Leitenberg (Ed.), *Handbook of social and evaluation anxiety* (pp. 47-82). New York: Plenum.

Cheng, C. (1999). Gender-role differences in susceptibility to the influence of support availability on depression. *Journal of Personality, 67,* 439-467.

Choi, S. H. (1991). Communicative socialization processes: Korea and Canada. In B. B. Schieffelin & E. Ochs (Eds.), *Language socialization across cultures* (pp. 213-250). Cambridge: Cambridge University Press.

Christensen, A. (1988). Dysfunctional interaction patterns in couples. In P. Noller & M. A. Fitzpatrick (Eds.), *Perspectives on marital interaction* (pp. 31-52). Clevedon, Eng.: Multilingual Matters.

Christie, R., & Geis, F. L. (1970). *Studies in Machiavellianism.* New York: Academic Press.

Ciarrochi, J. V., Chan, A. Y. C., & Caputi, P. (2000). A critical evaluation of the emotional intelligence construct. *Personality and Individual Differences, 28,* 539-561.

Collier, M. J. (1991). Conflict competence within African, Mexican, and Anglo American friendships. In S. Ting-Toomey & F. Korzenny (Eds.), *Cross-cultural interpersonal communication* (pp. 132-154). Newbury Park, CA: Sage.

Collier, M. J. (1996). Communication competence problematics in ethnic friendships. *Communication Monographs, 63,* 314-336.

Collier, M. J., & Shimizu, M. (1993, May). *Close friendships: A cross-cultural comparison of males and females in Japan and the United States.* Paper presented at the annual meeting of the International Communication Association, Washington, DC.

Collins, N. L., & Feeney, B. C. (2000). A safe haven: An attachment theory perspective on support-seeking and caregiving in adult romantic relationships. *Journal of Personality and Social Psychology, 78,* 1053-1073.

Comadena, M. E., & Prusank, D. T. (1988). Communication apprehension and academic achievement among elementary and middle school children. *Communication Education, 37,* 270-277.

Cooley, C. H. (1902). *Human nature and the social order.* New York: Scribner's.

Cooley, E. L., & Nowicki, S. (1989). Discrimination of facial expressions of emotion by depressed subjects. *Genetic, Social, and General Psychology Monographs, 115,* 451-465.

Costa, P. T., Terracciano, A., & McCrae, R. R. (2001). Gender differences in personality traits across cultures: Robust and surprising findings. *Journal of Personality and Social Psychology, 81,* 322-331.

Costanzo, M., & Archer, D. (1989). Interpreting the expressive behavior of others: The interpersonal perception task. *Journal of Nonverbal Behavior, 13,* 225-245.

Cote, S., & Moskowitz, D. S. (1998). On the dynamic covariation between interpersonal behavior and affect: Prediction from neuroticism, extraversion, and agreeableness. *Journal of Personality and Social Psychology, 75,* 1032-1046.

Cotterell, N., Eisenberger, R., & Speicher, H. (1992). Inhibiting effects of reciprocation wariness on interpersonal relationships. *Journal of Personality and Social Psychology, 62,* 658-668.

Coupland, N., & Coupland, J. (2001). Language, ageing, and ageism. In W. P. Robinson & H. Giles (Eds.), *The new handbook of language and social psychology* (pp. 465-488). New York: John Wiley.

Coyne, J. C. (1976). Toward an interactional description of depression. *Psychiatry, 39,* 28-40.

Cross, S. E., & Madson, L. (1997). Models of the self: Self-construals and gender. *Psychological Bulletin, 122,* 5-37.

Crowne, D. P., & Marlowe, D. (1964). A new scale of social desirability independent of psychopathology. *Journal of Consulting Psychology, 24,* 349-354.

Cummings, E. M., & Davies, P. T. (1994). Maternal depression and child development.

Journal of Child Psychology and Psychiatry, 35, 73-112.

Cummings, E. M., & Davies, P. T. (1999). Depressed parents and family functioning: Interpersonal effects and children's functioning and development. In T. Joiner & J. C. Coyne (Eds.), *The interactional nature of depression: Advances in interpersonal approaches* (pp. 299-327). Washington, DC: American Psychological Association.

Dabady, M., Bell, M., & Kihlstrom, J. F. (1999). Person memory: Organization of behaviors by traits. *Journal of Research in Personality, 33,* 369-377.

Dabbs, J. M., Jr., Evans, M. S., Hopper, C. H., & Purvis, J. A. (1980). Self-monitors in conversation: What do they monitor? *Journal of Personality and Social Psychology, 39,* 278-284.

Dabbs, J. M., Jr., Strong, R., & Milun, R. (1997). Exploring the mind of testosterone: A beeper study. *Journal of Research in Personality, 31,* 577-587.

Daly, J. A. (1978). Communication apprehension and behavior: Applying a multiple act criteria. *Human Communication Research, 4,* 208-216.

Daly, J. A., & Bippus, A. (1998). Personality and interpersonal communication. In J. C. McCroskey, J. A. Daly, M. M. Martin, & M. J. Beatty (Eds.), *Communication and personality: Trait perspectives* (pp. 1-40). Cresskill, NJ: Hampton.

Daly, J. A., Caughlin, J. P., & Stafford, L. (1997). Correlates and consequences of social-communicative anxiety. In J. A. Daly, J. C. McCroskey, J. Ayres, T. Hopf, & D. M. Ayres (Eds.), *Avoiding communication: Shyness, reticence, and communication apprehension* (2nd ed., pp. 21-74). Cresskill, NJ: Hampton.

Daly, J. A., & Friedrich, G. (1981). The development of communication apprehension: A retrospective analysis of some contributory correlates. *Communication Quarterly, 29,* 243-255.

Daly, J. A., Kreiser, P. O., & Roghaar, L. A. (1994). Question-asking comfort: Explorations of the demography of communication in the eighth grade classroom. *Communication Education, 43,* 27-41.

Daly, J. A., & McCroskey, J. C. (1975). Occupational desirability and choice as a function of communication apprehension. *Journal of Counseling Psychology, 22,* 309-313.

Daly, J. A., McCroskey, J. C., Ayres, J., Hopf, T., & Ayres, D. M. (Eds.). (1997). *Avoiding communication: Shyness, reticence, and communication apprehension* (2nd ed.). Cresskill, NJ: Hampton.

Daly, J. A., McCroskey, J. C., & Richmond, V. P. (1977). The relationship between vocal activity and perceptions of communicators in small group interaction. *Western Speech Communication Journal, 41,* 175-187.

Daly, J. A., Richmond, V. P., & Leth, S. (1979). Social-communicative anxiety and the personnel selection process: Testing the similarity effect in selection decisions. *Human Communication Research, 6,* 18-32.

Daly, J. A., & Street, R. L., Jr. (1980). Measuring social-communicative anxiety: Social desirability and the fakability of scale responses. *Human Communication Research, 6,* 185-189.

Daly, J. A., Vangelisti, A. L., & Daughton, S. (1987). The nature and structure of conversational sensitivity. *Human Communication Research, 14,* 167-202.

Daly, J. A., Vangelisti, A. L., & Lawrence, S. (1989). Public speaking anxiety and self-focused attention. *Personality and Individual Differences, 10,* 903-913.

Daly, J. A., Vangelisti, A. L., & Weber, D. J. (1995). Speech anxiety affects how people prepare speeches: A protocol analysis of the preparation processes of speakers. *Communication Monographs, 62,* 383-397.

Daniels, D., & Plomin, R. (1985). Origins of individual differences in infant shyness. *Developmental Psychology, 21,* 118-121.

Darling, N., & Steinberg, L. (1993). Parenting style as context: An integrative model. *Psychological Bulletin, 113,* 487-496.

Davies, M., Stankov, L., & Roberts, R. D. (1998). Emotional intelligence: In search of an elusive construct. *Journal of Personality and Social Psychology, 75,* 989-1015.

Davies, P. T., Dumenci, L., & Windle, M. (1999). The interplay between maternal depressive symptoms and marital distress in the prediction of adolescent adjustment. *Journal of Marriage and the Family, 61,* 238-254.

Davila, J., Burge, D., & Hammen, C. L. (1997). Why does attachment style change? *Journal of Personality and Social Psychology, 73,* 826-838.

Davis, A. (1998). Age differences in dating and marriage: Reproductive strategies or social preferences? *Current Anthropology, 39,* 374-380.

Davis, M. H. (1983). Measuring individual differences in empathy: Evidence for a multidimensional approach. *Journal of Personality and Social Psychology, 44,* 113-126.

Day, L., & Maltby, J. (2000). Can Kinderman and Bentalls' suggestions for a personal and situational attributions questionnaire be used to examine all aspects of attributional style? *Personality and Individual Differences, 29,* 1047-1055.

Deaux, K., & LaFrance, M. (1998). Gender. In D. T. Gilbert, S. T. Fiske, & G. Lindzey (Eds.), *Handbook of social psychology* (4th ed., pp. 788-827). New York: McGraw-Hill.

DeBono, K., & Klein, C. (1993). Source expertise and persuasion: The moderating role of recipient dogmatism. *Personality and Social Psychology Bulletin, 19,* 167-173.

DeNeve, K. M., & Cooper, H. (1998). The happy personality: A meta-analysis of 137 personality traits and subjective well-being. *Psychological Bulletin, 124,* 197-229.

Depue, R. A., & Collins, P. F. (1999). Neurobiology of the structure of personality: Dopamine, facilitation of incentive motivation, and extraversion. *Behavioral and Brain Sciences, 22,* 491-569.

Depue, R. A., Luciana, M., Arbisi, P., Collins, P., & Leon, A. (1994). Dopamine and the structure of personality: Relation of agonist-induced dopamine activity to positive emotionality. *Journal of Personality and Social Psychology, 67,* 485-498.

Dew, M. A., & Bromet, E. J. (1991). Effects of depression on social support in a community sample of women. In J. Eckenrode (Ed.), *The social context of coping* (pp. 189-219). New York: Plenum.

Dewaele, J., & Furnham, A. (2000). Personality and speech production: A pilot study of second language learners. *Personality and Individual Differences, 28,* 355-365.

Dillehay, R. (1978). Authoritarianism. In H. London & J. E. Exner (Eds.), *Dimensions of personality* (pp. 85-127). New York: John Wiley.

Dindia, K., & Allen, M. (1992). Sex differences in self-disclosure: A meta-analysis. *Psychological Bulletin, 112,* 106-124.

Dion, K. L., & Dion, K. K. (1973). Correlates of romantic love. *Journal of Consulting and Clinical Psychology, 41,* 51-56.

DiTommaso, E., & Spinner, B. (1997). Social and emotional loneliness: A reexamination of Weiss' typology of loneliness. *Personality and Individual Differences, 22,* 417-427.

Dobson, K. S. (1989). Real and perceived responses to subclinically anxious and depressed targets. *Cognitive Therapy and Research, 13,* 37-47.

Doherty, W. J. (1983). Locus of control and marital interaction. In H. M. Lefcourt (Ed.), *Research with the locus of control construct: Vol. 2. Developments and social problems* (pp. 155-183). New York: Academic Press.

Downey, G., & Feldman, S. I. (1996). Implications of rejection sensitivity for intimate relationships. *Journal of Personality and Social Psychology, 70,* 1327-1343.

Downey, G., Freitas, A. L., Michaelis, B., & Khouri, H. (1998). The self-fulfilling prophecy in close relationships: Rejection sensitivity and rejection by romantic partners. *Journal of Personality and Social Psychology, 75,* 545-560.

Dsilva, M. U. (1999). Individual differences and choice of information source: Sensation seeking in drug abuse prevention. *Communication Reports, 12,* 51-57.

Duck, S., Pond, K., & Latham, G. (1994). Loneliness and the evaluation of relational events. *Journal of Social and Personal Relationships, 11,* 253-276.

Duggan, E. S., & Brennan, K. A. (1994). Social avoidance and its relation to Bartholomew's adult attachment typology. *Journal of Social and Personal Relationships, 11,* 147-153.

Dumlao, R., & Botta, R. A. (2000). Family communication patterns and the conflict styles young adults use with their fathers. *Communication Quarterly, 48,* 174-189.

Duran, R. L., & Spitzberg, B. H. (1995). Toward the development and validation of a measure of cognitive communication competence. *Communication Quarterly, 43,* 259-275.

Dykman, B. M., Horowitz, L., Abramson, L. Y., & Usher, M. (1991). Schematic and situational determinants of depressed and non-depressed students' interpretation of feedback. *Journal of Abnormal Psychology, 100,* 45-55.

D'Zurilla, T. J., Maydeu-Olivares, A., & Kant, G. L. (1998). Age and gender differences in social problem-solving ability. *Personality and Individual Differences, 25,* 241-252.

Eagly, A. H., & Carli, L. L. (1981). Sex of researchers and sex-typed communications as determinants of sex differences in influence-ability: A meta-analysis of social influence studies. *Psychological Bulletin, 90,* 1-20.

Eagley, A. H., & Johnson, B. T. (1990). Gender and leadership style: A meta-analysis. *Psychological Bulletin, 108,* 233-256.

Eagley, A. H., & Karau, S. J. (1991). Gender and the emergence of leaders: A meta-analysis. *Journal of Personality and Social Psychology, 60,* 685-710.

Eddy, G., & Sinnett, E. (1973). Behavior setting utilization by emotionally disturbed college students. *Journal of Consulting and Clinical Psychology, 40,* 210-216.

Eiden, R. D., Teti, D. M., & Corns, K. M. (1995). Maternal working models of attachment, marital adjustment, and the parent-child relationship. *Child Development, 66,* 1504-1518.

Eisenberg, N., Fabes, R. A., Schaller, M., & Miller, P. A. (1989). Sympathy and personal distress: Development, gender differences, and interrelations of indexes. *New Directions for Child Development, 44,* 107-126.

Emmons, R. A., Diener, E., & Larson, R. J. (1986). Choice and avoidance of everyday situations and affect congruence: Two models of reciprocal interactionism. *Journal of Personality and Social Psychology, 51,* 815-826.

Epstein, S. (1979). The stability of behavior: I. On predicting most of the people most of the time. *Journal of Personality and Social Psychology, 37,* 1097-1126.

Eronen, S., & Nurmi, J. (1999). Social reaction styles, interpersonal behaviours and person perception: A multi-informant approach. *Journal of Social and Personal Relationships, 16,* 315-333.

Fandt, P. M., & Ferris, G. R. (1990). The management of information and impressions: When employees behave opportunistically. *Organizational Behavior and Human Performance, 45,* 140-158.

Feeney, B. C., & Collins, N. L. (2001). Predictors of caregiving in adult intimate relationships: An attachment theoretical perspective. *Journal of Personality and Social Psychology, 80,* 972-994.

Feeney, B. C., & Kirkpatrick, L. A. (1996). Effects of adult attachment and presence of romantic partners on physiological responses to stress. *Journal of Personality and Social Psychology, 70,* 255-270.

Feingold, A. (1994). Gender differences in personality: A meta-analysis. *Psychological Bulletin, 116,* 429-456.

Fiske, D. W. (1949). Consistency of the factorial structure of personality ratings from different sources. *Journal of Abnormal and Social Psychology, 44,* 329-344.

Flora, J., & Segrin, C. (1998). Joint leisure time in friend and romantic relationships: The role of activity type, social skills, and positivity. *Journal of Social and Personal Relationships, 15,* 711-718.

Flora, J., & Segrin, C. (2000). Relationship development in dating couples: Implications for relationship satisfaction and loneliness. *Journal of Social and Personal Relationships, 17,* 811-825.

Forsyth, D., Schlenker, B. R., Leary, M. R., & McCown, N. E. (1985). Self-presentational determinants of sex differences on leadership behavior. *Small Group Behavior, 16,* 197-210.

Fraley, R. C., & Shaver, P. R. (1998). Airport separations: A naturalistic study of adult attachment dynamics in separating couples. *Journal of Personality and Social Psychology, 75,* 1198-1212.

Fujita, F., Diener, E., & Sandvik, E. (1991). Gender differences in negative affect and well-being: The case for emotional intensity. *Journal of Personality and Social Psychology, 61,* 427-434.

Funder, D. C. (2001). Personality. *Annual Review of Psychology, 52,* 197-221.

Funder, D. C., & Colvin, C. R. (1988). Friends and strangers: Acquaintanceship, agreement, and accuracy of personality judgments. *Journal of Personality and Social Psychology, 55,* 149-158.

Funder, D. C., & Colvin, C. R. (1991). Explorations in behavioral consistency: Properties of persons, situations, and behaviors. *Journal of Personality and Social Psychology, 60,* 773-794.

Funder, D. C., & Ozer, D. J. (1983). Behavior as a function of the situation. *Journal of Personality and Social Psychology, 44,* 107-112.

Furnham, A. (1981). Personality and activity preference. *British Journal of Social Psychology, 20,* 57-68.

Furnham, A., & Medhurst, S. (1995). Personality correlates of academic seminar behaviour: A study of four instruments. *Personality and Individual Differences, 19,* 197-208.

Gable, M., & Topol, M. T. (1991). Machiavellian managers: Do they perform better? *Journal of Business and Psychology, 5,* 355-365.

Gable, S. L., & Shean, G. D. (2000). Perceived social competence and depression. *Journal* of Social and Personal Relationships, 17, 139-150.

Gangestad, S. W., & Simpson, J. A. (1990). Toward an evolutionary history of female sociosexual variation. *Journal of Personality, 58,* 69-96.

Gangestad, S. W., & Snyder, M. (2000). Self-monitoring: Appraisal and reappraisal. *Psychological Bulletin, 126,* 530-555.

Garcia, S., Sinson, L., Ickes, W. J., Bissonnette, V., & Briggs, S. R. (1991). Shyness and physical attractiveness in mixed-sex dyads. *Journal of Personality and Social Psychology, 61,* 35-49.

Gardner, H. (1993). *Multiple intelligences.* New York: Basic Books.

Garland, J., & Beard, J. F. (1979). Relationship between self-monitoring and leader emergence across two task situations. *Journal of Applied Psychology, 64,* 72-76.

Gauvain, M., & Huard, R. D. (1999). Family interaction, parenting style, and the development of planning: A longitudinal analysis using archival data. *Journal of Family Psychology, 13,* 75-92.

Gavazzi, S. M., McKenry, P. C., Jacobson, J. A., Julian, T. W., & Lohman, B. (2000). Modeling the effects of expressed emotion, psychiatric symptomatology, and marital quality levels on male and female verbal aggression. *Journal of Marriage and the Family, 62,* 669-682.

Geis, F. L. (1978). Machiavellianism. In H. London & J. E. Exner (Eds.), *Dimensions of personality* (pp. 305-363). New York: John Wiley.

George, C., Kaplan, N., & Main, M. (1984). *The attachment interview for adults.* Unpublished manuscript.

Gilbert, P., & Miles, J. N. V. (2000). Sensitivity to social put-down: Its relationship to perceptions of social rank, shame, social anxiety, depression, anger, and self-other blame. *Personality and Individual Differences, 29,* 757-774.

Giordano, C., Wood, J. V., & Michela, J. L. (2000). Depressive personality styles, dysphoria, and social comparisons in everyday life. *Journal of Personality and Social Psychology, 79,* 438-451.

Goldberg, L. R. (1993). The structure of phenotypic personality traits. *American Psychologist, 48,* 26-34.

Goleman, D. (1995). *Emotional intelligence: Why it can matter more than IQ.* New York: Bantam.

Gotlib, I. H., & Asarnow, R. F. (1979). Interpersonal and impersonal problem-solving skills in mildly and clinically depressed university students. *Journal of Consulting and Clinical Psychology, 47,* 86-95.

Gottman, J. M., & Levenson, R. W. (1988). The social psychophysiology of marriage. In P. Noller & M. A. Fitzpatrick (Eds.), *Perspectives on marital interaction* (pp. 182-200). Clevedon, Eng.: Multilingual Matters.

Gray, M. R., & Steinberg, L. (1999). Unpacking authoritative parenting: Reassessing a multidimensional construct. *Journal of Marriage and the Family, 61,* 574-587.

Graziano, W. G., Jensen-Campbell, L. A., & Hair, E. C. (1996). Perceiving interpersonal conflict and reacting to it: The case for agreeableness. *Journal of Personality and Social Psychology, 70,* 820-835.

Greenberg, B. D., Li, Q., Lucas, F. R., Hu, S., Sirota, L. A., Benjamin, J., et al. (2000). Association between the serotonin transporter polymorphism and personality traits in a primarily female population sample. *American Journal of Medical Genetics, 96,* 202-216.

Grob, L. M., Meyers, R. A., & Schuh, R. (1997). Powerful/powerless language use in group interactions: Sex differences or similarities. *Communication Quarterly, 45,* 282-303.

Gudjonsson, G. H., & Clark, N. K. (1986). Suggestibility in police interrogation: A social psychological model. *Social Behaviour, 1,* 83-104.

Gudykunst, W. B., Matsumoto, Y., Ting-Toomey, S., Nishida, T., Kim, K., & Heyman, S. (1996). The influence of cultural individualism-collectivism, self-construals, and individual values on communication styles across cultures. *Human Communication Research, 22,* 510-543.

Gudykunst, W. B., & Ting-Toomey, S. (1988). *Culture and interpersonal communication.* Newbury Park, CA: Sage.

Guerrero, L. K. (1996). Attachment-style differences in intimacy and involvement: A test of the four-category model. *Communication Monographs, 63,* 269-292.

Haas, S., & Stafford, L. (1998). An initial examination of maintenance behaviors in gay and lesbian relationships. *Journal of Social and Personal Relationships, 15,* 846-855.

Hackman, M. Z., Ellis, K., Johnson, C. E., & Staley, C. (1999). Self-construal orientation: Validation of an instrument and a study of the relationship to leadership communication style. *Communication Quarterly, 47,* 183-195.

Hagestad, G. O., & Smyer, M. A. (1982). Dissolving long-term relationships: Patterns of divorcing in middle age. In S. Duck (Ed.), *Personal relationships 4: Dissolving relationships* (pp. 115-188). New York: Academic Press.

Hall, E. T. (1976). *Beyond culture.* Garden City, NY: Doubleday.

Hall, J. A. (1984). *Nonverbal sex differences: Communication accuracy and expressive style.* Baltimore: Johns Hopkins University Press.

Hamer, D. H., Greenberg, B. D., Sabol, S. Z., & Murphy, D. L. (1999). Role of the serotonin transporter gene in temperament and character. *Journal of Personality Disorders, 13,* 312-327.

Hamer, R. J., & Bruch, M. A. (1997). Personality factors and inhibited career development: Testing the unique contributions of shyness. *Journal of Vocational Behavior, 50,* 382-400.

Hammen, C. L., & Peters, S. D. (1978). Interpersonal consequences of depression: Responses to men and women enacting a depressed role. *Journal of Abnormal Psychology, 87,* 322-332.

Hample, D., & Dallinger, J. M. (1995). A Lewinian perspective on taking conflict personally: Revision, refinement, and validation of the instrument. *Communication Quarterly, 43,* 297-319.

Hart, R. P., Carlson, R. E., & Eadie, W. F. (1980). Attitudes towards communication and the assessment of rhetorical sensitivity. *Communication Monographs, 47,* 1-22.

Haslett, B. (1990). Social class, social status, and communicative behavior. In H. Giles & W. P. Robinson (Eds.), *Handbook of language and social psychology* (pp. 329-344). New York: John Wiley.

Hazen, C., & Hutt, M. J. (1990, July). *Continuity and change in inner working models of attachment.* Paper presented at the Fifth International Conference on Personal Relationships, Oxford.

Hazen, C., & Shaver, P. (1987). Conceptualizing romantic love as an attachment process. *Journal of Personality and Social Psychology, 52,* 511-524.

Hecht, M. L., Marston, P. J., & Larkey, L. K. (1994). Love ways and relationship quality in heterosexual relationships. *Journal of Social and Personal Relationships, 11,* 25-43.

Helgeson, V. S., & Fritz, H. L. (1999). Unmitigated agency and unmitigated communion: Distinctions from agency and communion. *Journal of Research in Personality, 33,* 131-158.

Helgeson, V. S., Shaver, P., & Dyer, M. (1987). Prototypes of intimacy and distance in same-sex and opposite-sex relationships. *Journal of Social and Personal Relationships, 4,* 195-233.

Hendricks, C., & Hendricks, S. (1986). A theory and method of love. *Journal of Personality and Social Psychology, 50,* 392-402.

Higgins, E. T. (1987). Self-discrepancy: A theory relating self and affect. *Psychological Review, 94,* 319-340.

Hildebrand-Saints, L., & Weary, G. (1989). Depression and social information gathering. *Personality and Social Psychology Bulletin, 15,* 150-160.

Hofstede, G. (1980). *Culture's consequences: International differences in work-related values.* Beverly Hills, CA: Sage.

Hofstede, G. (2001). *Culture's consequences: Comparing values, behaviors, institutions, and organizations across nations* (2nd ed.). Thousand Oaks, CA: Sage.

Hogan, R. (1998). Reinventing personality. *Journal of Social and Clinical Psychology, 17,* 1-10.

Hokanson, J. E., & Butler, A. C. (1992). Cluster analysis of depressed college students' social behaviors. *Journal of Personality and Social Psychology, 62,* 273-280.

Hooley, J. W., & Hahlweg, K. (1986). The marriages and interaction patterns of depressed patients and their spouses: Comparing high and low EE dyads. In M. J. Goldstein, I. Hand, & K. Hahlweg (Eds.), *Treatment of schizophrenia: Family assessment and intervention* (pp. 85-96). Berlin: Springer-Verlag.

Hope, D. A., & Heimberg, R. G. (1990). Dating anxiety. In H. Leitenberg (Ed.), *Handbook of social and evaluative anxiety* (pp. 217-246). New York: Plenum.

Hops, H., Biglan, A., Sherman, L., Arthur, J., Friedman, L., & Osteen, R. (1987). Home observations of family interactions of depressed women. *Journal of Consulting and Clinical Psychology, 55,* 341-346.

Huang, L. (1999). Family communication patterns and personality characteristics. *Communication Quarterly, 47,* 230-243.

Hummert, M. L., Shaner, J. L., Garstka, T. A., & Henry, C. (1998). Communication with older adults: The influence of age stereotypes, context, and communicator age. *Human Communication Research, 25,* 124-151.

Ickes, W. J. (1985). Sex role influences in dyadic interaction: A theoretical model. In W. J. Ickes (Ed.), *Compatible and incompatible relationships* (pp. 187-208). New York: Springer-Verlag.

Ickes, W. J., & Barnes, R. D. (1977). The role of sex and self-monitoring in unstructured dyadic interactions. *Journal of Personality and Social Psychology, 35,* 315-330.

Ickes, W. J., Snyder, M., & Garcia, S. (1997). Personality influences on the choice of situations. In R. Hogan, J. Johnson, & S. R. Briggs (Eds.), *Handbook of personality psychology* (pp. 165-195). San Diego, CA: Academic Press.

Infante, D. A. (1981). Trait argumentativeness as a predictor of communicative behavior in situations requiring argument. *Central States Speech Journal, 32,* 265-277.

Infante, D. A. (1985). Inducing women to be more argumentative: Source credibility effects. *Journal of Applied Communication Research, 13,* 33-44.

Infante, D. A. (1995). Teaching students to understand and control verbal aggression. *Communication Education, 44,* 51-63.

Infante, D. A., Chandler, T. A., & Rudd, J. E. (1989). Test of an argumentative skill deficiency model of interspousal violence. *Communication Monographs, 56,* 163-177.

Infante, D. A., & Gorden, W. I. (1985). Superiors' argumentativeness and verbal aggressiveness as predictors of subordinates' satisfaction. *Human Communication Research, 12,* 117-125.

Infante, D. A., & Gorden, W. I. (1989). Argumentativeness and affirming communicator style as predictors of satisfaction/dissatisfaction with subordinates. *Communication Quarterly, 37,* 81-90.

Infante, D. A., & Rancer, A. S. (1982). A conceptualization and measure of argumentativeness. *Journal of Personality Assessment, 45,* 72-80.

Infante, D. A., Riddle, B. L., Horvath, C. L., & Tumlin, S. A. (1992). Verbal aggressiveness: Messages and reasons. *Communication Quarterly, 40,* 116-126.

Infante, D. A., Trebing, J. D., Shepherd, P. E., & Seeds, D. E. (1984). The relationship of argumentativeness to verbal aggression. *Southern Speech Communication Journal, 50,* 67-77.

Infante, D. A., & Wigley, C. J. (1986). Verbal aggressiveness: An interpersonal model and measure. *Communication Monographs, 53,* 61-69.

Ingram, R. E. (1989). Affective confounds in social-cognitive research. *Journal of Personality and Social Psychology, 57,* 715-722.

Izard, C. E., Fine, S., Schultz, D., Mostow, A., Ackerman, B., & Youngstrom, E. (2001). Emotion knowledge as a predictor of social behavior and academic competence in children at risk. *Psychological Science, 12,* 18-23.

Jaccard, J., & Daly, J. A. (1980). Personality traits and multiple act criteria. *Human Communication Research, 6,* 367-377.

Jacob, T., & Johnson, S. L. (2001). Sequential interactions in the parent-child communications of depressed fathers and depressed mothers. *Journal of Family Psychology, 15,* 38-52.

Jang, K. L., Hu, S., Livesley, W. J., Angleitner, A., Rieman, R., Ando, J., et al. (2001). Covariance structure of neuroticism and agreeableness: A twin and molecular genetic analysis of the role of the serotonin transporter gene. *Journal of Personality and Social Psychology, 81,* 295-304.

Jockin, V., McGue, M., & Lykken, D. T. (1996). Personality and divorce: A genetic analysis. *Journal of Personality and Social Psychology, 71,* 288-299.

Joiner, T. E. (1996). Likeability of those in relationships with low positive affect people: (Dis)liking by association or contrast. *Journal of Research in Personality, 30,* 179-188.

Joiner, T. E., & Metalsky, G. I. (2001). Excessive reassurance seeking: Delineating a risk factor involved in the development of depressive symptoms. *Psychological Science, 12,* 371-378.

Jones, E. E., & Baumeister, R. F. (1976). The self-monitor looks at the ingratiator. *Journal of Personality, 44,* 654-674.

Jones, R. E., & White, C. S. (1983). Relationship between Machiavellianism, task orientation, and team effectiveness. *Psychological Reports, 53,* 859-866.

Jones, W. H. (1982). Loneliness and social behaviour. In L. A. Peplau & D. Perlman (Eds.), *Loneliness: A sourcebook of current theory, research and therapy* (pp. 238-254). New York: John Wiley.

Jones, W. H., & Carpenter, B. N. (1986). Shyness, social behavior, and relationships.

In W. H. Jones, J. M. Cheek, & S. R. Briggs (Eds.), *Shyness: Perspectives on treatment and research* (pp. 227-238). New York: Plenum.

Jones, W. H., Hobbs, S. A., & Hockenbury, D. (1982). Loneliness and social skills deficits. *Journal of Personality and Social Psychology, 42,* 682-689.

Josephs, R. A., Markus, H. R., & Tafarodi, R. W. (1992). Gender and self-esteem. *Journal of Personality and Social Psychology, 63,* 391-402.

Karney, B., & Bradbury, T. N. (1995). The longitudinal course of marital quality and stability: A review of theory, methods, and research. *Psychological Bulletin, 118,* 3-34.

Kassing, J. W., Pearce, K. J., & Infante, D. A. (2000). Corporal punishment and communication in father-son dyads. *Communication Research Reports, 17,* 237-249.

Kazoleas, D. (1993). The impact of argumentativeness on resistance to persuasion. *Human Communication Research, 20,* 118-137.

Keelan, J. P. R., Dion, K. L., & Dion, K. K. (1994). Attachment style and heterosexual relationships among young adults: A short-term panel study. *Journal of Social and Personal Relationships, 11,* 201-214.

Kelly, E. L., & Conley, J. J. (1987). Personality and compatibility: A prospective analysis of marital stability and marital satisfaction. *Journal of Personality and Social Psychology, 52,* 27-40.

Kendler, K. S., & Prescott, C. A. (1999). A population-based twin study of depression in men and women. *Archives of General Psychiatry, 56,* 39-44.

Kenny, D. A., & DePaulo, B. M. (1993). Do people know how others view them? An empirical and theoretical account. *Psychological Bulletin, 114,* 145-161.

Kenrick, D. T., Gabrielidis, C., Keefe, R. C., & Cornelius, J. S. (1996). Adolescents' age preferences for dating partners: Support for an evolutionary model of life-history strategies. *Child Development, 67,* 1499-1511.

Kernis, M. H., Brown, A. C., & Brody, G. H. (2000). Fragile self-esteem in children and its associations with perceived patterns of parent-child communication. *Journal of Personality, 68,* 225-252.

Kerr, M., Lambert, W. W., & Bem, D. J. (1996). Life course sequelae of childhood shyness in Sweden: Comparison with the United States. *Developmental Psychology, 32,* 1100-1105.

Kiesler, D. J. (1996). *Contemporary interpersonal theory and research: Personality, psychopathology, and psychotherapy.* New York: John Wiley.

Kilduff, M., & Day, D. (1994). Do chameleons get ahead? The effects of self-monitoring on managerial careers. *Academy of Management Journal, 37,* 1047-1060.

Kilman, R., & Thomas, K. (1977). Developing a forced-choice measure of conflict-handling behavior: The MODE instrument. *Educational and Psychological Measurement, 37,* 309-325.

Kim, M.-S., Aune, K. S., Hunter, J. E., Kim, H.-J., & Kim, J. S. (2001). The effect of culture and self-construals on predispositions toward verbal communication. *Human Communication Research, 27,* 382-408.

Kline, S. L., Pelias, R., & Delia, J. G. (1991). The predictive validity of cognitive complexity measures on communication relevant abilities. *International Journal of Personal Construct Psychology, 4,* 347-357.

Kling, K. C., Hyde, J. S., Showers, C. J., & Buswell, B. N. (1999). Gender differences in self-esteem: A meta analysis. *Psychological Bulletin, 125,* 470-500.

Klohnen, E. C., & Bera, S. J. (1998). Behavioral and experiential patterns of avoidantly and securely attached women across adulthood: A 31-year longitudinal perspective. *Journal of Personality and Social Psychology, 74,* 211-223.

Klopf, D. W. (1984). Cross-cultural apprehension research: A summary of Pacific Basin studies. In J. A. Daly & J. C. McCroskey (Eds.), *Avoiding communication: Shyness, reticence, and communication apprehension* (pp. 157-169). Beverly Hills, CA: Sage.

Knowles, E. D., Morris, M. W., Chiu, C., & Hong, Y. (2001). Culture and the process of person perception: Evidence for automaticity among East Asians in correcting for situational influences on behavior. *Personality and Social Psychology Bulletin, 27,* 1344-1356.

Kobak, R. R., & Sceery, A. (1988). Attachment in late adolescence: Working models, affect regulation, and representations of self and others. *Child Development, 95,* 135-146.

Kochanska, G. (1997). Mutually responsive orientation between mothers and their young children: Implications for early socialization. *Child Development, 68,* 94-112.

Koestner, R., Bernieri, F., & Zuckerman, M. (1989). Trait-specific versus person-specific moderators of cross-situational consistency. *Journal of Personality, 57,* 1-16.

Kohler, G., & Ruch, W. (1996). Sources of variance in current sense of humor inventories: How much substance, how much method variance? *Humor: International Journal of Humor Research, 9,* 363-397.

Kowalski, R. M., & Brown, K. J. (1994). Psychosocial barriers to cervical cancer screening: Concerns with self-presentation and social evaluation. *Journal of Applied Social Psychology, 24,* 941-958.

Kraut, R. E., & Price, J. D. (1976). Machiavellianism in parents and their children. *Journal of Personality and Social Psychology, 33,* 782-786.

Kring, A. M., & Gordon, A. H. (1998). Sex differences in emotion: Expression, experience, and physiology. *Journal of Personality and Social Psychology, 74,* 686-703.

Kunkel, A. W., & Burleson, B. R. (1999). Assessing explanations for sex differences in emotional support: A test of the different cultures and skills specialization accounts. *Human Communication Research, 25,* 307-340.

Lamborn, S. D., Mounts, N. S., Steinberg, L., & Dornbusch, S. M. (1991). Patterns of competence and adjustment among adolescents from authoritative, authoritarian, indulgent, and neglectful families. *Child Development, 62,* 1049-1065.

Lamke, L. (1989). Marital adjustment among rural couples: The role of expressiveness. *Sex Roles, 21,* 579-590.

Lamke, L., & Bell, N. (1982). Sex role orientation and relationship development in same-sex dyads. *Journal of Research in Personality, 16,* 343-354.

Lane, J. D., & DePaulo, B. M. (1999). Completing Coyne's cycle: Dysphorics' ability to detect deception. *Journal of Research in Personality, 33,* 311-329.

Larson, J. H., Anderson, S. M., Holman, T. B., & Niemann, B. K. (1998). A longitudinal study of the effects of premarital communication, relationship stability, and self-esteem on sexual satisfaction in the first year of marriage. *Journal of Sex and Marital Therapy, 24,* 193-206.

Leary, M. R. (1983). *Understanding social anxiety.* Beverly Hills, CA: Sage.

Leary, M. R., Knight, P. D., & Johnson, K. A. (1987). Social anxiety and dyadic conversation: A verbal response analysis. *Journal of Social and Clinical Psychology, 5,* 34-50.

Leary, T. (1957). *The interpersonal diagnosis of personality.* New York: Ronald.

Leck, K., & Simpson, J. A. (1999). Feigning romantic interest: The role of self-monitoring. *Journal of Research in Personality 33,* 69-91.

Lee, J. A. (1973). *The colors of love: An exploration of the ways of loving.* Don Mills, ON: New Press.

Lefcourt, H. M., Martin, R. A., & Fick, C. M. (1985). Locus of control for affiliation and behavior in social interactions. *Journal of Personality and Social Psychology, 48,* 755-759.

LePine, J. A., & Van Dyne, L. (2001). Voice and cooperative behavior as contrasting forms of contextual performance: Evidence of differential relationships with Big Five personality characteristics and cognitive ability. *Journal of Applied Psychology, 86,* 326-336.

Le Poire, B. A., Haynes, J., Driscoll, J., Driver, B. N., Wheelis, T. F., Hyde, M. K., et al. (1997). Attachment as a function of parental and partner approach-avoidance tendencies. *Human Communication Research, 23,* 413-444.

Le Poire, B. A., Shepard, C. A., & Duggan, A. (1999). Nonverbal involvement, expressiveness, and pleasantness as predicted by parental and partner attachment style. *Communication Monographs, 66,* 293-311.

Lewin, K. (1935). *Dynamic theory of personality.* New York: McGraw-Hill.

Lippa, R. (1978). Expressive control, expressive consistency, and the correspondence between expressive behavior and personality. *Journal of Personality, 46,* 438-461.

Loehlin, J. C., & Nichols, R. C. (1976). *Heredity, environment, and personality: A study of 850 sets of twins.* Austin: University of Texas Press.

Long, E. C. J., & Andrews, D. W. (1990). Perspective taking as a predictor of marital adjustment. *Journal of Personality and Social Psychology, 59,* 126-131.

Lundy, J. R. (1972). Some personality correlates of contraceptive use among unmarried female college students. *Journal of Psychology, 80,* 9-14.

Lynn, R., & Martin, T. (1997). Gender differences in extraversion, neuroticism, and psychoticism in 37 countries. *Journal of Social Psychology, 137,* 369-373.

Maccoby, E. E., & Jacklin, C. N. (1974). *The psychology of sex differences.* Stanford, CA: Stanford University Press.

Maccoby, E. E., & Martin, J. (1983). Socialization in the context of the family: Parent-child interaction. In P. H. Mussen (Series Ed.) & E. M. Hetherington (Vol. Ed.), *Handbook of child psychology: Vol. 4. Socialization, personality, and social development* (4th ed., pp. 1-101). New York: John Wiley.

Magai, C., Distel, N., & Liker, R. (1995). Emotion socialization, attachment, and patterns of adult emotional traits. *Cognition and Emotion, 9,* 461-481.

Magnusson, D., & Endler, N. S. (1977). *Personality at the crossroads: Current issues in interactional psychology.* Hillsdale, NJ: Lawrence Erlbaum.

Maltby, J., & Day, L. (2000). The reliability and validity of a susceptibility to embarrassment scale among adults. *Personality and Individual Differences, 29,* 749-756.

Markus, H. R., & Kitayama, S. (1991). Culture and self: Implications for cognition, emotion, and motivation. *Psychological Review, 98,* 224-253.

Marsh, H. W. (1989). Age and sex effects in multiple dimensions of self-concept. Preadolescence to early adulthood. *Journal of Educational Psychology, 81,* 417-430.

Martin, M. M., & Anderson, C. M. (1995). Roommate similarity: Are roommates who are similar in the communication traits more satisfied? *Communication Research Reports, 12,* 46-52.

Martin, M. M., Anderson, C. M., Burant, P. A., & Weber, K. (1997). Verbal aggression in sibling relationships. *Communication Quarterly, 45,* 304-317.

Martin, M. M., Anderson, C. M., & Thweatt, K. S. (1998). Aggressive communication traits and their relationships with the cognitive flexibility scale and the communication flexibility scale. *Journal of Social Behavior and Personality, 13,* 531-540.

Martin, R. A. (2001). Humor, laughter, and physical health: Methodological issues and research findings. *Psychological Bulletin, 127,* 504-519.

Mayer, J. D., DiPaulo, M., & Salovey, P. (1990). Perceiving affective content in ambiguous visual stimuli: A component of emotional intelligence. *Journal of Personality Assessment, 54,* 772-781.

Mayer, J. D., & Salovey, P. (1997). What is emotional intelligence? In P. Salovey & D. J. Sluyter (Eds.), *Emotional development and emotional intelligence: Educational implications* (pp. 3-34). New York: Basic Books.

McAdams, D. P. (1980). A thematic coding system for the intimacy motive. *Journal of Research in Personality, 14,* 413-432.

McAdams, D. P. (1992). The intimacy motive. In C. P. Smith (Ed.), *Motivation and personality: Handbook of thematic content analysis* (pp. 224-228). New York: Cambridge University Press.

McClelland, D. C. (1986). *Human motivation.* New York: Cambridge University Press.

McClure, E. B. (2000). A meta-analytic review of sex differences in facial expression processing and their development in infants, children, and adolescents. *Psychological Bulletin, 126,* 424-453.

McCrae, R. R., Costa, P. T., del Pilar, G. H., Rolland, J. P., & Parker, W. D. (1998). Cross-cultural assessment of the five-factor model: The revised NEO Personality Inventory. *Journal of Cross-Cultural Psychology, 29,* 171-188.

McCrae, R. R., & John, O. P. (1992). An introduction to the five-factor model and its applications. *Journal of Personality, 60,* 175-215.

McCroskey, J. C., & Andersen, J. (1976). The relationship between communication apprehension and academic achievement among college students. *Human Communication Research, 3,* 214-226.

McCroskey, J. C., Andersen, J., Richmond, V. P., & Wheeless, L. R. (1981). Communication apprehension of elementary and secondary students and teachers. *Communication Education, 30,* 122-132.

McCroskey, J. C., Daly, J. A., Richmond, V. P., & Falcione, R. L. (1977). Studies of the relationship between communication apprehension and self-esteem. *Human Communication Research, 3,* 269-277.

McCroskey, J. C., Fayer, J. M., & Richmond, V. P. (1985). Don't speak to me in English: Communication apprehension in Puerto Rico. *Communication Quarterly, 33,* 185-192.

McCroskey, J. C., & Richmond, V. P. (1979). The impact of communication apprehension on individuals in organizations. *Communication Quarterly, 27,* 55-61.

McCroskey, J. C., & Richmond, V. P. (1998). Willingness to communicate. In J. C. McCroskey, J. A. Daly, M. M. Martin, & M. J. Beatty (Eds.), *Communication and personality: Trait perspectives* (pp. 119-132). Cresskill, NJ: Hampton.

McCullough, M. E. (2001). Forgiveness: Who does it and how do they do it. *Current Directions in Psychological Science, 10,* 194-197.

McGuire, S., & Clifford, J. (2000). Genetic and environmental contributions to loneliness in children. *Psychological Science, 11,* 487-491.

McGuire, W. J., & McGuire, C. V. (1981). The spontaneous self-concept as affected by personal distinctiveness. In M. Lynch, A. A. Norem-Hebeisen, & K. J. Gergen (Eds.), *Self-concept: Advances in theory and research.* Cambridge: Cambridge University Press.

McLeod, J. M., & Chaffee, S. H. (1972). The construction of social reality. In J. T. Tedeschi (Ed.), *The social influence process* (pp. 50-99). Chicago: Aldine.

Meleshko, K. G. A., & Alden, L. E. (1993). Anxiety and self-disclosure: Toward a motivational model. *Journal of Personality and Social Psychology, 64,* 1000-1009.

Messer, S. C., & Gross, A. M. (1995). Childhood depression and family interaction: A naturalistic observation study. *Journal of Clinical Child Psychology, 24,* 77-88.

Messman, S., & Jones-Corley, J. (2001). Effects of communication environment, immediacy, and communication apprehension on cognitive and affective learning. *Communication Monographs, 68,* 184-200.

Mikulincer, M. (1998). Attachment working models and the sense of trust: An exploration of interaction goals and affect regulation. *Journal of Personality and Social Psychology, 74,* 1209-1224.

Mikulincer, M., Florian, V., & Weller, A. (1993). Attachment styles, coping strategies, and posttraumatic psychological stress: The impact of the Gulf War in Israel. *Journal of Personality and Social Psychology, 64,* 817-826.

Miller, J. B., & Noirot, M. (1999). Attachment memories, models, and information processing. *Journal of Social and Personal Relationships, 16,* 147-173.

Miller, J. G. (1984). Culture and the development of everyday social explanation. *Journal of Personality and Social Psychology, 46,* 961-978.

Miller, P. C., Lefcourt, H. M., Holmes, J. G., Ware, E. E., & Saleh, W. E. (1986). Marital locus of control and marital problem solving. *Journal of Personality and Social Psychology, 51,* 161-169.

Miller, P. C., Lefcourt, H. M., & Ware, E. E. (1983). The construction and development of the Miller Marital Locus of Control Scale. *Canadian Journal of Behavioral Science, 15,* 266-279.

Mills, J., & Clark, M. S. (1994). Communal and exchange relationships: Controversies and research. In R. Erber & R. Gilmour (Eds.), *Theoretical frameworks for personal relationships* (pp. 29-42). Hillsdale, NJ: Lawrence Erlbaum.

Mischel, W. (1968). *Personality and assessment.* New York: John Wiley.

Mischel, W. (1999). Personality coherence and dispositions in a cognitive-affective personality system (CAPS) approach. In D. Cervone & Y. Shoda (Eds.), *The coherence of personality: Social-cognitive bases of consistency, variability, and organization* (pp. 37-60). New York: Guilford.

Morrow, G. D., Clark, E. M., & Brock, K. F. (1995). Individual and partner love styles: Implications for the quality of romantic involvement. *Journal of Social and Personal Relationships, 12,* 363-387.

Moskowitz, D. S., Suh, E. J., & Desaulniers, J. (1994). Situational influences on gender differences in agency and communion. *Journal of Personality and Social Psychology, 66,* 753-761.

Mount, K. L., & Barrick, M. R. (1995). The Big Five personality dimensions: Implications for the research and practice of human resource management. In G. R. Ferris (Ed.), *Research in personnel and human resources management* (Vol. 13, pp. 153-200). Stamford, CT: JAI.

Mulac, A., Bradac, J. J., & Gibbons, P. (2001). Empirical support for the gender-as-culture hypothesis. *Human Communication Research, 27,* 121-152.

Myers, S. A. (1998). Instructor socio-communicative style, argumentativeness, and verbal aggressiveness in the classroom. *Communication Research Reports, 15,* 141-150.

Myers, S. A., & Knox, R. L. (2000). Perceived instructor argumentativeness and verbal aggressiveness and student outcomes. *Communication Research Reports, 17,* 299-309.

Myers, S. M., & Booth, A. (1999). Marital strains and marital quality: The role of high and low locus of control. *Journal of Marriage and the Family, 61,* 423-436.

Nardi, P. M., & Sherrod, D. (1994). Friendships in the lives of gay men and lesbians. *Journal of Social and Personal Relationships, 11,* 185-200.

Neuliep, J. W., & Ryan, D. J. (1998). The influence of intercultural communication apprehension and socio-communicative orientation on uncertainty reduction during initial cross-cultural interaction. *Communication Quarterly, 46,* 88-99.

Newsome, S., Day, A. L., & Catano, V. M. (2000). Assessing the predictive value of emotional intelligence. *Personality and Individual Differences, 29,* 1005-1016.

Nezlek, J. B., Imbrie, M., & Shean, G. D. (1994). Depression and everyday social interaction. *Journal of Personality and Social Psychology, 67,* 1101-1111.

Ng, S. H., & Bradac, J. J. (1993). *Power in language: Verbal communication and social influence.* Newbury Park, CA: Sage.

Ng, S. H., Liu, J. H., Weatherall, A., & Loong, C. S. (1997). Younger adults' communication experiences and contact with elders and peers. *Human Communication Research, 24,* 82-108.

Nicotera, A. M., & Rancer, A. S. (1994). The influence of sex on self-perceptions and social stereotyping of aggressive communication predispositions. *Western Journal of Communication, 58,* 283-307.

Nolen-Hoeksema, S. (1987). Sex differences in unipolar depression: Evidence and theory. *Psychological Bulletin, 101,* 259-282.

Nolen-Hoeksema, S. (2001). Gender differences in depression. *Current Directions in Psychological Science, 10,* 173-176.

Noller, P., Feeney, J. A., Bonnell, D., & Callan, V. J. (1994). A longitudinal study of conflict in early marriage. *Journal of Social and Personal Relationships, 11,* 233-252.

Noller, P., & Fitzpatrick, M. A. (1990). Marital communication in the eighties. *Journal of Marriage and the Family, 52,* 832-843.

Norman, W. T. (1963). Toward a taxonomy of personality attributes. *Journal of Abnormal and Social Psychology, 66,* 574-583.

Norton, R. W. (1978). Foundations of a communicator style construct. *Human Communication Research, 4,* 99-112.

Notarius, C. I., Benson, S., Sloane, D., Vanzetti, N., & Hornyak, L. (1989). Exploring the interface between perception and behavior: An analysis of marital interactions in distressed and nondistressed couples. *Behavioral Assessment, 11,* 39-64.

Oetzel, J. G. (1998). Explaining individual communication processes in homogeneous and heterogeneous groups through individualism-collectivism and self-construals. *Human Communication Research, 25,* 202-224.

O'Keefe, B. J. (1988). The logic of message design: Individual differences in reasoning about communication. *Communication Monographs, 55,* 80-103.

O'Keefe, B. J., Delia, J. G., & O'Keefe, D. J. (1977). Construct individuality, cognitive complexity, and the formation and remembering of interpersonal impressions. *Social Behavior and Personality, 5,* 229-240.

O'Keefe, B. J., & Lambert, B. L. (1995). Managing the flow of ideas: A local management approach to message design. In B. R. Burleson (Ed.), *Communication yearbook 18* (pp. 54-82). Thousand Oaks, CA: Sage.

O'Keefe, B. J., & Shepherd, G. J. (1989). The communication of identity during face-to-face persuasive interactions: Effects of perceiver's construct differentiation and target's message strategies. *Communication Research, 16,* 375-404.

Okun, M. A., Shepard, S. A., & Eisenberg, N. (2000). The relations of emotionality and regulation to dispositional empathy-related responding among volunteers-in-training. *Personality and Individual Differences, 28,* 367-382.

Olson, J. M., Vernon, P. A., Harris, J. A., & Jang, K. L. (2001). The heritability of attitudes: A study of twins. *Journal of Personality and Social Psychology, 80,* 845-861.

Ones, D. S., & Viswesvaran, C. (1996). Bandwidth-fidelity dilemma in personality measurement for personnel selection. *Journal of Organizational Behavior, 17,* 609-626.

Onyekwere, E. O., Rubin, R. B., & Infante, D. A. (1981). Interpersonal perception and communication satisfaction as a function of argumentativeness and ego-involvement. *Communication Quarterly, 39,* 35-47.

Page, J. R., Stevens, H. B., & Galvin, S. L. (1997). Relationships between depression, self-esteem, and self-silencing behavior. *Journal of Social and Clinical Psychology, 15,* 381-396.

Paley, B., Cox, M. J., Burchinal, M. R., & Payne, C. C. (1999). Attachment and marital functioning: Comparison of spouses with continuous-secure, earned-secure, dismissing, and preoccupied attachment stances. *Journal of Family Psychology, 13,* 580-597.

Park, H. S., & Levine, T. R. (1999). The theory of reasoned action and self-construal: Evidence from three cultures. *Communication Monographs, 66,* 199-218.

Paunonen, S. V., & Ashton, M. C. (2001). Big Five factors and facets and the prediction of behavior. *Journal of Personality and Social Psychology, 81,* 524-539.

Paunonen, S. V., & Jackson, D. N. (2000). What is beyond the Big Five? Plenty! *Journal of Personality, 68,* 821-835.

Paunonen, S. V., Rothstein, M. G., & Jackson, D. N. (1999). Narrow reasoning about the use of broad personality measures in personnel selection. *Journal of Organizational Behavior, 20,* 389-405.

Pavot, W., Diener, E., & Fujita, F. (1990). Extraversion and happiness. *Personality and Individual Differences, 11,* 1299-1306.

Pearson, J. L., Cohn, D. A., Cowan, P. A., & Cowan, C. P. (1994). Earned- and continuous-security in adult attachment: Relation to depressive symptomatology and parenting style. *Development and Psychopathology, 6,* 359-373.

Perlman, D., & Peplau, L. A. (1981). Towards a social psychology of loneliness. In S. Duck & R. Gilmour (Eds.), *Personal relationships in disorders* (pp. 31-56). London: Academic Press.

Persad, S. M., & Polivy, J. (1993). Differences between depressed and nondepressed individuals in the recognition of and response to facial emotional cues. *Journal of Abnormal Psychology, 102,* 358-368.

Pfau, M., Van Bockern, S., & Kang, J. G. (1992). Use of inoculation to promote resistance to smoking initiation among adolescents. *Communication Monographs, 59,* 213-230.

Pilkonis, P. A., Heape, C., & Klein, R. H. (1980). Treating shyness and other psychiatric difficulties in psychiatric outpatients. *Communication Education, 29,* 250-255.

Pincus, A. L., & Gurtman, M. B. (1995). The three faces of interpersonal dependency: Structural analysis of self-report dependency measures. *Journal of Personality and Social Psychology, 69,* 744-758.

Plomin, R., DeFries, J. C., & McClearn, G. E. (1990). *Behavioral genetics: A primer.* New York: Freeman.

Powers, W. G., & Love, D. E. (2000). Communication apprehension in the dating partner context. *Communication Research Reports, 17,* 221-228.

Rahim, M., & Magner, N. (1995). Confirmatory factor analysis of the styles of handling interpersonal conflict: First-order factor model and its invariance across groups. *Journal of Applied Psychology, 80,* 122-132.

Rancer, A. S. (1998). Argumentativeness. In J. C. McCroskey, J. A. Daly, M. M. Martin, & M. J. Beatty (Eds.), *Communication and personality: Trait perspectives* (pp. 149-170). Cresskill, NJ: Hampton.

Rancer, A. S., Kosberg, R. L., & Baukus, R. A. (1992). Beliefs about arguing as predictors of trait argumentativeness: Implications for training in argument and conflict management. *Communication Education, 41,* 375-387.

Rancer, A. S., Kosberg, R. L., & Silvestri, V. N. (1992). The relationship between self-esteem and aggressive communication predispositions. *Communication Research Reports, 9,* 23-32.

Regan, P. C. (1998). Minimum mate selection standards as a function of perceived mate value, relationship context, and gender. *Journal of Psychology and Human Sexuality, 10,* 53-73.

Rhodes, N., & Wood, W. (1992). Self-esteem and intelligence affect influenceability: The mediating role of message reception. *Psychological Bulletin, 111,* 156-171.

Rholes, W. S., Simpson, J. A., Campbell, L., & Grich, J. (2001). Adult attachment and the transition to parenthood. *Journal of Personality and Social Psychology, 81,* 421-435.

Rholes, W. S., Simpson, J. A., & Orina, M. M. (1999). Attachment and anger in an anxiety-provoking situation. *Journal of Personality and Social Psychology, 76,* 940-957.

Richmond, V. P., & Martin, M. M. (1998). Sociocommunicative style and sociocommunicative orientation. In J. C. McCroskey, J. A. Daly, M. M. Martin, & M. J. Beatty (Eds.), *Communication and personality: Trait perspectives* (pp. 133-147). Cresskill, NJ: Hampton.

Rickman, M. D., & Davidson, R. J. (1994). Personality and behavior in parents of temperamentally inhibited and uninhibited children. *Developmental Psychology, 30,* 346-354.

Riggio, R. E. (1986). Assessment of basic social skills. *Journal of Personality and Social Psychology, 51,* 649-660.

Riggio, R. E., & Friedman, H. S. (1982). The interrelationships of self-monitoring factors, personality traits, and nonverbal social skills. *Journal of Nonverbal Behavior, 7,* 33-45.

Ritchie, L. D., & Fitzpatrick, M. A. (1990). Family communication patterns: Measuring intrapersonal perceptions of interpersonal relationships. *Communication Research, 17,* 523-544.

Roberts, J. E., Gotlib, I. H., & Kassel, J. D. (1996). Adult attachment security and symptoms of depression: The mediating role of dysfunctional attitudes and low self-esteem. *Journal of Personality and Social Psychology, 70,* 310-320.

Robins, C. J., Ladd, J., Welkowitz, J., Blaney, P. H., Diaz, R., & Kutcher, G. (1994). The Personal Style Inventory: Preliminary validation studies of a new measure of sociotropy and autonomy. *Journal of Psychopathology and Behavioral Assessment, 16,* 277-300.

Robins, R. W., Caspi, A., & Moffitt, T. E. (2000). Two personalities, one relationship: Both partners' personality traits shape the quality of their relationship. *Journal of Personality and Social Psychology, 79,* 251-259.

Roger, D., & Najarian, B. (1989). The construction and validation of a new scale for measuring emotion control. *Personality and Individual Differences, 10,* 845-853.

Rokeach, M. (1960). *The open and closed mind: Investigations into the nature of belief systems and personality systems.* New York: Basic Books.

Rosenstein, P. (1995). Parental levels of empathy as related to risk assessment in child protective services. *Child Abuse & Neglect, 19,* 1349-1360.

Ross, M., & Holmberg, D. (1990). Recounting the past: Gender differences in the recall of events in the history of a close relationship. In J. M. Olson & M. P. Zanna (Eds.), *The Ontario Symposium: Vol. 6. Self-inference processes* (pp. 135-152). Hillsdale, NJ: Lawrence Erlbaum.

Rotenberg, K. J., Shewchuk, V., & Kimberly, T. (2001). Loneliness, sex, romantic jealousy, and powerlessness. *Journal of Social and Personal Relationships, 18,* 55-79.

Rotter, J. B. (1966). Generalized expectancies for internal and external control of reinforcement. *Psychological Monographs, 80,* 1-28.

Rubin, M., & Hewstone, M. (1998). Social identity theory's self-esteem hypothesis: A review and some suggestions for clarification. *Personality and Social Psychology Review, 2,* 40-62.

Rudd, J. E., Vogl-Bauser, S., Dobos, J. A., Beatty, M. J., & Valencic, K. M. (1998). Interactive effects of parents' trait verbal aggressiveness and situational frustration on parents' self-reported anger. *Communication Quarterly, 46,* 1-11.

Russell, D. W., Cutrona, C. E., & Jones, W. H. (1986). A trait-situational analysis of shyness. In W. H. Jones, J. M. Cheek, & S. R. Briggs (Eds.), *Shyness: Perspectives on research and treatment* (pp. 239-249). New York: Plenum.

Ryan, E. B., Hummert, M. L., & Boich, L. H. (1995). Communication predicaments of aging: Patronizing behavior toward older adults. *Journal of Language and Social Psychology, 14,* 144-166.

Sabourin, T. C., Infante, D. A., & Rudd, J. E. (1993). Verbal aggression in marriages: A comparison of violent, distressed but nonviolent, and nondistressed couples. *Human Communication Research, 20,* 245-267.

Salovey, P., & Mayer, J. D. (1990). Emotional intelligence. *Imagination, Cognition, and Personality, 9,* 185-211.

Saucier, G., & Goldberg, L. R. (1998). What is beyond the Big Five? *Journal of Personality, 66,* 495-524.

Scarr, S., Webber, P. L., Weinberg, R. A., & Wittig, M. A. (1981). Personality resemblance among adolescents and their parents in biologically related and adoptive families. *Journal of Personality and Social Psychology, 40,* 885-898.

Scarr, S., & Weinberg, R. A. (1981). The transmission of authoritarianism in families: Genetic resemblance in social-political attitudes. In S. Scarr (Ed.), *Race, social class, and individual differences in I.Q.* (pp. 399-427). Hillsdale, NJ: Lawrence Erlbaum.

Scherwitz, L., Perkins, L., Chesney, M., & Hughes, G. (1991). Cook-Medley Hostility Scale and subsets: Relationship to demographic and psychosocial characteristics in young adults in the CARDIA study. *Psychosomatic Medicine, 53,* 36-49.

Schmidt, L. A., & Fox, N. A. (1995). Individual differences in young adults' shyness and sociability: Personality and health correlates. *Personality and Individual Differences, 19,* 455-462.

Schneier, F. R., Johnson, J., Hornig, C. D., Liebowitz, M. R., & Weissman, M. M. (1992). Social phobia: Comorbidity and morbidity in an epidemiologic sample. *Archives of General Psychiatry, 49*, 282-288.

Schroeder, J. E., & Ketrow, S. M. (1997). Social anxiety and performance in an interpersonal perception task. *Psychological Reports, 81*, 991-996.

Schultz, B. (1982). Argumentativeness: Its effect in group decision-making and its role in leadership perceptions. *Communication Quarterly, 30*, 368-375.

Schultz, N. R., & Moore, D. (1986). The loneliness experience of college students: Sex differences. *Personality and Social Psychology Bulletin, 12*, 111-119.

Schwartz, S. H. (1999). A theory of cultural values and some implications for work. *Applied Psychology, 48*, 23-47.

Segrin, C. (1990). A meta-analytic review of social skills deficits in depression. *Communication Monographs, 57*, 292-308.

Segrin, C. (1996). The relationship between social skills deficits and psychosocial problems: A test of the vulnerability model. *Communication Research, 23*, 425-450.

Segrin, C., & Abramson, L. Y. (1994). Negative reactions to depressive behaviors: A communication theories analysis. *Journal of Abnormal Psychology, 103*, 655-668.

Shields, C. G., Franks, P., Harp, J. J., Campbell, T. L., & McDaniel, S. H. (1995). Family emotional involvement and criticism scale (FEICS): II. Reliability and validity studies. *Family Systems Medicine, 12*, 361-377.

Shoda, Y., Mischel, W., & Wright, J. C. (1994). Intra-individual stability in the organization and patterning of behavior: Incorporating psychological situations into the idiographic analysis of personality. *Journal of Personality and Social Psychology, 67*, 674-687.

Simpson, J. A., Rholes, S. W., & Nelligan, J. S. (1992). Support seeking and support giving within couples in an anxiety-provoking situation. *Journal of Personality and Social Psychology, 62*, 434-446.

Simpson, J. A., Rholes, S. W., & Phillips, D. (1996). Conflict in close relationships: An attachment perspective. *Journal of Personality and Social Psychology, 71*, 899-914.

Singelis, T. M., & Brown, W. J. (1995). Culture, self, and collectivist communication: Linking culture to individual behavior. *Human Communication Research, 21*, 354-389.

Slesnick, N., & Waldron, H. B. (1997). Interpersonal problem-solving interactions of depressed

adolescents and their parents. *Journal of Family Psychology, 11*, 234-245.

Smalley, R. L., & Stake, J. E. (1996). Evaluating sources of ego-threatening feedback: Self-esteem and narcissism effects. *Journal of Research in Personality, 30*, 483-495.

Smith, R. H., Parrott, W. G., Diener, E. F., Hoyle, R. H., & Kim, S. H. (1999). Dispositional envy. *Personality and Social Psychology Bulletin, 25*, 1007-1020.

Smith-Lovin, L., & Brody, C. (1989). Interruptions in group discussions: The effects of gender and group composition. *American Sociological Review, 54*, 424-435.

Smolen, R. C., & Spiegel, D. A. (1987). Marital locus of control as a modifier of the relationship between the frequency of provocation by spouse and marital satisfaction. *Journal of Research in Personality, 21*, 70-80.

Snyder, M. (1974). Self-monitoring of expressive behavior. *Journal of Personality and Social Psychology, 30*, 526-537.

Snyder, M. (1987). *Public appearances, private realities: The psychology of self-monitoring*. New York: Freeman.

Snyder, M., & Gangestad, S. W. (1986). On the nature of self-monitoring: Matters of assessment, matters of validity. *Journal of Personality and Social Psychology, 51*, 125-139.

Snyder, M., Gangestad, S. W., & Simpson, J. A. (1983). Choosing friends as activity partners: The role of self-monitoring. *Journal of Personality and Social Psychology, 45*, 1061-1072.

Snyder, M., & Simpson, J. A. (1984). Self-monitoring and dating relationships. *Journal of Personality and Social Psychology, 47*, 1281-1291.

Snyder, M., & Simpson, J. A. (1987). Orientations toward romantic relationships. In D. Perlman & S. Duck (Eds.), *Intimate relationships: Development, dynamics, and deterioration* (pp. 45-62). Newbury Park, CA: Sage.

Solano, C. H., Batten, P. G., & Parish, E. A. (1982). Loneliness and the patterns of self-disclosure. *Journal of Personality and Social Psychology, 43*, 524-531.

Solano, C. H., & Koester, N. H. (1989). Loneliness and communication problems: Subjective anxiety or objective skills? *Personality and Social Psychology Bulletin, 15*, 126-133.

Spence, J. (1993). Gender-related traits and gender ideology: Evidence for a multifactorial theory. *Journal of Personality and Social Psychology, 64,* 624-635.

Spitzberg, B. H. (1993). The dialectics of (in)competence. *Journal of Social and Personal Relationships, 10,* 137-158.

Spitzberg, B. H., & Canary, D. (1985). Loneliness and relationally competent communication. *Journal of Social and Personal Relationships, 2,* 387-402.

Spitzberg, B. H., & Hurt, H. T. (1987). The measurement of interpersonal skills in instructional contexts. *Communication Education, 36,* 29-45.

Steinfatt, T. M. (1987). Personality and communication: Classical approaches. In J. C. McCroskey & J. A. Daly (Eds.), *Personality and interpersonal communication* (pp. 42-126). Newbury Park, CA: Sage.

Stephenson, M. T., & Palmgreen, P. (2001). Sensation seeking, perceived message sensation value, personal involvement, and processing of anti-marijuana PSAs. *Communication Monographs, 68,* 49-71.

Stewart, S., Stinnett, H., & Rosenfeld, L. B. (2000). Sex differences in desired characteristics of short-term and long-term relationship partners. *Journal of Social and Personal Relationships, 17,* 843-853.

Stokes, J. P. (1987). The relation of loneliness and self-disclosure. In V. J. Derlega & J. H. Berg (Eds.), *Self-disclosure: Theory, research, and therapy* (pp. 175-201). New York: Plenum.

Sulloway, F. J. (1996). *Born to rebel: Birth order, family dynamics, and creative lives.* New York: Pantheon.

Tarlow, E. M., & Haaga, D. A. F. (1996). Negative self-concept: Specificity to depressive symptoms and relation to positive and negative affectivity. *Journal of Research in Personality, 30,* 120-127.

Tasaki, K., Kim, M.-S., & Miller, M. D. (1999). The effects of social status on cognitive elaboration and post-message attitude: Focusing on self-construals. *Communication Quarterly, 47,* 196-212.

Taylor, D. A., & Belgave, F. Z. (1986). The effects of perceived intimacy and valence on self-disclosure reciprocity. *Personality and Social Psychology Bulletin, 12,* 247-255.

Tellegen, A., Lykken, D. T., Bouchard, T. J., Jr., Wilcox, K. J., Segal, N. L., & Rich, S. (1988). Personality similarity in twins reared apart and together. *Journal of Personality and Social Psychology, 54,* 1031-1039.

Thoits, P. A. (1995). Stress, coping, and social support processes: Where are we? What next? *Journal of Health and Social Behavior* [extra issue], pp. 53-79.

Thompson, J. M., Whiffen, V. E., & Blain, M. D. (1995). Depressive symptoms, sex, and perceptions of intimate relationships. *Journal of Social and Personal Relationships, 12,* 49-66.

Thorndike, E. L. (1920). Intelligence and its uses. *Harper's Magazine, 140,* 227-235.

Ting-Toomey, S., Gao, G., Trubinsky, P., Yang, Z., Kim, H. S., Lin, S. L., & Nishida, T. (1991). Culture, face maintenance, and styles of handling interpersonal conflict: A study of five cultures. *International Journal of Conflict Management, 2,* 275-296.

Triandis, H. C. (1995). *Individualism and collectivism.* Boulder, CO: Westview.

Trobst, K. K., Collins, R. L., & Embree, J. M. (1994). The role of emotion in social support provision: Gender, empathy, and expressions of distress. *Journal of Social and Personal Relationships, 11,* 45-62.

Turner, R. J., & Noh, S. (1983). Class and psychological vulnerability among women: The significance of social support and personal control. *Journal of Health and Social Behavior, 33,* 10-24.

Turner, S. M., Beidel, D. C., & Larkin, K. T. (1986). Situational determinants of social anxiety in clinic and nonclinic samples: Physiological and cognitive correlates. *Behavioral Research and Therapy, 24,* 56-64.

Turnley, W. H., & Bolino, M. C. (2001). Achieving desired images while avoiding undesired images: Exploring the role of self-monitoring in impression management. *Journal of Applied Psychology, 86,* 351-360.

Twenge, J. M. (2001). Changes in women's assertiveness in response to status and role: A cross-temporal meta-analysis, 1931-1993. *Journal of Personality and Social Psychology, 81,* 133-145.

Umberson, D. (1993). Sociodemographic position, world views, and psychological distress. *Social Science Quarterly, 74,* 576-589.

Valencic, K. M., Beatty, M. J., Rudd, J. E., Dobos, J. A., & Heisel, A. D. (1998). An empirical test of a communibiological model of trait verbal aggressiveness. *Communication Quarterly, 46,* 327-341.

van der Zee, K. I., & van Oudenhoven, J. P. (2001). The multicultural personality questionnaire: Reliability and validity of self- and other ratings of multicultural effectiveness. *Journal of Research in Personality, 35,* 278-288.

Vangelisti, A. L., & Daly, J. A. (1988). Correlates of speaking skills in the United States: A national assessment. *Communication Education, 38,* 132-144.

Vangelisti, A. L., & Daly, J. A. (1997). Gender differences in standards for romantic relationships. *Personal Relationships, 4,* 203-219.

Vangelisti, A. L., Knapp, M. L., & Daly, J. A. (1990). Conversational narcissism. *Communication Monographs, 57,* 251-274.

Vassend, O., & Skrondal, A. (1997). Validation of the NEO Personality Inventory and the five-factor model: Can findings from exploratory and confirmatory factor analysis be reconciled? *European Journal of Personality, 11,* 147-166.

Vikers, K. S., & Vogeltanz, N. D. (2000). Dispositional optimism as a predictor of depressive symptoms over time. *Personality and Individual Differences, 28,* 259-272.

Vitkus, J., & Horowitz, L. M. (1987). Poor social performance of lonely people: Lacking a skill or adopting a role? *Journal of Personality and Social Psychology, 52,* 1266-1273.

Wagner, H. L., MacDonald, C. J., & Manstead, A. S. R. (1986). Communication of individual emotions by spontaneous facial expressions. *Journal of Personality and Social Psychology, 50,* 737-743.

Wallston, K. A., & Wallston, B. S. (1981). Health locus of control scales. In H. M. Lefcourt (Ed.), *Research with the locus of control construct* (Vol. 1, pp. 189-243). New York: Academic Press.

Watson, A. K., & Cheek, J. M. (1986). Shyness situations: Perspectives of a diverse sample of shy females. *Psychological Reports, 59,* 1040-1042.

Watson, A. K., Monroe, E. E., & Atterstrom, H. (1989). Comparison of communication apprehension across cultures: American and Swedish children. *Communication Quarterly, 37,* 67-76.

Watson, D., & Clark, L. A. (1997). Extraversion and its positive emotional core. In R. Hogan, J. Johnson, & S. R. Briggs (Eds.). *Handbook of personality psychology* (pp. 751-793). San Diego, CA: Academic Press.

Watson, D., Clark, L. A., & Tellegen, A. (1988). Development and validation of brief measures of positive and negative affect: The PANAS Scales. *Journal of Personality and Social Psychology, 54,* 1063-1070.

Watson, D., Hubbard, B., & Wiese, D. (2000). General traits of personality and affectivity as predictors of satisfaction in intimate relationships: Evidence from self- and partner ratings. *Journal of Personality, 68,* 413-449.

Weiss, R. S. (1975). *Loneliness: The experience of emotional and social isolation.* Cambridge: MIT Press.

Wheeless, L. R. (1975). An investigation of receiver apprehension and social context dimensions of communication apprehension. *Speech Teacher, 24,* 261-268.

Wheeless, L. R. (1978). A follow-up study of the relationship among trust, disclosure, and interpersonal solidarity. *Human Communication Research, 4,* 143-157.

Wheeless, L. R., Preiss, R. W., & Gale, B. M. (1997). Receiver apprehension, informational receptivity, and cognitive processing. In J. A. Daly, J. C. McCroskey, J. Ayres, T. Hopf, & D. M. Ayres (Eds.), *Avoiding communication: Shyness, reticence, and communication apprehension* (2nd ed., pp. 151-187). Cresskill, NJ: Hampton.

White, G. L., & Mullen, P. E. (1989). *Jealousy: Theory, research, and clinical strategies.* New York: Guilford.

Wiggins, J. S. (1979). A psychological taxonomy of trait-descriptive terms: The interpersonal domain. *Journal of Personality and Social Psychology, 37,* 395-412.

Wiggins, J. S., & Trobst, K. K. (1997). When is a circumplex an "interpersonal circumplex"? The case of supportive actions. In R. Plutchik & H. Conte (Eds.), *Circumplex models of personality and emotions* (pp. 57-80). Washington, DC: American Psychological Association.

Wigley, C. J. (1995). Disclosiveness, willingness to communicate, and communication apprehension as predictors of jury selection in felony trials. *Communication Quarterly, 43,* 342-352.

Wigley, C. J. (1998). Verbal aggressiveness. In J. C. McCroskey, J. A. Daly, M. M. Martin, & M. J. Beatty (Eds.), *Communication and personality: Trait perspectives* (pp. 191-214). Cresskill, NJ: Hampton.

Wigley, C. J. (1999). Verbal aggressiveness and communicator style characteristics of summoned jurors as predictors of actual jury selection. *Communication Monographs, 66,* 265-275.

Wigley, C. J., Pohl, G. H., & Watt, M. G. S. (1989). Conversational sensitivity as a correlate of trait verbal aggressiveness and the predisposition to verbally praise others. *Communication Reports, 2,* 92-95.

Winkler, I., & Doherty, W. J. (1983). Communication styles and marital satisfaction in Israeli and American couples. *Family Process, 22,* 221-228.

Wittenberg, M. T., & Reis, H. T. (1986). Loneliness, social skills, and social perception. *Personality and Social Psychology Bulletin, 12,* 121-130.

Wolfson, S. L. (1981). Effects of Machiavellianism and communication on helping behavior during an emergency. *British Journal of Social Psychology, 20,* 189-195.

Wood, W. (1987). Meta-analytic review of sex differences in group performance. *Psychological Bulletin, 102,* 53-71.

Woods, E. (1996). Association of nonverbal decoding ability with indices of person-centered communicative ability. *Communication Reports, 9,* 13-22.

Wright, T. M., & Reise, S. P. (1997). Personality and unrestricted sexual behavior: Correlations of sociosexuality in Caucasian and Asian college students. *Journal of Research in Personality, 31,* 166-192.

Yamada, H. (1990). Topic management and turn distribution in business meetings: American versus Japanese strategies. *Text, 10,* 271-295.

Zaccaro, S. J., Foti, R. J., & Kenny, D. A. (1991). Self-monitoring and trait-based variance in leadership: An investigation of leader flexibility across multiple group situations. *Journal of Applied Psychology, 76,* 308-315.

Zahn-Waxler, C. (2000). The development of empathy, guilt, and internalization of distress: Implications for gender differences in internalizing and externalizing problems. In R. Davidson (Ed.), *Wisconsin Symposium on Emotion: Vol. 1. Anxiety, depression, and emotion* (pp. 222-265). Oxford: Oxford University Press.

Zellars, K. L., & Perrewe, P. L. (2001). Affective personality and the content of emotional social support: Coping in organizations. *Journal of Applied Psychology, 86,* 459-467.

Goals and Knowledge Structures in Social Interaction

CHARLES R. BERGER

Few would dispute the postulates that social interaction is a goal-directed activity and that various kinds of knowledge are vital to the achievement of the goals people pursue in their daily encounters with others. Knowing what to do and say and when and how to do and say it while conversing with a specific individual or a group of individuals is crucial to interaction success. In fashioning their actions, verbal messages, and nonverbal messages to achieve their goals, communicators must have knowledge about the backgrounds, habits, preferences, opinions, dispositions and interaction proclivities of their interaction partners. Moreover, they must have a substantial fund of knowledge about interaction procedures and strategies and the social contexts within which they are

interacting in order to reach their goals successfully. The idea that interaction skills can be taught and learned is itself predicated on the twin assumptions that these skills are both knowable and can be acquired.

The notion that those involved in social relationships may co-construct relationship realities as they interact in no way diminishes the importance of individuals' funds of knowledge to the successful conduct of social interaction (Murray & Holmes, 1996). People do not enter each new conversation as tabulae rasae. They employ prior knowledge to produce and interpret messages in current social interactions, even though they have access to new information revealed during the interactions (Fussell & Krauss, 1992). Even individuals meeting for the first time, who have no specific prior knowledge about each other, rely on general knowledge about people and interaction procedures to guide them during these initial encounters. Consequently, the notion of a conversational amnesiac relying solely on current information gleaned from the processing of others' discourse and actions to guide his or her own understanding, actions, and message production is highly implausible. Of course, knowledge bases are constantly being altered and updated by interactions with the physical and social environment, including interactions that involve other people (Planalp, 1987; Planalp & Honeycutt, 1985; Planalp & Rivers, 1996; Planalp, Rutherford, & Honeycutt, 1988). Nonetheless, the understanding and interpretation of others' discourse and actions, as well as the production of actions and verbal and nonverbal messages, depend to a significant degree upon the knowledge that has accumulated to that point in the current interaction.

A purview similar to this one has motivated research on the development of common ground during interactions. When individuals engage in joint activities in which they must coordinate their actions, they must make assumptions about each other. The totality of the presuppositions individuals have concerning shared beliefs, assumptions, and knowledge constitutes their common ground (Clark, 1994; Clark & Carlson, 1982; Clark & Marshall, 1981; Lewis, 1969; Schiffer, 1972; Stalnaker, 1978). There are two types of common ground. Communal common ground is found in the knowledge, beliefs, and assumptions held in the communities to which the interacting parties belong. This kind of common ground is especially important during initial encounters, when the parties know relatively little about each other. However, communal common ground may also be important in guiding interpretations, actions, and message production in other kinds of interactions. Personal common ground stems from inferences made by the parties based on personal experiences with each other (Clark, 1994, 1996; Clark & Marshall, 1981). This common ground includes knowledge about the preferences and beliefs of specific individuals, for example, "Joe likes deep-dish pizza" and "Mary listens to Debussy." Common ground accretes with each succeeding conversational exchange, and each conversational exchange is interpreted with respect to the common ground that has accumulated to that point.

Considerable research demonstrates that as common ground accumulates, communication becomes both more accurate and more efficient (e. g., Clark & Schaefer, 1987; Clark & Wilkes-Gibbs, 1986; Isaacs & Clark, 1987; Krauss & Weinheimer, 1964, 1966; Schober & Clark, 1989; Wilkes-Gibbs & Clark, 1992). In referential communication studies involving the matching of arrangements of symbols, matching accuracy increased over time and fewer speaking turns and words were required to achieve correct solutions. Presumably, these increases in accuracy and efficiency over trials were the result of increased common ground. Other studies have demonstrated the consequences of differences in common ground. For example, the content of conversations between friends demonstrates more evidence of mutual knowledge than does the content of strangers' conversations (Planalp, 1993). Naive observers are able to differentiate reliably between friends' and strangers' conversations because they recognize that friends' conversations manifest more evidence of mutual knowledge (Planalp & Benson, 1992). This mutual knowledge includes background information, habits, and dispositions. Friends also know about each other's activities and plans, and they refer to other people and events without having to explain them, thus suggesting greater communication efficiency. Apparently, not only does increased common ground promote greater communication accuracy and efficiency among interactants, naive observers can detect differences in the degree to which interaction participants share a common fund of knowledge.

Although common-ground research provides useful insights into how the accretion of common ground affects communication accuracy and efficiency, it does not provide a detailed account of the specific types of knowledge that are implicated in promoting effective interaction. Here, effective interaction is viewed simply as interaction that brings about desired instrumental and communication goals. Moreover, although communication accuracy and efficiency are frequently integral to effective interaction, these potentially desirable states are not the only determinants of interaction success. For example, an accurate understanding of another's negative emotional state does not necessarily guarantee that one will be able to generate actions and messages that bring about the goal of comforting the distressed other (Burleson & Goldsmith, 1998). Furthermore, the production of low-quality comforting messages might serve to undermine the goal of comforting the other and thus undermine efficiency. Consequently, it is useful to identify types of knowledge that are important to the attainment of goals across a wide spectrum of communication contexts.

There are at least five general classes of knowledge that are critical to effectiveness in social interactions: role knowledge, person knowledge, emotion knowledge, procedural knowledge, and context knowledge. Role knowledge includes knowledge about the actions and beliefs that are typical of individuals who play such social roles as brother, sister, mother, father, uncle, aunt, high school teacher, professor, dean, provost, and doctor. This knowledge acts to structure individuals' role expectations for themselves and others. These role expectations not only serve as standards for evaluating the adequacy of specific incumbents' role enactments—for example, "Dr. Evans is a very good professor" or "Dr. Howard is a terrible physician"—they also influence interpretations of role players' actions and messages and help to guide the production of messages directed toward those who are playing various roles. Person knowledge includes knowledge about people's dispositions and the relationship between these dispositions and action. Thus people who are judged to be introverted are expected to be relatively quiet and retiring in social situations, and observers take such behaviors as verbal reticence and lack of social contact to be diagnostic of introversion. Knowledge about cointeractants' dispositions, including such characteristics as intelligence and ability, significantly influences the kinds of messages individuals are likely to generate and the ways they interpret others' actions and messages.

Emotion knowledge structures organize individuals' knowledge about various emotional states (Burleson & Planalp, 2000; Fitness, 1996; Planalp, 1999; Shaver, Schwartz, Kirson, & O'Connor, 1987). This type of knowledge not only enables individuals to understand others' emotional states, it serves to guide the production of the individuals' own emotional responses. Procedural knowledge encompasses knowledge about the actions necessary to accomplish instrumental and social interaction goals. This knowledge simultaneously enables perceivers to understand why individuals act the way they do and guides goal-directed action. Finally, the physical and social context within which human interaction takes place can exert significant effects on the actions of the persons in those contexts. An interaction that takes place between a professor and a student during a lecture will probably differ significantly from an interaction on the same topic between the same two people that takes place in the professor's office or in the student union. And interactions between a romantically involved couple will differ significantly depending upon the presence or absence of others. Because social interaction is frequently context sensitive and sometimes highly so, individuals must have knowledge that enables them to alter their individual actions and their interactions in response to a multitude of contextual exigencies.

Table 6.1   Social Interaction Knowledge Types

	Level of Specificity	
Knowledge Type	General	Specific
Role	Role expectations for people in general	Role expectations for specific role incumbents
Person	General personality and dispositional prototypes and behaviors associated with them	Knowledge of specific dispositional qualities unique to the individual
Emotion	Knowledge of emotional states and their blends; knowledge of behavior associated with emotions	Knowledge about specific emotional expressions and the conditions under which they will be displayed
Procedural	Knowledge of action sequences that will bring about desired end states for people in general	Knowledge of action sequences that will bring about desired goals with specific individuals
Context	Knowledge of contextual variables that condition interaction behavior across situations	Knowledge of situational features that condition interaction behavior in specific situations

An important dimension that cuts across these five knowledge types is the degree to which knowledge is general or specific. These relationships are depicted in Table 6.1. As the table shows, within each of the five knowledge types, individuals may possess knowledge about "people in general," knowledge about specific individuals, or both. It is one thing to have general knowledge about professors' typical role behaviors; it is quite another to have detailed knowledge about Professor Farquar's behaviors as a result of having taken three of her classes. There are individual differences in the ways people enact social roles, but there are limits to the degree role incumbents can deviate from role expectations and still be perceived by others to be playing the role. Too much deviation from expectations will render the role enactment unrecognizable, for example, a teacher who consistently fails to teach. Nonetheless, repeated interactions with the same role occupants enable individuals to develop detailed knowledge about the idiosyncrasies with which they carry out their roles.

Moreover, interactions with a variety of individuals who play the same role enable social actors to detect commonalities among individuals' role enactments. These commonalities give rise to generalized knowledge about roles. The same processes of discrimination and generalization occur within each of the other knowledge types.

Knowledge about roles, people, emotions, interaction procedures, and strategies for attaining goals and social contexts may be of little use to individuals unless it is organized in such a way that it can be retrieved from memory when it is needed (Hammond, 1989; Schank, 1982). Books in a library are useful only if one can find them; consequently, they must be organized in some way and indexed in order to maximize their retrievability. With considerable luck, one might locate a specific book in a library stocked with 250,000 unindexed volumes; however, on average this would be a highly inefficient and frustrating way to find a desired book. To be useful, knowledge must be organized and indexed so that it is easily retrievable from memory when needed. The notion of retrieving knowledge from memory does not mean that this process is carried out consciously; however, in order to be accessible when needed, knowledge must be structured and indexed in some way. Knowledge structures serve this organizational function. The role these structures play in social interaction is the focus of this chapter.

Because social interaction is a goal-directed activity, I begin this chapter with a consideration of the roles that goals play in social interaction and cognition about interaction. Individuals have knowledge about goals and this knowledge is also structured, and individuals have procedural knowledge about action sequences that may bring about these desired end states. After considering the nature of the goals and action sequences, I shift attention to the roles these knowledge structures play in the interpretation of social interaction and the production of action and discourse. The focus here is on social interaction rather than on the more restricted domain of personal relationship development, although some researchers have considered the roles knowledge structures play in this domain (see Fletcher & Thomas, 1996). Nonetheless, in the crucible of everyday life, probably most social interactions are highly routine and impersonal (Aarts & Dijksterhuis, 2000). Within the large domain of commercial activity there are increasing efforts to routinize service interactions to the point of scripting the actions and the lines spoken by employees (Ford, 1999; Leidner, 1993). Although these routine interactions generally do not involve close friends, romantic partners, spouses, or family members, interactions between and among parties involved in such close relationships can become infused with routinized communication sequences (Coulmas, 1981a). In any case, like their less mundane counterparts, routine interactions are understood by their participants by reference to knowledge structures, and knowledge structures guide participants'

actions in them. Thus, to restrict the discussion of knowledge structures exclusively to the domain of close personal relationships and their development would be to ignore a much larger set of social interactions among nonintimates in which knowledge structures play an equally vital role.

Individuals vary in the degree to which they possess the types of knowledge adumbrated above. Even with considerable verbal capabilities, young children generally are unable to carry out the kinds of highly nuanced social interactions that some adults are capable of conducting. Although social interaction skill differences between adults and children may hinge on significant knowledge differentials, the ways in which knowledge is organized can also influence the skill with which people are able to perform in social interactions. Two adults might have about the same amounts and kinds of knowledge but differ with respect to the level of organization of that knowledge. To echo a previous theme, knowledge that lacks organization and is thus not highly retrievable and highly integrated may contribute little to social interaction skill. Because social interaction trajectories sometimes unfold rapidly and change directions abruptly, it is crucial that both interaction parties detect these changing goals and be able to bring relevant knowledge to bear on them quickly. Failure at one or both of the tasks of goal detection and knowledge retrieval is almost sure to undermine social interaction skill (Berger, in press).

THE NATURE AND SIGNIFICANCE OF GOALS IN SOCIAL INTERACTION AND COGNITION

Adaptation and Goal-Directed Action

The fundamental postulate that human action is goal directed and that human cognition is shaped by this goal-directedness receives support from a number of different quarters (see Austin & Vancouver, 1996; Pervin, 1989). In addressing the broad question of why human cognitive capacities have evolved, Bogdan (1994) argues:

> The ability to pursue specific ends by specific means enables an organism not only to specialize and focus its efforts but also to terminate them at some opportune point, thus saving energy and wear when the results are good or to continue its efforts or try something else when they are not. The more efficient an organism's ability to identify and get beneficial results and the more accurate the information gained from the results, the better off the organism and its ability to spread its genetic heritage will be. (p. 20)

He explains that guidance toward goals is necessary because organisms "are material systems or complexities that are genetically programmed to maintain and replicate themselves in goal-directed ways" (p. 1). He further argues that the overarching strategy of life is that of having and satisfying goals. Thus, in Bogdan's view, human cognition evolved as a way of increasing the efficiency with which humans attain goals.

Although communicating with others may occasionally be a goal unto itself, students of language have observed that individuals use language in order to reach goals (Austin, 1962; Clark, 1994; Wittgenstein, 1953). Wittgenstein (1953) avers that "language is an instrument" (para. 569), and Clark (1994) argues:

> People engage in discourse not merely to use language, but to accomplish things. They want to buy shoes or get a lost address or arrange a dinner party or trade gossip or teach a child improper fractions. Language is simply a tool for achieving these aims. (p. 1018)

In a similar vein, Hauser (1996) observes, "The design features of a communication system are the result of a complex interaction between the constraints of the system and the demands of the job required" (p. 1).

Although most would agree that language has evolved into a potentially powerful tool for attaining goals, Wittgenstein (1953) and others (Levinson, 1992; Sanders, 1997) have cautioned that in many instances language is used in the context of broadly defined goal-directed activities. Wittgenstein (1953) calls these activities "language games," and Levinson (1992) dubs them "activity types." In the pursuit of many everyday goals, language use may assume only a subsidiary role. Such activity types as rituals and routine service encounters may require little if any verbal interaction for their successful execution. By contrast, other activity types, such as counseling, negotiating, and teaching, place very heavy communication demands on those who participate in them. Unfortunately, theories of language use generally have ignored variations in activity types (Levinson, 1992; Sanders, 1997). Not only have interpersonal communication researchers failed to appreciate the large amount of variability in communication load across activity types, but they have focused little attention on the issue of how individuals coordinate actions with verbal behavior to achieve goals, especially in social contexts where communication demands are relatively low.

Just as language use is usually not a goal unto itself, individuals do not engage each other in social interaction simply for the purpose of carrying out turn-taking routines or showing behavioral adaptation (Burgoon, Stern, & Dillman, 1995; Giles, Mulac, Bradac, & Johnson, 1987; Shepard, Giles, & Le Poire, 2001). Behavioral coordination of social interaction and mutual adaptation are not merely interesting phenomena; rather, they may be instrumental in the achievement of such important goals as attachment and rapport (Cappella, 1998). Although verbal and nonverbal messages exchanged during social encounters and the mechanisms that coordinate these exchanges may indeed be critical for goal achievement, they generally do not constitute the raison d'être for social interaction. People use social interaction to achieve goals. Like language, social interaction is simply a tool.

That social interaction is a goal-directed process that sometimes involves the simultaneous pursuit of multiple goals is a fact that has not been lost on communication researchers and social psychologists (Austin & Vancouver, 1996; Dillard, 1990, 1997; Dillard, Segrin, & Harden, 1989; Greene, 1995; Greene & Lindsey, 1989; Greene, Lindsey, & Hawn, 1990; O'Keefe, 1988; Tracy, 1984; Tracy & Coupland, 1990; Tracy & Moran, 1983; Wiemann & Daly, 1994). However, attempts to delineate the strategies individuals use to attain goals during social interactions usually have focused on the words people utter to achieve their goals and the fluency with which they do so, while ignoring the actions that are necessary to attain the same goals. Clearly, the achievement of many everyday goals depends more heavily on the mute execution of action sequences than it does on protracted talk between people. That is, many important everyday goals, like buying groceries, obtaining gas for one's car, procuring already prepared comestibles, getting money from an ATM, or shopping for clothes, can be attained with minimal or no social interaction. Consequently, in order to understand how individuals use verbal messages to achieve goals, it is crucial to understand how these verbal messages are embedded within and coordinated with streams of ongoing goal-directed actions.

The ideas that human action and cognition are fundamentally goal directed and that language may be an instrument for attaining these goals speak to the issue of action generation, but the goal-directedness of human action can also account for the evolution of human interpretive capacities. Bogdan (1997) suggests that the ability to "read" others, or the ability to interpret others' intentions and actions, evolved from our need to understand others' goals in order to attain our own. If others'

goals potentially interfere with the satisfaction of our own, it is vital that we know others' intentions. The ability to make inferences concerning others' goals and plans is at the heart of this interpretive process. Within the more limited domain of language use, Green (1996) has asserted, "Understanding a speaker's intention in saying what she said the way she said it amounts to inferring the speaker's plan, in all of its hierarchical glory, although there is room for considerable latitude regarding the details" (p. 13). Considerable evidence suggests that narrative comprehension depends on story consumers' ability to make necessary goal and plan inferences about story characters' actions (Black & Bower, 1979, 1980; Bower, Black, & Turner, 1979; Bruce & Newman, 1978; Carberry, 1990; Hammond, 1989; Mandler, 1984; Schank & Abelson, 1977, 1995). Similar inferential processes subserve the comprehension of both discourse and nonverbal action sequences.

That human cognitive and interpretive capacities evolved to render guidance toward goals more efficient suggests the significance of goals for understanding human social interaction. Because the emergences of human intelligence, language, and technology are related, language too is a potentially important tool for improving the ease and consistency with which important goals are achieved (Hewes, 1993). Thus, by extension, the ability to coordinate goal-directed actions with others through social interaction is one that potentially augments the human capacity to recognize and get beneficial results. Having considered the adaptive significance of guidance toward goals and its relevance to the development of language and cognition, I now turn to a discussion of the nature and organization of goals.

Goal Structures in Cognition and Action

There is substantial evidence from several different research traditions to support the claim that human cognition about action is organized around hierarchies of goals. Within the cognitive domain, Lichtenstein and Brewer (1980) demonstrated how researchers could analyze the actions involved in the achievement of simple goals, such as setting up a movie projector or writing and mailing a letter, by identifying subgoals that enable superordinate goals. In the case of mailing a letter, the individual's achievement of the superordinate goal of affixing a stamp to an envelope would be enabled by his or her achieving the subgoals of tearing and licking a stamp. These researchers found that when subjects recalled videotapes of people pursuing the goal of setting up a movie projector or writing a letter, they showed better recall for superordinate goals than for subgoals. Similar patterns of recall were obtained when the same action sequences were described in written form. The finding that people show better memory for superordinate goals has been replicated in the research on story memory (Mandler, 1984). In this case, those who have read simple narratives demonstrate better memory for goals that are directly related to the development of the story's plot. They tend not to recall detailed actions that have been presented in the story. Similarly, actions that are part of the story's causal structure are better recalled than details that are not part of it (Trabasso, Secco, & van den Broek, 1984; van den Broek, 1994).

Newtson's (1973, 1976) work on the perception of goal-directed action sequences suggests that the perception of such sequences is hierarchically organized. In these studies, individuals observed videotapes of solo individuals engaging in various goal-directed activities. While subjects viewed these tapes, they pressed a button at the onset of a meaningful action and pressed the button again when the meaningful action ceased. Subjects were not told what constituted a "meaningful" action. Although subjects viewing the same action sequence showed considerable variability in the frequency with which they unitized the

sequence, the patterns of unitization suggested that the perceptual units employed by observers were hierarchically organized. That is, the perceptual units of the fine unitizers generally fit within the boundaries of the more abstract units of the gross unitizers. This research also revealed that individual observers are capable of controlling the degree to which they engage in fine or gross unitization.

Finally, proponents of action identification theory argue that observers can identify human action at various levels of abstraction in much the same way that individuals can vary with respect to the fineness with which they unitize ongoing action sequences (Vallacher & Wegner, 1985). One observer might characterize a long and complex interaction sequence involving two people simply as "a fight," whereas another observer of the same interaction sequence might provide a much more detailed account of the episode, including the specific words and actions exchanged by the disagreeing parties. Action identification theory explicates the conditions that promote more or less detailed identification of action sequences and the consequences that follow from identifying action at various levels of abstraction (Vallacher, Wegner, & Somoza, 1989). Thus both the work on the unitization of ongoing action and action identification suggest that observers of action sequences perceive and identify ongoing action hierarchically; consequently, they are capable of processing ongoing action at different levels of abstraction.

Although the lines of research mentioned above strongly support the assertion that human cognition about goal-directed action is organized around goal hierarchies, the question is whether goal-directed human action is itself hierarchically organized. Given the adaptive significance of guidance toward goals (Bogdan, 1994), the development of an interpretive capacity designed to detect potential sources of interference with goal attainment (Bogdan, 1997), and the evidence adduced above, it is reasonable to suppose that the hierarchical organization of cognition about human action reflects the hierarchical organization of goal-directed action itself. Barker's (1963) naturalistic studies of the behavior stream generally support this view.

Barker's research involved unobtrusive observation of children engaging in everyday activities. These studies revealed that the behavior units identified in these studies exhibit two important properties. First, behavioral units are frequently organized around the pursuit of a goal or a set of goals. Second, molar behavioral units often manifest hierarchical organization in which smaller behavioral units are essential for the production of larger, more abstract units. In describing this property of the behavior stream, Barker (1963) asserts, "These facts point to a fundamental structural feature of the behavior stream: behavior units occur in enclosing-enclosed structures; small units form the components of larger units" (p. 11). Research on narrative production suggests that beginning at age 5, children organize the content and structure of stories according to a hierarchical set of goals and a sustained plan of action. The stories of younger children do not manifest evidence of this conceptual framework (Trabasso & Nickels, 1992). Thus children organize both goal-directed actions themselves and narratives about goal-directed action sequences hierarchically at relatively young ages.

Goals and the Meaning of Social Interaction

Although the ways individuals conceptualize and talk about previous social interactions constitute an under-studied aspect of interpersonal communication, it is clear that when such conversations occur, previous social interactions are frequently characterized in terms of the presumed goals the individuals involved in those interactions were trying to

achieve. Consider, for example, two individuals conversing about the marital problems being experienced by a mutually known couple. Such comments as "She is trying to get him to stop drinking," "He is trying to get her to be more careful with money," and "She wants him to spend more time at home and less time at work" have at least one feature in common: They are about the presumed goals individuals in the relationship are trying to achieve. They are highly abstract summaries; that is, each of them might characterize multiple and highly complex interactions carried out over a lengthy period of time. Of course, the assertions themselves could be more elaborate and could include inferences about the plans the spouses are using to achieve their goals, for example, "She is trying to get him to stop drinking by encouraging him to go to Alcoholics Anonymous." Or they could be more concrete and detailed; for instance, "Yesterday, she picked up the phone and called AA to find out the next meeting date." Statements like these also could be made about one's own previous conversations; for example, "I was trying to get her to follow our budget."

As these examples amply demonstrate, the meanings individuals have of their own and others' social interactions are at least partially determined by inferences about goals being pursued during interactions. Inferences concerning interaction goals provide natural answers to the question, "Why were they talking to each other?" or even "Why were they together?" Whether these goals were successfully achieved or not may also become the focus of these explanatory gists. Of course, verbal characterizations of previous interactions may include more than inferences about goals and plans and whether goals were attained. Statements about emotional states displayed during previous interactions and the degree to which partners seemed to be getting along may also become grist for such commentaries. Nonetheless, inferences about goals and intentions provide observer-commentators with an important conceptual scaffolding for understanding what their own and others' social interactions are all about.

Goal Embeddedness

Because goals are organized hierarchically in both thought and action, and because individuals have limited attention capacities (Fiske & Taylor, 1991), at any given point in time those involved in social interactions can consciously focus their attention on only limited portions of goal hierarchies. Those interested in understanding the roles goals play in human striving and individual feelings of well-being have found that some individuals report that they strive to attain highly abstract goals (Emmons, 1986, 1989, 1996; Little, 1989; Sheldon & Kasser, 1995, 1998). Such personal strivings may include personal growth, affiliation, social recognition, and financial success. These goals resemble some of Rokeach's (1973) 18 terminal values. These highly abstract, regnant goals subsume the more concrete goals individuals seek to achieve in their everyday lives, for example, gaining entrance into an elite university, successfully completing classes, and attaining a degree, which, in turn, may promote the more abstract goals of financial success, social recognition, or both. Of course, the goal of successfully completing a particular course is itself a regnant goal that subsumes a number of more concrete goals, such as passing tests and writing passing papers, that an individual must achieve in order to receive credit for the class. Under extreme conditions, individuals may become quite cognizant of highly abstract goals such as social recognition or financial success (Kasser & Sheldon, 2000); however, in their everyday lives, their attention is generally focused on the less abstract goals that enable the achievement of higher-level goals.

Of course, there are individuals who characteristically focus their attention on very concrete goals and who pay little attention to potential higher-level goals (Emmons, 1996; Little, 1989). Those who characteristically focus on such highly concrete goals are less likely to find overall meaning in their lives because they are too preoccupied with "trivial pursuits" (Little, 1989). By contrast, those who focus exclusively on highly abstract goals may be less likely to be able to attain the necessary lower-level enabling goals; thus they may be disappointed because their ideal states are never achieved. Consequently, it may be that individuals who focus primarily on midrange goals experience the most positive subjective states of well-being (Emmons, 1996).

The hierarchical organization of goals combined with the limits of human attention sets up some problematic situations that have implications for the conduct of social interaction. First, the abstract goals that individuals move toward by satisfying a series of concrete subgoals may lose their activation over time. This may leave the individuals in the potentially embarrassing situation of having executed sequences of actions that have achieved concrete goals but not remembering why they undertook those action sequences in the first place (Norman, 1981; Reason, 1990). This is not unlike finding oneself in a room but being unable to remember why one came to the room, or approaching another individual to ask a question and then not being able to remember the question that one intended to ask. In the context of ongoing social interaction, this loss of goal activation may explain why individuals sometimes find themselves drifting off of the intended conversational topic and having to remind themselves about the original goal or goals of the conversation. The locution "getting off the topic" may be just another way of saying that because higher-order goals have lost activation, conversationalists have forgotten the overriding goal or goals of their conversation.

A second consequence of this hierarchical organization is the potential intrusion of automatically activated goals that interfere with goals being pursued during the interaction. There is ample evidence that goals can be automatically activated by stimuli about which individuals show little or no conscious awareness (Aarts & Dijksterhuis, 2000; Bargh, 1997; Bargh & Barndollar, 1996; Bargh & Gollwitzer, 1994; Gollwitzer, 1993, 1996). Although such automatic activation could potentially involve higher-level goals embedded in a currently active goal hierarchy, thus potentially facilitating goal attainment, simultaneous activation of goals could undermine communicative performance, especially if the activated goals subserve different higher-order goals. There is ample evidence to suggest that the simultaneous pursuit of multiple discourse goals places communicators under greater cognitive load, which, in turn, reduces the fluency with which they produce discourse (Greene & Lindsey, 1989; Greene et al., 1990). Although planning before such multiple-goal situations can facilitate performance (Greene & Lindsey, 1989), automatic activation of goals may occur so abruptly that even rapidly executed planning during discourse may not reduce the degree to which the newly activated goals interfere with ongoing interaction.

The automatic activation of goals may not only partially explain instances of conversational drift explicated above, such activation may also explain why, in some conflictive interactions, individuals find themselves involved in "kitchen sink" arguments. Parties to such interactions may begin their arguments consciously focused on one or two main issues, only to find that as they speak other issues and problems mysteriously find their way into the argument, thus giving the argument an "everything but the kitchen sink" quality. This overwhelming cascade of issues and problems may be partially explained by the automatic activation of subgoals nested under the more general goal, such as "marital problems to be solved." In such instances, external intervention by outside parties may be required to counteract the automatic activation of these goals and to

keep the interacting parties focused on only the most significant problems. In general, the seeming disorganization and "noise" exhibited by some social interactions may be at least partially explained by the intrusion of automatically activated goals.

Variations in activity types may be related to the likelihood that automatic activation of goals occurs. Highly mundane social interactions that are themselves propelled by the automatic activation of goals and plans may be less susceptible to such interfering automatic activation than less routine interactions. When a customer approaches the counter of the garden-variety fast-food restaurant, both the service provider and the customer have a firm grasp of each other's goals without uttering a single word. The context itself activates relevant goals and plans outside of conscious awareness. Of course, the service provider and any other customers present would experience considerable shock if the apparent customer were to reach into her pocket, take out a handgun, and demand all of the cash in the register. These nonroutine possibilities notwithstanding, under typical circumstances, the fast-food service goal hierarchy is so well rehearsed, it is unlikely that automatic activation that interferes with its successful execution will occur. By contrast, consider a conversation between two friends or spouses who are "checking in" with each other. Because the goals of such a conversation may not be very well defined for either individual, there are many more opportunities for automatic activation of goals to occur. Cues present in the environment of such an informal interaction, including those given off by conversational participants themselves, may have much more opportunity to activate goals and plans automatically and thus promote considerable conversational drift.

Although I have emphasized here the potential interfering effects of automatically activated goals, the unconscious and automatic activation of goals is vital to the carrying out of social interaction (Bargh, 1997;

Bargh & Barndollar, 1996; Gollwitzer, 1993, 1996). Because social interaction is at once complex and highly dynamic, it is important that verbal and action routines be retrieved, activated, and implemented rapidly, as interaction goals transmute over time. It is not simply a matter of activating relevant routines; these routines must be performed at the proper times and in the appropriate sequences (Lashley, 1951; MacKay, 1987). These timing and sequencing requirements alone preclude the possibility of a great deal of conscious decision making during social interactions, especially those that unfold rapidly. Automatic activation of goals helps to minimize the need for conscious processing that would interfere with the fluent production of action and speech. This is especially the case in highly routine goal-directed social interactions such as service encounters; however, automatic activation may also be important to the successful execution of discourse routines embedded within less mundane social encounters (Coulmas, 1981a, 1981b; Keller, 1981).

Finally, the hierarchical organization of goals may promote disappointment even when regnant goals are achieved. Individuals may be so focused on attaining the subgoals necessary to achieve an abstract goal that they may not consider the degree to which achieving the regnant goal will result in feelings of satisfaction. Individuals who achieve highly desired fame and fortune may find themselves no happier or more satisfied, even though the achievement of the required subgoals involved considerable time and effort (Emmons, 1996). The issue here is not necessarily one of loss of activation of a regnant goal or the automatic activation of competing goals; rather, the problem is one of knowing the degree to which the attainment of an abstract goal will bring one satisfaction before the goal is achieved. Certainly, there are instances in which people express considerable disappointment even when their social interactions result in the attainment of desired goals.

The successful conduct of social interaction requires that participants be able to make relatively accurate inferences about each other's intentions (Cohen, Morgan, & Pollack, 1990). As previously noted, Bogdan (1997) has argued that human interpretive capacity arose from our need to understand others' goals in order to ensure the achievement of our own. A fundamental inference that social interactants must make concerns the degree to which cointeractants intend to help or hinder their goal achievement. In the extreme, this inference might involve the degree to which one believes the others present threaten one's physical or psychological well-being. In a somewhat less ominous vein, once one is assured that others pose no physical or psychological threat, there remains the possibility that others' intentions are at variance with one's own. To answer all of these questions, individuals must be able to detect others' goals.

Given the nature of goal hierarchies, one might be able to detect successfully the goals that are in play at a given point in time; however, this may not ensure interaction success for at least two reasons. First, the hierarchical organization of goals may allow one to understand the specific lower-level goals currently being pursued by others, but may not allow one to understand the higher-level goals others are attempting to achieve. Those who are skilled at achieving their own goals during social interactions have to know not only where their fellow interlocutors currently are in their goal hierarchies, but what higher-order goals others are pursuing and where the present interaction is going. Evidence suggests that those people who think and plan ahead during conversations perform more competently than those who do not (Waldron, 1997; Waldron & Applegate, 1994). Second, because some interactions are highly dynamic, interactants' goals may change rapidly and abruptly. Consequently, in order to adapt one's messages to these changing circumstances, one must continually track others' goals (Berger, in press). Failure to detect these changes probably contributes to interaction failure in the sense that desired goals are not achieved. Goal-tracking demands vary considerably by activity type. Routine service encounters demand little in the way of goal detection and goal tracking, and only minimal attention to the progress of the encounter is required. By contrast, success in complex bargaining situations and situations involving interpersonal conflict probably requires high levels of attention to goal dynamics. Unfortunately, at this juncture we do not have a great deal of information about how individuals go about detecting and tracking each other's goals during social interactions. This fundamental and critical interaction process deserves much more research attention.

ORGANIZATION OF INTERACTION-RELEVANT KNOWLEDGE

To endorse the postulate that social interaction is organized around the pursuit of individual and mutual goals is to deal with only part of the larger question of how knowledge influences social interaction processes. Goals are end states for which individuals and groups strive. When desired goals require social interaction for their achievement, the knowledge necessary to attain these goals must involve not only actions but discourse as well. It is one thing to desire certain end states; it is quite another to attain them. The question is how knowledge about the actions and discourse required to reach goals is organized and how it is activated, accessed, and used to guide goal-directed social interaction. Furthermore, the role that knowledge about action and discourse plays in the processes that enable individuals to understand each other's actions is an equally important issue. However, before I present an explication of the details of these

processes, a consideration of the degree to which social interaction and discourse are organized is in order.

Communication Routines

The fact that many daily social encounters are highly routinized has been noted previously. To characterize a particular social interaction sequence simply as routine overlooks the fact that the concept of a routine is itself hierarchical. One could characterize the actions involved in a coffee-ordering routine at Starbucks as follows: Go to the counter, order, pay, pick up the coffee, sit down, and drink the coffee. More abstractly, the same sequence could be characterized as "going to Starbucks to get coffee." Or, more concretely, the utterances that are typically part of ordering coffee and paying for it could be specified as follows:

Counter person: May I help you?

Customer: Could I please have a tall Frappuccino?

Counter person: Would you like whipped cream?

Customer: Yes please. How much will that be?

Counter person: That will be $3.95, please.

Note that these specific utterances could be subsumed under the more abstract activity labels of "ordering" and "paying."

In addition to these kinds of macro routine sequences are more microscopic linguistic routines that are used in many different social contexts, including those that are nonroutine. Keller (1981) has identified some 500 conversational gambits that are semifixed expressions, including "The main point is," "I have something to add to that," "What I really meant was this," and "First of all." These kinds of routine expressions could be used in interactions that are not themselves routinized. Keller argues that gambits like these serve the following four functions: (a) semantic framing ("That reminds me"; "My guess is"), (b) social signaling ("May I interrupt you for a moment?" "That's about all I have to say"), (c) state-of-consciousness ("I'd like to hear all about it"; "I didn't know that"), and (d) communicative signaling ("Are you following me?" "Sorry, I didn't get that last part"). In addition to these kinds of gambits, there are formulaic discourse sequences associated with greetings, leave-takings, compliments, and apologies. Although Americans sometimes minimize the importance of communication routines like these, and sometimes mock them while at the same time using them frequently, in Japanese society, proper and frequent use of routine apologies is vital for observing politeness norms (Coulmas, 1981b).

Fixed expressions, like gambits and other formulaic utterances, are prevalent in English conversations and serve to organize and coordinate them in a number of different ways (Goffman, 1967, 1971). Coulmas (1981a) explains the frequent occurrence of these ritual-like conversation sequences as follows:

> The recurrence of communicative goals in everyday life has led to the evolution of standardized strategies for their accomplishment. Many speech events are very similar, and essentially of the same kind. The wording may not be identical from one performance to the next, but the sequential organization is more or less constant. . . . In some cases, strategies have turned into full rituals. . . . In other cases, only the order is fixed and the wording is flexible. (p. 3)

Given this characterization, it would be a mistake to take the narrow view that communication routines are discourse sequences that are invariant with respect to the utterances that make them up. Religious rituals and parts of the ceremonies surrounding the pledges and oaths taken by various officials are some examples of extremely rigid discourse routines that use the same words every time they are enacted. But even in these cases, the rendering of the ritualized speech may vary with respect to paralinguistic features from person to person. In everyday social commerce, this degree of rigidity is rarely observed. Yet, even with substantial variations in wording, observers usually can easily recognize the routines that subserve greetings, leave-takings, compliments, ritualized conflict episodes, and apologies. Moreover, certain gambits may give rise to very clear discourse expectations. When someone utters such gambits as "I would like to be more encouraging, but . . ." or "I wish there was another way to say this, but . . . ," the person being spoken to probably would anticipate hearing bad news, across a wide variety of social contexts, even though the two gambits are worded differently. Thus the variability of surface language is not necessarily diagnostic of the absence of underlying discourse organization and dissimilarity with respect to communicative function.

Some might blanch at the notion that much of daily social interaction and interpersonal communication is routine in either the macro or the micro sense explicated above. However, because social interaction is a goal-directed activity and because the goals that social interaction subserves frequently recur, for the sake of attaining these recurring goals efficiently, action sequences and the communication sequences that accompany them must become routine. Of course, unique goals may arise in the conduct of everyday affairs; however, even when these goals appear, one may resort to communication routines to meet these unusual communicative challenges. Thus, when one is suddenly put in the position of having to provide comfort to extremely distraught others and having to provide the comfort immediately, one may resort to a comforting routine. This is not to say that the routine will necessarily be effective; however, it may be the only readily available option to the comfort provider on such short notice. The alternative of taking time to generate discourse goals and detailed plans on-line may defeat the goal of providing relief as quickly as possible. Thus the degree to which the social context is unique and demands urgency is probably related to deployment of communication routines in such circumstances (Berger, in press).

Plans, Scripts, and Memory Organization Packets

If one accepts the idea that human cognition has evolved in response to the goal-directedness of human action (Bogdan, 1994, 1997), and if one accepts the notions that many everyday goals are recurrent, and that, as a consequence, much of social interaction is routine (Coulmas, 1981a), then sequences of actions and discourse associated with goal attainment should be represented cognitively. Cognitive representations of routines, especially those routines that have worked well in the past, are necessary for guiding goal-directed conduct in ways that will reliably produce desired end states as efficiently as possible. Moreover, cognitive representations of goals by themselves are not sufficient for the efficient satisfaction of those goals; the actions by which goals can be achieved must also be represented.

A number of theorists have argued that cognitive representations of knowledge about goal-directed action sequences, like representations of goals, are organized in hierarchical fashion, with abstract actions at the tops of these hierarchies and more concrete actions nested below them. Action philosophers have accorded these plan hierarchies a central role in explaining intentional action (Brand, 1984; Bratman, 1987, 1990), and those interested in the production of action and discourse have also found the plan construct to be of considerable purchase (Berger, 1995, 1997; Hobbs & Evans, 1980; Levelt, 1989; Meyer, 1997, 2000; Miller, Galanter, & Pribram, 1960;

Pea & Hawkins, 1987; Waldron, 1990, 1997; Wilson, 2000; Zammuner, 1981). Moreover, such planlike constructs as procedural records are part of action assembly theory, a theory that aims to explain the production of action and discourse (Greene, 1984a, 1997).

Natural language processing researchers have identified plan recognition as a key element in the understanding of spoken discourse and text (Carberry, 1990; Cohen et al., 1990; Green, 1989; Litman & Allen, 1987; Schank, 1982; Schank & Abelson, 1977; Schmidt, 1976; Wilensky, 1983). According to these accounts, discourse and text understanding hinge on the ability of listeners and readers to make inferences about the goals others are pursuing and the plans they are using to achieve them. As indicated previously, in many everyday situations, individuals may attain desired goals primarily through the execution of action sequences that involve little if any communication. In these situations as well, plan recognition is vital to understanding the goals being realized by those enacting these action sequences and the strategies they are using to achieve their goals.

Plans that are used repeatedly to achieve specific goals may become rigidified if they successfully produce desired end states. These highly specific plans have been labeled *scripts* (Abelson, 1976, 1981; Galambos, Abelson, & Black, 1986; Schank & Abelson, 1977). One would not speak of "the plan" to go from San Francisco to New York, as if there is only one possible way to accomplish this goal. Several alternative plans involving different modes of transportation and different routes could be devised to get from San Francisco to New York. However, if one habitually took the same flight from San Francisco to New York, one would develop a script for so doing. Plans are more general and flexible than scripts, although some have argued that successfully used plans for achieving goals can become "canned" and used in the future even when they must be altered to accommodate new exigencies (Hammond, 1989).

Schank (1982) attempted to add flexibility to the script concept (Abelson, 1976, 1981; Schank & Abelson, 1977) by invoking the notion of a memory organization packet (MOP). A MOP is a memory unit that organizes various scenes. Thus a "trip MOP" might include such scenes as purchasing tickets, checking in, boarding a mode of transportation, and disembarking after arrival at a destination. Within each of these scenes, scripts might specify the unique actions necessary to achieve the primary goal for a particular mode of transportation. Because scenes are general (for example, one might check in when traveling by airplane, boat, or train), they provide more processing flexibility than do highly particularistic and rigid scripts by themselves. Furthermore, scenes eliminate the redundancies that arise from having unique scripts for similar activities. For example, many of the actions required to achieve the goal of checking in to travel by airplane, boat, and train are similar. Thus a scene can be used to characterize a general action sequence necessary to attain a specific goal, while specific scripts attached to the scene can fill in the detailed actions that are unique to each transportation mode's check-in procedure.

The MOP construct has been invoked to characterize conversational exchanges, particularly initial conversations between strangers (Kellermann, 1991, 1995; Kellermann, Broetzmann, Lim, & Kitao, 1989; Kellermann & Lim, 1990). Kellermann (1995) suggests that there is a "conversational MOP" that is flexible but shows underlying order. She argues that this MOP can explain why conversations exhibit evidence of both routinization and uniqueness simultaneously. For example, the conversational MOP for informal, initial encounters includes such scenes as greeting, introduction, where one lives, hometowns, and good-byes. These kinds of scenes are general in the sense that they could be used

in other conversational MOPs, such as job interviews or formal introductions. However, because the job interview context might differ in some ways from the informal initial encounter, more specific scripts attached to the scenes would be necessary to provide the nuances necessary to differentiate an informal initial interaction introduction from a job interview introduction.

A critical aspect of Schank's (1982) dynamic memory theory is the idea that knowledge structures such as plans, scripts, and MOPs are constantly being updated by experience. Thus, when an individual encounters actions that are unique with respect to a well-established routine, these actions are tagged in memory. If these tagged actions occur several times, they may force revision of the knowledge structure. Moreover, when individuals pursue new goals, they may encounter action sequences that resemble those already represented in extant knowledge structures. Individuals who check in for an ocean cruise for the first time may recognize certain similarities between the cruise check-in procedure and the one used for airlines. The recognition of such similarities gives rise to generalized representations like check-in scenes.

Some researchers have questioned the utility of plan-based, problem-solving models of message design on the grounds that messages designed to achieve specific goals sometimes do not evidence a unitary or coherent structure (O'Keefe, 1997; O'Keefe & Lambert, 1995). Based on their analyses of goal-directed messages, these researchers suggest that although recurrent themes may appear in messages designed to reach goals, "messages are sometimes not functionally unified" (O'Keefe & Lambert, 1995, p. 64). Consequently, they suggest that theories offering "only a global characterization of message structure will face difficulty in explaining variability of message forms to message functions" (p. 64). In response to these arguments, I have observed that the mere fact that the surface structure of verbal messages does not exhibit strategic organization does not necessarily imply that abstract knowledge structures did not guide their generation (Berger, 1997). First, as we have already seen, some goal-directed action sequences may consist of an admixture of verbal messages and actions, and the achievement of other goals may be considerably more related to actions taken than to words uttered. In such cases, the study of verbal messages by itself may not reveal any underlying strategic structure even though it is manifestly present. Second, analyses of verbal messages do not provide a direct conduit to the thought processes that generated them (see Greene, 1990). Thus it is possible that verbal messages exhibiting an apparent lack of structure could be the product of well-articulated knowledge structures and highly organized thought processes. Finally, some social interaction contexts may call for the production of strategically ambiguous messages—that is, message sequences that may make discourse appear to be nonstrategic. Strategically ambiguous messages sequences may themselves emanate from a plan (Eisenberg, 1984).

KNOWLEDGE STRUCTURES IN SOCIAL INTERACTION

It is one thing to postulate the existence of such knowledge structures as goal hierarchies, plans, scripts, and MOPs and to describe them; it is quite another to demonstrate that these knowledge structures are implicated in social interaction processes in general and in skillful interaction performance in particular. In this section I consider evidence that links planning processes and knowledge structures to performance in social interaction.

Imagined Interactions

There is considerable evidence that, on occasion, individuals spend time imagining their interactions with others (Honeycutt, 1989, 1991; Honeycutt, Edwards, & Zagacki, 1989-1990; Honeycutt, Zagacki, & Edwards, 1992-1993). These imagined interactions may occur before actual interactions, or they may be recollections of prior interactions. Although studies of imagined interactions do not directly address issues related to the organization of knowledge, they indicate that the activity of imagining interactions has demonstrable effects on behavior. Allen and Edwards (1991) found that individuals who imagined interactions before engaging in them displayed shorter speech onset latencies and fewer silent pauses during the encounter than did those who did not first imagine the interaction. Similarly, Allen and Honeycutt (1997) found that those who imagined future interactions displayed fewer object-focused adaptors during their interactions than did individuals who were distracted from imagining the future encounter. Object-focused adaptors may be indicative of anxiety and stress.

Imagining an interaction either before or after it has occurred requires that relevant knowledge be activated and accessed from long-term memory. That is, the imagining process itself requires that relevant knowledge about people and interaction processes be consulted for imagination to occur. Imagining interactions before they take place may be much like planning them. Thus it is not surprising that imagining impending interactions reduces hesitations and speech disfluencies once the interaction commences. Several additional studies have demonstrated that planning before speaking reduces both speech onset latencies and hesitations once phonation begins (Berger, Knowlton, & Abrahams, 1996, Experiment 2; Greene, 1984b, 1995; Greene & Geddes, 1993; Greene & Lindsey, 1989; Greene et al., 1990; Lindsey, Greene, Parker, & Sassi, 1995). Presumably, precommunication planning activates relevant knowledge structures such that they are more accessible when individuals begin to speak, thus facilitating the fluency of their speech performance. Although the studies just considered show that imagining or planning interactions in advance can increase verbal fluency and potentially reduce visible signs of discomfort, they do not directly address the issue of plans and interaction effectiveness.

Planning, Plans, and Interaction Performance

Evidence gathered outside of the social interaction domain suggests that planning before undertaking a task may improve the efficiency of task performance. Individuals who planned before trying to arrange a hypothetical traveling salesman's stops produced more efficient plans for the travel route than did those who did not plan in advance (Battmann, 1989). Similarly, schoolchildren given the opportunity to replan the order in which various classroom cleanup tasks would be done produced more efficient plans for so doing (Pea & Hawkins, 1987). In addition, the children tended to alter lower-level, more concrete elements of their plans rather than more abstract and difficult-to-modify plan elements. These studies suggest that plans may become more efficient when individuals have the opportunity to plan in advance or to alter previous plans. These observed increments in plan efficiency could have been prompted by opportunistic planning (Hayes-Roth & Hayes-Roth, 1979). Planners who have the opportunity to reconsider plans may become aware of ways in which they can streamline already formulated plans without undermining their effectiveness.

Knowing when to pursue a pending goal is an important cognitive skill. When people plan for goals to be pursued later, they are more sensitive to future opportunities to achieve these goals when these opportunities arise (Patalano & Seifert, 1997). Moreover, individuals whose plans include implementation intentions—that is, intentions concerning

when and where they will use the plans to achieve their goals—are more likely to achieve the planned-for goals than are those whose plans do not include implementation intentions (Gollwitzer, 1993, 1996). Thus the activity of planning not only sensitizes individuals to opportunities to achieve goals as they arise spontaneously, it also increases the likelihood of goal attainment when plans include implementation intentions.

As noted previously, planning before engaging in verbal communication tends to increase the verbal fluency with which individuals perform once they begin to produce speech. The onset of planned speech tends to be more rapid and, once it begins, it is faster and contains fewer pauses and hesitations (Berger et al., 1996, Experiment 2; Greene, 1984b, 1995; Greene & Geddes, 1993; Greene & Lindsey, 1989; Greene et al., 1990; Lindsey et al., 1995). This is not only the case with nonduplicitous messages; Greene, O'Hair, Cody, and Yen (1985) found that individuals who planned before engaging in deceptive communication demonstrated higher levels of verbal fluency than did those who told spontaneous lies. Although these findings do not directly address the question of whether planned lies were any more difficult to detect than those told spontaneously, they suggest that performances of planned lies may provide fewer cues that are potentially indicative of anxiety, thus creating less suspicion in those who are lied to. Other studies suggest that preconversational planning produces observable effects on subsequent conversational content (Hjelmquist, 1991; Hjelmquist & Gidlund, 1984; Jordan, 1993). Ideas that appear in preconversational plans are manifested in later conversational discourse (Hjelmquist & Gidlund, 1984). Although these studies do not speak directly to the effectiveness of interactions so planned, they demonstrate that content elements of plans developed before interaction are integrated into subsequent conversational discourse.

Very few studies have examined direct links between characteristics of plans formulated before interaction and communication effectiveness. However, it appears that the propensity to devise complex and specific plans may enhance the likelihood that goals will be achieved. A study of mostly indigent clients enrolled in a welfare-to-work program revealed that those who obtained full-time employment and remained in their jobs devised significantly more specific job interview plans before their job interviews than did those who were not successful in obtaining employment and those who found jobs but lost them (Waldron & Lavitt, 2000). In addition, people who obtained full-time jobs and remained in them tended to generate more complex job interview plans than did those in the other groups. Among several communication competence measures administered to the clients, job interview plan specificity proved to be the most potent predictor of employment success. Not only are plan attributes implicated in such practical outcomes as job interviewing success, some theorists have suggested that parents' plans for dealing with their children's misbehavior may partially explain why some parents are predisposed to abuse their children (Wilson, 2000). Parents whose plans lack prosocial actions for dealing with children may resort to violent means to control their children's behavior. Although there are no data currently available to assess these possibilities, this topic obviously deserves research attention.

One might discount the significance of the studies noted above for increasing our understanding of the roles knowledge structures play in social interaction because in each case individuals had opportunities to plan actions before pursuing goals. Some communication contexts, such as public speaking and job interviewing, may allow for such preinteraction preparation; however, many informal social interaction situations do not allow such preparation before they are undertaken, although individuals may sometimes have opportunities to plan and rehearse less formal interactions with acquaintances, friends, and family members. Preinteraction planning opportunities aside, there is compelling evidence that individuals engaged in conversations think about their goals and plans on-line as their interactions progress. In one investigation, participants individually reviewed videotapes of their just-concluded interactions (Waldron, 1990). They were instructed to stop the videotape and record their thoughts whenever they could recall what they were thinking during the conversation. Analyses of the 2,273 thoughts generated by participants revealed that 44% were concerned with the goals the participants were pursuing in the conversations and the plans they were using or would use to achieve their goals. These findings suggest strongly that cognitions about conversational goals, plans, and planning are not solely preinteraction phenomena, and they apparently occur relatively frequently during conversations. Moreover, as we have already seen, because goals and plans can be activated and exert effects completely outside of conscious awareness (Bargh, 1997; Bargh & Barndollar, 1996; Gollwitzer, 1993, 1996), these figures probably underestimate the extent to which goals and plans guide ongoing interaction.

It is one thing to demonstrate that individuals think about goals and plans during conversations, but it is quite another to show that differences in plans affect interaction outcomes. Several studies have demonstrated that the attributes of plans generated on-line are related to success in achieving interaction goals. In one study, after conversing about an issue over which they disagreed, subjects individually reviewed a videotape of their conversation and indicated what actions they were planning to take and what actions they decided against taking when they were speaking (Waldron & Applegate, 1994). The researchers used these responses to construct indices of plan complexity, plan sophistication, plan specificity, and editing. The degree to which each individual used competent verbal disagreement tactics during the conversation was coded from the videotapes. Individuals also completed a cognitive complexity measure that tapped the degree to which they perceive people in relatively complex ways.

This study revealed that those whose plans were judged to be more complex, sophisticated, and specific and those who showed more evidence of editing during their interactions deployed significantly more competent verbal disagreement tactics than did those who scored lower on these plan and editing measures. Cognitive complexity was not significantly related to competence in the use of verbal disagreement tactics, although those with higher levels of cognitive complexity tended to devise more complex and sophisticated plans and to engage in more editing. Apparently, individuals' levels of cognitive complexity potentiate the degree to which their interaction plans will be complex and sophisticated; however, it is the nature of the interaction plans themselves that promotes effective communication.

Another study demonstrated that plans formulated during conversations may enhance performance, depending upon the nature of the plans (Waldron, Caughlin, & Jackson, 1995). In this study, one individual was given the task of eliciting as much AIDS-related information as possible from a conversational partner. At the conclusion of the discussion, participants individually reviewed the videotape of their conversation. The conversational plans were coded for their level of abstraction, ranging from implementation-level plans (highly concrete) to undifferentiated plans (highly abstract). The videotapes of the discussions were also scored for the degree to which the information seekers obtained specific AIDS-related information. The results indicated that individuals whose plans were more concrete and complex elicited more specific AIDS-related information from their partners

than did those whose plans were more abstract and simple or those who did not plan.

As the studies reviewed above indicate, not all plans devised during conversations necessarily result in more effective interaction performance. Apparently, individuals whose plans are both more concrete and more complex are more effective in achieving interaction goals; however, there may be trade-offs between the efficiency with which goals are achieved and the degree to which they are attained in a socially appropriate manner (Berger, 2000, in press). For example, information seekers whose plans for obtaining information from conversational partners were more direct were judged to be less socially appropriate than individuals whose information-seeking plans were less direct. However, information seekers who used less direct information-seeking plans sometimes failed to obtain the information they were seeking; that is, they were less efficient in reaching their interaction goal (Waldron, 1990). Another study revealed that when conversational success was defined as a combination of efficiency (information-seeking success) and perceived social appropriateness, planning was a strong determinant of positive outcomes (Cegala & Waldron, 1992).

In addition to these findings, Waldron (1997) has emphasized that in order for individuals' interaction plans to promote effective interaction outcomes, they must take into account the plans of cointerlocutors. Being able to detect others' goals and plans is vital for achieving interaction goals (Berger, in press); however, mere recognition of others' goals and plans is not sufficient for effectiveness in achieving goals. One must take others' goals and plans into account with respect to one's own. Consistent with this notion, Waldron and Applegate (1994) found that individuals who accommodated others' plans into their own were more effective in achieving mutually agreeable solutions to verbal disagreements. Given the demonstrated importance of the interplay between cointerlocutors' goals and plans during interactions, more research attention must be directed toward the study of interactive planning (Bruce & Newman, 1978; Carbonell, 1981), even though the methodological problems associated with such research are formidable (Waldron, 1997).

Although not collected within the context of ongoing interactions, some data suggest that the quality of individuals' plans to reach social goals is related to such feeling states as social loneliness (Berger & Bell, 1988; Berger & diBattista, 1992). In these studies, participants generated plans for achieving the goals of asking someone out for a date and ingratiating themselves with a new roommate. Participants also completed a revised version of the UCLA Loneliness Scale (Russell, Peplau, & Cutrona, 1980). The plans were subsequently judged for their likely effectiveness by a panel of judges who received no specific criteria for judging plan effectiveness. These studies revealed that men whose date-request plans were judged to be more effective reported significantly lower levels of felt loneliness than did their male counterparts who devised less effective date-request plans. No relationship was found between date-request plan effectiveness and loneliness among women. This sex difference is probably due to the fact that within the population studied, men tended to ask women for dates more often than women asked men. Thus the women's date-request skills were not germane to the women's social success. However, among both men and women, those who wrote more effective plans for ingratiating themselves with a new roommate reported significantly lower levels of felt loneliness. Because most college men and women both face the task of getting along with new roommates, plan effectiveness should be equally important for both sexes.

In an effort to determine judges' criteria for differentiating between more and less effective plans, Berger and Bell (1988) found that effective plans were longer and more complex than those judged to be less effective. Date-request plans that included such actions as seeking similarities between oneself and the prospective date were judged to be more effective. Roommate ingratiation plans containing such units as setting rules for living together, engaging in a social activity, and presenting a positive image were judged to be more effective. These correlational studies cannot address questions of causality, but we might speculate that the plans of socially lonely people may put others off. Reduced social contact with others, in turn, may prevent socially lonely people from developing more effective plans. Whether one could break this spiral by teaching lonely individuals to devise effective social interaction plans is an important question.

Plan Complexity

The studies just considered suggest that complex plans are judged to be more effective than simple plans (Berger & Bell, 1988), and complex plans developed on-line appear to be more effective than simple plans when implemented in ongoing interaction episodes (Waldron & Applegate, 1994; Waldron et al., 1995). Of course, under some conditions, simple plans might prove to be superior to more complex plans, for example, when the situation within which individuals are interacting is urgent and requires immediate action (Berger, in press). Nonetheless, because complex plans often appear to be more effective than simple ones in bringing about desired goals, I consider here some factors that influence the complexity of plans. Plans may be rendered more complex by virtue of both the sheer number of actions they contain and the extent to which they contain contingent actions that might be deployed in case specific planned actions fail.

Studies of children's planning have revealed that as children progress through their school years they develop more complex plans for achieving a variety of goals (Kreitler & Kreitler, 1987). Moreover, the same investigations have revealed that children display considerable variation in the degree to which they believe that planning is itself a useful activity. Children who believe in the efficacy of planning as an activity develop more complex plans to achieve future goals than do children who think that planning is generally not a useful activity. As noted earlier, individuals who display higher levels of cognitive complexity about people also devise more complex plans on-line than do their less cognitively complex counterparts (Waldron & Applegate, 1994).

In addition to these more or less stable dispositional correlates of plan complexity are situational factors that promote greater plan complexity. One of these is the degree to which the efficacy of planned actions is questioned. In one study, immediately after individuals wrote plans to persuade others to adopt their opinion on an issue, they were asked what they would do in the event that each of four randomly selected planned actions failed to bring about the intended result. Other individuals wrote plans but were not subsequently questioned. Subjects in both groups were then given the opportunity to write a second plan to achieve the same persuasion goal. Comparison of the two plans revealed that the second plans of those who were questioned contained significantly more new arguments than did the plans of those who were not questioned (Berger, Karol, & Jordan, 1989, Experiment 3). Thus when individuals are forced to entertain the possibility that planned actions may fail, they tend to generate unique alternatives in subsequent plans. Incorporating new alternatives in subsequent plans increases their complexity.

Another factor related to the complexity of plans is the degree to which planners seek information about the person or persons who will be the subject of their planned actions. In a study in which individuals wrote plans to request a date or induce their new roommate to like them, participants were given the opportunity to indicate information they would like to have about the person or the situation that would enable them to develop a more effective plan to achieve their assigned goal (Berger & diBattista, 1992). Half of the participants made these information requests before they wrote their plans, and the other half made their requests after they had already written their plans. Although none of the participants received any of the requested information, those who requested more items of information and those who requested information from more diverse information categories before they wrote their plans devised significantly more complex plans than did those who requested fewer items of information and those who used fewer information categories. There were no significant relationships between the amount of information requested and information diversity and plan complexity among those individuals who made their information requests after they wrote their plans. Apparently, the act of requesting relevant person and situation information is itself sufficient to prompt more complex planning, even if the requested information is not provided.

A final factor that influences the degree to which plans will be complex is the degree to which individuals are committed to the goals for which they are devising plans. In one study, students were asked to indicate their attitudes toward two salient issues (Berger, 1988). They were then asked to devise plans to persuade someone to accept their position on each of the two issues. The number of action units contained in each plan was used as an index of plan complexity and was correlated with the degree to which the opinions deviated from the neutral points of the attitude scales. The correlation between attitude commitment and plan complexity was .40 ($p < .001$). Those who were more committed to their attitude positions wrote more complex persuasion plans.

Although the individual-differences studies involving beliefs in the efficacy of planning and cognitive complexity are of somewhat limited practical use, the three experiments just discussed suggest some useful strategies for increasing plan complexity. Questioning planned actions, encouraging individuals to seek information about the potential targets of plans and the situations within which they will be enacted, and increasing commitment to desired goals all appear to be potential routes for encouraging the development of more complex plans. However, one must remain cognizant of the caveat that complex plans are not necessarily harbingers of successful interaction outcomes. Simple plans may be not only adequate but optimal for some kinds of communication situations, and, as we shall see presently, complex plans may actually debilitate performance under certain conditions.

Goal Failure

Whether message planning occurs before interaction or on-line as it unfolds, the actions guided by plans may fail to bring about desired superordinate goals and subgoals. One response to goal failure is to suspend efforts to reach current goals; however, if one chooses to continue to pursue goals, how does one go about altering plans? Artificial intelligence researchers have recognized the need for natural-language-understanding systems to adapt plans in the face of failed expectations (Schank, 1986), unmet goals (Alterman, 1988), and changing circumstances (Hammond, 1989). Schank (1986) has argued that human learning is failure driven; that is, when expectations are violated, individuals must develop explanations for these failures. Developing these explanation patterns requires learning.

Given goal failure, there are a number of possible ways individuals might alter message plans in order to circumvent the failure. For example, one might reiterate the same actions and words after goal failure, but alter certain paralinguistic features, such as speech rate, vocal intensity, or vocal intonation, during the second enactment of the same plan. Or,

because plans are hierarchically organized, one might reiterate the abstract features of the plan during a second attempt but modify the more concrete actions in the plan. For example, one might still offer a reward for compliance, but change the nature of the specific reward during the second rendition of the plan. Finally, one might respond to failure by altering abstract plan features: Instead of offering rewards for compliance, one might proffer threats.

As noted previously, giving individuals the opportunity to reconsider already formulated plans generally improves the plans' efficiency (Hayes-Roth & Hayes-Roth, 1979; Pea & Hawkins, 1987). Moreover, it appears that the preferred general strategy for modifying plans when opportunities arise is to leave abstract plan elements intact and to change more concrete plan elements (Pea & Hawkins, 1987). This strategy makes considerable sense in terms of cognitive economy, because modifications of more abstract plan elements related to the overall organization of the plan are more demanding of cognitive resources than are alterations to more concrete plan elements. Alterations to more abstract plan elements cascade down the plan hierarchy and force changes at more concrete plan levels. By contrast, modifications of concrete plan elements do not necessarily reverberate upward to more abstract plan features. This line of reasoning led to the development of the hierarchy principle (Berger, 1997; Berger et al., 1996; Knowlton & Berger, 1997), which states that when individuals continue to pursue failed goals, their subsequent plans will reflect alterations of concrete plan elements rather than modifications to abstract plan features.

Considerable empirical support has been adduced for the hierarchy principle. Berger and diBattista (1992) found that when experimental confederates indicated to direction givers that they had difficulty understanding their directions to a location several blocks away, the direction givers spoke more loudly and in some cases more slowly when providing the second rendition of their directions. However, almost no direction givers altered the walk routes of their directions during their second renditions. Because walk route representations are more abstract than speech features like rate and intensity, these plan modification choices comport with those predicted by the hierarchy principle. However, this experiment did not demonstrate directly that alterations to more abstract plan elements are more cognitively demanding than changes to concrete plan elements.

In recent years, my colleagues and I have undertaken a series of experiments designed to determine whether changes to abstract plan elements potentiate higher levels of cognitive load (Berger, 1997; Berger et al., 1996). In these experiments, direction givers were again asked by confederates to provide their directions a second time; however, the source of the understanding failure was varied. In some cases the confederates located the understanding failure at abstract plan levels, by indicating they could not follow the route given in the first rendition of the directions. By contrast, other direction givers were told that the reason for the understanding failure was that they spoke too quickly when giving their directions the first time. Cognitive load was determined by the amount of time it took the direction giver to provide the second set of directions after being informed of the locus of the failure for the receiver's not understanding the first rendition of the directions. Laboratory and field experiments both revealed that the speech onset latencies of direction givers who were asked to provide a new route, an abstract alteration, were from two to four times longer than those who were asked to speak more slowly, a concrete alteration (Berger, 1997; Berger et al., 1996). Moreover, direction givers asked to provide a second set of directions that included more specific landmarks showed speech onset latencies that were intermediate between these extremes (Berger et al.,

1996, Experiments 2, 3). Because inclusion of landmarks in directions does not require walk route alterations, these plan modifications were considered to be less abstract than route representations but more abstract than the speech rate feature. Thus the rank order of the speech onset latencies supports the supposition that alterations to abstract plan elements are more demanding of cognitive resources.

When individuals fail to reach their goals, those who have readily available alternative actions or alternative plans should have an advantage over those who have no alternative courses of action available to them. Consistent with this reasoning, individuals who responded more quickly when asked what they would do in the event that specific actions in their persuasion plans failed were judged to be significantly more fluent in trying to persuade a disagreeing confederate on the planned issue one week later (Berger, 1988). This result suggests that individuals with speedier access to alternative actions perform more fluently in the face of goal failure. However, another study revealed that among individuals whose persuasion plans were questioned in a similar way, those whose plans contained more specific arguments to support their position were less fluent when they attempted to persuade a disagreeing confederate (Berger et al., 1989, Experiment 1). Thus, in this case, persuaders with more complex persuasion plans were less fluent than those whose plans were less complex. The results of these two studies are not necessarily contradictory, because in the first case the critical parameter was speed of access to arguments, not the sheer number of alternative arguments in the plan. However, the second study raises the question of whether it is necessarily optimal to have a large number of alternative actions or plans available to deploy in the event of goal failure.

Knowlton and Berger (1997) addressed this issue in a series of experiments in which individuals prepared varying numbers of maps or persuasive arguments before attempting to provide directions or to persuade another, respectively. Confederates expressed either a lack of understanding of the directions or disagreement with the argument, depending upon the speaker's goal. Again, speech onset latencies were used to index the amount of cognitive load experienced by the speaker, depending upon the number of alternative plans/actions prepared. Two of the three experiments in this series revealed that in both the direction-giving and persuasion tasks, those who prepared either one or six maps or arguments showed significantly longer speech onset latencies than did those who prepared three alternative maps or three arguments (Knowlton & Berger, 1997, Experiments 2, 3). Thus having too few or too many alternatives in one's repertoire may prove to be debilitating to performance in the face of goal failure.

Although it is true that these studies do not speak to the issue of the quality of the alternatives generated in terms of their potential effectiveness, the fact that verbal fluency may be undermined when too few or too many alternatives are available is itself significant. Apparently, verbal fluency is a major determinant of judged source credibility; that is, verbally disfluent individuals tend to be judged by others to be less competent and dynamic (Burgoon, Birk, & Pfau, 1990; Miller & Hewgill, 1964). Finding oneself unable to respond quickly and perhaps decisively when goal failure occurs during interaction may well spell the difference between continued progress toward a desired superordinate goal and ultimate failure to reach the goal. Cointerlocutors who observe lengthy delays in others' responses to instances of goal failure are likely to conclude that those displaying long speech onset latencies are not knowledgeable, are ill prepared, or both. This is not to say that rapid verbal recovery from goal failure will necessarily be decisive. A rapidly accessed alternative might not be very effective. However, under most conditions elongated response times in the event of goal failure are probably

not helpful in cultivating perceptions of credibility.

CONCLUSION

Social interaction is an instrument for attaining a wide panorama of goals. The verbal, nonverbal, and action sequences that enable individuals to achieve their goals are guided by and understood with reference to general and specific knowledge about people, the social roles they play, their emotions, the procedures they use to strive toward goals, and the contexts within which interactions take place. Not only are many daily social encounters highly routine, ostensibly novel interactions may have many highly routine sequences embedded within them. The knowledge structures that subserve these conversation and action sequences and the goals that drive them are frequently activated automatically. This automatic activation may explain why the trajectory of some social interactions is both discontinuous and nonlinear. However, surface disorganization should not be confused with conversational chaos and lack of abstract structure.

Although many types of knowledge are vital to the successful conduct of social interaction, in this chapter I have focused on goals and procedural knowledge. This focus has been driven by the postulate that much of the meaning individuals have for their interactions with others is organized in terms of the goals they are currently pursuing or have pursued in the past. Moreover, as this chapter has revealed, the ways individuals organize and the levels at which they conceptualize the procedural knowledge that makes up plans have impacts on their ability to understand others' actions and to reach their own interaction goals. The complexity of plans and the availability of alternative actions and plans have significant impacts on verbal fluency and the speed with which individuals recover from goal failures. Research in this area has the potential to find ways to help individuals develop more effective plans for achieving such fundamental goals as obtaining jobs and disciplining their children in more humane ways; these are reasons enough for scholars to take seriously the knowledge structures that enable individuals to reach their social interaction goals.

REFERENCES

Aarts, H., & Dijksterhuis, A. (2000). Habits as knowledge structures: Automaticity in goal-directed behavior. *Journal of Personality and Social Psychology, 78,* 53-63.

Abelson, R. P. (1976). Script processing in attitude formation and decision-making. In J. S. Carroll & J. W. Payne (Eds.), *Cognition and social behavior* (pp. 33-45). Hillsdale, NJ: Lawrence Erlbaum.

Abelson, R. P. (1981). The psychological status of the script concept. *American Psychologist, 36,* 715-729.

Allen, T. H., & Edwards, R. (1991, November). *The effects of imagined interaction and planning on speech fluency.* Paper presented at the annual meeting of the Speech Communication Association, Chicago.

Allen, T. H., & Honeycutt, J. M. (1997). Planning, imagined interaction, and the nonverbal display of anxiety. *Communication Research, 24,* 64-82.

Alterman, R. (1988). Adaptive planning. *Cognitive Science, 12,* 393-421.

Austin, J. L. (1962). *How to do things with words.* Oxford: Oxford University Press.

Austin, J. T., & Vancouver, J. B. (1996). Goal constructs in psychology: Structure, process, and content. *Psychological Bulletin, 120,* 338-375.

Bargh, J. A. (1997). The automaticity of everyday life. In R. S. Wyer, Jr. (Ed.), *Advances in social cognition: Vol. 10. The automaticity of everyday life* (pp. 1-61). Mahwah, NJ: Lawrence Erlbaum.

Bargh, J. A., & Barndollar, K. (1996). Automaticity in action: The unconscious as repository of chronic goals and motives. In P. M. Gollwitzer & J. A. Bargh (Eds.), *The psychology of action: Linking cognition and motivation to behavior* (pp. 457-481). New York: Guilford.

Bargh, J. A., & Gollwitzer, P. M. (1994). Environmental control of goal-directed action: Automatic and strategic contingencies between situations and behavior. In W. D. Spaulding (Ed.), *Nebraska Symposium on Motivation: Vol. 41. Integrative views of motivation, cognition, and emotion* (pp. 71-124). Lincoln: University of Nebraska Press.

Barker, R. G. (1963). The stream of behavior as an empirical problem. In R. G. Barker (Ed.), *The stream of behavior: Explorations of its structure and content* (pp. 1-22). New York: Appleton-Century-Crofts.

Battmann, W. (1989). Planning as a method of stress prevention: Will it pay off? In C. D. Spielberger, I. G. Sarason, & J. Strelau (Eds.), *Stress and anxiety* (Vol. 12, pp. 259-275). New York: Hemisphere.

Berger, C. R. (1988, May). *Communication plans and communicative performance.* Paper presented at the annual meeting of the International Communication Association, New Orleans.

Berger, C. R. (1995). A plan-based approach to strategic communication. In D. E. Hewes (Ed.), *The cognitive bases of interpersonal communication* (pp. 141-179). Hillsdale, NJ: Lawrence Erlbaum.

Berger, C. R. (1997). *Planning strategic interaction: Attaining goals through communicative action.* Mahwah, NJ: Lawrence Erlbaum.

Berger, C. R. (2000). Goal detection and efficiency: Neglected aspects of message production. *Communication Theory, 10,* 156-166.

Berger, C. R. (in press). Message production skill in social interaction. In J. O. Greene & B. R. Burleson (Eds.), *Handbook of communication and social interaction skills.* Mahwah, NJ: Lawrence Erlbaum.

Berger, C. R., & Bell, R. A. (1988). Plans and the initiation of social relationships. *Human Communication Research, 15,* 217-235.

Berger, C. R., & diBattista, P. (1992). Information seeking and plan elaboration: What do you need to know to know what to do? *Communication Monographs, 59,* 368-387.

Berger, C. R., Karol, S. H., & Jordan, J. M. (1989). When a lot of knowledge is a dangerous thing: The debilitating effects of plan complexity on verbal fluency. *Human Communication Research, 16,* 91-119.

Berger, C. R., Knowlton, S. W., & Abrahams, M. F. (1996). The hierarchy principle in strategic communication. *Communication Theory, 6,* 111-142.

Black, J. B., & Bower, G. H. (1979). Episodes as chunks in narrative memory. *Journal of Verbal Learning and Verbal Behavior, 18,* 309-318.

Black, J. B., & Bower, G. H. (1980). Story understanding as problem-solving. *Poetics, 9,* 223-250.

Bogdan, R. J. (1994). *Grounds for cognition: How goal-guided behavior shapes the mind.* Hillsdale, NJ: Lawrence Erlbaum.

Bogdan, R. J. (1997). *Interpreting minds: The evolution of a practice.* Cambridge: MIT Press.

Bower, G. H., Black, J. B., & Turner, T. J. (1979). Scripts in memory for text. *Cognitive Psychology, 11,* 177-220.

Brand, M. (1984). *Intending and acting: Toward a naturalized theory of action.* Cambridge: MIT Press.

Bratman, M. E. (1987). *Intentions, plans, and practical reason.* Cambridge, MA: Harvard University Press.

Bratman, M. E. (1990). What is intention? In P. R. Cohen, J. Morgan, & M. E. Pollack (Eds.), *Intentions in communication* (pp. 15-31). Cambridge: MIT Press.

Bruce, B., & Newman, D. (1978). Interacting plans. *Cognitive Science, 2,* 195-233.

Burgoon, J. K., Birk, T., & Pfau, M. (1990). Nonverbal behaviors, persuasion, and credibility. *Human Communication Research, 17,* 140-169.

Burgoon, J. K., Stern, L. A., & Dillman, L. (1995). *Interpersonal adaptation: Dyadic interaction patterns.* New York: Cambridge University Press.

Burleson, B. R., & Goldsmith, D. J. (1998). How the comforting process works: Alleviating emotional distress through conversationally induced reappraisals. In P. A. Anderson & L. K. Guerrero (Eds.), *Handbook of communication and emotion: Theory, research, applications, and contexts* (pp. 245-289). San Diego, CA: Academic Press.

Burleson, B. R., & Planalp, S. (2000). Producing emotion(al) messages. *Communication Theory, 10,* 221-250.

Cappella, J. N. (1998). The dynamics of nonverbal coordination and attachment: Problems of causal direction and causal mechanism. In M. T. Palmer & G. A. Barnett (Eds.), *Progress in communication sciences* (Vol. 14, pp. 19-37). Stamford, CT: Ablex.

Carberry, S. (1990). *Plan recognition in natural language dialogue.* Cambridge: MIT Press.

Carbonell, J. G. (1981). Counterplanning: A strategy-based model of adversary planning in real-world situations. *Artificial Intelligence, 16,* 295-329.

Cegala, D. J., & Waldron, V. R. (1992). A study of the relationship between communication performance and conversation participants' thoughts. *Communication Studies, 43,* 105-125.

Clark, H. H. (1994). Discourse in production. In M. A. Gernsbacher (Ed.), *Handbook of psycholinguistics* (pp. 985-1021). San Diego, CA: Academic Press.

Clark, H. H. (1996). Communities, commonalities, and communication. In J. J. Gumperz & S. C. Levinson (Eds.), *Rethinking linguistic relativity* (pp. 324-355). Cambridge: Cambridge University Press.

Clark, H. H., & Carlson, T. B. (1982). Hearers and speech acts. *Language, 58,* 332-373.

Clark, H. H., & Marshall, C. R. (1981). Definite reference and mutual knowledge. In A. K. Joshi, B. Webber, & I. A. Sag (Eds.), *Elements of discourse understanding* (pp. 10-63). Cambridge: Cambridge University Press.

Clark, H. H., & Schaefer, E. F. (1987). Concealing one's meaning from overhearers. *Journal of Memory and Language, 26,* 209-225.

Clark, H. H., & Wilkes-Gibbs, D. (1986). Referring as a collaborative process. *Cognition, 22,* 1-39.

Cohen, P. R., Morgan, J., & Pollack, M. E. (Eds.). (1990). *Intentions in communication.* Cambridge: MIT Press.

Coulmas, F. (1981a). Introduction: Conversational routine. In F. Coulmas (Ed.), *Conversational routine: Explorations in standardized communication situations and prepatterned speech* (pp. 1-17). The Hague: Mouton.

Coulmas, F. (1981b). "Poison to your soul": Thanks and apologies contrastively viewed. In F. Coulmas (Ed.), *Conversational routine: Explorations in standardized communication situations and prepatterned speech* (pp. 69-91). The Hague: Mouton.

Dillard, J. P. (1990). The nature and substance of goals in tactical communication. In M. J. Cody & M. L. McLaughlin (Eds.), *The psychology of tactical communication* (pp. 70-90). Clevedon, Eng.: Multilingual Matters.

Dillard, J. P. (1997). Explicating the goal construct: Tools for theorists. In J. O. Greene (Ed.),

Message production: Advances in communication theory (pp. 47-69). Mahwah, NJ: Lawrence Erlbaum.

Dillard, J. P., Segrin, C., & Harden, J. M. (1989). Primary and secondary goals in the production of interpersonal influence messages. *Communication Monographs, 56,* 19-38.

Eisenberg, E. M. (1984). Ambiguity as a strategy in organizational communication. *Communication Monographs, 51,* 227-242.

Emmons, R. A. (1986). Personal striving: An approach to personality and subjective well-being. *Journal of Personality and Social Psychology, 51,* 1058-1068.

Emmons, R. A. (1989). The personal striving approach to personality. In L. A. Pervin (Ed.), *Goal concepts in personality and social psychology* (pp. 87-126). Hillsdale, NJ: Lawrence Erlbaum.

Emmons, R. A. (1996). Striving and feeling: Personal goals and well-being. In P. M. Gollwitzer & J. A. Bargh (Eds.), *The psychology of action: Linking cognition and motivation to behavior* (pp. 313-337). New York: Guilford.

Fiske, S. T., & Taylor, S. E. (1991). *Social cognition* (2nd ed.). New York: McGraw-Hill.

Fitness, J. (1996). Emotion knowledge structures in close relationships. In G. J. O. Fletcher & J. Fitness (Eds.), *Knowledge structures in close relationships: A social psychological approach* (pp. 195-217). Mahwah, NJ: Lawrence Erlbaum.

Fletcher, G. J. O., & Thomas, G. (1996). Close relationship lay theories: Their structure and function. In G. J. O. Fletcher & J. Fitness (Eds.), *Knowledge structures in close relationships: A social psychological approach* (pp. 3-24). Mahwah, NJ: Lawrence Erlbaum.

Ford, W. S. Z. (1999). Communication and customer service. In M. E. Roloff (Ed.), *Communication yearbook 22* (pp. 341-375). Thousand Oaks, CA: Sage.

Fussell, S. R., & Krauss, R. M. (1992). Coordination of knowledge in communication: Effects of speakers' assumptions about what others know. *Journal of Personality and Social Psychology, 62,* 378-391.

Galambos, J. A., Abelson, R. P., & Black, J. B. (1986). Goals and plans. In J. A. Galambos, R. P. Abelson, & J. B. Black (Eds.), *Knowledge structures* (pp. 101-102). Hillsdale, NJ: Lawrence Erlbaum.

Giles, H., Mulac, A., Bradac, J. J., & Johnson, P. (1987). Speech accommodation theory:

The first decade and beyond. In M. L. McLaughlin (Ed.), *Communication yearbook 10* (pp. 13-48). Newbury Park, CA: Sage.

Goffman, E. (1967). *Interaction ritual: Essays on face-to-face behavior.* Garden City, NY: Anchor.

Goffman, E. (1971). *Relations in public: Microstudies of the public order.* Harmondsworth: Penguin.

Gollwitzer, P. M. (1993). Goal achievement: The role of intentions. In W. Stroebe & M. Hewstone (Eds.), *European review of social psychology* (Vol. 4, pp. 141-185). Chichester: John Wiley.

Gollwitzer, P. M. (1996). The volitional benefits of planning. In P. M. Gollwitzer & J. A. Bargh (Eds.), *The psychology of action: Linking cognition and motivation to behavior* (pp. 287-312). New York: Guilford.

Green, G. M. (1996). *Pragmatics and natural language understanding* (2nd ed.). Hillsdale, NJ: Lawrence Erlbaum.

Greene, J. O. (1984a). A cognitive approach to human communication: An action assembly theory. *Communication Monographs, 51,* 289-306.

Greene, J. O. (1984b). Speech processes and verbal fluency. *Human Communication Research, 11,* 61-84.

Greene, J. O. (1990). Tactical social action: Towards some strategies for theory. In M. J. Cody & M. L. McLaughlin (Eds.), *The psychology of tactical communication* (pp. 31-47). Clevedon, Eng.: Multilingual Matters.

Greene, J. O. (1995). Production of messages in pursuit of multiple social goals: Action assembly theory contributions to the study of cognitive encoding processes. In B. R. Burleson (Ed.), *Communication yearbook 18* (pp. 26-53). Thousand Oaks, CA: Sage.

Greene, J. O. (1997). A second generation action assembly theory. In J. O. Greene (Ed.), *Message production: Advances in communication theory* (pp. 151-170). Mahwah, NJ: Lawrence Erlbaum.

Greene, J. O., & Geddes, D. (1993). An action assembly theory on social skill. *Communication Theory, 3,* 26-49.

Greene, J. O., & Lindsey, A. E. (1989). Encoding processes in the production of multiple-goal messages. *Human Communication Research, 16,* 120-140.

Greene, J. O., Lindsey, A. E., & Hawn, J. J. (1990). Social goals and speech production:

Effects of multiple goals on pausal phenomena. *Journal of Language and Social Psychology, 9,* 119-134.

Greene, J. O., O'Hair, H. D., Cody, M. J., & Yen, C. (1985). Planning and control of behavior during deception. *Human Communication Research, 11,* 335-364.

Hammond, K. J. (1989). *Case-based planning: Viewing planning as a memory task.* New York: Academic Press.

Hauser, M. D. (1996). *The evolution of communication.* Cambridge: MIT Press.

Hayes-Roth, B., & Hayes-Roth, F. (1979). A cognitive model of planning. *Cognitive Science, 3,* 275-310.

Hewes, G. W. (1993). A history of speculation on the relation between tools and language. In K. R. Gibson & T. Ingold (Eds.), *Tools, language and cognition in human evolution* (pp. 20-31). Cambridge: Cambridge University Press.

Hjelmquist, E. (1991). Planning and execution of discourse in conversation. *Communication and Cognition, 24,* 1-17.

Hjelmquist, E., & Gidlund, A. (1984). Planned ideas versus expressed ideas in conversation. *Journal of Pragmatics, 8,* 329-343.

Hobbs, J. R., & Evans, D. A. (1980). Conversation as planned behavior. *Cognitive Science, 4,* 349-377.

Honeycutt, J. M. (1989). A functional analysis of imagined interaction activity in everyday life. In J. E. Shorr, P. Robin, J. A. Connelia, & M. Wolpin (Eds.), *Imagery: Current perspectives* (pp. 13-25). New York: Plenum.

Honeycutt, J. M. (1991). Imagined interactions, imagery and mindfulness/mindlessness. In R. G. Kunzendorf (Ed.), *Mental imagery* (pp. 121-128). New York: Plenum.

Honeycutt, J. M., Edwards, R., & Zagacki, K. S. (1989-1990). Using imagined interaction features to predict measures of self-awareness: Loneliness, locus of control, self-dominance, and emotional intensity. *Imagination, Cognition and Personality, 9,* 17-31.

Honeycutt, J. M., Zagacki, K. S., & Edwards, R. (1992-1993). Imagined interaction, conversational sensitivity and communication competence. *Imagination, Cognition and Personality, 12,* 139-157.

Isaacs, E., & Clark, H. H. (1987). References in conversation between experts and novices. *Journal of Experimental Psychology: General, 116,* 26-37.

Jordan, J. M. (1993). *An exploration of executive control processes in conversations: Extending a plan-based model of communication.* Unpublished doctoral dissertation, Northwestern University, Department of Communication Studies.

Kasser, T., & Sheldon, K. M. (2000). Of wealth and death: Materialism, mortality salience, and consumption behavior. *Psychological Science, 11,* 348-351.

Keller, E. (1981). Gambits: Conversational strategy signals. In F. Coulmas (Ed.), *Conversational routine: Explorations in standardized communication situations and prepatterned speech* (pp. 93-113). The Hague: Mouton.

Kellermann, K. (1991). The conversation MOP II: Progression through scenes in discourse. *Human Communication Research, 17,* 385-414.

Kellermann, K. (1995). The conversation MOP: A model of patterned and pliable behavior. In D. E. Hewes (Ed.), *The cognitive bases of interpersonal communication* (pp. 181-221). Hillsdale, NJ: Lawrence Erlbaum.

Kellermann, K., Broetzmann, S., Lim, T., & Kitao, K. (1989). The conversation MOP: Scenes in the stream of discourse. *Discourse Processes, 12,* 27-62.

Kellermann, K., & Lim, T. (1990). The conversation MOP: III. Timing scenes in discourse. *Journal of Personality and Social Psychology, 59,* 1163-1179.

Knowlton, S. W., & Berger, C. R. (1997). Message planning, communication failure, and cognitive load: Further explorations of the hierarchy principle. *Human Communication Research, 24,* 4-30.

Krauss, R. M., & Weinheimer, S. (1964). Changes in reference phrases as a function of usage in social interaction: A preliminary study. *Psychonomic Science, 1,* 113-114.

Krauss, R. M., & Weinheimer, S. (1966). Concurrent feedback, confirmation, and the encoding of referents in verbal communication. *Journal of Personality and Social Psychology, 4,* 343-346.

Kreitler, S., & Kreitler, H. (1987). Plans and planning: Their motivational and cognitive antecedents. In S. L. Friedman, E. K. Skolnick, & R. R. Cocking (Eds.), *Blueprints for thinking: The role of planning in cognitive development* (pp. 110-178). New York: Cambridge University Press.

Lashley, K. S. (1951). The problem of serial order in behavior. In L. A. Jeffress (Ed.), *Cerebral mechanism in behavior* (pp. 112-146). New York: John Wiley.

Leidner, R. (1993). *Fast food, fast talk: Service work and the routinization of everyday life.* Berkeley: University of California Press.

Levelt, W. J. M. (1989). *Speaking: From intention to articulation.* Cambridge: MIT Press.

Levinson, S. C. (1992). Activity types and language. In P. Drew & J. Heritage (Eds.), *Talk at work: Interaction in institutional settings* (pp. 66-100). Cambridge: Cambridge University Press.

Lewis, D. (1969). *Convention.* Cambridge, MA: Harvard University Press.

Lichtenstein, E. H., & Brewer, W. F. (1980). Memory for goal directed events. *Cognitive Psychology, 12,* 412-445.

Lindsey, A. E., Greene, J. O., Parker, R., & Sassi, M. (1995). Effects of advanced message formulation on message encoding: Evidence of cognitively based hesitation in the production of multiple-goal messages. *Communication Quarterly, 43,* 320-331.

Litman, D. J., & Allen, J. F. (1987). A plan recognition model for subdialogues in conversation. *Cognitive Science, 11,* 163-200.

Little, B. R. (1989). Personal projects analysis: Trivial pursuits, magnificent obsessions, and the search for coherence. In D. M. Buss & N. Cantor (Eds.), *Personality psychology: Recent trends and emerging directions* (pp. 15-31). New York: Springer-Verlag.

MacKay, D. G. (1987). *The organization of perception and action: A theory for language and other cognitive skills.* New York: Springer-Verlag.

Mandler, J. M. (1984). *Stories, scripts, and scenes: Aspects of schema theory.* Hillsdale, NJ: Lawrence Erlbaum.

Meyer, J. R. (1997). Cognitive influences on the ability to address interaction goals. In J. O. Greene (Ed.), *Message production: Advances in communication theory* (pp. 71-90). Mahwah, NJ: Lawrence Erlbaum.

Meyer, J. R. (2000). Cognitive models of message production: Unanswered questions. *Communication Theory, 10,* 176-187.

Miller, G. A., Galanter, E., & Pribram, K. H. (1960). *Plans and the structure of behavior.* New York: Holt, Rinehart & Winston.

Miller, G. R., & Hewgill, M. A. (1964). The effect of variations in nonfluency on audience ratings of source credibility. *Quarterly Journal of Speech, 50,* 36-44.

Murray, S. L., & Holmes, J. G. (1996). The construction of relationship realities. In G. J. O. Fletcher & J. Fitness (Eds.), *Knowledge structures in close relationships: A social psychological approach* (pp. 91-120). Mahwah, NJ: Lawrence Erlbaum.

Newtson, D. (1973). Attribution and the unit of perception of ongoing behavior. *Journal of Personality and Social Psychology, 28,* 28-38.

Newtson, D. (1976). Foundations of attribution: The perception of ongoing behavior. In J. H. Harvey, W. J. Ickes, & R. F. Kidd (eds.), *New directions in attribution research* (Vol. 1, pp. 223-247). Hillsdale, NJ: Lawrence Erlbaum.

Norman, D. A. (1981). Categorization of action slips. *Psychological Review, 88,* 1-15.

O'Keefe, B. J. (1988). The logic of message design: Individual differences in reasoning about communication. *Communication Monographs, 55,* 80-103.

O'Keefe, B. J. (1997). Variation, adaptation, and functional explanation in the study of message design. In G. Philipsen & T. L. Albrecht (Eds.), *Developing communication theories* (pp. 85-118). Albany: State University of New York Press.

O'Keefe, B. J., & Lambert, B. L. (1995). Managing the flow of ideas: A local management approach to message design. In B. R. Burleson (Ed.), *Communication yearbook 18* (pp. 54-82). Thousand Oaks, CA: Sage.

Patalano, A. I., & Seifert, C. M. (1997). Opportunistic planning: Being reminded of pending goals. *Cognitive Psychology, 34,* 1-36.

Pea, R. D., & Hawkins, J. (1987). Planning in a chore-scheduling task. In S. L. Friedman, E. K. Skolnick, & R. R. Cocking (Eds.), *Blueprints for thinking: The role of planning in cognitive development* (pp. 273-302). New York: Cambridge University Press.

Pervin, L. A. (Ed.). (1989). *Goal concepts in personality and social psychology.* Hillsdale, NJ: Lawrence Erlbaum.

Planalp, S. (1987). Interplay between relational knowledge and events. In R. Burnett, P. McGhee, & D. Clarke (Eds.), *Accounting for relationships: Explanation, representation and knowledge* (pp. 175-191). London: Methuen.

Planalp, S. (1993). Friends' and acquaintances' conversations II: Coded differences. *Journal of Social and Personal Relationships, 10,* 339-354.

Planalp, S. (1999). *Communicating emotion: Social, moral, and cultural processes.* New York: Cambridge University Press.

Planalp, S., & Benson, A. (1992). Friends' and acquaintances' conversations I: Perceived differences. *Journal of Social and Personal Relationships, 9,* 483-506.

Planalp, S., & Honeycutt, J. M. (1985). Events that increase uncertainty in personal relationships. *Human Communication Research, 11,* 593-604.

Planalp, S., & Rivers, M. (1996). Changes in knowledge of personal relationships. In G. J. O. Fletcher & J. Fitness (Eds.), *Knowledge structures in close relationships: A social psychological approach* (pp. 299-324). Mahwah, NJ: Lawrence Erlbaum.

Planalp, S., Rutherford, D. K., & Honeycutt, J. M. (1988). Events that increase uncertainty in personal relationships: II. Replication and extension. *Human Communication Research, 14,* 516-547.

Reason, J. (1990). *Human error.* New York: Cambridge University Press.

Rokeach, M. (1973). *The nature of human values.* New York: Free Press.

Russell, D. W., Peplau, L. A., & Cutrona, C. E. (1980). The revised UCLA Loneliness Scale: Concurrent and discriminant validity evidence. *Journal of Personality and Social Psychology, 39,* 472-480.

Sanders, R. E. (1997). The production of symbolic objects as components of larger wholes. In J. O. Greene (Ed.), *Message production: Advances in communication theory* (pp. 245-277). Mahwah, NJ: Lawrence Erlbaum.

Schank, R. C. (1982). *Dynamic memory: A theory of reminding in computers and people.* New York: Cambridge University Press.

Schank, R. C. (1986). *Explanation patterns: Understanding mechanically and creatively.* Hillsdale, NJ: Lawrence Erlbaum.

Schank, R. C., & Abelson, R. P. (1977). *Scripts, plans, goals, and understanding: An enquiry into human knowledge structures.* Hillsdale, NJ: Lawrence Erlbaum.

Schank, R. C., & Abelson, R. P. (1995). Knowledge and memory: The real story. In R. S. Wyer, Jr. (Ed.), *Advances in social cognition: Vol. 8. Knowledge and memory: The real story* (pp. 1-85). Mahwah, NJ: Lawrence Erlbaum.

Schiffer, S. R. (1972). *Meaning.* Oxford: Basil Blackwell.

Schmidt, C. F. (1976). Understanding human action: Recognizing the plans and motives of other persons. In J. S. Carroll & J. W. Payne (Eds.), *Cognition and social behavior* (pp. 47-67). Hillsdale, NJ: Lawrence Erlbaum.

Schober, M. F., & Clark, H. H. (1989). Understanding by addressees and overhearers. *Cognitive Psychology, 21,* 211-232.

Shaver, P. R., Schwartz, J., Kirson, D., & O'Connor, C. (1987). Emotion knowledge: Further explorations of a prototype approach. *Journal of Personality and Social Psychology, 52,* 1061-1086.

Sheldon, K. M., & Kasser, T. (1995). Coherence and congruence: Two aspects of personality integration. *Journal of Personality and Social Psychology, 68,* 531-543.

Sheldon, K. M., & Kasser, T. (1998). Pursuing personal goals: Skills enable progress, but not all progress is beneficial. *Personality and Social Psychology Bulletin, 24,* 1319-1331.

Shepard, C. A., Giles, H., & Le Poire, B. A. (2001). Communication accommodation theory. In W. P. Robinson & H. Giles (Eds.), *The new handbook of language and social psychology* (pp. 33-56). New York: John Wiley.

Stalnaker, R. C. (1978). Assertion. In P. Cole (Ed.), *Syntax and semantics 9: Pragmatics* (pp. 315-332). New York: Academic Press.

Trabasso, T., & Nickels, M. (1992). The development of goal plans of action in the narration of a picture story. *Discourse Processes, 15,* 249-275.

Trabasso, T., Secco, T., & van den Broek, P. W. (1984). Causal cohesion and story coherence. In H. Mandl, N. L. Stein, & T. Trabasso (Eds.), *Learning and comprehension of text* (pp. 83-111). Hillsdale, NJ: Lawrence Erlbaum.

Tracy, K. (1984). The effect of multiple goals on conversational relevance and topic shift. *Communication Monographs, 51,* 274-287.

Tracy, K., & Coupland, N. (Eds.). (1990). *Multiple goals in discourse.* Clevedon, Eng.: Multilingual Matters.

Tracy, K., & Moran, J. P. (1983). Conversational relevance in multiple-goal settings. In R. T. Craig & K. Tracy (Eds.), *Conversational coherence: Form, structure, and strategy* (pp. 116-135). Beverly Hills, CA: Sage.

Vallacher, R. R., & Wegner, D. M. (1985). *A theory of action identification.* Hillsdale, NJ: Lawrence Erlbaum.

Vallacher, R. R., Wegner, D. M., & Somoza, M. (1989). That's easy for you to say: Action identification and speech fluency. *Journal of Personality and Social Psychology, 56,* 199-208.

van den Broek, P. W. (1994). Comprehension and memory of narrative texts: Inferences and coherence. In M. A. Gernsbacher (Ed.), *Handbook of psycholinguistics* (pp. 539-588). San Diego, CA: Academic Press.

Waldron, V. R. (1990). Constrained rationality: Situational influences on information acquisition plans and tactics. *Communication Monographs, 57,* 184-201.

Waldron, V. R. (1997). Toward a theory of interactive conversational planning. In J. O. Greene (Ed.), *Message production: Advances in communication theory* (pp. 195-220). Mahwah, NJ: Lawrence Erlbaum.

Waldron, V. R., & Applegate, J. L. (1994). Interpersonal construct differentiation and conversational planning: An examination of two cognitive accounts for the production of competent verbal disagreement tactics. *Human Communication Research, 21,* 3-35.

Waldron, V. R., Caughlin, J. P., & Jackson, D. W. (1995). Talking specifics: Facilitating effects of planning on AIDS talk in peer dyads. *Health Communication, 7,* 247-264.

Waldron, V. R., & Lavitt, M. R. (2000). "Welfare-to-work": Assessing communication competencies and client outcomes in a job training program. *Southern Communication Journal, 66,* 1-15.

Wiemann, J. M., & Daly, J. A. (1994). Introduction: Getting your own way. In J. A. Daly & J. M. Wiemann (Eds.), *Strategic interpersonal communication* (pp. vii-xiv). Hillsdale, NJ: Lawrence Erlbaum.

Wilensky, R. (1983). *Planning and understanding: A computational approach to human reasoning.* Reading, MA: Addison-Wesley.

Wilkes-Gibbs, D., & Clark, H. H. (1992). Coordinating beliefs in conversation. *Journal of Memory and Language, 31,* 183-194.

Wilson, S. R. (2000). Developing planning perspectives to explain parent-child interaction patterns in physically abusive families. *Communication Theory, 10,* 210-220.

Wittgenstein, L. (1953). *Philosophical investigations.* Oxford: Basil Blackwell.

Zammuner, V. L. (1981). *Speech production: Strategies in discourse planning.* Hamburg: Helmut Buske Verlag.

7

Language and Interpersonal Communication

SCOTT JACOBS

The concepts of language and communication, although intimately related, have never really been happily married. Communication scholars will readily recognize that the use of language to formulate messages and to perform social actions is the paradigm case of communication. Almost all cases of communication that interest communication researchers involve talk or writing in some way. Still, the effort to ground notions of "message meaning" or "symbolic action" in a detailed account of the organization of linguistic forms and functions has always seemed to be so technical and tedious a task that it has been generally bypassed in the process of building communication theory. Likewise, students of language have often been reluctant to integrate

their theories of language structure with what is manifestly the paradigm function of language, that of communication. Knowing what language does has commonly been thought to be superfluous to knowing what language is. While this attitude has begun to fade, the term *language* has been so thoroughly appropriated by the technical structural interests of sentence grammarians that any effort to study the uses of language or the structures of language beyond the sentence requires use of a whole new term: *discourse*.

Discourse analysis is an effort to close the gap between conceptions of communication process and language structure and function. Its research questions center on the role of language in constructing an "architecture

---

EDITORS' NOTE: This chapter is reprinted from the second edition of the *Handbook of Interpersonal Communication*.

of intersubjectivity" (Heritage, 1984; Rommetveit, 1974): How do you decide what to say when you talk? And how is it that when I speak words, you understand me? How do we assemble linguistic units and place them into the interactional stream to produce fitting messages and sensible patterns of social interaction? It is generally assumed by discourse analysts that these sorts of questions will be answered through specification of the content and operational properties of a shared system of knowledge that informs linguistic choice and enables linguistic interpretation. Although well-developed, detailed models of this system of knowledge are beyond the reach of most areas of contemporary discourse analysis, there is a growing catalog of discursive forms and patterns that have become susceptible to systematic description. Analysis of these forms and patterns has led to an emerging consensus that any model of discourse must be compatible with certain fundamental properties. This chapter first summarizes those basic properties of discourse, then shows how they are manifested in the organization of conversational interaction. As we shall see, the effort to come to grips with these properties has led to a basic shift in the conceptual framework of discourse analysis from a "normative/code" model of discourse knowledge to a more "inferential/ strategic" model.

CENTRAL PROBLEMS AND BASIC PROPERTIES

Language is systematically organized in a variety of ways beyond the units of word and sentence, all of which contribute to the information conveyed and the actions performed by a message. Linguistic organization can be described at various levels of conceptual structure that organize linguistic content (texts, stories, conversational topics, and so on), at various levels of pragmatic structure that organize linguistic action and interaction

(speech acts, adjacency pairs, conversational episodes, and so on), or at levels of stylistic structure that integrate linguistic features with the characteristics of person and situation (for example, styles, codes, or message design logics). Discourse analysts are concerned with isolating these various structures and formulating principles for their construction and use. In analyzing these levels of organization, discourse analysts address three interrelated puzzles. From these puzzles have emerged some very general principles that operate across levels.

The Problem of Meaning

What sort of information is expressed by discourse structures, and what derivational operations enable people to express and interpret that information? How do we know facts about our language such as the following?

(1) "Is Sybil there?" can be used to request that the addressee call Sybil to the telephone.

(2) "You sure are hot" can literally refer to the addressee's body temperature or metaphorically refer to his or her streak of success or emotional state; and the utterance may also be used ironically to express just the opposite of the literal or metaphorical reference.

(3) Using *title plus last name* to address someone (for example, Dr. Welby) conveys that the addressee is someone of high power, status, and/or social distance.

(4) "John subscribes to *SPY*" ordinarily conveys that John reads *SPY*.

Somehow people are able to refer to events and to describe states of affairs. They can convey attitudes, beliefs, and desires. They express relationships to situation and addressee. They may speak plainly and explicitly or they may speak indirectly and figuratively. And they are very good at saying just enough for the hearer to be able to "fill in" what is left unsaid.

The Problem of Action

How do speakers and writers assemble messages? What kinds of choices and assessments enter into the decision of what to say, how to say it, and when? Why, for example, is it odd to introduce oneself just to ask for directions from a passerby on the sidewalk?

(5) Hi, my name is Scott Jacobs. Could you tell me where I could find a public telephone?

And what is it about sentence 6 that makes it a more fitting response than 7 or 8 when writing a thank-you note to a friend for a gift that is awful (Bavelas, Black, Chovil, & Mullett, 1990)?

(6) I appreciate your thoughtfulness.

(7) The gift is perfect; I really love it.

(8) I don't like the gift and am going to exchange or return it.

Along another line, no one would think that uttering sentence 9 would ever fry the egg.

(9) I hereby fry this egg.

So how is it that, given the right circumstances, uttering sentence 10 will marry Ralph and Linda, and uttering 11 will place the speaker under an obligation to be there Friday (Searle, 1989)?

(10) I hereby pronounce you husband and wife.

(11) I promise to be there Friday.

In producing messages, people decide what will make sense and what won't, what will work and what will not. They are more or less sensitive to the need to be polite. They know how to do things with words like *bet, beg,* and *complain.* There is a consequentiality to language use that speakers and writers more or less successfully take into account when constructing messages. And this consequentiality is intimately related to what any message means (Sanders, 1987).

The Problem of Coherence

The problems of meaning and action converge in the problem of coherence. What are the recognizably sensible and orderly patterns and relations among linguistic elements, and what principles govern the formation of those patterns? Clearly, all natural language users show great facility in finding the ways in which the elements of language "hang together" and in seeing to it that their own contributions do so. Such impressions are central to the sense of orderliness, meaningfulness, and appropriateness we find in language structure and use. But it is not at all clear how we construct coherent discourse. Why is it, for example, that we find it difficult to keep track of the topic in the following conversation (adapted from the musical comedy *The Music Man*)?

(12) *A:* Mama, a man with a suitcase followed me home.

B: Did he say anything?

A: He tried.

B: Did you say anything?

A: Of course not, mama.

B: If you don't mind my saying so, it wouldn't have hurt to find out what the gentleman wanted.

A: I know what the gentleman wanted.

B: What, dear?

A: You'll find it in Balzac.

B: Well, excuse me for living, but I've never read it.

A: Neither has anyone else in this town.

B: There you go again with the same old comment about the low mentality of River City people, and taking it too much to heart.

A: Since the Madison County Library was entrusted to me for the purpose of improving River City's cultural level, you can't blame me for considering that the ladies of River City keep ignoring all my counsel and advice.

B: When a woman's got a husband and you've got none, why should she take advice from you, even if you can quote Balzac and Shakespeare, and all them other high-falutin' Greeks?

A: If you don't mind my saying so, you have a bad habit of changing every subject.

B: I haven't changed the subject. We were talking about that stranger.

A: What stranger?

B: With the suitcase. Who may be your very last chance.

We can recognize "topic drift," but it is not obvious how to define it (Hobbs, 1990b; Jacobs & Jackson, 1992). Alternatively, how is it that we are able to hear an utterance like that in example 13, but not an utterance like that in 14, as belonging in a conversational closing (Schegloff & Sacks, 1974, p. 249)?

(13)   Well, I'll letchu go.

(14)   What's up?

Somehow, natural language users can see in a string of sentences a story. They know how to make topically relevant contributions to conversations. They know how to reply to questions and offers, and they can organize arguments and lead up to invitations. They can open and close conversations. All of these skills involve the application of a system of knowledge for how discourse units fit together into well-formed wholes at higher levels of order.

Properties of Linguistic Communication

So what kind of knowledge enables people to produce and understand discourse that is coherent, fitting, and meaningful? It is

becoming increasingly apparent that any theory of language structure and use must be compatible with certain core facts, or basic principles.

1. Linguistic communication requires shared principles for inference beyond information given by a "surface" reading. Whereas students of interpersonal communication have commonly emphasized the idiosyncratic and personal qualities of message interpretation, discourse analysts have started from the massive fact of the generally reliable and public quality of much interpretation. When people use language, they usually understand one another, and do so at an exceedingly intricate level of detail. And where there is ambiguity, vagueness, deception, confusion, or the like, this too results from public qualities of the discourse. Moreover, the message communicated may not be connected in any obvious way to what is directly and literally said. An adequate representation of the "message" conveyed may bear no obvious correspondence to the string of signs, or signals, that serve as the vehicle for that message. To see this, consider just some of the commonplace intuitions about what is being communicated in the following two-turn exchange.

(15)   *Ruth Anne:* These are beautiful plants. The leaves are so waxy and green.

Sally: Well, uh (.) actually Scott's the one who takes care of them. Hehhh. I don't do much of the housework.

Among the more obvious meanings that can be seen by any native language user are the following: Ruth Anne and Sally are having a casual conversation. Sally knows Scott and believes that Ruth Anne knows Scott—or at least knows who Scott is. Scott does not have any pertinent formal status over Ruth Anne or Sally.

The leaves mentioned by Ruth Anne are the leaves of the plants that are beautiful. Part of what makes the plants appear beautiful is the waxy and green appearance of their leaves. What Scott takes care of are the plants (and not the leaves, or the cats, or the old people next door), and his taking care of the plants is the reason they are beautiful.

Ruth Anne is issuing a compliment to Sally. In doing so, Ruth Anne awards positive value to the plants' appearing beautiful; Ruth Anne assumes that Sally is responsible for that appearance, and Ruth Anne thereby expresses approval of Sally.

Sally is not accepting Ruth Anne's compliment. Instead, Sally deflects the compliment to Scott. The reason for the rejection is that Sally does not take care of the plants (as Ruth Anne seems to think), and so Sally cannot claim responsibility for their beauty. Sally also believes that Ruth Anne believes that Sally occupies the role of houseworker. Scott does most of the housework. Taking care of the plants is part of the housework.

Information like this is part of what we would want to call the meaning of the exchange. It is what gets communicated. Yet, strictly speaking, none of this information is literally and explicitly said. In effect, messages must be identified with the context that is constructed for a text, and not just with the meaning of the words themselves.

All of what is noted above is the product of inferences made in the process of constructing a sensible interpretation of what was said. That interpretation involves the construction of inferences based on finding the functional significance of what could have been said but wasn't (not saying "Thank you" or not saying "Mr. Jacobs" or "my husband" instead of "Scott"). It involves inferences guided by principles for designing coherent discourse. For example, Brown and Yule's (1983) *principle of local interpretation* (p. 59) instructs hearers not to expand or change a context any more than is needed to arrive at an interpretation. Thus we ordinarily assume that Ruth Anne and Sally maintain the same topic, and so we infer that the leaves referred to are the leaves

of the same plant that is beautiful and that taking care of the plants has something to do with the appearance of the plants.

Of course, these inferences are all defeasible. They can change given additional information. But the point is that these are the kinds of inferences that people make, and these inferences are quite detailed, highly reliable, and far beyond the explanatory capacity of any correspondence theory of symbolic meaning. Any theory that equates message meaning with the literal meaning of what is said will miss how coherent and meaningful messages are produced and understood. Inference beyond the information given in the text is a characteristic process invited by all natural language use. A theory of linguistic communication needs to model the different types of inferences that people make and explain how people are able to derive such information from language. Most discourse analysts today take it for granted that the coherence of interactional patterns and the sense of messages must be explained in terms of a rich conceptual structure—a constructed context for the surface structure of what is actually said or written.

2. Linguistic communication requires generative principles. The intricacy of our system for linguistic communication is all the more remarkable when one considers the creative capacity for language use. Chomsky (1959, 1972, pp. 11-12) first drew widespread attention to this aspect of language. He noted that any natural language user can spontaneously and effortlessly produce and understand a potentially infinite number of sentences that are completely novel—discourse that is not a repetition of anything we have ever heard before and is not in any obvious way similar in pattern to discourse we have spoken in the past.

Although Chomsky had in mind syntactic structures of sentences, similar observations could be made at a variety of levels of language organization. Theories that try to account for language production and understanding by appeal to sets of standardized patterns quickly exhaust themselves when they attempt to model seriously the flexibility of language use and the wide variety of possible structures. Consider as an example the variety of ways you might communicate to your spouse that you wish to leave a party.

(16) Let's go home.

(17) I want to leave.

(18) What time is it?

(19) This sure is boring.

(20) Don't you have to be up early tomorrow?

(21) Are you going to have another drink?

(22) Do you think the Millers would give you a ride home?

(23) You look ready to party all night.

(24) Did you get a chance to talk to everyone you wanted to?

(25) Is it starting to rain?

(26) It looks like it's stopped raining.

Although some ways to get your spouse to leave are more or less standardized and may be widely used, it would be seriously misleading to suggest that knowledge of such forms sufficiently characterizes the productive and interpretive capacities of a natural language user. The list could go on indefinitely. And the problem becomes even more unmanageable for patterns of interactional exchange and episodes. Certainly discourse is filled with standardized usages, recurrent patterns, and conventionalized forms of expression. And their occurrence is a matter of considerable interest (compare Hopper, 1992; Kellermann, Broetzmann, Lim, & Kitao, 1989).

But once the creative potential for language use is taken seriously, the basic problem confronted by the discourse analyst becomes one of explaining the massive fact of variability, innovation, and novelty in language patterning (compare Cappella, 1990; Jacobs, 1990). Discourse analysts today have begun to abandon the idea that discourse knowledge consists of some sort of behavioral repertoire or closed set of response types (see O'Keefe, 1990). If modeling discourse knowledge is to be a finite enterprise, standardized patterns alone cannot be the basis for its characterization. Such characterizations would be inherently incomplete. Rather than specifying a list of patterns that people are motivated to follow regularly, discourse models need to postulate a system of principles that enable people to generate an open-ended set of patterns, only some of which become what Cushman and Whiting (1972) term "standardized usages."

3. Communicative meaning is context determined. If theories of action must somehow accommodate the generativity of language, then theories of meaning must acknowledge the contextualization of meaning. The meaning of any particular utterance is fixed with respect to a context of knowledge brought to bear in the process of interpretation. As Bransford and Johnson (1972) showed in very early studies, people must activate a relevant field of world knowledge in order to comprehend a text. Searle (1980) makes a similar point with sentences like the following:

(27) Bill cut the grass.

(28) The barber cut Tom's hair.

(29) Sally cut the cake.

(30) The tailor cut the cloth.

The word *cut* has the same literal meaning in all four sentences (Sanders, 1987). Nevertheless, the sense of the term changes depending upon what we know about the activity being indexed by the sentence. Cutting grass is not the same as cutting hair, cake, or cloth. And even the sense of "cut the grass" may change depending on whether Bill is understood to be, say, mowing a lawn or preparing a floral arrangement. And it is this need to activate a context of knowledge that makes it difficult to understand sentences 31-33.

(31)   Mary cut the sand.

(32)   Bill cut the mountain.

(33)   Pat cut it.

We simply have no clear knowledge of what is involved in cutting mountains or sand. Likewise, even if we assume that "cut" in sentence 33 is meant literally, the lack of clear context leaves its sense incomplete and underdetermined.

A straightforward implication of context determination is that any particular utterance may mean multiple things depending upon its context of occurrence. There can be no simple assignment of meaning, given an utterance. Consider the following exchange overheard in a Mexican restaurant:

(34)   *Customer:*   Did you say sopapillas come with the chiles rellenos?

   Waitress: I'll get it right away sir.

Here, the customer's utterance occurred as the waitress was serving the orders for the table. His question called attention to the fact that no sopapillas had been delivered, served to check his expectation that his order would come with sopapillas, communicated that he wanted the sopapillas to be served at the same time as the chiles rellenos, and functioned to request the waitress to bring them. But the question would have been taken to mean something altogether different if the waitress had just placed sopapillas next to the customer's chiles rellenos. In that case, the customer could have been taken to communicate that he did not expect sopapillas and, perhaps, that he was concerned with whether they had been mistakenly served to him, whether he would be billed for them, and

so on. And we can easily imagine an identical utterance being asked as the customer is ordering food. And here again the meaning would be quite different.

Once the importance of context in determining meaning is recognized, the idea that symbolic forms contain their own meanings quickly loses its attractiveness. It becomes impossible to sustain a project that tries to model inference by the kind of self-contained operations suggested below:

(35)   "John is a bachelor" implies that John is not married.

(36)   "Barbara is older than Carol. Carol is older than Mary" implies that Barbara is older than Mary.

There are meanings that are conventionally or logically determined in ways like this. But contextually inferred meanings are never logically or conventionally necessary in these ways because contextual inference requires hearers to assume premises in addition to what is said, and these premises are never necessarily relevant and are always to some degree uncertain. Rather than looking simply for ways to unpack meaning from symbolic containers, theories of discourse need to model the way in which meaning emerges by integrating text with context.

4. Language structures are functional designs. The structures found in discourse are intimately related to the functional design of those structures. What "pattern" is found to exist in discourse depends on what functions are performed by that discourse. So, for example, the waiter's response in example 37 creates a meaningful and coherent exchange only by seeing how the customer's question is being used to gain information to decide on a possible order and how the waiter's utterance— while not an answer to the question—is being used as a reason for not being able to comply with that possible upcoming order.

(37) *Customer:* What's the chicken marsala like?

      Waiter: I'm sorry, we're all out of that tonight.

Any model of language use and structure must come to grips with a difficult problem: The functional design of language structure means that the principles of linguistic structuring are not just followed; they are used. The paradox this presents is that deviating from structural expectations and principles of order may make sense in a deeper functional representation of that order. Insult and humor often work precisely because natural language users recognize the existence of structural principles that are being apparently violated in the service of making some point (Ervin-Tripp, 1971). And language choice may reflect the demands of literal reference or the most obliquely metaphorical social meanings (Fitch, 1991). All this suggests that models of discourse knowledge must reflect how meaning and coherence emerge from the interplay of strategy and structure.

5. *Language use is multifunctional.* What people say, how they say it, and where they say it in the stream of discourse all reflect the ways in which individuals manage multiple goals and situational demands to convey an assembly of information. In part, the multifunctionality of language use reflects the relevance of multiple levels of organization and order that apply to any utterance. All utterances, for example, participate in procedural and ritual orders, convey both topical and relational information, and contribute to varying aspects of discourse coherence (Clark & Delia, 1979; Ellis, 1992; Sigman, 1987). But functional organization also reflects communicators' ongoing assessments of locally emergent demands and possibilities in a situation (Mandelbaum & Pomerantz, 1991). What counts as a fitting contribution to a situation will depend upon the communicator's definition of it.

The important thing to see, however, is that the processes providing for multifunctionality may not simply be an additive organization of unifunctional processes. There is an *integrative* process that does not decompose into elementary functions. Thus an utterance like sentence 6 reflects one way of responding in a unified way to the demand to acknowledge a gift while avoiding telling a falsehood or making the friend feel bad. Utterances like sentences 7 and 8 are less successful in reconciling these goals. A great deal of what constitutes communicative "skill" in producing a message is the ability to formulate situational demands, to see the potential for pursuing goals, to imagine alternative definitions of a situation, and to construct messages so as to maximally satisfy those demands and goals (O'Keefe, 1991).

These properties of language structure and use exist at virtually all levels of discourse organization. How to model these properties is a recalcitrant puzzle that has shaped the direction of theory development.

THE NORMATIVE CODE MODEL

Although discourse analysis owes a historical debt to early work in anthropology (Malinowski, 1923, 1935) and analytic philosophy (Austin, 1962; Wittgenstein, 1953), the major impetus for contemporary studies of discourse must be traced to the achievements and limitations of contemporary linguistics and Noam Chomsky's theory of transformational generative grammar. With the publication of *Syntactic Structures* (1957) from his dissertation, Chomsky started a revolution in linguistics (Newmeyer, 1980). It was largely through the philosophical and psychological controversies generated by his work that the analytic concepts and techniques of linguistics came to be disseminated throughout the social sciences and humanities (see Hook, 1969). Though the theory of transformational generative grammar applied strictly to certain formal properties of the syntax of sentences, the theory supplied a general paradigm for conceptualizing structure at any level of discourse and a motivation for expanding the initially narrow domain of "linguistic competence" to include aspects of communicative knowledge previously relegated to "performance" considerations.

Linguistics and Grammar

The goal of linguistic analysis is to specify those rules that constitute the grammar of a language. Put simply, a grammar describes the logical structure of relations between meanings and signals that are created by a code. The rules of a grammar are computational procedures that combine the elements of a language so as to specify the forms in which a "message" may acceptably appear. Linguists have generally analyzed the grammar of human languages into three components, or subsystems of rules. The rules governing the combinatorial relations among words in sentences are syntax. Semantics is the component of grammar that assigns meaning representations to the words and specifies the logical form of sentences. The rules that specify the sounds of a language and their permissible combinations constitute phonology.

Following Saussure's (1916/1983) distinction between *langue* and *parole*, Chomsky (1965) argued that the subject matter of a theory of grammar is not language behavior per se but the linguistic competence of an idealized speaker-hearer of the language. That is, a grammar formally describes an isolatable system of knowledge restricted to the grammatical properties of sentences. Within this technical delimitation of the subject matter of "language," a theory of grammar would be capable of reproducing all the permissible sentences in a language (and none of the impermissible ones) and formally representing the distinctions and relations that natural language users can be brought to recognize intuitively within and among those sentences.

So, for example, at the level of syntactic organization, any adequate theory of English grammar should be capable of distinguishing between examples 38 and 39.

(38)   Colorless green ideas sleep furiously.

(39)   Furiously sleep ideas green colorless.

Even though sentence 38 is nonsensical and bizarre, by comparing it with 39, any speaker of English can be brought to recognize that 38 has a kind of word order to it (i.e., it is grammatical)—a fact that demonstrates that speakers of a language seem to have a relatively autonomous knowledge of syntax (Chomsky, 1957, p. 15).

Such a system of knowledge is abstracted from actual performance considerations where restrictions on memory and attention, operation of extralinguistic beliefs about the speaker and the situation, and other aspects of knowledge and cognitive structure interact with the grammatical system in the process of actual discourse production and comprehension (Chomsky, 1972, pp. 115-116). The competence-performance distinction focuses attention on the principles of organization in the formation of sentences rather than on the factors influencing when and how people will actually recognize and exhibit behaviors of that type (Sanders, 1987). Johnson-Laird (1983) illustrates the distinction with a sentence from a book review:

(40)   This book fills a much-needed gap in the
        literature.

Many readers, at first glance, will take this sentence to be complimenting the book as being much needed. But that would be a mistaken reading. And the fact that we can recognize our mistake shows that we have a knowledge of language that is not always exhibited in practice.

While the "data" for much linguistic analysis are intuitions about hypothetical sentences, linguists recognize that not just any property can be directly intuited. Intuitions need to be clarified and disciplined through comparative analysis. It would probably be useless (even positively misleading) to ask a native speaker directly, for example, whether or not sentences 41 and 42 are syntactically identical.

(41)   I left, for he made me nervous.

(42)   I left, because he made me nervous.

Nevertheless, persons can see a grammatical and an ungrammatical sentence (marked by an asterisk) in each of the following pairs.

(43a)   It was because I was nervous that I left.

(43b)   *It was for I was nervous that I left.

(44a)   Did you leave because he made you nervous?

(44b)   *Did you leave for he made you nervous?

(45a)   I left, because I was nervous and because I wanted to go.

(45b)   *I left, for I was nervous and for I wanted to go.

On the basis of these asymmetries, one can reasonably conclude that a theory of English grammar should not treat *because* clauses and *for* clauses as syntactically identical, despite their similarity in semantic meaning (Smith & Wilson, 1990, p. 39).

Likewise, an adequate theory of English syntax should be able to represent that John is the object of sentence 46 but the subject of sentence 47, that sentences 48, 49, and 50 are structurally related, and that 51 is structurally ambiguous (between "flying a plane" and "a flying plane").

(46)   John is easy to please.

(47)   John is eager to please.

(48)   John hit the ball.

(49)   The ball was hit by John.

(50)   Did John hit the ball?

(51)   Flying planes can be dangerous.

Syntactic theory after Chomsky has produced exceedingly subtle and sophisticated formal analyses of the structure of language (compare with Soames & Perlmutter, 1979). The power of these analyses has led many to take them as exemplars for normative code modeling.

In advancing an exceedingly powerful theory of syntactic structure, Chomsky also called attention to three fundamental properties of syntax that demanded a wholesale reassessment of the complexity of the system. First, as mentioned earlier, Chomsky pointed out the infinite generativity of syntax. Just as with mathematical equations, natural language sentences are generated by a finite system of rules that can operate in combination with one another and recursively to produce an infinite range of possibilities. Consider, for example, the scope of the operation implied by sentences 52 and 53:

(52)   The man runs the store on 59th Street.

(53)   The man who took the cat that ate the mouse that ran down the stairs of the big white house that stands next to the church . . . runs the store on 59th Street.

Second, Chomsky called attention to the special way in which syntactic structures are hierarchically organized. As Lyons (1970, p. 60) points out, traditional grammarians had long recognized that the linear string of words in a sentence exhibits a hierarchical structure. For example, sentence 54 has a structural relation between a subject and a predicate.

(54) The girl reads the book.

The subject of the sentence (S) is a noun phrase (NP) that specifies a relation between a noun (N) and a definite article (T). The predicate is a verb phrase (VP) in which there is a relation between a verb (V) and its object, which is also a noun phrase consisting of a structural relation between a noun and a definite article. Such a hierarchical structure can be formally represented by means of the

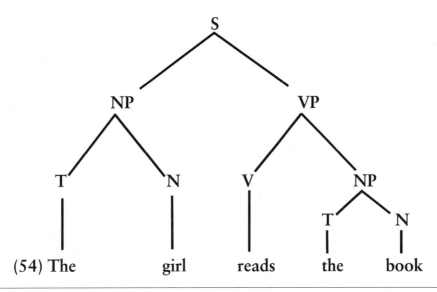

Figure 7.1   Tree Diagram

following rewrite rules (adapted from Chomsky, 1957, p. 28):

a. S → NP + VP
b. NP → T + N
c. VP → V + NP
d. T → the
e. N → girl, book, . . .
f. V → reads, eats, . . .

Each rule (X → Y) is to be interpreted as the instruction "Rewrite X as Y" and provides the phrase structure representation of sentence 54 found in Figure 7.1.

The contribution that Chomsky made to understanding this hierarchical organization was to show that syntax consists of *structure-dependent* operations that cannot be modeled by any system that defines structural dependencies through linear relations between words (for example, "finite state grammar" of the sort illustrated by Shannon & Weaver's, 1949, information theory or by any Markov process). Chomsky argued that the syntactic rules operate on hierarchically defined units so that structural dependencies among units are maintained over an indefinitely large series of intervening elements. So the relation between

"The girl" and "reads" obtains at the level of structure defined by the main NP and VP in the sentence and is completely indifferent to the number of words and clauses that might be inserted between them. (Compare also sentences 52 and 53.) One striking possibility, which Chomsky (1957) argues, is that finite state grammars are in principle incapable of handling operations like those expressed in g:

g. S → NP + S, VP

Because S is also a sentence, it too can have an embedded sentence and so on indefinitely, being restricted only by performance limitations of human memory. Thus we can generate the following:

(55)   The girl reads the book.

(56)   The girl the cat scratched reads the book.

(57)   The girl the cat the dog ate scratched reads the book.

The third property of syntactic structure that Chomsky pointed out was its dual structure: Every sentence has a "surface structure" and a "deep structure." The surface structure consists of the words of the sentence in their order of occurrence in actual sentences. The deep structure corresponds to the level of representation on which a semantic mapping is made. The two levels are related through transformational rules. The postulation of some sort of "deep structure" appears necessary to explain the intuition that sentences 48, 49, and 50 all embody a common propositional structure, "John hit the ball." Likewise, the ambiguity of sentence 51 can be explained through generation of a common surface structure from two different deep structures. While Chomsky's particular version of deep structure has lost its widespread popularity (Sells, 1985), the concept was mainly taken metaphorically by discourse analysts to warrant a distinction between the linear structure of what is explicitly said and the conceptual structure of what is implicitly conveyed.

The General Model

By far the most popular approach to developing models of discourse has been to pick out from discourse some relatively manageable level of structural organization and, in Levinson's (1981, p. 93) phrase, "do a Chomsky" on it. "Doing a Chomsky" means showing how the organization of linguistic communication reflects a normatively regulated code for structuring and using linguistic categories. In this paradigm, discourse knowledge is taken to consist of a self-contained rule system that organizes the various levels of structure in a message in a way akin to a kind of "supergrammar." It amounts to a "rules and units" approach to modeling discourse (Taylor & Cameron, 1987).

Perhaps the real popularity of the Chomskyan vision of grammar is due to the way that it formalizes a commonsense model of communication. Reddy (1979) calls it the "conduit metaphor" and locates its principles in the very fabric of ordinary language usage. The intellectual foundations of a code model can be traced back to Locke (1690/1975;

see Harris, 1987; Taylor, 1992). Akmajian, Demers, Farmer, and Harnish (1990, pp. 307-354) and Sperber and Wilson (1986, pp. 1-31) describe its appearance in information theory and linguistics in ways that bear a striking resemblance to Berlo's (1960) linear model. Wilson (1970) clearly articulates the normative aspects of code use.

The normative code model portrays linguistic communication as the transmission of a message in which a sender encodes meanings into a physical signal and a receiver decodes the message to derive a meaningful representation of it. Decoding and encoding occur through the application of a code. A code is a system of rules that specifies derivational relations between the elements at various structural levels (thus connecting meanings with public signs, or signals) and combinatorial relations among the elements at any given structural level (thus providing coherent configurations in the arrangement of signs). In encoding, senders consult the rules to determine what signal to transmit, given an intended meaning. In decoding, receivers consult the rules to determine the intended meaning, given a received signal.

Senders decide what messages to send by consulting normative rules and conforming to their behavioral specifications. Norms are standing social expectations known and adhered to by members of a linguistic community, or internalized dispositions shared by members of that community. They can be stated in the form, "Given condition(s) C, act A is obligated (or permitted or prohibited)." The given conditions for action are contextual features that exist prior to the action. The act is any structural unit or combination of units defined by the language code. By recognizing relevant contextual features, actors call up the corresponding norms and decide what to do by following the behaviors associated with those conditions (Cushman & Whiting, 1972; Shimanoff, 1980).

Normative code models predict that communication will be successful just in case the receiver employs the same rules to decode the message that the sender employs to encode the message. Communication breakdowns will occur to the degree that the sender and receiver fail to share the same code rules. Indeed, one of the features of this model is that, in the absence of noise, proper application of code rules *guarantees* the meaning of a message, just as the rules of mathematics guarantee a determinate (or indeterminate) solution to an equation. Likewise, regularities in the production and patterning of messages will occur to the degree that normative rules are strongly internalized or sanctioned by members of a linguistic community and the relevant contextual features are clearly recognizable.

The following subsection examines the logic and prospects of this kind of model for the analysis of conversational interaction. Modeling the way in which the use of language creates and regulates interactional structure supplies a clear and obvious bridge between theories of language and theories of interpersonal communication. As will be shown, a normative code model runs into intractable problems—problems intimately connected to the properties of discourse discussed earlier. These problems have led discourse analysts to develop an alternative framework to be discussed in the concluding section of the chapter.

Extensions of the Normative Code Model to Conversational Interaction

By far the most influential approach to modeling meaning and coherence in conversation is one that assumes that coherent structural patterns consist of a series of moves or act types and that the functional meanings communicated by utterances can be typified in terms of these acts. It has been widely assumed that when analyzed in this way conversation will reveal a "grammar of natural conversation" (Schenkein, 1978, p. 3) or "social syntax" (Gumperz & Hymes, 1972, p. 348). The

kinds of problems that cast doubt on the adequacy of such a conceptualization will be presented below through a consideration first of the ways in which discourse analysts have attempted to model conversational sequencing and then of the ways in which they have attempted to model the expression and interpretation of conversational acts.

Sequencing rule approaches. In its simplest form, the orderliness of conversational sequencing might be modeled on the assumptions that (a) the units of conversational structure consist of utterances, (b) these utterances correspond to speech act types, and (c) the succession of utterances in conversation is regulated by rules that specify the range of speech act types that may appropriately follow any given speech act (Levinson, 1981; Mohan, 1974). In such a model, the assignment of speech act types is assumed to be essentially nonproblematic, the main problem being to account for their order of appearance. The advantage of such an assumption is that one may construct a model by specifying irreducible conventions that operate directly on the surface structure of turns at talk.

The most familiar version of such a model grows out of the system of turn-taking rules proposed by Sacks, Schegloff, and Jefferson (1974). According to this rule system, one of the basic techniques for allocating turns is by initiating an adjacency pair. Adjacency pairs are action sequences such as question-answer, greeting-greeting, offer-acceptance/refusal, request-acceptance/rejection. Schegloff and Sacks (1974) argue that they are the basic constructional units for creating sequentially implicated turns at talk. Adjacency pairs are two turns long, having two parts said by different speakers in adjacent turns at talk. By using the first part of an adjacency pair (a "first pair part," or FPP), a speaker establishes a "next turn position" that casts the recipient into the role of respondent and structures the range of appropriate next moves to those second pair parts (SPPs) that are congruent with the FPP. Schegloff and Sacks suggest that this pairing is regulated by the following rule: "Given the recognizable production of a first pair part, on its first possible completion its speaker should stop and a next speaker should start and produce a second pair part from the pair type the first is recognizably a member of" (p. 239). Through such a rule, adjacency pairs create a sense of coherence in sequential structure that has been described by Schegloff (1972) in terms of conditional relevance: "By conditional relevance of one item on another we mean: Given the first, the second is expectable; upon its occurrence it can be seen to be a second item to the first; upon its nonoccurrence it can be seen to be officially absent" (p. 111).

Adjacency pairs are also regulated by a structural preference between the pair parts. Of the SPPs that can coherently combine with an FPP, there is usually one SPP that is preferred and one that is dispreferred. For example, Pomerantz (1978, 1984) has argued that evaluations are built to prefer an agreement with the evaluation ("Nice day today." "Yes, isn't it?"). And Atkinson and Drew (1979) argue that accusations prefer denials ("Who made this mess?" "It wasn't me").

Now, what is meant exactly by *structural preference* is not always clear. Bilmes (1988) has done the most careful exegesis, and his analysis suggests three more or less discrete senses that could be applied to adjacency pair structure. The first sense of preference follows from the notion of conditional relevance—if something is not done, it is noticeably absent, so that the absence of a preferred SPP would imply the performance of a dispreferred SPP. Silence in response to an accusation, for example, would be taken as a tacit admission of guilt.

Another sense of preference often used by conversation analysts parallels the linguistic concept of "markedness" (Levinson, 1983, p. 333). In this sense, preferred SPPs are

"unmarked" while dispreferred SPPs tend to be avoided by the discourse system and, when they occur, are "marked" in various ways as structurally irregular. Thus Levinson (1983) reviews literature suggesting that the components of adjacency pairs tend to be constructed in ways that avoid dispreferred SPPs and that dispreferred SPPs tend to be done in formats that are more complex than preferred SPPs. Dispreferred SPPs are characteristically indirect or mitigated, may be accompanied by accounts and explanations, and are often prefaced by various filler material and otherwise delayed.

A third sense of preference is similar to a functional principle of ordering and is related to a concept of repair. Certain SPPs, given an FPP, are normal and are what the FPP is designed to get, while other SPPs are what the FPP is designed to avoid. This latter sense leads Jacobs and Jackson (1989) to postulate a general preference for agreement and to treat argument as a way of preparing for and repairing disagreements. Sacks (1987) also seems to point to this sense when suggesting that individuals phrase questions to get agreements (as in example 58) and answers to appear agreeable (as in example 59).

(58) A: They have a good cook there?

         ((pause))

         Nothing special?

      B: No, everybody takes their turns.

(59) A: 'N they haven't heard a *word* huh?

      B: Not a word, *uh*-uh. Not- Not a word. Not at all. *Except*- Neville's mother got a call . . .

It is also this sense that seems to lead Heritage (1984) to equate structural preference with a kind of principle of social solidarity. Regardless of particular sense, however, structural preference does not refer to the psychological desires or personal motivations of the participants but to institutional properties "built into" the rule system itself.

The plausibility of a sequencing rule approach is further strengthened by the possibility for modeling broader stretches of conversation in the form of embedded or insertion sequences and presequences (Jefferson, 1972; Schegloff, 1972, 1980). Presequences are adjacency pairs whose component parts are interpreted relative to some adjacency pair yet to come. This prefatory character is part of their meaning (Jacobs & Jackson, 1983b; Sacks, 1967; Schegloff, 1980).

(60) *A:* You going to be finished soon?

    B: No, why?

    A: Well, it's getting pretty near the time we need to go pick up Curtie.

    B: OK. Well just give me a couple seconds to clean up and then we can go.

Insertion and embedded sequences are adjacency pairs that occur between an FPP and its SPP. These too are interpreted with respect to their position relative to the superordinate adjacency pair. Thus certain questions and statements can be understood as objections or contingent queries by virtue of their structural position between the FPP and SPP (Labov & Fanshel, 1977, p. 91).

(61) *A:* Can I have a pack of Merits?

    B: Regulars or hundreds?

    A: Regulars.

    B: Here you go.

These patterns of sequential expansion suggest rules permitting the repeated and recursive placement of subsidiary adjacency pairs before, within, and after any adjacency pair.

This analysis of adjacency pair relations and sequential expansion would appear to suggest, then, that the properties of conversational sequencing can be modeled on the basis of a three-component system of rules strikingly akin to that of a sentence grammar. Such a model requires (a) a turn-taking system for generating turn slots into which utterances may be placed, a procedure for assigning act meanings to utterances, and a set of rules for the "syntax" of conversation that can be formally expressed in terms of the basic adjacency pair relation where the subscripts designate pair parts drawn from the same type;

A. $AP_i \rightarrow FPP_i + SPP_i$

(b) a specification of the types of adjacency pair parts where the subscripts indicate the adjacent pair type of which they can be a part; (c) an ordering of preference among the SPPs of each adjacency pair type in which dispreferred SPPs are lowest (as marked by asterisks);

B. $FPP_i \rightarrow Greeting_A, Request_B, Question_C, Offer_D, \ldots$
C. $SPP_i \rightarrow Greeting_A, Grant_B, *Refusal_{BD}, Answer_C, Acceptance_D, \ldots$

and (d) a rewriting rule that permits the optional expansion of adjacency pairs.

D. $AP \rightarrow (AP) + FPP + (AP) + SPP + (AP)$

When applied as a system, these sorts of rules appear capable of representing many powerful intuitions natural language users have for sequential patterns as well as accommodating observable regularities in their use (Jose, 1988). By following such rules, the analyst can generate well-formed patterns and explain why the patterns in examples 62 and 63 appear ill formed and why sequences like those in examples 64 and 65 appear to lack closure:

(62) *A:* How are you doing?

    B: No.

(63) *A:* How old are you?

    B: All right.

(64) *A:* Are you busy tonight?

    B: No, not really.

(65) A: Have you read this article?

      B: Which one is that?

Such rules can also represent the structural subordination of insertion sequences and pre-sequences relative to some dominant adjacency pair by associating this with their derivative appearance through rewrite rules even though in the surface structure of talk they occur before the production and/or completion of the main adjacency pair. The rules can also represent hierarchical relations among utterances separated by indefinitely long stretches of conversation, and can generate indefinite embeddings analogous to those identified by Chomsky for sentence structures. Thus Schegloff (1972, p. 79) suggests that the following hypothetical exchange of questions and answers can be analyzed in the fashion of Figure 7.2.

(66) A: Are you coming tonight?

      B: Can I bring a guest?

      A: Male or female?

      B: What difference does that make?

      A: An issue of balance.

      B: Female.

      A: Sure.

      B: I'll be there.

So a sequencing rule approach appears to offer a promising way to model conversational structure. Through a straightforward application of code rules and normative regulations, a variety of interesting structures and interpretations can be represented and explained. But numerous problems appear upon closer inspection.

First, there are a variety of ways to coherently fill the slot made for the appearance of an SPP that are not themselves SPPs to that FPP (Jacobs & Jackson, 1983a; Levinson, 1981; Sinclair & Coulthard, 1975). Consider what might coherently follow a straightforward question about time:

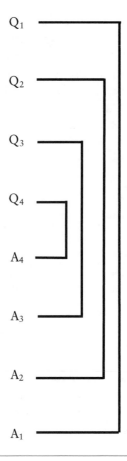

Figure 7.2   Recursive Embedding

(67) *FPP:*   What time is it?

   ??SPP: (i)   It's noon.

              (ii)   Ask Cal. He has a watch.

              (iii) I'm sure it's still early.

              (iv)   Forget about the time and just do your work.

              (v)   Sorry, I don't have a watch.

              (vi)   It's just three minutes before class starts.

In addition to (i) direct answers, questions can also coherently receive (ii) passes that redirect the question, (iii) disagreeable responses that attempt to satisfy the demands of the question as well as possible, (iv) alternative proposals for action, (v) accounts for not answering, and (vi) iDIrect answers that primarily set up other information. And there are numerous other ways to respond coherently, including just showing the face of a wristwatch and saying nothing. To call all such acts "answers" reduces the sequencing rule to the empty claim that anything that is a coherent response is an answer. To drop back to the claim that "answers" are expected even if they do not occur does not explain what counts as an "answer" and still fails to explain what else can and cannot coherently follow a question. Either way, sequencing rules provide no obvious way to characterize the broad array of acts that can be coherent replies. At best, the adjacency pair relation appears to be a normatively standardized pattern, not a general principle of sequential coherence.

Similar problems emerge in defining the constituents of structurally expanded sequences. Why, for example, are some sequences structurally subordinate expansions whereas others are digressions or wholly unrelated intrusions into an exchange (see Dascal & Katriel, 1979; Jacobs & Jackson, 1992)? What is it about some acts that places them within the structural environment of a dominant adjacency pair while excluding other temporally contiguous utterances? Sequential structure appears to be inextricably bound up in considerations of thematic content and topical continuity.

Difficulties also emerge when one tries to extend the analysis of sequential expansions to account for the full range of possible structural variations. For example, the presequential patterning of request-grant/refusal sequences may involve preemptive offers, hints, and counters, none of which is easily represented in terms of any surface structuring (Jacobs & Jackson, 1983b). Similarly, insertion sequences may exhibit complex structural relations that are not captured through rules of embedding. Notice that example 68 does not really contain an embedded sequence at all (Merritt, 1976,

would argue the same for example 61). The "thanks" by B is directed at A's offer and not to the initial suggestion. So accepting the offer as a solution to a potential objection obviates the need to produce an SPP to the initial suggestion. Contrast this with the hypothetical alternative in example 69, where "OK" would be heard to respond to the initial suggestion (because it is A's treat).

(68) A: Let's go eat.

     B: Well, it can't be anyplace very expensive.

     A: It's my treat today.

     B: Thanks.

(69) A: Let's go eat.

     B: Well, it can't be anyplace very expensive.

     A: It's my treat today.

     B: OK.

Both examples are coherent, but only example 69 can be represented by the sequential rules discussed so far.

The most immediate way out of these problems would be to postulate the existence of "transformational rules" that, like Chomskyan grammar, would provide a reading of "surface structure" utterances in terms of relations among act types represented in a kind of "deep structure." Such rules might permit operations of substitution, deletion, combination, and the like, so that whatever appeared in actual utterances may be only indirectly related to the acts being performed at several hierarchically layered levels of functioning. Early efforts took this direction (Churchill, 1978; Goffman, 1981; Labov, 1972; Merritt, 1976). But this approach has generally been abandoned. In part, this is because even this kind of representation exhausts itself in the face of the sequential complexities of actual interaction (Jacobs & Jackson, 1983b, pp. 293-295; Levinson, 1981).

But it is also because such an approach, as we shall see, relies on a unifunctional and decontextualized notion of the acts as elements of those sequential structures.

At this point, it is worth noting a characteristic feature of all the reasoning about sequential structure so far: A sequencing rule approach uses act types as the labels for the structural units upon which relations of coherence are defined, but the functional properties of those acts do not enter into the characterization of why the relation should obtain. Strictly speaking, sequencing rules treat relations of coherence as essentially arbitrary and irreducible conventions of form. The meaning of an act is, at best, a derivative quality of the way it functions in grammatical relations with other acts. The sense and function of an utterance is determined by its sequential location. In other words, an answer is simply that class of utterances that can recognizably fill the slot of an SPP to a question, and a question is simply that class of utterances that can recognizably combine with answers. A request is simply the class of utterances that takes grants and refusals as its SPP. A refusal is just that class of utterances that tends to occupy structurally dispreferred positions in relation to a request. As far as defining relations of coherence is concerned, question-answer or request-grant/refusal pairs might just as well be termed FPP_1-SPP_1 and FPP_2-SPP_{2p}/SPP_{2d} without any further specification of their meaning. Of course, there is nothing wrong with this sort of self-containment so long as there exists some independent procedure by which utterances can be assigned to, and generated from, act categories. The parallel here would be to a grammatical category such as definite article, which can be straightforwardly assigned to a word like *the*. The grammatical function of the category is defined relative to nouns within noun phrases (Ellis, 1992). Unfortunately, little clear progress has been made in identifying rules linking utterances to act types.

Utterances-act rules. The most straightforward approach to defining utterance-act linkages is to attempt to make the act type dependent upon the propositional content and syntactic form of the utterance. This corresponds to our intuitions that, for example, questions are characteristically associated with interrogative form, commands with imperative form, and statements with declarative form. Utterance content may also more or less explicitly contain information about the act being uttered.

(70)   I promise not to talk with my mouth full.

(71)   I bet it snows tonight.

(72)   We find the defendant guilty as charged.

Such an approach does seem to be extendable to the description of a large class of standardized formulas and grammatical markers that are conventionally associated with the expression of a speech act (see Bach & Harnish, 1979, pp. 173-233, for an extensive review). For example, the formulas in 73 and 74 are conventionally associated with the performance of a request (Bach & Harnish, 1979), while the formulas in 75 and 76 are conventional ways to make a compliment (Knapp, Hopper, & Bell, 1984; Manes & Wolfson, 1981).

(73)   Can/Will + (NEGATIVE) + (SUBJUNCTIVE) + You + IMPERATIVE? [Can you pass the salt? Would you open the door? Won't you come here? Can't you sit still? Couldn't you move?]

(74)   How about VP-ing? [How about lending me a dime?]

(75)   NP is/looks (really) POSITIVE ADJECTIVE. [Your house looks really nice.]

(76)   I (really) like/love NP. [I like your haircut.]

Such an approach to identifying act-utterance linkages, however, quickly runs into insurmountable difficulties. One problem is the generativity in patterning. As the requests to leave the party in sentences 16 through 26 indicate, an indefinite range of nonstandardized forms may be employed to perform an act. Another problem is that none of these formulas can guarantee the meaning of the utterance as a matter of rule. "How about telling him yourself?" can be a suggestion, but in other contexts it can be a challenge, a criticism, a rhetorical answer, or a simple hypothetical question. "I like this shirt" can be a compliment, but it can justify wearing the shirt the speaker has on or it can be an act of selecting a shirt in a store.

Sensitive to these problems, a number of discourse analysts have suggested that utterance-act assignment rules must specify context so that utterance-act linkages are established only when certain contextual features are present. The contextual features most frequently appealed to are the felicity conditions associated with the valid performance of a speech act.

According to mainstream speech act theory (Austin, 1962; Searle, 1969), actions in language are regulated and defined by a set of rules that specify the necessary preconditions for validly performing those actions. Differences in these conditions will reflect differences in the kind of speech act being performed. In expressing a speech act, the speaker commits herself by rule to the wants and beliefs associated with the valid performance of the act. (See Searle, 1969, for an initial typology of these conditions and later revisions by Searle & Vanderveken, 1985, and Vanderveken, 1990.) So, for example, requests are subject to the requirement that the hearer is willing in principle to perform the requested act, while orders require that the speaker have authority over the hearer. Information questions require that the speaker does not know the information asked for, while test questions require that the speaker does know the information but does not know whether the hearer knows the information. Or, again, promises

commit the speaker to believing that the projected action is desired by the hearer; warnings commit the speaker to believing that the projected action is not desired by the hearer. And speech acts typically communicate some point or intent—what speech act the utterance "counts as" performing. For requesting, the utterance counts as an effort to get the hearer to do the desired action. For questioning, the utterance counts as an attempt to elicit the information from the hearer. The essential condition is satisfied just in those cases in which the other felicity conditions obtain.

The notion of felicity conditions has suggested to many speech act theorists that a speech act will be heard in those cases where it could be validly performed and not in those cases where its performance would be infelicitous. In other words, assuming that a speaker is encoding a message in accordance with the regulative constraints on linguistic action, a hearer can check whether or not a particular decoding would be consistent with a valid action. Along these lines, Gordon and Lakoff (1975) and Searle (1975) suggest that an utterance may trigger an indirect reading beyond its literal meaning in just those cases in which it is implausible that the speaker intends to be (simply) performing the act literally expressed in the utterance (that is, a simple statement, question, or imperative). The point that the speaker is really trying to make is cued by the fact that the propositional content of the utterance refers to a felicity condition for the indirect speech act, and this indirect reading is made if the other felicity conditions for that act are satisfied. Labov and Fanshel (1977) have proposed a similar rule for the specific case of requests. Under their rule, however, a request reading is an omnirelevant possibility. A request is searched for whenever reference is made to aspects of the proposed action or the preconditions for a request, regardless of whether or not the literal speech act is performed felicitously.

Neither of these rules is a fully satisfactory account of how act types get assigned to utterances. First, if we assume, like Searle (1975) and Gordon and Lakoff (1975), that a literal reading must be implausible in order to trigger an indirect reading of an utterance, how are we to handle cases in which a speaker means to perform both a direct and an indirect act? Consider example 77, where an instructor (me) asked an overtime student about his exam:

(77) How much longer will you be?

Not only did this utterance serve as an indirect request to finish up, it was also intended (and responded to) as an information question. Moreover, it also functioned as criticism. So a "triggering" model based on the infelicitous performance of a literal act does not appear to be powerful enough, because it would never represent multiple acts. Alternatively, if we take Labov and Fanshel's (1977) proposal and presume the omnirelevant potential of any speech act (and not just requests), multiple act interpretations are possible, but we are faced with the problem that there is no clear way to stop the process of searching for additional indirect meanings. Talking to Labov and Fanshel's model natural language user would be like writing to a literary critic. Although natural language users do go beyond validly performed acts that are immediately apparent, they stop long before considering all possible interpretations (Clark, 1977).

A second, deeper problem for these models is that the determination of what is referred to by the propositional content of an utterance does not appear to be a rule-governed process at all. Both models assume that the propositional content of the utterance leads to an indirect reading by reference to a felicity condition for the indirect act. But, as Labov and Fanshel (1977, p. 84) note, this connection can be established only after the fact. Any propositional content can refer to any other proposition given a circuitous enough route. Because of this, Labov and Fanshel argue that a generative grammar connecting speech action to utterance forms cannot be written. One is left with the position that expectations and interpretations are guided by the context of activity. And while there is good evidence for this (Clark, 1979; Ervin-Tripp, 1976; Ervin-Tripp, Strage, Lampert, & Bell, 1987; Lecouteur, 1988; Levinson, 1979), at best this points to a jumble of cues for what is going on at any moment—a rather discouraging prospect for developing a grammar of conversation.

TOWARD AN INFERENTIAL/ STRATEGIC MODEL

Problems like those discussed for a "grammar of conversational interaction" can be found at virtually all levels of discourse organization. The problem that repeatedly surfaces is that a normative code model is insufficient to explain the basic properties of language structure and use outlined at the beginning of this chapter—inference beyond the information given, generativity of patterning, contextual determination of meaning, functional design of structure, and multifunctionality. Extending a Chomskyan grammar for sentences to other domains of structure and use, which appeared to provide such a promising exemplar, has repeatedly run into a wall of resistance.

So, for example, the notion that topical coherence in texts and dialogue might be modeled by rules linking utterance form and content to the form and content of prior discourse (see Halliday & Hasan, 1976) has generally been given up by discourse analysts. Researchers in this area are instead turning to models assuming active constructive processes that bring to bear assumptions about speaker plans and strategies, general principles of rationality, and coherent representations of the world (Clark & Schaefer, 1989; Ellis, 1992; Grosz &

Sidner, 1990; McLaughlin, 1984). From the very beginning, studies of stylistic code choice have encountered the phenomenon of blatant rule violation that is nevertheless meaningful and coherent (Brown & Gilman, 1960; Ervin-Tripp, 1971). These analysts are increasingly emphasizing the strategic basis for meaning in language choice (Brown & Levinson, 1987; Gumperz, 1982). Likewise, models of "story grammars" (Mandler & Johnson, 1977; Rumelhart, 1975) have given way to problem-solving approaches that integrate text with world knowledge and assumptions about speaker strategy (Hobbs, 1990a).

While current approaches take several directions, all share certain core assumptions that are at odds with those of a normative code model. Within an inferential/strategic model, messages are not understood to be transmitted through an encoding and decoding process that applies self-sufficient code rules to determine meaning. The process is viewed instead as a kind of problem-solving activity involving the assessment of mutual knowledge in the generation of speaker plans and hearer inferences as to the most plausible solution for what that speaker plan might be (Clark, 1992). In this view, apparent violations of normative expectations are "normalized" by the hearer seeing how those acts are rational solutions to the achievement of communicative ends and by the speaker assessing the likelihood that the hearer will find such a solution. Understanding a message is a matter of constructing a context of beliefs in which the speaker's utterance would make sense (Sperber & Wilson, 1986). And expressing a message is a matter of embodying through utterance that aspect of the intended context most likely to cue construction of that context for an addressee (Hermann, 1983; Lambert & O'Keefe, 1990). Rather than looking for messages in symbolic vehicles, for strategic/inferential models the context is the message (Sperber & Wilson, 1986).

How such a model might work can best be seen through an illustration of its application to the problems of conversational interaction. Inferential/strategic models capitalize on the insight that utterances have points to them and preconditions for achieving those points (see Schank et al., 1982; Tracy, 1984). Conversations are coherent not because they conform to conventions of form defined across structural units of action but because they reflect a functionally sensible progression through joint activity. Rather than following rules of sequential form, people are assumed to reason from general principles of instrumental (i.e., means-ends) rationality (Jacobs & Jackson, 1983a; Levinson, 1981; Mohan, 1974; Pollack, 1990).

From an inferential/strategic perspective, it is this sort of functional design that underlies the structural coherence found by the sequencing rule approach. The adjacency pair is a standardized solution to the problem of communicating goals that an addressee must satisfy and then the addressee responding in a way that promotes or obstructs those goals. The properties of conditional relevance and structural preference find a general rationale in the functional design of the intended goal communicated by the FPP and in the way the SPP contributes to that goal. So, for example, questions have as part of their goal the intention to obtain information from the hearer, a goal achieved when an answer is supplied. Requests have as their intended goal the performance of an action, a goal whose achievement is promised by a grant or denied by a refusal. (Notice that a refusal takes up the goal of the FPP, which is why it is conditionally relevant, but it obstructs that goal, which is why it is structurally dispreferred.) Such an analysis also accounts for the broad range of acts that are not SPPs but are still coherent replies (as in example 67). Such acts take up the point of the FPP in some way or another by trying to satisfy it by means other than an SPP, by supplying partial satisfaction, by renegotiating goals, by identifying the lack of relevant preconditions for achieving the goal, and so on.

The regularities and irregularities of sequential expansion can also be seen as the unfolding and interlocking of broader plan-like structures. Presequences and insertion sequences are placed within the structural environment of a dominant adjacency pair in just those cases in which the acts are designed to establish or cancel a precondition necessary for the valid performance of an action (see Cohen & Perrault, 1979; Jacobs & Jackson, 1983a). Presequences and contingent queries are recognized as such just when their contribution to an underlying plan is recognized. Furthermore, the occurrence of a wide variety of irregular forms of expansion can be understood as coherent once it is seen how the conversationalists position their actions relative to the underlying goals of the conversation (Jacobs & Jackson, 1983b).

Similarly, an inferential/strategic account provides a promising way to model the communication of utterance meaning. The essential insight in the analyses of indirect speech acts discussed above is that the meaning of an utterance is discovered through the construction of contexts in which an utterance can be found to have a rational functional design. One major line of analysis follows the direction charted by H. P. Grice (1989) and emphasizes how linguistic expression and interpretation are guided by very general background assumptions about rational communicative activity.

According to Grice, communication is guided by a *cooperative principle* (CP): "Make your contribution such as is required, at the stage in which it occurs, by the accepted purpose or direction of the talk exchange in which you are engaged" (p. 26). Speakers are expected to observe the CP in constructing messages, and listeners assume speakers are doing so when interpreting those messages. Messages are sensible when it is understood how they pursue the accepted purpose of the

talk exchange. Grice suggests that in addition to the CP messages are regulated by four classes of conversational maxims: quality (say what is true), quantity (be as informative as necessary, but not more so), relation (be relevant), and manner (be clear, efficient, orderly, and to the point). These maxims provide guides for constructing inferences (what Grice calls "implicatures") so that the message will be seen to satisfy the CP. According to Grice (1989), "To calculate a conversational implicature is to calculate what has to be supposed in order to preserve the supposition that the CP is being observed" (pp. 39-40). When the literal and direct meaning of what is said seems to violate the CP or one of its maxims, listeners do not simply conclude that the message is false, uninformative, irrelevant, unintelligible, or otherwise defective. Instead, listeners look beyond the face value of the message to construct plausible meanings that would satisfy the CP and its maxims.

This type of analysis of communicative meaning can be found in substance or form in a diverse set of models that apply to speech act inference and a variety of other discourse information (Bach & Harnish, 1979; Brown & Levinson, 1987; Clark & Haviland, 1977; Horn, 1984; Kasher, 1982; Leech, 1983; Levinson, 1983; Searle, 1975; Sperber & Wilson, 1986). While many of these approaches continue to privilege some notion of literal meaning as a first and simplest guess, many do not, and it is generally recognized in any case that contextual expectations interact with linguistic information to determine the meaning of the act performed.

The picture emerging, then, is one in which multiple sources of information are simultaneously weighed and assessed in relation to one another on the assumption that a rational solution to what is meant should be found. Rather than looking like a linear deductive process starting from linguistic input and ending, by rule, in a determinate meaning, the process of interpretation appears to look much more like a solution to an equation with several unknown values (Dascal, 1977). By juggling the unknowns in various ways, we may obtain more than one solution—a theoretically derived conclusion that accords well with the real-life uncertainties of human communication.

This framework also shows how conventional expectations about meaning may be deliberately exploited for communicative effect. As Levinson (1983) points out, theories like Grice's show

> a fundamental way in which a full account of the communicative power of language can never be reduced to a set of conventions for the use of language. The reason is that wherever some convention or expectation about the use of language arises, there will also therewith arise the possibility of the non-conventional exploitation of that convention or expectation. It follows that a purely conventional or rule-based account of natural language usage can never be complete, and that what can be communicated always exceeds the communicative power provided by the conventions of language and its use. (p. 112)

These models of conversational sequencing and utterance meaning also dovetail with recent calls to abandon speech acts as analytic categories altogether. Arguments by Levinson (1979), Jacobs (1989), and Schegloff (1988) all suggest that there is no principled way to restrict the functions served by utterances. One can posit a finite set of functions only by ignoring the situated distinctions in function drawn by ordinary language users. And for any speech act category that can be specified, there is no necessary and sufficient set of preconditions that define their valid performance. Analysts such as Sanders (1987) and Sperber and Wilson (1986) question whether speech act categories have any representational role to play as participants interpret and respond

to many kinds of utterances. Levinson (1981) and Jacobs and Jackson (1989) point to cases like the responses in examples 34 and 37 to suggest that what is represented are not speech acts per se but plans and goals pursued in the utterance. Indeed, if what participants attend to are the points of an utterance and the preconditions for achieving those points, this can be preserved in conversational models without taking on the conventional baggage of speech act categories. As Cohen and Levesque (1990) comment regarding their own model, "The view that illocutionary acts are not primitive and therefore need not be recognized explicitly is a liberating one" (p. 244).

CONCLUSION

This chapter has charted a general shift in the way discourse analysts think about the nature of language use and structure. Approaches to the problems of meaning and coherence were dominated by a normative code model of communication. That model cannot handle the manifest properties of linguistic communication and interaction, and promotes a misleading view of language meaning and language choice. Expression and interpretation are not matters of encoding and decoding meaning by determinate rules applied to signals, and language choice is not something dictated by normative regulations. In place of this model has emerged a view of linguistic communication as a process of strategic design and constructive inference. Messages are located in the interplay of text and context. Rather than a process mechanically played out by rule, discourse analysts have come to see linguistic communication as creative problem solving.

REFERENCES

Akmajian, A., Demers, R. A., Farmer, A. K., & Harnish, R. M. (1990). *Linguistics* (3rd ed.). Cambridge: MIT Press.

Atkinson, J. M., & Drew, P. (1979). *Order in court: The organization of verbal interaction in judicial settings.* London: Macmillan.

Austin, J. L. (1962). *How to do things with words.* Oxford: Clarendon.

Bach, K., & Harnish, R. M. (1979). *Linguistic communication and speech acts.* Cambridge: MIT Press.

Bavelas, J. B., Black, A., Chovil, N., & Mullett, J. (1990). *Equivocal communication.* Newbury Park, CA: Sage.

Berlo, D. K. (1960). *The process of communication.* New York: Holt, Rinehart & Winston.

Bilmes, J. (1988). The concept of preference in conversation analysis. *Language in Society, 17,* 161-181.

Bransford, J. D., & Johnson, M. K. (1972). Contextual prerequisites for understanding: Some investigations of comprehension and recall. *Journal of Verbal Learning and Verbal Behavior, 11,* 717-726.

Brown, G., & Yule, G. (1983). *Discourse analysis.* Cambridge: Cambridge University Press.

Brown, P., & Levinson, S. C. (1987). *Politeness: Some universals in language usage.* Cambridge: Cambridge University Press.

Brown, R., & Gilman, A. (1960). The pronouns of power and solidarity. In T. A. Sebeok (Ed.), *Style in language* (pp. 253-276). Cambridge: MIT Press.

Cappella, J. N. (1990). The method of proof by example in interaction analysis. *Communication Monographs, 57,* 236-242.

Chomsky, N. (1957). *Syntactic structures.* The Hague: Mouton.

Chomsky, N. (1959). Review of verbal behavior. *Language, 35,* 26-58.

Chomsky, N. (1965). *Aspects of the theory of syntax.* Cambridge: MIT Press.

Chomsky, N. (1972). *Language and mind.* New York: Harcourt Brace Jovanovich.

Churchill, L. (1978). *Questioning strategies in sociolinguistics.* Rowley, MA: Newbury House.

Clark, H. H. (1977). Bridging. In P. N. Johnson-Laird & P. C. Wason (Eds.), *Thinking: Readings in cognitive science* (pp. 411-420). Cambridge: Cambridge University Press.

Clark, H. H. (1979). Responding to indirect requests. *Cognitive Psychology, 11,* 430-477.

Clark, H. H. (1992). *Arenas of language use.* Chicago: University of Chicago Press.

Clark, H. H., & Haviland, S. E. (1977). Comprehension and the given-new contact. In R. O. Freedle (Ed.), *Discourse production and comprehension* (pp. 1-40). Norwood, NJ: Ablex.

Clark, H. H., & Schaefer, E. F. (1989). Contributing to discourse. *Cognitive Science, 13,* 259-294.

Clark, R. A., & Delia, J. G. (1979). Topoi and rhetorical competence. *Quarterly Journal of Speech, 65,* 187-206.

Cohen, P. R., & Levesque, H. J. (1990). Rational interaction as the basis for communication. In P. R. Cohen, J. Morgan, & M. E. Pollack (Eds.), *Intentions in communication* (pp. 221-255). Cambridge: MIT Press.

Cohen, P. R., & Perrault, C. R. (1979). Elements of a plan-based theory of speech acts. *Cognitive Science, 3,* 177-212.

Cushman, D., & Whiting, G. C. (1972). An approach to communication theory: Toward consensus on rules. *Journal of Communication, 22,* 217-238.

Dascal, M. (1977). Conversational relevance. *Journal of Pragmatics, 1,* 309-328.

Dascal, M., & Katriel, T. (1979). Digressions: A study in conversation coherence. *Poetics and Theory of Literature, 4,* 203-232.

Ellis, D. G. (1992). *From language to communication.* Hillsdale, NJ: Lawrence Erlbaum.

Ervin-Tripp, S. M. (1971). Sociolinguistics. In J. A. Fishman (Ed.), *Advances in the sociology of language* (Vol. 1, pp. 15-91). The Hague: Mouton.

Ervin-Tripp, S. M. (1976). Is Sybil there? The structure of some American English directives. *Language in Society, 5,* 25-66.

Ervin-Tripp, S. M., Strage, A., Lampert, M., & Bell, N. (1987). Understanding requests. *Linguistics, 25,* 107-143.

Fitch, K. L. (1991). The interplay of linguistic universals and cultural knowledge in personal address: Colombian *madre* terms. *Communication Monographs, 58,* 254-272.

Goffman, E. (1981). *Forms of talk.* Philadelphia: University of Pennsylvania Press.

Gordon, D., & Lakoff, G. (1975). Conversational postulates. In P. Cole & J. L. Morgan (Eds.), *Syntax and semantics: Vol. 3. Speech acts* (pp. 83-106). New York: Academic Press.

Grice, H. P. (1989). *Studies in the way of words.* Cambridge, MA: Harvard University Press.

Grosz, B. J., & Sidner, C. L. (1990). Plans for discourse. In P. R. Cohen, J. Morgan, & M. E. Pollack (Eds.), *Intentions in communication* (pp. 417-444). Cambridge: MIT Press.

Gumperz, J. J. (1982). *Discourse strategies.* Cambridge: Cambridge University Press.

Gumperz, J. J., & Hymes, D. (1972). [Editors' introduction to *Sequencing in conversational openings*, by E. A Schegloff, pp. 349-380]. In J. J. Gumperz & D. Hymes (Eds.), *Directions in sociolinguistics: The ethnography of communication* (pp. 346-348). New York: Holt, Rinehart & Winston.

Halliday, M. A. K., & Hasan, R. (1976). *Cohesion in English*. London: Longman.

Harris, R. (1987). *The language machine*. London: Duckworth.

Heritage, J. (1984). *Garfinkel and ethnomethodology*. Cambridge: Polity.

Hermann, T. (1983). *Speech and situation*. Berlin: Springer-Verlag.

Hobbs, J. (1990a). *Literature and cognition*. Stanford, CA: Center for the Study of Language and Information.

Hobbs, J. (1990b). Topic drift. In B. Dorval (Ed.), *Conversational organization and its development* (pp. 3-22). Norwood, NJ: Ablex.

Hook, S. (Ed.). (1969). *Language and philosophy*. New York: New York University Press.

Hopper, R. E. (1992). *Telephone conversation*. Bloomington: Indiana University Press.

Horn, L. R. (1984). Toward a new taxonomy for pragmatic inference: Q-based and R-based implicature. In D. Schiffrin (Ed.), *Meaning, form, and use in context* (pp. 11-42). Washington, DC: Georgetown University Press.

Jacobs, S. (1989). Speech acts and arguments. *Argumentation, 3*, 23-43.

Jacobs, S. (1990). On the especially nice fit between qualitative analysis and the known properties of conversation. *Communication Monographs, 57*, 243-249.

Jacobs, S., & Jackson, S. (1983a). Speech act structure in conversation: Rational aspects of pragmatic coherence. In R. T. Craig & K. Tracy (Eds.), *Conversational coherence* (pp. 47-66). Beverly Hills, CA: Sage.

Jacobs, S., & Jackson, S. (1983b). Strategy and structure in conversational influence attempts. *Communication Monographs, 50*, 285-305.

Jacobs, S., & Jackson, S. (1989). Building a model of conversational argument. In B. Dervin, L. Grossberg, B. J. O'Keefe, & E. Wartella (Eds.), *Rethinking communication: Vol. 2. Paradigm exemplars* (pp. 153-171). Newbury Park, CA: Sage.

Jacobs, S., & Jackson, S. (1992). Relevance and digressions in argumentative discussion: A pragmatic approach. *Argumentation, 6*, 161-172.

Jefferson, G. (1972). Side sequences. In D. Sudnow (Ed.), *Studies in social interaction* (pp. 294-338). New York: Free Press.

Johnson-Laird, P. N. (1983). *Mental models*. Cambridge, MA: Harvard University Press.

Jose, P. E. (1988). Sequentiality of speech acts in conversational structure. *Journal of Psycholinguistic Research, 17*, 65-88.

Kasher, A. (1982). Gricean inference revisited. *Philosophica, 29*, 25-44.

Kellermann, K., Broetzmann, S., Lim, T., & Kitao, K. (1989). The conversation MOP: Scenes in the stream of discourse. *Discourse Processes, 12*, 27-62.

Knapp, M. L., Hopper, R., & Bell, R. A. (1984). Compliments: A descriptive taxonomy. *Journal of Communication, 34*, 12-31.

Labov, W. (1972). *Sociolinguistic patterns*. Philadelphia: University of Pennsylvania Press.

Labov, W., & Fanshel, D. (1977). *Therapeutic discourse: Psychotherapy as conversation*. New York: Academic Press.

Lambert, B. L., & O'Keefe, B. J. (1990, November). *Modelling message design*. Paper presented at the annual meeting of the Speech Communication Association, Chicago.

Lecouteur, A. J. (1988). Understanding unconventional requests. *Linguistics, 26*, 873-877.

Leech, G. (1983). *Principles of pragmatics*. London: Longman.

Levinson, S. C. (1979). Activity types and language. *Linguistics, 17*, 365-399.

Levinson, S. C. (1981). Some pre-observations on the modeling of dialogue. *Discourse Processes, 4*, 93-116.

Levinson, S. C. (1983). *Pragmatics*. Cambridge: Cambridge University Press.

Locke, J. (1975). *Essay concerning human understanding* (P. H. Nidditch, Ed.). Oxford: Clarendon. (Original work published 1690)

Lyons, J. (1970). *Noam Chomsky*. New York: Viking.

Malinowski, B. (1923). The problem of meaning in primitive languages. In C. K. Ogden & I. A. Richards (Eds.), *The meaning of meaning* (pp. 296-336). New York: Harcourt, Brace & World.

Malinowski, B. (1935). *Coral gardens and their magic* (2 vols.). New York: Dover.

Mandelbaum, J., & Pomerantz, A. (1991). What drives social action? In K. Tracy (Ed.), *Understanding face-to-face interaction: Issues linking goals and discourse* (pp. 151-166). Hillsdale, NJ: Lawrence Erlbaum.

Mandler, J. M., & Johnson, N. S. (1977). Remembrance of things parsed: Story structure and recall. *Cognitive Psychology, 9,* 111-151.

Manes, J., & Wolfson, N. (1981). The compliment formula. In F. Coulmas (Ed.), *Conversational routine* (pp. 115-132). The Hague: Mouton.

McLaughlin, M. L. (1984). *Conversation: How talk is organized.* Beverly Hills, CA: Sage.

Merritt, M. (1976). On questions following questions in service encounters. *Language in Society, 5,* 315-357.

Mohan, B. J. (1974). Do sequencing rules exist? *Semiotica, 12,* 75-96.

Newmeyer, F. J. (1980). *Linguistic theory in America.* New York: Academic Press.

O'Keefe, B. J. (1990). The logic of regulative communication: Understanding the rationality of message designs. In J. P. Dillard (Ed.), *Seeking compliance: The production of interpersonal influence messages* (pp. 87-104). Scottsdale, AZ: Gorsuch Scarisbrick.

O'Keefe, B. J. (1991). Message design logic and the management of multiple goals. In K. Tracy (Ed.), *Understanding face-to-face interaction: Issues linking goals and discourse* (pp. 131-150). Hillsdale, NJ: Lawrence Erlbaum.

Pollack, M. E. (1990). Plans as complex mental attitudes. In P. R. Cohen, J. Morgan, & M. E. Pollack (Eds.), *Intentions in communication* (pp. 77-103). Cambridge: MIT Press.

Pomerantz, A. (1978). Compliment responses: Notes on the cooperation of multiple constraints. In J. Schenkein (Ed.), *Studies in the organization of conversational interaction* (pp. 79-112). New York: Academic Press.

Pomerantz, A. (1984). Agreeing and disagreeing with assessments: Some features of preferred/dispreferred turn shapes. In J. M. Atkinson & J. Heritage (Eds.), *Structures of social action: Studies in conversation analysis* (pp. 57-101). Cambridge: Cambridge University Press.

Reddy, J. J. (1979). The conduit metaphor: A case of frame conflict in our language about language. In A. Ortony (Ed.), *Metaphor and thought* (pp. 284-324). Cambridge: Cambridge University Press.

Rommetveit, R. (1974). *On message structure.* London: John Wiley.

Rumelhart, D. E. (1975). Notes on a schema for stories. In D. G. Bobrow & A. Collins (Eds.), *Representation and understanding* (pp. 211-236). New York: Academic Press.

Sacks, H. (1967). [Unpublished lectures], University of California, Los Angeles.

Sacks, H. (1987). On the preferences for agreement and contiguity in sequences in conversation. In G. Button & J. R. E. Lee (Eds.), *Talk and social organization* (pp. 54-69). Clevedon, Eng.: Multilingual Matters.

Sacks, H., Schegloff, E. A., & Jefferson, G. (1974). A simplest systematics for the organization of turn taking in conversation. *Language, 50,* 696-735.

Sanders, R. E. (1987). *Cognitive foundations of calculated speech.* Albany: State University of New York Press.

Saussure, F. de. (1983). *A course in general linguistics* (R. Harris, Trans). London: Duckworth. (Original work published 1916)

Schank, R. C., Collins, G. C., Davis, E., Johnson, P. N., Lytinen, S., & Reiser, B. J. (1982). What's the point? *Cognitive Science, 6,* 255-275.

Schegloff, E. A. (1972). Notes on a conversational practice: Formulating place. In D. Sudnow (Ed.), *Studies in social interaction* (pp. 75-119). New York: Free Press.

Schegloff, E. A. (1980). Preliminaries to preliminaries: "Can I ask you a question?" *Sociological Inquiry, 50,* 104-152.

Schegloff, E. A. (1988). Presequences and indirection. *Journal of Pragmatics, 12,* 55-62.

Schegloff, E. A., & Sacks, H. (1974). Opening up closings. In R. Turner (Ed.), *Ethnomethodology* (pp. 223-264). Harmondsworth: Penguin Education.

Schenkein, J. (1978). Sketch of an analytic mentality for the study of conversational interaction. In J. Schenkein (Ed.), *Studies in the organization of conversational interaction* (pp. 1-6). New York: Academic Press.

Searle, J. R. (1969). *Speech acts: An essay in the philosophy of language.* Cambridge: Cambridge University Press.

Searle, J. R. (1975). Indirect speech acts. In P. Cole & J. L. Morgan (Eds.) *Syntax and semantics: Vol. 3. Speech acts* (pp. 59-78). New York: Academic Press.

Searle, J. R. (1980). The background of meaning. In J. R. Searle, F. Kiefer, & M. Bierwisch (Eds.), *Speech act theory and pragmatics* (pp. 221-232). Dordrecht, Netherlands: D. Reidel.

Searle, J. R. (1989). How performatives work. *Linguistics and Philosophy, 12,* 535-558.

Searle, J. R., & Vanderveken, D. (1985). *Foundations of illocutionary logic.* Cambridge: Cambridge University Press.

Sells, P. (1985). *Lectures on contemporary syntactic theories.* Stanford, CA: Center for the Study of Language and Information.

Shannon, C. E., & Weaver, W. (1949). *The mathematical theory of communication.* Urbana: University of Illinois.

Shimanoff, S. B. (1980). *Communication rules.* Beverly Hills, CA: Sage.

Sigman, S. J. (1987). *A perspective on social communication.* Lexington, MA: Lexington.

Sinclair, J. M. C. H., & Coulthard, R. M. (1975). *Toward an analysis of discourse.* Oxford: Oxford University Press.

Smith, N., & Wilson, D. (1990). *Modern linguistics.* London: Penguin.

Soames, S., & Perlmutter, D. M. (1979). *Syntactic argumentation and the structure of English.* Berkeley: University of California Press.

Sperber, D., & Wilson, D. (1986). *Relevance.* Cambridge, MA: Harvard University Press.

Taylor, T. J. (1992). *Mutual misunderstanding.* Durham, NC: Duke University Press.

Taylor, T. J., & Cameron, D. (1987). *Analyzing conversation.* Oxford: Pergamon.

Tracy, K. (1984). Staying on topic: An explication of conversational relevance. *Discourse Processes, 7,* 447-464.

Vanderveken, D. (1990). *Meaning and speech acts* (2 vols.). Cambridge: Cambridge University Press.

Wilson, T. P. (1970). Normative and interpretive paradigms in sociology. In J. D. Douglas (Ed.), *Understanding everyday life* (pp. 57-79). Chicago: Aldine.

Wittgenstein, L. (1953). *Philosophical investigations* (G. E. M. Anscombe, Trans.). New York: Macmillan.

8

Nonverbal Signals

JUDEE K. BURGOON
GREGORY D. HOOBLER

For centuries, poets and pundits, sages and songwriters have waxed lyrical about the powers of nonverbal communication, their sentiments captured well by this famous quotation from Edward Sapir (1949): "We respond to gestures with an extreme alertness and, one might almost say, in accordance with an elaborate and secret code that is written nowhere, known to none, and understood by all" (p. 556). The claim that the code is understood by all may be hyperbole, but it underscores the universality of nonverbal signals as a communication coding system. That the code may be known to none is a deficiency we aim to remedy in part with this chapter.

THE IMPORTANCE OF NONVERBAL BEHAVIOR

In some respects, the importance of nonverbal communication should be patently obvious.

After all, not only are nonverbal signals ubiquitous in interpersonal exchanges, they have always laid claim to communicative primacy—in our evolutionary development as a species, in our ontological development as individuals, and in our initial encounters with others. The designation of nonverbal signals as "fundamental units" also is intended to signify their centrality in interpersonal communication. Yet recognition of this importance remains unmatched by the space devoted to it in the extant literature. Nonverbal communication too often remains "ground" to the "figure" that is verbal communication. Thus, despite our strong commitment to viewing nonverbal and verbal communication as highly integrated constituents of the total communication system, we must temporarily divorce them to illuminate the breadth and depth of the contributions made by nonverbal behavior to interpersonal communication processes and outcomes.

Some Illustrations

To make this point more concrete, we offer the following observations regarding some popular lines of research and the risks involved in ignoring the nonverbal signals that accompany verbal behavior:

1. *Development of relational intimacy.* Is relational closeness fostered by partners reciprocating intimacies? Researchers have typically studied this question by observing whether one person's intimate verbal disclosures are matched by a partner's disclosures. Problematic with this approach is the assumption that an actor's verbal behavior is what influences a partner's verbal responses, when in fact sensitive, embarrassing, or hurtful verbal disclosures may be tempered and downplayed by accompanying nonverbal displays. Claims made about the extent of reciprocity from examination of the verbal channel alone overlook possible nonverbal compensation, resulting in misleading conclusions.

2. *Relational control strategies.* How people signal and establish relational dominance is a core interpersonal issue. Often, scholars examine it by using a verbal coding scheme that identifies who is "in control" according to one-up, one-cross, and one-down moves. A one-up move, such as a command, followed by a one-down move, such as a supportive reply, qualifies as an instance of dominance by the person engaging in the one-up behavior. Researchers who rely strictly on verbal criteria to classify dominant and submissive (or symmetrical and complementary) behaviors risk missing vocal behavior that may alter significantly the function and meaning of an utterance. For example, a reply that appears supportive on the surface—such as "I'll be happy to do it"—may actually mean the opposite if said in a sarcastic voice. Numerous other nonverbal signals of dominance or submission may also neutralize or radically modify the total meaning of an utterance.

3. *Conflict and negotiation strategies.* As in research on relational control, most systems for classifying conflict and negotiation rely on verbal behaviors, with the same attendant problems. A regressive-appearing statement such as "Your point is well taken" can actually be a nonsupportive defending move if accompanied by backward lean, indirect body orientation, gaze aversion, and facial impassivity. Failure to take account of the concomitant "nonverbal text" of a confrontation may lead to inaccurate conclusions about which tactics are successful or how confrontative a particular strategy is.

4. *Public self-presentation.* When it comes to forming impressions of others, how people present themselves nonverbally often carries far more import than what they say. A case in point: The microphone-amplified sighs that Al Gore emitted during his televised debates with George Bush in the 2000 presidential campaign made Gore seem patronizing and impatient. In the realm of social perceptions, the nonverbal content of messages often *is* the message.

Skill in Nonverbal Encoding and Decoding

The importance of nonverbal signals to interpersonal communication can also be seen in the centrality of nonverbal encoding (sending) and decoding (receiving) skills to successful individual and interpersonal functioning, as underscored by the mushrooming awareness of "emotional intelligence" (see, e.g., Goleman, 1995; Mayer, Caruso, & Salovey, 2000; Mayer & Salovey, 1997), itself a constellation of nonverbal and verbal social skills. Because Spitzberg and Cupach address this topic in Chapter 15 of this *Handbook* and far more comprehensive treatments are available elsewhere (e.g., Burgoon & Bacue, in press), we provide here only a brief synopsis of some of the more robust research findings.

1. Nonverbal encoding and decoding skills are strong predictors of popularity, attraction, and psychosocial well-being. This may be partly due to the associations between social skills and personality. Encoding skill is greater among those who are expressive, extraverted, nonreticent, high in self-esteem, outgoing, high in self-monitoring, not socially anxious, non-dogmatic, persuasive, and physically attractive. Decoding skill is greater among those who are gregarious, sociable, nondogmatic, and low on Machiavellianism. Research specifically on self-reported expressivity reveals that expressives' nonverbal behaviors are easier to decode because they include a higher rate of "meaningful" gestural, head, and eye movements; are seen as more salient (novel, intense, complex, and changeable); and are more noticeable (Sullins, 1989). Thus expressive individuals are more animated and engaging.

2. *Nonverbally skilled senders are more successful in deceiving and influencing others.* The same skills that lead to perceptions of attractiveness enable senders to evade detection while deceiving because they exhibit an honest-appearing demeanor and are more persuasive.

3. *Encoding and decoding skills are related to sex and gender.* Female encoding superiority exists regardless of age but may be limited to visual cues and to nondeceptive messages (Hall, 1979, 1984, 1998). Of 21 relevant studies in Hall's (1998) most recent meta-analysis, 71% favored women as the better senders. (The only qualification was that results were too variable to support a consistent vocal effect.) The decoding superiority also exists regardless of age and gender of the stimulus person. Of 61 relevant studies, 84% percent showed women to be more accurate interpreters than men. However, the magnitude of the encoding and decoding advantage is small. We address other gender-related effects below in our discussion of emotional expression and management. Although a number of hypotheses have been advanced for female social skill advantages, many, including the possibility that female subordination and powerlessness make women more vigilant and attuned to the signals of more powerful conspecifics, have been ruled out. Other tentative hypotheses include women's socialization to be more accommodating than men and to attend to intentional cues, as well as various differences between men and women: innate differences, cognitive processing differences, differences in degree of linguistic involvement, differences in hemispheric lateralization (with concomitant differences in processing skill), and biologically based differences in expressiveness, with women more inclined to externalize their feelings and men more inclined to internalize them. To the extent that women manifest their emotional states externally, their expressions are more readily understood, whereas men are more likely to experience high internal physiological arousal but outwardly to display less, making decoding of their expressions more difficult.

4. *Race, education, and intelligence do not appear to be related to encoding and decoding skills, but age, occupation, and training do.* People with better nonverbal skills tend to gravitate toward people-oriented occupations. Maturation and social development also contribute to skill improvements up to a point, then begin to decline as hearing and visual acuity, concentration, and memory decline, producing a curvilinear relationship with age. Practice and training also can aid accuracy in interpreting nonverbal expressions (and can even eliminate the female advantage over several trials). Additionally, research in the deception arena suggests that highly experienced decoders (e.g., customs agents, police investigators, interrogators) are often no better than novices at detecting deception, and may actually do more poorly than novices, perhaps because their experience makes them overly suspicious. Experience thus is not necessarily the best teacher.

5. Encoding and decoding abilities are correlated. Those who are better senders tend to be better receivers and vice versa, but the relationship is a modest one. Also, vocal encoding skill tends to correlate with visual encoding skill. The same is often, although not always, true of decoding skills. We discuss other, more focused skills, such as those related to empathic accuracy, below.

In sum, the skillful creation, transmission, and comprehension of nonverbal signals underpins successful communication generally. Able communicators are those who not only employ semantic and syntactic nonverbal signals to elicit intended meanings in message recipients, and do so in pragmatically appropriate ways, but also decipher accurately the nonverbal signals of others.

THE DOMAIN OF NONVERBAL COMMUNICATION

Defining Nonverbal Communication

Most people have an intuitive sense of what is included as nonverbal communication. Called *body language* in the popular vernacular, it is assumed to encompass gestures, body movements, facial expressions, gaze, dress, and the like. But this lay interpretation is both too vague and potentially too restrictive. It omits a number of important communicative nonverbal elements, such as use of the voice, touch, distancing, time, and physical objects as messages. Taking a broader view are experts who define nonverbal communication as the "transmission of information and influence by an individual's physical and behavioral cues" (e.g., Patterson, in press). Broader still are popularized books with such titles as *How to Read a Person Like a Book*, which equate all human behavior with communicative behavior.

The variability in definitions of nonverbal communication presages innumerable controversies surrounding this topic, starting with where nonverbal communication stops and other aspects of human behavior begin. There are three distinctly different perspectives on this topic, the broadest of which is the *receiver (decoder) orientation*, familiarized in the oft-heard claim that "one cannot not communicate." Originating in a classic work by Watzlawick, Beavin, and Jackson titled *Pragmatics of Human Communication* (1967) and now deeply entrenched in many basic communication texts, the claim, reinterpreted as "All nonverbal behavior is communicative," places the locus for deciding what is communication with the receiver. If the receiver thinks a behavior is a message, it is. This makes all human action potentially communicative. For example, an ear tug can be interpreted as discomfort or deception if an observer chooses to "read" it as that. Even the act of sleeping can be regarded as a "message" of inaccessibility to others. The only requirements are that the action must occur in the presence of a receiver, and the receiver must be aware of it to form some interpretation of it. Aside from the fact that this position privileges the perspective of receivers over that of senders, a serious pragmatic disadvantage of this position is that it becomes very difficult to arrive at any general principles about human communication if all human behavior counts as communication. Further, it makes the term *communication* completely redundant with the term *behavior* and, therefore, dispensable.

At the other extreme is the *source (encoder) orientation*, which holds that only actions intended as communication by a source qualify as communication. This narrows the domain of nonverbal communication considerably. The rub comes in the issue of intent. Apart from the practical obstacles to determining just which nonverbal behaviors are intentional and which are not, the issue of whether intentionality is a legitimate criterion for defining communication has been hotly contested (see, e.g., Andersen, 1991; Clevenger, 1991; Kellermann, 1992; Motley,

1986, 1990a, 1991; Stamp & Knapp, 1990). Some argue that communication need not be intentional or even symbolic. Others insist that communicative behavior must be differentiated from that which is informative or expressive but not intentional (Ekman & Friesen, 1969b). Thus more restrictive definitions limit communication to (a) *other-directed behavior* that is (b) *encoded* (i.e., transformed from a cognition into some code), (c) *symbolic* (including symptomatic behaviors that function as symbols), and (d) part of a *two-way, interactive process* (see, e.g., Motley, 1990b). The apparent restrictiveness of this definition evaporates, however, if one accepts Bavelas's (1990) contention that in interactive situations, one cannot not communicate because one's behavior at minimum sends messages about availability for communication.

A third alternative that is compatible with Motley's and Bavelas's views but shifts focus from senders and receivers to the nonverbal behaviors themselves is the *message orientation* (Burgoon, 1980; see also Wiener, Devoe, Rubinow, & Geller, 1972), which defines as nonverbal communication those behaviors that could reasonably function as messages within a given speech community. More specifically, it includes *those behaviors other than words themselves that form a socially shared coding system;* that is, they are typically sent with intent, are typically interpreted as intentional, are used with regularity among members of a speech community, and have consensually recognizable interpretations. This approach emphasizes socially shared rather than idiosyncratic behavior patterns but broadens nonverbal communication to include habitual behaviors that have well-recognized meanings among members of the social system. The operative word is *typically.* If a behavior is commonly encoded deliberately and interpreted as meaningful by receivers or observers, it does not matter if, on a given occasion, it is performed unconsciously or unintentionally.

For example, an "unintended" frown can be regarded as a message because the behavior is one that people typically encode as a signal of displeasure and typically decode as an intentional signal of displeasure. If much nonverbal communication is well-practiced, routinized behavior that is "run off" in a semi-automatic, largely mindless, unmonitored fashion (Burgoon, Berger, & Waldron, 2000), then it becomes more productive to identify the "vocabulary" of nonverbal communication than to divine intent on each occasion of a behavior's enactment. The stipulation that a behavior be used with regularity implies that it is frequently selected to convey a particular meaning and regarded by recipients or observers as a purposive and meaningful signal. Intent still enters into the equation in that mutually recognized nondeliberate and incidental behaviors are excluded. For example, a frown prompted by stubbing one's toe would unlikely be regarded as a message by sender or receiver. In this respect, the message orientation shares some commonality with Stamp and Knapp's (1990) *interaction perspective,* in which sender and receiver negotiate meanings within the context of particular interactions.

A related definitional distinction is between spontaneous nonverbal signal systems (variously labeled as *signs, symptoms, indicative behavior, expressive behavior,* and *rituals*) and symbolic (or socially shared) signal systems (e.g., Buck, 1988, 1997; Cronkhite, 1986; Ekman & Friesen, 1969b; Liska, 1986; Mahl, 1987). The former include involuntary and biologically based signals such as fight-or-flight responses, emotional expressions, monitoring behaviors, and courtship cues that form an innate, rudimentary, and universally shared communication system. The latter include voluntary, complex, and symbolic forms of communication that are context dependent, have an arbitrary relationship between sign and referent, and are acquired through learning and practice. However, the line between these two classes of nonverbal communication is easily blurred when behaviors originating as "symptoms" or "signs" take on more deliberate and symbolic properties (see Motley, 1991). Both biologically and socially based nonverbal behaviors become communicative to the extent that they exhibit the properties of other coding systems—that is, they have semantic, syntactic, and pragmatic rules governing their use. As with our verbal lexicon, interpretations for a given behavior or behavioral set are constrained by the context in which it occurs and by concurrent or preceding verbal and nonverbal behaviors. So, for example, a squint in the presence of bright sunlight might be regarded merely as an adaptive reaction to the environment (i.e., symptomatic) rather than as communicative. The same squint in the midst of a heated discussion about politics might be taken as a display of puzzlement or disagreement. If the squint is accompanied by head shaking and the question, "Where did you ever get such an idea?" the latter meaning would become increasingly probable.

When this message-centered approach is applied, some classes of nonverbal signals more readily qualify as communication than do others. For example, natural body odors, although a potential signal system (much as nonhuman species use them), do not meet the criteria of a coding system because they are not intentional, voluntarily encoded signals, nor do they typically evoke consistent interpretations from receivers. Similarly, body type doesn't qualify as a message in itself because individuals are unable to manipulate their body types at will to encode particular meanings, although dieting, bodybuilding, and clothing choices emphasizing thinness or height might be seen as individuals' deliberate acts to modify the images they project. Other behaviors, such as gestures, facial expressions, vocalizations of affective states, touch, and choice of attire, have clear communication potential.

Nonverbal Codes, Contexts, and Functions

Guided by this orientation, we have identified seven classes of nonverbal signals as codes—vehicles for communication. These encompass most of the codes or channels traditionally regarded as part of nonverbal communication (although some, such as olfactics and oculesics, are omitted or folded into others). The seven classes are as follows:

1. *Kinesics:* visual bodily movements, including gestures, facial expressions, trunk and limb movements, posture, gaze, and gait

2. *Vocalics or paralanguage:* use of vocal cues other than the words themselves, including such features as pitch, loudness, tempo, pauses, and inflection

3. *Physical appearance:* manipulable features such as clothing, hairstyle, cosmetics, fragrances, and adornments; excludes nonmanipulable features such as physiognomy and height

4. *Haptics:* use of touch, including the frequency, intensity, and type of contact

5. *Proxemics:* use of interpersonal distance and spacing relationships

6. *Chronemics:* use of time as a message system, including such code elements as punctuality, waiting time, lead time, and amount of time spent with someone

7. *Artifacts:* manipulable objects and environmental features that may convey messages from their designers or users

Although it is common for summaries of nonverbal communication scholarship to be organized according to these individual codes, such approaches imply that the codes operate in relatively independent fashion when, in reality, the evidence is quite compelling that nonverbal codes typically work in concert as multichannel messages that are also highly integrated with the verbal channel.

An alternative approach to organizing this enormous body of literature might be to follow traditional contextual categories (e.g., interpersonal, small group, organizational, media). Although contextual variation unquestionably invokes different constraints, usage patterns, and unique interpretations, a contextual approach implies that knowledge best coheres around structural properties. Apart from overemphasizing static qualities at the expense of dynamic ones, such an approach is out of step with contemporary agentive and goal-oriented perspectives on human communication, because it glosses over fundamental differences in the purposes being served within a given context while overlooking commonalities in nonverbal functions that cut across contexts. We have therefore chosen to organize what is admittedly a selective sampling rather than an exhaustive census of the latest theorizing and research according to the communicative functions that nonverbal behaviors serve. A functional perspective organizes knowledge according to the communication functions that a constellation of verbal and nonverbal behaviors accomplish or are intended to accomplish within a given situation or context. By definition, then, functional approaches are goal directed, episodic, and time-bound. A functional approach points up the equipotentiality and equifinality in the nonverbal means by which various goals are accomplished while calling attention to the multifunctional character of any given nonverbal behavior or set of behaviors in the performance of goal-directed behavior.

Functions can be grouped according to whether they satisfy personal or social goals. Accordingly, we first examine *individual functions*. These functions include comprehending and producing comprehensible messages, expressing and managing emotional and affective states, and creating and projecting personal identities. Other nonverbal functions are truly interpersonal and social in nature. These we divide according to those dedicated to

interpersonal functions, which include forming impressions of others, and managing desired impressions, managing interpersonal relationship definitions; *interactional functions,* which include the structuring and regulation of conversations; and *influence functions,* which include persuasion, compliance, modeling, and other unidirectional and bidirectional influence processes. The remainder of this chapter is devoted to a review of the major theories and pertinent research associated with each of these functions as they relate to interpersonal communication. For those topics covered in detail in other chapters in this volume or elsewhere, we offer a relatively cursory treatment and direct the reader to the other sources. We largely omit yet other topics, such as developmental aspects of nonverbal communication, from mention not because they lack importance but because the literature is too extensive for us to be able to do it justice here. We conclude with some directions for future research, which include investigation of the role of nonverbal cues in new communication technologies. Throughout, the research citations that we include represent a sampling rather than an exhaustive review of the available literature; for information on earlier and classic studies, see the versions of this chapter in the previous editions of the *Handbook of Interpersonal Communication* (Burgoon, 1985a, 1994).

INDIVIDUAL FUNCTIONS

Message Production and Processing

That nonverbal signals are integral to the creation of meaning in human encounters is indisputable and attested to by experimental and meta-analytic research evidence showing that approximately 60-65% of all meaning in human encounters derives from nonverbal cues (Birdwhistell, 1955; Hegstrom, 1979; Philpott, 1983; compare Mehrabian & Wiener, 1967). In their seminal analysis of nonverbal behavior, Ekman and Friesen (1969b) underscore the interrelatedness between verbal and nonverbal cues in message production by noting that nonverbal acts may repeat, augment, illustrate, accentuate, or contradict the words they accompany. Although these categories, repeated in dozens of textbooks on nonverbal communication, tend to relegate nonverbal cues to a collateral role, Ekman and Friesen also observe that nonverbal acts can precede the words, substitute for them, or be unrelated to them. Contemporary work exploring these various interrelationships has piqued controversies over the extent to which nonverbal cues operate independent of or as intrinsic components of verbally encoded messages; the extent to which they are biological, social, and/or symbolic signals; and the extent to which they have a one-to-one correspondence with ascribed meanings (see, e.g., Buck, 1995, 1997; Fridlund, 1994, 1995; Kendon, 1994; Krauss, Fussell, & Chen, 1995; McNeill, 1992; Rimé & Schiaratura, 1991). Notwithstanding these important (although somewhat esoteric) distinctions, the empirical evidence is persuasive that nonverbal cues are not only essential to verbal message encoding and decoding, they are also "message bearers" in their own right. The ability to encode and decode nonverbal messages, therefore, is critically important to successful communication.

Message Encoding

On the encoding or message production side, certain nonverbal cues "set the stage" by indicating whether a context is to be understood as an interactional one or not and, consequently, what may count as a message. The mere presence of others does not create an "interpersonal communication" context; some level of "engagement" is necessary. Nonverbal cues perform this role. The "minimalist" hypothesis, as Bavelas (1990) calls it, is that people rely on nonverbal cues to signal, at minimum, their accessibility or inaccessibility

to communication. Among the behaviors she cites (many taken from empirical studies) are gaze (whether one makes or avoids gaze, the latency before it occurs, and its duration), postural rigidity, vocal cues of concentration such as sighing or groaning, smiling, and looking at one's watch. Staring straight ahead, focusing intently on one's work, and closing eyes communicate that one doesn't want to be bothered and relegate the other to the status of a "nonperson." Other behaviors such as increasing the physical distance between self and another, indirect body orientation, crossed arms, body blocks, and shielding one's eyes may likewise inhibit approach by others. Conversely, smiling and eye contact signal willingness to interact.

In defining situations as interactional or noninteractional, nonverbal cues also determine whether other nonverbal behaviors should be regarded as messages. The importance of this framing function should not be underestimated. With verbal communication, the act of uttering words in another's presence is usually sufficient to signal an intent to communicate. With nonverbal communication, intent is not as obvious. Many nonverbal messages such as flirtations occur in the absence of verbalizations. Yet merely "behaving" in another's presence isn't sufficient to qualify as communication. Nonverbal cues of accessibility reduce ambiguity and distinguish potentially communicative behaviors from expressive or indicative ones.

This framing role is only the beginning. Nonverbal cues perform semantic, pragmatic, and syntactic functions (Ekman & Friesen, 1969b; Ricci Bitti & Poggi, 1991; Liska, 1986; Scherer, 1980), conveying messages themselves or aiding the production of verbal messages. In their semantic and pragmatic roles, they may take the form of *emblems,* symbolic behaviors that have direct verbal translations; *illustrators,* gestures that accompany and clarify the verbal stream; *affect displays,* facial, postural, vocal, or tactile behaviors that convey primary emotional states; *regulators,* behaviors that manage conversational turn taking; *adaptors,* autistic actions such as scratching or rubbing the self, picking at clothing, or manipulating objects that relieve private, personal needs but may be used to show disrespect (such as filing fingernails in a meeting); *relational messages* that define the nature of the interpersonal relationship; and other *rituals* that have clear meaning within a given culture and can stand alone. Syntactically, nonverbal cues may function to *segment* and *synchronize* the flow of speech. The amusing practice of someone on the telephone gesturing dramatically and making exaggerated facial expressions, supposedly for the benefit of the unseeing listener, may be partly a matter of habit but may assist the speaker in punctuating and coordinating the verbal stream.

In fact, the extent to which nonverbal behaviors are integral to senders' encoding of messages or merely designed to facilitate recipient decoding and whether they serve communicative functions in their own right or are merely indicative of effort in producing a verbal message remain controversial issues. According to the *social meaning model* (e.g., Burgoon, Coker, & Coker, 1986; Burgoon & Newton, 1991) and Bavelas and Chovil's *integrated message model* (see Chovil, 1991), many nonverbal signals are truly communicative in the sense of regularity in usage and consensus in admissible interpretations. They thus represent intrinsic features of a total message that are integrated into meaning production at the inception of the encoding process. This view, adumbrated by Darwin's (1872/1965) observations of more than 130 years ago, is bolstered by ethologists' claims that many nonverbal behaviors have a uniquely communicative purpose. That communicative role may sometimes operate independent of the verbal content but is often an integral part of fashioning a meaningful utterance. Extensive research (e.g., Bavelas, Black, Chovil, Lemery, & Mullett, 1988; Birdwhistell, 1970;

Cappella, 1984; Cohen, 1977; Costo, Dinsbach, Manstead, & Ricci Bitti, 2002; Goldman-Eisler, 1968; Krauss, Morrel-Samuels, & Colasante, 1991; Mahl, 1987; McNeill, 1985; McNeill, Cassell, & McCullough, 1994; Poyatos, 1993; Siegman, 1978), much of it summarized by Rimé and Schiaratura (1991), has led to the following conclusions.

1. Gestures are present regardless of the presence and visibility of a message recipient. This implies that gestures are not produced solely for the benefit of a recipient but must also facilitate message production for the sender. That said, the interpersonal context serves to intensify some of this nonverbal activity and to suppress other behavior. Many gestures, such as emphatic arm and hand movements, gestures depicting the train of thought, pointing, shrugging, and facial displays such as smiling and motor mimicry (expressions indicating empathy for another's plight), are more likely to occur when a receiver is visibly present or imagined; other gestures, such as adaptors, decrease. The fact that the former class of nonverbal cues often occurs in abbreviated fashion or not at all when other people are absent implies that those cues serve primarily a social or communicative function.

2. Gestures, vocal fluency, and gaze are not solely indicators of arousal or cognitive effort. That is, they are not merely incidental by-products of producing a message, although they may index the degree of effort that is expended. The amount of gestures accompanying speech does not differ, for example, according to degree of arousal.

3. Gestures closely parallel and synchronize with verbal output, typically preceding or occurring simultaneously with, rather than following, verbal utterances. This supports the contention that gestures and speech originate together as part of the same communicative intention, the resultant encoding process activating both a verbal-vocal utterance and a motoric (gestural) representation that may serve a priming function in helping the individual to access and assemble the verbal features of a message.

4. Nonverbal cues facilitate message production by (a) providing encoders an efficient mode in which to express content (such as spatial or visual information) and (b) facilitating the activation of words, concepts, ideas, and images used in utterance construction.

5. Nonverbal cues reveal encoding difficulty. When verbal utterances are complex, difficult to construct, or occur under stress (e.g., divulging highly personal information, expressing an abstract idea, responding during an embarrassing situation, giving complicated directions, delivering bad news, or making one's case during an argument), nonverbal performances suffer. Speech fluency is disrupted, adaptor use increases, and silent pauses become more numerous and lengthy. Thus nonverbal cues may signal difficulty in message production. Because these same cues may arise for other reasons—such as transitory emotional or mood states, anxiety, or restless disinterest—their significance is often ambiguous and "misread." Moreover, concurrent gestures and other nonverbal behaviors may be intended to compensate for encoding difficulties. However, if cues fluctuate consistently with conditions that could reasonably be interpreted as cognitively demanding, they may be taken as legitimate signs of "heavy cognitive load."

Message Decoding

Regarding the decoding of nonverbal signals, early message-processing research considered the impact of congruence between verbal and nonverbal channels on interpretations and comprehension. Illustrative are experiments conducted by Argyle and associates in which friendly, neutral, and unfriendly verbal passages were paired with friendly, neutral, and unfriendly nonverbal presentations or superior, neutral, and inferior attitudinal statements were combined with parallel nonverbal behaviors (Argyle, Alkema, & Gilmour, 1971; Argyle, Salter, Nicholson, Williams, & Burgess, 1970). Even though the verbal and nonverbal presentations were seen as relatively equal in strength when rated separately, once combined, the nonverbal cues accounted for as much as 12 times as much variance in meaning as did the verbal statements. These and numerous other investigations have found that adults tend to place greater reliance on nonverbal cues than on verbal cues under such varied circumstances as job interviews, assessments of leadership, therapeutic sessions, expressions of attitudes, and judgments of first impressions. Moreover, cues are not weighted according to a straight additive or averaging strategy whereby each cue is weighted equally. Rather, numerous other factors influence the weighting of information. The research conclusions can be framed as propositions regarding reliance on nonverbal information compared with verbal information (see Burgoon, 1985b; Burgoon, Buller, & Woodall, 1996; Church, Kelly, & Lynch, 2000; LaPlante & Ambady, 2000; McNeil, Alibali, & Evans, 2000; Thompson, Driscoll, & Markson, 1998).

1. Adults generally rely more on nonverbal cues than on verbal cues in determining social meaning. As a broad generalization, this principle holds but must be qualified by the propositions that follow.

2. Age and stage of development influence channel reliance. For example, children's patterns in reliance on nonverbal cues differ from those of adults. As children acquire language, they shift from total reliance on nonverbal messages to greater attention to literal verbal meanings. For example, they do not interpret sarcasm well. Prior to puberty, however, they revert to greater belief in nonverbal signals. Research on memory for mixed messages also suggests a U-shaped function in which recognition for mismatched gestures and speech is higher in early childhood and adulthood than among 9- and 10-year-olds. Changes in visual and auditory acuity and tactile sensitivity may also shift reliance on verbal versus nonverbal channels among the elderly.

3. Adult reliance on nonverbal cues is greatest when the verbal and nonverbal messages conflict. Verbal cues become increasingly important as the messages become more congruent. Some research has found that under congruent message conditions, verbal messages are believed over nonverbal ones. But more commonly, congruence among channels just makes the verbal and nonverbal coding systems more equal in their contribution to meaning.

4. Channel reliance depends on what communication function is primary. Verbal cues are more important for factual, abstract, and persuasive communications, whereas nonverbal cues are more important for relational, attributional, affective, and attitudinal messages. Not surprisingly, people rely on verbalizations for the denotative or "objective" meaning of a message. But for connotations, metamessages, emotional expressions, and meanings about the interpersonal relationship between speaker and auditor, people largely depend on nonverbal signals, making nonverbal behavior especially important in interpersonal contexts.

5. Channel congruence or incongruence influences how verbal and nonverbal information is weighted. When content across channels is congruent, the information from all contributing channels tends to be averaged together equally; when content is incongruent, channels and cues may be weighted differently. Sometimes a single cue or channel will be discounted if two or more other cues are consistent with

each other. For example, direct gaze coupled with close proximity may be sufficient to convey conversational involvement even if a person uses a monotone voice. However, a single cue can also override multiple cues, such as physical closeness taking precedence over indirect body posture and averted gaze. Sometimes, people believe the most extreme or negative cue. But nonverbal cues still tend to be believed over verbal ones, even if the verbal message is more extreme.

6. Incongruence does not impair comprehension and may actually improve it. Evidence is mixed on whether anomalous and incongruent messages produce deeper cognitive processing or less recall. Some research indicates that expressions in which all channels convey redundant or congruent information are no better recognized or understood than incongruent ones. Reinforcing (consistent) gestures also do not necessarily improve comprehension of verbal content relative to conflicting ones. In fact, compound expressions (ones in which multiple meanings across or within channels are blended together) may actually produce higher recognition accuracy than singular or totally congruent expressions. The implication is that the distinctiveness or salience of different cues may aid an individual in arriving at a more refined interpretation than a unitary display might supply. Further, some evidence suggests that channel incongruencies may arouse attention and deeper processing.

7. Individuals have consistent biases in channel reliance. Some individuals consistently depend on verbal information, some consistently depend on nonverbal information, and some are situationally adaptable. Although individuals have personal predilections for which channels of information they attend to most often, the prevailing pattern is still one of relying more frequently and for more purposes on the nonverbal codes.

A variety of reasons have been offered for adults' significant dependence on nonverbal channels in interpreting and expressing interpersonal messages. These include possible innate origins for nonverbal attention and expression, phylogenetic and ontogenetic primacy of nonverbal cues as coding systems, belief in the veridicality and spontaneity of nonverbal displays, the ability of such displays to reveal psychological and emotional information about the interactants, their special suitability to handling interpersonal business while the verbal channel is simultaneously occupied with transmitting other information, and their substantial role in clarifying verbal content.

Regardless of which reasons are most correct, accumulating evidence substantiates that nonverbal signals are critical in several respects to the processing, comprehension, recall, and understanding of interpersonal messages (Abele, 1986; Birdwhistell, 1970; Boomer, 1978; Folger & Woodall, 1982; Kendon, 1983; McNeill, 1992; Rimé & Schiaratura, 1991; Riseborough, 1981; Woodall & Burgoon, 1981; Woodall & Folger, 1985). First, nonverbal cues may draw attention to a message. For example, a primary function of a speaker's gaze and gesture is to monitor and secure others' attention. Second, visible articulatory cues in the face may facilitate comprehension by helping receivers access lexical items, while the rhythmic synchronization and coordination of the speaker's verbal-vocal stream with his or her other nonverbal cues (self-synchrony) and with the nonverbal cues of auditors (interactional synchrony) adds its own lubricant to the processing of verbal inputs. Third, nonverbal cues supply semantic and syntactic information that facilitates comprehension and recall. At the semantic level, emblematic and illustrator gestures add redundancy or semantic elaboration to specific utterances as well as depict and reflect the larger meanings of extended utterances. At the syntactic level, vocalic cues such as tempo and prosody and kinesic cues such as stress kinemes supply nonverbal punctuation that "chunks" linguistic content into phonemic clauses—the form in which linguistic information is likely processed. Fourth, nonverbal cues supply contextual information that aids in information retrieval and in deepening the inference-making process so central to message comprehension. Emblematic gestures and, to a lesser extent, emphasizing gestures facilitate recall even of language not recognized on its own. Kinesic, physical appearance, and artifactual cues may lend visual vividness to the stimulus-cue complex, whereas haptic, proxemic, and vocalic cues may stimulate physiological arousal, thereby strengthening the associations in memory between content and context.

Nonverbal signals do not, however, exert only beneficent effects on message processing. They may also activate various social cognition processes and biases. The well-documented "seeing is believing" visual bias (see, e.g., Keeley-Dyreson, Burgoon, & Bailey, 1991; Noller, 1985) places a premium on nonverbal kinesic, proxemic, and physical appearance cues in interpersonal interactions. Such visual cues have been shown to increase the salience of speaker (rather than message) characteristics and, along with auditory cues, to moderate how language style affects message persuasiveness (Sparks, Areni, & Cox, 1998). Among the reasons proffered for this visual primacy are that visual cues may be more semantically distinctive, especially in conveying emotional and motivational information, and therefore able to transmit information more efficiently per unit of time; the face, because of its controllability, may offer more intentional information to a viewer; visual cues can be scanned for a longer time than can more fleeting, sequentially presented vocal and verbal cues; and vocal cues, which are automatically alerting, may be reserved as threat signals, leaving the visual channel as primary information carrier for routine matters.

Nonverbal cues may also distort information processing by distracting attention from the central message. A meta-analysis showing that auditory and visual distractions reduce comprehension (Buller, 1986) implies that nonverbal behaviors may be unsuspected and intrinsic sources of distraction in interpersonal interchanges. Nonverbal signals such as vocal nonfluencies, unpleasant voice qualities, extreme conversational distances, extremes in physical attractiveness, and excessive environmental stimulation may distract from, rather than center attention on, the verbal content of a message. Such findings support the claim that heuristic processing becomes more likely when nonverbal modes of information are available to message recipients (compared with receiving messages in written mode).

It should be noted that many factors may temper these nonverbal biases, including gender, culture, actual or suspected message content, and dimension of judgment. Females rely more on visual cues than do males; visual information from females is discounted more than that of males, especially by children. Westernized, industrial cultures may be more visually oriented, whereas non-Westernized cultures may be more oriented to auditory cues. Greater reliance may also shift to vocal information when deception or discrepant messages are being judged. Finally, whereas visual information is more important for judging positivity/negativity, vocal information is more important for judging dominance, assertiveness, fearfulness, and sincerity. We consider other ways in which nonverbal cues contribute to biased or accurate information processing later in this chapter, in our discussion of impression formation.

Emotional Expression and Management

It is perhaps one mark of the extent to which nonverbal scholarship has matured that nonverbal communication is no longer simplistically and exclusively equated with expressive behavior. That said, nonverbal codes are primary vehicles for expressing emotions and affective states as well as for managing emotional experiences. Indeed, "people express feelings through their communicative conduct in incredibly rich and diverse ways; understanding the processes through which they do so requires an appreciation of the biology, psychology, and sociology of emotion" (Burleson & Planalp, 2000, p. 244). Because an entire chapter of this volume is devoted to this topic, our focus here is on the twin issues of how nonverbal behaviors are employed in the communication of affective states (akin to Burleson & Planalp's, 2000, notion of how emotion is expressed as the content of messages) and how nonverbal resources are marshaled to control or alter those states. Moreover, whereas Metts and Planalp elaborate in more detail the interpersonal implications of *experienced* affect and emotion in Chapter 10 of this *Handbook,* we consider only the nonverbal *expressions* of emotion, that is, the external manifestations of those emotional states and people's abilities to detect and interpret them, which are clearly distinct from the internal physiological and subjective experiences.

Within the nonverbal literature the terms *emotion, affect,* and *arousal* are often used synonymously. However, it is possible to differentiate among these concepts. *Emotion* may be understood to refer to a discrete, relatively transitory state that entails both a valence dimension (positive to negative or pleasant to unpleasant) and some degree of physiological activation or arousal as an integral part of the emotional experience. Most of the work on nonverbal cues of emotion relates to these brief states, which are the primary focus of our attention here. *Affect* is sometimes also used as a synonym for *emotion* but sometimes merely refers to any subjective experiences that are hedonically toned on a good-bad or positive-negative continuum. These states may be short-lived or of long duration (as in the case of liking someone or being in a bad mood, both of which may or may not pass quickly). *Arousal* refers to physiological, cognitive, and/or behavioral activation, which is a central defining property of different emotions, but can also refer to states such as watchful readiness or boredom that are not thought of as emotions.

Emotional Expression

More theorizing surrounds the expressive function of nonverbal communication than any other, and nowhere is the nature/nurture controversy more central than here, its roots tracing back to Darwin's writings about emotional expressions in humans and other species. Among the primary issues being addressed in this corpus of work are the origins and development of nonverbal emotional displays, the relationship between internal states and their external manifestations, the dimensionality of emotions, and the manner in which meaning is assigned to overt behaviors. Due to space limitations, we focus here on the broad theoretical developments pertinent to the expression of emotion. For a recent and thorough review of the specific cues of emotional expression, see Planalp (1999).

Early theorists proposed three alternative possibilities regarding the nature of emotional expressions: (a) They arise from inborn neurological programs and feedback mechanisms that produce and/or elicit emotional displays; (b) they are manifestations of experiences common to all humans (such as the need to ward off danger or to withdraw from pain); or (c) they are shaped strictly by environmental and social factors (e.g., Eibl-Eibesfeldt, 1972; Izard, 1971; LaBarre, 1947; Plutchik, 1984; Tomkins, 1984). The first two positions reflect a *universalist perspective*—that at least certain primary affect displays are produced and understood in the same way by all members of the species. The last position underpins the

cultural relativist perspective—that any cross-cultural similarities are only superficial and that actual use and interpretation are strictly functions of cultural and environmental influences. As a compromise between the two extremes, Ekman (1973, 1997; Ekman, Friesen, & Ellsworth, 1972) advanced *neurocultural theory,* which holds that all humans are endowed with the same innate neuromuscular programs but that social factors not only filter what stimuli will elicit different emotions but also introduce cultural display rules, which dictate when, how, with what meaning, and with what consequences emotional displays will occur. Subsequent theorizing has tended to maintain these three perspectives but to cast them under new terminology (e.g., Barrett, 1993). *Differential emotions theory* and other biologically grounded positions hold that specieswide, inherited facial configurations are used to express the same emotions across all cultures and exhibit a one-to-one correspondence between the external display and internal experience. The *behavioral ecology approach* (e.g., Fridlund, 1991) holds that facial expressions evolved to serve social rather than emotional motives and that they lack isomorphism with internal emotional states. Emotional labels are thought to be convenient shorthand for whatever facial displays happen to be associated with socially evoked experiences, and an enormously large number of displays may all signal the same meaning, so that any given display cannot be assumed to represent a particular emotional state. A *functional perspective* (e.g., Barrett, 1993; Buck, 1984) views the latter alternative as creating a false dichotomy between social and emotional responses. It holds, among other things, that facial expressions are not the exclusive site for communicating emotions and that "emotion-relevant movements" function to accomplish both intraindividual regulation (of physiology and behavior) and social regulation. Buck and Ginsburg's (1997) communicative gene hypothesis comports with this perspective in contending that emotional displays are part and parcel of social interaction. Visual, auditory, and chemical signals are thought to constitute a direct and spontaneous communication system to which species mates are preattuned, but the system also requires shaping or "education" to be used appropriately in social contexts.

It can be seen that these various positions reflect distinct controversies related to (a) the competing merits of biological (innate) versus social (learned) explanations, (b) the degree to which nonverbal emotional displays represent voluntary and adaptable versus involuntary and fixed behavior, (c) whether biologically based expressions are communicative, (d) whether social signals are manifestations of underlying emotions or other social functions, (e) the degree of authenticity of emotional social signals, (f) universality versus cultural relativism in display, and (g) universality versus context-dependence in interpretation.

As attempting to address these issues in a concrete and substantial way is beyond the scope of this chapter, we offer only a cursory review of some of the evidentiary support for these various alternatives, which derives from widely varying sources. Physiological studies, including research on the facial feedback hypothesis, have demonstrated that voluntarily posing a given emotion in the face can actually elicit the felt experience, thereby linking internal experiences closely to their external manifestations (Buck, 1984; Levenson, Ekman, & Friesen, 1990). Relatedly, studies examining the configurations associated with emotional expressions (e.g., diagonal lines, angularity, roundness) have shown that the same configural properties convey meanings of threat, anger, warmth, happiness, and so on (Aronoff, Barclay, & Stevenson, 1988; Aronoff, Woike, & Hyman, 1992). These "configural properties" point to an evolutionary process whereby humans have become hardwired to express emotion though nonverbal communication (Andersen & Guerrero, 1998; Dillard, 1998).

Comparative studies of nonhuman primates showing that many human behaviors bear a striking similarity to those of other primates imply an evolutionary continuity and innate origins based on survival value. Cross-cultural research showing a high degree of similarity of emotional expression across cultures (e.g., Ekman, 1993; Scherer & Wallbott, 1994) tacitly supports the likelihood that such behavior is at least biologically based. Research in child development demonstrating that infants and toddlers follow the same stages of emotional development and exhibit the same expressions at each successive stage offers further indirect support for a biological explanation. More definitive evidence comes from studies of blind, deaf, and limbless children, who, lacking the ability to learn emotional displays through sensory experience, still exhibit universally recognized expressions.

From the opposite perspective, cultural relativists (e.g., Birdwhistell, 1970; Mead, 1975) assert that individuals learn to express emotion in the same way that they learn a language. This argument rests upon the claim that any pancultural similarities are superficial at best and regulated by cultural practices; cultural relativists cite cross-cultural variability and the strong influence of socialization practices on nonverbal expressions to bolster their position.

Taken together, the aforementioned bodies of literature make either a purely biological or a purely sociocultural theory of emotion expression rather implausible. The principles proposed by Ekman (1984) remain a useful framework for organizing the emotion expression literature most relevant to interpersonal communication.

1. There is a distinctive pancultural signal for each emotion. Although researchers have proposed various labels and estimates for the number of distinctive affects that exist, the cross-cultural work of Ekman and his associates offers definitive support for these six:

happiness, sadness, fear, anger, disgust, and surprise. Other affect displays are proposed to be blends of these basic ones. To the extent that these expressions are part of our genetic heritage as humans, they form an elemental universal language that can supplant or augment more ambiguous messages and can cross cultural barriers. Nevertheless, significant differences exist in the form and intensity of these displays across cultures and social groups. For example, collectivist cultures may display more emotions that promote group cohesion and harmony than do individualist cultures, whereas cultures with significant power differences may display more of those emotions that preserve such differences.

2. *Emotional expressions involve multiple signals.* Within the kinesic code, the body is responsible for signaling the intensity of affect, whereas the face signals the specific evaluative state, with various regions of the face differentially salient to sending and interpreting feeling states (Ekman & Friesen, 1975). However, the extensive attention to the face overlooks the extremely important place of vocal cues in emotional expression, perhaps best articulated in Scherer's (1986) component process model of emotion. Acoustic features such as amplitude, fundamental frequency (pitch), tempo, breathing, intonation pattern, and stress contours differentiate specific emotions as well as their intensity and valence (Banse & Scherer, 1996). (Other codes, such as haptics, although intuitively relevant, have received little systematic analysis for their contributions to coordinated, multichannel emotional displays.)

3. *There are limits on the duration of an emotion.* "Real" emotions typically last from half a second to 4 seconds; expressions of shorter or longer duration than this range are usually false or mock expressions. This is probably one basis for "intuitive" reactions to some expressions as insincere or suspicious.

4. *The timing and intensity of an emotional expression reflects the specifics of a particular emotional experience.* That is, the latency and duration of the manifest expression correlate with the strength and positivity or negativity of the experience.

5. *Emotional expression can be controlled, simulated, or inhibited.* This principle presages the related function of affect management, discussed below. Just as people can intensify or deintensify emotions, they can also completely conceal or fabricate them and do so convincingly (although false emotions are detectable by the muscle groups that are enlisted as well as by their duration; Ekman, Friesen, & O'Sullivan, 1988). This principle is especially relevant to interpersonal interactions, because people may regulate their expressive behaviors during face-to-face encounters as part of self-presentation and are capable, with varying levels of success, of becoming more or less expressive (DePaulo, Blank, Swaim, & Hairfield, 1992). Although some theorists propose that social factors inhibit certain emotional expressions, especially spontaneous ones (e.g., Ekman & Friesen, 1969a; Friedman & Miller-Herringer, 1991), an alternative position is that the presence of others facilitates and potentiates some emotional expressivity (Chovil, 1991). Undoubtedly, both processes are operative (Buck, 1991), pointing to the important social and communicative nature of emotional expression.

Although the argument for the universality of emotional expression might imply that emotions are easily recognized by all members of the human species, such is not the case. This leads to a final principle not articulated by Ekman.

6. *Decoding accuracy is highly variable.* Extensive research examining how accurately various emotions can be detected has revealed that people have difficulty accurately decoding many primary facial affects and most vocal

emotions (e.g., Davitz & Davitz, 1959; Zuckerman, Lipets, Koivumaki, & Rosenthal, 1975). Especially relevant to interpersonal communication is Motley and Camden's (1988) finding that spontaneously expressed emotions in interpersonal interactions are much more ambiguous and difficult to decode than the posed expressions so often studied in the emotions literature. Coupled with the greater frequency of "affect blends"—combinations of emotions displayed simultaneously—in normal interaction and the likelihood that people may attempt to manage many emotional expressions to foster favorable impressions, these findings lead to the inescapable conclusion that a major stumbling block in many interpersonal encounters is the parties' deciphering of one another's true emotional states. Fortunately, there is some evidence that people are more facially expressive with friends than with strangers, making their emotional states easier to identify (Wagner & Smith, 1991).

One factor that is particularly influential in determining decoding as well as encoding accuracy is sex or gender. The empirical evidence supports commonly held beliefs that women are more nonverbally expressive than men, which aids accuracy among observers, and women demonstrate greater accuracy in decoding emotion and affect (for reviews, see Guerrero & Reiter, 1998; Hall, Carter, & Horgan, 2000). Other factors likely to have impacts on decoding and encoding accuracy include context, channel integration, commensurability of verbal and nonverbal expression, correspondence to relational outcomes, and multiplicity of meanings associated with a given display (Burgoon, 1994). For example, emotion displays may also convey interpersonal intentions such as affiliation and dominance (Hess, Blairy, & Kleck, 2000), and congruence of affect/emotion displays has surplus implications for identity and power perceptions (Robinson & Smith, 1999).

With few exceptions (e.g., Gottman, 1994; Huston & Vangelisti, 1991), there is a paucity of research on nonverbal emotional expressions that takes a longitudinal and dynamic perspective. Thus knowledge of how displays change over time in ongoing interpersonal interactions, how context moderates those displays, and the accuracy with which they are judged remains limited.

Arousal Expression

Several theories that we discuss later in this chapter in the section on conversation management invoke arousal as a primary mediator or moderator of communication behavior. Of interest here is the degree to which arousal is manifested overtly and nonverbally. Two different forms of arousal may be evident: an orientation or alertness response that entails cognitive activation but limited physical activation and a defensive response that entails strong physiological reactivity (Le Poire & Burgoon, 1996). Both may range from pleasant to aversive. Research on a bidimensional perspective on arousal expression has successfully distinguished between nonverbal cues associated with the intensity of arousal and cues associated with its valence (Burgoon, Kelley, Newton, & Keeley-Dyreson, 1989; Burgoon, Le Poire, Beutler, Bergan, & Engle, 1992). Specifically, research has generally supported three conclusions. First, as arousal intensity increases, speech performance is increasingly impaired. Second, immediacy, kinesic activation, and kinesic attentiveness follow an inverted-U pattern (highest arousal change associated with moderation in the nonverbal cues). And third, as negatively valenced arousal increases, immediacy, activity, and attentiveness decrease; expressiveness decreases; tension increases; communication performances become more awkward; and negative affect increases.

Presumably, interpersonal interactants rely on these cues to infer the arousal levels of their partners. Such cues may serve as useful diagnostics in assessing the extent to which other aspects of interactions, such as intimacy escalation, expectancy violations, or alterations in power and status relations, are accompanied by intense positive or negative arousal (see Kemper, 1984; Matsumoto, 1991). Yet the communicative nature of arousal expression can be seen as bringing both clarity and confusion to interaction. Although physiological arousal associated with emotional experiences may offer additional behavioral cues, it is nonetheless difficult to make precise and accurate attributions as to the underlying causes of such arousal. Physiological changes due to emotional activation may be indistinguishable from arousal due to exercise, chemical drugs, and so forth (Berscheid, 1990). Similarly, considering the controversy of cognitive or affective primacy in emotion (e.g., Lazarus, 1984; Zajonc, 1984), expressions of arousal cannot be regarded as reliable and precise indicators of emotion (Frijda, 1986), a difficulty exacerbated by the human capacity to control, regulate, and manage physiological reactions to arousal.

Affect Management

A related aspect of emotional experience is the individual's regulation of the experience of strong affect, a function Patterson (1987) labels affect management, Cappella (1991) addresses under the rubric of stimulation regulation and emotional responsiveness patterns, DePaulo (1991) includes as part of self-presentation and identity management, and Barrett (1993) describes as internal regulation. Regardless of the label applied, the principle is an important one. People use their overt nonverbal behavior to regulate their internal emotional experiences. By voluntarily controlling nonverbal immediacy and expressive behaviors, people can intensify or dampen feeling states.

Affect management is largely achieved through cultural socialization. DePaulo (1991) identifies a host of factors governing the degree to which spontaneous and posed emotions are presented during interpersonal interaction. Five primary display rules that simultaneously facilitate internal regulation are (a) *simulation*, which occurs when we show emotion(s) that we are not feeling; (b) *intensification*, which calls for expressing an amplified version of an experienced emotion; (c) *miniaturization*, the opposite of intensification, in which the expression of felt emotion is minimized; (d) *inhibition*, which is the attempt to show no affect; and (e) *masking*, which is the attempt to show a different emotion than what is experienced. These display rules are highly salient not only in the realm of emotional expression but also in such interpersonal functions as relational communication and deception. Kemper (1984) proposes that the motivation for employing such management of affect displays comes from a desire to communicate integrating emotions and immediacy behaviors to bind people together or differentiating emotions and nonimmediacy behaviors in order to distance them. When facing threats or crises, people may engage in approach behaviors or display distress, which should prompt reciprocal closeness and comforting from others, thereby alleviating fears and anxieties. When elated, people may express happiness and seek greater involvement to intensify the experience. When embarrassed or ashamed, they may eschew involvement and exhibit embarrassed smiles to elicit sympathy and lessen the aversive emotional state. Thus people may fulfill basic needs such as security, affiliation, and social comparison by regulating nonverbal involvement and emotional experience.

Identification and Identity Management

A core objective for communicators in interpersonal contexts is identification and identity management (Clark & Delia, 1979; Schlenker, 1985). Manifest indications of one's cultural, social, demographic, and personal characteristics serve as "identity badges," enabling one to project one's own identification with various personal and social categories while simultaneously enabling observers to use the same cues as an instant means of classification. As the example of Sherlock Holmes ably demonstrates, detectives often rely on combinations of seemingly inconsequential nonverbal cues to identify their quarry. This is because nonverbal demeanor is often an "embodiment" of a person vis-à-vis his or her social relationships (Mahl, 1987). Not only may individuals rely on their own nonverbal behaviors as affirmation or self-verification of their identities (see Swann, 1987), but others may also treat such information as outward reflections of the inner self (notwithstanding that such judgments may be fraught with errors, such as overgeneralizing from insufficient cues and using a stereotypical "average person" as a benchmark for comparisons to others).

Although the line between identity management and impression management may be blurry, we make a subtle distinction between the two. The former involves the presentation of the "phenomenological" self—that is, the individual's self-perceived "true" identity—whereas the latter involves the strategic presentation of image for the benefit of an audience, a presentation that may depart from the individual's "inner self" (see Jones & Pittman, 1982). The former is typically reflected in fairly unconscious, highly internalized, and highly consistent patterns of verbal and nonverbal actions that reflect a person's own sense of self. Because such presentations may emanate from biological forces, acculturation, and learning processes, they may be more "indicative" than "communicative." Nevertheless, because individuals may also deliberately emphasize or de-emphasize features of their identities (e.g., having plastic surgery, wearing native dress, suppressing a dialect), it is useful to analyze how nonverbal cues convey social identities,

especially as they are adapted in particular interpersonal relationships.

Scholars of self-image and identity increasingly acknowledge that our personal identities are partly social constructions; that is, they are shaped and negotiated through interactions with others (McCall, 1987). According to *social identity theory* (Tajfel, 1981), our self-construals influence our communication patterns very directly. The "self" is defined primarily through five classes of factors: culture, race and ethnicity, age, gender, and personality. We take up each in turn below. Given that the available information on cultural, biosocial, and personality differences far exceeds the space that we can devote to it here, what follows is necessarily just a sampling of some major trends, all of which could be examined from the standpoint of individual-difference variables but take on greater significance if recognized for their identification potential.

Indicators of Culture and Subculture

Cultures differ radically in their use of space, touch, time, and artifacts; in the symbolism of their attire; in their use of kinesic and vocalic cues—in short, in all the nonverbal codes (see, e.g., Gudykunst & Ting-Toomey, 1988; Hall, 1977; Morris, Collett, Marsh, & O'Shaughnessy, 1979; Ricci Bitti & Poggi, 1991). Cultural differences are not random events; they occur because cultures develop with different geographies, climates, economies, religions, and histories, all exerting their own unique influences (Andersen, Hecht, Hoobler, & Smallwood, 2002). These differences in interaction and communication have been categorized into a number of dimensions, such as individualism/collectivism, power distance, high and low context (Hofstede, 1980, 2001), and pace of life (Levine & Norenzayan, 1999), to name but a few. As one illustration, a distinction is often made between "contact cultures"—the members of which prefer close interaction distances, frequent use of touch, higher rates of gaze, and more gestural animation—and their opposites, "noncontact cultures" (Hall, 1966). These distinctions have been criticized as overly simplistic, as not reflecting cultural shifts that have occurred in the past two decades, and as less predictive of communicative style than self-construals (e.g., Burgoon, Buller, & Woodall, 1996; Fernandez, Carlson, Stepina, & Nicholson, 1997; Gudykunst et al., 1996; McDaniel & Andersen, 1998).

That said, the extant data unmistakably reveal systematic differences in interpersonal nonverbal behaviors arising from cultural practices, differences that become a vehicle for making one's identity manifest. By adhering to a culture's or subgroup's norms, one may signal identification with that culture or subgroup, thereby invoking all the characteristics, expectations, and behaviors stereotypically associated with its members (Manusov, Winchatz, & Manning, 1997), regardless of whether that is one's intent or not, and externalizing one's "collective self" (see Triandis, 1989). By violating a culture's norms (for example, wearing Western dress in a Muslim culture), one may likewise send a message distancing oneself from that culture and repudiating that identity. Conversely, sharing verbal, vocalic, kinesic, proxemic, and physical appearance similarities helps individuals identify themselves as in-group members (Mulac, Studley, Wiemann, & Bradac, 1987) while distinguishing them from out-group members. As prolific research on in-group–out-group relations testifies (Fiske & Taylor, 1991), such distinctions can influence all manner of interpersonal interactions, ranging from in- and out-group communication patterns in organizations (e.g., Suzuki, 1998) to communication between people with and without disabilities (e.g., Fox, Giles, Orbe, & Bourhis, 2000). One theory that addresses this process explicitly is *communication accommodation theory* (e.g., Giles, Coupland, & Coupland, 1991;

Giles & Smith, 1979), which postulates that people converge their speech patterns toward those of in-group members and diverge from those of out-group members. These outward manifestations of association solidify identification with primary groups.

We discuss general methodological advances in the study of nonverbal communication later in this chapter, but there is at least one advance concerning culture that is worthy of note here. Paunonen, Zeidner, Engvik, Oosterveld, and Maliphant (2000) have developed a personality assessment tool that they call the Nonverbal Personality Questionnaire. Researchers have been using verbally based methods of personality assessment for years, but the difficulty of translation and back-translation as well as other cultural and linguistic issues make a nonverbal tool for assessing cultural personality and communicative differences a welcome methodological advance.

Closely related to cultural differences are racial and ethnic identifiers. Despite lip service paid to the importance of researching these differences, the amount of published work remains sparse (for exceptions, see Blascovich, Wyer, Swart, & Kibler, 1997; Hecht, LaFrance, & Haertl, 1993) and limited largely to normative differences between members of U.S. minority groups (blacks, Hispanics) and Caucasians. Findings remain too mixed, and the amount of research too spotty, to warrant definitive conclusions.

Indicators of Sex and Gender

A central ingredient of a person's self-image is her or his sex and/or gender identity. The nonverbal literature is rife with evidence of sex and gender differences (see, e.g., Canary & Dindia, 1998; Gallaher, 1992; Hall, 1984; Hall & Halberstadt, 1986). Some of these are rooted in primary (genetic) and secondary (physiological and anatomical) features associated with sexual functioning. Other biological differences between males and females likewise produce observable "nonverbal" differences in such physical characteristics as physical appearance and voice and may influence entire patterns of responding. Haviland and Malatesta (1981), citing male infants' greater emotional lability, propose that biobehavioral predispositions, in interaction with environmental influences and social learning processes, affect a whole range of nonverbal encoding and decoding patterns. When these sex-linked differences take behavioral form, they become part of what Birdwhistell (1970) labels *tertiary gender displays*. Some feminine and masculine gender behavior patterns may stem from biological or cultural needs to distinguish the sexes and promote sexual attraction. Provocative walking and standing postures, grooming and adornment practices that emphasize female or male physical attributes, and vocal qualities that connote strength or weakness may fit this category. Other behavioral differences, such as sitting with crossed ankles or crossed legs, may be due in large part to socially prescribed sex role expectations for female and male behavior. Among the differences, many of which are enumerated in the version of this chapter that appears in the previous edition of this *Handbook*, are that women display all of the following, relative to men: more gaze during listening and speaking; more smiling; more vocal and facial expressivity; more gestures that suggest submissiveness, such as the open palm; more head tilts; more close postures and sitting positions that take up less space; closer interaction distances and greater tolerance of others' approach; less talk and more listening; recipients of more interruptions; rising vocal intonations; more hesitations; more laughter; and more accommodation to their partners' interaction styles (see Burgoon, 1994). Although considerable evidence has suggested that women give and receive more touch, and although touch is stereotypically perceived as appropriate for females and inappropriate for males, there is little evidence to support this claim, and where sex differences have been found, they are often very small (e.g., Guerrero & Andersen, 1994; Hall & Veccia, 1990).

One controversial aspect of these basic display patterns, alluded to earlier, is the extent to which they reflect differences in power. Recent evidence has put the dominance explanation in doubt. Although sex differences based in cultural and socioeconomic power may have some credence (Cashdan, 1998; Noller, 1993), these explanations likely oversimplify the observed differences, and rival explanations have been offered. One is that women are more affiliative, communal, and socially sensitive than men. Consistent with Bem's (1981) *gender schema theory* and Eagly's (1987) *gender role theory,* which assert that many gender differences are attributable to women's and men's conforming to culturally defined gender role expectations, women have been found to have greater sensitivity and responsivity to the communication of others (Eagly & Karau, 1991; Snodgrass, 1992; Street & Murphy, 1987). The validity of this perspective relative to the power interpretation remains a contentious argument (see, e.g., LaFrance, Henley, Hall, & Halberstadt, 1997), but in support of it, Hall (1998) recently found that "sex differences for smiling and nonverbal sensitivity are relatively large" (p. 169) and that these differences are closely linked to people's gender identity. Another proposed explanation for observed sex differences is LaFrance and Hecht's (2000) *expressivity demand theory.* These authors conclude, based on reviews and meta-analyses, that sex, type of relationship, and situational factors all interact to create expected levels of expressivity in behavior. Women are generally expected to be more expressive and particularly when they are in caregiving roles. On the other hand, when status and power differ, the sexes behave the same: Both men and women smile more in the low-power position and smile less in the high-power position.

The literature on sex differences in nonverbal behavior reveals both disagreement and confusion, but three additional principles can be stated regarding how individuals display their sexual identities: (a) Sex differences vary by culture and subculture, (b) individuals differ in their acceptance of and adherence to sex and gender role expectations and norms, and (c) gender differences are minimized with age (Burgoon, Buller, & Woodall, 1996).

Indicators of Age

Recent work in communication has applied social identity theory to the communication of age (e.g., Harwood, Giles, & Ryan, 1995). All of the major nonverbal codes provide identifiers of age. Changes in physical appearance include wrinkled skin, graying hair, modified clothing style, and stooped posture. Reductions in motor control and coordination affect gesturing (O'Hair, Allman, & Gibson, 1991), and older persons may use closer interpersonal distance to compensate for hearing loss (Nussbaum, Thompson, & Robinson, 1989). Physiological changes to the respiratory and phonatory systems can also change speech patterns and vocal styles (O'Hair et al., 1991), and those changes reliably indicate cues for the identification of age (Hummert, Mazloff, & Henry, 1999). Some of these and other issues are addressed by the contributors to a 1999 special issue of the *Journal of Nonverbal Behavior* devoted to aging and nonverbal behavior (e.g., Montepare & Tucker, 1999).

Indicators of Personality

The psychoanalytic, psychological, and communication literatures have produced nonverbal profiles associated with personality traits such as extraversion-introversion, Machiavellianism, anxiety, authoritarianism, and need for affiliation; disorders such as schizophrenia, paranoia, depression, and hysteria; and communication predispositions such as communication apprehension, unwillingness to communicate, self-monitoring, social skills, and touch avoidance. The relationships are sufficiently stable to warrant the conclusion that nonverbal style "may be regarded as an aspect of personality rather than merely as a cue to it" (Gallaher, 1992, p. 143). If this notion carries truth, then nonverbal indicators of personality should likewise identify individuals according to the "Big Five" traits—neuroticism, extraversion, agreeableness, conscientiousness, and openness to experience (see, e.g., Asendorpf, 1998; Digman, 1990). Although Lippa and Dietz (2000) recently found that, except for openness, these primary personality dimensions were generally unrelated to accurate judgments of strangers' personality traits from video segments, future research may establish more connections. Certainly, the number of nonverbal codes and cues implicated as manifestations of personality suggests that there should be strong linkages. More specifically, talk time, loudness, speech errors, pitch, voice quality, vocal characterizers (such as crying or laughing), silences, interruptions, response latencies, amount of eye contact, head orientation and nods, leg movements, object adaptors, coordination of movement, amount of gesticulation, postural relaxation, amount of physical movement, conversational distance, amount of touch, personal grooming, and colorfulness of clothing all have been implicated. Nonverbal behavior patterns such as gaze, loudness, speaking tempo, laughter, smiling, expressiveness, nervous mannerisms, conventionality of appearance, and general interpersonal style show impressive cross-situational consistency in interpersonal situations (Funder & Colvin, 1991; Gallaher, 1992).

A plethora of nonverbal signals serve as "identity badges" that reveal culture, sex and gender, age, and personality. These vary from expressiveness, touch, and chronemic orientation to gaze, physical features, and vocalic cues. Indeed, an individual's full repertoire of nonverbal behaviors acts to provide markers or clues to his or her identity, and observers need not possess the investigative talents of a Sherlock Holmes to decode and make meaning of them.

INTERPERSONAL FUNCTIONS

Impression Formation and Management

Whereas the function of identification and identity management is grounded in an encoder perspective, examining how communicators manifest "who they are" through nonverbal signals, impression formation is grounded in a decoder perspective, examining how receivers use the same signals to form judgments of communicators. Impression management returns to an encoder perspective, examining the ways in which communicators strategically craft their nonverbal performances to create desired images, projecting "who they want to be."

Impression Formation

When people first meet or talk, they rapidly categorize one another on such characteristics as gender, age, socioeconomic status, political affiliation, nationality, and geographic residence. At the same time, they begin to draw inferences about political, social, and religious attitudes, personality traits, and global qualities such as attractiveness, likability, and credibility. This subconscious but instantaneous process of impression formation is highly stereotypic and fraught with misjudgments. Nonetheless, people rely on it, perhaps because the pressure to reduce uncertainty is great (see Berger & Calabrese, 1975), because initially available information is accurate at some levels, and because, as Freud (1915-1917/1963) cautions, even feeble indicators can reveal important information. Given that initial verbal exchanges are often constrained by convention, the nonverbal cues, especially stable physical appearance and kinesic and vocalic cues, take on particular importance in

shaping interpersonal expectations and in generating a frame for the parties' interpretation of subsequent behavior. Our review of the relevant research on impression formation suggests the following basic principles.

1. Judgments are formed rapidly. As seen in the recent development of "thin slice" methodology (Ambady, Hallahan, & Conner, 1999; Ambady & Rosenthal, 1993), people need only very brief samples of behavior to form fairly accurate and strong judgments of actors. Three primary reasons support the rapidity of judgments from limited information, particularly nonverbal behavior, and the development of consensual standards. First, humans are driven by an underlying need for uncertainty reduction. Social interaction theories such as balance theory (Heider, 1958) and uncertainty reduction theory (Berger & Calabrese, 1975) are premised on the basic human avoidance of uncertainty and drive to find methods of reducing uncertainty. Second, humans are likewise driven by a basic need for sense making. Various attribution theories (e.g., Weiner, 1986) are premised on individuals' tendency to overgeneralize to dispositions based on information from isolated and/or unique impressions. Third, individuals are subject to information-processing biases whereby cognitive miserliness, cognitive busyness, and mindlessness lead them to take mental shortcuts in impression formation (Burgoon et al., 2000; Pendry & Macrae, 1994). Readily available or anecdotal cues of nonverbal behavior operate as simple but often inappropriate decision rules by which people form generalizable judgments from limited information.

2. Judgments are based on limited and external information. Evolutionary and biological imperatives probably required humans to develop the mental shortcuts, or heuristics, that encourage us to construct relatively complete judgments about objects from limited amounts of information. Whereas internal characteristics become more important when individuals are transforming impressions into relational knowledge, initial judgments rely upon readily accessible cues that make such judgments akin to viewing others as objects. This imparts primacy to visual nonverbal cues in initial interactions. Human vision has developed as a phylogenetically stronger sense than the auditory channel, and the richness in the visual field, coupled with the greater number of visual nonverbal codes, may reinforce attunement to visual information.

3. Judgments are based on stereotyping and biases. A number of inaccuracies and distortions are common, including the aforementioned *visual primacy effect* and the *"what is beautiful is good" stereotype* (Dion, Berscheid, & Walster, 1972), by which attractive individuals are credited with more positive attributes, such as intelligence, persuasiveness, poise, sociability, warmth, power, and employment success, than unattractive individuals. These halo effects are triggered by both facial and vocal attractiveness, and favorable judgments in one channel elicit similarly favorable judgments in the other, causing innumerable impressions to be influenced by attractiveness (Berry, 1992; Semic, 1999; Zebrowitz, 1990; Zuckerman, Hodgins, & Miyake, 1990; Zuckerman, Miyake, & Hodgins, 1991). Although the "what is beautiful is good" stereotype has continued to draw empirical support across different cultures (e.g., Wheeler & Kim, 1997) and age groups (Larose & Standing, 1998), emerging evidence suggests that this heuristic is not as strong or as general as first thought (Eagly, Ashmore, Makhijani, & Longo, 1991), and "what is beautiful" occasionally is "bad" (Tseelon, 1992). In some cases, highly attractive individuals may be at a disadvantage in a hiring process (Farley, Chia, & Allred, 1998) and may be lied to more often by prospective romantic partners (Rowatt, Cunningham, & Druen, 1999). In addition,

these effects become attenuated when people are familiar with one another or gain other relevant information (Berry, 1990; Morrow & McElroy, 1984), bolstering the contention that the potency of attractiveness biases should diminish once people begin to interact and shift from category-based to person-based judgments (Fiske & Neuberg, 1990; Knapp, 1985).

4. Consensus in judgments of strangers is high; accuracy is more variable. The term *consensus* here refers to people's ability to make judgments of communicators that are, at minimum, consistent across multiple judges and, at maximum, accurate reflections of the persons' "true" characteristics (Kenny, 1991). As a species, and perhaps due to phylogenetic development, humans tend to share common impressions of unfamiliar others and objects. Although some evidence indicates that agreement outstrips accuracy (i.e., observers share the same perceptions, but those perceptions are often erroneous), research has documented that people's "hunches" can also be remarkably accurate (Smith, Archer, & Costanzo, 1991). Accuracy tends to be highest for judgments concerning sex, age, occupation, and social status, which are derivable from external and emblematic appearance and vocal cues (Ambady & Rosenthal, 1993; Kenny, Horner, Kashy, & Chu, 1992). Judgments of attitudes, values, and personality traits are much more variable and subject to stereotyping; however, some personal and interpersonal characteristics can be judged accurately. The high degree of accuracy in some judgments can be accounted for by (a) direct link(s) between personality and behavior, (b) self-fulfilling prophecies, and (c) permanent appearance features resulting from repetitive expressions of affect (Berry, 1991). The redundancy of nonverbal cues likely acts to increase accuracy in judgments (Smith et al., 1991).

5. First impressions are persistent. First impressions based on nonverbal cues tend to be highly persistent, even in the face of subsequent contradictory cues (Burgoon & Le Poire, 1993; Kenny et al., 1992). People are biased toward seeking information that confirms first impressions, and this serves to solidify and perpetuate those impressions. As relationships progress, static or slow signals such as physical attractiveness diminish in importance, and dynamic nonverbal cues rise in prominence. Cues that are novel, unexpected, or extreme also have greater impact.

6. *A premium is placed on nonverbal communication cues.* As mentioned above, of the two primary information sources, verbal and nonverbal cues, nonverbal cues are much more important, partly because of the stronger constraints placed upon verbal communication by cultural and social norms, but also because of all the previously cited reasons nonverbal cues carry such import in social interactions generally.

Physical appearance, which is clearly instrumental to impression formation, includes some less obvious features, such as facial babyishness or maturity, in addition to such obvious ones as physical attractiveness, height, weight, and grooming (Berry, 1991). In keeping with the visual primacy and beauty biases, the visual channel appears to be more important than the auditory channel in forming impressions of attractiveness (Raines, Hechtman, & Rosenthal, 1990; Zuckerman et al., 1991). Other codes strongly implicated in impression formation are kinesics, vocalics, and proxemics. Relatively unchanging features, such as vocal maturity, and dynamic cues of expressivity and positivity, such as smiling, gaze, pleasant facial expressions, gait, vocal loudness, pitch and pitch variety, tempo, fluency, silence, immediacy, and self-touch, all contribute to perceived attractiveness (Berry, 1992; Brownlow, 1992; DePaulo, 1992; Gallaher, 1992; Raines et al., 1990). Unlike negative behaviors, which are often discounted, positive behaviors tend to be regarded as

intentional (Manusov, 1990, 1991; Manusov & Rodriguez, 1989).

In an attempt to integrate many of the issues involved in impression formation, and nonverbal exchange in general, Patterson (1995, 1999) has developed the *parallel process model,* which focuses on the interdependence of behavioral and person-perception processes from a functional perspective on social interaction. This model presupposes that individuals engage in both social behavior and social cognition simultaneously. One of the features of this model suggests that impressions based on appearance and nonverbal cues will be generally unaffected by limited cognitive resources and effort, making cognitive demand an important moderator of judgment and perception accuracy (Patterson & Stockbridge, 1998). This theoretical proposition exemplifies recent advances in nonverbal scholarship as theorists create increasingly complex and holistic models to describe biological, sociological, cognitive, affective, and behavioral influences on interpersonal communication.

Impression Management

The flip side of impression formation is impression management: How can communicators use nonverbal cues to foster desired impressions? Impression management is often, but not always, strategic (Palmer & Simmons, 1995). At the theory level, emphasis is on what macro-level strategies a communicator can use to project desired images along dimensions of believability, expertise, attraction, status, prestige, and the like. At the research level, emphasis is typically on what micro-level nonverbal cues actually encourage favorable impressions or are judged as appropriate or inappropriate in particular contexts, the implication being that inappropriate or unacceptable behavior leads to failed performances. Thus, much of the impression formation literature can be recast as revealing what nonverbal strategies enhance self-presentation.

Theories with special relevance to nonverbal impression management are Jones and Pittman's (1982) *strategic self-presentation theory,* which centers on "those features of behavior affected by power augmentation motives designed to elicit or shape others' attributions of the actor's dispositions" (p. 233); Ting-Toomey's (1988, 1994) *face-negotiation theory,* which focuses on facework, or "communicative behaviors that people use to regulate their social identity and to support or challenge the other's social dignity" (Ting-Toomey & Kurogi, 1998, p. 188) and the ways in which people can prevent face threats or restore face; the progenitor of face-negotiation theory, Goffman's (1959) theory of *the presentation of self in everyday life,* a dramaturgic perspective on the individual's management of his or her public face that includes specific strategies for successful and spoiled performances; and Burgoon's (1983, 1993) *expectancy violations theory,* which is explicitly designed to predict and explain the positive and negative consequences of individuals' violating expectations.

This last theory offers propositions that predict when nonverbal behaviors will produce positive outcomes, such as heightened credibility and attraction, or negative outcomes. Central to this theory are two premises: (a) Nonverbal behaviors engender strong expectations that govern interaction patterns and outcomes, and (b) nonverbal behaviors have message value. When meanings are unequivocal and/or congruent (in the case of multiple meanings), a social meaning model prevails such that interpretations and evaluations associated with the behaviors are predicted to influence outcomes directly. When meanings are ambiguous or conflicting, communicator reward valence is posited to moderate the cognitive-affective assessment process. *Communicator reward valence* is a summary term for all the combined communicator characteristics that, on balance, cause the communicator to be regarded positively or

negatively. The interpretation and evaluation process results in a net valence for the nonverbal act. Positively valenced acts are posited to produce positive outcomes, and negatively valenced acts, negative outcomes. Violations of expectations are hypothesized to intensify this process by causing an attentional shift to the source of the violations and the behaviors themselves, thus making communicator and message characteristics more salient.

A substantial amount of research to date on expectancy violations theory (e.g., Burgoon & Dillman, 1995; Burgoon & Hale, 1988; Burgoon & Le Poire, 1993; Burgoon, Le Poire, & Rosenthal, 1995; Burgoon & Walther, 1990; Burgoon, Walther, & Baesler, 1992; Le Poire & Burgoon, 1994) has produced the following conclusions, condensed and summarized here in terms of impression management strategy:

1. *Proxemic violations and nonintimate touch promote favorable impressions of positively valenced communicators but undermine impressions of negatively valenced communicators.*

2. *Increases beyond normative levels in conversational involvement and immediacy behaviors such as gaze are positive violations that improve impressions, regardless of communicator valence, whereas reduced involvement and gaze aversion are negative violations. However, there may be an upper threshold for immediacy-related cues that, if exceeded, accrues diminishing and possibly negative returns.*

3. *Hypo- and hyperrelaxation are negative violations that produce largely unfavorable social judgments, although hyperrelaxation may engender impressions of power and dominance.*

Other relevant research on appropriateness or acceptability speaks to the likelihood of success of specific nonverbal tactics (e.g., Storrs & Kleinke, 1990; von Raffler-Engel, 1983). In keeping with Goffman's (1959) claims about successful self-presentation, much of this research leads to the conclusion that doing what is appropriate is successful. However, the expectancy violations work is challenging the assumption that the route to success is always conformity to expectations. The conditions under which violations are the more efficacious choice for impression management remain a focal area for research.

Common to the predominant theories of impression management are two basic aims: managing impressions of attractiveness and likability, and managing impressions of credibility and power. Four general classes of nonverbal cues instrumental to impression management of attractiveness and likability are (a) *physical attractiveness* (apparel, hairstyle, grooming), (b) *warmth and pleasantness* (expressive behaviors such as smiling, head nods, eyebrow raises, vocal pleasantness), (c) *immediacy* (eye contact or gaze, touch, close proximity, open body positions, direct body orientation, forward lean), and (d) *dominance* (e.g., relaxed, asymmetrical posture with slight backward leaning and frequent gesturing but infrequent nodding; louder, faster, more fluent voice with shorter response latencies and longer turn lengths). It is unclear whether dominance cues work similarly for both females and males to promote attractiveness. Many of these cues are employed to manage impressions of credibility and power in a like manner. Credibility, a multidimensional construct that includes judgments of competence, character, sociability, dynamism, and composure, can be thought of as an end unto itself but is often activated in concert with interpersonal implications for power, such as in social influence and deception. Vocal behaviors that are most relevant to fostering impressions of credibility and power include moderately high loudness, greater pitch and tempo variety, and absence of a distinguishable accent (e.g., Burgoon, Birk, & Pfau, 1990; Giles, Henwood, Coupland, Harriman, & Coupland, 1992). Faster speaking tempo has generally been found to gain greater perceptions of competence,

status, knowledge, and power (e.g., Buller & Aune, 1988; Giles & Street, 1985), but these findings are tempered by research documenting that slow or moderately paced speech increases impressions of honesty, benevolence, and composure (e.g., Ray, 1986; Woodall & Burgoon, 1983). Many of the kinesic and proxemic cues that convey dominance, which we summarize below in our discussion of relational communication, also foster impressions of credibility, as do height, a mesomorphic body build, and other physical appearance cues signifying status, maturity, and professional accomplishment. Timeliness, defined as adhering to a scheduled meeting time without being noticeably early or late, brings about the impression of competence. Taken together, these cues help speakers to manage others' impressions of their poise, competence, trustworthiness, credibility, and power. The number of relevant cues points to the powerful and dramatic effects of nonverbal signals in fostering desired impressions.

Relational Communication and Relationship Management

Relational communication bears a close resemblance to identity and impression management, particularly at the level of the specific nonverbal cues used to signal evaluations and self-images. However, relational communication is distinct in at least four respects:

1. Relational communication follows a participant, as opposed to an observer, perspective.

2. A relational message is directed toward a specific target as opposed to a generalized audience.

3. Relational communication typically focuses on dyadic interaction between sender and receiver and may use the dyad as the unit of analysis, whereas impression management focuses on the individual sender.

4. Relational communication focuses on meanings attached to nonverbal behavior, as

opposed to the common cause-effect approach of identity and impression management.

Traditional approaches to relational communication have identified only two or three dimensions (e.g., dominance, affection, inclusion or involvement) along which messages may be exchanged. Such perspectives can underestimate the variety and richness of message themes that are present in interpersonal encounters. Based on a review of ethological, anthropological, sociological, psychological, and communication literature, Burgoon and Hale (1984) have proposed 12 orthogonal but distinctive topoi, or themes, of relational messages, themes that are intended to reflect more fully the nuances and variegation of relational communication. Many of these themes, however, are interdependent and, when parsimony is the objective, can be combined into fewer message composites (Burgoon, 1991; Burgoon & Hale, 1987; Burgoon & Dillman, 1995). We describe the major themes and their associated nonverbal messages below.

Intimacy/Similarity

Every relationship can be characterized according to a horizontal and a vertical dimension. The horizontal dimension is captured by a superordinate cluster of intimacy and similarity themes, which include messages of affection, depth, trust, inclusion, and involvement. This cluster of themes is defined largely by nonverbal behavior—physical closeness, touches, lingering gazes, smiling and laughing, prolonged time spent together (e.g., Burgoon & Le Poire, 1999; Le Poire, Shepard, Duggan, & Burgoon, in press; Register & Henley, 1992). Some of the experience of intimacy can be understood as a function of one major ingredient, *nonverbal involvement*. Involvement per se neither implies nor includes positivity, but when accompanied by *positive affect* (smiling, nodding, vocal pleasantness, relaxed laughter), which is often the case, it connotes greater attraction, liking, trust, affiliation, depth, and

similarity. Other cues contributing to intimacy messages include touch to more "intimate" body regions, softer voices, postural openness, motor mimicry and mirroring (exhibiting the same behavior as another), wearing similar apparel and "identification symbols" (tie-signs), punctuality, monochronic use of time, and sharing of territories and possessions. Involvement may also, however, combine with negative affect, in which case it may create an intense message of hostility. Noninvolvement and nonimmediacy cues signal detachment and/or desire for privacy. It is important to note that many of the individual behaviors, if viewed singly, might be ambiguous in meaning because they have multiple relational interpretations. But when these behaviors are combined with other cues into a pattern, the appropriate interpretation becomes clear.

Two other closely related message themes are empathy and rapport. Buck and Ginsburg (1997) present a biologically based model that proposes that empathy is a spontaneous, communicative process fundamental to all living creatures and entails innate transmission and attendance to visual, auditory, and chemical displays. Empathic accuracy, or the ability to convey relational messages effectively, depends upon (a) the individual's ability to engage in nonverbal behavior that sufficiently reflects his or her thoughts and feelings, and (b) the ability of other interactants to observe this behavior and derive accurate judgments (Thomas & Fletcher, 1997). A second element of empathy relies upon emotional contagion— the ability to feel *with* someone. In this way, individuals are expected to perceive another's emotional state(s) from that person's nonverbal behavior and summarily internalize the other person's position and feelings (Planalp, 1999). Although the ability to "step into someone else's shoes" is specifically outside the realm of nonverbal communication, the ability to recognize and successfully decode another's emotional state is clearly dependent upon nonverbal receiving ability and attunement.

Rapport is usually considered to be a combination of involvement, positivity, and interactional synchrony. Research employing thin-slice methodology (e.g., Bernieri & Gillis, 1995; Bernieri, Gillis, Davis, & Grahe, 1996; Grahe & Bernieri, 1999) has led Bernieri and colleagues to assert that "interactant rapport must have been expressed and communicated nonverbally rather than verbally in order for observers to detect it in such brief exposures" (Grahe & Bernieri, 1999, p. 255). In situations where observers have only limited exposure to behavioral episodes, nonverbal signals allow more accurate judgment than does the verbal content of messages (Grahe & Bernieri, 1999). The apparent strength of visual cues in communicating rapport is best exemplified by nonverbal behaviors that indicate involvement and synchrony. These include gesturing, interactional coordination, proximity, postural mirroring, and facial mimicry (Bernieri et al., 1996; Levenson & Ruef, 1997). The overlap of behavioral indicators between empathy and rapport signifies the interrelatedness of these concepts and also denotes their contribution to intimacy.

Dominance

The vertical dimension of relationship is captured by the theme of dominance or power. Whereas *power* may refer to potential for influence or perceptions of influence, *dominance* refers to actual interactional behaviors by which power and influence can be accomplished, although dominance constitutes only one and not the exclusive route to influence (Berger, 1994; Burgoon & Dunbar, 2000). Interpersonal dominance is a relational construct, thus requiring that when one person is dominant, there must then be someone else who is not. Although dominance has often carried a negative connotation at the construct level, such an attribution is not entirely accurate, nor does it reflect the multiple components of interpersonal dominance. Components of

dominance displays include aggressiveness, threat, strength, persuasiveness, dynamism, and self-control. These components manifest themselves in nonverbal behaviors that communicate poise, panache, and self-assurance and that permit individuals to exert influence and conversational control (Burgoon & Dillman, 1995; Burgoon, Johnson, & Koch, 1998). There is a strong positive correlation between social skills and dominance such that more skilled individuals are more likely to evidence dominance displays in service of their goals and in response to the demands of the particular circumstances. However, fairly intense emotional displays can be confounded with relational messages of dominance (Hess et al., 2000), reminding scholars and students alike of the complexity of interpreting nonverbal signals in interpersonal communication.

Regarding micro-level indicators, dominance is expressed by all the behaviors cited in our discussion of impression management as cues of power, status, and prestige, as well as by the expressiveness facet of involvement. Submissiveness is expressed by the opposites of these, along with some specific gestures, such as the head tilt and open palms, that convey vulnerability and some involvement and affiliative cues. Dominance/submissiveness is also expressed vocally through such cues as relaxed voice and laughter, pitch variety and animation, loudness, amplitude, intensity, and rate (Burgoon & Le Poire, 1999; Tusing & Dillard, 2000). Preliminary evidence suggests that kinesic cues—such as facial expression (Aguinis, Simonsen, & Pierce, 2000)—may be better predictors of perceptions of dominance than vocalic cues (Burgoon & Le Poire, 1999).

Underlying the numerous forms by which dominance and submission are expressed are some common principles, including threat, elevation, size, initiation and precedence, expectancy violations, privileged access, activity, relaxation, and task-related expectation advantages. For example, physical height, upright stance, and expansive gesturing all draw upon the principle of elevation to convey superiority. Sitting at the head of the table, walking ahead of others, initiating touch, changing conversational tempo, and similar "going first" behaviors reflect the principle of initiation or precedence (for elaboration on these principles, see Burgoon, 1994).

Arousal and Composure

The arousal and composure cluster and the cluster noted in the next subsection perform somewhat auxiliary functions to the primary dimensions of intimacy and dominance. Emotional arousal and lack of composure are conveyed by a host of vocalic, kinesic, and proxemic cues, some of which we have discussed above in relation to emotional expression and management. Research has substantiated that composure and relaxation are communicated by such behaviors as asymmetrical limb and postural positions, less body tonus and tension, less vocal tract tension, closer- or farther-than-usual interpersonal distancing, and smiling. Greater kinesic expressiveness and faster tempo also connote composure. Although it is likely that people intentionally manipulate these cues to send relational messages of poise and composure, the converse may not be true. Noncomposure may merely reflect a person's current emotive state irrespective of the relationship.

Formality and Task Versus Social Orientation

The dimensions of formality and task versus social orientation demonstrate that not all nonverbal messages need carry romantic meaning or connotation. They are interrelated in that part of being task oriented is being more formal, and formality often connotes more of a task orientation than a social orientation. Formality is conveyed by decreased vocal expressiveness, increased resonance and precise articulation, postural tension or erectness, and greater distance. The task cues

identified in expectation states theory (discussed below) serve as indicators of a group member's inferred task competence and confidence. They include response latency, gaze, loudness, fluency, posture, gestures, and seating position (Ridgeway, Berger, & Smith, 1985). Although verbal content and language style are prime means for expressing this dimension, the nonverbal codes can powerfully reinforce the degree of focus on formality and on task or social relations.

Relationship Management

The features that unify research on nonverbal behavior in interpersonal relationships are a macroscopic perspective—looking at entire relationships rather than single encounters—and carry a consequent concern with longitudinal factors. One strand of research and theorizing examines how nonverbal cues function in the development, maintenance, and dissolution of interpersonal relationships. Work on relationship development has long recognized that nonverbal behaviors signify the state of the relationship and can promote or obstruct the development of intimacy (e.g., Altman & Taylor's, 1973, social penetration theory; Knapp's, 1984, dimensions of communication in relationship development). The other strand of research examines the connection between nonverbal behavior and such measures of relationship state as intimacy, commitment, and satisfaction.

Within the first strand are developmental theories that consider the role of nonverbal cues in the progression of relational trajectories from initiation through escalation and maintenance to dissolution. One perspective, *uncertainty reduction theory* (Berger, 1979), postulates that people have a strong need to reduce uncertainty about others and will engage in a variety of communication strategies, including use of nonverbal behaviors, to reduce that uncertainty over time. Reduced uncertainty is posited to be positively related to relationship development. A related theory, *predicted outcome value theory* (Sunnafrank, 1986), posits that relational escalation or termination depends on whether the uncertainty reduction process leads to predictions that the relationship and future interactions in it will be rewarding or nonrewarding. In either case, nonverbal signals are instrumental to this process and are foundational to the creation and development of intimate relationships (Afifi & Burgoon, 2000; Andersen & Guerrero, 1998). Many of the relevant nonverbal behaviors—involvement, expressivity, smiling, gaze, and positivity of facial expressions—coincide with judgments of attractiveness in impression formation. Related empirical work has bolstered the importance of nonverbal cues in relationship development. Research on initial attraction has confirmed that kinesic and vocal behaviors mediate attitudinal similarity effects, signaling that communication similarities during interaction are more potent indicators of attraction than are preinteractional attitudinal similarities (Cappella & Palmer, 1990). Research on courtship stages and rituals has identified different nonverbal cues associated with each stage and has differentiated courtship cues from quasi-courtship ones (e.g., Givens, 1978, 1983; Scheflen, 1965; Simpson, Gangestad, & Biek, 1993). Research on romantic touch has shown that increasingly intimate touch signifies increasing levels of relational commitment (Johnson & Edwards, 1991). Additionally, research on relationship stages and types has found significant differences across various relationships (e.g., acquaintance, friend, romantic, superior-subordinate, parent-child, doctor-patient) in nonverbal intimacy, play, and emotional expressivity and continues to refine profiles of how nonverbal cues signal relational states (Baxter, 1992; Guerrero & Andersen, 1991; Morman & Floyd, 1999; Noller, Feeney, Sheehan, & Peterson, 2000; Planalp & Benson, 1992; Trees, 2000; Wagner & Smith, 1991). Researchers studying

relational escalation, maintenance, and de-escalation have developed typologies of the combined verbal and nonverbal strategies and tactics relational partners employ (e.g., Cupach & Metts, 1986; Shea & Pearson, 1986; Tolhuizen, 1989) and have estimated their frequency of use.

Among the theoretical perspectives relevant to the maintenance phase of relationships is *attachment theory* (Ainsworth, 1982; Bowlby, 1982). Results from work utilizing the four-category model of attachment (Bartholomew, 1990) indicate that more socially adjusted types ("secures" and "preoccupieds") generally display more pleasant nonverbal behaviors, such as facial and vocal attentiveness, receptivity, gaze, interest, and attentiveness, and more physical closeness (Guerrero, 1996; Guerrero & Burgoon, 1996; Tucker & Anders, 1998). Preoccupieds and fearful avoidants display more vocal anxiety, whereas fearful avoidants display the least vocal fluency. Preoccupieds also exhibit the strongest pattern of reciprocity and compensation in response to partner behavior.

Research on nonverbal cues in the waning and de-escalation stages of relationships has centered largely on signals of negative affect and conflict. The most successful of these research programs has been Gottman's work on differentiating successful from failed marriages (Carrere & Gottman, 1999; Gottman, 1994; Gottman & Levenson, 1992; Levenson & Gottman, 1983). This line of research has culminated in the *cascade model of relational dissolution,* which focuses on nonverbal displays of negative affect in the form of criticism, contempt, defensiveness, and stonewalling (Gottman labels these the four horsemen of the apocalypse). According to the model, as behavior follows a linear procession through these affective displays, negative physiological arousal leads to withdrawal. Research summarized by Gottman (1994) indicates that an approximately five-to-one ratio of positive to negative behaviors is necessary to sustain a healthy relationship, whereas a ratio approaching one-to-one predicts further de-escalation leading to dissolution. This model's focus on nonverbal expressions of affect and the instruments used to assess them, such as the Specific Affect Coding System (Gottman & Krokoff, 1989), should serve as a foundation for further research in this area. Additional marital conflict research has uncovered nonverbal profiles that accompany different conflict strategies, shown that conflicts often take the form of reciprocal escalating spirals of nonverbal hostility, confirmed that nonverbal expressions of affect are a deciding factor in whether conflicts are resolved or not, and conducted cross-cultural comparisons (Alberts, 1989; Bodenmann, Kaiser, Hahlweg, & Fehm-Wolfsdorf, 1998; Huston & Vangelisti, 1991; Julien, Markman, & Lindahl, 1989; Newton & Burgoon, 1990). Finally, research has identified relational message themes and conflict resolution patterns that promote satisfaction or dissatisfaction in physician-patient and marital relationships (Burgoon et al., 1987; Kelley & Burgoon, 1991; Rusbult, Verett, Whitney, Slovik, & Lipkus, 1991). Among the important conclusions to be drawn from these lines of work are that nonverbal cues are important barometers of, and influences on, attraction and intimacy; relationship type or stage does indeed mediate forms of nonverbal expression; and nonverbal patterns significantly influence relational trajectories and outcomes.

It is our hope that the continuing evolution of research on relationships in contexts such as turning points—a kiss, an act of aggression, the absence of an expected handshake—and longitudinal processes will continue to draw further theoretical attention to the meanings of nonverbal behaviors in relationships of all types across various stages. One specific area that may bear fruit is that of nonverbally "mixed" messages—when the verbal content of a message is in conflict with the nonverbal

behavior accompanying it. Although far short of the complications inherent to the "double-bind" messages that Bateson (1972) has associated with schizophrenia, misunderstandings arising from incongruent messages have clear relational implications.

Deception

The function of deception concerns the ways in which people send messages that are designed to foster beliefs contrary to what the message senders believe is the true state of affairs and to convince others of their truthfulness. It is thus part self-presentation, part relational communication, and part social influence (Buller & Burgoon, 1994; DePaulo, 1992; Miller & Stiff, 1993). Broadly construed, deception is not confined to outright lies; it may take a variety of forms, such as equivocations, evasions, hyperbole, white lies, and omissions, which makes it a commonplace event in day-to-day interactions. The literally hundreds of studies in this area have typically focused on either the sender's deception displays and related cognitions or the receiver's detection accuracy, but the past decade has witnessed increasing emphasis on the dynamic interplay between the two as well as inclusion of receiver behaviors in the mix. What follows is a brief overview of those theories and lines of deception research that are most relevant to interpersonal interaction.

Theoretical Perspectives

Contemporary psychological approaches to deception are well encapsulated in Ekman and Friesen's (1969a) *leakage hypothesis,* which was founded on the belief that deception is an emotionally charged and arousing activity that generates involuntary and unbidden indicators that it is occurring, despite deceivers' attempts to the contrary. The hypothesis is that involuntary nonverbal actions escape control, "leaking" out of the body and serving as telltale signs of deception. Because deceivers are thought to focus more on managing their facial expressions than their body and limb movements, and because many vocal and kinesic cues are thought to be beyond conscious control, Ekman and Friesen hypothesized that the least controllable or controlled channels and cues would be the best indicators of deceit. Expanding upon this hypothesis, Zuckerman, DePaulo, and Rosenthal (1981, 1986) advanced the *four-factor theory,* which posits that changes in deceivers' behavior are the result of four psychological processes: *physiological arousal* (due to detection apprehension), *emotional reactions* (arising from guilt or fear of detection), *cognitive effort* (required to formulate deceptive messages), and *attempted control* (to create a truthful demeanor and suppress cues stereotypically associated with deception). Zuckerman et al. theorized that these four factors account for deception displays (see also Hocking & Leathers, 1980). Moreover, they posited that deception cues and channels form a leakage hierarchy, from most to least amenable to control. This principle of a hierarchy of controllability is featured prominently in DePaulo's *motivation impairment effect,* which asserts that the harder people try to control nonverbal deception leakage, the worse it backfires, so that when receivers have access to nonverbal channels, the lies of highly motivated senders are more readily detected than the lies of less motivated senders. DePaulo has argued that, comparatively, the verbal channel is the most controllable and therefore less amenable to detection under conditions of high motivation (see DePaulo & Kirkendol, 1989; DePaulo, LeMay, & Epstein, 1991; DePaulo, Stone, & Lassiter, 1985).

Although the psychological approach has brought considerable coherence to the deception literature and prompted much research, its reliance on highly controlled and brief experimental manipulations, strangers as subjects, and observers rather than participants as

detectors overlooks the deliberate and strategic nature of most deception episodes and the skills brought to bear by communicators in perpetrating deceit; underestimates the agency of the receiver as a communication participant; and ignores the dynamic changes in deception that are likely to occur when deceiver and receiver are acquainted or actually interact with one another. To remedy these shortcomings, emerging communication perspectives have begun examining the message exchange process itself, including such factors as the ways in which verbal and nonverbal message features can be manipulated to produce different types of deceptions, the impact of receivers' asking probing questions of deceivers, what sender behaviors pique receiver suspicion, the impact of relational and behavioral familiarity on deceit and suspicion, and the patterns of sender and receiver adaptation to one another over time (Buller, Comstock, Aune, & Strzyzewski, 1989; Buller, Stiff, & Burgoon, 1996; Buller, Strzyzewski, & Comstock, 1991; Burgoon, Buller, Dillman, & Walther, 1995; Levine & McCornack, 1996; Stiff, Kim, & Ramesh, 1992).

One theory that attempts to capture the deliberative, dynamic, and adaptive nature of deception episodes is *interpersonal deception theory* (Buller & Burgoon, 1996; Burgoon & Buller, 1996, in press). Drawing upon a goal-oriented approach to communication, this theory begins with the premise that deception invokes all the communication functions identified in this chapter (identity management, self-presentation, relational communication, emotion management, conversation management, social influence). Deceivers are usually motivated to protect their image and self-identities while also successfully influencing others. To do so, they need to manage their communication performances so as to avoid negative relational messages that spoil their identities or relationships while sending positive relational messages that promote trust. They also need to manage their emotions so as to minimize clues to arousal or anxiety prompted by the deceit. And they need to maintain their conversational responsibilities so that their interactions proceed smoothly. Receivers, in turn, have similar responsibilities that may include masking any suspicions they have. Consequently, deception displays and their detection reflect not only inadvertent, or nonstrategic, activity but also intentional and planned, or strategic, behavior by both sender and receiver to manage the content and style of their messages and overall demeanor. Moreover, the cognitions and behaviors of both sender and receiver are postulated to change dynamically as the conversation unfolds and each adapts to his or her own and the other's nonverbal and verbal behaviors. The significance of these findings is that deception displays, detection accuracy, and interactants' beliefs about each other's honesty or suspicion are not static but transient and variable over the course of an interaction.

Empirical Evidence

Tests of the nearly 20 propositions of this theory, as well as other communication research with direct relevance to nonverbal signals, have produced a number of important conclusions regarding how deception is played out in interpersonal contexts (e.g., Anolli & Ciceri, 1997; Buller et al., 1991; Burgoon & Buller, 1994; Burgoon, Buller, Dillman, & Walther, 1995; Burgoon, Buller, Ebesu, & Rockwell, 1994; Burgoon, Buller, Ebesu, White, & Rockwell, 1996; Burgoon, Buller, & Floyd, 2001; Burgoon, Buller, Floyd, & Grandpre, 1996; Burgoon, Buller, & Guerrero, 1995; Burgoon, Buller, White, Afifi, & Buslig, 1999; Burgoon & Floyd, 2000; deTurck & Miller, 1990; Ekman, O'Sullivan, Friesen, & Scherer, 1991; Feeley & deTurck, 1995, 1998; Fiedler & Walka, 1993; Horvath, Jayne, & Buckley, 1994; Inbau, Reid, & Buckley, 1986; Kalbfleisch, 1992; Levine et al., 2000; Memon, Vrij, & Bull, 1998; Rockwell, Buller, & Burgoon,

1997; Vrij, 2000; Vrij, Edward, & Bull, 2001; Vrij, Edward, Roberts, & Bull, 2000; White & Burgoon, 2001; Zuckerman & Driver, 1985). A brief summary follows.

1. Deception and suspicion are manifested through a combination of strategic and nonstrategic behaviors. Although far more nonverbal cues are stereotypically associated rather than reliably associated with deceit, there are several nonverbal signals, most vocal, that distinguish truth from deception. These include involuntary and inadvertent actions such as longer response latencies and elevated pitch as well as strategic actions such as restraint of random gestures and movements. Whether deceit is planned or unplanned, sanctioned or unsanctioned, also affects the behavioral profile. Like deceivers, receivers also engage in strategic and nonstrategic activity when their suspicions have been piqued. Arousal (in this case engendered by uncertainty), emotional reactions (engendered by negative reactions to being deceived as well as distress over how to proceed), and task complexity (engendered by the need to detect without alerting the deceiver) all may produce receiver "leakage," accompanied by more deliberate management of a skeptical or accepting interaction style.

2. Initial deception displays show some impairment, but over time, deceivers adapt to a truthful standard. Early on, deceivers may show depressed involvement, overly stiff, rigid postures, less genuine smiles, shorter responses, longer response latencies, nonfluencies, and other behaviors that deviate from normalcy. Over time, however, they are able, with the benefit of receiver feedback, to repair their performances and achieve a more normal-appearing, truthful demeanor.

3. Receivers unwittingly aid deceivers in producing more credible performances. Not only do receivers begin with a *truth bias* (a tendency to regard others as truthful) that gives deceivers an advantage, especially if senders and receivers are familiar with one another, and not only do they telegraph their suspicions to deceivers, which allows the deceivers to make needed adjustments, they also typically respond to deceivers' increased submissiveness by picking up more of the conversational load and helping the deceivers construct plausible accounts. If receivers adopt an accepting demeanor, they may also elicit a reciprocal involved and pleasant demeanor from deceivers that looks honest and sincere.

4. Sender deception success, defined either as believable nonverbal and verbal performances or as low detection accuracy, is improved by social skill and motivation. Deception success is variable across individuals. Beyond some personality differences, senders scoring higher on emotional and social expressivity and control and those who report higher motivation to succeed are more successful, often producing an honest demeanor bias.

5. Receiver detection accuracy is improved when interactivity between sender and receiver is reduced; when the receiver has access to, or focuses on, vocal rather than visual channels; when the receiver is trained in deception detection; and when the receiver embraces a nonconfrontative interviewing style rather than an interrogative one. When senders are forced to speak at length without the benefit of engaging their receivers in dialogue, and when receivers shift from the role of participant to that of observer, detection accuracy improves. Although greater familiarity with deception—be it through exposure to previous samples of behavior (behavioral) or training (knowledge)—can confer a modest boost in detection success, there is growing evidence that too much experience with deception can lead to a lie bias and concomitant reduction in deception success. This may explain why law enforcement and military professionals charged with distinguishing deceit from truth often are no more accurate at doing so than laypersons. Additionally, when receivers attend to more diagnostic vocal cues and ignore less reliable visual ones, their accuracy benefits. The lack of correspondence between the cues and channels that receivers use to make judgments and the ones they should use partly accounts for the generally poor success rate in the detection of deception. Use of an apparently accepting communication style can also put senders at ease, engender their trust, and lead them to drop their guard so that they inadvertently reveal incriminating information. But the same style can also elicit a reciprocal interaction style that makes senders appear more truthful. Conversely, an intimidating interrogator's style can produce an "Othello error," causing truthful senders to appear nervous and dishonest. And the use of probing questions may backfire by leading receivers to view any answers as acceptable.

This brief compilation of findings from a voluminous body of research testifies to the complexity of interpersonal deception and to the growing recognition of its highly changeable nature, which depends on a host of communication-relevant factors. It also testifies to communicators' capacity to capitalize on the properties of interpersonal interaction and the interdependence between sender and receiver to achieve their goals, including successful duplicity.

INTERACTIONAL FUNCTIONS

Conversation Structuring and Management

A sizable share of the nonverbal literature has tackled the issue of how nonverbal behaviors influence the progression and patterning of conversation. Three main foci in the literature are the ways in which nonverbal cues set the stage for interaction, the ways in which they segment and regulate conversational turn taking, and the ways in which interactants come to coordinate their ongoing interaction patterns within and across episodes.

Setting the Stage

Contextual nonverbal features shoulder major responsibility for defining the nature of interactional episodes and actors' roles within those episodes. Prior to any interaction commencing, architectural features and other artifacts, spatial arrangements, actors' attire and grooming, and other static features are already signaling what kind of communication is expected (for example, formal or informal, social or task oriented, public or private) and any constraints dictated by task requirements and the physical setting itself (Altman, 1975; Goffman, 1963). Other dynamic features, such as kinesic and vocalic demeanor, clarify such role-related considerations as who occupies high-status and authoritative versus stigmatized or illegitimate positions. Together, these features define the nature of the social situation. By clarifying the purposes of an interpersonal encounter and the programs of behavior that are to be invoked in it, they assist in regulating the interaction that follows. Goffman (1974) describes this process as *framing*—creating a perspective through which the social interaction that occurs may be understood. For example, a male physician's white lab coat, the medical paraphernalia in an examining room, and the presence of a nurse all serve to frame a gynecological exam as an impersonal, professional medical procedure rather than a sexual encounter. In the absence of nonverbal framing cues, the physician's behaviors could take on very different connotations.

Beyond defining the situation, many static proxemic, artifactual, and physical appearance features influence the amount, frequency, and nature of conversation. For example, sheer propinquity and physical attractiveness increase the probability that contact will occur; small volumes of space and horizontal linear perspectives in an environment promote casual conversation; and group seating arrangements govern who speaks to whom, how often, and how cooperatively (for summaries, see Burgoon, Buller, & Woodall, 1996; Kendon, Harris, & Key, 1975; Knapp & Hall, 1992; Patterson, 1978, 1983).

A particularly potent way in which nonverbal cues not only define interactional situations but also influence the extent and nature of communication is by establishing the public versus private nature of the setting and interactional episode within it. Individuals seek to manage the boundaries of privacy in many areas of their lives. Although it is possible to conceptualize privacy in many different ways (see, e.g., Rosenfeld, 2000), four major types or dimensions of privacy are perhaps most relevant to nonverbal communication and conversational management (Burgoon, 1982; see also Burgoon, Buller, & Woodall, 1996). *Physical privacy* refers to the degree to which an individual, dyad, or group is physically accessible to others. Individuals seek to structure and manage interactions to maintain desired physical proximity, crowding, and availability to the amount and location of touch. They attain greater amounts of privacy by limiting their accessibility through any and all of these channels. *Social privacy* refers to the ability to control the degree of social contacts at the individual, dyad, or group level; this includes the capacity to control the who, when, and where of communication. Communicators will seek to retreat from situations when social contacts become excessive. This is manifested by persons, dyads, or groups when they seek to maximize togetherness within the group (or isolation of the individual) and maximize exclusion of others by offering nonverbal signals intended to indicate social unavailability. *Psychological privacy* refers to an individual's ability to control affective and cognitive inputs and outputs. On the input side, a person seeks freedom from external sources of influence or distraction, whereas on the output side a person desires control over when, where, and with whom he or she shares personal thoughts, feelings, and disclosure of personal information. *Informational privacy* refers to individual desires concerning the release and availability of personal information (some of which is a legal issue). Informational and psychological privacy differ in the degree to which personal information such as financial, medical, legal, and lifestyle records is increasingly available without individuals' consent or control, and individuals' ability to regulate informational privacy increasingly will be a matter of computerized precautions.

One theoretical explanation of the balancing of secrecy and disclosure is *communication boundary management* (Petronio, 1991, 2000). This theory proposes that people manage private information through the intersection of boundary structures and a rule-based management system. The term *boundary structures* refers to an individual's degree of ownership of information sharing, control over the dissemination of personal information, the permeability of boundaries (or degree of desired secrecy), and levels of privacy. Boundary structures help individuals to balance their risks, vulnerability, and personal desire for privacy and may be regulated nonverbally through general cues of conversational management. *Rule-based management* refers to how individuals form, use, and coordinate boundaries, and the turbulence stemming from boundary rule conflict or transgression. These rules drive the individual's strategy of privacy management. Individuals can use nonverbal signals to erect, maintain, or diminish "boundaries" to communication; such signals are most effective for achieving multiple personal and relational goals when they take the form of moderately aggressive nonverbal tactics. Nonaggressive tactics may be insufficient to achieve personal goals of privacy, and overly aggressive tactics may be perceived as interpersonally or relationally inappropriate (Burgoon, Parrott, et al., 1989; Buslig & Burgoon, 2000).

Conversation Management

Nonverbal signals regulate the onset, flow, and termination of interpersonal interchanges, first, by forming the core of greeting and leave-taking rituals. The behaviors and sequences through which people initiate and end conversations, and the cultural variability in those patterns, have been cataloged by several researchers (Kellermann, Reynolds, & Chen, 1991; Kendon, 1990; Knapp, Hart, Friedrich, & Schulman, 1973; Krivonos & Knapp, 1975; Morris, 1977; Morris et al., 1979; O'Leary & Gallois, 1985; Pittinger, Hockett, & Darehy, 1960). Although specific rituals vary significantly by culture, greeting and termination patterns have in common the degree to which they signal impending accessibility or inaccessibility and reinforce the intimacy level of the relationship.

Second, many of the same nonverbal signals mark changes in the tone or topic within episodes. Extralinguistic behaviors such as postural shifts, proxemic adjustments, and manipulation of objects may signify, for example, that the topic under discussion is concluding or that interest in it has waned. Five clusters of cues also indicate degree of actor involvement in the conversation: (a) *nonverbal immediacy* (proximity, gaze, touch, lean, and facial/body orientation); (b) gestural, facial, and vocal *expressivity;* (c) attentiveness cues that convey *altercentrism* (e.g., postural stillness); (d) *composure* (absence of nervous behaviors and moderate rather than hyper- or hyporelaxation); and (e) *interaction coordination* (fluent, synchronized speech and smooth turn switches) (Burgoon, 1994; Coker & Burgoon, 1987).

Third, once conversations have commenced, nonverbal cues function as "traffic cops" governing floor holding and turns at talk. Substantial research has verified the classes of cues that speakers employ to yield versus maintain the conversational floor and that auditors use to request or refuse a turn (e.g., Drummond, 1989; Duncan, 1974, 1975; Erickson, 1975; Feldstein & Welkowitz, 1978; Gurevitch, 1989; Hodgins & Zuckerman, 1990; Jaffe, 1978; Kendon, 1990; Rosenfeld, 1978; Sharkey & Stafford, 1990; Wiemann & Knapp, 1975). For example, back-channel cues—cues used by auditors to encourage the speaker to continue occupying the "front" channel—include smiling, nodding, and "uh-huh's." Three theoretical approaches have been advanced to explain how people manage to accomplish smooth turn taking: a *signaling approach,* in which sender nonverbal cues operate in a fairly deterministic way to mark turns at talk; a *sequential production model,* which relies more heavily on verbal indicators of appropriate junctures for turn switching; and a *resource model,* which combines the other two and views turn-taking signals as conversational resources to be used as needed, especially to gain interpersonal control (see Duncan & Fiske, 1977; Wiemann, 1985).

Finally, the influence of dynamic cues on the flow of conversation has been examined in the context of patterns of adaptation in dyadic interaction, that is, the manner in which two (or more) individuals match, synchronize, or offset each other's interaction styles. Among the various forms of coordinated action that have been distinguished from one another are matching, motor mimicry, mirroring, reciprocity, convergence, synchrony, divergence, complementarity, and compensation (see Bernieri & Rosenthal, 1991; Burgoon, Stern, & Dillman, 1995; Condon, 1980; Ross, Cheyne, & Lollis, 1988). As noted earlier, the very capacity of living organisms for social organization may be rooted in a fundamental and automatic proclivity to produce nonverbal visual, auditory, proxemic, and chemical signs to which members of the same species are preattuned and that they "pick up" and "know"

through direct sensory experience but that are also amenable to voluntary and strategic modification (Buck & Ginsburg, 1997; Levenson & Ruef, 1997). Cappella (1991) asserts that, "in combination with evidence from neonatal and infant development, physiological structures, and ethological parallels, the arguments for adaptive selection and genetic endowment . . . produce a highly suggestive, if not airtight, case" (p. 12).

Theorizing in this area has been abundant. Among the models and theories that have been advanced to predict and explain intimacy and involvement patterns specifically are Argyle and Dean's (1965; Argyle & Cook, 1976) *affiliative conflict theory, the norm of reciprocity* (Gouldner, 1960), the *arousal-labeling model* and subsequent *sequential functional model* (Patterson, 1976, 1983), *expectancy violations theory* (Burgoon, Le Poire, & Rosenthal, 1995), *discrepancy arousal theory* (Cappella & Greene, 1982, 1984), *arousal valence theory* (Andersen, 1985), *communication accommodation theory* (Giles et al., 1991; Giles, Mulac, Bradac, & Johnson, 1987), and *interaction adaptation theory* (Burgoon, Stern, & Dillman, 1995; Burgoon & White, 1997). Although no single theory has garnered unequivocal support—studies have yielded evidence of both matching/reciprocity and compensation within the same experiment—the preponderance of research evidence confirms that humans have strong tendencies to synchronize and adapt their nonverbal and linguistic behaviors to one another in both reciprocal and compensatory ways (e.g., Beebe, Stern, & Jaffe, 1979; Cappella, 1981; Cappella & Planalp, 1981; Chapple, 1970; Condon, 1980; Erickson & Shultz, 1982; Gregory, Dagan, & Webster, 1997; Gregory & Webster, 1996; Guerrero, Jones, & Burgoon, 2000; Kempton, 1980; Kendon, 1990; Le Poire & Yoshimura, 1999; Warner, Malloy, Schneider, Knoth, & Wilder, 1987). Reciprocity and matching appear to be the rule, and probably the default pattern, to which there are important exceptions, including moderating impacts of attachment style, social skills, and sex composition of a pair (Bilous & Krauss, 1988; Guerrero, 1996, 1998; Guerrero & Burgoon, 1996; Hubbard, 2000; Le Poire, Shepard, & Duggan, 1999; Tucker & Anders, 1998).

Adaptation patterns are linked to relationship definitions such as affection, attraction, similarity, and power; to trajectories of relational escalation or de-escalation; and to outcomes such as satisfaction (e.g., Grammer, Kruck, & Magnusson, 1998; Gregory, 1994; Gregory, Webster, & Huang, 1993). Intermediate levels of patterning appear to be beneficial to comprehension, smooth interaction, bonding, interpersonal attraction, and stress reduction, whereas extreme degrees of patterning may reflect rigidity and produce negative affect and dysfunction. Yet it is negatively valenced adaptation patterns that show the strongest associations within pairs (Levenson & Ruef, 1997).

The advent of the Internet and other forms of computer-mediated communication has revived interest in how the presence or absence of various nonverbal modalities affects interpersonal and small group interaction. Whereas early modality research employed text transcripts, audio recordings, and videotape as tools for parsing out the effects of verbal and nonverbal modalities in face-to-face interaction, contemporary work has been interested in communication under mediated conditions and utilizes face-to-face interaction merely as a control comparison. Still, the work illuminates how adding various nonverbal features to verbal ones alters communication practices and outcomes. Beyond the impact of vocalic, physical appearance, and kinesic cues, other nonverbal features being investigated are proxemics, in the form of interactants being geographically proximal (located in the same place) or distal (interacting at a distance), and chronemics, in the form of synchronicity

(whether interactions take place in real time or in delayed fashion). Of particular relevance here are theories and studies that examine whether new technologies need to incorporate nonverbal cues to create *social presence* (a sense of being physically, socially, and emotionally copresent; Lombard & Ditton, 1997); whether minimal social cues—verbal or nonverbal—are sufficient to elicit social responses from humans, even when they are interacting with computers (Moon & Nass, 1996; Nass, Fogg, & Moon, 1996; Nass & Moon, 2000; Nass, Moon, Morkes, Kim, & Fogg, 1997); and whether new technologies such as immersive virtual reality can not only offset any perceived deficits but intensify and augment the channels that are present (Biocca & Delaney, 1995).

Initial approaches such as *media richness theory, social identity-deindividuation theory,* and other *cues-filtered-out* perspectives (e.g., Culnan & Markus, 1987; Daft & Lengel, 1986; Krauss & Fussell, 1990; Lea & Spears, 1991, 1992, 1995; Short, Williams, & Christie, 1976; Sproull & Kiesler, 1986, 1991) tended toward technological determinism in proposing that the elimination of nonverbal visual and auditory channels from new technologies removed essential nonverbal social cues, with detrimental consequences to interpersonal relationships and task performance accompanying lost "social presence." For instance, "flaming"—engaging in disinhibited and hostile verbal exchanges—and depersonalization were attributed to the reduced awareness of social identities and attention to face needs associated with the use of "leaner" media. Subsequent theorizing has been shifting emphasis from the technologies themselves to what actors do with new media. Emerging models such as the *rational actor model, social information processing theory,* the *hyperpersonal perspective, channel expansion theory, social presence theory,* and *the principle of interactivity,* bolstered by related empirical work, are demonstrating not only that humans are highly responsive to whatever social cues are present and adapt to so-called impoverished communication modalities, but that the leaner audio channel may have unique benefits without the drawbacks that accompany having visual cues present (see, e.g., Adkins & Brashers, 1995; Biocca, Harms, & Burgoon, in press; Burgoon et al., 1999-2000; Burgoon et al., in press; Carlson & Zmud, 1999; Doherty-Sneddon et al., 1997; Harmon, 1998; Jensen, Farnham, Drucker, & Kollock, 2000; Kayani, Wotring, & Forrest, 1996; O'Malley, Langton, Anderson, Doherty-Sneddon, & Bruce, 1996; Parks & Floyd, 1996; Parks & Roberts, 1998; Reeves & Nass, 1996; Utz, 2000; Walther, 1992, 1993, 1996; Walther & Burgoon, 1992; Whittaker, 1995). Prosodic and paralinguistic cues may gain the synchronicity, back-channeling, and capacity for relational and emotional messages without the distractions, self-focus, and greater cognitive load that come when interactants have visual access to one another. Also, opportunities are greater for more selective, planned, and enhancing self-presentations when there are fewer channels to manage. With greater social distances comes the prospect of keeping unintended emotional and relational statements in check when dealing with disliked others or conflict. Removal of visible status differences also creates a greater sense of equality that those in subordinate and low-power positions may find beneficial.

As for synchronicity and proximity, interacting in real time, perhaps by capitalizing on conversational synchrony, creates a greater sense of connection, similarity, and involvement; asynchronous interaction has the advantage of allowing time for greater editing and control by senders and thoughtful processing by receivers. Geographic distance appears to be a double-edged sword that can facilitate interactants' holding onto idealized perceptions of one another but can also create a sense

of detachment (Burgoon et al., 1999-2000, in press).

INFLUENCE FUNCTIONS

We discuss the functions of social influence only briefly, because other chapters in this *Handbook* cover this topic in depth. Nonverbal interest in this area has centered on the pragmatics of nonverbal behavior, specifically on how such behavior alters the attitudes and overt actions of message recipients. The types of dependent variables that have been studied run the gamut from expressed changes in attitude, petition-signing behavior, and task performance to helping behavior (for example, making change for someone), aggression (for example, shocking someone), and compliance with orders, as well as persuasion.

The literature related to this function comes from highly diverse disciplines and is not easily synthesized because it lacks unifying theoretical perspectives and covers research in which nonverbal signals are of only ancillary interest. Among the theories pertaining directly to nonverbal behavior are three that relate to expectations or their violations—expectancy signaling, expectation states, and expectancy violations theory (described above)—as well as the other theories we have addressed above in our discussion of impression management.

Expectancy signaling (Harris & Rosenthal, 1985; Rosenthal, 1985) concerns the ways in which humans inadvertently signal through nonverbal clues what they expect from others and elicit behavioral conformity to those expectations by targets, producing self-fulfilling prophecies (also referred to as behavioral confirmation). These expectations, which may be signaled within the first 30 seconds of interaction, include vocal and kinesic signals of warmth, attentiveness, dominance, and—in the case of classroom expectancies—more opportunities for the target to respond and receive feedback. Influence is thus created by use of subtle nonverbal cues that typically exert their impact outside conscious awareness on the part of either expector or target but exert significant influence nonetheless.

Expectation states theory (Berger, Conner, & Fisek, 1974; Berger, Rosenholtz, & Zelditch, 1980; Ridgeway & Berger, 1986; Ridgeway & Walker, 1995) relatedly concerns how nonverbal (and verbal) cues create expectations in group interactions and enable those for whom expectations are more favorable to exert more influence on the group. Nonverbal cues serve to create a power and prestige order by providing manifest indicators of status and other indicators of likely contributions to the group's performance that together create *performance expectations* and confer an "expectation advantage or disadvantage" on actors, depending on whether they are expected to contribute favorably or unfavorably to successful task completion. Status cues may include the diffuse characteristics associated with age, sex, race, ethnicity, education, occupation, physical attractiveness, and intelligence discussed previously in relation to identity management and impression formation that signify higher status (e.g., being male, older, nonminority, educated, attractive) as well as actual interaction styles, such as dominance/submission or task/social orientation, that connote expertise and socially valued skills. Thus many of the behaviors that we have covered in our discussion of impression management and relational communication are germane. Expectation advantages are thought to create self-fulfilling prophecies by creating more opportunities for individuals to initiate ideas and problem-solving performances, to hold the conversational floor and thus gain hearing of their ideas, to receive more favorable feedback, and to be less influenced when there are disagreements. As in expectancy violations theory, many of the same cues are responsible for establishing communicators' *reward valence* or *reward expectations*, which moderate or augment actors' ability to exert influence. For example, an actor's being physically attractive, tall and muscular, or graying may activate stereotypical expectations that the actor is credible, capable, and commanding, whereas visible physical handicaps, short stature, or a babyish visage may trigger the opposite expectations. Similarly, a task-oriented and somewhat dominant interaction style—for example, direct eye contact and body orientation, brief touch, high-energy and louder voice, shorter response latencies, and fluent speech—may convey authoritativeness, whereas a submissive style may undermine credibility and, hence, the actor's capacity to influence.

Research testing these theories and the general persuasive efficacy of nonverbal behavior has yielded two conclusions with special implications for interpersonal communication (for research summaries and recent findings, see Berger, Ridgeway, Fisek, & Norman, 1998; Brownlow, 1992; Buller, Le Poire, Aune, & Eloy, 1992; Burgoon et al., 1990; Burgoon, Segrin, & Dunbar, 2002; Carli, LaFleur, & Loeber, 1995; Edinger & Patterson, 1983). First, *contrary to the view that their influence is only indirect and weak, nonverbal cues have direct impacts on persuasion, compliance, helping, and hiring decisions, in addition to indirect impacts through enhanced credibility and attraction.* Constellations of objective nonverbal cues (sometimes referred to as distal indicators) create more subjective judgments (sometimes referred to as proximal percepts) that qualify as strategies or types of nonverbal appeals. The impact of single indicators is thus best understood as part of larger strategies that enable interpersonal influence. Among the strategies documented recently as effective in promoting influence are dominance, power, and status appeals (tempo, gestural activity, facial expressivity, mature facial appearance, touch); affiliation, attractiveness, and pleasantness appeals (immediacy, smiling, fluency, vocal pleasantness, touch, speech rate similarity, physical attractiveness); and relaxation (vocal, postural). Dominance and power strategies may be more advisable when the speaker does not benefit from compliance; attractiveness strategies are more advisable when the speaker is the main beneficiary of compliance. Although verbal content is a central component of the strategies people use in persuading others and gaining compliance, the research findings signal that those who neglect the role of nonverbal cues do so at their peril.

Second, *contrary to the view that expectancy confirmation is the preferred route to successful influence, positive expectancy violations produce more persuasion, compliance, and endorsements for hiring than does conformity to expectations.* Examples of positive violations include close or far conversational distance, touch, and high degree of gaze. Sometimes, communicator reward valence moderates these effects, but often, both well-regarded and ill-regarded communicators profit from engaging in violations. According to expectancy violations theory, negative violations (such as nonimmediacy, reduced involvement, and gaze aversion) should be detrimental to influence, relative to conformity to expectations, but recent findings suggest that they may actually have some residual benefit, possibly because they increase uncertainty and information processing, motivate efforts to "win over" the violator, and leave open the prospect that the violation is a transitory event. Thus the popular injunction, also advocated by Goffman (1959), to conform to norms and expectations may be poor advice when the objective is to gain influence.

SUMMARY

Nonverbal signals are essential ingredients in the interpersonal communication mix. Research substantiates that rather than being mere auxiliaries to the verbal stream, they carry a significant, and often dominant, portion of the social meaning in face-to-face interchanges. In analyzing the role of nonverbal signals in interpersonal communication,

we have emphasized here those behaviors that form a socially shared coding system. According to this message orientation, codes of greatest interest are kinesics, vocalics, haptics, proxemics, chronemics, and manipulable features of physical appearance and artifacts. These codes and their constituent cues are coordinated with one another and with the verbal stream to achieve particular functions or purposes, several of which may be operative simultaneously and, although ambiguous or unpredictable when viewed singly, become meaningful when viewed as part of a collective and systematic pattern.

Social functions for which such patterns have been identified include message production and processing, identification and identity management, impression formation and management, relational communication and relationship management, emotion expression and management, deception, conversation structuring and management, and social influence. The research is impressive in documenting how much responsibility is shouldered by the nonverbal codes in accomplishing these fundamental communication objectives.

Although a substantial amount of research has addressed these social functions, it has often failed to look at the nonverbal behaviors as an integrated system; to study their occurrence in natural, diverse, and cross-cultural interpersonal contexts; to examine them dyadically; or to consider how patterns might differ when interactions occur among familiar others rather than strangers. Our knowledge of interpersonal nonverbal communication will advance exponentially as researchers increasingly embrace a truly interpersonal perspective. Finally, just as the interpersonal communication area in general needs more theorizing and research on processual features of interchange, so must nonverbal researchers be enjoined to devote more future effort to the sequential and longitudinal aspects of nonverbal communication. As cycles, developmental patterns, and temporal adjustments receive greater scrutiny, nonverbal behavior may take on added significance in interpersonal communication.

REFERENCES

Abele, A. (1986). Functions of gaze in social interaction: Communication and monitoring. *Journal of Nonverbal Behavior, 10,* 83-101.

Adkins, M., & Brashers, D. E. (1995). The power of language in computer-mediated groups. *Management Communication Quarterly, 8,* 289-323.

Afifi, W. A., & Burgoon, J. K. (2000). The impact of violations on uncertainty and consequences for attractiveness. *Human Communication Research, 26,* 203-233.

Aguinis, H., Simonsen, M. M., & Pierce, C. A. (2000). Effects of nonverbal behavior on perceptions of power bases. *Journal of Social Psychology, 138,* 455-469.

Ainsworth, M. D. S. (1982). Attachment: Retrospect and prospect. In C. M. Parks & J. Stevenson-Hinde (Eds.), *The place of attachment in human behavior* (pp. 3-30). New York: Basic Books.

Alberts, J. K. (1989). A descriptive taxonomy of couples' complaint interactions. *Southern Communication Journal, 54,* 125-143.

Altman, I. (1975). *The environment and social behavior.* Monterey, CA: Brooks/Cole.

Altman, I., & Taylor, D. A. (1973). *Social penetration: The development of interpersonal relationships.* New York: Holt, Rinehart & Winston.

Ambady, N., Hallahan, M., & Conner, B. (1999). Accuracy of judgments of sexual orientation from thin slices of behavior. *Journal of Personality and Social Psychology, 77,* 538-547.

Ambady, N., & Rosenthal, R. (1993). Half a minute: Predicting teacher evaluations from thin slices of nonverbal behavior and physical attractiveness. *Journal of Personality and Social Psychology, 64,* 431-441.

Andersen, P. A. (1985). Nonverbal immediacy in interpersonal communication. In A. W. Siegman & S. Feldstein (Eds.), *Multichannel integrations of nonverbal behavior* (pp. 1-36). Hillsdale, NJ: Lawrence Erlbaum.

Andersen, P. A. (1991). When one cannot not communicate: A challenge to Motley's traditional communication postulates. *Communication Studies, 42,* 309-325.

Andersen, P. A., & Guerrero, L. K. (1998). Principles of communication and emotion in social interaction. In P. A. Andersen & L. K. Guerrero (Eds.), *Handbook of communication and emotion: Research, theory, applications, and contexts* (pp. 49-96). San Diego, CA: Academic Press.

Andersen, P. A., Hecht, M. L., Hoobler, G. D., & Smallwood, M. (2002). Nonverbal communication across cultures. In W. B. Gudykunst & B. Mody (Eds.), *Handbook of international and intercultural communication* (2nd ed., pp. 89-106). Thousand Oaks, CA: Sage.

Anolli, L., & Ciceri, R. (1997). The voice of deception: Vocal strategies of naive and able liars. *Journal of Nonverbal Behavior, 21,* 259-284.

Argyle, M., Alkema, F., & Gilmour, R. (1971). The communication of friendly and hostile attitudes by verbal and non-verbal signals. *European Journal of Social Psychology, 1,* 385-402.

Argyle, M., & Cook, M. (1976). *Gaze and mutual gaze.* Cambridge: Cambridge University Press.

Argyle, M., & Dean, J. (1965). Eye contact, distance and affiliation. *Sociometry, 28,* 289-304.

Argyle, M., Salter, V., Nicholson, H., Williams, M., & Burgess, P. (1970). The communication of interior and superior attitudes by verbal and nonverbal signals. *British Journal of Social and Clinical Psychology, 9,* 221-231.

Aronoff, J., Barclay, A. M., & Stevenson, L. A. (1988). The recognition of threatening facial stimuli. *Journal of Personality and Social Psychology, 54,* 647-655.

Aronoff, J., Woike, B. A., & Hyman, L. M. (1992). Which are the stimuli in facial displays of anger and happiness? Configurational bases of emotion recognition. *Journal of Personality and Social Psychology, 62,* 1050-1066.

Asendorpf, J. B. (1998). Personality effects on social relationships. *Journal of Personality and Social Psychology, 74,* 1531-1544.

Banse, R., & Scherer, K. R. (1996). Acoustic profiles in vocal emotion expression. *Journal of Personality and Social Psychology, 7,* 614-636.

Barrett, K. C. (1993). The development of nonverbal communication of emotion: A functionalist perspective. *Journal of Nonverbal Behavior, 17,* 145-169.

Bartholomew, K. (1990). Avoidance of intimacy: An attachment perspective. *Journal of Social and Personal Relationships, 7,* 147-178.

Bateson, G. (1972). *Steps to an ecology of mind.* New York: Ballantine.

Bavelas, J. B. (1990). Behaving and communicating: A reply to Motley. *Western Journal of Speech Communication, 54,* 593-602.

Bavelas, J. B., Black, A., Chovil, N., Lemery, C. R., & Mullett, J. (1988). Form and function in motor mimicry: Topographic evidence that the primary function is communicative. *Human Communication Research, 14,* 275-300.

Baxter, L. A. (1992). Forms and functions of intimate play in personal relationships. *Human Communication Research, 18,* 336-363.

Beebe, B., Stern, D., & Jaffe, J. (1979). The kinesic rhythm of mother-infant interactions. In A. W. Siegman & S. Feldstein (Eds.), *Of speech and time: Temporal patterns in interpersonal contexts* (pp. 23-34). Hillsdale, NJ: Lawrence Erlbaum.

Bem, S. L. (1981). Gender schema theory: A cognitive account of sex typing. *Psychological Review, 88,* 354-364.

Berger, C. R. (1979). Beyond initial interaction: Uncertainty, understanding, and the development of interpersonal relationships. In H. Giles & R. St. Clair (Eds.), *Language and social psychology* (pp. 122-144). Oxford: Blackwell.

Berger, C. R. (1994). Power, dominance, and social interaction. In M. L. Knapp & G. R. Miller (Eds.), *Handbook of interpersonal communication* (2nd ed., pp. 450-507). Thousand Oaks, CA: Sage.

Berger, C. R., & Calabrese, R. J. (1975). Some explorations in initial interaction and beyond: Toward a developmental theory of interpersonal communication. *Human Communication Research, 1,* 99-112.

Berger, J., Conner, T. L., & Fisek, M. H. (1974). *Expectation states theory: A theoretical research program.* Cambridge, MA: Winthrop.

Berger, J., Ridgeway, C. L., Fisek, M. H., & Norman, R. Z. (1998). The legitimation and delegitimation of power and prestige orders. *American Sociological Review, 63,* 379-405.

Berger, J., Rosenholtz, S. J., & Zelditch, M., Jr. (1980). Status organizing processes. *Annual Review of Sociology, 6,* 479-508.

Bernieri, F. J., & Gillis, J. S. (1995). The judgment of rapport: A cross-cultural comparison between Americans and Greeks. *Journal of Nonverbal Behavior, 19,* 115-130.

Bernieri, F. J., Gillis, J. S., Davis, J. M., & Grahe, J. E. (1996). Dyad rapport and the accuracy of its judgment across situations: A lens model analysis. *Journal of Personality and Social Psychology, 71,* 110-129.

Bernieri, F. J., & Rosenthal, R. (1991). Interpersonal coordination: Behavior matching and interactional synchrony. In R. S. Feldman & B. Rimé (Eds.), *Fundamentals of nonverbal behavior* (pp. 401-432). Cambridge: Cambridge University Press.

Berry, D. S. (1990). Vocal attractiveness and vocal babyishness: Effects on stranger, self, and friend impressions. *Journal of Nonverbal Behavior, 14,* 141-154.

Berry, D. S. (1991). Accuracy in social perception: Contributions of facial and vocal information. *Journal of Personality and Social Psychology, 61,* 298-307.

Berry, D. S. (1992). Vocal types and stereotypes: Joint effects of vocal attractiveness and vocal maturity on person perception. *Journal of Nonverbal Behavior, 16,* 41-54.

Berscheid, E. (1990). Contemporary vocabularies of emotion. In B. S. Moore & A. M. Isen (Eds.), *Affect and social behavior* (pp. 22-38). Cambridge: Cambridge University Press.

Bilous, F. R., & Krauss, R. M. (1988). Dominance and accommodation in the conversational behaviors of same- and mixed-gender dyads. *Language & Communication, 8,* 183-194.

Biocca, F., & Delaney, B. (1995). Immersive virtual reality technology. In F. Biocca & M. R. Levy (Eds.), *Communication in the age of virtual reality* (pp. 57-124). Mahwah, NJ: Lawrence Erlbaum.

Biocca, F., Harms, C., & Burgoon, J. K. (in press). Criteria and scope conditions for a theory and measure of social presence. *Presence: Teleoperators and Virtual Environments.*

Birdwhistell, R. L. (1955). Background to kinesics. *Etc., 13,* 10-18.

Birdwhistell, R. L. (1970). *Kinesics and context: Essays on body motion communication.* Philadelphia: University of Pennsylvania Press.

Blascovich, J., Wyer, N. A., Swart, L. A., & Kibler, J. L. (1997). Racism and racial categorization. *Journal of Personality and Social Psychology, 72,* 1364-1372.

Bodenmann, G., Kaiser, A., Hahlweg, K., & Fehm-Wolfsdorf, G. (1998). Communication patterns during marital conflict: A cross-cultural replication. *Personal Relationships, 5,* 343-356.

Boomer, D. S. (1978). The phonemic clause: Speech unit in human communication. In

A. W. Siegman & S. Feldstein (Eds.), *Nonverbal behavior and communication* (pp. 245-262). Hillsdale, NJ: Lawrence Erlbaum.

Bowlby, J. (1982). *Attachment and loss: Vol. 1. Attachment* (2nd ed.). New York: Basic Books.

Brownlow, S. (1992). Seeing is believing: Facial appearance, credibility, and attitude change. *Journal of Nonverbal Behavior, 16,* 101-115.

Buck, R. (1984). *The communication of emotion.* New York: Guilford.

Buck, R. (1988). Nonverbal communication: Spontaneous and symbolic aspects. *American Behavioral Scientist, 31,* 341-354.

Buck, R. (1991). Social factors in facial display and communication: A reply to Chovil and others. *Journal of Nonverbal Behavior, 15,* 155-161.

Buck, R. (1995). Emotional and social factors in communication via facial expression: A rejoinder to Fridlund's reply. *Communication Theory, 5,* 398-401.

Buck, R. (1997). From DNA to MTV: The spontaneous communication of emotional messages. In J. O. Greene (Ed.), *Message production: Advances in communication theory* (pp. 313-349). Mahwah, NJ: Lawrence Erlbaum.

Buck, R., & Ginsburg, B. (1997). Communicative genes and the evolution of empathy. In W. Ickes (Ed.), *Empathic accuracy* (pp. 17-43). New York: Guilford.

Buller, D. B. (1986). Distraction during persuasive communication: A meta-analytic review. *Communication Monographs, 53,* 91-114.

Buller, D. B., & Aune, K. (1988). The effects of vocalics and nonverbal sensitivity on compliance: A speech accommodation theory explanation. *Human Communication Research, 14,* 301-332.

Buller, D. B., & Burgoon, J. K. (1994). Deception: Strategic and nonstrategic communication. In J. A. Daly & J. M. Wiemann (Eds.), *Strategic interpersonal communication* (pp. 191-223). Hillsdale, NJ: Lawrence Erlbaum.

Buller, D. B., & Burgoon, J. K. (1996). Interpersonal deception theory. *Communication Theory, 6,* 203-242.

Buller, D. B., Comstock, J., Aune, R. K., & Strzyzewski, K. D. (1989). The effect of probing on deceivers and truth tellers. *Journal of Nonverbal Behavior, 13,* 155-169.

Buller, D. B., Le Poire, B. A., Aune, R. K., & Eloy, S. V. (1992). Social perceptions as mediators of the effect of speech rate similarity on compliance. *Human Communication Research, 19,* 286-311.

Buller, D. B., Stiff, J. B., & Burgoon, J. K. (1996). Behavioral adaptation in deceptive transactions: Fact or fiction? *Human Communication Research, 22,* 589-603.

Buller, D. B., Strzyzewski, K. D., & Comstock, J. (1991). Interpersonal deception: I. Deceivers' reactions to receivers' suspicions and probing. *Communication Monographs, 58,* 1-24.

Burgoon, J. K. (1980). Nonverbal communication in the 1970s: An overview. In D. Nimmo (Ed.), *Communication yearbook 4* (pp. 179-197). New Brunswick, NJ: Transaction.

Burgoon, J. K. (1982). Privacy and communication. In M. Burgoon (Ed.), *Communication yearbook 6* (pp. 206-249). Beverly Hills, CA: Sage.

Burgoon, J. K. (1983). Nonverbal violations of expectations. In J. M. Wiemann & R. P. Harrison (Eds.), *Nonverbal interaction* (pp. 11-77). Beverly Hills, CA: Sage.

Burgoon, J. K. (1985a). Nonverbal signals. In M. L. Knapp & G. R. Miller (Eds.), *Handbook of interpersonal communication* (pp. 344-390). Beverly Hills, CA: Sage.

Burgoon, J. K. (1985b). The relationship of verbal and nonverbal codes. In B. Dervin & M. J. Voigt (Eds.), *Progress in communication sciences* (Vol. 6, pp. 263-298). Norwood, NJ: Ablex.

Burgoon, J. K. (1991). Relational message interpretations of touch, conversational distance, and posture. *Journal of Nonverbal Behavior, 15,* 233-259.

Burgoon, J. K. (1992). Applying a comparative approach to nonverbal expectancy violations theory. In J. Blumler, K. E. Rosengren, & J. M. McLeod (Eds.), *Comparatively speaking: Communication and culture across space and time* (pp. 53-69). Newbury Park, CA: Sage.

Burgoon, J. K. (1993). Interpersonal expectations, expectancy violations, and emotional communication. *Journal of Language and Social Psychology, 12,* 30-48.

Burgoon, J. K. (1994). Nonverbal signals. In M. L. Knapp & G. R. Miller (Eds.), *Handbook of interpersonal communication* (2nd ed., pp. 229-285). Thousand Oaks, CA: Sage.

Burgoon, J. K., & Bacue, A. (in press). Nonverbal skills. In J. O. Greene & B. R. Burleson (Eds.), *Handbook of communication and social interaction skills.* Mahwah, NJ: Lawrence Erlbaum.

Burgoon, J. K., Berger, C. R., & Waldron, V. R. (2000). Mindfulness and interpersonal communication. *Journal of Social Issues, 56*(1), 105-127.

Burgoon, J. K., Birk, T., & Pfau, M. (1990). Nonverbal behaviors, persuasion, and credibility. *Human Communication Research, 17,* 140-169.

Burgoon, J. K., Bonito, J., Bengtsson, B., Ramirez, A., Jr., Dunbar, N. E., & Miczo, N. (1999-2000). Testing the interactivity model: Communication processes, partner assessments, and the quality of collaborative work. *Journal of Management Information Systems, 16,* 35-58.

Burgoon, J. K., Bonito, J., Ramirez, A., Jr., Dunbar, N. E., Kam, K., & Fischer, J. (in press). Testing the interactivity principle: Effects of mediation, propinquity, and verbal and nonverbal modalities in interpersonal interaction. *Journal of Communication.*

Burgoon, J. K., & Buller, D. B. (1994). Interpersonal deception: III. Effects of deceit on perceived communication and nonverbal behavior dynamics. *Journal of Nonverbal Behavior, 18,* 155-184.

Burgoon, J. K., & Buller, D. B. (1996). Reflections on the nature of theory building and the theoretical status of interpersonal deception theory. *Communication Theory, 6,* 311-328.

Burgoon, J. K., & Buller, D. B. (in press). Interpersonal deception theory. In J. S. Seiter & R. H. Gass (Eds.), *Readings in persuasion, social influence and compliance-gaining.* New York: Allyn & Bacon.

Burgoon, J. K., Buller, D. B., Dillman, L., & Walther, J. B. (1995). Interpersonal deception: IV. Effects of suspicion on perceived communication and nonverbal behavior dynamics. *Human Communication Research, 22,* 163-196.

Burgoon, J. K., Buller, D. B., Ebesu, A. S., & Rockwell, P. A. (1994). Interpersonal deception: V. Accuracy in deception detection. *Communication Monographs, 61,* 303-325.

Burgoon, J. K., Buller, D. B., Ebesu, A. S., White, C. H., & Rockwell, P. A. (1996). Testing interpersonal deception theory: Effects of suspicion on communication behaviors and

perceptions. *Communication Theory, 6,* 243-267.

Burgoon, J. K., Buller, D. B., & Floyd, K. (2001). Does participation affect deception success? A test of the interactivity principle. *Human Communication Research, 27,* 503-534.

Burgoon, J. K., Buller, D. B., Floyd, K., & Grandpre, J. (1996). Deceptive realities: Sender, receiver, and observer perspectives in deceptive conversations. *Communication Research, 23,* 724-748.

Burgoon, J. K., Buller, D. B., & Guerrero, L. K. (1995). Interpersonal deception: IX. Effects of social skill and nonverbal communication on deception success and detection accuracy. *Journal of Language and Social Psychology, 14,* 289-311.

Burgoon, J. K., Buller, D. B., White, C. H., Afifi, W. A., & Buslig, A. L. S. (1999). The role of conversational involvement in deceptive interpersonal communication. *Personality and Social Psychology Bulletin, 25,* 669-685.

Burgoon, J. K., Buller, D. B., & Woodall, W. G. (1996). *Nonverbal communication: The unspoken dialogue* (3rd ed.). New York: McGraw-Hill.

Burgoon, J. K., Coker, D. A., & Coker, R. A. (1986). Communicative effects of gaze behavior: A test of two contrasting explanations. *Human Communication Research, 12,* 495-524.

Burgoon, J. K., & Dillman, L. (1995). Gender, immediacy, and nonverbal communication. In P. J. Kalbfleisch & M. J. Cody (Eds.), *Gender, power, and communication in human relationships* (pp. 63-81). Mahwah, NJ: Lawrence Erlbaum.

Burgoon, J. K., & Dunbar, N. E. (2000). An interactionist perspective on dominance-submission: Interpersonal dominance as a dynamic, situationally contingent social skill. *Communication Monographs, 67,* 96-121.

Burgoon, J. K., & Floyd, K. (2000). Testing for the motivation impairment effect during deceptive and truthful interaction. *Western Journal of Communication, 64,* 243-267.

Burgoon, J. K., & Hale, J. L. (1984). The fundamental topoi of relational communication. *Communication Monographs, 51,* 193-214.

Burgoon, J. K., & Hale, J. L. (1987). Validation and measurement of the fundamental themes of relational communication. *Communication Monographs, 54,* 19-41.

Burgoon, J. K., & Hale, J. L. (1988). Nonverbal expectancy violations: Model elaboration and application to immediacy behaviors. *Communication Monographs, 55,* 58-79.

Burgoon, J. K., Johnson, M. L., & Koch, P. T. (1998). The nature and measurement of interpersonal dominance. *Communication Monographs, 65,* 309-335.

Burgoon, J. K., Kelley, D. L., Newton, D. A., & Keeley-Dyreson, M. P. (1989). The nature of arousal and nonverbal indices. *Human Communication Research, 16,* 217-255.

Burgoon, J. K., & Le Poire, B. A. (1993). Effects of communication expectancies, actual communication, and expectancy disconfirmation on evaluations of communicators and their communication behavior. *Human Communication Research, 20,* 75-107.

Burgoon, J. K., & Le Poire, B. A. (1999). Nonverbal cues and interpersonal judgments: Participant and observer perceptions of intimacy, dominance, composure, and formality. *Communication Monographs, 66,* 105-124.

Burgoon, J. K., Le Poire, B. A., Beutler, L. E., Bergan, J., & Engle, D. (1992). Nonverbal behaviors as indices of arousal: Extension to the psychotherapy context. *Journal of Nonverbal Behavior, 16,* 159-178.

Burgoon, J. K., Le Poire, B. A., & Rosenthal, R. (1995). Effects of preinteraction expectancies and target communication on perceiver reciprocity and compensation in dyadic interaction. *Journal of Experimental Social Psychology, 31,* 287-321.

Burgoon, J. K., & Newton, D. A. (1991). Applying a social meaning model to relational messages of conversational involvement: Comparing participant and observer perspectives. *Southern Communication Journal, 56,* 96-113.

Burgoon, J. K., Parrott, R., Le Poire, B. A., Kelley, D. L., Walther, J. B., & Perry, D. (1989). Maintaining and restoring privacy through communication in different types of relationships. *Journal of Social and Personal Relationships, 6,* 131-158.

Burgoon, J. K., Pfau, M., Parrott, R., Birk, T., Coker, R. A., & Burgoon, M. (1987). Relational communication, satisfaction, compliance-gaining strategies and compliance in communication between physicians and patients. *Communication Monographs, 54,* 307-234.

Burgoon, J. K., Segrin, C., & Dunbar, N. E. (2002). Nonverbal communication and social influence. In J. P. Dillard & M. Pfau (Eds.), *The persuasion handbook: Developments in theory and practice.* Thousand Oaks, CA: Sage.

Burgoon, J. K., Stern, L. A., & Dillman, L. (1995). *Interpersonal adaptation: Dyadic interaction patterns.* New York: Cambridge University Press.

Burgoon, J. K., & Walther, J. B. (1990). Nonverbal expectancies and the consequences of violations. *Human Communication Research, 17,* 232-265.

Burgoon, J. K., Walther, J. B., & Baesler, E. J. (1992). Interpretations and consequences of interpersonal touch. *Human Communication Research, 19,* 237-263.

Burgoon, J. K., & White, C. A. (1997). Researching nonverbal message production: A view from interaction adaptation theory. In J. O. Greene (Ed.), *Message production: Advances in communication theory* (pp. 279-312). Mahwah, NJ: Lawrence Erlbaum.

Burleson, B. B., & Planalp, S. (2000). Producing emotion(al) messages. *Communication Theory, 10,* 221-250.

Buslig, A. L. S., & Burgoon, J. K. (2000). Aggressiveness in privacy-seeking behavior. In S. Petronio (Ed.), *Balancing the secrets of private disclosures* (pp. 181-196). Mahwah, NJ: Lawrence Erlbaum.

Canary, D. J., & Dindia, K. (Eds.). (1998). *Sex differences and similarities in communication: Critical essays and empirical investigations of sex and gender in interaction.* Mahwah, NJ: Lawrence Erlbaum.

Cappella, J. N. (1981). Mutual influence in expressive behavior: Adult-adult and infant-adult interaction. *Psychological Bulletin, 89,* 101-132.

Cappella, J. N. (1984). The relevance of microstructure of interaction to relationship change. *Journal of Social and Personal Relationships, 1,* 239-264.

Cappella, J. N. (1991). The biological origins of automated patterns of human interaction. *Communication Theory, 1,* 4-35.

Cappella, J. N., & Greene, J. O. (1982). A discrepancy-arousal explanation of mutual influence in expressive behavior in adult- and infant-adult interaction. *Communication Monographs, 49,* 89-114.

Cappella, J. N., & Greene, J. O. (1984). The effects of distance and individual differences in arousability on nonverbal involvement: A test of discrepancy-arousal theory. *Journal of Nonverbal Behavior, 8,* 259-286.

Cappella, J. N., & Palmer, M. T. (1990). Attitude similarity, relational history, and attraction: The mediating effects of kinesic and vocal behaviors. *Communication Monographs, 57,* 161-183.

Cappella, J. N., & Planalp, S. (1981). Talk and silence sequences in informal conversations III: Interspeaker influence. *Human Communication Research, 7,* 117-132.

Carli, L. L., LaFleur, S. J., & Loeber, C. C. (1995). Nonverbal behavior, gender, and influence. *Journal of Personality and Social Psychology, 68,* 1030-1041.

Carlson, J., & Zmud, R. (1999). Channel expansion theory and the experiential nature of media richness perceptions. *Academy of Management Journal, 42,* 153-170.

Carrere, S., & Gottman, J. M. (1999). Predicting divorce among newlyweds from the first three minutes of a marital conflict discussion. *Family Process, 38,* 293-301.

Cashdan, E. (1998). Smiles, speech, and body posture: How women and men display sociometric status and power. *Journal of Nonverbal Behavior, 22,* 209-228.

Chapple, E. D. (1970). *Culture and biological man: Explorations in behavioral anthropology.* New York: Holt, Rinehart & Winston.

Chovil, N. (1991). Social determinants of facial displays. *Journal of Nonverbal Behavior, 15,* 141-154.

Church, R. B., Kelly, S. D., & Lynch, K. (2000). Immediate memory for mismatched speech and representational gesture across development. *Journal of Nonverbal Behavior, 24,* 151-174.

Clark, R. A., & Delia, J. G. (1979). Topoi and rhetorical competence. *Quarterly Journal of Speech, 65,* 187-206.

Clevenger, T., Jr. (1991). Can one not communicate? A conflict of models. *Communication Studies, 42,* 340-353.

Cohen, A. A. (1977). The communicative functions of hand illustrators. *Journal of Communication, 27*(4), 54-63.

Coker, D. A., & Burgoon, J. K. (1987). The nature of conversational involvement and nonverbal communication, and expectancy disconfirmation on evaluations of communicators and their communication behavior. *Human Communication Research, 20,* 75-107.

Condon, W. S. (1980). The relation of interactional synchrony to cognitive and emotional processes. In M. R. Key (Ed.), *The relationship of verbal and nonverbal communication* (pp. 49-65). The Hague: Mouton.

Costo, M., Dinsbach, W., Manstead, A. S. R., & Ricci Bitti, P. E. (2002). Social presence, embarrassment, and nonverbal behavior. *Journal of Nonverbal Behavior, 25,* 225-240.

Cronkhite, G. (1986). On the focus, scope, and coherence of the study of human symbolic activity. *Quarterly Journal of Speech, 72,* 231-246.

Culnan, M. J., & Markus, M. L. (1987). Information technologies. In F. M. Jablin, L. L. Putnam, K. H. Roberts, & L. W. Porter (Eds.), *Handbook of organizational computing: An interdisciplinary perspective* (pp. 420-443). Newbury Park, CA: Sage.

Cupach, W. R., & Metts, S. (1986). Accounts of relational dissolution. *Communication Monographs, 53,* 311-334.

Daft, R. L., & Lengel, R. H. (1986). Organizational information requirements, media richness, and structural design. *Management Science, 32,* 554-571.

Darwin, C. (1965). *The expression of the emotions in man and animals.* Chicago: University of Chicago Press. (Original work published 1872)

Davitz, J. R., & Davitz, L. J. (1959). The communication of feelings by content-free speech. *Journal of Communication, 9,* 6-13.

DePaulo, B. M. (1991). Nonverbal behavior and self-presentation: A developmental perspective. In R. S. Feldman & B. Rimé (Eds.), *Fundamentals of nonverbal behavior* (pp. 351-397). Cambridge: Cambridge University Press.

DePaulo, B. M. (1992). Nonverbal behavior and self-presentation. *Psychological Bulletin, 111,* 203-243.

DePaulo, B. M., Blank, A. L., Swaim, G. W., & Hairfield, J. G. (1992). Expressiveness and expressive control. *Personality and Social Psychology Bulletin, 18,* 276-285.

DePaulo, B. M., & Kirkendol, S. E. (1989). The motivational impairment effect in the communication of deception. In J. Yuille (Ed.), *Credibility assessment* (pp. 51-70). Deurne, Belgium: Kluwer.

DePaulo, B. M., LeMay, C. S., & Epstein, J. A. (1991). Effects of importance of success and expectations for success on effectiveness at deceiving. *Personality and Social Psychology Bulletin, 17,* 14-24.

DePaulo, B. M., Stone, J. I., & Lassiter, G. D. (1985). Deceiving and detecting deceit. In B. R. Schlenker (Ed.), *The self and social life* (pp. 323-370). New York: McGraw-Hill.

deTurck, M. A., & Miller, G. R. (1990). Training observers to detect deception effects of self-differences. *Journal of Social and Personal Relationships, 9,* 483-506.

Digman, J. (1990). Personality structure: Emergence of the five-factor model. *Annual Review of Psychology, 41,* 417-440.

Dillard, J. P. (1998). Foreword: The role of affect in communication, biology, and social relationships. In P. A. Andersen & L. K. Guerrero (Eds.), *Handbook of communication and emotion: Research, theory, applications, and contexts* (pp. xvii-xxxii). San Diego, CA: Academic Press.

Dion, K. K., Berscheid, E., & Walster, E. (1972). What is beautiful is good. *Journal of Personality and Social Psychology, 24,* 285-290.

Doherty-Sneddon, G., O'Malley, C., Garrod, S., Anderson, A., Langton, S., & Bruce, V. (1997). Face-to-face and video-mediated communication: A comparison of dialogue structure and task performance. *Journal of Experimental Psychology: Applied, 3,* 105-125.

Drummond, K. (1989). A backward glance at interruptions. *Western Journal of Speech Communication, 53,* 150-166.

Duncan, S., Jr. (1974). On signaling that it's your turn to speak. *Journal of Personality and Social Psychology, 10,* 234-247.

Duncan, S., Jr. (1975). Interaction units during speaking turns in dyadic, face-to-face conversations. In A. Kendon, R. M. Harris, & M. R. Key (Eds.), *Organization of behavior in face-to-face interaction* (pp. 199-213). The Hague: Mouton.

Duncan, S., Jr., & Fiske, D. W. (1977). *Face-to-face interaction: Research, methods, and theory.* Hillsdale, NJ: Lawrence Erlbaum.

Eagly, A. H. (1987). *Sex differences in social behavior: A social-role interpretation.* Hillsdale, NJ: Lawrence Erlbaum.

Eagly, A. H., Ashmore, R. D., Makhijani, M. G., & Longo, L. C. (1991). What is beautiful is good, but . . . : A meta-analytic review of research on the physical attractiveness stereotype. *Psychological Bulletin, 110,* 109-128.

Eagly, A. H., & Karau, S. J. (1991). Gender and the emergence of leaders: A meta-analysis. *Journal of Personality and Social Psychology, 60,* 685-710.

Edinger, J. A., & Patterson, M. L. (1983). Nonverbal involvement and social control. *Psychological Bulletin, 93,* 30-56.

Eibl-Eibesfeldt, I. (1972). Similarities and differences between cultures in expressive movements. In R. Hinde (Ed.), *Non-verbal communication* (pp. 297-314). Cambridge: Cambridge University Press.

Ekman, P. (1973). Cross-cultural studies of facial expression. In P. Ekman (Ed.), *Darwin and facial expression: A century of research in review* (pp. 169-222). New York: Academic Press.

Ekman, P. (1984). Expression and the nature of emotion. In K. R. Scherer & P. Ekman (Eds.), *Approaches to emotion* (pp. 319-343). Hillsdale, NJ: Lawrence Erlbaum.

Ekman, P. (1993). Facial expression and emotion. *American Psychologist, 48,* 384-392.

Ekman, P. (1997). Expression or communication about emotion. In N. L. Segal, G. E. Weisfeld, & C. C. Weisfeld (Eds.), *Uniting psychology and biology: Integrative perspectives on human development* (pp. 315-338). Washington DC: American Psychological Association.

Ekman, P., & Friesen, W. V. (1969a). Nonverbal leakage and clues to deception. *Psychiatry, 32,* 88-105.

Ekman, P., & Friesen, W. V. (1969b). The repertoire of nonverbal behavior: Categories, origins, usage, and coding. *Semiotica, 1,* 49-98.

Ekman, P., & Friesen, W. V. (1975). *Unmasking the face: A guide to recognizing emotions from facial clues.* Englewood Cliffs, NJ: Prentice Hall.

Ekman, P., Friesen, W. V., & Ellsworth, P. (1972). *Emotion in the human face: Guidelines for research and an integration of findings.* New York: Pergamon.

Ekman, P., Friesen, W. V., & O'Sullivan, M. (1988). Smiles when lying. *Journal of Personality and Social Psychology, 54,* 414-420.

Ekman, P., O'Sullivan, M., Friesen, W. V., & Scherer, K. R. (1991). Face, voice, and body in encoding patterns. *Human Communication Research, 13,* 463-494.

Erickson, F. (1975). One function of proxemic shifts in face-to-face interaction. In A. Kendon, R. M. Harris, & M. R. Key (Eds.), *Organization of behavior in face-to-face interaction* (pp. 175-187). The Hague: Mouton.

Erickson, F., & Shultz, J. J. (1982). *The counselor as gatekeeper: Social interaction in interviews.* New York: Academic Press.

Farley, S. D., Chia, R. C., & Allred, L. J. (1998). Stereotypes about attractiveness: When beautiful is not better. *Journal of Social Behavior and Personality, 13,* 479-492.

Feeley, T. H., & deTurck, M. A. (1995). Global cue usage in behavioral lie detection. *Communication Quarterly, 43,* 420-430.

Feeley, T. H., & deTurck, M. A. (1998). The behavioral correlates of sanctioned and unsanctioned deceptive communication. *Journal of Nonverbal Behavior, 22,* 189-204.

Feldstein, S., & Welkowitz, J. (1978). A chronography of conversation: In defense of an objective approach. In A. W. Siegman & S. Feldstein (Eds.), *Nonverbal behavior and communication* (pp. 329-378). Hillsdale, NJ: Lawrence Erlbaum.

Fernandez, D. R., Carlson, D. S., Stepina, L. P., & Nicholson, J. D. (1997). Hofstede's country classification 25 years later. *Journal of Social Psychology, 137,* 43-54.

Fiedler, K., & Walka, I. (1993). Training lie detectors to use nonverbal cues instead of global heuristics. *Human Communication Research, 20,* 199-223.

Fiske, S. T., & Neuberg, S. L. (1990). A continuum of impression formation from category-based to individuating processes: Influences of information and motivation on attention and interpretation. In M. P. Zanna (Ed.), *Advances in experimental social psychology* (Vol. 23, pp. 1-74). New York: Academic Press.

Fiske, S. T., & Taylor, S. E. (1991). *Social cognition.* New York: McGraw-Hill.

Folger, J. P., & Woodall, W. G. (1982). Nonverbal cues as linguistic context: An information-processing view. In M. Burgoon (Ed.), *Communication yearbook 6* (pp. 63-91). Beverly Hills, CA: Sage.

Fox, S. A., Giles, H., Orbe, M. P., & Bourhis, R. Y. (2000). Interability communication: Theoretical perspectives. In D. O. Braithwaite & T. L. Thompson (Eds.), *Handbook of communication and people with disabilities: Research and application* (pp. 193-222). Mahwah, NJ: Lawrence Erlbaum.

Freud, S. (1963). Introductory lectures on psychoanalysis. In J. Strachey (Ed.), *The standard edition of the complete psychological works of Sigmund Freud* (J. Strachey, Trans.) (Vols. 15-16). London: Hogarth. (Original works published 1915-1917)

Fridlund, A. J. (1991). Evolution and facial action in reflect, social motive, and paralanguage. *Biological Psychology, 32,* 3-100.

Fridlund, A. J. (1994). *Human facial expression: An evolutionary view.* San Diego, CA: Academic Press.

Fridlund, A. J. (1995). Reply to Buck's review of *Human facial expression: An evolutionary view. Communication Theory, 5,* 396-398.

Friedman, H. S., & Miller-Herringer, T. (1991). Nonverbal display of emotion in public and in private: Self-monitoring, personality, and expressive cues. *Journal of Personality and Social Psychology, 61,* 766-775.

Frijda, N. H. (1986). *The emotions.* Cambridge: Cambridge University Press.

Funder, D. C., & Colvin, C. R. (1991). Explorations in behavioral consistency: Properties of persons, situations, and behaviors. *Journal of Personality and Social Psychology, 60,* 773-794.

Gallaher, P. E. (1992). Individual differences in nonverbal behavior: Dimensions of style. *Journal of Personality and Social Psychology, 63,* 133-145.

Giles, H., Coupland, J., & Coupland, N. (Eds.). (1991). *Contexts of accommodation: Developments in applied sociolinguistics.* New York: Cambridge University Press.

Giles, H., Henwood, K., Coupland, N., Harriman, J., & Coupland, J. (1992). Language attitudes and cognitive mediation. *Human Communication Research, 18,* 500-527.

Giles, H., Mulac, A., Bradac, J. J., & Johnson, P. (1987). Speech accommodation theory: The first decade and beyond. In M. L. McLaughlin (Ed.), *Communication yearbook 10* (pp. 13-48). Newbury Park, CA: Sage.

Giles, H., & Smith, P. M. (1979). Accommodation theory: Optimal levels of convergence. In H. Giles & R. N. St. Clair (Eds.), *Language and social psychology* (pp. 45-65). Baltimore: University Park.

Giles, H., & Street, R. L., Jr. (1985). Communicator characteristics and behavior. In M. L. Knapp & G. R. Miller (Eds.),

Handbook of interpersonal communication (pp. 205-261). Beverly Hills, CA: Sage.

Givens, D. B. (1978). The nonverbal basis of attraction: Flirtation, courtship, and seduction. *Psychiatry, 41,* 346-359.

Givens, D. B. (1983). *Love signals.* New York: Crown.

Goffman, E. (1959). *The presentation of self in everyday life.* Garden City, NY: Doubleday/ Anchor.

Goffman, E. (1963). *Behavior in public places: Notes on the social organization of gatherings.* New York: Free Press.

Goffman, E. (1974). *Frame analysis: An essay on the organization of experience.* Cambridge, MA: Harvard University Press.

Goldman-Eisler, F. (1968). *Psycholinguistics: Experiments in spontaneous speech.* New York: Academic Press.

Goleman, D. (1995). *Emotional intelligence: Why it can matter more than IQ.* New York: Bantam.

Gottman, J. M. (1994). *What predicts divorce? The relationship between marital processes and marital outcomes.* Hillsdale, NJ: Lawrence Erlbaum.

Gottman, J. M., & Krokoff, L. J. (1989). Marital interaction and satisfaction: A longitudinal view. *Journal of Consulting and Clinical Psychology, 57,* 47-52.

Gottman, J. M., & Levenson, R. W. (1992). Marital processes predictive of later dissolution: Behavior, physiology, and health. *Journal of Personality and Social Psychology, 63,* 221-233.

Gouldner, A. W. (1960). The norm of reciprocity: A preliminary statement. *American Sociological Review, 25,* 161-178.

Grahe, J. E., & Bernieri, F. J. (1999). The importance of nonverbal cues in judging rapport. *Journal of Nonverbal Behavior, 23,* 253-269.

Grammer, K., Kruck, K. B., & Magnusson, M. S. (1998). The courtship dance: Patterns of nonverbal synchronization in opposite-sex encounters. *Journal of Nonverbal Behavior, 22,* 3-29.

Gregory, S. W., Jr. (1994). Sounds of power and deference: Acoustic analysis of macro social constraints on micro interaction. *Sociological Perspectives, 37,* 497-526.

Gregory, S. W., Jr., Dagan, K., & Webster, S. (1997). Evaluating the relation of vocal accommodation in conversation partners' fundamental frequencies to perceptions of communication quality. *Journal of Nonverbal Behavior, 21,* 23-43.

Gregory, S. W., Jr., & Webster, S. (1996). A nonverbal signal in voices of interview partners effectively predicts communication accommodation and social status perceptions. *Journal of Personality and Social Psychology, 70,* 1231-1240.

Gregory, S. W., Jr., Webster, S., & Huang, G. (1993). Voice pitch and amplitude convergence as a metric of quality in dyadic interviews. *Language & Communication, 13,* 195-217.

Gudykunst, W. B., Matsumoto, Y., Ting-Toomey, S., Nishida, T., Kim, K., & Heyman, S. (1996). Influence of cultural individualism-collectivism, self-construals, and individual values on communication styles across cultures. *Human Communication Research, 22,* 510-543.

Gudykunst, W. B., & Ting-Toomey, S. (1988). *Culture and interpersonal communication.* Newbury Park, CA: Sage.

Guerrero, L. K. (1996). Attachment-style differences in intimacy and involvement: A test of the four-category model. *Communication Monographs, 63,* 269-292.

Guerrero, L. K. (1998). Attachment-style differences in the experience and expression of romantic jealousy. *Personal Relationships, 5,* 273-291.

Guerrero, L. K., & Andersen, P. A. (1991). The waxing and waning of relational intimacy: Touch as a function of relational stage, gender, and touch avoidance. *Journal of Social and Personal Relationships, 8,* 147-166.

Guerrero, L. K., & Andersen, P. A. (1994). Patterns of matching and initiation: Touch behavior and avoidance across romantic relationship stages. *Journal of Nonverbal Behavior, 18,* 137-153.

Guerrero, L. K., & Burgoon, J. K. (1996). Attachment styles and reactions to nonverbal involvement change in romantic dyads: Patterns of reciprocity and compensation. *Human Communication Research, 22,* 335-370.

Guerrero, L. K., Jones, S. M., & Burgoon, J. K. (2000). Responses to nonverbal intimacy change in romantic dyads: Effects of behavioral valence and degree of behavioral change on nonverbal and verbal reactions. *Communication Monographs, 67,* 325-346.

Guerrero, L. K., & Reiter, R. L. (1998). Expressing emotion: Sex differences in social skills and communicative responses to anger, sadness, and jealousy. In D. J. Canary & K. Dindia (Eds.), *Sex differences and similarities in communication: Critical essays and empirical investigations of sex and gender in interaction* (pp. 321-350). Mahwah, NJ: Lawrence Erlbaum.

Gurevitch, Z. D. (1989). Distance and conversation. *Symbolic Interaction, 12,* 251-263.

Hall, E. T. (1966). *The silent language.* Garden City, NY: Anchor/Doubleday.

Hall, E. T. (1977). *Beyond culture.* Garden City, NY: Anchor.

Hall, J. A. (1979). Gender, gender roles, and nonverbal communication skills. In R. Rosenthal (Ed.), *Skill in nonverbal communication: Individual differences* (pp. 32-67). Cambridge, MA: Oelgeschlager, Gunn & Hain.

Hall, J. A. (1984). *Nonverbal sex differences: Communication accuracy and expressive style.* Baltimore: Johns Hopkins University Press.

Hall, J. A. (1998). How big are nonverbal sex differences? The case of smiling and sensitivity to nonverbal cues. In D. J. Canary & K. Dindia (Eds.), *Sex differences and similarities in communication: Critical essays and empirical investigations of sex and gender in interaction* (pp. 155-178). Mahwah, NJ: Lawrence Erlbaum.

Hall, J. A., Carter, J. D., & Horgan, T. G. (2000). Gender differences in nonverbal communication of emotion. In A. H. Fischer (Ed.), *Gender and emotion: Social psychological perspectives* (pp. 97-117). Cambridge: Cambridge University Press.

Hall, J. A., & Halberstadt, A. G. (1986). Smiling and gazing. In J. S. Hyde & M. Linn (Eds.), *The psychology of gender: Advances through meta-analysis* (pp. 136-158). Baltimore: Johns Hopkins University Press.

Hall, J. A., & Veccia, E. M. (1990). More "touching" observations: New insights on men, women, and interpersonal touch. *Journal of Personality and Social Psychology, 59,* 1155-1162.

Harmon, J. (1998). Electronic meetings and intense group conflict: Effects of a policy-modeling performance support system and an audio communication support system on satisfaction and agreement. *Group Decision and Negotiation, 7,* 131-155.

Harris, M. J., & Rosenthal, R. (1985). Mediation of interpersonal expectancy effects: 31 meta-analyses. *Psychological Bulletin, 97,* 363-386.

Harwood, J., Giles, H., & Ryan, E. B. (1995). Aging, communication, and intergroup theory: Social identity and intergenerational communication. In J. F. Nussbaum & J. Coupland (Eds.), *Handbook of communication and aging research* (pp. 133-159). Mahwah, NJ: Lawrence Erlbaum.

Haviland, J. J., & Malatesta, C. Z. (1981). The development of sex differences in nonverbal signals: Fallacies, facts, and fantasies. In C. Mayo & N. M. Henley (Eds.), *Gender and nonverbal behavior* (pp. 183-208). New York: Springer-Verlag.

Hecht, M. A., LaFrance, M., & Haertl, J. C. (1993, August). *Gender differences in smiling: A meta-analysis of archival data.* Paper presented at the 101st Annual Meeting of the American Psychological Association, Toronto.

Hegstrom, T. G. (1979). Message impact: What percentage is nonverbal? *Western Journal of Speech Communication, 43,* 134-142.

Heider, F. (1958). *The psychology of interpersonal relations.* New York: John Wiley.

Hess, U., Blairy, S., & Kleck, R. E. (2000). The influence of facial emotion displays, gender, and ethnicity on judgments of dominance and affiliation. *Journal of Nonverbal Behavior, 24,* 265-283.

Hocking, J. E., & Leathers, D. G. (1980). Nonverbal indicators of deception: A new theoretical perspective. *Communication Monographs, 47,* 119-131.

Hodgins, H. S., & Zuckerman, M. (1990). The effect of nonverbal sensitivity on social interaction. *Journal of Nonverbal Behavior, 14,* 155-170.

Hofstede, G. (1980. *Culture's consequences: International differences in work-related values.* Beverly Hills, CA: Sage.

Hofstede, G. (2001). *Culture's consequences: Comparing values, behaviors, institutions, and organizations across nations* (2nd ed.). Thousand Oaks, CA: Sage.

Horvath, F. S., Jayne, B. C., & Buckley J. P. (1994). Differentiation of truthful and deceptive criminal suspects in behavior analysis interviews. *Journal of Forensic Sciences, 39,* 793-807.

Hubbard, A. S. E. (2000). Interpersonal coordination in interactions: Evaluations and social skills. *Communication Research Reports, 17,* 95-104.

Hummert, M. L., Mazloff, D., & Henry, C. (1999). Vocal characteristics of older adults and stereotyping. *Journal of Nonverbal Behavior, 23,* 111-132.

Huston, T. L., & Vangelisti, A. L. (1991). Socioemotional behavior and satisfaction in marital relationships: A longitudinal study. *Journal of Personality and Social Psychology, 61,* 721-733.

Inbau, F. E., Reid, J. E., & Buckley, J. P. (1986). *Criminal interrogations and confessions* (3rd ed.). Baltimore: Williams & Wilkins.

Izard, C. E. (1971). *The face of emotion.* Englewood Cliffs, NJ: Prentice Hall.

Jaffe, J. (1978). Parliamentary procedure and the brain. In A. W. Siegman & S. Feldstein (Eds.), *Nonverbal behavior and communication* (pp. 55-66). Hillsdale, NJ: Lawrence Erlbaum.

Jensen, C., Farnham, S. D., Drucker, S. M., & Kollock, P. (2000). The effect of communication modality on cooperation in online environments. In ACM SIGCHI, *Proceedings of CHI 2000* (pp. 470-477). The Hague: ACM SIGCHI.

Johnson, K. L., & Edwards, R. (1991). The effects of gender and type of romantic touch on perceptions of relational commitment. *Journal of Nonverbal Behavior, 15,* 43-55.

Jones, E. E., & Pittman, T. S. (1982). Toward a general theory of strategic self-presentation. In J. Suls (Ed.), *Psychological perspectives on the self* (Vol. 1, pp. 231-262). Hillsdale, NJ: Lawrence Erlbaum.

Julien, D., Markman, H. J., & Lindahl, K. M. (1989). A comparison of a global and a microanalytic coding system: Implications for future trends in studying interactions. *Behavioral Assessment, 11,* 81-100.

Kalbfleisch, P. J. (1992). Deceit, distrust and the social milieu: Application of deception research in a troubled world. *Journal of Applied Communication Research, 20,* 308-334.

Kayani, J. M., Wotring, C. E., & Forrest, E. J. (1996). Relational control and interactive media choice in technology-mediated communication situations. *Human Communication Research, 22,* 399-421.

Keeley-Dyreson, M. P., Burgoon, J. K., & Bailey, W. (1991). The effect of stress on decoding kinesic and vocalic communication. *Human Communication Research, 17,* 584-605.

Kellermann, K. (1992). Communication: Inherently strategic and primarily automatic. *Communication Monographs, 59,* 288-300.

Kellermann, K., Reynolds, R., & Chen, J. B. (1991). Strategies of conversational retreat: When parting is not sweet sorrow. *Communication Monographs, 58,* 362-383.

Kelley, D. L., & Burgoon, J. K. (1991). Understanding marital satisfaction and couple type as functions of relational expectations. *Human Communication Research, 18,* 40-69.

Kemper, T. D. (1984). Power, status, and emotions: A sociological contribution to a psychophysiological domain. In K. R. Scherer & P. Ekman (Eds.), *Approaches to emotion* (pp. 369-383). Hillsdale, NJ: Lawrence Erlbaum.

Kempton, W. (1980). The rhythmic basis of interactional micro-synchrony. In M. R. Key (Ed.), *The relationship of verbal and nonverbal communication* (pp. 67-75). The Hague: Mouton.

Kendon, A. (1983). Gesture and speech: How they interact. In J. M. Wiemann & R. P. Harrison (Eds.), *Nonverbal interaction* (pp. 13-45). Beverly Hills, CA: Sage.

Kendon, A. (1990). *Conducting interaction: Patterns of behavior in focused encounters.* Cambridge: Cambridge University Press.

Kendon, A. (1994). Do gestures communicate? A review. *Research on Language and Social Interaction, 27,* 175-200.

Kendon, A., Harris, R. M., & Key, M. R. (Eds.). (1975). *Organization of behavior in face-to-face interaction.* The Hague: Mouton.

Kenny, D. A. (1991). A general model of consensus and accuracy in interpersonal perception. *Psychological Review, 98,* 155-163.

Kenny, D. A., Horner, C., Kashy, D. A., & Chu, L. (1992). Consensus at zero acquaintance: Replication, behavioral cues, and stability. *Journal of Personality and Social Psychology, 62,* 88-97.

Knapp, M. L. (1984). The study of nonverbal behavior vis-à-vis human communication theory. In A. Wolfgang (Ed.), *Nonverbal behavior: Perspectives, applications, and intercultural insights* (pp. 15-40). Toronto: Hogrefe.

Knapp, M. L. (1985). The study of physical appearance and cosmetics in Western culture. In J. A. Graham & A. M. Kligman (Eds.), *The psychology of cosmetic treatments* (pp. 45-76). New York: Praeger.

Knapp, M. L., & Hall, J. A. (1992). *Nonverbal communication in human interaction* (3rd ed.). Ft. Worth, TX: Holt, Rinehart & Winston.

Knapp, M. L., Hart, R. P., Friedrich, G. W., & Schulman, G. M. (1973). The rhetoric of goodbye: Verbal and nonverbal correlates of human leave-taking. *Speech Monographs, 40,* 182-198.

Krauss, R. M., & Fussell, S. R. (1990). Mutual knowledge and communication effectiveness. In J. Galegher, R. E. Kraut, & C. Egido (Eds.), *Intellectual teamwork: Social and technological foundations of cooperative work* (pp. 111-145). Hillsdale, NJ: Lawrence Erlbaum.

Krauss, R. M., Fussell, S. R., & Chen, Y. (1995). Coordination of perspective in dialogue: Intrapersonal and interpersonal processes. In I. Marková, C. Graumann, & K. Foppa (Eds.), *Mutualities in dialogue* (pp. 124-145). Cambridge: Cambridge University Press.

Krauss, R. M., Morrel-Samuels, P., & Colasante, C. (1991). Do conversational hand gestures communicate? *Journal of Personality and Social Psychology, 61,* 743-754.

Krivonos, P. D., & Knapp, M. L. (1975). Initiating communication: What do you say when you say hello? *Central States Speech Journal, 26,* 115-125.

LaBarre, W. (1947). The cultural basis of emotions and gestures. *Journal of Personality, 16,* 49-68.

LaFrance, M., & Hecht, M. A. (2000). Gender and smiling: A meta-analysis. In A. H. Fischer (Ed.), *Gender and emotion: Social psychological perspectives* (pp. 118-142). New York: Cambridge University Press.

LaFrance, M., Henley, N. M., Hall, J. A., & Halberstadt, A. G. (1997). Nonverbal behavior: Are women's superior skills caused by their oppression? In M. R. Walsh (Ed.), *Women, men, and gender: Ongoing debates* (pp. 101-133). New Haven, CT: Yale University Press.

LaPlante, D., & Ambady, N. (2000). Multiple messages: Facial recognition advantage for compound expressions. *Journal of Nonverbal Behavior, 24,* 211-224.

Larose, H., & Standing, L. (1998). Does the halo effect occur in the elderly? *Social Behavior and Personality, 26,* 147-150.

Lazarus, R. S. (1984). On the primacy of emotion. *American Psychologist, 39,* 124-129.

Lea, M., & Spears, R. (1991). Computer-mediated communication, de-individuation and group decision-making. *International Journal of Man-Machine Studies, 34,* 283-301.

Lea, M., & Spears, R. (1992). Paralanguage and social perception in computer-mediated communication. *Journal of Organizational Computing, 2,* 321-341.

Lea, M., & Spears, R. (1995). Love at first byte? Building personal relationships over computer networks. In J. T. Wood & S. Duck (Eds.), *Under-studied relationships: Off the beaten track* (pp. 197-233). Thousand Oaks, CA: Sage.

Le Poire, B. A., & Burgoon, J. K. (1994). Two contrasting explanations of involvement violations: Expectancy violations theory and discrepancy arousal theory. *Human Communication Research, 20,* 560-591.

Le Poire, B. A., & Burgoon, J. K. (1996). Usefulness of differentiating arousal responses within communication theories: Orienting response of defensive arousal within theories of expectancy violation. *Communication Monographs, 63,* 208-230.

Le Poire, B. A., & Yoshimura, S. M. (1999). The effects of expectancies and actual communication on nonverbal adaptation and communication outcomes: A test of interaction adaptation theory. *Communication Monographs, 66,* 1-30.

Le Poire, B. A., Shepard, C. A., & Duggan, A. (1999). Nonverbal involvement, expressiveness, and pleasantness as predicted by parental and partner attachment style. *Communication Monographs, 66,* 293-311.

Le Poire, B. A., Shepard, C. A., Duggan, A., & Burgoon, J. K. (in press). Relational messages associated with nonverbal involvement, pleasantness, and expressiveness in romantic couples. *Communication Research Reports.*

Levenson, R. W., Ekman, P., & Friesen, W. V. (1990). Voluntary facial action generates emotion-specific autonomic nervous system activity. *Psychophysiology, 27,* 363-384.

Levenson, R. W., & Gottman, J. M. (1983). Marital interaction: Physiological linkage and affective exchange. *Journal of Personality and Social Psychology, 45,* 587-597.

Levenson, R. W., & Ruef, A. M. (1997). Physiological aspects of emotional knowledge and rapport. In W. Ickes (Ed.), *Empathic accuracy* (pp. 44-72). New York: Guilford.

Levine, R. V., & Norenzayan, A. (1999). The pace of life in 31 countries. *Journal of Cross-Cultural Psychology, 30,* 178-205.

Levine, T. R., Anders, L. N., Banas, J., Baum, K. L., Endo, K., Hu, A. D. S., & Wong, N. C. H.

(2000). Norms, expectations, and deception: A norm violation model of veracity judgments. *Communication Monographs, 67,* 123-137.

Levine, T. R., & McCornack, S. A. (1996). A critical analysis of the behavioral adaptation explanation of the probing effect. *Human Communication Research, 22,* 575-588.

Lippa, R. A., & Dietz, J. K. (2000). The relation of gender, personality, and intelligence to judges' accuracy in judging strangers' personality from brief video segments. *Journal of Nonverbal Behavior, 24,* 25-43.

Liska, J. (1986). Symbols: The missing link? In J. G. Else & P. Lee (Eds.), *Proceedings of the Tenth Annual Congress on the International Primatological Society: Vol. 3. Primate ontology, cognition, and social behavior.* Cambridge: Cambridge University Press.

Lombard, M., & Ditton, T. (1997). At the heart of it all: The concept of presence. *Journal of Computer-Mediated Communication, 3*(2). Retrieved March 25, 2002, from http://www. ascusc.org/jcmc/vol3/issue2/lombard.html

Mahl, G. F. (1987). *Explorations in nonverbal and vocal behavior.* Hillsdale, NJ: Lawrence Erlbaum.

Manusov, V. (1990). An application of attribution principles to nonverbal behavior in romantic dyads. *Communication Monographs, 57,* 104-118.

Manusov, V. (1991). Perceiving nonverbal messages: Effects of immediacy and encoded intent on receiver judgments. *Western Journal of Speech Communication, 55,* 235-253.

Manusov, V., & Rodriguez, J. S. (1989). Intentionality behind nonverbal messages: A perceiver's perspective. *Journal of Nonverbal Behavior, 13,* 15-24.

Manusov, V., Winchatz, M. R., & Manning, L. M. (1997). Acting out our minds: Incorporating behavior into models of stereotype-based expectancies for cross-cultural interactions. *Communication Monographs, 64,* 119-139.

Matsumoto, D. (1991). Cultural influences on facial expressions of emotion. *Southern Communication Journal, 56,* 128-137.

Mayer, J. D., Caruso, D. R., & Salovey, P. (2000). Selecting a measure of emotional intelligence: The case for ability scales. In R. Bar-On & J. D. A. Parker (Eds.), *The handbook of emotional intelligence: Theory, development,* assessment, and application at home, school, and in the workplace (pp. 320-342). San Francisco: Jossey-Bass.

Mayer, J. D., & Salovey, P. (1997). What is emotional intelligence? In P. Salovey & D. J. Sluyter (Eds.), *Emotional development and emotional intelligence: Educational implications* (pp. 3-34). New York: Basic Books.

McCall, G. J. (1987). The self-concept and interpersonal communication. In M. E. Roloff & G. R. Miller (Eds.), *Interpersonal processes: New directions in communication research* (pp. 63-76). Newbury Park, CA: Sage.

McDaniel, E., & Andersen, P. A. (1998). International patterns of interpersonal tactile communication: A field study. *Journal of Nonverbal Behavior, 22,* 59-75.

McNeil, N. M., Alibali, M. W., & Evans, J. L. (2000). The role of gesture in children's comprehension of spoken language: Now they need it, now they don't. *Journal of Nonverbal Behavior, 24,* 131-150.

McNeill, D. (1985). So you think gestures are nonverbal? *Psychological Review, 92,* 350-371.

McNeill, D. (1992). *Hand and mind: What gestures reveal about thought.* Chicago: University of Chicago Press.

McNeill, D., Cassell, J., & McCullough, K. (1994). Communicative effects of speech-mismatched gestures. *Research on Language and Social Interaction, 27,* 223-237.

Mead, M. (1975). Review of *Darwin and facial expression: A century of research in review* by P. Ekman. *Journal of Communication, 25*(1), 209-213.

Mehrabian, A., & Wiener, M. (1967). Decoding of inconsistent communications. *Journal of Personality and Social Psychology, 6,* 109-114.

Memon, A., Vrij, A., & Bull, R. (1998). *Psychology and law: Truthfulness, accuracy, and credibility.* Maidenhead, Eng.: McGraw-Hill.

Miller, G. R., & Stiff, J. B. (1993). *Deceptive communication.* Newbury Park, CA: Sage.

Montepare, J. M., & Tucker, J. S. (1999). Aging and nonverbal behavior: Current perspectives and future directions. *Journal of Nonverbal Behavior, 23,* 105-110.

Moon, Y., & Nass, C. I. (1996). How "real" are computer personalities? Psychological responses to personality types in human computer interaction. *Communication Research, 23,* 651-674.

Morman, M. T., & Floyd, K. (1999). Affectionate communication between fathers and young adult sons: Individual- and relational-level correlates. *Communication Studies, 50,* 294-309.

Morris, D. (1977). *Manwatching: A field guide to human behavior.* New York: Abrams.

Morris, D., Collett, P., Marsh, P., & O'Shaughnessy, M. (1979). *Gestures.* New York: Stein & Day.

Morrow, P. C., & McElroy, J. C. (1984). The impact of physical attractiveness in evaluative contexts. *Basic and Applied Social Psychology, 5,* 171-182.

Motley, M. T. (1986). Consciousness and intentionality in communication: A preliminary model and methodological approaches. *Western Journal of Speech Communication, 50,* 3-23.

Motley, M. T. (1990a). Communication as interaction: A reply to Beach and Bavelas. *Western Journal of Speech Communication, 54,* 613-623.

Motley, M. T. (1990b). On whether one can(not) communicate: An examination via traditional communication postulates. *Western Journal of Speech Communication, 54,* 1-20.

Motley, M. T. (1991). How one may not communicate: A reply to Andersen. *Communication Studies, 42,* 326-339.

Motley, M. T., & Camden, C. T. (1988). Facial expression of emotion: A comparison of posed expressions versus spontaneous expressions in an interpersonal setting. *Western Journal of Speech Communication, 52,* 1-22.

Mulac, A., Studley, L. B., Wiemann, J. M., & Bradac, J. J. (1987). Male/female gaze in same-sex and mixed-sex dyads. *Human Communication Research, 13,* 323-343.

Nass, C. I., Fogg, B. J., & Moon, Y. (1996). Can computers be teammates? *International Journal of Human-Computer Studies, 45,* 669-678.

Nass, C. I., & Moon, Y. (2000). Machines and mindlessness: Social responses to computers. *Journal of Social Issues, 56*(1), 81-103.

Nass, C. I., Moon, Y., Morkes, J., Kim, E.-Y., & Fogg, B. J. (1997). Computers are social actors: A review of current research. In B. Friedman (Ed.), *Human values and the design of computer technology* (pp. 137-162). Cambridge: Cambridge University Press.

Newton, D. A., & Burgoon, J. K. (1990). Nonverbal conflict behaviors: Functions, strategies, and tactics. In D. D. Cahn (Ed.), *Intimates in conflict: A communication perspective* (pp. 77-104). Hillsdale, NJ: Lawrence Erlbaum.

Noller, P. (1985). Video primacy: Another look. *Journal of Nonverbal Behavior, 9,* 28-47.

Noller, P. (1993). Gender and emotional communication in marriage: Different cultures or different social power? *Journal of Language and Social Psychology, 12,* 92-112.

Noller, P., Feeney, J. A., Sheehan, G., & Peterson, C. (2000). Marital conflict patterns: Links with family conflict and family members' perceptions of one another. *Personal Relationships, 7,* 79-94.

Nussbaum, J. F., Thompson, T., & Robinson, J. D. (1989). *Communication and aging.* New York: Harper & Row.

O'Hair, D., Allman, J., & Gibson, L. A. (1991). Nonverbal communication and aging. *Southern Communication Journal, 56,* 147-160.

O'Leary, M. J., & Gallois, C. (1985). The last ten turns: Behavior and sequencing in friends' and strangers' conversational findings. *Journal of Nonverbal Behavior, 9,* 8-27.

O'Malley, C., Langton, S., Anderson, A., Doherty-Sneddon, G., & Bruce, V. (1996). Comparison of face-to-face and video-mediated interaction. *Interacting With Computers, 8,* 177-192.

Palmer, M. T., & Simmons, K. B. (1995). Communication intentions through nonverbal behaviors: Conscious and nonconscious encoding of liking. *Human Communication Research, 22,* 128-160.

Parks, M. R., & Floyd, K. (1996). Making friends in cyberspace. *Journal of Communication, 46*(1), 80-97.

Parks, M. R., & Roberts, L. D. (1998). "Making MOOsic": The development of personal relationships on line and a comparison to their off-line counterparts. *Journal of Social and Personal Relationships, 15,* 517-537.

Patterson, M. L. (1976). An arousal model of interpersonal intimacy. *Psychological Review, 83,* 235-245.

Patterson, M. L. (1978). The role of space in social interaction. In A. W. Siegman & S. Feldstein (Eds.), *Nonverbal behavior and communication* (pp. 265-290). Hillsdale, NJ: Lawrence Erlbaum.

Patterson, M. L. (1983). *Nonverbal behavior: A functional perspective.* New York: Springer-Verlag.

Patterson, M. L. (1987). Presentational and affect-management functions of nonverbal involvement. *Journal of Nonverbal Behavior, 11,* 110-122.

Patterson, M. L. (1995). A parallel process model of nonverbal communication. *Journal of Nonverbal Behavior, 19,* 3-29.

Patterson, M. L. (1999). The evolution of a parallel process model of nonverbal communication. In P. Philippot, R. S. Feldman, & E. J. Coats (Eds.), *The social context of nonverbal behavior* (pp. 317-347). New York: Cambridge University Press.

Patterson, M. L. (in press). Nonverbal communication. In A. S. R. Manstead & M. Hewstone (Eds.), *The Blackwell encyclopedia of social psychology* (2nd ed.). Oxford: Basil Blackwell.

Patterson, M. L., & Stockbridge, E. (1998). Effects of cognitive demand and judgment strategy on person perception accuracy. *Journal of Nonverbal Behavior, 22,* 253-263.

Paunonen, S. V., Zeidner, M., Engvik, H. A., Oosterveld, P., & Maliphant, R. (2000). The nonverbal assessment of personality in five cultures. *Journal of Cross-Cultural Psychology, 31,* 220-239.

Pendry, L. F., & Macrae, C. N. (1994). Stereotypes and mental life: The case of the motivated but thwarted tactician. *Journal of Experimental Social Psychology, 30,* 303-325.

Petronio, S. (1991). Communication boundary management: A theoretical model of managing disclosure of private information between married couples. *Communication Theory, 1,* 311-335.

Petronio, S. (2000). The boundaries of privacy: Praxis of everyday life. In S. Petronio (Ed.), *Balancing the secrets of private disclosures* (pp. 37-49). Mahwah, NJ: Lawrence Erlbaum.

Philpott, J. S. (1983). *The relative contribution to meaning of verbal and nonverbal channels of communication: A meta-analysis.* Unpublished master's thesis, University of Nebraska.

Pittinger, R., Hockett, C., & Darehy, J. (1960). *The first five minutes.* Ithaca, NY: Martineau.

Planalp, S. (1999). *Communicating emotion: Social, moral, and cultural processes.* Cambridge: Cambridge University Press.

Planalp, S., & Benson, A. (1992). Friends' and acquaintances' conversations I: Perceived differences. *Journal of Social and Personal Relationships, 9,* 483-506.

Plutchik, R. (1984). Emotions: A general psychoevolutionary theory. In K. R. Scherer & P. Ekman (Eds.), *Approaches to emotion* (pp. 197-219). Hillsdale, NJ: Lawrence Erlbaum.

Poyatos, F. (1993). *Paralanguage: A linguistic and interdisciplinary approach to interactive speech and sounds.* Amsterdam: John Benjamins.

Raines, R. S., Hechtman, S. B., & Rosenthal, R. (1990). Nonverbal behavior and gender as determinants of physical attractiveness. *Journal of Nonverbal Behavior, 14,* 253-267.

Ray, G. B. (1986). Vocally cued personality prototypes: An implicit personality theory approach. *Communication Monographs, 53,* 266-276.

Reeves, B., & Nass, C. I. (1996). *The media equation: How people treat computers, television, and new media like real people and places.* New York: Cambridge University Press.

Register, L. M., & Henley, T. B. (1992). The phenomenology of intimacy. *Journal of Social Relationships, 8,* 147-165.

Ricci Bitti, P. E., & Poggi, I. (1991). Symbolic nonverbal behavior: Talking through gestures. In R. S. Feldman & B. Rimé (Eds.), *Fundamentals of nonverbal behavior* (pp. 433-457). Cambridge: Cambridge University Press.

Ridgeway, C. L., & Berger, J. (1986). Expectations, legitimation, and dominance behavior in task groups. *American Sociological Review, 62,* 218-235.

Ridgeway, C. L., Berger, J., & Smith, L. (1985). Nonverbal cues and status: An expectation states approach. *American Journal of Sociology, 90,* 955-978.

Ridgeway, C. L., & Walker, H. A. (1995). Status structures. In K. S. Cook, G. A. Fine, & J. S. House (Eds.), *Sociological perspectives on social psychology* (pp. 281-310). Boston: Allyn & Bacon.

Rimé, B., & Schiaratura, L. (1991). Gesture and speech. In R. S. Feldman & B. Rimé (Eds.), *Fundamentals of nonverbal behavior* (pp. 239-281). Cambridge: Cambridge University Press.

Riseborough, M. G. (1981). Physiographic gestures as decoding facilitators: Three experiments exploring a neglected facet of communication. *Journal of Nonverbal Behavior, 5,* 172-183.

Robinson, D. T., & Smith, L. L. (1999). Emotion display as a strategy for identity negotiation. *Motivation and Emotion, 23,* 73-104.

Rockwell, P., Buller, D. B., & Burgoon, J. K. (1997). The voice of deceit: Refining and expanding vocal cues to deception. *Communication Research Reports, 14,* 451-458.

Rosenfeld, H. M. (1978). Conversational control functions of nonverbal behavior. In A. W. Siegman & S. Feldstein (Eds.), *Nonverbal behavior and communication* (pp. 291-328). Hillsdale, NJ: Lawrence Erlbaum.

Rosenfeld, L. B. (2000). Overview of the ways privacy, secrecy, and disclosure are balanced in today's society. In S. Petronio (Ed.), *Balancing the secrets of private disclosures* (pp. 3-17). Mahwah, NJ: Lawrence Erlbaum.

Rosenthal, R. (1985). Nonverbal cues in the mediation of interpersonal expectancy effects. In A. W. Siegman & S. Feldstein (Eds.), *Multichannel integrations of nonverbal behavior* (pp. 105-128). Hillsdale, NJ: Lawrence Erlbaum.

Ross, H. S., Cheyne, J. A., & Lollis, S. P. (1988). Defining and studying reciprocity in young children. In S. Duck (Ed.), *Handbook of personal relationships: Theory, research and interventions* (pp. 143-160). New York: John Wiley.

Rowatt, W. C., Cunningham, M. R., & Druen, P. B. (1999). Lying to get a date: The effect of facial physical attractiveness on the willingness to deceive prospective dating partners. *Journal of Social and Personal Relationships, 16,* 209-223.

Rusbult, C. E., Verett, J., Whitney, G. A., Slovik, L. F., & Lipkus, I. (1991). Accommodation processes in close relationships: Theory and preliminary empirical evidence. *Journal of Personality and Social Psychology, 60,* 53-78.

Sapir, E. (1949). The unconscious patterning of behavior in society. In D. Mandelbaum (Ed.), *Selected writings of Edward Sapir in language, culture and personality* (pp. 544-559). Berkeley: University of California Press.

Scheflen, A. E. (1965). Quasi-courtship behavior in psychotherapy. *Psychiatry, 28,* 245-257.

Scherer, K. R. (1980). The functions of nonverbal signs in conversation. In R. N. St. Clair & H. Giles (Eds.), *The social and psychological contexts of language* (pp. 225-244). Hillsdale, NJ: Lawrence Erlbaum.

Scherer, K. R. (1986). Vocal affect expression: A review and a model for future research. *Psychological Bulletin, 99,* 143-165.

Scherer, K. R., & Wallbott, H. G. (1994). Evidence for universality and cultural variation of differential emotion response patterning. *Journal of Personality and Social Psychology, 66,* 310-328.

Schlenker, B. R. (1985). Identity and self-identification. In B. R. Schlenker (Ed.), *The self and social life* (pp. 65-99). New York: McGraw-Hill.

Semic, B. (1999). Vocal attractiveness: What sounds beautiful is good. In L. K. Guerrero, J. A. DeVito, & M. L. Hecht (Eds.), *The nonverbal communication reader: Classic and contemporary readings* (pp. 149-155). Prospect Heights, IL: Waveland.

Sharkey, W. F., & Stafford, L. (1990). Turn-taking resources employed by congenitally blind conversers. *Communication Studies, 41,* 161-182.

Shea, B. C., & Pearson, J. C. (1986). The effects of relationship type, partner intent, and gender on the selection of relationship maintenance strategies. *Communication Monographs, 53,* 352-364.

Short, J., Williams, E., & Christie, B. (1976). *The social psychology of telecommunication.* London: John Wiley.

Siegman, A. W. (1978). The telltale voice: Nonverbal messages of verbal communication. In A. W. Siegman & S. Feldstein (Eds.), *Nonverbal behavior and communication* (pp. 183-243). Hillsdale, NJ: Lawrence Erlbaum.

Simpson, J. A., Gangestad, S. W., & Biek, M. (1993). Personality and nonverbal social behavior: An ethological perspective of relationship initiation. *Journal of Experimental Social Psychology, 29,* 434-461.

Smith, H. J., Archer, D., & Costanzo, M. (1991). "Just a hunch": Accuracy and awareness in person perception. *Journal of Nonverbal Behavior, 15,* 3-18.

Snodgrass, S. E. (1992). Further effects of role versus gender on interpersonal sensitivity. *Journal of Personality and Social Psychology, 62,* 154-158.

Sparks, J. R., Areni, C. S., & Cox, K. C. (1998). An investigation of the effects of language style and communication modality on persuasion. *Communication Monographs, 65,* 108-125.

Sproull, L. S., & Kiesler, S. (1986). Reducing social context cues: Electronic mail in organizational communication. *Management Science, 32,* 1492-1512.

Sproull, L. S., & Kiesler, S. (1991). *Connections: New ways of working in the networked organization.* Cambridge: MIT Press.

Stamp, G. H., & Knapp, M. L. (1990). The construct of intent in interpersonal communication. *Quarterly Journal of Speech, 76,* 282-299.

Stiff, J. B., Kim, H. J., & Ramesh, C. N. (1992). Truth-biases and aroused suspicion in relational deception. *Communication Research, 19,* 326-345.

Storrs, D., & Kleinke, C. L. (1990). Evaluation of high and equal status male and female touchers. *Journal of Nonverbal Behavior, 14,* 87-95.

Street, R. L., Jr., & Murphy, T. L. (1987). Interpersonal orientation and speech behavior. *Communication Monographs, 54,* 42-62.

Sullins, E. S. (1989). Perceptual salience as a function of nonverbal expressiveness. *Personality and Social Psychology Bulletin, 15,* 584-595.

Sunnafrank, M. (1986). Predicted outcome value during initial interactions: A reformulation of uncertainty reduction theory. *Human Communication Research, 13,* 3-33.

Suzuki, S. (1998). In-group and out-group communication patterns in international organizations: Implications for social identity theory. *Communication Research, 25,* 154-182.

Swann, W. B. (1987). Identity negotiation: Where two roads meet. *Journal of Personality and Social Psychology, 53,* 1038-1051.

Tajfel, H. (1981). *Human groups and social categories: Studies in social psychology.* Cambridge: Cambridge University Press.

Thomas, G., & Fletcher, G. J. O. (1997). Empathic accuracy in close relationships. In W. Ickes (Ed.), *Empathic accuracy* (pp. 194-217). New York: Guilford.

Thompson, L. A., Driscoll, D., & Markson, L. (1998). Memory for visual-spoken language in children and adults. *Journal of Nonverbal Behavior, 22,* 167-187.

Ting-Toomey, S. (1988). Intercultural conflict styles: A face-negotiation theory. In Y. Y. Kim & W. B. Gudykunst (Eds.), *Theories in intercultural communication* (pp. 213-235). Newbury Park, CA: Sage.

Ting-Toomey, S. (1994). *The challenge of face work: Cross-cultural and interpersonal issues.* Albany: State University of New York Press.

Ting-Toomey, S., & Kurogi, A. (1998). Face work competence in intercultural conflict: An updated face-negotiation theory. *International Journal of Intercultural Relations, 22,* 187-225.

Tolhuizen, J. H. (1989). Communication strategies for intensifying dating relationships: Identification, use and structure. *Journal of Social and Personal Relationships, 6,* 413-434.

Tomkins, S. S. (1984). Affect theory. In K. R. Scherer & P. Ekman (Eds.), *Approaches to emotion* (pp. 163-195). Hillsdale, NJ: Lawrence Erlbaum.

Trees, A. (2000). Nonverbal communication and the support process: Interactional sensitivity in interactions between mothers and young adult children. *Communication Monographs, 67,* 239-261.

Triandis, H. C. (1989). The self and social behavior in differing cultural contexts. *Journal of Personality and Social Psychology, 96,* 506-520.

Tseelon, E. (1992). What is beautiful is bad: Physical attractiveness as stigma. *Journal for the Theory of Social Behavior, 22,* 295-309.

Tucker, J. S., & Anders, S. L. (1998). Adult attachment style and nonverbal closeness in dating couples. *Journal of Nonverbal Behavior, 22,* 109-124.

Tusing, K. J., & Dillard, J. P. (2000). The sounds of dominance: Vocal precursors of perceived dominance during interpersonal influence. *Human Communication Research, 26,* 148-171.

Utz, S. (2000). Social information processing in MUDs: The development of friendships in virtual worlds. *Journal of Online Behavior, 1*(1). Retrieved March 25, 2002, from http://www.behavior.net/job/v1n1/utz.html

von Raffler-Engel, W. (1983). *The perception of nonverbal behavior in the career interview.* Amsterdam: John Benjamins.

Vrij, A. (2000). *Detecting lies and deceit: The psychology of lying and its implications for professional practice.* Chichester: John Wiley.

Vrij, A., Edward, K., & Bull, R. (2001). Police officers' ability to detect deceit: The benefit of indirect deception detection measures. *Legal and Criminological Psychology, 6,* 185-196.

Vrij, A., Edward, K., Roberts, K. P., & Bull, R. (2000). Detecting deceit via analysis of verbal and nonverbal behavior. *Journal of Nonverbal Behavior, 24,* 239-263.

Wagner, H. L., & Smith, J. (1991). Facial expression in the presence of friends and strangers. *Journal of Nonverbal Behavior, 15,* 201-214.

Walther, J. B. (1992). Interpersonal effects in computer-mediated interaction: A relational perspective. *Communication Research, 19,* 52-89.

Walther, J. B. (1993). Impression development in computer-mediated communication. *Western Journal of Communication, 57,* 381-398.

Walther, J. B. (1996). Computer-mediated communication: Impersonal, interpersonal, and hyperpersonal interaction. *Communication Research, 23,* 3-43.

Walther, J. B., & Burgoon, J. K. (1992). Relational communication in computer-mediated interaction. *Human Communication Research, 19,* 50-88.

Warner, R. M., Malloy, D., Schneider, K., Knoth, R., & Wilder, B. (1987). Rhythmic organization of social interaction and observer ratings of positive affect and involvement. *Journal of Nonverbal Behavior, 11,* 57-74.

Watzlawick, P., Beavin, J. H., & Jackson, D. D. (1967). *Pragmatics of human communication: A study of interactional patterns, pathologies, and paradoxes.* New York: W. W. Norton.

Weiner, B. (1986). *An attributional theory of motivation and emotion.* New York: Springer-Verlag.

Wheeler, L., & Kim, Y. (1997). What is beautiful is culturally good: The physical attractiveness stereotype has different content in collectivistic cultures. *Personality and Social Psychology Bulletin, 23,* 795-800.

White, C. H., & Burgoon, J. K. (2001). Adaptation and communicative design: Patterns of interaction in truthful and deceptive conversations. *Human Communication Research, 27,* 9-37.

Whittaker, S. (1995). Rethinking video as a technology for interpersonal communications: Theory and design implications. *International Journal of Human-Computer Studies, 42,* 501-529.

Wiemann, J. M. (1985). Interpersonal control and regulation in conversation. In R. L. Street, Jr., & J. N. Cappella (Eds.), *Sequence and pattern in communicative behaviour* (pp. 85-102). London: Edward Arnold.

Wiemann, J. M., & Knapp, M. L. (1975). Turn-taking in conversations. *Journal of Communication, 25*(2), 75-92.

Wiener, M., Devoe, S., Rubinow, S., & Geller, J. (1972). Nonverbal behavior and nonverbal communication. *Psychological Review, 79,* 185-214.

Woodall, W. G., & Burgoon, J. K. (1981). The effects of nonverbal synchrony on message comprehension and persuasiveness. *Journal of Nonverbal Behavior, 5,* 207-223.

Woodall, W. G., & Burgoon, J. K. (1983). Talking fast and changing attitudes: A critique and clarification. *Journal of Nonverbal Behavior, 8,* 126-142.

Woodall, W. G., & Folger, J. P. (1985). Nonverbal cue context and episodic memory: On the availability and endurance of nonverbal behaviors as retrieval cues. *Communication Monographs, 52,* 319-333.

Zajonc, R. B. (1984). On the primacy of affect. *American Psychologist, 39,* 117-123.

Zebrowitz, L. A. (1990). *Social perception.* Pacific Grove, CA: Brooks/Cole.

Zuckerman, M., DePaulo, B. M., & Rosenthal, R. (1981). Verbal and nonverbal communication of deception. In L. Berkowitz (Ed.), *Advances in experimental social psychology* (Vol. 14, pp. 2-59). New York: Academic Press.

Zuckerman, M., DePaulo, B. M., & Rosenthal, R. (1986). Humans as deceivers and lie-detectors. In P. D. Blanck, R. Buck, & R. Rosenthal (Eds.), *Nonverbal communication in the clinical context* (pp. 13-35). University Park: Pennsylvania State University Press.

Zuckerman, M., & Driver, R. E. (1985). Telling lies: Verbal and nonverbal correlates of deception. In A. W. Siegman & S. Feldstein (Eds.), *Multichannel integrations of nonverbal behavior* (pp. 129-148). Hillsdale, NJ: Lawrence Erlbaum.

Zuckerman, M., Hodgins, H. S., & Miyake, K. (1990). The vocal attractiveness stereotype: Replication and elaboration. *Journal of Nonverbal Behavior, 14,* 97-112.

Zuckerman, M., Lipets, M. S., Koivumaki, J. H., & Rosenthal, R. (1975). Encoding and decoding nonverbal cues of emotion. *Journal of Personality and Social Psychology, 32,* 1068-1076.

Zuckerman, M., Miyake, K., & Hodgins, H. S. (1991). Cross-channel effects of vocal and physical attractiveness and their implications for interpersonal perception. *Journal of Personality and Social Psychology, 60,* 545-554.

Culture, Meaning, and Interpersonal Communication

JÜRGEN STREECK

THE CHANGING STATUS OF CULTURE

What is culture? The word *culture* in the anthropological sense in which we use it today is an invention of the second half of the 19th century and is roughly equivalent with *civilization:* It denotes all the "stuff" that distinguishes humanity from other species, the "set of prosthetic devices by which human beings ... exceed ... the '*natural* limits' of human functioning" (Bruner, 1990, p. 21; emphasis added), that are the product of invention and tradition, not biology. E. B. Tylor (1871), one of the founders of modern anthropology, defined culture as "that complex whole which includes knowledge, belief, art, law, morals, custom, and any other capabilities and habits acquired by man as a member of society" (p. 21). *Webster's College Dictionary* defines it as "the sum total of ways of living built up by a group of human beings and transmitted from one generation to another." These definitions continue to be useful, as long as we take into account that "capabilities and habits" and "ways of living" also and prominently include media, practices, and skills for communication. What is problematic, however, and becoming more and more so, is the easy association of "culture" and "group" (or "society"), the tacit assumption that cultures "belong" to groups and occupy pieces of land with them—islands, valleys, states, or perhaps just city blocks—that "cultures," in other words, are expanses in space.

Two linguistic phenomena apparently play a part in our tendency to think about culture in this fashion. One is the grammar of the word *culture* itself, which exists, in English, in two versions, but in versions whose differences are covert: They manifest themselves only in the grammatical behavior of the terms. The term *culture* exists in the form of both a mass noun and a count noun. As a mass noun ("culture in the singular"), the term does not admit an article and denotes all the "stuff" that the above definitions designate. This stuff is unbounded, does not come in discrete units, and is therefore not countable; it bears more resemblance to the weather than to a piece of land. We don't always know where it comes from, how far it reaches, and where it will go. The count noun variety of *culture* ("culture in the plural," admitting articles) is an even more recent terminological invention. The word *cultures* is generally used more or less interchangeably with *groups* or *societies* and presumes that cultures are discrete and bounded—that they can, in other words, be individualized and thus counted.

We apparently understand the relationship between "culture" and "cultures" (and make sense of the latter) by analogy to "language" and "languages" (*language* is another word that comes in both mass noun and count noun form): "Language" is something that all of humanity possesses, a faculty (an acquired faculty no less); "languages" are bounded entities, and there are thousands of them. Although it may not always be possible to draw the boundaries between languages with precision, there is generally little doubt to which language a word belongs. The faculty "language" thus is always instantiated as mastery of an individual language (or a small set of languages). By analogy, the possession of culture is construed as mastery of (or membership in) "a culture," an individual one, even though the reference of that term may be anything but clear. The cultural "stuff" that is indexed by

the mass noun *culture* does not easily cluster into segregated, bounded units, as language does; it is often difficult to identify the communities (or "cultures") to which particular kinds of cultural stuff belong (say, chairs or winks).

The other cultural artifacts that mediate our imagination of culture are maps on which nation-states appear as bounded territories, distinct, and in different colors. We regard this representation—which became popular during the late 19th century, when administrators of the British Empire began to shade the crown's possessions on world maps in a single color (red)—as an embodiment of the natural order of things, of the world in which we have acquired our identities and customs: Being socialized in one territory makes us brown (or German), whereas our neighbors are orange (or Dutch).

Thus, as soon as we begin to use *culture* as a count noun and divide the world into a finite set of cultures, and as soon as we take the convention by which nation-states are represented on maps as an equally valid representation of culture, we are deeply mired in stereotypical thinking. We assume discreteness and distinction where in reality there are only fuzzy boundaries; we inadvertently homogenize the entities that we call *cultures;* we abstract from history, notably histories of migration, as well as its effects, such as cultural borrowing and hybridization; and we massively underestimate the extent to which human beings share the stuff that is indexed by *culture,* the mass noun.

However, the old model of the patchwork of cultures and cultural identities, which is to a large extent a product of late-19th-century anthropology and its context, colonialism, has now begun to recede, giving way to a mode of thinking about culture and social life that, in the first place, regards cultural difference as a product of human agency, not as part of a seemingly natural order of things, and is utterly aware of the contested and shifting nature of cultural identity and cultural borders: cultural studies. Where 10 years ago in communication studies the prevailing view of the influence of culture on communication was modeled after the difficulties that Japanese and American businesspeople might experience in their negotiations with one another because of their countries' different traditions and values regarding communicative conduct, today we are much more likely to encounter accounts of ways in which communication is used as a mechanism for achieving distinction, for the individual or the group— that is, identity. In other words, cultural identity and membership are more likely to be regarded as products than as antecedents of communicative relations.

The academic study of culture and communication is thus trying to catch up with a rapidly changing and deeply contradictory world in which ethnicity and cultural differences play multiple, incommensurable, and very unstable roles. As the contributions to the second edition of this *Handbook* (Knapp & Miller, 1994) were being written, "ethnic cleansing" and genocide were ravaging Bosnia. Now, the 19th-century idea of the nation-state has finally asserted itself in formerly multiethnic Yugoslavia (pending a Greater Albania), but as soon as that was accomplished, the perpetrators and the masses supporting them began to lose interest in their own distinction, realizing instead that they had thwarted their own advance toward participation in a unified Europe. There is a constant push and pull between the forces of globalization and cultural homogeneity on the one hand and those of cultural and ethnic segregation on the other. Although ethnic violence is unabated and has increased sharply in some parts of the world, more and more people seem to be becoming aware that, behind their nationalist or ethnocentric veils, they all use the same communication technologies and have similar aspirations, making

cultural differences seem very shallow. Anthropology's romantic vision of a mosaic of distinct, bounded, and equally worthy cultures gives way to weariness vis-à-vis a messy world in which *culture* has become a fighting word, but where it is impossible to predict how intercultural relations will develop in different places. Scholars in cultural studies, which does not share anthropology's colonial heritage and has from the outset been aligned with the struggle for economic fairness and social and political recognition of immigrants from the former colonies (for example, West Indians in the United Kingdom), seem better equipped to observe and theorize the contested and fluctuating roles of culture in contemporary society, not least because of their refusal to "essentialize" culture and their interest in cultural hybridity.

In the United States, black-white cultural relations changed quite dramatically during the presidency of Bill Clinton, whom the African American sociologist Orlando Patterson labeled "the first black president." What is most noteworthy is a new celebration of cultural hybridity: Among American youth, it is now "cool to be black," and not only for blacks; rather, black idioms of speech and social interaction have become entirely commonplace, and adolescents have become adept at the game of "crossing" (Rampton, 1995), borrowing and playing with each other's styles. It is too early to tell how deep and persistent this change, which is not least a product of the popularity of hip-hop culture, will prove to be, or if it is perhaps only a contemporary version of "blackface," as Spike Lee suggests in his film *Bamboozled*.

The anthropological tradition in the study and theorizing of human relations and interpersonal communication, which is the topic of this chapter, thus finds itself in a tense and problematic relation to its subject matter. However, cultural studies scholars have largely devoted themselves to the study of symbolic embodiments and representations of cultural identity and their interaction with relations of power; cultural studies more or less excludes the psychological realm, the "cultural programming" of the human psyche, which is at the center of this overview.

AN ANTHROPOLOGICAL VIEW OF CULTURE

We will uncouple *culture* from *ethnicity, identity,* and *group* and use the term in two senses, both of them lucidly synthesized by Bruner in his book *Acts of Meaning* (1990). First of all, culture is what distinguishes the human species from other species (or most other species—some animals, such as apes and whales, have been shown to have limited bodies of tradition) and enables it to survive in a world for which it is biologically maladapted. Humanity was condemned to develop culture because it was not naturally designed to survive; it lacked a biosphere. This is a theme that various philosophical and biological anthropologists have expounded, beginning during the Age of Enlightenment (Herder, 1772/1966; Kant, 1798/1977); more recent contributions have been made by, among others, Gehlen (1958), Plessner (1964/1980), and Donald (1991). Culture includes humanity's material creations—symbols, shelter, technology, and so on—but also its mental abilities to operate them; it is both external and internal.

Culture, then, is "a set of prosthetic devices by which human beings can exceed or even redefine the 'natural limits' of human functioning" (Bruner, 1990, p. 21). Of chief importance among these prosthetic devices are *symbolic* or *representation systems,* systems "used in constructing meaning" (p. 11). Although the modern world consists in a multitude of overlapping, moving, shifting local meaning systems, at its roots culture is a human universal, acquired by the species in the process of evolution. Contemporary representation systems, languages, and systems of social interaction

are built upon and contain structures developed at previous evolutionary stages.

> The modern mind has evolved from the primate mind through a series of major adaptations, each of which led to the emergence of a new representation system. Each ... new ... system has remained intact within our current mental architecture, so that the modern mind is a mosaic structure of cognitive vestiges from earlier stages of human emergence. (Donald, 1991, p. 3)

Each cultural form—symbol, behavior, artifact—can therefore be "read" in its contemporary, local, "cultural" web of meanings or as a reflection and instantiation of older, more global human achievements. Different languages have different morphologies to inflect verbs and nouns (some have no inflection whatsoever), but some version of the verb-noun (or process-thing) dichotomy is found in all of them. Similarly, politeness is marked by many different devices, but in all speech communities, there are ways to be polite (Brown & Levinson, 1987).

There is another reason for looking at cultural meaning systems from the point of view of their dual nature as partly universal, partly diverse: Independent findings from several disciplines, in particular population genetics and linguistic typology (Cavalli-Sforza, 1991; Greenberg & Ruhlen, 1992), suggest that human language—and thus culture—originated in only one place ("monogenesis") in Africa and spread from there around the globe with humanity's migrations. In the process, languages diversified and developed various independent lineages. All languages, in other words, are at one level "dialects" of one another; however diverse they might be, they are of common origin. This invites us to see cultural phenomena as if through a telescope: Depending on the age we focus upon, we can variously see them as local and diverse or as global and unified. In so doing, we can gain a sense of their ongoing evolution.

The most important feature of representation systems is that they enable, structure, represent, and communicate *meaning*. Only by using representation systems within which we can represent something *as* something (Goodman, 1976) are we able to "make common sense" of experience. For example, we can communicate emotional experience by casting it within the metaphorical webs of our common language, likening it to phenomena that are overt, public, tangible: "I felt *shattered.*"

As Bruner (1990) notes: "By virtue of participation in culture, meaning is rendered *public* and *shared*. Our . . . way of life depends upon shared meanings and shared concepts and depends as well upon shared modes of discourse for negotiating differences in meaning and interpretation" (p. 11). In other words, by calling something a "cultural phenomenon" (this is the second aspect of our working definition of culture), we make a commitment to describing it as a *meaningful* thing. We commit ourselves to *meaning analysis* as our preferred type of research practice, and we subscribe to a particular type of *description*. As Geertz (1973) puts it: "Culture is not a power, something to which social events, behaviors, institutions, or processes can be causally attributed; it is a context, something within which they can be intelligibly . . . described" (p. 14).

It is important to note, however, that culture involves more than meaning in the representational or cognitive sense. Rather,

> meanings in general, and cultural meaning systems in particular, do at least four different things. Meanings represent the world, create cultural entities, direct one to do certain things, and evoke certain feelings. These four functions of meaning—the *representational*, the *constructive*, the *directive*, and the *evocative*—are differently elaborated in particular cultural meaning systems but are always present to some degree in any system. . . .
>
> . . . Analytically, cultural meaning systems can be treated as a very large diversified pool of knowledge, or partially shared clusters of norms, or as intersubjectively shared, symbolically created realities. (D'Andrade, 1984, pp. 96, 116)

PRECURSORS TO SYMBOLIC APPROACHES TO CULTURE AND COMMUNICATION

Keeping our definition of culture in the back of our minds for a moment, let us now take a brief look at the history of Western intellectuals' interest in other cultures. The first descriptions of other people's interpersonal behaviors and customs can be found in the travelogues of Herodotus (1949) and Xenophon (1962) and in Tacitus's "ethnography" *Germania* (1970). These reports, along with later ones by European explorers (e.g., Columbus, 1492-1493/1966; for an overview, see Hewes, 1974), astonish the reader not only because of their detailed accounts of first encounters and different customs, but also because they report the facility with which the explorers managed to communicate with the "Indians." It was gesture that served as lingua franca for intercultural exchange. And when the explorers, motivated by the spirit of enlightenment that had taken hold of their own societies, began to make more systematic attempts to record native cultures, communication by gesture even enabled them to engage in detailed ethnographic and linguistic fieldwork (Forster, 1777). At this time, the study of distant cultures was regarded as an important avenue toward an understanding of humanity's essence. Again and again in these travelogues we find the writers wondering whether the emotional lives of the others resemble their own, whether there is a psychic unity to humankind. Rousseau (1755/1967), "the founder of the sciences of man" (Lévi-Strauss, 1976), suggested: "When one wants to study men, one must look around oneself; but to study man, one must first learn to look into the distance; one must first see differences in order to discover characteristics" (chap. 8).

In the 18th century, an evolutionary account of the diversity of cultures began to emerge. Montesquieu (1901) had introduced a three-stage model of the development of human communities from "primitive" to "savage" to "civilized." This model survived even into the beginnings of modern anthropology (Mallery, 1880/1978; Tylor, 1856), until it was finally replaced by cultural relativism (which made any reference to degrees of development or civilization obsolete). The idea of evolution was thus already popular before Darwin began his studies. In particular, Locke (1690/1959) and Condillac (1746) conceived of human knowledge as a product of the evolution of *material* sign systems (languages) that register, store, and enable the manipulation of "information"—that is, thought (see also Aarsleff, 1974; Lane, 1976). Sign systems, according to Condillac, evolve in the communication among groups of people; he recognized the nexus of communication, cognition, and language. However, while he and some other philosophers during the Enlightenment were keenly aware of the relationship between knowledge and language, *communication* did not become a topic of scientific attention until much later, approximately the 1930s and 1940s. One reason for this is that, whereas a technology for recording spoken language (alphabetic writing) had existed for more than 2,000 years, technologies for recording visual communication (photography and cinematography) emerged only in the 19th and 20th centuries (Edwards, 1992). The existence of such technologies is arguably a precondition for the appearance of organized and systematic scientific inquiry.

However, in the aftermath of the "romantic" period in the European arts and literature, the "soft," subjective domains of human life—interpersonal relations, communication, the emotions—became the dominating theme of a flourishing body of literature, particularly in France, for example, in the works of Balzac, Flaubert, and later Proust. For most of the 19th century, there existed thus a division of labor between the increasingly empirical, observational sciences of man and the increasingly introspective literary accounts of human experience. When Freud (1949) finally suspended this division and made subjective, psychic experience the subject of rigorous analysis, this was perceived as a revolution. Freud's discoveries would eventually lead to an altogether new way of thinking about human relationships. The patterns of relationships and interactions in which adult persons engage are seen as "transferences" from primary childhood relationships and interaction patterns. The transference is mediated by our complex psychic organization, in particular its unconscious part, the "id," and the "primary processes" governing it.

Of great interest to the student of communication is the symbol theory inherent in Freud's view of the unconscious. In his analyses of symbolic productions such as dreams and jokes, Freud (1955, 1960) not only discovered universal processes of symbolization, such as displacement and condensation, but described their role in psychic organization and the structuring of experience (Jones, 1913). The human psyche's symbolic organization makes it a cultural phenomenon that is structured not unlike a language (Lacan, 1977). In contrast to some contemporary "symbols and meanings" approaches to culture, Freud never lost sight of the *repressive* character of all culture: There will always be an essential and insurmountable difference between the desires of the human psyche and the social forms of human action and relationship that culture dictates or allows. Human beings do not acquire culture without experiencing pain and frustration (Freud, 1958; for a critique, see Marcuse, 1955).

The other great breakthrough of the 19th century—aside from Freud's discovery of the unconscious—was of course Darwin's (1859/ 1964) discovery of the evolution of the species. With this discovery, the stage was set for the understanding of the *continuities* between human structures and abilities and their precursors on the evolutionary ladder. In this regard, Darwin's (1872/1955) own study of the evolution of *facial expression* is of paradigmatic importance. Darwin demonstrated how a genuinely *communicative* type of behavior—along with the anatomical and physiological structures that enable it—has developed from more fundamental, purely instrumental behaviors and structures. The instrumental substructure explains the particular shape of the later, specialized communicative adaptation: The shape of a threat display is derived from direct, noncommunicative attack behavior. There is thus a continuity between forms of interaction that are developed prior to the emergence of specialized communicative displays and the shapes that these displays eventually take. Communication behavior reflects its precommunicative origins. Darwin's study, in many ways still uncontested (see Ekman, 1973; Izard, 1971), was a very powerful demonstration that the human organism has evolved to its present shape partly in response to the needs to communicate and to maintain viable social groups (see also Ingold, 1986; Smith, 1977). *Culture,* however, was rather a nuisance to Darwin. In his eyes, it only obscured the true nature of man, and this he saw as its wicked purpose: to conceal our true emotions from others. Thus, although Darwin took great care to obtain information on facial displays from as many as 20 different cultures—he corresponded with missionaries and travelers, and drew from their reports—in his interpretation of these data he aimed exclusively at laying bare the natural order of things underneath the veil of normative cultural rules. In contemporary adaptations of Darwin's theory, however, his thesis of the continuity between human and earlier life forms has been extended so that culture and symbol systems as well the cognitive architecture they produce can be seen as products of the same evolutionary dynamics

that produced the human body (Donald, 1991; Maturana & Varela, 1987/1992).

Of particular interest in this regard is the contemporary debate about language origins (see, e.g., Hurford, Studdert-Kennedy, & Knight, 1998), which centers in part on the question of the social matrix of the hominid groups in which language evolved: It is astonishing that language evolved at all, given the ease with which one can lie with it and given also the "Machiavellian" nature of primate intelligence (Byrne & Whitten, 1988), the propensity of our predecessors for deception. Language would have been ill adapted to hominid society if there had not been a context of trustful social relationships within which linguistic messages could be believed and their social potential could unfold and evolve. Some researchers therefore assume that language must first have emerged within groups of females, who, because of their asynchronous reproductive cycles, have a *collective* interest in male protection (Power, 1998). One account, known as the "grooming and gossip" hypothesis, assumes that language first evolved as an exchange of social information among females ("gossip") while at the same time serving as a mechanism for "vocal grooming at a distance" (see Dunbar, 1998; Knight, 1998), a mechanism that enabled the formation and maintenance of larger hominid groups.

The period from the late 19th century to the early 20th century was an era of the emergence of the empirical sciences—and their often arbitrary disciplinary boundaries. In Germany, Wundt established psychology as an experimental science by postulating the parallel organization of physiological and psychological processes. In France, Durkheim secured a place for sociology by proposing that there is a realm of *social facts* that cannot be reduced to any other order of phenomena. Saussure (1964) used similar arguments to claim the independent status of *langue*—the system of rules and contrasts underlying actual speech performance—and thus linguistics. And in

England, and later in the United States, Tylor, Frazer, Malinowski, and Boas created two separate versions of the "science of customs" (Benedict, 1934), that is, (social and cultural) anthropology. All of these disciplinary frameworks contributed to our present understanding of communication, but their separation made it—and continues to make it—difficult to integrate this knowledge into a unified science. Today, the divisions separating individual psychological approaches in the tradition of Wundt, sociological approaches in the tradition of Durkheim, and symbol-theoretic approaches in the tradition of linguistics and cultural anthropology can be felt as clearly as ever.

Wilhelm Wundt's *Völkerpsychologie* (1911/1975) was a monumental attempt to explain language, myth, and customs (i.e., culture) by reference to what Wundt considered universal psychological laws of affect and expression. But despite Wundt's fame during his lifetime (his Institute of Experimental Psychology in Leipzig, the first in the world, attracted such luminaries as the anthropologist Malinowski and the sociologist G. H. Mead), today his work is largely forgotten. Despite the psychological bias of much work on communication and culture, it is all too obvious that cultural organization cannot be explained solely in terms of psychic organization. After Wundt, psychologists other than those of psychoanalytic orientation have generally refrained from any *cultural* analysis of psychic phenomena; the emergence of "cultural psychology" is a recent development (Stigler, Shweder, & Herdt, 1990).

At the same time in France, Émile Durkheim developed an explanatory framework of interpersonal relations and communications as *social facts,* to be described in macrosocial categories of status, class, power, and so on. From a Durkheimian perspective, patterns of communication appear as phenomena that are shaped by, and derive their meaning from, the particular places they inhabit within the *totality* of social phenomena (Durkheim, 1895/1982). Action—particularly communicative action—is intelligible only by virtue of its determination by shared norms. In Durkheim's framework, there is a direct link between a society's moral consensus and the single actions that ultimately make up that society's daily life. Action is a direct manifestation of a society's norms. In other words, there is no place in this framework for the individual actor who has internalized these norms and faces the constant need to reconcile them with his or her individual goals and motives. It was the American sociologist Talcott Parsons (1937; Parsons & Shils, 1951) who later bridged this gap by combining the Durkheimian view of social macrostructure with a "model of the actor." Durkheim's and Parsons's normative sociology became the dominating paradigm for sociologists in the 20th century, until it was subjected to a penetrating methodological critique by ethnomethodologists who argued that reference to normative rules is always a situated, interpretive, and open-ended process, not a mindless operation that automatically produces socially accepted behavior (Cicourel, 1964; Garfinkel, 1967; see also Heritage, 1984). Actors appeal to normative rules to *demonstrate* the rationality and rule-guided character of their everyday actions. Norms should therefore be studied as *cognitive* phenomena, that is, as components of members' social knowledge and practical sociological reasoning.

Durkheim also made important contributions to ethnology (it is a general characteristic of the "French school" that sociology and ethnology are not fully separated; see Bourdieu, 1977). Of great interest to students of culture and communication, although currently not widely read, is the work of Durkheim's nephew Marcel Mauss (e.g., Durkheim & Mauss, 1903/1963). Mauss (1950/1966, 1935/1973, 1938/1979) subjected information provided by a broad range of ethnographic literature, especially by American cultural anthropologists (see below), to a comparative analysis of elementary social forms: self-hood and personhood, gift exchange, and "techniques of the body." His work demonstrates how total and pervasive the influence of culture and society on human behavior is:

> I think I can . . . recognize a girl who has been raised in a convent. In general she will walk with her fists closed. And I can still remember my third-form teacher shouting at me: 'Idiot! why do you walk around the whole time with your hands flapping wide open?' Thus there exists education in walking. (Mauss, 1935/1973, p. 72)

Every bit of human behavior is subject to normative social control and thus becomes an element in a *code*: It is this normative structuration that gives human behavior its communicative power.

Interpersonal relations, conceived as social forms, figure prominently in the work of Durkheim's German contemporary Georg Simmel. To Simmel (1950), society was "merely the name for a number of individuals connected by interaction" (p. 10); accordingly, "the description of the forms of interaction is the science of society in its strictest and most essential sense" (pp. 20-21). In some of Simmel's large, scattered, complex, and little-known oeuvre (as a Jew in Germany, Simmel had considerable difficulty gaining professional recognition), he addresses phenomena at the boundary of individual and society—"skin phenomena," one might say—in which individual and social determinations intersect, for example, shame (a social emotion, typically felt in public) and secrecy (a form of individuation, the withholding of knowledge from "the public domain"). Simmel published a large number of studies of just the kinds of entities contemporary ethnographers of communication and practitioners of "cultural studies" are fond of: meals, arguing, jewelry, gratitude, letters, female culture, and the "sociology of the senses" (Simmel, 1924). Some of his articles appeared in the *American Journal*

of Sociology (Simmel, 1902, 1903-1904, 1905-1906).

The last intellectual movement originating around the end of the 19th century that should be mentioned here before we turn to the "symbols and meanings" approaches is *social anthropology* (Stocking, 1968, 1987). (Conventional wisdom labels British anthropology "social" and American anthropology "cultural." The terminology is not without merit, because it reflects the intellectual roots of the British school in Durkheimian and Marxian sociology, where ideational phenomena are considered "superstructure": reflections of "material," economic, and power relations and the roots of cultural anthropology in 18th- and 19th-century philosophical idealism. See Kant, 1798/1977; von Humboldt, 1836/1988.) Social anthropology is "sociological" in that it interprets cultural phenomena as social forms cum symbolic representations. Elementary relationships in a society (e.g., kin relations) constitute social forms that are defined by mutual rights and obligations, and they are symbolically represented in rituals, forms of address, kinship terms, and so on. Representations, however, are not simple reflections of the social world; they are themselves subject to social determinations. For example, how rigidly an individual must follow the rules of address for kin is a function of the degree of "ritualism" in a society at a given point in time—which is itself a sociological state of affairs (Douglas, 1970; Evans-Pritchard, 1964).

Malinowski's (1922, 1935/1965) classic ethnographies, as well as his statement of functionalism in anthropology (Malinowski, 1944), are among the better-known examples of early work in social anthropology. An important contribution to the study of communication is Radcliffe-Brown's (1952/1965) analysis of the *joking relationship,* in which he suggests that in many relationships that involve contradictory social obligations (e.g., social proximity and avoidance, as in the relationship between son-in-law and mother-in-law), humor and joking serve as institutionalized conflict resolution mechanisms; they allow the concurrent enactment of ambivalent sentiments. Among more recent contributions to social anthropology, Leach (1976) and Douglas (1970) have further explored the relationships between "economic transactions and acts of communication" and the social structural shaping of symbolic universes.

CULTURE, LANGUAGE, AND RELATIVITY

Whereas there is much affinity between British social anthropology and the "French school," American cultural and linguistic anthropology has roots in the German idealist and romantic philosophies of the 18th and 19th centuries (e.g., Herder, 1772/1966; Kant, 1798/1977; von Humboldt, 1836/1988). Franz Boaz, the person who is generally considered to be the founder of these disciplines in the United States, and the linguist Edward Sapir were German-born Jews who brought this tradition with them when they immigrated to America. Boas and Sapir developed Wilhelm von Humboldt's ideas into an empirical science and transformed the linguistic study of "mentality" into an analysis of "culture." What is common to both versions of the program is the analysis of categories of grammar as categories of experience.

Boas undertook his first linguistic "fieldwork" experience by studying the language of three Bella Coola Indians who were exhibited in Berlin during the 1886 World's Fair. Motivated by this initial work, he subsequently traveled to the Pacific Northwest and eventually launched one of the major projects of linguistic research, the *Handbook of American Indian Languages* (see Boas, 1911/1966a). This project secured invaluable linguistic and ethnological information about Native Americans at a time when some speakers of most of the languages were still alive. At the same time, these languages proved to be so fundamentally different from the Indo-European languages that the 19th-century linguists in Germany had so successfully reconstructed that the conventional grammatical categories that were previously used in linguistic description—most of which had been taken from Latin grammars—turned out to be of little use in organizing the American materials. For hundreds of years, missionaries had confidently misrepresented "exotic" languages in these terms, but now it became clear that new categories were needed to describe languages such as Kwakiutl and Bella Coola. Moreover, the categories that would properly organize the data would first have to be *discovered* in the process of analysis. Not even concepts as fundamental and seemingly universal as "word" and "sentence" could be taken for granted: There are languages in North America (e.g., Apache and Inuit) that can express entire propositions in single, compound words. Or take the noun category *case* (nominative, accusative, and so on): Some languages have case sets other than those found in Latin (e.g., ergative, absolutive), others have no nominal case marking at all (e.g., English). Similarly, there are languages without the category *gender* and others with different gender sets (animate/inanimate, rather than masculine/feminine, or animate moving, animate at rest, inanimate long, inanimate round, inanimate high, and inanimate collective, as is the case in Sioux). It is important to note that languages differ not only in what they *allow* one to say (readily), but in what they *require* one to say, that is, in the distinctions that are *obligatory* in the language. Finally these categories are not just empty forms but categories of *experience*—that is, *meanings*. "Languages differ not only in the character of their constituent phonetic elements and sound-clusters, but also in the groups of ideas that find expression in fixed phonetic groups" (Boas, 1911/1966a, p. 20; see also Malinowski, 1923).

The study of "exotic" languages is thus the single most important paradigm for the study of "other cultures." It provides us with a method for understanding different categories of experience without imposing our own categories in the process of description. Linguistic analysis thus shows one way out of ethnocentrism; it enables the researcher to study "other mentalities" using methodical procedures with agreed-upon standards of adequacy and validity. The promise is that, by organizing our linguistic data properly so that they can "speak for themselves," we will be enabled to grasp the worldviews of others and thus come to understand, if only to a limited extent, the minds of others. The condition is that we relinquish our own preconceived cultural categories, such as "noun/verb," "masculine/feminine," and even "we/they." In other words, understanding other cultures, in this view, is not at all a mystical experience, nor does it have much to do with empathy. It means being able to explicate conceptual distinctions and categories of experience that are encoded in a language.

Although this view of "linguistic relativity" was already implicit in Boas's approach to culture, it was fully articulated not by Boas but by Sapir (1921) and Benjamin Lee Whorf (1956). Sapir (1921) observes:

> The relation between language and experience is often misunderstood. Language is not merely a more or less systematic inventory of the various items of experience which seem relevant to the individual, . . . , but is also a self-contained, creative symbolic organization, which not only refers to experience largely acquired without its help but actually defines experience for us. (p. 221)

The "Sapir-Whorf hypothesis" has been and continues to be of considerable influence in linguistics and linguistic anthropology (for recent contributions, see Gumperz & Levinson, 1996; Lucy, 1992a, 1992b; Silverstein, 1976; for overviews, see Hill & Mannheim, 1992;

Rosch, 1987). Much of the most recent research has considered levels of language structure other than the grammatical categories Whorf was interested in, and context—that is, cultural procedures for signaling and assessing the contextual frames within which linguistic messages are to be interpreted—has been given central consideration (Gumperz, 1996; Hanks, 1996a; Haviland, 1996). Research by a growing number of scholars who refer to their work as "prototype theory" (see Taylor, 1989) or "cognitive linguistics" (Langacker, 1987; Rudzka-Ostyn, 1988) shows that relativism can live in a happy marriage with universalism: Although linguistic structures at all levels (vocabulary, syntax, and so on) show a great deal of variation, they also reveal a considerable amount of cross-linguistic similarity, in particular in central or basic constructions. For example, research on color terms has shown that these must have evolved according to a universal sequence: The first distinction is black/white (or dark/light), then red is added, then blue/green, and so on (Berlin & Kay, 1969).

In all languages, the most basic sentence pattern centers on an animate subject—typically human—that acts upon an inanimate object; active sentences are universally less complex than passive ones; animate nouns are more easily made the heads of relative sentences than inanimate ones; and so on (Comrie, 1981). These linguistic facts indicate that there are indeed universal, basic human experiences—bodily experiences such as gravity, erect posture, movement, agency, manipulation, as well as sensory perception—and that these figure prominently in language structure (Johnson, 1987; Lakoff, 1987). Roughly, the type of event that is most easily encoded in any language is a human event, one brought about and experienced *subjectively* by a human being. Cultural diversity is always an elaboration of these universal foundations. This is in line with what appears to be the historical record, namely, that humanity and its various cultures developed during thousands and thousands of years of migration away from a common birthplace in Africa.

Is linguistic relativity of interest to students of culture and interpersonal communication? Yes, in several respects. First of all, of course, most communication involves language, and whenever that is the case cultural comparison raises the issue of *translation* across language systems. One-to-one translations of terms will not do, because we have to take into account the "values" that terms have within the "systems" of particular languages. For example, a simple kinship term such as *brother* can have different values, such as when members of the same age grade (or initiation cohort) are also considered brothers. The framework of analysis that Boas established allows us to account for these differences systematically. Second, interpersonal communication and relations are themselves *conceptualized* in different ways in different cultures, and the concepts involved are in need of the same kind of unbiased cultural explication. Whenever human conduct is subjected to interpretive analysis, linguistic relativity becomes an issue.

But Boas's work far transcended the study of culture as language. Another program of research that he helped initiate has been called "culture and personality." It was actually Sapir (1934/1991a, 1927/1991b) who first suggested that language should be seen as only one among various cultural communication systems; he also suggested that "personality" should be an object of cultural analysis.

Before we turn to the "culture and personality" school, we must ascertain the *nature* of Boas's contribution. The most important aspect of his work is the demonstration that anything that can properly be called "cultural" is *learned,* and not hereditary (Boas, 1940). Thus there is no *genetic* basis to differences in human traits, customs, or "mentalities"; even physical traits can in part be environmentally induced (Boas, 1912). The only important process involved in the survival of cultures is

therefore *transmission;* thus interactions between the generations—the "knowing" and the "novices"—are of particular interest. Culture is dependent on communication; only what can be communicated has a chance to survive in the realm of culture (see D'Andrade, 1981). There is no merit at all to the notion of "racial character" or to the claim, propagated especially by Nazi "anthropologists," that "racial descent is the determining cause for the character of a people" (Boas, 1932). Much of Boas's scientific energy was spent on clarifying this. The scientific study of culture thus emerged from the intellectual fight against the racial ideology of the Nazis and of the "eugenics" movement in the United States. What Boas could neither anticipate nor prevent was that, over time, the term *culture* would be put to ideological uses not unlike those of *race.* "Ethnic cleansing" is a machinery for cultural purification. Boas himself was very aware that there is no more cultural "purity" than there is "purity" of race. In 1928 he wrote, "We should remember that people of pure descent or of a pure racial type are not found in any part of Europe" (p. 85). Every human being alive is a "racial" and cultural hybrid.

CULTURE AND PERSONALITY

The study of "culture and personality," of the acquisition of "national character" by individual members of societies, was initiated by a small circle of intimately related anthropologists with the energetic Margaret Mead at its center and including Sapir, Ruth Benedict, Reo Fortune, and Gregory Bateson (see also Kluckhohn & Murray, 1948). I describe this school of thought in this section by reviewing three representative studies: Benedict's extremely popular book *Patterns of Culture* (1934) and two far less popular, but nevertheless highly influential, studies by Bateson, *Naven* (1958) and the "photographic analysis" *Balinese Character,* which he produced with Mead (1942). In all of these works, the

authors—and the culture and personality
school as a whole—sought to analyze cultures
as *integrated wholes* that manifest themselves
equally in symbols, customs, and patterns of
thought, feeling, and behavior.

Benedict (1934) uses the term *configuration,* a term she adopted from Gestalt psychology, to refer to patterns of cultural integration.
Human communities, she suggests, select their
cultural institutions from a "great arc" of
possibilities (p. 24). It is the particular configuration of choices from this common matrix
that makes for the "pattern" of a culture.
A "pattern of culture" is thus analogous to the
sound pattern of a language—its selection
from among possible human sounds and
sound sequences that makes up its phonological structure. Patterning is needed in both
cases to bring about *intelligibility.*

> A culture that capitalized even a considerable
> proportion of these [possibilities] would be as
> unintelligible as a language that used all the
> clicks, all the glottal stops, all the labials, dentals, sibilants, and gutturals from voiceless to
> voiced and from oral to nasal. Its identity as
> a culture depends upon the selection of some
> segments of this arc. (Benedict, 1934, p. 24)

But, of course, the "great arc" of possibilities contains much more than possible language sounds. It embraces all the possible
human ways of dealing with life's circumstances and crises, such as coming of age,
marriage, child rearing, and death; all possible
ways of dealing with emotion, frustration, and
sexual desire; all possible cultural definitions
of "normality" and deviance (p. 258); all cultural institutions, such as initiation, marriage,
kinship, and government; and, finally, all possible ways of conducting oneself and interacting with others. The selections that a culture
makes from these sets form consistent clusters;
only certain selections "go together":

> Cultures . . . are more than the sum of their
> parts. . . . A culture, like an individual, is a
> more or less consistent pattern of thought

and action. . . . This integration of cultures is
not in the least mystical. It is the same process
by which a style in art comes into being and
exists. (pp. 46-47)

Benedict's comparison with style in art points
to one of the sources of her work, the analysis
of *Weltanschauungen* by the philosopher
Wilhelm Dilthey (1977), the founder of
"hermeneutics." Dilthey's studies of worldviews in both philosophical and everyday
thinking was framed as cultural history and
modeled after art history.

Geertz (1988) has pointed out that to
Benedict, "culture" really means "personality
writ large." The best way to characterize a
cultural configuration, therefore, is to describe
the prevailing personality type, the prevailing
way for the culture's members of carrying
themselves, of feeling, and of relating to one
another. Benedict drew upon a simple two-way typology that Nietzsche (1927) had
devised in his study of the ancient Greeks to
mark the poles of the arc of possible cultural
personality types: the "Appolonian" versus
the "Dionysian."

The Appolonian is a quintessential middle-of-the-roader, bound by tradition, striving for
measure and balance, distrustful of individualism and of any form of ecstatic experience.
The Dionysian seeks to find the value of
existence in experiences that *transcend* the
mundane order of things—trance, ecstasy,
visionary experiences, and so on. Most cultures fall somewhere between these poles,
taking elements from both.

In *Patterns of Culture,* Benedict (1934)
reinterprets three ethnographic accounts in
light of this typology: Bunzel's (1932/1992)
study of the Zuñi, a Pueblo people of the
American Southwest; Fortune's (1932)
description of the Dobu islanders off the
southern coast of New Guinea; and Boas's
(1966b) work on the Kwakiutl of the Pacific
Northwest. I will briefly review her account of
the first two groups to flesh out her view of
cultural "configurations." The measured Zuñi

of the American Southwest are an Appolonian people in the largely Dionysian world that was native North America. Whereas the Dionysian Dakota, for example, may show their grief over the death of a child by "coming naked into the camp, wailing" (Benedict, 1934, p. 112), the Zuñi

> do not . . . convert mourning for a near relative into an ambitious display or a terror situation. They treat it as loss, and as important loss. But they provide detailed techniques for getting past it as quickly and with as little violence as possible. The emphasis is upon making the mourner forget. (p. 109)

Among the Zuñi, the cultural emphasis, thus, is upon *containing* the emotions so that the individual can continue to participate in the moderate, unemotional ways of the community. The Zuñi attribute intrinsic value to these communal practices; in their "Hellenic" view (p. 79), communal life per se is civilizing. Among the Zuñi, thus, the "internal" life of the person is subsumed to the survival needs of the community. The "folk psychology" of the people and the values they place upon felt emotions and their external expression is centered on the requirements of harmonious social life; a premium is placed on social accommodation.

On the island of Dobu, the relationship between individual and society is conceptualized almost in opposite terms, and this has much to do with the structure of the society. Whereas Zuñi society is highly integrated, Dobu society is fragmented, and social life is potentially explosive. Accordingly, folk psychology and philosophy place the individual— that is, one's own needs—at the center of attention, and others are primarily seen as potential dangers to one's well-being. The Dobu islanders count as the savages in the otherwise Appolonian archipelago off southern New Guinea where they live: "They are lawless and treacherous. . . . The social forms which obtain in Dobu put a premium upon ill-will and treachery and make of them the recognized virtues of their society" (p. 131).

The hostile tendencies in Dobuan communicative and community life are maximized by bizarre lineage and residence patterns. The Dobu are matrilineal; the *susu* (mother's milk), the matrilineal group, is the most stable social unit, and most of Dobu social life takes place inside its boundaries. But the groups are so small that exogamy is required; one's spouse is therefore always from a hostile group. The person who marries into the unit is met with all the hostility that an intruder should expect. He or she is subjected to constant humiliation. But this ordeal befalls both spouses in alternating years, for this is how the Dobuans, curiously, resolve the problem of locality and lineage: the couple lives in her village in one year, in his the next. Add to this the fact that adultery is "a favourite pastime" (p. 138), and one has all the ingredients for a regime of terror and suspicion even in the most intimate of human relationships. "The person with whom one shares the bed is the person to charge with one's fatal illness" (p. 160). The Dobuans live in a world of constant terror, fear, and insecurity.

> Behind a show of friendship, behind the evidences of co-operation, in every field of life, the Dobuan believes that he has only treachery to expect. Everyone else's best endeavours . . . are directed toward bringing his own plans to confusion and ruin. (p. 171)

For Dobuans, morality is a kind of zero-sum game: "Any man's gain is another's loss" (p. 146). And the formula equivalent to our saying "thank you" when we receive a gift is, "If you now poison me, how should I repay you?" (p. 166).

Lineage and residence rules thus create a context that produces and admits only certain types of emotions; every experience is mediated by a pervasive feeling of fear and paranoia. The configuration necessitates internal and external safeguards to enable social interaction at all: a world of maneuvering, strong-arming, and deceit, where "sincerity" and "authenticity" would be impossible moral standards.

The comparison of Zuñi and Dobu societies shows the interdependence of social structure and organization on the one hand and prevailing personality type on the other. The two are mediated by forms of interaction that are, in any society, shaped by societal norms and that have pervasive influence on individual psychology. However, all of these forms are possibilities that constitute human nature; each culture represents a selection.

> Dionysian behaviour is stressed in the institutions of certain cultures because it is a permanent possibility in individual psychology, but it is stressed in certain cultures and not in others because of historical events that have in one place fostered its development and in others have ruled it out. (p. 233)

Cultural patterns are local phenomena. The Zuñi are local exceptions from the Dionysian principles that otherwise characterize aboriginal North America, and the Dobuans are savages among their neighbors. There is, in other words, no connection between culture and place (or climate), or between culture and genetic relationships between peoples. Cultural patterns develop and change via *diffusion*.

For Benedict, analyzing the cultural patterns of other societies was also a way of critically reflecting upon the patterns of her own. Anthropology, to her, is *cultural critique* (Marcus & Fischer, 1986). Geertz (1988) has said about her work that "the culturally at hand is made odd and arbitrary, the culturally distant, logical and straightforward. Our own forms of life become strange customs of a strange people" (p. 106). Benedict (1934) herself describes the critical intentions of her work in these words:

> There is no royal road to Utopia. There is, however, one difficult exercise to which we may accustom ourselves as we become

increasingly culture-conscious. We may train ourselves to pass judgment upon the dominant traits of our own civilization. (p. 249)

THE CONCEPT OF "ETHOS"

In his book *Naven*, Bateson (1958) suggests a conceptual subdivision of Benedict's concept of "configuration." He distinguishes the *eidos* from the *ethos* of a culture: "The eidos of a culture is an expression of the standardised cognitive aspects of the individuals, while the ethos is the corresponding expression of their standardized affective aspects" (p. 33). But he also points out that these are only "alternative ways of arranging the data" (p. 296). Bateson has always been very conscious of the fact that explanations of the data are first of all *abstractions*. To say that a behavior is "culturally motivated" means to subject it to a *class* of descriptions; it is not a reference to a cause. "If 'ethos', 'social structure', 'economics', etc. are words in that language which describes how scientists arrange data, then these words cannot be used to 'explain' phenomena" (p. 281).

In their study of the Iatmul in New Guinea, Bateson and Mead (1942) addressed their *ethos,* the ways "in which [their] emotional life . . . is organized in culturally standardized forms" (p. xi). *Organization,* however, in Bateson's view, refers to a *process;* the term is more than just another name for "structure." It means the *process* of shaping personality in contexts of interaction. Among Bateson's many contributions to the study of culture, communication, and personality, his conceptualizations of phenomena in processual terms are perhaps the most important. In *Naven* he interprets a ritual (*Naven* is its name) in terms of its adaptive functions within the ongoing structuration of Iatmul society. The ritual is based upon transvestism. Men and women exchange not only clothes, but also roles. The function of the ritual, thus, is that of a self-corrective mechanism that counteracts "schismogenetic" forces operating within Iatmul society and interaction. The Iatmul have a divided ethos: Men strive to present themselves in spectacular acts of performance; women, in contrast, are resigned to an ethos of admiration and spectatorship. The two patterns of behavior, thus, stand in complementary relation to one another. And each interaction between men and women that follows this pattern further reinforces the differences and thus narrows the range of possibilities of action for both. Bateson (1958) calls this process of cumulative interaction *complementary schismogenesis*. Schismogenesis is

> a process of differentiation in the norms of individual behavior resulting from cumulative interaction between individuals. . . .
>
> . . . Many systems of relationship, either between individuals or groups of individuals, contain a tendency towards progressive change. . . . A must necessarily become more and more assertive, while B will become more and more submissive. . . . Progressive changes of this sort we may describe as *complementary* schismogenesis. (pp. 175-176)

The more Iatmul men interact with Iatmul women, the more exaggerated and spectacular their actions become and the more passive and admiring the behavior of the women. However, wherever such schismogenetic, cumulative interactions become habitual and binding, personality distortions result.

> The distortion is a progressive specialization in certain directions and results in a corresponding under-development of other sides of the personality. Thus the members of each group see the stunted parts of their own affective life fully developed—indeed overdeveloped—in the members of the other group. It is in such situations that mutual envy arises. (p. 188)

The very structure of Iatmul interaction, then, bears the seed of destruction of Iatmul society. The *Naven* ceremony, with its exchange of roles and identities, suspends and counteracts this schismogenetic process; it provides both groups with contrasting experiences, in effect allowing both to "see" themselves from within the identity of the other—and thus to see the "latent," unexpressed, complementary part of the self.

Bateson presents in *Naven* the fundamentals of a theory of character formation. Personality is formed by the cumulative patterning of interaction, which is itself an adaptation to the overarching needs of group integration.

> The individual in a symmetrical relationship with another will tend, perhaps unconsciously, to form the habit of acting as if he expected symmetry in further encounters with all other individuals. The ground is thus laid for progressive change. As a given individual learns patterns of symmetrical behavior he not only comes to expect this type of behavior in others, but also acts in such a way that others will experience those contexts in which they in turn will learn symmetrical behavior. . . . They will act back upon the initial individual to produce further change in him in the same direction. (p. 286)

"Personality" is thus a sedimentation of the patterning of interactional contexts. It is one manifestation of a larger system that relevantly includes all the other "personalities" with whom someone regularly interacts, especially the other members of his or her primary group or family. Bateson later applied this framework of analysis, which he first developed in the study of the *Naven* ritual, to the study of personality disorders, in particular schizophrenia, which he interpreted as an individual's adaptation to persistent, inescapable paradoxes in his or her primary relationships (Bateson, 1972).

The viability and value of Bateson's "formal" method of analyzing communication and culture had already become apparent in *Balinese Character* (Bateson & Mead, 1942). In this study, Bateson and Mead used photographs as their main body of data. This was a completely innovative way of gathering and analyzing data on human interaction and cultural life,

> a new method of stating the intangible relationships among different types of culturally standardized behavior by placing side by side mutually relevant photographs. Pieces of behavior—a trance dancer being carried in procession, a man looking up at an aeroplane, a servant greeting his master in a play, the painting of a dream—may all be relevant to a single discussion: the same emotional thread may run through them. (p. xii)

The resulting account of Balinese culture is the product of *visual abstraction*. By selecting 700 from among 25,000 photographs, and by juxtaposing photographs taken in different contexts and representing different domains of social life, as well as simply by focusing on the often neglected *visual* aspects of human behavior, Bateson and Mead show how "the Balinese—[through] the way in which they, as living persons, moving, standing, eating, sleeping, dancing, and going into trance, embody that abstraction which (after we have abstracted it) we technically call culture" (p. xii).

Among the features of the Balinese ethos that are revealed by the photographs (and their arrangement) are the preference for crowds and the resulting limited possibilities for withdrawal and individuation. The Balinese prefer being in crowds to being alone, but while they are in a crowd, they might withdraw. They fall into a trancelike state of "awayness." The "social organization of attention" (Chance & Larsen, 1976) in Balinese society explains an important feature of mother-child interaction, which in turn has important adaptive functions for the survival of Balinese culture. Unlike the Iatmul culture that Bateson had previously studied, Balinese culture is free of schismogenetic processes. In contrast to Iatmul culture, Balinese culture—behavior, music, feeling—is "anticlimactic." The Balinese *avoid* cumulative processes altogether. The patterning of mother-child interaction is the paradigmatic experience

in which the Balinese acquire this disposition. A characteristic sequence involves the mother's physical and emotional stimulation of her infant to the point that the child begins to become excited; at that moment, the mother withdraws her attention from the child, in effect invalidating the child's experience. Although children initially react with frustration and bewilderment to this pattern, they later internalize it and adapt to it via "unresponsiveness," that is, the avoidance of overly stimulating moments. This disposition, according to Bateson and Mead, is an essential foundation of Balinese society.

Balinese Character has suffered from the "logocentric" bias of Western science. It is only recently that visual research has begun to play a notable role in the study of communication and culture (Collier & Collier, 1986).

SYMBOLIC ANTHROPOLOGY

We will now make a big leap and review a very different approach to the study of culture and communication, the "symbolic anthropology" of Clifford Geertz (1973, 1984). Like his predecessors who took a "configurational" approach to anthropology, Geertz aims at accounts of cultures as integrated wholes. His approach concentrates on the *symbolic* aspects of culture. In contrast to advocates of other contemporary versions of the "symbols and meanings" approach to culture (e.g., cognitive anthropology), Geertz insists that "culture," "meaning," and "mind" (i.e., culture as "ideation") are *overt, public* phenomena. "Culture is public because meaning is," Geertz (1973, p. 12) states. "Thinking is a matter of trafficking in the symbolic forms available in one or another community. . . . The community is the shop where thoughts get constructed or deconstructed" (Geertz, 1983, p. 153). Meaning and intention are available to us in the symbols that the natives use: in the language they speak, the art they appreciate, the names they give one another. What we in effect do when we study conduct in its cultural context is to "sort out [its] structures of signification" (Geertz, 1973, p. 9) and to "freeze" its communicated sense into an enduring text.

> Ethnographic description . . . is interpretive; what it is interpretive of is the flow of social discourse; and the interpreting involved consists in trying to rescue the "said" of such discourse from its perishing occasions and fix it in perusable terms. . . . [Another] characteristic of such description [is] . . . it is microscopic. (Geertz, 1973, p. 20)

Studying human behavior in its cultural context is therefore in some respects like interpreting a poem.

> The anthropologist has to . . . tack between . . . two sorts of descriptions—between increasingly fine-comb observations (of how Javanese distinguish feelings, Balinese name children, Moroccans refer to acquaintances) and increasingly synoptic characterizations ("quietism", "dramatism", "contextualism")—in such a way that, held in the mind together, they present a credible, fleshed-out picture of a human form of life. . . . A conception which . . . brings it rather closer to what a critic does to illumine a poem than what an astronomer does to account for a star. (Geertz, 1983, p. 10)

One of the things we must know about in order to understand properly how the natives conduct their communicative dealings with one another is what, to them, is "personhood." What we call "the self" is not the same thing everywhere, and people's varying conceptions of what it means to be a human person affect the ways they relate to and communicate with one another. Interaction styles, in other words, have "folk-philosophical" and "folk-psychological" (Bruner, 1990) underpinnings. For example, the Javanese conception of the person is predicated upon two pairs of conceptual opposites: "inside" and "outside," and "refined" and "vulgar." In contrast to Western conceptions, which regard the

"outside" as a symptom or expression of processes going on "inside" the person, in Java the two realms are seen as independent. Each is subject to its own laws and rules, but neither is in any way indicative of what Westerners perceive as "individuality." "Subjective feeling . . . is considered to be . . . identical across all individuals," and "external actions, movements, postures, speech . . . [are also] conceived as in . . . essence invariant from one individual to the next" (Geertz, 1984, p. 127).

> The goal is to be *alus* (pure, refined, polished, civilized) in both the separated realms of the self. . . . Through meditation, the civilized man thins out his emotional life to a kind of constant hum; through etiquette, he both shields that life from external disruptions and regularizes his outer behavior in such a way that it appears to others as a predictable, undisturbing, elegant, and rather vacant set of choreographed motions and settled forms of speech. (p. 128)

What appears as "cultural style," then, is intimately interwoven with metapsychological and metasocial beliefs of a people. Cultural analysis must go beyond mere description and capture the underlying meaning systems that motivate the style.

Java stands in sharp contrast to the small island of Bali just off its eastern shore, which has retained and developed its flamboyant Hindu traditions. As Geertz (1984) puts it, "What is philosophy in Java is theater in Bali" (p. 128). But the Balinese symbolic universe, too, can be understood through a focus on the concept of the self (or its local equivalent). Among the symbolic phenomena pertaining to it are *naming practices,* which constitute "symbolic orders of person-definition" (p. 368). In Bali, these practices are depersonalizing: The Balinese bear birth-order names (they are called "the second," "the third," and so on), titles, and—once they become parents—technonyms (e.g., "the mother of . . ."). Nothing in their names leads the Balinese to believe that they are "someone special."

Rather, each time someone calls them by their names, they are reminded that they are "perishing" (p. 390), mere moments in the passage of time, "dramatis personae" in an eternal, spiritual play.

> There is in Bali a persistent and systematic attempt to stylize all aspects of personal expression to the point where anything idiosyncratic, anything characteristic of the individual . . . is muted in favor of his assigned place in the continuing . . . pageant that is Balinese life. (Geertz, 1984, p. 128)

This cultural configuration—"theater of status," as Geertz calls it—is complemented by appropriate kinds of emotion. The Balinese, according to Geertz, are haunted by stage fright, *lek,* the fear that they might botch their acts, that "an esthetic illusion will not be maintained that the actor will show through his part and the part thus dissolve into the actor. When this occurs . . . , the immediacy of the moment is felt with an excruciating intensity, and men become unwilling consociates locked in mutual embarrassment, as though they had inadvertently intruded upon one another's privacy. *Lek* is the fear of *faux pas"* (Geertz, 1973, p. 402).

Balinese social intercourse is "studied game and drama" (p. 400), but it is drama without climax and overt passion. Passion and violence (very much part of the Balinese psyche, as the 1965 massacres showed) are enacted in a segregated, symbolic domain, the cockfight. Like the transvestism of the *Naven* ceremonies, the Balinese cockfight "brings to imaginative realization a dimension of Balinese experience normally well-obscured from view" (p. 444), namely, the violent emotional underpinnings of the rigid status hierarchy. The function of the cockfight is to interpret this hidden dimension. "It provides a metasocial commentary. . . . It is a Balinese reading of Balinese experience, a story they tell themselves about themselves" (p. 448).

Ritual, ceremony, gambling, and cockfights are all constitutive of the overall symbolic configuration that is Balinese culture. The existence of the dramatic realm of "gambling" relinquishes the expressive requirements made upon other sectors of social intercourse. This is to say that, unless we analyze a culture's self-representation in all of its rituals and theatrical performances, we may be reading only half the story, for everyday life always represses certain aspects of social and psychic organization and obscures them from our view. These find their way to the surface in circumscribed domains of theatrical action.

THE PERSON BEHIND THE SMILE

Geertz presents us with a highly integrated account of Bali, and, not unlike Benedict, he makes Bali appear very exotic: Balinese selves, values, and forms of life are entirely different from ours. The Balinese not only live in a different culture, they are different *persons.* Our only chance to make sense of them is not through empathy, but through the explication of the structures of signification in their symbolic productions.

However, yet another account of Balinese culture challenges Geertz's "theatrical" image. The Norwegian anthropologist Unni Wikan (1990) has taken a very different approach. She has written a book about one Balinese woman, Suriati, in an attempt to explain one single public expression on Suriati's part: In line with what her culture demanded of her, Suriati smiled when she told Wikan that her fiancé had died the night before. How did Suriati manage? And what does this management of emotion and expression imply for the conduct of interpersonal communication in Bali?

Wikan's analysis exhibits a pervasive dilemma of Balinese interpersonal life. The dilemma is that, according to the assumptions of their own culture, the Balinese are inscrutable to one another. The culture puts a premium on keeping a "bright face." There are many reasons for this. One is that the Balinese have a strong fear of black magic, and they believe that anger causes it. Accordingly, they must constantly reassure one another that they are not angry—which they do by maintaining a bright face. But they also realize that in this fashion, they hide their feelings from one another. There is a paradoxical logic to the Balinese rules of emotional expression.

> Balinese are perpetually preoccupied to decipher each other's hidden hearts. So frightful are the consequences that anger or offense may work, it is necessary to be deeply preoccupied. So the "bright" face and composure, while pleasing to humans and gods, also, paradoxically, encapsulate people's fears. For the will to do magic is set in motion by feeling-thoughts that may never be expressed. This sobering realization, that the true feelings of others are inscrutably hidden behind their bright faces and polite demeanors, presents Balinese with an everyday existential problem. (Wikan, 1990, p. 43)

Such paradoxes of expression are not unique to Balinese society; they occur in all societies that conceptualize and organize expression as public performance.

The three accounts of Bali reviewed above all concentrate on similar situations and experiences in daily life: What does a Balinese experience in a crowd? What is involved in the attitude that Bateson and Mead call "away"? What is the meaning of smiling in public and private situations? What is the Balinese "inner experience" in this context, and what is the nature of the social forces that shape Balinese subjective experience? What, in sum, is the nature of the relationships among affect, social interaction, expression, and public life?

The titles of these three texts are evocative of the different ways in which their authors seek to capture the subtle interfaces of culture, affect, and interpersonal relations. *Balinese Character: A Photographic Analysis* represents an effort to capture personality as visible style, as an *aesthetic* phenomenon. The "character" emerges in the data during the process of visual records. This is an aesthetic analysis, based upon a notion of culture as style. The title of Geertz's study (which is part of his larger volume *The Interpretation of Cultures*) is "Person, Time, and Conduct," and thus refers to very general experiential categories, which are then synthesized into a comparative "philosophical" account of the entire cultural configuration. Geertz uncovers these categories through the analysis of symbolic systems: naming, calendars, rituals, and so on. The nexus that makes the culture what it is appears in each and every cultural domain. Wikan, finally, has given her book a title that includes a verb marked for ongoing action and thus indexes an ongoing practical concern: *Managing Turbulent Hearts: A Balinese Formula for Living*. Her book shows the individual member of the culture in the *process* of the ongoing struggle that is her life in the culture, a process in which she is asked to manage her emotions so that she can genuinely show a bright face. In Wikan's account, culture reveals its repressive nature as the flip side of the bright face. There is nothing glamorous about the theatricality of Balinese life as seen from Suriati's perspective. Nor is Suriati such a stranger to us; although we do not share her experiences, we can "picture" them and we can identify with the pain that she feels while she smiles and hides her sadness.

How distant and strange another culture, its members, and their actions appear to us is thus to a great extent dependent upon the perspective and the "unit of analysis" that we choose. *People* can easily be made to seem familiar to us; ceremonies, beliefs, and customs are easily made to appear strange. The title of Wikan's book also suggests that the human concern that it expresses is not restricted to a particular culture. It is a play on the title of Arlie Hochschild's book *The Managed*

Heart (1983), a study of American airline stewardesses. Airline companies sell the flight attendant's smile as a commodity, and the feelings of the flight attendant become commercialized: The company subsumes the flight attendant's emotions and makes them components of the process of service delivery. The boundary separating self and social world is driven deeper inside the person; the self is no longer "private." As a result, the regulative interpersonal concept of "authenticity" loses its meaning. The logic of interpersonal relations changes when this happens. In Hochschild's view, we lose our natural ability to feel and to learn "how we are doing" in interpersonal relations. The commercialization of feeling alters the selves that participate in interaction and destroys human sensibilities acquired in the process of evolution. The social contexts—Bali versus Delta Airlines—differ, but the processes involved and the alienation caused by them are similar: Human expression is modified and expropriated under the influence of repressive sociocultural demands.

To Hochschild and other critical researchers of human communication, the professionalization of communication involves a process of *alienation* of self and body, self and expression, and self and other. Others scholars, however, notably Elias (1978, 1983), have interpreted the historical development of normative rules of expression and conduct as a "civilizing process" in which we acquire techniques of *autonomous* expressive and affective control. Elias's work—sometimes referred to as "configurational sociology"—can be compared to Benedict's analysis of cultural configurations: Whereas Benedict places societies and the prevailing social forms of conduct, feeling, and communication in a cross-culturally comparative perspective, Elias shows the historical variation of human behavior as it unfolds along with changing modes of production, power, and social control. Elias is particularly interested in the representational aspects of interpersonal behavior, that is, in the question how social formations of interaction are used to display social structure. An enlightening example is his analysis of the *levée*, the daily ceremony enacted when King Louis XIV of France got up in the morning: Every movement in this ceremony was used as a codified symbolic resource to express the current status hierarchy at the court. Court societies are of particular interest to those who study the historical origins of manners and rules of interpersonal conduct, because they have often been the birthplaces from which these norms have subsequently trickled down into societies at large; note the root of the term *courtesy*.

In contrast to the current interest in cultural variations in human conduct and communication, only a few scholars in recent years have devoted their research to historical development; an important explanatory dimension is thereby lost. One other name that deserves to be mentioned here is that of Richard Sennett (1977, 1990), who has provided penetrating analyses of the changing character of the public self and its interactions in the large European cities during the 18th and 19th centuries. The cities were agglomerations of strangers, and this created problems of credibility for the people; the meanings of their respective expressions and actions were no longer embedded in and guaranteed by intimate mutual knowledge. Codes of public behavior therefore had to generate their own criteria of credibility, and these were dramatically different from those that we rely upon today. Today, we associate authenticity with spontaneity: An expression is the more authentic the less it is premeditated. We expect to be *overcome by* emotion, otherwise the emotion is perceived as shallow if not "fake." In contrast, in 18th-century France, for example, it was common for people, men and women alike, to break out in tears and weep loudly during theater performances. When the actors managed to elicit particularly strong emotions, the audience often interrupted the play to have the scene performed again—often several times, each time with the same overwhelming emotional effects. The authenticity of the audience's emotional response, "unnatural" though it may seem to us, was never in question.

THE ANTHROPOLOGY OF EMOTION

Emotions are at the center of various contemporary research programs in the social sciences, and the cultural variability of emotions and emotional expression is one of the main themes of this research. One program—which in some ways continues the tradition of the "culture and personality" framework, is the *anthropology of emotions* (Lutz & White, 1986). Within this program, emphasis is placed upon the *cognitive* and *conceptual* aspects of emotions. When we communicate, we do not transmit "brute," "natural" feelings. Rather, we communicate emotions that we have interpreted in light of the categories that our culture provides, and the expressed emotions are interpreted by the audience by reference to these same categories (Carbaugh, 1993). Emotions have names. Every culture theorizes them. They are conceptually linked to particular kinds of interpersonal circumstances and are invoked to justify or criticize actions. In a word, emotions are "unnatural" (Lutz, 1988). They are cultural institutions.

Rosaldo (1984) describes emotions as *embodied thoughts:*

> What differentiates thought and affect, differentiating a "cold" cognition from a "hot", is fundamentally a sense of the engagement of the actor's self. Emotions are thoughts somehow "felt" in flushes, pulses, "movements" of our livers, minds, hearts, stomachs, skin. They are *embodied* thoughts, thoughts seeped with the apprehension that "I am involved." (Rosaldo, 1984, p. 143; see also Rosaldo, 1980)

Emotions thus tell us "how we are doing" in a social situation; they give us information about our well-being in the context of interaction with others. They are social cognitions. Lutz (1988; Lutz & White, 1986) emphasizes the *conceptual* structure of emotions. "Emotions may be construed as ideas"; they are "judgments" (Lutz & White, 1986, p. 407). Lutz (1988) proposes to view "emotions as a form of discourse" (p. 7): "Emotion can be viewed as a cultural and interpersonal process of naming, justifying, and persuading by people in relationship to each other" (p. 5). This implies that the categorical distinction between thought and emotion is not a given, but a cultural construct, characteristic of Western rationalism in the aftermath of Descartes.

Emotions are conceptually tied to social scenarios (scripts) that involve actors, others, and prototypical interaction problems: frustration of expectations, social incompetence, awareness of the possibility of social failure, danger to oneself or one's significant others, loss of significant relationships (Lutz & White, 1986, p. 427). Through their connection to typified social scenarios, emotions are embedded in the moral order of the community; they link somatic experience with action, rules, and interpersonal as well as intrapsychic coping strategies. We have seen above that the Balinese emotion *lek* (stage fright) can exist only in a world where social life is experienced as a theatrical performance and where people's main preoccupation is not to botch their parts. Lutz (1988) describes the Ifaluk (Micronesian) emotion *song* (justifiable anger), which is tied to a scenario that involves offense, moral condemnation, fear/anxiety, and a standardized process of counseling. The emotion—the way it is felt and conceptualized—thus has all the features of an institutionalized, embodied conflict-regulating procedure.

The imagined, metaphorical seat of the emotions varies from culture to culture as well. Whereas we locate love in the heart, the

Philippine Ilongot feel *liget* (anger) in the liver (Rosaldo, 1980). Americans imagine anger according to a "hydraulic" model: It is like a hot liquid in a closed container, building up pressure under increasing heat, coming closer and closer to the point of explosion unless its cause—the energy source—is removed (Lakoff & Kövecses, 1987).

The anthropology of emotion suggests that it is not sufficient to ask how a set of presumably basic, universal emotions is *expressed* differently in different cultures. We should not assume that others "feel the same way," because we cannot presuppose that our respective conceptual schemata are commensurable and that emotions and emotion terms mean the same across cultures. We need to subject emotions to the scrutiny of conceptual analysis (Gerber, 1985) and explicate how experiential, expressive, cognitive, and regulative aspects are integrated in the various emotions that a culture recognizes.

Emotions provide a nexus between various components of interaction processes. They are cognitions about interactive events. They tell us how we experience interactions; they provide us with information about ourselves in the company of others. But they also regulate interactions, because they get expressed, displayed, or performed and thus enable mutual awareness about how everyone subjectively experiences the interactions.

Independent of the question of whether there are, as Ekman (1992) has argued, universal basic emotions, one might object that the anthropology of emotions, with its emphasis on cross-cultural diversity, loses sight of the functions that emotions serve in all societies. Certainly, emotions are components of overall cultural configurations, and they are subject to conceptual structuring. But everywhere, emotions serve important functions in the regulation of interpersonal conduct. They inform us whether or not we feel we are being treated fairly or are treating others fairly; whether we

experience our failure as guilt or as shame is of secondary importance. In other words, emotions might be an expression of a universal human "passion for justice" (Solomon, 1990). Another criticism that must be leveled against some of the work in the anthropology of emotions is its excessively "textualist" bent and its corresponding abstraction away from the feeling body. Although scholars have recognized, even emphasized, the embodied nature of emotions, they have largely studied emotions as purely conceptual-discursive phenomena and failed to develop research methods that would enable us to investigate emotions as body-mind processes within contexts of social interaction.

EMPIRICAL STUDIES OF COMMUNICATION IN ITS CULTURAL CONTEXT

So far in this chapter, I have dealt with culture and communication at abstract levels and in the broadest possible terms. In particular, I have paid little attention to research practice and methodology. This neglect has been deliberate: My goal has been to review in very general terms a number of schools of thought that can easily escape the attention of today's communication scholar, partly because they are dated, and partly because they have been developed in other academic disciplines. I nevertheless believe that they are of paradigmatic interest to students of culture and interpersonal communication, in particular because they make reference, in one way or another, to the "person" who communicates and to the cultural construction of personhood.

The approaches reviewed thus point up a dimension of interpersonal communication that is difficult to operationalize and not necessarily accessible to direct observation: We can perceive emotion only in its effects or through its expression, and we can become aware of the cultural constitution of self only when we analyze the language that is spoken in a culture. All of these themes thus transcend to a higher or lesser degree the legitimate limitations of existing observational and descriptive methods in the analysis of communication. It is not yet clear whether and how we will eventually be able to subject the affective or expressive dimension of communication to the same rigorous scrutiny with which we currently describe its referential aspects.

Among the existing empirical approaches to interpersonal communication, three in particular are in line with the "symbols and meanings" view of culture that I have adopted in this chapter. These are the *ethnography of communication, microethnography* (or *context analysis*), and *conversation analysis*. There are no agreed-upon boundaries separating these methods, because "ethnography" does not entail a commitment to a school of thought, only to descriptive methods, and conversation analysis is certainly an ethnographic method (Goodwin, 1990; Hopper, 1990-1991; Moerman, 1988). Microethnography" is named for the order of phenomena described, and context analysis indexes the conviction, held by practitioners of all these approaches, that symbols and behaviors have meaning only within contexts (Scheflen, 1974). There are certainly differences among these methods, but their complementarity has been demonstrated many times (Auer & diLuzio, 1992; Duranti & Goodwin, 1992). Most recently, there have been very promising attempts to link the cultural analysis of interaction to the cultural analysis of language (Hanks, 1996b; Urban, 1991). Detailed accounts of all of these methods are available: Duranti (1988) and Saville-Troike (1989) for the ethnography of communication, Kendon (1990, chap. 2) for context analysis, Heritage (1984) and Levinson (1983) for conversation analysis, and Streeck (in press) for microethnography. (Several of these approaches are reviewed and integrated by Duranti, 1997.) My review can therefore be brief.

The *ethnography of communication* began as a belated implementation of Sapir's call for language to be studied within the entire ensemble of symbol systems that are in use in a society. Speech is a form of human behavior that is embedded in other forms, an activity among activities, and itself is made up of a multitude of different acts. The research program, when it was finally launched (Bauman & Sherzer, 1989; Gumperz & Hymes, 1972), reflected the history of methods of analysis that had developed since Sapir's initial call (in 1927): Structural analysis and taxonomic description were its initial tools. The ethnography of communication began as an application of methods developed in the study of grammatical forms to phenomena of language use and social interaction (Hymes, 1962). It was a structural description of social practices and situations. The descriptions have since become less taxonomic and more dynamic, and researchers have moved from the classification of units of behavior to the description of their unfolding over time.

Researchers have studied various kinds of units of communication behavior: speech communities, speech events, speech acts, and speech genres, among others. Each level of social integration poses its own set of questions and points up phenomena of different kinds. The study of *speech communities* (Carbaugh, 1988, 1990; Phillipsen, 1990; Sherzer, 1983) deals with internal variation and linguistic differentiation, with the maintenance and symbolization of a community's integrity, and with issues of social and cultural identity among its members, but also with the "cycle of situational frames" (Hall, 1977) that these travel through in their daily lives and with the shifting demands each situation makes on the participants' communicative repertoires. This program of study has yielded a far richer and more differentiated model of linguistic competence than the predominant Chomskyan one, which assumes an idealized homogeneous community of language; the ethnographic account of competence accommodates the real variability of linguistic behavior (Hymes, 1972a, 1972b). The description of *speech events* (Bauman, 1986; Katriel, 1990; Phillips, 1982, 1989)—the ethnography of situated linguistic action—focuses on the impact that variable social factors, such as status and rank, situated role, and gender, have upon, and the ways in which they are symbolized by, speech behavior (see the contributions in Bauman & Sherzer, 1989; Gumperz & Hymes, 1972). *Event* is the "basic level" unit in many of these studies (Rosch, 1987); a culture's members can typically identify and label events quite easily. Events provide coherence, integration, and functional meaning-in-context for lower-level units such as speech acts, as well as for stylistic choices (Agar, 1974; Frake, 1977). Goffman's (1961, 1963, 1974, 1981) sociology of "situations and their men" has been a strong influence in this line of research (see also Drew & Wootton, 1988; Levinson, 1988). The ethnography of *speech acts,* or "culturally contexted" speech act analysis (see Moerman, 1988), includes the study of culturally specific kinds of speech acts (Abrahams, 1989), the procedural rules for performing them (Frake, 1964, 1975), and the underlying metalinguistic and philosophical folk conceptions of speech, such as truth and sincerity (Albert, 1972; Duranti, 1984; Goody, 1978; Hill & Irvine, 1992; Rosaldo, 1990). The study of *speech genres*, finally, explores the constitutive features of kinds of discourse across individual events, settings, and so on (Atkinson & Drew, 1979; Conley & O'Barr, 1990). Recently, the importance of Bakhtin's (1952-1953/1986) theory of oral intertextuality for understanding the nature of genre has been recognized (Briggs & Bauman, 1992). New visions of language are beginning to emerge from the practice of ethnography as a result of the recognition of the primordially *discursive* existence of all linguistic and cultural forms (Hanks, 1996a; Urban, 1991).

Langue (Saussure, 1964) is thus "repositioned" (Urban, 1991); it is no longer seen as the real reality behind the fleeting appearances of *parole,* but as an ongoing production, produced by the discursive practices of face-to-face communication (and other discourse genres).

The ethnography of communication typically deals with *labeled* acts and events. But not all unit acts of social interaction in a culture are labeled. As soon as we begin to explore the structures of the smaller unit acts—say, the utterance of a sentence or the assembly of a complex gesture—we enter a realm without much linguistic codification. Yet units at this level are essential components of social interaction. Microunits of behavior—tone groups, hand movements, and so on—have no names, but they make up things that have names: cheers, greetings, and the like.

This is the realm of *microethnography*. What changes when we enter the microcosm of the single utterance, sequence, or visual act is not just the size of the phenomenon under study. Inevitably, our perspective on the phenomenon also changes, from form to process, from "communicational structure" (Scheflen, 1973) to "behaving and making sense" (Bremme & Erickson, 1977). What comes into view are the processes through which communicative acts are assembled. In practical terms, microethnographers study small segments of audio- or videotapes (often in the context of observational studies of macrophenomena), reviewing these segments again and again *as they unfold over time.* These research experiences reposition the structural categories that have previously been used for the description of communication. Traditional descriptive categories (e.g., sentence, posture configuration) identify phenomena through *hindsight* (Good, 1995); they identify structures that *have already been assembled.* In the study of language, this orientation to *langue* and its units as atemporal objects is a result of, and partly justified by, the material abstraction of language from its unfolding in time in writing.

But in the study of body behavior no such abstraction is possible; a gesture, for example, exists *only* as an object-in-time.

The move into the realm of the microethnographic thus naturally leads to a revolution in the conceptualization of communication. Communication and interaction begin to take on the appearance of *living processes,* and the concepts used to describe them are necessarily becoming more reflective of communication's unfolding over time. Microethnography can thus be described as the study of the ways in which acts and events are assembled over time in the interaction of mutually copresent people (McDermott & Roth, 1978). Its premise is contextualism (Duranti & Goodwin, 1992; Erickson & Shultz, 1977): Meaning is seen as a "relation between an act and the context in which it regularly occurs" (Scheflen, 1974, p. 14). All of the units involved—acts, their components, contexts—are *cultural units,* elements from a repertoire shared by the members and enabling them to configure the larger units of social integration. Microethnographers have provided very detailed descriptions of interaction processes (Goodwin, 1995), especially in social institutions such as schools, and have exposed the subtle misarticulations that occur when participants bring different cultural repertoires and interpretive methods to a situation (Erickson, 1979; Erickson & Mohatt, 1982; Phillips, 1982; Streeck, 1984; Streeck & Mehus, in press).

In this world of microscopic appearances, the customary distinctions between disciplines and approaches disappear. Whether a study is "ethnographic" (targeting just one culture) or "basic research" (dealing with generic or universal practices) is a question that only the phenomena themselves can answer. We can never know in advance how widely distributed a communication phenomenon is. The most comprehensive oeuvre in context analysis— the work of Adam Kendon—includes strictly local cultural phenomena such as the ritual sign language of an Australian aboriginal society (Kendon, 1988) or codified South Italian gestures (Kendon, 1992), but also presumably universal mechanisms such as self- and interactional synchrony (Kendon, 1990).

Microethnography intersects with another, small research tradition that goes back to the work of Boas—the study of *expressive culture.* One of the projects that Boas launched in his fight against racist theories of human behavior was a study of gestures in New York City that compared the conversational gestures of southern Italian and Jewish immigrants of Eastern European descent (Efron, 1942). The immediate aim of this study was to show that patterns of embodied behavior—such as the moving of the hands in gesticulation—are not innate. In a painstaking comparison of the gestures of first- and second-generation Jewish and Italian immigrants, Efron (1942) demonstrated the slow "hybridization" of the gestural style as immigrants moved into the American mainstream. Like all other cultural forms of expression, gestures are learned.

Efron's study could have laid the groundwork for a field devoting itself to empirical study of expressive "behavior in public places" (Goffman, 1963) had it not for a long time remained an isolated attempt; the focus of most research on human expression was almost exclusively psychological. Gesture has alternatively been thought of as a window into *cognitive* or *affective* processes "inside" the person, only rarely as a mode of public behavior. Although there have been many interesting studies of the *representation* of expressive behavior in the fine arts (Barash, 1987; Baxandall, 1988; Bremmer & Roodenburg, 1991), only a few researchers have subjected expressive behavior to microanalytic *cultural* scrutiny (Calbris, 1990; Creider, 1986; Kendon, 1995). In recent years, however, there has been an outpouring of research on social interaction that focuses on the coordinated deployment of multiple communication resources in highly complex interaction settings, especially workplaces, and on the multiple roles that an interactant's body can simultaneously play within such a setting (Goodwin, 1998; Goodwin & Goodwin, 1996; Heath & Luff, 1993, 1996; Hutchins & Palen, 1997; LeBaron & Streeck, 1997, 2000; Streeck, 1996; Streeck & Kallmeyer, 2001).

Whatever units and structures there are in communication behavior, they are units and structures *in time.* They do not appear "at once," but "step by step," in the presence and within reach of other participants who can invite, discourage, or preempt them. That these units unfold over time thus implies that they unfold *in a process of interaction* in which every move made or not made by the interlocutor can influence the further shape of the unit (Goodwin, 1979). "Real time" is "shared time," and it is nonlinear. Rather, utterances and other communicative acts are produced and received with a *prospective-retrospective* orientation (Cicourel, 1973).

Conversation analysts describe "the procedures by which conversationalists produce their own behavior and understand and deal with the behavior of others" (Heritage, 1984, p. 1; see also Atkinson & Heritage, 1984). Among these procedures are those that enable conversational participants to take turns and produce a "linear" series of conversational utterances with a minimum of overlap, so that mutual hearing and understanding can be secured (Sacks, Schegloff, & Jefferson, 1974), procedures for the sequencing of conversational actions (Schegloff & Sacks, 1979), and procedures for the "repair" of interactional and conversational "trouble" (correcting mishaps in speaking, addressing problems in hearing and understanding, and so on; Schegloff, 1979). Conversation analysis can be regarded as an account of the highly adaptive, systematic organization that allows society's members to sustain social order and relationships in a routine fashion. This organization is designed to let the participants *progress* in their interaction with one another. It is a set of *enabling, forward-looking* rules, not a set of restrictions.

Some of these rules or practices have important social-organizational implications that go beyond the realm of conversation. For example, so-called *preference organizations* (Drew, 1984; Pomerantz, 1978, 1984) reveal a "systematic 'bias' in favour of conflict avoidance" (Heritage, 1984, p. 280). Prosocial solution types to problems of interactional and social coordination have become parts of the interactional *langue,* of the "prosthetic devices" that we routinely employ in our dealings with one another.

Conversation analysts have reported their findings in culture-free terms and have defined conversational organization as a set of "generic," "context-free" practices for the production of "particular," "contextual" scenes (Schegloff, 1972). Charges have therefore been brought that these analysts are oblivious to the cultural variation of these practices. But this debate is ill framed. Conceiving the issue in terms of the traditional "nature/nurture" dichotomy ("learned" or "cultural" versus "innate" or "universal") obscures the fact that interaction patterns, languages, and other symbol systems have evolved over time; although some are vestiges of rather ancient times, they are nevertheless part of our *tradition,* not "hardwired" into our genes. Only when we understand the human repertoires of interaction and communication abilities and resources as products of a *continuing* process of evolution and history, as layered sets of imprints and vestiges from various developmental stages, some very old, some more recent, can we begin to think about their relative order of appearance and ask questions such as, How does the structure of natural language reflect the needs of face-to-face interaction? or Which features of conversational organization are universal, and which show cultural variation? For example, human beings very likely accumulated experiences in turn taking long before the invention of language—for example, in the context of food sharing. To the extent that humanity developed viable, routine solutions to recurrent social organization problems of this kind, these became "entrenched" in the culture and subsequently available for the management of more advanced systems or tasks, such as turn taking during vocal communication (which requires the sharing of a "channel"). The solution patterns have likely became part of the human tradition—*culture*—long before any separation of languages and *cultures*. Not everything that is universal has to be innate.

CONCLUSION: WHERE IS CULTURE?

We have thus returned to our initial reflections on the definition of *culture:* It is a "prosthetic device." At one level, culture is just a way of organizing our data, a framing of experience (Goffman, 1974). But we can frame the phenomena of culture and communication in many ways and interpret the very same set of phenomena at various levels of generality or local specificity. For example, we can discover in an elaborate, status-symbolizing ceremony that involves a differential distribution of speaking turns an example of the local culture with its peculiar emphasis on decorum and rank, but we can also see it as a local variant of a very old, vestigial human achievement, namely, the exploitation of a management system for scarce resources (e.g., the speech "channel") for secondary social-organizational resources (e.g., the negotiation and symbolic representation of differential rank). The phenomena of interpersonal communication— language, embodied behavior, interactional organization—as well as any other cultural achievement are always "local" and "generic," "specific" and "universal" at the same time. The difference is one of research focus. If by some crazy twist of history the study of conversation had first begun in the Amazon basin—or maybe Bosnia-Herzegovina—the local variety of conversational organization would have served equally well to make the

point: that talking requires the exchange of turns. This does not mean, of course, that it is all the same—that all languages resemble English (as the Chomskyans used to pretend) or that there is not a tremendous amount of variation. The variation, however, is always variation around a universal core, or, rather, away from an older, common core, for this is how humanity evolved.

An altogether different level of cultural organization and symbolic representation has remained almost completely overlooked by students of human communication: the realm of cultural artifacts—the things we act with, that we build, rebuild, write with and upon, and so on. Cultural meanings do not reside only in symbols, and the human mind and its cultural manifestations are not located only in brains. We are accustomed to making a categorical distinction between person and environment and to attributing everything that is "mental" or "ideational"—meaning, knowledge, symbols—to the "mind," which we locate inside the brain. But this is a very partial view, motivated perhaps by the antimaterialist, individualist conception of mind and soul that is so much part of our tradition. But cultural meanings are distributed across many locations, both internal and external, and they are quite obviously embodied in part in *material culture* (Norman, 1988, 1993; Resnick, Levine, & Behrend, 1990). Culture is a vast information pool, transmitted from generation to generation and increasing constantly in size for the past 50,000 years. But this pool is transmitted not only by symbols (language, graphic signs, and so on) but by the entire "culturally constituted reality," which includes such things as "buildings, roads, vehicles, lawns, furniture, appliances" (D'Andrade, 1981, p. 180). When we use these things, the meanings that we have stored in our minds articulate with the meanings embodied in them, which are themselves inscriptions of years and years of intelligent human action. It is only recently that psychologists and communication researchers have begun to recognize and investigate the distribution of meaning and mind (or "cognition") across different locations and to study the processes of communication within such "systems of distributed cognition" (Hutchins & Klausen, 1996). These systems include human actors, material representation systems, built spaces, and so on, but, importantly, also "other actors." Human competence typically relies upon the presence of other actors who have partly similar, partly complementary competences: Couples share memory through a distribution of labor, families develop differential communication roles, and of course workers and learners everywhere depend upon experts.

We thus rely on our material environment to serve as a stock of ready-made symbolic structures that we can manipulate to externalize cognitive functions and to represent, in an enduring kind of way, interactively assembled conceptual structures: Pens, cups, pieces of paper, and lines in the sand can represent the features of an agreement, doodles can stand for action plans. Increasingly, machines and sophisticated symbol-processing technology are becoming routine settings for human communication (Goodwin, 1993; Suchman, 1987). The distribution of meaning and mind across various locations, however, is very old. Rain forest dwellers, for example, have for a long time been using the sounds of their environments—the calls of birds and the noise of waterfalls—as external symbolic structures within which to embed their songs and thus their communal knowledge (Feld, 1982). Culture, meaning, and mind cannot be kept within territories or containers, but they can be endangered, destroyed, and extinguished.

REFERENCES

Aarsleff, H. (1974). The tradition of Condillac: The problem of the origin of language in the eighteenth century and the debate in the Berlin Academy before Herder. In D. Hymes (Ed.), *Studies in the history of linguistics* (pp. 93-156). Bloomington: Indiana University Press.

Abrahams, R. D. (1989). Black talking on the streets. In R. Bauman & J. Sherzer (Eds.), *Explorations in the ethnography of speaking* (2nd ed., pp. 240-262). Cambridge: Cambridge University Press.

Agar, M. (1974). Talking about doing: Lexicon and event. *Language in Society, 3,* 83-89.

Albert, E. (1972). Cultural patterning of speech behavior in Burundi. In J. J. Gumperz & D. Hymes (Eds.), *Directions in sociolinguistics: The ethnography of communication* (pp. 106-129). New York: Holt, Rinehart & Winston.

Atkinson, J. M., & Drew, P. (1979). *Order in court: The organization of verbal interaction in judicial settings.* London: Macmillan.

Atkinson, J. M., & Heritage, J. (Eds.). (1984). *Structures of social action: Studies in conversation analysis.* Cambridge: Cambridge University Press.

Auer, P., & diLuzio, A. (Eds.). (1992). *The contextualization of language.* Amsterdam: John Benjamins.

Bakhtin, M. M. (1986). The problem of speech genres. In M. M. Bakhtin, *Speech genres and other late essays* (C. Emerson & M. Holquist, Eds.; V. W. McGee, Trans.) (pp. 60-103). Austin: University of Texas Press. (Original work published 1952-1953)

Barash, M. (1987). *Giotto and the language of gesture.* Cambridge: Cambridge University Press.

Bateson, G. (1958). *Naven* (2nd ed.). Stanford, CA: Stanford University Press.

Bateson, G. (1972). *Steps to an ecology of mind.* New York: Ballantine.

Bateson, G., & Mead, M. (1942). *Balinese character: A photographic analysis.* New York: New York Academy of Sciences.

Bauman, R. (1986). *Story, performance, and event: Contextual studies of oral narrative.* Cambridge: Cambridge University Press.

Bauman, R., & Sherzer, J. (Eds.). (1989). *Explorations in the ethnography of speaking* (2nd ed.). Cambridge: Cambridge University Press.

Baxandall, M. (1988). *Painting and experience in fifteenth-century Italy* (2nd ed.). New York: Oxford University Press.

Benedict, R. (1934). *Patterns of culture.* Boston: Houghton Mifflin.

Berlin, B., & Kay, P. (1969). *Basic color terms.* Berkeley: University of California Press.

Boas, F. (1912). Changes in the bodily form of descendants of immigrants. *American Anthropologist, 14,* 530-562.

Boas, F. (1928). *Anthropology and modern life.* New York: Dover.

Boas, F. (1932). Rasse und Charakter. *Anthropologischer Anzeiger, 8,* 280-284.

Boas, F. (1940). *Race, language and culture.* New York: Free Press.

Boas, F. (1966a). Introduction to *Handbook of American Indian languages.* In F. Boas & J. W. Powell, *American Indian languages* (P. Holder, Ed.). Lincoln: University of Nebraska Press. (Original work published 1911)

Boas, F. (1966b). *Kwakiutl ethnography.* Chicago: University of Chicago Press.

Bourdieu, P. (1977). *Outline of a theory of practice.* Cambridge: Cambridge University Press.

Bremme, D. W., & Erickson, F. (1977). Behaving and making sense. *Theory Into Practice, 16,* 153-160.

Bremmer, J., & Roodenburg, H. (Eds.). (1991). *A cultural history of gesture.* Ithaca, NY: Cornell University Press.

Briggs, C. L., & Bauman, R. (1992). Genre, intertextuality, and social power. *Journal of Linguistic Anthropology, 2,* 131-172.

Brown, P., & Levinson, S. C. (1987). *Politeness: Some universals in language usage.* Cambridge: Cambridge University Press.

Bruner, J. (1990). *Acts of meaning.* Cambridge, MA: Harvard University Press.

Bunzel, R. (1992). *Zuñi ceremonialism.* Albuquerque: University of New Mexico Press. (Original work published 1932)

Byrne, R. W., & Whiten, A. (Eds.). (1988). *Machiavellian intelligence: Social expertise and the evolution of intellect in monkeys, apes, and humans.* Oxford: Clarendon.

Calbris, G. (1990). *The semiotics of French gestures* (O. Doyle, Trans.). Bloomington: Indiana University Press.

Carbaugh, D. (1988). *Talking American: Cultural discourses on Donahue.* Norwood, NJ: Ablex.

Carbaugh, D. (Ed.). (1990). *Cultural communication and intercultural contact.* Hillsdale, NJ: Lawrence Erlbaum.

Carbaugh, D. (1993). "Soul" and "self": Soviet and American cultures in conversation. *Quarterly Journal of Speech, 79,* 182-200.

Cavalli-Sforza, L. L. (1991). Genes, peoples and languages. *Scientific American, 263*(5), 104-111.

Chance, M. R. A., & Larsen, R. R. (Eds.). (1976). *The social structure of attention.* New York: John Wiley.

Cicourel, A. V. (1964). *Method and measurement in sociology.* New York: Free Press.

Cicourel, A. V. (1973). *Cognitive sociology.* Harmondsworth: Penguin.

Collier, J., Jr., & Collier, M. (1986). *Visual anthropology: Photography as a research method* (Rev. ed.). Albuquerque: University of New Mexico Press.

Columbus, C. (1966). *Across the ocean sea; a journal of Columbus' voyage.* New York: Harper & Row. (Original work published 1492-1493)

Comrie, B. (1981). *Language universals and linguistic typology.* Chicago: University of Chicago Press.

Condillac, E. (1746). *An essay on the origin of human knowledge, being a supplement to Mr. Locke's essay on the human understanding.* London: J. Noursse.

Conley, J., & O'Barr, W. (1990). *Rules versus relationships: The ethnography of legal discourse.* Chicago: University of Chicago Press.

Creider, C. A. (1986). Interlanguage comparisons in the study of the interactional use of gesture. *Semiotica, 62,* 147-164.

D'Andrade, R. G. (1981). The cultural part of cognition. *Cognitive Science, 5,* 179-195.

D'Andrade, R. G. (1984). Cultural meaning systems. In R. A. Shweder & R. A. LeVine (Eds.), *Culture theory: Essays on mind, self, and emotion* (pp. 88-120). Cambridge: Cambridge University Press.

Darwin, C. (1955). *The expression of emotions in animals and man.* New York: Philosophical Society. (Original work published 1872)

Darwin, C. (1964). *On the origin of species.* Cambridge, MA: Harvard University Press. (Original work published 1859)

Dilthey, W. (1977). *Descriptive psychology and historical understanding.* The Hague: Martinus Nijhoff.

Donald, M. (1991). *Origins of the modern mind: Three stages in the evolution of culture and cognition.* Cambridge, MA: Harvard University Press.

Douglas, M. (1970). *Natural symbols: Explorations in cosmology.* London: Barrie & Jenkins.

Drew, P. (1984). Speakers' reportings in invitation sequences. In J. M. Atkinson & J. Heritage (Eds.), *Structures of social action: Studies in conversation analysis.* Cambridge: Cambridge University Press.

Drew, P., & Wootton, A. (Eds.). (1988). *Erving Goffman: Exploring the interaction order.* Oxford: Polity.

Dunbar, R. (1998). Theory of mind and the evolution of language. In J. R. Hurford, M. Studdert-Kennedy, & C. Knight (Eds.), *Approaches to the evolution of language* (pp. 92-110). Cambridge: Cambridge University Press.

Duranti, A. (1984). *Intentions, self, and local theories of meaning: Words and social action in a Samoan context.* San Diego, CA: University of California, Center for Human Information Processing.

Duranti, A. (1988). Ethnography of speaking: Toward a linguistics of the praxis. In F. J. Newmeyer (Ed.), *Linguistics: The Cambridge Survey: II. Linguistic theory: Extensions and implications* (pp. 210-228). Cambridge: Cambridge University Press.

Duranti, A. (1997). *Linguistic anthropology.* Cambridge: Cambridge University Press.

Duranti, A., & Goodwin, C. (Eds.). (1992). *Rethinking context: Language as an interactive phenomenon.* Cambridge: Cambridge University Press.

Durkheim, E. (1982). *The rules of sociological method.* London: Macmillan. (Original work published 1895)

Durkheim, E., & Mauss, M. (1963). *Primitive classification.* Chicago: University of Chicago Press. (Original work published 1903)

Edwards, E. (Ed.). (1992). *Anthropology and photography 1860-1920.* New Haven, CT: Yale University Press.

Efron, D. (1942). *Gesture, race and culture.* The Hague: Mouton.

Ekman, P. (Ed.). (1973). *Darwin and facial expression: A century of research in review.* New York: Academic Press.

Ekman, P. (1992). Are there basic emotions? *Psychological Review, 99,* 550-554.

Elias, N. (1978). *The civilizing process: The history of manners.* New York: Urizen.

Elias, N. (1983). *The court society.* Oxford: Basil Blackwell.

Erickson, F. (1979). Talking down: Some cultural sources of miscommunication in interracial interviews. In A. Wolfgang (Ed.), *Nonverbal behavior: Applications and cultural*

implications (pp. 99-126). New York: Academic Press.

Erickson, F., & Mohatt, G. (1982). Cultural organization of participation structures in two classrooms with Indian students. In G. Spindler (Ed.), *Doing the ethnography of schooling* (pp. 132-175). New York: Holt, Rinehart & Winston.

Erickson, F., & Shultz, J. J. (1977). When is a context? Some issues in the analysis of social competence. *Quarterly Newsletter of the Institute for Comparative Human Development, 1*(2), 5-10.

Evans-Pritchard, E. (1964). Nuer modes of address. In D. Hymes (Eds.), *Language in culture and society* (pp. 221-225). New York: Harper & Row.

Feld, S. (1982). *Sound and sentiment: Birds, weeping, poetics, and sons in Kaluli expression.* Philadelphia: University of Pennsylvania Press.

Forster, G. (1777). *A voyage round the world.* London.

Fortune, R. F. (1932). *Sorcerers of Dobu.* London: Routledge.

Frake, C. (1964). How to ask for a drink in Subanun. *American Anthropologist, 66,* 127-132.

Frake, C. (1975). How to enter a Yakan house. In M. Sanchez & B. Blount (Eds.), *Sociocultural dimensions of language use* (pp. 25-40). New York: Academic Press.

Frake, C. (1977). Plying frames can be dangerous: An assessment of methodology in cognitive anthropology. *Quarterly Newsletter of the Institute for Comparative Human Development, 1*(3), 1-7.

Freud, S. (1949). *An outline of psychoanalysis.* New York: W. W. Norton.

Freud, S. (1955). *The interpretation of dreams.* New York: Basic Books.

Freud, S. (1958). *Civilization and its discontents.* Garden City, NY: Doubleday.

Freud, S. (1960). *Jokes and their relation to the unconscious.* New York: W. W. Norton.

Garfinkel, H. (1967). *Studies in ethnomethodology.* Englewood Cliffs: Prentice Hall.

Geertz, C. (1973). *The interpretation of cultures: Selected essays.* New York: Basic Books.

Geertz, C. (1983). *Local knowledge: Further essays in interpretive anthropology.* New York: Basic Books.

Geertz, C. (1984). "From the native's point of view": On the nature of anthropological understanding. In R. A. Shweder & R. A. LeVine (Eds.), *Culture theory: Essays on mind, self, and emotion* (pp. 123-136). Cambridge: Cambridge University Press.

Geertz, C. (1988). *Works and lives: The anthropologist as author.* Stanford, CA: Stanford University Press.

Gehlen, A. (1958). *Der Mensch. Seine Natur und seine Stellung in der Welt.* Frankfurt: V. Klostermann.

Gerber, E. R. (1985). Rage and obligation: Samoan emotion in conflict. In G. M. White & J. T. Kirkpatrick (Eds.), *Person, self, and experience: Exploring Pacific ethnopsychologies* (pp. 121-167). Berkeley: University of California Press.

Goffman, E. (1961). *Encounters: Two studies in the sociology of interaction.* Indianapolis: Bobbs-Merrill.

Goffman, E. (1963). *Behavior in public places: Notes on the social organization of gatherings.* New York: Free Press.

Goffman, E. (1974). *Frame analysis: An essay on the organization of experience.* New York: Harper & Row.

Goffman, E. (1981). *Forms of Talk.* Oxford: Basil Blackwell.

Good, D. (1995). Where does foresight end and hindsight begin? In E. N. Goody (Ed.), *Social intelligence and interaction: Expressions and implications of the social bias in human intelligence* (pp. 139-150). Cambridge: Cambridge University Press.

Goodman, N. (1976). *Languages of art* (2nd ed.). Indianapolis: Hackett.

Goodwin, C. (1979). The interactive construction of a sentence in natural conversation. In G. Psathas (Ed.), *Everyday language: Studies in ethnomethodology* (pp. 97-122). New York: Irvington.

Goodwin, C. (1993). *Perception, technology and interaction on a scientific research vessel.* Unpublished manuscript.

Goodwin, C. (1995). Co-constructing meaning in conversations with an aphasic man. *Research on Language and Social Interaction, 28,* 233-260.

Goodwin, C. (1998, June). *Action and embodiment within situated human interaction.* Paper presented at the International Graduate School in Language and Communication, Odense University, Odense, Denmark.

Goodwin, C., & Goodwin, M. H. (1996). Seeing as situated activity: Formulating planes. In Y. Engeström & D. Middleton (Eds.), *Cognition and communication at work* (pp. 61-95). Cambridge: Cambridge University Press.

Goodwin, M. H. (1990). *He-said-she-said: Talk as social organization among black children.* Bloomington: Indiana University Press.

Goody, E. N. (Ed.). (1978). *Questions and politeness: Strategies in social interaction.* Cambridge: Cambridge University Press.

Greenberg, J. H., & Ruhlen, M. (1992). Linguistic origins of Native Americans. *Scientific American, 267*(5), 94-99.

Gumperz, J. J. (1996). The linguistic and cultural relativity of inference. In J. J. Gumperz & S. C. Levinson (Eds.), *Rethinking linguistic relativity* (pp. 374-406). Cambridge: Cambridge University Press.

Gumperz, J. J., & Hymes, D. (Eds.). (1972). *Directions in sociolinguistics: The ethnography of communication.* New York: Holt, Rinehart & Winston.

Gumperz, J. J., & Levinson, S. C. (Eds.). (1996). *Rethinking linguistic relativity.* Cambridge: Cambridge University Press.

Hall, E. T. (1977). *Beyond culture.* Garden City, NY: Anchor.

Hanks, W. F. (1996a). *Language and communicative practices.* Boulder, CO: Westview.

Hanks, W. F. (1996b). Language form and communicative practices. In J. J. Gumperz & S. C. Levinson (Eds.), *Rethinking linguistic relativity* (pp. 232-270). Cambridge: Cambridge University Press.

Haviland, J. B. (1996). Projections, transpositions, and relativity. In J. J. Gumperz & S. C. Levinson (Eds.), *Rethinking linguistic relativity* (pp. 271-323). Cambridge: Cambridge University Press.

Heath, C., & Luff, P. (1993). Disembodied conduct: Interactional asymmetries in video-mediated communication. In G. Button (Ed.), *Technology in working order: Studies of work, interaction, and technology* (pp. 35-54). London: Routledge.

Heath, C., & Luff, P. (1996). Convergent activity: Line control and passenger information on the London underground. In Y. Engeström & D. Middleton (Eds.), *Cognition and communication at work* (pp. 96-129). Cambridge: Cambridge University Press.

Herder, J. G. (1966). *Abhandlung über den Ursprung der Sprache.* Stuttgart: Reclam. (Original work published 1772)

Heritage, J. (1984). *Garfinkel and ethnomethodology.* Cambridge: Polity.

Herodotus. (1949). *Herodotus.* Oxford: Clarendon.

Hewes, G. (1974). Gesture language in culture contact. *Sign Language Studies, 4,* 1-34.

Hill, J. H., & Irvine, J. T. (Eds.). (1992). *Responsibility and evidence in oral discourse.* Cambridge: Cambridge University Press.

Hill, J. H., & Mannheim, B. (1992). Language and world view. *Annual Review of Anthropology, 21,* 381-406.

Hochschild, A. (1983). *The managed heart: Commercialization of human feeling.* Berkeley: University of California Press.

Hopper, R. (Ed.). (1990-1991). Ethnography and conversation analysis after *Talking culture* [Special section]. *Research on Language and Social Interaction, 24,* 161-387.

Hurford, J. R., Studdert-Kennedy, M., & Knight, C. (Eds.). (1998). *Approaches to the evolution of language.* Cambridge: Cambridge University Press.

Hutchins, E., & Klausen, T. (1996). *Distributed cognition in an airline cockpit.* In Y. Engeström & D. Middleton (Eds.), *Cognition and communication at work* (pp. 15-34). Cambridge: Cambridge University Press.

Hutchins, E., & Palen, L. (1997). Constructing meaning from space, gesture, and speech. In L. B. Resnick, R. Säljö, C. Pontecorvo, & B. Burge (Eds.), *Discourse, tools, and reasoning: Essays on situated cognition* (pp. 23-40). New York: Springer-Verlag.

Hymes, D. (1962). The ethnography of speaking. In T. Gladwin & W. Sturtevant (Eds.), *Anthropology and human behavior* (pp. 13-53). Washington, DC: Anthropological Society of Washington.

Hymes, D. (1972a). Models of the interaction of language and social life. In J. J. Gumperz & D. Hymes (Eds.), *Directions in sociolinguistics: The ethnography of communication* (pp. 35-71). New York: Holt, Rinehart & Winston.

Hymes, D. (1972b). *Towards communicative competence.* Philadelphia: University of Pennsylvania Press.

Ingold, T. (1986). *Evolution and social life.* Cambridge: Cambridge University Press.

Izard, C. (1971). *The face of emotion.* New York: Appleton.

Johnson, M. (1987). *The body in the mind: The bodily basis of meaning, imagination, and reason.* Chicago: University of Chicago Press.

Jones, E. (1913). *Papers on psycho-analysis.* New York: Wood.

Kant, I. (1977). *Anthropologie in pragmatischer Absicht.* Frankfurt: Suhrkamp. (Original work published 1798)

Katriel, T. (1990). "Griping" as a verbal ritual in some Israeli discourse. In D. Carbaugh (Ed.), *Cultural communication and intercultural contact* (pp. 99-114). Hillsdale, NJ: Lawrence Erlbaum.

Kendon, A. (1988). *Sign languages of Aboriginal Australia.* Cambridge: Cambridge University Press.

Kendon, A. (1990). *Conducting interaction: Patterns of behavior in focused encounters.* Cambridge: Cambridge University Press.

Kendon, A. (1992). Some recent work from Italy on quotable gestures (emblems). *Journal of Linguistic Anthropology, 2,* 92-108.

Kendon, A. (1995). Gestures as illocutionary and discourse structure markers in southern Italian conversation. *Journal of Pragmatics, 23,* 247-279.

Kluckhohn, C., & Murray, H. A. (Eds.). (1948). *Personality in nature, society, and culture.* New York: Alfred A. Knopf.

Knapp, M. L., & Miller, G. R. (Eds.). (1994). *Handbook of interpersonal communication* (2nd ed.). Thousand Oaks, CA: Sage.

Knight, C. (1998). Ritual/speech coevolution: A solution to the problem of deception. In J. R. Hurford, M. Studdert-Kennedy, & C. Knight (Eds.), *Approaches to the evolution of language* (pp. 68-91). Cambridge: Cambridge University Press.

Lacan, J. (1977). *Ecrits: A selection.* New York: W. W. Norton.

Lakoff, G. (1987). *Women, fire, and dangerous things: What categories reveal about the mind.* Chicago: University of Chicago Press.

Lakoff, G., & Kövecses, Z. (1987). The cognitive model of anger inherent in American English. In D. Holland & N. Quinn (Eds.), *Cultural models in language and thought* (pp. 195-221). Cambridge: Cambridge University Press.

Lane, H. (1976). *The Wild Boy of Aveyron.* Cambridge, MA: Harvard University Press.

Langacker, R. W. (1987). *Foundations of cognitive grammar: Vol. 1. Theoretical prerequisites.* Stanford, CA: Stanford University Press.

Leach, E. (1976). *Culture and communication: The logic by which symbols are connected.* Cambridge: Cambridge University Press.

LeBaron, C., & Streeck, J. (1997). Built space and the interactional framing of experience during a murder interrogation. *Human Studies, 20,* 1-25.

LeBaron, C., & Streeck, J. (2000). Gestures, knowledge, and the world. In D. McNeill

(Ed.), *Language and gesture* (pp. 118-140). Cambridge: Cambridge University Press.

Levinson, S. C. (1983). *Pragmatics.* Cambridge: Cambridge University Press.

Levinson, S. C. (1988). Putting linguistics on a proper footing: Explorations in Goffman's concepts of participation. In P. Drew & A. Wootton (Eds.), *Erving Goffman: Exploring the interaction order* (pp. 161-227). Oxford: Polity.

Lévi-Strauss, C. (1976). *Structural anthropology.* Chicago: University of Chicago Press.

Locke, J. (1959). *An essay concerning human understanding.* New York: Dover. (Original work published 1690)

Lucy, J. A. (1992a). *Grammatical categories and cognition: A case study of the linguistic relativity hypothesis.* Cambridge: Cambridge University Press.

Lucy, J. (1992b). *Language diversity and thought: A reformulation of the linguistic relativity hypothesis.* Cambridge: Cambridge University Press.

Lutz, C. A. (1988). *Unnatural emotions: Everyday sentiments on a Micronesian atoll and their challenge to Western theory.* Chicago: University of Chicago Press.

Lutz, C. A., & White, G. M. (1986). The anthropology of emotions. *Annual Review of Anthropology, 15,* 405-436.

Malinowski, B. (1922). *Argonauts of the Western Pacific: An account of native enterprise and adventure in the archipelagoes of Melanesian New Guinea.* London: Routledge & Kegan Paul.

Malinowski, B. (1923). The problem of meaning in primitive languages. In C. K. Ogden & I. A. Richards, *The meaning of meaning* (pp. 296-336). New York: Harcourt, Brace.

Malinowski, B. (1944). *A scientific theory of culture.* Chapel Hill: University of North Carolina Press.

Malinowski, B. (1965). *Coral gardens and their magic.* Bloomington: Indiana University Press. (Original work published 1935)

Mallery, G. (1978). Introduction to the study of sign language among the North American Indians as illustrating the gesture speech of mankind. In D. J. Umiker-Sebeok & T. A. Sebeok (Eds.), *Aboriginal sign languages of the Americas and Australia* (pp. 291-310). New York: Plenum. (Original work published 1880)

Marcus, G. E., & Fischer, M. M. J. (1986). *Anthropology as cultural critique: An experimental moment in the human sciences.* Chicago: University of Chicago Press.

Marcuse, H. (1955). *Eros and civilization.* New York: Vintage.

Maturana, H. R., & Varela, F. J. (1992). *The tree of knowledge: The biological roots of human understanding.* Boston: Shambala. (Original work published 1987)

Mauss, M. (1966). *The gift.* London: Cohen & West. (Original work published 1950)

Mauss, M. (1973). The techniques of the body. *Economy and Society, 2,* 70-88. (Original work published 1935)

Mauss, M. (1979). A category of the human mind: The notion of person; the notion of self. In M. Mauss, *Sociology and psychology: Essays* (B. Brewster, Trans.) (pp. 57-94). London: Routledge & Kegan Paul.

McDermott, R. P., & Roth, D. (1978). Social organization of behavior: Interactional approaches. *Annual Review of Anthropology, 7,* 321-345.

Moerman, M. (1988). *Talking culture: Ethnography and conversation analysis.* Philadelphia: University of Pennsylvania Press.

Montesquieu, C. de. (1901). *The citizen of the world.* Washington, DC: M. Walter Dunne.

Nietzsche, F. (1927). *The birth of tragedy.* New York: Modern Library.

Norman, D. A. (1988). *The design of everyday things.* Garden City, NY: Doubleday.

Norman, D. A. (1993). *Things that make us smart: Defending human attributes in the age of the machine.* Reading, MA: Addison-Wesley.

Parsons, T. (1937). *The structure of social action.* New York: McGraw-Hill.

Parsons, T., & Shils, E. A. (1951). *Towards a general theory of action.* Cambridge, MA: Harvard University Press.

Phillips, S. (1982). *The invisible culture: Communication in classroom and community on the Warm Springs Indian reservation.* New York: Longman.

Phillips, S. (1989). Warm Springs "Indian time": How the regulation of participation affects the progress of events. In R. Bauman & J. Sherzer (Eds.), *Explorations in the ethnography of speaking* (2nd ed., pp. 92-109). Cambridge: Cambridge University Press.

Phillipsen, G. (1990). Speaking "like a man" in Teamsterville: Culture patterns of role enactment in an urban neighborhood. In D. Carbaugh (Ed.), *Cultural communication and intercultural contact* (pp. 11-20). Hillsdale, NJ: Lawrence Erlbaum.

Plessner, H. (1980). *Conditio humana.* Frankfurt: Suhrkamp. (Original work published 1964)

Pomerantz, A. (1978). Compliment responses: Notes on the cooperation of multiple constraints. In J. Schenkein (Ed.), *Studies in the organization of conversational interaction* (pp. 79-112). New York: Academic Press.

Pomerantz, A. (1984). Agreeing and disagreeing with assessments: Some features of preferred/dispreferred turn shapes. In J. M. Atkinson & J. Heritage (Eds.), *Structures of social action: Studies in conversation analysis* (pp. 57-100). Cambridge: Cambridge University Press.

Power, C. (1998). Old wives' tales: The gossip hypothesis and the reliability of cheap signals. In J. R. Hurford, M. Studdert-Kennedy, & C. Knight (Eds.), *Approaches to the evolution of language* (pp. 111-129). Cambridge: Cambridge University Press.

Radcliffe-Brown, A. R. (1965). *Structure and function in primitive society.* New York: Free Press. (Original work published 1952)

Rampton, B. (1995). *Crossing: Language and ethnicity among adolescents.* London: Longman.

Resnick, L. B., Levine, J. M., & Behrend, S. D. (Eds.). (1990). *Perspectives on socially shared cognition.* New York: American Psychological Association.

Rosaldo, M. Z. (1980). *Knowledge and passion: Ilongot notions of self and social life.* New York: Cambridge University Press.

Rosaldo, M. Z. (1984). Toward an anthropology of self and feeling. In R. A. Shweder & R. A. LeVine (Eds.), *Culture theory: Essays on mind, self, and emotion* (pp. 137-157). Cambridge: Cambridge University Press.

Rosaldo, M. Z. (1990). The things we do with words: Ilongot speech acts and speech act theory in philosophy. In D. Carbaugh (Ed.), *Cultural communication and intercultural contact* (pp. 373-408). Hillsdale, NJ: Lawrence Erlbaum.

Rosch, E. (1987). Linguistic relativity. *Etc., 44,* 254-279.

Rousseau, J.-J. (1967). *Discourse on the origin of inequality.* New York: Pocket Books. (Original work published 1755)

Rudzka-Ostyn, B. (1988). *Topics in cognitive linguistics.* Amsterdam: John Benjamins.

Sacks, H., Schegloff, E. A., & Jefferson, G. (1974). A simplest systematics for the organization of turn-taking in conversation. *Language, 50,* 696-735.

Sapir, E. (1921). *Language.* New York: Harcourt, Brace.

Sapir, E. (1991a). The emergence of the concept of personality in a study of cultures. In E. Sapir, *Selected writings of Edward Sapir* (D. Mandelbaum, Ed.). Berkeley: University of California Press. (Original work published 1934)

Sapir, E. (1991b). The unconscious patterning of behavior in society. In E. Sapir, *Selected writings of Edward Sapir* (D. Mandelbaum, Ed.). Berkeley: University of California Press.

Saussure, F. de. (1964). *Cours de linguistique générale.* Paris: Payot.

Saville-Troike, M. (1989). *The ethnography of communication: An introduction* (2nd ed.). Oxford: Basil Blackwell.

Scheflen, A. (1973). *Communicational structure: Analysis of a psychotherapy transaction.* Bloomington: Indiana University Press.

Scheflen, A. (1974). *How behavior means.* Garden City, NY: Anchor.

Schegloff, E. A. (1972). Notes on a conversational practice: Formulating place. In D. Sudnow (Ed.), *Studies in social interaction* (pp. 75-119). New York: Free Press.

Schegloff, E. A. (1979). On the relevance of repair to syntax-for-conversation. In T. Givon (Ed.), *Discourse and syntax* (pp. 261-288). New York: Academic Press.

Schegloff, E. A., & Sacks, H. (1979). Opening up closings. *Semiotica, 7,* 289-327.

Sennett, R. (1977). *The fall of public man: On the social psychology of capitalism.* New York: Alfred A. Knopf.

Sennett, R. (1990). *The conscience of the eye: The design and social life of cities.* New York: Alfred A. Knopf.

Sherzer, J. (1983). *Kuna ways of speaking: An ethnographic perspective.* Austin: University of Texas Press.

Silverstein, M. (1976). Shifters, linguistic categories, and cultural description. In K. Basso & H. Selby (Eds.), *Meaning in anthropology* (pp. 11-55). Albuquerque: University of New Mexico Press.

Simmel, G. (1902). The number of members as determining the sociological form of the group. *American Journal of Sociology, 8,* 1-46, 158-196.

Simmel, G. (1903-1904). The sociology of conflict. *American Journal of Sociology, 9,* 490-525, 672-698, 798-811.

Simmel, G. (1905-1906). The sociology of secrecy and of the secret societies. *American Journal of Sociology, 11,* 441-498.

Simmel, G. (1924). The sociology of the senses: Visual interaction. In R. E. Park & E. W. Burgess (Eds.), *Introduction to the science of sociology* (pp. 356-361). Chicago: University of Chicago Press.

Simmel, G. (1950). *The sociology of Georg Simmel* (K. H. Wolff, Ed.). New York: Free Press.

Smith, W. J. (1977). *The behavior of communicating: An ethological approach.* Cambridge, MA: Harvard University Press.

Solomon, R. C. (1990). *A passion for justice.* Reading, MA: Addison-Wesley.

Stigler, J. W., Shweder, R. A., & Herdt, G. (Eds.). (1990). *Cultural psychology: Essays on comparative human development.* Cambridge: Cambridge University Press.

Stocking, G. W. (1968). *Race, culture, and evolution: Essays in the history of anthropology.* New York: Free Press.

Stocking, G. W. (1987). *Victorian anthropology.* New York: Free Press.

Streeck, J. (1984). Embodied contexts, transcontextuals, and the timing of speech acts. *Journal of Pragmatics, 8,* 113-137.

Streeck, J. (1996). How to do things with things: Objets trouvés and symbolization. *Human Studies, 19,* 365-384.

Streeck, J., and Mehus, S. (in press). Microethnography: The study of practices. In K. L. Fitch &
R. E. Sanders (Eds.), *Handbook of language and social interaction.* Mahwah, NJ: Lawrence Erlbaum.

Streeck, J., & Kallmeyer, W. (2001). Interaction by inscription. *Journal of Pragmatics, 33,* 465-490.

Suchman, L. A. (1987). *Plans and situated actions: The problem of human-machine communication.* Cambridge: Cambridge University Press.

Tacitus, C. (1970). *Germania.* London: Heinemann.

Taylor, J. R. (1989). *Linguistic categorization: Prototypes in linguistic theory.* Oxford: Clarendon.

Tylor, E. B. (1856). *Researches into the early history of mankind.* Chicago: University of Chicago Press.

Tylor, E. B. (1871). *Primitive culture.* London: J. Murray.

Urban, G. (1991). *A discourse-centered approach to culture: Native South American myths and rituals.* Austin: University of Texas Press.

von Humboldt, W. (1988). *On language.* Cambridge: Cambridge University Press. (Original work published 1836)

Whorf, B. L. (1956). *Language, thought, and reality.* Cambridge: MIT Press.

Wikan, U. (1990). *Managing turbulent hearts: A Balinese formula for living.* Chicago: University of Chicago Press.

Wundt, W. (1975). *Völkerpsychologie. Eine Untersuchung der Entwicklungsgesetze von Sprache, Mythus und Sitte.* Aalen, Germany: Scientia Verlag. (Original work published 1911)

Xenophon. (1962). *Anabasis.* Norman: University of Oklahoma Press.

PART IV

Processes and Functions

10

Emotional Communication

SANDRA METTS
SALLY PLANALP

The period since the chapter on emotion was written for the first edition of the *Handbook of Interpersonal Communication* has been an exciting and expansive one. Recent work on emotion has flourished in large part because it has grown from the well-established roots of research traditions described in earlier reviews. The research on message variables and pragmatics reviewed by Bowers, Metts, and Duncanson in 1985 still serves as a solid basis for current work on how emotion is communicated in face-to-face interaction. Emotional communication in intimate relationships, as reviewed by Metts and Bowers in 1994, continues to be studied with increasing sophistication and realism. Developments in the field of communication are part of a broadly interdisciplinary revival of interest and research in emotion; some have called this the "emotion revolution," although perhaps *evolution* would be a more appropriate term.

We recognize that any attempt to review and integrate this large body of scholarship is necessarily selective. Therefore, we limit ourselves in this chapter to three primary objectives. First, we believe it is important to provide an overview of recent developments in approaches to emotion that characterize both interpersonal communication and related disciplines. A number of books and review articles and chapters have appeared recently that summarize current thinking about and approaches to emotion. These perspectives are informative for those who wish to understand the broad scope of emotion theory and/or to extend their own research efforts. We therefore provide a brief review of these works.

Second, however, we attempt to provide a more focused integration of empirical research on emotional communication in social and personal relationships by drawing on the organizing principles of the contextual model of interaction (Bradbury & Fincham, 1989, 1991). We present research relevant to both distal and proximal contexts that influence the processes of emotional communication. Finally, we offer several suggestions for research on emotional communication that hold promise as agenda items for future research in interpersonal communication.

RECENT DEVELOPMENTS

Interpersonal Communication

In the past 15 to 20 years, but especially in the past decade, dozens of major books and reviews on emotion have appeared in several academic disciplines. Among interpersonal communication scholars, the second half of the 1990s generated the first books on emotional communication, most notably Andersen and Guerrero's *Handbook of Communication and Emotion* (1998a), which showcases important and varied programs of research conducted by many of the prominent scholars in interpersonal communication. That volume contains chapters on basic principles, strategic embarrassment, communication strategies used to manage negative emotions, communication problems associated with depression, the communication of social support, the role of emotion in persuasion, and more. It was preceded by Omdahl's *Cognitive Appraisal, Emotion, and Empathy* (1995), which investigates empirical links among the three factors named in the title and shows how individuals use appraisal information to decode emotional messages and how this contributes to empathy. Andersen and Guerrero's handbook was followed by Planalp's book *Communicating Emotion* (1999), which synthesizes a range of interdisciplinary research around basic issues

that bear upon emotional communication, not only in dyadic interaction but also in social, moral, and cultural systems.

Not only have the seeds planted by earlier research dispersed in the field of interpersonal communication, they have also taken root in a number of other fields of inquiry and have yielded a variety of new concepts, interesting ideas, surprising facts, and intriguing questions. In the next subsection we provide a brief overview of developments in those disciplines, with an emphasis on issues and perspectives that have been informative to communication scholars and that offer promise for future research.

Interdisciplinary Approaches

Multi- and interdisciplinary efforts abound, although the bulk of the work is still done by psychologists, as shown in the brief but authoritative reviews in the two editions of the *Handbook of Emotions* (Lewis & Haviland, 1993; Lewis & Haviland-Jones, 2000). The second edition includes introductory chapters on interdisciplinary foundations written by a philosopher, a historian, an anthropologist, a sociologist, a psychiatrist, an artist, and three psychologists (general, clinical, and evolutionary). Several of these authors recognize explicitly the interdisciplinary nature of emotion research and emotion processes. Solomon (2000) writes of a "serious effort to join forces with psychologists, neurologists, anthropologists, and moral philosophers to obtain a more holistic theory of emotion" (p. 9). Stearns (2000, p. 24) bemoans the fact that links between history and the other social sciences, especially psychology, are not well developed. White (2000, p. 30) contrasts the popular scientific notion of emotion residing in the brain with the commonsense understandings of emotion in terms of social relations and situations that anthropologists typically investigate. Kemper (2000, p. 45) says that psychologists "own" emotion but that many other disciplines, including his own home discipline of sociology, are concerned with affective life. Tan (2000, p. 116) takes up the argument that we need art to understand emotion more deeply. Interestingly, the psychologists in this collection do not address interdisciplinary efforts as directly, although Frijda's (2000) title implies that "the psychologists' point of view" is only one of several. The range of outlets for publication of emotion research is expanding, not only within academic circles but beyond them to best-sellers. The primary journal dedicated to emotion research, *Motivation and Emotion* (from the 1970s), has been joined by *Cognition and Emotion* (from the 1980s), and more recently by *Emotion* and *Consciousness and Emotion*. The bulk of the research is still to be found in the journals of specific disciplines and interdisciplinary journals, but the numbers of books published on the topic have increased dramatically in the past decade. The long-standing book series Studies in Emotion and Social Interaction, published by Cambridge University Press (formerly the "green books") has continued into a second phase (now a rainbow of colors) and has been joined by the impressive Affective Science series published by Oxford University Press and the Emotions and Social Behavior series published by Guilford. Popular books have also brought emotion to the attention of the reading public in ways that would have been unimaginable a decade ago. The best-seller *Emotional Intelligence,* by Daniel Goleman (1995), comes to mind, but so do *The Art of Happiness,* by the Dalai Lama and Howard Cutler (1998), and *The Care of the Soul,* by Thomas Moore (1992). Antonio Damasio has become a kind of Oliver Sachs of the emotion world, relating wild tales of strange and intriguing neurological disorders that have received some popular attention (*Descartes' Error,* 1994; *The Feeling of What Happens,* 1999).

Although each discipline brings a distinctive perspective to bear on the problems of emotion, many scholars in a variety of fields have engaged issues that have concerned communication scholars all along. In the subsections that follow we offer a brief tour of some of the primary developments in each of these academic disciplines (ordered alphabetically), especially as they serve to frame, inform, and pose further questions for research from a communication perspective.

Anthropology

More than any other discipline, anthropology has moved emotion out of the head and body and into the social world, prompted by the recognition that people in many cultures consider emotion to occur *between* people, not *inside* them (Lutz, 1988), and so do Americans, perhaps more than we realize (Andersen & Guerrero, 1998b; Shaver, Wu, & Schwartz, 1992). Studies have leaned toward the lexical (for a review, see Besnier, 1990), including work on several emotion lexicons (e.g., for Indonesian languages, Heider, 1991; for Ifaluk, Lutz, 1986; for Chinese, Shaver et al., 1992), work that attempts to avoid translation problems by finding a natural semantics metalanguage to capture the essential meanings of emotions (Wierzbicka, 1995), and analyses of emotion metaphors across cultures (Kövecses, 2000, pp. 139-181). In the nonverbal domain, the big news for teachers who have presented Ekman's work on universal facial expressions of emotion as gospel in basic interpersonal communication classes is that it may not be so (more on this point later).

Interpersonal communication in its richest sense is enacted through social episodes, which have received a great deal of attention from anthropologists. They focus "on the institutionalized, even ritualized, practices that express and transform the social emotional problems of everyday life" (White, 1993, p. 36). In this literature we can find intriguing alternatives for handling conflict from the

Ifaluk islanders (Lutz, 1988), for controlling anger from the Inuit Eskimos (Briggs, 1970), for spreading contagious joy from the Balinese (Wikan, 1990), for creating and sustaining moods from Fijian Indians (Brenneis, 1990), for managing improper feelings through gossip from Nukulaelae islanders (Besnier, 1995), for appreciating feeling as a vital force in social relations from the Ilongots of the Philippine jungles (Rosaldo, 1980), for managing expressiveness from the Wolof of Senegal (Irvine, 1990), and for challenging social arrangements through passionate song from Egyptian Bedouins (Abu-Lughod, 1990).

Managing emotionally charged conflict through "disentangling," as practiced by many of the South Pacific island groups, is an intriguing and instructive example of cultural practices used to straighten out tangled relationships (Watson-Gegeo & White, 1990). Disentangling takes place when a problematic event draws the protagonists and an audience of community members together to (re)construct an account of the event that heals relationships. The goal is not so much to describe emotions and thoughts accurately as it is to shape them in ways that open channels of communication and reconciliation. For example, sadness and shame are more commonly expressed than anger, signaling that repair is valued over retribution (White, 1990, pp. 56-57). Interpretations of problematic events (both rational and emotional) are seen as flexible and are shaped to foster fellowship rather than fairness or face. Scholars and practitioners in more Westernized cultures have used a related procedure called "reintegrative shaming" to push people or organizations to come to terms with the wrong they have done and yet to reintegrate offending parties back into the community (Braithwaite & Mugford, 1994; Makkai & Braithwaite, 1994a, 1994b).

Art

As a conglomerate of academic disciplines, art has just begun to examine several ways in which artists' own concerns link up with the rest of emotion scholarship. Obviously, people have emotional reactions to objects of art, including the visual arts, music, dance, literature, theater, and film (Plantinga & Smith, 1999; Tan, 2000). When we view movies and theater, we experience terror, disgust, and sadness vicariously by identifying with characters, but through our exposure to many different media we may also experience more subtle aesthetic emotions, such as awe or the love of beauty (Lazarus & Lazarus, 1994, pp. 129-136). Songs and movies especially may teach us in subtle ways what emotions are typical or expected in interpersonal situations, such as suffering for love or violent anger in conflict. Always controversial is the issue of whether experiencing feelings vicariously serves to indulge, purge, or educate our emotions (Scheff, 1979).

Emotion is also involved in the production of creative works of all kinds. Actors are called upon to portray emotions, and the Stanislavski method requires actors to use their imaginations to conjure up not just the expressions but the feelings as well (Hochschild, 1983). Creativity is also associated with flow experiences, in which the ego is lost in the task at hand, the sense of time is altered, and the experience is remembered later as deep enjoyment sometimes bordering on ecstasy (Csikszentmihalyi, 1990). Interestingly, conversation is often reported as a "flow" experience, even though it is no longer widely considered an art form.

Art can also be used as a form of evidence in work aimed at understanding emotion. Certainly, compelling literary quotes have enlivened many a dry scientific paper, but some authors have used works of art as their primary bases of evidence. Oatley (1992) uses Tolstoy's *Anna Karenina* and other literary texts to illustrate and develop his theory. Spacks (1995) analyzes boredom as it is described in a wide variety of literary texts. In one book, Miller (1993) analyzes codes of honor and shame in ancient Icelandic sagas; in another, he turns his attention to disgust, examining it through scientific work and literary texts (Miller, 1997). Of course, historians have long relied heavily on literary texts as evidence, and they continue to do so (see below). Because interpersonal relationships are so frequently the subject matter of art, there is much to be learned from film, music, and other art forms about how emotions function in close relationships.

Business

Business has contributed little original work on its own, but it has been quick to pick up on the "emotional intelligence" paradigm developed by Salovey and Mayer (1990; for a more recent summary, see Salovey, Bedell, Detweiler, & Mayer, 2000) and popularized by Goleman (1995). The basic thrust of this concept is that people in business, especially leaders, have been overly rational and have neglected critical emotional skills. They will "work smarter" if they embrace or at least become reconciled with the intuitive, the emotional, and the social (Cooper & Sawaf, 1996). Much of the literature on emotional intelligence has a decidedly practical, airport-reading style (Goleman, 1998; Ryback, 1998; Weisinger, 1998), but more scholarly collections can also be found (e.g., Ashkanasy, Härtel, & Zerbe, 2000; Fineman, 1993, 2000).

Among the important contributions to interpersonal communication scholarship made by this work are (a) the shifting of emotion out of the ghetto of personal relationships into professional relationships as well; (b) the legitimation of the role of emotion in decision making, commitment, and creative problem solving, whether done interpersonally, impersonally, or alone; (c) the emphasis on emotional and social skills as extremely important "added value" beyond technical skills in the workplace, especially for jobs that require workers to have substantial interaction with other people; and (d) the recognition of the roles of empathy, persuasion, and interpersonal sensitivity in effective leadership and teamwork.

Nearly all of the books mentioned above have chapters or extended sections on communication skills. For example, Weisinger's 1998 book *Emotional Intelligence at Work* includes topics such as sensitivity, self-disclosure, assertiveness, dynamic listening, criticism, team communication, and analyzing relationships. Goleman's 1998 book *Working With Emotional Intelligence* is as much about social skills as it is about emotional skills. A cynical interpretation might be that the new emotional tornado sucks up every related idea in its path; a more generous one is that communication scholars have failed to recognize the essential emotional underpinnings of many basic interpersonal processes. Certainly, work in business focuses attention on the links between emotional processes and everyday communication skills in ways that are less obvious in the work being done in other disciplines.

History

History has taught us that writing about emotion changes over time, and, presumably, so do the emotions and the emotional standards described in written texts. Two themes appear to be prominent sources of lessons for interpersonal communication scholars (Stearns, 2000). The first is that standards and strategies for emotion control have changed over the centuries, and not uniformly in the direction of increasing control. Among the most intriguing ideas for interpersonal scholars is Stearns's (1994) description of American "cool," the modern emotion standard that requires moderation and control, at least in public and at least most of the time. Interpersonal scholars might ask whether the standard applies to close relationships (or perhaps just its opposite), what effect the public standard has on private life, and how the standard guides our discourse about personal problems as clinicians, as scholars, and as people.

The second theme in historical work is that changes in family, social class, and gender roles are accompanied by changes in emotional expectations. Feelings dear to the hearts of interpersonal researchers—love, jealousy, loneliness, anger, grief—are shaped by historical forces in ways that have interesting parallels for communication issues. We cannot assume that current ways of communicating love, methods for socializing and controlling children (through fear, shame, and the like), or strategies for managing jealousy or grief have always been or always will be what they are now. In particular, historical work should remind us of the sensitivity of emotional communication to changes in social roles, power dynamics, gender roles, access to privacy, and other life circumstances (Lofland, 1985; Stephen, 1994).

Philosophy

Philosophers have engaged the question of what makes a good life and how emotion contributes to or detracts from such a life. Solomon (2000) describes how emotion has been viewed historically, from Aristotle's belief in moderation to the Stoics' denial, to the deadly sins of the Middle Ages, to emotion's enslavement to reason during the Enlightenment, to ambivalence about the value of emotion in the modern era, to cautious respect in the past few decades. De Sousa (1987), Greenspan (1995), and Stocker (1996) have argued that emotion is essential in decision making, especially moral decision making, because it is a source of values. These authors are concerned with individual decision making, but emotion is equally important for interpersonal decision making, in ways that have yet to be explored. Solomon (1989) has argued for a variety of emotions as the foundations of

justice that goes well beyond the simple anger and guilt of equity theory.

Another important concern for philosophers and communication scholars alike is the morality of emotion. For philosophers, the problem is framed as whether we are responsible for our emotions; communication scholars would frame the problem as whether we are responsible for our emotional discourse—the effects on others of emotionally charged messages (e.g., shame appeals; Planalp, Hafen, & Adkins, 2000) and the morality of the general cultural discourse on emotion. For example, we might consider whether there is a link between modern anger (in the forms of road rage and youth anger) and public discourses of entitlement, the premium put on strength and action, and the general belief that emotions "happen" and are largely beyond our control, all of which promote acting out of anger (Averill, 1993) and using harmful speech as a weapon (Leets & Giles, 1997).

Psychology

Psychologists have devoted themselves primarily to understanding emotion as an intrapersonal phenomenon, but certainly not exclusively so. One of the most promising developments from the point of view of interpersonal communication is that psychologists have increasingly recognized emotions as interpersonal and social phenomena (Frijda & Mesquita, 1994; Parkinson, 1995). Because the work in psychology is so extensive, we highlight below only two major strains of research that are most directly relevant to communication: the expression and suppression of emotion, and the manifestation and effects of emotion in interpersonal contexts. For useful collections containing classical works in psychology, we recommend the recent volumes edited by Jenkins, Oatley, and Stein (1998) and Parrott (2001); for engaging debates about fundamental issues, see Ekman and Davidson (1994) and Mayne and Bonanno (2001).

Expression and suppression of emotion. The view of emotional expression so commonly held that it is embedded in our vocabularies is that we are "gripped," "seized," or "overcome" by emotion (Kövecses, 1990), and we feel compelled to "express" or "vent" it. Although there is no doubt some truth to this view (e.g., Christophe & Rimé, 1997), it has probably been exaggerated, and it may be a self-fulfilling prophecy (Bushman, Baumeister, & Stack, 1999); based on this view, emotional control has taken the high ground. Interpersonal scholars take for granted that we often make choices about whether and how to express or suppress feelings, and the scholarly literature gives us some grounds for making wise ones. Pennebaker (1995, 1997) has tackled the question of whether it is therapeutic to express feelings resulting from trauma through writing. Kennedy-Moore and Watson (1999) have pulled together an excellent collection of articles analyzing the pros and cons of expression and nonexpression of emotion in a number of contexts. We have also become aware of how expressed emotion can be contagious (Cappella, 1995; Hatfield, Cacioppo, & Rapson, 1994), and several scholars have raised the question of what exactly is expressed (see chapters in Russell & Fernández-Dols, 1997; see also Fridlund, 1994).

Although all emotions are social to some degree, certain ones inhabit almost exclusively social territory. The so-called social emotions have received a great deal of research attention, with interpersonal implications drawn clearly and explicitly. Baumeister, Stillwell, and Heatherton's (1994) analysis of guilt is explicitly "an interpersonal approach"; these authors argue that the principal purpose of guilt is to maintain and repair relationships. Some researchers are studying other members of the shame family, embarrassment (Miller, 1996) and shame itself (Tangney & Fischer, 1995), in the interest of understanding everyday experience and improving clinical practice. Jealousy is a mainstay (Salovey, 1991; White & Mullen, 1989). Leary and Kowalski (1995) have analyzed social anxiety, or what they call "stage fright in everyday life."

Manifestation and effects of emotion. There have been some interesting new research developments regarding the manifestation and effects of emotion in interpersonal contexts (Richards & Gross, 2000). Clark and Taraban (1991), for example, have explored the influence of type of relationship (exchange or communal) on emotion expression and have found that emotion expression is greater in communal than in exchange relationships. Gottman's (1994) work on physiological entrainment between married couples is familiar to many interpersonal scholars; his work on how families communicate emotional styles or philosophies to children is less well-known but just as important (Gottman, Katz, & Hooven, 1997). In a controversial book fostering the spirit of empathy, Christensen and Jacobson (2000) suggest that trying to change one's spouse may be less fruitful than trying to understand and accept his or her feelings and behavior. Also surprisingly social are Saarni's (1999) formulation of the components of and development of emotional competence and Salovey et al.'s (2000) notion of "emotional intelligence."

Sociology

Sociologists focus on the role of emotion in social interaction, but especially as influenced by social structure, power, connection, and social change (Kemper, 2000). For example, Scheff (1990) places shame, especially unacknowledged shame, at the crux of micro- and macroprocesses in social control and conformity. As Retzinger (1995a) states so simply, "Shame tells us that we are both separate and social beings" (p. 1105). Clark's (1997) analysis of sympathy should serve as a model for multifaceted research questions and multimethod research, including extensive use of texts such as newspaper articles, blues songs, and greeting cards. Hochschild (1990) has analyzed how emotions, like earthquakes, reveal stresses as the tectonic plates of social life drift, shift, and come into tension. Sociologists also share concerns for the politics and power dynamics of emotion with anthropologists (Lutz, 1990) and business scholars (several chapters in Ashkanasy et al., 2000).

Hochschild's (1983) early work on emotion management in the workplace is a natural topic for communication scholars, who have applied and extended it into new types of workplaces and new issues (see the review by Waldron, 1994; see also Krone, Chen, Sloan, & Gallant, 1997; Tracy & Tracy, 1998), as have researchers in other fields (see Planalp, 1999). Most of this work has a decidedly organizational bent, but interpersonal scholars can learn from it about shared emotional dynamics, strategies to control emotions, empathy burnout, dilemmas of self-control and sincerity, and, of course, the influence of social context on emotional issues in dyads. Work in interpersonal communication has been criticized for treating the dyad as an isolated social unit, and the accusation holds true for most studies of emotional communication. Emotionally charged issues are usually framed as problems for a dyad (especially a couple) to work out, with little attention to the social politics of those issues and how private practice and public discourse shape expectations. What counts as unfairness, lack of supportiveness, or excessive dependence depends on social norms as well as dyadic rules.

It should be evident by this point that the extensive interest in emotion experience and expression available in disciplines outside of communication has much to contribute to our understanding of emotional communication. The question that remains to be answered, however, is what unique insights interpersonal communication theory can contribute to the discourse on emotion. We turn now to that question.

INTEGRATING CURRENT RESEARCH: AN INTERPERSONAL COMMUNICATION PERSPECTIVE

Before we address the types of research questions, methods, assumptions, and applications suggested by interpersonal communication theory for the study of emotion, we begin with a caveat. Interpersonal communication theory can do little to help us understand some aspects of emotion experience, such as physiological qualities of arousal. It can, however, significantly inform the efforts of scholars and clinicians who are attempting to chart the implications of the claim that emotions are social phenomena (for a review, see Parkinson, 1996). Clearly, emotions are often experienced outside of social relations, as when a stunning sunrise evokes awe, an unfamiliar sound startles, or a busy traffic intersection induces fear. Yet even when people are alone, memories of prototypical experiences and the influence of imagined others guide emotional expressions and probably the feelings themselves (Fridlund, 1994). When people interact with others, the nature of their contact (face-to-face, one observing the other, speaking on the telephone) and the nature of the relationship (friends or strangers) influence emotional expressions such as smiling or wincing (Bavelas, Black, Lemery, & Mullett, 1986; Jakobs, Manstead, & Fischer, 1999). Indeed, most of the time emotions emerge from interactions between people, and they find their meaning within social and personal relationships (Averill, 1980; de Rivera & Grinkis, 1986; Schwartz & Shaver, 1987). As such, emotions are both motivational systems and contextualized communication challenges. In this section we hope to contribute to the scholarly dialogue on emotions as social phenomena by showing how our knowledge of message features in relationship contexts might inform current thinking about emotions and open up avenues for future research.

This is not the first summary chapter to address this issue. In 1993, Gallois presented a summary of research on the language (linguistic features) of emotion communication comparing interpersonal and intergroup contexts. More recently, Guerrero and Andersen (2000) have offered an excellent summary of the role of several emotion families (affectionate emotions, self-conscious emotions, melancholic emotions, and hostile emotions) in the three stages of relationship development (early stage, maintenance, and dissolution). Our approach is complementary to these existing reviews, but more specifically focused on interaction features. We take as our organizing framework the model of relational interaction known as the contextual model of interaction (Bradbury & Fincham, 1989, 1991). This model enables us to explore preexisting influences on interaction processes and outcomes in social and personal relationships (elements in the "distal context") as well as emergent and contingent features of the interaction (elements of the "proximal context"). Our concern is not so much with types of emotions that might be salient in relationships at different times as it is with the process of emotion communication more generally. We therefore begin with a discussion of how emotional expression can be conceptualized as emotional communication. We then move to a more detailed discussion of how principles of interpersonal communication can serve as a framework to integrate current research on emotion and forecast future explorations.

Characterizing Emotional Expression

Although it may not seem controversial to state that emotions are communicative, the implications of this claim are complex. Depending upon disciplinary focus and scholarly tradition, researchers employ various terms to describe the visible and/or auditory manifestation of emotional experience, including *emotional signaling, emotional display, emotional expression,* and *emotional communication* (see Planalp, 1998). The preference for particular definitional terms reflects, in part, a scholar's position on the questions of whether there is isomorphism between the experience of any particular emotion and its expression and whether social controls on emotion expression can override the isomorphism if it does exist.

In early investigations of emotion display, Ekman and Friesen (1975) found that several basic emotions (e.g., fear, disgust, anger, sadness, surprise, and joy) could be recognized from facial expressions at levels better than chance across cultures (especially across Western and non-Western cultures with little exposure to Western influences). Ekman and his colleagues continued to generate further evidence over the years (e.g., Ekman et al., 1987), and the universality of facial expressions of emotion became accepted truth. In 1994, however, Russell looked at the work critically and drew complicated and subtle conclusions that questioned the methodological approach and conceptual premises of the existing work. He concluded, for example, that it is easy to distinguish positive from negative expressions (joy versus sadness), but much more difficult to distinguish among negative expressions (anger, fear, disgust, sadness). He even challenged the assumption that facial expressions are interpreted as emotions with specific labels (fear, surprise, and so on) rather than as responses to situations ("She looks the way you look at a small child playing") or as instrumental actions ("She is shielding herself from something") (see also Bavelas & Chovil, 1997; Frijda & Tcherkassof, 1997). Ekman (1994) has, of course, defended his findings, but what seemed to be unquestioned truth is now debatable.

Indeed, recent empirical research continues to demonstrate inconsistencies in the so-called coherence hypothesis. This research offers convincing evidence that posed facial expressions may not always be interpreted as the emotions they are intended to portray, and, conversely, primary emotions are not invariably manifested in the facial expressions one would expect. In a laboratory study, Fernández-Dols, Sánchez, Carrera, and Ruiz-Belda (1997) asked participants to watch emotion-arousing films and videotaped their facial expressions. Results indicated that only 2 out of the 35 participants who reported basic emotions exhibited the prototypical facial expressions, and another 3 participants actually showed prototypical facial expressions predicted for different basic emotions. Thus the participants' self-reported emotional experiences (i.e., sadness, fear, anger, disgust, surprise, happiness) did not reliably predict facial expressions even in a laboratory setting with no other persons present. Outside the laboratory, at the Olympic Games in Barcelona, some gold medal winners who were very happy (as we would expect and as they reported) showed facial expressions closer to anger or sadness than to joy (Fernández-Dols & Ruiz-Belda, 1995).

It appears, then, that although there may be a "natural" display pattern at some level for the primary emotions, the utility of this link for scholars and laypersons who seek to understand emotional communication as an interpersonal process may be limited. The experience and expression of emotions, both primary and social emotions, are enmeshed with normative expectations and constraints. For example, the happy gold medal winners were more likely to smile while greeting the crowd than when backstage (Fernández-Dols & Ruiz-Belda, 1995). Particularly within the complex environment of ongoing interaction, social and relational norms moderate the direct influence from innate display patterns (e.g., Averill, 1980, 1993; Heise & Calhan, 1995; Kemper, 1978). With little or no conscious effort, speakers respond to situational cues of appropriateness or "display rules."

They interrupt the actions of their facial muscles so that no emotion display is visible and create facial patterns that look like emotions when no emotions are felt (Ekman, 1997). Ekman and Friesen (1975) have identified five ways in which persons alter their emotional expressions to conform to the display rules: inhibition (suppressing the expression of a felt emotion), simulation (expressing an emotion when no arousal is felt), intensification (expressing emotion to a greater degree than it is felt), deintensification (expressing an emotion to a lesser degree than it is felt), and masking (expressing one emotion when another emotion is actually felt). Deep socialization may take the process one step further, so that not only are expressions controlled but the actual feelings are as well (Hochschild, 1983; Planalp, 1999, pp. 71-103). In some situations, such as when danger lurks or when support is needed, it may be more important for an individual to suppress emotion or enact an emotion (whether felt fear or faked sympathy) than to feel it.

The fact that people can and do alter the expression of even the primary emotions suggests that *emotion display* or *emotion expression* may be more aptly termed *emotional communication,* in the sense that emotional information, like other types of information, is shaped for audiences. This does not discount the fact that "leakage" of arousal sometimes occurs (Ekman, 1982), particularly for strongly felt and/or socially inappropriate emotions (Gallois, 1993). But leakage can be seen as the individual's unsuccessful but nonetheless informative attempt to control information about his or her feelings in the presence of other people. More specifically, we view emotion information manifested in the presence of other people as a message for three reasons.

First, the nature of its manifestation, both nonverbally and linguistically, is *constrained* by historical, cultural, relational, and situational circumstances. Emotions may (or may not) be activated internal states, but when they are communicated, they are packaged in ways that are consistent with other communication practices. For example, Shimanoff (1985) examined the expression of emotion during naturally occurring conversations recorded by participants with their friends and relational partners. She found a "preferential hierarchy regarding references to emotions" that followed the broader social norm of politeness (i.e., expressing more regard for a listener's positive face than for one's own). Similarly, Zammuner (2000) found that respondents frequently mentioned trying to control negative emotional expressions and reactions but trying sincerely to show and talk about positive experiences.

Second, the manifestation of emotional information has a *pragmatic* dimension. Whether intended or not (e.g., blushing or trembling), emotional signals stimulate responses from others, be they cognitive, affective, or behavioral. Cognitive responses may take the form of certain types of attributions: dispositional (e.g., "What a hothead!"), situational ("That comment must have really upset him"), or relational ("She is jealous because she loves me"). Affective responses may be complementary (feeling shame in response to contempt), symmetrical (feeling anger when confronted with anger), or shared (catching another person's depression), as is the case with emotional contagion (Hatfield, Cacioppo, & Rapson, 1992) and empathy (Thomas & Fletcher, 1997). Finally, behavioral responses may be nonverbal (smiling, frowning, hugging, hitting, wincing, or silence when a speaking turn is mandated), verbal ("I know how you must feel" or "I'm sorry, I didn't mean to hurt you"), or action ("Let me outta here!").

Whatever the particular response elicited, expression of positive affect is more likely to meet with approval and expression of negative affect is more likely to meet with disapproval (Sommers, 1984), even unconsciously (Monahan, 1998). The ability to anticipate this consequence is apparently acquired early. In a study of elementary school children, Zeman and Garber (1996) found that their subjects were more likely to control anger, sadness, and physical pain in their expression when they were interacting with peers than when they were interacting with mother or father. Presumably, children want to avoid negative (and possibly dispositional) attributions from others in voluntary relationships, but believe that parents are less judgmental. It is important to note that other people's cognitive, affective, and behavioral responses to emotional expressions are often what facilitate or impede interpersonal and interactional goals. As Karasawa (1995) advises at the conclusion of a report on three studies that examined negative emotion expression and attributions, those who seek relief from depression or seek social support for emotional stress will likely encounter more productive responses if they frame their emotions as situational rather than dispositional.

Third, the manifestation of emotion in the presence of others functions to meet personal and interactional goals and, in this sense, is *strategic,* whether or not it is consciously intended to be (Thoits, 1985). Messages serve multiple goals, often distinguished as primary and secondary (e.g., Dillard, 1990; Dillard & Schrader, 1998; Schrader & Dillard, 1998). In actual practice, specific goals are often difficult to separate, and the goals of emotional messages are no exception. For example, an individual might express strong negative emotions primarily to vent and dispel the intensity, but if another person is present, the expression might also serve to gain the individual social support, increase understanding, or bring about change (Barbee, Rowatt, & Cunningham, 1998; Burleson & Goldsmith, 1998; Kennedy-Moore & Watson, 1999). Conversely, an individual may express emotion to achieve relational control ("I feel jealous when you go out with someone else"), relational repair ("I am so sorry I hurt your feelings"), relational enhancement ("I am so happy being with you"), and so forth, but in the process of meeting these primary goals, a secondary goal of venting restrained emotions may also be served.

Most researchers implicitly consider the inhibition of felt emotions to be a secondary goal in the service of a primary one (e.g., controlling one's irritation with a coworker in order to work on a task), but several scholars have investigated how emotional displays may be conjured up or at least released in the service of interactional goals. For example, respondents have reported concocting inauthentic displays of guilt in order to avoid or minimize punishment or negative evaluation by others (e.g., Tsoudis & Smith-Lovin, 1998). In a series of studies, Clark, Pataki, and Carver (1996) found that people reported using expressions of happiness to get others to like them, sadness to get help from others, and anger to get their way. This is due, no doubt, to the pragmatic consequences of emotion manifestation. That is, displays of happiness and anger tend to elicit attributions of dispositional affiliation and dominance, respectively, although a much stronger display (e.g., strong frown) is required to achieve dominance than is needed to achieve affiliation (e.g., a slight smile; Hess, Blairy, & Kleck, 2000). These attributions then enable a person to accomplish self-presentational goals of ingratiation and intimidation. Likewise, sad and fearful displays elicit low ratings on dominance but neutral (rather than low) ratings on affiliation (Knutson, 1996). This combination, then, apparently enables a person to accomplish the goal of supplication.

Although we tend to privilege practical goals and behavior over emotional goals, the practical often serves the emotional. O'Keefe and Figgé (1997) found that people did not manage their feelings in order to pursue their preestablished goals, but just the reverse. Where people were confronted with a large initial request, which they refused, followed by a smaller second request (the door-in-the-face persuasive strategy), they tended to grant the second request in the hopes of alleviating their guilt (although it didn't work). Similarly, Boster et al. (1999) found that experimental participants who were induced to feel guilty were more likely to volunteer to help in an experiment and were more likely to recruit friends when they were told that "it's something that you could feel really good about." In both cases, feelings of guilt and hope that the guilt could be overcome guided action, not vice versa.

In summary, emotional communication is constrained, pragmatic, and strategic in the same ways that all communication is. When emotional information is complex, particularly in the case of the so-called social emotions (e.g., jealousy, envy, hurt, guilt, shame, pride, lust, and love), emotional communication reflects and responds even more strongly to social/relational norms and interactional contingencies. When social goals are at stake (as they often are), the intensity, duration, and quality of emotions that are experienced and communicated are emergent and negotiable. We take this proposition seriously and explore its implications below.

Principles of Interpersonal Communication

More than 25 years ago, Miller and Steinberg (1975) formulated a view of interpersonal communication that moved it from a structural model to a developmental model. They began with the now widely accepted premise that not all face-to-face interactions are interpersonal. Some are noninterpersonal in the sense that they are guided by role expectations and generalized social norms. But as interactions become more frequent and varied, and as the breadth and depth of self-disclosure increase, partners begin to predict and explain behaviors based on their knowledge of each other as unique individuals.

In recent years, interpersonal scholars have begun to explore a similar developmental process under the rubric of *script theory*, suggesting that the idiosyncratic interaction patterns, routines, and expectations that characterize interpersonal communication emerge from and are adaptations of more broadly shared cultural knowledge structures, or scripts (Fitness, 2000). As interactions between individuals are sustained over a period of time, knowledge of how people in general are expected to act in certain situations is particularized to knowledge of how "this person," in "our relationship," in "this type of situation" is expected to act. These adaptations emerge through a process of negotiation as the rituals, routines, and language patterns of the broader culture become increasingly idiosyncratic and as couples develop their own relational cultures (Burleson, Metts, & Kirch, 2000) and interaction scripts (Planalp & Rivers, 1996).

Embedded within the developmental perspective are two important principles that serve as useful frameworks for discussing emotional communication. The first principle is that cultural or social-level knowledge is not abandoned during more interpersonal interactions, but continues to inform and guide participants. Not only does it facilitate attraction through the coordination of initial interactions, it also continues to guide expectations about how relationships in general, and this relationship in particular, should be enacted. Thus, for example, the expectation that social support should be provided when needed would be recognized as a prevailing social norm. This is no less true when the support is being sought by a relative stranger or acquaintance than when it is sought by a loved one. However, the means by which support is requested and the type of support provided become adapted to the informality of relationships over time, emerging seamlessly and inconspicuously during ordinary interaction (Leatham & Duck, 1990) and being expressed in idiosyncratic idioms such as "Hey, Ms. Whiney, just get over it" (Klingbeil-Parker, 1998). Similarly, husbands and wives draw on cultural assumptions about

what emotions are legitimate (traditionally, husbands' anger and wives' guilt, not vice versa). However, those assumptions may be adapted to the emerging relational scripts of particular couples. For example, recognizing women's anger and hurt as legitimate reasons for negotiation, even if it leads to conflict, can be a powerful way to realign social power and change assumptions about how marriages work (Benjamin, 1998), at least for those couples who tend to have positive (rather than negative) interaction patterns (Gottman & Levenson, 1992).

In sum, the norms that guide emotion communication at the broader social level are not abandoned as relationships develop. Rather, they are adapted in unique ways to the needs and exigencies of particular relationships (Planalp & Fitness, 1999), and those adaptations themselves, ironically, become resistant to change over time. Such mutually constructed expectations then become one aspect of the "distal context" of relational interaction (e.g., Bradbury & Fincham, 1989, 1991). That is, they exist prior to any particular interaction, but they shape the communicative messages, attributions, and expectations that constitute the interaction processes and outcomes in the more immediate or "proximal context."

A second principle that is derived from a developmental perspective is the recognition that interactions, including those involving emotional communication, are characterized by emergent and contingent features as well as preexisting relational patterns. Although distal factors exert some influence on the processes of interaction, influences that arise during the interaction (e.g., moods, message forms, attributions) necessarily constrain and/or facilitate emotional communication.

In the following section we turn our attention to the distal and proximal aspects of interpersonal communication that influence emotion expression. Relationship scholars have identified a number of elements operative in the distal context, but for our purposes, we examine three that are commonly associated with emotional communication: cultural-level knowledge structures or emotion scripts, sex role expectations, and preexisting individual differences (e.g., affective orientation, attachment style). We then explore elements of the proximal context and their role in the emotional interactions of persons in close relationships.

DISTAL FACTORS

Emotion Prototypes and Scripts

The coordination of social interaction derives largely from culturally shared knowledge structures that provide individuals with information about how to conduct themselves and how to interpret the actions of others when engaged in various activities. For example, when we dine in a restaurant, we expect that a server will bring menus, leave the table, return and allow us to make our dinner choices, leave again, return with the meals, leave again, and finally bring the check (Schank & Abelson, 1977). When certain elements in such a sequence of actions are different, we recognize that we are involved in a different "scene." For example, if we go to a counter, order food, pay for it, stand at the counter until we receive the food in paper wrappers, and carry it to a table ourselves, we are not "dining out" but rather "eating at a fast-food place." The same holds true for coordinating the activities that cumulatively engender a relationship (Baldwin, 1992, 1995). In Western culture, for example, first dates among college students tend to include certain activities (e.g., dinner and a movie) but exclude others (e.g., spending the evening with parents). (Indeed, when meeting parents is a central aspect of a date, the definition of the relationship has likely moved from casual to committed.)

Emotion scholars have recently used similar lenses to understand the coordination of emotional communication (e.g., Fehr, Baldwin,

Collins, Patterson, & Benditt, 1999; Fitness, 1996; Heise & Calhan, 1995; Lazarus & Lazarus, 1994; Shaver, Schwartz, Kirson, & O'Connor, 1987). They suggest that emotion schemata, prototypes, or scripts are defined as knowledge structures that represent a culture's view of the critical features of an emotion, including (a) the type of event, behavior, or other stimulus that is expected to trigger a certain type of emotion ("prescriptive norms"); (b) how, and with what intensity, that emotion should (or should not) be revealed, exhibited, or otherwise communicated to others ("reactive norms"); (c) the nature of the relationship with relevant others (i.e., those who serve as targets of the emotion and those who are present when it is experienced or communicated); and (d) status or power constraints (Conway, Di Fazio, & Mayman, 1999). Systematic combinations of elements across these domains constitute emotion scripts or prototypes. For example, although it is generally the norm that generous or kind actions evoke feelings of affection that can be overtly displayed, the norm against overt displays of affection between men constrains overt expression to certain contexts (e.g., sporting events) and certain types of relationships (e.g., father and son or brother relationships; Floyd & Morman, 1997).

The "romantic love script," which has been studied most intensively in Canadian college students but is widely held in the West, has features such as caring, good times, feeling free to talk about anything, and doing things together (Fehr, 1994). Those features prescribe as well as describe, at least in a general way, what is to be expected and how one is to act when "in love." Love scripts vary, of course, across history and cultures (Cancian, 1987; Dion & Dion, 1996; Singer, 1984a, 1984b, 1987) and have various permutations, such as passionate and companionate love (Fehr & Broughton, 2001; Hatfield & Walster, 1978); friendly, erotic, practical, altruistic, game-playing, and manic love (Hendrick & Hendrick, 1989); and maternal love, puppy love, and committed love versus infatuation (Fehr, 1994). Given that there are many varieties of love scripts, it is not surprising that there are "love problematics" when partners fail to recognize that their own ideas or preferences about love do not match their partners' ("If you loved me you would[n't] . . .") (Marston & Hecht, 1994).

Sex Role Expectations

A good deal of scholarship has been devoted to understanding the nature and extent of sex differences in emotional communication. Unfortunately, as with all research on emotional communication, this inquiry is complicated by operational difficulties. For example, if researchers assess recall and self-reports of emotions experienced and expressed, there is the possibility that individuals (perhaps unwittingly) may report sex role expectations, stereotypes, or gendered emotional scripts (Fischer, 2000). If researchers use stimulus materials (e.g., scenes from movies) to elicit emotional responses, there is the possibility that the ecological validity for findings in ordinary, situated interaction may be compromised. If researchers attempt to record and code actual interactions, they must determine how to code emotional expressions (e.g., linguistic references, paralinguistic cues, facial expressions), how to distinguish emotional from nonemotional expressions (happy smiles from merely polite smiles), how to distinguish emotional expressions that refer to other persons' emotional experiences from expressions referring to the participants' own emotional experiences (e.g., wincing in sympathy with another's distress), and how to distinguish emotional references or displays currently felt from those that are recalled from previous events ("I have fond memories of her").

Cutting across all of these research designs is the challenge of how to categorize emotions (Canary & Emmers-Sommer, 1997). Some scholars examine a limited range of emotions,

typically the primary emotions, whereas others are interested more broadly in positive emotions versus negative emotions or generalized positive and negative affect (Cacioppo & Gardner, 1999; Dillard & Peck, 2001). Some scholars distinguish levels of intensity for emotional experience, whereas others do not. Researchers interested in sex differences in emotional communication must also contend with the fact that any interaction under scrutiny is embedded within a relational context that may reformulate social expectations. Sex role expectations and behaviors are confounded with such sociological variables as power, status, and situational expectations, which may or may not be salient during a given interaction. Finally, regardless of the particular design used to collect data, researchers face the challenge of controlling for individual differences in emotional experience and expression. In sum, when reporting findings on sex differences in emotional communication, researchers must struggle to untangle the relative contributions of any innate or inherent patterns of emotional experience and/or expression that might reside in the intrapersonal level from the cultural, relational, and situational fabric of the interpersonal level in which they are embedded (Brody, 1997).

Needless to say, offering definitive conclusions about the presence or absence of sex differences in the experience or expression of emotion is problematic. Even comparisons of findings from studies using similar methods reveal inconsistent results. For example, in analyses of naturally occurring conversations, Anderson and Leaper (1998) found no difference in emotion references between male and female college students. By contrast, Goldshmidt (2000) found substantial differences in emotional references in the conversations of men and women at a community center, of boys and girls in a kindergarten, of men and women at family gatherings, and of men and women in interactions among friends. Indeed, she also found differences when she conducted "hidden" observations of switchboard operators in a tile manufacturing plant.

However, in order to further our discussion of sex role expectations as a distal factor in emotional communication, we offer two general claims: (a) Whether or not actual differences exist, the assumption that men and women enact different emotional scripts is a pervasive heuristic in American society; and (b) observed differences in emotional communication patterns between men and women, both in expressing emotions and in decoding the emotions of others, are probably better framed in terms of different social motives than in terms of different ability or biology.

Support for the presence of a gender-emotion heuristic can be found in a number of studies in which respondents were asked to rate hypothetical others or to imagine themselves in emotion-producing hypothetical situations. Kelly and Hutson-Comeaux (1999), for example, used 24 scenarios that depicted a target person over- or underreacting to happy, sad, or angry events in either an interpersonal (friend) or an achievement (work or occupation) context. Undergraduate judges rated how characteristic they believed these reactions to be for women and men. Results demonstrated that overreactions to happy and sad events were perceived to be more characteristic of women in the interpersonal context but were perceived to be more characteristic of men in the achievement context. Overreactions to angry scenarios, however, were rated as more characteristic of men, regardless of context. Using a similar design, Blier and Blier-Wilson (1989) asked respondents to rate their confidence in expressing certain emotions and the perceived consequences to same- and opposite-sex targets in hypothetical scenarios (using the Efficacy and Consequences Expectation for Social Skills Scale). The findings revealed stereotypical gender patterns: Males reported lower confidence in expressing anger to females in the scenario than to males, and

females reported higher confidence than did males in expressing liking/love/affection to males in the scenario. Female respondents were more confident in expressing fear and sadness than were male respondents, regardless of the gender of the person in the scenario. Respondents also judged females and recipients of negative emotions to feel worse and less powerful than their male counterparts. Overall, Blier and Blier-Wilson conclude that "subjects perceived that actors and recipients feel better when they behave in ways consistent with gender role stereotypes" (p. 292).

Perhaps even more compelling evidence that gendered emotion stereotypes exist as an organizing principle is found in studies comparing respondents' ratings of hypothetical others with their own self-reports in similar situations. Robinson and Johnson (1997) used 13 problematic hypothetical situations that were ambiguous in terms of what types of affective responses might be appropriate. When asked to rate the feelings of the "average person" in the situation, respondents characterized reactions of the average female as emotional, but the average male as feeling stressed. However, the labels that participants chose to describe their own subjective experiences were not affected by gender. Robinson, Johnson, and Shields (1998) conducted two studies using a word game as a stimulus. They divided participants into those who imagined the emotions in the game, those who observed players in the game, and those who actually participated in the game. All participants rated the perceived (or imagined) intensity of 17 feelings: socially desirable emotions oriented toward the self (e.g., satisfaction, pride), socially desirable emotions oriented toward others (e.g., sympathy for opponent, gratitude toward partner), socially undesirable emotions oriented toward self (e.g., disappointment, embarrassment), and socially undesirable emotions oriented toward others (e.g., anger toward partner or opponent). Ratings of the feelings of hypothetical players and ratings made by players a week later tended to exhibit gender stereotypes, but those made during the actual playing of the game did not.

The second claim regarding sex role expectations is that because emotions are socially embedded, observed sex differences are more likely a result of different social motives than of different ability or biology. For example, the long-accepted belief in women's greater empathic ability and interpersonal sensitivity compared with men has recently been recast in terms of differential motivation stemming from sex role expectations rather than differential ability. For example, Graham and Ickes (1998) speculate that as part of a self-presentational strategy, men learn to "tune out" or ignore other people's feelings and "effectively mask or suppress a social sensitivity which—if expressed—could cause them to be perceived as insufficiently strong and masculine" (p. 140). In support of this speculation, Ickes, Gesn, and Graham (2000) later concluded from a meta-analysis of 15 empathy studies that the relatively stronger performance of women on empathy measures occurs when subjects are aware that they are being evaluated on empathy-related measures and when gender role expectations relevant to empathy are made salient. These authors suggest that although the question of ability and motivation is still open to debate, it seems likely that the stereotype of "women's intuition" and greater "interpersonal sensitivity" is due more to women's willingness to invest effort to attend to relational cues.

This conclusion is further supported by the results of a broader study of male and female motives for emotion expression conducted by Timmers, Fischer, and Manstead (1998). These researchers employed scenarios that depicted emotion-evoking events and asked respondents to report the intensity of emotion they would feel, the probable types of expressions they would use (e.g., I would walk away,

I would say to my friend that I am angry, I would cry, I would yell, I would be silent), and their motives for expressing or not expressing emotions in each scenario. Their findings indicate, among other things, that men and women report different motives for either expressing or suppressing emotion. In general, the women in Timmers et al.'s sample were less reluctant than the men to display powerless emotions because they were more concerned than the men with the effect of expression on the relationship and less concerned with being judged as emotional. The men, on the other hand, exhibited more concern with power-based motives, such as being seen to be in control over the situation and creating a self-confident impression.

Overall, the research on sex differences in emotion is difficult to summarize because it is such a mixed bag of similarities, differences, and contingencies. The working Western assumption, and the heuristic that likely guides many interpersonal interactions, seems to be that women are more emotional than men, both in experience and in expression. This belief endures in spite of the fact that it is rarely upheld empirically, as assessed in Fischer's (2000) collection of reviews. A few elements of the broader gender stereotype have, however, received support; these include the findings that women, compared with men, tend to feel more comfortable with emotional discourse (Fivush & Buckner, 2000; Shields, 2000); are better judges of nonverbal cues to emotion (Hall, Carter, & Horgan, 2000), at least when motivated to attend to them (Ickes et al., 2000); and tend both to smile (LaFrance & Hecht, 2000) and to cry more (Vingerhoets & Scheirs, 2000). Otherwise, gender differences, if found at all, depend on a number of factors, including the emotion at issue and factors arising in particular situations (Canary & Emmers-Sommer, 1997; Kring, 2000; Kring & Gordon, 1998; Zammuner, 2000). As a result of the contingencies and variations, nearly all explanations center on social and cultural expectations associated with sex roles rather than on biological factors.

Individual Differences

The literature on individual differences in emotion experience and expression is extremely large and often interfaces with that on gender differences. Space does not permit a full review of this literature here, but we will discuss briefly two broad approaches to individual differences that are relevant to emotional communication because they are important features of the distal context. The first is that people do differ in how they process and express emotional information. The second is that people also differ in personality features that indirectly influence the coordination of emotional communication with relational partners.

Gohm and Clore (2000) provide a particularly comprehensive overview of existing dispositional responsiveness and expression measures. These authors systematize the numerous measures of individual differences into several categories to represent the conceptual foci of the measures and then submit the scales to hierarchical cluster analysis. Their findings suggest four clusters of individual differences in experience and expression of emotion: (a) absorption and attention, (b) clarity (in understanding, labeling, and/or articulating emotions), (c) intensity (in feelings and mood changes), and (d) expression (tendencies to be open in expression, inhibited, or ambivalent about expression). In various ways, the research on individual differences in emotion and emotional communication (expression and display) tends to reflect these general areas.

In a study of whether the dispositional tendency to be expressive is consistent across positive and negative affect, Gross, John, and Richards (2000) found that respondents' own ratings of their "habitual" emotional experiences were related to their expression of positive emotions when measured both by peer ratings of expressiveness and by observer ratings of videotaped responses to films. However, respondents' ratings of their "habitual" negative emotional experiences were related to peer ratings and observer ratings of expressiveness only for those respondents who were highly emotionally expressive. In other words, people are generally prone to match their expression of positive affect with its experience, but only dispositionally expressive people are likely to exhibit negative affect to others when they experience it.

Other researchers have examined individual differences in sensitivity to positive or negative affect cues in the environment that contribute to a characteristic emotional profile. In a diary study in which students reported their emotions three times a day for a month, Zelenski and Larsen (2000) found that positive emotions were experienced with greater frequency and intensity than negative emotions and were more highly intercorrelated than were the negative emotions. More relevant to our discussion here is their finding of high intersubject correlations; that is, people who were afraid a lot were also sad a lot. Zelenski and Larsen suggest that certain personality features influence vulnerability to valenced affect in that some people are sensitive to cues of reward and thus positive emotionality, whereas others are sensitive to cues of punishment and thus negative emotionality. In a similar vein, in examining the specific emotion of envy, Smith, Parrott, Diener, Hoyle, and Kim (1999) found strong support for the existence of a dispositional tendency to feel envy across a variety of situations independent of level of self-esteem. In a study of vengefulness, McCullough, Bellah, Kilpatrick, and Johnson (2001) found that it was a characteristic affective reaction to perceived wrongful acts by others. Individual differences in jealousy have also been established, although these differences appear to be confounded with other personality (e.g., self-esteem) and relational factors (e.g., trust, perceived equity) (Guerrero & Andersen, 1998), as well as with the nature of the jealousy-inducing situation (i.e., sexual involvement or emotional involvement of partner) (Nannini & Meyers, 2000).

Several personality variables that are not themselves emotional but appear to be relevant to emotional communication have also been identified. Primary among these is attachment style (Bartholomew & Horowitz, 1991; Bowlby, 1969, 1973, 1980; Shaver, Collins, & Clark, 1996; Simpson, 1990). Based on the interaction experiences that infants have with their primary caregivers, attachment theory suggests that individuals move into adulthood with characteristic emotional sensitivities or "working models" of how they expect relationships to unfold for them (e.g., Feeney, Noller, & Roberts, 1998, 2000). As might be expected, secure attachment individuals tend to report higher relationship satisfaction, happiness, and trust (Hazan & Shaver, 1987). In an examination of the viability of a two-dimensional model of attachment styles (i.e., positive/negative view of self/other), Bartholomew and Horowitz (1991) found that certain emotional expression profiles are associated with attachment types; for example, secure individuals are moderately expressive, dismissive individuals are not typically emotionally expressive, and preoccupied individuals are highly expressive. Becker-Stoll, Delius, and Scheitenberger (2001) found a similar pattern among adolescents during interactions with their mothers: Secure attachment style was associated with open and positive emotional expression (coded from facial expression), and dismissive attachment style was associated with inhibited emotional expression.

In emotionally salient events that sometimes occur in the context of intimate relationships, attachment styles also appear to function as interpretive screens (Feeney, 1995). In a study of relationship breakups, Barbara and Dion (2000) found that preoccupied individuals (compared with individuals

with other attachment styles) reported that their partners had initiated the breakups, that they had trouble adjusting to the termination, and that they experienced more negative emotions and fewer positive emotions associated with the breakups. These findings are consistent with those from earlier work by Feeney and Noller (1992), who found that ambivalent attachment orientation (particularly in preoccupied individuals) was associated with greater distress and less relief, whereas avoidant attachment orientation (particularly in dismissive individuals) was negatively associated with distress. Sprecher, Felmlee, Metts, Fehr, and Vanni (1998) also found that the fearful attachment style was positively associated with all measures of distress at the time of the breakup and currently, whereas the dismissing style was negatively associated with distress at the time of the breakup and currently. Attachment style may serve as a behavioral control (or lack of control) mechanism during intense negative arousal as well. In a study of reciprocally aggressive relationships, Bookwala and Zdaniuk (1998) found that after relationship problems were controlled for, preoccupied attachment style was still strongly associated with aggressive behavior in the relationship.

Other individual-differences variables that have received less systematic investigation but appear to be related to emotions such as love and relationship satisfaction include romantic beliefs (Jones & Cunningham, 1996; Sprecher & Metts, 1999) and the tendency to display accommodation toward one's partner (i.e., to refrain from responding destructively when one's partner acts badly and instead respond constructively; Rusbult, Yovetich, & Verette, 1996). In addition, several of the "Big Five" personality variables have shown consistent associations with emotion feelings, display, and regulation. For example, extraversion is associated with happiness and joy (Emmons & Diener, 1985), and openness (to novel experiences) is associated with greater felt intensity of emotion, both positive and negative (McCrae & Costa, 1991). In studies of facial displays, neuroticism has been found to be predictive of negative emotions and extraversion to be predictive of positive emotions (Keltner, 1996).

In summary, it appears that people share socially constructed scripts, or knowledge structures, about the nature and expression of various emotions in social and interpersonal contexts. There is also a belief that men and women differ in their tendencies to express certain types of emotions and to respond to the emotion displays of others, although there is perhaps more validity to the claim that men and women are simply motivated by different types of concerns in some contexts. Finally, there is convincing evidence that some people are dispositionally more expressive and perhaps more "emotional" in their tendency to respond to cues enhancing positive or negative affect. We turn now to a discussion of how these distal influences affect and are affected by emotional communication during relational interactions.

The Proximal Context

Although the distal factors we have described—knowledge of emotion prototypes or scripts, sex role parameters, and individual differences—are relatively stable features that frame expectations for given interactions, they are not immutable properties. They are, in fact, subject to modification from the reciprocal influence of interactions over time, including messages exchanged, attributions made, perceptions drawn, and consequences experienced. This process of adaptation engenders a couple's characteristic emotional communication patterns (Fitness, 1996). We suggest five ways in which these adaptations are manifested.

First, as relationships develop, the persons involved in them encounter increasingly complex levels of interconnectedness (Baxter,

1990; Hinde, 1997). They may feel more open about disclosing personal information, including information that is affectively valenced. This is particularly evident in the domain of the negative emotions, which are disfavored in both experience and expression in Western cultures (Metts & Bowers, 1994). Ironically, because negative affect is generally unexpected, it is more salient or informative to others than positive affect. In some cases, this information encourages greater relational understanding and more open communication; in other circumstances, however, it can strain or destabilize a relationship (Thomas & Fletcher, 1997). In a discussion of empathic accuracy, Ickes and Simpson (1997) note that during interactions where negative affect is threatening to self or the viability of the relationship, persons experience low motivation to perceive their partners' emotional communication accurately, a response that might actually be beneficial to the long-term stability of the relationship.

As a relationship develops, the partners also need to test and refine display rules that will guide their emotion experience and expression (Aune, 1997; Aune, Aune, & Buller, 1994; Aune, Buller, & Aune, 1996). Interestingly, although the experience and expression of positive emotions are more common than negative emotions across all stages of development, couples who are in midstage dating relationships report feeling and displaying more negative emotions than do couples in early- or late-stage development (Aune et al., 1996). This pattern suggests two possibilities. Compared with couples in the other stages, midstage couples may be more actively engaged in the negotiation of the cultural mandate against displaying negative emotions. Alternatively, perhaps couples who cannot use negative emotional information constructively or cannot counterbalance it with positive affect break up and consequently do not appear in cross-sectional samples. Gottman and Levenson's (2000) longitudinal analysis of married couples lends some support for the latter hypothesis and provides important information about the long-term effects of negative and positive emotion displays both in conflict interactions and in ordinary, "events of the day" conversations. Gottman and Levenson found that negative emotion during conflict is a strong predictor of early divorce (during the first 7 years of marriage), but that lack of positive affect during both conflict and events-of-the-day interactions predicts later divorce (after the first 7 years of marriage).

Second, although individuals enter relationships with a shared understanding of what emotions are considered negative and what emotions are considered positive, this a priori classification of families of emotional experience is responsive to reinterpretation during the interactional process of emotional communication. That is, even though jealousy, anger, fear, and grief are uniformly classified as negative emotions, scholars have begun to recognize that although they may be "painful" for the person experiencing them, they may not necessarily be negative in their consequences (Retzinger, 1995b). Indeed, expressions of jealousy may be flattering, and may be perceived as signaling value and regard for one's partner that is not communicated fully in expressions of love.

Evidence that negative emotions can be managed constructively in interaction comes from two detailed analyses of naturally occurring conversations between friends (both same-sex and opposite-sex pairs) and romantic partners. Staske (1998) found that during "emotional talk," partners were able to "normalize" problematic emotional communication through a variety of responses. Some were direct strategies that assured others that their feelings were, in those situations, to be expected (i.e., invoking clarification of normative scripts), and some were indirect, relating similar emotions or identifying positive outcomes. It is important to note, although Staske does not develop this point, that the conversational partners in the study were not explicitly offering "social support" but rather acknowledging the latitude available through discourse to redefine the very quality of the emotional experience. In a second study, Staske (1999) examined the collaborative construction of the specific emotion of jealousy. As might be expected, most of the friendship pairs (all but one) constructed jealousy as a negative and destructive emotion, consistent with cultural prototypes. However, many of the romantic partners who had actually experienced jealousy constructed it positively, viewing it as a stimulus for negotiating the "rights, obligations, and rules" that should prevail in that relationship. Thus the experience was difficult for the one who felt the emotion, but the communication process constructed positive consequences. Furthermore, Staske's transcription indicates that several speakers referred to themselves as "just a jealous person." Without realizing it, these speakers were invoking a distal factor, their dispositional jealousy, as a way to protect their partners' positive face (at their own expense) and thereby facilitate a more open dialogue.

Third, because attributions and perceptions are made during interactions and influence subsequent interactions, and because messages are contingent, couples tend to construct habitualized sequences of emotional communication over time (Gottman, Coan, Carrere, & Swanson, 1998; Retzinger, 1995b). The partners often enact these routines to achieve interactional or relational goals. As Buck (1989) describes it: "Partners in developing relationships are involved in a social biofeedback process in which the partner's response to an expression becomes an increasingly potent control mechanism" (p. 156). Partners come to realize what behaviors will be followed by what responses. This knowledge is represented in the form of "if-then contingencies," such as "If I sulk, then my partner will give in," or "If I express anger, my partner will respond in kind," or "If I appear sad, my partner will help me with a task." This suggests that persons who know each other well become adept at using emotional messages to achieve their goals (Laux & Weber, 1991).

Fourth, habitualized sequences seem to entail characteristic interpretive patterns as well. Gaelick, Bodenhausen, and Wyer (1985) found that during conflict, men interpreted their partners' failure to express love as hostility, but women interpreted the absence of hostility from their partners as an expression of love. In a more systematic exploration of this phenomenon, Krokoff (1990) examined the "hidden agendas" that marital partners develop and subsequently deploy during discussions of troublesome issues in their relationships. Krokoff defines hidden agendas as perceptual filters that influence how messages are decoded but that are not explicitly discussed. For example, a love agenda might filter messages in ways that confirm a partner's lack of affection, caring, attraction, or interest (e.g., when a distracted partner apologizes for not listening, his or her partner assumes that this signals lack of interest). After examining observer ratings of audiotapes and videotapes, scores on the Hidden Agenda Checklist for love and respect, and couples' self-reports of marital satisfaction, Krokoff offers the following conclusion, noting that the findings emerged across levels of satisfaction:

> As predicted, disgust and contempt are at the core of both love and respect agendas, although these affects are manifested somewhat differently for husbands and wives. For wives, hidden agendas are found in those who seem to be fearful of being criticized and put down by a contemptuous husband. The wife who has a respect hidden agenda might feel especially dominated because (unlike the wife with a love agenda) she will not strike back at him with blame, only with fear. For husbands, hidden agendas (especially respect) are found in those who appear to be disgusted with a contemptuous wife who does not back down, even when the husband gets nasty. (p. 494)

Fifth, although seldom examined by emotion scholars, relationship-destabilizing events are often managed in the moment, although partners may be drawing on cultural scripts. Clearly, the realization that a valued and trusted other has been unfaithful, deceptive, or otherwise broken a relational rule evokes hurt, sadness, and/or anger. These reactions are inherent in the cultural-level script. No doubt, individual differences in such personality features as neuroticism, agreeableness, and the tendency to ruminate (McCullough et al., 2001) influence whether initial emotional reactions are transformed into revenge or forgiveness.

However, when a relational transgression occurs, the future of the relationship in terms of quality or continuation depends critically on the remedial efforts of the offending person (Fincham, 2000). Although occasionally forgiveness is accomplished independently, in most cases, the process of reappraising initial feelings of hurt and anger to achieve forgiveness is facilitated by the actions of the offending partner. Evidence that strongly supports the importance of the transgressor's communicative efforts in enabling the victim to achieve forgiveness is found in a series of studies using both hypothetical scenarios (Metts & Cupach, 1999) and respondent descriptions of their own transgression experiences (Cupach & Metts, 2000; Metts, Cupach, & Morse, 2001; Metts, Pensinger, & Cupach, 2001). Even after variance attributable to other factors (e.g., severity of the offense, personality factors such as the tendency to ruminate, attachment style, affective orientation, and romantic beliefs) was accounted for, the willingness of the offending person to address the problem emerged as a significant predictor of forgiveness. Most notably, in those situations where the transgressor offered a fully developed apology and accepted responsibility for his or her behavior, forgiveness was more likely; in those situations where the transgressor denied responsibility, shifted blame, or simply refused to engage in remedial efforts, lingering resentment was more likely. Remarkably, this pattern holds across transgression type and relationship outcome (i.e., terminated or still intact). It appears, then, that forgiveness is, ironically, both necessitated by the hurtful actions of those we trust and dependent on the ability of those persons to help us through the process.

What is yet to be examined is the question of whether repeated infractions within the same relationship generate habitualized patterns of coping. We might surmise, for example, that in families or marriages where separation is not easy, repeated harmful behaviors may lead eventually to desensitization or emotional distance, such that these events are no longer appraised as harmful to well-being. Or a pattern of attributions may develop that somehow exonerates the offender (he/she is just that way; he/she speaks without thinking; he/she is just forgetful). Indirect support for these speculations is provided by investigations of a type of transgression commonly known as hurtful messages. Vangelisti and Young (2000) found that people were likely to distance themselves from the sources of hurtful messages when the messages were part of "an ongoing pattern of hurtful communication" and when they believed the messages were unintentional but self-serving and/or indicative of a dispositional tendency to be hurtful (p. 421).

Other research on hurtful messages indicates that responses to such messages depend not only on the attributions of the person hurt by the messages but also on the type and quality of the relationship between the producer and the receiver of the hurt. In a study of acquaintances, for example, Snapp and Leary (2001) found that people were more hurt when they were ignored by someone who barely knew them than they were when ignored by someone with whom they had already had a brief interaction, although in other studies respondents reported being hurt more by people who know them exceptionally well

(Vangelisti, 1994). In long-term relationships, satisfied partners are more likely than dissatisfied partners to interpret hurtful messages as unintentional (Vangelisti, 1994), rendering them less damaging to the relationship. Vangelisti and Crumley (1998) found that people responded to hurtful messages in three general ways: active verbal responses (such as attacking the other or defending themselves), acquiescing (such as crying or apologizing), or acting invulnerable (ignoring the message or laughing). Compared with less satisfied partners, partners in more satisfied relationships reported messages that were less hurtful and had less impact on their relationships; they also reported using more active verbal responses to hurtful messages.

As many studies of emotional communication illustrate, the emotional meaning of messages is a flexible substance that is shaped and negotiated in the moment (the proximal context) and yet built from resources developed by the participants through their experiences, predispositions, and cultures (the distal context). Scholars are beginning to understand this process, but it is immensely rich and complex, and there is much more to know than is known.

RECOMMENDATIONS FOR FUTURE RESEARCH ON EMOTIONAL COMMUNICATION

Based on our review of the existing literature on emotional communication, we come away with a clearer sense of what research problems and possibilities for studying emotion are the special responsibilities of interpersonal communication scholars. They reflect the commitments, sensitivities, and perspectives on the world that come from thinking of emotional communication as constrained, pragmatic, strategic, and especially important in close relationships. This review also invites speculation about possibilities for continued investigation. The list we offer below is not meant to be exhaustive, of course; rather, it is expansive.

We need research on *implicit theories of emotional communication*. Under what circumstances do people feel compelled by their feelings or able to control them? Under what circumstances are emotional displays acceptable, encouraged, or prohibited? When do people find that their feelings seem to facilitate their communicative goals or obstruct them? To what extent do people feel responsible for managing their own feelings in order to minimize or optimize the impact on other people? To what extent do they feel responsible for and capable of influencing the feelings of others, and in what situations (embarrassment, comforting, and the like)?

We need research on *scripts of emotional communication episodes*. What kinds of emotional episodes do people deal with on a daily basis? We need a typology of emotional episodes, if possible, along the lines of Goldsmith and Baxter's (1996) typology of speech events. How do anger episodes in close relationships typically play out? What do people believe are constructive or destructive anger episodes? What is the usual scenario for comforting (if there is one)? What happens when there is an inappropriate public outburst? What kinds of episodes do people feel well or ill equipped to handle? How do experts, compared with novices, handle such episodes?

We need research on the *unique emotional patterns* that partners in close relationships work out between themselves, along the lines of idiomatic expressions (Bell, Buerkel-Rothfuss, & Gore, 1987). Planalp, DeFrancisco, and Rutherford (1996) have found some evidence that people recognize idiosyncratic emotional expressions in others they know well ("My father's neck always turns red when he is angry"). Probably more interesting are dyadic patterns that customize cultural scripts for handling transgressions ("I always apologize, and he hugs me"), irritation ("She stomps around until I turn off the music"), dueling preferences ("He keeps bringing it up until I give in"), or mood discrepancies ("When she's in a bad mood, she won't join my friends and me playing cards"). What effects do the patterns have on the task at hand, the relationship, and both partners' feelings?

We need more studies of *real interactions where emotions are negotiated* in the moment, using all available channels, responding to situational constraints, and the like. Gottman's (1994) work on the recorded interactions of married couples serves as a good model, although a communication scholar would probably put more emphasis on topics and verbal statements and less on the physiological states of participants. A trend in this direction is evident in the detailed analyses of naturally occurring conversations of relational partners provided by Staske (1996, 1998, 1999). As she argues theoretically and demonstrates empirically, not only is the expression of emotion influenced by the presence of relational partners, but "the nature and function of the feelings themselves—that is the emotional experience—are also fashioned from and constrained by the pragmatic, social requirements of human interaction" (Staske, 1996, p. 112). Perhaps researchers could develop a repertoire of scenarios that represent the construction of emotional experiences during ordinary talk or that challenge partners' emotional skills and reveal dyadic patterns.

We need more longitudinal studies *linking relational development, emotion, and communication*. That includes not only the obvious questions of how each person's feelings about the partner (especially love) change as intimacy develops and how partners communicate those changes to each other, but also how other feelings (such as anger or joy) change and get negotiated as interdependence develops and coordination increases. It should be obvious from the start that emotions influence relationships, especially through communication, and relationships influence emotion and how it is communicated, but much descriptive work needs to be done before cause and effect can be unraveled.

CONCLUSION

Three objectives have guided the construction of this chapter. First, we wanted to provide a review of current approaches to emotion across related disciplines, highlighting the particular utility of selected pieces for interpersonal communication scholarship. Second, we wanted to integrate research findings that would bring factors that influence emotional communication in social and personal relationships more sharply into focus. And, third, we wanted to offer suggestions concerning several avenues for additional research in emotional communication. In moving toward these objectives, we have sometimes been overwhelmed by the sheer volume and the remarkable diversity of scholarly writing on emotion. We have also, however, been encouraged by what we see as new developments in how emotion and its role in ordinary daily life are currently conceptualized.

The most striking new development in the study of emotion and communication during the past decade or more has been the increasing recognition that emotion is an integral part of social interaction and vice versa (e.g., Oatley, 1992; Oatley & Johnson-Laird, 1996; Parkinson, 1995). Emotional expression is no longer seen as a bizarre event in social life, probably problematic, perhaps pathological, but nothing that need concern us as we go about disentangling the basic processes of interaction. Instead, it is now seen as essential to interaction, always present, always influential, braided inextricably with all the other threads that make up social life. Conversely, social interaction is no longer seen as an optional feature of emotion or as important to only some types of emotions (e.g., guilt and love but not fear and disgust). Now we see social interaction as by far the most common trigger for nearly all emotions, the most common setting in which emotion is felt, the most common way of managing emotion, and, in fact, one of the most important reasons for having emotions in the first place, at least in social species (with all due respect to acrophobia and arachnophobia) (Andersen & Guerrero, 1998a).

It follows quite naturally, of course, that emotional communication is increasingly viewed less often in terms of signs (external indicators of internal processes) and more often in terms of speech acts (conscious or nonconscious attempts to influence the social world). The difference is revealed in Bergmann's (1979) clever analysis:

> If you still believe that shame is a feeling inside you and that you principally announce the presence of that feeling when you say "I am ashamed," then you might for consistency's sake interpret "I am sorry" in the same way. You would then assume that the man is merely telling you how he feels, so that you could perfectly well reply, "Enough is enough! First you kick me, and then you give me an account of your internal life." (as quoted in Campbell, 1997, p. 103)

Nobody much believes it works that way anymore. Emotion functions in the social world to change things, not just to report on things—or, more likely, to do both (Planalp & Knie, in press). Probably its most important job is to act as a mediator between the demands of the individual mind and body and those of the personal, social, and political mind and body (Planalp, 1999, pp. 146-158). The only way emotion can do its job is to be present in every conversation, every meeting, and every family reunion, urging people to speak out, back off, make amends, give aid, and do all the other things we do in our personal and social lives.

REFERENCES

Abu-Lughod, L. (1990). Shifting politics in Bedouin love poetry. In C. A. Lutz & L. Abu-Lughod (Eds.), *Language and the politics of emotion* (pp. 24-45). Cambridge: Cambridge University Press.

Andersen, P. A., & Guerrero, L. K. (Eds.). (1998a). *Handbook of communication and emotion: Research, theory, applications, and contexts.* San Diego, CA: Academic Press.

Andersen, P. A., & Guerrero, L. K. (1998b). Principles of communication and emotion in social interaction. In P. A. Andersen & L. K. Guerrero (Eds.), *Handbook of communication and emotion: Research, theory, applications, and contexts* (pp. 49-96). San Diego, CA: Academic Press.

Anderson, K. J., & Leaper, C. (1998). Emotion talk between same- and mixed-gender friends: Form and function. *Journal of Language and Social Psychology, 17,* 419-448.

Ashkanasy, N. M., Härtel, C. E. J., & Zerbe, W. J. (Eds.). (2000). *Emotions in the workplace: Research, theory, and practice.* Westport, CT: Quorum.

Aune, K. S. (1997). Self and partner perceptions of the appropriateness of emotions. *Communication Reports, 10,* 133-145.

Aune, K. S., Aune, R. K., & Buller, D. B. (1994). The experience, expression, and perceived appropriateness of emotions across levels of relationship development. *Journal of Social Psychology, 134,* 141-150.

Aune, K. S., Buller, D. B., & Aune, R. K. (1996). Display rule development in romantic relationships: Emotion management and perceived appropriateness of emotions across relationship stages. *Human Communication Research, 23,* 115-146.

Averill, J. R. (1980). A constructivist view of emotion. In R. Plutchik & H. Kellerman (Eds.), *Emotion: Theory, research, and experience* (pp. 305-339). New York: Academic Press.

Averill, J. R. (1993). Illusions of anger. In R. B. Felson & J. T. Tedeschi (Eds.), *Aggression and violence: Social interactionist perspectives* (pp. 171-192). Washington, DC: American Psychological Association.

Baldwin, M. W. (1992). Relational schemas and the processing of social information. *Psychological Bulletin, 112,* 461-484.

Baldwin, M. W. (1995). Relational schemas and cognition in close relationships. *Journal of Social and Personal Relationships, 12,* 547-552.

Barbara, A. M., & Dion, K. L. (2000). Breaking up is hard to do, especially for strongly "preoccupied" lovers. *Journal of Personal and Interpersonal Loss, 5,* 315-343.

Barbee, A. P., Rowatt, T. L., & Cunningham, M. R. (1998). When a friend is in need: Feelings about seeking, giving, and receiving social support. In P. A. Andersen & L. K. Guerrero (Eds.), *Communication and emotion: Theory, research, and applications* (pp. 281-301). San Diego, CA: Academic Press.

Bartholomew, K., & Horowitz, L. A. (1991). Attachment styles among young adults: A test of a four-category model. *Journal of Personality and Social Psychology, 61,* 226-244.

Baumeister, R. F., Stillwell, A. M., & Heatherton, T. F. (1994). Guilt: An interpersonal approach. *Psychological Bulletin, 115,* 243-267.

Bavelas, J. B., Black, A., Lemery, C. R., & Mullett, J. (1986). "I *show* how you feel": Motor mimicry as a communicative act. *Journal of Personality and Social Psychology, 50,* 322-329.

Bavelas, J. B., & Chovil, N. (1997). Faces in dialogue. In J. A. Russell & J. M. Fernández-Dols (Eds.), *The psychology of facial expression* (pp. 334-346). Cambridge: Cambridge University Press.

Baxter, L. A. (1990). Dialectical contradictions in relationship development. *Journal of Social and Personal Relationships, 7,* 69-88.

Becker-Stoll, F., Delius, A., & Scheitenberger, S. (2001). Adolescents' nonverbal emotional expressions during negotiation of a disagreement with their mothers: An attachment approach. *International Journal of Behavioral Development, 25,* 344-353.

Bell, R. A., Buerkel-Rothfuss, N. L., & Gore, K. E. (1987). "Did you bring the yarmulke for the Cabbage Patch Kid?" The idiomatic communication of young lovers. *Human Communication Research, 14,* 47-67.

Benjamin, O. (1998). Therapeutic discourse, power, and change: Emotion and negotiation in marital conversations. *Sociology, 32,* 771-793.

Bergmann, F. (1979). A monologue on the emotions. In F. D. Miller & T. W. Attig (Eds.),

Understanding human emotions (pp. 1-17). Bowling Green, OH: Bowling Green State University, Department of Philosophy.

Besnier, N. (1990). Language and affect. *Annual Review of Anthropology, 19,* 419-451.

Besnier, N. (1995). The politics of emotion in Nukulaelae gossip. In J. A. Russell, J. M. Fernández-Dols, A. S. R. Manstead, & J. C. Wellenkamp (Eds.), *Everyday conceptions of emotion: An introduction to the psychology, anthropology, and linguistics of emotion* (pp. 221-240). Dordrecht, Netherlands: Kluwer.

Blier, M. J., & Blier-Wilson, L. A. (1989). Gender differences in self-rated emotional expressiveness. *Sex Roles, 21,* 287-295.

Bookwala, J., & Zdaniuk, B. (1998). Adult attachment styles and aggressive behavior within dating relationships. *Journal of Social and Personal Relationships, 15,* 175-190.

Boster, F. J., Mitchell, M. M., Lapinski, M. K., Cooper, H., Orrego, V. O., & Reinke, R. (1999). The impact of guilt and type of compliance-gaining message on compliance. *Communication Monographs, 66,* 168-177.

Bowers, J. W., Metts, S. M., & Duncanson, W. T. (1985). Emotion and interpersonal communication. In M. L. Knapp & G. R. Miller (Eds.), *Handbook of interpersonal communication* (pp. 502-559). Beverly Hills, CA: Sage.

Bowlby, J. (1969). *Attachment and loss: Vol. 1. Attachment.* New York: Basic Books.

Bowlby, J. (1973). *Attachment and loss: Vol. 2. Separation: Anxiety and anger.* New York: Basic Books.

Bowlby, J. (1980). *Attachment and loss: Vol. 3. Loss: Sadness and depression.* New York: Basic Books.

Bradbury, T. N., & Fincham, F. D. (1989). Behavior and satisfaction in marriage: Prospective mediating processes. In C. Hendrick (Ed.), *Close relationships* (pp. 119-143). Newbury Park, CA: Sage.

Bradbury, T. N., & Fincham, F. D. (1991). A contextual model for advancing the study of marital interaction. In G. J. O. Fletcher & F. D. Fincham (Eds.), *Cognition in close relationships* (pp. 127-147). Hillsdale, NJ: Lawrence Erlbaum.

Braithwaite, J., & Mugford, S. (1994). Conditions of successful reintegration ceremonies: Dealing with juvenile offenders. *British Journal of Criminology, 34,* 139-171.

Brenneis, D. (1990). Shared and solitary sentiments: The discourse of friendship, play, and anger in Bhatgaon. In C. A. Lutz & L. Abu-Lughod (Eds.), *Language and the politics of emotion* (pp. 113-125). Cambridge: Cambridge University Press.

Briggs, J. L. (1970). *Never in anger: Portrait of an Eskimo family.* Cambridge, MA: Harvard University Press.

Brody, L. R. (1997). Gender and emotion: Beyond stereotypes. *Journal of Social Issues, 53*(2), 369-393.

Buck, R. (1989). Emotional communication in personal relationships: A developmental-interactionist view. In C. Hendrick (Ed.), *Close relationships* (pp. 144-163). Newbury Park, CA: Sage.

Burleson, B. R., & Goldsmith, D. J. (1998). How the comforting process works: Alleviating emotional distress through conversationally induced reappraisals. In P. A. Andersen & L. K. Guerrero (Eds.), *Handbook of communication and emotion: Research, theory, applications, and contexts* (pp. 245-280). San Diego, CA: Academic Press.

Burleson, B. R., Metts, S., & Kirch, M. W. (2000). Communication in close relationships. In C. Hendrick & S. S. Hendrick (Eds.), *Close relationships: A sourcebook* (pp. 245-258). Thousand Oaks, CA: Sage.

Bushman, B. J., Baumeister, R. F., & Stack, A. D. (1999). Catharsis, aggression, and persuasive influence: Self-fulfilling or self-defeating prophecies? *Journal of Personality and Social Psychology, 76,* 367-376.

Cacioppo, J. T., & Gardner, W. L. (1999). Emotion. *Annual Review of Psychology, 50,* 191-214.

Campbell, S. (1997). *Interpreting the personal: Expression and the formation of feelings.* Ithaca, NY: Cornell University Press.

Canary, D. J., & Emmers-Sommer, T. M. (1997). *Sex and gender differences in personal relationships.* New York: Guilford.

Cancian, F. M. (1987). *Love in America: Gender and self-development.* New York: Cambridge University Press.

Cappella, J. N. (1995). Inoculating against emotional contagion. *Contemporary Psychology, 40,* 636-637.

Christensen, A., & Jacobson, N. S. (2000). *Reconcilable differences.* New York: Guilford.

Christophe, V., & Rimé, B. (1997). Exposure to the social sharing of emotion: Emotional impact, listener responses and secondary social sharing. *European Journal of Social Psychology, 27,* 37-54.

Clark, C. (1997). *Misery and company: Sympathy in everyday life.* Chicago: University of Chicago Press.

Clark, M. S., Pataki, S. P., & Carver, V. H. (1996). Some thoughts and findings on self-presentation of emotions in relationships. In G. J. O. Fletcher & J. Fitness (Eds.), *Knowledge structures in close relationships: A social psychological approach* (pp. 247-274). Mahwah, NJ: Lawrence Erlbaum.

Clark, M. S., & Taraban, C. (1991). Reactions to and willingness to express emotion in communal and exchange relationships. *Journal of Experimental Social Psychology, 27,* 324-336.

Conway, M., Di Fazio, R., & Mayman, S. (1999). Judging others' emotions as a function of the others' status. *Social Psychology Quarterly, 62,* 291-305.

Cooper, R. K., & Sawaf, A. (1996). *Executive EQ: Emotional intelligence in leadership and organizations.* New York: Perigee.

Csikszentmihalyi, M. (1990). *Flow: The psychology of optimal experience.* New York: Harper & Row.

Cupach, W. R., & Metts, S. (2000, February). *Test of a contextual model of relational transgressions: Distal and proximal factors predicting forgiveness.* Paper presented at the annual meeting of the Western States Communication Association, Sacramento, CA.

Dalai Lama & Cutler, H. C. (1998). *The art of happiness: A handbook for living.* New York: Penguin.

Damasio, A. R. (1994). *Descartes' error: Emotion, reason, and the human brain.* New York: G. P. Putnam's Sons.

Damasio, A. R. (1999). *The feeling of what happens: Body and emotion in the making of consciousness.* New York: Harcourt Brace.

de Rivera, J., & Grinkis, C. (1986). Emotions as social relationships. *Motivation and Emotion, 10,* 351-369.

de Sousa, R. (1987). *The rationality of emotion.* Cambridge: MIT Press.

Dillard, J. P. (1990). A goal-driven model of interpersonal influence. In J. P. Dillard (Ed.), *Seeking compliance: The production of interpersonal influence messages* (pp. 41-56). Scottsdale, AZ: Gorsuch Scarisbrick.

Dillard, J. P., & Peck, E. (2001). Persuasion and the structure of affect. *Human Communication Research, 27,* 38-68.

Dillard, J. P., & Schrader, D. (1998). On the utility of the goals-plans-action sequence. *Communication Studies, 49,* 300-305.

Dion, K. K., & Dion, K. L. (1996). Cultural perspectives on romantic love. *Personal Relationships, 3,* 5-17.

Ekman, P. (Ed.). (1982). *Emotion in the human face* (2nd ed.). Cambridge: Cambridge University Press.

Ekman, P. (1994). Strong evidence for universals in facial expressions: A reply to Russell's mistaken critique. *Psychological Bulletin, 115,* 268-287.

Ekman, P. (1997). Should we call it expression or communication? *Innovation, 10,* 333-344.

Ekman, P., & Davidson, R. J. (1994). *The nature of emotion: Fundamental questions.* Oxford: Oxford University Press.

Ekman, P., & Friesen, W. V. (1975). *Unmasking the face: A guide to recognizing emotions from facial clues.* Englewood Cliffs, NJ: Prentice Hall.

Ekman, P., Friesen, W. V., O'Sullivan, M., Chan, A., Diacoyanni-Tarlatzis, I., Heider, K., et al. (1987). Universals and cultural differences in the judgments of facial expressions of emotion. *Journal of Personality and Social Psychology, 53,* 712-717.

Emmons, R. A., & Diener, E. (1985). Personality correlates of subjective well-being. *Personality and Social Psychology Bulletin, 11,* 89-97.

Feeney, J. A. (1995). Adult attachment and emotional control. *Personal Relationships, 2,* 143-159.

Feeney, J. A., & Noller, P. (1992). Attachment style and romantic love: Relationship dissolution. *Australian Journal of Psychology, 44,* 69-74.

Feeney, J. A., Noller, P., & Roberts, N. (1998). Emotion, attachment, and satisfaction in close relationships. In P. A. Andersen & L. K. Guerrero (Eds.), *Handbook of communication and emotion: Research, theory, applications, and contexts* (pp. 473-505). San Diego, CA: Academic Press.

Feeney, J. A., Noller, P., & Roberts, N. (2000). Attachment and close relationships. In C. Hendrick & S. S. Hendrick (Eds.), *Close relationships: A sourcebook* (pp. 185-201). Thousand Oaks, CA: Sage.

Fehr, B. (1994). Prototype-based assessment of laypeople's views of love. *Personal Relationships, 1,* 309-331.

Fehr, B., Baldwin, M., Collins, L., Patterson, S., & Benditt, R. (1999). Anger in close relationships: An interpersonal script analysis. *Personality and Social Psychology Bulletin, 25,* 299-312.

Fehr, B., & Broughton, R. (2001). Gender and personality differences in conceptions of love: An interpersonal theory analysis. *Personal Relationships, 8,* 115-136.

Fernández-Dols, J. M., & Ruiz-Belda, M.-A. (1995). Are smiles a sign of happiness? Gold medal winners at the Olympic Games. *Journal of Personality and Social Psychology, 69,* 1113-1119.

Fernández-Dols, J. M., Sánchez, F., Carrera, P., & Ruiz-Belda, M.-A. (1997). Are spontaneous expressions and emotions linked? An experimental test of coherence. *Journal of Nonverbal Behavior, 21,* 163-177.

Fincham, F. D. (2000). The kiss of the porcupines: From attributing responsibility to forgiving. *Personal Relationships, 7,* 1-23.

Fineman, S. (Ed.). (1993). *Emotion in organizations.* London: Sage.

Fineman, S. (Ed.). (2000). *Emotion in organizations* (2nd ed.). London: Sage.

Fischer, A. H. (Ed.). (2000). *Gender and emotion: Social psychological perspectives.* Cambridge: Cambridge University Press.

Fitness, J. (1996). Emotion knowledge structures in close relationships. In G. J. O. Fletcher & J. Fitness (Eds.), *Knowledge structures in close relationships: A social psychological approach* (pp. 195-217). Mahwah, NJ: Lawrence Erlbaum.

Fitness, J. (2000). Anger in the workplace: An emotion script approach to anger episodes between workers and their superiors, co-workers, and subordinates. *Journal of Organizational Behavior, 21,* 147-162.

Fivush, R., & Buckner, J. P. (2000). Gender, sadness, and depression: The development of emotional focus through gendered discourse. In A. H. Fischer (Ed.), *Gender and emotion: Social psychological perspectives* (pp. 232-253). Cambridge: Cambridge University Press.

Floyd, K., & Morman, M. T. (1997). Affectionate communication in nonromantic relationships:

Influences of communicator, relational, and contextual factors. *Western Journal of Communication, 61,* 279-298.

Fridlund, A. J. (1994). *Human facial expression: An evolutionary view.* San Diego, CA: Academic Press.

Frijda, N. H. (2000). The psychologists' point of view. In M. Lewis & J. M. Haviland-Jones (Eds.), *Handbook of emotions* (2nd ed., pp. 59-74). New York: Guilford.

Frijda, N. H., & Mesquita, B. (1994). The social roles and functions of emotions. In S. Kitayama & H. R. Markus (Eds.), *Emotion and culture: Empirical studies of mutual influence* (pp. 51-87). Washington, DC: American Psychological Association.

Frijda, N. H., & Tcherkassof, A. (1997). Facial expressions as modes of action readiness. In J. A. Russell & J. M. Fernández-Dols (Eds.), *The psychology of facial expression* (pp. 78-102). Cambridge: Cambridge University Press.

Gaelick, L., Bodenhausen, G. V., & Wyer, R. S., Jr. (1985). Emotional communication in close relationships. *Journal of Personality and Social Psychology, 49,* 1246-1265.

Gallois, C. (1993). The language and communication of emotion: Universal, interpersonal, or intergroup? *American Behavioral Scientist, 36,* 309-338.

Gohm, C. L., & Clore, G. L. (2000). Individual differences in emotional experience: Mapping available scales to processes. *Personality and Social Psychology Bulletin, 26,* 679-697.

Goldshmidt, O. T. (2000). "Talking emotions": Gender differences in a variety of conversational contexts. *Symbolic Interaction, 23,* 117-135.

Goldsmith, D. J., & Baxter, L. A. (1996). Constituting relationships in talk: A taxonomy of speech events in social and personal relationships. *Human Communication Research, 25,* 87-114.

Goleman, D. (1995). *Emotional intelligence: Why it can matter more than IQ.* New York: Bantam.

Goleman, D. (1998). *Working with emotional intelligence.* New York: Bantam.

Gottman, J. M. (1994). *What predicts divorce? The relationship between marital processes and marital outcomes.* Hillsdale, NJ: Lawrence Erlbaum.

Gottman, J. M., Coan, J., Carrere, S., & Swanson, C. (1998). Predicting marital happiness and stability from newlywed interactions. *Journal of Marriage and the Family, 60,* 5-22.

Gottman, J. M., Katz, L. F., & Hooven, C. (1997). *Meta-emotion: How families communicate emotionally.* Mahwah, NJ: Lawrence Erlbaum.

Gottman, J. M., & Levenson, R. W. (1992). Marital processes predictive of later dissolution: Behavior, physiology, and health. *Journal of Personality and Social Psychology, 63,* 221-233.

Gottman, J. M., & Levenson, R. W. (2000). The timing of divorce: Predicting when a couple will divorce over a 14-year period. *Journal of Marriage and the Family, 62,* 737-745.

Graham, T., & Ickes, W. (1998). When women's intuition isn't greater than men's. In W. Ickes (Ed.), *Empathic accuracy* (pp. 117-143). New York: Guilford.

Greenspan, P. S. (1995). *Practical guilt: Moral dilemmas, emotions, and social norms.* New York: Oxford.

Gross, J. J., John, O. P., & Richards, J. M. (2000). The dissociation of emotion expression from emotion experience: A personality perspective. *Personality and Social Psychology Bulletin, 26,* 712-726.

Guerrero, L. K., & Andersen, P. A. (1998). Jealousy experience and expression in romantic relationships. In P. A. Andersen & L. K. Guerrero (Eds.), *Handbook of communication and emotion: Research, theory, applications, and contexts* (pp. 155-188). San Diego, CA: Academic Press.

Guerrero, L. K., & Andersen, P. A. (2000). Emotion in close relationships. In C. Hendrick & S. S. Hendrick (Eds.). *Close relationships: A sourcebook* (pp. 171-183). Thousand Oaks, CA: Sage.

Hall, J. A., Carter, J. D., & Horgan, T. G. (2000). Gender differences in nonverbal communication of emotion. In A. H. Fischer (Ed.), *Gender and emotion: Social psychological perspectives* (pp. 97-117). Cambridge: Cambridge University Press.

Hatfield, E., Cacioppo, J. T., & Rapson, R. L. (1992). Primitive emotional contagion. M. S. Clark (Ed.), *Emotion and social behavior* (pp. 151-177). Newbury Park, CA: Sage.

Hatfield, E., Cacioppo, J. T., & Rapson, R. L. (1994). *Emotional contagion.* Cambridge: Cambridge University Press.

Hatfield, E., & Walster, G. W. (1978). *A new look at love.* Reading, MA: Addison-Wesley.

Hazan, C., & Shaver, P. R. (1987). Attachment as an organizational framework for research on close relationships. *Journal of Psychological Inquiry, 5,* 1-22.

Heider, K. G. (1991). *Landscapes of emotion: Mapping three cultures of emotion in Indonesia.* Cambridge: Cambridge University Press.

Heise, D. R., & Calhan, C. (1995). Emotion norms in interpersonal events. *Social Psychology Quarterly, 58,* 223-240.

Hendrick, C., & Hendrick, S. S. (1989). Research on love: Does it measure up? *Journal of Personality and Social Psychology, 56,* 784-794.

Hess, U., Blairy, S., & Kleck, R. E. (2000). The influence of facial emotion displays, gender, and ethnicity on judgments of dominance and affiliation. *Journal of Nonverbal Behavior, 24,* 265-283.

Hinde, R. A. (1997). *Relationships: A dialectical perspective.* Brighton, Eng.: Psychology Press.

Hochschild, A. R. (1983). *The managed heart: Commercialization of human feeling.* Berkeley: University of California Press.

Hochschild, A. R. (1990). Ideology and emotion management: A perspective and path for future research. In T. D. Kemper (Ed.), *Research agendas in the sociology of emotions* (pp. 117-142). Albany: State University of New York Press.

Ickes, W., Gesn, P. R., & Graham, T. (2000). Gender differences in empathic accuracy: Differential ability or differential motivation? *Personal Relationships, 7,* 95-109.

Ickes, W., & Simpson, J. A. (1997). Managing empathic accuracy in close relationships. In W. Ickes (Ed.), *Empathic accuracy* (pp. 218-250). New York: Guilford.

Irvine, J. T. (1990). Registering affect: Heteroglossia in the linguistic expression of emotion. In C. A. Lutz & L. Abu-Lughod (Eds.), *Language and the politics of emotion* (pp. 126-161). Cambridge: Cambridge University Press.

Jakobs, E., Manstead, A. S. R., & Fischer, A. H. (1999). Social motives, emotional feelings, and smiling. *Cognition and Emotion, 13,* 321-345.

Jenkins, J. M., Oatley, K., & Stein, N. L. (Eds.). (1998). *Human emotions: A reader.* Malden, MA: Blackwell.

Jones, J. T., & Cunningham, J. D. (1996). Attachment styles and other predictors of relationship satisfaction in dating couples. *Personal Relationships, 3,* 387-399.

Karasawa, K. (1995). An attributional analysis of reactions to negative emotions. *Personality and Social Psychology Bulletin, 21,* 456-467.

Kelly, J. R., & Hutson-Comeaux, S. L. (1999). Gender-emotion stereotypes are context specific. *Sex Roles, 40,* 107-120.

Keltner, D. (1996). Facial expressions of emotion and personality. In C. Malatesta-Magai & S. H. McFadden (Eds.), *Handbook of emotion, adult development, and aging* (pp. 385-401). New York: Academic Press.

Kemper, T. D. (1978). *A social interactional theory of emotion.* New York: John Wiley.

Kemper, T. D. (2000). Social models in the explanation of emotions. In M. Lewis & J. M. Haviland-Jones (Eds.), *Handbook of emotions* (2nd ed., pp. 45-58). New York: Guilford.

Kennedy-Moore, E., & Watson, J. C. (1999). *Expressing emotion: Myths, realities, and therapeutic strategies.* New York: Guilford.

Klingbeil-Parker, K. J. (1998, November). *Relational idiosyncrasies: The nature of married couples' comforting communication.* Paper presented at the annual meeting of the National Communication Association, New York.

Knutson, B. (1996). Facial expression of emotion influence interpersonal trait inferences. *Journal of Nonverbal Behavior, 20,* 165-182.

Kövecses, Z. (1990). *Emotion concepts.* New York: Springer-Verlag.

Kövecses, Z. (2000). *Metaphor and emotion: Language, culture, and body in human feeling.* Cambridge: Cambridge University Press.

Kring, A. M. (2000). Gender and anger. In A. H. Fischer (Ed.), *Gender and emotion: Social psychological perspectives* (pp. 211-231). Cambridge: Cambridge University Press.

Kring, A. M., & Gordon, A. H. (1998). Sex differences in emotion: Expression, experience, and physiology. *Journal of Personality and Social Psychology, 74,* 686-703.

Krokoff, L. J. (1990). Hidden agendas in marriage. *Communication Research, 17,* 483-500.

Krone, K. J., Chen, L., Sloan, D. K., & Gallant, L. M. (1997). Managerial emotionality in Chinese factories. *Management Communication Quarterly, 11,* 6-50.

LaFrance, M., & Hecht, M. (2000). Gender and smiling: A meta-analysis. In A. H. Fischer (Ed.), *Gender and emotion: Social psychological perspectives* (pp. 118-142). Cambridge: Cambridge University Press.

Laux, L., & Weber, H. (1991). Presentation of self in coping with anger and anxiety: An intentional approach. *Anxiety Research, 3,* 233-255.

Lazarus, R. S., & Lazarus, B. N. (1994). *Passion and reason: Making sense of our emotions.* Oxford: Oxford University Press.

Leary, M. R., & Kowalski, R. M. (1995). *Social anxiety.* New York: Guilford.

Leatham, G., & Duck, S. (1990). Conversations with friends and the dynamics of social support. In S. Duck (Ed.). *Personal relationships and social support* (pp. 1-29). London: Sage.

Leets, L., & Giles, H. (1997). Words as weapons—When do they wound? Investigations of harmful speech. *Human Communication Research, 24,* 260-301.

Lewis, M., & Haviland, J. M. (Eds.). (1993). *Handbook of emotions.* New York: Guilford.

Lewis, M., & Haviland-Jones, J. M. (Eds.). (2000). *Handbook of emotions* (2nd ed.). New York: Guilford.

Lofland, L. H. (1985). The social shaping of emotion: The case of grief. *Symbolic Interaction, 8,* 171-190.

Lutz, C. (1986). The domain of emotion words in Ifaluk. In R. Harré (Ed.), *The social construction of emotions* (pp. 267-288). Oxford: Basil Blackwell.

Lutz, C. A. (1988). *Unnatural emotions: Everyday sentiments on a Micronesian atoll and their challenge to Western theory.* Chicago: University of Chicago Press.

Lutz, C. A. (1990). Engendered emotion: Gender, power, and the rhetoric of emotional control in American discourse. In C. A. Lutz & L. Abu-Lughod (Eds.), *Language and the politics of emotion* (pp. 69-91). Cambridge: Cambridge University Press.

Makkai, T., & Braithwaite, J. (1994a). The dialectics of corporate deterrence. *Journal of Research in Crime and Delinquency, 31,* 347-374.

Makkai, T., & Braithwaite, J. (1994b). Reintegrative shaming and compliance with regulatory standards. *Criminology, 32,* 361-385.

Marston, P. J., & Hecht, M. L. (1994). Love ways: An elaboration and application to relational maintenance. In D. J. Canary & L. Stafford (Eds.), *Communication and relational maintenance* (pp. 187-202). San Diego, CA: Academic Press.

Mayne, T. J., & Bonanno, G. A. (Eds.). (2001). *Emotions: Current issues and future directions*. New York: Guilford.

McCrae, R. R., & Costa, P. T. Jr. (1991). Adding *Liebe und Areit:* The full five-factor model and well-being. *Personality and Social Psychology Bulletin, 17,* 227-232.

McCullough, M. E., Bellah, C. G., Kilpatrick, S. D., & Johnson, J. L. (2001). Vengefulness: Relationships with forgiveness, rumination, well-being, and the Big Five. *Personality and Social Psychology Bulletin, 27,* 601-611.

Metts, S., & Bowers, J. W. (1994). Emotion in interpersonal communication. In M. L. Knapp & G. R. Miller (Eds.), *Handbook of interpersonal communication* (2nd ed., pp. 508-541). Thousand Oaks, CA: Sage.

Metts, S., & Cupach, W. R. (1999, February). *Linking, rumination, and redressive action as predictors of forgiveness following a relational transgression.* Paper presented at the annual meeting of the Western States Communication Association, Vancouver.

Metts, S., Cupach, W. R., & Morse, C. (2001, July). *Dispositional and communicative factors predicting forgiveness in close relationships.* Paper presented at the International Conference on Personal Relationships (sponsored by the International Network on Personal Relationships and the International Society for the Study of Personal Relationships), Prescott, AZ.

Metts, S., Pensinger, A., & Cupach, W. R. (2001, April). *How could you? Relational transgressions, redressive actions, and forgiveness.* Paper presented at the annual meeting of the Central States Communication Association, Cincinnati, OH.

Miller, G. R., & Steinberg, M. (1975). *Between people: A new analysis of interpersonal communication.* Chicago: Science Research.

Miller, R. S. (1996). *Embarrassment: Poise and peril in everyday life.* New York: Guilford.

Miller, W. I. (1993). *Humiliation.* Ithaca, NY: Cornell University Press.

Miller, W. I. (1997). *The anatomy of disgust.* Cambridge, MA: Harvard University Press.

Monahan, J. L. (1998). I don't know it but I like you. *Human Communication Research, 24,* 480-500.

Moore, T. (1992). *The care of the soul: A guide for cultivating depth and sacredness in everyday life.* New York: HarperCollins.

Nannini, D. K., & Meyers, L. S. (2000). Jealousy in sexual and emotional infidelity: An alternative to the evolutionary explanation. *Journal of Sex Research, 37,* 117-123.

Oatley, K. (1992). *Best laid schemes: The psychology of emotions.* Cambridge: Cambridge University Press.

Oatley, K., & Johnson-Laird, P. N. (1996). The communicative theory of emotions: Empirical tests, mental models, and implications for social interaction. In L. L. Martin & A. Tesser (Eds.), *Striving and feeling: Interactions among goals, affect, and self-regulation* (pp. 363-393). Mahwah, NJ: Lawrence Erlbaum.

O'Keefe, D. J., & Figgé, M. (1997). A guilt-based explanation of the door-in-the-face influence strategy. *Human Communication Research, 24,* 64-81.

Omdahl, B. L. (1995). *Cognitive appraisal, emotion, and empathy.* Mahwah, NJ: Lawrence Erlbaum.

Parkinson, B. (1995). *Ideas and realities of emotion.* New York: Routledge.

Parkinson, B. (1996). Emotions are social. *British Journal of Psychology, 87,* 663-684.

Parrott, W. G. (Ed.). (2001). *Emotions in social psychology.* Philadelphia: Psychology Press.

Pennebaker, J. W. (Ed.). (1995). *Emotion, disclosure, and health.* Washington, DC: American Psychological Association.

Pennebaker, J. W. (1997). *Opening up: The healing power of expressing emotions* (Rev. ed.). New York: Guilford.

Planalp, S. (1998). Communicating emotion in everyday life: Cues, channels, and processes. In P. A. Andersen & L. K. Guerrero (Eds.), *Communication and emotion: Theory, research, and applications* (pp. 29-48). San Diego, CA: Academic Press.

Planalp, S. (1999). *Communicating emotion: Social, moral, and cultural processes.* New York: Cambridge University Press.

Planalp, S., DeFrancisco, V., & Rutherford, D. (1996). Varieties of cues to emotion in naturally occurring situations. *Cognition and Emotion, 10,* 137-153.

Planalp, S., & Fitness, J. (1999). Thinking/feeling about social and personal relationships. *Journal of Social and Personal Relationships, 16,* 731-750.

Planalp, S., Hafen, S., & Adkins, A. D. (2000). Messages of shame and guilt. In M. E. Roloff

(Ed.), *Communication yearbook 23* (pp. 1-65). Thousand Oaks, CA: Sage.

Planalp, S., & Knie, K. (in press). Verbal and non-verbal cues to emotion. In S. Fussell (Ed.). *The verbal communication of emotions: Interdisciplinary perspectives.* Mahwah, NJ: Lawrence Erlbaum.

Planalp, S., & Rivers, M. (1996). Changes in knowledge of personal relationships. In G. J. O. Fletcher & J. Fitness (Eds.), *Knowledge structures in close relationships: A social psychological approach* (pp. 299-324). Hillsdale, NJ: Lawrence Erlbaum.

Plantinga, C., & Smith, G. M. (Eds.). (1999). *Passionate views: Film, cognition, and emotion.* Baltimore: Johns Hopkins University Press.

Retzinger, S. M. (1995a). Identifying shame and anger in discourse. *American Behavioral Scientist, 38,* 1104-1113.

Retzinger, S. M. (1995b). Shame and anger in personal relationships. In S. Duck & J. T. Wood (Eds.), *Personal relationships 4: Confronting relationship challenges* (pp. 22-42). Thousand Oaks, CA: Sage.

Richards, J. M., & Gross, J. J. (2000). Emotion regulation and memory: The cognitive costs of keeping one's cool. *Journal of Personality and Social Psychology, 79,* 410-424.

Robinson, M. D., & Johnson, J. T. (1997). Is it emotion or is it stress? Gender stereotypes and the perception of subjective experience. *Sex Roles, 36,* 235-258.

Robinson, M. D., Johnson, J. T., & Shields, S. A. (1998). The gender heuristic and the data-base: Factors affecting the perception of gender-related differences in the experience and display of emotions. *Basic and Applied Social Psychology, 20,* 206-29.

Rosaldo, M. Z. (1980). *Knowledge and passion: Ilongot notions of self and social life.* New York: Cambridge University Press.

Rusbult, C. E., Yovetich, N. A., & Verette, J. (1996). An interdependence analysis of accommodation processes. In G. J. O. Fletcher & J. Fitness (Eds.), *Knowledge structures in close relationships: A social psychological approach* (pp. 63-90). Mahwah, NJ: Lawrence Erlbaum.

Russell, J. A. (1994). Is there universal recognition of emotion from facial expression? A review of the cross-cultural studies. *Psychological Bulletin, 115,* 102-141.

Russell, J. A., & Fernández-Dols, J. M. (Eds.). (1997). *The psychology of facial expression.* Cambridge: Cambridge University Press.

Ryback, D. (1998). *Putting emotional intelligence to work: Successful leadership is more than IQ.* Boston: Butterworth-Heinemann.

Saarni, C. (1999). *The development of emotional competence.* New York: Guilford.

Salovey, P. (Ed.). (1991). *The psychology of jealousy and envy.* New York: Guilford.

Salovey, P., Bedell, B. T., Detweiler, J. B., & Mayer, J. D. (2000). Current directions in emotional intelligence research. In M. Lewis & J. M. Haviland-Jones (Eds.), *Handbook of emotions* (2nd ed., pp. 504-520). New York: Guilford.

Salovey, P., & Mayer, J. D. (1990). Emotional intelligence. *Imagination, Cognition and Personality, 9,* 185-211.

Schank, R. C., & Abelson, R. P. (1977). *Scripts, plans, goals, and understanding: An enquiry into human knowledge structures.* Hillsdale, NJ: Lawrence Erlbaum.

Scheff, T. J. (1979). *Catharsis in healing, ritual, and drama.* Berkeley: University of California Press.

Scheff, T. J. (1990). *Microsociology: Discourse, emotion and social structure.* Chicago: University of Chicago Press.

Schrader, D. C., & Dillard, J. P. (1998). Goal structures and interpersonal influence. *Communication Studies, 49,* 276-293.

Schwartz, J. C., & Shaver, P. R. (1987). Emotions and emotion knowledge in interpersonal relations. In W. H. Jones & D. Perlman (Eds.), *Advances in personal relationships* (Vol. 1, pp. 197-241). Greenwich, CT: JAI.

Shaver, P. R., Collins, N., & Clark, C. L. (1996). Attachment styles and internal working models of self and relationship partners. In G. J. O. Fletcher & J. Fitness (Eds.), *Knowledge structures in close relationships: A social psychological approach* (pp. 25-62). Mahwah, NJ: Lawrence Erlbaum.

Shaver, P. R., Schwartz, J., Kirson, D., & O'Connor, C. (1987). Emotion knowledge: Further exploration of a prototype approach. *Journal of Personality and Social Psychology, 52,* 1061-1086.

Shaver, P. R., Wu, S., & Schwartz, J. C. (1992). Cross-cultural similarities and differences in emotion and its representation: A proto-type approach. In M. S. Clark (Ed.),

Emotion (pp. 175-212). Newbury Park, CA: Sage.

Shields, S. A. (2000). Thinking about gender, thinking about theory: Gender and emotional experience. In A. H. Fischer (Ed.), *Gender and emotion: Social psychological perspectives* (pp. 3-23). Cambridge: Cambridge University Press.

Shimanoff, S. B. (1985). Expressing emotions in words: Verbal patterns of interactions. *Journal of Communication, 35*(3), 16-31.

Simpson, J. A. (1990). The influence of attachment style on romantic relationships. *Journal of Personality and Social Psychology, 59,* 971-980.

Singer, I. (1984a). *The nature of love* (Vol. 1, 2nd ed.). Chicago: University of Chicago Press.

Singer, I. (1984b). *The nature of love* (Vol. 2). Chicago: University of Chicago Press.

Singer, I. (1987). *The nature of love* (Vol. 3). Chicago: University of Chicago Press.

Smith, R. H., Parrott, W. G., Diener, E. F., Hoyle, R. H., & Kim, S. H. (1999). Dispositional envy. *Personality and Social Psychology Bulletin, 25,* 1007-1020.

Snapp, C. M., & Leary, M. R. (2001). Hurt feelings among new acquaintances: Moderating effects of interpersonal familiarity. *Journal of Social and Personal Relationships, 18,* 315-326.

Solomon, R. C. (1989). The emotions of justice. *Social Justice Research, 3,* 345-374.

Solomon, R. C. (2000). The philosophy of emotions. In M. Lewis & J. M. Haviland-Jones (Eds.), *Handbook of emotions* (2nd ed., pp. 3-15). New York: Guilford.

Sommers, S. (1984). Reported emotions and conventions of emotionality among college students. *Journal of Personality and Social Psychology, 46,* 207-215.

Spacks, P. M. (1995). *Boredom: The literary history of a state of mind.* Chicago: University of Chicago Press.

Sprecher, S., Felmlee, D., Metts, S., Fehr, B., & Vanni, D. (1998). Factors associated with distress following the breakup of a close relationship. *Journal of Social and Personal Relationships, 15,* 791-809.

Sprecher, S., & Metts, S. (1999). Romantic beliefs: Their influence on relationships and patterns of change over time. *Journal of Social and Personal Relationships, 16,* 834-851.

Staske, S. A. (1996). Talking feelings: The collaborative construction of emotion in talk between close relational partners. *Symbolic Interaction, 19,* 111-136.

Staske, S. A. (1998). The normalization of problematic emotion in conversations between close relational partners: Interpersonal emotion work. *Symbolic Interaction, 21,* 59-87.

Staske, S. A. (1999). Creating relational ties in talk: The collaborative construction of relational jealousy. *Symbolic Interaction, 22,* 213-247.

Stearns, P. N. (1994). *American cool: Constructing a twentieth-century emotional style.* New York: New York University Press.

Stearns, P. N. (2000). History of emotions: Issues of change and impact. In M. Lewis & J. M. Haviland-Jones (Eds.), *Handbook of emotions* (2nd ed., pp. 16-29). New York: Guilford.

Stephen, T. (1994). Communication in the shifting context of intimacy: Marriage, meaning, and modernity. *Communication Theory, 4,* 191-218.

Stocker, M. (1996). *Valuing emotions.* New York: Cambridge University Press.

Tan, E. S. (2000). Emotion, art, and the humanities. In M. Lewis & J. M. Haviland-Jones (Eds.), *Handbook of emotions* (2nd ed., pp. 116-134). New York: Guilford.

Tangney, J. P., & Fischer, K. W. (1995). *Self-conscious emotions: The psychology of shame, guilt, embarrassment, and pride.* New York: Guilford.

Thoits, P. A. (1985). Social support and psychological well-being: Theoretical possibilities. In I. G. Sarason & B. R. Sarason (Eds.), *Social support: Theory, research, and application* (pp. 51-72). Dordrecht, Netherlands: Martinus Nijhoff.

Thomas, G., & Fletcher, G. J. O. (1997). Empathic accuracy in close relationships. In W. Ickes (Ed.), *Empathic accuracy* (pp. 194-217). New York: Guilford.

Timmers, M., Fischer, A. H., & Manstead, A. S. R. (1998). Gender differences in motives for regulating emotions. *Personality and Social Psychology Bulletin, 24,* 974-985.

Tracy, S. J., & Tracy, K. (1998). Emotion labor at 911: A case study and theoretical critique. *Journal of Applied Communication Research, 26,* 1-22.

Tsoudis, O., & Smith-Lovin, L. (1998). How bad was it? The effects of victim and perpetrator emotion on responses to criminal court vignettes. *Social Forces, 77,* 695-722.

Vangelisti, A. L. (1994). Messages that hurt. In W. R. Cupach & B. H. Spitzberg (Eds.), *The dark side of interpersonal communication* (pp. 53-82). Hillsdale, NJ: Lawrence Erlbaum.

Vangelisti, A. L., & Crumley, L. P. (1998). Reactions to messages that hurt: The influence of relational contexts. *Communication Monographs, 65,* 173-197.

Vangelisti, A. L., & Young, S. L. (2000). When words hurt: The effects of perceived intentionality on interpersonal relationships. *Journal of Social and Personal Relationships, 17,* 393-424.

Vingerhoets, A., & Scheirs, J. (2000). Sex differences in crying: Empirical findings and possible explanations. In A. H. Fischer (Ed.), *Gender and emotion: Social psychological perspectives* (pp. 143-165). Cambridge: Cambridge University Press.

Waldron, V. R. (1994). Once more, *with feeling:* Reconsidering the role of emotion in work. In S. A. Deetz (Ed.), *Communication yearbook 17* (pp. 388-416). Thousand Oaks, CA: Sage.

Watson-Gegeo, K. A., & White, G. M. (1990). *Disentangling: Conflict discourse in Pacific societies.* Stanford, CA: Stanford University Press.

Weisinger, H. (1998). *Emotional intelligence at work.* San Francisco: Jossey-Bass.

White, G. L., & Mullen, P. E. (1989). *Jealousy: Theory, research, and clinical strategies.* New York: Guilford.

White, G. M. (1990). Moral discourse and the rhetoric of emotions. In C. A. Lutz & L. Abu-Lughod (Eds.), *Language and the politics of emotion* (pp. 46-68). Cambridge: Cambridge University Press.

White, G. M. (1993). Emotions inside out: The anthropology of affect. In M. Lewis & J. M. Haviland (Eds.), *Handbook of emotions* (pp. 29-39). New York: Guilford.

White, G. M. (2000). Representing emotional meaning: Category, metaphor, schema, discourse. In M. Lewis & J. M. Haviland-Jones (Eds.), *Handbook of emotions* (2nd ed., pp. 30-44). New York: Guilford.

Wierzbicka, A. (1995). Everyday conceptions of emotion: A semantic perspective. In J. A. Russell, J. M. Fernández-Dols, A. S. R. Manstead, & J. C. Wellenkamp (Eds.), *Everyday conceptions of emotion: An introduction to the psychology, anthropology, and linguistics of emotion* (pp. 19-47). Dordrecht, Netherlands: Kluwer.

Wikan, U. (1990). *Managing turbulent hearts: A Balinese formula for living.* Chicago: University of Chicago Press.

Zammuner, V. L. (2000). Men's and women's lay theories of emotion. In A. H. Fischer (Ed.), *Gender and emotion: Social psychological perspectives* (pp. 48-70). Cambridge: Cambridge University Press.

Zelenski, J. M., & Larsen, R. J. (2000). The distribution of basic emotions in everyday life: a state and trait perspective from experience sampling data. *Journal of Research in Personality, 34,* 178-197.

Zeman, J., & Garber, J. (1996). Display rules for anger, sadness, and pain: It depends on who is watching. *Child Development, 67,* 957-974.

11

Supportive Communication

BRANT R. BURLESON
ERINA L. MACGEORGE

For many of us, the terrorist attacks on the World Trade Center and the Pentagon on September 11, 2001, stimulated a renewed appreciation for family, friends, and other social contacts whose presence makes our lives happier and healthier. Millions coped with the horror of crashing planes and imploding towers by seeking contact with loved ones, benefiting from the reassurance brought by familiar voices, faces, and touch. Subsequently, as grief and anger filled households worldwide, our interactions with those close to us created spaces for us to try to comprehend and cope with the terrible sense of threat that had entered our world. As we strive to resume living normal lives in the midst of a far-reaching, potentially lengthy war, many of us have recognized anew how much our joy in living depends on our interactions with those around us. In scholarly terms, the events of 9/11 highlight the phenomenon of *supportive communication* and its impact on human well-being.

In this chapter, we define supportive communication as verbal and nonverbal behavior produced with the intention of providing assistance to others perceived as needing that aid. Supporting others is a fundamental form of human interaction, just as central to the human experience as persuading, informing, or entertaining one another. For better or worse, the tragedy of 9/11 has made us more mindful of this essential form of human communication and the ways in which it is conducted through varied messages, within ordinary (and extraordinary) interactions and relationships, and in response to myriad life events. Supportive interactions are ubiquitous in human life, beginning early (as caregivers seek to soothe distressed newborns) and extending to our final moments (where, if we are fortunate, we are comforted by loving others after we have lived long and full lives). At a multitude of points in our lives, all of us are seekers and providers of support.

The ubiquity of supportive communication, however, is only an incidental reason for its study. There are several more substantive warrants for scholarship in this arena (Burleson, Albrecht, Goldsmith, & Sarason, 1994). One warrant is pragmatic. Over the past 30 years, a massive body of research findings has accumulated documenting the positive effects of supportive interactions and social relationships on the health and well-being of individuals. For example, effective support fosters psychological adjustment and perceptions of self-efficacy (Krause, Liang, & Yatomi, 1989; Lackner et al., 1993), improves coping with upsetting events (Cunningham & Barbee, 2000), and enhances task performance under stressful conditions (Pierce, Sarason, & Sarason, 1996; Tardy, 1994). It also improves resistance to and recovery from disease (Cohen, 2001; Seeman, 2001; Spiegel & Kimerling, 2001) and even reduces mortality (Berkman, 1995; House, Landis, & Umberson, 1988). Clearly, we need to understand supportive processes if we are to facilitate these beneficial outcomes (e.g., Gottlieb, 2000). A second warrant for the study of supportive communication is theoretical. Like other forms of discourse, supportive communication is a venue for exploring fundamental communication processes, including message production (e.g., Burleson, 1985; MacGeorge, 2001), message reception (e.g., Burleson & Goldsmith, 1998; Kunkel, 2002), and conversational interaction (Jefferson, 1988; Jefferson & Lee, 1992). Moreover, because supportive interactions are a primary means through which social connections are created and sustained (Gottlieb & Wagner, 1991; Reis, 2001), research on supportive

communication contributes to theory on the formation and development of personal relationships. A third warrant is moral in character. Supportive communication frequently displays the highest expressions of the human spirit, so by studying this behavior we better acquaint ourselves with the nature and practice of virtue in everyday life. Surely the events of 9/11 only deepen the importance of scholarship that explores the character of moral action and fosters a sense of community.

Despite the ubiquity and relevance of supportive communication, its formal study has a relatively short history. Arguably, the initial critical mass was not reached until the late 1980s or early 1990s, when a spate of articles, special issues of journals, and books focused attention on this subject (Albrecht & Adelman, 1984, 1987a; Albrecht, Burleson, & Goldsmith, 1994; Albrecht, Burleson, & Sarason, 1992; Burleson, Albrecht, & Sarason, 1994; Duck, 1990; Hobfoll, 1990; Hobfoll & Stokes, 1988; Sarason, Sarason, & Pierce, 1990a). Since that time, research on supportive communication has grown considerably, making it entirely possible for us to focus this review chapter within the confines of this still-young area. However, as many readers will be aware, to do so would ignore the fact that the recent focus on supportive communication owes much to an older and broader tradition of interdisciplinary scholarly inquiry centered on the concept of *social support*. In this latter tradition, which continues with considerable vigor, social support has typically been conceptualized and measured as generalized perceptions of the availability and adequacy of supportive behaviors or relationships (the psychological perspective) or as the enmeshment of individuals in social roles and networks (the sociological perspective). Thus this work does not focus on the role that communication plays when individuals provide assistance to others. However, we believe that understanding, evaluating, and contributing to the scholarship on supportive communication requires an appreciation of this broader literature, including its concepts, measurement choices, findings, and theoretical directions. More specifically, we believe that research on supportive communication can benefit from attention to this literature's focus on linking social support to psychological and physical health.

Accordingly, we pursue a threefold purpose here. Initially, we provide a broad overview of research on social support conducted in the sociological and psychological traditions. At the heart of this chapter is a thorough review of theory and research focused on supportive communication. This work coheres in its focus on messages and interactions associated with communicative efforts directed at assisting others in need. Although space does not permit us to provide an entirely comprehensive review, we address many of the major issues, research paradigms, and findings so that scholars new to the area will find this a useful introduction. In the final section, we examine the limitations of the supportive communication perspective, emphasizing directions for future research and how such research can connect more functionally with the sociological and psychological traditions.

SOCIAL SUPPORT: AN OVERVIEW

The earliest work on "social support" appeared more than a century ago, when English and French demographers argued from statistical data that marriage is a health-promoting institution (Bertillion, 1879; Farr, 1885/1975). Subsequently, Durkheim's (1897/1951) analyses indicated that suicides were more frequent among those with fewer social ties, and similar findings were reported in a scattering of subsequent studies (e.g., Park & Burgess, 1926; Thomas & Znaniecki, 1920). However, today's thriving research tradition on social support and well-being was given its primary stimulus by several essays and books published in the mid-1970s (Caplan, 1974, 1976; Cassel,

1976; Cobb, 1976; Moss, 1973). Drawing on sociological, psychological, biological, epidemiological, and medical studies from the 1940s through the 1970s, these writers argued for a coherent, comprehensive explanation of findings that ranged from the greater incidence of ulcers in rats subjected to electric shock without the presence of littermates to the higher rate of depression among elderly individuals with less social interaction. Informed by such studies, these scholars argued that stressful conditions place individuals at greater risk for psychological disorder, disease, and mortality, but that protection from these risks can be obtained from social relationships that provide support.

In these early formulations, social support was conceptualized and defined in a variety of overlapping but somewhat distinctive ways. For example, Caplan (1974) emphasized the types of relationships that constitute a support network (marriage; parenthood; other intimate ties; friendships; relationships with colleagues at work; membership in religious congregations and in social, cultural, political, and recreational associations; and acquaintanceships with neighbors, shopkeepers, and providers of services). He also identified distinct forms of supportive behavior, noting that significant others "help the individual mobilize his psychological resources and master his emotional burdens; they share his tasks; and they provide him with extra supplies of money, materials, tools, skills, and cognitive guidance to improve his handling of the situation" (p. 7). Taking an approach that focused more closely on the experience of the support recipient, Cobb (1976) defined social support as information "leading the subject to believe that he is cared for and loved . . . esteemed and valued . . . [and] belongs to a network of communication and mutual obligation" (p. 300). Similarly, Moss (1973) defined social support as "the subjective feeling of belonging, of being accepted or being loved, of being needed all for oneself and for what one can do" (p. 237).

(For a review of other early definitions of social support, see Albrecht & Adelman, 1987b.)

Stimulated by the formation of a theoretical and definitional framework, large numbers of researchers began to examine the relationship between social support and well-being. Because these researchers came from diverse disciplinary backgrounds, they conceptualized and operationalized social support in varying ways, emphasizing different aspects of the definitions provided by theorists. Accordingly, subsequent research took a variety of directions from which two major perspectives gradually emerged. The first perspective, dominated by epidemiologists and sociologists, conceptualized and assessed social support in ways that were consistent with macrostructural sociological theory. Congruent with Caplan's descriptions of the relationships that constitute supportive networks and Cobb's "network of communication and mutual obligation," social support was understood as being (or resulting from) participation in a social network. A second perspective, dominated by psychologists, defined and measured social support in ways that were consistent with psychology's focus on individual cognitive processes. Informed by Cassel's (1976) and Moss's (1973) descriptions of social support as information or acts that influence another's feelings, work in the psychological perspective has largely conceptualized support as the perceived availability of helpful persons or behaviors.

The Sociological Perspective

Research Approaches and Findings

In an early and influential study, epidemiologists Berkman and Syme (1979) examined the association between social support and morbidity in a 9-year follow-up of a representative sample of residents ($N = 6,928$) of Alameda County, California. Social support was measured as a composite of diverse indicators of social integration, including whether the individual was married, had contacts with extended family and close friends, attended church, and was involved in other formal or informal social groups. Those who were more socially integrated at the study's beginning (in 1965) were found to have lower mortality 9 years later, and this effect remained even when the researchers controlled for a range of potentially confounding factors. The more socially integrated were also less likely to have experienced various health-related problems, such as heart, digestive, and respiratory illnesses.

Berkman and Syme's (1979) study illustrates two key characteristics of social support investigations in the sociological tradition. First, social support was operationalized as social integration, or "the extent to which individuals belong to different groups (e.g., marital status, church membership, friendship) and the actual use they make of these group memberships (e.g., activities)" (Stroebe & Stroebe, 1996, p. 598). Measures of social integration typically tap role differentiation (the number of social roles an individual routinely enacts), social participation (the frequency with which the individual engages in various social activities), perceived integration (the individual's feelings of community and belonging), or some combination of these three constructs—the so-called complex indicators—such as those employed by Berkman and Syme (for a review of social integration measures, see Brissette, Cohen, & Seeman, 2000). A few researchers have employed measures derived from social network analysis (e.g., network size and density) as assessments of social support (e.g., Hirsch, 1980); however, these measures appear less reliably associated with assessments of well-being than social integration measures (Brissette et al., 2000; Stroebe & Stroebe, 1996), perhaps because these purely structural indices fail to capture the quality of social relationships.

A second characteristic of the Berkman and Syme study is its methodological strength in the domains of sampling, design, and statistical controls. Epidemiological and sociological studies typically are large scale, use representative regional or national samples, and control for multiple factors that might confound associations between social support and health. Moreover, many of these studies employ longitudinal, prospective designs to assess whether social support at one point in time predicts well-being at a future date. The methodological rigor of studies in the sociological tradition thus provides some of the best empirical evidence linking social support and well-being.

Since Berkman and Syme's work, the association between social integration and longevity has been documented repeatedly in prospective studies (see reviews by Berkman, Glass, Brissette, & Seeman, 2000; House et al., 1988; Schwarzer & Leppin, 1991). In addition, a large body of work has documented positive effects of social integration on disease outcomes, including resistance to infectious disease (see Cohen, 2001) and recovery from heart attacks, strokes, and cancer (recent reviews include Berkman, 1995; Cohen, Gottlieb, & Underwood, 2000; Helgeson, Cohen, & Fritz, 1998; Reifman, 1995). Additional research has documented ties between social integration and underlying physiological and biological mechanisms that influence health (Cohen, 1988; Uchino, Cacioppo, & Kiecolt-Glaser, 1996), including cardiovascular function (Seeman, 2001), immune system function (Cohen, 1994), and neuroendocrine function (Seeman, Berkman, Blazer, & Rowe, 1994). Greater social integration is also associated with a variety of important psychological outcomes, including depression and general mental health (Biegel, McCardle, & Mendelson, 1985; Schwarzer & Leppin, 1992).

Theoretical Development

As findings continued to corroborate the relationship between social integration and well-being, researchers in the sociological tradition largely accepted that social integration could be good for health (at least under some circumstances) and turned their attention increasingly to several theoretical issues. One early controversy concerned whether social support has a "main" or "buffering" effect on well-being (see Cohen & Wills, 1985). The issue here concerns whether social support exercises its positive influence primarily in the context of stressful events ("buffering" the individual against the negative impacts of those events) or whether it has a beneficial effect regardless of stress levels (a main effect). Reviews of studies that were methodologically suited to distinguishing these effects have indicated that both models are valid, albeit they are appropriate to different conceptualizations and measures of social support. Buffering effects are most likely to be observed when research assesses perceptions of support availability or adequacy in the presence of stressful conditions (see the discussion of "perceived support" later in this chapter). In contrast, social integration typically has a main rather than buffering effect on well-being (Cohen & Wills, 1985; Schwarzer & Leppin, 1989, 1991), a finding consistent with the fact that social integration measures are ill suited to capturing network qualities or network member behaviors that are specifically relevant to stressful events. Accordingly, most theorizing about the mechanisms through which social integration affects health has been informed by the main effect model, concentrating on factors that should be operative across the broad spectrum of life events (Brissette et al., 2000; Cohen et al., 2000).

A second theoretical issue concerns whether increases in social integration, participation, and interaction consistently facilitate health or can also be damaging to health. As several theorists have observed, the mere existence of social connections does not necessarily mean that these connections are supportive (e.g., Antonucci, 1990). In particular, research by Rook and her colleagues has demonstrated that many social relationships are sources of stress, even when they also provide support (e.g., Rook, 1984, 1990; Rook & Pietromonaco, 1987). Thus research has increasingly focused on identifying means by which particular social ties function both to promote and to undermine health (see Rook & Underwood, 2000).

A third theoretical issue concerns the nature of the causal mechanisms linking social integration with health outcomes. Some theoretical accounts of the effects of social participation on health focus on the behavioral consequences of social integration. For example, greater social integration may cause individuals to experience more *social control,* in which social roles act as restraints on health-relevant behaviors (e.g., drug use, sexual activity) or members of the social network actively monitor and influence behavior through compliance-gaining efforts. Alternatively, those who are more socially integrated may have more access to *social resources*—"goods" such as information, money, and direct forms of assistance. Those with greater access to such goods should be able to draw from them to maintain physical and psychological well-being. Other causal mechanisms focus on cognitive and emotional factors that may directly influence psychological well-being and in turn influence physiology or health behaviors. For example, greater social involvement and activity may produce higher levels of *positive affect,* promoting positive psychological states (e.g., optimism) that benefit physiological functioning or promote the individual's motivation to protect his or her health. Alternatively, greater social integration may result in a more *differentiated self-concept,* making negative events in any particular domain of life less important, and thereby reducing the impacts of such events. Additional explanatory mechanisms and pathways for the health benefits of social integration, including direct effects on biological functioning, have been reviewed by many authors (Brissette et al., 2000; Cohen, 1988; Uchino et al., 1996).

Determining the merit of proposed explanatory mechanisms is complicated by the fact that both social integration and health are multidimensional constructs. Most likely, different aspects of social integration promote specific health outcomes through the operation of distinct causal mechanisms. For example, it seems reasonable to hypothesize that integration in social systems such as the family facilitates social control of the individual's lifestyle and health behaviors, resulting in lower rates of morbidity and mortality from accidents, risky behaviors, drug abuse, eating disorders, and other lifestyle-related causes. In contrast, recovery from debilitating conditions such as stroke, heart attack, and cancer might be particularly facilitated by the social resources made available through a large social network. A third hypothesis is that participation in diverse social roles may diminish the affective impact of negative events while enhancing opportunities for positive affective experiences; enhanced positive affect and decreased negative affect may afford protection from stress-related illnesses such as hypertension, cardiovascular disease, and depression.

As Brissette et al. (2000) state: "The association between social integration and health is clear. However, determining [the nature of] this relation . . . remains a chief research priority" (p. 76). Thus, for scholars working within the sociological perspective, the research agenda increasingly is focused on determining precisely which aspects of social integration influence particular aspects of health through specific causal mechanisms.

The Psychological Perspective

Whereas scholars in the sociological tradition have conceptualized social support in terms of integration within a social network, psychologists have developed approaches consistent with their discipline's traditional concern with the cognitive and emotional processes of individuals. Most of the research informed by the psychological perspective has been loosely tied together by its focus on the *perceived availability of support.* Broadly, the perception that support is available (and, sometimes, that the available support is adequate) is viewed as buffering the individual against stress and its health-damaging effects, as well as enhancing the individual's coping performance (Lakey & Cohen, 2000). However, the focus on perceived availability represents an evolution from a focus on *enacted and received support*, more behaviorally based ways of conceptualizing and measuring support. As will be seen, this evolution has been important to the development of the supportive communication tradition, as well as to current theoretical controversies within the psychological tradition.

Enacted Support

Some of the earliest work in the psychological tradition (e.g., Barrera, 1981) was based on the plausible hypothesis that those who experience a stressful event but receive high levels of assistance from their social networks will be happier and healthier than those who experience such an event and receive low levels of assistance. Consistent with Caplan's (1974) idea that support consists of "supplies of money, materials, tools, skills, and cognitive guidance," this early work conceptualized social support as resources or commodities given or exchanged in the effort to assist others (e.g., Gore, 1978).

Various classifications of support resources or functions were proposed, with the typology presented by House (1981) being both typical and influential: emotional support (affection, trust, esteem), appraisal support (confirmation, validation, affirmation), informational support (advice, information, guidance), and instrumental or tangible support (money, labor, material assistance) (for a review of related typologies, see Cutrona & Russell, 1990). The intuitive notion underlying this "supportive actions" perspective (Lakey & Cohen, 2000) is that by providing these resources, a helper assists a target in coping more effectively with

environmental demands, thereby reducing stress and protecting the target's health. Researchers who employed more complex versions of this approach proposed that, to be effective, the type of support enacted by the helper needs to match the type of stressor experienced by the target (e.g., Cohen & McKay, 1984). (We review such "matching models" in more detail below, in the section on supportive communication.)

Despite the intuitive appeal of this approach, very few studies were conducted in which researchers actually observed helpers as they enacted supportive behaviors and then assessed the effects of these enacted behaviors on the coping and well-being of the targets. Researchers were quick to recognize the practical difficulties associated with observing the provision of support in real-world settings, as well as the possibility that behaviors enacted by helpers might not be perceived as supportive by their recipients. This led researchers to develop self-report questionnaires to be completed by support recipients, giving rise to the "received support" tradition.

Received Support

As a convenient alternative to observational data, self-report measures were designed to obtain participants' perceptions of how much supportive behavior they had received from their social networks in the recent past. For example, the popular Inventory of Socially Supportive Behaviors, developed by Barrera, Sandler, and Ramsey (1981), has respondents indicate how often during the previous 4 weeks they perceived (or recall) receiving each of 40 behaviors providing emotional, tangible, and informational support. Wills and Shinar (2000) review several common measures of received support.

Research utilizing received support measures has encountered substantial conceptual and methodological challenges. Some studies indicate that correlations between enacted support (measured from the perspective of the support provider) and received support (measured from the perspective of the support recipient) are modest at best (e.g., Antonucci & Israel, 1986). Even more disenchanting to scholars in the psychological tradition, many early studies reported *positive* correlations between measures of received support and measures of stress and health problems (e.g., Cohen & Hoberman, 1983; Sandler & Barrera, 1984), indicating that increased levels of received support were associated with *higher* levels of stress and *more* physical or mental health problems. Although these findings are meaningful, suggesting that people actively marshal support resources when they are stressed (Barrera, 1986; Dunkel-Schetter & Bennett, 1990), most psychologists were disinclined to embrace an approach indicating that more support is associated with more stress. Finally, early comparative studies suggested that the competing construct of perceived availability of support explained more variance in physical and mental health outcomes than did measures of received support (e.g., Antonucci & Israel, 1986; Wethington & Kessler, 1986).

Perceived Support

Concurrent with, and in response to, the empirical "failures" of received support measures, influential researchers argued that the critical element of social support is the *perception* that it is *available if needed* (Cohen & Wills, 1985; Kessler, 1992). This conceptual movement was presaged by early social support definitions that emphasized perceptions of care, value, or positive regard over the behaviors that may produce such perceptions (e.g., Cassel, 1976; Cobb, 1976; see also Sarason, Sarason, & Pierce, 1990b). Instruments designed to measure perceived support have respondents indicate the likely availability to them of various types of support, should the need arise (for a review of measures, see Wills & Shinar, 2000).

The conceptual and methodological shift from enacted or received support to perceived support availability was part and parcel of an evolution in theorizing about the mechanisms through which social support affects well-being. The concepts of enacted support and received support fit most naturally within a "coping assistance" model (in which experienced supportive behaviors help stressed individuals deal more effectively with problems). In contrast, the construct of perceived support availability is future oriented and de-emphasizes the empirically problematic role of supportive behavior. Correspondingly, cognitive mechanisms such as appraisal processes were invoked to account for the effects of perceived support availability on well-being. Appraisal theory explains stress as arising not from events themselves, but from their interpretation or "appraisal," including evaluations of available coping resources (Lazarus & Folkman, 1984). Thus, to the extent that people perceive support as available to help with coping, they experience less stress from negatively appraised events (Wethington & Kessler, 1986), regardless of whether they actually seek supportive behaviors from others or such behaviors are provided.

This theoretical conceptualization of how social support functions raises questions about the etiology of perceptions of support availability. Most researchers appear to have assumed (albeit implicitly) that perceptions of availability are founded upon the receipt of past supportive behaviors. However, measures of received support and perceived support frequently correlate only weakly (Dunkel-Schetter & Bennett, 1990), raising doubt about whether perceptions of support received in the recent past are the basis for more global beliefs that support is available if needed (see Kessler, 1992). A very different possibility is that the perception of support availability constitutes a stable personality characteristic (Lakey & Cassady, 1990; Sarason, Sarason, & Shearin, 1986). According to Barbara Sarason and her colleagues, perceptions of support availability reflect the individual's fundamental "sense of acceptance," or the extent to which he or she feels loved, valued, and accepted by others (Sarason, Pierce, & Sarason, 1990). This sense of acceptance is hypothesized to develop as a function of attachment experiences in infancy and childhood. Evidence supporting this trait view of perceived support availability includes findings that individuals' reports of support experiences and expectations (a) tend to be highly consistent over time (Sarason, Sarason, & Gurung, 1997), (b) are correlated with several relevant personality traits (Lakey & Lutz, 1996), and (c) are correlated with measures of attachment style (Asendorpf & Wilpers, 2000). Consistent with this trait view of perceived support, some experimental evidence indicates that perceptions of the supportiveness of standardized behaviors vary as a function of stable individual differences, including personality traits (e.g., Pierce, Sarason, & Sarason, 1992). However, other research suggests that characteristics of both behavior and the perceiver influence perceptions of support-intended behaviors and their providers (e.g., Lakey, McCabe, Fiscaro, & Drew, 1996; Samter, Burleson, & Basden-Murphy, 1989).

Regardless of how it is conceptualized, perceived support availability has been found to be associated with a wide array of physical and psychological outcomes. Studies have been conducted with respect to a diversity of stressors and populations, and have employed a vast array of research designs and means of measuring perceived support availability. In fact, the relevant literature is now so large that most reviews are either impressionistic or specific to particular stressors, populations, outcomes, or some combination thereof. As one might expect from such a large and heterogeneous literature, there is considerable variation in the sizes and cross-study consistency of the observed effects, but taken together, the findings overwhelmingly support the positive influence of perceived support availability on physical and mental health (for reviews, see Cunningham & Barbee, 2000; Sarason et al., 1997; Schwarzer & Leppin, 1992; Stroebe & Stroebe, 1996; Wills, 1991).

Current Issues

Researchers working within the psychological perspective are currently focused on several issues critical to an understanding of the connections between the perceived availability of support and well-being. Although enacted support continues to be largely ignored in this tradition, the other conceptions of support and their associations with health outcomes continue to fuel theoretical controversy. Some theorists believe that only the trait-based conception of perceived availability has shown consistent, appropriate outcomes with assessments of well-being, discounting any influence of "enacted" or "received" supportive behaviors (Kessler, 1992; Sarason, Pierce, & Sarason, 1990). However, several recent studies of received support have used improved measures focused on types of supportive behavior especially relevant to given stressors; these studies have detected positive (and even strong) associations between received support and various well-being outcomes (e.g., Collins, Dunkel-Schetter, Lobel, & Scrimshaw, 1993; Krause, 1987). Additional studies employing longitudinal designs have measured both received and perceived support, showing that the latter is affected by the former across time (e.g., Cohen & Lichtenstein, 1990; Norris & Kaniasty, 1996), something that should not occur if perceived support is exclusively a personality trait established in childhood. Findings such as these strongly suggest that the study of received support—or, more generally, supportive behaviors—should not be abandoned just because the effects of received support on coping, perceived support, and well-being are complex and challenging to document (Barrera, 1986; Norris & Kaniasty, 1996).

Another issue currently receiving considerable attention concerns the precise mechanism, or mechanisms, through which perceived support availability influences well-being. Theorists have articulated with growing specificity different explanatory mechanisms, suggesting that perceived support may affect well-being through the mediation of appraisal processes, self-esteem, relational schemata, and self-conceptions, among others (Lakey & Cohen, 2000; Stroebe & Stroebe, 1996; Wills & Shinar, 2000). Thus far, however, few empirical studies have evaluated the operation of these proposed mechanisms. This remains an important area for future research.

A final theoretical issue concerns the origins or sources of the individual's perceptions of support availability. Once again, the processes viewed as contributing to the sense that support is (or is not) available vary with different understandings of the perceived availability construct. Each conception of perceived availability implies a distinct set of interactional experiences underlying the belief that support is more or less available. To date, only limited inquiry has examined whether the implied interactional experiences actually contribute to the individual's sense that support is available; thus this also remains an area for future research.

Summary

Research in the sociological and psychological perspectives has clearly indicated the relevance of social support—however defined—to physical and mental well-being. Social integration generally enhances both physiological and psychological quality of life. Further, the perceived availability of support reduces the level of stress produced by negative events and, correspondingly, reduces the incidence of stress-related mental conditions and physical illnesses. These documented associations between well-being and assessments of social integration and perceived support availability

make the study of social support within the sociological and psychological frameworks both important and exciting; that a considerable number of theoretical issues remain to be addressed in these traditions only makes the work more intriguing and potentially valuable. However, in this chapter our primary focus is on an alternative to the sociological and psychological perspectives, one with a distinctive focus on social support as a *communication* process.

The sociological and psychological perspectives implicitly recognize that communication plays a role in the origin and impact of social support. The sociological perspective takes for granted that social networks are maintained through communication between network members, and many of the mechanisms through which social integration may affect well-being necessarily imply communication (e.g., communication is a primary means by which network members exert social control). In the psychological perspective, communication is an assumed but largely invisible vehicle through which perceptions of support availability are created. This is true regardless of whether perceived support availability is viewed as a situationally specific state (i.e., influenced by recent interactions in which support was or was not provided) or as a trait shaped in childhood (i.e., created by interactions with parents and other caregivers; see Albrecht et al., 1994). Despite these implicit assumptions, little research within the sociological and psychological traditions has directly examined these functions of communication, making it likely that that theoretical development could be enhanced if communication variables were included in studies of social integration and perceived support availability.

But communication also deserves a far more central place in the study of social support. We believe that "social support should be studied *as communication* because it is ultimately conveyed through messages directed by one individual to another in the context of a relationship that is created and sustained through interaction" (Burleson, Albrecht, Goldsmith, & Sarason, 1994, p. xviii; emphasis added).

SUPPORTIVE COMMUNICATION

At about the same time the sociological and psychological perspectives on social support were being articulated and refined (roughly 1975-1990), scholars in several different academic disciplines were developing research programs examining what eventually would be called *supportive communication*. The work of Albrecht and her colleagues within the academic discipline of communication provided much of the initial impetus for an articulation of a communication perspective on social support (Albrecht & Adelman, 1984, 1987a; Albrecht, Irey, & Mundy, 1982), but this emerging perspective was also informed by a variety of other empirical traditions, including research on altruism by both developmental and social psychologists (Batson & Oleson, 1991; Eisenberg, Fabes, & Losoya, 1997; Zahn-Waxler & Radke-Yarrow, 1990), research on psychotherapy by clinical psychologists (Elliott, 1985; Greenberg, 1993), research on "troubles talk" by ethnomethodologists (Jefferson, 1988; Pritchard, 1993), research on "comforting communication" by communication researchers (Burleson, 1984b, 1990), research on coping assistance by community and social psychologists (e.g., Gottlieb, 1978; Thoits, 1986), and research on interpersonal competence by scholars representing a variety of disciplines (e.g., Buhrmester, Furman, Wittenberg, & Reis, 1988), as well as work on "received support" in the psychological tradition (Kahn & Antonucci, 1980; Shumaker & Brownell, 1984).

These diverse literatures remained largely segregated through the early 1990s. Since that time, however, growing numbers of scholars have appreciated the common focus in these varied research traditions on communicative

efforts directed at helping others in need. As a result, a distinctive communication or interactional perspective on social support has emerged over the past 10 years (see Albrecht et al., 1994; Barbee & Cunningham, 1995; Burleson & Goldsmith, 1998; Dunkel-Schetter, Blasband, Feinstein, & Herbert, 1992; Reis & Collins, 2000). In this section we examine an increasingly extensive and sophisticated body of research centered on the concept of supportive communication. We begin by explicating the distinctive conceptual and theoretical commitments of this emerging perspective. We then review two major traditions of research that explore different facets of supportive communication: supportive messages and supportive interactions.

Distinctive Features of the Communication Perspective

The communication perspective on social support is distinct from the sociological and psychological perspectives in several respects. First and foremost among these is the *centrality of the role allotted to communication*. Most variants of the sociological and psychological perspectives assume (at least implicitly) that communication contributes to the origins or effects of social support. In contrast, the communication perspective conceptualizes social support as assistance that people seek to convey to those they perceive as needing some form of help (Dunkel-Schetter et al., 1992). In this perspective, social support is not a by-product or perceptual outcome of social interactions; rather, it is fundamentally communicative in character. Thus, from a communication perspective, the study of "social support" *is the study of supportive communication*: verbal (and nonverbal) behaviors intended to provide or seek help. The object of study here thus resembles what the psychological perspective has termed "enacted support," a phenomenon largely abandoned by researchers working in that perspective due to methodological challenges.

A second distinguishing feature of the communication perspective is the assumption of a relatively *direct connection between communication and well-being*. The sociological perspective assumes that integration within a social network leads to a variety of interactions that are not necessarily intended to provide assistance but nonetheless serve to influence cognition, emotion, behavior, and physiological processes in ways that facilitate physical and mental health. The psychological perspective assumes that the individual's sense of support availability, a product of either recent or distant interactions, provides a buffer against stress and related health problems and facilitates functional coping and adaptation. Thus in both of these perspectives the connection between communication and well-being is indirect. In contrast, the communication perspective takes as its primary focus those communicative acts specifically intended to improve the well-being of another person who is currently experiencing a problematic or emotionally distressing situation. Thus the communication perspective examines behaviors enacted in pursuit of such objectives as reducing emotional upset and promoting the resolution of problems.

A third way in which the communication perspective differs from the sociological and psychological is in its focus on *helpers' intentional responses to targets' perceived needs*. In the sociological perspective, social integration is implicitly understood to result from roles, relationships, and interactions, but it is not seen as an intentional creation or as a response to particular stressors. Similarly, in the psychological perspective, perceived support availability is assumed to have a basis in past interactions (either distant or recent), but is not viewed as produced by the current stressful event or the behaviors of helpers relative to that stressor. In contrast, the communication perspective emphasizes the study of intentional responses to currently observed needs. Such needs may stem from a variety of acute or chronic stressful experiences, ranging from major losses and challenges (e.g., bereavement, loss of a job, moving to a new home, poverty) to the myriad upsets and hassles that arise in everyday life. Emphasis is placed on understanding intentional helping in response to the perception of such events in others' lives, with research examining how and why "a 'provider' attempts to proffer support and a 'recipient' may be helped or benefited by the attempt" (Dunkel-Schetter & Skokan, 1990, p. 437). Several theorists provide detailed discussions of the character of supportive intentions (see Albrecht et al., 1994, p. 421; Burleson, 1994b, pp. 136-137; Dunkel-Schetter et al., 1992, pp. 86-88).

A fourth distinctive characteristic of the communication perspective is that research within it typically *exhibits a normative focus*. Both the sociological and psychological perspectives exhibit a "more is better" orientation (Vaux, 1990) with respect to how well-being is affected by social support. Specifically, the implication in each of these perspectives is that well-being will be enhanced by an increase in the quantity of social integration or perceived support availability. In contrast, the communication perspective does *not* assume that well-being (and other outcomes of interest) will be improved simply by *more* supportive communication. Rather, the communication perspective appreciates that not everything individuals say or do when seeking or providing support is equally effective (Burleson & Goldsmith, 1998; Dunkel-Schetter et al., 1992). Some forms of supportive communication are better than others—at least in some situations, with respect to certain goals, and as evaluated by certain criteria. The appreciation that there are functional differences in forms of supportive communication motivates researchers' efforts to determine which forms of support are more effective than others, to identify the features distinguishing more and less effective forms, and to develop theory that explains why these features are effective.

A fifth distinguishing characteristic of the communication perspective is its emphasis on *interaction and relationship outcomes.* Most research stemming from the sociological and psychological perspectives has focused on the outcomes of physical and psychological health. In contrast, supportive communication research has focused primarily on other classes of outcomes. Of particular interest in this research tradition is whether communication behaviors achieve "primary goals" (Wilson, 1997)—the relatively immediate effects for which supportive communication is typically sought and provided. For example, does a particular communication behavior actually reduce emotional distress or improve problem-solving ability? Attention has also been given to the effects of supportive communication on the quality of relationships between helpers and targets. These effects are of special interest because support—especially emotional support—is viewed as a key provision of close relationships (Cunningham & Barbee, 2000; Cutrona & Russell, 1987; Weiss, 1974). People place high value on the supportive communication skills of their partners (Buhrmester et al., 1988; Burleson, Kunkel, Samter, & Werking, 1996; Westmyer & Myers, 1996), and the receipt of support, especially quality emotional support, is associated with relationship satisfaction and commitment (Acitelli & Antonucci, 1994; Sprecher, Metts, Burleson, Hatfield, & Thompson, 1995).

In sum, the communication perspective focuses on more or less explicit communicative efforts by one person to improve the well-being of another who is perceived as in need or under stress. These efforts are assumed to be goal directed or intentional (although it is not assumed that people are necessarily conscious or reflectively aware of their supportive intentions; see Dillard, 1997). Research on supportive communication is further informed by the assumption that support efforts differ in their effectiveness and that the features of more and less effective support efforts can be specified. The effectiveness of supportive communication has been examined primarily with respect to interaction and relationship outcomes.

We turn now to a more detailed review of the supportive communication literature. As an organizing framework, we note the suggestion by Burleson, Albrecht, Goldsmith, and Sarason (1994) that researching social support as communication "means studying the *messages* through which people both seek and express support; studying the *interactions* in which supportive messages are produced and interpreted; and studying the *relationships* that are created by and contextualize the supportive interactions in which people engage" (p. xviii; for a largely similar view, see Reis & Collins, 2000, p. 139). Although a very broad array of phenomena have been subjected to research under the general rubric of "supportive communication," most of these can be classified as messages or interactions. Thus we adopt this structure and present our review in terms of work examining supportive messages and interactions.

SUPPORTIVE MESSAGES

The preponderance of research concerned with "supportive communication" has focused on supportive messages. We define supportive messages as *specific lines of communicative behavior enacted by one party with the intent of benefiting or helping another.* Viewed as such, supportive messages are but one part of "supportive interactions," the latter of which can be understood as extended conversational sequences or episodes that also include seeking, receiving, processing, and responding to supportive efforts. In this section, we (a) discuss criteria for evaluating supportive messages; (b) describe and critique research methods used to investigate supportive message properties; (c) summarize findings regarding the features of more and less effective messages, considering the extent to which these findings are qualified by various moderating factors; and (d) review emerging theoretical explanations for the effectiveness of certain message features.

Criteria for Evaluating Supportive Messages

Consistent with the normative focus of the communication perspective on social support, research on supportive messages is grounded in the recognition that not everything said or done by a support provider is equally successful. Some messages or acts intended to provide assistance do so quite effectively, but others are of questionable value, and still others may be counterproductive (Burleson & Goldsmith, 1998; Dunkel-Schetter et al., 1992). Consequently, the major aims in research on supportive messages have been (a) to identify more and less effective message forms and (b) to specify the features that distinguish the more effective forms from those that are less effective. Noting that messages vary in their effectiveness raises an issue that pervades the study of supportive messages but has not always been addressed explicitly: What criteria should we use to determine message effectiveness?

Matching Models

Much of the early work on features of effective supportive messages was informed by "matching models" of the support process (Cohen & McKay, 1984; Cutrona, 1990; Cutrona & Russell, 1990; Wills, 1985). The key idea underlying these models is that the type of support offered must be *relevant* to the particular stressor experienced by the target if it is to be effective. Lakey and Cohen (2000) describe the central thesis of matching models in the following terms: "The hypothesis is that social support will be effective in promoting coping and reducing the effects of a stressor, insofar as the form of assistance matches the demands of the stressor. According to this

view, each stressful circumstance places specific demands on the affected individual" (p. 31). This has strong intuitive appeal; after all, offering sympathy to a traveler who has run out of gas is "obviously" less effective than providing directions (or a ride) to a gas station.

Categories of stressors and "types" of supportive communication become crucial in attempts to test this hypothesis. Several theorists working in the psychological tradition have proposed classifications of stressors and support types (e.g., Cutrona & Russell, 1987; House, 1981; Weiss, 1974), and although there are differences in these, most include largely similar sets of categories (for a review, see Cutrona & Russell, 1990). This work has directly influenced category systems for types of supportive messages. A representative classification system is that developed by Cutrona and Suhr (1994), who distinguish among *emotional support* (expressions of care, concern, and sympathy), *esteem support* (reassurance of worth, expressions of liking for or confidence in the other), *network support* (expressions of connection and belonging), *informational support* (information and advice), and *tangible assistance* (offers of money, physical intervention, material aid).

Despite their intuitive appeal, matching models have not fared well empirically. For example, Cutrona and Suhr (1994), leading proponents of matching models, found little support for the matching hypothesis in a detailed study of supportive messages exchanged by married couples coping with diverse stressors. These researchers conclude that "the optimal matching model was a significant oversimplification of a complex phenomenon" (p. 132). Numerous conceptual problems have contributed to the empirical inadequacy of matching models. First, many stressors are complex, creating multiple challenges for those facing them. The loss of one's job, for example, may result not only in financial problems, but also sadness or depression, loss of self-esteem, a disrupted social network, and the need to locate a new position. Thus no single type of support is sufficient to address this situation. Second, communication scholars have increasingly realized that messages are often, even typically, multifunctional, addressing a variety of objectives (O'Keefe & Delia, 1982; Wilson, 1997) and producing multifaceted effects (e.g., Bingham & Burleson, 1989). Thus it is problematic to classify a message as providing a single type of support or to assume a one-to-one correspondence between particular message types and their impacts (e.g., emotional support may influence problem-solving motivation or capacity, and instrumental support may influence emotional states) (Burleson & Goldsmith, 1998; Tardy, 1994).

But the third and most important limitation of matching models is the assumption of functional equivalence among messages of a "type" relevant to the stressor. This is, quite simply, naive and detrimental to the explication of message effectiveness. Many different messages can be equally relevant to a stressor (e.g., expressions of sympathy to someone suffering a bereavement) but differ dramatically in other important ways (e.g., the sensitivity with which sympathy is conveyed). Thus matching models have probably failed empirically because (a) many messages will be "matches" to some aspect of a stressor, and (b) such messages may vary on other, more specific and critical dimensions.

A Multiple-Objectives Framework

An alternative to the matching model framework is provided by Burleson's (1994b) distinction between proximal (immediate) and distal (long-term) objectives that are either instrumental or relational in character. This framework assumes that supportive messages can be evaluated in terms of their success at achieving these different objectives. To some extent, the framework borrows from, and elaborates, the distinction made by communication theorists between primary goals (those that define and give rise to messages and interactions) and secondary goals (typical interaction concerns that constrain the manner in which primary goals are pursued) (Clark & Delia, 1979; Dillard, 1997). However, it also recognizes that criteria for evaluating supportive messages cannot rest entirely on the actual or typical intentions of the support provider; some outcomes of theoretical and pragmatic interest may not be consciously recognized or pursued.

In Burleson's framework, instrumental objectives are those having primary influence on the target of the supportive messages, whereas relational objectives affect both the target and the support provider. Such objectives can be further distinguished into immediate (taking place in closer proximity to the message behavior and more likely to be affected by single messages or interactions) and distal (observable at some distance from message behaviors and more likely to be influenced by accumulated messages and interactions). Thus supportive messages can be evaluated for their success at fulfilling *immediate instrumental objectives*, such as reducing distress or promoting problem-solving actions, and *immediate relational objectives*, such as protecting or managing the interpersonal relationship with the target, responding to relevant concerns for identity and self-presentation, and maintaining coherent interaction. (For a detailed explication of various instrumental objectives relevant to supportive messages and interactions, see MacGeorge, 2001.) Supportive messages can also be evaluated for their impact on *distal instrumental objectives*, including the development of targets' coping capacities, enhancement of targets' psychological and physical health, heightening of targets' perceptions of availability of support, and even influencing individuals' capacity to provide support for others. Similarly, evaluation of supportive messages can be made with respect to *distal relational objectives,* including satisfaction, stability, and commitment in the relationship between support provider and target.

In sum, stressful events create multiple needs, so supportive messages are frequently multifunctional, seeking to service multiple goals. Matching models fail to capture this richness, focusing exclusively on the relevance of message content to a stressor. The relevance of message content is obviously important, but it is only one basis for evaluating the effectiveness of messages. Approaches that evaluate supportive messages in terms of multiple outcomes, particularly those tied to the goals pursued by helpers, should provide more useful information about message effects.

Methods for Assessing the Effectiveness of Supportive Messages

In this subsection we review methods that are useful for identifying more and less effective supportive messages and determining their distinguishing features. Researchers confront at least three analytically distinct tasks when pursuing this objective: (a) generating a sample of messages to evaluate, (b) evaluating these messages according to some standard of effectiveness, and (c) describing the features that differentiate more and less effective message forms. Logically, the tasks of message generation, evaluation, and description are independent of one another, so it is conceivable that researchers could use many different combinations of procedures in developing approaches to message assessment (for a detailed review of these procedural options, see Burleson, in press). In practice, however, four approaches have been adopted, each exhibiting a distinctive integration of message generation, evaluation, and description procedures. We provide an overview of these approaches, describe recent applications of them, and discuss their strengths and

limitations as vehicles for assessing the effectiveness of supportive messages.

The Naturalistic Paradigm

The most frequently used approach in studies of support message effectiveness is what Dunkel-Schetter et al. (1992) term the "naturalistic paradigm." Participants in such research typically are coping with some acute or chronic stressor (e.g., the death of a child, a serious medical condition). Through interviews or questionnaires, participants provide retrospective self-reports regarding "helpful" and "unhelpful" messages they have received from others. For example, Clark and Stephens (1996) asked 55 stroke patients to report on helpful and unhelpful behaviors by their spouses. These actions were coded within several broad categories, with helpful actions including "assistance with instrumental activities of daily living" and "emotional support," and unhelpful actions including "criticism/demandingness" and "lack of emotional involvement." Participants' perceptions of their spouses' helpful and unhelpful actions were then used to predict measures of psychosocial well-being. (For additional examples of this paradigm, see Dakof & Taylor, 1990; Metts, Geist, & Gray, 1994.)

The strength of this paradigm is its ecological validity; it examines instances of naturally occurring supportive communication in the context of real (and substantial) stressors and frequently preserves aspects of participants' natural language categories for these acts. However, there are serious limitations inherent in this paradigm as a device for identifying and theorizing about features of effective supportive messages. People are far better at recalling the perceived intentions of others and episode outcomes than they are at recalling the details of what others actually said (e.g., Benoit, Benoit, & Wilkie, 1995), a circumstance that is only exacerbated by the typical procedure of obtaining data well after the supportive encounter took place (weeks or months, if not longer). Thus "messages" obtained in the naturalistic paradigm are frequently descriptions of perceived intentions and outcomes, and participants' recollections of verbal and nonverbal behaviors lack precision (see Goldsmith, 1992).

The message classification systems employed in this perspective also contribute to a lack of specificity in the findings. Although many typologies have been employed (see Wortman & Dunkel-Schetter, 1987), most are implicitly informed by "matching models" and focus on the "type" of support offered by a message (e.g., emotional support, informational support). This approach to coding embodies the problematic assumption that broad categories of content are the primary influence on message effectiveness. The selection of "helpfulness" as the single dimension of evaluation similarly detracts from the value of the findings. What this term signifies is undertheorized in these studies. Does it refer to immediate or more distal outcomes? To instrumental or relational effects? Thus, despite their prevalence, naturalistic paradigm studies provide little precise knowledge about supportive message effectiveness.

The Interaction Analysis Paradigm

A second approach, the interaction analysis paradigm, focuses on conversations between pairs of participants (often spouses, sometimes friends) in a laboratory during which one discusses a current stressor and the other responds. These interactions are typically recorded and subsequently transcribed and coded for varied types of support, with frequencies of supportive acts then being correlated with outcomes of interest. Thus critical features of this paradigm are the elicitation of quasi-natural supportive interactions in controlled settings and the subsequent coding of those interactions for instances of specific behaviors. For example, Cutrona and Suhr (1994) had 50 married couples report to their laboratory and complete a measure of marital satisfaction. The couples then discussed, for 10 minutes, an "important stressor" currently faced by one spouse; subsequently, the disclosing spouse completed a measure of interaction satisfaction and depressive mood. The supporting spouses' behaviors were coded into the categories of emotional support, esteem support, informational support, social network support, and tangible aid, and frequencies in each of these categories were correlated with measures of marital satisfaction, interaction satisfaction, and mood.

Messages obtained through laboratory interactions obviously do not suffer from the recall problems inherent in the retrospective self-reports generated by the naturalistic paradigm. The realism and abundance of message data available in these interactions is clearly a strength, although researchers do have to be concerned with participant reactivity to the lab environment (Reis & Collins, 2000), as well as with effects that are specific to the nature of problems chosen for discussion. Another significant strength of this paradigm is its use of measures that tap a range of outcomes, instrumental and relational as well as proximal and distal. In addition to the measures employed by Cutrona and Suhr (1994), other researchers have examined reductions in negative affect, subsequent task performance, and perceived social support as measures of message effectiveness (e.g., Hill, 1996; Winstead, Derlega, Lewis, Sanchez-Hucles, & Clarke, 1992).

The most fundamental limitation of interaction analysis studies is that they have used coding procedures very similar to those employed in the naturalistic paradigm. Coding for broad content categories (support "types") obscures other dimensions on which messages vary and their effects on important outcomes, resulting in frustratingly vague and inconsistent findings (some of which we review below). Of course, messages obtained through the interaction analysis paradigm can be analyzed with more sophisticated coding systems (for one such possibility, see the coding system developed by Samter & Burleson, 1984), but this has generally not occurred (see Goldsmith, 1995).

The Message Perception Paradigm

In a third approach, the message perception paradigm, researchers present participants with sets of supportive messages designed to instantiate features of theoretical interest. The messages are presented in lists or embedded in constructed conversations, and participants evaluate the messages (and, in some cases, the message producer) on certain criteria (e.g., effectiveness or sensitivity of the message, kindness or likableness of the helper). Assessments of message effectiveness are thus obtained from third-party observers who read about (or "witness") the use of supportive messages by others. For example, Burleson and Samter (1985a, Study 2) had college students read four hypothetical situations depicting a friend as experiencing some form of emotional distress; accompanying each situation was a list of nine supportive messages written to vary systematically in their "person-centered" quality. Participants read and rated each message for perceived sensitivity and perceived effectiveness. Applications of this paradigm are widespread (e.g., Caplan & Samter, 1999; Samter, Burleson, & Murphy, 1987).

The defining strength of the message perception paradigm is its capacity to allow the researcher to isolate, control, and observe the effects of specific message features such as "person centeredness." For this reason, the paradigm has been the primary source of precise information about effective features of supportive messages. Researchers employing this paradigm must be concerned with the reliability and generalizability of their results, issues they routinely address by using multiple message versions and stimulus situations

(which are assessed for realism) both within and across studies (see Goldsmith & MacGeorge, 2000).

Despite its strengths, this paradigm is not without important limitations. One of these is an issue of external validity; there is obviously a difference (of unknown magnitude) between actually experiencing a supportive message when upset and making judgments about messages directed at hypothetical others. Another important issue is the use of message evaluations as the primary dependent variable. Some studies have obtained global ratings of "helpfulness" (Caplan & Samter, 1999), others have used criteria such as perceived "sensitivity" and "effectiveness" (e.g., Kunkel & Burleson, 1999), and still others have obtained assessments of "message quality" that include these characteristics and others such as appropriateness and supportiveness (Goldsmith & MacGeorge, 2000; MacGeorge, Lichtman, & Pressey, in press). Despite typically high correlations among "helpfulness," "sensitivity," and the like, some research indicates that these items tap somewhat distinctive judgments (Bippus, 2001; Goldsmith, McDermott, & Alexander, 2000). A still more important concern is the relationship between these message *evaluations* and their likely *outcomes*. Obtaining a message evaluation is not the same as directly examining the effects of messages, such as their capacity to reduce emotional distress (an immediate, instrumental outcome) or avoid damaging self-image (an immediate, relational outcome). This is not to say that message evaluation studies could not utilize more outcome-oriented measures, such as "likelihood that this would make me feel better." Few have done so, however, with the primary exception being liking for the producer of the message (e.g., Samter et al., 1987).

The Experimental Paradigm

In a fourth approach, the experimental paradigm, researchers use varied procedures to induce stress or upset (typically of a mild sort) in participants. Participants are then exposed to supportive messages generated by the researcher or by experimental confederates. Subsequently, participants provide postexposure assessments of relevant message outcomes (e.g., change in emotional state). Tardy (1994) has employed a simple variant of this paradigm in several studies; participants were assigned to complete a challenging anagram task under stressful conditions, and the experimenter gave them brief messages designed to convey no support, emotional support, instrumental support, or both forms of support. Task performance and participant ratings of perceived experimenter supportiveness served as the dependent variables. In a more elaborate application of this paradigm, Jones and Guerrero (2001) had 216 college students think about and then disclose to a confederate a recent situation that they found emotionally upsetting. While talking with participants, the trained confederates used messages reflecting specific combinations of nonverbal immediacy (behaviors such as smiling and eye gaze that reflect warmth and psychological closeness) and verbal person centeredness (the explicit acknowledgment, elaboration, and legitimation of the other's feelings and perspective). Following these interactions, participants completed scales assessing their perceptions of the confederates' appropriateness, helpfulness, sensitivity, and effectiveness.

The experimental paradigm combines the strengths of the interaction analysis and message evaluation paradigms, permitting the systematic manipulation of specific features of supportive messages and the evaluation of message effects on multiple outcomes. However, this paradigm has yet to fulfill its inherent promise because relatively few studies of this type have been conducted. The dearth of studies likely stems from the challenges of this paradigm, which center on the manipulations. Not only do the messages need to be valid and believable instantiations of selected

features (as in the message evaluation paradigm), they must also be delivered in a consistent (reliable) manner by the researcher or a confederate. (For a discussion of the training and monitoring procedures researchers need to use when employing confederates in supportive message research, see Jones & Guerrero, 2001.)

The experimental paradigm also has limitations that should not be overlooked. Clearly, the character of the experimental situation may limit the generalizability of the results. Perhaps the most important concern of this type is the extent to which the message recipient's distressed emotional state is artificially induced (and there are obvious ethical concerns about this as well). Further, this paradigm permits the researcher to manipulate only limited numbers of features in a limited number of messages at one time. Finally, research using this paradigm is expensive in terms of both time and resources, and that makes it difficult for researchers to conduct multiple studies. Still, considerable improvement in the precision of our knowledge about the outcomes of supportive messages could result from greater use of the experimental paradigm.

Summary

The naturalistic paradigm examines recollections of "real-world" supportive messages in response to significant stressors, whereas the interaction analysis paradigm trades some of the realism of the naturalistic paradigm for message data untainted by recall methods. However, both of these paradigms are handicapped by the classification of messages into broad categories of supportive message "types." The message perception and experimental paradigms have proved more useful for testing the effects of specific (and theoretically derived) message features, but there are limitations associated with the type of message evaluations obtained (e.g., "effectiveness," "sensitivity") as the outcome measure, and generalizability is necessarily a recurrent concern. Because all assessment procedures have limitations, the best evidence regarding the effectiveness of different message types and features is obtained through the use of multiple methods.

In addition to the four paradigms reviewed above, at least three other approaches have received limited use or should be considered as potential resources for future studies. Diary methods (Reis & Collins, 2000), in which participants complete brief questionnaires on a regular (e.g., daily) basis, can allow researchers to examine the effects of naturally occurring supportive messages on a wide range of outcomes, such as mood and coping behaviors (see Cutrona, 1986). Field observation of real-world instances of supportive behaviors and their effects (as manifested in target responses) is possible with some populations, such as children (e.g., Farver & Branstetter, 1994; Strayer, 1980). Researchers should also consider using stimulated- or cued-recall procedures (see Waldron & Cegala, 1992) in applications of the interaction analysis and experimental paradigms. This method involves videotaping supportive interactions and then conducting interviews with the interactants in which the videotape is played and selectively paused to "cue" participants' memories about their earlier cognitive and emotional responses.

Features of More and Less Effective Supportive Messages: Research Findings

In this subsection we summarize research findings concerning more and less effective supportive messages. Data generated by applications of the naturalistic and interaction analysis paradigms generally provide information about the "types" of supportive messages (e.g., emotional, instrumental) that people find more and less helpful when coping with stressors. In contrast, data generated through applications of the experimental and message perception paradigms provide much more precise information about the effectiveness of specific features in messages intended to comfort or advise.

Effectiveness of Support "Types" and Intents

Researchers employing the naturalistic and interaction analysis paradigms have typically coded message behavior into broad content/function categories such as emotional support (e.g., expressions of sympathy, care, and concern) and informational support (e.g., statements of information or advice) (see Cutrona & Suhr, 1994; Dunkel-Schetter et al., 1992). Different researchers have classified messages in somewhat different ways, with the result that category systems differ across studies. For example, some researchers have classified expressions of affection for, or confidence in, the distressed person as emotional support, whereas others using more differentiated systems of classification have placed them in the category of "esteem support" (e.g., compare Barbee & Cunningham, 1995; Cutrona & Suhr, 1994). Nonetheless, if one generalizes broadly across studies, there is consistency in the findings with respect to emotional (including esteem) support and instrumental support (including information and advice), as well as with respect to a set of behaviors that might be loosely classified as "negative" in character (for a review, see Dunkel-Schetter et al., 1992).

In studies employing the naturalistic paradigm, messages coded as conveying emotional support have regularly been identified by participants as either the most or one of the most helpful forms of assistance they recall receiving from others (e.g., Barbee, Derlega, Sherburne, & Grimshaw, 1998; Clark & Stephens, 1996; Dakof & Taylor, 1990; Lehman, Ellard, & Wortman, 1986; Sullivan, 1996). And in studies employing the interaction analysis paradigm, frequencies for messages coded in the emotional support category typically exhibit the highest and most consistent correlations with outcomes such as perceived supportiveness, stress reduction, interaction satisfaction, and relationship satisfaction (e.g., Cutrona, Hessling, & Suhr, 1997; Hill, 1996; Pasch, Bradbury, & Davila, 1997; Yankeelov, Barbee, Cunningham, & Druen, 1995). Further underscoring the value of emotional support are findings indicating that its absence is viewed as particularly unhelpful (e.g., Dakof & Taylor, 1990; Lehman et al., 1986; Sullivan, 1996) and is associated with negative relational outcomes (e.g., Barbee & Yankeelov, as cited in Cunningham & Barbee, 2000; Hill, 1996).

Numerous factors moderate the reported helpfulness of emotional support and its impact on coping and relational outcomes. Some of these moderators include demographic factors such as gender (e.g., Dakof & Taylor, 1990), personality traits of the recipient (e.g., Cutrona et al., 1997), the type of relationship between the recipient and helper (e.g., Metts et al., 1994), the type of stressor (e.g., Yankeelov et al., 1995), the specific outcome examined (e.g., Winstead et al., 1992), and the timing of the support effort (e.g., Jacobson, 1986). For the most part, however, these moderators are mild in their effects and do not result in emotional support's having negative outcomes. Thus there is broad evidence indicating that emotional support (a) is viewed by recipients as especially helpful and (b) positively influences long-term relational outcomes as well as more immediate outcomes (for additional reviews of these and related findings, see Barbee & Cunningham, 1995; Burleson & Goldsmith, 1998; Dunkel-Schetter et al., 1992).

The effects of informational support are much less consistent. In some studies, it has been found to be helpful or to result in beneficial coping and relational outcomes (Cutrona, Suhr, & MacFarlane, 1990; Sullivan, 1996; Winstead et al., 1992). However, the findings from an equal or greater number of studies indicate that informational support may be viewed as unhelpful (e.g., Lehman et al., 1986)

or may fail to have any effect on desirable outcomes (e.g., Cutrona et al., 1997; Cutrona & Suhr, 1994). The effects of informational support messages also appear to be strongly qualified by factors such as the expertise of the support provider (e.g., Dakof & Taylor, 1990), the extent to which the support provider has control over the recipient's problem (e.g., Cutrona & Suhr, 1994), and whether the informational support is accompanied by emotional support (e.g., Sullivan, 1996).

Studies from the naturalistic and interaction analysis paradigms coalesce to suggest that there are a diverse group of behaviors unified by observable negativity in content and negative outcomes. Such behaviors include minimizing or exaggerating a support recipient's problem, indicating that a support recipient is perceived as incompetent or blameworthy, and exhibiting "overinvolvement, intrusiveness, oversolicitousness, and overconcern" (Dunkel-Schetter et al., 1992, p. 97). Not only are these behaviors viewed as unhelpful, they have detrimental consequences for relationships (Clark & Stephens, 1996; Dakof & Taylor, 1990; Lehman et al. 1986; Sullivan, 1996).

In contrast, research employing the naturalistic paradigm regularly finds that a clear expression or manifestation of supportive intent by the provider is perceived as helpful (e.g., Dakof & Taylor, 1990; Lehman & Hemphill, 1990). Helpers' supportive intentions are most commonly accompanied by substantive statements intended to assist the targets. Sometimes, however, helpers express supportive intentions but indicate their inability to provide substantive assistance (e.g., "I know there is nothing I can say that will make a difference, but I just want you to know that I care"; or "I really want to help, but I just don't know what to say or do!"). Such statements are recalled by their recipients as helpful, as is the mere presence of others who are assumed to have caring intent. Moreover, on some occasions targets may experience helpers' supportive intentions as the only aspect of helpers' behavior that actually facilitates coping (e.g., Lehman et al., 1986). This is nicely illustrated by a remark made by one of our students in her evaluation of her mother's efforts to be supportive: "Even when she's being pushy, makes me feel like a dope, and gives bad advice, I can tell that she's trying to help and cares for me." Thus perception of an underlying supportive intention can help mitigate the effects of insensitive or unhelpful comments (see Lehman & Hemphill, 1990). Obviously, targets may not recognize the supportive intentions of helpers even when those intentions are present. However, some recent research suggests that targets may imagine supportive intentions and attribute them to "helpers" even when such intentions do not exist; such illusory supportive intentions appear to provide some benefit to targets (Bolger, Zuckerman, & Kessler, 2000).

The findings of studies using the naturalistic and interaction analysis paradigms tell us that helpers' supportive intentions and emotional support are very important to those coping with stressful situations, whereas informational support appears to be more of a double-edged sword. Further, some types of "negative" messages are virtually always viewed as unhelpful. Some researchers employing these paradigms have used their findings to suggest more specific features of emotional and instrumental support that targets appreciate or find valuable (see Dunkel-Schetter et al., 1992). However, most researchers using these paradigms have not provided (or cannot provide) detailed examinations of the message features that underlie judgments of helpfulness or cause message outcomes such as reduced emotional distress. Research employing the message perception and experimental paradigms is critical to addressing these concerns. We next review two research traditions that have utilized these latter paradigms, one that has extensively tested a theoretically derived model of effectiveness in comforting messages and one that has more recently assessed a model of effectiveness for advice messages.

Features of Effective Comforting Messages

One line of work exploring the features of effective emotional support has focused on comforting behaviors, messages having the goal of alleviating or lessening the emotional distress experienced by others. Applegate (1980) and Burleson (1982) have proposed that comforting messages can be scaled hierarchically for the extent to which they reflect a person-centered orientation to discourse. *Person centeredness* refers to the extent to which message behavior "reflects an awareness of and adaptation to the subjective, affective, and relational aspects of communicative contexts" (Burleson, 1987, p. 305). Thus messages low in person centeredness deny the other's feelings and perspective by criticizing the other's feelings, challenging the legitimacy of those feelings, or telling the other how he or she should act and feel. Messages displaying a moderate degree of person centeredness afford an implicit recognition of the other's feelings by attempting to distract the other's attention from the troubling situation, offering expressions of sympathy and condolence, or presenting explanations of the situation intended to reduce the other's distress. Highly person-centered comforting messages explicitly recognize and legitimate the other's feelings by helping the other to articulate those feelings, elaborating reasons the other might feel those feelings, and assisting the other to see how those feelings fit in a broader context. In addition, highly person-centered comforting messages project a greater degree of involvement with the other and tend to be more listener centered, accepting, emotion focused, and evaluatively neutral. (For detailed descriptions of this approach to the analysis of comforting messages, see Burleson, 1994a, 1994b.)

In several studies utilizing the message perception paradigm, Burleson and his colleagues have developed evidence that highly person-centered comforting messages are viewed as more sensitive and effective methods of managing another's distressed emotions than are less person-centered messages (e.g., Burleson & Samter, 1985a; Samter et al., 1987). Subsequent studies employing variants of the message perception paradigm have demonstrated that the effect of person-centeredness on message evaluations is moderated only slightly (and sometimes nonsignificantly) by factors such as (a) sex of the evaluator (Kunkel & Burleson, 1999; Samter et al., 1987), (b) ethnicity and culture of the evaluator (Burleson & Mortenson, in press; Samter, Whaley, Mortenson, & Burleson, 1997), (c) personality traits (Burleson & Samter, 1985b), and (d) situational variables such as target responsibility for the problem (Jones & Burleson, 1997) and sex of the depicted helpers and recipients (Samter et al., 1987). Thus the person-centeredness construct appears to do a good job of representing people's notions about what constitutes sensitive, effective comforting messages. Moreover, recent work by Jones and Guerrero (2001) indicates that highly person-centered comforting messages are not just perceived as more sensitive and effective; they actually do a better job of reducing emotional distress than less person-centered forms of comforting. Using the experimental paradigm, these researchers had participants think about an upsetting event and then disclose it to a confederate; confederates responded with messages exhibiting combinations of low, moderate, or high levels of person-centeredness and low, moderate, or high levels of nonverbal immediacy. Analyses detected a strong, linear effect for the person-centered quality of the confederate's message on the participant's assessment of comforting quality. Further, this effect was not moderated by the nonverbal immediacy of the confederate.

Several studies show that, in addition to affecting observer judgments and recipient emotion, the person-centered quality of comforting messages can influence the social acceptance of helpers as well as have long-term effects on the cognitive and communicative abilities of their targets. For example, Samter et al. (1987) found that the person-centered quality of the messages used by a helper predicted observers' liking for and attraction to the helper. Consistent with these findings, other studies indicate that the ability to produce highly person-centered comforting messages is associated with measures of peer acceptance (e.g., Burleson, Delia, & Applegate, 1992; Samter & Burleson, 1990). Other research indicates that the person-centered quality of the comforting messages employed by parents and peers predicts the developing child's social-cognitive and functional communication skills, including comforting skills (Applegate, Burleson, & Delia, 1992; Burleson & Kunkel, in press). In sum, the person-centered quality of comforting messages has been found to influence varied outcomes of support situations, both short- and long-term and both instrumental and relational.

Although the person-centered quality of comforting messages appears to capture an important aspect of effective emotional support, recent research indicates some significant limitations in this model of effective comforting and suggests other important dimensions along which more and less effective comforting messages may vary. For example, Jones and Burleson (1997) found that the person-centered quality of comforting messages explained more variance in judges' evaluations when the target was not responsible for the problematic situation than when the target bore some responsibility for the problem and its alleviation, a finding suggesting that the person-centered quality of comforting messages is more important in some situations than in others (see also Range, Walston, & Pollard,

1992). And in two recent studies employing the message perception paradigm, Clark and her colleagues found that participants varied substantially in the degree to which they endorsed comforting messages focusing on distressed feelings (Clark & Delia, 1997; Clark et al., 1998).

These findings suggest the need for expanded conceptual models of comforting messages—models developed with respect to a much wider range of situations. Goldsmith (1994) has proposed a broad-scale alternative analysis of the features of effective emotional support messages grounded in Brown and Levinson's (1987) politeness theory. Disclosing a problem and expressing negative feelings can threaten an individual's public "face" or status as a competent and independent social actor. Moreover, messages intended to reduce emotional distress can further threaten face by conveying incompetence and dependency (e.g., "You poor baby . . ."). Thus Goldsmith suggests that comforting efforts can be scaled for the degree of support they provide for the target's "positive face wants" (i.e., desire to be treated as likable and competent) and "negative face wants" (desire to be free from constraint or imposition). A few studies utilizing the message perception paradigm provide some support for this view, indicating that expressions of sympathy containing attention to positive face wants are preferred to those not containing this element (Caplan & Samter, 1999; Goldsmith, 1994). Thus factors such as facework may be essential components of effective efforts to provide relief from emotional distress.

Features of Effective Advice Messages

Goldsmith's (1992, 1994) analysis of face threat in the context of supportive interactions was intended to apply to any type of supportive communication, but it has primarily informed research on features that distinguish more and less effective forms of advice. Theories of face and facework, especially politeness theory (Brown & Levinson, 1987), indicate that advice is intrinsically threatening to negative face wants (i.e., the desire to be unimpeded). This is because advice messages, as directives to engage in some action, impose symbolic constraints on a support seeker's autonomy. Research indicates that the extent to which advice is actually perceived as face threatening depends on the imputed goals of the advice giver. Specifically, advice messages may be experienced as threatening to negative face if the advice giver's goal is interpreted as "being nosy" or "butting in," or threatening to positive face (the desire to be positively evaluated) when the adviser's intention is viewed as critical, blaming, or "unsupportive" in nature (Goldsmith & Fitch, 1997; Wilson & Kunkel, 2000). Because of the value that people typically place on protecting (and enhancing) their face, Goldsmith has argued that advice perceived as more face threatening will also be perceived as generally less effective. This claim has received substantial support from a recent study in which the perceived regard for face (an index combining both positive and negative face wants) associated with an advice message was found to be positively correlated with an index of advice quality (a composite measure of helpfulness, supportiveness, sensitivity, appropriateness, and effectiveness) (Goldsmith & MacGeorge, 2000).

Key features of effective advice thus include message elements that influence perceptions of face threat. A handful of studies using the message evaluation paradigm have sought to test models specifying such features. Most of these studies have been grounded in politeness theory (Brown & Levinson, 1987), which distinguishes between bald-on-record message strategies (in which the propositional content of a message is delivered bluntly) and polite or mitigating strategies (in which language is used as facework to "redress" the threat posed by the propositional content). Mitigating facework strategies are further divided into

(a) positive politeness strategies, which attend to positive face wants (e.g., advice given with expressions of solidarity, compliments); (b) negative politeness strategies, which attend to negative face wants (e.g., advice given with expressions of deference or uncertainty); and (c) off-record strategies, which use indirect language to make the existence of any face threat plausibly deniable (e.g., advice couched within a story of what someone did in similar circumstances). Following Brown and Levinson, Goldsmith and colleagues hypothesized that off-record strategies would produce the greatest protection for face, and that negative politeness strategies would be more face protective than positive politeness strategies (because the affiliative nature of positive politeness strategies may itself threaten negative face wants); they expected perceived advice quality to vary correspondingly (Goldsmith, 1994; Goldsmith & MacGeorge, 2000).

Support for these hypotheses has been mixed. Goldsmith (1994) found that advice with mitigation strategies was perceived as more effective than bald-on-record messages, but positive politeness was perceived as more effective than negative politeness or off-record strategies. Caplan and Samter (1999) did not include a "bald-on-record" condition, but compared advice messages designed to mitigate or aggravate positive face and negative face threat. Messages that mitigated positive face were perceived as higher in quality than messages aggravating positive face threat, but no difference was detected between messages mitigating negative face threat and those aggravating it. Goldsmith and MacGeorge (2000) conducted a comprehensive evaluation of effects produced by Brown and Levinson's facework strategies, obtaining evaluations of all four strategies across advice messages that were (a) relevant to multiple problems, (b) produced within various relationships, and (c) representative of diverse advice content. Despite (or perhaps because of) the methodological rigor of this study, the researchers found no

significant differences in the perceived face threat or perceived quality of advice consistently associated with any of the facework strategies.

One probable explanation for the diversity of these findings is the complexity of the connections among specific language choices, facework strategies as defined by politeness theory, situational factors, and perceptions of face threat (for a more detailed discussion, see Goldsmith & MacGeorge, 2000). Does this mean that nothing specific can be said about means of reducing perceived face threat (and thereby enhancing perceived advice quality)? Not necessarily. In a recent study, MacGeorge et al. (in press) compared perceptions of advice messages that overtly threatened both positive and negative face in multiple ways (aggravating facework), bald-on-record messages, and those that included redress to both positive and negative face (mitigating facework). As predicted, mitigating messages were evaluated more positively than blunt messages, which in turn were evaluated more positively than aggravating messages, and these findings were only slightly qualified by a variety of contextual factors (e.g., men evaluated aggravating messages somewhat more positively than did women). These findings suggest that relatively overt facework strategies may reliably affect perceptions of advice.

In sum, perceived face threat influences evaluations of advice messages, although much remains to be determined about the precise features of advice that explain variance in perceptions of face threat. To date, research on advice effectiveness has been dominated by politeness theory and the use of the message perception paradigm. Future research needs to examine not only face-relevant perceptions of advice messages, but other message features, such as the comprehensibility, relevance, and feasibility of the proposals contained in these messages (see MacGeorge et al., in press). Researchers also need to supplement their use of the message perception paradigm by examining how "real" advice is perceived (for one effort in this direction, see Goldsmith & Fitch, 1997) and to probe the effects of advice forms on outcomes such as compliance, distress relief, problem-solving success, and relational satisfaction.

Summary

Research shows that several features of supportive messages contribute to their effectiveness. Messages exhibiting clear supportive intent are perceived as helpful even when the providers are able to say or do little else of value. The content of supportive messages is also important; message recipients appear to derive benefit consistently from messages expressing care, concern, and sympathy, whereas messages providing information or advice are helpful only in certain contexts. Facework can enhance the effectiveness of messages conveying both emotional and instrumental support. Finally, the person-centered quality of comforting messages strongly influences their perceived and actual effectiveness.

Explaining Why Supportive Messages Work: Some Theoretical Mechanisms

We have identified several features that distinguish more and less effective supportive messages. Here we ask, *why* do these features make a difference? More specifically, what are the theoretical mechanisms that link messages having these features to certain outcomes? Almost no research has directly addressed these questions, explicitly testing alternative theoretical mechanisms that might explain message effectiveness. Thus the proposals we offer here are necessarily speculative; we hope these speculations prompt much-needed research on the underlying mechanisms through which supportive messages have their effects.

Both classical rhetorical theory (e.g., Murphy, 1972) and contemporary cognitive analyses of message production (e.g., Greene, 1997) suggest that explanatory models for supportive messages must account for relationships among three elements: message features, theoretical mechanisms, and outcomes. *Message features* are verbal and nonverbal components of a helper's behavior directed at assisting a target; these are isolatable units of behavior that have a characteristic structure. *Theoretical mechanisms* describe the actions performed by message features; such mechanisms identify what the enactment or presence of message components does. Finally, *outcomes* are the events or states that follow (more or less reliably) from the action of some mechanism; when messages are successful, outcomes reflect the goals helpers seek to achieve.

As we have shown above, at least four features influence the effectiveness of supportive messages: (a) the presence of a discernible supportive intention, (b) the use of politeness or facework, (c) the informative or propositional content of the message, and (d) the person-centered quality of the message. It appears unlikely that a single mechanism can explain how such diverse message features produce a variety of outcomes. Thus we suggest that multiple theoretical mechanisms serve to link specific message features (or combinations of features) with particular outcomes. Here, we discuss each feature in conjunction with the particular outcomes and theoretical mechanisms with which it appears most associated.[1]

Supportive Intentions

Supportive intentions are helpers' underlying desires to provide aid or assistance to targets perceived as needing help. The intention to "be supportive" is a feature common to all supportive messages; indeed, the existence of this intention is what makes a message "supportive" (at least from the vantage point of the illocutionary force of the message; see

Searle, 1969).[2] The supportive intentions of helpers may be more or less clear (ranging from vaguely discernible to overtly obvious), intense (ranging from mild to deep), and pure (combined with other intentional elements such as blame and avoidance or exclusively focused on providing help). Variations in the quality of helpers' supportive intentions almost certainly affect targets. Most often, supportive intentions are "read off" or inferred from the behavior of the helper. However, helpers can make their supportive intentions explicit through overt statements of availability (e.g., "I'm here for you"), desire to help ("I really want to help however I can"), and focus ("I'm only trying to help"); these overt statements appear to be aimed at enhancing targets' perceptions of the clarity, intensity, purity, and sincerity of the helpers' intentions.

Several outcomes are likely to follow from a target's recognition of a helper's supportive intention. Most important, the target should comprehend that, at least in the context of the ongoing episode, the helper is concerned and wants to provide assistance. The target may view the helper's supportive intention as a reflection of more general motivations or sentiments (e.g., the helper's affection for the target), and any such contextualization by the target may be consequential. At a minimum, however, the target's recognition of the helper's supportive intention should carry with it an appreciation of the helper's immediate interest and involvement. Recognition of the helper's supportive intention should also establish an interpretive context within which the target can make sense of the helper's concurrent and subsequent actions (e.g., "I know he was trying to help even though some of the things he said hurt terribly").

Targets' detection of helpers' supportive intentions may lead to several other outcomes. For example, because people are more likely to help liked than disliked others (Cialdini, 2001), targets may infer that helpers like them and value their relationship. However, less benign consequences are also possible. As several researchers have suggested, the existence of supportive intentions implies a belief on the part of the helper that the target cannot manage the problem on his or her own (e.g., Goldsmith, 1992). This implication can negatively affect the target's self-esteem and sense of self-efficacy (see Nadler, 1986). Exhibiting supportive intentions also implies the helper's right and, perhaps, duty to assist the target, which may constrain the target by making it necessary for him or her at least to consider (if not actually accept) aid offered by the helper. In sum, supportive intentions can lead to several relational and identity-relevant outcomes.

How do supportive intentions achieve these outcomes? The expression of a supportive intention (whether implicit or explicit) conveys to the target (to a greater or lesser extent) the helper's care, concern, interest, and involvement, at least in the context of the current episode. The action of conveying the desire to help, and the accompanying implication that there is at least a modicum of concern for the target, is the mechanism through which this message feature realizes the outcomes with which it is associated (Grice, 1975).

Facework or Politeness Strategies

Supportive intentions and actions can—however implicitly—convey negative evaluations of the target and impose on the target's autonomy. Supportive intentions may imply that the target needs help, is unable (or not competent) to solve his or her problem, or acted unwisely in creating (or failing to avoid) a problematic situation. Many helper actions following from supportive intentions have the potential to threaten the target's autonomy or positive self-image: Asking questions can challenge privacy, offering advice may undermine autonomy, and making suggestions can imply criticism.

Facework or politeness strategies are communicative devices for redressing the face threats inherent in supportive messages. As discussed previously, positive facework aims to protect the target's desire to be evaluated positively; it includes verbal devices that express positive regard for the target, admiration for the courage or effort shown by the target, respect for the target's pluck, understanding of the difficulty of the target's plight, confidence that the target will prevail, belief that the target possesses the qualities needed to succeed, and the like. In contrast, negative facework aims to protect the target's desire to be free from constraint or imposition; it includes verbal devices that hedge and qualify, suggest rather than insist or command, mention possibilities, hint, describe hypothetical options, and otherwise indicate respect for the target's autonomy (e.g., "I don't mean to be pushy, but have you considered . . .").

If the redressive facework employed by the helper successfully prevents or buffers threats to the target's face, then several desirable outcomes may follow, including increases in the target's (a) willingness to consider the substance of the helper's message (something that a target may find difficult if he or she feels criticized or imposed upon); (b) interest in interacting with the helper, revealing potentially sensitive thoughts and feelings; and (c) liking of the helper. Facework achieves these and related outcomes through the mechanism of conveying the helper's positive regard and respect for the target while inhibiting expressions that might call such regard and respect into question. As Rogers (1975) and other client-centered therapists (e.g., Greenberg, 1993) have underscored, expressions of positive regard and respect by a helper can heighten the target's feelings of acceptance and trust, which, in turn, enhance the target's willingness to discuss sensitive concerns.

When coupled with clear supportive intentions, sensitive facework helps cultivate what Burleson and Goldsmith (1998) term a "supportive conversational environment," an arena in which upsetting and potentially face-threatening matters can be explored openly. Moreover, these message features should contribute to the target's "sense of being supported" or "sense of support availability"—a sense that abundant research indicates contributes to effective coping (Sarason et al., 1997). This sense of support may be curative (or helpful) in itself (Carkhuff & Berenson, 1977; Rogers, 1957). However, maximally effective support messages do more than cultivate trust, acceptance, and openness; they also address specific tasks in the effort to facilitate more effective coping by the target (see Greenberg, Rice, & Elliott, 1993). We next consider message features that are potentially helpful in this latter regard.

Informative Content of Support Messages

A third feature of support messages influencing effectiveness is informative content. Many supportive messages contain *declaratives* (factual statements, observations, opinions) intended to enhance the target's awareness or understanding of a problematic situation or *directives* (advice, suggestions, proposals) intended to enhance the target's appreciation of (and, perhaps, motivation to undertake) courses of action that may improve the situation. Helpful declaratives present informationally adequate statements that contain appropriate quantities of relevant, truthful information expressed in a clear manner (Grice, 1975). Helpful directives present sound proposals that are relevant to the problem at hand, will solve the problem effectively and efficiently, and can be implemented successfully by the target (Rogers, 1983; Witte, 1998).

Typically, the target's information deficits are related to some substantive problem or task, with the provided information or advice constituting "instrumental support" that facilitates task accomplishment. Occasionally, however, helpers may see targets as lacking information, or having incorrect information, about themselves or their social status; targets sometimes doubt their competence and self-efficacy or their likability and social acceptance. In these latter cases, helpers may produce declarations that the targets are able and competent (appraisal support) or accepted and loved (emotional support). Helpers may also see targets as needing advice about how to manage their distressed feelings (although research suggests that such advice is rarely effective or well received; see Burleson & Goldsmith, 1998).

Targets who receive adequate information and sound advice should be better able to manage current difficulties and, perhaps, minimize future problems. Thus the primary outcome achieved through informative declarations and sound directives is improved coping by the target. Of course, the target's coping will be affected not only by the intrinsic quality of the offered information (i.e., its adequacy or soundness), but also by the extent to which the target comprehends, believes, and applies the information offered by the helper.

The declarations and directives generated by the helper achieve the intended outcome of improved target coping by conveying a needed resource to the target: information of various types. Matching models (Cohen & McKay, 1984; Cutrona & Russell, 1990) have long invoked this mechanism to explain the effectiveness of support, underscoring that the type of support (or information) offered must be relevant to the particular stressor faced by the target if it is to be helpful. However, controversy currently surrounds the characterization of social support as a "resource" or "commodity" that can be conveyed. Although the resource view has its proponents (see Cohen et al., 2000, p. 4; Veiel & Baumann, 1992, p. 2), other authorities argue that "social support is not a commodity or a resource that can be delivered; rather, it arises through the interactions occurring in our relationships" (Gottlieb, 1994, p. 318; see also

Burleson & Goldsmith, 1998, p. 259). Quite apart from concerns associated with viewing social support as providing needed resources, there are serious limitations in conceptualizations of communication that represent it as a conduit for transferring information (Reddy, 1979). Nonetheless, it seems useful for certain ends to regard people as communicating for the purpose of conveying ideas, information, and opinions to others. If people become distressed because they lack information needed to reach conclusions, or because their current information leads to untenable or undesirable conclusions, it appears sensible to view "conveying information" as one mechanism through which supportive messages effectively help their targets.

The Person-Centered Quality of Supportive Messages

A final feature of helpful supportive messages is their person-centered quality. Components of highly person-centered support messages include acknowledgments of the target's emotional and cognitive states, inquiries about the problematic situation and the target's affective reactions, expressions of compassion and understanding, and, especially, utterances (statements, questions, and conversational continuers) that encourage the target to elaborate his or her feelings and perspective regarding the problematic situation (see Burleson, 1994b; Burleson & Samter, 1985a). Just as important, highly person-centered support messages avoid evaluating targets and their feelings or telling targets how they should feel or act in the situation; such acts undermine the reflective processes that highly person-centered messages seek to engage.

Highly person-centered support messages assist the target in developing greater comprehension of the problematic situation and improved perspective on it. These messages may also lead the target to modify personal goals and feelings as a result of increased appreciation for the character of the situation and possibilities inherent within it. Ultimately, these messages may facilitate the target's acceptance of losses and reorientation to existing challenges and opportunities. Over the long term, the enhanced understanding, acceptance, and adjustment facilitated by these message elements contribute to the reduction of anxiety (e.g., Sgoutas-Emch & Johnson, 1998), lowered physical stress (e.g., Smyth, 1998; Smyth & Pennebaker, 1999), and improvements in health (King & Miner, 2000; Pennebaker, 1993).

Through what mechanisms do highly person-centered messages produce these outcomes? By fostering the target's elaboration of detailed, emotion-focused narratives pertaining to the problematic situation, these messages facilitate the target's sense-making processes (Burleson & Goldsmith, 1998). Many features of highly person-centered support messages elicit from the target detailed descriptions of troubling events and accompanying emotions, making these thoughts and feelings more available and coherent to the target. Describing these thoughts and feelings in narrative form further contributes to their coherence (Clark, 1993; Harber & Pennebaker, 1992). The increased accessibility of coherent thoughts and feelings about upsetting events helps the target to develop appraisals (and reappraisals) of the events' significance and meanings, allowing the target to see the events in a broader perspective (e.g., Gross, 1998). Overall, these message elements serve to prompt and maintain the target's sense-making processes, resulting in greater insight, understanding, and meaning.

Implications

Several observations follow from our consideration of the mechanisms through which features of supportive messages may generate certain outcomes. First, because different message features accomplish different things,

particular features are more or less relevant to specific exigencies. For example, a target attempting to cope with a shocking, hurtful loss will not be helped as much by information, advice, or facework as by highly person-centered messages. Second, most of the message features discussed here can (and do) work well in combination with each other. To extend the previous example, although attending to a hurting target's face may not be as helpful as person-centered comforting, lack of attention to face concerns may exacerbate the target's distress and make him or her unwilling to interact with the helper. Third, the independence of the message features analyzed here means that a single message can contain both helpful and unhelpful elements that compete with, undermine, or otherwise interfere with each other. Inattention to face concerns (e.g., forcefully telling the target what he or she should do in a situation) may undermine the helpfulness of clear supportive intentions and sound advice. Fourth, different components of supportive messages may be relevant at different points in the support process (Jacobson, 1986). Thus when seeking to assist a target in coping with a shocking, hurtful loss, a helper will probably want initially to establish a "supportive conversational environment" by making his or her supportive intentions evident and attending to face concerns. Once this is accomplished, person-centered comforting may assist the target in making sense of the situation; subsequently, the helper may find it fruitful to offer information and advice.

Summary

Research on supportive messages has pursued several clear objectives through a variety of well-developed research paradigms, resulting in an impressive body of findings regarding the features of more and less effective messages. Most generally, messages exhibiting an emotion focus are viewed as broadly helpful, especially when they reflect a descriptive (rather than evaluative) orientation to the problem situation. More concretely, supportive messages are experienced as most helpful when they (a) exhibit a clear supportive intent, (b) use politeness strategies to manage face threats inherent in support provision, (c) contain adequate information and sound proposals, and (d) take a person-centered approach in providing support, especially with respect to facilitating the target's sense-making processes. We have proposed several mechanisms through which these features achieve desirable outcomes. These proposals should be assessed empirically in future research.

Thus far, most research on supportive messages has examined them "extracted" from their natural context in supportive interactions. This has been understandable, and perhaps necessary, given the goals of identifying features that distinguish more and less effective messages and understanding how these features produce certain outcomes. However, exclusively considering supportive messages apart from the interactions in which they figure may foster a "magic bullet" view of the support process (Burleson & Goldsmith, 1998), the problematic notion that helpers can change the internal states of targets merely by using messages that contain the "right words" (i.e., magic bullets). Supportive messages are produced during the course of interactions, are almost certainly influenced by characteristics of these interactions, achieve their effects in the course of interaction, and therefore need to be examined and understood within the context of these interactions. Moreover, there is a very important sense in which support is an interactional accomplishment—something realized through multiturn exchanges rather than through a single, isolated message (Gottlieb, 1994). Thus the dynamics of supportive interactions are deserving of study in their own right, and we now turn our attention to them.

SUPPORTIVE INTERACTIONS

Supportive interactions can be understood as multiturn conversational sequences or episodes focused on support seeking, provision, receipt, processing, and response. Two sets of issues pertaining to supportive interactions have captured the attention of theorists: (a) the structure of supportive interactions, especially the nature and sequence of the events composing these interactions; and (b) the factors that influence the behavior of both helpers and targets during the course of supportive interactions.

The Structure of Supportive Interactions

Social psychologists and communication researchers have studied supportive interactions intensively, both groups using a standard suite of social scientific research methods (e.g., experiments, self-reports, observation of behavior elicited in the laboratory). Other scholars have studied supportive interactions under the rubric of "troubles talk" and "advice giving," using the methods of conversation analysis, an inductive, microanalytic approach grounded in ethnomethodology (e.g., Heritage & Sefi, 1992; Jefferson, 1988). Remarkably, these two very different approaches converge in suggesting that supportive interactions have a typical structure composed of four phases or events that are sequenced in a characteristic order. These events, in the order in which they typically occur, are (a) support activation by a target, (b) support provision by a helper, (c) support receipt and accompanying reactions by the target, and (d) responses to the target's reactions by the helper.

Barbee and Cunningham (1995) provide the most explicit characterizations of these four events. *Support activation* by the target can be intentional (e.g., the target asks for help) or unintentional (the helper notices that the target appears upset and indicates concern). The term *support seeking* is often used to describe support activation when it appears that the target is intentionally acting so as to elicit support from the helper. *Support provision* involves the helper's producing messages directed at assisting the target (i.e., supportive messages); we have discussed this event extensively above. *Target reactions* encompass the target's immediate behavioral replies (both verbal and nonverbal) to the helper's supportive message. These reactions reflect the target's receipt and processing of the helper's support attempt and may be either spontaneous (i.e., minimally mediated by cognition) or symbolic (i.e., reflective of deeper interpretation and planning) (Buck, 1984). Finally, *helper responses* reference and respond to the reactions of the target. These serve to continue the supportive episode (e.g., commenting on the target's reactions, offering additional supportive comments) or close it (e.g., acknowledging changes in the target, redirecting the focus of the interaction).

Several aspects of the proposed interactional sequence and its constituent events merit comment. First, the proposed sequence of events for supportive interactions is ideal-typical or schematic in that it describes a common series of actions characteristic of these episodes. But this sequence is certainly not necessary or invariant; supportive interactions are characterized by false starts, interruptions, topic changes, recycles, competing definitions of the interaction focus, and numerous other occurrences that can complicate and disrupt the overall process (Jefferson & Lee, 1992). The occurrence of each event later in the sequence is made relevant and more or less probable by antecedent events, but is not guaranteed by them (e.g., a target may seek support but go unnoticed or be ignored by a potential helper). Of course, the occurrence of events later in the sequence assumes that antecedent events have transpired, or at least are perceived to have transpired (e.g., helper responses to target

reactions should not occur in the absence of those target reactions). Thus this four-event sequence is a logical structure for supportive interactions; it may also be a routine empirical sequence. As such, this event sequence may be a commonly held schema, script, or memory organization packet (MOP) that channels actors' expectations, interpretations, and actions in support episodes (Kellermann, 1995).

Second, few studies have examined the full sequence of events composing supportive interactions, focusing instead on just a single event (e.g., either support seeking or support provision). The vast majority of studies have examined support provision, and a growing body of work focuses on support seeking or activation (e.g., Barbee, Gulley, & Cunningham, 1990; Hill, 1991), but only limited research has examined target reactions to support efforts (Barrera & Baca, 1990; Fisher, Nadler, & Witcher-Alagna, 1982) and helper responses to those reactions (Cheuk & Rosen, 1992; Jung, 1989). Regardless of the event examined, most researchers have collected data using the same methods employed in research on supportive messages (i.e., the naturalistic, interaction analysis, experimental, and message perception paradigms). In the rare cases where researchers have examined contingencies in helper-target behavior, they have employed data-analytic procedures permitting assessments of dependencies in behavior, including lag sequential analysis, hierarchical log-linear analysis, and structural equation modeling (e.g., DeGarmo & Forgatch, 1997; Saitzyk, Floyd, & Kroll, 1997).

Third, each of the four support events has a variable internal structure and may consist of anything from a brief bit of behavior to long, complex behavioral sequences. For example, support activation may consist of a single simple sigh or a very long multiturn narrative ("You're not going to believe what happened at work today! I'm in such trouble. Sit down and let me tell you the whole story; I really need your help with this"). Further, multiple conversational turns may be used (or needed) to accomplish a particular event. Consider how support activation extends over multiple turns in the following exchange:

Target: [Sigh]

Helper: Everything okay?

Target: Oh, well, I guess so.

Helper: You sure?

Target: Well . . . [pause].

Helper: What's up?

Target: Well, I've been thinking about work again. I can't get it off my mind.

Notice here that the target and helper collaboratively construct the support activation event; in this case, the actions of both parties are required to complete support activation and set the stage for support provision.

Fourth, the events identified in this analysis are open structures, or slots, that can be filled appropriately by a variety of content. That is, actors may pursue each of these broad events by performing several possible actions. Barbee and Cunningham (1995) propose for each event a four-category classification of possible act types. For example, support seeking or activation can occur through direct verbal acts (asking), indirect verbal acts (hinting or complaining), direct nonverbal acts (crying or pouting), or indirect nonverbal acts (sighing or sulking). Helpers can provide support by engaging in problem-focused approach acts, which suggest solutions to problems (solve); emotion-focused approach acts, which strive to elicit positive emotions (solace); problem-focused avoidance acts, which minimize the significance of the problem (dismiss); or emotion-focused avoidance acts, which distract the target or discourage the expression of negative emotion (escape). Although these typologies have heuristic value, they also have

significant limitations; as Goldsmith (1995) notes, they lack a systematic, coherent theoretical foundation. Further, different versions of each act identified in these typologies can be performed, often with different outcomes: Questions can be more or less nosy, advice can be more or less imposing, and expressions of concern can be more or less demeaning. Thus it is important for researchers to identify not only the general types of acts relevant to each event in support episodes, but also the different versions of relevant acts as well as the behavioral features that distinguish more and less effective versions of these acts. Researchers must undertake a multitude of tasks, including specifying appropriate theoretical bases for generating typologies of actions, identifying dimensions for arraying versions of various acts, determining appropriate standards for assessing the quality or effectiveness of different act versions, and developing coding systems that permit the reliable capture of relevant theoretical distinctions in message forms.

Fifth, there is some limited, but intriguing, evidence that the actions that take place in one event influence the interpretations, experiences, and actions occurring in subsequent events. For example, in one recent study, Goldsmith (2000) found that the conversational sequence in which advice was offered (e.g., whether it was solicited, given in response to disclosure of a problem, or simply presented "out of the blue") affected perceived face threat. Barbee and Cunningham (1995) summarize evidence indicating that helper use of approach behaviors (solve, solace) is more likely to follow target use of direct (compared with indirect) support activation behaviors. Saitzyk et al. (1997) found that the giving of advice by helpers tended to elicit "autonomy" reactions from targets in which they expressed problem-solving ideas of their own. These researchers also found that helper expressions of confidence in and esteem for the target increased the likelihood of reactions in which the target disclosed thoughts and feelings about the problem situation. These results are largely suggestive, but they serve to illustrate that some actions occurring in support episodes are contingent on antecedent actions. Deeper insights about behavioral contingencies await the development of coding systems that embody more sophisticated understandings of relevant actions in different phases of support episodes and the dimensions along which these acts may differ.

Finally, every phase of supportive interactions is filled with perils, pitfalls, paradoxes, and predicaments for both helpers and targets. These problematics of supportive interactions stem from a variety of sources, including threats to face inherent in both seeking and providing support (Goldsmith, 1992, 1994), self-presentational dilemmas of targets and helpers (Coates & Winston, 1987; Silver, Wortman, & Crofton, 1990), equity concerns arising from seeking and providing help (DePaulo, 1982), threats to independence inherent in seeking or offering support (Coyne, Ellard, & Smith, 1990), the very real difficulties associated with both expressing and managing negative affect (Herbert & Dunkel-Schetter, 1992; Segrin, 1998), individuals' concerns about perceptions of their social competence (Nadler, 1986, 1991), and the costs of caring, including the drain on personal resources and risks of distress contagion (Cahill & Sias, 1997; Perrine, 1993; for reviews, see Albrecht & Adelman, 1987c; Albrecht et al., 1994; Fisher, Goff, Nadler, & Chinsky, 1988; La Gaipa, 1990). Communicative strategies are available for managing many of these problematics (Burleson & Goldsmith, 1998; Dunkel-Schetter et al., 1992; Goldsmith & Parks, 1990), but the incidence of "support attempts that fail" (e.g., Lehman & Hemphill, 1990), "miscarried helping" (e.g., Coyne, Wortman, & Lehman, 1988), and "unsupportive responses" (e.g., Davis, Brickman, & Baker, 1991) documented in the literature suggests that many people lack, or do not employ, effective strategies.

One is left with the impression that virtually every phase of supportive interactions—seeking, providing, reacting, and responding—represents a challenging task, and that many people lack the skills necessary to meet the challenges successfully. Further, many features of support situations increase the difficulty of seeking and providing support, even for skilled communicators. We next consider some of the individual and contextual factors that influence communicative activities in support situations, particularly the success of efforts to seek and provide support.

Individual and Contextual Factors Influencing Communication in Supportive Interactions

What factors lead people to employ various behaviors when they seek and provide support—especially more and less effective forms of these actions? As we have seen, seeking and providing emotional support are complicated, challenging tasks. Maximally effective behavioral strategies for seeking and supplying support must, in many cases, simultaneously pursue multiple goals and service multiple rhetorical demands (e.g., signaling intent, attending to face concerns, incorporating appropriate information, exhibiting person-centeredness). Highly effective messages for seeking and providing support thus represent complex, sophisticated behavioral structures. Producing such structures requires considerable skill, including the ability to retrieve relevant knowledge from memory (of persons, situations, and message options), acquire new information, and integrate new information with existing knowledge so as to generate optimal (or at least appropriate) messages. In addition, producing sophisticated behavioral strategies can require considerable effort; hence both seekers and providers of support must possess the *motivation* to initiate and pursue what may prove to be challenging tasks. Further, the motivation to seek and provide support can be affected by a host of situational factors. Appreciation of these facts has led to a broad consensus among theorists that adequate accounts of message behavior by helpers and their targets must incorporate both competence and performance factors (i.e., both skill and desire or knowledge and motivation factors) (Barbee & Cunningham, 1995; Burleson, 1984b; Burleson & Kunkel, 1996; Feeney & Collins, 2001; Zahn-Waxler & Radke-Yarrow, 1990).

But what are the relevant competence and performance factors involved in support activation, provision, reaction, and response? What attributes of individuals enable them to seek and supply support skillfully? And what attributes of situations make the seeking and provision of support more or less challenging activities? Considerable research has addressed these questions in recent years, especially with respect to the support provision process. Smaller, but growing, literatures have developed with respect to individual and situational influences on support seeking, reactions to support provision, and responses to these reactions.

Studies examining individual and situational influences on support-related behaviors have largely employed one of two methodological paradigms (for detailed discussion of these paradigms, see Burleson, 1984b). In one paradigm, participants respond to hypothetical support situations created by researchers, providing either (a) open-ended descriptions of what they would say or do in these situations or (b) selections or evaluations of behavioral options provided by the researcher. For example, Burleson (1984a) had children and adolescents respond orally to four hypothetical situations, stating what they would say in each situation to help a distressed peer feel better. These messages were subsequently coded for the degree of person-centeredness exhibited, and these codings were correlated with independent assessments of interpersonal cognitive complexity and social

perspective-taking skill. This methodological approach has several advantages, including the use of multiple situations to enhance reliability and generalizability, the capacity to tailor stimulus situations so as to manipulate variables of interest, and economy in collecting large quantities of data quickly through mass-administered questionnaires. However, the ecological validity of this procedure remains a concern: Do factors found to influence responses to hypothetical situations similarly influence behavior in the real world?

A second method used to investigate influences on behavior in support situations closely resembles what we previously termed the interaction analysis paradigm. Here, a participant interacts with another participant (or an experimental confederate) in a support situation created by the researcher in a laboratory environment. For example, Hill (1996) had pairs of college students discuss intimate personal problems; these interactions were recorded, transcribed, and coded for frequencies of various support behaviors. Several personality variables (e.g., affiliative need, social skill) were used to predict frequencies of helpful and unhelpful behaviors. Confidence about the validity of results obtained through this paradigm is comparatively strong given the reasonably close approximation to real-world conditions. Moreover, depending on how it is structured, this procedure can generate data relevant to multiple events in support episodes (support activation, support provision, reactions to support efforts, and so on). However, the generalizability and reliability of results remain questionable due to the use of a single stimulus situation. Further, this is an expensive procedure for collecting data.

Varied forms of these paradigms have been productively employed by a host of researchers. Studies have found that behavior by both helpers and their targets is influenced by numerous variables, including *demographic factors* (e.g., sex, age, social class), *personality traits* (e.g., attachment styles, trait empathy, prosocial values, gender orientations), *cognitive variables* (cognitive complexity, social perspective taking, attribution processes), *affective states* (e.g., helper mood, target mood, specific emotional states of helpers and targets), *relationship factors* (e.g., type of relationship between the participants, quality of the relationship, length of the relationship), *interactional contingencies* (e.g., type of support activation behavior, success of helping efforts, costs of helping), and *situational variables* (e.g., problem severity, responsibility for the problem, interaction setting). (For reviews, see Barbee & Cunningham, 1995; Barbee, Rowatt, & Cunningham, 1998; Dunkel-Schetter et al., 1992; Stroebe & Stroebe, 1996; Vaux, 1988.) Indeed, so many findings have accumulated that the available data appear to exceed the explanatory capacity of existing theory.

Most existing models of factors that influence behavior in support situations (Barbee & Cunningham, 1995; Burleson, 1984b; Burleson & Kunkel, 1996; Feeney & Collins, 2001; Zahn-Waxler & Radke-Yarrow, 1990) provide typologies that classify variables with respect to (a) the support event in which they figure (e.g., variables influencing support seeking versus support provision), (b) their underlying nature (e.g., personality trait, cognitive process, situation feature), or (c) their global function (e.g., competence factor, motivational factor). Although such typologies have organizational and heuristic value, they do not provide much in the way of explanation. In particular, these typologies shed little light on the character of underlying message production and reception processes in support situations, nor do they indicate how certain variables influence the operation of these processes and thereby affect their outcomes. More adequate explanations of individual and situational influences on behavior in support situations must be grounded in general theories of message production and reception, particularly theories that provide detailed analyses of the cognitive structures

and processes that contribute to message generation and processing.

Currently available theories of message reception largely focus on specific communicative contexts, such as the processing of persuasive messages (e.g., Petty & Wegener, 1999) or problematic messages (e.g., Hewes, 1995b). General theories of message reception remain underdeveloped, so applications of these theories to the reception and processing of behaviors seeking and providing support would not bear much fruit. In contrast, the general character of the message production process has been detailed extensively in recent years (see Greene, 1997; Hewes, 1995a), with most theorists proposing similar outlines of the cognitive structures and processes figuring in the generation of messages. Abstracting across particular models, it appears that processes implicated in message production minimally involve

(1) *interpretation* (e.g., defining the situation; making attributions about the causes of others' actions; inferring others' internal states; noting relevant aspects of the setting; determining situationally relevant roles and rules), which gives rise to (2) *goal generation* (forming intentions pertaining to primary and secondary instrumental objectives; forming intentions pertaining to relational and identity objectives), which serves as the impetus to (3) *planning or action assembly* (building "behavioral programs" or cognitive representations of action lines), which eventuates in (4) *enactment* (executing behavioral plans or output representations), which is followed by (5) *monitoring* (observing and evaluating the outcomes of one's behavior—a directed form of interpretation), the results of which may lead to (6) *re-encoding* (recycling processes 2 through 5 in light of monitored outcomes). (Burleson & Planalp, 2000, p. 222)

This analysis of message production processes needs to be supplemented by a parallel analysis specifying the cognitive and affective structures that are generated by one set of processes and, subsequently, execute another set of processes. Specifically, interpretation proceeds through the application of cognitive schemata or constructs, the activation and operation of which are influenced by features of the current situation as well as enduring interpretive abilities (e.g., the social information-processing capacity of the individual) and motivational orientations (e.g., personality dispositions). The output of the interpretive process is a situational representation or definition of the situation; this gives rise, both directly and through the mediation of aroused emotional states, to interaction goals. Goals (in conjunction with underlying situational representations and emotions) activate elements of procedural memory that contain action-outcome specifications; these elements are selectively synthesized through an "action assembly" or planning process into specific behavioral plans (i.e., representations of action lines). Subsequently, the enactment process produces the behavioral structure that we call the *act*, or *message*.

This sketch of the message production process provides a framework for the integration of substantial research examining individual and situational influences on the generation of behaviors used to seek and provide support. For example, numerous studies have found that individual differences in interpersonal cognitive complexity and perspective-taking skills are associated with the use of person-centered supportive messages (for reviews, see Burleson, 1985; Burleson & Caplan, 1998). These variables reflect social information-processing capacity, which should influence message behavior primarily by influencing the complexity of situational representations and, through these, the complexity of interaction goals (O'Keefe & Delia, 1982; Wilson, 1995).

A second set of individual differences, personality traits or dispositions, should influence behavior in support episodes primarily through their impact on the situationally

specific desire (i.e., motivation) to provide or seek support. These traits should be activated by perceptions of target need (Feeney & Collins, 2001); once activated, they should affect the degree of effort persons are willing to expend in pursuit of support-related goals. Selected personality traits exhibiting these motivational implications in support situations include affiliative need (Hill, 1991, 1996), emotional empathy (e.g., Tamborini, Salomonson, & Bahk, 1993; Trobst, Collins, & Embree, 1994), self-efficacy for providing support (MacGeorge, Clark, & Gillihan, 2002), trait communication apprehension (Samter & Burleson, 1984), and prosocial orientation (Feeney & Collins, 2001).

A large number of contextual variables should also influence behavior in support episodes primarily through their impact on the situationally specific desire to provide or seek support. Some of these contextual variables include ambient mood states (Barbee, Rowatt, & Cunningham, 1998; Salovey, Mayer, & Rosenhan, 1991), relationship qualities such as satisfaction (Dunkel-Schetter et al., 1992) and intimacy or closeness (Feeney & Collins, 2001; Hobfoll & Lerman, 1988), and the helper's thoughts and feelings aroused by perceptions of (a) his or her own personal responsibility for the target's problem (Carlson & Miller, 1987); (b) target responsibility for the problem (Jones & Burleson, 1997; MacGeorge, 2001); (c) target effort to solve the problem (Dunkel-Schetter, Folkman, & Lazarus, 1987; Schwarzer & Weiner, 1991); (d) problem severity or apparent target need (Hale, Tighe, & Mongeau, 1997); (e) intensity of target affect (Gottlieb & Wagner, 1991; Hobfoll & Lerman, 1988); (f) type of target affect (e.g., sorrow versus hostility; see Lane & Hobfoll, 1992); (g) target gender (Goldsmith & Dun, 1997; Reevy & Maslach, 2001); (h) target responses to prior support efforts by the helper, especially indications that helping efforts were unsuccessful (Cheuk & Rosen, 1992; Jung, 1989;

Notarius & Herrick, 1988); and (i) risks and costs associated with providing support (Chesler & Barbarin, 1984; Perrine, 1993). The level of motivation aroused by factors such as these should influence an individual's willingness to expend effort in pursuit of support-related goals; such motivation should be manifest not only in the quality or sophistication of the messages produced, but also in the persistence of supportive efforts, especially in the face of resistance.

Another set of factors appears to affect behavior in support episodes by generating emotions that have disruptive effects on the processes of message generation (i.e., planning or action assembly) and message enactment. Research on *cognitive interference* (Sarason, Pierce, & Sarason, 1996) indicates that certain emotions can undermine the functioning of complex cognitive operations involved in message generation and enactment, resulting in degraded behaviors (Burleson & Planalp, 2000). Some of the emotions that can cause such cognitive interference, and the features of support situations eliciting these emotions, include (a) anxiety stemming from confronting upset and potentially volatile targets (e.g., Lehman et al., 1986); (b) discomfort or embarrassment aroused by engaging in behavior (e.g., explicit talk about distressed feelings) viewed as inconsistent with central aspects of the self-concept, such as gender identity (Copenhaver, Lash, & Eisler, 2000; Saurer & Eisler, 1990); and (c) depression created by interacting with a depressed target (Coyne, 1976; Segrin, 1998).

The model sketched here of contextual influences on communication in support situations is largely speculative. It organizes existing findings in a theoretically informed way, but it needs to be evaluated in terms of its predictive power and capacity to generate novel insights. Further, this model, as well as the research it organizes, focuses primarily on one event in support episodes, the production of supportive messages. Both theory and research

need to expand their focus to encompass behavior in other phases of support episodes (support activation, reactions to supportive messages). Finally, the model developed here is limited to message production processes; it needs to be supplemented by and integrated with models providing analyses of contextual influences on the reception and processing of support-related behaviors.

CONCLUSION

In this chapter, we have reviewed the scholarly literature on supportive communication, positioning it in the context of the larger, older research tradition of social support. We have emphasized the distinctive questions, methods, and findings of the supportive communication perspective, as well as various limitations that need to be addressed in future theorizing and research. In concluding, we underscore some key limitations in existing work on supportive communication, identify areas in which our knowledge needs to be expanded, advocate reconnection with the sociological and psychological perspectives, and encourage application of what is known about supportive communication in intervention and training programs.

The chapter of this same title in the previous edition of this *Handbook* looked toward "a future where research methods illumine . . . aspects of social support that are unquestionably a cornerstone for the quality of human life" (Albrecht et al., 1994, p. 441). Certainly, research since 1994 has broadened and deepened our understanding of supportive messages and interactions, but considerable work remains to be done. We have an improved understanding of the features contributing to message helpfulness, but only informed speculation about why these features work as they do. Researchers need to go beyond examining how characteristics of messages influence evaluations of effectiveness and sensitivity to more direct investigation of emotional, cognitive, behavioral, and social outcomes, giving special attention to the message reception processes through which message characteristics have their effects.

The study of supportive messages needs to be supplemented by much more intensive study of supportive interactions, focusing on how these interactions unfold, are collaboratively constructed by the participants, and shape the outcomes of the messages produced within them (one research agenda is outlined in Burleson & Goldsmith, 1998). In particular, more research is needed on support seeking, as well as on the contingent responses targets and helpers make to one another over the course of their interactions. Moreover, the study of supportive interactions needs to be more deeply embedded in examinations of the social relationships in which these interactions transpire. Supportive interactions occur in many different kinds of human relationships, and properties of relationships almost certainly influence these interactions in numerous ways (Reis & Collins, 2000). Researchers have illuminated support processes in selected kinds of relationships, such as marriage (e.g., Cutrona, 1996), but considerably more work needs to address just how supportive interactions shape, and are shaped by, the diverse relationships in which they occur.

In our discussions of the sociological and psychological perspectives on social support, we have noted that greater attention to communication processes should enhance theoretical understanding of how support contributes to health. Attention to several features of these perspectives can also improve supportive communication research. The sociological and psychological perspectives are focally concerned with the effects of social support on mental and physical health. Research on supportive communication has given relatively little attention to these health outcomes, detracting from the theoretical and pragmatic value of this research. More studies should

examine how exposure to supportive messages and interactions exhibiting various features influences diverse aspects of well-being. For example, research could investigate how variations in support messages (naturally occurring or experimentally manipulated) produced by helpers during interactions in a laboratory affect target physiological responses such as cardiovascular and neuroendocrine function; these techniques are increasingly common in research on interpersonal conflict. Researchers could also obtain data on individuals' exposure to supportive messages across time (perhaps through diary methods) and examine how patterns of stress and support influence health outcomes such as physical symptomatology or visits to health practitioners.

Scholars can better integrate the research on supportive communication with the sociological and psychological perspectives by treating social integration and perceived support availability as contextual factors potentially influencing the effects of supportive messages and interactions. As a variable indicative of the social context in which supportive interactions occur, social integration may have important effects on patterns of support seeking and provision both within and across relationships. Similarly, perceived support availability may influence ways in which support is sought and received, as well as affect how people interpret, experience, and respond to specific supportive messages.

Applications of what we know about helpful supportive messages and interactions not only offer the hope of improving people's lives, but also provide a vehicle for testing theories about more and less helpful forms of support in the context of particular stressors. Given the real risks associated with supportive communication—for both helpers and targets—researchers should exercise caution in conducting intervention research. However, we possess considerable data concerning the features of helpful messages, and these data can inform the development of careful interventions. Research findings regarding effective forms of supportive communication can also be incorporated in educational and training programs; studies documenting the widespread incidence of unhelpful support efforts underscore the need for and potential value of such efforts.

The events of September 11, 2001, have given many of us a stronger appreciation for the support others provide in times of sadness, anxiety, and anger. Supportive communication obviously cannot mend all the hardships people experience; tangible support also has its place in helping people to manage problems and cope with stress. Yet much of what we can do for one another, whether in response to crises or everyday upsets, is intangible, conveyed through messages and interactions that add warmth, love, and meaning to life.

NOTES

1. Our discussion of these constructs and their interconnections necessarily proceeds in a linear fashion, and thus runs the risk of implying that there are only limited, one-to-one connections among these elements. We reject this implication and underscore that particular message features may be occasioned by a variety of exigencies and have multiple outcomes through diverse mechanisms. Despite the very real complexity that almost surely exists, we nonetheless believe there is merit in suggesting some primary linkages among various constructs; these hypothesized linkages should provide a basis for research and subsequent conceptual refinement.

2. The current approach to characterizing the critical feature of supportive behavior follows a Gricean route in making behavior "supportive" by virtue of the helper's intention to provide assistance (see Grice, 1975); the helper accomplishes a central aspect of this objective by getting the target to recognize that his or her intent is to provide assistance. The current approach thus differs somewhat from that suggested by Goldsmith (1994), who lets "the term 'supportive communication' refer to a category of speech acts and events that are culturally recognized as intending to convey assistance" (p. 35). If the current approach is

indebted to Grice, it appears that Goldsmith's approach, with its emphasis on culturally conventional devices for conveying supportive intentions, is more influenced by Searle (1969). Both of these approaches appear superior to tautological approaches that define supportive behaviors by virtue of the outcomes they produce (i.e., supportive behaviors cause supportive outcomes). For critiques of this latter position, see Thoits (1986).

REFERENCES

Acitelli, L. K., & Antonucci, T. C. (1994). Gender differences in the link between marital support and satisfaction in older couples. *Journal of Personality and Social Psychology, 67,* 688-698.

Albrecht, T. L., & Adelman, M. B. (1984). Social support and life stress: New directions for communication researchers. *Human Communication Research, 11,* 3-32.

Albrecht, T. L., & Adelman, M. B. (Eds.). (1987a). *Communicating social support.* Newbury Park, CA: Sage.

Albrecht, T. L., & Adelman, M. B. (1987b). Communicating social support: A theoretical perspective. In T. L. Albrecht & M. B. Adelman (Eds.), *Communicating social support* (pp. 18-39). Newbury Park, CA: Sage.

Albrecht, T. L., & Adelman, M. B. (1987c). Dilemmas of supportive communication. In T. L. Albrecht & M. B. Adelman (Eds.), *Communicating social support* (pp. 240-254). Newbury Park, CA: Sage.

Albrecht, T. L., Burleson, B. R., & Goldsmith, D. (1994). Supportive communication. In M. L. Knapp & G. R. Miller (Eds.), *Handbook of interpersonal communication* (2nd ed., pp. 419-449). Thousand Oaks, CA: Sage.

Albrecht, T. L., Burleson, B. R., & Sarason, I. G. (1992). Meaning and method in the study of communication and social support: An introduction. *Communication Research, 19,* 149-153.

Albrecht, T. L., Irey, K. V., & Mundy, A. K. (1982). Integration in a communication network as a mediator of stress. *Social Work, 27,* 229-234.

Antonucci, T. C. (1990). Social support and social relationships. In R. H. Binstock & L. K. George (Eds.), *Handbook of aging and the social sciences* (3rd ed., pp. 205-226). Orlando, FL: Academic Press.

Antonucci, T. C., & Israel, B. A. (1986). Veridicality of social support: A comparison of principal and network members' responses. *Journal of Consulting and Clinical Psychology, 54,* 432-437.

Applegate, J. L. (1980). Adaptive communication in educational contexts: A study of teachers' communicative strategies. *Communication Education, 29,* 158-170.

Applegate, J. L., Burleson, B. R., & Delia, J. G. (1992). Reflection-enhancing parenting as antecedent to children's social-cognitive and communicative development. In I. E. Sigel, A. V. McGillicuddy-Delisi, & J. J. Goodnow (Eds.), *Parental belief systems: The psychological consequences for children* (2nd ed., pp. 3-39). Hillsdale, NJ: Lawrence Erlbaum.

Asendorpf, J. B., & Wilpers, S. (2000). Attachment security and available support: Closely linked relationship qualities. *Journal of Social and Personal Relationships, 17,* 115-138.

Barbee, A. P., & Cunningham, M. R. (1995). An experimental approach to social support communications: Interactive coping in close relationships. In B. R. Burleson (Ed.), *Communication yearbook 18* (pp. 381-413). Thousand Oaks, CA: Sage.

Barbee, A. P., Derlega, V. J., Sherburne, S. P., & Grimshaw, A. (1998). Helpful and unhelpful forms of social support for HIV-positive individuals. In V. J. Derlega & A. P. Barbee (Eds.), *HIV and social interaction* (pp. 83-105). Thousand Oaks, CA: Sage.

Barbee, A. P., Gulley, M. R., & Cunningham, M. R. (1990). Support seeking in close relationships. *Journal of Social and Personal Relationships, 7,* 531-540.

Barbee, A. P., Rowatt, T. L., & Cunningham, M. R. (1998). When a friend is in need: Feelings about seeking, giving, and receiving social support. In P. A. Andersen & L. K. Guerrero (Eds.), *Handbook of communication and emotion: Research, theory, applications, and contexts* (pp. 281-301). San Diego, CA: Academic Press.

Barrera, M., Jr. (1981). Social support in the adjustment of pregnant adolescents. In B. H. Gottlieb (Ed.), *Social networks and social support* (pp. 69-96). Beverly Hills, CA: Sage.

Barrera, M., Jr. (1986). Distinctions between social support concepts, measures, and models. *American Journal of Community Psychology, 14,* 413-445.

Barrera, M., Jr., & Baca, L. M. (1990). Recipient reactions to social support: Contributions of enacted support, conflicted support, and network orientation. *Journal of Social and Personal Relationships, 7,* 541-551.

Barrera, M., Jr., Sandler, I. N., & Ramsey, T. B. (1981). Preliminary development of a scale of social support: Studies on college students. *American Journal of Community Psychology, 9,* 435-447.

Batson, C. D., & Oleson, K. C. (1991). Current status of the empathy-altruism hypothesis. In M. S. Clark (Ed.), *Prosocial behavior* (pp. 62-85). Newbury Park, CA: Sage.

Benoit, W. L., Benoit, P. J., & Wilkie, J. (1995). Participants' and observers' memory for conversational behavior. *Southern Communication Journal, 61,* 139-155.

Berkman, L. F. (1995). The role of social relations in health promotion. *Psychosomatic Medicine, 57,* 245-254.

Berkman, L. F., Glass, T., Brissette, I., & Seeman, T. E. (2000). From social integration to health: Durkheim in the new millennium. *Social Science and Medicine, 51,* 843-857.

Berkman, L. F., & Syme, S. L. (1979). Social networks, host resistance, and mortality: A nine-year follow-up study of Alameda County residents. *American Journal of Epidemiology, 109,* 186-204.

Bertillion, M. J. (1879, February). Les celibataires, les veufs and les divorces au point de vue du mariage. *Revue Scientifique,* pp. 776-783.

Biegel, D. E., McCardle, E., & Mendelson, S. (1985). *Social networks and mental health: An annotated bibliography.* Beverly Hills, CA: Sage.

Bingham, S. G., & Burleson, B. R. (1989). Multiple effects of messages with multiple goals: Some perceived outcomes of responses to sexual harassment. *Human Communication Research, 16,* 184-216.

Bippus, A. M. (2001). Recipients' criteria for evaluating the skillfulness of comforting communication and the outcomes of comforting interactions. *Communication Monographs, 68,* 301-313.

Bolger, N., Zuckerman, A., & Kessler, R. C. (2000). Invisible support and adjustment to stress. *Journal of Personality and Social Psychology, 79,* 953-961.

Brissette, I., Cohen, S., & Seeman, T. E. (2000). Measuring social integration and social networks. In S. Cohen, L. G. Underwood, & B. H. Gottlieb (Eds.), *Social support measurement and intervention: A guide for health and social scientists* (pp. 53-85). New York: Oxford University Press.

Brown, P., & Levinson, S. C. (1987). *Politeness: Some universals in language usage.* Cambridge: Cambridge University Press.

Buck, R. (1984). *The communication of emotion.* New York: Guilford.

Buhrmester, D., Furman, W., Wittenberg, M. T., & Reis, H. T. (1988). Five domains of interpersonal competence in peer relations. *Journal of Personality and Social Psychology, 55,* 991-1008.

Burleson, B. R. (1982). The development of comforting communication skills in childhood and adolescence. *Child Development, 53,* 1578-1588.

Burleson, B. R. (1984a). Age, social-cognitive development, and the use of comforting strategies. *Communication Monographs, 51,* 140-153.

Burleson, B. R. (1984b). Comforting communication. In H. E. Sypher & J. L. Applegate (Eds.), *Communication by children and adults: Social cognitive and strategic processes* (pp. 63-104). Beverly Hills, CA: Sage.

Burleson, B. R. (1985). The production of comforting messages: Social-cognitive foundations. *Journal of Language and Social Psychology, 4,* 253-273.

Burleson, B. R. (1987). Cognitive complexity. In J. C. McCroskey & J. A. Daly (Eds.), *Personality and interpersonal communication* (pp. 305-349). Newbury Park, CA: Sage.

Burleson, B. R. (1990). Comforting as everyday social support: Relational consequences of supportive behaviors. In S. Duck (Ed.), *Personal relationships and social support* (pp. 66-82). London: Sage.

Burleson, B. R. (1994a). Comforting communication: Significance, approaches, and effects. In B. R. Burleson, T. L. Albrecht, & I. G. Sarason (Eds.), *Communication of social support: Messages, interactions, relationships, and community* (pp. 3-28). Thousand Oaks, CA: Sage.

Burleson, B. R. (1994b). Comforting messages: Features, functions, and outcomes. In J. A. Daly & J. M. Wiemann (Eds.), *Strategic interpersonal communication* (pp. 135-161). Hillsdale, NJ: Lawrence Erlbaum.

Burleson, B. R. (in press). Emotional support skills. In J. O. Greene & B. R. Burleson (Eds.), *Handbook of communication and social interaction skills.* Mahwah, NJ: Lawrence Erlbaum.

Burleson, B. R., Albrecht, T. L., Goldsmith, D. J., & Sarason, I. G. (1994). The communication of social support. In B. R. Burleson, T. L. Albrecht, & I. G. Sarason (Eds.), *Communication of social support: Messages, interactions, relationships, and community* (pp. xi-xxx). Thousand Oaks, CA: Sage.

Burleson, B. R., Albrecht, T. L., & Sarason, I. G. (Eds.). (1994). *Communication of social support: Messages, interactions, relationships, and community.* Thousand Oaks, CA: Sage.

Burleson, B. R., & Caplan, S. E. (1998). Cognitive complexity. In J. C. McCroskey, J. A. Daly, M. M. Martin, & M. J. Beatty (Eds.), *Communication and personality: Trait perspectives* (pp. 230-286). Cresskill, NJ: Hampton.

Burleson, B. R., Delia, J. G., & Applegate, J. L. (1992). Effects of maternal communication and children's social-cognitive and communication skills on children's acceptance by the peer group. *Family Relations, 41,* 264-272.

Burleson, B. R., & Goldsmith, D. J. (1998). How the comforting process works: Alleviating emotional distress through conversationally induced reappraisals. In P. A. Andersen & L. K. Guerrero (Eds.), *Handbook of communication and emotion: Research, theory, applications, and contexts* (pp. 245-280). San Diego, CA: Academic Press.

Burleson, B. R., & Kunkel, A. W. (1996). The socialization of emotional support skills in childhood. In G. R. Pierce, B. R. Sarason, & I. G. Sarason (Eds.), *Handbook of social support and the family* (pp. 105-140). New York: Plenum.

Burleson, B. R., & Kunkel, A. W. (in press). Parental and peer contributions to the emotional support skills of the child: From whom do children learn to express support? *Journal of Family Communication.*

Burleson, B. R., Kunkel, A. W., Samter, W., & Werking, K. J. (1996). Men's and women's evaluations of communication skills in personal relationships: When sex differences make a difference—and when they don't.

Journal of Social and Personal Relationships, 13, 201-224.

Burleson, B. R., & Mortenson, S. R. (in press). Explaining cultural differences in evaluations of emotional support behaviors: Mediating influences of value systems and interaction goals. *Communication Research.*

Burleson, B. R., & Planalp, S. (2000). Producing emotion(al) messages. *Communication Theory, 10,* 221-250.

Burleson, B. R., & Samter, W. (1985a). Consistencies in theoretical and naive evaluations of comforting messages. *Communication Monographs, 52,* 103-123.

Burleson, B. R., & Samter, W. (1985b). Individual differences in the perception of comforting messages: An exploratory investigation. *Central States Speech Journal, 36,* 39-50.

Cahill, D. J., & Sias, P. M. (1997). The perceived social costs and importance of seeking emotional support in the workplace: Gender differences and similarities. *Communication Research Reports, 14,* 231-240.

Caplan, G. (1974). *Support systems and community mental health.* New York: Behavioral Publications.

Caplan, G. (1976). The family as a support system. In G. Caplan & M. Killilea (Eds.), *Support systems and mutual help* (pp. 19-36). New York: Grune & Stratton.

Caplan, S. E., & Samter, W. (1999). The role of facework in younger and older adults' evaluations of social support messages. *Communication Quarterly, 47,* 245-264.

Carkhuff, R. R., & Berenson, B. G. (1977). *Beyond counseling and therapy* (2nd ed.). New York: Holt, Rinehart & Winston.

Carlson, M., & Miller, N. (1987). Explanation of the relation between negative mood and helping. *Psychological Bulletin, 102,* 91-108.

Cassel, J. (1976). The contribution of the social environment to host resistance. *American Journal of Epidemiology, 104,* 107-123.

Chesler, M. A., & Barbarin, O. A. (1984). Difficulties of providing help in a crisis: Relationships between parents of children with cancer and their friends. *Journal of Social Issues, 40*(4), 113-134.

Cheuk, W. H., & Rosen, S. (1992). Helper reactions: When help is rejected by friends or strangers. *Journal of Social Behavior and Personality, 7,* 47-63.

Cialdini, R. B. (2001). *Influence: Science and practice* (4th ed.). Boston: Allyn & Bacon.

Clark, L. F. (1993). Stress and the cognitive-conversational benefits of social interaction. *Journal of Social and Clinical Psychology, 12,* 25-55.

Clark, R. A., & Delia, J. G. (1979). *Topoi* and rhetorical competence. *Quarterly Journal of Speech, 65,* 187-206.

Clark, R. A., & Delia, J. G. (1997). Individuals' preferences for friends' approaches to providing support in distressing situations. *Communication Reports, 10,* 115-122.

Clark, R. A., Pierce, A. J., Finn, K., Hsu, K., Toosley, A., & Williams, L. (1998). The impact of alternative approaches to comforting, closeness of relationship, and gender on multiple measures of effectiveness. *Communication Studies, 49,* 224-239.

Clark, S. L., & Stephens, M. A. P. (1996). Stroke patients' well-being as a function of caregiving spouses' helpful and unhelpful actions. *Personal Relationships, 3,* 171-184.

Coates, D., & Winston, T. (1987). The dilemma of distress disclosure. In V. J. Derlega & J. H. Berg (Eds.), *Disclosure: Theory, research, and therapy* (pp. 229-255). New York: Plenum.

Cobb, S. (1976). Social support as a moderator of life stress. *Psychosomatic Medicine, 38,* 300-314.

Cohen, S. (1988). Psychosocial models of the role of social support in the etiology of physical disease. *Health Psychology, 7,* 269-297.

Cohen, S. (1994). Psychosocial influences on immunity and infectious disease in humans. In R. Glaser & J. K. Kiecolt-Glaser (Eds.), *Handbook of human stress and immunity* (pp. 301-319). San Diego, CA: Academic Press.

Cohen, S. (2001). Social relationships and susceptibility to the common cold. In C. D. Ryff & B. H. Singer (Eds.), *Emotion, social relationships, and health* (pp. 221-233). New York: Oxford University Press.

Cohen, S., Gottlieb, B. H., & Underwood, L. G. (2000). Social relationships and health. In S. Cohen, L. G. Underwood, & B. H. Gottlieb (Eds.), *Social support measurement and intervention: A guide for health and social scientists* (pp. 3-25). New York: Oxford University Press.

Cohen, S., & Hoberman, H. N. (1983). Positive events and social supports as buffers of life change stress. *Journal of Applied Social Psychology, 13,* 99-125.

Cohen, S., & Lichtenstein, E. (1990). Partner behaviors that support quitting smoking. *Journal of Consulting and Clinical Psychology, 58,* 304-309.

Cohen, S., & McKay, G. (1984). Social support, stress, and the buffering hypothesis: A theoretical analysis. In A. Baum, J. E. Singer, & S. E. Taylor (Eds.), *Handbook of psychology and health* (Vol. 4, pp. 253-263). Hillsdale, NJ: Lawrence Erlbaum.

Cohen, S., & Wills, T. A. (1985). Stress, social support, and the buffering hypothesis. *Psychological Bulletin, 98,* 310-357.

Collins, N. L., Dunkel-Schetter, C., Lobel, M., & Scrimshaw, S. C. M. (1993). Social support in pregnancy: Psychosocial correlates of birth outcomes and postpartum depression. *Journal of Personality and Social Psychology, 65,* 1243-1258.

Copenhaver, M. M., Lash, S. J., & Eisler, R. M. (2000). Masculine gender-role stress, anger, and male intimate abusiveness: Implications for men's relationships. *Sex Roles, 42,* 405-416.

Coyne, J. C. (1976). Depression and the response of others. *Journal of Abnormal Psychology, 85,* 186-193.

Coyne, J. C., Ellard, J., & Smith, D. (1990). Social support, interdependence, and the dilemmas of helping. In B. R. Sarason, I. G. Sarason, & G. R. Pierce (Eds.), *Social support: An interactional view* (pp. 129-149). New York: John Wiley.

Coyne, J. C., Wortman, C. B., & Lehman, D. R. (1988). The other side of social support: Emotional overinvolvement and miscarried helping. In B. H. Gottlieb (Ed.), *Marshalling social support: Formats, processes, and effects* (pp. 305-330). Newbury Park, CA: Sage.

Cunningham, M. R., & Barbee, A. P. (2000). Social support. In C. Hendrick & S. S. Hendrick (Eds.), *Close relationships: A sourcebook* (pp. 272-285). Thousand Oaks, CA: Sage.

Cutrona, C. E. (1986). Behavioral manifestations of social support: A microanalytic investigation. *Journal of Personality and Social Psychology, 51,* 201-208.

Cutrona, C. E. (1990). Stress and social support: In search of optimal matching. *Journal of Social and Clinical Psychology, 9,* 3-14.

Cutrona, C. E. (1996). *Social support in couples.* Thousand Oaks, CA: Sage.

Cutrona, C. E., Hessling, R. M., & Suhr, J. A. (1997). The influence of husband and wife personality on marital support interactions. *Personal Relationships, 4,* 379-393.

Cutrona, C. E., & Russell, D. W. (1987). The provisions of social relationships and adaptations to stress. In W. H. Jones & D. Perlman (Eds.), *Advances in personal relationships* (Vol. 1, pp. 37-67). Greenwich, CT: JAI.

Cutrona, C. E., & Russell, D. W. (1990). Types of social support and specific stress: Toward a theory of optimal matching. In B. R. Sarason, I. G. Sarason, & G. R. Pierce (Eds.), *Social support: An interactional view* (pp. 319-366). New York: John Wiley.

Cutrona, C. E., & Suhr, J. A. (1994). Social support communication in the context of marriage: An analysis of couples' supportive interactions. In B. R. Burleson, T. L. Albrecht, & I. G. Sarason (Eds.), *Communication of social support: Messages, interactions, relationships, and community* (pp. 113-135). Thousand Oaks, CA: Sage.

Cutrona, C. E., Suhr, J. A., & MacFarlane, R. (1990). Interpersonal transactions and the psychological sense of support. In S. Duck (Ed.), *Personal relationships and social support* (pp. 30-45). London: Sage.

Dakof, G. A., & Taylor, S. E. (1990). Victims' perceptions of support attempts: What is helpful from whom? *Journal of Personality and Social Psychology, 58,* 80-89.

Davis, R. C., Brickman, E., & Baker, T. (1991). Supportive and unsupportive responses of others to rape victims: Effects on concurrent victim adjustment. *American Journal of Community Psychology, 19,* 443-451.

DeGarmo, D. S., & Forgatch, M. S. (1997). Confidant support and maternal distress: Predictors of parenting practices for divorced mothers. *Personal Relationships, 4,* 304-317.

DePaulo, B. M. (1982). Social-psychological processes in informal help seeking. In T. A. Wills (Ed.), *Basic processes in helping relationships* (pp. 255-279). New York: Academic Press.

Dillard, J. P. (1997). Explicating the goal construct: Tools for theorists. In J. O. Greene (Ed.), *Message production: Advances in communication theory* (pp. 47-69). Mahwah, NJ: Lawrence Erlbaum.

Duck, S. (Ed.). (1990). *Personal relationships and social support.* London: Sage.

Dunkel-Schetter, C., & Bennett, T. L. (1990). Differentiating the cognitive and behavioral aspects of social support. In B. R. Sarason,

I. G. Sarason, & G. R. Pierce (Eds.), *Social support: An interactional view* (pp. 267-296). New York: John Wiley.

Dunkel-Schetter, C., Blasband, D., Feinstein, L., & Herbert, T. (1992). Elements of supportive interactions: When are attempts to help effective? In S. Spacapan & S. Oskamp (Eds.), *Helping and being helped: Naturalistic studies* (pp. 83-114). Newbury Park, CA: Sage.

Dunkel-Schetter, C., Folkman, S., & Lazarus, R. S. (1987). Social support received in stressful situations. *Journal of Personality and Social Psychology, 58,* 80-89.

Dunkel-Schetter, C., & Skokan, L. A. (1990). Determinants of social support provision in personal relationships. *Journal of Social and Personal Relationships, 7,* 437-450.

Durkheim, E. (1951). *Suicide: A study in sociology.* New York: Free Press. (Original work published 1897)

Eisenberg, N., Fabes, R. A., & Losoya, S. (1997). Emotional responding: Regulation, social correlates, and socialization. In P. Salovey & D. J. Sluyter (Eds.), *Emotional development and emotional intelligence: Educational implications* (pp. 129-163). New York: Basic Books.

Elliott, R. (1985). Helpful and nonhelpful events in brief counseling interviews: An empirical taxonomy. *Journal of Counseling Psychology, 32,* 307-322.

Farr, W. (1975). Marriage and mortality. In N. Humphreys (Ed.), *Vital statistics: A memorial volume of selections from the reports and writings of William Farr.* Metuchen, NJ: Scarecrow. (Original work published 1885)

Farver, J. M., & Branstetter, W. H. (1994). Preschoolers' prosocial responses to their peers' distress. *Developmental Psychology, 30,* 334-341.

Feeney, B. C., & Collins, N. L. (2001). Predictors of caregiving in adult intimate relationships: An attachment theoretical perspective. *Journal of Personality and Social Psychology, 80,* 972-994.

Fisher, J. D., Goff, B., Nadler, A., & Chinsky, J. M. (1988). Social psychological influences on help-seeking and support from peers. In B. H. Gottlieb (Ed.), *Marshalling social support: Formats, processes, and effects* (pp. 267-304). Newbury Park, CA: Sage.

Fisher, J. D., Nadler, A., & Witcher-Alagna, S. (1982). Recipient reactions to aid. *Psychological Bulletin, 91,* 27-54.

Goldsmith, D. J. (1992). Managing conflicting goals in supportive interaction: An integrative theoretical framework. *Communication Research, 19,* 264-286.

Goldsmith, D. J. (1994). The role of facework in supportive communication. In B. R. Burleson, T. L. Albrecht, & I. G. Sarason (Eds.), *Communication of social support: Messages, interactions, relationships, and community* (pp. 29-49). Thousand Oaks, CA: Sage.

Goldsmith, D. J. (1995). The communicative microdynamics of support. In B. R. Burleson (Ed.), *Communication yearbook 18* (pp. 414-433). Thousand Oaks, CA: Sage.

Goldsmith, D. J. (2000). Soliciting advice: The role of sequential placement in mitigating face threat. *Communication Monographs, 67,* 1-19.

Goldsmith, D. J., & Dun, S. A. (1997). Sex differences and similarities in the communication of social support. *Journal of Social and Personal Relationships, 14,* 317-337.

Goldsmith, D. J., & Fitch, K. L. (1997). The normative context of advice as social support. *Human Communication Research, 23,* 454-476.

Goldsmith, D. J., & MacGeorge, E. L. (2000). The impact of politeness and relationship on perceived quality of advice about a problem. *Human Communication Research, 26,* 234-263.

Goldsmith, D. J., McDermott, V. M., & Alexander, S. C. (2000). Helpful, supportive, and sensitive: Measuring the evaluation of enacted support in personal relationships. *Journal of Social and Personal Relationships, 17,* 369-391.

Goldsmith, D. J., & Parks, M. (1990). Communicative strategies for managing the risks of seeking social support. In S. Duck (Ed.), *Personal relationships and social support* (pp. 104-121). London: Sage.

Gore, S. (1978). The effect of social support in moderating the health consequences of unemployment. *Journal of Health and Social Behavior, 19,* 157-165.

Gottlieb, B. H. (1978). The development and application of a classification scheme of informal helping behaviours. *Canadian Journal of Behavioural Science, 10,* 105-115.

Gottlieb, B. H. (1994). Social support. In A. L. Weber & J. H. Harvey (Eds.), *Perspectives on close relationships* (pp. 307-324). Boston: Allyn & Bacon.

Gottlieb, B. H. (2000). Selecting and planning support interventions. In S. Cohen, L. G. Underwood, & B. H. Gottlieb (Eds.), *Social support measurement and intervention: A guide for health and social scientists* (pp. 195-220). New York: Oxford University Press.

Gottlieb, B. H., & Wagner, F. (1991). Stress and support processes in close relationships. In J. Eckenrode (Ed.), *The social context of coping* (pp. 165-188). New York: Plenum.

Greenberg, L. S. (1993). Emotion and change processes in psychotherapy. In M. Lewis & J. M. Haviland (Eds.), *Handbook of emotions* (pp. 499-508). New York: Guilford.

Greenberg, L. S., Rice, L. N., & Elliott, R. (1993). *Facilitating emotional change: The moment-by-moment process*. New York: Guilford.

Greene, J. O. (Ed.). (1997). *Message production: Advances in communication theory*. Mahwah, NJ: Lawrence Erlbaum.

Grice, H. P. (1975). Logic and conversation. In P. Cole & J. L. Morgan (Eds.), *Syntax and semantics 3: Speech acts* (pp. 41-58). New York: Academic Press.

Gross, J. J. (1998). Antecedent and response-focused emotion regulation: Divergent consequences for experience, expression, and physiology. *Journal of Personality and Social Psychology, 74*, 224-237.

Hale, J. L., Tighe, M. R., & Mongeau, P. A. (1997). Effects of event type and sex on comforting messages. *Communication Research Reports, 14*, 214-220.

Harber, K. D., & Pennebaker, J. W. (1992). Overcoming traumatic memories. In S.Å. Christianson (Ed.), *The handbook of emotion and memory: Research and theory* (pp. 359-387). Hillsdale, NJ: Lawrence Erlbaum.

Helgeson, V. S., Cohen, S., & Fritz, H. L. (1998). Social ties and cancer. In J. C. Holland (Ed.), *Psycho-oncology* (pp. 99-109). New York: Oxford University Press.

Herbert, T., & Dunkel-Schetter, C. (1992). Negative social reactions to victims: An overview of responses and their determinants. In L. Montada, S. Filipp, & M. Lerner (Eds.), *Life crises and experiences of loss in adulthood* (pp. 497-518). Hillsdale, NJ: Lawrence Erlbaum.

Heritage, J., & Sefi, S. (1992). Dilemmas of advice: Aspects of the delivery and reception of advice in interactions between health visitors and first-time mothers. In P. Drew & J. Heritage (Eds.), *Talk at work: Interaction in institutional settings* (pp. 359-417). Cambridge: Cambridge University Press.

Hewes, D. E. (Ed.). (1995a). *The cognitive bases of interpersonal communication*. Mahwah, NJ: Lawrence Erlbaum.

Hewes, D. E. (1995b). Cognitive processing of problematic messages: Reinterpreting to "unbias" texts. In D. E. Hewes (Ed.), *The cognitive bases of interpersonal communication* (pp. 113-138). Mahwah, NJ: Lawrence Erlbaum.

Hill, C. A. (1991). Seeking emotional support: The influence of affiliative need and partner warmth. *Journal of Personality and Social Psychology, 60*, 112-121.

Hill, C. A. (1996). Interpersonal and dispositional influences on problem-related interactions. *Journal of Research in Personality, 30*, 1-22.

Hirsch, B. J. (1980). Natural support systems and coping with major life events. *American Journal of Community Psychology, 8*, 159-172.

Hobfoll, S. E. (1990). Introduction: The importance of predicting, activating, and facilitating social support. *Journal of Social and Personal Relationships, 7*, 435-436.

Hobfoll, S. E., & Lerman, M. (1988). Personal relationships, personal attitudes, and stress resistance: Mothers' reactions to their child's illness. *American Journal of Community Psychology, 16*, 565-589.

Hobfoll, S. E., & Stokes, J. P. (1988). The process and mechanics of social support. In S. Duck (Ed.), *Handbook of personal relationships: Theory, research and interventions* (pp. 497-518). New York: John Wiley.

House, J. S. (1981). *Work stress and social support*. Reading, MA: Addison-Wesley.

House, J. S., Landis, K. R., & Umberson, D. (1988). Social relationships and health. *Science, 241*, 540-545.

Jacobson, D. E. (1986). Types and timing of social support. *Journal of Health and Social Behavior, 27*, 250-264.

Jefferson, G. (1988). On the sequential organization of troubles-talk in ordinary conversation. *Social Problems, 35*, 418-441.

Jefferson, G., & Lee, J. R. E. (1992). The rejection of advice: Managing the problematic convergence of a "troubles-telling" and a "service encounter." In P. Drew & J. Heritage (Eds.), *Talk at work: Interaction in institutional settings* (pp. 521-548). Cambridge: Cambridge University Press.

Jones, S. M., & Burleson, B. R. (1997). The impact of situational variables on helpers' perceptions of comforting messages: An attributional analysis. *Communication Research, 24,* 530-555.

Jones, S. M., & Guerrero, L. A. (2001). The effects of nonverbal immediacy and verbal person centeredness in the emotional support process. *Human Communication Research, 27,* 567-596.

Jung, J. (1989). Social support rejection and reappraisal by providers and recipients. *Journal of Applied Social Psychology, 19,* 159-173.

Kahn, T. L., & Antonucci, T. C. (1980). Convoys over the life course: Attachment, roles, and social support. *Life Span Development and Behavior, 3,* 202-218.

Kellermann, K. (1995). The conversation MOP: A model of patterned and pliable behavior. In D. E. Hewes (Ed.), *The cognitive bases of interpersonal communication* (pp. 181-221). Mahwah, NJ: Lawrence Erlbaum.

Kessler, R. C. (1992). Perceived support and adjustment to stress. In H. O. F. Veiel & U. Baumann (Eds.), *The meaning and measurement of social support* (pp. 259-271). New York: Hemisphere.

King, L. A., & Miner, K. N. (2000). Writing about the perceived benefits of traumatic events: Implications for physical health. *Personality and Social Psychology Bulletin, 26,* 220-230.

Krause, N. (1987). Life stress, social support, and self-esteem in an elderly population. *Psychology and Aging, 2,* 349-356.

Krause, N., Liang, J., & Yatomi, N. (1989). Satisfaction with social support and depressive symptoms: A panel analysis. *Psychology and Aging, 4,* 88-97.

Kunkel, A. W. (2002). Explaining sex differences in the evaluation of comforting messages: The mediating role of interaction goals. *Communication Reports, 15,* 29-42.

Kunkel, A. W., & Burleson, B. R. (1999). Assessing explanations for sex differences in emotional support: A test of the different cultures and skill specialization accounts. *Human Communication Research, 25,* 307-340.

Lackner, J. B., Joseph, J. G., Ostrow, D. G., Kessler, R. C., Eshleman, S., Wortman, C. B., et al. (1993). A longitudinal study of psychological distress in a cohort of gay men: Effects of social support and coping strategies. *Journal of Nervous and Mental Disease, 181,* 4-12.

La Gaipa, J. J. (1990). The negative effects of informal support systems. In S. Duck (Ed.), *Personal relationships and social support* (pp. 122-139). London: Sage.

Lakey, B., & Cassady, P. B. (1990). Cognitive processes in perceived social support. *Journal of Personality and Social Psychology, 59,* 337-348.

Lakey, B., & Cohen, S. (2000). Social support theory and measurement. In S. Cohen, L. G. Underwood, & B. H. Gottlieb (Eds.), *Social support measurement and intervention: A guide for health and social scientists* (pp. 29-52). New York: Oxford University Press.

Lakey, B., & Lutz, C. J. (1996). Social support and preventive and therapeutic interventions. In G. R. Pierce, B. R. Sarason, & I. G. Sarason (Eds.), *Handbook of social support and the family* (pp. 435-465). New York: Plenum.

Lakey, B., McCabe, K. M., Fiscaro, S., & Drew, J. B. (1996). Environmental and personal determinants of support perceptions: Three generalizability studies. *Journal of Personality and Social Psychology, 70,* 1270-1280.

Lane, C., & Hobfoll, S. E. (1992). How loss affects anger and alienates potential supporters. *Journal of Consulting and Clinical Psychology, 60,* 935-942.

Lazarus, R. S., & Folkman, S. (1984). *Stress, appraisal, and coping.* New York: Springer.

Lehman, D. R., Ellard, J. H., & Wortman, C. B. (1986). Social support for the bereaved: Recipients' and providers' perspectives on what is helpful. *Journal of Consulting and Clinical Psychology, 54,* 438-446.

Lehman, D. R., & Hemphill, K. J. (1990). Recipients' perceptions of support attempts and attributions for support attempts that fail. *Journal of Social and Personal Relationships, 7,* 563-574.

MacGeorge, E. L. (2001). Support providers' interaction goals: The influence of attributions and emotions. *Communication Monographs, 68,* 72-97.

MacGeorge, E. L., Clark, R. A., & Gillihan, S. J. (2002). Sex differences in the provision of skillful emotional support: The mediating role of self-efficacy. *Communication Reports, 15,* 17-28.

MacGeorge, E. L., Lichtman, R., & Pressey, L. (in press). The evaluation of advice in supportive interactions: Facework and contextual factors. *Human Communication Research*.

Metts, S., Geist, P., & Gray, J. L. (1994). The role of relationship characteristics in the provision and effectiveness of supportive messages among nursing professionals. In B. R. Burleson, T. L. Albrecht, & I. G. Sarason (Eds.), *Communication of social support: Messages, interactions, relationships, and community* (pp. 229-246). Thousand Oaks, CA: Sage.

Moss, G. E. (1973). *Illness, immunity, and social interaction*. New York: John Wiley.

Murphy, J. J. (1972). *A synoptic history of classical rhetoric*. New York: Random House.

Nadler, A. (1986). Self-esteem and the seeking and receiving of help: Theoretical and empirical perspectives. In B. Maher & W. Maher (Eds.), *Progress in experimental personality research* (Vol. 14, pp. 115-163). New York: Academic Press.

Nadler, A. (1991). Help-seeking behavior: Psychological costs and instrumental benefits. In M. S. Clark (Ed.), *Prosocial behavior* (pp. 290-311). Newbury Park, CA: Sage.

Norris, F. H., & Kaniasty, K. (1996). Received and perceived social support in times of stress: A test of the social support deterrence deterrence model. *Journal of Personality and Social Psychology, 71*, 498-511.

Notarius, C. I., & Herrick, L. R. (1988). Listener response strategies to a distressed other. *Journal of Social and Personal Relationships, 5*, 97-108.

O'Keefe, B. J., & Delia, J. G. (1982). Impression formation and message production. In M. E. Roloff & C. R. Berger (Eds.), *Social cognition and communication* (pp. 33-72). Beverly Hills, CA: Sage.

Park, R. E., & Burgess, E. W. (Eds.). (1926). *The city*. Chicago: University of Chicago Press.

Pasch, L. A., Bradbury, T. N., & Davila, J. (1997). Gender, negative affectivity, and observed social support behavior in marital interaction. *Personal Relationships, 4*, 361-378.

Pennebaker, J. W. (1993). Putting stress into words: Health, linguistic, and therapeutic implications. *Behavior Research and Therapy, 31*, 539-548.

Perrine, R. M. (1993). On being supportive: The emotional consequences of listening to another's distress. *Journal of Social and Personal Relationships, 10*, 371-384.

Petty, R. E., & Wegener, D. T. (1999). The elaboration likelihood model: Current status and controversies. In S. Chaiken & Y. Trope (Eds.), *Dual-process theories in social psychology* (pp. 41-72). New York: Guilford.

Pierce, G. R., Sarason, B. R., & Sarason, I. G. (1992). General and specific support expectations and stress as predictors of perceived supportiveness: An experimental study. *Journal of Personality and Social Psychology, 63*, 297-307.

Pierce, G. R., Sarason, I. G., & Sarason, B. R. (1996). Coping and social support. In M. Zeidner & N. S. Endler (Eds.), *Handbook of coping: Theory, research, applications* (pp. 434-451). New York: John Wiley.

Pritchard, C. R. (1993). Supportive devices in language and paralanguage in the achievement of affiliation in troubles talk. *Australian Review of Applied Linguistics, 16*, 57-70.

Range, L. M., Walston, A. S., & Pollard, P. M. (1992). Helpful and unhelpful comments after suicide, homicide, accident, or natural death. *Omega: Journal of Death and Dying, 25*, 25-31.

Reddy, M. J. (1979). The conduit metaphor: A case of frame conflict in our language about language. In A. Ortony (Ed.), *Metaphor and thought* (pp. 285-310). New York: Cambridge University Press.

Reevy, G. M., & Maslach, C. (2001). Use of social support: Gender and personality differences. *Sex Roles, 44*, 437-459.

Reifman, A. (1995). Social relationships, recovery from illness, and survival: A literature review. *Annals of Behavioral Medicine, 17*, 124-131.

Reis, H. T. (2001). Relationship experiences and emotional well-being. In C. D. Ryff & B. H. Singer (Eds.), *Emotion, social relationships, and health* (pp. 57-86). New York: Oxford University Press.

Reis, H. T., & Collins, N. (2000). Measuring relationship properties and interactions relevant to social support. In S. Cohen, L. G. Underwood, & B. H. Gottlieb (Eds.), *Social support measurement and intervention: A guide for health and social scientists* (pp. 136-192). New York: Oxford University Press.

Rogers, C. R. (1957). The necessary and sufficient conditions of therapeutic personality change. *Journal of Consulting Psychology, 21*, 95-103.

Rogers, C. R. (1975). Empathic: An unappreciated way of being. *Counseling Psychologist, 5*(2), 2-10.

Rogers, R. W. (1983). Cognitive and physiological processes in fear appeals and attitude change: A revised theory of protection motivation. In J. T. Cacioppo & R. E. Petty (Eds.), *Social psychophysiology* (pp. 153-176). New York: Guilford.

Rook, K. S. (1984). The negative side of social interaction: Impact on psychological well-being. *Journal of Personality and Social Psychology, 46*, 1097-1108.

Rook, K. S. (1990). Parallels in the study of social support and social strain. *Journal of Social and Clinical Psychology, 9*, 118-132.

Rook, K. S., & Pietromonaco, P. (1987). Close relationships: Ties that heal or ties that bind? In W. H. Jones & D. Perlman (Eds.), *Advances in personal relationships* (Vol. 1, pp. 1-35). Greenwich, CT: JAI.

Rook, K. S., & Underwood, L. G. (2000). Social support measurement and interventions: Comments and future directions. In S. Cohen, L. G. Underwood, & B. H. Gottlieb (Eds.), *Social support measurement and intervention: A guide for health and social scientists* (pp. 311-334). New York: Oxford University Press.

Saitzyk, A. R., Floyd, F. J., & Kroll, A. B. (1997). Sequential analysis of autonomy-interdependence and affiliation-disaffiliation in couples' social support interactions. *Personal Relationships, 4*, 341-360.

Salovey, P., Mayer, J. D., & Rosenhan, D. L. (1991). Mood and helping: Mood as a motivator of helping and helping as a regulator of mood. In M. S. Clark (Ed.), *Prosocial behavior* (pp. 213-237). Newbury Park, CA: Sage.

Samter, W., & Burleson, B. R. (1984). Cognitive and motivational influences on spontaneous comforting behavior. *Human Communication Research, 11*, 231-260.

Samter, W., & Burleson, B. R. (1990, May). *The role of affectively oriented communication skills in the friendships of young adults: A sociometric study.* Paper presented at the annual meeting of the International Communication Association, Dublin.

Samter, W., Burleson, B. R., & Basden-Murphy, L. (1989). Behavioral complexity is in the eye of the beholder: Effects of cognitive complexity and message complexity on impressions of the source of comforting messages. *Human Communication Research, 15*, 612-629.

Samter, W., Burleson, B. R., & Murphy, L. B. (1987). Comforting conversations: Effects of strategy type on evaluations of messages and message producers. *Southern Speech Communication Journal, 52*, 263-284.

Samter, W., Whaley, B. B., Mortenson, S. R., & Burleson, B. R. (1997). Ethnicity and emotional support in same-sex friendship: A comparison of Asian-Americans, African-Americans, and Euro-Americans. *Personal Relationships, 4*, 413-430.

Sandler, I. N., & Barrera, M., Jr. (1984). Toward a multimethod approach to assessing the effects of social support. *American Journal of Community Psychology, 12*, 37-52.

Sarason, B. R., Pierce, G. R., & Sarason, I. G. (1990). Social support: The sense of acceptance and the role of relationships. In B. R. Sarason, I. G. Sarason, & G. R. Pierce (Eds.), *Social support: An interactional view* (pp. 95-128). New York: John Wiley.

Sarason, B. R., Sarason, I. G., & Gurung, R. A. R. (1997). Close personal relationships and health outcomes: A key to the role of social support. In S. Duck (Ed.), *Handbook of personal relationships: Theory, research and interventions* (2nd ed., pp. 547-573). New York: John Wiley.

Sarason, B. R., Sarason, I. G., & Pierce, G. R. (Eds.). (1990a). *Social support: An interactional view.* New York: John Wiley.

Sarason, B. R., Sarason, I. G., & Pierce, G. R. (1990b). Traditional views of social support and their impact on assessment. In B. R. Sarason, I. G. Sarason, & G. R. Pierce (Eds.), *Social support: An interactional view* (pp. 9-25). New York: John Wiley.

Sarason, I. G., Pierce, G. R., & Sarason, B. R. (Eds.). (1996). *Cognitive interference: Theories, methods, and findings.* Mahwah, NJ: Lawrence Erlbaum.

Sarason, I. G., Sarason, B. R., & Shearin, E. N. (1986). Social support as an individual difference variable: Its stability, origins, and relational aspects. *Journal of Personality and Social Psychology, 50*, 845-855.

Saurer, M. K., & Eisler, R. M. (1990). The role of masculine gender role stress in expressivity and social support network factors. *Sex Roles, 23*, 261-271.

Schwarzer, R., & Leppin, A. (1989). Social support and health: A meta-analysis. *Psychology and Health, 3,* 1-15.

Schwarzer, R., & Leppin, A. (1991). Social support and health: A theoretical and empirical overview. *Journal of Social and Personal Relationships, 8,* 99-127.

Schwarzer, R., & Leppin, A. (1992). Social support and mental health: A conceptual and empirical overview. In L. Montada, S. H. Filipp, & M. J. Lerner (Eds.), *Life crises and experiences of loss in adult life* (pp. 435-458). Hillsdale, NJ: Lawrence Erlbaum.

Schwarzer, R., & Weiner, B. (1991). Stigma controllability and coping as predictors of emotions and social support. *Journal of Social and Personal Relationships, 8,* 133-140.

Searle, J. R. (1969). *Speech acts: An essay in the philosophy of language.* Cambridge: Cambridge University Press.

Seeman, T. E. (2001). How do others get under our skin? Social relationships and health. In C. D. Ryff & B. H. Singer (Eds.), *Emotion, social relationships, and health* (pp. 189-210). New York: Oxford University Press.

Seeman, T. E., Berkman, L. F., Blazer, D., & Rowe, J. W. (1994). Social ties and support and neuroendocrine function: The MacArthur studies of successful aging. *Annals of Behavioral Medicine, 16,* 95-106.

Segrin, C. (1998). Interpersonal communication problems associated with depression and loneliness. In P. A. Andersen & L. A. Guerrero (Eds.), *Handbook of communication and emotion: Research, theory, applications, and contexts* (pp. 215-242). San Diego, CA: Academic Press.

Sgoutas-Emch, S. A., & Johnson, C. J. (1998). Is journal writing an effective method of reducing anxiety towards statistics? *Journal of Instructional Psychology, 25,* 49-57.

Shumaker, S. A., & Brownell, A. (1984). Toward a theory of social support: Closing conceptual gaps. *Journal of Social Issues, 40*(1), 11-36.

Silver, R. C., Wortman, C. B., & Crofton, C. (1990). The role of coping in support provision: The self-presentational dilemmas of victims of life crises. In B. R. Sarason, I. G. Sarason, & G. R. Pierce (Eds.), *Social support: An interactional view* (pp. 397-426). New York: John Wiley.

Smyth, J. M. (1998). Written emotional expression: Effect sizes, outcome types, and moderating variables. *Journal of Consulting and Clinical Psychology, 66,* 174-184.

Smyth, J. M., & Pennebaker, J. W. (1999). Sharing one's story: Translating emotional experiences into words as a coping tool. In C. R. Snyder (Ed.), *Coping: The psychology of what works* (pp. 70-89). New York: Oxford University Press.

Spiegel, D., & Kimerling, R. (2001). Group psychotherapy for women with breast cancer: Relationships among social support, emotional expression, and survival. In C. D. Ryff & B. H. Singer (Eds.), *Emotion, social relationships, and health* (pp. 97-123). New York: Oxford University Press.

Sprecher, S., Metts, S., Burleson, B. R., Hatfield, E., & Thompson, A. (1995). Domains of expressive interaction in intimate relationships: Associations with satisfaction and commitment. *Family Relations, 44,* 203-210.

Strayer, J. (1980). A naturalistic study of empathic behaviors and their relation to affective states and perspective-taking skills in preschool children. *Child Development, 51,* 815-822.

Stroebe, W., & Stroebe, M. (1996). The social psychology of social support. In E. T. Higgins & A. W. Kruglanski (Eds.), *Social psychology: Handbook of basic principles* (pp. 597-621). New York: Guilford.

Sullivan, C. F. (1996). Recipients' perceptions of support attempts across various stressful life events. *Communication Research Reports, 13,* 183-190.

Tamborini, R., Salomonson, K., & Bahk, C. (1993). The relationship of empathy to comforting behavior following film exposure. *Communication Research, 20,* 723-738.

Tardy, C. H. (1994). Counteracting task-induced stress: Studies of instrumental and emotional support in problem-solving contexts. In B. R. Burleson, T. L. Albrecht, & I. G. Sarason (Eds.), *Communication of social support: Messages, interactions, relationships, and community* (pp. 71-87). Thousand Oaks, CA: Sage.

Thoits, P. A. (1986). Social support as coping assistance. *Journal of Counseling and Clinical Psychology, 54,* 416-423.

Thomas, W., & Znaniecki, F. (1920). *The Polish peasant in Europe and America.* New York: Alfred A. Knopf.

Trobst, K. K., Collins, R. L., & Embree, J. J. (1994). The role of emotion in social support provision: Gender, empathy, and expressions of distress. *Journal of Social and Personal Relationships, 11,* 45-62.

Uchino, B. N., Cacioppo, J. T., & Kiecolt-Glaser, J. K. (1996). The relationship between social support and physiological processes: A review with emphasis on underlying mechanisms and implications for health. *Psychological Bulletin, 119,* 488-531.

Vaux, A. (1988). *Social support: Theory, research, and intervention.* New York: Praeger.

Vaux, A. (1990). An ecological approach to understanding and facilitating social support. *Journal of Personal and Social Relationships, 7,* 507-518.

Veiel, H. O. F., & Baumann, U. (1992). The many meanings of social support. In H. O. F. Veiel & U. Baumann (Eds.), *The meaning and measurement of social support* (pp. 1-12). New York: Hemisphere.

Waldron, V. R., & Cegala, D. J. (1992). Assessing conversational cognition: Levels of cognitive theory and associated methodological requirements. *Human Communication Research, 18,* 599-622.

Weiss, R. S. (1974). The provisions of social relationships. In Z. Rubin (Ed.), *Doing unto others* (pp. 17-26). Englewood Cliffs, NJ: Prentice Hall.

Westmyer, S. A., & Myers, S. A. (1996). Communication skills and social support messages across friendship levels. *Communication Research Reports, 13,* 191-197.

Wethington, E., & Kessler, R. C. (1986). Perceived support, received support, and adjustment to stressful life events. *Journal of Health and Social Behavior, 27,* 78-89.

Wills, T. A. (1985). Supportive functions of interpersonal relationships. In S. Cohen & S. L. Syme (Eds.), *Social support and health* (pp. 61-82). New York: Academic Press.

Wills, T. A. (1991). Social support and interpersonal relationships. In M. S. Clark (Ed.), *Prosocial behavior* (pp. 265-289). Newbury Park, CA: Sage.

Wills, T. A., & Shinar, O. (2000). Measuring perceived and received social support. In S. Cohen, L. G. Underwood, & B. H. Gottlieb (Eds.), *Social support measurement and intervention: A guide for health and social scientists* (pp. 86-135). New York: Oxford University Press.

Wilson, S. R. (1995). Elaborating the cognitive rules model of interaction goals: The problem of accounting for individual differences in goal formation. In B. R. Burleson (Ed.), *Communication yearbook 18* (pp. 3-25). Thousand Oaks, CA: Sage.

Wilson, S. R. (1997). Developing theories of persuasive message production: The next generation. In J. O. Greene (Ed.), *Message production: Advances in communication theory* (pp. 15-43). Mahwah, NJ: Lawrence Erlbaum.

Wilson, S. R., & Kunkel, A. W. (2000). Identity implications of influence goals: Similarities in perceived face threats and facework across sex and close relationships. *Journal of Language and Social Psychology, 19,* 195-221.

Winstead, B. A., Derlega, V. J., Lewis, R. J., Sanchez-Hucles, J., & Clarke, E. (1992). Friendship, social interaction, and coping with stress. *Communication Research, 19,* 193-211.

Witte, K. (1998). Fear as motivator, fear as inhibitor: Using the extended parallel process model to explain fear appeal successes and failures. In P. A. Andersen & L. K. Guerrero (Eds.), *Handbook of communication and emotion: Research, theory, applications, and contexts* (pp. 423-450). San Diego, CA: Academic Press.

Wortman, C. B., & Dunkel-Schetter, C. (1987). Conceptual and methodological issues in the study of social support. In A. Baum & J. E. Singer (Eds.), *Handbook of psychology and health* (Vol. 5, pp. 63-108). Hillsdale, NJ: Lawrence Erlbaum.

Yankeelov, P. A., Barbee, A. P., Cunningham, M. R., & Druen, P. B. (1995). The influence of negative medical diagnoses and verbal and nonverbal support activation strategies on the interactive coping process. *Journal of Nonverbal Behavior, 19,* 243-260.

Zahn-Waxler, C., & Radke-Yarrow, M. (1990). The origins of empathic concern. *Motivation and Emotion, 14,* 107-130.

12

Interpersonal Influence

JAMES PRICE DILLARD
JASON W. ANDERSON
LEANNE K. KNOBLOCH

Let us begin with the premise that individuals uniformly possess needs and desires that they wish to satisfy. From that simple claim flow powerful ramifications for how the functions of communication should be conceptualized. Consider that because we are social creatures to our very core (Dunbar, 1998), need satisfaction is highly contingent on the actions of others. If we wish to slake our thirst for relatedness (Alderfer, 1972), for inclusion or affection (Schutz, 1966), for esteem or belongingness (Maslow, 1968), the means by which we bring about those ends are inescapably interpersonal. Although the desires we have mentioned thus far are distinctly social, the essential claim regarding need satisfaction extends to all forms of human motivation, social or otherwise.

Kellermann (1992) speaks to this point with characteristic clarity when she writes that "no reason to communicate exists apart from a dependence on others for need satisfaction. All communication is, consequently, purposive and goal-directed" (p. 289). And need satisfaction frequently involves changing the affects, cognitions, or behaviors of others.

DEFINING INTERPERSONAL INFLUENCE

There is much to appreciate in the foregoing logic and only one small, pragmatic point of reservation: Our embracing this perspective fully would render our task in this chapter impossibly large. Hence we gravitate toward a definition of interpersonal influence that will allow us to cleave existing research into manageable chunks while still permitting connections to the issues that characterize the communication literature more generally. For present purposes, we are concerned only with research that has focused on symbolic efforts designed (a) to preserve or change the behavior of another individual or (b) to maintain or modify aspects of another individual that are proximal to behavior, such as cognitions, emotions, and identities.

Several aspects of this definition invite elaboration. First, we use the term *efforts* to emphasize the fact that an influence episode is merely an attempt to change another person. The attempt does not guarantee the desired outcome. Indeed, the question of how compliance should be recognized is itself fraught with complexities (e.g., Shriver & Allen, 1997). And, of course, message techniques for enhancing compliance are one of the foci of our review.

That these efforts contain some degree of *symbolic* behavior is essential. Miller (1987) makes the point in this way: "To say that persuasion [or interpersonal influence] is symbolic underscores the primacy of *communication*; it stresses that primary interest is directed at the verbal and nonverbal code systems employed by the transactants" (p. 451). With respect to the practical task of cleaving the research corpus, this feature of the definition directs us to set aside certain aspects of the social influence literature, such as conformity and implicit group pressure.

The assertion that influence attempts are *designed* to achieve compliance follows from the position that individuals seek to satisfy their needs and desires. Yet simply recognizing that actions are imbued with purpose does not mean that influence attempts arise from unalloyed intention. In fact, much communication is routinized (Kellermann, 1992), and substantial portions of the message production process may occur with little or no awareness (Craig, 1986).

We emphasize *behavior* because, historically, that emphasis has been the sine qua non

for most research on interpersonal influence. However, rather than confine ourselves to behavioral *change* alone, we suggest that the *preservation* of existing lines of action also falls within the domain of interpersonal influence. Not only do individuals attempt to induce novel actions in their message targets, they also endeavor to reinforce existing patterns of behavior (e.g., "You can do it; you can keep up with your exercise program") and nonbehavior (e.g., "You'll regret it if you start smoking again"). As these examples suggest, preserving behavior may be as important as changing it.

It is also evident from our scope statement that we will not use the behavioral criterion strictly. Rather, in our consideration of both message production and message effects, we devote attention to the cognitive and emotional antecedents and consequents of behavior. Eliminating consideration of these processes, given that they play such an important role in theories of interpersonal influence, would produce a seriously distorted picture of the research literature. Finally, we focus on messages aimed at and exchanged between individuals rather than mass audiences. Collectively, these parameters constitute our concept of interpersonal influence.

DESCRIPTIVE ASPECTS OF INTERPERSONAL INFLUENCE

One place to begin our analysis of interpersonal influence is with basic descriptive questions. For example, it is surely the case that the success of different influence tactics varies greatly as a function of the context and propensities of the interactants. However, data reported by Cody, Canary, and Smith (1994) suggest that one generalization regarding effectiveness is possible: Influence attempts are successful more often than not. Our secondary analysis of Cody et al.'s recall data reveals that self-reported success rates ranged from 49% to 73%, with a mean of 59% across target roles that included family members, friends, roommates, strangers, and bureaucrats (p. 76). Similar analysis of diary data on the same target roles reveals a range of 64% to 76% with a mean of 69%. Although these summary statistics tell us nothing about the relative efficacy of the many tactics available to individuals, they do suggest that people choose their persuasive battles carefully.

We might also ask about the nature of the relationship between interactants. A small body of research has attempted to address this question by asking individuals to report on interactions in which they took part (Baesler, 1995; Cody et al., 1994; Rule, Bisanz, & Kohn, 1985). In these investigations, researchers obtained recall and diary data by asking respondents to report whom they attempted to influence and/or who attempted to influence them. In the recall data, respondents described from memory the nature and situation surrounding some prior influence attempt. The scholars collected diary data by instructing respondents to log influence attempts that they encountered on a daily basis. Collectively, the data from these studies consist of more than 9,000 influence attempts reported by 384 respondents.

In each of the individual studies, the researchers classified the episodes in terms of the source-target relationship. In a secondary analysis, we grouped them into two broader categories for the purpose of illustrating a simple point: Most influence attempts (roughly 80%) occur within the confines of close relationships. From this result, it can be inferred that social interaction provides a forum for expressing and seeking fulfillment of needs. Although very important forms of influence occur in nonintimate dyads, close relationships are constructed from and maintained through reciprocal, ongoing influence interactions. Not only do individuals possess needs that they wish to satisfy, but they enter into relationships of varying duration and intimacy in order to do so. Thus interpersonal influence is a fundamental feature of human existence

and one that is intimately bound up in social relationships. Understanding variation in the nature of those relationships is essential to understanding influence (Brown & Levinson, 1987; Roloff & Janiszewski, 1989).

The Structure of This Review

In our judgment, the contemporary literature on interpersonal influence is best understood as the result of several historical and theoretical trends. Consequently, we provide a history of the area beginning about 80 years ago. With that backdrop in place, we offer a more detailed analysis of three aspects of the literature: message production, action-interaction, and message effects. These are not perfect categories because the contents connect to one another in a variety of theoretical and practical ways. Still, they serve adequately to partition and illuminate the large and vibrant literature on interpersonal influence.

A HISTORY OF INTERPERSONAL INFLUENCE

The Roots of Interpersonal Influence

For many years, the study of rhetoric was largely synonymous with the study of persuasion in public venues. Thus when members of speech departments first sought to apply the scientific model to the study of communication, it was only natural that they would embrace questions concerned with the operation of ethos, pathos, and logos in one-to-many contexts (Knower, 1936; Woolbert, 1920). But this rhetorically grounded focus splintered as scholars began to recognize that change in behavior or opinion might reflect a number of underlying processes (Festinger, 1953). In an analysis of considerable historical significance, Kelman (1961) drew distinctions among three such processes, defining *internalization* as genuine belief change, *identification* as change resulting from attraction to the message source, and *compliance* as behavior change resulting from the agent's ability to control outcomes desired by the target (for some similar distinctions, see French, 1956). Whereas internalization shows a rough conceptual correspondence with logos, and identification with ethos, the notion of compliance stands apart from the rhetorical canon. Since these distinctions were drawn, internalization and identification have remained the province of attitude and persuasion researchers. The study of compliance subsequently developed into an area all its own.

Compliance

During the 1960s, compliance began to emerge as a distinct area of inquiry. However, the term was not strictly equated with the exercise of power, as in Kelman's usage. In practice, it came to mean the study of behavior change, usually as a function of some brief message. Freedman and Fraser's (1966) classic article titled "Compliance Without Pressure: The Foot-in-the-Door Technique" offers a well-known case in point. That report presented startling (at the time) evidence that a compliance seeker could double the likelihood of a target's compliance with a request by first securing agreement with an initial request that was trivial in magnitude. Perhaps in part because of the dramatic findings, the paper also made a substantial contribution to the establishment of behavior as *the* dependent variable of interest in the study of compliance.

Two other aspects of Freedman and Fraser's (1966) investigation are also notable. In fact, they serve as distinguishing characteristics of compliance studies to this day (e.g., Carlsmith & Gross, 1969; Cialdini, Wosinska, Barrett, Butner, & Gornik-Durose, 1999). One is the tendency to give folksy labels to compliance techniques. In this regard, the descendants of the foot-in-the-door study include the "door-in-the-face" technique

(Cialdini et al., 1975), the "even-a-penny" technique (Cialdini & Schroeder, 1976), the "lure" (Joule, Gouilloux, & Weber, 1989), the "foot-in-the-mouth" technique (Howard, 1990), the "that's-not-all" technique (Burger, 1986), and the "low-ball" technique (Burger & Petty, 1981), all of which we examine in more detail later in this chapter. Another, more substantive feature of the compliance paradigm is that it is unabashedly dyadic. It has, almost exclusively, examined only two-person interactions. As the communication discipline, which was traditionally focused on persuasion in one-to-many contexts, began to broaden itself so as to include more one-to-one contexts, the interpersonal aspects of the compliance paradigm showed a natural affinity for these developments.

The Beginnings of Compliance-Gaining Research

In 1967, Marwell and Schmitt published two papers that introduced the term *compliance-gaining behavior,* a phrase meant to describe message strategies intended to produce behavior change (these might more accurately be called compliance-*seeking* strategies). Both papers were motivated by the assumption that the political and economic disadvantages suffered by certain segments of society might arise from lack of persuasive skills (Marwell & Schmitt, 1990). While Marwell and Schmitt were drifting away from the study of compliance gaining and toward questions that they thought more answerable (Marwell & Schmitt, 1990, p. 5), their work was discovered by investigators at Michigan State University.

In 1977, Miller, Boster, Roloff, and Seibold entered a report into the research literature that had a profound impact on communication inquiry for the following two decades. The "MBRS study" (an acronym derived from the authors' initials) asked participants to indicate the likelihood of their using each of Marwell and Schmitt's (1967b) 16 compliance-gaining techniques in four hypothetical scenarios. Although the findings do not lend themselves to quick summary, neither are they especially important to the history of interpersonal influence. The paper itself, however, remains a landmark for at least three reasons (Wilson, 1997). For one, it drove home the emerging view that persuasion takes place in interpersonal relationships as well as in public contexts, and so should be studied therein. Of equal importance, the paper set a research agenda and provided a specific methodology for attaining it. The message selection methodology, in which participants used closed-ended scales to indicate the likelihood that they would use each strategy, became a distinguishing feature of the compliance-gaining tradition and, later, the basis for much controversy. A third contribution of the MBRS study was that it made it plain that an effects-only orientation to the study of communication was too limiting: Such an orientation necessarily excluded phenomena that were properly of interest to the developing discipline (Miller & Burgoon, 1978).

Although strong theory was not a prevalent feature of the compliance-gaining literature in the 10 to 15 years following MBRS, it is impossible for research to proceed in the absence of theoretical assumptions. This is true even when those assumptions are unspoken. During and prior to that time, researchers in communication and allied disciplines were engaged in work guided by the family of cognitive theories known as expectancy-valence or subjective expected utility models. Regardless of disciplinary context—organizational behavior (Vroom, 1964), social psychology (Fishbein & Ajzen, 1975; Rogers, 1975), or public health (Sutton & Eiser, 1984)—the basic form of the theories specified that some overall evaluation of a choice or action follows from consideration of all foreseeable outcomes and their associated probabilities (Babrow, 2001, offers a contemporary application of these ideas). In large measure, the theories embraced a human-as-computer metaphor, with all of its attendant presumptions.

Essentially the same suppositions were identified as characteristic of the influence literature prior to 1985 (Seibold, Cantrill, & Meyers, 1985). In their review of the literature, Seibold et al. (1985) outline the strategic choice model. It is not a theory per se, but rather a set of assumptions implicit in the influence literature at the time. In the strategic choice model, individuals are cast as highly conscious actors, oriented toward reward maximization, blessed with immense information-processing capacity, and armed with more or less complete knowledge of the behavioral options available to them and the consequences of each. Thus the basic presumptions of compliance-gaining research, although often unarticulated, were quite in line with theoretical trends in social science broadly construed.

The Beginnings of Constructivism

At the same time the compliance-gaining tradition was beginning to blossom, researchers at the University of Illinois were setting the agenda for a prolific research program on constructivism (Clark & Delia, 1977). At the core of this perspective were the twin notions that (a) individuals differ in terms of their domain-specific social-cognitive abilities, and (b) variation in these abilities explain variation in message production. With regard to the first notion, the phrase *interpersonal cognitive complexity* refers to the domain of interest to the constructivists while also expressing the belief that this complexity is the fundamental dimension on which cognitive ability should be characterized. The most commonly used means of assessing interpersonal cognitive complexity was the Role Category Questionnaire (RCQ; Crockett, 1965), an instrument that asks participants to articulate their impressions of two peers, one liked and one disliked. Although it is possible to derive a variety of indices of complexity from such data, the number of unique terms was most often interpreted to measure one form of complexity, that is, interpersonal construct differentiation (Gastil, 1995).

To examine the impact of cognitive complexity on message behavior, most constructivist researchers asked participants what they would say in response to one or more hypothetical scenarios (e.g., Clark & Delia, 1977). Then they used a hierarchically arranged coding scheme to categorize the resulting message data in terms of the degree to which the data reflected an awareness of and concern for the message target (i.e., the *person-centeredness* of the message). Thus the important question of how to classify influence behavior was settled by a priori identification of *the* dimension of interest. Clark and Delia's (1977) work on persuasive skill in children provided a model for constructivist inquiry that would be re-created many times over in the years following its appearance. In that investigation, boys and girls enrolled in the second through ninth grades described what they would say in three hypothetical influence episodes. The researchers scored the children's verbal output using a hierarchical coding scheme that ranged from (a) messages that indicated no awareness of the target's perspective to (b) messages that manifested awareness and understanding of the target's point of view. The children also responded to the RCQ and a measure of social perspective taking. Both of these measures were positively correlated with the degree of listener adaptation in the persuasive appeals. These relationships held even after the researchers controlled for the influence of chronological age. Just as the MBRS investigation served as a model for compliance-gaining research, the Clark and Delia (1977) study became paradigmatic to the constructivist tradition (Wilson, 1997).

The Rise and Fall of Compliance-Gaining Research

The 1980s saw an enormous outpouring of influence research, such that by the end of the decade, Boster (1990) estimated that 100 papers on the topic had been presented or published. This corpus of research is readily subdivided into four areas (see Seibold et al., 1985): (a) efforts to develop, analyze, or apply a message classification system; (b) descriptive studies of perceptions of compliance-gaining situations; (c) studies that related situational or individual difference variables to strategy selection; or (d) work aimed at gaining a better understanding of the methods used to study compliance gaining. The first problem—how best to characterize and study influence behavior—is a problem of critical importance because it must be resolved before research of any sort can proceed. Consequently, it is a challenge faced by every influence tradition and one that emerges repeatedly as a source of contention.

As Marwell and Schmitt's (1967b) list of compliance-gaining techniques appeared in research more frequently, so did an awareness of the shortcomings of that and other lists (e.g., Plax, Kearney, & Tucker, 1986). The 16 techniques were too numerous to permit efficient theorizing, but too limited to be considered exhaustive. Moreover, they varied greatly in their conceptual width (e.g., there are many more ways to threaten than to engage in positive or negative altercasting), and they were not united or differentiated in any principled manner. In short, the techniques constituted a list, not a taxonomy. This was a crucial problem for compliance-gaining research because it was impossible for scholars to develop theory or gather data in the absence of some consensus as to how to characterize the domain of compliance-seeking behavior. Three different data-driven solutions were attempted, the first of which was factor analysis. Whereas Marwell and Schmitt's (1967b) factor analysis suggested that the 16 techniques could be reduced to five groupings reminiscent of French and Raven's (1960) bases of power, application of essentially the same statistical algorithm to other data sets produced solutions that ranged from two to as many as eight factors (see Roloff & Barnicott, 1978; Miller et al., 1977). Due to the difficulty of cumulating knowledge about an ever-changing set of message categories, this approach proved unsatisfactory.

Hunter and Boster (1978, 1987) offered a different solution in their elegant reconceptualization of the message selection data as representative of a single underlying factor. Secondary analysis of three data sets provided the basis for their claim that likelihood data are best viewed as a unidimensional stage model, or, in the terminology of factor analysis, a Guttman simplex. Initially, it was thought that the likelihood data represented estimates of the probable affective impact of each strategy on the message target (Hunter & Boster, 1978), ranging from positive to negative. Later interpretations were more circumspect: "These responses may provide both a reliable and valid indicator of verbal aggression, argumentativeness, or some other trait" (Hunter & Boster, 1987, p. 82). Although this effort did resolve the matter of how best to treat likelihood data, it left open the question of what the data meant. Perhaps because of researchers' reluctance to reduce the complexities of communication to a single dimension, this solution never achieved widespread acceptance.

Wiseman and Schenck-Hamlin (1981) offered a third alternative with their 14-strategy model. In this model, compliance-gaining research had a genuine typology as these researchers were able to generate the categories logically from a combination of four overarching dimensions: explicitness of the

persuader's intent, manipulation of rewards/punishments, source control over the rewards/punishments, and explicitness of the rationale for compliance (Schenck-Hamlin, Wiseman, & Georgacarakos, 1982). Best of all, Wiseman and Schenck-Hamlin provided evidence that language users themselves make use of these four perceptual dimensions for organizing compliance-seeking messages. However, the strategies bore considerable resemblance to Marwell and Schmitt's (1967b) list. In fact, when treated as Guttman simplexes, the two sets of strategies produced results that were indistinguishable (Boster, Stiff, & Reynolds, 1985). Thus, despite its many laudable features, this solution never gained acceptance as a wholly satisfactory resolution to the problem of message classification.

In retrospect, it is apparent that the collective research effort was very much a bottom-up enterprise. Although the work was not entirely bereft of theory, the theory was most frequently implicit. On the face of it, the work was often purely descriptive and rarely more than variable analytic. That state of affairs prompted one reviewer to characterize the literature as having simultaneously too many and too few data (Boster, 1995). That is, although many studies were conducted, they were not sufficiently uniform in method or question to permit cumulation. Many other writers also bemoaned the difficulty of integrating work in this area (e.g., Baxter, 1984a). Three failings of the compliance-gaining approach were frequently voiced: (a) the reliance on paper-and-pencil measures in lieu of communication behavior, (b) the utilization of "one-message-then-done" designs, and (c) the absence of viable theory (Berger, 1985; Miller, 1987). Although some researchers made efforts to address each of these shortcomings (e.g., Boster & Stiff, 1984; deTurck, 1985), they form a distinct minority when viewed against the tradition as a whole.

Initial Influences of Discourse Perspectives

While constructivist and compliance-gaining researchers were pursuing their own agendas, sociolinguists were tackling remarkably similar questions of message production from a decidedly different standpoint. Brown and Levinson (1978) were surely the most influential of these researchers, as can be seen in the enormous impact of their ambitious theory of politeness (but see also Ervin-Tripp, 1976; Searle, 1976). They begin their theoretical exercise by proposing the existence of a "model person" who is possessed of three characteristics: (a) linguistic fluency, (b) rationality, and (c) face. By *rationality,* they mean a specific mode of means-end reasoning that enables speakers to achieve their goals even though they cannot necessarily fully articulate that reasoning (i.e., a very different kind of rationality than is implied by subjective expected utility models). *Face* consists of the desire to be approved by others as well as the desire to be unimpeded. Brown and Levinson refer to these two face wants as *positive* and *negative* face, respectively. Although the labels are so broad as to lack any intuitive meaning whatsoever, they are now securely (and unfortunately) lodged in the literature (see Lim, 1990; Lim & Bowers, 1991).

Politeness theory resolved the question of how to characterize influence behavior by positing the existence of five superstrategies arrayed along a continuum of politeness. Brown and Levinson's painstaking, multicultural ethnographic work provided extensive examples of utterances in four of the superstrategies (the fifth was "Don't communicate"). But more important, politeness theory offered a theoretical framework within which interpersonal influence could be studied. Concepts drawn from that perspective began to make their way into the communication literature not long after the theory was initially published (Kline, 1981), but it wasn't until 1984 that Baxter (1984a) offered the first

full-blown examination of it in the communication literature. Other researchers provided thoughtful applications, reinterpretations, and commentary on the limits and virtues of politeness theory (Craig, Tracy, & Spisak, 1986; Tracy, Craig, Smith, & Spisak, 1984). Subsequently, Barbara J. O'Keefe and her colleagues devised a system of message analysis that melded many of Brown and Levinson's ideas with extensions of constructivist thinking (O'Keefe, 1988; O'Keefe & McCornack, 1987; O'Keefe & Shepherd, 1987). Their use of the concepts of face and practical reasoning followed from politeness theory and its predecessors (e.g., Goffman, 1959). And their claim that an individual's communication behavior is the product of developmentally distinct "message design logics" can be viewed as an elaboration of the central person variable in the constructivist tradition: cognitive complexity.

Message Effects in Interpersonal Influence: Principles of Compliance

All the while that message production research was blossoming (as compliance-gaining research, constructivism, and politeness theory), research on compliance techniques continued its slow and steady growth pattern. One notable event was the appearance of Cialdini's book *Influence: How and Why People Agree to Things* (1984). Although written in a breezy style and intended for a mass audience, the work drew on social scientific research and appeared in shortened form in scholarly venues (e.g., Cialdini, 1987). Cialdini delineated six psychological principles of compliance from which a variety of techniques could be derived: reciprocation, commitment/consistency, social proof, liking, authority, and scarcity. The principles were more akin to empirical generalizations than theoretical propositions. Nonetheless, the work was a significant attempt to define the study of interpersonal message effects as an area unto itself.

The Methodology Wars

Differences between the compliance-gaining and constructivist traditions were numerous, but the one point on which proponents of the two perspectives openly disagreed was methodology. Whereas compliance-gaining researchers typically collected likelihood-of-use data by employing one or another set of preformulated strategies, constructivists preferred to use message construction tasks in which participants, when presented with a hypothetical scenario, spoke or wrote out what they would say. The most pointed attack was launched by Burleson and his colleagues (1986, 1988), who presented seven studies that compared the two procedures. Their conclusion that "the checklist methodology produces garbage" (Burleson et al., 1986, p. 1) was based, in part, on their belief that the selection procedure suffered from item desirability effects. This prompted swift and spirited rebuttal (Beatty, 1987; Boster, 1988; Hunter, 1988; Seibold, 1988). Even in conjunction with other studies that contrasted the two methods (Burke & Clark, 1982; Plax, Kearney, & Sorensen, 1990) or assessed the selection procedure against actual behavior (Dillard, 1988), it would be difficult to conclude that either side emerged the clear victor. Nonetheless, the debate marked an important turning point in the history of interpersonal influence scholarship. To the extent that compliance-gaining research was defined by the selection methodology, it was decidedly on the wane. Constructivism was undergoing a transformation that would give it a different look and a new set of assumptions. The two traditions were soon to be replaced by a perspective on message production that emphasized goal pursuit (Seibold et al., 1985; Wilson, 1997).

The Onset of Goals Research

Research concerning goals assumes that social actors possess wants, desires, and needs that they attempt to satisfy. Some researchers lean toward a conception of "goal" as a psychological entity that is in principle, although often not in practice, accessible to conscious awareness (Dillard, 1990a; Kellermann, 1988; Meyer, 1990; Wilson, 1995). In this view, goals are future states of affairs that an individual is committed to maintaining or bringing about (Klinger, 1985). Wilson (1997) echoes and refines this definition when he writes that "*interaction goals* are states of affairs that individuals want to attain/maintain through talk" (p. 22; emphasis added). Broadly speaking, research in this arena is allied with the principles of cognitivism.

Other authors, especially those engaged in the development of rational models, mean something rather different by the term *goal* (see Craig, 1986). Work on message design logics presents a case in point:

> Goals are not conceived to be clear, consciously recognized objectives that originate in moral values and individual character; rather goals are conceptualized and analyzed as the central elements in social codified representations of situations. . . . Thus, rational goal analyses interpret message structures as efforts to meet the demands of social situations, and not as efforts to meet an individually selected and consciously recognized set of goals. (O'Keefe, 1988, p. 82)

No doubt because of the deep differences between these two concepts of goals, this tradition lacks a single, exemplar study that is analogous to Miller et al.'s (1977) for compliance-gaining research or Clark and Delia's (1977) for constructivism. Conceptual differences aside, however, all models of goal pursuit agree on at least two points. First, they recognize that individuals may possess multiple goals simultaneously and that they try to achieve them through talk. This point has become so well accepted in the field of communication that it is now taken for granted. Some allied disciplines have yet to discover the research that the multiple-goal premise has prompted in the field of communication:

"Multiple goal striving appears to be the rule, *yet little empirical research addresses the topic*" (Austin & Vancouver, 1996, p. 362; emphasis added). In reality, the goal-pursuit models all address precisely that topic.

A second feature those models share is that they view goals as imposing strictures on the message behavior of interactants. However, there is considerable variation in the ways in which constraints are conceptualized and operationalized. In short, although the utility of the goal concept is not without its critics (e.g., Shepherd, 1998), it figures prominently and productively in several ongoing research programs (Kellermann & Shea, 1996; Meyer, 1997; Schrader & Dillard, 1998; Wilson, 1995). As a group, these programs reflect much of the contemporary landscape of interpersonal influence, at least with regard to message production (Hample, 1997, p. 188). However, to round out our description of current research on influence, one other emerging strain of inquiry deserves mention.

Discourse Perspectives Again

Although many would take issue with our definition, we use *discourse perspectives* as an umbrella term for all of those interpretive approaches that emphasize close analysis of talk and build their arguments from examples (e.g., discourse analysis, conversation analysis, ethnography). Work on interpersonal influence using these methods is becoming more common (e.g., Clark, Drew, & Pinch, 1994; Clark & Pinch, 1992; Pudlinski, 1998). However, the absolute number of publications that explicitly address issues of historical concern to communication scholars remains quite small (e.g., Fitch, 1994; Fitch & Sanders, 1994; Sanders & Fitch, 2001; Wilson, Cameron, & Whipple, 1997).

Owing to their dependence on convenience samples and argument by example, it is unlikely that the discourse approaches can produce

knowledge claims that would be widely regarded as scientific or even generalizable. Yet they very effectively vivify influence behavior in naturalistic contexts and enable the study of communicative sequences in ways that have proven challenging to other traditions. On both counts, the discourse approaches offer an appealing complement to the ways in which influence has traditionally been studied. How they will continue to contribute to our understanding of interpersonal influence processes remains to be seen.

At Present

Currently, research on interpersonal influence can be loosely grouped into three categories. Message production research, which derives from the compliance-gaining, constructivist, and politeness traditions, is reasonably abundant. The body of work on interaction, although smaller, utilizes a diverse array of perspectives and methods. Finally, message effects research continues to search for and explain techniques that enhance behavior change. We examine each of these three areas in greater detail below.

MESSAGE PRODUCTION

Research on Situation Perception and Goals

Perceiving Influence Interactions

In the 1980s, a brief spurt of research sought to understand how social actors naturally perceive influence interactions (Cody & McLaughlin, 1980, 1985; Cody, Woelfel, & Jordan, 1983; Hertzog & Bradac, 1984). These efforts were presumably motivated by the belief that individuals act on their perceptions of given situations, and understanding how social actors perceive situations would illuminate the immediate causes of message production. As it turned out, there was remarkable similarity in the results of the various investigations. Cody and McLaughlin's (1980) investigation is typical. These researchers recovered six dimensions: (a) the degree of intimacy between the source and the target, (b) the extent to which the outcome of the attempt would personally benefit the source, (c) the consequences of the attempt for the source-target relationship, (d) the rights of the source, (e) the power differential between the source and the target, and (f) the degree of resistance the source anticipates from the target (see also Hample & Dallinger, 2002; Miller, Cody, & McLaughlin, 1994).

The results of the situation perception investigations were important for at least two reasons. First, they presumably provided an exhaustive map of the perceived structure of influence episodes. This was valuable in that it presented the pieces that would need to be incorporated into a theory of compliance seeking, were one to be developed. Any such effort that ignored the results would presumably be incomplete. Second, identification of the situational dimensions prompted research that used these dimensions as predictors of message production (Cody et al., 1986) or selection (Dillard & Burgoon, 1985). Surprisingly, the dimensions did not predict either very well (but see Hample & Dallinger, 2002). The relatively weak associations between situation and the indices of message behavior, coupled with erratic relationships between individual differences and message behavior (e.g., Roloff & Barnicott, 1978), prompted researchers to search for explanations that were more proximal to message behavior. They turned to goals as constructs that were closely aligned with message production and reception.

Goals That Motivate Interpersonal Influence

At first glance, it might appear that people seek to persuade others for an enormous variety of reasons. Yet research on interpersonal influence goals has revealed that perceptions of immense diversity are more illusory than real (Cody et al., 1994; Dillard, 1989; Rule et al., 1985). These studies have embraced a data-driven approach to the identification of influence goals that (a) asks individuals why they seek to influence others and then (b) groups the resulting data through statistical or interpretive means (Cody et al., 1994; Dillard, 1989; Rule et al., 1985). The most frequently identified reasons for influencing others are listed in Table 12.1, along with a description and an example of each (see Kellermann, 1992). Although this list is based on data from studies that utilized a variety of methods and data sources, its contents are hardly definitive. These are distinctions that are grounded in the subjective experience of young adults living in North America and attending public universities. Depending on one's research agenda, this feature of the list may or may not be desirable. Studies of influence in organizations, for example, indicate that individuals hold goals that are unlikely to exist outside their own task arena, such as initiating changes in work procedures and improving another's job performance (Kipnis, Schmidt, & Wilkinson, 1980).

In contrast, one can easily imagine more parsimonious groupings of goals involving only two or three categories. For instance, we might distinguish between goals that substantially advance the interests of the individual and those that remedy a problem. Similarly, any one of the seven goals might be parsed more finely. Perhaps the best example of this point is the "change relationship" goal. Even if one assumes that the communicative processes involved in relational escalation and de-escalation bear some similarity, the experiences of the two events are quite distinct and the utterances associated with them are markedly different (Battaglia, Richard, Datteri, & Lord, 1998; Baxter, 1984b; Honeycutt, Cantrill, Kelly, & Lambkin, 1998). Hence alternative

Table 12.1   Influence Goals

Type	Description	Example
Gain assistance	Obtain material or nonmaterial resources.	"Can I borrow your class notes?"
Give advice	Provide counsel (typically about health or relationships).	"I think that you should quit smoking."
Share activity	Promote joint endeavors between source and target.	"Let's do something tonight."
Change orientation	Alter target's stance toward a sociopolitical issue.	"Here's why you are wrong about gun control."
Change relationship	Alter the nature of the source-target relationship.	"We should agree not to date other people."
Obtain permission	Secure the endorsement of the (more powerful) target.	"Hey, Dad, can I use the car?"
Enforce rights and obligations	Compel target to fulfill commitment or role requirement.	"You promised that you would take out the trash. So, how about it?"

goal lists are quite conceivable and may be desirable, depending on the aims of the researcher. Nonetheless, the goals displayed in Table 12.1 are valuable to the degree that they strike a balance between the competing needs for generality and specificity within the domain of nontask relationships.

Wilson (1997) defines interaction goals as "states of affairs that individuals want to attain/maintain through talk" (p. 22). It is important to note that the idea of interaction goals is not limited to the range shown in Table 12.1. Rather, individuals may have a number of other concerns to which they attend during interpersonal influence episodes. In other words, at the same time message sources are trying to induce compliance in their targets, they may be attempting to achieve other ends as well. The belief that speakers must juggle multiple goals is incorporated into cognitive and discourse perspectives in a variety of ways, which may be best understood through close examination of those models. We provide a discussion of cognitive models next, followed by a consideration of discourse perspectives.

Models of Influence Message Production

Conceptual frameworks intended to shed light on message production might reasonably be composed of at least four stages: (a) situation comprehension, (b) goal formation, (c) planning, and (d) the enactment of behavior (Dillard & Solomon, 2000). Although general models of message production exist (e.g., Berger, 1997; Greene, 1997; Hermann, 1983), our focus here is limited to theoretical perspectives expressly designed to understand influence attempts. Each of them addresses one or more of the four stages of message production. Within the subsections below on cognitive and discourse models, we present the models in roughly chronological order. However, because much of the work was contemporaneous, there is also an element of arbitrariness to the order of our presentation. For each of the models, we sketch its essential features, briefly summarize associated research, and offer some evaluation of its current status.

Cognitive Models

With varying degrees of specificity, the cognitive models of message production distinguish themselves by their interest in the thought processes that precede and accompany communication. Thus they tend to emphasize psychological activities over social ones. And, although most of these models at least pay lip service to interaction (as opposed to action), they have most often been tested using research designs that examine the determinants of only the first utterance. This move enhances experimental control, but it has also led to criticism of these models as mechanical and egoistic (Shepherd, 1998).

Cognitive editing. Following Cicero, Hample and Dallinger's (1990) cognitive editing research presumes that invention occurs in two phases: the creation of possible arguments and their evaluation. The model further assumes that individuals typically create more communicative options than they can exercise. Thus the task faced by the message source is that of how to eliminate or suppress unwanted message possibilities. As its name implies, the cognitive editing model focuses on the evaluation phase of the message production process.

The first step in this extensive research program was to identify the editing criteria that individuals use for making message choices (reviewed in Hample & Dallinger, 1990). Although research isolated eight distinct criteria for editing, these criteria can be usefully and compactly grouped into four overarching categories (Hample & Dallinger, 1992). The *effectiveness criterion* focuses on the likelihood of success (e.g., "This message wouldn't work"). Messages are also rejected due to *principled objections* (e.g., "This is too negative to use"). *Person-centered standards* are concerned with threats to the speaker's face, the hearer's face, or the relationship (e.g., "This message might make me look bad or hurt the other person's feelings"). The *discourse competence criterion* attends to issues of truth and relevance (e.g., "This is untrue or doesn't make sense in this situation").

The second and ongoing step in the research program has been to link the editing criteria to various situational and individual-difference variables. Hample and Dallinger's (2002) most recent work presents an elegant secondary analysis of nine previous investigations of situational variables. Drawing explicitly on the situation perception studies of the early 1980s, the researchers first replicated Cody, McLaughlin, and Jordan's (1980) scaling of situation dimensions (plus a seventh dimension, situation apprehension) and then used mean judgments of the hypothetical situations from their earlier work to predict editing for the 1,692 participants who took part in those studies. The particulars of the results are complex, but the general conclusion that emerges from the data is that each of the situation dimensions predicts the use of one or more of the editing criteria. (The research on the correspondence between individual differences and editing criteria does not lend itself to the brief summary necessary here; overviews of the findings appear in Hample & Dallinger, 1987, 1990; see also Dallinger & Hample, 1994.) These efforts to link editing to situational and individual-difference variables speak clearly to the goal formation portion of the message production process. Moreover, because editing involves the evaluation of different courses of action, it can readily be viewed as a form of planning.

Implicit rules. The cornerstone concept of Meyer's (1990, 1997) implicit rules model is that of schemata, which are defined as "cognitive structures that organize information about situations, goals, and the kinds of communication behavior that can be used to achieve goals in particular types of situations" (Meyer, 1990, p. 57). Situation schemata organize information about the influence goal as well as relevant features of the situation. Although the contents of any individual's schema is dependent on his or her experience, Meyer (1990) draws on situation perception studies (e.g., Cody et al., 1980) to propose that situation schemata contain information on resistance, intimacy, dominance, and so on. Strategy schemata consist of structured knowledge about particular communicative options and their degree of success or failure in past interactions. Compliance-seeking strategies are cognitive representations of the propositional content, relational implications, and sequence of behaviors that define a course of action.

Several information-acquisition and -processing principles are specified by the implicit rules model. For example, the model is premised on the belief that individuals have learning histories. That is, individuals participate in a variety of influence attempts, in a variety of situations, and have a variety of strategies available to them. From these experiences, they abstract the contents of situation and strategy schemata and the possible relationships between the two. These relationships, which exist below the level of consciousness, are the implicit rules for which the model is named.

In subsequent interactions, implicit rules guide behavior via a three-step process (Meyer, 1990). First, in any given circumstance, the speaker constructs a representation of the situation in working memory. This is sufficient to trigger activation of the appropriate situation schema. Next, the situation schema prompts activation of one or more corresponding strategy schemata. Third, the strategy that appears most appropriate to the situation at hand is selected (i.e., "comes to mind"). When the speaker possesses both ability and motivation, cognitive editing may occur at this juncture (Meyer, 1997). The implicit rules model has spawned a number of investigations, most of which have been supportive of the theory's predictions (Meyer, 1992, 1994a, 1994b, 1996). And, in principle, the model speaks to

all four phases of the message production process in various ways.

Cognitive rules. Because it is also firmly grounded in cognitive science, Wilson's (1990) cognitive rules (CR) model shares various features with the implicit rules model. For example, both theories assume that knowledge of communication is stored in a hierarchical associative network that is composed of nodes representing oneself and others, traits, roles, contexts, relational qualities, and desired outcomes. And, like implicit rules, cognitive rules are patterns of association between nodes that represent goals and nodes that represent situational features.

Activation of a cognitive rule is a necessary condition for goal formation, although not a sufficient one. The likelihood that a rule will be triggered is a function of three parameters. One of these is fit, or the degree to which the situational features match the rule. However, assessment of fit is qualified by the presence of ambiguity. The likelihood that a rule will be triggered also varies as a function of its frequency and recency of activation (see Meyer, 1990).

Much of the research carried out under the banner of the CR model has sought to understand the role of interpersonal construct differentiation as assessed by the role category questionnaire (Crockett, 1965) and studied so vigorously by constructivists. Because constructivist inquiry had shown cognitive complexity to be a consistent predictor of person-centered messages, Wilson (1990) initially reasoned that construct differentiation would be positively associated with chronic accessibility of rules for forming supportive interaction goals. However, unexpected findings prompted him to reconceptualize interpersonal construct differentiation as "the degree to which individual's social judgments are responsive to information from the immediate situation" (Wilson, 1995, p. 9). Subsequent studies provided data favorable to this revised conceptualization (Wilson,

Cruz, & Kang, 1992; Wilson & Kang, 1991) and suggested directions for extending the theory (Wilson, 1995). The CR model addresses all four stages of the message production process (i.e., situation perception, goal formation, planning, and enactment), although much of the research has emphasized situation perception and goal formation.

Goals-planning-action. The kernel ideas of the goals-planning-action (GPA) model can be expressed in just a few sentences. First, with regard to components of the model, goals are defined so as to align with the cognitive perspectives (Klinger, 1985). Plans are representations of verbal and nonverbal behaviors and behavior sequences that may result in behavior change in the message target. Actions are behaviors. Second, with regard to process, goals precede plans and, in turn, plans precede actions.

In the explication of the GPA model, each of the basic concepts is elaborated and several additional processes are delineated (Dillard, 1990a). For example, message output may be the result of processes that occur in different orders. A source might first decide to engage the target, then generate a plan. Or a source might first generate a number of plans and then, after assessing their viability, choose and act on one. Further, as is standard in cybernetic models, a feedback loop returns information to earlier stages of the model in order to compare the situation and the goal(s) (see Miller, Galanter, & Pribram, 1960). Because both speaker and hearer can be modeled in terms of the GPA sequence, with each one providing feedback to the other, the theory can be applied to interaction (Dillard, 1990a; Dillard & Schrader, 1998). However, it is best known for its treatment of individuals' goals.

The GPA model distinguishes between two types of goals. *Primary or influence goals* are those that motivate the speaker to engage in interaction (see Table 12.1). As the target gains awareness of the source's goal, that goal

serves to punctuate the episode by topically marking the beginning and the end. Moreover, the influence goal provides an explanation for interaction; it provides a theme and tells the interactants what the episode is about. In contrast, *secondary goals* are those concerns of the speaker that logically arise from consideration of the influence attempt (e.g., concern for the relationship). As in the other cognitive models, secondary goals will most often serve as constraints, although the GPA model recognizes that on certain occasions both types of goals may be advanced simultaneously. Research prompted by GPA theory has focused primarily on the ways in which primary and secondary goals shape situation perception (Dillard, Kinney, & Cruz, 1996; Schrader & Dillard, 1998), message output (Dillard, Segrin, & Harden, 1989), and judgments of message behavior (Schrader, 1999; Trost & Langan, 1999). The GPA model focuses mainly on the goal formation, planning, and enactment phases of message production.

Planning and metagoals. As they have been discussed thus far, goals are desired end states. The notion of metagoals shifts the focus away from outcome and onto process (Kellermann & Park, 2001; Kellermann & Shea, 1996). Kellermann (1988) explains:

> Metagoals are cross-situational concerns, that is, constraints that influence the selection of tactical goals in the service of primary goals. Unlike primary and tactical goals, metagoals cannot be said to be achieved at a particular moment in the conversation; rather they serve as ongoing constraints on the achievement of primary goals. (p. 3)

In this line of research, two metagoals are specified (Berger & Kellermann, 1983). *Efficiency* may be conceptualized as the ratio of outcome to effort, where higher values are more efficient. Less formally, speakers achieve efficiency by realizing their goals with a minimum of wasted effort. *Social appropriateness* is the degree to which a behavior is suitable or fitting in a specific interaction. It is synonymous with politeness.

Kellermann's (1988) explication of the role of metagoals in message production hinges on the degree of tension between the two goals as well as their absolute levels of importance. With regard to tension, she notes that the relationship between the two metagoals is variable. Depending on the primary goal and the circumstances at hand, the relationship might be one of conflict, independence, or compatibility. Goal importance derives from a multiplicity of conditions, including urgency, publicity, and formality (Kellermann & Park, 2001). Kellermann and Shea (1996) present evidence of the conceptual independence of the metagoals as well as their importance for an understanding of message production. Although the main theoretical machinery of Kellermann's metagoals work is concerned with the goal formation and planning aspects of message production, it also links planning to a number of situational variables.

Discourse Models of Message Design

Discourse models conceive of message production as a means of coordinating message features to meet interaction goals (O'Keefe, 1997). They have been termed *rational models* due to their assumption that people reason from means to ends within interactions (e.g., Brown & Levinson, 1978, 1987; Francik & Clark, 1985; O'Keefe & Shepherd, 1987). Because rational models characterize message production as an adaptive process of constructing messages to achieve goals (O'Keefe, 1997), they devote particular attention to understanding the correspondence between message form and function. Unlike the cognitive models reviewed above, they give virtually no attention to the cognitive processes that underlie behavior production.

Politeness theory. Brown and Levinson's (1978, 1987) politeness theory argues that people are motivated to achieve three aims within influence attempts: (a) gain compliance, (b) be efficient, and (c) preserve the face of both the speaker and the hearer (compare Kellermann's, 1988, metagoals). The theory defines *face* as the public image an individual conveys to others. People possess two specific face wants: (a) positive face, which is the desire to gain approval from others; and (b) negative face, which is the desire to maintain autonomy from others. Because they recognize the mutual benefits of preserving face, individuals endeavor to communicate in ways that minimize face threat but maintain message clarity. Politeness theory argues that influence attempts unavoidably threaten face because, by definition, they intrude on the hearer (but see Wilson, Kim, & Meischke, 1991-1992).

How is politeness accomplished? According to Brown and Levinson (1978), individuals employ one of five strategies to manage the competing wants of being clear and efficient versus protecting face. The least polite approach is *bald-on-record*, that is, simply issuing the request with no obvious concern for the hearer (e.g., "Bring me the book!"). *Positive politeness* is evident whenever the message source softens the influence attempt by showing respect or liking for the target (e.g., "Hey, old friend, would you bring me the book?"). A third strategy, *negative politeness,* deals with the imposition of the request itself (e.g., "I'm sorry to bother you, but would you bring me the book?"). *Going off-record* means being indirect (e.g., "Are you using that book?"). These indirect messages offer the hearer the opportunity to refuse the request without having to acknowledge explicitly that it has been made. The final strategy is *not making the request at all.* This choice most clearly privileges the target's desires over those of the potential message source.

Brown and Levinson (1978) argue that these five strategies are (a) mutually exclusive and (b) ordered on a unidimensional continuum running from most polite (not making the request) to least polite (bald-on-record). The theory assumes that speakers redress each face threat with one and only one politeness strategy, that strategies can be rank ordered for degree of politeness on conceptual grounds, and that hearers' subjective perceptions of politeness match this rank ordering (see Brown & Levinson, 1987, pp. 17-21).

These claims have not gone uncontested. In contradiction to the exclusivity assumption, several studies have shown that speakers often redress face threats with complex combinations of positive and negative politeness, both sequentially and simultaneously within the same utterances (Aronsson & Sätterlund-Larsson, 1987; Craig et al., 1986; Lim & Bowers, 1991; Penman, 1990; Shimanoff, 1977).

Brown and Levinson's (1978) ranking of strategies has also been a target of criticism. On conceptual grounds, scholars have argued that the desire for approval and the desire for autonomy are distinct and orthogonal phenomena (Lim, 1990; Scollon & Scollon, 1995). By implication, then, the corresponding constructs of positive and negative politeness are not themselves ordered either. Instead, they must be considered independent concepts. Empirically, scholars evaluating the match between Brown and Levinson's ranking and subjective perceptions of politeness have generated both supportive and conflicting findings. For example, people do not always perceive off-record strategies as more polite than negative politeness strategies (Holtgraves & Yang, 1990).

Although not easily accounted for by the theory, it is clear that the perceived politeness of any strategy can vary dramatically depending on its conversational and relational context and the intentions attributed to the speaker (Becker, Kimmel, & Bevill, 1989; Coupland,

Grainger, & Coupland, 1988; Penman, 1990; Wilson, 1992). Moreover, scholars have questioned the usefulness of equating politeness with indirectness (Blum-Kulka, 1987), the accuracy of the predicted link between social distance and politeness (Baxter, 1984a; Lim, 1990; Solomon, 1997), and the exhaustiveness of the parameters that determine the degree of face threat within a request (Craig et al., 1986; Holtgraves & Yang, 1990; Slugoski & Turnbull, 1988). There can be no doubt that politeness theory has contributed enormously to research on message production, but that same research has generated many findings that are incompatible with the theory's original formulation. Politeness theory will need to undergo a thorough reworking if it is to account for the corpus of research that it was instrumental in producing. Lim (1990) presents one such effort. Like all discourse perspectives, politeness theory largely ignores the situation comprehension (it is simply "context") and planning stages of message production. Goals, however, flow from general wants. Behavior is enacted not through the specification of cognitive machinery, but simply because that is what is on the speaker's mind.

Obstacles. According to the obstacle hypothesis, individuals anticipate potential impediments to target compliance and attempt to craft their requests in ways that address those obstacles (Francik & Clark, 1985; Gibbs, 1986). Moreover, the logic of the obstacle hypothesis predicts that when multiple obstacles are present, speakers will look for the most serious barriers to compliance and design their requests to deal with those barriers. When no obstacles are present, message sources will tend to produce unqualified requests. Obviously, speakers' ability to produce requests that address obstacles is limited by the speakers' own understanding of the context. But, apart from ability, there are good reasons for sources to address obstacles when they are aware that obstacles exist. For one, to the extent that speakers identify specific obstacles, they save targets the cognitive effort of doing so themselves. Additionally, when speakers direct attention toward obstacles and away from their requests, they provide targets with a means of declining the requests that protects the face of both interactants. In other words, such speakers behave politely.

Obstacles may assume a variety of forms. For example, a target's complying with a request for information might be hindered by any of the following: (a) The target may not know the information, (b) the target may be unwilling to offer the desired information, or (c) the target may not remember the desired information (Francik & Clark, 1985; Gibbs, 1986). Similarly, obstacles to favor-seeking requests include unwillingness, inability, and imposition (i.e., prior commitment) (Ifert & Roloff, 1996). (For more elaborate taxonomies of obstacles, see Gibbs, 1987; Ifert & Roloff, 1994.)

Consistent with the obstacle hypothesis, research suggests that people tailor the forms of their requests to address potential impediments to compliance. For example, individuals make their requests conditional on the obstacles that they perceive to be most likely to prevent the targets from complying with the requests (Francik & Clark, 1985). They also tailor the phrasing of their requests to the specific obstacles present in a variety of situations (Gibbs, 1986). In addition, Roloff and Janiszewski (1989) found that the type of help people seek influences the linguistic features of their requests. For example, they found that when people asked to borrow an object, a request likely to produce concerns about when the object will be returned, they included contractual clauses that specified the duration of the loan. When people asked for a favor, a request that corresponds with concerns about costs to the target, they included both inquiries about the target's ability to comply and inducements for help.

Individuals also vary the directness of their requests based on the presence of obstacles. Indeed, research suggests that people generally produce indirect requests that are contingent upon the presence of the obstacles to compliance they perceive (Francik & Clark, 1985; Gibbs, 1986). For example, an individual may say to a bartender, "Do you serve martinis?" rather than "Are you willing to bring me a martini?" Clearly, the availability of drink ingredients is a more relevant obstacle to the bartender's compliance than is willingness to serve a potential customer (e.g., Francik & Clark, 1985). Notably, people are likely to use direct requests when they do not perceive any obstacles to compliance (Francik & Clark, 1985).

Research in which individuals have been asked to judge requests has also documented the effects of requests that reference obstacles. For example, people perceive requests that address obstacles as more conventional, typical, and common (Gibbs, 1986; Paulson & Roloff, 1997), more polite (Paulson & Roloff, 1997), and more comprehensible (Gibbs, 1986) than requests that do not address obstacles. In addition, people view requests that address unwillingness obstacles to be more polite than those that address inability obstacles within the context of date requests, perhaps because these requests acknowledge that the target may not want to spend time with the source (Paulson & Roloff, 1997). Messages that address obstacles also influence the tone of the subsequent refusals (Paulson & Roloff, 1997). In turn, the obstacles mentioned in request refusals predict the amount of persistence the requester will engage in (Ifert & Roloff, 1996). The obstacle research can be viewed as illuminating the planning stage of the message production process.

Message design logic. Message design logics are particular ways of thinking about interaction (O'Keefe, 1988, 1990, 1997). Individuals who construct messages using an *expressive design logic* view communication as a vehicle for expressing thoughts and feelings. Because their aim is to convey information honestly and accurately, expressive communicators devote little attention to the social context that surrounds an interaction episode. In contrast, individuals who employ a *conventional design logic* conceive of communication as a cooperative game played according to rules dictated by social norms. Conventional communicators strive to achieve social appropriateness, fulfill normative expectations, and obtain specific responses from their conversational partners within interaction. Finally, those who utilize a *rhetorical design logic* engage in the negotiation of social selves and situations. Rhetorical communicators are motivated to create social consensus and interpersonal harmony within interaction; when discord is present in conversation, persons using a rhetorical design typically reconcile the competing desires of the interactants by redefining the situation. Examined as a set, the three message design logics differ in both the numbers and types of goals they encompass.

The three message design logics are thought to be developmentally ordered such that they reflect increasing degrees of sophistication and ability to manage multiple goals (O'Keefe, 1997; O'Keefe & Delia, 1988). Thus the three logics might be viewed as a single individual-difference variable, akin to cognitive complexity. In fact, a positive association exists between the ordered logics and interpersonal construct differentiation (O'Keefe & McCornack, 1987). The three logics are not, however, conceptualized as traitlike differences. Rather, the logics are situation specific. Even in complex situations that would seem to require individuals to make an effort to optimize their outcomes, persons who are capable of more advanced design logics may not employ them. Because the theory eschews reliance on cognitive explanation, it is not clear when individuals might choose to employ suboptimal logics or what may motivate this action.

The theory of message design logics shares fundamental assumptions with Brown and Levinson's (1978, 1987) politeness theory. In fact, it may be considered a direct extension of politeness theory (O'Keefe, 1997). Whereas Brown and Levinson's theory assumes that all people produce requests according to the principles of conventional message design logic (e.g., striving to be socially appropriate by taking into account the social distance between communicators, their distribution of power, and the degree of imposition posed by the request), O'Keefe's (1997) theory suggests that some people adhere to principles of expressiveness or rhetorical sensitivity in producing requests. Thus the model of message design logics adds an individual-difference component to politeness theory. Additionally, it emphasizes appreciation of situational complexity and goal formation, the first two stages of the message production process.

Conversational constraints. Kim and her colleagues (e.g., Kim, 1994; Kim & Bresnahan, 1994; Kim, Sharkey, & Singelis, 1994; Kim & Wilson, 1994) have undertaken a research program focused on conversational constraints that derives, in part, from research on metagoals (Kellermann & Kim, 1991). In terms of theoretical focus and methodological scope, the body of work closely resembles Hample and Dallinger's (2002) cognitive editing research. However, we locate the conversational constraint research among the discourse models simply because the constraints themselves draw so directly from these theories. Kim proposes the existence of five issues that are assumed to guide message production: (a) concern for clarity, (b) concern for minimizing opposition, (c) concern for avoiding damage to the hearer's feelings, (d) concern for avoiding negative evaluation by the hearer, and (e) concern for effectiveness (Kim & Bresnahan, 1996; Kim & Wilson, 1994). Although this line of research does not directly assess message production, a likelihood-of-use measure is usually included that is intended to capture a portion of individuals' implicit theories of requesting (e.g., Kim & Wilson, 1994). In so doing, conversational constraint research gives a nod to the cognitive underpinnings of message production. But, because there is no further theoretical explication of "implicit theory," the body of work looks very much like the other discourse models discussed in this section.

Unlike cognitive editing research, which has focused on situational and individual-difference predictors of editing criteria, Kim's conversational constraint studies seek to generate knowledge about the cultural precursors of constraints. Hence the research program is distinguished by its use of multiple-culture samples. Some of the research treats cultural membership as the independent variable and the importance of the constraints as the dependent variables. This work has yielded some interesting findings. For example, Americans perceive clearer tactics as more effective, whereas Koreans believe just the opposite (Kim & Wilson, 1994). In other papers, Kim et al. (1994, 1996) have attempted to trace the effects of cultural membership through self-concept variables and onto judgments of constraint importance. Because goals arise from culture and self-concept, the model highlights the goal formation portion of the message production process. In addition, because conversation constraints limit message choice prior to enactment, the model speaks to the planning stage as well.

Summary

The turn away from situational and individual-difference predictors of message production led researchers toward the notion of goals. Although cognitive and discourse models conceive of goals differently, the essence of the concept—striving—appears in both lines of thought. Further, both perspectives grapple with when and how individuals form and manage multiple goals, which may or may not exist in conflict with one another. As researchers in both camps have begun to appreciate the value of the other's perspective, there is a growing tendency to incorporate elements of the social into the cognitive and vice versa. For example, cognitive researchers now regularly invoke the concept of face (e.g., Meyer, 1997; Wilson, Aleman, & Leatham, 1998), and socially oriented researchers have been forced to confront certain forms of cognitive questions (e.g., O'Keefe & Lambert, 1995). Although it is not clear that the fundamentally different premises on which these research endeavors are built will permit genuine integration, it is certain that the exchange of ideas has benefited both perspectives.

ACTION AND INTERACTION

Classifying Influence and Resistance Messages

Regardless of what theoretical perspective motivates inquiry or what applied question lies behind the research, it is impossible to examine interpersonal influence without some means of formally characterizing the behavior of interest. Thus message classification is *the* critical issue that must be resolved before inquiry can move forward. Two choices affect the way in which the problem of message classification is solved. First, which is more appropriate, a thinking-first approach or a data-first approach? Second, should one seek to develop message categories or to identify message dimensions?

Some researchers prefer a thinking-first, or top-down, approach. Potentially, this has the advantage of tying the system to some larger conceptual framework. Others seek to characterize message behavior using a bottom-up approach. The appeal of this tack is that it is grounded in the subjective reality of the social actors whose communication researchers seek to explain. The category versus dimension question involves other issues.

Perhaps categories correspond to natural units of cognition, but they may proliferate to such a degree as to inhibit ready cumulation of knowledge. Dimensions can be parsimonious, but they may gloss over important nuances.

When juxtaposed, these two issues—top-down versus bottom-up approach and categories versus dimensions—define four pure means of resolving the problem of message classification. Although perfectly pure approaches are rarely seen in practice, we nonetheless use the four types to illustrate our review of message classification schemes. Readers interested in more comprehensive reviews should consult Kellermann and Cole (1994) or Wheeless, Barraclough, and Stewart (1983) on compliance seeking and Ifert (2000) on compliance resisting. In our brief review we emphasize compliance seeking.

Top-Down Category Schemes

Top-down classification schemes are the result of some a priori conceptual work. However, the degree of conceptualization and the extent to which it is linked to theory vary tremendously. In their classic paper, French and Raven (1960; see also Collins & Raven, 1969; Raven, 1965) identify five types of power. *Coercive power* derives from the source's ability to mediate punishments, whereas *reward power* refers to the source's ability to mediate rewards. *Referent power* arises from the source's use of a group as a frame of reference for making judgments about behavior. *Expert power* is based on the hearer's belief that the source possesses specialized knowledge. The successful exercise of *information power* depends on the arguments that constitute the influence message.

Overall, French and Raven's scheme is marvelously clear and inarguably the result of a priori thought. However, it does not rise to the level of theory because it fails to specify the processes that give rise to different forms of power or the effects they might be expected to produce. In other words, it lacks the kind of interlocking propositional statements that are needed for a theory. More broadly, *top-down* is not a synonym for *theoretical.*

Bottom-Up Category Schemes

Bottom-up classification efforts are data-first approaches. The basic strategy is quite simple: The researcher gathers a sample of influence behaviors (or behavior surrogates) and then devises categories at some higher level of abstraction into which these behaviors can be assigned. The means by which the categories themselves are created can be interpretive (e.g., Rule et al., 1985) or quantitative (Wiseman & Schenck-Hamlin, 1981). Possibly the best-known example is the widely used and much-criticized list of 16 compliance-gaining behaviors reported by Marwell and Schmitt (1967b), presented here in Table 12.2. These researchers assembled their list of compliance-gaining techniques by examining prior research and theory. They then asked study participants to rate the likelihood that they would use each technique in four different situations that varied in terms of source-target power and intimacy. The resulting five-factor model bears substantial resemblance to the French and Raven (1960) typology discussed above.

One minor historical point requires mention here. Although the Marwell and Schmitt (1967b) study is often cited as an example of a "deductive" approach (e.g., Wiseman & Schenck-Hamlin, 1981), that label is certainly inaccurate. In terms of generating the 16 techniques, the researchers engaged in no deduction whatsoever. Rather, they generated a sample of influence behaviors and then proceeded to group them into five categories. Although Wiseman and Schenck-Hamlin (1981) argue for the superiority of "inductive" methods, in reality both their project and Marwell and Schmitt's were inductive: The two studies simply drew their samples of messages from different sources.

Table 12.2   Marwell and Schmitt's (1967b) Compliance-Gaining Techniques

Strategy/Technique	Definition	Example
Rewarding activity		
Pregiving	Source provides some sort of reward to the target just prior to the influence attempt.	"I just bought us all tickets to the ballgame. . . . Now, I want you to go to your room and study for that big exam."
Liking	Source acts nicely toward the target in an effort to create a positive mind-set.	A parent smiles and presents a sunny disposition toward a child, then asks, "Would you please eat your vegetables?"
Promise	Source offers the target a reward in return for compliance.	"I will do the laundry if you do the dishes."
Punishing activity		
Threat	Source suggests that the target will lose resources if he or she should fail to comply.	"If you don't wash those dishes this instant, you are going to bed right now."
Aversive stimulation	Source informs the target that some punishment will be enforced until the target is in compliance.	"I have decided to withhold your allowance until your grades improve."
Expertise		
Positive expertise	Source informs the target that compliance shall be rewarded due to the "nature of things."	"If you eat your vegetables, you will grow up to be big and strong."
Negative expertise	Source informs the target that failure to comply will lead to punishment due to the "nature of things."	"If you don't eat your vegetables, you will never grow up to be big and strong."
Activation of impersonal commitments		
Positive self-feelings	Source advises the target that compliance will make him or her feel better.	"If you study harder, you will feel much prouder of yourself as a student."
Negative self-feelings	Source advises the target that noncompliance will make the target feel worse.	"If you don't study harder, you will only feel worse about yourself as a student."
Positive altercasting	Source informs the target that those with positive qualities would comply.	"Good boys and girls do their chores when they are told."
Positive esteem	Source tells the target that valued others will think well of the target if he or she complies.	"If you do your homework, your brothers and sisters will be so proud of you."
Moral appeal	Source advises the target that lack of compliance would indicate a moral flaw in his or her character.	"It's a sin to not eat your vegetables when others are starving."

Table 12.2 (continued)

Strategy/Technique	Definition	Example
Activation of personal commitments		
Altruism	Source asks the target to comply out of respect for the source's wishes.	"I really want you to be the best student that you can be. So, for me, will you please study harder?"
Debt	Source makes the target aware of past favors that oblige the target to comply.	"I slaved all night over a hot stove for you. Now, eat your vegetables."
Negative altercasting[a]	Source informs the target that only those with negative qualities would fail to comply.	"Only bad boys and girls neglect their chores."
Negative esteem	Source tells the target that valued others will think less of the target if he or she does not comply.	"Do your homework. You don't want to disappoint your grandparents."

NOTE: The strategies shown here are the groupings of techniques identified by Marwell and Schmitt's (1967b) factor analysis.

a. This technique loaded on both the personal and impersonal commitment clusters, but here the technique is noted in terms of activation of personal commitment strategy.

Top-Down Dimensional Schemes

Hoffman (1960; Hoffman & Saltzstein, 1967) advances a distinction between two forms of parental discipline. *Power-assertion* is direct, coercive, and geared toward immediate behavior change. In contrast, *induction* appeals to the child's internalized standards by providing reasons and explanations. Applegate, Burke, Burleson, Delia, and Kline (1985) extended this two-part idea in their explication of reflection-enhancing parental communication. The resulting six-level, hierarchical coding scheme highlights the degree to which parents give or elicit reasons involving psychological consequences as justifications for why children should change their behavior. As Table 12.3 shows, parents employing low-level strategies use explicit language to dominate the child. Each step up the hierarchy moves toward greater focus on psychological consequences while simultaneously granting greater autonomy to the child.

Although this scheme springs from Hoffman's simple distinction, it is clearly infused with constructivist principles. As is typical of that tradition, the coding scheme captures variation in sophistication or complexity. In addition, there is a clear evaluative implication such that higher levels of reflection are preferable and should be expected to produce more desirable outcomes. Thus it is a good example of a top-down dimensional scheme.

Bottom-Up Dimensional Schemes

One of the earliest bottom-up dimensional schemes appears in the work of Falbo (1977). Eight individuals were provided with 16 influence message types and were asked to judge the similarity of all possible pairs. When the similarity data were submitted to a multidimensional scaling analysis, two dimensions were recovered, which Falbo labels *direct versus indirect* and *rational versus irrational*. Several other studies, using similar procedures but larger numbers of judges and messages, yielded similar results (Cody et al., 1980; Falbo & Peplau, 1980; Harkness, 1990; Kemper & Thissen, 1981; Wiseman & Schenck-Hamlin, 1981). One review of those

Table 12.3   Applegate, Burke, Burleson, Delia, and Kline's (1985) Scheme for Coding Degree of
Reflection-Enhancement in Parental Communication

Level	Definition	Example
1	Messages that explicitly discourage reflection by the child	"Go to your room."
2	Messages that implicitly discourage reflection by the child	"We don't run in the house."
3	Messages that implicitly encourage reflection by explaining physical consequences	"It works better this way."
4	Messages that implicitly encourage reflection by providing behavioral choices and associated consequences	"If you clean up now you can have a cookie later."
5	Messages that explicitly encourage reflection by explaining the psychological consequences or suggesting alternative behaviors	"Instead of yelling, if you asked nicely he would feel better."
6	Messages that explicitly encourage reflection by asking the child to consider consequences or generate alternative behaviors	"How do you think he would feel if you asked nicely instead of yelling?"

NOTE: The examples in this table are adapted from Wilson et al. (1997).

studies has concluded that there was strong evidence for at least three dimensions (Dillard, Wilson, Tusing, & Kinney, 1997). *Explicitness* references the extent to which the source's influence goal is made clear in the utterance itself (as opposed to the utterance in context). *Dominance-submissiveness* describes the perceived relative power of the source vis-à-vis the target as that power is expressed in the message. Finally, *argument* is defined as the extent to which a rationale for the sought-after action is presented in the message (not the quality of that rationale). One implication of these findings is that a multidimensional characterization of influences messages is *required* if we are to achieve a full understanding of their operation. Research on a single dimension, that does not control for the others, runs the risk of producing distorted results (Dillard et al., 1997).[1]

Evaluating Categorical Message Classification Schemes

Just prior to the appearance of the second edition of this *Handbook,* Kellermann and

Cole (1994) published an in-depth analysis of existing schemes for categorizing influence messages. Their review and integration of 74 existing classification schemes yielded a list of 64 unique strategies. However, Kellermann and Cole's intent was not to develop a master list, but rather to illustrate general challenges to the cumulation of knowledge. They identified three particular problems:

1. Strategies, both within and between classification systems, were defined using a variety of atheoretical criteria. This had a twofold effect: The resulting lists were neither mutually exclusive nor exhaustive, which, in turn, produced research findings that appeared chaotic and inconsistent.

2. "Conceptual definitions of the strategies were unclear, nonspecific, nonexclusive, and nondelimiting" (p. 3). This made it difficult to understand the strategies and to classify messages as instances of those strategies.

3. Many of the operationalizations that appeared in the literature were invalid representatives of the strategies they were intended to embody (but see O'Keefe, 1994).

This difficulty is, of course, a natural out-growth of the two preceding problems.

Given Kellermann and Cole's detailed and comprehensive analysis of the literature, the problems themselves are not much in dispute (but see Burgoon, 1994). The causes and implications of those problems, however, warrant closer examination. Roloff (1994) locates their roots in the sociology of science. He notes tendencies toward provincialism at the levels of both disciplines and areas within disciplines. For example, social psychologists lean toward Falbo's (1977) scheme, whereas organizational researchers utilize Kipnis et al.'s (1980) list of strategies. The same general sort of phenomenon is apparent between groups of researchers within a single field. Groups, at the level of disciplines or areas, develop assumptions and preferences that facilitate comparisons within groups but inhibit comparisons across groups.

Another problem derives from the impact of context (Roloff, 1994). A great deal of influence research takes place in specialized contexts, such as drug resistance programs (Trost & Langan, 1999), organizations (Krone & Ludlum, 1990), and personal relationships (Miller & Boster, 1988). The available means of persuasion vary from context to context, precisely because context renders some means possible and others impossible, even nonsensical.

What is most notable about these two issues—provincialism and context—is their durability. Among human beings, the formation of preferences is inevitable. And the limitations and opportunities introduced by context are a fundamental and unalterable feature of social life. Should influence research, therefore, abandon categorical approaches altogether? Not at all. Categorical classifications possess at least two desirable features that inform research in ways that no alternative can offer. For one, a categorical approach is well suited to enumerating the universe of strategies that individuals *could* use to gain or resist compliance *within a given context.* Second, and perhaps more important, a categorical approach has the potential to offer nuanced information about communication behavior that is otherwise unattainable. When categories are used *within clearly specified contextual boundaries,* they are quite meaningful. However, for the reasons discussed previously, transcontextual category schemes are unlikely ever to yield clear and unambiguous research findings. Kellermann and Cole's (1994) analysis is a case in point.

Evaluating Dimensional Message Classification Schemes

Advantages and disadvantages of dimensional schemes should also be made explicit. First, because dimensions are usually fewer in number than categories, they offer a parsimonious means of classification. Of course, the corresponding danger is that communication will be characterized in ways that gloss over important distinctions. But, second, whereas categories exist only in context, message dimensions have the potential to transcend context. For instance, researchers might pursue questions concerning the causes and effects of message explicitness in any of a multitude of contexts. However, it is important to recognize that contexts may limit the range of any dimension. To draw a statistical analogy, correlations are important, but they are a product of variances that may be restricted in any given context. Overall, then, there is value in both dimensional and categorical approaches. Each one hides and highlights different aspects of communication behavior.

The Role of Theory in the Development of Message Classification Schemes

As we have noted, top-down approaches should not be equated with theory. We wish to make a parallel point regarding bottom-up approaches: They are not theory-free. In fact, bottom-up approaches embrace a whole set of assumptions regarding the ability of social actors to report on or evaluate social stimuli in meaningful ways. For example, evidence of the psychological reality of a classification scheme may be a necessary condition for validity (Poole & Folger, 1981). However, psychological reality alone cannot guarantee that these are the dimensions utilized by the cognitive or social machinery that are, in fact, responsible for message production, because humans lack insight into all of the causes of their actions. So, although the theory associated with bottom-up approaches may not be explicitly articulated, it is operative nonetheless.

Dimensional schemes that are derived more straightforwardly from theory run a different type of risk. They may identify a dimension that has no real bearing on message behavior, or they may unwittingly intermingle multiple dimensions. Evidence of this latter difficulty may be seen in the Applegate et al. (1985) scheme, which conflates content variation (i.e., power assertion versus enhancement) with linguistic variation (explicitness versus implicitness).

Conclusion

The development of some means of classifying communication behavior is the sine qua non of empirical influence research. And, certainly, the way in which such classification is done delimits the conclusions that can emerge from the findings. All of the schemes we have discussed in this section constrain what can be found along two lines. First, by defining the domain of interest as either compliance gaining or compliance resisting, they effectively exclude other possible types of behavior that may take place during an influence episode. Surely, an individual might contest a point, seek more information, or generate some other kind of utterance that would not be seen as an effort to seek or resist compliance. Second, the schemes are essentially static. They have

nothing to say about the sequence in which people enact influence moves or how they deploy resistance tactics to counter attempts at influence. Researchers can address both limitations by focusing less on individual actions and more on interaction.

INTERACTION: RESEARCH AND THEORY

The Rebuff Phenomenon

While observing that many writers have lamented the lack of coherence in the compliance-gaining literature, Hample and Dallinger (1998) note the existence of what appears to be a durable empirical regularity. The *rebuff phenomenon*, as they label it, can be described simply: "When an initial persuasive effort is rebuffed, follow-up persuasive messages are ruder, more aggressive, and more forceful than the first one" (p. 305). Conceived in this way, the rebuff is clearly an interactive phenomenon. Empirical evidence of it can be found in message selection studies (Bisanz & Rule, 1990; deTurck, 1985; Kim, Shin, & Cai, 1998), message generation studies (Roloff & Janiszewski, 1989; Wilson, Cruz, Marshall, & Rao, 1993), recall studies (Yukl, Falbe, & Youn, 1993), and laboratory interaction studies (Lim, 1990; Mikolic, Parker, & Pruitt, 1997).

Lim (1990) contends that the effect may be explained by the norm of reciprocity. In fact, his experiment suggests two important findings: (a) Resistance alone leads to an increase in source aggressiveness, and (b) variations in how resistance is expressed (i.e., strong versus weak, friendly versus unfriendly) produce corresponding variations in the verbal aggressiveness of the source. These results imply a content aspect to reciprocity that is manifested as persistence in the face of resistance, as well as a stylistic aspect that can be seen in the aggressiveness with which compliance is pursued.

Hample and Dallinger (1998) have attempted to understand the rebuff phenomenon through the lens of their cognitive editing model. Two possibilities present themselves: Individuals may become more aggressive because they exhaust their supply of prosocial appeals, or message sources may alter their editing standards such that more aggressive messages are seen as acceptable. Although Hample and Dallinger did not address the first explanation in their hypothetical scenario study, they did find evidence to support the second. They documented that people's concern for effectiveness increased as a positive function of number of rebuffs, while their concern for principles and their concern for harming the hearer declined. This account can be viewed as illustrating the cognitive operations that underlie Lim's (1990) more social explanation of the rebuff phenomenon.

The Content and Sequencing
of Influence Interactions

Several studies that have explicitly examined message sequences reveal that there is more to influence interactions than simply compliance seeking and compliance resisting. For example, in a study in which participants solicited blood donations, 18% of initial responses to the request were either a "conditional yes or a maybe" rather than some form of compliance or refusal (Wilson, Levine, Humphreys, & Peters, 1994). In two investigations that were more qualitative in nature, researchers have observed other types of talk that are seemingly necessary to coordinate an influence episode. Specifically, when Bylund (2000) examined how physicians seek to induce behavior change in their patients, she found that resistance might result in a physician's temporarily dropping the effort only to return to it later in the interaction. Sanders and Fitch (2001) view this latter finding as an instance of the same phenomenon they observed in their own data, that is, the tendency for interlocutors to cycle in and out of explicit talk about a sought-after behavior change. They also note the existence

of an ending sequence to an episode in which the target has agreed to comply. In this "coda," the source seeks to firm up the target's commitment to the behavior.

Discourse-focused work has also shed some light on the sequencing of influence episodes. Application of Applegate et al.'s (1985) reflection-enhancing coding scheme to parent-child interactions (see Table 12.3) revealed the intermingling of strategies coded at different levels in a single conversational turn (Wilson et al., 1997). Further, they provide some evidence of a reverse rebuff sequence in which increased politeness followed resistance. Such findings illustrate the value of sequential analysis. And a surprising result that can be seen as evidence in support of the same claims derives from Clark et al.'s (1994) analysis of salespersons and their potential customers. Those scholars report that targets may signal resistance, albeit indirectly, *prior* to sources' requests for compliance.

Other researchers have discerned two basic forms of compliance-seeking interactions (Sanders & Fitch, 2001). In the *regressive form,* the source begins with a relatively direct solicitation, then offers inducements and removes obstacles as the target expresses them. The *progressive form* can be seen in a sequence in which the source attempts to identify and counter sources of resistance prior to making the request explicit. The two forms are reminiscent of Scollon and Scollon's (1995) characterization of Western (i.e., direct) and Eastern (i.e., indirect) preferences for influence patterns, thereby suggesting the possibility of cultural variations in their frequency of enactment.

These investigations show that interpersonal influence is necessarily an interactive process (Sanders & Fitch, 2001), a conclusion anticipated by researchers more or less aligned with the compliance-gaining tradition (e.g., Boster & Stiff, 1984; Miller, 1987; Wilson et al., 1993). However, the contributions of the research cited in this section on other issues is quite clear. Interpersonal influence researchers do need to recognize the important role played by messages and message sequences that are not strictly focused on compliance seeking or resisting. Moreover, a greater appreciation for the temporal and sequential elements of influence episodes has the potential to lead to important insights into this form of communication behavior.

Inconsistent nurturing as control theory. The recently developed inconsistent nurturing as control (INC) model offers a dyadic-system analysis grounded in learning theory (Le Poire, 1995). It is also highly contextualized in that it attempts to explain influence behavior targeted at reducing or eliminating substance abuse in close relationships. The theory recognizes that an individual whose relational partner is a substance abuser faces a dilemma of a very specific sort. The functional partner wishes to *nurture* the afflicted partner, especially in times of crisis, even though the crises are often drug induced. The functional partner also desires to eliminate the destructive behavior—that is, to *control* the substance-abusing partner. Nurturing behaviors are rewarding to the afflicted partner and serve to maintain the relationship. However, because nurturing occurs as a result of the afflicted partner's substance abuse, it may reinforce the problem. Controlling behaviors are needed to extinguish the substance abuse, but controlling must often include withdrawal of affection, with its attendant relational risks. In this way, the functional partner is caught between the desire to nurture and the desire to control. Competing goals cause the functional partner to intermittently reward and punish the afflicted partner's substance abuse, a pattern that is almost guaranteed to maintain that behavior (Skinner, 1974).

The research base associated with INC theory is relatively small, but the results are intriguing and largely supportive of the model. For example, there is evidence that consistent punishment for substance abuse coupled with consistent reinforcement for alternative behaviors is the most effective means of preventing relapse (Le Poire, Hallett, & Erlandson, 2000). This pattern is unlikely to manifest itself when the other partner is him- or herself a substance user (Le Poire, Erlandson, & Hallett, 1998). But, to the extent that afflicted partners do not relapse, functional partners themselves report reduced levels of depression (Le Poire et al., 2000). Jointly, these results point toward the need for dyadic-level interventions as a means of addressing this socially significant problem.

Abusive mothers. A similar conclusion readily emerges from Oldershaw, Walters, and Hall's (1986, 1989) analyses of physically abusive mothers and matched nonabusive control mothers. Compared with the nonabusive mothers, the abusive mothers used more strong, negative tactics in their efforts to control their offspring. However, the children of abusive mothers themselves displayed far more noncompliant behaviors than did children in the control group. As in the INC research, these findings underscore the value of that long-standing principle of interpersonal communication: Interaction is a reciprocal process in which the dyad is usefully viewed as system.

Summary

Designing message classification schemes is an essential undertaking. Fortunately, there are a variety of means available to help researchers accomplish this task. Efforts to classify compliance-seeking and compliance-resisting messages have proven quite useful, but influence episodes consist of more than exchanges of these two message types. Greater attention to message sequencing holds much promise for adding to our understanding. Tension exists between social and cognitive approaches, but we believe that the two approaches have the potential to complement rather than contradict one another.

MESSAGE EFFECTS

Compliance Techniques

The term *compliance technique* is intended to convey the fact that research in this area emphasizes planned and scripted methods for enhancing compliance, not spontaneous, top-of-the-head utterances. Implicitly, compliance technique research assumes a linear model of communication in which the source and target are clearly differentiated and influence flows in one direction. The source seeks to control the interaction for the purpose of producing behavior change in target, often with the aim of garnering tangible resources.

Some influence attempts are quite brief, consisting of no more than a request and a response. Others unfold in stages, with each segment of the interaction establishing the grounds for what follows. Accordingly, we partition the research literature on compliance techniques based on the degree of interaction between the message source and the target. Single-interact compliance techniques are those in which the source makes a single utterance and the target either complies or refuses. In other words, the source and the target each produce one communicative act, and together these acts constitute a single interact.

Triple-interact techniques are those in which, prior to making the request for compliance, the source utilizes some type of set-up that requires engagement on the part of the target. A total of four acts—request 1, response 1, request 2, response 2—yields three pairs of acts, or a triple interact. Compliance procedures that fall into this category are also known as sequential request techniques because they include two ordered requests. Finally, multi-interact techniques are defined as interaction sequences in which *more than two* ordered requests are planned as the means of achieving compliance.

Single-Interact Techniques

The that's-not-all technique. In the that's-not-all (TNA) sales technique, a salesperson presents a prospective buyer with a product, a price, and a request to purchase, but before the target can respond, the salesperson sweetens the deal, either by reducing the price or by adding something else of value. In the original research on this compliance technique, Burger (1986) demonstrated the superiority of TNA over a direct request in six experiments. He went on to argue that the effect might be accounted for either by a felt need for reciprocity or by perceptual contrast. Subsequent work on TNA has found that its effectiveness is probably limited to conditions in which the message recipient is processing superficially (Pollock, Smith, Knowles, & Bruce, 1998). This finding implies that TNA is unlikely to be effective in big-ticket transactions, where individuals are motivated to evaluate messages carefully, unless systematic processing can be reduced by some other means.

The lure. Joule et al. (1989) call this technique *the lure,* but another label that is equally apt is *bait-and-switch*. As both descriptors suggest, the technique is one in which the target is offered and agrees to an attractive deal. Once the decision is made, he or she is told that circumstances have changed: "We are out of that shoe in your size." Next, the target is provided with an opportunity to execute a substitute course of action, but one that lacks the advantages of the original offer: "We do stock some very similar shoes that would fit you, but they are not on sale." In the only scientific test of the technique known to us, Joule et al. report mixed evidence of the technique's effectiveness.

The disrupt-then-reframe technique. In the disrupt-then-reframe (DTR) technique, the message source momentarily confuses the target (Knowles, Butler, & Linn, 2001). The underlying logic of the approach is that individuals possess scripts for request interactions, and if a message source can mildly disrupt a target's script, the target will be rendered more vulnerable to reframing the episode in a way suggested by the message source. In one application of the DTR technique, control participants were asked, "Would you be interested in donating some money to the Richardson Center [for developmentally delayed adults]?" This request was followed immediately by a persuasive reframing: "You could make a difference!" In the DTR condition, a syntactically illegal construction of the request was produced, in which the words "money" and "some" were reversed; the researchers contend that this manipulation disrupted the interaction script. In any case, compliance went from 30% in the control group to 65% in the DTR group. A third condition, in which the words "Center" and "Richardson" were reversed in addition to "money" and "some," produced only 25% compliance. From this the researchers concluded that anything more than a very mild disruption reduces the effectiveness of the technique. Although research on the DTR technique is still in its infancy, the results of several experiments testify to the technique's efficacy in producing compliance (Knowles et al., 2001). If a more elaborated account of the underlying mechanism(s) were to be developed, it might well account for other techniques that also appear to operate through the disruption of message-processing scripts (e.g., Santos, Leve, & Pratkanis, 1994).

The even-a-penny technique. It seems self-evident that likelihood of compliance should be an inverse function of the size of the request. This presents a decision point for the compliance agent: Can one best maximize resource acquisition by gathering many small donations or by obtaining a few larger ones? Cialdini and Schroeder (1976; see also Weyant, 1984) suggest that one can avoid the apparent dilemma by legitimating small contributions. By adding the phrase "Even a penny will help" to their standard door-to-door solicitation, they were able to increase the frequency of contributions without affecting the size of donations. Subsequent research has generally indicated that the technique is superior to direct request (e.g., Fraser, Hite, & Sauer, 1988; Reingen, 1978; but see Fraser & Hite, 1989; Perrine & Heather, 2000). There is some evidence that face-to-face contact is needed, and that the appeal must seek on-the-spot, rather than delayed, compliance (Brockner, Guzzi, Kane, Levine, & Shaplen, 1984; Reeves, Macolini, & Martin, 1987; Reeves & Saucer, 1993; Weyant & Smith, 1987). The account given for this latter result—and, indeed, for the technique itself—is referred to as the *image-maintenance explanation.* It proposes simply that the desire to avoid appearing stingy or cheap is sufficient to motivate compliance. Once the requester can no longer observe the target's behavior, the target has no motivation to acquiesce (as was found in studies that attempted, and failed, to induce delayed compliance).

Triple-Interact Techniques

Pregiving. Throughout the history of humankind, every society has embraced a norm of reciprocity (Gouldner, 1960). This norm directs individuals to return in kind the actions, objects, and, to a lesser extent, affections that are provided to them by others: tit for tat, an eye for an eye. Application of the reciprocity principle is apparent in the marketing efforts of charitable organizations that send small, unsolicited gifts such as calendars and address labels along with their appeals for funds. These are examples of a strategy dubbed *pregiving* (Bell, Cholerton, Davison, Fraczek, & Lauter, 1996; Bell, Cholerton, Fraczek, Rohlfs, & Smith, 1994). One necessary condition for the effective implementation of pregiving is that the message recipient actually accept the initial offering. Without the indebtedness created by acceptance, a recipient would have no need to reciprocate. Conversely, if the gift is too large, the recipient may balk at accepting it, presumably because he or she would become indebted past the point of comfort (Bell et al., 1994).

A second variable that moderates the effectiveness of the pregiving technique is whether or not the target believes that the influencing agent will learn of his or her compliance (Whately, Webster, Smith, & Rhodes, 1999). That individuals apparently feel compelled to discharge the debt even when the pregivers will not know of their actions points toward an internalized norm of reciprocity. But compliance is further enhanced when the target expects that the source will learn of his or her compliance. This latter finding implies the operation of social concerns that extend beyond an internalized norm.

Research reported by Boster, Rodriguez, Cruz, and Marshall (1995) suggests a third moderator variable. In an experiment in which they varied the intimacy of the source-recipient relationship, these researchers found that pregiving produced more compliance than a direct request only when the influencing agent and recipient were strangers. In fact, one of the defining features of friendship is that reciprocity takes place in an extended time frame (Hatfield, Utne, & Traupmann, 1979; Rusbult & Buunk, 1993; Van Lange & Rusbult, 1996). If a source uses pregiving and also indicates a desire for immediate reciprocity, he or she signals that the relationship is *not* one of friendship. Conversely, there is evidence that pregiving produces liking (Whately et al., 1999).

Relational obligations. Whereas pregiving may be a means of establishing a relationship, compliance rates may be enhanced when message sources remind targets of an existing relationship between them, even when the two interactants are previously unknown to one another. Using a sample of college students, Aune and Basil (1994) report a fivefold increase in compliance relative to a single-request control group when the request was preceded by this interact: "Hi! Are you a student here at _____ ? Oh, that's great, so am I." In line with Roloff's (1987) thinking on relational obligations, the authors speculate that calling explicit attention to the role relationship is sufficient to stimulate a sense of obligation in the message target. A sense of group membership probably also contributes to the efficacy of this technique (Pratkanis & Aronson, 2000, chap. 25) as well as the attraction generated by a perception of similarity (Burger, Soroka, Gonzago, Murphy, & Somervell, 2001).

The door-in-the-face technique. The door-in-the-face (DITF) technique begins with a request large enough that it will be rejected by most individuals. That initial appeal is then followed by a smaller, but still substantial, request (Cialdini et al., 1975). Early efforts to explain the DITF effect posited a reciprocal concessions corollary to the general principle of reciprocity: "You should make concessions to those who make concessions to you" (Cialdini et al., 1975, p. 206). Although that view has been criticized as vague and incompatible with the research findings (e.g., O'Keefe, 1999; Tusing & Dillard, 2000), it retains many adherents (Cialdini, 1985; Hale & Laliker, 1999). One alternative account of the effect is the *perceptual contrast* explanation, which holds that large requests cause the target to perceive the request as less costly, thereby making compliance more likely (Abrahams & Bell, 1994; Cantrill & Seibold, 1986). The *self-presentation* perspective contends that when targets reject the first request, they become concerned that they will be evaluated negatively by the requesters. Complying with the second request allows targets to alleviate this concern (Bell, Abrahams, Clark, & Schlatter, 1996; Pendleton & Batson, 1979). The *availability hypothesis* asserts that a concession on the part of the requester is recorded as favorable information in working memory, subsequently informing the receiver to comply with the second request (Tybout, Sternthal, & Calder, 1983).

However, the data have not been kind to any of these alternatives; none is currently seen to be a viable explanation of the DITF effect (Cantrill & Seibold, 1986; Dillard, Hunter, & Burgoon, 1984; Fern, Monroe, & Avila, 1986; O'Keefe & Hale, 1998).

O'Keefe and Figge (1997) offer a *guilt-based explanation* of the DITF effect. They suggest that guilt arises from the juxtaposition of the moral or social standard (made salient by the first request) and the target's awareness that he or she has failed to behave in accordance with that standard by virtue of refusing the first request. Although this explanation is seemingly consistent with previous data, direct measures of guilt have not supported the notion that felt guilt mediates compliance (deTurck & Derme, 1999; O'Keefe & Figge, 1999). There is some preliminary evidence that *anticipated* guilt may instead function in that role (O'Keefe & Figge, 1999), but more research is needed to establish the veracity of this position.

Amid all of the theoretical controversy, one issue remains clear: The DITF technique *does* enhance compliance. Ceteris paribus, it increases compliance 10-15% over a single-message control group. Five well-identified scope conditions govern the potency of the DITF effect (Dillard et al., 1984; Fern et al., 1986; O'Keefe & Hale, 1998). Specifically, the two requests must be delivered (a) close together in time (b) in a face-to-face interaction (c) by the same requester and (d) on behalf of the same (e) prosocial beneficiary. When any of these elements is absent, the efficacy of the technique is diminished and may even be reversed.

The foot-in-the-door technique. The foot-in-the-door (FITD) technique begins with a small request to which almost anyone would be likely to acquiesce (e.g., "Would you mind displaying a small sign in the window of your home that reads 'Be a safe driver'?"). This is followed by a second request that is not so innocuous. In the initial investigation of the FITD effect, the second request asked study participants if they would be willing to have an imposing billboard erected in their front yard for a period of one week (Freedman & Fraser, 1966). Those who had previously committed to the first request complied at a rate twice that of those who had not been exposed to the initial request. Although subsequent work has shown the effect in the original study to be unusually large, there is little doubt as to the efficacy of the technique as a means of enhancing compliance (Burger, 1999; Dillard et al., 1984; Fern et al., 1986).

The most commonly invoked explanation for the FITD effect is self-perception theory (Bem, 1972) or some variant thereof (Dillard, 1990b; but see Gorassini & Olson, 1995; Guadagno, Asher, Demaine, & Cialdini, 2001). The essential premise of the theory is that individuals infer their attitudes from their actions. Although self-perception theory is silent concerning what might prompt compliance with the FITD initial request, it straightforwardly suggests that the target infers the existence of a favorable attitude from compliance that, in turn, serves as a guide to action upon presentation of the second request. From that general premise it is possible to deduce several factors that should increase the potency of the technique: (a) actually performing the initial request (rather than simply agreeing to do so), (b) labeling the target as helpful or supportive of the cause, (c) requiring more than a minimal amount of effort to enact the initial request, and (d) making the second request topically similar to the first. In fact, Burger (1999) presents meta-analytic evidence supportive of each of these hypotheses. However, direct evidence of a change in self-perception has proven elusive (Rittle, 1981; Scott, 1977). Whereas Dillard (1990b) found evidence consistent with a self-inference process in a between-subjects design, Gorassini and Olson (1995) did not find support for self-concept as a mediator in their within-subjects investigation.

The low-ball technique. Development of the low-ball technique is generally attributed to automobile dealerships (Carlson, 1973). In the first step of the sequence, the salesperson offers to sell the target a car at an unexpectedly low price. After securing a commitment to purchase from the target, the salesperson leaves the target, ostensibly to clear the transaction with management. When the salesperson returns, he or she tells the target that management has rejected the deal because the dealership would lose money at that price. Thus the salesperson can only offer to sell the car at a new, higher price. In addition to this technique's apparent effectiveness for selling cars, systematic evidence has been found for its potency in other contexts (Cialdini, Cacioppo, Bassett, & Miller, 1978). However, the effectiveness of the low-ball technique may be limited to circumstances in which the same person makes both the first and the second requests (Burger & Petty, 1981). Some research suggests that the low-ball technique is likely to produce higher rates of compliance than the FITD technique (Brownstein & Katzev, 1985; Hornik, Zaig, & Shadmon, 1991; Joule, 1987), but lower rates than the DITF technique (Wang, Brownstein, & Katzev, 1989; but see Brownstein & Katzev, 1985). The relative paucity of comparative data suggests that such conclusions should be drawn cautiously.

The foot-in-the-mouth technique. The foot-in-the-mouth (FITM) technique involves the requester's asking the target how he or she feels prior to making a request. Howard (1990) found that this technique resulted in heightened effectiveness relative to a single-request control group (see also Fointiat, 2000). He reasons that when an individual publicly claims to feel good—as the majority of individuals do when asked this common question—he or she experiences internal pressure to behave consistently with that statement, and that pressure results in enhanced compliance. Although there may be merit to this argument,

Howard's data show declining compliance rates when targets are grouped according to the favorability of their responses (e.g., "I feel good" versus "I'm fine" versus "I'm making it"). This pattern suggests that mood state may be responsible for variations in compliance, and that these statements are simply accurate self-reports of those moods (see Bless & Schwarz, 1999). If true, this would either undermine the commitment account or point toward the need for a multiple-process understanding of the FITM effect. Howard suggests that the FITM technique's effectiveness, like that of the DITF technique, is limited to prosocial requesters.

A Multi-interact Compliance Technique

One relatively new technique, called the *high-probability* (or *high-p*) *procedure* (Mace et al., 1988), bears some superficial resemblance to the FITD technique, but rather than using a single initial request, the high-p procedure calls for the source to pose *a series* of questions, each one of which is likely to produce compliance. These high-probability requests are followed by the target appeal, which is, relatively speaking, a low-probability request. Although no one, to our knowledge, has undertaken a quantitative synthesis of this literature, a substantial number of individual investigations have indicated that the procedure does reliably increase compliance (e.g., Davis, Brady, Williams, & Hamilton, 1992; Harchik & Putzier, 1990; Kennedy, Itkonen, & Lindquist, 1995; Mace et al., 1988; Sanchez-Fort, Brady, & Davis, 1996).

Despite similarities in appearance and effectiveness between the high-p procedure and the FITD technique, research on the high-p procedure is notably different from FITD inquiry in four main respects. First, whereas the FITD effect has been examined in the general population, most high-p research has targeted special populations, such as toddlers (McComas, Wacker, & Cooper, 1998), second-grade children (Ardoin, Martens, & Wolfe, 1999), emotionally disordered children (Davis & Reichle, 1996), developmentally disabled children (Ducharme & Worling, 1994), and mentally retarded adolescents (Mace, Mauro, Boyajian, & Eckert, 1997). The difference in target populations is a manifestation of the distinct aims of the researchers. As such, it directs our attention to a second point of contrast between the two research endeavors. FITD researchers are essentially concerned with one-episode interactions designed to benefit the requesters. High-p researchers, in contrast, study how to use longer-term behavior-shaping methods to prevent self-injurious behavior or promote socially appropriate action. Low-probability behaviors that clinical researchers wish to change to high-probability behaviors include sharing (e.g., "Hand [peer] a soda") and cooperation (e.g., "Help build the city with [peer]") (Davis & Reichle, 1996, p. 474). This goal has ramifications for research design and highlights a third way in which high-probability research is distinct from FITD research. In contrast to the large-sample, between-subjects FITD work, high-p research typically utilizes within-subject designs on a very small number of subjects, sometimes as few as one (e.g., McComas et al., 1998).

A final difference, which extends beyond population, research goals, and design, concerns conceptual explanations for the two techniques. Whereas scholars typically reference consistency or commitment when called upon to explain the FITD effect, researchers account for the high-p procedure in terms of reinforcement principles. Expanding on this tradition, Nevin's (1996) behavioral momentum metaphor equates rate of responding with velocity and resistance to extinction with mass. Although the metaphor is not without its critics (Houlihan & Brandon, 1996), it has provided the basis for much research into conditions that moderate the effect. In particular, the effectiveness of the high-probability procedure for increasing the frequency of

low-probability behaviors is enhanced by (a) shorter intervals between the first series of requests (Mace et al., 1988), (b) the use of "do" (versus "don't") requests (Ducharme & Worling, 1994), (c) the use of a variant sequence rather than an invariant sequence (Davis & Reichle, 1996), (d) a greater number of high-probability requests (Eckert, Boyajian, & Mace, 1995, as cited in Mace, 1996), and (e) the use of "higher-quality reinforcers" (e.g., food is more effective than praise when used to reinforce high-probability behaviors) (Mace et al., 1997).

Reflections on Compliance Technique Research

If one marks the beginning of technique research with Freedman and Fraser's (1966) classic foot-in-the-door study, it is easy to discern prolific growth in this research area since that time. Not only have a number of new techniques been developed (e.g., relational obligations, the disrupt-then-reframe technique), but our understanding of procedures developed earlier has deepened considerably (e.g., regarding the foot-in-the-door and door-in-the-face techniques), especially with regard to the scope conditions of their effectiveness.

Among the many moderator variables that variously limit the domains of effectiveness of the compliance techniques, two in particular stand out. First, because of the typical trade-off between request size and compliance, magnitude of the request is clearly important from the applied standpoint. But it also figures importantly into basic theory, in that it has long been viewed as a determinant of depth of message processing (Langer, Blank, & Chanowitz, 1978) and of message production (Brown & Levinson, 1987). For persons interested in questions of resource acquisition, magnitude of request is an inescapably important aspect of any compliance scenario. Second, the prosocialness of the requester serves as a side condition to some techniques (e.g., the even-a-penny and door-in-the-face techniques), although apparently not to others (e.g., the lure, pregiving). However, reasonable people may disagree as to what is for the good of society and what is not. For instance, a person's general attitudes toward ecology and business may determine whether he or she sees a pro-environment group as a positive influence on the world or a hindrance to the economy. As a consequence, our understanding of compliance techniques might gain greater theoretical precision if the social-level concept of pro*social*, which assumes agreement among message targets, were replaced with the psychological-level notion of pro*attitudinal*, which does not (Dillard & Hale, 1992; see also Millar, 2001).

The most significant development in the study of compliance techniques is surely the growing appreciation of the value of multiprocess accounts. The work of Bell and his colleagues is seminal in that those researchers attended to the multiple simultaneous processes that may be required to explain the DITF effect (Abrahams & Bell, 1994; Bell, Abrahams, et al., 1996). On the basis of his meta-analytic work, Burger (1999) advances an important conclusion regarding the FITD effect that echoes Bell's point: A single-process explanation of the FITD effect is inadequate because multiple processes determine the effectiveness of the technique. In fact, it is likely that this conclusion can be drawn with regard to all compliance techniques. Although planned and scripted by sources, interactions employing such techniques are conversations from the perspective of targets. As a consequence, they are subject to the same complex set of considerations that govern all interactions: Gricean maxims, politeness, reactance, impression management, and so on. Research that appreciates the potential for multiple social and psychological processes, operating in parallel, would be especially valuable for illuminating the bases and limitations of the compliance techniques.

Other Issues in Message Effects

Affect

Moderator effects. Moods and emotions that exist prior to the utterance of a suasive appeal and have no logical linkage to that appeal have been called *message-irrelevant affects* (Dillard & Meijnders, 2002; Dillard & Wilson, 1993). There is good evidence that such feelings can substantially alter the likelihood of compliance with a request. For example, preexisting sadness shows a positive correlation with compliance to helping requests, presumably because providing assistance provides relief from that dysphoria (Cialdini & Fultz, 1990). Similarly, when individuals are made to feel guilty and then are asked to comply, they do so more frequently than persons who are not experiencing guilt (O'Keefe, 2000). Although these are general effects, recent research suggests that the influence of affect on compliance may be moderated by message type. Boster et al. (1999) contend that message sources can enhance compliance by using messages that make salient the link between compliance and the reduction of negative affect. Indeed, the literature on persuasion and message-irrelevant affect suggests that individuals in good and bad moods consume or reject messages differentially if those messages have the potential to alter their moods (Wegener & Petty, 1996).

Affect as an outcome. Research designed to explore the relationships among emotion, cognition, and the dimensions of influence messages suggests several possible conclusions. For one, perceived dominance is associated with the arousal of negative emotions, including surprise, anger, and annoyance, especially when the message is highly explicit (Dillard & Harkness, 1992; Dillard & Kinney, 1994). These feelings apparently follow from the perception that the source has created an illegitimate and negatively valenced obstacle that will require effort to overcome (Dillard et al., 1996).

But the effects of explicitness are more variable. When dominance is controlled, highly explicit speech seems to signal relational closeness and generates correspondingly positive emotional responses (Dillard et al., 1996).

On the Concept of Compliance

The vast majority of the research reviewed in this chapter has tended to treat compliance as a dichotomous variable that can be observed in the conversational turn immediately following the target request. Although this operationalization has proven suitable to a multitude of studies, even a moment's reflection reveals that it represents an overly simple view of social influence. For example, research in the medical realm suggests that noncompliance is a multifaceted concept that can manifest itself in a variety of ways: "(1) failure to fill the prescription; (2) filling the prescription, but failing to take the medication; (3) taking only a portion of the medication; and (4) not following the frequency or dose instructions of the prescription" (Buckalew & Sallis, 1986, p. 49). Further, applied communication research shows us that compliance with a "do" request may be fundamentally different from compliance with a "don't" request (Adelinis & Hagopian, 1999). Perhaps this is because "do" requests are processed by the approach system, whereas "don't" requests are processed by the inhibition system (Gray, 1990). A greater emphasis on compliance as a complex construct would point the way to richer theoretical accounts of interpersonal influence. The two examples used here only highlight some of the numerous ways in which compliance research might be extended.

The Impact of Compliance Seeking on the Message Source

Standing in contrast to the large and active body of research on compliance techniques is a smaller and more diffuse literature on the effects of compliance seeking on the message source. It offers an interesting complement to the technique research. In this vein, Smith, Limon, Gallo, and Ngu (1996) demonstrate that effortful attempts to influence others, especially dominant-hostile attempts, yield increases in blood pressure and heart rate that may contribute to cardiovascular disease (see also Smith, Baldwin, & Christensen, 1990). Furthermore, message sources experience clear sets of emotional responses subsequent to interactions that are shaped by the outcomes (Segrin & Dillard, 1991): They react to success with feelings of competence and gratitude, and to failure with anger and guilt. This latter result is exacerbated among persons who are dysphoric (i.e., mildly depressed) prior to the influence attempt.

Finally, Kipnis and his colleagues have shed light on the long-term effects of powerful messages. In matching field investigations of conjugal dyads and employer-employee dyads, they found that high-power persons who used controlling strategies devalued the message targets and increased psychological distance from them (Kipnis, Castell, Gergen, & Mauch, 1976). An experimental study that assigned participants to different leadership styles (i.e., democratic versus authoritarian) verified the causal relationship between source behavior and evaluation of the other (Kipnis, Schmidt, Price, & Stitt, 1981). Similarly, O'Neal, Kipnis, and Craig (1994) found that individuals who were trained to use the DITF or the FITD technique to gain compliance judged their targets as less cognitively competent than targets who complied with a rational appeal. On the whole, this research reminds us that influence affects both interactants and points to the value of examining a variety of outcomes for each of them.

Summary

Much of the research we have reviewed above in the sections on preinteraction and action-interaction considered relatively spontaneous influence messages between persons in close relationships. In contrast, the research we have examined in this section on message effects sought to illuminate scripted sequences that took place, typically, between relative strangers. This general area of research (i.e., the compliance tradition) has grown slowly and steadily over the years by maintaining a focus on resource acquisition in this particular relational context. It could be broadened by a more complex definition of compliance and by the more explicit incorporation of affect into its theorizing.

GENERAL SUMMARY AND CONCLUSIONS

Since the beginning of the 20th century, many deep theoretical currents have moved through interpersonal influence research. Each one has invigorated the area by casting the fundamental question—How do individuals alter and maintain the actions of others?—in some new light. Many of the compliance studies demonstrate that apparently trivial language choices can produce surprising effects on behavior. The message production models flow in the opposite direction, focusing attention on how individuals prepare and enact strings of words. Social perspectives and interaction researchers insist on pairing production and effect in order to examine the interplay between the two. Across these traditions, certain changes, issues, and tensions are evident.

One ongoing change in the interpersonal influence literature is a trend toward increasingly complex conceptions of the human actor. For example, during the heyday of subjective expected utility models, individuals were seen as economically oriented toward maximizing rewards and minimizing punishments. Work in a more recent vein (that is, constructivism) has viewed individuals as having only one important feature: the ability to take the perspectives of others. In contrast

to both of these earlier positions, current models of message production, with their emphasis on multiple goals, highlight the many distinct aims that interlocutors attempt to achieve in interaction. Coming to this realization somewhat more recently and a great deal less uniformly, researchers in the compliance tradition are now beginning to recognize the need for multiple-process accounts of message effects. Surely, this trend toward a more complex image of communicators is desirable. Although Mr. Occam and his razor always stand ready to eliminate undue complexity, surely even he recognizes that our theories should be no *less* complex than the phenomena that we seek to understand.

Concern with explication and classification is another hallmark of the interpersonal influence research enterprise. This issue manifested itself clearly and vigorously in message production research during the methodology wars. But, as we have emphasized, the question is of such a fundamental nature that every research endeavor must resolve it regardless of its place in the history of interpersonal influence. And students of message production are currently armed with a variety of rigorous options for developing new message classification schemes. Concern with identifying and classifying sequences of talk arouses the interest of interaction-oriented scholars, and it certainly contributes to a clearer picture of interpersonal influence. Apart from Cialdini's (1987) compliance principles, the matter of how to classify compliance techniques has not been examined in any systematic way, nor has a thorough explication of compliance itself appeared in the literature. In our view, both issues merit attention.

In a variety of forms in the preceding pages, we have seen the classic tension between the desire for general theory and the belief that actions can be understood only in the context of the circumstances in which they occur. The difficulties of constructing general theory have sometimes led to open-ended models that wave their hands at context without ever specifying its nature or components. In contrast, some research is so highly contextualized that it serves to illustrate what *can* occur, but ultimately speaks to very small audiences. Yet socially significant problems often constitute contexts. Research conducted in their confines has the potential to raise the visibility of the field as well as contribute to theory. In our view, the strain between the need for general statements and the desire for contextualized knowledge is an enduring tension that provides the basis for enlightening dialogue between the two views. Because it stimulates research on interpersonal influence, it is valuable.

The nature of interpersonal relationships, broadly construed, and their place in our understanding of influence remains a topic of the utmost importance. Near the beginning of this chapter, we presented data that addressed the question of who attempts to influence whom. The response was that influence most frequently takes place in close relationships. Of course, this is not an argument for studying only close relationships, and it is most assuredly not an effort to conflate frequency with importance. But it should serve to remind researchers that interpersonal influence is not an area unto itself. Rather, it is part of a broader project that targets interpersonal interaction more generally. Accordingly, it is imperative that we locate questions of influence in a framework that attends to relational status and, particularly, relational development. Doing so promises to lead us to some insight into the forms and functions by which individuals accomplish the most essential of all activities: changing and maintaining the behavior of others.

NOTE

1. Roskos-Ewoldsen (1997) has reported results that seem somewhat at odds with previous work. Although one dimension, *acceptability*, resembles dominance-submissiveness or social appropriateness (compare metagoals), the other dimension

appears unique in the literature. It contrasts *association-oriented* strategies (e.g., "Refer to friends") with *message-oriented* strategies (e.g., "Detailed arguments"). These findings may result from the inclusion of stimuli that do not appear in the earlier studies (e.g., "Use statistics," "Lots of examples") or from the higher level of abstraction of the stimuli. Regarding the latter point, whereas previous investigations used utterances that varied in explicitness, Roskos-Ewoldsen's project employed stimuli such as "Be vague" and "Straightforward even if offend."

REFERENCES

Abrahams, M. F., & Bell, R. A. (1994). Encouraging charitable contributions: An examination of three models of the door-in-the-face compliance. *Communication Research, 21,* 131-153.

Adelinis, J. D., & Hagopian, L. P. (1999). The use of symmetrical "do" and "don't" requests to interrupt ongoing activities. *Journal of Applied Behavior Analysis, 32,* 519-523.

Alderfer, C. (1972). *Existence, relatedness, growth: Human needs in organizational settings.* New York: Free Press.

Applegate, J. L., Burke, J. A., Burleson, B. R., Delia, J. G., & Kline, S. L. (1985). Reflection-enhancing parental communication. In I. E. Sigel (Ed.), *Parental belief systems: The psychological consequences for children* (pp. 107-142). Hillsdale, NJ: Lawrence Erlbaum.

Ardoin, S. P., Martens, B. K., & Wolfe, L. A. (1999). Using high-probability instruction sequences with fading to increase student compliance during transitions. *Journal of Applied Behavior Analysis, 32,* 339-351.

Aronsson, K., & Sätterlund-Larsson, U. (1987). Politeness strategies and doctor-patient communication: On the social choreography of collaborative thinking. *Journal of Language and Social Psychology, 6,* 1-27.

Aune, R. K., & Basil, M. D. (1994). A relational obligations approach to the foot-in-the-mouth effect. *Journal of Applied Social Psychology, 24,* 546-556.

Austin, J. T., & Vancouver, J. B. (1996). Goal constructs in psychology: Structure, process, and content. *Psychological Bulletin, 120,* 338-375.

Babrow, A. S. (2001). Uncertainty, value, communication, and problematic integration. *Journal of Communication, 51*, 553-573.

Baesler, E. J. (1995, May). *Mapping and assessing the influence of interpersonal compliance-gaining attempts in everyday life.* Poster session presented at the annual meeting of the International Network on Personal Relationships, Williamsburg, VA.

Battaglia, D. M., Richard, F. D., Datteri, D. L., & Lord, C. G. (1998). Breaking up is (relatively) easy to do: A script for the dissolution of close relationships. *Journal of Social and Personal Relationships, 15*, 829-845.

Baxter, L. A. (1984a). An investigation of compliance-gaining as politeness. *Human Communication Research, 10*, 427-456.

Baxter, L. A. (1984b). Trajectories of relationship disengagement. *Journal of Social and Personal Relationships, 1*, 29-48.

Beatty, M. J. (1987). Erroneous assumptions underlying Burleson's critique. *Communication Quarterly, 35*, 329-333.

Becker, J. A., Kimmel, H. D., & Bevill, M. J. (1989). The interactive effects of request form and speaker status on judgments of requests. *Journal of Psycholinguistic Research, 18*, 521-531.

Bell, R. A., Abrahams, M. F., Clark, C L., & Schlatter, C. (1996). The door-in-the-face compliance strategy: An individual difference analysis of two models in an AIDS fundraising context. *Communication Quarterly, 44*, 107-124.

Bell, R. A., Cholerton, M., Davison, V., Fraczek, K. E., & Lauter, H. (1996). Making health communication self-funding: Effectiveness of pregiving in an AIDS fundraising/education campaign. *Health Communication, 8*, 331-352.

Bell, R. A., Cholerton, M., Fraczek, K. E., Rohlfs, G. S., & Smith, B. A. (1994). Encouraging donations to charity: A field study of competing and complementary factors in tactic sequencing. *Western Journal of Communication, 58*, 98-115.

Bem, D. J. (1972). Constructing cross-situational consistencies in behavior: Some thoughts on Alker's critique of Mischel. *Journal of Personality, 40*, 17-26.

Berger, C. R. (1985). Social power and communication. In M. L. Knapp & G. R. Miller (Eds.), *Handbook of interpersonal communication* (pp. 439-499). Beverly Hills, CA: Sage.

Berger, C. R. (1997). *Planning strategic interaction: Attaining goals through communicative action.* Mahwah, NJ: Lawrence Erlbaum.

Berger, C. R., & Kellermann, K. (1983). To ask or not to ask: Is that a question? In R. N. Bostrom (Ed.), *Communication yearbook 7* (pp. 342-368). Beverly Hills, CA: Sage.

Bisanz, G. L., & Rule, B. G. (1990). Children's and adults' comprehension of narratives about persuasion. In M. J. Cody & M. L. McLaughlin (Ed.), *The psychology of tactical communication* (pp. 48-69). Clevedon, Eng.: Multilingual Matters.

Bless, H., & Schwarz, N. (1999). Sufficient and necessary conditions in dual-process models: The case of mood and information processing. In S. Chaiken & Y. Trope (Eds.), *Dual-process theories in social psychology* (pp. 423-440). New York: Guilford.

Blum-Kulka, S. (1987). Indirectness and politeness in requests: Same or different? *Journal of Pragmatics, 11*, 131-146.

Boster, F. J. (1988). Comments on the utility of compliance-gaining message selection tasks. *Human Communication Research, 15*, 169-177.

Boster, F. J. (1990). An examination of the state of compliance-gaining message behavior research. In J. P. Dillard (Ed.), *Seeking compliance: The production of interpersonal influence messages* (pp. 7-17). Scottsdale, AZ: Gorsuch Scarisbrick.

Boster, F. J. (1995). Commentary on compliance-gaining message behavior research. In C. R. Berger & M. Burgoon (Eds.), *Communication and social influence processes* (pp. 91-113). East Lansing: Michigan State University Press.

Boster, F. J., Mitchell, M. M., Lapinski, M. K., Cooper, H., Orrego, V. O., & Reinke, R. (1999). The impact of guilt and type of compliance-gaining message on compliance. *Communication Monographs, 66*, 168-177.

Boster, F. J., Rodriguez, J. I., Cruz, M. G., & Marshall, L. (1995). The relative effectiveness of a pre-giving message on friends and strangers. *Communication Research, 22*, 475-484.

Boster, F. J., & Stiff, J. B. (1984). Compliance-gaining message selection behavior. *Human Communication Research, 10*, 539-556.

Boster, F. J., Stiff, J. B., & Reynolds, R. A. (1985). Do persons respond differently to inductively-derived and deductively-derived lists of compliance-gaining message strategies? A reply to Wiseman and Schenck-Hamlin. *Western Journal of Speech Communication, 49,* 177-187.

Brockner, J., Guzzi, B., Kane, J., Levine, E., & Shaplen, K. (1984). Organizational fundraising: Further evidence on the effects of legitimizing small donations. *Journal of Consumer Research, 11,* 611-614.

Brown, P., & Levinson, S. C. (1978). Universals in language use: Politeness phenomena. In E. N. Goody (Ed.), *Questions and politeness: Strategies in social interaction* (pp. 56-289). London: Cambridge University Press.

Brown, P., & Levinson, S. C. (1987). *Politeness: Some universals in language usage.* Cambridge: Cambridge University Press.

Brownstein, R., & Katzev, R. (1985). The relative effectiveness of three compliance techniques in eliciting donations to a cultural organization. *Journal of Applied Social Psychology, 15,* 564-574.

Buckalew, L. W., & Sallis, R. E. (1986). Patient compliance and medication perception. *Journal of Clinical Psychology, 42,* 49-53.

Burger, J. M. (1986). Increasing compliance by improving the deal: The that's-not-all technique. *Journal of Personality and Social Psychology, 51,* 277-283.

Burger, J. M. (1999). The foot-in-the-door compliance procedure: A multiple process analysis. *Personality and Social Psychology Review, 3,* 303-325.

Burger, J. M., & Petty, R. E. (1981). The low-ball compliance technique: Task or person commitment? *Journal of Personality and Social Psychology, 40,* 492-500.

Burger, J. M., Soroka, S., Gonzago, K., Murphy, E., & Somervell, E. (2001). The effect of fleeting attraction on compliance to requests. *Personality and Social Psychology Bulletin, 27,* 1578-1586.

Burgoon, M. (1994). Paths II: The garden variety. *Communication Theory, 4,* 81-92.

Burke, J. A., & Clark, R. A. (1982). An assessment of methodological options for investigating the development of persuasive communication skills across childhood. *Central States Speech Journal, 33,* 437-445.

Burleson, B. R., Wilson, S. R., Waltman, M. S., Goering, E. M., Ely, T. K., & Whaley, B. B. (1986, November). *Item desirability effects in compliance-gaining research: Seven empirical studies showing why the checklist methodology produces garbage.* Paper presented at the annual meeting of the Speech Communication Association, Chicago.

Burleson, B. R., Wilson, S. R., Waltman, M. S., Goering, E. M., Ely, T. K., & Whaley, B. B. (1988). Item desirability effects in compliance-gaining research: Seven studies documenting artifacts in the strategy selection procedure. *Human Communication Research, 14,* 429-486.

Bylund, C. L. (2000, November). *Physicians' and new patients' talk about health risk behaviors: Form, forcefulness, and face.* Paper presented at the annual meeting of the National Communication Association, Seattle, WA.

Cantrill, J. G., & Seibold, D. R. (1986). The perceptual contrast explanation of sequential request strategy effectiveness. *Human Communication Research, 13,* 253-267.

Carlsmith, J. M., & Gross, A. E. (1969). Some effects of guilt on compliance. *Journal of Personality and Social Psychology, 11,* 232-239.

Carlson, M. D. (1973). *How to get your car repaired without getting gypped.* New York: Harrow.

Cialdini, R. B. (1984). *Influence: How and why people agree to things.* New York: Morrow.

Cialdini, R. B. (1985). *Influence: Science and practice.* Glenview, IL: Scott, Foresman.

Cialdini, R. B. (1987). Compliance principles of compliance professionals: Psychologists of necessity. In M. P. Zanna, J. M. Olson, & C. P. Herman (Eds.), *The Ontario Symposium: Vol. 5. Social influence* (pp. 165-184). Hillsdale, NJ: Lawrence Erlbaum.

Cialdini, R. B., Cacioppo, J. T., Bassett, R., & Miller, J. A. (1978). Low-ball procedure for producing compliance: Commitment then cost. *Journal of Personality and Social Psychology, 36,* 463-476.

Cialdini, R. B., & Fultz, J. (1990). Interpreting the negative mood-helping literature via "mega" analysis: A contrary view. *Psychological Bulletin, 107,* 210-214.

Cialdini, R. B., & Schroeder, D. A. (1976). Increasing compliance by legitimizing paltry contributions: When even a penny helps. *Journal of Personality and Social Psychology, 34,* 599-604.

Cialdini, R. B., Vincent, J. E., Lewis, S. K., Catalan, J., Wheeler, D., & Darby, B. L. (1975). Reciprocal concessions procedure for inducing compliance: The door-in-the-face technique. *Journal of Personality and Social Psychology, 31,* 206-215.

Cialdini, R. B., Wosinska, W., Barrett, D. W., Butner, J., & Gornik-Durose, M. (1999). Compliance with a request in two cultures: The differential influence of social proof and commitment/consistency on collectivists and individualists. *Personality and Social Psychology Bulletin, 25,* 1242-1253.

Clark, C., Drew, P., & Pinch, T. (1994). Managing customer "objections" during real-life sales negotiations. *Discourse and Society, 5,* 437-462.

Clark, C., & Pinch, T. (1992). The anatomy of a deception: Fraud and finesse in the mock auction sales "con." *Qualitative Sociology, 15,* 151-175.

Clark, R. A., & Delia, J. G. (1977). Cognitive complexity, social perspective-taking, and functional persuasion skills in second- to ninth-grade children. *Human Communication Research, 3,* 128-134.

Cody, M. J., Canary, D. J., & Smith, S. W. (1994). Compliance-gaining goals: An inductive analysis of actors' and goal types, strategies, and successes. In J. A. Daly & J. M. Wiemann (Eds.), *Strategic interpersonal communication* (pp. 33-90). Hillsdale, NJ: Lawrence Erlbaum.

Cody, M. J., Greene, J. O., Marston, P. J., O'Hair, H. D., Baaske, K. T., & Schneider, M. J. (1986). Situation perception and message strategy selection. In M. L. McLaughlin (Ed.), *Communication yearbook 9* (pp. 390-420). Beverly Hills, CA: Sage.

Cody, M. J., & McLaughlin, M. L. (1980). Perceptions of compliance gaining situations: A dimensional analysis. *Communication Monographs, 47,* 132-148.

Cody, M. J., & McLaughlin, M. L. (1985). Models for the sequential construction of accounting episodes: Situational and inter-actional constraints on message selection and evaluation. In R. L. Street, Jr., & J. N. Cappella (Eds.), *Sequence and pattern in communicative behaviour* (pp. 50-69). London: Edward Arnold.

Cody, M. J., McLaughlin, M. L., & Jordan, W. J. (1980). A multi-dimensional scaling of three sets of compliance-gaining strategies. *Communication Quarterly, 28,* 34-46.

Cody, M. J., Woelfel, M. L., & Jordan, W. J. (1983). Dimensions of compliance-gaining situations. *Human Communication Research, 9,* 99-113.

Collins, B. E., & Raven, B. H. (1969). Group structure: Attraction, coalitions, communication, and power. In G. Lindzey & E. Aronson (Eds.), *Handbook of social psychology* (Vol. 4, pp. 102-204). Reading, MA: Addison-Wesley.

Coupland, N., Grainger, K., & Coupland, J. (1988). Politeness in context: Intergenerational issues. *Language and Society, 17,* 253-262.

Craig, R. T. (1986). Goals in discourse. In D. G. Ellis & W. A. Donohue (Eds.), *Contemporary issues in language and discourse processes* (pp. 257-273). Hillsdale, NJ: Lawrence Erlbaum.

Craig, R. T., Tracy, K., & Spisak, F. (1986). The discourse of requests: Assessment of a politeness approach. *Human Communication Research, 9,* 99-113.

Crockett, W. H. (1965). Cognitive complexity and impression formation. In B. A. Maher (Ed.), *Progress in experimental personality research* (Vol. 2, pp. 47-90). New York: Academic Press.

Dallinger, J. M., & Hample, D. (1994). The effects of gender on compliance-gaining strategy endorsement and suppression. *Communication Reports, 7,* 43-49.

Davis, C. A., Brady, M., Williams, R., & Hamilton, R. (1992). Effects of high-probability requests on the acquisition and generalization of responding to requests in young children with behavior disorders. *Journal of Applied Behavior Analysis, 25,* 905-916.

Davis, C. A., & Reichle, J. (1996). Variant and invariant high-probability requests: Increasing appropriate behaviors in children with emotional-behavioral disorders. *Journal of Applied Behavior Analysis, 29,* 471-482.

deTurck, M. A. (1985). A transactional analysis of compliance-gaining behavior: Effects of non-compliance, relational contexts, and actors' gender. *Human Communication Research, 12,* 54-78.

deTurck, M. A., & Derme, C. A. (1999, November). *A guilt-based interpretation of door-in-the-face.* Paper presented at the annual meeting of the National Communication Association, Chicago.

Dillard, J. P. (1988). Compliance-gaining message selection: What is our dependent variable? *Communication Monographs, 55,* 162-183.

Dillard, J. P. (1989). Types of influence goals in close relationships. *Journal of Personal and Social Relationships, 6,* 293-308.

Dillard, J. P. (1990a). A goal-driven model of interpersonal influence. In J. P. Dillard

(Ed.), *Seeking compliance: The production of interpersonal influence messages* (pp. 41-56). Scottsdale, AZ: Gorsuch Scarisbrick.

Dillard, J. P. (1990b). Self-inference and the foot-in-the-door technique: Quantity of behavior and attitudinal mediation. *Human Communication Research, 16,* 422-447.

Dillard, J. P., & Burgoon, M. (1985). Situational influences on the selection of compliance-gaining messages: Two tests of the predictive utility of the Cody-McLaughlin typology. *Communication Monographs, 52,* 289-304.

Dillard, J. P., & Hale, J. L. (1992). The prosocial parameter of sequential request strategies: Limits on the foot-in-the-door and the door-in-the-face? *Communication Studies, 43,* 220-232.

Dillard, J. P., & Harkness, C. D. (1992). Exploring the affective impact of influence messages. *Journal of Language and Social Psychology, 11,* 179-191.

Dillard, J. P., Hunter, J. E., & Burgoon, M. (1984). Sequential request persuasive strategies: Meta-analysis of foot-in-the-door and door-in-the-face. *Human Communication Research, 10,* 461-488.

Dillard, J. P., & Kinney, T. A. (1994). Experiential and physiological responses to interpersonal influence. *Human Communication Research, 20,* 502-528.

Dillard, J. P., Kinney, T. A., & Cruz, M. G. (1996). Influence, appraisals, and emotions in close relationships. *Communication Monographs, 63,* 105-130.

Dillard, J. P., & Meijnders, A. (2002). Persuasion and the structure of affect. In J. P. Dillard & M. Pfau (Eds.), *The persuasion handbook: Developments in theory and practice* (pp. 309-328). Thousand Oaks, CA: Sage.

Dillard, J. P., & Schrader, D. C. (1998). On the utility of the goals-plans-action sequence: Commentary reply. *Communication Studies, 49,* 300-304.

Dillard, J. P., Segrin, C., & Harden, J. M. (1989). Primary and secondary goals in the production of interpersonal influence messages. *Communication Monographs, 56,* 19-38.

Dillard, J. P., & Solomon, D. H. (2000). Conceptualizing context in message-production research. *Communication Theory, 10,* 167-175.

Dillard, J. P., & Wilson, B. J. (1993). Communication and affect: Thoughts, feelings, and issues for the future. *Communication Research, 20,* 637-646.

Dillard, J. P., Wilson, S. R., Tusing, K. J., & Kinney, T. A. (1997). Politeness judgments in personal relationships. *Journal of Language and Social Psychology, 16,* 297-325.

Ducharme, J. M., & Worling, D. E. (1994). Behavioral momentum and stimulus fading in the acquisition and maintenance of child compliance in the home. *Journal of Applied Behavior Analysis, 27,* 639-647.

Dunbar, R. (1998). *Grooming, gossip, and the evolution of language.* Cambridge, MA: Harvard University Press.

Ervin-Tripp, S. (1976). Is Sybil there? The structure of some American English directives. *Language in Society, 5,* 25-66.

Falbo, T. (1977). Multidimensional scaling of power strategies. *Journal of Personality and Social Psychology, 35,* 537-547.

Falbo, T., & Peplau, L. A. (1980). Power strategies in intimate relationships. *Journal of Personality and Social Psychology, 38,* 618-628.

Fern, E. F., Monroe, K. B., & Avila, R. A. (1986). Effectiveness of multiple request strategies: A synthesis of research results. *Journal of Marketing Research, 23,* 144-152.

Festinger, L. (1953). An analysis of compliant behavior. In M. Sherif & M. O. Wilson (Eds.), *Group relations at the crossroads* (pp. 232-256). New York: Harper.

Fishbein, M., & Ajzen, I. (1975). *Belief, attitude, intention, and behavior: An introduction to theory and research.* Reading, MA: Addison-Wesley.

Fitch, K. L. (1994). A cross-cultural study of directive sequences and some implications for compliance-gaining research. *Communication Monographs, 61,* 185-209.

Fitch, K. L., & Sanders, R. E. (1994). Culture, communication, and preferences for directness in expression of directives. *Communication Theory, 4,* 219-245.

Fointiat, V. (2000). "Foot-in-the-mouth" versus "door-in-the-face" requests. *Journal of Social Psychology, 140,* 264-266.

Francik, E. P., & Clark, H. H. (1985). How to make requests that overcome obstacles to compliance. *Journal of Memory and Language, 24,* 560-568.

Fraser, C., & Hite, R. E. (1989). The effect of matching contribution offers and legitimization of paltry contributions on compliance. *Journal of Applied Social Psychology, 19,* 1010-1018.

Fraser, C., Hite, R. E., & Sauer, P. L. (1988). Increasing contributions in solicitation campaigns: The use of large and small anchorpoints. *Journal of Consumer Research, 15,* 284-287.

Freedman, J. L., & Fraser, S. C. (1966). Compliance without pressure: The foot-in-the-door technique. *Journal of Personality and Social Psychology, 4,* 195-202.

French, J. R. P., Jr. (1956). A formal theory of social power. *Psychological Review, 63,* 181-194.

French, J. R. P., Jr., & Raven, B. (1960). The bases of social power. In D. Cartwright & A. Zander (Eds.), *Group dynamics* (pp. 607-623). New York: Harper & Row.

Gastil, J. (1995). An appraisal and revision of the constructivist research program. In B. R. Burleson (Ed.), *Communication yearbook 18* (pp. 83-104). Thousand Oaks, CA: Sage.

Gibbs, R. W., Jr. (1986). What makes some indirect speech acts conventional? *Journal of Memory and Language, 25,* 181-196.

Gibbs, R. W., Jr. (1987). Memory for requests in conversation revisited. *American Journal of Psychology, 100,* 179-191.

Goffman, E. (1959). *The presentation of self in everyday life.* Garden City, NY: Doubleday.

Gorassini, D. R., & Olson, J. M. (1995). Does self-perception change explain the foot-in-the-door effect? *Journal of Personality and Social Psychology, 69,* 91-105.

Gouldner, A. W. (1960). The norm of reciprocity: A preliminary statement. *American Sociological Review, 25,* 161-178.

Gray, J. A. (1990). Brain systems that mediate both emotion and cognition. *Cognition and Emotion, 4,* 269-288.

Greene, J. O. (1997). A second generation action assembly theory. In J. O. Greene (Ed.), *Message production: Advances in communication theory* (pp. 151-170). Mahwah, NJ: Lawrence Erlbaum.

Guadagno, R. E., Asher, T., Demaine, L. J., & Cialdini, R. B. (2001). When saying yes leads to saying no: Preference for consistency and the reverse foot-in-the-door effect. *Personality and Social Psychology Bulletin, 27,* 859-867.

Hale, J. L., & Laliker, M. (1999). Explaining the door-in-the-face: Is it really time to abandon reciprocal concessions? *Communication Studies, 50,* 203-210.

Hample, D. (1997). Framing message production research with field theory. In J. O. Greene (Ed.), *Message production: Advances in communication theory* (pp. 171-194). Mahwah, NJ: Lawrence Erlbaum.

Hample, D., & Dallinger, J. M. (1987). Individual differences in cognitive editing standards. *Human Communication Research, 14,* 123-144.

Hample, D., & Dallinger, J. M. (1990). Arguers as editors. *Argumentation, 4,* 153-169.

Hample, D., & Dallinger, J. M. (1992). The use of multiple goals in cognitive editing of arguments. *Argumentation and Advocacy, 28,* 109-122.

Hample, D., & Dallinger, J. M. (1998). On the etiology of the rebuff phenomenon: Why are persuasive messages less polite after rebuffs? *Communication Studies, 49,* 305-321.

Hample, D., & Dallinger, J. M. (2002). The effects of situation on the use or suppression of possible compliance-gaining appeals. In M. Allen, R. W. Preiss, B. M. Gayle, & N. Burrell (Eds.), *Interpersonal communication research: Advances through meta-analysis* (pp. 187-212). Mahwah, NJ: Lawrence Erlbaum.

Harchik, A., & Putzier, V. (1990). The use of high-probability requests to compliance with instructions to take medication. *Journal of the Association for Persons With Severe Handicaps, 15,* 40-43.

Harkness, C. D. (1990). Competition for resources and the origins of manipulative language. In J. P. Dillard (Ed.), *Seeking compliance: The production of interpersonal influence messages* (pp. 21-40). Scottsdale, AZ: Gorsuch Scarisbrick.

Hatfield, E., Utne, M. K., & Traupmann, J. (1979). Equity theory and intimate relationships. In R. L. Burgess & T. L. Huston (Eds.), *Social exchange in developing relationships* (pp. 99-133). New York: Academic Press.

Hermann, T. (1983). *Speech and situation: A psychological conception of situated speaking.* Berlin: Springer-Verlag.

Hertzog, R. L., & Bradac, J. J. (1984). Perceptions of compliance-gaining situations: An extended analysis. *Communication Research, 11,* 363-391.

Hoffman, M. L. (1960). Power assertion by the parent and its impact on the child. *Child Development, 31,* 129-143.

Hoffman, M. L., & Saltzstein, H. D. (1967). Parent discipline and child's moral development.

Journal of Personality and Social Psychology,
5, 45-57.

Holtgraves, T., & Yang, J. N. (1990). Politeness as universal: Cross-cultural perceptions of request strategies and inferences based on their use. *Journal of Personality and Social Psychology, 59,* 719-729.

Honeycutt, J. M., Cantrill, J. G., Kelly, P., & Lambkin, D. (1998). How do I love thee? Let me consider my options: Cognition, verbal strategies, and the escalation of intimacy. *Human Communication Research, 25,* 39-63.

Hornik, J., Zaig, T., & Shadmon, D. (1991). Reducing refusals in telephone surveys on sensitive topics. *Journal of Advertising Research, 31,* 49-56.

Houlihan, D., & Brandon, P. K. (1996). Compliant in a moment: A commentary on Nevin. *Journal of Applied Behavior Analysis, 29,* 549-555.

Howard, D. J. (1990). The influence of verbal responses to common greetings on compliance behavior: The foot-in-the-mouth effect. *Journal of Applied Social Psychology, 20,* 1185-1196.

Hunter, J. E. (1988). Failure of the social desirability response set hypothesis. *Human Communication Research, 15,* 162-168.

Hunter, J. E., & Boster, F. J. (1978, November). *An empathy model of compliance-gaining message strategy selection.* Paper presented at the annual meeting of the Speech Communication Association, San Antonio, TX.

Hunter, J. E., & Boster, F. J. (1987). A model of compliance-gaining message selection. *Communication Monographs, 54,* 63-84.

Ifert, D. E. (2000). Resistance to interpersonal requests: A summary and critique of recent research. In M. E. Roloff (Ed.), *Communication yearbook 23* (pp. 125-161). Thousand Oaks, CA: Sage.

Ifert, D. E., & Roloff, M. E. (1994). Anticipated obstacles to compliance: Predicting their presence and expression. *Communication Studies, 45,* 120-130.

Ifert, D. E., & Roloff, M. E. (1996). Responding to rejected requests: Persistence and response type as functions of obstacles to compliance. *Journal of Language and Social Psychology, 15,* 40-58.

Joule, R. V. (1987). Tobacco deprivation: The foot-in-the-door technique versus the low-ball technique. *European Journal of Social Psychology, 17,* 361-365.

Joule, R. V., Gouilloux, G., & Weber, F. (1989). The lure: A new compliance procedure. *Journal of Social Psychology, 129,* 741-749.

Kellermann, K. (1988, March). *Understanding tactical choice: Metagoals in conversation.* Paper presented at the Temple University Discourse Conference, Philadelphia.

Kellermann, K. (1992). Communication: Inherently strategic and primarily automatic. *Communication Monographs, 59,* 288-300.

Kellermann, K., & Cole, T. (1994). Classifying compliance gaining messages: Taxonomic disorder and strategic confusion. *Communication Theory, 4,* 3-60.

Kellermann, K., & Kim, M.-S. (1991, May). *Working within constraints: Tactical choices in the pursuit of social goals.* Paper presented at the annual meeting of the International Communication Association, Miami, FL.

Kellermann, K., & Park, H. S. (2001). Situational urgency and conversational retreat: When politeness and efficiency matter. *Communication Research, 28,* 3-47.

Kellermann, K., & Shea, B. C. (1996). Threats, suggestions, hints, and promises: Gaining compliance efficiently and politely. *Communication Quarterly, 44,* 145-165.

Kelman, H. C. (1961). Processes of opinion change. *Public Opinion Quarterly, 25,* 57-78.

Kemper, S., & Thissen, D. (1981). Memory for the dimensions of requests. *Journal of Verbal Learning and Verbal Behavior, 20,* 552-563.

Kennedy, C., Itkonen, T., & Lindquist, K. (1995). Comparing interspersed requests and social comments as antecedents for increasing student compliance. *Journal of Applied Behavior Analysis, 28,* 97-98.

Kim, M.-S. (1994). Cross-cultural comparisons of perceived importance of conversational constraints. *Human Communication Research, 21,* 128-151.

Kim, M.-S., & Bresnahan, M. (1994). A process model of request tactic evaluation. *Discourse Processes, 18,* 317-344.

Kim, M.-S., & Bresnahan, M. (1996). Cognitive basis of gender communication: A cross-cultural investigation of perceived constraints in requesting. *Communication Quarterly, 44,* 53-69.

Kim, M.-S., Hunter, J. E., Miyahara, A., Horvath, A. M., Bresnahan, M., & Yoon, H.-J. (1996). Individual- vs. culture-level dimensions of individualism and collectivism: Effects on preferred conversational styles. *Communication Monographs, 63,* 29-49.

Kim, M.-S., Sharkey, W. F., & Singelis, T. M. (1994). The relationship between individuals' self-construals and perceived importance of interactive constraints. *International Journal of Intercultural Relations, 18,* 117-140.

Kim, M.-S., Shin, H. C., & Cai, D. A. (1998). Cultural influences on the preferred forms of requesting and re-requesting. *Communication Monographs, 65,* 47-66.

Kim, M.-S., & Wilson, S. R. (1994). A cross-cultural comparison of implicit theories of requesting. *Communication Monographs, 61,* 210-235.

Kipnis, D., Castell, P. J., Gergen, M., & Mauch, D. (1976). Metaphoric effects of power. *Journal of Applied Psychology, 61,* 127-135.

Kipnis, D., Schmidt, S. M., Price, K., & Stitt, C. (1981). Why do I like thee: Is it your performance or my orders? *Journal of Applied Psychology, 66,* 324-329.

Kipnis, D., Schmidt, S. M., & Wilkinson, I. (1980). Intraorganizational influence tactics: Explorations in getting one's way. *Journal of Applied Psychology, 65,* 440-452.

Kline, S. L. (1981, May). *Construct system development and face support in persuasive messages: Two empirical investigations.* Paper presented at the annual meeting of the International Communication Association, Minneapolis.

Klinger, E. (1985). Missing links in action theory. In M. Frese & J. Sabini (Eds.), *Goal-directed behavior: The concept of action in psychology* (pp. 134-160). Hillsdale, NJ: Lawrence Erlbaum.

Knower, F. H. (1936). Experimental studies in changes in attitude: II. A study of the effects of printed argument on changes of attitude. *Journal of Abnormal and Social Psychology, 30,* 522-532.

Knowles, E., Butler, S., & Linn, J. (2001). Increasing compliance by reducing resistance. In J. P. Forgas & K. D. Williams (Eds.), *Social influence: Direct and indirect processes* (pp. 41-60). Philadelphia: Taylor & Francis.

Krone, K. J., & Ludlum, J. T. (1990). An organizational perspective on interpersonal influence. In J. P. Dillard (Ed.), *Seeking compliance: The production of interpersonal influence messages* (pp. 123-142). Scottsdale, AZ: Gorsuch Scarisbrick.

Langer, E. J., Blank, A., & Chanowitz, B. (1978). The mindlessness of ostensibly thoughtful action: The role of "placebic" information in interpersonal interaction. *Journal of Personality and Social Psychology, 36,* 635-642.

Le Poire, B. A. (1995). Inconsistent nurturing as control theory: Implications for communication-based research and treatment programs. *Journal of Applied Communication Research, 22,* 60-74.

Le Poire, B. A., Erlandson, K. T., & Hallett, J. S. (1998). Punishing versus reinforcing strategies of drug discontinuance: Effects of persuaders' drug use. *Health Communication, 10,* 293-316.

Le Poire, B. A., Hallett, J. S., & Erlandson, K. T. (2000). An initial test of inconsistent nurturing as control theory: How partners' of drug abusers assist their partners' sobriety. *Human Communication Research, 26,* 432-457.

Lim, T. S. (1990). Politeness behavior in social influence situations. In J. P. Dillard (Ed.), *Seeking compliance: The production of interpersonal influence messages* (pp. 75-86). Scottsdale, AZ: Gorsuch Scarisbrick.

Lim, T. S., & Bowers, J. W. (1991). Facework: Solidarity, approbation, and tact. *Human Communication Research, 17,* 415-450.

Mace, F. C. (1996). In pursuit of general behavioral relations. *Journal of Applied Behavior Analysis, 29,* 557-563.

Mace, F. C., Hock, M. L., Lalli, J. S., West, B. J., Belfiore, P., Pinter, E., & Brown, D. K. (1988). Behavioral momentum in the treatment of non-compliance. *Journal of Applied Behavior Analysis, 21,* 123-141.

Mace, F. C., Mauro, B. C., Boyajian, A. E., & Eckert, T. L. (1997). Effects of reinforcer quality on behavioral momentum: Coordinated applied and basic research. *Journal of Applied Behavior Analysis, 30,* 1-20.

Marwell, G., & Schmitt, D. R. (1967a). Compliance-gaining behavior: A synthesis and model. *Sociological Quarterly, 8,* 317-328.

Marwell, G., & Schmitt, D. R. (1967b). Dimensions of compliance-gaining behavior: An empirical analysis. *Sociometry, 30,* 350-364.

Marwell, G., & Schmitt, D. R. (1990). An introduction. In J. P. Dillard (Ed.), *Seeking compliance: The production of interpersonal influence messages* (pp. 3-5). Scottsdale, AZ: Gorsuch Scarisbrick.

Maslow, A. H. (1968). *Toward a psychology of being* (2nd ed.). Princeton, NJ: Van Nostrand.

McComas, J. J., Wacker, D. P., & Cooper, L. J. (1998). Increasing compliance with medical procedures: Application of the high-probability request procedure to a toddler. *Journal of Applied Behavior Analysis, 31,* 287-290.

Meyer, J. R. (1990). Cognitive processes underlying the retrieval of compliance-gaining strategies: An implicit rules model. In J. P. Dillard (Ed.). *Seeking compliance: The production of interpersonal influence messages* (pp. 57-74). Scottsdale, AZ: Gorsuch Scarisbrick.

Meyer, J. R. (1992). Fluency in the production of requests: Effects of degree of imposition, schematicity and instruction onset. *Journal of Language and Social Psychology, 11,* 233-251.

Meyer, J. R. (1994a). Effects of situational features on the likelihood of addressing face needs in requests. *Southern Communication Journal, 59,* 240-254.

Meyer, J. R. (1994b). Formulating plans for requests: An investigation of retrieval processes. *Communication Studies, 45,* 131-144.

Meyer, J. R. (1996). Retrieving knowledge in social situations: A test of the implicit rules model. *Communication Research, 23,* 342-351.

Meyer, J. R. (1997). Cognitive influences on the ability to address interaction goals. In J. O. Greene (Ed.), *Message production: Advances in communication theory* (pp. 71-90). Mahwah, NJ: Lawrence Erlbaum.

Mikolic, J. M., Parker, J. C., & Pruitt, D. G. (1997). Escalation in response to persistent annoyance: Groups versus individuals and gender effects. *Journal of Personality and Social Psychology, 72,* 151-163.

Millar, M. G. (2001). Promoting health behaviours with door-in-the-face: The influence of the beneficiary of the request. *Psychology, Health, and Medicine, 6,* 115-119.

Miller, G. A., Galanter, E., & Pribram, K. H. (1960). *Plans and the structure of behavior.* New York: Holt, Rinehart & Winston.

Miller, G. R. (1987). Persuasion. In C. R. Berger & S. H. Chaffee (Eds.), *Handbook of communication science* (pp. 446-483). Newbury Park, CA: Sage.

Miller, G. R., & Boster, F. J. (1988). Persuasion in personal relationships. In S. Duck (Ed.), *Handbook of personal relationships: Theory, research and interventions* (pp. 275-288). New York: John Wiley.

Miller, G. R., Boster, F. J., Roloff, M. E., & Seibold, D. R. (1977). Compliance-gaining message strategies: A typology and some findings concerning effects of situational differences. *Communication Monographs, 44,* 37-51.

Miller, G. R., & Burgoon, M. (1978). Persuasion research: Review and commentary. In B. D. Ruben (Ed.), *Communication yearbook 2* (pp. 29-47). New Brunswick, NJ: Transaction.

Miller, L. C., Cody, M. J., & McLaughlin, M. L. (1994). Situations and goals as fundamental constructs in interpersonal communication research. In M. L. Knapp & G. R. Miller (Eds.), *Handbook of interpersonal communication* (2nd ed., pp. 162-198). Thousand Oaks, CA: Sage.

Nevin, J. A. (1996). The momentum of compliance. *Journal of Applied Behavior Analysis, 29,* 535-547.

O'Keefe, B. J. (1988). The logic of message design: Individual differences in reasoning about communication. *Communication Monographs, 55,* 80-103.

O'Keefe, B. J. (1990). The logic of regulative communication: Understanding the rationality of message designs. In J. P. Dillard (Ed.), *Seeking compliance: The production of interpersonal influence messages* (pp. 87-104). Scottsdale, AZ: Gorsuch Scarisbrick.

O'Keefe, B. J. (1997). Variation, adaptation, and functional explanation in the study of message design. In G. Phillipsen & T. L. Albrecht (Eds.), *Developing communication theories* (pp. 85-118). Albany: State University of New York Press.

O'Keefe, B. J., & Delia, J. G. (1988). Communicative tasks and communicative practices: The development of audience-centered message production. In B. A. Rafoth & D. L. Rubin (Eds.), *The social construction of written communication: Writing research* (pp. 70-98). Stamford, CT: Ablex.

O'Keefe, B. J., & Lambert, B. L. (1995). Managing the flow of ideas: A local management approach to message design. In B. R. Burleson (Ed.), *Communication yearbook 18* (pp. 54-82). Thousand Oaks, CA: Sage.

O'Keefe, B. J., & McCornack, S. A. (1987). Message design logic and message goal structure: Effect on perceptions of message quality in regulative communication situations. *Human Communication Research, 14,* 68-92.

O'Keefe, B. J., & Shepherd, G. J. (1987). The pursuit of multiple objectives in face-to-face persuasive interactions: Effects of construct differentiation on message organization. *Communication Monographs, 54,* 396-419.

O'Keefe, D. J. (1994). From strategy-based to feature-based analyses of compliance-gaining message classification and production. *Communication Theory, 4,* 61-69.

O'Keefe, D. J. (1999). Three reasons for doubting the adequacy of the reciprocal concessions explanation of door-in-the-face effects. *Communication Studies, 50,* 211-220.

O'Keefe, D. J. (2000). Guilt and social influence. In M. E. Roloff (Ed.), *Communication yearbook 23* (pp. 67-101). Thousand Oaks, CA: Sage.

O'Keefe, D. J., & Figge, M. (1997). A guilt-based explanation of the door-in-the-face influence strategy. *Human Communication Research, 24,* 64-81.

O'Keefe, D. J., & Figge, M. (1999). Guilt and expected guilt in the door-in-the-face technique. *Communication Monographs, 66,* 312-324.

O'Keefe, D. J., & Hale, S. L. (1998). The door-in-the-face influence strategy: A random-effects meta-analytic review. In M. E. Roloff (Ed.), *Communication yearbook 21* (pp. 1-33). Thousand Oaks, CA: Sage.

Oldershaw, L., Walters, G. C., & Hall, D. K. (1986). Control strategies and noncompliance in abusive mother-child dyads: An observational study. *Child Development, 57,* 722-732.

Oldershaw, L., Walters, G. C., & Hall, D. K. (1989). A behavioral approach to the classification of different types of physically abusive mother-child dyads. *Merrill-Palmer Quarterly, 35,* 255-279.

O'Neal, E. C., Kipnis, D., & Craig, K. M. (1994). Effects on the persuader of employing a coercive influence technique. *Basic and Applied Social Psychology, 15,* 225-238.

Paulson, G. D., & Roloff, M. E. (1997). The effect of request form and content on constructing obstacles to compliance. *Communication Research, 24,* 261-290.

Pendleton, M. G., & Batson, C. D. (1979). Self-presentation and the door-in-the-face technique for reducing compliance. *Personality and Social Psychology Bulletin, 5,* 77-81.

Penman, R. (1990). Facework and politeness: Multiple goals in courtroom discourse. *Journal of Language and Social Psychology, 9,* 15-38.

Perrine, R. M., & Heather, S. (2000). Effects of a picture and even-a-penny-will-help appeals on anonymous donations to charity. *Psychological Reports, 86,* 551-559.

Plax, T. G., Kearney, P., & Sorensen, G. (1990). The strategy selection-construction controversy II: Comparing pre- and experienced teachers' compliance-gaining message constructions. *Communication Education, 38,* 128-141.

Plax, T. G., Kearney, P., & Tucker, L. K. (1986). Prospective teachers' use of behavioral alteration techniques on common student behaviors. *Communication Education, 35,* 32-42.

Pollock, C. L., Smith, S. D., Knowles, E. S., & Bruce, H. J. (1998). Mindfulness limits compliance with the that's-not-all technique. *Personality and Social Psychology Bulletin, 24,* 1153-1157.

Poole, M. S., & Folger, J. P. (1981). A method for establishing the representational validity of interaction coding systems: Do we see what they see? *Human Communication Research, 8,* 26-42.

Pratkanis, A., & Aronson, E. (2000). *The age of propaganda: The everyday use and abuse of persuasion.* New York: Freeman.

Pudlinski, C. (1998). Giving advice on a consumer-run warm line: Implicit and dilemmatic practices. *Communication Studies, 49,* 322-341.

Raven, B. H. (1965). Social influence and power. In I. D. Steiner & M. Fishbein (Eds.), *Current studies in social psychology* (pp. 371-382). New York: Holt, Rinehart & Winston.

Reeves, R. A., Macolini, R. M., & Martin, R. C. (1987). Legitimizing paltry contribution: On-the-spot vs. mail-in requests. *Journal of Applied Social Psychology, 17,* 731-738.

Reeves, R. A., & Saucer, P. R. (1993). A test of commitment in legitimizing paltry contributions. *Journal of Social Behavior and Personality, 8,* 537-544.

Reingen, P. H. (1978). On inducing compliance with requests. *Journal of Consumer Research, 5,* 551-562.

Rittle, R. H. (1981). Changes in helping behavior: Self- versus situational perceptions as mediators of the foot-in-the-door effect. *Personality and Social Psychology Bulletin, 7,* 431-437.

Rogers, R. W. (1975). A protection motivation theory of fear appeals and attitude change. *Journal of Psychology, 91,* 93-114.

Roloff, M. E. (1987). *Interpersonal communication: The social exchange approach.* Newbury Park, CA: Sage.

Roloff, M. E. (1994). Validity assessments of compliance-gaining exemplars. *Communication Theory, 4,* 69-80.

Roloff, M. E., & Barnicott, E. (1978). The situational use of pro- and anti-social compliance-gaining strategies by high and low Machiavellians. In B. D. Ruben (Ed.), *Communication yearbook 2* (pp. 193-208). New Brunswick, NJ: Transaction.

Roloff, M. E., & Janiszewski, C. A. (1989). Overcoming obstacles to interpersonal compliance: A principle of message construction. *Human Communication Research, 16,* 33-61.

Roskos-Ewoldsen, D. R. (1997). Implicit theories of persuasion. *Human Communication Research, 24,* 31-63.

Rule, B. G., Bisanz, G. L., & Kohn, M. (1985). Anatomy of a persuasion schema: Targets, goals, and strategies. *Journal of Personality and Social Psychology, 48,* 1127-1140.

Rusbult, C. E., & Buunk, B. P. (1993). Commitment processes in close relationships: An interdependence analysis. *Journal of Social and Personal Relationships, 10,* 175-204.

Sanchez-Fort, M., Brady, M., & Davis, C. (1996). Using behavioral momentum to increase the use of signed vocabulary words of young children with moderate to severe disabilities. *Education and Training in Mental Retardation and Developmental Disabilities, 30,* 151-165.

Sanders, R. E., & Fitch, K. L. (2001). The actual practice of compliance-seeking. *Communication Theory, 11,* 263-289.

Santos, M. D., Leve, C., & Pratkanis, A. R. (1994). Hey, buddy, can you spare seventeen cents? Mindful persuasion and the pique technique. *Journal of Applied Social Psychology, 24,* 755-764.

Schenck-Hamlin, W. J., Wiseman, R. L., & Georgacarakos, G. N. (1982). A model of properties of compliance-gaining strategies. *Communication Quarterly, 30,* 92-100.

Schrader, D. C. (1999). Goal complexity and the perceived competence of interpersonal influence message. *Communication Studies, 50,* 188-202.

Schrader, D. C., & Dillard, J. P. (1998). Goal structures and interpersonal influence. *Communication Studies, 49,* 276-293.

Schutz, W. C. (1966). *The interpersonal world.* Palo Alto, CA: Science and Behavior.

Scollon, R., & Scollon, S. W. (1995). *Intercultural communication: A discourse approach.* Oxford: Blackwell.

Scott, C. A. (1977). Modifying socially conscious behavior: The foot-in-the-door technique. *Journal of Consumer Research, 4,* 156-164.

Searle, J. (1976). A classification of illocutionary acts. *Language in Society, 5,* 1-23.

Segrin, C., & Dillard, J. P. (1991). (Non)depressed persons' cognitive and affective reactions to (un)successful interpersonal influence. *Communication Monographs, 58,* 115-134.

Seibold, D. R. (1988). A response to "Item desirability in compliance-gaining research." *Human Communication Research, 15,* 152-161.

Seibold, D. R., Cantrill, J. G., & Meyers, R. A. (1985). Communication and interpersonal influence. In M. L. Knapp & G. R. Miller (Eds.), *Handbook of interpersonal communication* (pp. 551-611). Beverly Hills, CA: Sage.

Shepherd, G. J. (1998). The trouble with goals. *Communication Studies, 49,* 294-299.

Shimanoff, S. B. (1977). Investigating politeness. In E. O. Keenan & T. L. Bennett (Eds.), *Discourse across time and space* (pp. 213-241). Los Angeles: University of Southern California Press.

Shriver, M. D., & Allen, K. D. (1997). Defining child noncompliance: An examination of temporal parameters. *Journal of Applied Behavior Analysis, 30,* 173-176.

Skinner, B. F. (1974). *About behaviorism.* New York: Alfred A. Knopf.

Slugoski, B. R., & Turnbull, W. (1988). Cruel to be kind and kind to be cruel: Sarcasm, banter and social relations. *Journal of Language and Social Psychology, 7,* 101-121.

Smith, T. W., Baldwin, M., & Christensen, A. (1990). Interpersonal influence as active coping: Effects of task difficulty on cardiovascular reactivity. *Psychophysiology, 27,* 429-437.

Smith, T. W., Limon, J. P., Gallo, L. C., & Ngu, L. Q. (1996). Interpersonal control and cardiovascular reactivity: Goals, behavioral expression, and the moderating effects of sex. *Journal of Personality and Social Psychology, 70,* 1012-1024.

Solomon, D. H. (1997). A developmental model of intimacy and date request explicitness. *Communication Monographs, 64,* 99-118.

Sutton, S. R., & Eiser, J. R. (1984). The effect of fear-arousing communications on cigarette smoking: An expectancy-value approach. *Journal of Behavioral Medicine, 7,* 13-33.

Tracy, K., Craig, R. T., Smith, M., & Spisak, F. (1984). The discourse of requests: Assessment of a compliance-gaining approach. *Human Communication Research, 10,* 513-538.

Trost, M., & Langan, E. J. (1999). Not everyone listens when you "just say no": Drug resistance is a relational context. *Journal of Applied Communication Research, 27,* 120-138.

Tusing, K. J., & Dillard, J. P. (2000). The psychological reality of the door-in-the-face: It's helping, not bargaining. *Journal of Language and Social Psychology, 19,* 5-25.

Tybout, A., Sternthal, B., & Calder, B. J. (1983). Information availability as a determinant of multiple request effectiveness. *Journal of Marketing Research, 20,* 280-290.

Van Lange, P. A. M., & Rusbult, C. E. (1996). Interdependence processes. In E. T. Higgins & A. W. Kruglanski (Eds.), *Social psychology: Handbook of basic principles* (pp. 564-596). New York: Guilford.

Vroom, V. H. (1964). *Work and motivation.* New York: John Wiley.

Wang, T., Brownstein, R., & Katzev, R. (1989). Promoting charitable behavior with compliance techniques. *Applied Psychology, 38,* 165-183.

Wegener, D. T., & Petty, R. E. (1996). Effects of mood on persuasion processes: Enhancing, reducing, and biasing scrutiny of attitude-relevant information. In L. L. Martin & A. Tesser (Eds.), *Striving and feeling: Interactions among goals, affect, and self-regulation* (pp. 329-362). Mahwah, NJ: Lawrence Erlbaum.

Weyant, J. M. (1984). Applying social psychology to induce charitable donations. *Journal of Applied Social Psychology, 14,* 441-447.

Weyant, J. M., & Smith, S. L. (1987). Getting more by asking for less: The effects of request size on donations to charity. *Journal of Applied Social Psychology, 17,* 392-400.

Whately, M. A., Webster, J. M., Smith, R. H., & Rhodes, A. (1999). The effect of a favor on public and private compliance: How internalized is the norm of reciprocity? *Basic and Applied Social Psychology, 21,* 251-259.

Wheeless, L. R., Barraclough, R., & Stewart, R. (1983). Compliance-gaining and power in persuasion. In R. N. Bostrom (Ed.), *Communication yearbook 7* (pp. 105-145). Beverly Hills, CA: Sage.

Wilson, S. R. (1990). Development and test of a cognitive rules model of interaction goals. *Communication Monographs, 57,* 81-103.

Wilson, S. R. (1992). Face and facework in negotiation. In L. L. Putnam & M. E. Roloff (Eds.), *Communication and negotiation* (pp. 176-205). Newbury Park, CA: Sage.

Wilson, S. R. (1995). Elaborating the cognitive rules model of interaction goals: The problem of accounting for individual differences in goal formation. In B. R. Burleson (Ed.), *Communication yearbook 18* (pp. 3-25). Thousand Oaks, CA: Sage.

Wilson, S. R. (1997). Developing theories of persuasive message production: The next generation. In J. O. Greene (Ed.), *Message production: Advances in communication theory* (pp. 15-43). Mahwah, NJ: Lawrence Erlbaum.

Wilson, S. R., Aleman, C. G., & Leatham, G. B. (1998). Identity implications of influence goals: A revised analysis of face-threatening acts and application to seeking compliance with same-sex friends. *Human Communication Research, 25,* 64-96.

Wilson, S. R., Cameron, K. A., & Whipple, E. E. (1997). Regulative communication strategies within mother-child interactions: Implications for the study of reflection-enhancing parental communication. *Research on Language and Social Interaction, 30,* 73-92.

Wilson, S. R., Cruz, M. G., & Kang, K. H. (1992). Is it always a matter of perspective? Construct differentiation and variability in attributions about compliance gaining. *Communication Monographs, 59,* 350-367.

Wilson, S. R., Cruz, M. G., Marshall, L. J., & Rao, N. (1993). An attributional analysis of compliance-gaining interactions. *Communication Monographs, 60,* 352-372.

Wilson, S. R., & Kang, K. H. (1991). Communications and unfulfilled obligations: Individual differences in causal judgments. *Communication Research, 18,* 799-824.

Wilson, S. R., Kim, M.-S., & Meischke, H. (1991-1992). Evaluating Brown and Levinson's politeness theory: A revised analysis of directives and face. *Research on Language and Social Interaction, 25,* 215-252.

Wilson, S. R., Levine, K., Humphreys, L., & Peters, H. (1994, November). *Seeking and resisting compliance: Strategies and sequences in telephone solicitations for blood donations.* Paper presented at the annual meeting of the Speech Communication Association, New Orleans.

Wiseman, R. L., & Schenck-Hamlin, W. J. (1981). A multidimensional scaling validation of an inductively-derived set of compliance-gaining strategies. *Communication Monographs, 48,* 251-270.

Woolbert, C. (1920). The effects of various models of public reading. *Journal of Applied Psychology, 4,* 162-185.

Yukl, G., Falbe, C. M., & Youn, J. Y. (1993). Patterns of influence behavior for managers. *Group and Organization Management, 18,* 5-28.

13

Interpersonal Conflict

A Review

MICHAEL E. ROLOFF
KARI P. SOULE

Humanity reflects a dizzying array of diversity. Individuals vary with regard to their cultural memberships, age cohorts, socioeconomic statuses, and myriad other personality characteristics and traits. Whether biologically or socially based, many of these characteristics carry with them somewhat unique values and preferred behaviors. Some observers rejoice in the richness of humanity and believe that it strengthens the human condition, but such diversity also has harmful potential. To the degree that individuals with different values and preferences must coordinate their actions, conflict is inevitable. Although conflict has the potential to increase understanding, stimulate positive change, and facilitate human relations, all too often conflict leads to intolerance and physical and psychological harm. The dysfunctional consequences of conflict are evident in terrorist activities and warfare between groups and nations, but they are not confined to interactions between members of such macroentities. Individuals often experience everyday conflicts with strangers, acquaintances, friends, and family members. In some cases, these conflicts escalate into psychological and physical abuse. Hence humans face the challenge of managing their everyday conflicts so as to maximize positive consequences while minimizing negative ones.

Interpersonal communication scholars have conducted research related to this challenge, and in this chapter we review the results of their investigations. Like the literature in many areas of inquiry, the conflict literature is voluminous, multidisciplinary, and heterogeneous with regard to theory and method. All of the aforementioned features constitute serious organizational challenges for anyone who wishes to make sense of the extant literature. Prior reviewers have created coherence by organizing the literature according to theoretical perspective (Cahn, 1992), relational type (Canary, Cupach, & Messman, 1995), or unit of analysis (Roloff, 1988). Although each of these organizational schemes has yielded useful insights, we have chosen a somewhat different perspective. As is often the case in scholarly inquiry, researchers concerned with conflict have focused on somewhat distinct phenomena. Each of these phenomena is thought to stimulate conflict, influence the manner in which conflict is conducted, and/or determine the impact of conflict. In most cases, scholars have generated several theories to help them understand the roles of given conflict phenomena, and they have studied these phenomena in multiple relational contexts. Hence our scheme provides information similar to that found in prior reviews, but we organize this information around the factors that are thought to play key roles in most conflicts.

To identify the various conflict phenomena, we looked at books and journal articles written about conflict from a variety of disciplines and fields. However, we did impose limits on our search. Because this volume is focused on interpersonal communication, we concentrate here on studies that examined conflict in informal relationships, such as those occurring between acquaintances, roommates, friends, and family members. Consequently, we do not review the literature that examines intraindividual conflict or conflicts between nations or groups, nor do we look at conflicts between individuals who have formal role relationships, such as those found in many organizations. Moreover, the bulk of the research we reviewed used survey or experimental methods

to generate data. Thus we do not discuss here the rather large body of research in clinical and counseling psychology that is based on case studies or informal observations. Even with these limitations, the resulting body of research is large.

Although researchers have studied a variety of conflict-related phenomena, we focus here on six areas that have received the greatest attention: (a) types of incompatibility, (b) relational contexts, (c) social networks, (e) perceptions, (f) conflict management styles, and (g) argumentation patterns. We examine each in turn in the sections that follow.

TYPES OF INCOMPATIBILITY

Over the years, scholars have advanced a variety of definitions of conflict (see Fink, 1968); these definitions vary on two dimensions: (a) whether conflict is conceived as episodic or pervasive and (b) whether it involves specific behaviors or is a general state of affairs (Canary et al., 1995). Although there is no single agreed-upon definition of conflict, scholars concur that incompatibility is its central characteristic. For example, Deutsch (1973) notes: "Conflict exists whenever incompatible activities occur.... An action that is incompatible with another action prevents, obstructs, interferes, injures or in some way makes the latter less likely or less effective" (p. 73). Similarly, Hocker and Wilmot (1995) define interpersonal conflict as "an expressed struggle between at least two interdependent parties who perceive incompatible goals, scarce resources, and interference from the other party in achieving their goals" (p. 21). Because of the defining nature of incompatibility, it is not surprising that researchers have studied it. In doing so, they have relied mostly on one of the following perspectives in deducing their hypotheses: principled/communal conflict, realistic/nonrealistic conflict, personal/superindividual conflict, unexpressed/expressed conflict, behavioral/attributional conflict, transgression/ nontransgression-based conflict, antagonistic/ dialectical conflict, and conflict issues. We review the research associated with each of these approaches below.

Principled/Communal Conflict

In 1956, Coser noted that conflicts vary with regard to their relevance to the ongoing relationship between the disputants. In some cases, conflicts are about principles, and, if unresolved, they may call into question whether there is sufficient consensus to justify the continuation of the relationship. Wheaton (1974) built upon this notion by distinguishing between two types of conflict: Principled conflict concerns disagreements about ideals and reflects value differences; communal conflict assumes that the disputants agree as to their values, but differ concerning how they should be acted upon. For example, spouses who disagree about whether or not to have children are considered to be in a principled conflict, whereas spouses who both want children but disagree about when to have them are involved in a communal conflict. From this perspective, principled conflicts constitute a more serious threat to a relationship than do communal ones. Indeed, Wheaton argues that communal conflict often forces the disputants to reaffirm and recognize their value agreement and thereby strengthen their relationship. However, this expectation is qualified by whether the conflict issue is internal or external to the relationship. An internal issue is implied by the relationship itself and constitutes a basic expectation for it, whereas an external issue is grounded in the group membership of the disputants. Thus disagreement about whether or not to have children might be perceived as an internal issue for marriage, whereas some might judge disagreements about political viewpoints as external issues. In Wheaton's view, the negative relational impact of principled conflict and the positive

relational impact of communal conflict are of greater magnitude when the issue is internal rather than external to the relationship. Wheaton conducted a survey of college roommates that confirmed these expectations: After several factors were controlled for, the number of principled conflicts occurring between roommates was negatively related to relational cohesiveness. Wheaton also found that the number of communal conflicts was positively related to relational cohesiveness, but this association was statistically significant only when the issues were internal to the relationship.

In spite of its promising beginning, this perspective did not produce subsequent research. In part, this lack of research may reflect the difficulty of assessing types of conflicts and issues, in that people may have difficulty categorizing them. Indeed, Wheaton relied on self-categorizations by the roommates in his study and had to adjust for anomalies in their responses. Moreover, the correlational nature of this design prohibits the making of definitive inferences about causality. Finally, Wheaton did not include measures that would make it possible to verify why communal conflicts seemed to enhance relational quality. However, notwithstanding these limitations, Wheaton's is one of the few studies that has found a positive relationship between the number of conflicts and relational quality.

Realistic/Nonrealistic Conflict

Coser (1956) argues that conflicts arise from feelings of frustration, but that the source of the frustration need not be the contentious parties:

> Conflicts which arise from frustration of specific demands within the relationship and from estimates of gains of the participants, and which are directed at the presumed frustrating object, can be called *realistic conflicts,* insofar as they are means toward a specific result. *Nonrealistic conflicts,* on the other hand, although still involving interaction

between two or more persons, are not occasioned by the rival ends of the antagonists, but by the need for tension release of at least one of them. In this case, the choice of antagonists depends on determinants not directly related to a contentious issue and is not oriented toward the attainment of specific results. (p. 49)

Coser argues that nonrealistic conflicts often arise from situations in which individuals are unable to confront the causes of their frustration and subsequently take out their anger on others. This implies that circumstances that prevent a realistic conflict from being expressed may stimulate nonrealistic conflict between a disputant and a party who was not directly involved in the original dispute. Moreover, because the source of frustration in a nonrealistic conflict has little to do with the issue at hand, it is unlikely that constructive resolution can be reached. Indeed, from Coser's perspective, the primary goal in nonrealistic conflict is tension release through aggression.

In some respects, Coser's conception of nonrealistic conflict is evident in research conducted on displaced aggression (Miller & Marcus-Newhall, 1997). In displaced aggression, individuals who are prevented from retaliating against the sources of their frustration subsequently act aggressively toward other persons or things. Indeed, a recent meta-analysis of four decades of experimental research has verified the existence of this phenomenon (Marcus-Newhall, Pedersen, Carlson, & Miller, 2000). The results of this meta-analysis indicate that displaced aggression is more likely to take place when subsequent encounters occur in a negative setting (e.g., the victim made many errors on a test conducted by the frustrated individual) than when they occur in a positive one (e.g., the victim correctly answered most of the questions). Other researchers have even found that displaced aggression occurs regardless of whether the frustrated individuals are directly

provoked (e.g., insulted) by their victims (Baron & Bell, 1975). Moreover, displaced aggression may actually be self-reinforcing. Bushman, Baumeister, and Stack (1999) conducted a study in which individuals who were frustrated by another person engaged in aggression toward an inanimate object (hitting a punching bag) prior to interacting again with the source of frustration. They found that the majority of subjects reported that punching the bag was highly pleasurable, and this increased their aggression in the subsequent interaction with the source of frustration. Therefore, some individuals may take out their frustrations on nonprovoking others because they believe it improves their mood (see Bushman, Baumeister, & Phillips, 2001).

Research on marital conflict provides evidence of both realistic and nonrealistic conflict. Often spouses encounter frustrations arising from sources outside of the marriage, and these negative feelings may spill over into their marital interactions. One such external frustration may arise from the state of the economy. During economic downturns, spouses may find their economic security threatened by reduced work hours, declining wages, and layoffs. As might be expected, these economic pressures are reflected in marital interaction. Using a longitudinal data set that followed married couples from the late 1920s through the 1940s, Liker and Elder (1983) examined the impact on marital interaction of income loss and economic hardship arising from the Great Depression. Their research indicates that the greater the negative economic consequences experienced by a family, the greater the number of conflicts that occur over financial issues. This pattern seems to constitute realistic conflict in that tight finances stimulate conflict over spending habits and priorities as well as the need for more revenue. Moreover, Liker and Elder found that among husbands in their sample, economic pressures were positively related to marital tensions (i.e., couples appeared to observers to disagree about most issues) and hostility (i.e., extreme irritability and emotional instability). Although the latter patterns were evident across the sample, they were strongest among marriages that were problematic prior to the Depression. This suggests a degree of nonrealistic conflict. Some individuals seem prone to conflict and hostility regardless of economic conditions, but these behaviors are more common during times of financial stress.

In a similar vein, Conger et al. (1990) found that as family economic hardships increased, husbands were more likely to treat their wives in a hostile fashion and less likely to act warmly, even during general discussions and problem-solving interactions unrelated to financial issues. Not surprisingly, such behavior decreased wives' sense of marital quality and increased their consideration of divorce. On the other hand, economic hardships seemed to have little impact on how hostile or warm wives were toward their husbands. Regardless of its source, however, wives' hostility toward their husbands decreased the husbands' perceptions of marital quality, which prompted the husbands to consider divorce. In contrast to Conger et al.'s findings, Vinokur, Price, and Caplan (1996) found that the impacts of economic difficulties on relationships may not be gender-bound. They report that, regardless of gender, being unemployed and having difficulty finding work increased the likelihood that an individual and his or her partner would become depressed. Furthermore, it increased the likelihood that the partner would socially undermine (e.g., act angry, criticize, insult) the unemployed individual, which reduced that person's relational satisfaction.

Thus there is some evidence that realistic and nonrealistic conflicts might exist and can both occur within the same relationship. However, this conclusion must be qualified. Most studies have not directly measured the degree to which conflicts are realistic or nonrealistic. For example, as a result of arguments about finances, spouses may become more sensitive to or perhaps uncover other real sources of disagreement. Hence what would appear to be a general tendency toward tension release (i.e., arguing about irrelevant issues) might reflect the discovery of other areas of realistic conflict. Moreover, tensions in an individual's life might translate into social withdrawal rather than an increased propensity to engage in conflict. For example, Repetti (1989) examined the relationship between daily workload and the marital interactions of married male air traffic controllers. On highly demanding and difficult workdays, the controllers were more socially withdrawn and less angry with their wives than they were on less demanding days. Moreover, these patterns were strongest when the controllers' wives acted in a supportive fashion. These data indicate that withdrawing from interaction helps to decrease the frustration of a difficult day and that spouses are most helpful when they allow such withdrawal to take place. In a follow-up study, Repetti and Wood (1997) found similar results among a sample of working mothers. On highly stressful days, these mothers were more socially withdrawn when interacting with their children than they were on less stressful days. Moreover, these trends were strongest among mothers suffering from depression and trait anxiety, or who had Type A characteristics. Although social withdrawal is not necessarily a desirable outcome of stress, nonrealistic conflict does not inevitably result from frustration.

Personal/Superindividual Conflict

Conflict arises whenever a person's actions have an adverse impact on another individual. In such a case, the victim might confront the provocateur with the goal of stopping the objectionable action. However, some provocations harm more than a single individual, and a person might confront another not simply on his or her own behalf, but with the goal of protecting other victims. Coser (1956) labels the first case *personal conflict,* that is, conflict in which an individual is acting in his or her own self-interest. In the second type of case, *superindividual conflict,* the individual is serving the interests of the collectivity. Coser asserts that the two forms of conflict differ with regard to how they might be resolved. When individuals act on behalf of others rather than merely for themselves, they tend to harden and radicalize their positions. Such individuals see themselves as engaged in noble crusades aimed at helping the disadvantaged. They may feel that they cannot make any accommodation without selling out their interests, and so they single-mindedly muster their resources in an effort to attain victory, often through the use of aggression.

Although one might expect that personal conflict is the predominant form in interpersonal relationships, evidence of superindividual conflict exists. For example, Scanzoni (1978) found both types of conflicts in wives' reports of their marital conflicts. Two kinds of conflicts seem especially personal: Some wives reported marital conflicts over their autonomy/independence and others experienced conflict arising from their husbands' lack of emotional expressiveness and supportiveness. One kind of conflict seems superindividual: Some wives reported conflicts over their husbands' treatment of the children. The two different conflict types were correlated with different processes. Scanzoni asked each wife about the reasons she gave her husband to justify why he should change his behavior. The two forms of personal conflict were positively related to the wife's arguing that the husband should change because it would benefit her. Among working wives, conflict over the husband's lack of expressivity was positively related to making self-interest appeals, whereas among nonworking wives, conflict over the wife's autonomy increased her use of self-interest arguments. Scanzoni also found that conflict about the husband's treatment of the children was positively related to the wife's

arguing that the husband's changing his behavior would benefit the entire family. Clearly, personal conflicts elicit self-interested appeals, whereas superindividual conflicts prompt arguments based on collective interests. Interestingly, Scanzoni found that collective appeals were correlated with measures of conflict escalation. Among nonworking wives, collective appeals were positively correlated with both their resentment and the degree to which they acted aggressively toward their husbands. Among working wives, the use of collective appeals was positively related only to the wife's aggressiveness. The use of self-interested appeals was not significantly related to either resentment or aggressiveness.

A key question concerns why superindividual conflict is more likely than personal conflict to be aggressive. Simmel (1955) suggests that this flows from the greater legitimacy afforded someone who acts on behalf of others rather than for his or her own selfish interests. However, some evidence implies that this may not be true. Edmonds (1978) had individuals evaluate the same physically aggressive act in different contexts. In general, the study participants evaluated aggression enacted to defend another person more favorably than aggression intended to gain rewards or that resulted from hostility. However, they evaluated both aggression intended to defend another person and aggression intended to defend oneself positively. Although this study provides no information about the mind-set of a person involved in a superindividual conflict, it does suggest that, normatively, such disputes provide no greater justification for aggression than do personal conflicts.

Unexpressed/Expressed Conflict

The existence of incompatibility does not always result in a confrontation. In some cases, individuals withhold their complaints and conflict is unexpressed. Coser (1956) argues that individuals withhold their complaints because they are fearful that the relationship might end should the complaints be disclosed. However, expressed conflict may actually increase relational stability. Expressed conflict allows individuals to vent their anger and may lead to dispute resolution, both of which enhance the stability of relationships. Unexpressed conflict is thought to create relational ambivalence or even hostility toward the partner that could eventually lead to violent confrontation.

Research verifies the existence of unexpressed conflict. For example, Roloff and Cloven (1990) asked college students to list the things about their dating partners they found irritating and then to identify which of these irritations they had disclosed to their partners. On average, the students were withholding about two irritations, or about 40% of those listed. Using the same assessment method, Makoul and Roloff (1998) found that about 35% of the individuals in their undergraduate sample were withholding irritations from their dating partners. In a study by Solomon and Roloff (1996), undergraduates reported that they withhold complaints for the following reasons: (a) The irritation is unimportant, (b) negative relational consequences would result from complaining, (c) the discloser's self-image would be damaged, (d) communication about the irritation would be futile, (e) the relationship is insufficiently intimate to justify disclosure, (f) the complaint is illegitimate, (g) indirect complaining is preferred, and (h) situational cues inhibit disclosure. Similarly, Lundgren and Rudawsky (2000) studied circumstances in which individuals who were angered by peers chose to express their anger. Expressed conflict was most likely when (a) there was a close relationship between the individuals, (b) the issue was important, (c) the angry feelings were intense, and (d) the angered individual expected the peer to react positively to the confrontation.

There is limited information available about the effects of unexpressed conflict. The research suggests that under certain circumstances,

unexpressed conflict could be harmful. For example, Baumeister, Stillwell, and Wotman (1990) examined accounts of what happened when an angered individual confronted a provocateur. Angry individuals described their confrontations as occurring only in response to multiple provocations. Thus the angry individuals did not express their displeasure in response to the initial and following provocations. Interestingly, the provocateurs tended to view the confronting individuals' anger as a gross overreaction. Although in this study the accounts of the provocateurs and angry individuals were about different confrontations, they imply that unexpressed anger could result in emotional encounters that the persons confronted may see as unjustified.

There is tentative evidence that unexpressed conflict could lay the groundwork for destabilizing a relationship, but only for some individuals. Solomon and Roloff (1996) found a negative correlation between the proportion of unexpressed conflict and relational satisfaction. However, this correlation was moderated by the reason for withholding complaints. When individuals withheld complaints because they preferred indirect forms of communication or they felt they had no right to complain, the negative association between unexpressed conflict and satisfaction was greater than it was among individuals who did not cite these reasons. Conversely, among those withholding complaints because they felt the problem was unimportant, a weak but positive association existed between unexpressed conflict and satisfaction. It is possible that satisfied individuals find benefits to being in a relationship that offset the undesirable by-products of conflict, so, essentially, they see little reason to confront their partners. Moreover, Ruvolo, Fabin, and Ruvolo (2001) found in a longitudinal study among dating couples that conflict avoidance influenced how secure some individuals were in their attachment to others (i.e., trust and feel comfortable in a relationship). Among women, conflict avoidance reduced their security, but the pattern was more complex among men. For men whose dating relationships remained intact during the study, conflict avoidance was not significantly related to security; but among those men whose relationships broke up, conflict avoidance increased their level of security. Ruvolo et al. speculate that conflict avoidance prevents women from understanding their partners and reinforces a negative view of relationships, whereas it allows men to dodge distressing relational issues and thereby maintain a generally secure view of relationships. Indeed, Buysse et al. (2000) found that among men, avoidance results from their desire to distract themselves from their own transgressions and thereby reduce the likelihood that their relationships might be destabilized.

Limited research has been conducted on expressed versus unexpressed conflict. Furthermore, most of the research that has been undertaken has been cross-sectional, making it difficult to infer causality. Indeed, longitudinal studies might determine whether conflict avoidance in relationships results in growing anger that leads to outbursts or whether, for some individuals, it represents a long-term strategy for maintaining relationships.

Behavioral/Attributional Conflict

When incompatible actions occur, individuals often try to make sense of them. Victims may construct causal explanations for what has happened to them, and, if confronted, perpetrators may provide their own accounts for the objectionable behavior. When individuals attribute different causes to behavioral incompatibility, a behavioral conflict becomes an attributional conflict (Horai, 1977). Kelley (1979) characterizes this transformation as conflict escalation, in that the issues have expanded from the problematic action to the reasons for it. As a result of this transgression, the victim may raise other problematic instances that are consistent with his or her preferred explanation or causal attribution, which the provocateur

may try to refute or counter in some way. Orvis, Kelley, and Butler (1976) speculate that, because the evidence for such causal explanations is inherently subjective and unclear, attributional conflicts will generally be irresolvable.

Researchers have found several instances of attributional conflicts. For example, Orvis et al. (1976) asked heterosexual couples to report instances in which the partners had disagreed over explanations for each other's behavior. Their reports indicate that attributional conflict often centers on the following behaviors: (a) passivity, (b) poor affectionate or sex role behavior, (c) insensitivity or unyielding actions, (d) irresponsible or annoying behavior, (e) emotional or aggressive actions, (f) avoidance of particular activities, (g) situational ineptness or social rejection, (h) habitual engagement in activities disliked by the other partner, and (i) overly caring or demanding behavior. Across these conflicts, partners commonly disagreed as to whether the behaviors should be attributed to (a) circumstances or the actor's characteristics, (b) the actor's preferences/beliefs or the actor's characteristics, (c) the desirability of the behavior or the actor's characteristics, (f) the partner's or the actor's characteristics, (g) different actors' characteristics, and (h) positive or negative attitudes toward the partner. A multidimensional analysis of the causal explanations indicates that both actors and their partners perceive that the accounts vary in the degree to which they reflect the actor's positive or negative attitude toward the partner. Actors also differentiate among the accounts based on the degree to which they reflect their intentionality, whereas partners distinguish them based on the degree to which they reflect the actors' stable traits versus temporary circumstances or states (Passer, Kelley, & Michela, 1978). Kelley (1979) notes that actors generally prefer explanations that reflect their positive attitudes toward their partners, but that partners seem to prefer explanations that reflect the partners' negative traits and negative attitude toward the partner.

Also, there is evidence that attributional conflict is common during the interactions of individuals in unhappy relationships. Ting-Toomey (1983) coded discussions about relational problems involving spouses who varied in their marital adjustment. Couples who were not well adjusted enacted a highly structured interaction pattern in which one individual complained that his or her partner caused a relational problem, which prompted the partner to respond defensively by refuting these claims. Interestingly, a defensive statement also prompted complaining. Hence partners do not always accept each other's causal explanations for behavioral conflicts. Better-adjusted couples engaged in information seeking and disclosure in addition to actions that acknowledged and confirmed each other's statements. There is also evidence that marital adjustment may be related to whether husbands and wives perceive their conflicts to be behavioral versus attributional. Alberts (1988) found that during complaining interactions, well-adjusted husbands and wives were more likely than maladjusted ones to make specific complaints about their spouses' behaviors. However, the opposite pattern was observed for complaints about personal characteristics, such as a spouse's personality, attitudes, or emotional nature. Moreover, among maladjusted couples, these complaints were often met with counter-complaints, which could expand the issues at hand and escalate the dispute.

In spite of the evidence supporting its general existence, attributional conflict may be confined to certain kinds of relational events. For attributional conflict to occur, an individual must think about causal explanations. Holtzworth-Munroe and Jacobson (1985) asked spouses who varied in marital satisfaction to think about each other's positive and negative behaviors. Attributional thinking was most common among distressed husbands and wives, who focused on their spouses' frequently occurring negative behavior. Regardless of the valence of the behavior, attributional thinking was less common among satisfied husbands and wives. Moreover, regardless of marital satisfaction, attributional thinking was less frequent for positive behaviors.

On a dyadic basis, attributional conflict may reflect similar processes for both relational partners. Schutz (1999) examined how husbands and wives viewed one of their conflicts and found that both felt victimized by the other. Typically, individuals felt that their partners engaged in inappropriate actions, which stimulated criticism. The partners, however, felt that the criticism was inappropriate or intolerant. For the same conflicts, individuals attributed their own behavior to good intentions and circumstances, but viewed their partners' behavior as irrational and inconsistent. Thus each spouse felt that the other started the conflict, and each felt that his or her intentions were more appropriate and legitimate than those of his or her partner.

Although attributional conflict is an observable phenomenon, why it occurs is unclear. It is possible that it results from self-focused attention. Thus, although individuals are aware of why they perform certain behaviors, they do not recognize that the same forces influence their partners. Alternatively, attributional conflict could result from a desire to project a positive self-image to both self and partner. Such impression management could maintain self-esteem as well as afford strategic value during an interaction. By deflecting responsibility from self to partner, a person might be in a stronger position to demand changes in the partner's behavior.

Transgression/ Nontransgression-Based Conflict

When entering into relationships, individuals face the problem of how best to coordinate their actions. One means of doing so is to create a set of rules specifying that certain behaviors should occur and others are prohibited (Argyle & Henderson, 1985). Such rules not only provide a guide for functional behaviors, but should serve as a basis for partners' predictions of how each other will act. However, rules are sometimes violated, and when this happens, a transgression has occurred and conflict results. Metts (1994) argues that transgression-based conflicts have three key characteristics: focus, salience, and consequences. We address the research associated with each below.

Focus

As we have noted, a transgression is a rule violation. Hence researchers have sought to identify the kinds of rules that guide relationships and the behaviors that violate them. For example, Argyle and Henderson (1985) examined the degree to which rules are applied to a wide variety of relationships. They found six universal rules: three aimed at preventing conflict (partners should respect each other's privacy, partners should not discuss with others things said in confidence, partners should not criticize each other in public), two regulating intimacy (partners should look each other in the eye while conversing, partners should/ should not have sex with each other), and one dictating reciprocal exchanges (partners should seek to repay debts, favors, or compliments, no matter how small). However, they found many more rules tied to specific types of relationships, with marriage having the largest number. In many instances, relationally specific rules are aimed at preventing common conflicts from arising within particular relationships. For example, arguing is a common activity among spouses (Argyle & Furnham, 1982), and researchers have identified a set of rules that guide how marital arguing should be enacted (Honeycutt, Woods, & Fontenot, 1993; Jones & Gallois, 1989). Shackelford and Buss (1996) offer insight into why such adaptation occurs. Basing their argument on the assumptions of evolutionary psychology, they assert that humans have learned that

relationships differ with regard to the particular resources and challenges experienced by relational partners. To help ensure that relationships run smoothly, humans have developed norms that guide relational conduct and have become sensitive to the degree to which given behaviors violate appropriate relational rules. Shackelford and Buss found that the degree to which certain behaviors (e.g., extrarelational intimacy) engender feelings of betrayal varies predictably according to the nature of the relationship (e.g., acquaintanceship, friendship, romantic involvement).

Although the aforementioned research has been quite successful in identifying the types of rules and highlighting their relationships to conflict prevention, it does not provide much information as to the specific behaviors that are considered transgressions. Other researchers have addressed this issue. Metts (1991) asked college students to describe actions or attitudes that they believed would constitute a transgression in an intimate relationship. The four most frequently described transgressions were (a) having extrarelational sexual intercourse, (b) wanting to or dating others, (c) deceiving the partner, and (d) flirting/necking/petting with others. Similarly, Roloff, Soule, and Carey (2001) asked undergraduates to recall transgressions committed against them by dating partners. The most frequently reported transgressions were romantic infidelity, lack of openness/honesty, inconsiderate/insensitive behavior, dominating behavior, and considering the relationship to be of low priority.

The research mentioned above has yielded useful insights, but it is limited. Although there is some correspondence between the results of research focused on rules and that examining the actions considered to be transgressions, the link is inferential rather than direct. In other words, researchers have not investigated the links between particular actions and the precise rules those actions violate. Because rules are thought to be prescriptions phrased in a rather broad fashion, their application to precise actions could be problematic for both researchers and relational partners.

Salience

Although a transgressor may attempt to hide his or her action, in some cases the partner will find out and the transgression will become salient. In the limited research that has been conducted on salience, researchers have focused on two issues. First, some have looked at how the transgression was discovered. Afifi, Falato, and Weiner (2001) asked undergraduates to recall dating relationships in which either they or their partners had been unfaithful, and to describe how the offense was discovered. Third parties such as friends or the person with whom the partner had been involved were the most frequent sources of information (42% of the cases). However, the study participants frequently reported that the unfaithful partner disclosed the indiscretion, either because the individual asked the partner about it (32%) or because the partner simply decided to volunteer the information (19%). In less than 10% of the cases, the partner was caught in the act. Although transgressions resulted in the greatest relational damage and were least likely to be forgiven when discovered through contact with third parties, relationships were more likely to terminate when the partner was caught in the act or admitted the transgression after being confronted. Unsolicited disclosures seem to be the least harmful mode of discovery. In part, this may result from the transgressor's honest admission, which reduces the likelihood that he or she will be perceived as deceptive and thereby guilty of another transgression (e.g., McCornack & Levine, 1990).

Second, in examining salience, researchers have studied factors that keep a discovered transgression salient. For example, Roloff et al. (2001) found that some victims reported mulling over the transgression by (a) frequently imagining the romantic partner committing the transgression, (b) recalling prior instances of a transgression, (c) plotting revenge, (d) considering breaking up with the partner, or (e) trying to understand the partner's perspective. Furthermore, some victims consulted their friends about what to do. Individuals who decided to stay with their transgressing partners because they had no better alternative relationships were more likely to recall prior instances of transgression, plot revenge, and consult friends. On the other hand, those who stayed because they were emotionally committed to the relationship were less likely to think about breaking up and more likely to consider the partner's perspective.

Obviously, the small number of research projects conducted to date limits our knowledge of salience. Moreover, most of the projects relied on recollections, which may be biased. On the other hand, this research does indicate that the salience of a transgression may affect future conflicts and even the future of a relationship.

Consequences

When entering into a relationship, individuals are implicitly—in some cases explicitly—committing themselves to obey certain rules. When these rules are violated, there is often a strong sense of betrayal that could even end the relationship (Davis & Todd, 1985). When investigating the consequences of these rules violations, researchers have explored the following four types of effects: (a) the impact on the transgressor (i.e., the person who committed the transgression), (b) the impact on the likelihood of a confrontation, (c) how the victim of a transgression responds to the transgressor, and (d) the impact of a transgression on the future of the relationship.

Investigators who have examined the impact of a transgression on the person who committed it have hypothesized that having committed an action that betrays another should induce substantial guilt (Baumeister, Stillwell, & Heatherton, 1995). Although guilt is a negatively experienced emotion (Baumeister, Reis, & Delespaul, 1995), it may produce some positive outcomes. Baumeister, Reis, and Delespaul (1995) found that guilty individuals were more likely than nonguilty ones to indicate that they had learned a lesson from their misdeeds, confessed them, apologized, and changed their behavior. Nonguilty individuals focused on mitigating factors, finding ways to blame their partners for the transgressions and justifying their misdeeds.

Researchers who have examined the impact of transgressions on the likelihood of confrontation have found that there is no guarantee that individuals who become aware that their partners have committed transgressions will confront them. Newell and Stutman (1991) found that confrontations are most likely to take place when individuals think that (a) it is their responsibility to say something to the transgressors, (b) the confrontation is in their self-interest, (c) they can influence the transgressors, (d) the problem cannot be handled better by someone else, and (e) they can no longer tolerate the offensive behavior. When deciding to confront a transgressor, an individual will often rehearse what he or she will say and formulate precise goals for the encounter (Stutman & Newell, 1990). In a sense, a confrontation is most likely to take place when an individual believes that he or she has legitimate concerns. This perception of legitimacy in turn promotes open expression, problem-solving behavior, and a willingness on the part of a partner to listen (Klein & Lamm, 1996).

Researchers have also examined how victims of transgressions respond to their partners. Not surprisingly, discovering a partner's transgression seems to prompt a rather cautious, risk-averse outlook, wherein the individual becomes less willing to accept the transgressor's excuses at face value (Boon & Holmes, 1999). Moreover, a victimized partner can legitimately seek retribution and restitution. McCullough, Bellah, Kilpatrick, and Johnson (2001) examined the degree to which individuals were vengeful after

being seriously offended by someone. In about 80% of the cases, the offender was a friend, romantic partner, or family member. Vengefulness was negatively related to forgiving and positively related to rumination about the offense and negative affectivity. Interestingly, individuals who were initially vengeful remained so over an 8-week period. Vengefulness may also lead to retaliation. Some vengeful individuals indicate that they have tried to make their partners jealous (White, 1980) or have reminded their partners of rule violations in an attempt to make them feel guilty (Vangelisti, Daly, & Rudnick, 1991). However, being vengeful can be costly to victims. Vengefulness is negatively related to life satisfaction (McCullough et al., 2001) and, relative to empathic responses, vengeful thinking prompts greater physiological stress and negative emotion (Witvliet, Ludwig, & Vander Laan, 2001).

Some victims choose to forgive their transgressors. McCullough, Worthington, and Rachal (1997) found that forgiveness results from a sequence that begins with the transgressor apologizing. This apology then prompts the victim to empathize with the transgressor. Empathy in turn produces forgiveness, which results in conciliatory behavior and less frequent avoidance of the transgressor. In a follow-up study, McCullough et al. (1998) found that forgiveness and vengefulness constitute independent causal sequences. Some individuals who were very close to their transgressors prior to the offensive actions experienced the above-outlined sequence, which ultimately led to the restoration of closeness. Other individuals who also had close relationships with their transgressors prior to the offenses ruminated about the transgressions. This rumination in turn prompted greater vengefulness and avoidance of the transgressors. Although the aforementioned research suggests that a partner's apology and the victim's empathy are key factors leading to forgiveness, Fincham (2000) offers an alternative sequence: When a transgression occurs, the victim attributes a degree of responsibility to the transgressor; the greater the degree of attributed responsibility, the less likely the victim is to forgive the partner. In support of this assertion, Fincham found that the negative relationship between the amount of responsibility attributed to a spouse for a transgression and positive marital interaction was fully mediated by the degree to which the victim forgave the transgressor.

Researchers have also been interested in the impact of transgressions on the future of relationships. Some have examined the kinds of rules that most frequently lead to relational harm. For example, Argyle and Henderson (1984) found that violations of nine rules were important causes of the breakup of friendships: (a) being jealous/critical of other relationships, (b) not keeping confidences, (c) not being tolerant of each other's friends, (d) criticizing each other in public, (e) not trusting/confiding in each other, (f) not volunteering help in a time of need, (g) not showing positive regard for each other, (h) not standing up for the other when he or she is not present, and (i) not providing emotional support. Baxter (1986) extrapolated the following seven primary rules from accounts of the breakups of heterosexual romantic relationships: (a) Partners should acknowledge each other's identities and lives outside of the relationship; (b) partners should express similar attitudes, values, and interests; (c) partners should enhance each other's self-worth/self-esteem; (d) partners should be open/genuine with each other; (e) partners should remain loyal/faithful to each other; (f) partners should gain relational rewards that are proportional to their investments; and (g) partners should experience an inexplicable magic when with each other.

The aforementioned research highlights that the type of transgression is a key determinant of whether the relationship continues. Alternatively, the key may be the reactions of the victim. We noted earlier that forgiveness rather than vengefulness seems critical to restoring the pretransgression closeness of a relationship. It is also possible that the degree to which a relationship survives a transgression results from the victim's reasons for staying in it. As discussed earlier, Roloff et al. (2001) found that those who were emotionally committed to relationships with transgressors were more likely to try to repair the relationships and stay with their partners. Those who were committed to transgressors because they had no better alternatives were likely to have more volatile and harmful confrontations about the transgressions. However, staying because there was no alternative was unrelated to terminating the relationship.

Summary

Research on transgressions adds an important element to the study of conflict: the degree to which a behavior is incompatible with social rules. Research associated with this topic has been more extensive than that examining other areas of conflict. However, this research is limited by two persistent methodological problems. First, although most scholars treat transgressions as a separate form of conflict, no research to date has compared transgression-based with nontransgression-based conflicts. Typically, researchers study transgressions in isolation. Hence we cannot tell whether the processes associated with rule violations are indeed unique to them. Second, in only a few studies have subjects actually been asked to report about transgressions per se. Most frequently, subjects are asked to describe conflicts in which someone has seriously offended them or they felt betrayed. Such assessment techniques could produce accounts of conflicts that are not rule violations.

Antagonistic/Dialectical Conflict

As we have previously discussed, conflict can emerge from incompatible individual and relational needs. Erbert (2000) argues that this incompatibility can take two forms, antagonistic and dialectical. Antagonistic incompatibility arises when relational partners have opposing needs, such as when an individual wishes greater personal autonomy within the relationship but his or her partner wants greater connection. Dialectical incompatibility occurs when partners pursue interdependent needs that at face value seem contradictory. For example, individuals may desire both autonomy and connectedness, but the fulfillment of one need (e.g., acting independent of one's partner) could undercut the ability to meet the other. Research has identified a number of dialectical contradictions, some of which are internal (e.g., autonomy/connection, predictability/novelty, and openness/closedness) and others of which are external to the relationship (e.g., third-party openness/closedness, integration/separation, and conventionality/uniqueness).

Erbert (2000) argues that interpersonal conflicts might reflect varying degrees of both types of incompatibility. A conflict that is both dialectical and antagonistic occurs when two individuals value both poles of a dialectical contradiction (e.g., both want autonomy and connectedness), but at the moment, the partners are advocating different positions (e.g., one is pursuing autonomy and the other connectedness). A dialectical and nonantagonistic conflict occurs when both partners value the opposing poles of a contradiction and are jointly seeking to achieve both. In such a case, their goal is to a find a means of achieving their mutual needs. A purely antagonistic conflict arises from pragmatic concerns, such as scarce resources. Finally, it is possible that a conflict might be neither antagonistic nor dialectical (e.g., arising from stress or misperception).

To assess the frequency of these conflicts, Erbert (2000) asked spouses to list conflicts in their marriages and to indicate the degree to which they were antagonistic and dialectical. The results indicated that 20% of all conflicts involved a combination of antagonism and dialectical contradiction, and 16% reflected only dialectical contradictions. Although some conflicts were indicative of unique contradictions, the most common contradictions were autonomy/connection and openness/closedness. Unfortunately, Erbert does not report the percentage of purely antagonistic conflicts separately from those that reflected neither antagonism nor dialectical contradiction.

This is a relatively new approach to studying interpersonal conflict, and many questions have not yet been addressed. It is unclear which processes cause conflicts to vary in antagonism or dialectical contradictions and whether such variance results in unique approaches to conflict management or different relational outcomes.

Conflict Issues

Inherently, conflict is about a particular topic or behavior. Often, researchers ask individuals to report on the issue at hand. In some cases, researchers inductively code the issues from responses to open-ended questions about a conflict (e.g., Buss, 1989; Roloff & Cloven, 1990; Steinmetz, 1977; Sternberg & Beier, 1977). Regardless of their origins, typologies of issues are typically restricted to single samples and often serve only as contextual information or as a data reduction technique rather than as a central focus of the investigation.

Contrary to the aforementioned norm, several researchers have focused on areas of interdependence as issues of conflict. Being in a relationship involves a degree of interdependence such that the typical behaviors enacted by each partner have impacts on the other (Kelley & Thibaut, 1978). When two partners have different preferences or liking for activities, these areas of interdependence can become conflict issues. For example, Surra and Longstreth (1990) asked dating couples to describe 45 activities in which they engaged as well as the degree to which they disagreed or felt tension about the activities. The activities were drawn from diaries kept by dating partners about their everyday activities (Surra, 1985). A cluster analysis of the frequency of these activities yielded 10 clusters: sex, relationship maintenance, foods/errands, housekeeping, exercise, secure stimulation, entertainment/cultural, partying, sports/games, and companionship. The researchers predicted the frequency of conflict over each activity based on (a) each partner's preference for the activity, (b) how similar the partners' preferences were, and (c) how frequently they performed the activity. Among women, similarity was negatively related to conflict over partying and sports/games, and frequency of participation was positively related to conflict over sex and sport/games. With regard to entertainment/cultural activities, among women who preferred these activities, the greater the joint participation, the greater the conflict; the same association was negative among women who did not strongly prefer the activity. Among men, similarity only reduced conflict about entertainment/cultural activities, and frequent joint participation increased conflict over relationship maintenance, housekeeping, and exercise. Although individuals in stable and satisfying relationships engaged in more joint activities and had less conflict about these activities than did those in problematic relationships, there was variance among the activities. Among women, conflicts about sex, relationship maintenance, partying, and companionship were negatively related to their relational satisfaction and to the stability of their relationships over a year's time. Among men, only conflict about relationship maintenance had an adverse impact on their relational satisfaction, and regardless of the activity, frequency of conflict was unrelated to the stability of the relationship.

Kurdek (1994a) studied the areas of behavioral and attitudinal interdependence in which heterosexual and homosexual couples experienced conflict, and related the frequency of these conflicts to changes in their relationship satisfaction. He found six areas of conflict arising from interdependence: power, social issues, personal flaws, distrust, intimacy, and personal distance. With regard to couple type, heterosexual couples reported more frequent conflict over social issues than did homosexual couples, whereas the opposite pattern was found for distrust. No other issues differed significantly among the couple types. Among all couple types, intimacy and power were the most frequent conflict issues, and relational satisfaction was negatively associated with frequent conflict about power, social issues, and distrust.

Clearly there are areas of interdependence in a relationship that become issues of conflict and, consequently, can reduce relational quality. However, it is unclear why only some become problematic. Indeed, in Surra and Longstreth's (1990) study, less than half of the regression equations predicting either the frequency of conflict or relational quality from relational activities were statistically significant. Furthermore, Kurdek (1994a) found that only three of the six conflict issues he established were significantly related to relational satisfaction. It is possible that some issues prompt the use of more harmful conflict management techniques. For example, in a study using diaries kept by spouses about their everyday interactions, Kirchler, Rodler, Holzl, and Meier (2001) found that conflict over economic matters—and, to a lesser degree, job requirements—more frequently prompted reasoned argument and factual presentation than did conflicts over children and relationship issues. Relationship and child-related conflicts more frequently produced negative emotion and withdrawal than did conflicts over economic and job-related issues. However, this study sheds no light on what features of these issues may have caused these differences. Thus, although researchers have speculated as to the critical features of issues that make them more or less problematic, we have no definitive evidence.

Summary

The research base associated with each of the perspectives on incompatibility is very thin. Some approaches have generated only one or two studies. Researchers have undertaken other studies that are indirectly related to the concepts under investigation here, but given that these studies were not directly constructed to examine particular types of conflict, their findings must be viewed with some caution. Hence the study of types of incompatibility has produced intriguing, but not definitive, findings.

RELATIONAL CONTEXTS

As we have noted, conflict is a state of incompatibility between individuals. This implies that the individuals' behaviors and outcomes are interdependent and that their differences are discovered and become evident through interaction. Because interactions are thought to be a core element of relationships (Hinde, 1979; McCall, 1970), conflict occurs within relational contexts. Many researchers have focused on the impact of conflict on relational quality, but there is another manner in which conflict and relationships are linked: Relational contexts may affect the types of conflicts that occur and the ways in which they are managed. In this section, we focus on two key relational elements that researchers have linked to conflict: intimacy and dependence.

Intimacy

Altman and Taylor (1973) hypothesized that "the more intimate a social relationship, the greater the possibility of conflict" (p. 168). Coser (1956) posited that "a conflict is more radical and more passionate when it arises out of close relationships" (p. 71). Many factors are thought to underlie the relationship between intimacy and conflict. For example, relative to nonintimates, intimates engage in more joint

activities and are more knowledgeable about each other, both of which increase the probability that incompatibilities will occur or be discovered (Altman & Taylor, 1973). Furthermore, in order to prevent damage to their relationship, intimates may withhold complaints until they finally erupt into an intense confrontation (Coser, 1956). Research testing the relationship between intimacy and conflict has focused on cross-relational and developmental comparisons.

Cross-Relational Comparisons

Researchers working within this perspective compare conflict across a variety of relationships. Argyle and Furnham (1982) asked individuals to report the kinds of activities in which they engaged with work colleagues, family members, and friends. They found that, relative to other relational types, arguing was most frequent between spouses. In a subsequent study, Argyle and Furnham (1983) had individuals describe the amount of criticism and emotional conflict they encountered with an adolescent in their family, a neighbor, a parent, an opposite-sex friend, a same-sex friend, a sibling, a spouse, a work associate, and a work superior. Criticism and emotional conflict were more frequent with a spouse than with any other type of relational partner. However, criticism was also frequent with an adolescent family member, a sibling, and a parent, and emotional conflict occurred frequently with a work superior. Compared with the aforementioned relationships, those with friends, neighbors, and work associates were relatively free of conflict. Jensen-Campbell and Graziano (2000) asked adolescents to keep diaries of their daily conflicts and found that, compared with conflicts with friends, disagreements with family members (parents and siblings) were more frequent, evoked more intense anger, and were less satisfactorily resolved. Similarly, Schoeneman (1983) asked undergraduates to keep diaries about the frequency with which they received feedback about themselves. The participants reported receiving criticism more frequently from family members than from friends and nonintimates (e.g., teachers, coaches, strangers), and the latter more frequently provided positive feedback. In contrast, Benoit and Benoit (1987), who also used a diary methodology, found that undergraduates most frequently argued with romantic partners, roommates, and friends, but rarely argued with teachers, siblings, or other family members. It is possible that the infrequency of family arguing found in this study may have stemmed from the students' living on campus and thus having infrequent contact and opportunity to argue with family members (see Schoeneman, 1983).

There is also evidence that conflicts with intimates can be especially destructive. When asked to report their most recent strong emotion, individuals often describe negative feelings (e.g., anger, sadness), which more often arise from difficulties with family members than from problems with work colleagues, friends, and strangers (Scherer & Tannenbaum, 1986). Furthermore, compared with nonintimates, intimates often say things that are more hurtful (Vangelisti & Crumley, 1998), and, not surprisingly, intimates often regret saying such things (Knapp, Stafford, & Daly, 1986). Finally, individuals are more likely to be victims of physical aggression enacted by family members than they are to be victims of aggression from individuals with whom they have nonfamily relationships (see Gelles, 1997).

The aforementioned research indicates qualified support for the claim that conflict is more frequent and intense in intimate than in nonintimate relationships. However, this pattern is most evident in comparisons of family and romantic relationships with other types. Friendships are intimate, but some studies indicate that there seem to be fewer problematic conflicts between friends than are found in other kinds of relationships. Indeed, in a study of third and fourth graders, Nelson and

Aboud (1985) found that friends were more likely to criticize each other than were nonfriends, but also provided more explanations for the criticism and were more likely to reach high-quality solutions to their disputes. Using a diary methodology with a sample of adolescents, Adams and Laursen (2001) discovered that, relative to conflicts with friends, the adolescents' disagreements with their parents were more likely to be coercive and angry and to end in win/lose solutions.

Developmental Comparisons

If intimacy prompts conflict, then as a relationship becomes more intimate, the level of conflict should also increase. To test this notion, researchers have asked individuals to recall the levels of conflict at certain development points in their romantic relationships. Braiker and Kelley (1979) asked spouses to recall the levels of conflict that occurred while they were casually dating, while they were seriously dating, and when they were engaged, as well as their current level of marital conflict. The reports indicated that the level of conflict increased significantly from casual to serious dating, but did not change at any stage after that. Using cross-sectional data, Stets (1993) found that when perspective taking was controlled for, conflict was lower among casual daters than among those daters who were somewhat serious, but the level of conflict among those who were somewhat serious did not differ from that among those who were seriously dating or engaged. Lloyd and Cate (1985) had individuals report the levels of conflict at various points in the histories of serious romantic relationships that had broken up. Their data indicate that the level of conflict increased across four relational stages (casual dating, becoming a couple, being committed to the relationship, and becoming uncertain about the future of the relationship), but leveled off after the respondents became certain that the relationship would break up. Interestingly, the frequency of conflict was not significantly correlated with love when respondents were casually dating, becoming a couple, or being committed to the relationship, but the correlation was significant and negative when they became uncertain about the future of the relationship and remained so after they concluded that the relationship would end.

A few studies have investigated conflict over the course of a marriage; most of these have employed cross-sectional designs. Swensen, Eskew, and Kohlhepp (1981) examined the frequency with which couples reported marital problems (e.g., expression of affection, problem solving/decision making) during different stages of their marriages. Problems increased significantly during the child-rearing years of marriage, but declined in a linear fashion as children aged and left the home. Zietlow and Sillars (1988) examined the extent of marital problems among young, middle-aged, and retired married couples and found that the frequency of conflict declined in a linear fashion. Although these data suggest that conflict lessens as marriage progresses, they may simply reflect how long-married couples deal with conflict. Swensen et al. (1981) found that couples at a later stage of marriage were actually less tolerant of one another, but also reported that they discussed fewer personal issues with each other and instead chose to keep their feelings to themselves. Zietlow and Sillars (1988) performed content analysis on the conflict conversations of retired couples and found that, relative to other groups, retired spouses were relatively noncommittal and equivocal in their conversations unless discussing highly salient problems, in which case they were extremely confrontational. Perhaps with relational longevity couples learn to pick their battles, letting small problems go unaddressed but fully engaging over salient ones.

There is also evidence that as a romantic relationship becomes more intimate, conflicts become more intense. Billingham and Sacks (1987) asked dating couples who were at one

of seven stages of emotional commitment to describe their conflict behaviors. Relative to casual daters who felt no emotional commitment, verbal aggressiveness was significantly greater among those respondents who (a) were in love with their partners, (b) were in love with their partners and wanted to marry them but had not discussed marriage, or (c) had discussed marriage with their partners but had no specific plans. However, among those who were engaged, the degree of verbal aggression was not significantly different from that reported by couples who had no emotional commitment. Furthermore, retrospective accounts indicate that the onset of physical abuse is associated with the point at which a dating relationship becomes serious (Cate, Henton, Koval, Christopher, & Lloyd, 1982; Henton, Cate, Koval, Lloyd, & Christopher, 1983).

Unfortunately, none of the aforementioned studies sheds light on why conflict seems to increase as intimacy grows. In part, this pattern might reflect problems associated with sexual activity. When dating, couples may have to reach consensus as to the onset, frequency, form, and exclusivity of sexual activity, and this could lead to conflict. Christopher and Cate (1985) asked individuals in serious dating relationships to recall the levels of conflict they experienced when on their first date, when casually dating, when considering becoming a couple, and after having become a couple. Moreover, the researchers asked about the level of sexual involvement at each stage. Among couples who were sexually intimate early in the relationship, conflict was high even at the time of the first date and remained so across relational stages. However, among those whose sexual intimacy developed gradually or was delayed, the level of conflict increased at later relational stages, when they were becoming more sexually intimate. Unfortunately, Christopher and Cate did not seek information about the specific topics of conflicts. Other research suggests that such conflicts could be related to a variety of sexual issues. Buss (1989) asked a sample of undergraduate daters and a sample of newlyweds to describe the frequency with which their partners engaged in behaviors that upset the respondents. Relative to newlyweds, daters more frequently complained that their partners were possessive, unfaithful, sexually aware of others, and sexually aggressive. However, this does not mean that increased intimacy resolves all sexual issues. For example, Buss found that regardless of relational status, men more so than women complained that their partners were sexually withholding. Nor does it imply that sexual activity does not reemerge as a source of conflict later in marriage. For example, Sternberg and Beier (1977) interviewed spouses when they were newlyweds and at their first wedding anniversaries, and found that sex was a more salient issue at the time of the second interviews than it had been when the spouses were newlyweds. Finally, even if sexual issues are resolved, nonsexual issues may emerge as a relationship becomes more intimate. Buss (1989) discovered that, relative to daters, newlyweds more frequently reported that their partners were abusive, inconsiderate, moody, and disheveled.

Increasing intimacy may also prompt confrontations. In other words, conflicts may exist at all stages of intimacy, but they are more likely to be expressed in intimate relationships, which in turn should increase the partners' awareness of them and the possibility that confrontations may escalate. Using a cross-sectional design, Cloven and Roloff (1994) found that the proportion of relational complaints a person was withholding from his or her dating partner was negatively related to love and stage of emotional commitment. In part, this reflected the belief among some individuals in nonintimate relationships that they should not express complaints until their relationships became closer. Hence norms might militate against a partner's complaining until a threshold of intimacy is reached. However, this does not mean that conflict avoidance never occurs in more intimate relationships. Cloven and Roloff found that individuals in more intimate relationships withheld complaints when they felt that such disclosures would lead to negative consequences or that their complaints were not important.

The positive link between intimacy and willingness to confront a partner might also reflect the increasing level of relational commitment that individuals often feel as a relationship grows closer. When individuals are generally satisfied with their relationship or have invested a great deal of time and resources in it, they have a stake in seeing it continue (see Rusbult & Buunk, 1993). Thus, when a problem occurs, intimates should be willing to voice their concerns as a means of protecting the relationship. Indeed, both relational satisfaction and investment are positively related to voicing relational concerns to a partner (Rusbult, Johnson, & Morrow, 1986a; Rusbult, Zembrodt, & Gunn, 1982).

It is also possible that the link between intimacy and conflict might result from control attempts. Stets (1995) argues that relational partners are more likely to attempt to control their partners when they feel their control over the relationship is threatened. In a cross-sectional study of daters, she found that as intimacy increased, so did both conflict and control attempts. Although Stets's model assumes that conflict causes control attempts, it is also possible that increased control attempts may stimulate conflict as one partner resists being controlled.

The aforementioned studies indicate that conflict becomes frequent and more aggressive when a dating relationship moves from casual to serious, especially after love emerges. However, with the exception of romantic involvements that ultimately break up, the frequency of conflict levels off (although some types of conflicts, such as those concerned with sexual intimacy, may increase in frequency).

Our confidence in these conclusions must be tempered by the nature of the data. Most of the studies we have reviewed employed retrospective accounts of relational conflict or cross-sectional designs that may be subject to a number of biases and confounds, such as memory distortions and cohort effects. Furthermore, the exclusive focus on the development of heterosexual romantic involvements leaves open the question of whether the results are generalizable to other forms of intimate relationships.

Summary

Although there is evidence that intimacy is linked to conflict, significant ambiguities remain. First, the causal mechanisms that produce this association are unclear. Does it emerge from the increased contact, knowledge, interdependence, and commitment that are the by-products of relational intimacy? Second, researchers have relied on relational categories that are thought to reflect different levels of intimacy rather than directly measuring intimacy. Hence romantic relationships are thought to be more intimate than friendships. Although this may typically be true, it is possible that a best friendship may be more intimate than a dating relationship or perhaps even a marriage. Thus our measures really provide a test only of the degree to which relational categories defined within our culture as having varying levels of intimacy are related to conflict. They do not directly test whether the amount of intimacy experienced within a given relationship is related to conflict.

Dependence

Although a given relationship may be quite rewarding, there is a sense in which it might be substitutable. In other words, either partner could find another partner or another type of relationship that could provide comparable rewards. To the degree that an individual perceives the rewards provided by alternatives to be of lesser quality than those received from the current relationship, that individual could become dependent on his or her partner. Moreover, should the partner have alternatives that are superior, the individual is in a state of relative dependence. As dependence increases, the individual should become more motivated to sustain the relationship or at least to avoid harming it. Because conflict could be harmful to a relationship, researchers have focused their attention on the role of dependence in conflict management. Two areas of research have emerged; these concern the chilling effect of dependence and responses to dissatisfaction.

The Chilling Effect

As we have noted, individuals sometimes do not express their grievances to their partners, and research indicates that dependence could have a chilling effect on the expression of complaints. Roloff and Cloven (1990) examined the degree to which dating partners were withholding complaints from their partners. They found that, consistent with a dependence hypothesis, as the quality of a person's relational alternatives declined, he or she withheld more complaints, but only when he or she perceived the partner's alternatives to be of higher quality than the current relationship. Furthermore, among those individuals whose alternatives were inferior, withholding complaints increased the perceived quality of the partner's alternatives. In such cases, the partner could easily replace the individual, so a confrontation could threaten the relationship. Thus the individual's perception of the partner plays a critical role in withholding. Indeed, when an individual perceived his or her partner's alternatives to be superior, withholding was greatest when the partner was not perceived to be committed to the current relationship or was engaging in extradyadic dating. Interestingly, the chilling effect was not related to whether the partner had ever threatened to end the relationship; thus it may result from the individual's perceptions rather than from the partner's pressure.

Obviously, the chilling effect could make it difficult for a person to address relational problems because, in effect, it renders him or her powerless. Indeed, the greater the perceived quality of a relational partner's alternatives, the greater the likelihood that an individual is withholding complaints about his or her lack of affection, excessive independence, lack of respect, and interest in other romantic partners (Roloff & Cloven, 1990). Furthermore, an individual who is involved with an aggressive partner is especially likely to withhold complaints about the partner's dominating/controlling behavior when the partner has superior relational alternatives or is not highly committed to the relationship (Cloven & Roloff, 1993). Dependence could also influence a person's appraisal of the seriousness of a relationship problem. Solomon and Samp (1998) found that among individuals who were highly committed to their relationships but who believed their partners were not highly committed, perceptions that the partner had superior alternatives decreased their perceptions that a relational problem was serious. It is possible that individuals who are dependent cope with their inability to express complaints by reducing their perception of the complaints' importance.

Although the aforementioned studies seem to suggest that dependence leads to conflict avoidance, there are anomalies in the data. In some cases, individuals who have superior relational alternatives withhold complaints. For example, Roloff and Cloven (1990) found that among those individuals whose partners had inferior alternatives, the quality of their own alternatives was positively related to withholding complaints. Furthermore, individuals who had good alternatives and were not committed to their relationships withheld dominance-related complaints from their aggressive partners (Cloven & Roloff, 1993). In part, this could reflect a tendency of individuals with good relational alternatives and low commitment to disengage from their relationships

rather than work to improve them. We examine this possibility next.

Dependence and Responses to Dissatisfaction

In close relationships, partners frequently engage in daily behaviors that have negative impacts on each other (Birchler, Weiss, & Vincent, 1975), and research indicates that dependence plays a role in determining how individuals respond to such impacts. In two studies, Rusbult and colleagues (1982, 1986a) found that having inferior relational alternatives decreased the likelihood that a person would respond to dissatisfaction by exiting from the relationship, and sometimes inhibited neglectful responses while increasing loyalty. These findings reflect the greater relational commitment and maintenance that come from an individual's perceiving that the current relationship is better than alternative ones. For example, Van Lange et al. (1997) found that commitment mediates the positive relationship between the willingness to sacrifice personally important activities for the good of the relationship and inferior relational alternatives. Furthermore, commitment also mediates how, relative to individuals with superior relational alternatives, persons with inferior alternatives respond more constructively (e.g., with voice and loyalty) and less destructively (e.g., by exiting or becoming neglectful) to their partners' negative behaviors.

One could argue that the aforementioned dependence effects could result in exploitation, such that individuals with inferior alternatives could be giving up more than their partners. However, research suggests that this may not always be the case. Using a measure of dependence that included quality of relational alternatives, Wieselquist, Rusbult, Foster, and Agnew (1999) identified a growth cycle that produces mutual rather than asymmetrical dependence. Specifically, a person's dependence prompts relational commitment and prosocial acts such as willingness to sacrifice and accommodation. The partner notices these actions, and this in turn increases his or her trust and dependence.

The aforementioned research indicates that dependence has a positive impact on relational functioning. Indeed, individuals who are highly committed to their relationships increase their dependence by being inattentive to relationship alternatives (Miller, 1997); when they do notice alternative partners, they tend to derogate the quality of those who are highly attractive (Johnson & Rusbult, 1989) or who are interested in them (Lydon, Meana, Sepinwall, Richards, & Mayman, 1999). However, there is evidence that dependence can have a negative impact on individuals. Spouses who believe that they have inferior relational alternatives are more likely to experience jealousy about their partners' extrarelational activities than are those whose alternatives are superior (Hansen, 1985). Moreover, women who have been physically abused by their male partners are more likely to remain committed to their relationships when they perceive that they have few structural alternatives, such as sources of income and transportation (Rusbult & Martz, 1995), and that their relational alternatives are inferior (Truman-Schram, Cann, Calhoun, & Vanwallendael, 2000). However, it should be noted that having poor structural alternatives increases the likelihood that a woman will return to her abuser (Rusbult & Martz, 1995), whereas the perception of inferior relational alternatives is unrelated to her decision (Truman-Schram et al., 2000).

Summary

Research suggests that dependence can have an important impact on conflict management. However, the nature of the data leaves some questions unanswered. Surprisingly, researchers have not directly assessed the degree to which individuals feel dependent on their partners. Instead, they have relied on indirect indicators such as the quality of individuals' alternatives or those of their partners. Hence we cannot speak to the degree to which feeling dependent emerges from the quality of an individual's alternatives or has an impact on conflict management. Furthermore, researchers have not fully addressed the nature of dependence. Most researchers have assumed that dependence entraps an individual by reducing his or her ability to form a better relationship or rewards source. Drigotas and Rusbult (1992) have argued that, rather than simply serving as an indicator of escape avenues, dependence may reflect a standard of comparison by which a person evaluates the vitality of his or her relationship. When a partner better satisfies an individual's needs than do alternative partners, the individual may view the relationship as more vital. When alternative partners are better sources of need satisfaction, the individual might end the relationship, even though he or she might not immediately move to form a new relationship with another partner.

SOCIAL NETWORKS

Individuals often have many relationships, and any given one can affect and be affected by others. This raises the possibility that social networks play a role in interpersonal conflict. Conflict research has focused on two ways in which social networks are influential: as causes of dyadic conflict and as shapers of conflict.

Social Networks as Causes of Dyadic Conflict

Social networks can create conflict in at least two ways. First, members of a person's social network may compete for that person's resources. Relationships require the commitment of time, attention, and often affection. In some cases, individuals may not be able to provide adequate resources for all of their relationships. Consequently, they redistribute their resources. When reallocation occurs, a partner who suffers a reduction in benefits may feel slighted, and conflict may result. For example, research indicates that as a romantic involvement grows more intimate, the partners withdraw from social contact with family and friends (Johnson & Leslie, 1982; Milardo, Johnson, & Huston, 1983), and their reallocation of contact can create conflict between the partners and those groups (Johnson & Milardo, 1984). Similarly, individuals report that they would become at least moderately jealous if their spouses were to reduce the amount of time spent with them so as to care for their baby, perform uncompensated work at their jobs, spend time with platonic opposite-sex friends, or do things on weekends with their families (Hansen, 1985). Furthermore, Kluwer, Heesink, and Van De Vliert (1996) found that when a husband's job requires more time commitment than expected by either spouse, both partners become dissatisfied about his workload, which results in more frequent marital conflict about paid labor.

Second, relational partners may disagree about how they should treat the members of their social networks. For example, Steinmetz (1977) found that husbands and wives frequently complained about how their spouses discipline their children. The repercussions of this conflict could be serious, given that spouses who disagree on child-rearing values have an increased risk of divorce (Block, Block, & Morrison, 1981). Furthermore, wives with children report less conflict with their own mothers and greater conflict with their mothers-in-law than do wives who are childless (Fischer, 1983). In part, this difference in the level of conflict between daughter-in-law and mother-in-law stems from greater disagreement over the treatment of the children. Such conflict between in-laws can have a negative impact on the future of a marriage. Indeed, in a longitudinal study, Bryant, Conger, and Meehan (2001) found that for both husbands and wives, conflict with

mothers-in-law decreased perceptions of marital success. For wives, conflict with fathers-in-law also decreased perceptions of marital success. However, among husbands, feelings of having an unsuccessful marriage increased their level of conflict with their fathers-in-law. It is possible that wives disclose their husbands' negative views of their marriages to their parents, thus prompting their fathers to confront their husbands.

Although the aforementioned research indicates that third parties can cause conflict within a relationship, often these outsiders are constrained by boundary rules. Boundary rules keep disruptive influences from entering into a relationship (McCall, 1970) and might prevent third parties from addressing potential problems they see in others' relationships. Wilson, Roloff, and Carey (1998) asked individuals to report what they found irritating in a friend's dating partner; they also asked whether the respondents had told the friend or his or her partner about this source of irritation. On average, the respondents had expressed about 50% of the irritations to the friend, but only about 10% of the irritations had been directly communicated to the dating partner. Often, their reluctance to express their irritations resulted from the belief that the problem was none of their business. These respondents did report, however, that they would be willing to confront the friend and/or partner if either of them brought up the irritation first, or if the friend was hurt by the irritation. Thus there appears to be a norm against interfering in the affairs of others unless invited to do so or unless the problem is serious. It is important to note, however, that some individuals reported they would never intervene in a friend's relationship.

Social Networks as Shapers of Conflict

Individuals may be reluctant to cause conflicts, but they may be willing to get involved in one that has already started. When they do get involved in a preexisting conflict, outsiders may shape the direction that it takes. Felson (1978) argues that when verbally attacked by another person, an individual loses face and consequently experiences a strong desire to retaliate in an aggressive fashion. However, the reaction of third parties determines whether retaliation actually occurs. Retaliation is most likely when third parties act in a way that signals they would approve of such a reaction, but it is inhibited when third parties act in a disapproving fashion. Consistent with this reasoning, Felson (1982) found that conflicts were more aggressive when third parties urged one party to continue the dispute rather than attempted to calm things down. Felson, Ribner, and Siegel (1984) examined presentencing reports on youths convicted of criminal assaults, and found that the assaults were more violent when family and friends were present and encouraged rather than mediated the disputes. Moreover, the mere presence of third parties may influence aggression. Feld and Robinson (1998) reasoned that there is a norm against stronger individuals acting aggressively against weaker ones and that this norm is more salient when third parties are present during a dispute. Consistent with their logic, their study participants' responses to hypothetical scenarios indicated that the presence of third parties increased the likelihood that a woman would physically retaliate against a boyfriend who insulted her, but decreased the likelihood that a male would physically retaliate against a verbally provocative girlfriend.

Analyses of family quarrels also demonstrate that third parties can shape disputes. Vuchinich, Emery, and Cassidy (1988) studied family quarrels at the dinner table and found that daughters and mothers most often intervened in the disagreements of other family members. Daughters typically attempted to distract the disputants by changing the subject, whereas mothers tried to mediate the disputes. In some cases, third parties formed alliances with one of the disputants, parents most frequently siding with each other and children forming alliances with one another. Interestingly, third-party intervention increased the likelihood that a dispute would end with one party withdrawing by refusing to talk any more or by leaving the table. Apparently, intervention did not resolve the issue, but simply prompted at least one of the parties to disengage.

As we have noted, boundary rules make friends leery of becoming involved in each other's conflicts. However, when asked, they do so. Thus researchers have studied the types of advice individuals receive and the impacts of such advice on conflicts. In a study of friendship conflicts, Healey and Bell (1990) discovered that the more a social network of friends opposed the dissolution of a given friendship, the less likely the disagreeing friends would be to exit from their relationship and the more likely they would be to attempt to talk through the problem. Moreover, Klein and Milardo (2000) found that individuals who were dating generally believed that their friends were more likely to support their positions in conflicts with their partners than were family members, but they also expected their same-sex friends to be more supportive than the friends they shared with their partners. When Klein and Milardo examined actual levels of support, they found that among women, the greater the number of supporters they had, the more legitimate they felt their position was. Men, however, perceived their legitimacy to be greatest when they had fewer critics. Women who had more support from their own networks were also less willing to compromise than were women with less support. For both sexes, support from the couple's joint network increased the partners' willingness to compromise, and among men, such support increased their willingness to be accommodative toward their girlfriends. Women who had support from their partners' networks were more contentious, and men who perceived that their partners were being criticized by their own networks were less willing to accommodate.

In another study of the impact of outsiders on conflict, Julien et al. (2000) investigated how the best friends of satisfied and dissatisfied spouses responded to disclosures about marital conflict. Not surprisingly, satisfied couples and their friends were more positive and less negative when discussing conflicts than were dissatisfied couples and their friends. Moreover, the friends of satisfied versus dissatisfied spouses, especially the friends of satisfied wives, seemed to be more effective at reframing relational concerns so as to make them less threatening to the relationship. Indeed, satisfied wives felt closer to their husbands after their conversations with their best friends.

Although the aforementioned research suggests that the direct involvement of social network members can significantly influence the course of conflict, it is also possible that social network members have an indirect influence. Research indicates that through socialization, individuals acquire preferences for modes of conflict resolution that are used in other contexts (e.g., Roloff & Greenberg, 1980). Recent research has shown that a child's exposure to intense conflict between his or her parents promotes pro-aggressive attitudes that subsequently lead to aggression at school (Marcus, Lindahl, & Malik, 2001).

Summary

Although research indicates that social networks can cause and shape relational conflicts, it does not address whether or how relational partners try to limit the intrusion of their social networks into their relationships. In effect, although there is evidence that relational boundaries prevent a degree of interference, we do not know whether those boundaries are explicitly negotiated, develop implicitly over time, or reflect normative patterns within a culture. Furthermore, it is unclear whether

individuals bring up the support they have from friends during relational arguments, and, if they do, what effect this has. Because individuals enact conflict behaviors that are similar to the ones performed by their significant others, they may view their own conflict actions to be normal and justified, which is a view that might not be shared by the persons with whom they are in conflict.

PERCEPTIONS

To a large extent, conflict is influenced by perceptions. For conflict to occur, individuals must perceive some sort of incompatibility and try to understand its source. These perceptions are thought to influence the ways in which individuals attempt to manage disputes. Hence substantial research has focused on how people make sense of their disputes. Researchers have examined the influence of knowledge structures on conflict and the factors that lead to perceptual biases.

Knowledge Structures

With experience, individuals develop expectations for events that help them understand and respond effectively to similar circumstances. Such is the case for conflict. Five general types of knowledge structures have been researched: conflict frames, conflict metaphors, conflict scripts, relational beliefs, and problem conceptualization.

Conflict Frames

Pinkley (1990) argues that when an individual encounters a conflict, a frame is elicited that partly determines how he or she will interpret and behaviorally respond to it. This conflict frame reflects the person's memory of past experiences as well as his or her perceptions of salient cues within the situation. A frame is thought to be composed of a set of interpretive dimensions. To assess these dimensions,

Pinkley asked respondents in a noncollege sample to describe a current conflict in which they were involved and then had a sample of undergraduates make similarity judgments among these conflict exemplars. A multidimensional analysis of these judgments uncovered three dimensions. The first was focused on the degree to which the conflict involved relationship issues (e.g., the ongoing interaction between two individuals) versus specific task issues (e.g., money, property, job requirements). The second reflected the degree to which the conflict had elicited intellectual (e.g., focus on facts or thoughts) or emotional responses (e.g., jealousy, hatred, anger). The final dimension concerned the degree to which the conflict required a win/lose (e.g., one party is right and the other is wrong) or compromise solution (e.g., both parties are to blame). In a follow-up study, Pinkley (1992) found that individuals who framed a current conflict as relational and intellectual believed that the conflict had been occurring over a long period and involved a number of issues. Similarly, those using an emotional compromise frame reported that their conflict involved a number of issues, but that it had emerged suddenly rather than developed gradually. The most serious and intense conflicts were reported by those who framed them as emotional and win/lose. There was also evidence that parties to a given conflict often share the same frame with regard to the relationship versus task and win/lose versus compromise dimensions. However, they do not always have a common perception of the intellectual versus task dimension.

These results are to some degree in accord with theorizing about conflict. For example, although he does not posit specific dimensions, Deutsch (1973) notes that conflicts can be about issues concerning the relationship between two parties as well as scarce resources. He further adds that disputants might use competitive (win/lose) or cooperative (compromise) approaches to solving

conflict. Little subsequent research has been generated on conflict frames, so the potential of this area of inquiry remains largely untapped.

Conflict Metaphors

Researchers often ask people to describe specific features of their conflicts, and the descriptions they offer include metaphors (i.e., figurative language in which one process is described as being like another). Many scholars believe that these metaphors provide information about the perceptual sets that individuals use to make sense of disputes, and that one might determine how individuals will act based on the metaphors they use. In effect, when a person characterizes one process as being similar to another, he or she may come to believe that the two processes are the same.

McCorkle and Mills (1992) asked undergraduates to provide written descriptions of up to four of their personal conflicts. The researchers then content analyzed the descriptions for their metaphors. Two important patterns emerged. First, 88% of the descriptions included metaphors, which indicates that individuals see connections between conflict and other processes. Second, all of the metaphors were negative. The most frequently occurring metaphors involved animals (e.g. "two rams butting heads"), natural processes (e.g., "a tornado"), one-way communication (e.g., "talking to a brick wall"), confinement (e.g., "tied up in chains"), and military- or war-related images (e.g., "never-ending battle"). Although many conflict scholars tout the benefits of conflict, these metaphors suggest that ordinary individuals experience conflict as negative.

The study of conflict metaphors can provide useful insights into how people make sense of their disputes. Unfortunately, the potential of this perspective remains untouched. Limited research has been conducted using this perspective, so we have no information about how conflict metaphors emerge, why individuals use the metaphors they do to characterize their disputes, or, especially, the degree to which the use of particular metaphors predicts conflict management.

Conflict Scripts

After repeated experience with certain kinds of situations, individuals may develop expectations for the behaviors typically enacted in those situations and the order in which those behaviors will occur. These scripts provide a means by which individuals can understand what will happen in given situations and what behaviors they should enact (Abelson, 1981).

Two studies have focused on conflict scripts. Miller (1991) explored the degree to which males and females differ with regard to the sequence of behaviors they expect to occur across friendship conflicts arising from broken promises, cumulative annoyances, criticism, rebuffs, and illegitimate demands. In relation to conflicts over broken promises, cumulative annoyances, criticism, and illegitimate demands, most individuals in Miller's sample expected that the offended party would initiate the confrontation with a question. In the case of rebuffs, they expected the offended party to start the confrontation with an accusation. After the conflict was initiated, Miller's respondents typically expected the offender to respond with excuses when the conflict was about broken promises, criticism, and illegitimate demands, but expected apologies when the conflict was over cumulative annoyances or rebuffs. In conflicts over broken promises, cumulative annoyances, and illegitimate demands, they expected the offended party to accept fully the account provided by the offender, but only begrudgingly so when the conflict was over criticisms or a rebuff. Finally, in conflicts over cumulative annoyances, criticism, rebuffs, and illegitimate demands, Miller's respondents expected the issues to be resolved, although only partially so when there was a broken promise. Generally, the individuals in

Miller's sample had positive conflict scripts. Moreover, very few gender differences in scripts were identified. The sequence of actions involved in a male's script was more positive when the offended party initiated the conflict with a question rather than an accusation, but for females the sequence was more positive when the offending party apologized. Apparently, males felt that the way the conflict was initiated was critical for determining how constructively the individuals managed it, whereas females were less sensitive to how it was initiated and more concerned about whether the offender apologized.

Fehr, Baldwin, Collins, Patterson, and Benditt (1999) investigated whether individuals have anger scripts for conflict situations. They examined the degree of anger and the reactions to it that were expected in dating conflicts arising from betrayal of trust, rebuffs, unwarranted criticism, negligence/lack of consideration, and cumulative annoyances. Regardless of gender, individuals in their sample reported that they would be most angry in a conflict arising from betrayal of trust, followed by a rebuff, criticism, negligence, and cumulative annoyance. Across all situations, females indicated that they would be angrier than males; the greatest gender difference occurred for conflicts over negligence and personal criticism. Although both males and females expected that anger would prompt them to talk through the dispute, females were more likely to report that they would express hurt feelings and respond aggressively, especially in conflicts over negligence and personal criticism. Finally, both males and females anticipated that if they approached their partners positively, the partners would reciprocate. However, females predicted that that if they aggressively confronted their partners, the partners would deny responsibility for the problem. Males expected that their aggressive initiation of conflict would prompt expressions of hurt feelings, avoidance, and rejection.

The aforementioned research indicates that individuals do indeed have expectations for what should happen in conflict. However, the research stops short of demonstrating that such scripts are accurate representations of what happens during conflict. For example, Kelley et al. (1978) found that some stereotypes of what males and females say and do during conflicts appear to be valid, but some are not. Furthermore, none of the research has focused on the degree to which individuals use scripts to guide their actions during conflict.

Relational Beliefs

Researchers have identified a number of beliefs that are negatively related to marital adjustment and satisfaction (Eidelson & Epstein, 1982). These include beliefs about sexual perfectionism and beliefs that the sexes are different, that mind reading is expected, that partners cannot change, and that disagreement is destructive. Metts and Cupach (1990) found that endorsement of each of these five beliefs was related to how individuals responded to dissatisfaction in their relationships. Indeed, the more strongly individuals endorsed these beliefs, the greater their likelihood of exit and neglect and the lesser their likelihood of voicing complaints. Not surprisingly, these responses (i.e., exit, neglect, voicing complaints) mediated the relationship between relational beliefs and relational satisfaction. These findings indicate that conflict-related beliefs (e.g., disagreement is destructive, partners cannot change) play a critical role in how individuals handle dissatisfaction in their relationships. In a longitudinal study, Crohan (1992) examined the relationship between marital satisfaction and consensus between spouses about whether conflicts are healthy and can be solved through discussion or should be avoided. Her data indicate that spousal agreement about these specific beliefs is not significantly related to marital satisfaction, but that holding negative beliefs

about conflict in general is negatively related to satisfaction. Thus negative beliefs about conflict seem dysfunctional.

Although useful, this research does not indicate how such beliefs are formed. It is possible that individuals who are involved with partners who respond destructively are more inclined to develop negative beliefs about conflict and respond to conflict in a dysfunctional way. Indeed, believing that disagreement is destructive and that partners cannot change is positively correlated with spouses' becoming critical or defensive during conflict (Epstein, Pretzer, & Fleming, 1987). Hence it is possible that such beliefs are grounded in the personal reality of the respondent.

Problem Conceptualization

Witteman (1988) argues that conflicts prompt cognitive activity aimed at understanding them. When an individual attempts to understand an interpersonal conflict, his or her thought processes focus on five dimensions. First, the person compares the conflict with other disagreements so as to gauge its uniqueness and relative frequency. Second, the person assesses the goal he or she wants to achieve in the conflict, including its importance, complexity (i.e., whether it is composed of subgoals), and mutuality (i.e., whether the conflict partner will allow them to achieve it). Third, the person considers the degree of uncertainty he or she is experiencing about the partner, the relationship, or how to manage the problem. Fourth, the person determines whether the problem should be attributed to self, the partner, the relationship, or the environment. Finally, the person considers his or her feelings for the partner. Each of these dimensions is thought to influence the manner in which the person will manage the dispute. Witteman examined how undergraduates perceived a current conflict on each of these dimensions and whether their responses were related to their conflict management behaviors. He found that individuals were more distributive (e.g., argued, threatened each other) when they perceived the conflict to be common and frequent, when they believed the other person intentionally caused the problem, and when they had negative feelings for the person. Individuals enacted more integrative behaviors (i.e., disclosed feelings, suggested solutions) when the problem was unique, when their goals were important, and when the environment caused the problem. Individuals preferred indirect confrontation strategies (e.g., waited to confront the person until he or she was in a good mood) when the conflict was frequent, when their goals were complex, when they were uncertain about the person and the relationship, when the relationship caused the problem, and when they had negative feelings toward the partner. Finally, individuals were avoidant when they were uncertain about the other person and how to manage the dispute, and when they felt the relationship caused the problem. In a follow-up study, Witteman (1992) replicated many of these findings with a different measure of conflict management.

This research suggests that when analyzing a conflict, individuals cue on certain features that predict how they will attempt to manage it. However, the nature of the research methods used cannot tell us whether these dimensions are always salient. For example, Witteman asked individuals to assess each of these dimensions, which may have highlighted their importance. Whether such dimensional judgments occur spontaneously has not been explored.

Perceptual Biases

Some researchers have been interested in the degree to which individuals form biased perceptions of disputes. Four approaches have been taken to studying bias; these are known as sentiment override, reactivity, positive illusions, and information processing.

Sentiment Override

Weiss (1980) has posited that during a conflict interaction, partners' emotional and cognitive responses to each other's behaviors may be biased by their general feelings toward each other. Although very few studies have tested this notion, there is partial support for it. Floyd (1988) discovered that husbands, but not wives, interpreted their partners' interaction behaviors in a manner that was not consistent with the evaluation ratings of outside observers, but judged their own behaviors in a manner consistent with that of the observers. Wives judged their husbands' behaviors in much the same way observers perceived those behaviors. Recently, Flora and Segrin (2000) examined the degree to which spouses' affective reactions to a complimenting and complaining interaction reflected their partners' behavior or their own relational satisfaction. They found that positive affect was not significantly correlated with relational satisfaction, but relational satisfaction reduced feelings of negative affect arising from the conversation. With one exception, a spouse's relational satisfaction was a better predictor of his or her negative affective response than was the actual behavior of the partner. The exception was that, regardless of their satisfaction, wives experienced more negative affect when their husbands were highly involved in a complaining interaction. Finally, Fincham, Garnier, Gano-Phillips, and Osborne (1995) found evidence of sentiment override, but only when sentiment toward a partner is highly accessible to the individual. Although the sentiment override hypothesis is intriguing, it has generated little research. Thus the findings from this small research base suggest that the effect is limited in scope.

Reactivity

Research indicates that, for some individuals, relational satisfaction varies from day to day (e.g., Jacobson, Waldron, & Moore, 1980) and that such fluctuations predict relational dissolution (Arriaga, 2001). To account for these patterns, Jacobson, Follette, and McDonald (1982) argue that couples vary in the degree to which they are reactive to daily events. In their sample, the daily marital satisfaction of distressed versus nondistressed couples was determined by the valence of the partners' behavior. Hence on days when the spouse was especially rewarding, the marital satisfaction of a distressed spouse increased, but when the spouse was punitive it decreased. The daily marital satisfaction of a nondistressed spouse was relatively uninfluenced by the spouse's behavior. It is important to note that reactivity effects were not artifacts of the frequency of positive and negative actions. However, some limitations to these findings were observed. The researchers found that some spouses were more reactive to positive events, others were more reactive to negative events, and some were equally reactive to both types.

Although the phenomenon of reactivity is intriguing, little research has examined it, and its nature remains largely unexplored. For example, it is unclear why distressed couples are more reactive to daily events. It is possible that in a distressed relationship, individuals are more likely to be actively questioning whether they wish to continue it, and hence they are more sensitive to current events. Alternatively, individuals in nondistressed marriages may be more committed to their partners, and hence have a long-term outlook on their relationships that render the outcomes of most daily activities inconsequential.

Positive Illusions

Although realistically viewing a partner's traits might appear to be beneficial to a relationship, there is a growing body of evidence that idealizing a partner might be more functional. When Murray, Holmes, and Griffin (1996a) asked intimates to rate each other's characteristics, they found that the ratings reflected the raters' own self-perceptions and idealizations to a greater extent than they did the partners' self-perceptions. Indeed, individuals rated their partners more positively than they rated themselves, and these idealized impressions were positively related to relational satisfaction. In a follow-up, Murray, Holmes, Dolderman, and Griffin (2000) found that happily married individuals rated their spouses more positively than the spouses rated themselves or than friends rated the spouses. Conversely, unhappily married individuals rated their spouses more negatively than did the spouses or friends. Having positive illusions such as idealized perceptions of one's partner and unrealistic optimism reduces the level of conflict in a relationship, mitigates doubt, and increases satisfaction (Murray & Holmes, 1997; Murray, Holmes, & Griffin, 1996b). In part, storytelling may play a role in creating and sustaining positive illusions. When creating narratives about their partners' negative conflict behaviors, intimates find ways of integrating those behaviors into larger positive views of their partners, such as linking faults to redeeming values or downplaying the faults' significance (Murray & Holmes, 1993, 1994). Moreover, such integration actually increases the stability of a relationship (Murray & Holmes, 1999). Paradoxically, this finding suggests that individuals may be prompted by their partners' faults to construct stories that will mitigate the impact of those faults and thereby strengthen their relationships.

Although much research on perceptual biases demonstrates that they have negative relational impacts, research on positive illusions indicates the opposite. Of course, the degree to which relational illusions are seen as positive may depend on the nature of the relationship. For example, although positive illusions might help individuals deal with their partners' minor flaws, such illusions might not be beneficial in abusive relationships.

Information Processing

The process by which individuals attempt to make sense of conflicts may also introduce bias. When conflicts occur, individuals may be motivated to think about why they happened, and two studies have found that frequent rumination about serious interpersonal offenses is positively related to reacting in a vengeful manner (McCullough et al., 1998, 2001). Vengeful motivations could results from biases that are linked to mulling over a conflict. When thinking about conflicts in isolation, individuals pay little attention to their partners' perspectives (Cloven, 1990); consequently, the more they mull over the conflicts, the more they should attribute responsibility to their partners and the more the conflicts should appear to be serious. In a study of roommate conflicts, Cloven and Roloff (1991) verified this relationship. However, they found that for major conflicts, the impact of mulling was lessened when the roommates communicated frequently with each other and especially when they enacted integrative strategies. On the other hand, having distributive interactions increased the impact of mulling.

Hence communication allows both partners' viewpoints to be aired and overcomes the singular focus of mulling, but other aspects of the communication situation also affect what individuals think about. In particular, individuals may be biased when processing communication events. Because conflict interactions often contain myriad cues, it is possible that individuals selectively attend to some cues and thus show processing biases. For example, Sillars, Roberts, Leonard, and Dun (2000) asked spouses to watch a tape of one of their conflicts and then reconstruct the thoughts they had during the exchange. They found that each person's thoughts rarely took into account the perspective of the partner, were of limited complexity, and were often focused on implicit relational issues rather than on the conflict issues. Moreover, each person viewed his or her own communication more favorably than the partner's. In addition, more severe conflicts reduced the correspondence between the strategies that wives reported using and the strategies that coders actually observed. Finally, severe conflicts and disputes between dissatisfied partners resulted in angrier, more pessimistic, and more blaming thoughts, with fewer thoughts focusing on the conflict issue.

Although the aforementioned research suggests inherent biases, there may be individual differences in people's tendencies to interpret cues in particular ways. Individuals, especially women, who are sensitive to social rejection are prone to interpret ambiguous interactions with or insensitive behavior enacted by their partners as rejection (Downey & Feldman, 1996). Furthermore, rejection-sensitive women are more negative during conflicts, which causes their partners to be less accepting and more withdrawn afterward (Downey, Freitas, Michaelis, & Khouri, 1998). This withdrawal then causes more conflict (Ayduk, Downey, Testa, Yen, & Shoda, 1999). In such cases, a person's misinterpretation of a partner's cues stimulates behavior that is consistent with the erroneous impressions.

Summary

Research indicates that people have knowledge structures related to conflict that sometimes direct their behavior. Moreover, individual's perceptions, particularly their misperceptions, influence conflict. However, scholarship does not clearly indicate the causes of these knowledge structures or perceptions. Generally, we assume that knowledge structures and perceptual biases are formed through experience, but rarely have researchers directly explored this link. Alternatively, some biases could result from human beings' limited ability to process the large number of cues embedded in a cluttered environment. Furthermore, Buss (2001) has argued that some cognitive biases, especially those related to male-female interactions, may result from adaptive reproduction-related responses arising from evolution. Hence males are prone to perceive greater sexual interest from certain females so as not to miss sexual opportunities, and females underestimate males' actual commitment early in relationships so as not to fall victim to sexual exploitation (Haselton & Buss, 2000).

CONFLICT MANAGEMENT STYLES

Some researchers have been interested in identifying and evaluating the effectiveness of clusters of conflict behaviors that reflect different styles of conflict management. Although a variety of measures of conflict strategies and styles have been developed, we focus here on four that have generated the greatest amount of research: responses to dissatisfaction, conflict resolution styles, conflict tactics, and avoidance-distributive-integrative strategies.

Responses to Dissatisfaction

Based on Hirschman's (1970) analysis of the decline of macroentities such as organizations, Rusbult et al. (1982) argue that relational partners may respond to dissatisfaction in four ways. First, they may exit from the relationship by threatening to and/or actually disengaging from the relationship. Second, they may neglect the relationship by being hostile/cruel, distancing themselves from their partner, and/or silently waiting for the relationship to end. Third, they may remain loyal to the partner by forgiving, submitting, or waiting for the relationship to improve. Finally, they may voice their concerns by suggesting solutions, talking about the problem, or somehow trying to fix the problem. Rusbult and Zembrodt (1983) solicited examples of responses to relational dissatisfaction from a sample of undergraduates and from a random sample of adults. A multidimensional analysis of the responses indicated that they clustered into the following categories: exit, neglect, loyalty, and voice. These categories were differentiated by active/passive and constructive/destructive dimensions. Voice was perceived to be constructive and active, whereas loyalty was seen as constructive and passive. Exit and neglect were both judged to be destructive, but the former was perceived to be active and the latter passive.

To assess the impact of each of these responses, Rusbult, Johnson, and Morrow (1986b) investigated the degree to which individuals perceived that their own and their partners' responses were related to relational distress. Regardless of whether enacted by the respondent or his or her partner, exit and neglect were positively related to distress, and voice was negatively related. However, exit and neglect were more powerful predictors of distress than voice. Furthermore, individuals who reciprocated their partners' destructive behaviors reported greater distress, whereas those who responded with voice reported less distress. Loyalty proved to be a weak and inconsistent predictor of distress. Indeed, subsequent analyses have shown that loyalty is not often noticed by a partner (Drigotas, Whitney, & Rusbult, 1995). Although loyalty produces a more constructive response than exit or neglect, it is less effective than voice.

Since Rusbult et al. (1986b) found that an individual's reaction to a partner's destructive response seems to be a powerful predictor of distress, subsequent researchers have combined voice/loyalty and neglect/exit into two indices. These indices reflect constructive and destructive responses, respectively. Taken together, they constitute the degree to which a person is willing to inhibit his or her initial impulse to reciprocate a partner's destructive response and instead respond constructively. Research suggests that such accommodation flows primarily from relational commitment (Rusbult, Verette, Whitney, Slovik, & Lipkus, 1991), but that accommodation processes are less likely to take place when individuals are under time pressure to react (Yovetich & Rusbult, 1994) and among individuals who are unable to exert self-control (Finkel & Campbell, 2001).

This approach to conflict styles has created a substantial amount of research and has produced useful insights. However, several issues have been neglected. Although research suggests that people differentiate among the responses based on the degree to which they are active or passive, researchers have rarely focused on this dimension. Other than the study conducted by Drigotas et al. (1995), most research has focused on the constructive/ destructive dimension. This dominant focus may be leading scholars to overlook intriguing possibilities. Because passive responses inherently involve less intervention, one might wonder why people choose to employ them. Does the use of passive responses stem from individuals' belief that the sources of their dissatisfaction are not under their control, and so intervention makes little sense? When uncontrollable problems also seem unstable, do individuals behave in a loyal fashion, and do they neglect their relationships when the problems are stable, waiting for the relationships' demise? Furthermore, researchers have not focused on the degree to which these four responses might occur in conjunction or, alternatively, in sequence. In other words, individuals may initially respond in passive fashion, engaging in active confrontation only after passive responses are no longer effective.

Conflict Resolution Styles

Based on behavioral observations of marital conflict (Gottman & Krokoff, 1989), Kurdek (1994b) created an instrument aimed at assessing four potential conflict resolution styles. The results of a confirmatory factor analysis indicated that there are indeed four distinct styles. The first of these styles, positive problem solving, involves compromise and negotiation. The second, conflict engagement, is

characterized by the use of personal attacks and losing control. The third, withdrawal, reflects the degree to which the individual refuses to discuss a problematic issue and tunes out the partner. The last style, compliance, occurs when the individual gives in and does not defend his or her own position. Kurdek found that the frequency of use of these four styles was similar among gay, lesbian, and heterosexual nonparent and parent couples. Across the various types of couples, relational satisfaction was positively correlated with positive problem solving and negatively related to conflict engagement and withdrawal. However, a compliant style was not consistently related to relational satisfaction. In predicting changes in relational satisfaction and dissolution over a 1-year period for all four types of couples, positive problem solving increased relational satisfaction and decreased the likelihood of dissolution. However, conflict engagement had the opposite effect. Withdrawal tended to reduce satisfaction over time, but had no effect on dissolution. Finally, the pattern of correlations for compliance was again inconsistent.

In a follow-up study, Kurdek (1995) examined the relationship between conflict style and changes in relational satisfaction among heterosexual couples over a 2-year period. A factor analysis yielded three styles instead of four. Although withdrawal and compliance emerged as distinct styles, the conflict engagement items loaded positively and the positive problem-solving items loaded negatively on the same dimension. This new factor was labeled *conflict engagement*. Changes in a wife's marital satisfaction were not strongly related to her husband's conflict style, but the wife's conflict style, sometimes in concert with her husband's, was significantly related to changes in his satisfaction. Regardless of the husband's conflict style, a wife's frequent use of conflict engagement decreased her husband's marital satisfaction. However, a husband's marital satisfaction increased when (a) he frequently used conflict engagement and his wife rarely withdrew, and (b) he frequently was compliant and his wife frequently withdrew. Finally, both spouses' marital satisfaction decreased when the wife engaged in conflict engagement and the husband withdrew.

This approach to conflict resolution styles has a great deal of utility. It not only seems to characterize styles across a variety of relationships, but the styles are related to long-term changes in a relationship as well. However, the inability to replicate a positive problem-solving style that is distinct from conflict engagement suggests that this notion of conflict styles requires revision.

Conflict Tactics

Straus (1979) has suggested that conflict is an inevitable part of human relations, but to understand its effects, one should not focus on its frequency, but should instead examine the modes of conflict management and resolution that are used. To help identify those modes, Straus created a scale that measures three clusters of conflict tactics. The first of these clusters, rationality, involves rational discussion, argument, and reasoning. The second, verbal aggression, includes verbal and nonverbal acts aimed at hurting or threatening the partner. The last, physical aggression, involves the use of physical force. Although various forms of Straus's Conflict Tactics Scale exist, several factor analyses have verified the existence of these three clusters (for a review, see Straus, 1990b). Although Straus's conceptualization suggests that three styles might be found, the greatest impact of his perspective arises from his focus on physical aggression. Indeed, the Conflict Tactics Scale has been used extensively to study abuse between dating partners, child abuse, and spouse abuse. However, its use in these domains has been controversial (for a discussion, see Straus, 1990a).

As a result of the dominant focus on physical aggression, little attention has been directed

toward the reasoning and verbal aggression tactics. However, a few useful insights related to these tactics have emerged. There is evidence that the three styles frequently occur within the same relationships. Billingham (1987) asked individuals in dating relationships that were at various stages of emotional commitment about the extent to which they had used reasoning, verbal aggression, and physical aggression to resolve their conflicts. He then compared the responses of individuals in nonaggressive relationships with those who had been victimized by their partners, were victimizers themselves, or were involved in mutually aggressive relationships. Across the stages of emotional commitment, individuals in the three groups that had experienced physical aggression generally reported higher levels of reasoning and verbal aggressiveness than did those in the nonaggressive groups. This finding could indicate that abusive couples have a greater prevalence of conflict and hence use a wider variety of tactics. In fact, they may even use reasoning and verbal aggression to try to end physical abuse. In addition, there is evidence that individuals' reactions vary according to which tactics are initially used. Stets and Henderson (1991) asked individuals to report how often they and their partners used the three sets of tactics and how they and their partners responded. They found that the use of reasoning in disputes produced a wide variety of reactions, including discussion of the issue, laughing, and arguing. Verbal aggression typically was reciprocated, but sometimes prompted avoidance and sulking. Physical aggression was often reciprocated, but also resulted in verbal aggression. An important finding was that if a partner responded to a tactic with discussion or with verbal or physical aggression, the initiator reciprocated.

The greatest strength of this approach to conflict styles stems from its inclusion of physical aggression as a separate style. However, this strength is also its greatest weakness, in that it has led researchers to focus most of their attention on the physically aggressive style, usually to the exclusion of the other two (see Straus, 1990a). Hence we have limited knowledge about the causes or effects of verbal aggression and reasoning, and how the three tactics interact.

Avoidance-Distributive-Integrative Strategies

Sillars (1980) argues that there are two dimensions to a person's response to a conflict: the degree to which the response directly discloses information, which facilitates more information exchange, and the degree to which the response reflects the attainment of individual or mutual goals. Sillars analyzed the descriptions of conflict provided by college roommates, then clustered them into three distinct kinds of strategies. The strategies in the first cluster, passive and indirect strategies, involve no direct discussion of a problem and reflect low information disclosure. Those in the second cluster, distributive strategies, include explicit acknowledgment and discussion of the conflict aimed at gaining concessions from the partner. Those in the last cluster, integrative strategies, openly acknowledge the conflict and the views of the partner with the aim of achieving mutual goals. In a follow-up study, Sillars, Coletti, Parry, and Rogers (1982) examined how conflict discussions that contained primarily avoidance, distributive, or integrative interaction behaviors were related to observer ratings of disclosiveness and competitiveness. As expected, integrative and distributive interactions were perceived to be more disclosive than avoidance discussions. Moreover, distributive discussions were perceived to be more competitive than integrative or avoidance discussions. Finally, integrative and distributive discussions did not differ in perceived disclosiveness, and avoidance and integrativeness did not differ with regard to perceived competitiveness.

Several studies have evaluated the impacts of these styles. First, Sillars (1980) found that

the self-reported use of avoidance strategies was negatively related to conflict resolution, but that the use of integrative strategies was positively related. The use of distributive strategies was not significantly related to resolution. Second, the competence model of interpersonal conflict has been used to evaluate these three strategies (Spitzberg, Canary, & Cupach, 1994). Essentially, the competence model assumes that the relational impacts of conflict strategies depend on the degree to which they are perceived to be situationally appropriate (i.e., relational and situation expectations are met) and effective (i.e., they meet personal goals). There is some support for this notion. Using data derived from a cross-sectional design, Canary and Spitzberg (1989) found that a partner's use of avoidance and distributive strategies was negatively related to perceived competence, whereas the use of integrative strategies was positively related to perceived competence. However, it should be noted that the impact of integrative strategies on judgments of competence was stronger than the impact of distributive or avoidant behaviors. Regardless, Canary and Spitzberg's data indicate that the relationship between conflict strategy and relational outcomes is mediated by perceived competence. However, using longitudinal data, Canary, Cupach, and Serpe (2001) found that perceived competence and communication satisfaction mediated the relationship between conflict strategies and initial trust and liking/love, but these relational evaluations were not related to the subsequent use of conflict strategies. Instead, subsequent conflict management strategies were related to those initially used by the respondent and his or her partner.

This approach to styles has several strengths. First, the styles can be assessed through general self-reported descriptions of behaviors or from coding interactions. Hence researchers can study them in a variety of settings. Second, there is evidence that they are linked to relational outcomes through competence. However, there are limitations to their use. For example, the relationship between a conflict partner's perceived use of a strategy and his or her perceived competence is stronger than the association between self-reported use and self-perceived competence (Canary & Spitzberg, 1990). Thus there is evidence of perceptual bias in the judging of the competence of those who use the tactics. Furthermore, research suggests that when judges examine the degree to which two parties in a conflict agree as to which styles they are using, greater consensus occurs for distributive behaviors, followed by avoidance, with the least consensus for integrative strategies (Canary & Spitzberg, 1990).

Summary

Interest in conflict styles has generated a great deal of research, and useful insights have emerged. However, with the exception of research conducted on avoidance-distributive-integrative strategies, most scholars have cast approaches to dealing with conflict as general responses rather than as specific actions that could be coded from particular conflict interactions. In other words, the links between specific styles and precise behaviors are not always clear.

ARGUMENTATION PATTERNS

Arguing is one of the most overt forms of conflict, and, not surprisingly, it has attracted a great deal of research. Arguing research has focused on five areas: defining features, argument sequences, argument escalation, serial arguing, and relational effects.

Defining Features

Researchers have taken several approaches in studying the features of everyday arguments. Some have tried to determine how individuals differentiate arguments from nonarguments. Resick et al. (1981) provided college students

with a vignette that involved a couple having a discussion. They then asked the students to select 10 nonverbal and 5 verbal traits, from among 77 nonverbal and 24 verbal items, that would best indicate whether the two people in the vignette were having a verbal disagreement or were agreeing with each other. The most frequently occurring nonverbal behaviors were speaking loudly, talking fast, and gesturing, and the most frequently occurring verbal behaviors were sarcasm, criticism, disagreement, and swearing. The researchers then coded marital interactions involving conflict or accord for each of the aforementioned behaviors. They found that individuals in verbal conflicts were indeed louder, more critical, more sarcastic, and more disagreeable than were those interactions in which the partners were in accord. Similarly, Jackson, Jacobs, Burrell, and Allen (1986) have suggested that individuals rely on more than simple linguistic disagreement when inferring that an argument is occurring. Individuals look to the degree to which aggravators (e.g., epithets, making statements rather than questions) or mitigators (e.g., no name-calling, relatively more questions than statements) are present when making these judgments. Consistent with this view, Jackson et al. found that a disagreement was more likely to be judged to be an argument when it contained many aggravators and was less likely to be perceived to be an argument when many mitigators were present. These studies suggest that although disagreement may be an obvious characteristic of an argument, other factors must be present before observers will make such an attribution.

Other researchers have focused on what typical arguments are like. Benoit and Benoit (1987) asked undergraduates to either keep diaries about their everyday arguments or complete a questionnaire about them. The results from both methods suggest that college students argue more with romantic partners, roommates, and friends and less often with family members and bosses. Moreover, the same topics are often the subjects of repeated arguments. Finally, these respondents reported that their arguments often ended with concession or compromise, but in many cases, they simply terminated arguments without resolution (38%). However, compared with the study participants who kept diaries, individuals who completed questionnaires reported that they had more arguments that lasted longer. Because none of the respondents completed both questionnaire and diary, it was difficult to determine why such differences occurred. A study in which married couples kept diaries of daily verbal disagreements and also provided summary reports of the frequency of conflict during that time suggests that global estimates slightly underestimate diary records, but only among those reporting that conflict never occurs, occurs less than once per month, or occurs once per month (McGonagle, Kessler, & Schilling, 1992). Those reporting that two to three arguments occur per month or that arguments occur weekly provided global estimates that were more consistent with those they recorded in their diaries. Perhaps frequent arguing is more salient to individuals, and so they more accurately report its occurrence.

Vuchinich (1987) observed family quarrels at the dinner table. He suggests that two conditions must exist for an argument to take place: First, one person negatively evaluates some action, opinion, characteristic, or significant other associated with another person; and second, the person who has received the attack resists. Vuchinich found that roughly one-third of the attacks he observed did not elicit resistance; instead, the person either submitted to the attack or ignored it. Most arguments were very short, averaging less than five speaking turns. Most arguments (61%) ended in standoffs in which neither party gave in; instead, they changed the topic of conversation. One party submitted in about 20% of the cases, and compromises and withdrawals were much less frequent.

Although the aforementioned studies used different methods and different kinds of samples, together they suggest that conflict is not a dominant form of interaction, and that when arguments do occur, they typically are short and sometimes end without resolution. Given the latter finding, it is not surprising that arguments often are repeated.

Argument Sequences

At its core, an argument is a form of interaction; hence there is a degree of dependence between the behaviors of the partners (i.e., one partner's action may prompt a particular response from the other). Researchers have explored the possibility that some sequences of behaviors might be more problematic than others. Surprisingly, few researchers have studied the kinds of arguments and responses that they generate. Canary, Weger, and Stafford (1991) conceive of an argument as a process aimed at achieving a convergence of ideas. They studied argument sequences in marital interaction and found four sets, but only those that reflected divergent patterns (i.e., reciprocal disagreement or responding to a complaint with a justification for one's own view) were significantly and negatively correlated with marital satisfaction. Similarly, Ting-Toomey (1983) found that marital couples who were low in marital adjustment were more likely than those of higher adjustment to engage in cycles of mutual confrontation over issues or to respond to confrontational statements and complaints by defending themselves.

More often, researchers have focused on sequences that reflect verbal or nonverbal behaviors enacted during arguments. Perhaps the most research has been conducted on a sequence called the "demand/withdraw pattern" (Sullaway & Christensen, 1983). Within this pattern, one partner confronts the other with criticism, complaints, and demands, to which the second partner responds by becoming defensive or passively withdrawing.

Research indicates that where this pattern is evident, the confrontational partner is often female and the partner who withdraws is male (Caughlin & Vangelisti, 1999; Christensen & Heavey, 1990; Terman, Buttenweiser, Ferguson, Johnson, & Wilson, 1938). In part, this pattern is thought to stem from the greater relational inequities that occur for women than for men; that is, women may be more confrontational as they attempt to effect change. Indeed, two studies have found that when a wife is unhappy with the distribution of housework and wishes her husband to do more, the wife-demand/husband-withdraw pattern frequently occurs and leads to destructive outcomes (Kluwer, Heesink, & Van De Vliert, 1997, 2000). Furthermore, the occurrence of the wife-demand/husband-withdraw pattern increases a wife's stress (Kiecolt-Glaser et al., 1996) and decreases her marital satisfaction over time (Heavey, Christensen, & Malamuth, 1995; Heavey, Layne, & Christensen, 1993). When enacted early in a marriage, the wife-demand/husband-withdraw pattern increases the odds of divorce (Gottman & Levenson, 2000). This also implies that, regardless of gender, the more a partner wants the other partner to change, the more demanding he or she is and the more withdrawn the partner will be. Hence the demand/withdraw pattern may occur when either partner wishes the other to change. Two studies found that when couples discussed an issue important to the husband, the wife-demand/husband-withdraw and the husband-demand/wife-withdraw patterns occurred with similar frequencies, but when they discussed an issue important to the wife, wife-demand/husband-withdraw was more frequent (Christensen & Heavey, 1990; Heavey et al., 1993). However, in a follow-up, Klinetob and Smith (1996) replicated the findings for the wife's issue, but found that on the husband's issue, husband-demand/wife-withdraw was more frequent. Holtzworth-Munroe, Smutzler, and Stuart (1998) recently uncovered a similar result.

Although the aforementioned research indicates that the desire for change predicts the particular form of the demand/withdraw pattern, not all research has verified this. Caughlin and Vangelisti (1999) found that regardless of gender, the more individuals wanted their partners to change, the greater the likelihood of wife-demand/husband-withdraw and husband-demand/wife-withdraw, and these relationships were especially strong on salient issues. Perhaps the answer to this anomaly lies in the manner in which the argument unfolds. An individual may initiate a sequence by being demanding, which prompts immediate withdrawal by the partner, but later in the conversation, the partner may rebound by countercomplaining (i.e., bringing up his or her own issue) or by pointing out that the demanding individual's problem is of his or her own making and that he or she should take action, either of which may prompt that individual to withdraw.

Another limitation to this approach arises from the possibility that the wife-demand/husband-withdraw pattern really is a husband-withdraw/wife-demand pattern. In a time-series analysis of marital interaction, Roberts and Krokoff (1990) found that dissatisfied wives responded to their husbands' withdrawal by becoming hostile. Perhaps this reflects the wives' perception that their husbands are uninvolved in their relationships or are acting disrespectfully toward them.

Other researchers have explored how the sequences of behaviors vary during the course of an argument. For example, Gottman, Markman, and Notarius (1977) found that married couples undergoing counseling began their arguments with cross-complaining (i.e., one person's complaint was countered with another by the partner), which was followed by a negative exchange wherein one partner made a mind-reading statement and the other responded with negative affect. Not surprisingly, these couples were unlikely to reach agreement by the end of the conversation. By contrast, couples who were not in counseling began with a validation loop wherein one partner complained and the partner explicitly acknowledged the complaint and did so with neutral affect. This allowed the couples to avoid negative exchanges and instead reach agreement by the end of their arguments. Overall, the couples undergoing counseling showed a stronger tendency to reciprocate negative affect than did those who were not in counseling.

Perhaps the most ambitious test of argument sequences was conducted by Gottman, Coan, Carrere, and Swanson (1998). These researchers coded the problem-solving interactions of newlyweds in such a manner that they could test seven different process models. They then used these variables to predict marital satisfaction and divorce 2 years into the future. Their data indicated that the most satisfied and stable marriages were those in which the wife reduced the intensity with which she initiated the confrontation and, during the argument, used humor to soothe her husband's arousal. Her husband was willing to be influenced by her and acted so as to de-escalate the confrontation and reduce his own arousal. Surprisingly, anger, active listening, and reciprocity of negative affect were not related to marital satisfaction and divorce.

Although researchers have learned a great deal from studying argument sequences, this research is to some degree limited by its focus on the surface meanings of interaction behaviors as opposed to the underlying issues they might reflect. For example, Krokoff (1990) argues that conflicts sometimes involve hidden agendas that reflect fundamental issues that drive the disagreement but are not discussed. Indeed, he found that in conflicts in which wives had hidden agendas involving the degree to which they felt that their husbands loved or respected them, the wives were more negative toward their husbands and the wives' marital satisfaction eroded over time.

Argument Escalation

In some cases, arguments escalate into aggression. Researchers who have explored the sequences of events involved in this process have focused primarily on three areas: escalation sequences, social control sequences, and argument attenuation.

Escalation Sequences

Mikolic, Parker, and Pruitt (1997) studied the sequences of actions that characterize how individuals respond to persons who persistently annoy them. Study participants were assigned to work on a task that required sharing resources with another (a confederate) who consistently resisted sharing. Analysis of their reactions indicated that in the face of continuing resistance, individuals' actions followed an escalating sequence: request compliance, impatient demands, complaints, angry statements, threats, harassment, and abuse. Although problem solving and appeals to third parties sometimes occurred, they did not appear as part of the typical sequence. In part because they perceived greater unfair treatment, females were more likely than males to escalate the dispute, and males were more frequently the target of escalation than were females. In a follow-up study that used a similar method, Pruitt, Parker, and Mikolic (1997) discovered that few people skipped steps in the sequence, verbal escalation was associated with disparaging the annoyer's character, and physical aggression resulted from frustration and anger.

Although there is clear evidence of an escalatory sequence, the cause is unclear. The researchers posit that the sequence might represent a script, but it is unclear how it was formed or what underlying factors produced the order of action contained in it. Alternatively, the sequence may reflect a lowering threshold of restraint that comes with frequent annoyance.

Social Control Sequences

Felson (1984) focused on the interplay between two individuals in producing escalatory sequences leading to violence. He compared accounts of incidents in which an angry person (a) kept his or her anger in and did not confront the source of the anger; (b) confronted the person who was the source of the anger, which resulted in an argument; (c) confronted the person and hitting occurred; or (d) confronted the person and someone used a knife or gun. Although not all of the accounts involved physical aggression, there was a general sequence of action that characterized confrontations: (a) An individual is observed engaging in a rule violation, (b) an observer orders the person to stop, (c) the observer reproaches or insults the rule violator, (d) the rule violator does not comply, (e) the rule violator provides accounts for his or her actions, (f) insults are exchanged, as are (g) threats, and (h) physical attacks occur, which are followed by (i) submission and (j) mediation by third parties. Felson found that angry observers frequently do not confront rule violators, and typically, an argument does not occur except when a reproach or insult has been made. Furthermore, providing accounts and making threats play critical roles in escalation. When a rule violator provides accounts, the argument is less likely to escalate to violence, but making threats significantly increases the chances of aggression. Interestingly, Felson found that males were more likely than females to be rule violators, and females are more likely than males to engage in reproaches, especially against male rule violators. Surprisingly, although reproaches often cause escalation to physical aggression, physical aggression was more common for males than for females. Hence females more frequently enter into confrontation than do males and often engage in insults, which are precursors of aggression, but they seem to end the sequence before aggression occurs. Finally, rule violators are less likely to engage in physical aggression than are the persons who confront them.

This analysis provides an interesting perspective on confrontations that escalate. The processes that lead to arguing, hitting, or use of weapons are quite similar at the earlier stages of the confrontation. However, something causes individuals to disengage before the more violent part of the sequence occurs. This implies that confrontations have the potential to escalate and hence could be viewed as dangerous behavior. Perhaps that is why so many rule violations go unaddressed. Furthermore, the likelihood of aggression seems to increase when individuals insult each other; hence aggression could reflect face-saving behavior.

Argument Attenuation

When, in his study of family quarrels, Vuchinich (1986) found that the typical argument is short, he hypothesized that some factor exists that decreases the likelihood that an argument will continue and escalate. He thought that this attenuation factor might reflect conflict avoidance or perhaps an attempt to keep the argument from spoiling or preventing other activities. Regardless, he noted that the family members he observed often tried to "cool out" an argument by shifting the topic, making a joke, or using some other mitigating device, although such actions did not result in resolution of the issue. Alberts and Driscoll (1992) found similar processes. They examined how the individuals in satisfied versus unsatisfied couples responded to each other's complaints. In happy relationships, the partners were more likely to pass on responding to complaints (i.e., ignore them), refocus the nature of complaints, or mitigate complaints by downgrading their seriousness. Dissatisfied couples were more likely to be unresponsive or to escalate disputes by expanding the complaint topics or expressing hostility. Furthermore, Burman, Margolin, and John (1993) observed that nondistressed, low-conflict couples were better able to de-escalate their conflicts than were physically aggressive, verbally aggressive, or withdrawing couples. The nondistressed couples often accomplished this de-escalation by interspersing positive statements in a noncontingent fashion during disputes. Finally, Gottman (1979) found that in marriage, spouses play different roles in dampening emotional reactions to conflict. The husband plays a key role when the dispute is relatively minor, whereas the wife is more involved in dampening serious conflicts.

This research suggests that individuals are aware of the potential for escalation that is inherent in confrontation and take actions to keep their arguments under control. However, the research does not indicate what cues signal to participants that an argument is escalating or what factors influence their decisions to disengage or to let the argument escalate.

Serial Arguing

As we have noted, undergraduates report that they often have arguments with others that are focused on the same issues as earlier arguments. Trapp and Hoff (1985) characterize this as serial arguing. Researchers have studied the impacts of serial arguing as well as processes that might attenuate those impacts. Some research suggests that males and females may respond differently to serial arguing. Lloyd (1987, 1990) asked individuals to keep diaries of their everyday disputes in which they kept track of the stability of particular conflict issues—that is, how often those issues were discussed. She found that for males, the stability of disputes was negatively related to their love and relational commitment and positively related to their feelings of ambivalence, but the same correlations were of much lower magnitude and not statistically significant among females. Also, among males but not females, the stability of disputes was negatively related to negotiation (i.e., talking about the problem, not responding with silence), and there was a

slight tendency for males to report that stable disputes resulted in hostile reactions. Unfortunately, the nature of the data does not allow us to gain any insight into why these differences were found or any causal direction among the variables. However, Kurdek (1994b) has developed a measure of ineffective arguing that includes many features of serial arguing, including fighting over repetitive issues, knowing how an argument will end before it is over, and ending an argument with resolution. In a longitudinal study, ineffective arguing predicted reductions in marital satisfaction and increased the chances of marital dissolution. Also, other data derived from marital diaries indicate that, regardless of the genders of the interactants, interpersonal conflicts that extend over several days have more adverse impacts on mood than do conflicts that do not recur (Bolger, DeLongis, Kessler, & Schilling, 1989). The only exception was found in mother-child conflicts, in which mood did not worsen as the conflict progressed.

In a recent study, Johnson and Roloff (2000b) found that an individual's typical role in a serial argument affects how he or she views the dispute. The person who typically initiates an argumentative episode reports that he or she had planned for the interaction, saw an urgent need for change, and demanded the partner should change; the partner typically responded by withdrawing. In addition, there is a weak tendency for initiators who have frequently confronted their partners to believe the problem can be resolved without relational harm. This is consistent with other research that suggests that individuals who want their partners to change expend greater cognitive effort focused on the problem than do their partners, and hence can point to specific partner-related causes of the conflict and changes that the partner should make (Sagrestano, Christensen, & Heavey, 1998). However, among those who are typically confronted, the more often argumentative episodes occur, the less resolvable they perceive a serial argument to be and the greater the relational harm attributed to it. Although some research suggests that confronted individuals often ask questions about why their behavior is problematic (Sagrestano et al., 1998), it is possible that with repeated confrontations, they shift from information seeking to expressing resistance.

Additional research has examined how individuals control their serial arguing. For example, Baxter and Wilmot (1985) discovered that declaring a topic taboo is one way to avoid raising conflict-inducing topics, and Roloff and Ifert (1998) found that the more often a topic had been discussed prior to its being declared taboo, the greater the likelihood that there was an explicit as opposed to implicit agreement never to talk about the topic again.

Finally, Johnson and Roloff (1998) found that being optimistic about the resolvability of a serial argument was a stronger predictor of relational quality than was the frequency with which argumentative episodes occur. Perceived resolvability was negatively related to countercomplaining, partner-demand/respondent-withdraw patterns, mulling over the dispute, and withdrawing after an episode. Moreover, Johnson and Roloff (2000a) found that perceived resolvability was positively correlated with making relationally affirming statements during an argumentative episode and coping with the dispute by making optimistic comparisons.

Research on serial arguing is relatively new, and the number of studies is limited. Moreover, researchers have typically studied dating couples, so we have relatively little knowledge about how these processes occur in other types of relationships. Finally, virtually all of the studies conducted to date have relied upon self-report measures and cross-sectional designs, which limits causal inference.

Relational Effects

Perhaps the most fundamental issue facing researchers concerns the effects that arguing has on relationships. Several approaches have been taken in this regard. McGonagle, Kessler, and Gotlib (1993) conducted a longitudinal study of marriage in which they examined the impacts of argument frequency, style of arguing, and conflict outcome on the probability of divorce. They found that the strongest predictors of divorce among couples married less than 8 years was how negatively they characterized their arguments (e.g., as cruel/intense, lacking in mutual appreciation, and with low levels of problem solving) and how frequently they disagreed. For those marriages that were of at least 8 years' duration, only frequency of arguing predicted divorce. This could reflect the degree to which individuals try to maintain their relationships after arguments. Kelly, Huston, and Cate (1985) found that the amount of premarital arguing occurring after a couple started dating seriously was positively related to subsequent marital arguing and negatively related to marital satisfaction. They also found that frequency of arguing and maintenance were positively related at early stages of courtship, but the correlation was nonsignificant at later stages of dating and in marriage. Hence, with time, partners may be less likely to try to repair any damage resulting from their arguments.

Gottman and Levenson (2000) found that negativity and positivity during an argument predict relational dissolution, but at different points in a marriage. In a longitudinal study, they found that the odds that a couple would divorce within the first 7 years of marriage increased when the partners expressed a great deal of negativity (i.e., husband was defensive, contemptuous, and stonewalling, and wife was critical, contemptuous, and defensive) during their arguments, but negativity did not predict later divorcing. However, the lack of positive affect during arguments and other everyday events was the best predictor of divorcing after the seventh year of marriage.

These data suggest that the frequency of arguing and certain aspects of arguing appear to be damaging to a relationship. Other researchers have investigated whether this association depends on the nature of the relationship. Research indicates that marital and family types differ in the ways they manage conflict (e.g., Fitzpatrick, 1988; Koerner & Fitzpatrick, 1997; Ridley, Wilhelm, & Surra, 2001; Segrin & Fitzpatrick, 1992; Williamson & Fitzpatrick, 1985) and that the relational impact of argumentative behavior may depend on the type of relationship in which it is enacted. For example, VanLear and Zietlow (1990) examined how conflict patterns are related to marital satisfaction in each of Fitzpatrick's (1988) marital types. They found that among spouses in traditional marriages (i.e., those having traditional notions of marriage and high interdependence), the frequency of deferential behavior and complimentary exchanges (one person makes a controlling statement that the other partner accepts) was positively related to marital satisfaction. This could reflect the tendency of traditional wives to offer solutions to problems disclosed by their husbands and to respond positively to their husbands' attempts to read their minds (Fitzpatrick, 1988). Also, among traditionals, a pattern in which one partner responded to a control attempt by simply disagreeing or trying to justify his or her behavior was negatively related to satisfaction. However, among couples in separate marriages (i.e., those in which the spouses are low in interdependence and prefer conflict avoidance), deference was negatively correlated with relational satisfaction, as was a pattern in which neither partner attempted to control the interaction. However, because of the cross-sectional nature of this design, it is not possible to determine the direction of the effect (i.e., does conflict behavior cause marital satisfaction, or vice versa?).

Gottman (1993, 1994) has proposed that the impact of negativity on a marriage depends on the spouses' ability to counter it with positive affect. In his research, he found that couples in stable relationships were able to maintain a ratio of five positive conflict behaviors to every one negative action. However, couples varied in how they maintained this ratio. During arguments, volatile couples were highly confrontational and negative, but they intermingled such behavior with a great many positive behaviors. Validating couples maintained the ratio by mixing moderate amounts of both positive and negative behaviors, and avoidant couples engaged in low levels of both positive and negative behaviors. Although their ways of dealing with conflict differed, all of these couples were stable and satisfied. Only when couples were unable to maintain the five-to-one ratio, such as in the case of hostile and hostile/detached couples, did relational quality suffer.

Summary

Thus, although there is evidence that arguing has a generally negative impact on relationships, this impact is moderated by a number of factors, including the style of conflict and relational orientation. However, researchers have spent far more time studying arguing in marriage than they have looking at how arguing affects other types of relationships. Perhaps this focus arises from the greater centrality of arguing to marriage than to other types of relationships. However, some research suggests that, on average, conflicts with family members are less distressing than conflicts with friends, neighbors, and coworkers, and this finding seems to hold regardless of the relative frequency of nonfamily conflicts (Bolger et al., 1989). Hence there is justification for expanding our relational focus. Furthermore, many studies seem to indicate that the relational effect of arguing is determined primarily by the degree to which negative behaviors are enacted rather than by the degree to which partners respond constructively to conflicts. Although an integrative response style seems to have immediate positive impacts on conflict resolution (Kluwer et al., 1997; Sillars, 1980), two longitudinal studies have found that the frequency of negative actions can have long-term impacts on relational quality, but that positive behaviors do not (McGonagle et al., 1993; Noller, Feeney, Bonnell, & Callan, 1994). The long-term relational harm from negative actions is easy to explain from prior research. However, reasons for the absence of long-term benefits from acting constructively are not obvious, particularly given that constructive actions would seem to predict constructive resolution of conflicts. It may well be that the ability to resolve everyday conflicts is a less important factor in relationships than the relational fallout that comes from consistently acting in a destructive fashion.

CONCLUSION

At this point, the reader may feel bewildered by the wide variety of phenomena that researchers have studied concerning interpersonal conflict. That feeling would likely be even greater had we not limited our coverage of the research in this chapter. However, we believe that certain generalizations are warranted based on this review.

First, conflict arises from incompatibility, but the nature of incompatibility varies considerably. Second, intimate relationships give rise to more opportunity for conflict, and especially intense conflict, than do nonintimate relationships, but this association occurs primarily for relationships between family members, relative to other types of relationships, and among individuals who move from casual to serious dating. Third, although constrained by boundary rules, a person's social network can be both a cause of conflict and a shaper of how conflict proceeds. Fourth, individuals have knowledge structures that guide their perceptions of conflict and that are related to their conflict behavior, but their perceptions of conflict may be biased in negative or positive ways. Fifth, researchers have identified a variety of conflict styles that seem to be related to

conflict outcomes and to relational quality. Finally, arguing appears to be negatively related to relational quality, although the strength of its impact varies.

Obviously, these generalizations are quite broad and undoubtedly ignore many subtle processes and limitations. Indeed, the reader may have noted that research has yielded a number of complex processes associated with particular types of conflicts, and that the methods, measures, and samples that researchers employ impose further limitations on the generalizability of the results. Moreover, researchers have not addressed how any of the phenomena are interrelated (e.g., how different incompatibilities are related to one another, and how any one of them might affect conflict styles or arguing, or how conflict styles are manifested in particular argument processes). In part, this reflects the disjointed nature of conflict inquiry. Typically, research programs focus on particular approaches to particular phenomena and pay little attention to other phenomena or to other approaches to the same phenomena. Indeed, a given approach is often associated with a particular scholar and his or her students, and little contribution is made by anyone who is not part of the core group. Although this way of conducting research has allowed us to uncover a great deal of knowledge about some features of conflict, it may have prevented us from developing a coherent picture of conflict.

At this point in a literature review, authors typically point to new topics that are emerging and that should be addressed by scholars. Although new approaches and phenomena will undoubtedly draw our attention, the greatest challenge facing conflict researchers is how to synthesize, integrate, and perhaps consolidate the findings of extant research. Unless we address this challenge, the sheer volume and diversity apparent in the literature will result in even greater incoherence. Although we are doubtful that a grand theory of interpersonal conflict is possible, we believe that broader-based and more integrative perspectives could be created that could result in a more coherent and comprehensible view of conflict. We hope that by providing this overview of many of the key areas of research, we will help such an integrative perspective to emerge.

REFERENCES

Abelson, R. P. (1981). Psychological status of the script concept. *American Psychologist, 36,* 715-729.

Adams, R., & Laursen, B. (2001). The organization and dynamics of adolescent conflict with parents and friends. *Journal of Marriage and Family, 63,* 97-110.

Afifi, W. A., Falato, W. L., & Weiner, J. L. (2001). Identity concerns following a severe relational transgression: The role of discovery method for the relational outcomes of infidelity. *Journal of Social and Personal Relationships, 18,* 291-308.

Alberts, J. K. (1988). An analysis of couples' conversational complaints. *Communication Monographs, 55,* 184-196.

Alberts, J. K., & Driscoll, G. (1992). Containment versus escalation: The trajectory of couples' conversational complaints. *Western Journal of Communication, 56,* 394-412.

Altman, I., & Taylor, D. A. (1973). *Social penetration: The development of interpersonal relationships.* New York: Holt, Rinehart & Winston.

Argyle, M., & Furnham, A. (1982). The ecology of relationships: Choice of situation as a function of relationship. *British Journal of Social Psychology, 21,* 259-262.

Argyle, M., & Furnham, A. (1983). Sources of satisfaction and conflict in long-term relationships. *Journal of Marriage and the Family, 45,* 481-493.

Argyle, M., & Henderson, M. (1984). The rules of friendship. *Journal of Social and Personal Relationship, 1,* 211-237.

Argyle, M., & Henderson, M. (1985). The rules of relationships. In S. Duck & D. Perlman (Eds.), *Understanding personal relationships: An interdisciplinary approach* (pp. 63-84). Beverly Hills, CA: Sage.

Arriaga, X. B. (2001). The ups and downs of dating: Fluctuations in satisfaction in newly formed romantic relationships. *Journal of Personality and Social Psychology, 80,* 754-765.

Ayduk, O., Downey, G., Testa, A., Yen, Y., & Shoda, Y. (1999). Does rejection elicit hostility in rejection-sensitive women? *Social Cognition, 17,* 245-271.

Baron, R. A., & Bell, P. A. (1975). Aggression and heat: Mediating effects of prior provocation and exposure to an aggressive model. *Journal of Personality and Social Psychology, 31,* 825-832.

Baumeister, R. F., Reis, H. T., & Delespaul, P. A. E. G. (1995). Subjective and experiential correlates of guilt in daily life. *Personality and Social Psychology Bulletin, 21,* 1256-1268.

Baumeister, R. F., Stillwell, A. M., & Heatherton, T. F. (1995). Personal narratives about guilt: Role in action control and interpersonal relationships. *Basic and Applied Social Psychology, 17,* 173-198.

Baumeister, R. F., Stillwell, A. M., & Wotman, S. R. (1990). Victim and perpetrator accounts of interpersonal conflict: Autobiographical narratives about anger. *Journal of Personality and Social Psychology, 59,* 991-1005.

Baxter, L. A. (1986). Gender differences in the heterosexual relationship rules embedded in break-up accounts. *Journal of Social and Personal Relationships, 3,* 289-306.

Baxter, L. A., & Wilmot, W. W. (1985). Taboo topics in close relationships. *Journal of Social and Personal Relationships, 2,* 253-269.

Benoit, W. L., & Benoit, P. J. (1987). Everyday argument practices of native social actors. In J. W. Wenzel (Ed.), *Argument and critical practices: Proceedings of the Fifth SCA/AFA Conference on Argumentation* (pp. 465-473). Annandale, VA: Speech Communication Association.

Billingham, R. E. (1987). Courtship violence: The patterns of conflict resolution strategies across seven levels of emotional commitment. *Family Relations, 36,* 283-289.

Billingham, R. E., & Sacks, A. R. (1987). Conflict tactics and the level of emotional commitment among unmarrieds. *Human Relations, 40,* 59-74.

Birchler, G. R., Weiss, R. L., & Vincent, J. P. (1975). Multimethod analysis of social reinforcement exchange between maritally distressed and nondistressed spouse and stranger dyads. *Journal of Personality and Social Psychology, 31,* 349-360.

Block, J. H., Block, J., & Morrison, A. (1981). Parental agreement-disagreement on child-rearing orientations and gender-related personality correlates in children. *Child Development, 52,* 965-974.

Bolger, N., DeLongis, A., Kessler, R. C., & Schilling, E. A. (1989). Effects of daily stress on negative mood. *Journal of Personality and Social Psychology, 57,* 808-818.

Boon, S. D, & Holmes, J. G. (1999). Interpersonal risk and the evaluation of transgressions in close relationships. *Personal Relationships, 6,* 151-168.

Braiker, H. B., & Kelley, H. H. (1979). Conflict in the development of close relationships. In R. L. Burgess & T. L. Huston (Eds.), *Social exchange in developing relationships* (pp. 135-168). New York: Academic Press.

Bryant, C., Conger, R. D., & Meehan, J. M. (2001). The influence of in-laws on change in marital success. *Journal of Marriage and Family, 63,* 614-626.

Burman, B., Margolin, G., & John, R. S. (1993). America's angriest home videos: Behavioral contingencies observed in home reenactments of marital conflict. *Journal of Consulting and Clinical Psychology, 61,* 28-39.

Bushman, B. J., Baumeister, R. F., & Phillips, C. M. (2001). Do people aggress to improve their mood? Catharsis beliefs, affect regulation opportunity, and aggressive responding. *Journal of Personality and Social Psychology, 81,* 17-32.

Bushman, B. J., Baumeister, R. F., & Stack, A. D. (1999). Catharsis, aggression, and persuasive influence: Self-fulfilling or self-defeating prophecies? *Journal of Personality and Social Psychology, 76,* 367-376.

Buss, D. M. (1989). Conflict between the sexes: Strategic interference and the evocation of anger and upset. *Journal of Personality and Social Psychology, 56,* 735-747.

Buss, D. M. (2001). Cognitive biases and emotional wisdom in the evolution of conflict between the sexes. *Current Directions in Psychological Science, 10,* 219-223.

Buysse, A., De Clercq, A., Verhofstadt, L., Heene, E., Roeyers, H., & Van Oost, P. (2000). Dealing with relational conflict: A picture in milliseconds. *Journal of Social and Personal Relationships, 17,* 574-597.

Cahn, D. D. (1992). *Conflict in intimate relationships.* New York: Guilford.

Canary, D. J., Cupach, W. R., & Messman, S. J. (1995). *Relationship conflict.* Thousand Oaks, CA: Sage.

Canary, D. J., Cupach, W. R., & Serpe, R. T. (2001). A competence-based approach to examining interpersonal conflict: Test of a longitudinal model. *Communication Research, 28,* 79-104.

Canary, D. J., & Spitzberg, B. H. (1989). A model of the perceived competence of conflict strategies. *Human Communication Research, 15,* 630-649.

Canary, D. J., & Spitzberg, B. H. (1990). Attribution biases and associations between conflict strategies and competence judgments. *Communication Monographs, 57,* 139-151.

Canary, D. J., Weger, H., Jr., & Stafford, L. (1991). Couples' argument sequences and their associations with relational characteristics. *Western Journal of Speech Communication, 55,* 159-179.

Cate, R. M., Henton, J. M., Koval, J., Christopher, F. S., & Lloyd, S. (1982). Premarital abuse: A social psychological perspective. *Journal of Family Issues, 3,* 79-90.

Caughlin, J. P., & Vangelisti, A. L. (1999). Desire for change in one's partner as a predictor of the demand/withdraw pattern of marital communication. *Communication Monographs, 66,* 66-89.

Christensen, A., & Heavey, C. L. (1990). Gender and social structure in the demand/withdraw pattern of marital conflict. *Journal of Personality and Social Psychology, 59,* 73-81.

Christopher, F. S., & Cate, R. M. (1985). Premarital sexual pathways and relationship development. *Journal of Social and Personal Relationships, 2,* 271-288.

Cloven, D. H. (1990). *Relational effects of interpersonal conflict: The role of cognition, satisfaction, and anticipated communication.* Unpublished master's thesis. Northwestern University.

Cloven, D. H., & Roloff, M. E. (1991). Sense-making activities and interpersonal conflict: Communicative cures for the mulling blues. *Western Journal of Speech Communication, 55,* 134-158.

Cloven, D. H., & Roloff, M. E. (1993). The chilling effect of aggressive potential on the expression of complaints in intimate relationships. *Communication Monographs, 60,* 199-219.

Cloven, D. H., & Roloff, M. E. (1994). A developmental mode of decisions to withhold relational irritations in romantic relationships. *Personal Relationships, 1,* 143-164.

Conger, R. D., Elder, G. H., Jr., Lorenz, F. O., Conger, K. J., Simons, R. L., Whitbeck, L. B., Huck, S., & Melby, J. N. (1990). Linking economic hardship to marital quality and instability. *Journal of Marriage and the Family, 52,* 634-656.

Coser, L. (1956). *The functions of social conflict.* New York: Free Press.

Crohan, S. E. (1992). Marital happiness and spousal consensus on beliefs about marital conflict: A longitudinal investigation. *Journal of Social and Personal Relationships, 9,* 89-102.

Davis, K. E., & Todd, M. J. (1985). Assessing friendships: Prototypes, paradigm cases, and relationship description. In S. Duck & D. Perlman (Eds.), *Understanding personal relationships: An interdisciplinary approach* (pp. 17-38). Beverly Hills, CA: Sage.

Deutsch, M. (1973). *The resolution of conflict: Constructive and destructive processes.* New Haven, CT: Yale University Press.

Downey, G., & Feldman, S. I. (1996). Implications of rejection sensitivity for intimate relationships. *Journal of Personality and Social Psychology, 70,* 1327-1343.

Downey, G., Freitas, A. L., Michaelis, B., & Khouri, H. (1998). The self-fulfilling prophecy in close relationships: Rejection sensitivity and rejection by romantic partners. *Journal of Personality and Social Psychology, 75,* 545-560.

Drigotas, S. M., & Rusbult, C. E. (1992). Should I stay or should I go? A dependence model of breakups. *Journal of Personality and Social Psychology, 62,* 62-87.

Drigotas, S. M., Whitney, G. A., & Rusbult, C. E. (1995). On the peculiarities of loyalty: A diary study of responses to dissatisfaction in everyday life. *Personality and Social Psychology Bulletin, 21,* 596-609.

Edmonds, G. (1978). Judgments of different types of aggressive behaviour. *British Journal of Social and Clinical Psychology, 17,* 121-125.

Eidelson, R. J., & Epstein, N. (1982). Cognition and relationship maladjustment: Development of a measure of dysfunctional beliefs. *Journal of Consulting and Clinical Psychology, 50,* 715-720.

Epstein, N., Pretzer, J. L., & Fleming, B. (1987). The role of cognitive appraisal in self-reports of marital conflict. *Behavior Therapy, 18,* 51-69.

Erbert, L. A. (2000). Conflict and dialectics: Perceptions of dialectical contradictions in marital conflict. *Journal of Social and Personal Relationships, 17,* 638-659.

Fehr, B., Baldwin, M., Collins, L., Patterson, S., & Benditt, R. (1999). Anger in close relationships: An interpersonal script analysis. *Personality and Social Psychology, 25,* 299-312.

Feld, S. L., & Robinson, D. T. (1998). Secondary bystander effects on intimate violence: When norms of restraint reduce deterrence. *Journal of Social and Personal Relationships, 15,* 277-285.

Felson, R. B. (1978). Aggression as impression management. *Social Psychology, 41,* 205-213.

Felson, R. B. (1982). Impression management and the escalation of aggression and violence. *Social Psychology Quarterly, 45,* 245-254.

Felson, R. B. (1984). Patterns of aggressive social interaction. In A. Mummendey (Ed.), *Social psychology of aggression: From individual behavior to social interaction* (pp. 107-126). New York: Springer-Verlag.

Felson, R. B., Ribner, S. A., & Siegel, M. S. (1984). Age and the effect of third parties during criminal violence. *Sociology and Social Research, 68,* 452-462.

Fincham, F. D. (2000). The kiss of the porcupines: From attributing responsibility to forgiving. *Personal Relationships, 7,* 1-12.

Fincham, F. D., Garnier, P. C., Gano-Phillips, S., & Osborne, L. N. (1995). Preinteraction expectations, marital satisfaction, and accessibility: A new look at sentiment override. *Journal of Family Psychology, 9,* 3-14.

Fink, C. F. (1968). Some conceptual difficulties in the theory of social conflict. *Journal of Conflict Resolution, 12,* 412-460.

Finkel, E. J., & Campbell, W. K. (2001). Self-control and accommodation in close relationships: An interference analysis. *Journal of Personality and Social Psychology, 81,* 263-277.

Fischer, L. R. (1983). Mothers and mothers-in-law. *Journal of Marriage and the Family, 45,* 187-192.

Fitzpatrick, M. A. (1988). *Between husbands and wives: Communication in marriage.* Newbury Park, CA: Sage.

Flora, J., & Segrin, C. (2000). Affect and behavioral involvement in spousal complaints and compliments. *Journal of Family Psychology, 14,* 641-657.

Floyd, F. J. (1988). Couples' cognitive/affective reactions to communication behaviors.

Journal of Marriage and the Family, 50, 523-532.

Gelles, R. J. (1997). *Intimate violence in families* (3rd ed.). Thousand Oaks, CA: Sage.

Gottman, J. M. (1979). *Marital interaction: Experimental investigations.* New York: Academic Press.

Gottman, J. M. (1993). The roles of conflict engagement, escalation, and avoidance in marital interaction: A longitudinal view of five types of couples. *Journal of Consulting and Clinical Psychology, 61,* 6-15.

Gottman, J. M. (1994). *What predicts divorce? The relationship between marital processes and marital outcomes.* Hillsdale, NJ: Lawrence Erlbaum.

Gottman, J. M., Coan, J., Carrere, S., & Swanson, C. (1998). Predicting marital happiness and stability from newlywed interactions. *Journal of Marriage and the Family, 60,* 5-22.

Gottman, J. M., & Krokoff, L. J. (1989). Marital interaction and satisfaction: A longitudinal view. *Journal of Consulting and Clinical Psychology, 57,* 47-52.

Gottman, J. M., & Levenson, R. W. (2000). The timing of divorce: Predicting when a couple will divorce over a 14-year period. *Journal of Marriage and the Family, 62,* 737-745.

Gottman, J. M., Markman, H. J., & Notarius, C. I. (1977). The topography of marital conflict: A sequential analysis of verbal and nonverbal behavior. *Journal of Marriage and the Family, 39,* 461-477.

Hansen, G. L. (1985). Perceived threats and marital jealousy. *Social Psychology Quarterly, 48,* 262-268.

Haselton, M. G., & Buss, D. M. (2000). Error management theory: A new perspective on biases in cross-sex mind reading. *Journal of Personality and Social Psychology, 78,* 81-91.

Healey, J. G., & Bell, R. A. (1990). Effects of social networks on individuals' responses to conflicts in friendship. In D. D. Cahn (Ed.), *Intimates in conflict: A communication perspective* (pp. 121-150). Hillsdale, NJ: Lawrence Erlbaum.

Heavey, C. L., Christensen, A., & Malamuth, N. M. (1995). The longitudinal impact of demand and withdrawal during marital conflict. *Journal of Consulting and Clinical Psychology, 63,* 797-801.

Heavey, C. L., Layne, C., & Christensen, A. (1993). Gender and conflict structure in marital interactions: A replication and extension. *Journal of Consulting and Clinical Psychology, 61,* 16-27.

Henton, J., Cate, R., Koval, J., Lloyd, S., & Christopher, S. (1983). Romance and violence in dating relationships. *Journal of Family Issues, 4,* 467-482.

Hinde, R. A. (1979). *Toward understanding relationships.* New York: Academic Press.

Hirschman, A. O. (1970). *Exit, voice, and loyalty: Responses to decline in firms, organizations and states.* Cambridge, MA: Harvard University Press.

Hocker, J. L., & Wilmot, W. E. (1995). *Interpersonal conflict* (4th ed.). Dubuque, IA: William C. Brown.

Holtzworth-Munroe, A., & Jacobson, N. S. (1985). Causal attributions of married couples: When do they search for causes? What do they conclude when they do? *Journal of Personality and Social Psychology, 48,* 1398-1412.

Holtzworth-Munroe, A., Smutzler, N., & Stuart, G. L. (1998). Demand and withdraw communication among couples experiencing husband violence. *Journal of Consulting and Clinical Psychology, 66,* 731-743.

Honeycutt, J. M., Woods, B. L., & Fontenot, K. (1993). The endorsement of communication conflict rules as a function of engagement, marriage and marital ideology. *Journal of Social and Personal Relationships, 10,* 285-304.

Horai, J. (1977). Attributional conflict. *Journal of Social Issues, 33*(1), 88-100.

Jackson, S., Jacobs, S., Burrell, N., & Allen, M. (1986). Characterizing ordinary argument: Substantive and methodological issues. *Journal of the American Forensic Association, 23,* 42-57.

Jacobson, N. S., Follette, W. C., & McDonald, D. W. (1982). Reactivity to positive and negative behavior in distressed and nondistressed married couples. *Journal of Consulting and Clinical Psychology, 50,* 706-714.

Jacobson, N. S., Waldron, H., & Moore, D. (1980). Toward a behavioral profile of marital distress. *Journal of Consulting and Clinical Psychology, 48,* 696-703.

Jensen-Campbell, L. A., & Graziano, W. G. (2000). Beyond the schoolyard: Relationships as moderators of daily interpersonal conflict. *Personality and Social Psychology Bulletin, 26,* 925-935.

Johnson, D. J., & Rusbult, C. E. (1989). Resisting temptation: Devaluation of alternative partners as a means of maintaining commitment in close relationships. *Journal of Personality and Social Psychology, 57,* 967-980.

Johnson, K. L., & Roloff, M. E. (1998). Serial arguing and relational quality: Determinants and consequences of perceived resolvability. *Communication Research, 25,* 327-343.

Johnson, K. L., & Roloff, M. E. (2000a). Correlates of the perceived resolvability and relational consequences of serial arguing in dating relationships: Argumentative features and the use of coping strategies. *Journal of Social and Personal Relationships, 17,* 676-686.

Johnson, K. L., & Roloff, M. E. (2000b). The influence of argumentative role (initiator vs. resistor) on perceptions of serial argument resolvability and relational harm. *Argumentation, 14,* 1-15.

Johnson, M. P., & Leslie, L. (1982). Couple involvement and network structure: A test of the dyadic withdrawal hypothesis. *Social Psychology Quarterly, 45,* 34-43.

Johnson, M. P., & Milardo, R. M. (1984). Network interference in pair relationships: A social psychological recasting of Slater's theory of social regression. *Journal of Marriage and the Family, 46,* 893-899.

Jones, E., & Gallois, C. (1989). Spouses' impressions of rules for communication in public and private marital conflicts. *Journal of Marriage and the Family, 51,* 957-967.

Julien, D., Tremblay, N., Belanger, I., Dube, M., Begin, J., & Bouthillier, D. (2000). Interaction structure of husbands' and wives' disclosure of marital conflict to their respective best friend. *Journal of Family Psychology, 14,* 286-303.

Kelley, H. H. (1979). *Personal relationships: Their structure and processes.* Hillsdale, NJ: Lawrence Erlbaum.

Kelley, H. H., Cunningham, J. D., Grisham, J. A., Lefebvre, L. M., Sink, C. R., & Yablon, G. (1978). Sex differences in comments made during conflict within close heterosexual pairs. *Sex Roles, 4,* 473-492.

Kelley, H. H., & Thibaut, J. W. (1978). *Interpersonal relations: A theory of interdependence.* New York: John Wiley.

Kelly, C., Huston, T. L., & Cate, R. M. (1985). Premarital relationship correlate of the erosion of satisfaction in marriage. *Journal of Social and Personal Relationships, 2,* 167-178.

Kiecolt-Glaser, J. K., Newton, T., Cacioppo, J. T., MacCallum, R. C., Glaser, R., & Malarkey, W. B. (1996). Marital conflict and endocrine function: Are men really more physiologically affected than women? *Journal of Consulting and Clinical Psychology, 64,* 324-332.

Kirchler, E., Rodler, C. Holzl, E., & Meier, K. (2001). *Conflict and decision-making in close relationships: Love, money, and daily routines.* Philadelphia: Psychology Press.

Klein, R. C. A., & Lamm, H. (1996). Legitimate interest in couple conflict. *Journal of Social and Personal Relationships, 13,* 619-626.

Klein, R. C. A., & Milardo, R. M. (2000). The social context of couple conflict: Support and criticism from informal third parties. *Journal of Social and Personal Relationships, 17,* 618-637.

Klinetob, N. A., & Smith, D. A. (1996). Demand-withdraw communication in marital interaction: Tests of interspousal contingency and gender role hypotheses. *Journal of Marriage and the Family, 58,* 945-958.

Kluwer, E. S., Heesink, J. A. M., & Van De Vliert, E. (1996). Marital conflict about the division of household labor and paid work. *Journal of Marriage and the Family, 58,* 958-969.

Kluwer, E. S., Heesink, J. A. M., & Van De Vliert, E. (1997). The marital dynamics of conflict over the division of labor. *Journal of Marriage and the Family, 59,* 635-653.

Kluwer, E. S., Heesink, J. A. M., & Van De Vliert, E. (2000). The division of labor in close relationships: An asymmetrical conflict issue. *Personal Relationships, 7,* 263-282.

Knapp, M. L., Stafford, L., & Daly, J. A. (1986). Regrettable messages: Things people wish they hadn't said. *Journal of Communication, 36*(4), 40-58.

Koerner, A. F., & Fitzpatrick, M. A. (1997). Family type and conflict: The impact of conversation orientation and conformity orientation on conflict in the family. *Communication Studies, 48,* 59-75.

Krokoff, L. J. (1990). Hidden agendas in marriage: Affective and longitudinal dimensions. *Communication Research, 17,* 483-499.

Kurdek, L. A. (1994a). Areas of conflict for gay, lesbian, and heterosexual couples: What couples argue about influences relationship satisfaction. *Journal of Marriage and the Family, 56,* 923-934.

Kurdek, L. A. (1994b). Conflict resolution styles in gay, lesbian, heterosexual nonparent, and heterosexual parent couples. *Journal of Marriage and the Family, 56,* 705-722.

Kurdek, L. A. (1995). Predicting change in marital satisfaction from husbands' and wives' conflict resolution strategies. *Journal of Marriage and the Family, 57,* 153-164.

Liker, J. K, & Elder, G. H., Jr. (1983). Economic hardship and marital relations in the 1930s. *American Sociological Review, 48,* 343-359.

Lloyd, S. A. (1987). Conflict in premarital relationships: Differential perceptions of males and females. *Family Relations, 38,* 290-294.

Lloyd, S. A. (1990). A behavioral self-report technique for assessing conflict in close relationships. *Journal of Social and Personal Relationships, 7,* 265-272.

Lloyd, S. A., & Cate, R. M. (1985). The developmental course of conflict in dissolution of premarital relationships. *Journal of Social and Personal Relationships, 2,* 179-194.

Lundgren, D. C., & Rudawsky, D. J. (2000). Speaking one's mind or biting one's tongue: When do angered persons express or withhold feedback in transactions with male and female peers? *Social Psychology Quarterly, 63,* 253-263.

Lydon, J. E., Meana, M., Sepinwall, D., Richards, N., & Mayman, S. (1999). The commitment calibration hypothesis: When do people devalue attractive alternatives? *Personality and Social Psychology Bulletin, 25,* 152-161.

Makoul, G., & Roloff, M. E. (1998). The role of efficacy and outcome expectations in the decision to withhold relational complaints. *Communication Research, 25,* 5-29.

Marcus, N. E., Lindahl, K. M., & Malik, N. M. (2001). Interparental conflict, children's social cognitions, and child aggression: A test of a mediational model. *Journal of Family Psychology, 15,* 315-333.

Marcus-Newhall, A., Pedersen, W. C., Carlson, M., & Miller, N. (2000). Displaced aggression is alive and well: A meta-analytic review. *Journal of Personality and Social Psychology, 78,* 670-689.

McCall, M. (1970). Boundary rules in relationships and encounters. In G. McCall, M. McCall, N. K. Denzin, G. Suttles & S. Kurth (Eds.), *Social relationships* (pp. 35-61). Chicago: Aldine.

McCorkle, S., & Mills, J. L. (1992). Rowboat in a hurricane: Metaphors of interpersonal conflict management. *Communication Reports, 5,* 57-66.

McCornack, S. A., & Levine, T. R. (1990). When lies are uncovered: Emotional and relational outcomes of discovered deception. *Communication Monographs, 57,* 119-136.

McCullough, M. E., Bellah, C. G., Kilpatrick, S. D., & Johnson, J. L. (2001). Vengefulness: Relationships with forgiveness, rumination, well-being, and the big five. *Personality and Social Psychology Bulletin, 27,* 601-610.

McCullough, M. E., Rachal, K. C., Sandage, S. J., Worthington, E. L., Jr., Brown, S. W., & Hight, T. L. (1998). Interpersonal forgiving in close relationships: II. Theoretical elaboration and measurement. *Journal of Personality and Social Psychology, 75,* 1586-1603.

McCullough, M. E., Worthington, E. L., Jr., & Rachal, K. C. (1997). Interpersonal forgiving in close relationships. *Journal of Personality and Social Psychology, 73,* 321-336.

McGonagle, K. A., Kessler, R. C., & Gotlib, I. H. (1993). The effects of marital disagreement style, frequency, and outcome on marital disruption. *Journal of Social and Personal Relationships, 10,* 385-404.

McGonagle, K. A., Kessler, R. C., & Schilling, E. A. (1992). The frequency and determinants of marital disagreements in a community of sample. *Journal of Social and Personal Relationships, 9,* 507-524.

Metts, S. (1991, February). *The wicked things you say, the wicked things you do: A pilot study of relation transgressions.* Paper presented at the annual meeting of the Western Speech Communication Association, Phoenix, AZ.

Metts, S. (1994). Relational transgression. In W. R. Cupach & B. H. Spitzberg (Eds.), *The dark side of interpersonal communication* (pp. 217-239). Hillsdale, NJ: Lawrence Erlbaum.

Metts, S., & Cupach, W. R. (1990). The influence of relationship beliefs and problem-solving responses on satisfaction in romantic relationships. *Human Communication Research, 17,* 170-185.

Mikolic, J. M., Parker, J. C., & Pruitt, D. G. (1997). Escalation in response to persistent annoyance: Groups versus individuals and gender effects. *Journal of Personality and Social Psychology, 72,* 151-163.

Milardo, R. M., Johnson, M. P., & Huston, T. L. (1983). Developing close relationships: Changing patterns of interactions between pair members and social networks. *Journal of Personality and Social Psychology, 44,* 964-976.

Miller, J. B. (1991). Women's and men's scripts for interpersonal conflict. *Psychology of Women Quarterly, 15,* 15-29.

Miller, N., & Marcus-Newhall, A. (1997). A conceptual analysis of displaced aggression. In R. Ben-Ari & Y. Riche (Eds.), *Enhancing education in heterogeneous schools* (pp. 69-108). Ramat-Gan, Israel: Bar-Ilan University Press.

Miller, R. S. (1997). Inattentive and contented: Relationship commitment and attention to alternatives. *Journal of Personality and Social Psychology, 73,* 758-766.

Murray, S. L., & Holmes, J. G. (1993). Seeing virtues in faults: Negativity and the transformation of interpersonal narratives in close relationships. *Journal of Personality and Social Psychology, 65,* 707-722.

Murray, S. L., & Holmes, J. G. (1994). Storytelling in close relationships: The construction of confidence. *Personality and Social Psychology Bulletin, 20,* 650-663.

Murray, S. L., & Holmes, J. G. (1997). A leap of faith? Positive illusions in romantic relationships. *Personality and Social Psychology Bulletin, 23,* 586-604.

Murray, S. L., & Holmes, J. G. (1999). The (mental) ties that bind: Cognitive structures that predict relationship resilience. *Journal of Personality and Social Psychology, 77,* 1228-1244.

Murray, S. L., Holmes, J. G., Dolderman, D., & Griffin, D. W. (2000). What the motivated mind sees: Comparing friends' perspectives to married partners' views of each other. *Journal of Experimental Social Psychology, 36,* 600-620.

Murray, S. L., Holmes, J. G., & Griffin, D. W. (1996a). The benefits of positive illusions: Idealization and the construction of satisfaction in close relationships. *Journal of Personality and Social Psychology, 70,* 79-86.

Murray, S. L., Holmes, J. G., & Griffin, D. W. (1996b). The self-fulfilling nature of positive illusions in romantic relationships: Love is not blind but prescient. *Journal of Personality and Social Psychology, 71,* 1155-1180.

Nelson, J., & Aboud, F. E. (1985). The resolution of social conflict between friends. *Child Development, 56,* 1009-1017.

Newell, S. E., & Stutman, R. K. (1991). The episodic nature of social confrontation. In J. A. Anderson (Ed.), *Communication yearbook 14* (pp. 359-392). Newbury Park, CA: Sage.

Noller, P., Feeney, J. A., Bonnell, D., & Callan, V. J. (1994). A longitudinal study of conflict in early marriage. *Journal of Social and Personal Relationships, 11,* 233-252.

Orvis, B. R., Kelley, H. H., & Butler, D. (1976). Attributional conflict in young couples. In J. H. Harvey, W. Ickes, & R. F. Kidd (Eds.), *New directions in attribution research* (Vol. 1, pp. 353-386). Hillsdale, NJ: Lawrence Erlbaum.

Passer, M. W., Kelley, H. H., & Michela, J. L. (1978). Multidimensional scaling of the causes for negative interpersonal behavior. *Journal of Personality and Social Psychology, 36,* 951-962.

Pinkley, R. L. (1990). Dimensions of conflict frame: Disputant interpretations of conflict. *Journal of Applied Psychology, 75,* 117-126.

Pinkley, R. L. (1992). Dimensions of conflict frame: Relation to disputant perceptions and expectations. *International Journal of Conflict Management, 3,* 95-113.

Pruitt, D. G., Parker, J. C., & Mikolic, J. M. (1997). Escalation as a reaction to persistent annoyance. *International Journal of Conflict Management, 8,* 252-270.

Repetti, R. L. (1989). Effects of daily workload on subsequent behavior during marital interaction: The roles of social withdrawal and spouse support. *Journal of Personality and Social Psychology, 57,* 651-659.

Repetti, R. L., & Wood, J. (1997). Effects of daily stress at work on mother's interactions with preschoolers. *Journal of Family Psychology, 11,* 90-108.

Resick, P. A., Barr, P. K., Sweet, J. J., Keiffer, D. M., Ruby, N. L., & Spiegel, D. K. (1981). Perceived and actual discriminators of conflict from accord in marital communication. *American Journal of Family Therapy, 9,* 58-68.

Ridley, C. A., Wilhelm, M. S., & Surra, C. (2001). Married couples' conflict responses and marital quality. *Journal of Social and Personal Relationships, 18,* 517-534.

Roberts, L. J., & Krokoff, L. J. (1990). A time-series analysis of withdrawal, hostility, and displeasure in satisfied and dissatisfied marriages. *Journal of Marriage and the Family, 52,* 95-105.

Roloff, M. E. (1988). Communication and conflict. In C. R. Berger & S. H. Chaffee (Eds.), *Handbook of communication science* (pp. 484-534). Newbury Park, CA: Sage.

Roloff, M. E., & Cloven, D. H. (1990). The chilling effect in interpersonal relationships: The reluctance to speak one's mind. In D. D. Cahn (Ed.), *Intimates in conflict: A communication perspective* (pp. 49-76). Hillsdale, NJ: Lawrence Erlbaum.

Roloff, M. E., & Greenberg, B. S. (1980). TV, peer, and parent models for pro- and anti-social conflict behaviors. *Human Communication Research, 6,* 340-351.

Roloff, M. E., & Ifert, D. E. (1998). Antecedents and consequences of explicit agreements to declare a topic taboo in dating relationships. *Personal Relationships, 5,* 191-206.

Roloff, M. E., Soule, K. P., & Carey, C. M. (2001). Reasons for remaining in a relationships and responses to relational transactions. *Journal of Social and Personal Relationships, 18,* 362-385.

Rusbult, C. E., & Buunk, B. P. (1993). Commitment processes in close relationships: An interdependence analysis. *Journal of Social and Personal Relationships, 10,* 175-204.

Rusbult, C. E., Johnson, D. J., & Morrow, G. D. (1986a). Determinants and consequences of exit, voice, loyalty, and neglect: Response to dissatisfaction in adult romantic involvements. *Human Relations, 39,* 45-63.

Rusbult, C. E., Johnson, D. J., & Morrow, G. D. (1986b). Impact of couple patterns of problem solving on distress and nondistress in dating relationships. *Journal of Personality and Social Psychology, 50,* 744-753.

Rusbult, C. E., & Martz, J. M. (1995). Remaining in an abusive relationship: An investment model analysis of nonvoluntary dependence. *Personality and Social Psychology Bulletin, 21,* 558-571.

Rusbult, C. E., Verette, J., Whitney, G. A., Slovik, L. F., & Lipkus, I. (1991). Accommodation processes in close relationships: Theory and preliminary empirical evidence. *Journal of Personality and Social Psychology, 60,* 53-78.

Rusbult, C. E., & Zembrodt, I. M. (1983). Responses to dissatisfaction in romantic involvements: A multidimensional scaling analysis. *Journal of Experimental Social Psychology, 19,* 274-293.

Rusbult, C. E., Zembrodt, I. M., & Gunn, L. K. (1982). Exit, voice, loyalty, and neglect: Responses to dissatisfaction in romantic involvements. *Journal of Personality and Social Psychology, 43,* 1230-1242.

Ruvolo, A. P., Fabin, L. A., & Ruvolo, C. M. (2001). Relationship experiences and change in attachment characteristics of young adults: The role of relationship breakups and conflict avoidance. *Personal Relationships, 8,* 265-281.

Sagrestano, L. M., Christensen, A., & Heavey, C. L. (1998). Social influence techniques during marital conflict. *Personal Relationships, 5,* 75-89.

Scanzoni, J. (1978). *Sex roles, women's work, and marital conflict.* Lexington, MA: Lexington.

Scherer, K. R., & Tannenbaum, P. H. (1986). Emotional experiences in everyday life: A survey approach. *Motivation and Emotion, 10,* 295-314.

Schoeneman, T. J. (1983). Frequency of social evaluation in self-observed daily interactions. *Social Behavior and Personality, 11,* 77-80.

Schutz, A. (1999). It was your fault! Self-serving biases in autobiographical accounts of conflicts in married couples. *Journal of Social and Personal Relationships, 16,* 193-208.

Segrin, C., & Fitzpatrick, M. A. (1992). Depression and verbal aggressiveness in different marital couple types. *Communication Monographs, 43,* 79-91.

Shackelford, T. K., & Buss, D. M. (1996). Betrayal in mateships, friendships, and coalitions. *Personality and Social Psychology Bulletin, 11,* 1151-1164.

Sillars, A. L. (1980). Attributions and communication in roommate conflicts. *Communication Monographs, 47,* 180-200.

Sillars, A. L., Coletti, S. F., Parry, D., & Rogers, M. A. (1982). Coding verbal conflict tactics: Nonverbal and perceptual correlates of the "avoidance-distributive-integrative" distinction. *Human Communication Research, 9,* 83-95.

Sillars, A. L., Roberts, L. J., Leonard, K. E., & Dun, T. (2000). Cognition during marital conflict: The relationship of thought and talk. *Journal of Social and Personal Relationships, 17,* 479-502.

Simmel, G. (1955). *Conflict* (K. H. Wulff, Trans.). New York: Free Press.

Solomon, D. H., & Roloff, M. E. (1996). *Conflict avoidance in personal relationships: Reasons for withholding complaints from romantic partners.* Unpublished manuscript.

Solomon, D. H., & Samp, J. A. (1998). Power and problem appraisal: Perceptual foundations of the chilling effect in dating relationships. *Journal of Social and Personal Relationships, 15,* 191-209.

Spitzberg, B. H., Canary, D. J., & Cupach, W. R. (1994). A competence-based approach to the study of interpersonal conflict. In D. D. Cahn (Ed.), *Conflict in personal relationships* (pp. 183-202). Hillsdale, NJ: Lawrence Erlbaum.

Steinmetz, S. K. (1977). *The cycle of violence: Assertive, aggressive and abusive family interaction.* New York: Praeger.

Sternberg, D. P., & Beier, E. G. (1977). Changing patterns of conflict. *Journal of Communication, 27*(3), 97-103.

Stets, J. E. (1993). Control in dating relationships. *Journal of Marriage and the Family, 55,* 673-685.

Stets, J. E. (1995). Modeling control in relationships. *Journal of Marriage and the Family, 57,* 489-501.

Stets, J. E., & Henderson, D. A. (1991). Contextual factors surrounding conflict resolution while dating: Results from a national study. *Family Relations, 40,* 29-36.

Straus, M. A. (1979). Measuring intrafamily conflict and violence: The Conflict Tactics (CT) Scales. *Journal of Marriage and the Family, 41,* 75-88.

Straus, M. A. (1990a). Measuring intrafamily conflict and violence: The Conflict Tactics (CT) Scales. In M. A. Straus & R. J. Gelles (Eds.), *Physical violence in American families: Risk factors and adaptations to violence in 8,145 families* (pp. 29-47). Brunswick, NJ: Transaction.

Straus, M. A. (1990b). The Conflict Tactics Scale and its critics: An evaluation and new data on validity and reliability. In M. A. Straus & R. J. Gelles (Eds.), *Physical violence in American families: Risk factors and adaptations to violence in 8,145 families* (pp. 49-73). Brunswick, NJ: Transaction.

Stutman, R. K., & Newell, S. E. (1990). Rehearsing for confrontation. *Argumentation, 4,* 185-198.

Sullaway, M., & Christensen, A. (1983). Assessment of dysfunctional interaction patterns in couples. *Journal of Marriage and the Family, 45,* 653-660.

Surra, C. A. (1985). Courtship types: Variations in interdependence between partners and social networks. *Journal of Personality and Social Psychology, 49,* 357-375.

Surra, C. A., & Longstreth, M. (1990). Similarity of outcomes, interdependence, and conflict in dating relationships. *Journal of Personality and Social Psychology, 59,* 501-516.

Swensen, C. H., Eskew, R. W., & Kohlhepp, K. A. (1981). Stage of family life cycle, ego development, and the marriage relationship. *Journal of Marriage and the Family, 43,* 841-853.

Terman, L. M., Buttenweiser, P., Ferguson, L. W., Johnson, W. B., & Wilson, D. P. (1938). *Psychological factors in marital happiness.* New York: McGraw-Hill.

Ting-Toomey, S. (1983). An analysis of verbal communication patterns in high and low marital adjustment groups. *Human Communication Research, 9,* 306-319.

Trapp, R., & Hoff, N. (1985). A model of serial argument in interpersonal relationships. *Journal of the American Forensic Association, 22,* 1-11.

Truman-Schram, D. M., Cann, A., Calhoun, L., & Vanwallendael, L. (2000). Leaving an abusive dating relationship: An investment model comparison of women who stay versus women who leave. *Journal of Social and Clinical Psychology, 19,* 161-183.

Vangelisti, A. L., & Crumley, L. P. (1998). Reactions to messages that hurt: The influence of relational contexts. *Communication Monographs, 65,* 173-196.

Vangelisti, A. L., Daly, J. A., & Rudnick, J. R. (1991). Making people feel guilty in conversations: Techniques and correlates. *Human Communication Research, 18,* 3-39.

Van Lange, P. A. M., Rusbult, C. E., Drigotas, S. M., Arriaga, X. B., Witcher, B. S., & Cox, C. L. (1997). Willingness to sacrifice in close relationships. *Journal of Personality and Social Psychology, 72,* 1373-1395.

VanLear, C. A., Jr., & Zietlow, P. H. (1990). Toward a contingency approach to marital interactions: An empirical integration of the three approaches. *Communication Monographs, 57,* 202-218.

Vinokur, A. D., Price, R. H., & Caplan, R. D. (1996). Hard times and hurtful partners: How financial strain affects depression and relationships satisfaction of unemployed persons and their spouses. *Journal of Personality and Social Psychology, 71,* 166-179.

Vuchinich, S. (1986). On attenuations in verbal family conflict. *Social Psychology Quarterly, 49,* 281-293.

Vuchinich, S. (1987). Starting and stopping spontaneous family conflicts. *Journal of Marriage and the Family, 49,* 591-601.

Vuchinich, S., Emery, R. E., & Cassidy, J. (1988). Family members as third parties in dyadic family conflict: Strategies, alliances, and outcomes. *Child Development, 59,* 1293-1302.

Weiss, R. L. (1980). Strategic behavioral marital therapy: Toward a model for assessment and intervention. In J. P. Vincent (Ed.), *Advances in family intervention, assessment, and theory* (Vol. 1, pp. 229-271). New York: Guilford.

Wheaton, B. (1974). Interpersonal conflict and cohesiveness in dyadic relationships. *Sociometry, 37,* 328-348.

White, G. L. (1980). Inducing jealousy: A power perspective. *Personality and Social Psychology Bulletin, 6,* 222-227.

Wieselquist, J., Rusbult, C. E., Foster, C. A., & Agnew, C. R. (1999). Commitment, pro-relationship behavior, and trust in close relationships. *Journal of Personality and Social Psychology, 77,* 942-966.

Williamson, R. N., & Fitzpatrick, M. A. (1985). Two approaches to marital interaction: Relational control patterns in marital types. *Communication Monographs, 52,* 236-252.

Wilson, L. L., Roloff, M. E., & Carey, C. (1998). Boundary rules: Favors that inhibit expressing concerns about another's romantic relationships. *Communication Research, 25,* 618-640.

Witteman, H. (1988). Interpersonal problem solving: Problem conceptualization and communication use. *Communication Monographs, 55,* 336-359.

Witteman, H. (1992). Analyzing interpersonal conflict: Nature of awareness, type of initiating event, situational perceptions, and management styles. *Western Journal of Communication, 56,* 248-280.

Witvliet, C. V., Ludwig, T. E., & Vander Laan, K. L. (2001). Granting forgiveness or harboring grudges: Implications for emotion, physiology, and health. *Psychological Sciences, 12,* 117-123.

Yovetich, N. A., & Rusbult, C. E. (1994). Accommodative behavior in close relationships: Exploring transformation of motivation. *Journal of Experimental Social Psychology, 30,* 138-164.

Zietlow, P. H., & Sillars, A. L. (1988). Life-stage differences in communication during marital conflicts. *Journal of Social and Personal Relationships, 5,* 223-245.

14

Cues Filtered Out, Cues Filtered In

*Computer-Mediated
Communication and Relationships*

JOSEPH B. WALTHER
MALCOLM R. PARKS

In August 1998, news of the results of a study soon to be published in the *American Psychologist* sent shock waves through the Internet community and, to no small extent, through public discourse about the social impact of the Internet. Robert Kraut and his colleagues (1998) had found that Internet use in a sample of 93 families had resulted in small but significant increases in loneliness, social isolation, and depression over a 2-year period. The researchers asserted that the cause of these decrements in well-being was that on-line relationships do not sustain social support, and the substitution of on-line relationships for stronger, off-line relationships led to these negative outcomes. The ensuing debate was a forceful reminder that the Internet has become a flash point for more general concerns about technology. For some, Kraut et al.'s findings were a direct challenge to their prized ideological positions about the Internet as a source of meaningful relationships, social support, therapeutic engagement, and identity growth. For others, the findings were striking confirmation of the dehumanizing, destructive potential of computer technology. We will present a thorough assessment of these findings later in this chapter, but for now the essential point is that the impact of Internet communication on personal relationships is a central issue in technology research, one that raises controversy in academic and public discussions. In doing so, it underscores the fact that, for good or ill, the Internet is a profoundly social medium.

The social nature of the Internet has been recognized, albeit unevenly, throughout the history of Internet research. Such research has drawn heavily on interpersonal constructs such as self-presentation, impression formation and management, socioemotional orientation, hierarchical role awareness and performance, deference, cooperation, intimacy, attraction, affection, and relational development. Moreover, even when the focus of Internet research moves beyond the immediate world of dyadic and small group relationships to consider features such as organizational communication, community dynamics, collective action, and educational developments, the work's theoretical underpinnings have often remained solidly rooted in the relational aspects of interaction.

In this chapter we examine the theoretical research about computer-mediated communication (CMC) and relational dynamics. We begin by reviewing several theories that have emerged from or have been applied to these issues. Recent reviews have covered some of the same ground (e.g., Postmes, Spears, Lea, & Reicher, 2000; Walther, 1996), but our assessment is both more far reaching and set more squarely in the context of interpersonal communication. Next, we explore the use of CMC in three contexts of particular relevance for interpersonal communication: mental health and social functioning, social support, and relationship development. Finally, we evaluate the adequacy of existing theories of CMC and interpersonal communication in light of the observation that any given relationship frequently exists in several different media at once. We contend that these "mixed-media relationships" create challenges for current theoretical approaches. We offer a potentially unifying approach to the phenomenon of relationships that develop on-line and migrate to off-line encounters, and identify

several approaches from previous interpersonal communication research that suggest promise for adaptation into the electronic domain.

Computer-mediated communication is a broad term, and it is growing broader with each technological innovation. We therefore limit our review to those features that are likely to hold the greatest relevance for students of interpersonal communication. First, although inquiry ranges from rigorous ethnographic, interpretive, and linguistic work (e.g., Baym, 1999; Herring, 1993) to psychoanalytic and postmodernist accounts (e.g., Bruckman, 1992; Turkle, 1995), we devote the bulk of our attention to work rooted in traditional social scientific approaches. In many cases, of course, this research has been stimulated and enriched by alternative perspectives. Our emphasis, however, is on efforts to provide more general, theoretical explanations for the interpersonal dynamics of on-line interaction. Second, we focus here on text-based messaging systems on the Internet. This might strike the reader as an overly restrictive stance, given the proliferation of sound and sight in recent Internet technologies (e.g., voice messaging, video and photographic displays). However, the fact remains that text-based systems still dominate interaction on the Internet. E-mail, chat rooms, multiuser discussions (popularly called "MOOs" or "MUDs"), and Listservs and other mailing lists, as well as the global system of Usenet newsgroups that hosts thousands of group discussions on myriad topics, continue to link millions of people in text-based interaction on a daily basis. And innovations in text-based communication continue to unfold beside or within their flashier technological cousins. Instant messaging and "chat boxes" that stand alone or that accompany on-line games or retail shopping sites illustrate the continuing expansion of text-based interaction on the Internet (see Nardi, Whittaker, & Bradner, 2000; Pew Internet & American Life Project, 2001a, 2001b). Another reason we focus on text-based systems is that they are the most interactive and hence the most engaging for scholars of interpersonal communication. Although Web pages providing personal information (see Miller, 1995) can be revised, and files containing photographs or video can obviously be exchanged, the real give-and-take of social life involving the Internet still occurs in text-based interaction.

THEORIES OF COMPUTER-MEDIATED COMMUNICATION

The dominant theories with implications for the interpersonal dynamics of CMC have not, as a rule, developed in the context of interpersonal relations. Some were based in small group communication, whereas others were concerned with message comprehension in organizations. Still others were imported from nondigital domains and adapted to explain on-line phenomena. Some observers have raised questions about the applicability of such theories to the interpersonal uses of the Internet (e.g., Baym, 1995), and it is true that we do not yet have a clear sense of what the boundary conditions of these theories may be. They may or may not be applicable to interpersonal behavior on the Internet. Certainly a few have been stretched so far from their original starting places that the value of their guidance is open to question. Nevertheless, rooted as they are in basic communication constructs, and without any theoretical competition in sight at present, these general theories continue to be applied to interpersonal dynamics and CMC. In one way or another, all deal with how the communicative cues available in on-line settings affect the ensuing interaction. They differ in terms of the cues they consider and their conceptions of how people use those cues. In this section we consider five approaches, which for convenience we label cues filtered out, cues to choose by, cues filtered in, cues about us, and cues bent and twisted.

Cues Filtered Out

The Internet is only one in a succession of new media spawned over the past 150 years. It is therefore not surprising that early attempts to account for social behavior on the Internet drew on theories that were originally focused on other media. Short, Williams, and Christie's (1976) social presence theory, for example, dealt with more traditional media in terms of their *bandwidth* and *social presence*. *Bandwidth* refers to the number of communication cue systems a technology can convey, specifically, the incremental addition to verbiage of voice, kinesics, and proxemics. Short and his colleagues argue that nonverbal cues make the presence of communicators more salient to one another and enhance the warmth and friendliness of interaction. Thus the greater the bandwidth a system affords, the greater the social presence of communicators.

Researchers used this theory to explain CMC's effects on group discussion (e.g., Hiltz, Johnson, & Agle, 1978) as well as to predict preferences among alternative media for various tasks (Rice & Case, 1983). Because of their low bandwidth, text-based systems were thought to result in low social presence. This in turn was hypothesized to increase task orientation and to facilitate group discussion (e.g., Turoff, 1991). Early studies partially supported these speculations. Task-oriented communication was more frequent in computer-mediated settings than in face-to-face (FtF) settings. However, it also appeared that groups using CMC reached consensus less frequently. The lack of nonverbal cues and lower social presence made it more difficult for leadership to emerge and for groups to reach agreement in socioemotional terms (for a review, see Walther, 1996).

Other researchers pointed to the lack of social context cues in on-line settings (Kiesler, Siegel, & McGuire, 1984; Siegel, Dubrovsky, Kiesler, & McGuire, 1986; Sproull & Kiesler, 1986). CMC was thought to lack the nonverbal cues that are typically used in FtF settings to express purpose, setting, decorum, roles, relative status, and affect. Without such cues, researchers argued, communicators would become absorbed in the task and the self, and become disinhibited and hostile. Without nonverbal cues, communicators should be less able to "alter the mood of a message, communicate a sense of individuality, or exercise dominance or charisma" (Kiesler, 1986, p. 48). Research supported these predictions; compared with people in FtF groups, CMC users were found to express greater hostility (commonly called "flaming") and to send more task-oriented messages.

These approaches have been combined in what is generally referred to as the *cues filtered out* model (Culnan & Markus, 1987). They share the assumption of a one-to-one correspondence between communicative *cues* and communicative *functions*. That is, they assume that the functions served by nonverbal cues in FtF interaction go unmet in computer-mediated interaction because the nonverbal cues are absent. If no other cues can perform the social functions that physical appearance, copresence, and dynamic nonverbal behavior can, then, as Culnan and Markus (1987) point out, CMC must always be impersonal.

In spite of its considerable intuitive appeal and early empirical support, the cues filtered out perspective came under heavy criticism as evidence came in from a wider range of on-line settings and theoretical conceptualizations became more sophisticated. One critique pointed to the relatively short time periods allowed for both CMC and FtF groups in the early studies and the possibility that it simply takes longer to achieve the same level of content exchange in CMC as in oral FtF communication (Walther, 1992). If time limits interrupt group and relational development, task orientation and lack of agreement may be the result of different rates of communication. Indeed, reanalyses of existing data as well as new studies supported the belief that it was

time limitations, rather than the ultimate capacity of CMC to convey relational dynamics, that accounted for the differences in early studies (Walther, Anderson, & Park, 1994). Recent research also suggests that time limits may affect CMC interactions and FtF groups in qualitatively different ways. Reid and colleagues found that CMC groups were more sensitive to time pressure than parallel FtF groups. When time was restricted, CMC users expressed less positive affective content relative to unhurried CMC groups and FtF groups (Reid, Ball, Morley, & Evans, 1997; Reid, Malinek, Stott, & Evans, 1996).

Another line of critique challenged the notion of the isomorphism of communicative cues and communicative functions. The problem with the isomorphism assumption, as Lea and Spears (1995) observe, is that more complex factors outside the exclusive domain of spatial and nonverbal cues might predict attraction and affect; factors such as group identity and attitude similarity are not considered. Observations in newsgroups and field settings demonstrated that people were clearly making strong judgments based on text alone. The cues filtered out perspective has fallen out of favor with many CMC researchers because of these objections. Although the original advocates have not explicitly recanted their positions, their subsequent work has reflected more positive assessments of CMC's relational potential (e.g., Galagher, Sproull, & Kiesler, 1998; Sproull & Faraj, 1997). Elsewhere, however, researchers continue to draw on the images of restricted interactions and restricted cues (e.g., Gunawardena, 1995; Gunawardena & Zittle, 1997).

Cues to Choose by

Some types of messages might be conveyed more efficiently in one medium than in another. This seemingly commonsense proposition is the premise upon which media richness theory (or information richness theory; Daft & Lengel, 1984, 1986) is based. Although the theory originated in work on information processing in organizations, it has the potential to help explain why people used computer-mediated channels and why these channels might be particularly appealing for certain types of tasks.

The core argument in media richness theory is that there is an optimal match between the equivocality of communication tasks and the communication media among which one may choose. It is important to note that the original theory proposed a single and simple outcome as a result of such matching: efficiency (in turn, the effective accomplishment of understanding within a specific time interval; Daft & Lengel, 1984). Thus the more equivocal the communication task and the richer the medium one uses, the more efficient the exchange. Conversely and ingeniously, when equivocality is low, it does not matter what medium is used for *effectiveness,* but a leaner medium is more *efficient.*

Richness of a medium is determined by four characteristics: multiplicity of cue systems (analogous to the concept of bandwidth), the availability of immediate feedback (i.e., whether the medium offers delayed interaction or full interruptibility), message personalization (whether messages can be tailored to a specific individual versus a large audience), and natural language or language variety (formal versus conversational language). CMC, particularly electronic mail, has been incorporated into the model as a relatively lean medium (e.g., Daft, Lengel, & Trevino, 1987).

Media richness theory draws on a straightforward definition of equivocality as the number of possible interpretations one can make, but then takes a turn of particular relevance to those interested in the relational aspects of on-line communication. Emotionally arousing, personally involving tasks are conceptualized as having high equivocality and thus are seen as more appropriate for richer media (Daft & Lengel, 1984; Dennis & Kinney, 1998). This implies that relatively lean media,

such as text-based messaging systems, should not lend themselves to efficient communication of emotionally complex matters. And this, of course, suggests that lean media should be poor carriers of interpersonal communication.

Empirical tests of this framework have yielded inconsistent results. When *projective* methods have been used, findings have generally been supportive. These methods typically involve asking respondents to indicate which media they would be most likely choose, from FtF through e-mail, for each of several kinds of communication episodes that vary in equivocality (see, e.g., Rice, 1993). These studies indicate, for example, that managers who make optimal matches between equivocality and medium tend to be rated more successful in their organizations than those who make less sensitive matches (Daft et al., 1987). Results from *observational and experimental* studies have not been as supportive. These studies demonstrate that people often make very effective use of lean media to accomplish highly equivocal tasks (e.g., Dennis & Kinney, 1998; Fulk, Schmitz, & Steinfield, 1990; Markus, 1994a).

The discrepancy between projective and observational results is testimony to the fact that actual media choices often do not match normative expectations. One reason for this is that media choices in the real world are not always made on the basis of optimal efficiency. Even if a FtF meeting would be most efficient, such meetings cannot always be held on the spur of the moment; we walk down the hall to pay someone a visit but find the office empty, and telephone calls go unanswered, leaving e-mail, perhaps the last choice, as the first among unequals. This is not to say that CMC is a preferred medium, the easiest, or the most efficient. It is likely, however, that an asynchronous medium wins the day when synchronous choices are not available (see Bozeman, 1996). How, then, does a lean medium overcome its restrictions? Although this suggestion has not appeared in the literature to date, the answer may be found in a root proposition of the theory: We must work less efficiently—communicate more effortfully, or at least more iteratively—to achieve the same relative effectiveness that FtF or other rich media afford with less difficulty.

In this respect, Korzenny's (1978) theory of electronic propinquity, which also predates the Internet, offers a different perspective: The fewer one's choices of media, the more psychological closeness one may experience, even through low-bandwidth channels. Korzenny does not state whether this phenomenon should result from perceptual or behavioral processes. That is, does a low-bandwidth medium merely seem richer when alternatives are limited? Or, if forced to rely on the structurally least expressive of media choices, does a user accommodate and expand the otherwise limited range of the medium through greater effort, greater application of communication skills, and the reduction of formality? Such a process would go far in explaining how lean media can be used for the effective performance of interpersonally demanding tasks. Unfortunately, the sole empirical test of electronic propinquity theory failed to support the framework (Korzenny & Bauer, 1981), although the experimental protocols may have been problematic. The theory has received less subsequent attention than it probably deserves, and new experimentation is currently under way.

Closer inspection of the core definitions and propositions of media richness theory illuminates other problems as well. It is apparent that the relationships among the four characteristics of media richness have never been specified with any level of precision. It is not clear how or whether changes in cue multiplicity, immediacy of feedback, message personalization, and linguistic form might be related to one another. Although the theory appears to assume that all four move in unison as we examine one medium or another, obvious exceptions abound (Markus, 1994a). E-mail, for example, offers little immediate feedback

but many opportunities for personalized language. Moreover, communicative efficiency may rest on sequences or combinations of media rather than on isolated choices about a single medium. It may be more efficient, for example, to raise discussion of a difficult, emotionally charged topic in e-mail in advance of a FtF conversation than to raise the topic out of the blue in conversation. People may make suboptimal media choices as part of larger strategies to optimize overall series of exchanges.

Despite media richness theory's problems, it is also apparent that the research to date has not directly tested the underlying claim of the theory. The fundamental claim is that *if* users select richer media for equivocal messages, *then* their efficiency will be greater. Researchers who have asked respondents what they might use or have assigned users to tasks and media in order to assess perceptions or effectiveness have not addressed that proposition. This is equivalent to refuting the lawlike proposition that greater fuel efficiency and reduced fatalities result when motorists drive at 55 rather than 65 miles per hour by arguing that many drivers don't think so and that many good drivers exceed 55 miles per hour. The basic proposition remains untested.

Examination of media selection in interpersonal contexts makes it clear that media selection also depends on situational and relational goals of the participants. Thus Kayany, Wotring, and Forrest (1996) found that e-mail and phone were preferred to FtF communication in relationally competitive situations as well as in situations in which the communicators wished to regulate the extent to which they imposed on each other. Moreover, in relationally complementary settings, e-mail and phone were advantageous because they reduced the amount of pressure placed on the other party, conveyed deference, and were thought to maintain goodwill. O'Sullivan (2000) explored how the presence of potential face threats to the sender or receiver in an interpersonal encounter might affect media choice. His initial assumptions were consistent with media richness theory; namely, that electronic media with fewer cues and less temporally immediate interaction would create less emotional impact than FtF speech. However, he turned one of the implicit assumptions of media richness theory on its head by drawing on other lines of research to argue that people do not always seek unambiguous or unequivocal communication (e.g., Bavelas, Black, Chovil, & Mullett, 1990). Subjects were presented with scenarios in which they were called upon to communicate in a way that would bolster or threaten either their own egos or their partners' egos. They were then instructed to choose between FtF interaction and one of several "partial-cue" media (e-mail, telephone, answering machine, or letter). Results confirmed that subjects preferred partial-cue media over FtF when a preferred impression was threatened, and especially when the impression at stake was the subject's rather than the partner's. These results lend credence to Markus's (1994b) speculation that different aspects of different media may promote secrecy, privacy, hostility, or openness, depending on their application by users. Such applications would not be apparent either from a unitary media richness hierarchy or from conceptualizations of choice in which the sole focus is the reduction of equivocality.

Cues Filtered in

The social information processing (SIP) theory of CMC interaction (Walther, 1992) departs from the theories discussed above by explicitly rejecting the view that the absence of nonverbal cues restricts communicators' capability to exchange individuating information. It assumes instead that communicators are just as motivated to reduce interpersonal uncertainty, form impressions, and develop affinity in on-line settings as they are in other settings. When denied the nonverbal cues

available in FtF interaction, communicators substitute the expression of impression-bearing and relational messages into the cues available through the CMC. Thus SIP theory posits that communicators exchange social information through the content, style, and timing of verbal messages on-line. The rate of information exchange is slower on-line, not only because both instrumental and relational information must be conveyed in a limited bandwidth, but because typing and reading are slower than speaking, looking, and listening. Time therefore becomes the critical predictive variable. When time limits are imposed in CMC, interaction should not go beyond impersonal and task-oriented behavior. When interaction time is not restricted, people in on-line settings should ultimately reach, although more slowly, levels of impression and relational development similar to what they would reach in FtF settings.

Support for SIP theory has been obtained in several settings. One was a test of impression development in which comparisons were made between CMC and FtF groups that met over a period of 6 weeks to discuss three decision-making tasks (Walther, 1993). The CMC groups used asynchronous computer conferencing at times of their own choosing, and the FtF groups met once every 2 weeks for 2 hours. Participants completed measures assessing their willingness to rate group members on a number of attributes after each task was completed. Repeated measures analyses supported SIP predictions by indicating that FtF participants formed more fully developed impressions sooner than CMC participants, but the impressions of CMC participants continued to develop over time until the end of the 6-week study period, at which point they were not significantly different from those of the FtF participants.

Walther and Burgoon (1992) used similar procedures in a more extensive study of relational communication (see Burgoon & Hale, 1984, 1987). It was predicted that immediacy, composure, receptivity, and social orientation would initially be greater in FtF settings, but that over time, relational communication levels in CMC would increase and converge with those in FtF settings. These predictions were partially supported, although not all of the relational levels differed after only the first task. Moreover, although both CMC and FtF communication became more socially oriented over time as predicted, social orientation was greater in CMC than in FtF settings across all time points, in stark contrast to the earlier cues filtered out findings about task-oriented CMC. In an earlier study, Rice and Love (1987) also found relatively high levels of socioemotional content in a longitudinal examination of electronic bulletin board use, but did not find an expected increase over time in this behavior.

Additional support for social information processing theory emerged from a meta-analysis of previous research in CMC (Walther et al., 1994). Comparisons were made between previous studies in which time limits were placed on groups, and experiments with no deliberate time limits as well as field studies with cross-sectional data on socioemotional tone in CMC. The comparisons demonstrated a significant effect for time limitation. Studies in which there were no time limits found significantly more positive socioemotional communication than did studies in which interaction was cut off at any point.

These results all suggest that people who communicate using computers must either place greater weight on the cues that remain in text-based CMC or use alternative cues as substitutes for those they would typically use in FtF interaction. The first possibility directs attention to the fact that text-based communication systems still carry at least one nonverbal code, chronemics: the nonverbal cue system regarding "how we perceive, structure, and react to time and . . . the messages we interpret from such usage" (Burgoon & Saine, 1978, p. 99). E-mail users, for example, regularly attend to the time stamps that are automatically placed on their messages (Rice, 1990). Time stamps allow e-mail users to determine when the messages they receive were sent and how much time passed before one of their messages received a response. Walther and Tidwell (1995) hypothesized that these cues are potent enough to affect judgments of affection and dominance. They tested this hypothesis by varying the time stamps on two pairs of apparent e-mail message transcripts. One pair was socially oriented (gossip and plans to visit), and the other pair was a task-oriented request. The time stamps were manipulated to vary the time of day (night versus day) the first message was sent and the time it took for the receiver of that message to respond (immediate versus one day later). As predicted, chronemic codes had a significant impact on subjects' interpretations of senders' dominance and affection. Nighttime, task-oriented messages were rated the most dominant and the lowest in relational equality compared with daytime task requests. Social messages sent in the day signaled less equality and more dominance than did those sent at night. The amount of affection subjects ascribed to messages resulted from a complex interaction of the time a message was sent, its content, and the promptness with which it received a reply. The messages that were rated most affectionate were those that replied quickly to a task message sent during the day; those that gave a prompt response to a nighttime task message were rated least affectionate. A slow reply to either day or night task messages signaled moderate affection. As for social messages, more affection was perceived in a slower reply to a daytime message than in a fast reply, but a fast reply at night showed more affection than a slow one.

Other studies have focused on the cue systems that are unique to CMC. Chief among these are "emoticons" (graphical smiles, frowns, and other facial expression simulations created with various keyboard symbols) and "scripts" (preprogrammed texts that narrate nonverbal actions among players). Utz (2000), for example, found that players of a German MUD not only used more emoticons and scripts as they became more experienced, they also believed that they were becoming more skillful at conveying relational and emotional messages using these cues. Utz also found that the use of such cues was a significant predictor of relationship development in MUDs, accounting for 14% of the variance in users' frequency of friendly or romantic relationships on-line.

Although there is no shortage of speculation about the role of emoticons (e.g., Godin, 1993; Rezabek & Cochenour, 1998), only a few researchers have made systematic attempts to understand exactly how these symbols function in on-line discourse. Instead, researchers have focused on who uses them, examining gender differences (Witmer & Katzman, 1997), regional influences (Rezabek & Cochenour, 1998), and how their usage diffuses in mixed-gender on-line groups (Wolf, 2000).

The two studies that have examined the communicative functions of emoticons have yielded engaging, if somewhat inconsistent, results. Thompson and Foulger (1996) found that the impact of a positive emoticon (presumably a happy face) varied with the perceived hostility of the accompanying verbal message. Whereas the emoticon diminished the perceived hostility of a message showing "tension," it increased the perceived hostility of more antagonistic verbiage. Walther and D'Addario (2001) conducted a controlled experiment in which familiar emoticons depicting a smiling face, a winking and smiling face, and a frowning face were inserted in simulated e-mail messages that contained either positive or negative evaluations about a college course. Based on the messages, subjects evaluated their own attitudes toward the course in question as well as the affective states of the supposed message senders. Although the subjects were familiar with the emoticons and interpreted them as intended, the impacts of the emoticons were

extremely limited. The smiling face emoticons had no effect on message interpretation. The frown emoticons, on the other hand, attenuated positive verbal messages, but failed to affect subjects' interpretations of negative verbal messages. These findings suggest that emoticons, by themselves, have only limited effects on the interpretation of verbal messages. However, it could be that emoticons help the writer more than the reader. Generating an emoticon may act "as a self-signaling cue, prompting the writer to write in such a way that is as expressive as s/he intends" (Walther & D'Addario, 2001, p. 343). Just as speakers sometimes use gestures to help them construct verbal messages in FtF settings (Freedman, 1977), individuals using CMC may employ emoticons to prompt the construction of other affective messages.

Researchers are only now beginning to move beyond analysis of isolated cues to consider the relative availability of higher-order information-seeking strategies in CMC and FtF. Studies of initial interactions in FtF settings have identified several distinct types and subtypes of information-seeking strategies (Berger, 1979; Berger, Gardner, Parks, Schulman, & Miller, 1976). Tidwell and Walther (2002) argue that, unlike FtF settings, on-line systems offer individuals only limited opportunities to observe others unobtrusively or to gain information about them indirectly (e.g., by questioning third parties). Although group-based CMC and MUDs with textually represented rooms and objects may offer some opportunities for observational strategies (Ramirez, Walther, Burgoon, & Sunnafrank, 2002), e-mail and dyadic computer chat offer little other than interactive strategies.

Tidwell and Walther (2002) further argue that if CMC users do indeed adapt available cues to perform interpersonal functions, then they would rely on interactive strategies to a greater extent in CMC than in FtF settings. They tested this hypothesis by examining the information-seeking strategies employed by CMC and FtF dyads engaged in either acquaintance or decision-making tasks. Their results support the adaptation contention. CMC users employed a greater proportion of self-disclosures and questions than did FtF partners. Additionally, the personal questions employed by CMC users showed greater depth than those used by their FtF counterparts, with FtF partners employing proportionally more superficial interrogations and CMC partners using more intermediate ones. Moreover, the correspondence between the frequency of these interactive strategies and partners' ratings of one another's communication effectiveness was significantly more positive in CMC than in FtF communication. Thus, consistent with SIP theory, it appears that whereas FtF partners draw on numerous visual, auditory, and verbal cues at their disposal, CMC users readily avail themselves of the remaining strategies for effective interpersonal information acquisition.

Anticipation: A Solution and a Problem

Although the studies to date generally support most aspects of SIP theory, at least one finding has created both a refinement as well as a question about the theory's integrity. As we have noted, Walther and Burgoon (1992) discovered that people in initial interactions in CMC settings were rated no less positively along some relational dimensions than were people in initial interactions in FtF settings. This finding was inconsistent with the SIP prediction that initial CMC interactions should be less personal than initial FtF interactions. In an effort to explain the inconsistency, Walther (1994) proposed that members of the CMC group might have had heightened anticipation concerning future interaction. We know, for instance, that anticipating future interaction prompts greater exchange of personal information, greater perceived similarity, and more friendliness (for a review, see Kellermann & Reynolds, 1990). We know also that the groups in the initial study were aware that

they would be interacting on several occasions in the future.

On this basis, Walther (1994) formed CMC and FtF experimental groups in which medium (CMC versus FtF) was crossed with anticipation of future interaction. Half the groups were told they would be working together on multiple projects over a period of time, and the other half were told they would work together only once. At the end of the first period, analyses confirmed that anticipation prompted more positive relational communication. Indeed, when the effect of anticipated future interaction was factored out, communication medium itself did not predict relational immediacy, similarity, trust, or composure. Results also revealed that anticipation had greater effects among the CMC groups than among the FtF groups. That is, anticipating future interaction had a large effect across media, but it had a particularly large effect on CMC. These findings may account for the positive initial ratings in CMC groups in Walther and Burgoon's (1992) study, particularly given the fact that these groups were well aware that they would be working together over an extended sequence of projects. This dynamic may also account for Rice and Love's (1987) finding that socioemotional content in an ongoing electronic bulletin board discussion was high but did not grow higher over time; the participants may have assumed their communication would be ongoing.

Although the anticipation factor clarifies some aspects of the conflicting results found in research on SIP, it points to at least two theoretical challenges, one that has been addressed and one that has not. First, social information processing theory did not originally consider variations in the motivation to reduce uncertainty across different types of media. Anticipation has been acknowledged as one such factor, as have general expectations about CMC's relational potency: As Utz (2000) has found, people who are skeptical about the relational potential of CMC are less likely to report that they have formed relationships on-line. Utz's results may indicate little more than a self-fulfilling prophecy, but they also suggest that general expectations for the medium could influence motivations to seek information and to develop relationships using CMC.

The second issue concerns precisely what kind of catalyst anticipated future interaction provides, in CMC as well as FtF settings. One possibility is that anticipation stimulates greater amounts of information exchange (as seen in Calabrese, 1975; Cline & Musolf, 1985). Alternatively (or simultaneously), anticipation may stimulate heuristic processing and positively bias interpretations of information (as seen in Berger & Douglas, 1981). The net effect of either dynamic can be more favorable impressions and relational communication, obscuring which underlying process is functioning. At a practical level, it matters little how anticipation operates. At a theoretical level, however, this paradox raises questions about the fundamental assumptions of both SIP theory and reformulations of uncertainty reduction theory (Berger, 1979; Berger & Bradac, 1982). Both theories assume that a relatively straightforward and linear accretion of social information leads to impression formation and relational development. A qualitative shift in interpersonal evaluations, although very plausible from other perspectives, is not consistent with these theories' specifications.

Cues About Us, Not You or Me

Social identity/deindividuation (SIDE) theory is another theory founded on the assumption that CMC's lack of nonverbal cues filters out interpersonal and individual identity information (Lea & Spears, 1992; Spears & Lea, 1992). However, in contrast to previous theories, SIDE theory focuses on the effects of contextual cues and cues that indicate the common social categories of CMC group members. Communicating without nonverbal information, and in physical isolation, promotes greater group identification and self-categorization in line with social identity. For instance, individuals' participation in particular groups—such as Usenet newsgroups on specific topics, corporate e-mail lists, or social psychology experiments among college students—provides others with clues about them based on the nature of those groups. According to SIDE theory, people use such clues about collectives as a basis for relating. They interpret the content of others' messages not as individuating characteristics, but as signals creating or reinforcing group norms (Lea, O'Shea, Fung, & Spears, 1992). Rather than temper their impressions and relations on the basis of so little information, CMC users overinterpret the information they have. When context makes group identity salient, CMC users overattribute similarity and common norms, resulting in social attraction to the group and thereby its members.

This positive group bias is nullified when users relate on the basis of individual instead of social identities. Individuating information may result in a broader range of partner evaluations or stimulate attributions of dissimilarity and negative evaluations. A recent study offers a good example of SIDE theory's approach and utility. Lea, Spears, and de Groot (2001) formed groups with students in two countries who communicated via CMC. Some groups used text-based messaging alone and were visually anonymous, whereas others augmented their interaction with videoconferencing, providing physical appearance and nonverbal cues, and were thus identifiable as individuals. Not only were members of the visually anonymous groups more attracted to the group at the distal outcome level, but results also supported SIDE theory's predictions about the underlying processes involved. Analyses revealed that the text-only users developed greater group-based self-categorizations, which structural equation modeling showed to affect group attraction; group attraction was also indirectly affected through increased stereotyping of out-group members. Interestingly, group identification overcame the prospective in-group/out-group influence of nationality, which had no effect on member evaluations.

SIDE theory has accumulated an impressive body of empirical support for its central claims and has extended its domain into gender categories, differences in power and status, and intergroup perceptions and behavior. Its originators acknowledge that more work is needed on the strategic, as opposed to the interpretive, components of the theory; work to date has generally focused on perceptual outcomes rather than on direct assessment of message behavior, although some progress has been made on the latter front (e.g., Postmes, Spears, & Lea, 2000). As our discussion here must be somewhat abbreviated, we are glad to note that several extensive reviews cover this work in depth (e.g., Postmes, Spears, & Lea, 1998; Postmes, Spears, Lea, & Reicher, 2000).

Although SIDE theory offers a powerful lens through which to view certain CMC relationships, its application to *interpersonal* relations (in the sense of dyadic or close personal relationships) is less clear. The implication that all on-line interaction stays fixed at the social or group level, never reaching the personal level, is particularly troubling. Almost all of the studies supporting SIDE theory have experimentally manipulated group identity or created contexts in which group identities were especially likely to be salient. This is a reasonable experimental approach, but the generalizability of the findings to a wide range of naturally occurring CMC relationships is unclear. For example, although SIDE theory may explain initial attraction between two users who meet in a topical Usenet group, it is somewhat more difficult to imagine its application when those users move to private e-mail as they pursue dyadic friendship or romance (e.g., Parks & Floyd, 1996). In spite of conceptual efforts to apply SIDE theory to on-line

romantic relationships (Lea & Spears, 1995), the theory dictates that all CMC use in which communicators are visually anonymous and geotemporally dispersed must focus on a group level of identification. It clearly differentiates between *interpersonal* cues and *social* cues, precluding the former and promoting the latter in its account of on-line attraction. Individuating information that might personalize impressions has no role in SIDE theory, except, perhaps, to conform to a possible local norm of personal information sharing (see Walther, 1997). Indeed, according to the theory, interpersonal information should undermine the group-based categorizations upon which attraction is predicated. The implications of these issues for relationships other than groups' have yet to be addressed by SIDE theory (see Walther, Slovacek, & Tidwell, 2001).

Cues Bent and Twisted

Reports of surprisingly close friendships, rapidly escalating romances, and inexplicably cohesive groups forming on-line cropped up with increasing frequency as Internet use exploded during the 1990s. It was clear that in many cases people were achieving levels of sociality and intimacy in on-line settings that they would never have achieved as rapidly, if at all, in comparable FtF settings. It was also clear that existing theoretical approaches to CMC could not account for these phenomena. In an effort to explain these observations, Walther (1996) pointed to four sets of effects operating in many on-line settings. These *sender, receiver, channel,* and *feedback* effects may create "hyperpersonal communication" that goes beyond the interpersonal levels typically achieved in FtF associations.

Receiver and source effects flow from the roles individuals play in the communication process. Although there are individual differences, these effects generally are created when receivers initially engage in stereotypically positive and idealized attributions of on-line partners. Receivers may overgeneralize based on a common group identity (as in SIDE theory), but they may also make such positive attributions because of anticipated future interaction or because they are deliberately seeking new relational partners (Roberts, Smith, & Pollock, 1996; Walther, 1997). For their part, senders regularly exploit CMC's absence of nonverbal cues for the purpose of selective self-presentation. CMC users may take advantage of their greater control over message construction to craft messages to reflect preferred characteristics, and they may time self-revelations in order to serve developing relational goals.

The *channel* itself facilitates goal-enhancing messages by allowing sources far greater control over message construction than is available in FtF settings. A CMC user may pause to review and edit during the initial construction of a message and may take advantage of an asynchronous channel to buy time to consider responses. Asynchronous channels also allow users to interject social comments more easily in task-oriented settings, as there is no shortage of time for both dimensions when partners communicate in temporal independence. Moreover, sources are freed from a number of distractions while using CMC and are thus able to concentrate on managing their self-presentations. They need not attend to ambient environmental stimuli, to multiple simultaneous cues from their partners, or to their own physical back-channeling.

Finally, hyperpersonal *feedback* effects may create self-fulfilling prophesies among senders and receivers. As idealizing receivers in turn send selective messages, behavioral confirmation processes may be cued (Snyder, Tanke, & Berscheid, 1977) wherein partners rather easily come to behave in ways that meet their partners' exaggerated interpersonal expectations.

Positive hyperpersonal effects have received the greatest attention, but "hypernegative" effects are possible as well. When coupled with time restrictions and no expectation of future interaction, the relatively effortful nature of CMC may trigger overly negative interpretations on the part of receivers, ill regard and hostile message construction by sources, failure to use the channel's positive capabilities, and amplifying cycles of disaffiliation (Walther et al., 2001).

The overall hyperpersonal model has been tested in two studies involving students on different sides of the Atlantic. E-mail was used for international communication, although group members local to one another had FtF conversations occasionally. In the first study, student groups were prompted to develop either a group or individual identity and given the expectation that they would have either short- or long-term interaction (Walther, 1997). Surveys conducted at the end of the students' projects revealed a number of interaction effects that supported the hyperpersonal model. Long-term, group-identity partners rated their CMC-only partners as higher in affectionate communication and as more socially and physically attractive (despite never seeing them) than those in the short-term, group-identity condition. Individual-identity groups scored in the middle range, presumably because they were less sensitive to the cognitive biases suggested by SIDE theory. Moreover, the groups' self-reported ratings of their efforts on their projects coincided with their relational patterns, suggesting a social facilitation of work by relational states. Ratings of FtF partners, on the other hand, showed no influence of these manipulations.

Several additional aspects of the hyperpersonal framework were addressed in a second study involving international student groups using CMC (Walther et al., 2001). Two factors were manipulated: previous interaction (zero history versus semester-long contact) and visual information (photo versus no photo). As predicted from a social presence approach, providing participants photographs of one another over the Internet tempered negative effects in zero-history, no-future groups.

Conversely, in line with the hyperpersonal perspective, providing photographs dampened positive affect in the long-term, hyperpersonal condition. Long-term groups who saw photographs reported less attraction than did those who communicated without seeing photographs. Across all conditions, short-term, no-photo groups related least positively, as predicted, and the long-term, no-photo groups were most positive, with both of the photo-showing conditions in the middle ranges. Additional analyses indicated that participants generally felt more successful in their self-presentations when they did not have photographs showing. Post hoc analysis further revealed that when no pictures were shown, greater familiarity was associated with more affection, and that subjects' perceived success at self-presentation predicted how physically attractive they were judged to have been. With actual physical appearance through photos, however, self-presentation was negatively associated with physical attractiveness, suggesting (among other conclusions) that attempts to impress may backfire when physical appearance gets in the way of selective self-presentation. Ultimately, it appears that when virtual partners are given the time and opportunity, and conditions facilitate their getting to know one another, they appear to do so selectively and, ultimately, more positively using CMC and CMC alone.

The hyperpersonal model has been used as an explanatory framework for findings across several different domains. In person perception research, for example, Hancock and Dunham (2001) found that CMC partners evaluated their partners more extremely, albeit on fewer criteria, than did FtF counterparts. Hyperpersonal predictions have been utilized in studies of on-line social support (Turner, Grube, & Meyers, 2001), on-line education (Chester & Gwynne, 1998), and relationship development in on-line settings (Parks & Floyd, 1996; Parks & Roberts, 1998; Wildermuth, 2000).

Perhaps the greatest appeal of the hyperpersonal model is that it accounts for behavior in computer-mediated settings in terms of variations among familiar communication components—the sender, receiver, channel, and feedback. Its utility has been demonstrated across a variety of relational contexts in CMC. Yet the model is open to significant criticism as well. It is not at all clear whether there are any necessary theoretical linkages among and between the four major components and the more detailed processes that the model specifies. In other words, its constructs and propositions are poorly interrelated, and its status as a robust theory is therefore tenuous. The danger of this, as with any theory, is that it is difficult to reconcile either supportive or inconsistent empirical results with the overall model, or to identify which aspect of the model may have been supported or disconfirmed. Furthermore, as the model now offers both hyperpersonal and hypernegative outcomes and assumptions that users adapt the media to their relational goals, it will be important for researchers to stimulate, specify, or discover the relational goals CMC users bring to their interactions, without which the model may become unnecessarily teleological. Even so, the hyperpersonal approach offers an agenda worth pursuing, not only because of its promise for increasing our understanding of relational processes in a variety of CMC settings, but also for its practical implications for the management of on-line education and virtual work teams.

INTERPERSONAL PROCESSES IN COMPUTER-MEDIATED COMMUNICATION

In this section we consider the role CMC may play in larger interpersonal contexts and processes. Our focus shifts from research on the availability of cues and the structure of messages to research on several broader social uses to which those cues and messages are put in the domains of the social basis of mental health and well-being, social support, and relationship development. It is important to note that the nature of the research shifts focus as these topics are explored. First, the predominant focus in this research is on the different social networks that individuals access via the Internet. Second, whereas most theoretical investigations have taken the form of controlled experiments that dichotomize CMC and FtF associations, the researchers who have conducted the field studies reviewed below have recognized to a greater extent the availability and interchangeability of multiple communication channels in pursuing relationships, and have raised the issue of complementarity between on-line and off-line interaction. This represents a significant and healthy shift in the applied value of the research, although, as we will see, the tension between descriptive and theoretical understandings waxes and wanes throughout these studies as a whole.

Internet Use and Mental Health

Mental health and social functioning have been central topics in interpersonal communication research for nearly 50 years. It is not surprising, then, that a great deal of attention has been directed toward the question of whether social use of the Internet promotes or damages mental health and social functioning. This brings us back to where we began—to Kraut et al.'s (1998) longitudinal study of Internet adoption and use in a sample of 93 families. Kraut and his colleagues tracked these families, who did not previously have computers or the Internet at home, over a period of 2 years, starting in 1995. The results of the study indicated that spending more time on the Internet was associated with a small but significant increase in scores on a self-administered measure of general depression. Greater Internet use was also associated with small reductions in the amount of communication with family members and with geographically proximate acquaintances. The researchers offered images

of relational displacement or substitution to explain these findings. Assuming that on-line relationships are inherently weaker and less supportive than FtF relationships, Kraut and his colleagues argued that substituting on-line interaction for FtF interaction should result in a reduction in the social support available to users. With less support available to them, Kraut and his colleagues reasoned, people would be more likely to experience depression.

Criticism of the study was immediate. Some dismissed the results on the basis of their own subjective experiences in using the Internet for personal growth. Some insisted that because Kraut et al. did not include a control group, their results were meaningless (which is refutable, although not completely, given the study's longitudinal design). Others noted that Kraut et al.'s explanation depended on a negative correlation between Internet use and social support—a correlation that they did not in fact find. Still others suggested that the sample was not representative of the self-motivated Internet-using public: The participants' reactions might have represented a "newbie effect"—that is, their behavior reflected their relative inexperience with the Internet rather than characteristics of the Internet itself.

But this was not the only study that raised questions about the effects of Internet use on family communication. Nie and Erbring's (2000) survey of 4,113 Internet users indicated that the more time individuals spend on-line, the less time they spend with family members in FtF or telephone communication, looking at television and newspapers, or shopping in physical stores. These findings, like Kraut et al.'s, were trumpeted in the press as demonstrating the social dangers of the Internet. Once again, however, there were good reasons to believe that the findings were not as clear as claimed. Nie and Erbring did not account for obvious alternative explanations for some of their findings (such as children growing more autonomous and spending less time with parents). Nor did they pay adequate attention to the fact that when the Internet users switched from phone communication to e-mail, their e-mail communications included members of their extended families.

A number of studies have corroborated the value of the Internet for family and friendship networks. Stafford, Kline, and Dimmick (1999), for example, found that the dominant use of e-mail in the home was for contact within family and friendships networks. Users reported that e-mail provided them with greater opportunities for satisfying their interpersonal needs, but the reasons for this were e-mail's speed, low cost, and convenience, rather than any favorable or unfavorable expressive capacities. Likewise, the first report by the Pew Internet & American Life Project (2000), which presents survey data from 1,690 Internet users, indicates that communication with family members and existing friends via e-mail accounts for a significant proportion of Internet use. A majority of respondents indicated that they now communicate with family members more often than they did before they had access to the Internet. Focusing on the *nature* of on-line communication, the report also states that more than a third of the sample agreed that they find it easier to communicate frankly with their family members via e-mail than by alternative modes, and that the ability to do so improves their relationships.

Sorting through the conflicting findings and claims requires a more rigorous theoretical stance than has been applied in most studies. LaRose, Eastin, and Gregg (2001) made a positive step in this direction when they examined Internet use and mental well-being using social cognitive theory (Bandura, 1997). They were particularly concerned with how differences in experience with the Internet might lead to differences in self-efficacy, competence, stress, social support, and depression. They found that more experienced users reported greater self-efficacy with respect to their abilities to use the Internet. And those who felt

greater self-efficacy and competence, they found, experienced less stress using the Internet, and hence less depression. Moreover, more frequent Internet use—especially e-mail—was associated with increased social support, also leading to less depression. LaRose et al. note that more experienced users know how to take advantage of the Internet's resources to obtain social support, and also, they use e-mail to stay in touch with family and friends who provide support. These findings help put those of previous studies in context. Instead of blaming on-line communication for depression, these results point to the stresses and lack of efficacy new users often experience and suggest that these often transitory factors might account for the depression that new users (such as those in the Kraut et al., 1998, study) experience.

Time and additional research have also led to revisions in the postures taken by previous researchers. Kraut and colleagues (2002) have revised their conclusions about the effects of Internet use on depression after conducting a follow-up study in which they accounted for the potential differences as Internet dynamics changed over time. In a follow-up study among Kraut et al.'s (1998) original subjects, they found that more frequent Internet use (especially e-mail) was associated with increased contact with both local and distant social partners, as well as with family members. Internet use was associated with more family contact and greater social support for teens. For adults, more frequent use was associated with more FtF communication with family and closer feelings toward extended family and friends. Further, Internet use was also found to interact with extraversion. Extraverts experienced more positive effects as their Internet use increased, including less depression, more positive affect, and increased self-esteem; but introverts declined on these indicators the more they were on-line (see also Wright, 2000, regarding similar effects of communication apprehension). For all users, the more they used the Internet, the more stress and hassles they reported in their lives.

Kraut et al. (2002) account for this dramatic difference in findings by observing that both the users they studied and the Internet itself had changed since the first study. The users became more experienced. More of their FtF-based friends and relatives had moved on-line, thus making it easier for them to communicate with strong ties (see Markus, 1987, for a "critical mass" explanation of technology adoption). Interestingly, Kraut and his colleagues did not revisit their assumption that relationships that exist exclusively on-line are necessarily "weak," nor did they attempt to explain why greater use of CMC was associated with more positive affect and closeness within those strong-tie relationships that exist both on- and off-line.

The potential importance of CMC in these "mixed-mode" relationships—relationships that exist in several different media—is further illuminated by a recent study of long-distance relationship maintenance conducted by Gunn and Gunn (2000). These researchers found that, compared with long-distance partners who did not use the Internet, those who communicated using CMC "reported greater love and felt closer to long distance relationship partners, [and] self-disclosed at greater depth and breadth" (p. 2). They also found that those who used the Internet generally preferred their long-distance relationships over their local relationships, whereas those who did not use the Internet generally preferred their local relationships to the long-distance relationships they maintained through letters and telephone calls.

Looking across the studies to date, it appears that for new Internet users, contact with close ties, as well as social and mental well-being, may suffer slightly while they learn to use the social potential of the Internet. Over time, however, they become adept at using the Internet to maintain contact with friends and family and to obtain social support. Individual differences, such as extraversion/introversion, may make it easier or harder for some people to reap the social benefits of the Internet. For those who wish to maintain long-distance contacts with friends and family, however, CMC may be a more satisfying choice than more traditional channels such as letters or the telephone.

Social Support On-Line

The Internet must be judged as a fabulously successful medium for social support. Understanding, reassurance, and advice flow out through literally thousands of on-line support groups (for an extensive list of on-line support venues and the topics they address, see "Emotional Support on the Internet V1.36" at www.cix.co.uk/~net-services/care/list.htm). No one can observe the discussions that take place among the members of such support groups and not be struck by their authenticity and intimacy. The question for researchers is not whether the Internet is capable of providing social support, but rather why it should be so effective as a support medium.

CMC and the Internet fundamentally change two structural aspects of social support: the cues/channels of communication and the sociometric relationships of the participants. Most studies of on-line support have concentrated on one of these two factors. Thus studies have examined the use of CMC by individuals who have few FtF sources who share their illness-related experiences or concerns (Scheerhorn, Warisse, & McNeilis, 1995), the types and functions of social support messages typical in on-line venues (Braithwaite, Waldron, & Finn, 1999), the levels of emotion and relational strength among sociometric weak ties (Egdorf & Rahoi, 1994), and rhetorical strategies that establish a communicator's authenticity and credibility in seeking or providing support on-line (Galagher et al., 1998).

Two studies provide particular comparisons between social support in FtF and on-line settings. Walther and Boyd (2002) observed that previous literature had identified several risks or difficulties with FtF social support, especially in close relationships. For example, individuals who make up support seekers' close personal networks may not have the requisite expertise to deal with support seekers' problems (La Gaipa, 1990). In efforts to reassure them, partners may attempt to minimize the severity of support seekers' concerns, or, out of regard, be less than frank in their assessments. For support seekers, disclosing concerns may create vulnerability and dependence; they may risk stigmatization and embarrassment that may spread among other members of their personal networks (Adelman, Parks, & Albrecht, 1987; La Gaipa, 1990). When support messages are not well matched to a seeker's needs, social support is ineffective, and the relationship between the seeker and provider can suffer (Cutrona & Russell, 1990; Goldsmith, 1992).

Reasoning that many of these problems might be overcome in on-line settings, Walther and Boyd (2002) surveyed users of Usenet support groups in order to explore which aspects of on-line support the users themselves found attractive. Their research yielded four dimensions of attraction to on-line support, highlighting both the sociometric and interactional characteristics of the Internet and CMC. First, a *social distance* dimension reflects users' appreciation for the greater expertise of on-line sources, compared with the expertise available to them from their personal networks. A man suffering from testicular cancer, for example, may very well not know anyone in his FtF network who can speak to his experience. This is especially likely to be true if he lives in a rural area. People with rare conditions may find it difficult to locate anyone with expertise or common experience within the range of FtF contact. Social distance also allows people in on-line settings to be less concerned about becoming dependent or stigmatized.

Second, users value *anonymity* because it expands their ability to avoid embarrassment. The nature of the social and the technological networks allows both relative anonymity, with respect to the chances of knowing anyone directly, and actual anonymity, through technologically enabled anonymous addressing. One can even obtain support without ever saying a thing. Individuals can, as Mickelson (1997) observes, "obtain comparison information or vicarious support without having to disclose anything about themselves . . . [and] obtain validation for their feelings of stigma without having to communicate those feelings to others" (p. 172).

A third factor, *interaction management,* reflects users' appreciation of being able to craft messages carefully, read messages at their convenience, and express themselves more effectively than they might typically do FtF. Additionally, this dimension reflects the value of being able to enter and exit support relationships opportunistically. One need not, for example, sit through an entire meeting of a support group just to have a question answered.

Finally, users find the night-and-day *access* to on-line support systems attractive, in comparison to the potential difficulty of engaging in support exchanges off-line. The Internet never sleeps. No matter what time it is, a potential supporter is likely to be awake and available somewhere in the world.

These findings may seem paradoxical with respect to assertions from the studies on mental health and Internet use discussed above. Although the report of the Pew Internet & American Life Project (2000) acknowledges the benefits that CMC confers in interaction management and message construction, that study and several others (especially Kraut et al., 2002; LaRose et al., 2001) have emphasized that the benefits of CMC for enhancing social support derive from the fact that Internet access makes it possible for people to connect more readily to preestablished partners, such as family and friends. Walther and

Boyd's research suggests that the support advantage of the Internet is conferred in exchanges with relative strangers. One recent study that examined differences in satisfaction between on-line and off-line support networks found that users favored on-line networks over FtF sources (Wright, 2000).

Recent research has begun to untangle this paradox and offers a glimpse at the strategic, opportunistic, and intelligent ways in which Internet users exploit both local and virtual resources. Turner et al. (2001) compared support provision by on-line sources and close FtF sources. They posited that the relational depth and perceived support from FtF partners and the relational depth and support experienced with regard to an e-mail-based support list would predict the amount of involvement with each source. They also predicted that deficiencies in support from one source would lead to greater involvement with the other. Responses from users of several cancer-related Listservs provided no support for the main effects on involvement with each source, but they did highlight several significant interactions. "Perceived support from the list predicted time spent reading only when support from their face-to-face partner was low," Turner et al. (2001, p. 245) note. Moreover, "when both the depth of the relationship with the list was high and the depth of the relationship with their face-to-face partner was low, subjects spent more time reading, and staying in contact via email." These patterns also predicted an increase in users' e-mail correspondence with members of the list on a dyadic basis and FtF meetings among list members.

The implications of these findings should not be underestimated. They suggest that media choice is not predicted by users' assessments of media characteristics and goals alone. Rather, individuals exploit the alternative social networks and communicator characteristics that are associated with different channels. These findings remind us that there is nothing sacrosanct about FtF communication

or personal relationships; nothing makes them inherently beneficial all of the time. Relational competence and mental health might have much to do with knowing with whom to communicate, in what way, and when. In this respect, CMC expands the range of competent choices rather than simply extending opportunities to communicate with the same old partners in the same old ways. Finally, Turner and colleagues (2001) offer a note of contingency and maturity to some of our own earlier positions when they point out that although the hyperpersonal perspective may

> help us to understand how CMC enables close relationships to develop and flourish, most relationships do not occur in a vacuum but in the context of a network of supportive relationships inside and outside the virtual community. It is these other relationships, the needs of the participants, and the common . . . experience of [the community] that appear to interact with and cumulatively influence the development of hyperpersonal relationships. (p. 246)

Relationship Development on the Internet

Views regarding the types of relationships people develop in on-line settings have been both polarized and politicized. For some, nostalgic stances about "real relationships" and warnings about restricted cues combine to portray the Internet as a relational wasteland. For others, the Internet is not only a good place for intimate relationships, it's too good a place. They see it as a dangerous or at least exotic breeding ground for intense sexual relationships (e.g., Cooper, Delmonico, & Burg, 2000; Lipton, 1996). Although the Internet is undoubtedly not relationally fertile enough for some and a bit too fertile for others, neither extreme yields a very accurate or useful view of relational development in on-line settings.

In one of the first studies to provide basic descriptive data on the relational potential of the Internet, Parks and Floyd (1996) surveyed participants in a stratified sample of Usenet newsgroups. They discovered that a clear majority (60.7%) of participants reported having formed at least one dyadic personal relationship on-line. These relationships took place marginally more often between cross-sex partners than between same-sex partners, but only 8% were described as romantic relationships. Most were described as friendships of one type or another. The best predictor of individuals' starting relationships on-line was the length of time they had been Internet users. Just as people start relationships with the people they meet over time as residents in an apartment building, people start relationships with others on-line as they become more familiar with their virtual environs.

On-line relationships may reach remarkably high levels of development. Parks and Floyd asked respondents to rate one of the relationships they had started on-line along a number of standard developmental dimensions. Approximately half of the respondents indicated a high degree of *interdependence* in their relationships, and half scored low on this dimension. They reported moderate to high levels of both *breadth* and *depth* in their on-line personal relationships, including items assessing intimacy and self-disclosure. These relationships did not in general reflect a high degree of *shared personal codes* and idioms, as other close relationships traditionally do.

Parks and Floyd (1996) also asked their respondents how they and their on-line friends use communication media. After meeting in Usenet groups, almost all partners augmented their communication with other media, including direct, dyadic e-mail (98%), the telephone (35%), and postal exchanges (28%). Fully a third of those who had developed relationships on-line progressed to eventual FtF meetings, in spite of the fact that they and their on-line friends were often separated by formidable distances.

A follow-up and extension of this study conducted by Parks and Roberts (1998) examined relationship formation in another Internet setting and asked about FtF relationships as well. This study examined MOOs (multiuser dimensions, object oriented), real-time discussions in which participants create names and descriptions for themselves and can create textual depictions of rooms and objects. Many MOOs are purposefully designed to foster free-ranging social interaction, whereas others foster on-line games or are mixtures of the two types. Unlike newsgroups, where all postings are available for public inspection, MOOs allow participants to take part in person-to-person messaging, either by privately messaging targets despite the virtual presence of other participants or by going to private virtual rooms. Some 94% of the respondents in this study reported forming personal relationships with other MOO users, with such relationships typically lasting just over a year; 86% of these were cross-sex relationships. Most were close friendships or friendships, although 26% were described as romantic in nature. Compared with friendship partners, romantic partners spent significantly more hours on-line with one another and met on-line more frequently. Concerning *interdependence, breadth* and *depth,* and *shared personal codes,* participants in MOO-based relationships rated higher on each of these characteristics than the Usenet respondents. When participants were asked to rate comparable FtF partners, scores on the same measures were slightly but significantly higher.

Of those in MOO-initiated relationships, 93% used other channels as they progressed, and 38% eventually met face-to-face. However, Parks and Roberts ascertained that only 8% went from MOO to FtF without engaging a sequence of other channels first, and these were primarily friendships, not romantic partners. In general, between MOO meeting and FtF meeting, these partners used e-mail, telephone, cards and letters, and photographs exchanged by mail. Although Parks and Roberts do not speak to the final step, these findings suggest there may be some truth to the folklore reported by Mitchell (1995): "Hacker lore has it that burgeoning cyberspace romances progress through broadening bandwidth and multiplying modalities—from exchange of e-mail to phone and photo, then taking the big step of going [FtF], then climbing into bed" (p. 19).

In other research, Baker's (1998) descriptive study implies such romantic consummation and works backward from there. In an effort to determine what elements predict successful romantic relationships that begin on-line, Baker interviewed 18 couples who had initiated their acquaintances via the Internet, met FtF, and were still (at that time) together. She reports that most of the couples had originally encountered each other in some venue facilitating a mutually shared interest, such as playing a trivia game or participating in an occupationally related discussion group; fewer met via on-line matchmaking services. Consistent with some of the perspectives reviewed above, they were attracted to one another on the basis of "sense of humor, response time, interests, qualities described online, and writing style" (p. 2), and several respondents acknowledged that they had found it easier to reveal thoughts and feelings, and that they disclosed more, on-line in comparison to their experiences FtF.

All of the couples in Baker's sample used multiple media prior to meeting, and all but one had exchanged photographs of themselves before meeting FtF. Several subjects commented, however, that the photos they received were not very accurate depictions of their partners' actual physical appearance. Men more often sent pictures that were out-of-date and more flattering than they currently appeared (see also Levine, 2000), whereas women more often sent pictures or issued self-descriptions that were less attractive than they actually looked. With respect to communication behavior, some partners seemed shier FtF than their more outgoing on-line interactions suggested

they would be. Baker concluded from these interviews that time was a critical factor in the success of these couples: Despite the discrepancies in appearance or shyness, they felt as though they had gotten to know each other very well before meeting FtF. Although they had exchanged photos, some respondents indicated, the significance of the photos was nil, because they had already fallen in love. In spite of the small size of Baker's sample, these findings point in a number of directions that might prove fruitful for future research. The shift from CMC to FtF interaction presents opportunities for communication researchers not only to address basic theoretical questions regarding media use, interaction management, and identity construction, but to develop practical guidance for those involved.

MIXED-MODE RELATIONSHIPS: THEORETICAL OPPORTUNITIES AND CHALLENGES

The research reviewed in the preceding section bears testimony to the fact that CMC has become one among many modalities in contemporary relationships. As more people have connected, it has become apparent that the Internet is a remarkably convenient, low-cost tool that people can use to stay in touch with people they already know—coworkers, friends, family members. The research on social support suggests that people are making complex decisions about intimate disclosure within the context of a combined network of on-line and off-line contacts. Other studies have demonstrated that relationships that start on-line rarely stay there. As they develop, many on-line relationships migrate to FtF settings.

At the same time, modern relationships may have outgrown our theories about them. Although some accounting has been given to long-distance relationships that began FtF and are maintained using personal media (e.g., Stafford & Reske, 1990; Stephen, 1986), existing theories certainly never anticipated *mixed-mode relationships* (MMRs), in which people meet on-line and migrate off-line. As Rheingold (1993) observes, "The way you meet people in cyberspace puts a different spin on affiliation: in traditional kinds of communities, we are accustomed to meeting people, then getting to know them; in virtual communities, you can get to know people and then choose to meet them" (pp. 26-27). Nor do extant theories address how we may be affected by the orchestration of multiple relationships that have been segmented into different channels (regarding the pros and cons of cyberaffairs, see, e.g., Levine, n.d.).

These new social arrangements not only pose challenges for existing theories, they also afford new opportunities for theory. We explore several of these challenges and opportunities in this section. First, we illustrate how the rise of MMRs reveals gaps or strains in influential theories of interpersonal communication and CMC. Second, we offer an alternative approach for thinking about how communicators manage identity in a world of variably connected contexts.

Leaving Virtuality:
A Paradigmatic Problem

For people who have met on-line, the decision to meet FtF is rich in risk and opportunity. It is a potentially defining relational move. As Mitchell (1995) observes, "I have found that it can be a jarring, dislocating experience actually to meet somebody I have long known through network interactions and for whom I have by virtue of these interactions, presumptively devised a persona" (p. 12). This observation is hardly unique. Interviews with people who have met their virtual friends FtF reveal a trail of inaccurate guesses and violated expectations (Jacobson, 1999). These dislocations are theoretical as well as experiential. Some of the most promising theories in CMC research that account for relational processes taking place exclusively on-line break down

when faced with relationships' movement toward continuation in physical FtF interaction. The implicit or explicit assumptions about physicality in extant theories of FtF and CMC may make them problematic with respect to this type of progression. To illustrate, we review some of the more potent theories from both traditions below.

Uncertainty reduction theory (URT) holds great prospects for MMRs that move from the virtual to the physical realm successfully, but it cannot accommodate those that are unsuccessful. In the uncertainty reduction process, according to Berger and Calabrese (1975), uncertainty reduction leads to greater affinity. As interaction progresses and information is obtained or disclosed over time, greater liking and intimacy should result. A great deal of uncertainty-reducing information should be presented upon an initial FtF encounter following a CMC-based acquaintanceship. We should therefore predict that affinity will rise dramatically due to a shift from virtual to physical contact. Although there are many cases of relationships spawned on-line that lead to ongoing friendships and even marriage (e.g., Landis, 1994), there are also abundant anecdotal reports of relational failure upon first physical encounter (e.g., Albright & Conran, 1995; "Romance and the Internet," 1994). Although some efforts have been made to recognize both favorable and unfavorable outcomes in FtF uncertainty reduction (Berger, 1986; Berger & Bradac, 1982), these models are less clear than the original. We qualify this critique by noting that URT speaks most directly to the context of initial interactions, and does not as often address ongoing relationships (although some researchers have introduced modifications to URT in attempts to do so; e.g., Gudykunst, Yang, & Nishida, 1985; Parks & Adelman, 1983). In general, however, URT may not be up to explaining mixed-mode relationship development.

Social information processing theory (Walther, 1992) suggests that uncertainty reduction and social penetration can ultimately be as effective in CMC as in FtF interaction. A strict SIP interpretation suggests very little impact or value of FtF-based information once a virtual relationship is formed. If one can truly get to know another on-line, physical appearance or other data that might uniquely become apparent FtF should be superfluous to impressions and relationships. This is consistent with Baker's (1998) report of respondents who discounted the impact of photos. In other cases, as Jacobson's (1999) research and Mitchell's (1995) observations suggest, "real-life" characteristics may depart substantially from virtual ones, in which case SIP theory is found wanting.

SIDE theory, in contrast to URT and SIP theory, might account for MMRs that fail upon physical meeting, but cannot account for ones that succeed. Although SIDE theory has been offered as a framework with which to understand virtual romantic relationships (Lea & Spears, 1995), it depends on CMC users' keeping hidden their individuating characteristics (especially their physical characteristics). When partners are seen they are individuated and differentiation occurs; in SIDE theory, this undermines social attraction. Thus when a virtual relationship becomes physical, it should immediately individuate and suffer as a result. Although there are probably more cases of on-line romances that do not culminate in marriage than there are of those that do—as is the case in off-line life as well—those that do are not explainable from a SIDE perspective.

The *hyperpersonal* perspective is predicated on users' taking advantage of the opportunities that CMC affords them to enhance self-presentation and nonvisual interaction's ability to inflate perceptions of others. Because attraction in this framework presumes a good degree of selective processing of input and output information, the position does not bode well for the success of a shift to substantially less controlled information sharing, especially considering the observed dampening of affect

of even a photo in otherwise hyperpersonal relations (Walther et al., 2001).

Identity Warranting in Mixed Modes

The link between the self and a given self-presentation offers one starting point for reformulating our approach to communication in relationships that move from virtual to physical. The connection between who we are and who we claim to be on the Internet is by no means obvious. According to the Pew Internet & American Life Project (2001b), "Fully 56% of online teens have more than one email address or screen name and most use different screen names or email addresses to compartmentalize different parts of their lives online, or so that they can experiment with different personas." This research found that most teen deceptions were for pranks or privacy, but that adults used subtle deceptions about age, appearance, occupation, or life circumstances to achieve a wider range of goals. Such fabrications are performed in the context of games or simple curiosity, as potentially self-therapeutic investigations of aspects of the personality, to avoid on-line harassment or elevate social standing, or merely to impress (Curtis, 1992; Donath, 1999; Roberts & Parks, 1999; Turkle, 1995).

Stone (1995) suggests that we may conceive of a *warrant* connecting the self with an on-line presentation. In FtF settings, she observes, we typically have a strong and generally unquestioned warrant between the presented identity and the body's self. This reflects, among other things, a political necessity of society: When a personality commits a crime, some body must be incarcerated; when an identity performs salable, taxable services, the government must warrant that person to a body to whom retirement benefits may be sent. In interpersonal interaction in the physical world, it is a commonplace to warrant a relatively stable identity to a physical entity. But in cyberspace, the connection between the self and the self-presentation becomes mutable.

This notion of warrant has powerful implications as a construct for the analysis of virtual identities and relationships. In identities and relationships that exist entirely on-line, there is no necessary warrant between identity and corporeal self. There may be no necessary connection between the typist and the typed. To make her case, Stone (1995) draws on a radical but logical extension of symbolic interactionism, which holds that the shapes and meanings of things emerge initially through the instigation of one person but primarily through the social interaction of many. It is social interaction that defines a thing, an idea, or a self, as it evolves over time. Thus a spark of personality that may even be peripheral or antithetical to an individual's normal proclivities may provide the beginnings of the evolution of an on-line entity that has little or no relationship to the typist. Although Stone's work offers a provocative starting point, it does not help us approach issues in the movement from virtual (potentially warrantless) relationships toward physical (warranted) ones.

We can do four things to transform this construct for the present purposes. First, we can reconceptualize warrant from a binary state (cyberself and physically presented self are unconnected) to a continuum (cyberself and physical self may be more or less connected). Second, we can recognize that the less a communication system requires a warrant between the text-presented self and the physical self, the greater the freedom of the actor to diverge the two presentations. In cases where the system allows great anonymity (such as MOOs), the on-line presentation may differ radically from the physical self, but in less anonymous systems, radical departures would be less likely without potential exposure and sanction. Third, we can posit that in systems where any degree of anonymity is offered, no matter how similar an individual's self-presentation on-line is to the presentation of self off-line, the

perceiver of the on-line presentation must still decide what degree of warrant to attribute to that presentation. This, of course, is where suspicion of another person's deceptive presentation emerges. We assume that people generally prefer that the personality of a partner be consistent between one mode and another, as a basis of trust and a foundation for interpersonal vulnerability. The recognition of this need drives the behavior of the fourth implication: Actors can undertake behaviors that may increase the apparent warrant of their performance for the receiver's benefit, through the presentation of warranting information. We define the warranting value of information about a person as being derived from the receiver's perception about the extent to which the content of that information is immune to manipulation by the person to whom it refers.

Warranting is potentially quite limited in CMC settings in which individuals do not know each other off-line and do not expect to meet outside of their virtual interaction. Face-to-face communication, on the other hand, generally promotes fully warranted relationships over time. It does so by providing frequent exposure to partners' relatively uncontrolled behavior. Although office partners or roommates certainly can and do employ CMC when they are not copresent, we would not expect radical transformations in personality or excessively hyperpersonal interactions between such partners. When relationships that originated FtF become primarily mediated (e.g., the partners go for long periods without physical exposure to one another), the frequency of warranting information over time declines, and warrant may lessen somewhat. So it is that long-distance premarital couples idealize their beloveds, especially the more they use low-bandwidth media (e.g., letters versus the phone or FtF; Stafford & Reske, 1990).

Although the characteristics of the communication system set limits on possible warrantlessness, the degree of warrant in a relationship is not determined by the communication system alone. We suggest that warrant is also affected by the social structures in which relationships are embedded and by the symbolic efforts partners undertake to make credible their self-presentations when their purposes make it desirable to do so.

Warranting and Social Structure

Being aware of and being able to access a partner's social network should limit the degree of warrantlessness in an on-line relationship. An example will help illustrate this situation: Two students become virtual friends as they interact with each other in a distributed college course involving classes at two universities, with no initial FtF meeting and no planned terminal FtF encounter. At first glance, these arrangements seem very similar to those facilitating no warrant whatsoever. However, in this case, each partner is aware that the other also operates in a social network (i.e., the distant students), which she can access. Contact with members of another person's social network has been shown to provide significant uncertainty-reducing information about relational partners (Parks & Adelman, 1983). Even the potential to access a partner's social network provides a known ability to corroborate some aspects of the partner's disclosures (is the partner male or female, tall or short, athletic or sedate, married or single?). The network also provides an audience in which a partner could be held accountable for misstatements, gross exaggerations, or false claims.

Warranting and Symbolic Efforts

Partial warranting in a potentially warrantless environment should involve an individual's proffering information that can be corroborated or used for corroboration. Simple examples might include a verifiable "real name," a traceable address, identification of biographical (not autobiographical) information in an information system (e.g., a directory), indication of

some matter of public record, or direct access to the individual's FtF social network. Reference to a Web page with an identifiable and accountable address (such as an address at a corporation or educational institution, more so than at an ISP of unknown origin) should provide some value. If an individual's home page appears to be created by someone other than the subject of the page, so much more the warrant value that information might provide. Even self-description may work if it is specific and verifiable (e.g., "five feet, nine inches tall" rather than "tall"). Such aspects would *not* include self-disclosure of ambiguous information or events that cannot be corroborated. Attitudinal statements or biographical/historical details that are not generally known in the individual's social circles should have little effect in increasing warrant, and are more likely to serve as the kind of selective self-disclosure posited to be part of the hyperpersonal process (see Tidwell & Walther, 2002). One might think that the provision of stereotypically socially *undesirable* information may have a warranting effect, but without the potential for corroboration, it should be no more useful than any other well-timed self-disclosure.

As for the observation of partners through incrementally expanded bandwidth, from private mail to phone and photos before FtF, we can conjecture that these activities, too, provide warranting information. We make many trait inferences from vocal qualities (Siegman, 1987) and physical appearance (Berscheid & Walster, 1974), and we rely on nonverbal cues to detect deception because we assume they are less controllable than language content. Which physical cues through which channels matter most in this context is not yet known. It may depend on the receiver's preferences and/or the sender's self-concept. Physical appearance can be important, but photographs can be retouched or may be outdated, whereas vocal qualities generally cannot be altered. Perhaps the characteristic that the sender would least want to share would therefore be the one about which the receiver most wants to know.

Warrant Invites Traditional Interpersonal Constructs

Whether or not this reformulated construct of warrant will ultimately illuminate how relational partners move from on-line to physical relationships remains to be seen. At the same time, the warrant notion does create intriguing opportunities to connect previous research on interpersonal communication and relational development to the domain of MMRs. For example, it suggests potential application of Sunnafrank's (1986) predicted outcome value theory to relationships moving from CMC to FtF. This theory argues that each bit of uncertainty-reducing information triggers a receiver's evaluations of the sender. If the information suggests continued potential for interpersonal reward, the relationship is pursued. If revelations are seen as negative, the relationship may be curtailed. We suggest that in an MMR context, from this perspective, incremental exchanges of higher-bandwidth cues, and other warranting information, act as break points for decisions about relational escalation or termination.

Similarly, the request and provision of warranting information may constitute "secret tests" of relationships that on-line partners make and may explain why they make them (Baxter & Wilmot, 1984). Cases in which warranting information deviates from virtual expectations create significant opportunities for researchers to study "uncertainty-increasing events" (Planalp & Honeycutt, 1985). Additionally, the progression from an exclusively on-line context through a series of additional media to arrive at a face-to-face meeting might be approached as a series of relationship "turning points" (Baxter & Bullis, 1986). Useful as they are, however, these approaches provide no clear guidelines for predicting the degree to which the weight of warranting information

may influence relationship judgments relative to the weight they might have had in normal FtF acquaintance processes.

Alternative Interpretive Frameworks

In this last subsection we want to speculate on alternative ways in which appearance and behavior characteristics presented FtF may be processed in the context of a preexisting on-line relationship. Although some laud cyberspace as "a realm in which physical markers such as sex, race, age, body type, and size will eventually lose their salience as a basis for the categorization of self/other" (O'Brien, 1999, p. 77), Jacobson's (1999) research indicates that CMC users often construct impressions of their on-line partners that include imagined physical characteristics. This raises the question of whether judgments made from these imagined characteristics have as much, more, or less impact on interpersonal judgments when they appear later rather than earlier in relationship development. Is physicality just one layer in the unpeeling onion of social penetration, or does it hold particular potency? To address this issue, we suggest three plausible interpretive frameworks that CMC partners might employ with respect to the treatment of warranting information, using exposure to a partner's physical appearance as the paradigm case.

One interpretive option is *indefinite postponement*. A certain kind of uncertainty is never resolved in the absence of physical data, and ultimate judgments are held in check until such data appear. (Sunnafrank, 1986, might call this the recognition of "limited outcome experiences"; p. 9.) Communication between the first encounter and the physical encounter transpires under a "willing suspension of disbelief," but the eventual encounter of physical appearance is evaluated against standard individual criteria for attractiveness, and evaluations have similar force on relational judgments as if they had happened during initial acquaintanceship. That is to say, physically related judgments of attraction will have as strong an effect on the desire to escalate or terminate interaction as if no other uncertainty reduction or affinity development had taken place.

This process is likely to vary due to two factors: the perceiver's gender (males tend to value physical attractiveness more than do females) and the type of relationship (i.e., intellectual/professional versus romantic/erotic). According to Baxter and Wilmot (1984), those who are becoming involved in romantic relationships tend to value and make greater effort to obtain information about their partners than those who are in platonic relationships.

Alternatively, the Internet allows users to prescreen for prospective partners who find exceptional characteristics acceptable. Cooper and Sportolari (1997) describe cases in which users canvass prospective partners in advance about whether they object to this or that physical characteristic. Such users then pursue relationships only with those for whom they are already likely to pass physical appearance tests when they meet FtF.

A second interpretive frame might be labeled *irrelevance/assimilation*. Uncertainty reduction through alternative data and media is entirely sufficient for the formation of impressions and relational development, and the eventual introduction of physical characteristics is irrelevant insofar as relational judgments are concerned. According to Cooper and Sportolari (1997), "By the time these people meet each other in person, an intimate bond can already be formed. . . . unappealing physical traits are then more likely to be mitigated by the overall attraction that exists" (p. 9). Drawing on schema theory, it is reasonable that an individual's cognitive representation of a partner can assimilate within it a range of particulars. Could a wide disparity between the virtual and physical on some characteristic be integrated in this fashion? The "schema-plus-tag" model (Graesser, Gordon, & Sawyer, 1979; Woll & Graesser, 1982) suggests that a particular anomaly

may be cognitively "appended" to a previous impression without disrupting the initial impression itself.

Expectancy violations offer a third framework. New information is compared against expectations, and if it contrasts significantly with preconceptions, a positive or negative relationship decision ensues (Burgoon & Hale, 1988). Although nonverbal expectancy violations theory specifies different outcome dynamics depending on whether or not the violator is previously held to be well regarded and socially attractive, we can confine ourselves in this case to the dynamics in which on-line partners feel positive (enough to want to meet FtF). In this application, expectations theoretically may be formed through virtual interaction for a range of attributes. Upon exposure, actual appearance and physical behavior may be compared against such expectations. The theory predicts extraordinary positive reactions and intimacy when expectations are violated positively. When a violation is negative, extraordinary disregard occurs. When expectations are met, positive regard continues. Although the original theory discusses active nonverbal behaviors (spatial movement), it may apply to more passive characteristics as well; the theory's incorporation of expectancy violations for conversation management and self-presentation (Burgoon, 1993) offers especially interesting possibilities for potentially unexpected behavior that may contrast with virtual preconceptions.

An interesting question is opened by this framework regarding the range of expected behaviors that result from virtual relationship development. Will the range of expectations be expanded or constricted and heightened? If partners idealize each other through hyperpersonal on-line interaction, this might constrict expectations to a very high and narrow range of acceptability (as is the case for high-reward communicators off-line as well; Burgoon & Walther, 1990). Thus the chances of creating a positive violation, or even of avoiding a negative violation, become more remote. This would also suggest that unless incremental increases in warrant are enacted on the path to FtF meeting, otherwise favorable impressions are likely to be disappointed and the relationship short-lived. It also suggests that, in the case of warranting, individuals might find it useful to attempt to lower their partners' expectations and to deprecate their own characteristics convincingly (as did some females in Baker's 1998 research). Whether it is to this end that partners exchange successively higher-bandwidth information or whether this serves some other relational function are questions awaiting additional exploration.

CONCLUSIONS

The research we have reviewed suggests that there are two primary aspects related to CMC and the Internet that have fundamental impacts on interpersonal communication: how we communicate (using typed text) and with whom (related to the sociometric structures of on-line interaction). The restriction or adaptation of relational communication without the nonverbal cues available in FtF interaction was originally thought to divert users' attention from social and emotional aspects of communication, dampening (positive) affect and interpersonal relations. Alternative perspectives indicate that the very lack of nonverbal cues affords users certain opportunities and potential liberation for the management of identity and the accentuation of interpersonal dynamics. The effects of the CMC channel depend not on bandwidth alone, but on the interactions of media characteristics with social contexts, relational goals, salient norms, and temporal frames that promote or inhibit the strategic use of CMC in relationally supportive or detrimental ways.

The social structures of on-line interaction are also affected by the Internet. The extent to which people interact with strangers or with preestablished relationship partners offers contingencies for benefit or detriment. Research involving social support makes this paradoxically clear. Some studies suggest that the extent to which we avail ourselves of new connections to established links can improve our mental well-being. Others suggest that access to strangers who share our concerns over health problems or other interests (in addition to the mathematical probability of finding like-minded acquaintances among a relatively huge pool of prospects) offers several advantages, including the availability of superior expertise, access to optimal support messages, and the potential for the development of meaningful relationships based on similarity rather than propinquity alone.

Recent surveys reflect what many of us already know with respect to the diffusion of CMC into our lives: It is increasingly common for people to use the Internet as one among many channels for communication with work partners, social partners, and family members. How this technology affects such relationships is not well understood. Our theoretical models and experimental tests force the separation of channels. Field research shows that this is becoming a false dichotomy in many instances, but most such research has yet to aspire to theoretically elegant propositions that can explain and predict how these combinations affect interaction and long-term relationship development. The topic of relationship maintenance may hold promise, but forays into this domain have not as yet evolved beyond descriptive research. Moving in the other direction, toward the development of relationships from on-line to off-line, also points to the need for new thinking and alterations in our existing theories of relationships. The closest we have come to studying the dynamics of MMRs has been, once again, in research concerning groups—in particular, distributed work groups in organizations. Conclusions coming out of this research suggest that "virtual teams" need at least one, and maybe more, FtF meetings in order to be effective (e.g., Hinds & Bailey, 2000; Lipnack & Stamps, 1997). Such proclamations, which are based on field observations of such teams, unfortunately do not specify theoretical reasons for the researchers' conclusions; at best, we are given lists of the myriad ways in which CMC differs from FtF meetings, without specific identification of the crucial variables involved in the relative success of such groups. In other words, CMC becomes a "black box." Without more specific theoretical specification, our ability to correct, improve, or replace human adaptation failings with alternative procedures, or technological substitutions, will remain thwarted.

REFERENCES

Adelman, M. B., Parks, M. R., & Albrecht, T. L. (1987). Beyond close relationships: Support in weak ties. In T. L. Albrecht & M. B. Adelman (Eds.), *Communicating social support* (pp. 40-63). Newbury Park, CA: Sage.

Albright, J. M., & Conran, T. (1995, April). *Online love: Sex, gender and relationships in cyberspace.* Paper presented at the annual meeting of the Pacific Sociological Association, San Francisco.

Baker, A. (1998, July). Cyberspace couples finding romance online then meeting for the first time in real life. *CMC Magazine.* Retrieved December 1, 2000, from http://www.december.com/cmc/mag/1998/jul/baker.html

Bandura, A. (1997). *Self-efficacy: The exercise of control.* New York: W. H. Freeman.

Bavelas, J. B., Black, A., Chovil, N., & Mullett, J. (1990). *Equivocal communication.* Newbury Park, CA: Sage.

Baxter, L. A., & Bullis, C. (1986). Turning points in developing romantic relationships. *Human Communication Research, 12,* 469-493.

Baxter, L. A., & Wilmot, W. (1984). Secret tests: Social strategies for acquiring information about the state of the relationship. *Human Communication Research, 11,* 171-201.

Baym, N. K. (1995). The emergence of community in computer-mediated interaction. In S. G. Jones (Ed.), *Cybersociety: Computer-mediated communication and community* (pp. 138-163). Thousand Oaks, CA: Sage.

Baym, N. K. (1999). *Tune in, log on: Soaps, fandom, and online community.* Thousand Oaks, CA: Sage.

Berger, C. R. (1979). Beyond initial interaction. In H. Giles & R. St. Clair (Eds.), *Language and social psychology* (pp. 122-144). Oxford: Blackwell.

Berger, C. R. (1986). Uncertain outcome values in predicted relationships: Uncertainty reduction theory then and now. *Human Communication Research, 13,* 34-38.

Berger, C. R., & Bradac, J. J. (1982). *Language and social knowledge: Uncertainty in interpersonal relations.* London: Edward Arnold.

Berger, C. R., & Calabrese, R. J. (1975). Some explorations in initial interaction and beyond: Toward a developmental theory of interpersonal communication. *Human Communication Research, 1,* 99-112.

Berger, C. R., & Douglas, W. (1981). Studies in interpersonal epistemology III: Anticipated interaction, self-monitoring, and observational context selection. *Communication Monographs, 48,* 183-196.

Berger, C. R., Gardner, R. R., Parks, M. R., Schulman, L., & Miller, G. R. (1976). Interpersonal epistemology and interpersonal communication. In G. R. Miller (Ed.), *Explorations in interpersonal communication* (pp. 149-171). Beverly Hills, CA: Sage.

Berscheid, E., & Walster, E. (1974). Physical attractiveness. In L. Berkowitz (Ed.), *Advances in experimental social psychology* (Vol. 7, pp. 157-215). New York: Academic Press.

Bozeman, D. P. (1996, August). *Managerial choice of communication channel in organizations: A literature review and proposed model.* Paper presented at the annual meeting of the Academy of Management, Cincinnati, OH.

Braithwaite, D. O., Waldron, V. R., & Finn, J. (1999). Communication of social support in computer-mediated groups for persons with disabilities. *Health Communication, 11,* 123-151.

Bruckman, A. (1992). *Identity workshop: Emergent social and psychological phenomena in text-based virtual reality.* Retrieved September 30, 2001, from ftp://ftp.cc.gatech.edu/pub/people/asb/papers/identity-workshop.rtf

Burgoon, J. K. (1993). Interpersonal expectations, expectancy violations, and emotional communication. *Journal of Language and Social Psychology, 12,* 30-48.

Burgoon, J. K., & Hale, J. L. (1984). The fundamental *topoi* of relational communication. *Communication Monographs, 51,* 193-214.

Burgoon, J. K., & Hale, J. L. (1987). Validation and measurement of the fundamental themes of relational communication. *Communication Monographs, 54,* 19-41.

Burgoon, J. K., & Hale, J. L. (1988). Nonverbal expectancy violations theory: Model elaboration and application to immediacy behaviors. *Communication Monographs, 55,* 58-79.

Burgoon, J. K., & Saine, T. (1978). *The unspoken dialogue: An introduction to nonverbal communication.* Boston: Houghton Mifflin.

Burgoon, J. K., & Walther, J. B. (1990). Nonverbal expectancies and the evaluative consequences of violations. *Human Communication Research, 17,* 232-265.

Calabrese, R. J. (1975). *The effects of privacy and probability of future interaction on initial interaction patterns.* Unpublished doctoral dissertation, Northwestern University.

Chester, A., & Gwynne, G. (1998). Online teaching: Encouraging collaboration through anonymity. *Journal of Computer-Mediated Communication, 4*(2). Retrieved September 1, 2001, from http://www.ascusc.org/jcmc/vol4/issue2/chester.html

Cline, R. J., & Musolf, K. E. (1985). Disclosure as social exchange: Anticipated length of relationship, sex roles, and disclosure intimacy. *Western Journal of Speech Communication, 49,* 43-56.

Cooper, A., Delmonico, D. L., & Burg, R. (2000). Cybersex users, abusers, and compulsives: New findings and implications. *Sexual Addiction and Compulsivity, 7,* 5-29.

Cooper, A., & Sportolari, L. (1997). Romance in cyberspace: Understanding online attraction. *Journal of Sex Education and Therapy, 22,* 7-14.

Culnan, M. J., & Markus, M. L. (1987). Information technologies. In F. M. Jablin, L. L. Putnam, K. H. Roberts, & L. W. Porter (Eds.), *Handbook of organizational communication: An interdisciplinary perspective* (pp. 420-443). Newbury Park, CA: Sage.

Curtis, P. (1992). Mudding: Social phenomena in text-based virtual realities. In D. Schuler (Ed.), *DIAC-92: Directions and implications of advanced computing* (pp. 48-68). Palo Alto, CA: Computer Professionals for Social Responsibility.

Cutrona, C. E., & Russell, D. W. (1990). Types of social support and specific stress: Toward a theory of optimal matching. In B. R. Sarason, I. G. Sarason, & G. R. Pierce (Eds.), *Social support: An interactional view* (pp. 319-366). New York: John Wiley.

Daft, R. L., & Lengel, R. H. (1984). Information richness: A new approach to managerial behavior and organization design. In B. M. Staw & L. L. Cummings (Eds.), *Research in organizational behavior* (Vol. 6, pp. 191-233). Greenwich, CT: JAI.

Daft, R. L., & Lengel, R. H. (1986). Organizational information requirements, media richness and structural design. *Management Science, 32,* 554-571.

Daft, R. L., Lengel, R. H., & Trevino, L. K. (1987). Message equivocality, media selection, and manager performance: Implications for information systems. *MIS Quarterly, 11,* 355-368.

Dennis, A. R., & Kinney, S. T. (1998). Testing media richness theory in the new media: The effects of cues, feedback, and task equivocality. *Information Systems Research, 9,* 256-274.

Donath, J. (1999). Identity and deception in the virtual community. In M. A. Smith & P. Kollock (Eds.), *Communities in cyberspace* (pp. 29-59). New York: Routledge.

Egdorf, K., & Rahoi, R. L. (1994, November). *Finding a place where "we all want to hear it": E-mail as a source of social support.* Paper presented at the annual meeting of the Speech Communication Association, New Orleans.

Freedman, N. (1977). Hands, words and mind: On the structuralization of body movements during discourse and the capacity for verbal representation. In N. Freedman & S. Grand (Eds.), *Communicative structures and psychic structures: A psychoanalytic interpretation of communication* (pp. 109-132). New York: Plenum.

Fulk, J., Schmitz, J. A., & Steinfield, C. W. (1990). A social influence model of technology use. In J. Fulk & C. W. Steinfield (Eds.), *Organizations and communication technology* (pp. 117-140). Newbury Park, CA: Sage.

Galagher, J., Sproull, L., & Kiesler, S. (1998). Legitimacy, authority, and community in electronic support groups. *Written Communication, 15,* 493-530.

Godin, S. (1993). *The smiley dictionary: Cool things to do with your keyboard.* Berkeley, CA: Peachpit.

Goldsmith, D. (1992). Managing conflicting goals in supportive interaction: An integrative theoretical framework. *Communication Research, 19,* 264-286.

Graesser, A. C., Gordon, S. E., & Sawyer, J. D. (1979). Recognition memory for typical and atypical actions in scripted activities: Tests of a script pointer + tag hypothesis. *Journal of Verbal Learning and Verbal Behavior, 18,* 319-332.

Gudykunst, W. B., Yang, S. M., & Nishida, T. (1985). A cross-cultural test of uncertainty reduction theory: Comparisons of acquaintances, friends, and dating relationships in Japan, Korea, and the United States. *Human Communication Research, 11,* 407-454.

Gunawardena, C. N. (1995). Social presence theory and its implications for interaction and collaborative learning in computer conferences. *International Journal of Educational Telecommunications, 1,* 147-166.

Gunawardena, C. N., & Zittle, F. J. (1997). Social presence as a predictor of satisfaction within a computer-mediated conferencing environment. *American Journal of Distance Education, 11*(3), 8-27.

Gunn, D. O., & Gunn, C. W. (2000, October). *Electronic relationship maintenance processes.* Paper presented at the annual meeting of the Association of Internet Researchers, Lawrence, KS.

Hancock, J. T., & Dunham, P. J. (2001). Impression formation in computer-mediated communication revisited. *Communication Research, 28,* 325-347.

Herring, S. C. (1993). Gender and democracy in computer-mediated communication. *Electronic Journal of Communication, 3*(2). Retrieved September 30, 2001, from http://www.cios.org/getfile/herring_v3n293

Hiltz, S. R., Johnson, K., & Agle, G. (1978). *Replicating Bales' problem solving experiments on a computerized conference: A pilot study* (Research Rep. No. 8). Newark: New Jersey Institute of Technology, Computerized Conferencing and Communications Center.

Hinds, P. J., & Bailey, D. E. (2000, August). *Cohesion, conflict, participation, and performance in geographically distributed teams.* Paper presented at the annual meeting of the Academy of Management, Toronto.

Jacobson, D. (1999). Impression formation in cyberspace: Online expectations and offline experiences in text-based virtual communities.

Journal of Computer-Mediated Communication, 5(1). Retrieved May 18, 2000, from http://www.ascusc.org/jcmc/vol5/issue1/jacobson.html

Kayany, J. M., Wotring, C. E., & Forrest, E. J. (1996). Relational control and interactive media choice in technology-mediated communication situations. *Human Communication Research, 22,* 399-421.

Kellermann, K., & Reynolds, R. (1990). When ignorance is bliss: The role of motivation to reduce uncertainty in uncertainty reduction theory. *Human Communication Research, 17,* 5-75.

Kiesler, S. (1986). The hidden messages in computer networks. *Harvard Business Review, 64*(3), 46-54, 58-60.

Kiesler, S., Siegel, J. & McGuire, T. W. (1984). Social psychological aspects of computer-mediated communication. *American Psychologist, 39,* 1123-1134.

Korzenny, F. (1978). A theory of electronic propinquity: Mediated communications in organizations. *Communication Research, 5,* 3-24.

Korzenny, F., & Bauer, C. (1981). Testing the theory of electronic propinquity. *Communication Research, 8,* 479-498.

Kraut, R., Kiesler, S., Boneva, B., Cummings, J., Helgeson, V., & Crawford, A. (2002). Internet paradox revisited. *Journal of Social Issues, 58*(1), 49-74.

Kraut, R., Lundmark, V., Patterson, M., Kiesler, S., Mukopadhyay, T., & Scherlis, W. (1998). Internet paradox: A social technology that reduces social involvement and psychological well-being? *American Psychologist, 53,* 1017-1031.

La Gaipa, J. J. (1990). The negative effects of informal support systems. In S. Duck (Ed.), *Personal relationships and social support* (pp. 122-139). London: Sage.

Landis, D. (1994, February 11). Cyberspace as a frontier for romance. *USA Today,* pp. D1-D2.

LaRose, R., Eastin, M. S., & Gregg, J. (2001). Reformulating the Internet paradox: Social cognitive explanations of Internet use and depression. *Journal of Online Behavior, 1*(2). Retrieved September 1, 2001, from http://www.behavior.net/job/v1n2/paradox.html

Lea, M., O'Shea, T., Fung, P., & Spears, R. (1992). "Flaming" in computer-mediated communication: Observations, explanations, implication. In M. Lea (Ed.), *Contexts of computer-mediated communication* (pp. 89-112). London: Harvester-Wheatsheaf.

Lea, M., & Spears, R. (1992). Paralanguage and social perception in computer-mediated communication. *Journal of Organizational Computing, 2,* 321-341.

Lea, M., & Spears, R. (1995). Love at first byte? Building personal relationships over computer networks. In J. T. Wood & S. Duck (Eds.), *Under-studied relationships: Off the beaten track* (pp. 197-233). Thousand Oaks, CA: Sage.

Lea, M., Spears, R., & de Groot, D. (2001). Knowing me, knowing you: Anonymity effects on social identity processes within groups. *Personality and Social Psychology Bulletin, 27,* 526-537.

Levine, D. (2000). Virtual attraction: What rocks your boat. *CyberPsychology & Behavior, 3,* 565-573.

Levine, K. (n.d.). Cyber-affairs survey: Early survey answers. *Self Help Magazine.* Retrieved October 1, 2000, from http://www.shpm.com/articles/cyber_romance/cbrsxsrv.html

Lipnack, J., & Stamps, J. (1997). *Virtual teams: Reaching across space, time, and organizations with technology.* New York: John Wiley.

Lipton, M. (1996). Forgetting the body: Cybersex and identity. In L. Strate, R. Jacobson, & S. B. Gibson (Eds.), *Communication and cyberspace: Social interaction in an electronic environment* (pp. 335-349). Cresskill, NJ: Hampton.

Markus, M. L. (1987). Toward a "critical mass" theory of interactive media: Universal access, interdependence, and diffusion. *Communication Research, 14,* 491-511.

Markus, M. L. (1994a). Electronic mail as the medium of managerial choice. *Organization Science, 5,* 502-527.

Markus, M. L. (1994b). Finding a happy medium: Explaining the negative effects of electronic communication on social life at work. *ACM Transactions on Information Systems, 12,* 119-149.

Mickelson, K. D. (1997). Seeking social support: Parents in electronic support groups. In S. Kiesler (Ed.), *Culture of the Internet* (pp. 157-178). Mahwah, NJ: Lawrence Erlbaum.

Miller, H. (1995, June). *The presentation of self in electronic life: Goffman on the Internet.* Paper presented at the conference Embodied Knowledge and Virtual Space, London. Retrieved April 8, 2000, from http://ess.ntu.ac.uk/miller/cyberpsych/goffman.htm

Mitchell, W. J. (1995). *City of bits: Space, place, and the Infobahn.* Cambridge: MIT Press.

Nardi, B., Whittaker, S., & Bradner, E. (2000). Interaction and outeraction: Instant messaging in action. In *Proceedings of the ACM Conference on Computer Supported Cooperative Work* (pp. 79-88). New York: Association for Computing Machinery.

Nie, N., & Erbring, L. (2000, February 17). *Internet and society: A preliminary report.* Retrieved September 1, 2001, from the Stanford Institute for the Quantitative Study of Society Web site: http://www.stanford.edu/group/siqss/press_release/preliminary_report.pdf

O'Brien, J. (1999). Writing in the body: Gender (re)production in online interaction. In M. A. Smith & P. Kollock (Eds.), *Communities in cyberspace* (pp. 76-104). New York: Routledge.

O'Sullivan, P. B. (2000). What you don't know won't hurt *me*: Impression management functions of communication channels in relationships. *Human Communication Research, 26,* 403-431.

Parks, M. R., & Adelman, M. B. (1983). Communication networks and the development of romantic relationships: An expansion of uncertainty reduction theory. *Human Communication Research, 10,* 55-79.

Parks, M. R., & Floyd, K. (1996). Making friends in cyberspace. *Journal of Communication, 46*(1), 80-97.

Parks, M. R., & Roberts, L. D. (1998). "Making MOOsic": The development of personal relationships on line and a comparison to their off-line counterparts. *Journal of Social and Personal Relationships, 15,* 517-537.

Pew Internet & American Life Project. (2000). *Tracking online life: How women use the Internet to cultivate relationships with family and friends.* Retrieved September 1, 2001, from http://www.pewinternet.org/reports/toc.asp?report=11

Pew Internet & American Life Project. (2001a). *More online, doing more: 16 million newcomers gain Internet access in the last half of 2000 as women, minorities, and families with modest incomes continue to surge online.* Retrieved September 1, 2001, from http://www.pewinternet.org/reports/toc.asp?report=30

Pew Internet & American Life Project. (2001b). Teenage life online: The rise of the instant-message generation and the Internet's impact on friendships and family relationships. Retrieved Sept. 1, 2001, from http://www. pewinternet.org/reports/toc.asp?report=36

Planalp, S., & Honeycutt, J. M. (1985). Events that increase uncertainty in personal relationships. *Human Communication Research, 11,* 593-604.

Postmes, T., Spears, R., & Lea, M. (1998). Breaching or building social boundaries? SIDE-effects of computer-mediated communication. *Communication Research, 25,* 689-715.

Postmes, T., Spears, R., & Lea, M. (2000). The formation of group norms in computer-mediated communication. *Human Communi cation Research, 26,* 341-371.

Postmes, T., Spears, R., Lea, M., & Reicher, S. D. (Eds.). (2000). *SIDE issues centre stage: Recent developments in studies of deindividuation in groups.* Amsterdam: Royal Netherlands Academy of Arts and Sciences.

Ramirez, A., Jr., Walther, J. B., Burgoon, J. K., & Sunnafrank, M. (2002). Information-seeking strategies, uncertainty, and computer-mediated communication: Toward a conceptual model. *Human Communication Research, 28,* 213-228.

Reid, F. J. M., Ball, L. J., Morley, A. M., & Evans, J. S. B. T. (1997). Styles of group discussion in computer-mediated decision making. *British Journal of Social Psychology, 36,* 241-262.

Reid, F. J. M., Malinek, V., Stott, C., & Evans, J. S. B. T. (1996). The messaging threshold in computer-mediated communication. *Ergonomics, 39,* 1017-1037.

Rezabek, L. L., & Cochenour, J. J. (1998). Visual cues in computer-mediated communication: Supplementing text with emoticons. *Journal of Visual Literacy, 18,* 210-215.

Rheingold, H. (1993). *The virtual community: Homesteading on the electronic frontier.* Reading, MA: Addison-Wesley.

Rice, R. E. (1990). Computer-mediated communication system network data: Theoretical concerns and empirical examples. *International Journal of Man-Machine Studies, 32,* 627-647.

Rice, R. E. (1993). Media appropriateness: Using social presence theory to compare traditional and new organizational media. *Human Communication Research, 19,* 451-484.

Rice, R. E., & Case, D. (1983). Electronic message systems in the university: A description of use and utility. *Journal of Communication, 33*(1), 131-154.

Rice, R. E., & Love, G. (1987). Electronic emotion: Socioemotional content in a computer-mediated network. *Communication Research, 14,* 85-108.

Roberts, L. D., & Parks, M. R. (1999). The social geography of gender-switching in virtual environments on the Internet. *Information, Communication, and Society, 2,* 521-540.

Roberts, L. D., Smith, L. M., & Pollock, C. (1996, September). *A model of social interaction via computer-mediated communication in real-time text-based virtual environments.* Paper presented at the meeting of the Australian Psychological Society, Sydney.

Romance and the Internet [Special issue]. (1994). *Arachnet Electronic Journal on Virtual Culture, 2*(3). Retrieved September 1, 2001, from http://www.monash.edu.au/journals/ejvc/sqarv2n3.netlove

Scheerhorn, D., Warisse, J., & McNeilis, K. (1995). Computer-based telecommunication among an illness-related community. *Health Communication, 7,* 301-325.

Short, J., Williams, E., & Christie, B. (1976). *The social psychology of telecommunications.* London: John Wiley.

Siegel, J., Dubrovsky, V., Kiesler, S., & McGuire, T. W. (1986). Group processes in computer-mediated communication. *Organizational Behavior and Human Decision Processes, 37,* 157-187.

Siegman, A. W. (1987). The telltale voice: Nonverbal messages of verbal communication. In A. W. Siegman & S. Feldstein (Eds.), *Nonverbal behavior and communication* (2nd ed., pp. 351-434). Hillsdale, NJ: Lawrence Erlbaum.

Snyder, M., Tanke, E. D., & Berscheid, E. (1977). Social perception and interpersonal behavior: On the self-fulfilling nature of social stereotypes. *Journal of Personality and Social Psychology, 35,* 656-666.

Spears, R., & Lea, M. (1992). Social influence and the influence of the "social" in computer-mediated communication. In M. Lea (Ed.), *Contexts of computer-mediated communication* (pp. 30-65). London: Harvester-Wheatsheaf.

Sproull, L., & Faraj, S. (1997). Atheism, sex, and databases: The Net as a social technology. In

S. Kiesler (Ed.), *Culture of the Internet* (pp. 35-51). Mahwah, NJ: Lawrence Erlbaum.

Sproull, L., & Kiesler, S. (1986). Reducing social context cues: Electronic mail in organizational communication. *Management Science, 32,* 1492-1512.

Stafford, L., Kline, S. L., & Dimmick, J. (1999). Home e-mail: Relational maintenance and gratification opportunities. *Journal of Broadcasting & Electronic Media, 43,* 659-669.

Stafford, L., & Reske, J. R. (1990, May). Idealization and communication in long-distance premarital relationships. *Family Relations, 39,* 274-279.

Stephen, T. (1986). Communication and interdependence in geographically separated relationships. *Human Communication Research, 13,* 191-210.

Stone, A. R. (1995). *The war of desire and technology at the close of the mechanical age.* Cambridge: MIT Press.

Sunnafrank, M. (1986). Predicted outcome value during initial interactions: A reformulation of uncertainty reduction theory. *Human Communication Research, 13,* 3-33.

Thompson, P. A., & Foulger, D. A. (1996). Effects of pictographs and quoting on flaming in electronic mail. *Computers in Human Behavior, 12,* 225-243.

Tidwell, L. C., & Walther, J. B. (2002). Computer-mediated communication effects on disclosure, impressions, and interpersonal evaluations: Getting to know one another a bit at a time. *Human Communication Research, 28,* 317-348.

Turkle, S. (1995). *Life on the screen: Identity in the age of the Internet.* New York: Simon & Schuster.

Turner, J. W., Grube, J. A., & Meyers, J. (2001). Developing an optimal match within online communities: An exploration of CMC support communities and traditional support. *Journal of Communication, 51,* 231-251.

Turoff, M. (1991). Computer-mediated communication requirements for group support. *Journal of Organizational Computing, 1,* 85-113.

Utz, S. (2000). Social information processing in MUDs: The development of friendships in virtual worlds. *Journal of Online Behavior, 1*(1). Retrieved April 7, 2000, from http://www.behavior.net/job/v1n1/utz.html

Walther, J. B. (1992). Interpersonal effects in computer-mediated interaction: A relational perspective. *Communication Research, 19,* 52-90.

Walther, J. B. (1994). Anticipated ongoing interaction versus channel effects on relational communication in computer-mediated interaction. *Human Communication Research, 20,* 473-501.

Walther, J. B. (1993). Impression development in computer-mediated interaction. *Western Journal of Communication, 57,* 381-398.

Walther, J. B. (1996). Computer-mediated communication: Impersonal, interpersonal, and hyperpersonal interaction. *Communication Research, 23,* 1-43.

Walther, J. B. (1997). Group and interpersonal effects in international computer-mediated collaboration. *Human Communication Research, 23,* 342-369.

Walther, J. B., Anderson, J. F., & Park, D. (1994). Interpersonal effects in computer-mediated interaction: A meta-analysis of social and anti-social communication. *Communication Research, 21,* 460-487.

Walther, J. B., & Boyd, S. (2002). Attraction to computer-mediated social support. In C. A. Lin & D. Atkin (Eds.), *Communication technology and society: Audience adoption and uses* (pp. 153-188). Cresskill, NJ: Hampton.

Walther, J. B., & Burgoon, J. K. (1992). Relational communication in computer-mediated interaction. *Human Communication Research, 19,* 50-88.

Walther, J. B., & D'Addario, K. P. (2001). The impacts of emoticons on message interpretation in computer-mediated communication. *Social Science Computer Review, 19,* 323-345.

Walther, J. B., Slovacek, C., & Tidwell, L. C. (2001). Is a picture worth a thousand words? Photographic images in long-term and short-term virtual teams. *Communication Research, 28,* 105-134.

Walther, J. B., & Tidwell, L. C. (1995). Nonverbal cues in computer-mediated communication, and the effect of chronemics on relational communication. *Journal of Organizational Computing, 5,* 355-378.

Wildermuth, S. (2000, July). *Technology and the future of interpersonal relationships: Explaining the growth of hyperpersonal on-line interaction.* Paper presented at the conference Communication: Organizing for the Future, sponsored by the National

Communication Association and International Communication Association, Rome.

Witmer, D., & Katzman, S. (1997). On-line smiles: Does gender make a difference in the use of graphic accents? *Journal of Computer-Mediated Communication, 2*(4). Retrieved May 23, 2000, from http://www.ascusc.org/jcmc/vol2/issue4/witmer1.html

Wolf, A. (2000). Emotional expression online: Gender differences in emoticon use. *Cyber-Psychology & Behavior, 3*, 827-833.

Woll, S. B., & Graesser, A. C. (1982). Memory discrimination for information typical or atypical of person schemata. *Social Cognition, 1*, 287-310.

Wright, K. B. (2000). Social support satisfaction, on-line communication apprehension, and perceived life stress within computer-mediated support groups. *Communication Research Reports, 17*, 139-147.

15

Interpersonal Skills

BRIAN H. SPITZBERG
WILLIAM R. CUPACH

Interpersonal skills are the sine qua non of social life, yet few things in life are so taken for granted. Like eating and walking, talking and interacting are part of the mundane landscape of everyday behavior. Ordinarily, we take notice of our own or someone else's interpersonal skills when they are exceptionally bad, exceptionally good, or simply not at all what we expect. The rest of the time, interpersonal skills tend to be the ground to whatever figure is the focus of our attention.

Despite the extent to which interpersonal skills occupy the status of "scenery" to our everyday experience, there are few characteristics as vital to our quality of life. Social and interpersonal skills are the means through which all human relationships are initiated, negotiated, maintained, transformed, and dissolved. They are the means through which conflicts are resolved, face is negotiated, and predicaments are managed. In short, interpersonal skills are the fulcrum upon which the levers of social life are maneuvered. In this chapter, we review the research and theory relevant to interpersonal skills and the role such skills play in interpersonal communication. Initially, it suffices to treat *interpersonal skills* and *social skills* as synonymous, and as primitive terms referring to behaviors that facilitate competence in interaction. We will explicate more precise definitions and distinctions later in this chapter.

THE RATIONALE OF INTERPERSONAL SKILLS

A Synoptic History of Interpersonal Skills

By most accounts, social scientific interest in interpersonal skills is relatively recent in origin. When the discipline of communication is traced to its historical origins, public speaking and persuasion are found to be the focal point of most literature. Again, this suggests the extent to which interpersonal skills serve as a mere backdrop to what are considered more important activities.

Nevertheless, intellectual interest in interpersonal skills can be found even among the pantheon of the most noted and influential communication scholars and philosophers. One of the earliest historical references to communication being treated as a skill is implicit in the characterization of the sophistic rhetorics of ancient Sicily (Kennedy, 1963). When property and status were made contingent upon a person's ability to persuade in a forensic context, teachers arose to instruct people in the arts and skills of communication. Aristotle (1926), the most influential early philosopher of rhetoric, wrote relatively little about the interpersonal context per se, but identified several important distinctions that would later be replicated in more contemporary discussions of interpersonal skills. For example, he noted that ultimately "the object of rhetoric is judgment," such that a communicator needs to "know how to put the judge into a certain frame of mind" (p. 169). The art and "skill" of rhetoric, therefore, was concerned with creating preferred impressions in the mind of the interlocutor or audience. This key notion presages the contemporary interest in impression management. Cicero (1959) briefly discussed "tact" in conversation, which was necessary to avoid talking excessively about oneself, ignoring the status of conversants, or simply being "in any way awkward or tedious" (p. 211). Quintillian (1903)

discussed several similar topics, including appropriateness of style, decorum, aptitude, and adaptation ("*one kind of style cannot suit every cause, or every auditor, or every character, or every occasion*"; X, 1, 4, p. 310), and specifically employs the phrase "skilled in speaking" in defining the competent rhetor.

Medieval literature is relatively silent regarding interpersonal skills (Menache, 1990). Wine (1981) suggests, however, that the dominant model of social competence during this era was predicated on a "defect" conception of behavior. People who were socially incompetent were literally defective. Defect was diagnosed through the manifestation of deviant behavior, which in turn was attributable to physical, mental, or demonological causes. Although attributions of specific causes have changed considerably through the ages since, the basic notion that social competence is tied to personal defect is still very much in evidence in modern conceptions of competence.

Western intellectual interest in interpersonal skills heightened considerably during the Renaissance. After the bubonic plague swept Europe, accumulated wealth was concentrated among a much smaller surviving population, which still operated according to feudal and hereditary status structures. Among the societal trends that developed was an acute elaboration of the code of conduct in the context of royalty and "the court." The "art of conversation" became a popular subject of writing and education (Burke, 1993). Writers such as Machiavelli emphasized the tactics through which a person could achieve and maintain status, whereas others, such as Stephano Guazzo, emphasized aptitudes such as "decorum." *Decorum* is a term applied to a style of conversation that adapts vocal quality and verbal content to the context (Mohrmann, 1972). European writers such as de Sculdéry, Bussy-Rabutin, de Sévigné, and Boursault created models of communication in the salon, in which "conversation was the best indicator of the worth of an individual or of an entire group, enabling members of society to both measure and construct their personal status" (Goldsmith, 1988, p. 12). The rhetoric of the banquet became an art unto itself (Jeanneret, 1991). Ehninger (1975) describes this era of rhetoric as one of ingratiation, the strategic attempt to create positive impressions of self by pleasing others. It is no accident that the development of elaborate codes of conduct concerning such things as mannerisms, forms of address, and formal table manners served to erect social barriers potentially stronger than economic ones. A person might be able to come into wealth, but "manner" is something learned through the long enculturation process of being "born into" royalty and wealth. Meanwhile, outside the gilded courts and palaces during this era, Wine (1981) suggests, explorations in biology and medicine altered the demonological defect model into a more "medical" defect model. The basic assumption of this model is that deviant behavior is the product of underlying structural defects of the body, and those who are prone to such behavior may be identified through surface manifestations such as lesions, skull shape, or illness.

The 18th century brought forth the elocutionary movement, which was concerned with the "just and graceful management of the voice, countenance, and gesture in speaking" (Sheridan, 1762, p. II, 1). Textbooks identified precise behavioral representations of emotional displays and gestural flourishes and meticulously mapped body movements designed to communicate specific messages and moods (e.g., Austin, 1966; Bulwer, 1974). While still focusing almost entirely on the public oratorical context, such approaches clearly presaged a "skills" philosophy of communication. Excellent communication consists of (a) a specific set of behaviors that (b) can be learned and refined.

By the time of the transition into the 20th century, the United States was experiencing its own renaissance. The Industrial

Revolution, combined with the natural resources of the now settled United States, established another concentration of wealth among a relative minority of society's populace. Once again, interest in interpersonal skills was revealed in an expanding literature oriented to educating people in the social graces. Manners and etiquette books taught proper behavior, and often, the more proper the behavior, the more elaborate, formal, and privileged the context (Ewbank, 1987). The aristocracy found ways not only of restricting the entry of the lower classes, but also of stigmatizing the nouveau riche (Bushman, 1992; Kasson, 1990).

Throughout the 20th century, other trends began to take hold that would significantly influence the academic interest in interpersonal skills. In perhaps the earliest social scientific analogue, Thorndike (1920) speculated on the nature of social intelligence, a concept that has become closely yoked to interpersonal and social skills (Marlowe, 1985). The social scientific interest in intelligence led to a series of studies that attempted to develop a measurable and developmental model of social competence that was an analogue to mental intelligence (see Bradway, 1937, 1938; Doll, 1935, 1939, 1953; Otness, 1941). If a social intelligence quotient could be identified and validly operationalized, then there would be a way of diagnosing mental illness and identifying appropriate interventions. Of course, most of the ideological biases that surround theories and measures of mental intelligence apply equally (see Gould, 1981; Howe, 1997), if not more so, to social intelligence. For example, it no longer seems reasonable to view *social idiot* (Bassett, Longwell, & Bulow, 1939) as an objective clinical term.

As social competence lost momentum as an exact analogue to mental intelligence, the clinical interest in interpersonal and communication skills found voice in other theories of mental health. Ruesch (1951) reviewed the role of communication in psychiatric trends and identified "successful communication" as "the only criterion" of mental health: "It is obvious that people are mentally healthy only when their means of communication permit them to manage their surroundings successfully" (p. 87). This perspective sowed the seeds of the Palo Alto group's conception of disturbed communication processes as underlying most mental illness and relational disorders. This mantle was taken up as well by other programs of research that presumed a social skills basis of mental health (Phillips & Zigler, 1961; Zigler & Levine, 1981; Zigler & Phillips, 1960, 1961, 1962). It also prefigured the movement in counseling theories toward a communication skills model of helping (e.g., Carkhuff & Truax, 1966; Truax, 1967).

If psychologists were viewing social skills as the foundation of mental health, others were viewing social skills as the basis for family and relational health. Terman (1938) conducted some of the earliest social scientific research on marital satisfaction and provided perhaps the first in a long line of studies revealing "communication" as a primary source of healthy marital functioning. As the study of marriage became virtually a discipline of its own, interpersonal skills and processes became increasingly recognized as central to marital success (e.g., Boland & Follingstad, 1987; Feeney, 1994; Feeney, Noller, & Ward, 1997; Fitzpatrick, 1987; Gottman, 1994).

This selective synopsis of scholarly interest in interpersonal skills throughout recorded history suggests that such conceptions are always subject to the prevailing ideological paradigms and societal praxis of a given era. Although interpersonal skills may not always be prominent in the writings of a given era, their importance to the everyday life of any era is indisputable. A brief review of the literature regarding the importance of interpersonal skills supports this claim.

Importance of Interpersonal Skills

The rationale for the importance of interpersonal skills is developed through the premises of an axiomatic syllogism: Interpersonal skills are vital to the development of human relationships; human relationships are vital to personal well-being; therefore, interpersonal skills are vital to well-being. We develop these axioms below.

Interpersonal Skills Are Vital to the Development of Human Relationships

Interpersonal communication is the means through which relationships are initiated, negotiated, maintained, and ended (Applegate & Leichty, 1984; Burleson, Metts, & Kirch, 2000; Prisbell, 1995). It follows, then, that skill in interpersonal communication is essential to an individual's ability to manage relationships. For example, research consistently reveals communication as one of the most important factors in determining the satisfaction and dissatisfaction of marriages (e.g., Gottman, 1994; Steggell & Harper, 1991) and close relationships (Boland & Follingstad, 1987; Meeks, Hendrick, & Hendrick, 1998). The skill of managing relational conflict, and negative affect in particular, appears to be immensely important to the developmental success of relationships (e.g., Gottman 1994; Sillars & Weisberg, 1987; Spitzberg, Canary, & Cupach, 1994). Table 15.1 displays a sampling of the interpersonal skills involved in the successful and satisfying management of close relationships, particularly marital relationships. The sheer complexity of this landscape has led some to search for a simpler schema for skills intervention (e.g., Gottman & Rushe, 1995). Indeed, it seems clear that there is likely to be a higher-order structure to the list of skills in Table 15.1. Regardless of the complexity, studies and reviews of varied communication intervention and training programs generally reveal significant subsequent improvements in marital satisfaction and duration (e.g., Butler & Wampler, 1999; Markman, Floyd, Stanley, & Storaasli, 1988; Wampler, 1982; compare Beach & Fincham, 2001).

Table 15.1   Selective Communication Skill Correlates of Relational/Marital Satisfaction
and/or Duration

Acceptance (Hooley & Hahlweg, 1989)
Acknowledgment/confirmation (Doane, 1978)
Active listening (Boyd & Roach, 1977)
Affection expressions (Huston & Vangelisti, 1991)
Affective affirmation (Veroff, Douvan, Orbuch, & Acitelli, 1998)
Affective disengagement (Smith, Vivian, & O'Leary, 1990)
Affiliation (Thomsen & Gilbert, 1998)
Agreement (Basco, Birchler, Kalal, Talbott, & Slater, 1991; Royce & Weiss, 1975)
Amount of communication (Richmond, 1995)
Anger (Cohan & Bradbury, 1997; Leonard & Roberts, 1998)
Annoyance (Huston & Vangelisti, 1991)
Argumentativeness (Payne & Sabourin, 1990; Sabourin, Infante, & Rudd, 1993)
Attention/attentiveness (Royce & Weiss, 1975; Thomsen & Gilbert, 1998)
Avoidant conflict management (Bodenmann, Kaiser, Hahlweg, & Fehm-Wolfsdorf, 1998;
    Canary & Cupach, 1988; Canary & Spitzberg, 1987, 1989)
Balancing positive/negative behavior ratio (Gottman & Levenson, 1992)
Boredom expression (Huston & Vangelisti, 1991)
Clarity/articulation (Basco et al., 1991; Boyd & Roach, 1977; Doane, 1978; Duran & Zakahi, 1988)
Communication competence (Davis & Oathout, 1987)
Communication effectiveness—fulfilling interactional intentions (Burleson & Denton, 1992;
    Denton, Burleson, & Sprenkle, 1995)
Compliments (Huston & Vangelisti, 1991)
Composure (Duran & Zakahi, 1988)
Compromise (Royce & Weiss, 1975)
Conflict amount (Markman & Hahlweg, 1993; Veroff et al., 1998)
Conflict escalation (Julien, Markman, & Lindahl, 1989)
Conflict management skill (Flora & Segrin, 1998)
Constructive conflict management (Canary & Cupach, 1988; Canary & Spitzberg, 1987;
    Veroff, Douvan, & Hatchett, 1993; Veroff et al., 1998)
Criticism/complaint (Hooley & Hahlweg, 1989; Huston & Vangelisti, 1991)
Defensiveness/whining (Basco et al., 1991; Gottman & Krokoff, 1989)
Demand-withdrawal (Gottman, 1994; Heavey, Christensen, & Malamuth, 1995; Noller, Feeney,
    Bonnell, & Callan, 1994)
Denial (Julien et al., 1989)
Destructive process (Noller et al., 1994)
Disagreements (Gottman & Krokoff, 1989)
Disclosure (Flora & Segrin, 1998; Huston & Vangelisti, 1991; Noller & Feeney, 1998;
    Veroff et al., 1993)
Disengagement (Noller et al., 1994)
Distributive conflict management (Canary & Cupach, 1988; Canary & Spitzberg, 1987, 1989;
    Johnson & Bradbury, 1999; Noller & Feeney, 1998; Veroff et al., 1993)
Dominance (Huston & Vangelisti, 1991; Thomsen & Gilbert, 1998)
Empathic concern (Davis & Oathout, 1987; Sanford, 1998)
Expressiveness/expressivity (Kurdek, 1998)
Feedback—expressing understanding (Basco et al., 1991)
Humor (Cohan & Bradbury, 1997)
Integrative conflict management (Canary & Cupach, 1988; Canary & Spitzberg, 1987, 1989)
Integrative jealousy expression (Andersen, Eloy, Guerrero, & Spitzberg, 1995)
Interest (Gottman & Levenson, 1999a, 1999b)
Laughter (Huston & Vangelisti, 1991; Royce & Weiss, 1975)
Mutuality of affective expression (Basco et al., 1991; Heavey et al., 1996)

Table 15.1 (continued)

Mutuality of attribution (Basco et al., 1991)
Mutuality of blame (Heavey et al., 1996)
Mutuality of discussion (Heavey, Larson, Zumtobel, & Christensen, 1996)
Mutuality of negotiation-solutions (Basco et al., 1991; Heavey et al., 1996)
Mutuality of threat (Heavey et al., 1996)
Negative affective behavior (Caughlin, Huston, & Houts, 2000; Gill, Christensen, & Fincham, 1999; Hooley & Hahlweg, 1989; Kurdek, 1998; Levenson, Cartensen, & Gottman, 1994; Noller & Feeney, 1998; Noller et al., 1994; Noller & Gallois, 1988; Wills, Weiss, & Patterson, 1974)

    Anger/disgust/contempt/hostility (Gottman & Krokoff, 1989; Gottman & Levenson, 1999b; Huston & Vangelisti, 1991; Krokoff, 1991; Mathews, Wickrama, & Conger, 1996)
    Negative affect escalation/reciprocity (Julien et al., 1989; Levenson et al., 1994; Markman & Hahlweg, 1993)
    Negative mood (Thomsen & Gilbert, 1998)
    Negative verbal (Hooley & Hahlweg, 1989)
    Physical aggression (Basco et al., 1991; Bookwala, Frieze, & Grote, 1994)
    Verbal aggression (Basco et al., 1991; Heavey et al., 1996; Venable & Martin, 1997)

Nonverbal decoding accuracy (Noller & Feeney, 1998; Noller & Gallois, 1988)
Perceptual accuracy (Burleson & Denton, 1992)

    Nonverbal accuracy (Gottman & Porterfield, 1981; Kahn, 1970)
    Physical affection (Huston & Vangelisti, 1991)

Physiological arousal (Thomsen & Gilbert, 1998)
Physiological interdependence (Thomsen & Gilbert, 1998)
Positive affective behavior (Gill et al., 1999; Hooley & Hahlweg, 1989; Julien et al., 1989; Levenson et al., 1994; Noller et al., 1994; Tolstedt & Stokes, 1983)

    Nonverbal positive expression (Basco et al., 1991)
    Verbal expression of affection (Tolstedt & Stokes, 1983)
    Warmth (Davis & Oathout, 1987; Matthews et al., 1996)

Positive physical behavior (Royce & Weiss, 1975)
Possessiveness (Davis & Oathout, 1987)
Power base/tactic (Richmond, McCroskey, & Roach, 1997)
Problem-solving facilitation/inhibition (Haefner, Notarius, & Pellegrini, 1991)
Respect/recognition (Boyd & Roach, 1977; Noller & Feeney, 1998)
Sexual interaction (Veroff et al., 1998)
Solution closure (Basco et al., 1991)
Stubbornness (Gottman & Krokoff, 1989)
Support provision (Flora & Segrin, 1998; Julien et al., 1989; Kurdek, 1998; Pasch & Bradbury, 1998; Veroff et al., 1998)
Support solicitation (Pasch & Bradbury, 1998)
Topic maintenance—avoiding digression (Basco et al., 1991)
Understanding (lack of) (Noller & Gallois, 1988; Veroff et al., 1998)
Validation (Haefner et al., 1991)
Withdrawal/disengagement (Bodenmann et al., 1998; Gottman & Krokoff, 1989; Markman & Hahlweg, 1993; Noller & Feeney, 1998)

NOTE: Most of the relationships among these skills were moderated in their relationship to satisfaction or duration of marriage by various factors. Moderating factors include which spouse performed the skill, whether the dependent variable was assessed at Time 1 or later time, whether the skill was predicting self or partner outcomes, and whether the skill was self-reported or observed directly. Interested readers are referred to the specific studies cited to identify specific relationships. Also, a few of the works cited here are reviews or meta-analyses of research rather than original studies. This list can be compared to the summaries provided by Basco et al. (1991), Boland and Follingstad (1987), and Gottman (1994).

*Human Relationships and Interpersonal
Skills Are Vital to Personal Well-Being*

Attachment theory has long placed considerable emphasis on the importance of bonding (e.g., Ainsworth, Blehar, Waters, & Wall,
1978; Bowlby, 1969, 1973, 1980). Most
theories of human motivation have also
posited interpersonal (Maslow, 1968), love
(Freedman, Leary, Ossorio, & Coffey, 1951;
Leary & Coffey, 1955), approach (Horney,
1945), belonging (Baumeister & Leary, 1995;
Schutz, 1966), and connection (Baxter &
Montgomery, 1996) or analogous intimacy
(McAdams, 1988) drives. Feeling "competent"
appears to be an important ingredient of daily
well-being (Sheldon, Ryan, & Reis, 1996).
It follows that to the extent relationships
are neither established nor sustained, or managed incompetently, well-being will suffer.
The extent to which well-being depends on
relational contact has been the subject of
several lines of investigation, a few of which
we examine next.

Risk behavior. People deficient in their interpersonal skills over time may experience a
pattern of disturbed relationships that distort
normal feedback processes, diminish self-
esteem, and create pathways to deviant and
risky behavior. Although the research has not
been very direct or extensive, there is evidence
that deficits of social skills are related to
various risk-oriented behavior patterns, such
as smoking, alcohol abuse, drug use (Anda
et al., 1999; Herrmann & McWhirter, 1997;
Wilsnack, Wilsnack, Kristjanson, & Harris,
1998), risky sexual activity (e.g., Anderson,
Reis, & Stephens, 1997; Nangle & Hansen,
1993; Reis, Wheeler, Kernis, Spiegel, &
Nezlek, 1985; Vanwesenbeeck, van Zessen,
Ingham, Jaramazovic, & Stevens, 1999;
Wilsnack, Wilsnack, Kristjanson, & Harris,
1998), delinquency and criminal activity (e.g.,
Bullis, Walker, & Stieber, 1998; Palmer &
Hollin, 1999; Parker & Asher, 1987; Swanson

et al., 1998; compare Renwick & Emler, 1991),
and intimate partner violence (Babcock,
Waltz, Jacobson, & Gottman, 1993; Infante,
Chandler, & Rudd, 1989; Roberts & Noller,
1998; Sabourin, Infante, & Rudd, 1993).

Health. The precise mechanisms by which the
social body affects the physical body are still
very much the source of speculation. What
is no longer considered particularly speculative
is the proposition that the two are integrally
related. Several lines of research have demonstrated some of these links (for a review, see
Bowling & Grundy, 1998). Specific traumatic
childhood relational experiences affect adult
health. Felitti et al. (1998) and Anda et al.
(1999) had more than 9,000 HMO patients
report on several childhood experiences,
including psychological (e.g., parent insulted
child), physical (e.g., parent pushed or hit
child), and sexual (e.g., parent sexually
touched child) abuse, interparental violence
(e.g., mother was hit), as well as some less
interactional factors (i.e., parental substance
abuse, mental illness, familial criminal behavior). Generally, odds ratios indicated that the
more these events were reported, the more
likely the adults were to smoke, be severely
obese, have experienced 2 or more weeks of
depression in the past year, attempted suicide,
report alcoholism, inject drugs, have had
a sexually transmitted disease, display ischemic
heart disease, be diagnosed with cancer,
experience a stroke, or report bronchitis or
emphysema. Interpersonal types of trauma in
childhood appear to have potentially devastat-
ing impacts on health in adulthood.

Research reviewed by Argyle (1986, 1991)
also demonstrates the health benefits afforded
by marital relationships. Compared with
married persons, single, widowed, and separated/
divorced persons tend to display greater odds
ratios of having been a psychiatric outpatient
or inpatient, having been imprisoned, having
committed suicide, or having died from any
cause. Similar results have been reported for

accidents and assaults (Cheung, 1998). It is important to note, however, that evidence shows that it is not just the existence of relational status but also the quality of the relationship that reveals significant health effects (Ren, 1997; see also McCabe, Cummins, & Romeo, 1996; Reis et al., 1985; Reis & Franks, 1994; compare Dalgard & Lund Håheim, 1998). Thus couples who are unhappy in their relationships, occasionally uncooperative, or sometimes violent during disagreements tend to report poorer health. Indeed, research indicates that relatively specific interaction skills, such as affect regulation, affective expressiveness, and avoiding defensiveness and withdrawal, may be associated with both marital stability and health (Gottman & Levenson, 1992). The health benefits of marriage may be moderated and complex, but they nevertheless appear to be resilient and real (Burman & Margolin, 1992).

If primary relationships such as marriage and childhood relations with parents demonstrate material effects on health, the more extended web of familial, social, organizational, and community relationships may also provide important benefits. The findings of several large-scale epidemiological studies bear this out (Bosworth & Schaie, 1997; Bowling & Grundy, 1998; Dalgard & Lund Håheim, 1998; Ford, Ahluwalia, & Galuska, 2000; Glass, de Leon, Marottoli, & Berkman, 1999; House, Landis, & Umberson, 1988; Su & Ferraro, 1997).

The mechanisms by which relationships benefit health are not well understood. Aside from being tangible sources of support, relational partners may provide beneficial models and may act as tangible facilitators of healthier behavior practices (Broman, 1993; Ford et al., 2000; Lewis & Rook, 1999) and recovery (de Leon et al., 1999; Regehr & Marziali, 1999). Socially skilled persons may be better able to mobilize support and facilitate healthier practices in themselves and others (Lewis & Rook, 1999). Research is also beginning to isolate specific stress-linked (Herzberg

et al., 1998) hormonal and physiological effects of communication and supportive relationships (Davis & Swan, 1999; Petrie, Booth, & Davison, 1995; Schwartz & Kline, 1995; Seeman, Berkman, Blazer, & Rowe, 1994; Straits-Tröster et al., 1994). Analogous studies are isolating the physiological influences of negative interaction patterns in marriages (e.g., Ewart, Taylor, Kraemer & Agras, 1991; Gottman & Levenson, 1999a, 1999b; Miller, Dopp, Myers, Stevens, & Fahey, 1999; Thomsen & Gilbert, 1998). These latter findings serve as an important reminder that it is rarely just the existence of relationships that determines the nature of the health benefit; the relationships' interactional quality is a crucial factor (Burg & Seeman, 1994; McCabe et al., 1996; Miller, Kemeny, Taylor, Cole, & Visscher, 1997; Rook, 1984, 1992, 1998).

Achievement. People with better communication skills may employ those skills to negotiate their education and subsequent career objectives. Research suggests that social skills and competence are positively related to indicators of educational achievement (Agostin & Bain, 1997; Burleson & Samter, 1992; Cairns, Leung, Gest, & Cairns, 1995; Rosenfeld, Grant, & McCroskey, 1995; Rubin & Graham, 1988; Rubin, Graham, & Mignerey, 1990; compare Landsheer, Maassen, Bisschop, & Adema, 1998). Once out of school, better communicators probably do better in employment interviews (Peterson, 1997; Waldron & Lavitt, 2000; compare Spano & Zimmerman, 1995) and are more likely to master their relational connections to achieve status and career success (Alexander, Penley, & Jernigan, 1992; Bahniuk, Kogler Hill, & Darus, 1996; Dobos, Bahniuk, & Kogler Hill, 1991; Kolb, 1996; Papa & Graham, 1991; Penley, Alexander, Jernigan, & Henwood, 1991; Shockley-Zalabak, Staley, & Morley, 1988; Sypher & Zorn, 1986). The finding that homeless people often attribute their homelessness to breakdowns in social ties (Muñoz, Vazquez,

Bermejo, & Vazquez, 1999) is suggestive that unemployment may also be related to interpersonal skills. It is not surprising, therefore, that communication competencies are viewed as among the most central and vital qualifications and needs of the workforce (Curtis, Winsor, & Stephens, 1989; Daly, 1994; DiSalvo, 1980; DiSalvo, Larsen, & Seiler, 1976; Glaser & Eblen, 1986; Hawkins & Fillion, 1999; Muchmore & Galvin, 1983; O'Neil, Allred, & Baker, 1997).

Psychological well-being. In 1981, Michael Argyle, one of the pioneers of social skills models, reviewed the relatively meager evidence to claim a link between social skills deficits and the development and maintenance of childhood disturbance, schizophrenia, depression, neurosis, and alcoholism. In the years since, research has excavated these and other links and is continuing to uncover ever greater complexity among them.

Interpersonal skills are the means through which individuals negotiate everyday social interactions. If a person's interpersonal skills are deficient, then his or her social relations are likely to be less effective and more negatively reinforcing. Such outcomes extended over a long period of time are likely to lower the person's self-esteem significantly (Franks & Marolla, 1976; Richmond, McCroskey, & McCroskey, 1989) and diminish his or her popularity and social status with peers (Burleson, 1986; Burleson, Delia, & Applegate, 1992; Newcomb, Bukowski, & Pattee, 1993); potentially, they may lead to mental illness (Procidano, 1992). Furthermore, if a family sustains distorted and deviant forms of interaction, the children of that family are likely to develop similarly distorted social skills, which also present risk factors for adult mental disorder (Argyle, 1981; Trower, Bryant, & Argyle, 1978). Not surprisingly, researchers have consistently identified correlations between various forms of mental disturbance and deficient social skills (e.g., Carpenter, 1987; Casey,

Tyrer, & Platt, 1985). Thus there are many interpersonal communication paths to mental health and illness.

Evidence is beginning to indicate very strong influences of family-of-origin communication dynamics and later adolescent and adult health. Children of parents who are depressed or schizophrenic, or who display deviant and negative patterns of communication with their children, tend to have a significantly increased risk of developing social incompetence, schizophrenia, and other mental disorders (Lewine, 1984; Wichstrøm, Anderson, Holte, & Wynne, 1996; Wynne, 1984). Many studies have found that measures of social "competence prove to be the most powerful predictors of course and outcome for adult schizophrenics" (Weintraub & Neale, 1984, p. 279). Such patterns of findings have led some to theorize that social skills are the primary means through which mental adjustment and health are achieved and maintained (Brokaw & McLemore, 1991). Longitudinal studies have also revealed that the amount and quality of social relationships are related to mental health. In one study, minimal angry behavior, satisfactory peer social adjustment, and having a mentor relationship at time one predicted over a quarter of the variance in overall mental health more than 30 years later (Westermeyer, 1998).

If interpersonal skills are vital to the initiation and maintenance of relationships, then it seems an axiomatic extension that these skills should be related to syndromes such as social anxiety, loneliness, and depression. Although there has been no shortage of researchers who have drawn such links (e.g., Gable & Shean, 2000; Garland & Fitzgerald, 1998; Shaver, Furman, & Buhrmester, 1985; Spitzberg & Canary, 1985), others have been far more circumspect and ambivalent in their conclusions (e.g., Flora & Segrin, 1998; Segrin, 1996, 1999; Shean & Heefner, 1995; Vandeputte et al., 1999). Generally, the more carefully researchers specify interpersonal skills, the more qualified their findings become. Thus it appears that there are causal connections between certain social skills deficits and depression, but they tend to be small in magnitude (e.g., Segrin, 1992; for reviews, see Segrin, 1998, 1999). Social skills may also play a fairly specific role in mediating interactant vulnerability to psychosocial problems (e.g., Segrin & Flora, 2000). In contrast, when the construct of psychological well-being is viewed generally, the available evidence indicates that interpersonal skills are likely very facilitative of psychological quality of life. For example, Reis, Sheldon, Gable, Roscoe, and Ryan (2000) found that daily well-being is best predicted by "meaningful talk and feeling understood and appreciated by interaction partners" (p. 419).

In summary, the vast majority of available research, across several disciplines, methodologies, and theoretical perspectives, evidences support for the conclusion that interpersonal skills facilitate well-being. Interpersonal skills are probably a necessary but not sufficient factor in this relationship. Being "interpersonal," any given person's skills are contingent in part upon the skills of those with whom he or she interacts. Thus, ceteris paribus, the more interpersonally skilled people are, the better their quality of life.

THE PREVALENCE
OF (IN)COMPETENCE

Given the conclusion that interpersonal skills are vital to the collective state of social and personal health, the natural question arises as to the extent to which people in general are competent in their everyday lives. Surprisingly little research has addressed this question directly. As a baseline of comparison, Bassett, Whittington, and Staton-Spicer (1978) found that approximately a third of the U.S. adult population was "functionally incompetent" in the basic skills of math, reading, and problem solving (see also Ilott, 2001). Compared to this, research across a variety of approaches to

operationalizing competence suggests that about 7-25% of the adult population is interpersonally incompetent (Bryant & Trower, 1974; Bryant, Trower, Yardley, Urbieta, & Letemendia, 1976; Curran, Miller, Zwick, Monti, & Stout, 1980; Hecht & Wittchen, 1988; Vangelisti & Daly, 1989). When further broken down into specific communication competencies, the prevalence of incompetence can be estimated to be substantially higher. In a study of college students presented with a set of 19 communication tasks, "22% of the students tested had problems asking a question; 33% could not give accurate directions; 35% could not adequately express and defend a point of view; . . . and 49% could not describe the point of view of a person who disagreed with them" (Rubin, 1981, p. 30). Thus the available evidence indicates that there is substantial need for better interpersonal skills among a significant proportion of the populace. Presumably, the rest of the population has room for meaningful improvement as well. Although there is evidence that good communication experiences outnumber bad communication experiences in everyday life (e.g., Drury, Catan, Dennison, & Brody, 1998; Duck, Rutt, Hurst, & Strejc, 1991), the less frequent negative communication encounters may have a disproportionate influence on well-being (Rook, 1984).

THE NATURE OF
INTERPERSONAL SKILLS

Digesting the available scholarship regarding interpersonal skills is challenging, and sometimes frustrating. The relevant literature is vast, and several overlapping terms are employed, including *social skill, interpersonal skill, social competence, interpersonal competence,* and *communicative competence.* As Hargie (1997) indicates, "Quite often researchers and theorists in this area have been working in differing contexts, with little cross-fertilisation between those involved in clinical,

professional and developmental settings"
(p. 10). As a consequence, numerous conceptualizations have been offered and terminology is inconsistent across authors. Different
authors use different terms to refer to roughly
the same phenomena, and authors using the
same terms often define them in very different
ways. Thus what one author calls *skill* another
might label *competence,* and vice versa.
Some argue that skill subsumes competence,
whereas others maintain that competence subsumes skill (Hargie, 1997). So it is not surprising that several authors have noted the lack
of consensus in skills/competence terminology (e.g., Bedell & Lennox, 1997; Conger &
Conger, 1982; Ford, 1985; E. L. Phillips,
1978; G. M. Phillips, 1984; Spitzberg &
Cupach, 1989). Rather than review a plethora
of overlapping and unique conceptualizations
of skills, we offer a set of definitions and distinctions that derive from our own model of
interpersonal competence (Spitzberg, 2000;
Spitzberg & Cupach, 1984). In the present discussion, we consider *social skills* to be synonymous with *interpersonal skills.*

Situating Interpersonal Skills:
A Model of Interpersonal Competence

Interpersonal skills are usefully situated
within a broader conceptualization of interpersonal competence. Specifically, an individual's
interpersonal skills, along with his or her
knowledge and motivation, enable the occurrence of certain outcomes that are judged
interpersonally competent in a particular interactional context. We define interpersonal skills
as repeatable goal-directed behaviors, behavioral patterns, and behavior sequences that
are appropriate to the interactional context
(Spitzberg, in press). Thus the domain of skills
is circumscribed to observable performance
(Bellack & Hersen, 1978; Curran, 1979),
although not all behaviors would be considered
skills. "Skilled behavior is therefore more complex than instinctive or reflexive movements"

(Hargie, 1997, p. 8). Because skilled behavior is
performed in the service of desired outcomes, it
is repeatable and intentional, not coincidental.

Interpersonal skills are performed at several
levels of abstraction. Similar to goals, skills are
organized hierarchically, with simpler, more
microscopic behaviors (e.g., smiling, nodding
the head) combining to form more abstract
behaviors (e.g., showing interest). Skills are
therefore structurally and temporally coordinated in complex ways.

Although interpersonal skills per se can be
viewed "as behavioral pathways or avenues to
an individual's goals" (Kelly, 1982, p. 3), they
are tied to, and distinguishable from, the
underlying cognitive and affective processes
that enable and generate them. This is akin to
Trower's (1980, 1982, 1984) distinction
between *social skills* and *social skill.* He proposes that *social skills* "are the actual normative component behaviors or actions," whereas
social skill "refers to the process of generating
skilled behavior" (Trower, 1982, p. 418).
These generative mechanisms include knowledge and motivation.

Two distinct types of knowledge appear in
the literature: content and procedural. *Content
knowledge* (i.e., knowing what) includes pos-
sessing information about relational partners,
conversational topics (Roloff & Kellermann,
1984), social contexts (Forgas, 1983b), the
rules of language (Chomsky, 1965), and the
rules of conversation (McLaughlin, 1984).
Competent communicators generally possess
more elaborate and discriminating representations of interaction episodes (Forgas, 1983b;
Hazleton, Cupach, & Canary, 1987).

Procedural knowledge (i.e., knowing how
to) includes processes such as formulating and
prioritizing goals (e.g., Bochner & Kelly, 1974),
solving problems (e.g., Shure, 1981; Spivack,
Platt, & Shure, 1976), explaining and predicting others' behavior (Hazleton & Cupach,
1986), and selecting, coordinating, and imple-
menting relevant skills. Greene's (1984, 1997)
action assembly theory, for example, explains

how performance deficits can be attributable to *functional properties of the cognitive system*. According to action assembly theory, the *procedural record*, a long-term memory structure acquired through social experience, contains symbolic representations of key elements of social interaction. Specifically, procedural records consist of nodes and associative pathways that represent contingencies among actions, outcomes, and salient features of social situations. "The task facing the communicator, then, is the integration of these various procedural records and activated knowledge from the conceptual store to form a coherent output representation of action to be taken" (Greene, 1984, p. 293). Unskilled performance can occur when a person fails to retrieve from memory the appropriate elements of procedural records, or when cognitive effort is diverted from "assembly of components of the output representation where it is needed" (Greene & Geddes, 1993, p. 40). In this way, performance deficits can be explained by glitches in cognitive processing.

Motivation is the affective force that energizes performance and guides a person's approach-avoidance orientation to a social situation. Possession of both knowledge and motivation enhances the likelihood of skilled performance, but does not ensure it. By analogy, a stage actor may be thoroughly familiar with the script, very knowledgeable about acting techniques, and highly motivated to do well, yet give a weak performance.

Interpersonal skills, along with knowledge and motivation, facilitate interpersonal competence. We define *interpersonal competence* as the evaluative impression of the quality of interaction (Spitzberg & Cupach, 1984). Thus competence is inferred, in large part, based on the observation of skills. In this sense, the judgment that an individual has given a "skilled performance" is tantamount to perceiving his or her behavior as interpersonally competent. When the possession of knowledge and motivation leads to the performance of appropriate skills, the likelihood of the individual's being seen as competent is enhanced. However, the performance of appropriate skills cannot guarantee that an actor will be seen as interpersonally competent. Characteristics of the observer, whether the actor is observing his or her own behavior or another person is observing the actor, and the criteria employed by the observer also influence judgments of competence. Below, we consider the criteria that individuals employ when making competence judgments. Later in the chapter we illustrate that such criteria are inherently tied to contextual dimensions that frame interaction.

Criteria of Interpersonal Skills

As suggested by the synoptic review above, interpersonal skills have been conceptualized in many different ways. One era seeks sincerity, whereas another seeks politeness. One era seeks conciseness, whereas another seeks elaborateness. These historical shifts reflect in part changes in the criteria by which the quality of behavior is evaluated (Spitzberg, 1994b). Skills are ultimately always evaluated in terms of some criterion or set of criteria (Spitzberg, 2000). A person may be skilled at making loud, high-pitched whistling noises by expelling air through the nose, but this skill is unlikely to be viewed as an interpersonal skill because its relation to higher criteria of competence and quality is unclear. Therefore, an examination of the criteria of competence in interpersonal interaction is in order. At least six criteria of quality interaction have been articulated in connection with interpersonal relations: fidelity, satisfaction, efficiency, effectiveness, appropriateness, and ethics.

Fidelity Criteria

A layperson's definition of competent communication is likely to refer to clear communication, or communication in which a person's meanings are clearly understood (McCroskey, 1982; Powers & Lowry, 1984). Communication is widely presumed to be a means of making one's intentions and meanings apparent to an audience (Grimshaw, 1980), and therefore a conduit metaphor of communication is implied (Axley, 1984; Reddy, 1979). Accuracy reflects the extent to which the meaning or information in one person's mind (i.e., location) is replicated in another person's mind (i.e., location). The extent to which meaning is incomplete, biased, or distorted represents error in the signal transfer and thus interference, inability, intentional misrepresentation, or some combination of these influences.

Many approaches to the study of competent communication—and, indeed, entire perspectives on communication—have stressed one or another version of these fidelity and veracity criteria (e.g., Cahn, 1990; Coupland, Wiemann, & Giles, 1991; Davis, 1999; Makau, 1991; Mieth, 1997; Mortensen, 1997; Powers & Lowry, 1984; Taylor, 1986; Wood, 1998). The underlying assumptions of these approaches provide indirect rationales for many of the constructs closely associated with competence, such as empathy, perspective taking, interpersonal sensitivity, and cognitive complexity (Zebrowitz, 2001). That is, constructs thought to facilitate adaptation of messages to the receiver, and to facilitate perception and interpretation of the partner, are likely to enhance fidelity, veracity, and co-orientation as well.

In order to be clear, the criteria associated with accuracy and understanding require some elucidation. The term *clarity*, or *fidelity*, is generally used to describe message characteristics, somewhat independent of receiver perceptions. A message is clear to the extent that it represents the information it is intended to represent or information available in a referent. As an example, in Rubin's (1985) measure of competence, one of the items prompts the student subject to give directions to a location on that person's campus. The directions

are then, in essence, coded to determine the extent to which they would actually get a person to that location. So there is an explicit assumption that there is an objective foundation of information relevant to the message, and competence is demonstrated by the message's representation of that information in a relatively error-free manner. Clarity also tends to imply aspects of Grice's (1989; see also Cappella, 1995; Wilson & Sperber, 1981) maxims, that messages should not only represent the information, but do so in a concise, efficient manner. That is, clear communication avoids unnecessary information. The assumption is that all communication involves certain promissory and consensual features, and therefore competence consists of using communication in a way that does justice and minimal damage to these features (Makau, 1991; Mieth, 1997).

Co-orientation, or understanding, is the extent to which Coactor comprehends the intended meaning(s) of Actor's message. Understanding has been operationalized in numerous ways, including as perceived understanding (i.e., Actor's perception of Coactor's and Actor's correspondence in meanings) and as actual understanding (i.e., Coactor's actual correspondence of meaning with Actor). These types of understanding can further be taken to "meta" levels, such as Actor's perception of Coactor's perception of Actor's meanings (see Allen & Thompson, 1984; Ickes, 1997; Kenny, 1994; Laing, Phillipson, & Lee, 1966).

Finally, accuracy and co-orientation need to be distinguished from agreement (Mortensen, 1997). Agreement is the extent to which Actor and Coactor possess similar attitudes or beliefs, independent of the source of those correspondences. Two people may simply hold similar beliefs even though they may never have communicated, or may have simply discovered (versus achieved) their agreement through communication. To the extent that agreement is achieved through communication, it becomes more of an effectiveness criterion

Table 15.2 Possible Combinations of Clarity, Agreement, and Understanding as Criteria of Competence

Clear/agreement/understanding: For example, Actor accurately encodes personal attitude and belief about the death penalty; Coactor shares this belief and comprehends meanings intended by Actor.

Clear/disagreement/understanding: For example, Actor accurately encodes personal attitude and belief about the death penalty; Coactor holds an oppositely valenced attitude based on beliefs divergent from Actor's but nonetheless comprehends meanings intended by Actor.

Clear/agreement/misunderstanding: For example, Actor accurately encodes personal attitude and belief about the death penalty; Coactor shares this belief, but misapprehends Actor's intended meanings.

Clear/disagreement/misunderstanding: For example, Actor accurately encodes personal attitude and belief about the death penalty; Coactor holds an oppositely valenced attitude based on beliefs divergent from Actor's and misapprehends Actor's intended meanings.

Unclear/agreement/understanding: For example, Actor inaccurately encodes personal attitude and belief about the death penalty, but Coactor shares same "underlying" belief as Actor and comprehends meanings intended by Actor despite the unclear encoding.

Unclear/disagreement/understanding: For example, Actor inaccurately encodes personal attitude and belief about the death penalty; Coactor holds an oppositely valenced attitude based on beliefs divergent from Actor's and comprehends meanings intended by Actor despite the unclear encoding.

Unclear/agreement/misunderstanding: For example, Actor inaccurately encodes personal attitude and belief about the death penalty; Coactor shares same "underlying" belief as Actor but misapprehends meanings intended by Actor because of the unclear encoding.

Unclear/disagreement/misunderstanding: For example, Actor inaccurately encodes personal attitude and belief about the death penalty; Coactor holds an oppositely valenced attitude based on beliefs divergent from Actor's but misapprehends meanings intended by Actor because of the unclear encoding.

than a meaning-based criterion, given that some form of persuasion is implied. Theoretically, all possible combinations exist among agreement/ disagreement, accurate/inaccurate, and under-stood/misunderstood (see Table 15.2).

Despite the intuitive cachet of fidelity, veracity, and co-orientation criteria, there are several problems with predicating inter-personal competence on their accomplishment (Spitzberg, 1993, 1994a, 1994b). First, the conduit metaphor reifies meaning as an objec-tifiable and static entity that has some implicit or explicit one-to-one correspondence with reality or an operational representation of that reality. Thus, for an individual to be clear in communicating a belief about the death penalty, it must be assumed that there is a

belief and that this belief has distinct charac-teristics that can be identified and objectively mapped by verbal and nonverbal behavior (see Wittgenstein, 1958, 1963). Understanding thereby presupposes that this mapping can be "back-translated" in the mind of the receiver. Such conduit metaphors vastly oversimplify the nature of cognitive processing as well as sym-bolic subtlety and complexity. Furthermore, such approaches tend to presuppose that people are aware of their intentions as well as able to articulate their intentions. These are clearly problematic suppositions (e.g., Levinson, 1995; Nisbett & Ross, 1980).

Second, the clarity criterion runs afoul of such useful and common forms of commu-nication as idiomatic messages (e.g., Bell,

Buerkel-Rothfuss, & Gore, 1987; Bell & Healey, 1992; Bruess & Pearson, 1993; Hopper, Knapp, & Scott, 1981); humor (e.g., Graham, Papa, & Brooks, 1992); teasing (Alberts, Kellar-Guenther, & Corman, 1996; Kowalski, 2000); equivocation, ambivalence, and ambiguity (e.g., Chovil, 1994; Eisenberg, 1984); paradox (Wilder & Collins, 1994); and the ineffable (Branham, 1980). Even forms of communication such as poetry, metaphor, and socioemotional interaction (e.g., small talk) seem ill represented by a clarity criterion.

Third, the understanding criterion shows mixed empirical support. Although many studies have revealed mutual understanding to be positively associated with relational satisfaction (see Allen & Thompson, 1984; Boland & Follingstad, 1987), some findings suggest that mutual understanding is either unrelated or negatively related to relational adjustment (e.g., Garland, 1981; Tucker & Anders, 1999). Certainly, understanding seems to play a complex role in the management of relationships (Burggraf & Pavitt, 1991; Noller & Gallois, 1988; Sanford, 1998; Sillars, 1998; Sillars, Pike, Jones, & Murphy, 1984; Sillars, Weisberg, Burggraf, & Zietlow, 1990; Simpson, Ickes, & Blackstone, 1995; Tucker & Anders, 1999), as it may reveal all the finer-grained points of difference between any two individuals, which then may engender both a sense of psychological distance and interactional conflict.

Fourth, ideologically such criteria seem to marginalize deception as an intrinsically incompetent form of communication. Yet deception is a common form of interpersonal communication (DePaulo, Kashy, Kirkendol, Wyer, & Epstein, 1996; O'Hair & Cody, 1994; Reiss, Anderson, & Sponaugle, 1980; Rodriguez & Ryave, 1990); it is often intended to benefit the person being deceived (Camden, Motley, & Wilson, 1984; Lippard, 1988; Metts, 1989) and may even fulfill a variety of positive relational functions (Hunt & Manning, 1991; LaFollette & Graham, 1986; Rodriguez & Ryave, 1990; Tooke & Camire, 1991). For example, much of politeness behavior, which is widely considered a universal pragmatic (Brown & Levinson, 1987), relies on deception as its modus operandi. Politeness is a key aspect of appropriate, and therefore competent, interaction, even though it trades on the social capital of equivocation and deception for its competence. Conversely, savage, mean-spirited, and even evil communication can be frighteningly clear and well understood, even though intuitively most interactants would be hesitant to consider such behavior competent.

In summary, although interpersonal skills are commonly associated with standards of clarity of expression and extent of understanding, these standards are inherently problematic as theoretical and pragmatic criteria. They are ideologically biased against some of the more appropriate and commonly used forms of communication. These criteria also oversimplify the nature of meaning and the process by which meanings are communicated. One of the implications of these limitations is that interpersonal skills should be conceptualized as including certain counterintuitive abilities, such as ambivalence, equivocation, and deception (Spitzberg & Cupach, 1998).

Satisfaction Criteria

Most people prefer communication that "feels good." Satisfaction is the extent to which a communication encounter produces or is associated with a psychological sense of positively valenced feeling(s). Hecht (1978) defines communication satisfaction more specifically, as the affective reaction to the extent of fulfillment of positively valenced interactional expectations. A communicator develops expectations regarding a given type of interpersonal encounter. Most of these expectations will have valences attached to them. To the extent that an encounter fulfills the communicator's positively valenced expectations, it will be satisfying. Furthermore, satisfaction sometimes arises from a person's doing the best he or she can under the circumstances, or through violation of negatively valenced expectations (Spitzberg & Brunner, 1991). Thus a college student may go on an information interview hoping to get a job offer, but end up satisfied with simply making a good impression. A married couple may dislike conflict, but they may be satisfied when a conflict is not nearly as bad as expected. Several researchers have employed satisfaction as a criterion of competent interaction (for a review, see Spitzberg & Cupach, 1984).

Satisfaction is also an intuitive criterion of interpersonal skill. It too, however, is a flawed criterion. First, satisfaction is a solipsist criterion. A person who enjoys being mean-spirited, evil, and savage in his or her communication can be defined as competent under a satisfaction criterion. Conversely, if satisfaction is reserved for the receiver of communication, then perfectly clear and normatively appropriate behavior may not satisfy any given coactor. Some people are harder to satisfy than others, and some people may never be satisfied. For example, lonely and depressed interactants, compared with nonlonely and nondepressed interactants, tend to view all others as less competent (Segrin, 1998). Such a solipsist criterion therefore relegates interpersonal skills to the whim and subjectivity of the individual.

Second, it is unclear what role satisfaction plays in novel interactions that have no expectations, or in interactions that have little or no affective valence. Unexpected and unfamiliar encounters as well as routine or administrative communication encounters are examples of interactions in which satisfaction may simply be relatively irrelevant. Yet interpersonal skills are presumably involved in such encounters.

Third, sometimes the most important interactions may be encounters that have little or no potential to be satisfying. Relational breakups, conflicts, criticisms, and other such rejections may be critical incidents or turning points and, in the long run, perhaps even life altering, but they are seldom viewed as intrinsically satisfying.

Efficiency Criteria

Efficiency refers to the extent to which skills are used to achieve some outcome with a minimum of effort, time, complexity, and investment of resources. Generally, "when individuals succeed in their endeavors, the ease and speed with which they do so may be used as bases for judging their skill" (Berger, 2000, p. 160). Interpersonal skills are efficient if they accomplish their intended function in a parsimonious manner. If presented with an interpersonal objective (e.g., ask a person out on a date), an interactant may be able to envision several different behavioral approaches to achieve that objective. As a criterion of interpersonal skill, efficiency would require that these approaches be arrayed in terms of relative time, effort, difficulty, and likelihood of success. Efficiency has been employed as a criterion of competence in several studies (e.g., Kellerman & Shea, 1996; Kellermann, Reynolds, & Chen, 1991).

Given that communication is functional, efficiency has an intuitive appeal. If one has a choice between two paths to fulfilling a certain function, it is more competent to select the path that requires less effort relative to its chance of success. However, there are several problems with efficiency. First, because efficiency is inherently comparative (i.e., relative to alternatives forgone), it is empirically problematic. Because communication is irreversible, there is no reasonable empirical way to determine what the relative success would have been had other paths been taken rather than the one that was.

Second, efficiency permits highly objectionable behavior to be considered competent. For example, it may be far more efficient to tell people to "take a hike" or "get out of my face" when interaction is unwanted than to use other strategies, but it is hardly what most people would consider competent. Politeness phenomena often involve more elaborate performance codes. It may be argued that such objectionable behaviors are not efficient if they do not achieve their function, but if the function is to communicate rejection, this argument fails. If the function is to communicate rejection in an appropriate manner, then efficiency becomes confounded or redundant with other criteria of competence (which we discuss below).

Third, efficiency seems relatively orthogonal to some types of interaction. For example, small talk, play, storytelling, humor, and social support seem rather difficult to evaluate in terms of their efficiency, given that part of the function of such episodes is to allow an individual to invest in the function of bonding with another. The investment of resources such as time and effort is itself part of the measure of the value of the encounter. Ideologically, therefore, efficiency seems wedded not only to a conduit metaphor, but also to an almost mechanical or physicalist model of communication that "corresponds more closely with the demands of our current industrialized, technical social reality where instrumental rationality is equated with efficiency and success" (Lannamann, 1991, p. 189). Computers communicate efficiently, but do we want people to be reduced to such instrumentality?

Fourth, efficiency seems too much an extension of the mechanical or computer analogue of human behavior. These analogues have been common (Vroon, 1987), but they risk considerable reductionism (Marshall, 1977) and seem too dependent on concepts of error and time, and they prioritize minimization and planning over creativity and spontaneity. Perhaps communication ultimately is a process analogous to processes carried out by machines and computers, but such engineering metaphors suggest a rationality and design that may not characterize the more unanticipated features of the human communication condition.

Effectiveness Criteria

Effectiveness refers to the extent to which an interactant accomplishes preferred outcomes through communication (Spitzberg & Cupach, 1984). In many senses, therefore, effectiveness is inclusive of satisfaction and superordinate to efficiency. Presumably, when people achieve preferred outcomes, they are likely to be satisfied. Further, the attainment of a preferred outcome is likely to be more important to most people than the efficiency with which it is accomplished, at least as long as inefficiencies do not outweigh the value of the outcome itself. The term *preferred* fits better than *desirable* because of the pragmatics of avoidance-avoidance types of conflicts. Specifically, there may be instances in which communicators are faced with "no-win" contexts. In such cases, selection of the "least punishing" communication tactic(s) will be more effective, even though the outcomes may be undesirable (Spitzberg, 2000).

Effectiveness is one of the oldest and most firmly established criteria of competence. Classical rhetoric was primarily concerned with issues surrounding persuasion, in which effectiveness is the point of communication. All functional approaches to communication implicitly or explicitly rely on notions of effectiveness because they assume that communication varies in its efficacy in accomplishing certain functions. Indirectly, attributional approaches to communication also imply effectiveness criteria. We can often resolve causal questions such as "Why did she or he say or do that?" only by addressing the issue of what outcome the communicator was attempting to accomplish. In terms of interpersonal communication, most if not all of the compliance-gaining literature is concerned with issues of effectiveness and therefore, indirectly, with issues of competence. Finally, any approaches to communication that are based on plans (e.g., Berger, 1997), goals (e.g., Argyle, 1986; O'Keefe & McCornack, 1987;

Renshaw & Asher, 1982; Tracy & Moran, 1983; Waldron, Cegala, Sharkey, & Teboul, 1990), or communicator intentions implicitly or explicitly incorporate an effectiveness criterion of competence. A communicator's competence is determined by the extent to which his or her preferred goals, plans, or intentions are fulfilled.

Like the other criteria, effectiveness has substantial intuitive appeal. Nevertheless, it runs afoul of a couple of problems. First and foremost, effectiveness as a sole criterion of competence presents any number of ethical and normative difficulties. Preferred outcomes can be accomplished through the use of force, coercion, threat, manipulation, deception, exploitation, and the rest of the entire communicative arsenal of the darker side of interaction (e.g., Cupach & Spitzberg, 1994; Kowalski, 1997; Spitzberg & Cupach, 1998). Although these forms of communication may have their functional and even preferred aspects, normatively they are widely considered incompetent and unethical (see Makau, 1991; Mieth, 1997). It seems that there is less concern over a theory of competence based on effectiveness (e.g., Parks, 1995) than there is a philosophy of communication implicit in such a theory. What does it say about the human condition if a theory of competence predicated exclusively on effectiveness envisions the darker side of communication as competent and skilled?

The second difficulty with the effectiveness criterion revolves around issues of intentions and empiricism. Preferred outcomes can occur for reasons that have little or nothing to do with a communicator's performance (McCroskey, 1982; compare Spitzberg, 1983). Communicators may receive preferred outcomes due to luck, circumstance, or coincidence. Should they be considered competent or skilled merely because desirable things happen to them? Unless communicators apply communicative behavior to the intention of producing such preferred outcomes, competence should not be attributed to them. However, intentions are formidably difficult to operationalize. For example, communicators tend to be biased in their retroactive attributions of intention to self for positively valenced outcomes (Seibold & Spitzberg, 1981), and on-line or real-time intentions are often relatively inaccessible. Thus effectiveness may become a proxy for satisfaction rather than represent actual performance-based accomplishment.

Finally, effectiveness is also a solipsist criterion of competence. Only a given individual can know whether or not the outcomes that occurred were the preferred outcomes. The individual therefore is the sole *arbiter elegantiarum* of any given communicative performance. Therefore, there is no necessary normative point of reference in this criterion of competence, and as such, it permits competence to be disconnected from the larger societal context in which communication occurs.

Appropriateness Criteria

Appropriateness refers to the extent to which a communicative performance is judged legitimate within a given context (Spitzberg & Cupach, 1984). Appropriateness may be the most common theoretical criterion of competent communication (e.g., Larson, Backlund, Redmond, & Barbour, 1978). Given that competent communication is viewed as inherently contextual in nature, it follows that the standards of appropriateness for any given context must be taken into account in the evaluation of competence. Generally, it is therefore assumed that contexts "possess" such standards of appropriateness. Although appropriateness often is defined in terms of behavior's "conforming" to the "rules" of a context, the notion of its being legitimate seems better suited (Spitzberg, 2000). To conform is to abide by *existing* standards of appropriateness. This standard would therefore imply a highly conservative standard of competence in which norms of acceptable behavior would be strongly based in the status quo. Creativity, innovation, evolution, and revolution of communicative behavior would implicitly be discouraged as modes of competence in such a perspective. Instead, the most competent communicators may be those who are able to renegotiate the applicable rules of conduct in a given context (Pearce & Cronen, 1980). Thus competence is viewed as appropriate to the extent it is viewed as legitimate within the *extant* rules of a context, including those rules that may have been newly negotiated as applicable.

If effectiveness is problematic in part because of its solipsism, appropriateness is problematic because it is based too much in the judgments of others. In any given situation, a communicator may have to choose between satisfying his or her own objectives and satisfying those of the other(s) in the context. In such situations, there is little a priori basis for giving preference to the judgments of others (see Linell, 1998). The rule of mob, the distortions of peer influence, and the sometimes coercive nature of group pressures (e.g., Fishbein, 1996; Stafford & Dainton, 1994) all warn against the automatic evaluation of competence in strict terms of the other. Appropriateness "glorifies the collective while diminishing the importance of the individual" (Burgoon, 1995, p. 469). Furthermore, even though legitimacy in terms of extant rules may permit creativity, appropriateness as a criterion still seems spring-loaded to preserve the status quo. If so, then appropriateness as a sole criterion is biased by a conformist and traditionalist ideology.

Finally, appropriateness, as an other-oriented criterion, becomes problematic because there often is no identifiable "other." That is, communication is often performed to multiple audiences, and these different audiences may apply very different standards of appropriateness even within a given context. Therefore, there is no obvious calculus for determining who is the appropriate judge of appropriateness, or how to reconcile conflicting evaluations of appropriateness, in a given context.

Ethical Criteria

To a large extent, the criteria we have discussed to this point have focused on functional, or ends-oriented, approaches to identifying skilled communication. In contrast, there are more means-oriented approaches (Penman, 1992). Various approaches have taken a moralistic stance to delimiting ideal communication. Often influenced by Buber's philosophy of dialogue as well as the critical theories of Habermas and feminism, these approaches can be broadly described as dialogic. Dialogic approaches tend to define communication as competent to the extent that it fulfills various values of equal access, confirmation of other(s), and veracity. According to one author, dialogue requires (a) an "exchange of rational arguments among (more or less) equal persons," (b) "joint action that ties people together and creates the temporary world they experience," (c) interaction that is "appealing to all participants," and (d) "the expression of individual and constantly changing perspectives and individual or shared inspirations, enchantments, and desires" (Riikonen, 1999, p. 141).

Several variations of the dialogic approach appear in the scholarly literature. Space limitations prevent us from reviewing the work of specific authors, but interested readers should consult the works of Ayim (1997), Habermas (1970, 1981, 1987), Johannesen (1971), Kristiansen and Bloch-Poulsen (2000), Linell (1998), McNamee and Gergen (1999), Pearce and Littlejohn (1997), and Pearce and Pearce (2000). Clearly there is a core of common principles in these writings. They represent notions of equality, otherness, and freedom. Such notions seem to envision both a theoretical and a metatheoretical framework. In such a framework, "good communication theory and practice would be those that enrich our experience and increase our options and opportunities for actions. Bad communication, conversely, restricts or negates our experiences and options" (Penman, 1992, p. 241). Communication as dialogue envisions interpersonal skills as means that should abide by a moral code. This moral code, in turn, envisions a world in which ideal speech situations could empower all and provide respect and voice to each person regardless of station or stereotype. Thus, unlike the criteria of competence that indicate what good communication accomplishes (i.e., the ends), these moral criteria focus instead on what good communication *is* (i.e., the means). Of course, being part of critical approaches, moral criteria also tend to envision the world that would result from the enactment of such dialogic communication, and thus build a vision of the ends into the means themselves.

These ethical criteria for competent communication have not received as much attention in the interpersonal skills literature as the other criteria noted above. The ethical approaches that employ these criteria are unabashedly ideological, and this may be both their strength and the reason for the relative lack of attention they have received in the interpersonal skills literature. These approaches may purport a "political ideology" in which "the prototypical competent communicator is described as open, warm, caring, and so on" (Burgoon, 1995, pp. 477, 469; see also Katriel & Philipsen, 1981). In doing so, they may reflect a "feminization" of interpersonal skills (Parks, 1995, p. 488) that merely replaces old ideological dilemmas with new ones. For example, to the extent that collectivist concerns are privileged over individualist concerns, the individual voice may be diminished. To the extent that interpersonal skills are constrained through feminization, communicators are likewise constrained in their abilities to construct new and divergent identities that may or may not accord with existing notions of feminine voice. Thus the ideological objective of moral behavior may clash with the postmodern objective of celebrating self-determination (Burgoon, 1995; Parks, 1995; Spitzberg, 1993, 1994a, 1994b, 2000).

Summary

A person's mere production of a behavior is rarely considered a sufficient basis for claiming the person is "skilled." Skills are generally viewed as performances that are put to given socially valued purposes. Once such evaluative and normative considerations are applied, issues of the underlying criteria of such considerations become paramount. By what standards should skilled or competent communication behavior be evaluated? This deceptively complex question leads to answers that unravel more completely the more carefully they are examined.

The above discussion of criteria of competence in communication suggests that any single criterion is flawed. It is because of the limitations of singular standards of evaluation that most theorists have incorporated multiple or hybrid criteria. The most common hybrid is the claim that competent communication is both appropriate *and* effective (e.g., Spitzberg & Cupach, 1984). Such a hybrid argues that communication that accomplishes preferred objectives in a manner judged legitimate by others is likely to be satisfying and ethical as well. In any given context, a communicator obviously may give preference to one criterion over another, and thereby sacrifice a degree of optimal competence to the pragmatics of a given encounter. Such sacrifices are suggestive of the central role of context in discussions of competent and skilled interaction.

CONTEXTUAL DIMENSIONS OF INTERPERSONAL SKILLS

The contextual nature of interpersonal skills is axiomatic. That is, what is presumed to be skilled in one context is not necessarily presumed to be skilled in another. This axiom is reasonable, but also overly vague. It is not very useful to claim that interpersonal skills are contextual unless the notion of context can be systematically unpacked.

Context here is defined as a subjective interpretation of the frame within which interaction occurs (Goffman, 1974). The boundaries of this frame are interpreted through the matrix or intersection of five dimensions: culture, time, relationship, place, and function (Spitzberg, 2000). These dimensions combine in various ways to both limit and be limited by interaction.

Culture

Culture represents the intergenerational patterns of beliefs, values, and behaviors that are relatively consensual and transferable within the group. Although several pancultural dimensions have been identified (e.g., Hofstede, 1980, 2001; Spitzberg, 1989; Triandis, 1995), it is generally accepted that each culture will have its own instantiations of these dimensions as they apply to competent interaction. That is, all cultures may employ the same criteria of competence and dimensions for comprehending communication, but the specific behaviors that fulfill these criteria or "load" on those dimensions differ considerably across cultures. For example, research has consistently demonstrated that in reference to certain behaviors, different ethnic and national groups differ significantly in their evaluations of competence (Hecht, Collier, & Ribeau, 1993; Nicotera, 1997; Wyatt, 1999). Furthermore, various models of interpersonal competence have presupposed the contextual relevance of culture by identifying skills of cultural openness and adaptability as key competencies (e.g., Abe & Wiseman, 1983; Chen, 1989, 1992; Gudykunst & Hammer, 1984; Hammer, 1987; Martin & Hammer, 1989; Milhouse, 1993; Olebe & Koester, 1989; Ruben, 1976; Ruben & Kealey, 1979; Schneider & Jordan, 1981; Ward & Kennedy, 1999; Zimmerman, 1995).

Time

Time refers to several features of context that are relevant to competent interaction.

First among these is the stability of skills. Skill in interaction has variously been viewed as either a set of epiphenomenal states or a set of dispositional traits (e.g., Cupach & Spitzberg, 1983; Spitzberg, 1990, 1991, 1994c; Spitzberg & Brunner, 1991; for a review, see Spitzberg & Cupach, 1989). Whether skills are viewed as strictly situational or more dispositional depends on whether they are assumed to generalize across space and time. Thus time as a dimension of context concerns the stability of skills over time. The second feature involving time is the timing of skilled performance. In this sense, time is concerned with such issues as synchronicity of behaviors (VanLear, 1991), the management of speaking turns and talk time (Fischetti, Curran, & Wessberg, 1977; Peterson, Fischetti, Curran, & Arland, 1981), the appropriateness of an individual's arrival and departure (Albert & Kessler, 1976; Kellermann et al., 1991; Knapp, Hart, Friedrich, & Shulman, 1973), and other aspects of behavior sequencing in the interactional time stream (Higginbotham & Wilkins, 1999). Research consistently demonstrates the importance of timing in terms of interaction management skills (e.g., Dillard & Spitzberg, 1984; Wiemann, 1977).

Relationship

Relationship refers to the subjective and structural pattern of interdependence and closeness between interactants (Kelley et al., 1983). Research has shown that type of relationship is a natural cognitive category for organizing social information (Baldwin, 1992; Sedikides, Olsen, & Reis, 1993) and significantly influences expectations and evaluations of appropriate interpersonal motivation (e.g., Graham, Barbato, & Perse, 1993) and behavior (e.g., Baxter & Simon, 1993; Hecht, 1984; Knapp, Ellis, & Williams, 1980). Researchers working within various perspectives have attempted to identify the relatively unique skills and competencies involved in initiating and maintaining close relationships (e.g., Buhrmester, Furman, Wittenberg, & Reis, 1988; Burleson, 1995; Burleson & Samter, 1994; Carpenter, 1993; Davis & Oathout, 1987; Hansson, Jones, & Carpenter, 1984; Rubin, Booth, Rose-Krasnor, & Mills, 1995). In addition, much of the marital satisfaction literature can be interpreted as investigating implicit models of relational competence in a particular relationship context (e.g., Gottman, 1979; Gottman & Porterfield, 1981; Kieren & Tallman, 1972), and contemporary dialectical models of relationships also implicitly suggest competencies unique to particular relational forms and needs (e.g., Baxter & Montgomery, 1996). As with culture, there may be common underlying dimensions involved in the comprehension of relationship types (e.g., Burgoon & Hale, 1984), but specific competencies vary significantly across these dimensions depending on the particular relationship type being evaluated.

Place

Place refers to the physical situation in which interaction occurs. Research on social situations shows that place is a significant influence on expectations and evaluations of appropriateness of behavior (e.g., Argyle, Furnham, & Graham, 1981; Forgas, 1978, 1982, 1983a; Pavitt, 1989; Smith-Lovin, 1979). As with culture and relationship, there may be common underlying dimensions along which place is comprehended (e.g., Forgas, 1979; Heise, 1979; Wish, D'Andrade, & Goodnow, 1980; Wish & Kaplan, 1977), but perceptions of the competence of any given behavior will vary significantly along these from one place to the next.

Function

Function refers to the motives (e.g., intentions, objectives, goals, purposes) or pragmatic influences of behavior in the interactional system in which they are enacted. Articulated in speech act theory (e.g., Austin, 1962; Searle, 1969) and systems conceptions (e.g., Bochner & Eisenberg, 1987) of interaction, the assumption is that communication behavior "does" rather than just "is." Communication has effects, and these effects represent how communication functions in an encounter. Communication is in the service of certain effects on interactants, and these effects, or outcomes, are indicators of interactional effectiveness and practical achievement. Communication in the service of conflict is likely to be quite distinct from communication in the service of a job interview. Researchers taking various approaches to communication have attempted to identify the competencies associated with primary functions (e.g., Burleson & Denton, 1992, 1997; Burleson, Kunkel, Samter, & Werking, 1996; Burleson, Samter, & Lucchetti, 1992) or motives (e.g., Rubin, Perse, & Barbato, 1988) of interaction. Research has demonstrated that what is considered competent varies according to which functions are being pursued or fulfilled (e.g., Anderson & Martin, 1995; Graham, Barbato, & Perse, 1993).

Summary

One of the least contextual claims about competent interaction is that it is contextual. What this means precisely, however, is rarely a subject of direct inquiry or conceptualization. Context reveals at least five socially relevant facets: culture, time, relationship, place, and function. The matrix of these intersecting facets produces relatively consensual expectations and guidelines for conducting interaction, and yet the facets are also relatively negotiable by the interactants. Competence is likely to result from a complex interplay between the extent to which interactants fulfill the expectancies associated with their context and their ability to negotiate the very relevance and nature of those expectations (Burgoon, Stern, & Dillman, 1995; Spitzberg & Brunner, 1991). Thus any approach to conceptualizing and operationalizing interpersonal skills must account for the role of context in the competence of those skills.

TOWARD A TAXONOMY OF INTERPERSONAL SKILLS

In an earlier review of the literature, we identified more than 100 conceptual constructs, and more than another 100 factor-analytically based constructs, associated with interpersonal competence (Spitzberg & Cupach, 1989; see Table 15.3). Although it is possible that this is an accurate reflection of the complexity of the terrain of interpersonal skills, many scholars have a strong intuitive and empirical sense that there are higher-order structures by which this panoply of skills could be organized (Spitzberg, 1989). There has been no shortage of efforts to identify a more parsimonious yet reasonably comprehensive taxonomy of skills (e.g., Bubaš, Bratko, & Marusic, 1999; Buhrmester et al., 1988; Burleson & Denton, 1992; Caldarella & Merrell, 1997; Riggio, 1986; Spitzberg, 1994b) and functions (e.g., Rubin et al., 1988; Wicker, Lambert, Richardson, & Kahler, 1984). Several problems, however, continue to plague such efforts.

Obstacles

First, skills vary considerably in their levels of abstraction. For example, eye contact, which is a fairly specific behavior, has been further operationalized in terms of micro-momentaries, gaze, aversions, mutual eye contact, and related constructs. Eye contact is significantly related to impressions of competence and social skill (e.g., Dillard & Spitzberg, 1984), yet relatively few interpersonal skills taxonomies identify "eye contact" as a major interpersonal skill. In contrast, assertiveness and empathy are ubiquitous in the interpersonal skills literature

(e.g., Spitzberg & Cupach, 1984, 1989), yet there is far from any consensus on what specific behavioral components constitute these skills (on assertiveness, see, e.g., Furnham & Henderson, 1983; Gervasio & Crawford, 1989; Gorecki, Dickson, & Ritzler, 1981; Henderson & Furnham, 1983; Kolotkin, Wielkiewicz, Judd, & Weiser, 1983; Linehan & Walker, 1983; Pachman, Foy, Massey, & Eisler, 1978; Pitcher & Meikle, 1980; Weeks & Lefebvre, 1982; Wildman & Clementz, 1986; Winship & Kelley, 1976; on empathy, see, e.g., Bryant, 1987; Chlopan, McCain, Carbonell, & Hagen, 1985; Davis, 1983; Elliott et al., 1982; Feldstein & Gladstein, 1980; Matarazzo & Wiens, 1977; Omdahl, 1985; Wenegrat, 1974). Both assertiveness and empathy are likely to depend in part upon eye contact. So which is the "skill," eye contact or assertion? Both are skills, but they exist at different levels of abstraction. Skills vary from the microscopic (e.g., eye contact, asking questions) to the mezzoscopic (e.g., expressiveness, composure) to the macroscopic (e.g., distributive, integrative, avoidant).

A second problem with organizing skills is the complexity of determining what concept should guide the organization. Most researchers have attempted to organize skills according to one or more of three approaches: contextual, functional, or topographical. *Contextual approaches* attempt to identify the types of skills involved in particular interaction contexts, such as heterosexual (e.g., Davis & Oathout, 1992; Faulstich, Jensen, Jones, Calvert, & Van Buren, 1985; Goldfried, Padawer, & Robins, 1984; Vanwesenbeeck et al., 1999), organizational (e.g., DeWine, 1987; Monge, Bachman, Dillard, & Eisenberg, 1982; Wellmon, 1988), marital (e.g., Bienvenu, 1971; Filsinger, 1980; Gottman, 1979; Gottman & Rushe, 1995; Kieren & Tallman, 1972), and health care (e.g., Cegala, McNeilis, McGee, & Jonas, 1995; Gruppen et al., 1997; Morse & Piland, 1981; Scherz,

Table 15.3 Factor-Analytic Skills and Competencies Attributed to the Macro Concepts of Social Skills, Interpersonal Competence, and Interpersonal Skills

Altercentrism
Acceptance
Affiliation
Aggressiveness/aggression (–)[a]
Altercentrism
Attention
Attentiveness
Boorishness (–)
Confirmation
Cooperativeness
Cultural empathy
Decoding
Disapproval/criticism of others (–)
Disdainfulness of others (–)
Distance (–)
Enhancement
Emotional sensitivity
Emotional support
Empathy
Enmeshment
Evaluation and acceptance of feedback
Friendliness/outgoingness
Helping
Hostile depression (–)
Hostile domination (–)
Interpersonal diplomacy
Intimacy/warmth
Listening
Negative assertion (–)
Other-orientation/directedness
Perceptiveness
Personality traits (empathy, tolerance)
Prosocial competence/skills
Reflectiveness
Responsiveness
Self-centeredness (–)
Social interaction (display respect, appropriate behavior)
Social offensiveness (–)
Social sensitivity
Understanding

Composure
Ability to deal with psychological stress
Anxiety (comfort, composure, confidence, nervous movements) (–)
Assertiveness
Autonomy
Avoidance/social withdrawal (–)
Commitment
Coping with feelings

Dominance (–)
Emotional control
Impersonal endeavors/perils
Initiation
Instrumental skills
Intentionality
Interpersonal skills (establish relationship, initiate talking)
Managerial ability (motivation, creativity)
Need for achievement
Persuasiveness
Pleading
Self-efficacy
Self-orientation
Social control
Social relaxation/ease
Social instrumental skills
Social manipulation
Social superiority

Coordination
Ability to communicate effectively (deal with misunderstandings, different styles)
Conversational skills
Decoding and encoding
Interaction management/skills
Message orientation
Verbal skills

Expressiveness
Ability to be understood
Activity in the conversation
Affective skills
Animation
Articulation
Body nonverbal behavior
Clarity
Confrontation/anger expression
Openness/confiding
Emotional control
Emotional expressivity
Emotionality
Encoding
Expressiveness/expressivity
Facial expressiveness and vocalic behavior
Nonverbal behavior
Personal appearance/physical attractiveness
Self-disclosure/expression
Social expressivity
Vocalic skills
Wit

(Continued)

Table 15.3 (continued)

Contextual competencies	Creativity
Conflict management/handling differences	Similarity
Heterosocial contact	Social ability/skill
Relations with authority figures	
Social activity/experience	**Outcomes**
	Appropriateness
Macro-level competencies	Communication satisfaction
Ability to establish interpersonal	Communicative competence
relationships	Effectiveness
Adaptability	Rewarding impression
Awareness	Task completion

SOURCE: Expanded from Spitzberg (1994b) and Spitzberg and Cupach (1989).

NOTE: We have excluded or adapted labels if they had minimal interactional or communicative referents (e.g., "self-concept" or "self-perception") or if their referents were unclear (e.g., "completion" or "corruption"). In addition, we have combined cognate labels (e.g., "social anxiety," "anxiety," and "apprehension" became "anxiety" and "confirmation" and "social confirmation" became "confirmation"). Studies added since the original source works were published include those by Bubaš, Bratko, and Marusic (1999); Burleson, Kunkel, Samter, and Werking (1996); Cui (1989); Farrell, Rabinowitz, Wallander, and Curran (1985); Hammer, Gudykunst, and Wiseman (1978); and Ward and Kennedy (1999).

a. Minus signs in parentheses indicate skills or competencies with negative loadings or predicted relationships to competence.

Edwards, & Kallail, 1995) contexts. *Functional approaches* attempt to identify the types of skills involved when individuals competently accomplish certain interaction functions, such as conflict (e.g., Sillars & Weisberg, 1987; Spitzberg et al., 1994), support (e.g., Cohen, Sherrod, & Clark, 1986; Hansson et al., 1984; Riggio, Watring, & Throckmorton, 1993; Riggio & Zimmerman, 1991; Sarason, Sarason, Hacker, & Basham, 1985), and affinity seeking (e.g., Bell & Daly, 1984; Bell, Tremblay, & Buerkel-Rothfuss, 1987; Rubin, Rubin, & Martin, 1993). Other functional approaches have attempted to locate more inclusive functions, such as instrumental and expressive functions (e.g., Ickes, 1981, 1985; Lamke, Sollie, Durbin, & Fitzpatrick, 1994; Newcomb et al., 1993; see also McQuail, 1987). *Topographical approaches* attempt to identify clusters of behaviors that seem to bear structural resemblance in form or function, such as self-disclosure and openness (e.g., Derlega & Grzelak, 1979; Miller, Berg, & Archer, 1983), empathy (e.g., Ickes, 1997), and assertiveness (e.g., Rakos, 1991).

To identify these as approaches to the study of interpersonal skills is a generous attribution to the literature. In practice, most scholarly approaches to interpersonal skills research have been piecemeal, poorly conceptualized, and surprisingly lacking in rationale. They reflect what we have referred to as the "list" technique, in which a researcher assembles a list of independently reasonable skills candidates (Spitzberg & Cupach, 1989). Given the daunting complexities of identifying a rationale for an appropriate underlying organizing set of structural or functional features, such bootstrap approaches are not surprising. This difficulty of identifying underlying features reflects the third, and closely related, problem in organizing interpersonal skills: multifunctionality.

Systems theory has identified two vexing principles: equifinality and multifinality. *Equifinality* refers to the idea that many means can lead to a given outcome. For example, one person may flirt using relatively blatant tactics, whereas another may flirt using rather subtle and manipulative tactics, but both tactics may succeed in achieving the outcome of gaining someone's attraction (Egland, Spitzberg, & Zormeier, 1996). *Multifinality* indicates that any given means can lead to multiple possible outcomes. Thus both obvious and subtle forms of flirtation may lead to outright rejection, feigned interest, genuine interest with caution, or outright attraction. If skills are multifunctional in these senses (McFall, 1982), then there can be no fixed underlying functional taxonomy of skills. That is, no single skill can be tethered to a single function. This has implications for topographical approaches as well. For example, characterizing certain skills as constituting "expressiveness" implicitly suggests that they serve the function of regulating affect display and disclosure. Yet, clearly, expressive skills can function in instrumental, persuasive, manipulative, and status-based ways as well.

The multifunctionality of skills is closely related to a final problem in organizing such skills: Skills have a "dark side" to them (Spitzberg, 1993, 1994a). Counseling psychologists have discovered that "dysfunctional behavior is typically enacted in a highly skilled manner" (Brokaw & McLemore, 1991, p. 73). Most scholars view self-disclosure as an important interpersonal skill (e.g., Derlega, Metts, Petronio, & Margulis, 1993), yet someone very skilled in self-disclosure may employ it in manipulative and exploitative ways. Deception is a skill as well, and it can be used in very competent, prosocial ways (e.g., LaFollette & Graham, 1986; Metts, 1989; Rodriguez & Ryave, 1990). Yet self-disclosure is frequently touted as a vital interpersonal skill, whereas deception is rarely so endorsed. Employing aggression so as to escalate a conflict might be a very useful skill, and one that is clearly overlooked by most approaches to the study of conflict management (Cupach & Canary, 2000). There are times when conflicts need to be escalated rather than reduced, and this escalation may involve one person's moving against another. Taxonomies of interpersonal skills, in other words, tend to be ideologically normative

and therefore incomplete. They identify only those skills that have a normatively positive valence or "bright side" connotation.

These problems make the construction of a taxonomy of interpersonal skills particularly difficult. The alternative of listing more than 100 skill components, however, seems equally flawed. Although there is no obvious resolution to this difficulty in sight, we believe it is possible to construct a heuristic model to bridge some of these problems and set the stage for future refinement of these taxonomic issues.

A Working Taxonomy of Interpersonal Skills

Figure 15.1 illustrates an approach to an interpersonal skills taxonomy. We do not present it here as a final or comprehensive taxonomy, but as a framework through which such a practical taxonomy could be empirically refined. The taxonomy attempts to incorporate facets of several previous approaches (Baxter & Montgomery, 1996; Bochner, 1984; Bubaš, 2000; Burgoon & Dunbar, 2000; Burgoon & Hale, 1984; Burleson, Delia, & Applegate, 1992; Burleson & Denton, 1992; Caldarella & Merrell, 1997; Clark & Delia, 1979; Greene, 1984, 1997; Horney, 1945; Patterson, 1994; Rubin et al., 1988; Spitzberg, 1994c; Wicker et al., 1984), including five decades of research on the fundamental dimensions of interpersonal behavior (e.g., Birtchnell, 1993; Brokaw & McLemore, 1991; Caldarella & Merrell, 1997; Heise, 1979; Florsheim, Henry, & Benjamin, 1996; Freedman et al., 1951; McAdams, 1988; Osgood, May, & Miron, 1975; Ralph, 1990; Ralph & Lee, 1994; Ralph & Thorne, 1993; for syntheses, see Dillard, Solomon, & Palmer, 1999; Spitzberg, 1989; Spitzberg & Brunner, 1991). At the highest level of abstraction, the taxonomy identifies three macro interaction functions. Skills can be employed to move with or toward another person, as with integrative, cooperative, and bonding moves (Horney, 1945; Newcomb et al., 1993;

FORM (TOPOGRAPHY)   **FUNCTION**

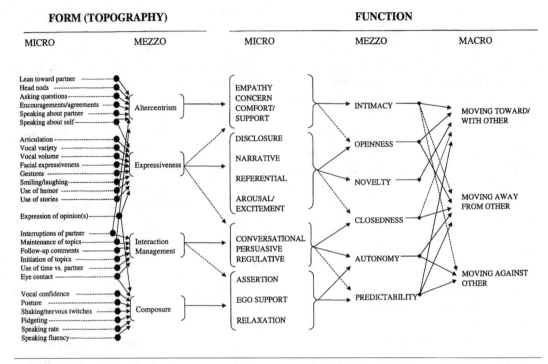

| MICRO | MEZZO | | MICRO | MEZZO | MACRO |

Figure 15.1   A Heuristic for Taxonomies of Interpersonal Skills

Santelli, Bernstein, Zborowski, & Bernstein, 1990). Skills can also be employed to move away from another person, as with avoidance, ambivalence, and equivocation. Finally, skills can be employed to move against another, as with aggression, coercion, and control. These macro functions represent a generic map of the ways in which behavior can function to affect an individual's relationship to another person. These functions need not be viewed as mutually exclusive. They represent interpersonal rather than personal functions because they are defined in terms of the effects of Actor's behavior on Coactor. Finally, the approach includes the overwhelming evidence of the importance of the affiliation and status dimensions of circumplex research, but adds the recognition that interpersonal behavior can be moving away from someone in addition to moving with or against that person.

Although skills are multifunctional, this taxonomy permits certain skills to have stronger links with certain functions than with others.

For example, skills associated with empathy and giving support tend to affect an individual's negotiation of intimacy and openness with another more so than negotiating autonomy in relation to that person. Offering support *could* be employed so as to affect autonomy, and may always have certain peripheral effects on autonomy, but it is functionally weighted more prominently in its effects on intimacy.

Similarly, microscopic skills have differential weightings in their linkage to mezzoscopic skills, which in turn have differential impacts on macroscopic skills. Any given microscopic skill can be employed in the service of any and all of the mezzo- and macroscopic skills, and by extension, therefore, to any of the mezzo- and macroscopic functions. It is expected, however, that research will reveal that some microscopic skills will be linked more to certain mezzo- and macroscopic skills than to others. Such anticipated weightings are illustrated in Figure 15.1 through the use of solid (primary link) versus dashed (peripheral linkage) lines.

Such a taxonomy is, in some ways, just as complex as a listing of 100 separate skills. But it helps unpack some of the conceptual and operational oversights of many discussions of social skills. First, it is flexible. It can accommodate additional terms and components in any column, so long as those components are distinguishable from those already noted. There may be a place in this taxonomy for other forms and functions, such as face management, self-expansion, trust, and altruism.

Second, it helps identify why so many measures reveal such distinct factor structures. Such measures often haphazardly mix items from several levels of abstraction, and thereby suggest empirically indeterminate factor interpretations (Spitzberg, 1994b). Recognition of these varying levels of abstraction should also lead to more conceptually rigorous and valid measures of interpersonal skills.

Third, this taxonomy reveals that topography (e.g., form) and function interrelate, but both are involved in identifying the nature of interpersonal skills. Form reduces to a more micro feature of interpersonal skills, whereas function concerns more mezzo and macro orientations to classifying skills. Both are important levels to a comprehensive conceptualization of interpersonal skills.

Finally, the taxonomy suggests areas of overlap and potential integration across interpersonal skill literatures. Showing support probably often looks like empathy, and both tend to enhance a sense of intimacy and closeness with another, thereby moving toward another. Thus lists of skills that are sometimes noted in current measures of social and interpersonal skills (e.g., Burleson & Denton, 1997; Carpenter, 1993) now have a higher-order structure within which the skills can be situated. Thus the question "Why is *this* skill included in a taxonomy of interpersonal skills rather than other skills?" can be answered

relative to its functional connection to the macro functions of interpersonal relations.

CONCLUSION

Local, state, and federal governments spend billions of dollars every year in attempts to eradicate crime, educational underachievement, smoking, obesity, and drug abuse. Although the available evidence suggests that modest improvements in people's interpersonal skills and ability to establish and maintain satisfying relationships stand to be a far more potent source of physical and psychological well-being, the issue of improving interpersonal skills is virtually absent from the public agenda. Several conclusions therefore bear emphasizing. First, large proportions of the U.S. population lack basic communication skills. Second, these deficits are associated with severe costs to society at large and to individual well-being in particular. Third, although there is little basis for a specific odds-ratio comparison, the evidence is at least suggestive that people's interpersonal skills related to the initiation, maintenance, and quality of relationships have substantially more impact on society in terms of social and personal well-being than whether or not people quit smoking, lose weight, or stop abusing drugs, than any program established to rehabilitate criminals, or than any improvement in educational expenditures. Despite the extensive evidence, the agenda of improving interpersonal skills is rarely if ever even mentioned in this public policy discourse, much less given the same weight as other societal agendas.

Perhaps one of the primary reasons for this is that the concept of interpersonal skills has lacked clarity. This lack of clarity, in turn, has been exacerbated by the sheer multiplicity of approaches and constructs associated with interpersonal skills. Certainly, the concept of interpersonal skills has seemed prismatic: The more one peers into the concept, the more facets and shades one discerns. In this chapter we have attempted to specify many of these facets, but with the intent of providing a relatively comprehensive and integrated approach. Although the approach we have discussed falls far short of a theory of interpersonal skills, we do believe it provides the conceptual parameters within which such a theory will eventually be formulated. Thus what this architecture lacks in theoretical detail we hope will be made up for by its theoretically heuristic nature and its integrative comprehensiveness.

REFERENCES

Abe, H., & Wiseman, R. L. (1983). A cross-cultural confirmation of the dimensions of intercultural effectiveness. *International Journal of Intercultural Relations, 7,* 53-67.

Agostin, T. M., & Bain, S. K. (1997). Predicting early school success with developmental and social skills screeners. *Psychology in the Schools, 34,* 219-228.

Ainsworth, M. D. S., Blehar, M. C., Waters, E., & Wall, S. (1978). *Patterns of attachment: A psychological study of the strange situation.* Hillsdale, NJ: Lawrence Erlbaum.

Albert, S., & Kessler, S. (1976). Processes for ending social encounters: The conceptual archaeology of a temporal place. *Journal for the Theory of Social Behavior, 6,* 147-170.

Alberts, J. K., Kellar-Guenther, Y., & Corman, S. R. (1996). That's not funny: Understanding recipients' responses to teasing. *Western Journal of Communication, 60,* 337-357.

Alexander, E. R., III, Penley, L. E., & Jernigan, I. E. (1992). The relationship of basic decoding skills to managerial effectiveness. *Management Communication Quarterly, 6,* 58-73.

Allen, A., & Thompson, T. (1984). Agreement, understanding, realization, and feeling understood as predictors of communicative satisfaction in marital dyads. *Journal of Marriage and the Family, 46,* 915-921.

Anda, R. F., Croft, J. B., Felitti, V. J., Nordenberg, D., Giles, W. H., Williamson, D. F., & Giovino, G. A. (1999). Adverse childhood experiences and smoking during adolescence and adulthood. *Journal of the American Medical Association, 282,* 1652-1658.

Andersen, P. A., Eloy, S. V., Guerrero, L. K., & Spitzberg, B. H. (1995). Romantic jealousy and relational satisfaction: A look at the impact of jealousy experience and expression. *Communication Reports, 8,* 77-85.

Anderson, C. M., & Martin, M. M. (1995). Communication motives of assertive and responsive communicators. *Communication Research Reports, 12,* 186-191.

Anderson, V., Reis, J., & Stephens, Y. (1997). Male and female adolescents' perceived interpersonal communication skills according to history of sexual coercion. *Adolescence, 32,* 419-427.

Applegate, J. L., & Leichty, G. B. (1984). Managing interpersonal relationships: Social cognitive and strategic determinants of competence. In R. N. Bostrom (Ed.), *Competence in communication: A multidisciplinary approach* (pp. 33-56). Beverly Hills, CA: Sage.

Argyle, M. (1981). Social competence and mental health. In M. Argyle (Ed.), *Social skills and mental health* (pp. 159-187). New York: Methuen.

Argyle, M. (1986). The skills, rules, and goals of relationships. In R. Gilmour & S. Duck (Eds.), *The emerging field of personal relationships* (pp. 23-39). Hillsdale, NJ: Lawrence Erlbaum.

Argyle, M. (1991). Benefits produced by supportive social relationships. In H. O. F. Veiel & U. Baumann (Eds.), *The meaning and measurement of social support* (pp. 13-32). New York: Hemisphere.

Argyle, M., Furnham, A., & Graham, J. A. (1981). *Social situations.* London: Cambridge University Press.

Aristotle. (1926). *The "art" of rhetoric* (J. H. Freese, Trans.). New York: Putnam's.

Austin, G. (1966). *Chironomia or, a treatise on rhetorical delivery.* Carbondale: Southern Illinois University Press.

Austin, J. L. (1962). *How to do things with words.* Cambridge, MA: Harvard University Press.

Axley, S. R. (1984). Managerial and organizational communication in terms of the conduit metaphor. *Academy of Management Review, 9,* 428-437.

Ayim, M. N. (1997). *The moral parameters of good talk: A feminist analysis.* Waterloo, ON: Wilfrid Laurier University Press.

Babcock, J. C., Waltz, J., Jacobson, N. S., & Gottman, J. M. (1993). Power and violence: The relation between communication patterns, power discrepancies, and domestic violence. *Journal of Consulting and Clinical Psychology, 61,* 40-50.

Bahniuk, M. H., Kogler Hill, S. E., & Darus, H. J. (1996). The relationship of power-gaining communication strategies to career success. *Western Journal of Communication, 60,* 358-378.

Baldwin, M. W. (1992). Relational schemas and the processing of social information. *Psychological Bulletin, 112,* 461-484.

Basco, M. R., Birchler, G. R., Kalal, B., Talbott, R., & Slater, M. A. (1991). The Clinician Rating of Adult Communication (CRAC): A clinician's guide to the assessment of interpersonal communication skill. *Journal of Clinical Psychology, 47,* 368-380.

Bassett, D. M., Longwell, S. G., & Bulow, H. V. (1939). Social and occupational competence of idiots. *American Association on Mental Deficiency, 44,* 97-102.

Bassett, R. E., Whittington, N., & Staton-Spicer, A. (1978). The basics in speaking and listening for high school graduates: What should be assessed? *Communication Education, 27,* 293-303.

Baumeister, R. F., & Leary, M. R. (1995). The need to belong: Desire for interpersonal attachments as a fundamental human motivation. *Psychological Bulletin, 117,* 497-529.

Baxter, L. A., & Montgomery, B. M. (1996). *Relating: Dialogues and dialectics.* New York: Guilford.

Baxter, L. A., & Simon, E. P. (1993). Relationship maintenance strategies and dialectical contradictions in personal relationships. *Journal of Social and Personal Relationships, 10,* 225-242.

Beach, S. R. H., & Fincham, F. D. (2001). Marital therapy and social psychology: Will we choose explicit partnership or cryptomnesia? In G. J. O. Fletcher & M. S. Clark (Eds.), *Blackwell handbook of social psychology: Interpersonal processes* (pp. 558-586). Malden, MA: Blackwell.

Bedell, J. R., & Lennox, S. S. (1997). *Handbook for communication and problem-solving skills training: A cognitive-behavioral approach.* New York: John Wiley.

Bell, R. A., Buerkel-Rothfuss, N. L., & Gore, K. E. (1987). "Did you bring the yarmulke for the Cabbage Patch Kid?" The idiomatic communication of young lovers. *Human Communication Research, 14,* 47-67.

Bell, R. A., & Daly, J. A. (1984). The affinity-seeking function of communication. *Communication Monographs, 51,* 91-115.

Bell, R. A., & Healey, J. G. (1992). Idiomatic communication and interpersonal solidarity in friends' relational cultures. *Human Communication Research, 18,* 307-335.

Bell, R. A., Tremblay, S. W., & Buerkel-Rothfuss, N. L. (1987). Interpersonal attraction as a communication accomplishment: Development of a measure of affinity-seeking competence. *Western Journal of Speech Communication, 51,* 1-18.

Bellack, A. S., & Hersen, M. (1978). Chronic psychiatric patients: Social skills training. In M. Hersen & A. S. Bellack (Eds.), *Behavior therapy in the psychiatric setting* (pp. 169-195). Baltimore: Williams & Wilkins.

Berger, C. R. (1997). *Planning strategic interaction: Attaining goals through communicative action.* Mahwah, NJ: Lawrence Erlbaum.

Berger, C. R. (2000). Goal detection and efficiency: Neglected aspects of message production. *Communication Theory, 10,* 156-166.

Bienvenu, M. J., Sr. (1971). An interpersonal communication inventory. *Journal of Communication, 21,* 381-388.

Birtchnell, J. (1993). *How humans relate: A new interpersonal theory.* Westport, CT: Praeger.

Bochner, A. P. (1984). The functions of human communication in interpersonal bonding. In C. C. Arnold & J. W. Bowers (Eds.), *Handbook of rhetorical and communication theory* (pp. 544-621). Boston: Allyn & Bacon.

Bochner, A. P., & Eisenberg, E. M. (1987). Family process: System perspectives. In C. R. Berger & S. H. Chaffee (Eds.), *Handbook of communication science* (pp. 540-563). Newbury Park, CA: Sage.

Bochner, A. P., & Kelly, C. W. (1974). Interpersonal competence: Rationale, philosophy, and implementation of a conceptual framework. *Speech Teacher, 23,* 270-301.

Bodenmann, G., Kaiser, A., Hahlweg, K., & Fehm-Wolfsdorf, G. (1998). Communication patterns during marital conflict: A cross-cultural replication. *Personal Relationships, 5,* 343-356.

Boland, J. P., & Follingstad, D. R. (1987). The relationship between communication and marital satisfaction: A review. *Journal of Sex and Marital Therapy, 13,* 286-313.

Bookwala, J., Frieze, I. H., & Grote, N. K. (1994). Love, aggression and satisfaction in dating relationships. *Journal of Social and Personal Relationships, 11*, 625-632.

Bosworth, H. B., & Schaie, K. W. (1997). The relationship of social environment, social networks, and health outcomes in the Seattle longitudinal study: Two analytical approaches. *Journal of Gerontology: Psychological Sciences, 52B*, P197-P205.

Bowlby, J. (1969). *Attachment and loss: Vol. 1. Attachment.* New York: Basic Books.

Bowlby, J. (1973). *Attachment and loss: Vol. 2. Separation: Anxiety and anger.* New York: Basic Books.

Bowlby, J. (1980). *Attachment and loss: Vol. 3. Loss: Sadness and depression.* New York: Basic Books.

Bowling, A., & Grundy, E. (1998). The association between social networks and mortality in later life. *Reviews in Clinical Gerontology, 8*, 353-361.

Boyd, L. A., & Roach, A. J. (1977). Interpersonal communication skills differentiating more satisfying from less satisfying marital relationships. *Journal of Counseling Psychology, 24*, 540-542.

Bradway, K. P. (1937). Social competence of exceptional children: II. The mentally subnormal. *Journal of Exceptional Children, 4*, 38-42.

Bradway, K. P. (1938). Social competence of grade school children. *Journal of Experimental Education, 6*, 326-331.

Branham, R. J. (1980). Ineffability, creativity, and communication competence. *Communication Quarterly, 28*, 11-21.

Brokaw, D. W., & McLemore, C. (1991). Interpersonal models of personality and psychopathology. In D. G. Gilbert & J. J. Connolly (Eds.), *Personality, social skills, and psychopathology: An individual differences approach* (pp. 49-83). New York: Plenum.

Broman, C. L. (1993). Social relationships and health-related behavior. *Journal of Behavioral Medicine, 16*, 335-350.

Brown, P., & Levinson, S. C. (1987). *Politeness: Some universals in language usage.* Cambridge: Cambridge University Press.

Bruess, C. J., & Pearson, J. C. (1993). "Sweet pea" and "pussy cat": An examination of idiom use and marital satisfaction over the life cycle. *Journal of Social and Personal Relationships, 10*, 609-615.

Bryant, B., & Trower, P. (1974). Social difficulty in a student sample. *British Journal of Educational Psychology, 44*, 13-21.

Bryant, B., Trower, P., Yardley, K., Urbieta, H., & Letemendia, F. J. (1976). A survey of social inadequacy among psychiatric outpatients. *Psychological Medicine, 6*, 101-112.

Bryant, B. K. (1987). Critique of comparable questionnaire methods in use to assess empathy in children and adults. In N. Eisenberg & J. Strayer (Eds.), *Empathy and its development* (pp. 361-373). Cambridge: Cambridge University Press.

Bubaš, G. (2000, March). *The structure of agency and communion dimensions in interpersonal communication interaction.* Paper presented at the European Communication Association Experts' Conference, Manchester, Eng.

Bubaš, G., Bratko, D., & Marusic, I. (1999, November). *The dimensions of interpersonal communication competence: An analysis of data collected by multiple self-rating scales.* Paper presented at the annual meeting of the National Communication Association, Chicago.

Buhrmester, D., Furman, W., Wittenberg, M. T., & Reis, H. T. (1988). Five domains of interpersonal competence in peer relations. *Journal of Personality and Social Psychology, 55*, 991-1008.

Bullis, M., Walker, H. M., & Stieber, S. (1998). The influence of peer and educational variables on arrest status among at-risk males. *Journal of Emotional and Behavioral Disorders, 6*, 141-152.

Bulwer, J. (1974). *Chirologia: Or the natural language of the hand* and *Chironomia: Or the art of manual rhetoric.* Carbondale: Southern Illinois University Press.

Burg, M. M., & Seeman, T. F. (1994). Families and health: The negative side of social ties. *Annals of Behavioral Medicine, 16*, 109-115.

Burggraf, C. S., & Pavitt, C. (1991, November). *Understanding on varying levels of abstraction and its association with marital satisfaction.* Paper presented at the annual meeting of the Speech Communication Association, Atlanta, GA.

Burgoon, J. K., & Dunbar, N. E. (2000). An interactionist perspective on dominance-submission: Interpersonal dominance as a dynamic, situationally contingent social skill. *Communication Monographs, 67*, 96-121.

Burgoon, J. K., & Hale, J. L. (1984). The fundamental topoi of relational communication. *Communication Monographs, 51*, 193-214.

Burgoon, J. K., Stern, L. A., & Dillman, L. (1995). *Interpersonal adaptation: Dyadic interaction patterns.* Cambridge: Cambridge University Press.

Burgoon, M. (1995). A kinder, gentler discipline: Feeling good about being mediocre. In B. R. Burleson (Ed.), *Communication yearbook 18* (pp. 464-479). Thousand Oaks, CA: Sage.

Burke, P. (1993). *The art of conversation.* Ithaca, NY: Cornell University Press.

Burleson, B. R. (1986). Communication skills and childhood peer relationships: An overview. In M. L. McLaughlin (Ed.), *Communication yearbook 9* (pp. 143-180). Beverly Hills, CA: Sage.

Burleson, B. R. (1995). Personal relationships as a skilled accomplishment. *Journal of Social and Personal Relationships, 12,* 575-581.

Burleson, B. R., Delia, J. G., & Applegate, J. L. (1992). Effects of maternal communication and children's social-cognitive and communication skills on children's acceptance by the peer group. *Family Relations, 41,* 264-272.

Burleson, B. R., & Denton, W. H. (1992). A new look at similarity and attraction in marriage: Similarities in social-cognitive and communication skills as predictors of attraction and satisfaction. *Communication Monographs, 59,* 268-287.

Burleson, B. R., & Denton, W. H. (1997). The relationship between communication skill and marital satisfaction: Some moderating effects. *Journal of Marriage and the Family, 59,* 884-902.

Burleson, B. R., Kunkel, A. W., Samter, W., & Werking, K. J. (1996). Men's and women's evaluations of communication skills in personal relationships: When sex differences make a difference—and when they don't. *Journal of Social and Personal Relationships, 13,* 201-224.

Burleson, B. R., Metts, M. W., & Kirch, M. W. (2000). Communication in close relationships. In C. Hendrick & S. S. Hendrick (Eds.), *Close relationships: A sourcebook* (pp. 244-258). Thousand Oaks, CA: Sage.

Burleson, B. R., & Samter, W. (1992). Are there gender differences in the relationship between academic performance and social behavior? *Human Communication Research, 19,* 155-175.

Burleson, B. R., & Samter, W. (1994). A social skills approach to relationship maintenance: How individual differences in communication skills affect the achievement of relationship functions. In D. J. Canary & L. Stafford (Eds.), *Communication and relational maintenance* (pp. 61-90). San Diego, CA: Academic Press.

Burleson, B. R., Samter, W., & Lucchetti, A. E. (1992). Similarity in communication values as a predictor of friendship choices: Studies of friends and best friends. *Southern Communication Journal, 57,* 260-276.

Burman, B., & Margolin, G. (1992). Analysis of the association between marital relationships and health problems: An interactional perspective. *Psychological Bulletin, 112,* 39-63.

Bushman, R. L. (1992). *The refinement of America: Persons, houses, cities.* New York: Alfred A. Knopf.

Butler, M. H., & Wampler, K. S. (1999). A meta-analytic update of research on the couple communication program. *American Journal of Family Therapy, 27,* 223-237.

Cahn, D. D. (1990). Perceived understanding and interpersonal relationships. *Journal of Social and Personal Relationships, 7,* 231-244.

Cairns, R. B., Leung, M.-C., Gest, S. D., & Cairns, B. D. (1995). A brief method for assessing social development: Structure, reliability, stability, and developmental validity of the interpersonal competence scale. *Behaviour Research and Therapy, 33,* 725-736.

Caldarella, P., & Merrell, K. W. (1997). Common dimensions of social skills of children and adolescents: A taxonomy of positive behaviors. *School Psychology Review, 26,* 264-278.

Camden, C., Motley, M. T., & Wilson, A. (1984). White lies in interpersonal communication: A taxonomy and preliminary investigation of social motivations. *Western Journal of Speech Communication, 48,* 309-325.

Canary, D. J., & Cupach, W. R. (1988). Relational and episodic characteristics associated with conflict tactics. *Journal of Social and Personal Relationships, 5,* 305-325.

Canary, D. J., & Spitzberg, B. H. (1987). Appropriateness and effectiveness in the perception of conflict strategies. *Human Communication Research, 13,* 93-118.

Canary, D. J., & Spitzberg, B. H. (1989). A model of competence perceptions of conflict strategies. *Human Communication Research, 13,* 630-649.

Cappella, J. N. (1995). An evolutionary psychology of Gricean cooperation. *Journal of Language and Social Psychology, 14,* 167-181.

Carkhuff, R. R., & Truax, C. B. (1966). Toward explaining success or failure in interpersonal experience. *Personnel and Guidance Journal, 44,* 723-728.

Carpenter, B. N. (1987). The relationship between psychopathology and self-disclosure. In V. J. Derlega & J. H. Berg (Eds.), *Self-disclosure: Theory, research, and therapy* (pp. 203-227). New York: Plenum.

Carpenter, B. N. (1993). Relational competence. In D. Perlman & W. H. Jones (Eds.), *Advances in personal relationships* (Vol. 4, pp. 1-28). Philadelphia: Jessica Kingsley.

Casey, P. R., Tyrer, P. J., & Platt, S. (1985). The relationship between social functioning and psychiatric symptomology in primary care. *Social Psychiatry, 20,* 5-9.

Caughlin, J. P., Huston, T. L., & Houts, R. M. (2000). How does personality matter in marriage? An examination of trait anxiety, interpersonal negativity, and marital satisfaction. *Journal of Personality and Social Psychology, 78,* 326-336.

Cegala, D. J., McNeilis, K. S., McGee, D. S., & Jonas, A. P. (1995). A study of doctors' and patients' perceptions of information processing and communication competence during the medical interview. *Health Communication, 7,* 179-203.

Chen, G.-M. (1989). Relationships of the dimensions of intercultural communication competence. *Communication Quarterly, 37,* 118-133.

Chen, G.-M. (1992). Communication adaptability and interaction involvement as predictors of cross-cultural adjustment. *Communication Research Reports, 9,* 33-42.

Cheung, Y.-B. (1998). Accidents, assaults, and marital status. *Social Science and Medicine, 47,* 1325-1329.

Chlopan, B. E., McCain, M. L., Carbonell, J. L., & Hagen, R. L. (1985). Empathy: Review of available measures. *Journal of Personality and Social Psychology, 48,* 635-653.

Chomsky, N. (1965). *Aspects of the theory of syntax.* Cambridge: MIT Press.

Chovil, N. (1994). Equivocation as an interactional event. In W. R. Cupach & B. H. Spitzberg (Eds.), *The dark side of interpersonal communication* (pp. 105-124). Hillsdale, NJ: Lawrence Erlbaum.

Cicero. (1959). *De oratore I, II* (E. W. Sutton, Trans.). Cambridge, MA: Harvard University Press.

Clark, R. A., & Delia, J. G. (1979). *Topoi* and rhetorical competence. *Quarterly Journal of Speech, 65,* 187-206.

Cohan, C. L., & Bradbury, T. N. (1997). Negative life events, marital interaction, and the longitudinal course of newlywed marriage. *Journal of Personality and Social Psychology, 73,* 114-128.

Cohen, S., Sherrod, D. R., & Clark, M. S. (1986). Social skills and the stress-protective role of social support. *Journal of Personality and Social Psychology, 50,* 963-973.

Conger, J. C., & Conger, A. J. (1982). Components of heterosocial competence. In J. P. Curran & P. M. Monti (Eds.), *Social skills training* (pp. 313-347). New York: Guilford.

Coupland, N., Wiemann, J. M., & Giles, H. (1991). Talk as "problem" and communication as "miscommunication": An integrative analysis. In N. Coupland, H. Giles, & J. M. Wiemann (Eds.), *"Miscommunication" and problematic talk* (pp. 1-17). Newbury Park, CA: Sage.

Cui, G. (1989, May). *Measuring intercultural effectiveness: An integrative approach.* Paper presented at the annual meeting of the International Communication Association, San Francisco.

Cupach, W. R., & Canary, D. J. (2000). *Competence in interpersonal conflict.* Prospect Heights, IL: Waveland.

Cupach, W. R., & Spitzberg, B. H. (1983). Trait versus state: A comparison of dispositional and situational measures of interpersonal communication competence. *Western Journal of Speech Communication, 47,* 364-379.

Cupach, W. R., & Spitzberg, B. H. (Eds.). (1994). *The dark side of interpersonal communication.* Hillsdale, NJ: Lawrence Erlbaum.

Curran, J. P. (1979). Social skills: Methodological issues and future directions. In A. S. Bellack & M. Hersen (Eds.), *Research and practice in social skills training* (pp. 319-354). New York: Plenum.

Curran, J. P., Miller, I. W., III, Zwick, W. R., Monti, P. M., & Stout, R. L. (1980). The socially inadequate patient: Incidence rate, demographic and clinical features, and hospital and posthospital functioning. *Journal of Consulting and Clinical Psychology, 48,* 375-382.

Curtis, D. B., Winsor, J. L., & Stephens, R. D. (1989). National preferences in business and communication education. *Communication Education, 38,* 6-14.

Dalgard, O. S., & Lund Håheim, L. L. (1998). Psychosocial risk factors and mortality: A prospective study with special focus on social support, social participation, and locus of control. *Journal of Epidemiology and Community Health, 52,* 476-481.

Daly, J. A. (1994). Assessing speaking and listening: Preliminary considerations for a national assessment. In A. Greenwood (Ed.), *The National Assessment of College Student Learning: Identification of the skills to be taught, learned, and assessed* (Report of the Proceedings of the Second Study Design Workshop, November 1992) (pp. 113-180). Washington, DC: U.S. Department of Education.

Davis, M. C., & Swan, P. D. (1999). Association of negative and positive social ties with fibrinogen levels in young women. *Health Psychology, 18,* 131-139.

Davis, M. H. (1983). Measuring individual differences in empathy: Evidence for a multidimensional approach. *Journal of Personality and Social Psychology, 44,* 113-126.

Davis, M. H., & Oathout, H. A. (1987). Maintenance of satisfaction in romantic relationships: Empathy and relational competence. *Journal of Personality and Social Psychology, 53,* 397-410.

Davis, M. H., & Oathout, H. A. (1992). The effect of dispositional empathy on romantic relationship behaviors: Heterosexual anxiety as a moderating influence. *Personality and Social Psychology Bulletin, 18,* 76-83.

Davis, O. (1999). Confusional consequences of illogical interaction. *Psychiatry, 62,* 250-264.

de Leon, C. F. M., Glass, T. A., Beckett, L. A., Seeman, T. E., Evans, D. A., & Berkman, L. F. (1999). Social networks and disability transitions across eight intervals of yearly data in the New Haven EPESE. *Journal of Gerontology: Social Sciences, 54B,* S162-S172.

Denton, W. H., Burleson, B. R., & Sprenkle, D. H. (1995). Association of interpersonal cognitive complexity with communication skill in marriage: Moderating effects of marital distress. *Family Process, 34,* 101-111.

DePaulo, B. M., Kashy, D. A., Kirkendol, S. E., Wyer, M. M., & Epstein, J. A. (1996). Lying in everyday life. *Journal of Personality and Social Psychology, 70,* 979-995.

Derlega, V. J., & Grzelak, J. (1979). Appropriateness of self-disclosure. In G. J. Chelune (Ed.), *Self-disclosure: Origins, patterns, and implications of openness in interpersonal relationships* (pp. 151-176). San Francisco: Jossey-Bass.

Derlega, V. J., Metts, S., Petronio, S., & Margulis, S. T. (1993). *Self-disclosure.* Newbury Park, CA: Sage.

DeWine, S. (1987). Evaluation of organizational communication competence: The development of the communication training impact questionnaire. *Journal of Applied Communication Research, 15,* 113-127.

Dillard, J. P., Solomon, D. H., & Palmer, M. T. (1999). Structuring the concept of relational communication. *Communication Monographs, 66,* 49-65.

Dillard, J. P., & Spitzberg, B. H. (1984). Global impressions of social skills: Behavioral predictors. In R. N. Bostrom (Ed.), *Communication yearbook 8* (pp. 446-463). Beverly Hills, CA: Sage.

DiSalvo, V. S. (1980). A summary of current research identifying communication skills in various organizational contexts. *Communication Education, 29,* 283-290.

DiSalvo, V. S., Larsen, D. C., & Seiler, W. J. (1976). Communication skills needed by persons in business organizations. *Communication Education, 25,* 269-275.

Doane, J. A. (1978). Family interaction and communicative deviance in disturbed and normal families: A review of research. *Family Process, 17,* 357-376.

Dobos, J., Bahniuk, M. H., & Kogler Hill, S. E. (1991). Power-gaining communication strategies and career success. *Southern Communication Journal, 57,* 35-48.

Doll, E. A. (1935). The measurement of social competence. *American Association on Mental Deficiency, 40,* 103-126.

Doll, E. A. (1939). Growth studies in social competence. *American Association on Mental Deficiency, 44,* 90-96.

Doll, E. A. (1953). *The measurement of social competence: A manual for the Vineland Social Maturity Scale.* Washington, DC: Educational Publishers.

Drury, J., Catan, L., Dennison, C., & Brody, R. (1998). Exploring teenagers' accounts of bad communication: A new basis for intervention. *Journal of Adolescence, 21,* 177-196.

Duck, S., Rutt, D. J., Hurst, M. H., & Strejc, H. (1991). Some evident truths about conversations in everyday relationships: All communications are not created equal. *Human Communication Research, 18,* 228-267.

Duran, R. L., & Zakahi, W. R. (1988). The influence of communicative competence upon roommate satisfaction. *Western Journal of Speech Communication, 52,* 135-146.

Egland, K. L., Spitzberg, B. H., & Zormeier, M. M. (1996). Flirtation and conversational competence in cross-sex platonic and romantic relationships. *Communication Reports, 9,* 105-118.

Ehninger, D. (1975). A synoptic view of systems of Western rhetoric. *Quarterly Journal of Speech, 61,* 448-453.

Eisenberg, E. M. (1984). Ambiguity as strategy in organizational communication. *Communication Monographs, 51,* 227-242.

Elliott, R., Filipovich, H., Harrigan, L., Gaynor, J., Reimschuessel, C., & Zapadka, J. K. (1982). Measuring response empathy: The development of a multicomponent rating scale. *Journal of Counseling Psychology, 29,* 379-387.

Ewart, C. K., Taylor, C. B., Kraemer, H. C., & Agras, W. S. (1991). High blood pressure and marital discord: Not being nasty matters more than being nice. *Health Psychology, 10,* 155-163.

Ewbank, H. L. (1987). The rhetoric of conversation in America: 1776-1828. *Southern Speech Communication Journal, 53,* 49-64.

Farrell, A. D., Rabinowitz, J. A., Wallander, J. L., & Curran, J. P. (1985). An evaluation of two formats for the intermediate-level assessment of social skills. *Behavioral Assessment, 7,* 155-171.

Faulstich, M. E., Jensen, B. J., Jones, G. N., Calvert, J. D., & Van Buren, D. J. (1985). Self-report inventories as predictors of men's heterosocial skill: A multiple regression analysis. *Psychological Reports, 56,* 977-978.

Feeney, J. A. (1994). Attachment style, communication patterns, and satisfaction across the life cycle of marriage. *Personal Relationships, 1,* 333-348.

Feeney, J. A., Noller, P., & Ward, C. (1997). Marital satisfaction and spousal interaction. In R. J. Sternberg & M. Hojjat (Eds.), *Satisfaction in close relationships* (pp. 160-189). New York: Guilford.

Feldstein, J. C., & Gladstein, G. A. (1980). A comparison of the construct validities of four measures of empathy. *Measurement and Evaluation in Guidance, 13,* 49-57.

Felitti, V. J., Anda, R. F., Nordenberg, D., Williamson, D. F., Spitz, A. M., Edwards, V., et al. (1998). Relationship of childhood abuse and household dysfunction to many of the leading causes of death in adults: The Adverse Childhood Experiences (ACE) study. *American Journal of Preventive Medicine, 14,* 245-257.

Filsinger, E. E. (1980). Social competence and marital adjustment. *Home Economics Research Journal, 9,* 158-162.

Fischetti, M., Curran, J. P., & Wessberg, H. W. (1977). Sense of timing: A skill deficit in heterosexual-socially anxious males. *Behavior Modification, 1,* 179-194.

Fishbein, H. D. (1996). *Peer prejudice and discrimination: Evolutionary, cultural, and developmental dynamics.* Boulder, CO: Westview.

Fitzpatrick, M. A. (1987). Marital interaction. In C. R. Berger & S. H. Chaffee (Eds.), *Handbook of communication science* (pp. 564-618). Newbury Park, CA: Sage.

Flora, J., & Segrin, C. (1998). Joint leisure time in friend and romantic relationships: The role of activity type, social skills, and positivity. *Journal of Social and Personal Relationships, 15,* 711-718.

Florsheim, P., Henry, W. P., & Benjamin, L. S. (1996). Integrating individual and interpersonal approaches to diagnosis: The structural analysis of social behavior and attachment theory. In F. W. Kaslow (Ed.), *Handbook of relational diagnosis and dysfunctional family patterns* (pp. 81-101). New York: John Wiley.

Ford, E. S., Ahluwalia, I. B., & Galuska, D. A. (2000). Social relationships and cardiovascular disease risk factors: Findings from the Third National Health and Nutrition Examination Survey. *Preventive Medicine, 30,* 83-92.

Ford, M. E. (1985). The concept of competence: Themes and variations. In H. A. Marlowe, Jr., & R. B. Weinberg (Eds.), *Competence development: Theory and practice in special populations* (pp. 3-49). Springfield, IL: Charles C Thomas.

Forgas, J. P. (1978). The effects of behavioural and cultural expectation cues on the perception of social episodes. *European Journal of Social Psychology, 8,* 203-213.

Forgas, J. P. (1979). *Social episodes: The study of interaction routines.* New York: Academic Press.

Forgas, J. P. (1982). Episode cognition: Internal representations of interaction routines.

Advances in Experimental Social Psychology, *15,* 59-101.

Forgas, J. P. (1983a). The effects of prototypicality and cultural salience on perceptions of people. *Journal of Research in Personality,* *17,* 153-173.

Forgas, J. P. (1983b). Social skills and the perception of interaction episodes. *British Journal of Clinical Psychology, 22,* 195-207.

Franks, D. D., & Marolla, J. (1976). Efficacious action and social approval as interacting dimensions of self-esteem: A tentative formulation through construct validation. *Sociometry, 39,* 324-341.

Freedman, M. B., Leary, T. F., Ossorio, A. G., & Coffey, H. S. (1951). The interpersonal dimension of personality. *Journal of Personality, 20,* 143-161.

Furnham, A., & Henderson, M. (1983). Assessing assertiveness: A content and correlational analysis of five assertiveness inventories. *Behavioral Assessment, 6,* 79-88.

Gable, S. L., & Shean, G. D. (2000). Perceived social competence and depression. *Journal of Social and Personal Relationships, 17,* 139-150.

Garland, D. R. (1981). Training married couples in listening skills: Effects on behavior, perceptual accuracy and marital adjustment. *Family Relations, 30,* 297-306.

Garland, M., & Fitzgerald, M. (1998). Social skills correlates of depressed mood in normal young adolescents. *Irish Journal of Psychological Studies, 15,* 19-21.

Gervasio, A. H., & Crawford, M. (1989). Social evaluations of assertiveness: A critique and speech act reformulation. *Psychology of Women Quarterly, 13,* 1-25.

Gill, D. S., Christensen, A., & Fincham, F. D. (1999). Predicting marital satisfaction from behavior: Do all roads lead to Rome? *Personal Relationships, 6,* 369-387.

Glaser, S. R., & Eblen, A. (1986). Organizational communication effectiveness: The view of corporate administrators. *Journal of Applied Communication Research, 14,* 119-132.

Glass, T. A., de Leon, C. M., Marottoli, R. A., & Berkman, L. F. (1999). Population based study of social and productive activities as predictors of survival among elderly Americans. *British Medical Journal, 319,* 478-483.

Goffman, E. (1974). *Frame analysis: An essay on the organization of experience.* Cambridge, MA: Harvard University Press.

Goldfried, M. R., Padawer, W., & Robins, C. (1984). Social anxiety and the semantic structure of heterosocial interactions. *Journal of Abnormal Psychology, 93,* 87-97.

Goldsmith, E. C. (1988). *Exclusive conversations: The art of interaction in seventeenth-century France.* Philadelphia: University of Pennsylvania Press.

Gorecki, P. R., Dickson, A. L., & Ritzler, B. (1981). Convergent and concurrent validation of four measures of assertion. *Journal of Behavioral Assessment, 3,* 85-91.

Gottman, J. M. (1979). *Marital interaction: Experimental investigations.* New York: Academic Press.

Gottman, J. M. (1994). *What predicts divorce? The relationship between marital processes and marital outcomes.* Hillsdale, NJ: Lawrence Erlbaum.

Gottman, J. M., & Krokoff, L. J. (1989). Marital interaction and satisfaction: A longitudinal view. *Journal of Consulting and Clinical Psychology, 57,* 47-52.

Gottman, J. M., & Levenson, R. W. (1992). Marital processes predictive of later dissolution: Behavior, physiology, and health. *Journal of Personality and Social Psychology, 63,* 221-233.

Gottman, J. M., & Levenson, R. W. (1999a). Rebound from marital conflict and divorce prediction. *Family Process, 38,* 287-292.

Gottman, J. M., & Levenson, R. W. (1999b). What predicts change in marital interaction over time? A study of alternative models. *Family Process, 38,* 143-158.

Gottman, J. M., & Porterfield, A. L. (1981). Communicative competence in the nonverbal behavior of married couples. *Journal of Marriage and the Family, 43,* 817-824.

Gottman, J. M., & Rushe, R. (1995). Communication and social skills approaches to treating ailing marriages: A recommendation for a new marital therapy called "minimal marital therapy." In W. O'Donohue & L. Krasner (Eds.), *Handbook of psychological skills training: Techniques and applications* (pp. 287-305). Boston: Allyn & Bacon.

Gould, S. J. (1981). *The mismeasure of man.* New York: W. W. Norton.

Graham, E. E., Barbato, C. A., & Perse, E. M. (1993). The interpersonal communication motives model. *Communication Quarterly, 41,* 172-186.

Graham, E. E., Papa, M. J., & Brooks, G. P. (1992). Functions of humor in conversation:

Conceptualization and measurement. *Western Journal of Communication, 56,* 161-183.

Greene, J. O. (1984). A cognitive approach to human communication: An action assembly theory. *Communication Monographs, 51,* 289-306.

Greene, J. O. (1997). A second generation action assembly theory. In J. O. Greene (Ed.), *Message production: Advances in communication theory* (pp. 151-170). Mahwah, NJ: Lawrence Erlbaum Associates.

Greene, J. O., & Geddes, D. (1993). An action assembly perspective on social skill. *Communication Theory, 3,* 26-49.

Grice, H. P. (1989). *Studies in the way of words.* Cambridge, MA: Harvard University Press.

Grimshaw, A. D. (1980). Mishearings, misunderstandings, and other nonsuccesses in talk: A plea for redress of speaker-oriented bias. *Sociological Inquiry, 50,* 31-74.

Gruppen, L. D., Garcia, J., Grum, C. M., Fitzgerald, J. T., White, C. A., Dicken, L., Sisson, J. C., & Zweifler, A. (1997). Medical students' self-assessment accuracy in communication skills. *Academic Medicine, 72* (Suppl. 1), S57-S59.

Gudykunst, W. B., & Hammer, M. R. (1984). Dimensions of intercultural effectiveness: Culture specific or culture general? *International Journal of Intercultural Relations, 8,* 1-10.

Habermas, J. (1970). Toward a theory of communicative competence. In H. P. Dreitzel (Ed.), *Recent sociology* (Vol. 2, pp. 115-148). New York: Macmillan.

Habermas, J. (1981). *The theory of communicative action: Vol. 1. Reason and the rationalization of society.* Boston: Beacon.

Habermas, J. (1987). *The theory of communicative action: Vol. 2. The critique of functionalist reason.* Cambridge: Polity.

Haefner, P. T., Notarius, C. I., & Pellegrini, D. S. (1991). Determinants of satisfaction with marital discussions: An exploration of husband-wife differences. *Behavioral Assessment, 13,* 67-82.

Hammer, M. R. (1987). Behavioral dimensions of intercultural effectiveness: A replication and extension. *International Journal of Intercultural Relations, 11,* 65-88.

Hammer, M. R., Gudykunst, W. B., & Wiseman, R. L. (1978). Dimensions of intercultural effectiveness: An exploratory study. *International Journal of Intercultural Relations, 2,* 382-393.

Hansson, R. O., Jones, W. H., & Carpenter, B. N. (1984). Relational competence and social support. *Review of Personality and Social Psychology, 5,* 265-284.

Hargie, O. D. W. (1997). Communication as skilled performance. In O. D. W. Hargie (Ed.), *The handbook of communication skills* (2nd ed., pp. 7-28). New York: Routledge.

Hawkins, K. W., & Fillion, B. P. (1999). Perceived communication skill needs for work groups. *Communication Research Reports, 16,* 167-174.

Hazleton, V., Jr., & Cupach, W. R. (1986). An exploration of ontological knowledge: Communication competence as a function of the ability to describe, predict, and explain. *Western Journal of Speech Communication, 50,* 119-132.

Hazleton, V., Jr., Cupach, W. R., & Canary, D. J. (1987). Situation perception: Interactions between competence and messages. *Journal of Language and Social Psychology, 6,* 57-63.

Heavey, C. L., Christensen, A., & Malamuth, N. M. (1995). The longitudinal impact of demand and withdrawal during marital conflict. *Journal of Consulting and Clinical Psychology, 63,* 797-801.

Heavey, C. L., Larson, B. M., Zumtobel, D. C., & Christensen, A. (1996). The communication patterns questionnaire: The reliability and validity of a constructive communication scale. *Journal of Marriage and the Family, 58,* 797-800.

Hecht, H., & Wittchen, H.-U. (1988). The frequency of social dysfunction in a general population sample and in patients with mental disorders: A comparison using the Social Interview Schedule (SIS). *Social Psychiatry and Psychiatric Epidemiology, 23,* 17-29.

Hecht, M. L. (1978). The conceptualization and measurement of interpersonal communication satisfaction. *Human Communication Research, 4,* 253-264.

Hecht, M. L. (1984). Satisfying communication and relationship labels: Intimacy and length of relationship as perceptual frames of naturalistic conversations. *Western Journal of Speech Communication, 48,* 201-216.

Hecht, M. L., Collier, M. J., & Ribeau, S. A. (1993). *African American communication.* Newbury Park, CA: Sage.

Heise, D. R. (1979). *Understanding events: Affect and the construction of social action.* New York: Cambridge University Press.

Henderson, M., & Furnham, A. (1983). Dimensions of assertiveness: Factor analysis of five assertion inventories. *Journal of Behavior Therapy and Experimental Psychiatry, 14,* 223-231.

Herrmann, D. S., & McWhirter, J. J. (1997). Refusal and resistance skills for children and adolescents: A selected review. *Journal of Counseling and Development, 75,* 177-187.

Herzberg, D. S., Hammen, C., Burge, D., Daley, S. E., Davila, J., & Lindberg, N. (1998). Social competence as a predictor of chronic interpersonal stress. *Personal Relationships, 5,* 207-218.

Higginbotham, D. J., & Wilkins, D. P. (1999). Slipping through the timestream: Social issues of time and timing in augmented interactions. In D. Kovarsky, J. F. Duchan, & M. Maxwell (Eds.), *Constructing (in)competence: Disabling evaluations in clinical and social interaction* (pp. 49-82). Mahwah, NJ: Lawrence Erlbaum.

Hofstede, G. (1980). *Culture's consequences: International differences in work-related values.* Beverly Hills, CA: Sage.

Hofstede, G. (2001). *Culture's consequences: Comparing values, behaviors, institutions, and organizations across nations* (2nd ed.). Thousand Oaks, CA: Sage.

Hooley, J. M., & Hahlweg, K. (1989). Marital satisfaction and marital communication in German and English couples. *Behavioral Assessment, 11,* 119-133.

Hopper, R., Knapp, M. L., & Scott, L. (1981). Couples' personal idioms: Exploring intimate talk. *Journal of Communication, 31*(1), 23-33.

Horney, K. (1945). *Our inner conflicts: A constructive theory of neurosis.* New York: W. W. Norton.

House, J. S., Landis, K. R., & Umberson, D. (1988). Social relationships and health. *Science, 241,* 540-545.

Howe, M. J. A. (1997). *IQ in question: The truth about intelligence.* Thousand Oaks, CA: Sage.

Hunt, J., & Manning, P. K. (1991). The social context of police lying. *Symbolic Interaction, 14,* 51-70.

Huston, T. L., & Vangelisti, A. L. (1991). Socioemotional behavior and satisfaction in marital relationships: A longitudinal study. *Journal of Personality and Social Psychology, 61,* 721-733.

Ickes, W. (1981). Sex-role influences in dyadic interaction: A theoretical model. In C. Mayo & N. M. Henley (Eds.), *Gender and nonverbal behavior* (pp. 95-128). New York: Springer-Verlag.

Ickes, W. (1985). Sex-role influences on compatibility in relationships. In W. Ickes (Ed.), *Compatible and incompatible relationships* (pp. 187-208). New York: Springer-Verlag.

Ickes, W. (Ed.). (1997). *Empathic accuracy.* New York: Guilford.

Ilott, I. (2001). Incompetence: An unspoken consensus. In J. Raven & J. Stephenson (Eds.), *Competence in the learning society* (pp. 57-66). New York: Peter Lang.

Infante, D. A., Chandler, T. A., & Rudd, J. E. (1989). Test of an argumentative skill deficiency model of interspousal violence. *Communication Monographs, 56,* 163-177.

Jeanneret, M. (1991). *A feast of words: Banquets and table talk in the Renaissance.* Chicago: University of Chicago Press.

Johannesen, R. L. (1971). The emerging concept of communication as dialogue. *Quarterly Journal of Speech, 57,* 373-382.

Johnson, M. D., & Bradbury, T. N. (1999). Marital satisfaction and topographical assessment of marital interaction: A longitudinal analysis of newlywed couples. *Personal Relationships, 6,* 19-40.

Julien, D., Markman, H. J., & Lindahl, K. M. (1989). A comparison of a global and a microanalytic coding system: Implications for future trends in studying interactions. *Behavioral Assessment, 11,* 81-100.

Kahn, M. (1970). Non-verbal communication and marital satisfaction. *Family Process, 9,* 449-456.

Kasson, J. F. (1990). *Rudeness and civility: Manners in nineteenth-century urban America.* New York: Hill & Wang.

Katriel, T., & Philipsen, G. (1981). "What we need is communication": "Communication" as a cultural category in some American speech. *Communication Monographs, 48,* 301-317.

Kellermann, K., Reynolds, R., & Chen, J. B. (1991). Strategies of conversational retreat: When parting is not sweet sorrow. *Communication Monographs, 58,* 362-383.

Kellermann, K., & Shea, B. C. (1996). Threats, suggestions, hints, and promises: Gaining compliance efficiently and politely. *Communication Quarterly, 44,* 145-165.

Kelley, H. H., Berscheid, E., Christensen, A., Harvey, J. H., Huston, T. L., Levinger, G., et al. (1983). *Close relationships.* New York: Freeman.

Kelly, J. (1982). *Social skills training: A practical guide for interventions.* New York: Springer.

Kennedy, G. (1963). *The art of persuasion in Greece.* Princeton, NJ: Princeton University Press.

Kenny, D. A. (1994). *Interpersonal perception: A social relations analysis.* New York: Guilford.

Kieren, D., & Tallman, I. (1972). Spousal adaptability: An assessment of marital competence. *Journal of Marriage and the Family, 34,* 247-255.

Knapp, M. L., Ellis, D. G., & Williams, B. A. (1980). Perceptions of communication behavior associated with relationship terms. *Communication Monographs, 47,* 262-278.

Knapp, M. L., Hart, R. P., Friedrich, G. W., & Shulman, G. M. (1973). The rhetoric of goodbye: Verbal and nonverbal correlates of human leave-taking. *Speech Monographs, 40,* 182-198.

Kolb, J. A. (1996). A comparison of leadership behaviors and competencies in high- and average-performance teams. *Communication Reports, 9,* 173-183.

Kolotkin, R. A., Wielkiewicz, R. M., Judd, B., & Weiser, S. (1983). Behavioral components of assertion: Comparison of univariate and multivariate assessment strategies. *Behavioral Assessment, 6,* 61-78.

Kowalski, R. M. (Ed.). (1997). *Aversive interpersonal behaviors.* New York: Plenum.

Kowalski, R. M. (2000). "I was only kidding!": Victims' and perpetrators' perceptions of teasing. *Personality and Social Psychology Bulletin, 26,* 231-241.

Kristiansen, M., & Bloch-Poulsen, J. (2000). The challenge of the unspoken in organizations: Caring container as a dialogic answer? *Southern Communication Journal, 65,* 176-190.

Krokoff, L. J. (1991). Communication orientation as a moderator between strong and negative affect and marital satisfaction. *Behavioral Assessment, 13,* 51-65.

Kurdek, L. A. (1998). Developmental changes in marital satisfaction: A 6-year prospective longitudinal study of newlywed couples. In T. N. Bradbury (Ed.), *The developmental course of marital dysfunction* (pp. 180-204). Cambridge: Cambridge University Press.

LaFollette, H., & Graham, G. (1986). Honesty and intimacy. *Journal of Social and Personal Relationships, 3,* 3-18.

Laing, R. D., Phillipson, H., & Lee, A. R. (1966). *Interpersonal perception: A theory and a method of research.* New York: Springer.

Lamke, L. K., Sollie, D. L., Durbin, R. G., & Fitzpatrick, J. A. (1994). Masculinity, femininity, and relationship satisfaction: The mediating role of interpersonal competence. *Journal of Social and Personal Relationships, 11,* 535-554.

Landsheer, H. A., Maassen, G. H., Bisschop, P., & Adema, L. (1998). Can higher grades result in fewer friends? A reexamination of the relation between academic and social competence. *Adolescence, 33,* 185-191.

Lannamann, J. W. (1991). Interpersonal communication research as ideological practice. *Communication Theory, 1,* 179-203.

Larson, C. E., Backlund, P., Redmond, M., & Barbour, A. (1978). *Assessing functional communication.* Falls Church, VA: Speech Communication Association.

Leary, T., & Coffey, H. S. (1955). Interpersonal diagnosis: Some problems of methodology and validation. *Journal of Abnormal and Social Psychology, 50,* 110-124.

Leonard, K. E., & Roberts, L. J. (1998). Marital aggression, quality, and stability in the first year of marriage: Findings from the Buffalo newlywed study. In T. N. Bradbury (Ed.), *The developmental course of marital dysfunction* (pp. 44-73). Cambridge: Cambridge University Press.

Levenson, R. W., Cartensen, L. L., & Gottman, J. M. (1994). Influence of age and gender on affect, physiology, and their interrelations: A study of long-term marriages. *Journal of Personality and Social Psychology, 67,* 56-68.

Levinson, S. C. (1995). Interactional biases in human thinking. In E. N. Goody (Ed.), *Social intelligence and interaction: Expressions and implications of the social bias in human intelligence* (pp. 221-260). Cambridge: Cambridge University Press.

Lewine, R. R. J. (1984). Stalking the schizophrenia marker: Evidence for a general vulnerability model of psychopathology. In N. F. Watt, E. J. Anthony, L. C. Wynne, & J. E. Rolf (Eds.), *Children at risk for schizophrenia: A longitudinal perspective* (pp. 545-550). Cambridge: Cambridge University Press.

Lewis, M. A., & Rook, K. S. (1999). Social control in personal relationships: Impact on health behaviors and psychological distress. *Health Psychology, 18,* 63-71.

Linehan, M. M., & Walker, R. O. (1983). The components of assertion: Factor analysis of a multimethod assessment battery. *British Journal of Clinical Psychology, 22,* 277-281.

Linell, P. (1998). *Approaching dialogue: Talk, interaction and contexts in dialogical perspectives.* Amsterdam: John Benjamins.

Lippard, P. V. (1988). "Ask me no questions, I'll tell you no lies": Situational exigencies for interpersonal deception. *Western Journal of Speech Communication, 52,* 91-103.

Makau, J. M. (1991). The principles of fidelity and veracity: Guidelines for ethical communication. In K. J. Greenberg (Ed.), *Conversations on communication ethics* (pp. 111-120). Norwood, NJ: Ablex.

Markman, H. J., Floyd, F. J., Stanley, S. M., & Storaasli, R. D. (1988). Prevention of marital distress: A longitudinal investigation. *Journal of Consulting and Clinical Psychology, 56,* 210-217.

Markman, H. J., & Hahlweg, K. (1993). The prediction and prevention of marital distress: An international perspective. *Clinical Psychology Review, 13,* 29-43.

Marlowe, H. A., Jr. (1985). Competence: A social intelligence perspective. In H. A. Marlowe, Jr., & R. B. Weinberg (Eds.), *Competence development: Theory and practice in special populations* (pp. 50-82). Springfield, IL: Charles C Thomas.

Marshall, J. C. (1977). Minds, machines and metaphors. *Social Studies of Science, 7,* 475-488.

Martin, J. N., & Hammer, M. R. (1989). Behavioral categories of intercultural communication competence: Everyday communicators' perceptions. *International Journal of Intercultural Relations, 13,* 303-332.

Maslow, A. H. (1968). *Toward a psychology of being* (2nd ed.). New York: D. Van Nostrand.

Matarazzo, J. D., & Wiens, A. N. (1977). Speech behavior as an objective correlate of empathy and outcome in interview and psychotherapy research: A review with implications for behavior modification. *Behavior Modification, 1,* 453-480.

Matthews, L. S., Wickrama, K. A. S., & Conger, R. D. (1996). Predicting marital instability from spouse and observer reports of marital interaction. *Journal of Marriage and the Family, 58,* 641-655.

McAdams, D. P. (1988). *Power, intimacy, and the life story: Personological inquiries into identity.* New York: Guilford.

McCabe, M. P., Cummins, R. A., & Romeo, Y. (1996). Relationship status, relationship quality, and health. *Journal of Family Studies, 2,* 109-120.

McCroskey, J. C. (1982). Communication competence and performance: A research and pedagogical perspective. *Communication Education, 31,* 1-8.

McFall, R. M. (1982). A review and reformulation of the concept of social skills. *Behavioral Assessment, 4,* 1-33.

McLaughlin, M. L. (1984). *Conversation: How talk is organized.* Beverly Hills, CA: Sage.

McNamee, S., & Gergen, K. J. (1999). *Relational responsibility: Resources for sustainable dialogue.* Thousand Oaks, CA: Sage.

McQuail, D. (1987). Functions of communication: A nonfunctionalist overview. In C. R. Berger & S. H. Chaffee (Eds.), *Handbook of communication science* (pp. 327-349). Newbury Park, CA: Sage.

Meeks, B. S., Hendrick, S. S., & Hendrick, C. (1998). Communication, love and relationship satisfaction. *Journal of Social and Personal Relationships, 15,* 755-773.

Menache, S. (1990). *Vox Dei: Communication in the middle ages.* New York: Oxford.

Metts, S. (1989). An exploratory investigation of deception in close relationships. *Journal of Social and Personal Relationships, 6,* 159-179.

Mieth, D. (1997). The basic norm of truthfulness: Its ethical justification and universality. In C. Christians & M. Traber (Eds.), *Communication ethics and universal values* (pp. 87-104). Thousand Oaks, CA: Sage.

Milhouse, V. H. (1993). The applicability of interpersonal communication competence to the intercultural context. In R. L. Wiseman & J. Koester (Eds.), *Intercultural communication competence* (pp. 184-203). Newbury Park, CA: Sage.

Miller, G. E., Dopp, J. M., Myers, H. F., Stevens, S. Y., & Fahey, J. L. (1999). Psychosocial predictors of natural killer cell mobilization during marital conflict. *Health Psychology, 18,* 262-271.

Miller, G. E., Kemeny, M. E., Taylor, S. E., Cole, S. W., & Visscher, B. R. (1997). Social relationships and immune processes in HIV seropositive gay and bisexual men. *Annals of Behavioral Medicine, 19,* 139-151.

Miller, L. C., Berg, J. H., & Archer, R. L. (1983). Openers: Individuals who elicit intimate self-disclosure. *Journal of Personality and Social Psychology, 44,* 1234-1244.

Mohrmann, G. F. (1972). The civile conversation: Communication in the Renaissance. *Speech Monographs, 39,* 193-204.

Monge, P. R., Bachman, S. G., Dillard, J. P., & Eisenberg, E. M. (1982). Communicator competence in the workplace: Model testing and scale development. In M. Burgoon (Ed.), *Communication yearbook 5* (pp. 505-528). Beverly Hills, CA: Sage.

Morse, B. W., & Piland, R. N. (1981). An assessment of communication competencies needed by intermediate-level health care providers: A study of nurse-patient, nurse-doctor, nurse-nurse communication relationships. *Journal of Applied Communication Research, 9,* 30-41.

Mortensen, C. D. (1997). *Miscommunication.* Thousand Oaks, CA: Sage.

Muchmore, J., & Galvin, K. (1983). A report of the task force on career competencies in oral communication skills for community college students seeking immediate entry into the work force. *Communication Education, 32,* 207-220.

Muñoz, M., Vazquez, C., Bermejo, M., & Vazquez, J. J. (1999). Stressful life events among homeless people: Quantity, types, timing, and perceived causality. *Journal of Community Psychology, 27,* 73-87.

Nangle, D. W., & Hansen, D. J. (1993). Relations between social skills and high-risk sexual interactions among adolescents. *Behavior Modification, 17,* 113-135.

Newcomb, A. F., Bukowski, W. M., & Pattee, L. (1993). Children's peer relations: A meta-analytic review of popular, rejected, neglected, controversial, and average sociometric status. *Psychological Bulletin, 113,* 99-128.

Nicotera, A. M. (1997). *The mate relationships: Cross-cultural applications of a rules theory.* Albany: State University of New York Press.

Nisbett, R., & Ross, L. (1980). *Human inference: Strategies and shortcomings of social judgment.* Englewood Cliffs, NJ: Prentice Hall.

Noller, P., & Feeney, J. A. (1998). Communication in early marriage: Responses to conflict, nonverbal accuracy, and conversational patterns. In T. N. Bradbury (Ed.), *The developmental course of marital dysfunction* (pp. 11-43). Cambridge: Cambridge University Press.

Noller, P., Feeney, J. A., Bonnell, D., & Callan, V. J. (1994). A longitudinal study of conflict in early marriage. *Journal of Social and Personal Relationships, 11,* 233-252.

Noller, P., & Gallois, C. (1988). Understanding and misunderstanding in marriage: Sex and marital adjustment differences in structured and free interaction. In P. Noller & M. A. Fitzpatrick (Eds.), *Perspectives on marital interaction* (pp. 53-77). Clevedon, Eng.: Multilingual Matters.

O'Hair, H. D., & Cody, M. J. (1994). Deception. In W. R. Cupach & B. H. Spitzberg (Eds.), *The dark side of interpersonal communication* (pp. 181-214). Hillsdale, NJ: Lawrence Erlbaum.

O'Keefe, B. J., & McCornack, S. A. (1987). Message design logic and message goal structure: Effects on perceptions of message quality in regulative communication situations. *Human Communication Research, 14,* 68-92.

Olebe, M., & Koester, J. (1989). Exploring the cross-cultural equivalence of the Behavioral Assessment Scale for Intercultural Communication. *International Journal of Intercultural Relations, 13,* 333-348.

Omdahl, B. L. (1985). *A multitrait-multimethod study of ten measures of empathy.* Paper presented at the annual meeting of the Speech Communication Association, Denver.

O'Neil, H. F., Jr., Allred, K., & Baker, E. L. (1997). Review of workforce readiness theoretical frameworks. In H. F. O'Neil, Jr. (Ed.), *Workforce readiness: Competencies and assessment* (pp. 3-25). Mahwah, NJ: Lawrence Erlbaum.

Osgood, C. E., May, W. H., & Miron, M. S. (1975). *Cross-cultural universals of affective meaning.* Urbana: University of Illinois Press.

Otness, H. R. (1941). Educating for social competence. *Training School Bulletin, 38,* 21-32.

Pachman, J. S., Foy, D. W., Massey, F., & Eisler, R. M. (1978). A factor analysis of assertive behaviors. *Journal of Consulting and Clinical Psychology, 46,* 347.

Palmer, E. J., & Hollin, C. R. (1999). Social competence and sociomoral reasoning in young offenders. *Applied Cognitive Psychology, 13,* 79-87.

Papa, M. J., & Graham, E. E. (1991). The impact of diagnosing skill deficiencies and assessment-based communication training on managerial performance. *Communication Education, 40,* 268-384.

Parker, J. G., & Asher, S. R. (1987). Peer relations and later personal adjustment: Are low-accepted children at risk? *Psychological Bulletin, 102,* 357-389.

Parks, M. R. (1995). Ideology in interpersonal communication: Beyond the couches, talk shows, and bunkers. In B. R. Burleson (Ed.), *Communication yearbook 18* (pp. 480-497). Thousand Oaks, CA: Sage.

Pasch, L. A., & Bradbury, T. N. (1998). Social support, conflict, and the development of marital dysfunction. *Journal of Consulting and Clinical Psychology, 66,* 219-230.

Patterson, M. L. (1994). Strategic functions of nonverbal exchange. In J. A. Daly & J. M. Wiemann (Eds.), *Strategic interpersonal communication* (pp. 273-293). Hillsdale, NJ: Lawrence Erlbaum.

Pavitt, C. (1989). Accounting for the process of communicative competence evaluation: A comparison of predictive models. *Communication Research, 16,* 405-433.

Payne, M. J., & Sabourin, T. C. (1990). Argumentative skill deficiency and its relationship to quality of marriage. *Communication Research Reports, 7,* 121-124.

Pearce, W. B., & Cronen, V. E. (1980). *Communication, action, and meaning.* New York: Praeger.

Pearce, W. B., & Littlejohn, S. W. (1997). *Moral conflict: When social worlds collide.* Thousand Oaks, CA: Sage.

Pearce, W. B., & Pearce, K. A. (2000). Combining passions and abilities: Toward dialogic virtuosity. *Southern Communication Journal, 65,* 161-175.

Penley, L. E., Alexander, E. R., Jernigan, I. E., & Henwood, C. I. (1991). Communication abilities of managers: The relationship to performance. *Journal of Management, 17,* 57-76.

Penman, R. (1992). Good theory and good practice: An argument in progress. *Communication Theory, 2,* 234-250.

Peterson, J., Fischetti, M., Curran, J. P., & Arland, S. (1981). Sense of timing: A skill deficit in heterosocially anxious women. *Behavior Therapy, 12,* 195-201.

Peterson, M. S. (1997). Personnel interviewers' perceptions of the importance and adequacy of applicants' communication skills. *Communication Education, 46,* 287-291.

Petrie, K. J., Booth, R. J., & Davison, K. P. (1995). Repression, disclosure, and immune function: Recent findings and methodological issues. In J. W. Pennebaker (Ed.), *Emotion, disclosure,*

and health (pp. 223-237). Washington, DC: American Psychological Association.

Phillips, E. L. (1978). *The social skills basis of psychopathology: Alternatives to abnormal psychology and psychiatry.* New York: Grune & Stratton.

Phillips, G. M. (1984). A competent view of "competence." *Communication Education, 32,* 25-26.

Phillips, L., & Zigler, E. (1961). Social competence: The action-thought parameter and vicariousness in normal and pathological behaviors. *Journal of Abnormal and Social Psychology, 63,* 137-146.

Pitcher, S. W., & Meikle, S. (1980). The topography of assertive behavior in positive and negative situations. *Behavior Therapy, 11,* 532-547.

Powers, W. G., & Lowry, D. N. (1984). Basic communication fidelity: A fundamental approach. In R. N. Bostrom (Ed.), *Competence in communication: A multidisciplinary approach* (pp. 57-73). Beverly Hills, CA: Sage.

Prisbell, M. (1995). Strategies for maintaining relationships and self-rated competence in ongoing relationships. *Psychological Reports, 76,* 63-64.

Procidano, M. E. (1992). The nature of perceived social support: Findings of meta-analytic studies. In C. D. Spielberger & J. N. Butcher (Eds.), *Advances in personality assessment* (Vol. 9, pp. 1-26). Hillsdale, NJ: Lawrence Erlbaum.

Quintillian. (1903). *Quintillian's institutes of oratory; or education of an orator* (J. S. Bell, Trans.). London: George Bell.

Rakos, R. F. (1991). *Assertive behavior: Theory, research, and training.* London: Routledge.

Ralph, A. (1990). Variations of verbal behaviour and the assessment of social competence in dyadic interactions. *Australian Journal of Psychology, 42,* 261-275.

Ralph, A., & Lee, E. (1994). The effects of interpersonal behaviour of varying participant role in initial dyadic conversations. *Scandinavian Journal of Behaviour Therapy, 23,* 155-175.

Ralph, A., & Thorne, E. (1993). Defining and enhancing competent interview behaviour using the verbal interaction analysis system. *Scandinavian Journal of Behaviour Therapy, 22,* 65-87.

Reddy, M. J. (1979). The conduit metaphor: A case of frame conflict in our language about language. In A. Ortony (Ed.), *Metaphor and thought* (pp. 284-324). Cambridge: Cambridge University Press.

Regehr, C., & Marziali, E. (1999). Response to sexual assault: A relational perspective. *Journal of Nervous and Mental Disease, 187,* 618-623.

Reis, H. T., & Franks, P. (1994). The role of intimacy and social support in health outcomes: Two processes or one? *Personal Relationships, 1,* 185-197.

Reis, H. T., Sheldon, K. M., Gable, S. L., Roscoe, J., & Ryan, R. M. (2000). Daily well-being: The role of autonomy, competence, and relatedness. *Personality and Social Psychology Bulletin, 26,* 419-435.

Reis, H. T., Wheeler, L., Kernis, M. H., Spiegel, N., & Nezlek, J. (1985). On specificity in the impact of social participation on physical and psychological health. *Journal of Personality and Social Psychology, 48,* 456-471.

Reiss, I. L., Anderson, R. E., & Sponaugle, G. C. (1980). A multivariate model of the determinants of extramarital sexual permissiveness. *Journal of Marriage and the Family, 42,* 395-411.

Ren, X. S. (1997). Marital status and quality of relationships: The impact on health perception. *Social Scientific Medicine, 44,* 241-249.

Renshaw, P. D., & Asher, S. R. (1982). Social competence and peer status: The distinction between goals and strategies. In K. H. Rubin & H. S. Ross (Eds.), *Peer relationships and social skills in childhood* (pp. 375-395). New York: Springer-Verlag.

Renwick, S., & Emler, N. (1991). The relationship between social skills deficits and juvenile delinquency. *British Journal of Clinical Psychology, 30,* 61-71.

Richmond, V. P. (1995). Amount of communication in marital dyads as a function of dyad and individual marital satisfaction. *Communication Research Reports, 12,* 152-159.

Richmond, V. P., McCroskey, J. C., & McCroskey, L. L. (1989). An investigation of self-perceived communication competence and personality orientations. *Communication Research Reports, 6,* 30-38.

Richmond, V. P., McCroskey, J. C., & Roach, K. D. (1997). Communication and decision-making styles, power base usage, and satisfaction in marital dyads. *Communication Quarterly, 45,* 410-426.

Riggio, R. E. (1986). Assessment of basic social skills. *Journal of Personality and Social Psychology, 51,* 649-660.

Riggio, R. E., Watring, K. P., & Throckmorton, B. (1993). Social skills, social support, and psychosocial adjustment. *Personality and Individual Differences, 15,* 275-280.

Riggio, R. E., & Zimmerman, J. (1991). Social skills and interpersonal relationships: Influences on social support and support seeking. In W. H. Jones & D. Perlman (Eds.), *Advances in personal relationships* (Vol. 2, 133-155). London: Jessica Kingsley.

Riikonen, E. (1999). Inspiring dialogues and relational responsibility. In S. McNamee & K. J. Gergen (Eds.), *Relational responsibility: Resources for sustainable dialogue* (pp. 139-150). Thousand Oaks, CA: Sage.

Roberts, N., & Noller, P. (1998). The associations between adult attachment and couple violence: The role of communication patterns and relationship satisfaction. In J. A. Simpson & W. S. Rholes (Eds.), *Attachment theory and close relationships* (pp. 317-350). New York: Guilford.

Rodriguez, N., & Ryave, A. (1990). Telling lies in everyday life: Motivational and organizational consequences of sequential preferences. *Qualitative Sociology, 13,* 195-210.

Roloff, M. E., & Kellermann, K. (1984). Judgments of interpersonal competence: How you know, what you know, and who you know. In R. N. Bostrom (Ed.), *Competence in communication: A multidisciplinary approach* (pp. 175-218). Beverly Hills, CA: Sage.

Rook, K. S. (1984). The negative side of social interaction: Impact on psychological well-being. *Journal of Personality and Social Psychology, 46,* 1097-1108.

Rook, K. S. (1992). Detrimental aspects of social relationships: Taking stock of an emerging literature. In H. O. F. Veiel & U. Baumann (Eds.), *The meaning and measurement of social support* (pp. 157-169). New York: Hemisphere.

Rook, K. S. (1998). Investigating the positive and negative sides of personal relationships: Through a lens darkly? In B. H. Spitzberg & W. R. Cupach (Eds.), *The dark side of close relationships* (pp. 369-393). Mahwah, NJ: Lawrence Erlbaum.

Rosenfeld, L. B., Grant, C. H., III, & McCroskey, J. C. (1995). Communication apprehension and self-perceived communication competence of academically gifted students. *Communication Education, 44,* 79-86.

Royce, W. S., & Weiss, R. L. (1975). Behavioral cues in the judgment of marital satisfaction: A linear regression analysis. *Journal of Consulting and Clinical Psychology, 43,* 816-824.

Ruben, B. D. (1976). Assessing communication competency for intercultural adaptation. *Group and Organization Studies, 1,* 334-354.

Ruben, B. D., & Kealey, D. J. (1979). Behavioral assessment of communication competency and the prediction of cross-cultural adaptation. *International Journal of Intercultural Relations, 3,* 15-47.

Rubin, K. H., Booth, C., Rose-Krasnor, L., & Mills, R. S. L. (1995). Social relationships and social skills: A conceptual and empirical analysis. In S. Shulman (Ed.), *Close relationships and socioemotional development* (pp. 63-94). Norwood, NJ: Ablex.

Rubin, R. B. (1981). *The development and refinement of a communication competency assessment instrument.* Paper presented at the annual meeting of the Speech Communication Association, Anaheim, CA.

Rubin, R. B. (1985). The validity of the Communication Competency Assessment Instrument. *Communication Monographs, 52,* 173-185.

Rubin, R. B., & Graham, E. E. (1988). Communication correlates of college success: An exploratory investigation. *Communication Education, 37,* 14-27.

Rubin, R. B., Graham, E. E., & Mignerey, J. T. (1990). A longitudinal study of college students' communication competence. *Communication Education, 39,* 1-14.

Rubin, R. B., Perse, E. M., & Barbato, C. A. (1988). Conceptualization and measurement of interpersonal communication motives. *Human Communication Research, 14,* 602-628.

Rubin, R. B., Rubin, A. M., & Martin, M. M. (1993). The role of self-disclosure and self-awareness in affinity-seeking competence. *Communication Research Reports, 10,* 115-128.

Ruesch, J. (1951). Communication and mental illness: A psychiatric approach. In J. Ruesch & G. Bateson, *Communication: The social matrix of psychiatry* (pp. 50-93). New York: W. W. Norton.

Sabourin, T. C., Infante, D. A., & Rudd, J. E. (1993). Verbal aggression in marriages: A comparison of violent, distressed but nonviolent, and nondistressed couples. *Human Communication Research, 20,* 245-267.

Sanford, K. (1998). Memories of feeling misunderstood, and a schema of partner empathic responding: New scales for marital research. *Journal of Social and Personal Relationships, 15,* 490-501.

Santelli, J., Bernstein, D. M., Zborowski, L., & Bernstein, J. M. (1990). Pursuing and distancing, and related traits: A cross-cultural assessment. *Journal of Personality Assessment, 55,* 663-672.

Sarason, B. R., Sarason, I. G., Hacker, T. A., & Basham, R. B. (1985). Concomitants of social support: Social skills, physical attractiveness, and gender. *Journal of Personality and Social Psychology, 49,* 469-480.

Scherz, J. W., Edwards, H. T., & Kallail, K. J. (1995). Communicative effectiveness of doctor-patient interactions. *Health Communication, 7,* 163-177.

Schneider, M. J., & Jordan, W. (1981). Perception of the communicative performance of Americans and Chinese in intercultural dyads. *International Journal of Intercultural Relations, 5,* 175-191.

Schutz, W. C. (1966). *The interpersonal underworld.* Palo Alto, CA: Science & Behavior.

Schwartz, G. E., & Kline, J. P. (1995). Repression, emotional disclosure, and health: Theoretical, empirical, and clinical considerations. In J. W. Pennebaker (Ed.), *Emotion, disclosure, and health* (pp. 177-193). Washington, DC: American Psychological Association.

Searle, J. R. (1969). *Speech acts: An essay in the philosophy of language.* Cambridge: Cambridge University Press.

Sedikides, C., Olsen, N., & Reis, H. T. (1993). Relationships as natural categories. *Journal of Personality and Social Psychology, 64,* 71-82.

Seeman, T. E., Berkman, L. F., Blazer, D., & Rowe, J. W. (1994). Social ties and support and neuroendocrine function: The MacArthur studies of successful aging. *Annals of Behavioral Medicine, 16,* 95-106.

Segrin, C. (1992). Specifying the nature of social skill deficits associated with depression. *Human Communication Research, 19,* 89-123.

Segrin, C. (1996). The relationship between social skills deficits and psychosocial problems: A test of a vulnerability model. *Communication Research, 23,* 425-450.

Segrin, C. (1998). The impact of assessment procedures on the relationship between paper and pencil and behavioral indicators of social skill. *Journal of Nonverbal Behavior, 22,* 229-251.

Segrin, C. (1999). Social skills, stressful life events, and the development of psychosocial problems. *Journal of Social and Clinical Psychology, 18,* 14-34.

Segrin, C., & Flora, J. (2000). Poor social skills are a vulnerability factor in the development of psychosocial problems. *Human Communication Research, 26,* 489-514.

Seibold, D. R., & Spitzberg, B. H. (1981). Attribution theory and research: Formalization, critique, and implications for communication. In B. Dervin & M. J. Voigt (Eds.), *Progress in communication sciences* (Vol. 3, pp. 85-125). Norwood, NJ: Ablex.

Shaver, P., Furman, W., & Buhrmester, D. (1985). Transition to college: Network changes, social skills, and loneliness. In S. Duck & D. Perlman (Eds.), *Understanding personal relationships: An interdisciplinary approach* (pp. 193-220). Beverly Hills, CA: Sage.

Shean, G. D., & Heefner, A. S. (1995). Depression, interpersonal style, and communication skills. *Journal of Nervous and Mental Disease, 183,* 485-487.

Sheldon, K. M., Ryan, R., & Reis, H. T. (1996). What makes for a good day? Competence and autonomy in the day and in the person. *Personality and Social Psychology Bulletin, 22,* 1270-1279.

Sheridan, T. (1762). *A course of lectures in elocution: Together with two dissertations on language; and some other tracts relative to those subjects.* London: W. Strahan.

Shockley-Zalabak, P., Staley, C. C., & Morley, D. D. (1988). The female professional: Perceived communication proficiencies as predictors of organizational advancement. *Human Relations, 41,* 553-567.

Shure, M. B. (1981). Social competence as a problem-solving skill. In J. D. Wine & M. D. Smye (Eds.), *Social competence* (pp. 158-188). New York: Guilford.

Sillars, A. L. (1998). (Mis)understanding. In B. H. Spitzberg & W. R. Cupach (Eds.), *The dark side of close relationships* (pp. 73-102). Mahwah, NJ: Lawrence Erlbaum.

Sillars, A. L., Pike, G. R., Jones, T. S., & Murphy, M. A. (1984). Communication and understanding in marriage. *Human Communication Research, 10,* 317-350.

Sillars, A. L., & Weisberg, J. (1987). Conflict as a social skill. In M. E. Roloff & G. R. Miller (Eds.), *Interpersonal processes: New directions in communication research* (pp. 140-171). Newbury Park, CA: Sage.

Sillars, A. L., Weisberg, J., Burggraf, C. S., & Zietlow, P. H. (1990). Communication and understanding revisited: Married couples' understanding and recall of conversations. *Communication Research, 17,* 500-522.

Simpson, J. A., Ickes, W., & Blackstone, T. (1995). When the head protects the heart: Empathic accuracy in dating relationships. *Journal of Personality and Social Psychology, 69,* 629-641.

Smith, D. A., Vivian, D., & O'Leary, K. D. (1990). Longitudinal prediction of marital discord from premarital expressions of affect. *Journal of Consulting and Clinical Psychology, 58,* 790-798.

Smith-Lovin, L. (1979). Behavior settings and impressions formed from social scenarios. *Social Psychology Quarterly, 42,* 31-43.

Spano, S., & Zimmerman, S. (1995). Interpersonal communication competence in context: Assessing performance in the selection interview. *Communication Reports, 8,* 18-26.

Spitzberg, B. H. (1983). Communication competence as knowledge, skill, and impression. *Communication Education, 32,* 323-328.

Spitzberg, B. H. (1989). Issues in the development of a theory of interpersonal competence in the intercultural context. *International Journal of Intercultural Relations, 13,* 241-268.

Spitzberg, B. H. (1990). The construct validity of trait-based measures of interpersonal competence. *Communication Research Reports, 7,* 107-116.

Spitzberg, B. H. (1991). An examination of trait measures of interpersonal competence. *Communication Reports, 4,* 22-29.

Spitzberg, B. H. (1993). The dialectics of (in)competence. *Journal of Social and Personal Relationships, 10,* 137-158.

Spitzberg, B. H. (1994a). The dark side of (in)competence. In W. R. Cupach & B. H. Spitzberg (Eds.), *The dark side of interpersonal communication* (pp. 25-49). Hillsdale, NJ: Lawrence Erlbaum.

Spitzberg, B. H. (1994b). Ideological issues in competence assessment. In S. Morreale, M. Brooks, R. Berko, & C. Cooke (Eds.), *Assessing college student competency in speech communication* (pp. 129-148). Annandale, VA: Speech Communication Association.

Spitzberg, B. H. (1994c). Instructional assessment of interpersonal competence: The Conversational Skills Rating Scale. In S. Morreale, M. Brooks, R. Berko, & C. Cooke (Eds.), *Assessing college student competency in speech communication* (pp. 325-352). Annandale, VA: Speech Communication Association.

Spitzberg, B. H. (2000). What is good communication? *Journal of the Association for Communication Administration, 29,* 103-119.

Spitzberg, B. H. (in press). Methods of interpersonal skills assessment. In J. O. Greene & B. R. Burleson (Eds.), *Handbook of communication and social interaction skills.* Mahwah, NJ: Lawrence Erlbaum.

Spitzberg, B. H., & Brunner, C. C. (1991). Toward a theoretical integration of context and communication competence inference research. *Western Journal of Speech Communication, 55,* 28-46.

Spitzberg, B. H., & Canary, D. J. (1985). Loneliness and relationally competent communication. *Journal of Social and Personal Relationships, 2,* 387-402.

Spitzberg, B. H., Canary, D. J., & Cupach, W. R. (1994). A competence-based approach to the study of interpersonal conflict. In D. D. Cahn (Ed.), *Conflict in personal relationships* (pp. 183-202). Hillsdale, NJ: Lawrence Erlbaum.

Spitzberg, B. H., & Cupach, W. R. (1984). *Interpersonal communication competence.* Beverly Hills, CA: Sage.

Spitzberg, B. H., & Cupach, W. R. (1989). *Handbook of interpersonal competence research.* New York: Springer-Verlag.

Spitzberg, B. H., & Cupach, W. R. (Eds.). (1998). *The dark side of close relationships.* Mahwah, NJ: Lawrence Erlbaum.

Spivack, G., Platt, J. J., & Shure, M. B. (1976). *The problem-solving approach to adjustment.* San Francisco: Jossey-Bass.

Stafford, L., & Dainton, M. (1994). The dark side of "normal" family interaction. In W. R. Cupach & B. H. Spitzberg (Eds.), *The dark side of interpersonal communication* (pp. 259-280). Hillsdale, NJ: Lawrence Erlbaum.

Steggell, G. L., & Harper, J. M. (1991). Family interaction patterns and communication processes. In S. J. Bahr (Ed.), *Family research: A sixty-year review, 1930-1990* (Vol. 1, pp. 97-170). New York: Lexington.

Straits-Tröster, K. A., Patterson, T. L., Semple, S. J., Temoshok, L., Roth, P. G.,

McCutchan, J. A., Chandler, J. L., & Grant, I. (1994). The relationship between loneliness, interpersonal competence, and immunologic status in HIV-infected men. *Psychology and Health, 9,* 204-219.

Su, Y.-P., & Ferraro, K. F. (1997). Social relations and health assessments among older people: Do the effects of integration and social contributions vary cross-culturally? *Journal of Gerontology: Social Sciences, 52B,* S27-S36.

Swanson, J., Swartz, M., Estroff, S., Borum, R., Wagner, R., & Hiday, V. (1998). Psychiatric impairment, social contact, and violent behavior: Evidence from a study of outpatient-committed persons with severe mental disorder. *Social Psychiatry and Psychiatric Epidemiology, 33*(Suppl.), S86-S94.

Sypher, B. D., & Zorn, T. E., Jr. (1986). Communication-related abilities and upward mobility: A longitudinal investigation. *Human Communication Research, 12,* 420-431.

Taylor, T. J. (1986). Do you understand? Criteria of understanding in verbal interaction. *Language & Communication, 6,* 171-180.

Terman, L. M. (1938). *Psychological factors in marital happiness.* New York: McGraw-Hill.

Thomsen, D. G., & Gilbert, D. G. (1998). Factors characterizing marital conflict states and traits: Physiological, affective, behavioral and neurotic variable contributions to marital conflict and satisfaction. *Personality and Individual Differences, 25,* 833-855.

Thorndike, R. L. (1920). Intelligence and its uses. *Harper's Monthly, 140,* 227-235.

Tolstedt, B. E., & Stokes, J. P. (1983). Relation of verbal, affective, and physical intimacy to marital satisfaction. *Journal of Counseling Psychology, 30,* 573-580.

Tooke, W., & Camire, L. (1991). Patterns of deception in intersexual and intrasexual mating strategies. *Ethology and Sociobiology, 12,* 345-364.

Tracy, K., & Moran, J. P., III. (1983). Conversational relevance in multiple-goal settings. In R. T. Craig & K. Tracy (Eds.), *Conversational coherence: Form, structure, and strategy* (pp. 116-135). Beverly Hills, CA: Sage.

Triandis, H. C. (1995). *Individualism and collectivism.* Boulder, CO: Westview.

Trower, P. (1980). Situational analysis of the components and processes of socially skilled and unskilled patients. *Journal of Consulting and Clinical Psychology, 48,* 327-339.

Trower, P. (1982). Toward a generative model of social skills: A critique and synthesis. In J. P. Curran & P. M. Monti (Eds.), *Social skills training* (pp. 399-427). New York: Guilford.

Trower, P. (1984). A radical critique and reformulation: From organism to agent. In P. Trower (Ed.), *Radical approaches to social skills training* (pp. 48-88). London: Croom Helm.

Trower, P., Bryant, B., & Argyle, M. (1978). *Social skills and mental health*. Philadelphia: University of Pennsylvania Press.

Truax, C. B. (1967). A scale for the rating of accurate empathy. In C. R. Rogers (Ed.), *The therapeutic relationship and its impact* (pp. 555-568). Madison: University of Wisconsin Press.

Tucker, J. S., & Anders, S. L. (1999). Attachment style, interpersonal perception accuracy, and relationship satisfaction in dating couples. *Personality and Social Psychology Bulletin, 25*, 403-412.

Vandeputte, D. D., Kemper, S., Hummert, M. L., Kemtes, K. A., Shaner, J., & Segrin, C. (1999). Social skills of older people: Conversations in same- and mixed-age dyads. *Discourse Processes, 27*, 55-76.

Vangelisti, A. L., & Daly, J. A. (1989). Correlates of speaking skills in the United States: A national assessment. *Communication Education, 38*, 132-143.

VanLear, C. A. (1991). Testing a cyclical model of communicative openness in relationship development: Two longitudinal studies. *Communication Monographs, 58*, 337-361.

Vanwesenbeeck, I., van Zessen, G., Ingham, R., Jaramazovic, E., & Stevens, D. (1999). Factors and processes in heterosexual competence and risk: An integrated review of the evidence. *Psychology and Health, 14*, 25-50.

Venable, K. V., & Martin, M. M. (1997). Argumentativeness and verbal aggressiveness in dating relationships. *Journal of Social Behavior and Personality, 12*, 955-964.

Veroff, J., Douvan, E., & Hatchett, S. (1993). Marital interaction and marital quality in the first year of marriage. In D. Perlman & W. H. Jones (Eds.), *Advances in personal relationships* (Vol. 4, pp. 103-138). Philadelphia: Jessica Kingsley.

Veroff, J., Douvan, E., Orbuch, T. L., & Acitelli, L. K. (1998). Happiness in stable marriages: The early years. In T. N. Bradbury (Ed.), *The developmental course of marital dysfunction* (pp. 152-179). Cambridge: Cambridge University Press.

Vroon, P. A. (1987). Man-machine analogs and theoretical mainstreams in psychology. In W. J. Baker, M. E. Hyland, H. Van Rappard, & A. W. Staats (Eds.), *Current issues in theoretical psychology* (pp. 393-414). New York: Elsevier North-Holland.

Waldron, V. R., Cegala, D. J., Sharkey, W. F., & Teboul, B. (1990). Cognitive and tactical dimensions of conversational goal management. *Journal of Language and Social Psychology, 9*, 101-118.

Waldron, V. R., & Lavitt, M. R. (2000). "Welfare-to-work": Assessing communication competencies and client outcomes in a job training program. *Southern Communication Journal, 66*, 1-15.

Wampler, K. S. (1982). The effectiveness of the Minnesota Couple Communication Program: A review of research. *Journal of Marital and Family Therapy, 8*, 345-355.

Ward, C., & Kennedy, A. (1999). The measurement of sociocultural adaptation. *International Journal of Intercultural Relations, 23*, 659-677.

Weeks, R. E., & Lefebvre, R. C. (1982). The assertive interaction coding system. *Journal of Behavioral Assessment, 4*, 71-85.

Weintraub, S., & Neale, J. M. (1984). Social behavior of children at risk for schizophrenia. In N. F. Watt, E. J. Anthony, L. C. Wynne, & J. E. Rolf (Eds.), *Children at risk for schizophrenia: A longitudinal perspective* (pp. 279-285). Cambridge: Cambridge University Press.

Wellmon, T. A. (1988). Conceptualizing organizational communication competence: A rules-based perspective. *Management Communication Quarterly, 1*, 515-534.

Wenegrat, A. (1974). A factor analytic study of the Truax Accurate Empathy Scale. *Psychotherapy: Theory, Research and Practice, 11*, 48-51.

Westermeyer, J. F. (1998). Predictors and characteristics of mental health among men at midlife: A 32-year longitudinal study. *American Journal of Orthopsychiatry, 68*, 265-273.

Wichstrøm, L., Anderson, M. C., Holte, A., & Wynne, L. C. (1996). Disqualifying family communication and childhood social competence as predictors of offspring's mental health and hospitalization. *Journal* of Nervous and Mental Disease, 184, 581-588.

Wicker, F. W., Lambert, F. B., Richardson, F. C., & Kahler, J. (1984). Categorical goal hierarchies and classification of human motives. *Journal of Personality, 52,* 285-305.

Wiemann, J. M. (1977). Explication and test of a model of communicative competence. *Human Communication Research, 3,* 195-213.

Wilder, C., & Collins, S. (1994). Patterns of interactional paradoxes. In W. R. Cupach & B. H. Spitzberg (Eds.), *The dark side of interpersonal communication* (pp. 83-104). Hillsdale, NJ: Lawrence Erlbaum.

Wildman, B. G., & Clementz, B. (1986). Assertive, empathic assertive, and conversational behavior. *Behavior Modification, 10,* 315-331.

Wills, T. A., Weiss, R. L., & Patterson, G. R. (1974). A behavioral analysis of the determinants of marital satisfaction. *Journal of Consulting and Clinical Psychology, 42,* 802-811.

Wilsnack, R. W., Wilsnack, S. C., Kristjanson, A. F., & Harris, T. R. (1998). Ten-year prediction of women's drinking behavior in a nationally representative sample. *Women's Health: Research on Gender, Behavior, and Policy, 4,* 199-230.

Wilson, D., & Sperber, D. (1981). On Grice's theory of conversation. In P. Werth (Ed.), *Conversation and discourse: Structure and interpretation* (pp. 155-178). New York: St. Martin's.

Wine, J. D. (1981). From defect to competence models. In J. D. Wine & M. D. Smye (Eds.), *Social competence* (pp. 3-35). New York: Guilford.

Winship, B. J., & Kelley, J. D. (1976). A verbal response model of assertiveness. *Journal of Counseling Psychology, 23,* 215-220.

Wish, M., D'Andrade, R. G., & Goodnow, J. E., II. (1980). Dimensions of interpersonal communication: Correspondences between structures for speech acts and bipolar scales. *Journal of Personality and Social Psychology, 39,* 848-860.

Wish, M., & Kaplan, S. J. (1977). Toward an implicit theory of interpersonal communication. *Sociometry, 40,* 234-246.

Wittgenstein, L. (1958). *The blue and brown books.* New York: Harper & Row.

Wittgenstein, L. (1963). *Philosophical investigations.* Oxford: Basil Blackwell.

Wood, J. T. (1998). *But I thought you meant . . . : Misunderstandings in human communication.* Mountain View, CA: Mayfield.

Wyatt, T. (1999). An Afro-centered view of communicative competence. In D. Kovarsky, J. F. Duchan, & M. Maxwell (Eds.), *Constructing (in)competence: Disabling evaluations in clinical and social interaction* (pp. 197-223). Mahwah, NJ: Lawrence Erlbaum.

Wynne, L. C. (1984). Communication patterns and family relations of children at risk for schizophrenia: The Stony Brook High-Risk Project. In N. F. Watt, E. J. Anthony, L. C. Wynne, & J. E. Rolf (Eds.), *Children at risk for schizophrenia: A longitudinal perspective* (pp. 551-556). Cambridge: Cambridge University Press.

Zebrowitz, L. A. (2001). Groping for the elephant of interpersonal sensitivity. In J. A. Hall & F. J. Bernieri (Eds.), *Interpersonal sensitivity theory and measurement* (pp. 333-350). Mahwah, NJ: Lawrence Erlbaum.

Zigler, E., & Levine, J. (1981). Premorbid competence in schizophrenia: What is being measured? *Journal of Consulting and Clinical Psychology, 49,* 96-105.

Zigler, E., & Phillips, L. (1960). Social effectiveness and symptomatic behaviors. *Journal of Abnormal and Social Psychology, 61,* 231-238.

Zigler, E., & Phillips, L. (1961). Social competence and outcome in psychiatric disorder. *Journal of Abnormal and Social Psychology, 63,* 264-271.

Zigler, E., & Phillips, L. (1962). Social competence and the process-reactive distinction in psychopathology. *Journal of Abnormal and Social Psychology, 65,* 215-222.

Zimmerman, S. (1995). Perceptions of intercultural communication competence and international student adaptation to an American campus. *Communication Education, 44,* 321-335.

PART V

Contexts

16

An Ecological Systems Perspective on Workplace Relationships

PATRICIA M. SIAS
KATHLEEN J. KRONE
FREDRIC M. JABLIN

Interpersonal relationships play an important role in human development. Throughout our lives, our relationships with others help us define ourselves (Bateson, 1980). Workplace relationships are unique interpersonal relationships with important implications for the individuals in those relationships and the organizations in which the relationships exist and develop. Workplace relationships function as information-sharing, decision-making, influence-sharing, and instrumental and emotional support systems. Healthy workplace relationships can increase employee satisfaction and commitment to the organization and can decrease turnover (Fritz, 1997; Kram & Isabella, 1985; Lincoln & Miller, 1979; Louis,

Posner, & Powell, 1983; Miller & Jablin, 1991; Rawlins, 1992). Unhealthy relationships can effect the opposite outcomes (e.g., Bingham & Burleson, 1989; Loy & Stewart, 1984; Taylor & Conrad, 1992; Tepper, 2000). Thus workplace relationships are important to both employees' work experience and organizational effectiveness.

Scholars have given a great deal of attention to the study of workplace relationships because of their important role in organizational processes. Beginning with systems theory (e.g., Katz & Kahn, 1978) and currently in "new science" and self-organizing systems approaches (Contractor & Grant, 1996; Wheatley, 2001), scholars have conceptualized organizations as systems of relationships. Such conceptualizations identify relationships as the locus of organizing and a crucial element in overall system functioning. It is through relationships that systems maintain balance (Katz & Kahn, 1978), chaos becomes order, and fragmentation is made whole (Wheatley, 1994).

In this chapter we focus on workplace relationships. Our goal is not to provide an encyclopedic review of the workplace relationship literature, but rather to offer an organizing framework that emphasizes the dynamic and developmental nature of these relationships. We address the progress that has been made in the study of workplace relationships and direct attention toward important voids in the literature. To that end, we rely on ecological systems theory to illuminate the mutual influence of relationships and the environments in which they develop.

CONCEPTUALIZING RELATIONSHIPS

Consistent with social construction approaches, we conceptualize relationships as social categories that are created, maintained, and altered through communication (Sigman, 1995). Relationships do not exist outside the partners involved; rather, they are social phenomena constituted in partners' interaction (Duck & Pittman, 1994). At the same time, partners' perceptions of their relationship influence their communication with one another. Thus communication between relationship partners is influenced by the partners' past interaction and influences their future interaction. As a consequence, relationships are defined by *patterned* interaction that occurs over *time*. Such a conceptualization emphasizes the dynamic nature of relationships, yet recognizes stability (patterned behavior over time) within that dynamism. This conceptualization also identifies interaction as the mechanism

for both relationship change and relationship maintenance.

Relationship Dimensions

Scholars have developed several methods for categorizing relationships, or for differentiating various types of relationships from one another. A typical category system might separate relationships into such types as romantic relationships, friendships, and family relationships. Our focus in this chapter is on a particular type of relationship—the workplace relationship. This and other types of relationships vary, however, on three primary dimensions: status, intimacy, and choice. We use these dimensions to organize our discussion of workplace relationships and the ways such relationships influence, and are influenced by, the various ecological systems in which they are embedded.

Status. Because virtually all organizations are at least somewhat hierarchical in nature, most treatments of workplace relationships differentiate among these relationships with respect to the relative statuses of the relationship partners. In particular, scholars have focused the bulk of their attention on supervisor-subordinate relationships, emphasizing the formal status and authority link between the partners. We use the term *equivalent status* to refer to workplace relationships in which partners have no formal authority over one another (e.g., peer relationships) and the term *different status* to refer to relationships in which one partner possesses formal authority over the other (e.g., supervisor-subordinate relationships).[1]

Intimacy. For decades, scholars have used intimacy as a metric for distinguishing and describing interpersonal relationships. Knapp's (1978) stage model of relationship development, for example, describes the way communication enables the development of increasingly intimate relationships. Similarly, Altman and Taylor's (1973) social penetration model depicts the role of self-disclosure in transforming relationships from superficial to intimate ties. These models identify communication as the central defining characteristic of relational intimacy; intimacy is reflected in deep and candid communication about personal topics. Intimacy is not a dichotomous variable, however. Rather, relationships can be more or less intimate, with less intimate relationships reflected in relatively superficial discussion of a relatively narrow and impersonal breadth of topics. Movement toward greater intimacy is reflected in increasingly deep and intense discussion of more varied and personal topics.

Choice. Not all relationships are freely chosen by individuals. Family relationships, for example, generally result from birth, not choice. In a similar vein, we usually are not provided the opportunity to choose our supervisors or peer coworkers; those relationships are assigned to us. Choice can come to characterize workplace relationships over time, however. Although we do not typically choose our peer coworkers, for example, we do choose which of those coworkers we befriend (Sias & Cahill, 1998). Similarly, although supervisors do not always choose their subordinate employees, they do choose which of those employees become members of the "in-group" (Graen & Scandura, 1987).

In the remainder of this chapter we discuss workplace relationships as they develop along these three dimensions within larger social systems. Consistent with our dynamic conceptualization of relationships, we use a theoretical framework for organizing our discussion that highlights developmental processes in human relationships. In particular, this framework, based on ecological systems theory, emphasizes the reciprocal influence of relationships and the environments in which they develop.

ECOLOGICAL SYSTEMS THEORY

Ecological systems theory (Bronfenbrenner, 1979; Johnson, Staton, & Jorgensen-Earp, 1995) proposes that human development results from the dynamic interaction of the environment and the developing person. Along these lines, the development of human relationships is influenced by, and influences, the environment and the various ecological systems that constitute the environment in which such development occurs.

The ecological systems perspective emphasizes the notion that "both individuals and environments change and interact as totalities [and] . . . changes do not take place in single aspects isolated from the totality" (Magnusson, 1995, p. 39). Consistent with this view, we suggest that workplace relationships influence, and are influenced by, a variety of environmental factors at different ecosystem levels. In particular, our discussion of workplace relationships revolves around four ecological system levels: (a) the microsystem, which contains the organizational member and his or her various relationships with other individuals (e.g., peer relationships, supervisor-subordinate relationships); (b) the mesosystem, which represents the interrelations among various microsystems (e.g., the nature of one's relationship with a supervisor affects the nature of one's relationships with peer coworkers); (c) the macrosystem, which does not represent the immediate context in which a workplace relationship exists, but does impinge upon that relationship (e.g., major divisions of an organization or the organization as a whole); and (d) the exosystem, which represents the overarching cultural belief system, forms of knowledge, and social, technological, and political ideologies that manifest themselves in the other subsystems (e.g., societal innovations in information technology and patriarchal beliefs concerning work roles and organizing).

An important feature of the ecological perspective is the notion of level embeddedness and reciprocal influence. The actions at one system level affect, and are affected by, the actions at other system levels. Thus each level in the total ecological system is an active, not passive, participant in the functioning of the entire system (Friedman & Wachs, 1999; Moen, Elder, & Luscher, 1995). An ecological approach to workplace relationships, therefore, conceptualizes such relationships as dynamic and effectual entities that do not exist in isolation from the larger system, but rather affect and are affected by other system elements in fundamental and consequential ways.

In the following sections we discuss workplace relationships along the three relational dimensions at each of the four ecological system levels described above. We begin with a focus on the microsystem, not to indicate the primacy of that system but because the vast majority of extant work focuses on microsystem relationship issues and concerns. Because existing work becomes increasingly limited as we move from the microsystem to the exosystem, our discussion becomes more speculative than descriptive. We hope that our speculations will provide fruitful directions for future research that more fully addresses the developmental nature of workplace relationships.

THE MICROSYSTEM

The microsystem most directly considers relationships among coworkers. Bronfenbrenner (1979) describes the microsystem as "a pattern of activities, roles, and interpersonal relations experienced by the developing person in a given setting with particular physical and material characteristics" (p. 22). The bulk of workplace relationship research focuses on such microsystem concerns as identifying and delineating different types of workplace relationships, the functions of these relationships for the partners, and the influence on these relationships of various microsystem elements, such as gender, age, and occupational role.

Research concerning the microsystem also most directly considers the role of interpersonal communication in workplace relationship development.

Equivalent Status Relationships

In general, the most prevalent type of relationship in an organization is the equivalent status relationship. Equivalent status relationships, typically referred to as *peer relationships* or *coworker relationships* in the organizational literature, are relationships between coworkers at the same hierarchical level with no formal authority over one another. These relationships represent the bulk of workplace relationships, as most employees have only one supervisor but several peer coworkers. Given their pervasiveness in organizations, however, these relationships have received surprisingly limited research attention.

Equivalent status relationships perform a variety of important functions in the workplace. Peer coworkers are the most likely, and most important, source of emotional and instrumental support for employees, primarily because coworkers possess knowledge and understanding about the workplace experience that external sources do not (Ray, 1987). Peers act as a second "set of eyes and ears" for one another, sharing important organizational information and gossip that may otherwise be unobtainable (Rawlins, 1992). Research also suggests that peers exert a significant amount of influence on employee job satisfaction, commitment, and turnover decisions (Cox, 1999; Fine, 1986; Kram & Isabella, 1985).

All peer relationships are not identical, however. Equivalent status relationships vary with respect to the intimacy and choice dimensions discussed earlier. In one of the earliest studies of peer relationships, Kram and Isabella (1985) identified three primary types of peer coworker relationships distinguished mainly by communication characteristics. *Information peer* relationships are characterized by communication regarding work and the organization and by low levels of self-disclosure and trust. Thus communication in these relationships focuses on limited, work-related content and reflects low levels of intimacy. According to Kram and Isabella, information peers represent the majority of equivalent status workplace relationships and are relationships employees do not freely choose but rather are assigned. *Collegial peer* relationships are characterized by communication regarding both work and personal issues and by moderate levels of trust, self-disclosure, emotional support, and friendship. Communication among collegial peers reflects broader content, including personal as well as work-related topics, and moderate levels of intimacy. Although all equivalent status relationships begin as information peer relationships, collegial peers are others with whom employees choose to develop closer relationships. Thus choice is a characteristic of these equivalent status relationships. Finally, the *special peer* relationship is characterized by communication regarding a wide variety of topics and high levels of emotional support, personal and career-related feedback, trust, self-disclosure, and friendship. Kram and Isabella describe the special peer as the equivalent of a "best friend" and the rarest equivalent status workplace relationship. Communication among special peers reflects an almost limitless breadth of content and high levels of intimacy. Similar to collegial peers, special peers are chosen by, not assigned to, employees. In addition, both collegial and special peers provide an important mentoring function and represent a primary type of workplace mentoring relationship.

Kram and Isabella's (1985) typology has been further developed and refined in subsequent research. Fritz and Dillard (1994) examined the three relationship types with respect to the characteristics of non-role-boundedness, honesty, self-disclosure, irreplaceability, and mutual dependence and found general support for the typology, with the exception of honesty

and self-disclosure, in which collegial and special peers were indistinguishable. Myers, Knox, Pawlowski, and Ropog (1999) examined the extent to which the three peer types are characterized by communication openness and functional communication skills. They found that among their study participants, information peers were perceived as less open and less communicatively skilled than collegial and special peers, who were indistinct from one another on these dimensions.

Extant research suggests that gender, a microsystem element, influences the development of equivalent status relationships. Odden and Sias (1997) found that men were likely to have a higher proportion of information peer relationships at work than were women, whereas women were more likely to have a higher proportion of collegial peer relationships. Fritz (1997) also found that men reported having more information peers at work than did women. Men and women also appeared to differ with respect to peer relationship functions. Specifically, Fritz found that men rated outside activities as a more important function of their information peer relationships than did women. Women, on the other hand, rated socioemotional functions, including emotional support, as more important than did men. In a related vein, Cahill and Sias (1997) found that women rated talking with a coworker about a work-related problem as much more important than did men. Women were also more likely than men to talk to their coworkers when faced with problems at work. Men, in contrast, were more likely to deal with work-related problems by engaging in activities (e.g., running, exercising) to relieve stress associated with the problems.

In sum, equivalent status relationships can be categorized as those low in intimacy, narrow in content, and assigned (i.e., information peers) and those more intimate, broad in content, and freely chosen (i.e., collegial and special peers). Many scholars characterize the latter relationships—collegial and special peers—as friendships (Fritz, 1997; Kram & Isabella, 1985; Odden & Sias, 1997).

Friendships among peer coworkers perform a unique role in the organizing process. Fine (1986), who was among the first to address this unique workplace relationship, found that friends in the workplace affect one another's enjoyment of, and commitment to, their work. Rawlins (1992) notes that workplace friends "help in finding jobs and opportunities for promotion, provide support and third party influence on important decisions, and convey warnings about policy changes and 'rumblings upstairs'" (pp. 165-166).

Workplace friendships are characterized by two qualities—voluntariness and personalistic focus (Sias & Cahill, 1998). *Voluntariness* refers to the concept of choice—although one cannot choose one's coworkers, one can choose which of those coworkers to befriend. *Personalistic focus* refers to the notion that friends treat one another as whole persons, rather than simply as workplace role occupants. Thus talk among friends is quite broad and encompasses both work and personal areas. Moreover, as a friendship develops, communication between the coworkers becomes increasingly intimate and less cautious (Sias & Cahill, 1998). Consistent with our conceptualization of relationships as entities constituted in interaction, such changes in communication change the relationship—as communication becomes more intimate, so does the relationship.

Several microsystem elements appear to influence the development of peer workplace friendships. In particular, cooperative or shared tasks and physical proximity appear to encourage the initial development of friendships among equivalent status employees (Sias & Cahill, 1998; Sias, Smith, & Avdeyeva, in press). These elements encourage frequent interaction among coworkers, and as this interaction becomes broader (e.g., personal topics) and more intimate, the coworkers

construct a relationship that exists beyond the workplace boundary.

Similar to other peer relationship types, peer friendships also appear to be affected by the genders of the relationship partners (Sias et al., in press). Specifically, cross-sex workplace friendships tend to be prompted and encouraged by workplace contextual variables such as shared tasks, proximity, and work-related problems. Same-sex close friendships, on the other hand, are more likely to be generated by extraorganizational factors, such as life events (problems and important changes in an individual's personal life) and socializing outside the workplace (Sias et al., in press). Thus, whereas same-sex friendships extend beyond the workplace boundary, cross-sex friendships tend to exist primarily within the workplace context. Such boundary maintenance likely serves to reduce the likelihood that other employees may perceive the relationship as a romantic one, which could harm the partners' job performance and careers (Sias et al., in press).

In a recent study, Sias (2000) examined why and how workplace friendships deteriorate. Among the reasons she found was the partners' inability to manage the dialectical tensions that individuals tend to experience in these unique relationships that "blend" the coworker and friend roles. These roles carry different, and often conflicting, expectations for appropriate behavior. Bridge and Baxter (1992) have identified five dialectics inherent in workplace friendships. The *instrumentality and affection* tension is that between the coworker role, which carries utilitarian and instrumental expectations, and the friend role, which assumes affinity based on affection rather than instrumentality. The *impartiality and favoritism* tension exists between organizational norms of impartial and objective treatment of employees and friendship expectations of unconditional support. The *openness and closedness* tension stems from expectations of openness and honesty among friends on the one hand and organizational expectations of confidentiality and caution about information sharing on the other. The *autonomy and connection* tension is that between the benefits of contact for friends and the possibility that ongoing and daily contact between coworkers may provide little autonomy for the relationship partners, "jeopardizing their friendship through excessive connection" (Bridge & Baxter, 1992, p. 204). The *judgment and acceptance* tension arises from expectations of mutual affirmation and acceptance among friends and organizational requirements of critical evaluation (although this dialectic applies primarily to different status relationships). If coworkers are unable to negotiate and manage these tensions consensually, the friendship will be affected and, most likely, terminated (Sias, 2000).

Other reasons for workplace friendship deterioration that Sias (2000) has identified include betrayal of trust, personality conflicts, and the promotion of one of the partners to a position of authority over the other. These relational transformations are accomplished with communication strategies, including avoidance of personal topics in conversation and nonverbal distancing. Avoidance of socializing outside the workplace also serves to alter the nature of these relationships. These strategies effectively reestablish the workplace boundary for the relationship so that it loses its "personalistic focus" and the coworkers once again treat each other solely as workplace role occupants (e.g., information peers).

Different Status Relationships

Despite contemporary trends toward less hierarchical forms, differential status relationships remain an enduring feature of organizational life. The most obvious such relationship in organizations is the supervisory relationship, in which one coworker formally outranks another in the organizational authority structure. In general, supervisory relationships are specified and, to some extent, held in place by differences in formal authority. They are less freely chosen than relationships between coworkers of equal status and are less likely to include the discussion of intimate topics that would allow them to grow into more personal relationships.

Not all supervisory relationships are equally differential, however. Some supervisory relationships begin as friendships, and others may evolve into friendships or more (Bridge & Baxter, 1992; Zorn, 1995). More than any other organizational relational type, however, supervisory relationships tend to begin as and remain "differential" (Fritz, 1997). Even when supervisors and employees also are friends, their formal status differences remain an ongoing force in the relationship (Zorn, 1995).

Perhaps because supervisory relationships are a manifestation of organizational hierarchy, in some sense required, and therefore restrained, organizational researchers tend to conceptualize and study them in ways that highlight their instrumental quality (e.g., as one more human resource to be managed, or, more recently, as a potential source of social capital; Nahapiet & Ghoshal, 1998). This tendency to view supervisory relationships as instruments of organizational effectiveness rather than as relationships in their own right underestimates their complexity and their significance in people's lives (Waldron, 2000). Clearly, differential supervisory relationships are an important source of meaning in organizational life and therefore worthy of study in and of themselves (Zorn, 1995). It is no accident that employees experience and manage intense emotion more often in relation to their supervisors than in relation to their coworker peers or to their own subordinates (Waldron & Krone, 1991).

Communication in supervisory relationships has been widely studied (for excellent reviews, see Fairhurst, 2001; Jablin, 1979, 1985, 2001; Jablin & Krone, 1994; Waldron, 1999), but not always with a sustained interest in the power and status differences that lie at the center of such relationships. Below, we turn our attention toward areas of research that speak most explicitly to the differential nature of supervisory relationships and the role of communication in the construction and maintenance of these relationships and the negotiation of status differences.

Developing and Maintaining Supervisory Relationships

Even though they seldom follow the same trajectories as intimate, freely chosen interpersonal relationships, involuntary, organizationally prescribed relationships still develop and are maintained. Not all supervisory relationships are differential to the same degree and in the same way, yet it wasn't until the mid-1970s that theorists and researchers began to address seriously how the supervisory relationships of a single supervisor may vary. For the past 25 years, leader-member exchange (LMX) theory has guided research investigating the antecedents, consequences, and nature of supervisory relationships of varying quality. (For a discussion of research and developments in leader-member exchange theory, see Fairhurst, 2000.) In general, leader-member relationships have been classified as either in-group or out-group. In-group relationships are characterized by high trust, mutual influence, supervisory support, and rewards, whereas out-group relationships are characterized by low trust, the use of formal authority, reduced supervisory support, and fewer rewards (Dienesch & Liden, 1986).

Beginning in the late 1980s and continuing into the 1990s, researchers began exploring the role of communication in the construction and maintenance of differential, supervisory relationships, guided to a large degree by LMX theory (Fairhurst, 1993; Fairhurst &

Chandler, 1989). The relational quality of supervisory relationships is, in part, socially constructed during routine conversations between supervisors and subordinates in which their use of language realizes and neutralizes power and social distance between them (Fairhurst & Chandler, 1989). For example, Fairhurst and Chandler (1989) found that social and power distance were minimized in a conversation between a leader and one of his in-group members, whereas the same supervisor and one of his out-group subordinates communicated in ways that reinforced their social and power differences. Discourse patterns also discriminate among high-, medium-, and low-quality leader-member relationships. Aligning behaviors such as values convergence, nonroutine problem solving, and insider markers minimize power differences and are most evident in the conversations found in high- and medium-quality leader-member relationships. Polarizing behaviors such as performance monitoring, face-threatening acts, and competitive conflict maximize power differences and are most evident in conversations found in medium- and low-quality leader-member relationships (Fairhurst, 1993).

Upward relational maintenance communication also appears to be affected by the quality of leader-member relationships and subsequently to affect the developmental trajectories of these relationships. Waldron (1991) has identified four relational maintenance tactic types that employees use differently depending on whether they are in-group or out-group members. In-group employees maintain their relationships with supervisors by relying on the use of personal (e.g., "talk with him/her frequently even though I have nothing important to discuss"; "ask about his/her personal life"), contractual (e.g., "I'm sure to follow the rules s/he has established"; "remain polite toward him/her"), and direct (e.g., "speak up when I feel s/he has treated me unjustly") upward maintenance tactics.

Out-group members rely more frequently on the use of regulative tactics (e.g., "talk only superficially to him/her"; "avoid appearing too ambitious when we talk"; "sometimes stretch the truth to avoid problems with him/her"). In-group relationships appear dynamic in that subordinates communicate with supervisors in ways that simultaneously maintain stability (e.g., contractual and personal tactics) and the capacity for change (e.g., direct tactics) in their relationships (Waldron, 1991). The narrow range of maintenance tactics used by out-group members, in contrast, suggests a kind of relational rigidity, making change in these relationships more necessary, but also more difficult to achieve.

In a study of relational maintenance strategies used by supervisors and subordinates, Lee and Jablin (1995) found that the use of strategies varied depending on whether the parties were involved in deteriorating, escalating, or routine situations. In routine maintenance situations, where the parties were unconcerned about becoming closer or more distant, in-group relational partners reported using more avoidance, restrained expression, and less supportiveness than did out-group relational partners. The routine maintenance situations that Lee and Jablin studied seem to parallel those assumed by Waldron (1991), and the patterns in use of maintenance tactic types under these conditions, although not identical, appear similar. Taken together, their results suggest that in-group members are more communicatively engaged in their supervisory relationships. Lee and Jablin also found that supervisors' perceptions of relational quality had no significant effect on their use of maintenance communication strategies, although subordinates' perceptions of relational quality did affect theirs. Subordinates may be more adaptive than supervisors in their maintenance communication behavior, and this appears to play a significant role in the developmental trajectory of leader-member relationships.

In a departure from the study of relational maintenance communication tactics, Zorn (1995) adopted an interpretive framework to study dialectical processes experienced among five respondents whose relationships with their supervisors or subordinates were simultaneously hierarchical and personal. Of the three primary dialectics that operate across personal relationships (Baxter, 1988), the autonomy-connection dialectic emerged most often in these respondents' descriptions of their relationships. Two additional relational dialectics also surfaced in their responses: the equality-superiority dialectic and the privilege-uniformity dialectic. Parties in supervisory relationships that were also personal simultaneously attempted to create a sense of equality and difference and to balance the sense of being special with the expectation of fair, uniform treatment (Zorn, 1995). For this group of respondents at least, personal friendships did not appear to eclipse the differential nature of their hierarchical relationships. When supervisory relationships are also personal, as opposed to simply hierarchical, this may intensify the relationships' importance and trigger more complex sets of relational dialectics. Recent developments in leader-member exchange theory emphasize that having both a close friendship and an in-group relationship offers the highest-quality work experience for leaders and their followers (Boyd & Taylor, 1998). Maintaining both, however, may be qualitatively different, on a communicative level, from simply maintaining an in-group work relationship.

To summarize, despite being organizationally prescribed and regulated, supervisory relationships still vary, and they do so in ways that both reflect and sustain differences in leader-member communication. Power, status, and social distance are not evenly maintained and communicated across all supervisory relationships; rather, they vary with relational quality.

*Maintaining Relational
Control and Harmony*

In general, supervisors are held accountable not only for their own performance but for the performance of their employees. Supervisors must maintain some degree of control over the performance of their employees, and this need is evident in supervisor-employee relationships. How to maintain control over the work process while simultaneously maintaining trouble-free relationships with employees is every supervisor's dilemma.

Maintaining relational control and harmony is one issue at stake as supervisors confront the classic dilemma of how to correct the performance of employees without alienating them. Because correcting employee performance can imply disapproval and can involve imposing constraints on future behavior, performance control situations are highly face threatening to employees. Supervisory relationships are more likely to withstand the pressures of performance evaluation to the extent that each party is sensitive to his or her own face as well as the face of the other (Morand, 1996). Through facework, interactants actively and cooperatively manage their own and others' face (Goffman, 1967). Researchers who have examined facework in performance control situations have focused mainly on ways in which *supervisors* communicate to support or threaten employees' negative face (i.e., desire for autonomy) and positive face (i.e., desire for approval and liking) (Brown & Levinson, 1987). During superior-subordinate interaction, individuals can engage in a number of politeness tactics to show consideration and support for the face of others (Morand, 1996).

The earliest research in this area suggests that a supervisor's use of face support appears to be most effective in controlling poor employee performance (Fairhurst, Green, & Snavely, 1984). Face-supportive communication includes demonstrating some degree of

approval of the employee (i.e., positive face) and providing him or her with the opportunity to make choices about how to solve the performance problem (i.e., negative face) (Fairhurst et al., 1984). A recent study further testifies to the importance of supervisors' offering face support while correcting employee performance. Employees who were the targets of face-threatening managerial reproaches were more likely to experience anger, more likely to perceive the reproach as unfair, less likely to view their supervisors as communicatively competent, and less likely to be satisfied with the outcome of the encounter (Carson & Cupach, 2000). Supervisors' failure to provide adequate positive and negative face support for employees can threaten relational harmony and control.

Communication accommodation theory (CAT) also has potential for exploring how relational control and harmony are accomplished in differential, supervisory relationships. CAT concerns itself with how relational partners modify their communication style to achieve a variety of goals, such as seeking approval or affinity, creating or maintaining social distance, signaling in-group or out-group membership, and simply making communication as smooth as possible (Giles, Coupland, & Coupland, 1991). In a recent application of CAT to supervisory communication, Willemyns, Gallois, and Callan (2000) examined subordinates' perceptions of the different patterns of in-group and out-group dynamics that occurred during self-described satisfactory and unsatisfactory interactions with their managers. Results demonstrated that social identity distinctiveness (i.e., intergroup perceptions emphasizing status and power differences) became salient in threatening, negative interactions with managers, but that in-group perceptions characterized positive interactions. It may be particularly important for supervisors to ameliorate intergroup perceptions during encounters with subordinates that are likely to include unsatisfactory interactions. The use of a more accommodative style may increase the likelihood that supervisors will achieve their goals in problematic situations, although more research is needed to determine the appropriate level of communicative accommodation.

Maintaining Distance

Relational distance is a consequence of all hierarchical relationships (Ferguson, 1984). Even among high-quality leader-member relationships, very few close friendships develop (Boyd & Taylor, 1998). The structural interdependence of leaders and members requires them to maintain contact, yet this contact, no matter how frequent, will seldom propel the parties toward greater closeness and friendship. Members of most supervisory relationships learn to maintain contact and distance simultaneously.

Interpersonal distancing is a particularly interesting area for research, not only because it counterbalances a bias toward the study of closeness in interpersonal relationships, but also because of its ethical and moral implications. Specifically, interpersonal distancing is associated with a tendency toward "blaming the victim" and with rationalizations that justify treating the other in callous and insensitive ways. Physical and interpersonal distancing also can result in a tendency to depersonalize others, which then makes it easier to harm them (Bandura, Barbaranelli, Caprara, & Pastorelli, 1996).

The study of interpersonal distancing in organizational settings has much merit. We located two studies that together address organizational conditions that prompt interpersonal distancing and the communication behaviors that convey it. Managers do not appear to distance themselves from employees routinely; rather, they appear to employ distancing tactics when they need to do so in order to avoid criticism and antagonism (Cameron, Freeman, & Mishra, 1993). Folger

and Skarlicki (1998) recently found that managers were more likely to distance themselves from victims of downsizing (e.g., spend less time in private meetings with them) when mismanagement, rather than external forces, was cited as the primary reason for the layoff. This pattern of individuals' distancing themselves from those they may be harming is consistent with the findings of previous research that has demonstrated that those who harm others the most tend to offer the shortest explanations for having done so (Hodgins, Liebeskind, & Schwartz, 1996).

Folger and Skarlicki (1998) used a fairly gross measure of interpersonal distancing (i.e., time spent in face-to-face meetings with employees), but Hess (2000) has recently reported a wide array of communication tactics that individuals use to maintain distance in nonvoluntary relationships with disliked partners. These include expressing detachment, avoiding involvement, and showing antagonism. *Expressing detachment* includes both feeling and showing detachment through the behaviors of ignoring the partner, treating the other person as a stranger, and presenting an image that matches the other's expectations rather than revealing the true self. *Avoiding involvement* includes reducing involvement and making the interaction less personal in a more active way than through detachment. Specifically, avoiding involvement includes not asking the other person questions, using superficial politeness and respect, using a less immediate channel of communication, and avoiding encountering the other person. *Showing antagonism* involves acting on the discomfort experienced in nonvoluntary relationships with disliked others and includes such behaviors as explicitly stating one's feelings for the other, showing hostility, and rejecting the disliked person from a conversation. Supervisory relationships may or may not be nonvoluntary relationships with disliked others. In those cases where they are, it may be particularly important for supervisors to balance maintaining and avoiding communicative contact so as to not trigger hostility or inflict harm (Bies, 1987).

The mirror image of maintaining a potentially damaging degree of distance in supervisory relationships would be maintaining a potentially harmful degree of closeness (e.g., demanding complete loyalty and obedience). To some extent, we address this supervisory relational pattern in the next subsection.

Maintaining Dominance

Like all human relationships, supervisory relationships have the potential to be harmful (e.g., Bies & Tripp, 1998; Hornstein, 1996). As the power disparity between supervisors and employees increases, so does the potential for harm in the relationship. Under these conditions, supervisors can more easily cross a line between using their power appropriately and using it in ways that harm and damage their employees. Research and anecdotal evidence both suggest that supervisors are perceived to be the most frequent perpetrators of workplace abuse (Hornstein, 1996; Keashly, Trott, & MacLean, 1994), including sexual harassment (Tangri, Burt, & Johnson, 1982).

Some have argued that instances of workplace abuse are on the rise, due in part to increasingly turbulent organizational circumstances. Increased competition, frequency of restructuring, and intensified pressure to improve performance can trigger the use of "tougher" managerial communication practices that too frequently cross the line into abusiveness (Folger & Skarlicki, 1998; Hornstein, 1996). Contributing to the problem is conventional managerial ideology that legitimates the use of harsh tactics in the interest of improving organizational performance (Bies & Tripp, 1998; Einarsen & Raknes, 1997). Researchers have been slow to identify workplace abuse for what it is. Perhaps the earliest attempts to illuminate the harmful side of supervisory relationships can be traced to sexual harassment research and scholars'

attempts to argue that men sexually harass women in organizations in order to control them and otherwise keep them "in their place" (Hearn & Parkin, 1987; Tancred-Sheriff, 1989). Communication researchers have joined in these efforts and have developed increasingly sophisticated explanations for how men and women experience, perpetuate, and respond to sexual harassment (e.g., Bingham, 1994; Clair, 1993, 1998; Kreps, 1993).

Consciousness concerning alternative forms of workplace abuse appears to be increasing and is inspiring a number of research efforts. Several of the researchers involved in these efforts begin by arguing that workplace abuse may be more damaging than sexual harassment, because it may be more frequent and more tolerated (e.g., Keashly et al., 1994). The studies reviewed here all conceptualized workplace abuse slightly differently, and the researchers all began by attempting to identify supervisory behaviors perceived by subordinates as abusive. They also attempted to associate frequency and type of workplace abuse with important individual and organizational outcomes.

Workplace abuse has been conceptualized as abusive work interactions involving hostile verbal and nonverbal, nonphysical behaviors directed by one person toward another (Keashly et al., 1994; Tepper, 2000) with the primary purpose of undermining the other to ensure compliance (Keashly et al., 1994). Bies and Tripp (1995) conceptualize workplace abuse as violations of a social contract shaped by commonly agreed-upon norms governing the legitimate use of power. Workplace abuse also has been conceptualized more generally as harassment. As such, it consists of behaviors that repeatedly torment, wear down, or frustrate another, or that provoke, frighten, intimidate, or cause another discomfort (Einarsen & Raknes, 1997).

Supervisory behaviors identified by employees as abusive include such things as intimidating employees with unreasonable demands (Keashly et al., 1994), intentionally putting employees down in front of others (Bies & Tripp, 1998; Keashly et al., 1994; Tepper, 2000), telling employees their thoughts or feelings are stupid, reminding employees of their past mistakes and failures, not giving employees credit for jobs requiring a lot of effort (Tepper, 2000), interacting overly harshly with employees over time, and being hypercritical of employees (Bies & Tripp, 1998). Abusive bosses also have been described as "micromanagers" and as having mercurial mood swings, being obsessed with loyalty and obedience, being capricious in their actions, and being prone to exercise "raw" power for personal gain (Bies & Tripp, 1998). Although researchers have yet to agree upon the best way to conceptualize and measure workplace abuse, it appears that employees are more likely to label personal or interpersonal behaviors (e.g., my supervisor ridicules me or my work in public) as abusive than global features of the work or work setting (e.g., an extraordinarily demanding work schedule).

It has been argued that, for a variety of reasons, organizations often will go to great lengths to protect abusive supervisors and managers (Hornstein, 1996). Scholars working from an organizational justice perspective, however, imply that such an approach may be shortsighted (Bies & Tripp, 1995, 1998). According to social justice researchers, abuses of power present organizations with "predicaments" that they must manage one way or another in order to restore a sense of justice and fairness (Bies & Tripp, 1995). Briefly, victims are likely to frame power abuse as a violation of the social contract (e.g., Donaldson & Dunfee, 1994; Rousseau & McLean-Parks, 1993) that implicitly and explicitly protects them from power abuse. Abusive treatment from supervisors violates the prevailing social norms concerning what is fair at work (Bies & Tripp, 1995). For institutions and perpetrators, the "predicament" involves facing the

potential loss of social legitimacy and the possibility of revenge, either from victims or from the communities that support them. Under these conditions, not only will victims be motivated to contain power abuse, but perpetrators and institutions will be as well. Bies and Tripp (1995) discuss ways in which institutions, perpetrators, and victims can respond reactively or proactively to manage predicaments triggered by power abuse.

Elsewhere, Bies and Tripp (1998) focus their attention more exclusively on victims of power abuse and present a two-by-two framework from which to understand the ways in which employees might cope with the behavior of "tyrannical" bosses. They identify four possible coping strategies that vary along a public-private dimension and a consent-dissent dimension. According to this framework, employees can cope with abusive supervision by surrendering to it (i.e., consenting both publicly and privately), by disguising their actual feelings in one of two ways (by publicly consenting with the supervisor's beliefs and policies while privately dissenting with them or by publicly dissenting while privately consenting), or by confronting their abusive supervisors directly (i.e., dissent both publicly and privately). Further research is necessary to determine how effective each of these strategies is for the victims and perpetrators of power abuse and their institutions.

In a study involving students, all of whom had paid work experience, Keashly et al. (1994) found that the most frequently reported strategy for dealing with abusive supervisors was trying to avoid or ignore them, which, of course, meant that the abusive behavior was unlikely to change. Although fewer respondents reported directly confronting their harassers, those who did also reported improvements in their subsequent interaction with them.

As might be expected, outcomes of abusive supervision mirror some of those found in abusive intimate relationships, especially decreased psychological health and well-being and higher levels of psychological distress (Einarsen & Raknes, 1997; Tepper, 2000). Tepper (2000) found that turnover was higher among subordinates who perceived their bosses as more abusive, and that job satisfaction was lower for those who did not quit their jobs, as were life satisfaction, normative commitment, and affective commitment. In addition to reporting higher levels of psychological distress, employees in Tepper's study who perceived their supervisors as more abusive also reported higher continuance commitment and higher conflict between work and family. Organizational justice (i.e., interactional, procedural, and distributive) moderated most of these effects, but interactional justice (Bies & Moag, 1986) moderated more of them than did the other two. Tepper also found that perceptions of higher job mobility moderated most of these negative effects, suggesting that subordinates were better able to cope with an abusive supervisor when they believed they could quit their present job and find another.

As the preceding discussion reveals, supervisory relationships are one site in which tensions related to control, distancing, and the use of power are likely to be experienced. Leaders and members bring different resources—which are rooted in power and status disparities—to bear on the working out of these tensions. It is no wonder, then, that encounters with supervisors are frequent sources of intense emotional experience for subordinates (Waldron & Krone, 1991).

Resistance in Supervisory Relationships

Where there is power, especially heavy-handed and abusive power, there is resistance (Ashforth & Mael, 1998; Clegg, 1994; Knights & Vurdubakis, 1994). Resistance occurs for many reasons, but it is motivated at least in part by acts of control that intrude upon valued aspects of an individual's identity (Ashforth & Mael, 1998). Resistance is not just a response to power, it is itself a form of power (Clair, 1998; Jermier, Knights, & Nord, 1994). Whether effective in altering an unjust status quo or not, the mere act of resisting can be very meaningful to the actors and their peers in that it signals a refusal to accept others' aggressive and self-interested attempts to classify, categorize, or label them (Ashforth & Mael, 1998).

Indeed, few forms of resistance actually result in meaningful changes in existing power relations (Ashforth & Mael, 1998; Clair, 1998; Clegg, 1994). Most often, power and resistance exist in dynamic tension such that each requires the other, but neither threatens the reproduction of the other (Ashforth & Mael, 1998; Clegg, 1994). If what we resist persists, why bother resisting? What is at stake in a person's participation in the power-resistance "drama" (Clegg, 1994)? Identities are constituted in systems of power relations (Clegg, 1994), and supervisory relationships provide ideal places to examine the micro-practices through which identities are formed, challenged, fought for, and sustained. In their everyday conversations, supervisors and subordinates make numerous identity claims that the other can honor or dispute. The ongoing interplay between power and resistance can be observed in the identity work of supervisory relationships.

Although this area has yet to be studied in any detail, some of the research discussed above is suggestive of how identity work may vary across leader-member relationships of differing quality (Fairhurst, 1993; Fairhurst & Chandler, 1989; Lee & Jablin, 1995; Waldron, 1991). The parties in medium- and high-quality leader-member relationships have been found to be more communicatively engaged than members of low-quality relationships. Because the discourse of high- and medium-quality relationships suggests an unsettledness in leader-member power differences (Fairhurst, 1993), this discourse may also represent the partners' more active struggle over their respective identity claims. Disengaging from a low-quality relationship may be one way for a leader and member to protect and maintain key features of their identities; in a sense, they are giving up on the struggle for interpretive control in that particular relational context.

A great deal of identity work is done in supervisory relationships that has yet to be explored. Reframing superior-subordinate communication as "identity talk" can help elucidate how this important relationship sustains the power-resistance drama of organizational life. Through their day-in, day-out conversations, leaders and members perform valued aspects of their identities. However, it also may be fruitful to locate particularly critical or consequential moments for "superior" and "subordinate" identity formation. Austrin (1994) identifies two such moments in his work on "identity talk."

Identity talk consists of structured occasions during which employees are required to talk about themselves in terms dictated by the supervisor or by organizational requirements. Identity talk is found in contexts in which the parties' identities as "superiors" and "subordinates" are made salient. Austrin (1994) characterizes these as "objective" conditions in which subjectivity is constituted. Examples include performance evaluation meetings and the act of filing a formal grievance when doing so requires that the subordinate have an official talk with the supervisor as a step in the process. Under such conditions, subordinates are required to account for themselves and their performances not in terms of their choosing, but in the organization's terms. Austrin found that subordinates learned to deploy the technical, dominant discourse to their own advantage during such meetings, thereby fueling the ongoing interplay between power and resistance.

In conclusion, although contemporary organizational theorizing de-emphasizes the importance of hierarchical relationships, the need to develop and maintain them remains a central feature of organizational life. Although the number of differential, supervisory relationships in which any given individual is embedded may be few, each of these relationships remains an important site for identity formation and the working out of tensions related to control and the use of power.

THE MESOSYSTEM

The mesosystem comprises the multiple roles an individual occupies both in and out of the workplace as well as the multiple micro-level relationships he or she forms in those various roles (e.g., an individual participates simultaneously in a supervisor-subordinate relationship and various peer coworker relationships). The mesosystem consists of the interrelations among these various microsystem relationships. As Vondracek, Lerner, and Schulenberg (1986) explain, the "primary building blocks of the mesosystem are the same as those for the microsystem: molar activities, interpersonal relations, and role transactions" (p. 57). The mesosystem is distinct from the microsystem "in that activities associated with the mesosystem occur across rather than within particular microsystem settings" (Jablin & Sias, 2001, p. 848). Thus consideration of relationships at the mesosystem level addresses the linkages among the various relationships in which an employee participates.

Equivalent Status Relationships

Although limited, extant research suggests some ways in which mesosystem linkages influence equivalent status relationships. Research suggests, for example, that the type of relationship an individual has with his or her supervisor can affect that individual's relationships with peer coworkers. Sias and Cahill (1998) found that employees who have problematic relationships with their supervisors often turn to their peer coworkers for support and feedback, which encourages the development of friendships among the coworkers. Similarly, Sias and Jablin (1995) found that employees in a supervisor's "out-group" tend to form more intimate and cohesive relationships with one another than with employees perceived to be in the "in-group." In contrast, employees perceived as supervisors' "pets" or favorites tend to become isolated from the rest of the work group. This isolation leaves them with a high proportion of information peer relationships and few, if any, friendships with their coworkers. Sias and Jablin note, however, that this impact is moderated by employee perceptions of the fairness of the differential supervisor-subordinate relationships. Thus, for example, if an employee has a "high-quality" relationship with the supervisor and the employee's coworkers perceive that the differential treatment is fair (e.g., the employee deserves it because she is highly competent), the employee is not likely to be isolated from her coworkers, but rather will be drawn into the relational network of the work group. These fairness perceptions are socially constructed by the coworkers, who discuss the differential treatment for sense-making and uncertainty reduction purposes (Sias, 1996).

An individual's equivalent status workplace relationships can also be influenced by his or her personal relationships outside the workplace. In particular, friendships among peer coworkers are often triggered by "life events" such as problems or important changes one of the coworkers experiences in his or her relationship with a spouse or partner outside the workplace. The employee with problems or changes in his or her life may talk to coworkers about them, seeking support and advice. This interaction contributes to the transformation of the coworker relationship into a friendship (Sias & Cahill, 1998; Sias et al., in press).

Different Status Relationships

Available research suggests several ways in which mesosystem linkages influence different status relationships. For example, employees' perceptions of the amount of influence their immediate supervisors have with their own supervisors can affect the employees' satisfaction with their supervisory relationships. Specifically, employees perceive their supervisory relationships to be most effective when they also perceive their supervisors to have moderate amounts, rather than inordinately large amounts, of upward influence (Pelz, 1952; Trempe, Rigny, & Haccoun, 1985). Although they've seldom been studied as such, supervisory relationships are nested within other supervisory relationships. So too, then, are processes of supervisory relational development. For instance, how the autonomy-connection dialectic is experienced and managed between a supervisor and his or her employees is influenced by and will influence how this same supervisor experiences and manages relational dialectics with his or her own supervisor.

The development and maintenance of supervisory relationships also can be influenced by either party's personal relationships outside the workplace. For example, traditional gender roles and interaction patterns learned outside the workplace can penetrate supervisory relationships in inappropriate and damaging ways (Gutek & Morasch, 1982; Nieva & Gutek, 1981; Sheffey & Tindale, 1992). When a male supervisor relates to a female employee as if she were a wife or a girlfriend, it becomes more difficult for him to see her also as a competent and committed employee, and the woman's attempts to meet the expectations associated with her work role are undermined (Gutek, 1992). A male supervisor might relate to a female subordinate sexually in a supervisory control move, with the intent of reminding her of her "proper place" in the relationship (Hearn & Parkin, 1987). Treating a female subordinate like a wife or girlfriend, however, also can make her more conscious of sexual harassment (DiTomaso, 1992). Just as relationships outside the workplace can influence those within, learning to confront harassing behaviors in supervisory relationships may influence the likelihood of individuals' confronting abusive behavior in their personal/romantic relationships.

THE MACROSYSTEM

The macrosystem includes elements of the overall system that do not directly contain the individual or immediate work group but that impinge on those entities. Thus the macrosystem encompasses major units or divisions of an organization and the organization as a whole.

Equivalent Status Relationships

Extant research suggests a number of ways in which equivalent status relationships are associated with organizational macrosystem elements such as organizational climate, organizational culture, and organizational structure/form. Odden and Sias (1997) found that employee peer relationships were associated with employee perceptions of the organizational climate, although these associations were moderated by the employee's sex (a microsystem element). Using Kram and Isabella's (1985) typology, they found that women with smaller proportions of information peer relationships and larger proportions of special peer relationships were more likely to perceive the organizational climate as cohesive but low in supervisor consideration (i.e., supervisors perceived as unsupportive, unfair, untrustworthy). On the other hand, men with larger proportions of information peer relationships reported *lower* perceptions of organizational cohesion, and men with larger proportions of special peer relationships perceived their organizations as having "low-pressure" climates (i.e., few time pressures and limited amounts of stress). These findings suggest that women are more likely than men to use their "special peers" as sounding boards and sources of emotional support (Odden & Sias, 1997).

Another macrosystem element likely associated with equivalent status relationships is organizational culture, or the shared values and beliefs of organizational members. Although no research has examined this possibility directly, Ashcraft (2000) recently conducted a study that provides some direction for speculation. She examined the formal and informal "cultural" rules and norms governing the formation and management of relationships among members of an organization devoted to helping survivors of domestic violence. This "feminist organization" was characterized by a culture that explicitly valued and encouraged the merging of "private matters" and "public life." To this end, the organizational culture explicitly encouraged intimate and personal communication that fostered relational development among the members (both staff and volunteer members). Thus the culture enhanced (at least initially) the formation of friendships and other intimate relationships among the coworkers.

Although research has not yet provided direct evidence in this area, it seems likely that the structural form of an organization has an impact on employees' equivalent status relationships. An organization's structural form carries with it explicit and implicit assumptions about the role of relationships in the organization. Feminist scholars, for example, criticize the "objectivity" that forms the foundation of bureaucratic/traditional organizations (Ferguson, 1984; Mumby & Putnam, 1992). These critics argue that the objective ideals of bureaucracy advocate separation of the individual members' private and public lives. This separation elevates rationality and objectivity (typically seen as masculine qualities) as the highest ideals and devalues emotion, affect, and intimacy (typically seen as feminine qualities). As a consequence, women tend to be relegated to lower-status positions (positions that require/value emotion and affect) in traditional organizations, whereas men occupy high-level positions (Ferguson, 1984). Thus equivalent status relationships characterized by intimacy, affect, and emotion (such as collegial and special peers, and friendships) would be devalued and discouraged in bureaucratic organizations. In contrast, these organizations would encourage peer relationships that remain exclusively within the workplace boundary (i.e., information peer relationships).

Human relations/functional and human resource/divisional organizational forms, on the other hand, view employee relationships as a primary element in the organizing process (Miles & Creed, 1995). In particular, human relations/functional organizations view employee relationships as a source of intrinsic reward and satisfaction for employees. Thus we would expect these types of organizations to encourage the formation and development of coworker relationships, perhaps through shared task assignments, social events, and the like. Human resource/divisional organizations would also encourage coworker relational development, primarily because these organizations would view such relationships as sites of creativity and innovation, as well as sources of intrinsic reward and satisfaction.

Finally, in new organizational forms such as collaborative organizations and feminist organizations, relationships are identified as a core value; these organizations develop structures that enhance relational development among organizational members. Along these lines, Ashcraft's (2000) study provides an example of the mutual influence processes that characterize the ecological systems foundation of this chapter. Interestingly (and quite ironically), the relationships formed among the members of the organization created tensions and perceptions (e.g., of favoritism and power imbalances) that affected the culture of the organization. The formation of close relationships among organizational members led to the development of explicit organizational rules governing coworker relationships. In particular, romantic relationships and friendships among members were explicitly forbidden, and

members in such relationships were instructed to discuss the situation with their supervisor for guidance and direction. Thus the close relationships among employees eventually led this "feminist organization" to exhibit a somewhat bureaucratic stance toward member relationships, explicitly severing personal from public life.

Different Status Relationships

Research suggests several ways in which supervisory relational processes are interdependent with macrosystem processes such as the centralization of organizational authority structures, organizational climate, sex ratio dynamics, and organizational policy. Employee perceptions of the extent to which authority is centralized in their organization are related to their perceptions of supervisory relational quality. Specifically, those employees who perceive their organizations as providing greater job autonomy and opportunities for participation in decision making also perceive themselves as having higher-quality leader-member relationships (Krone, 1994). The formation of supervisory relationships is embedded within the processes by which involvement in decision making is organized. Meaningful participation in decision making and control of one's work are likely to be associated with healthier supervisory relationships.

Although we might assume that lower-level subordinates would be more vulnerable to abuse in supervisory relationships, ascending the organizational hierarchy does not appear to protect women from an organizational climate that normalizes abusive supervisory relationships. When Sloan and Krone (2001) asked 30 high-level women managers to define and tell about their experiences with abusive communication, their respondents reported a variety of experiences with those who outranked them in the organizational hierarchy. These women described abusive communication as something that was intentional, forceful, ongoing, and gendered. Abusive communication was most often experienced not as a single, isolated incident, but as something associated with "the flavor of the place" that seemed to give male (and occasionally female) supervisors the right to communicate abusively. In such climates, these women reported having been the targets of explosive and violent behavior such as being yelled at or pushed down, or having objects thrown at them. When they attempted to discuss the difficulties they had experienced with their male managers, the managers reminded the women of their power to dress differently or to draw upon the use of "feminine wiles" so as not to appear too threatening. One woman was advised by her male supervisor not to confront a male coworker who repeatedly referred to her in public as "my work wife," on the grounds that doing so would only make life difficult for her and other women in the organization. For another woman, abusive communication took the form of "friendship harassment," in which her female manager discussed how they used to be friends, and how she thought they'd work together better if they were friends outside of work again, or if their children played together. The women in Sloan and Krone's study described their abusive communication experiences as isolating, as having a suppressing effect on their willingness to exert leadership in discussions, and as ever-present reminders that, even though they occupied organizational positions of authority, they also remained "outsiders within" (Collins, 1991).

Research also demonstrates that the overall gender balance in an organization or occupation is associated with "gendered" interaction in supervisory relationships. For instance, the sex role spillover effects we discussed earlier appear to be attenuated in more integrated work settings where the work itself is not associated with stereotypically male or female qualities. Women in these settings are less likely to feel that physical attractiveness is necessary for their success and are also less likely to experience sexual harassment (Gutek & Cohen, 1992). Similarly, Ely (1995) found that sex role stereotypes appeared to operate differently in shaping women's perceptions of themselves, their male colleagues, and the requirements for success in sex-integrated versus male-dominated law firms. Women in male-dominated firms appeared to see themselves as enacting stereotypical masculine characteristics and attempting to differentiate their behavior from that of other women, whereas women in sex-integrated firms appeared to see themselves as drawing creatively upon both masculine and feminine characteristics in order to succeed. Based on the results of these studies, we might conclude that supervisory relationships are more constrained by stereotypical sex role dynamics and therefore are a greater source of potential struggle when they are embedded in gender-imbalanced work settings.

Finally, organizational policy can be understood as a feature of organizations that influences and is influenced by supervisory relationships. These relationships are a significant site of the interpretation and negotiation of organizational policy, because their use often requires formal discussion between employees and their supervisors. For example, organizational culture and supervisory attitudes toward the use of family leave policies affect employees' willingness to use these policies (Thomas & Ganster, 1995). The findings of recent research conducted in a large federal organization illustrate how supervisors see themselves as needing to balance the tension between meeting employee needs to use these policies with their own need to meet pressing work deadlines (Kirby, 2000; Kirby & Krone, 2002). It is not surprising that the supervisors in the organization studied conveyed mixed messages to their employees about the availability and use of these policies, often letting employees know that although the policies do exist, they would prefer that employees take advantage of them only sparingly, if at all. These supervisors were also conscious of their need to maintain fairness among employees with differing work and family needs and of their need to use discretion when applying policies in order to adapt to particular situations, although the employees did not always perceive it that way. Although they have not been studied as such, required discussions between supervisors and subordinates concerning the use of organizational work-family leave policies are occasions in which supervisory and subordinate identities are made salient. Organizational policies penetrate the formation of supervisory relationships as both parties interpret the policies and communicate about their use. The form that the negotiation of the policies takes, whether harmonious or filled with resentment and struggle, influences and is influenced by supervisory relational dynamics and the health of those dynamics.

THE EXOSYSTEM

The exosystem comprises the overarching belief systems, forms of knowledge, and social, technological, and economic systems and trends as well as political ideologies of the larger society in which individuals and their relationships exist (Jablin & Sias, 2001). Although a limitless number of elements of the exosystem affect workplace relationships, for brevity's sake we address here a recent societal trend that we believe has important implications for workplace relationships: the growth of information/communication technologies.

Equivalent Status Relationships

Recent work has focused on the ways employee relationships may be affected by societal moves enabled by new communication technologies such as telecommuting and "virtual organizations," in which employees perform their work away from a central location and without the physical copresence of coworkers. Much of this research has focused on the social isolation telecommuters feel, particularly those for whom social support and interaction with coworkers is an important source of satisfaction (Kraut, 1987). Thus technologies that enable telecommuting and virtual organizations also affect member relationships. Sias and Cahill (1998), for example, note that physical proximity is an important influence in early stages of peer friendship development. Friendships may be more difficult to establish, therefore, among geographically dispersed coworkers. This impact may be mitigated, however, by communication technologies such as e-mail and other forms of computer-mediated communication (Ellison, 1999). Rice and Love (1987), among others, have noted the ability of computer-mediated communication technologies to enhance the development of social networks. Thus, rather than friendships becoming extinct in a society of virtual organizations, they may instead simply follow different developmental trajectories. Sias and Cahill (1998) suggest that among virtual coworkers, the importance of physical proximity to friendship development may simply be replaced by shared tasks that can be accomplished via technology and that require mediated interaction among the coworkers. In such cases, communication technologies enable "virtual coworkers" to become "virtual friends." To date, no research has examined these issues; scholars who undertake such studies would make important contributions to our understanding of workplace relationships in the 21st century.

A line of research by Fulk and her colleagues illustrates the reciprocal influence of relationships and environments in the area of new technologies, demonstrating how the implementation and adoption of new technologies in the workplace are embedded in existing social relationships (e.g., Fulk, 1993; Fulk, Steinfield, Schmitz, & Power, 1987). In particular, this research indicates that employees' adoption and use of new communication technologies are influenced in large part by coworker communication; that is, employees' attitudes toward and use of new technologies develop from their interaction with trusted coworkers. Thus, at the same time new communication technologies are likely to affect coworker relationships, coworker relationships also appear to affect the adoption and use of new technologies.

Different Status Relationships

The adoption and use of new communication technologies are likely to influence the formation of supervisory relationships and the use of power in those relationships. We might expect greater equality in supervisory relationships to the extent that communication technologies are used with the intention of flattening organizational hierarchy and reducing the number of layers of management (Cleveland, 1985; Davidow & Malone, 1992; Taylor & Van Every, 1993). Equality in supervisory relationships also may be enhanced when subordinates use communication technologies in ways that increase their power and centrality in social networks, thereby decreasing their dependence on supervisory relationships (Burkhardt & Brass, 1990; Hesse, Sproull, Kiesler, & Walsh, 1993).

Communication technologies can also be used, however, in ways that amplify power differences in organizations and supervisory relationships. Romm's (1999) recent collection of nine case studies illustrates how electronic mail has been used for political purposes in university settings. In these cases, Romm found that individuals used the speed of e-mail as well as selective patterns of forwarding, copying, and processing messages to exercise influence. Additional research is needed to explore patterns of dominance and resistance in e-mail usage. For example, a form of electronic harassment can occur when supervisors flood employees with e-mail messages throughout the workday and workweek,

closely monitor employee responses to these messages, and respond punitively if employees fail to open the messages and respond immediately. Dominant norms emerge for electronic mail usage, and others' unwillingness to conform to those norms can be used against them in supervisory relationships. Norms regarding e-mail use can become a site of struggle in which employees subtly resist, negotiate, or overtly challenge the dominant rules held in place by supervisory practices.

SUMMARY AND FUTURE DIRECTIONS

As we mentioned in the early part of this chapter, we chose an ecological systems framework to organize our discussion of workplace relationships not only because it is consistent with our conceptualization of relationships as dynamic entities, but also because such a framework highlights both the progress made by workplace relationships scholars and, perhaps more important, the issues scholars have overlooked or ignored. In this vein, our discussion reveals three primary biases in the research to date: (a) an emphasis on microsystem-level concerns, (b) an emphasis on *intra*level concerns rather than examination of mutual influence between system levels, and (c) an emphasis on how environmental factors affect relationships rather than on the reciprocal influences of relationships and their environments.

Microsystem Bias

First, scholars have focused almost exclusively on microsystem-level research. Thus we know a great deal about how and why workplace relationships develop, maintain, and change. We also know a great deal about the impacts of various microsystem elements in such development, including gender, occupation, proximity, and tasks. The research also reveals much about the role of communication in workplace relational processes. Such insights are very important, and we encourage scholars to continue such research. Little effort has been devoted, however, to research that would contribute to our understanding of relationships as they are associated with other ecological systems. In particular, we know very little about the role of mesosystem elements in relational development. As the ecological systems perspective highlights, relationships of one type affect and are affected by relationships of other types. Only a few studies have been explicitly directed at such concerns (e.g., Gutek & Morasch, 1982; Sias & Jablin, 1995). We encourage scholars to undertake research directed at examining mesosystem-level concerns. For example, as the line between personal and work lives becomes increasingly blurred with the advent of new technologies (Ashkenas, Ulrich, Jick, & Kerr, 1995), it would be very valuable to examine how employees' personal relationships outside the organization may be associated with their relationships at work.

We also know very little about workplace relationships as they develop at the exosystem level. Although we have discussed only one societal issue in this chapter (the changes brought about by new technologies), a limitless number of societal changes are occurring that are likely associated with workplace relationship development. Eisenberg and Goodall (2001), for instance, note that a new "social contract" is emerging in the United States in which old notions of corporate and employee loyalty and commitment are supplanted by more ephemeral and fleeting relationships. This shift is manifested in an increasingly "contingent" or nonpermanent workforce composed of temporary and limited-contract employees. Such a shift has serious implications for workplace relationships. For example, research on peer workplace relationship development suggests that the passage of time is an important developmental factor (Sias & Cahill, 1998) and that very close peer

relationships (e.g., "special peers") can take several years to develop (Odden & Sias, 1997). Such relationships may become less prevalent as individuals take jobs for finite periods. If this occurs, what, if anything, will replace these relationships in performing their mentoring and emotional support functions (Kram & Isabella, 1985)? Perhaps the new social contract, new technologies, and other societal shifts will alter the very way we conceptualize and define workplace relationships. Again, we encourage scholars to devote research attention to these and other important exosystem concerns.

Intralevel Bias

A second bias we have identified in the research is a tendency to examine relationship issues at one ecological system level in isolation from the other system levels. As we have mentioned, an important feature of the ecological systems perspective is the notion of level embeddedness and reciprocal systems influence. Activities at the various system levels mutually influence one another (Friedman & Wachs, 1999; Moen et al., 1995). A recent study by Kahn (2000), for instance, suggests that technological innovation (an exosystem element) can affect, and be affected by, organizational structure (a macrosystem element). In particular, Kahn found that the successful adoption of a new, more sophisticated record-keeping system at a university was influenced, in large part, by informal relationships between the archive office employees and other employees, such as those in the registrar's office. Moreover, the new system created an informal structure in the form of an alliance among these parties and employees in the university's graduate studies office. Thus the implementation of the new technology (exosystem) both was aided by an existing informal structure and enabled the creation of a new informal structure (macrosystem). Unfortunately, few studies have examined workplace relationships from the perspective of system-level embeddedness. Such research can provide important insights into the complexities of organizational phenomena such as structure, society, and relationships.

Unidirectional Influence Bias

A third bias in the research has been its almost exclusive focus on how environmental factors (e.g., proximity, organizational structure and culture) influence workplace relationships, rather than on the reciprocal influences of workplace relationships and the environments in which they develop. Organizations and environments are not static entities; they are dynamic and continually changing. And it is through relationships that systems such as organizations transform in incremental or quantum ways (Wheatley, 1994). As relationships grow closer or deteriorate, the entire system is affected—the relative impacts of individuals on decision making change, information distribution is altered, even the meanings derived from information differ depending upon with whom the information is discussed. Additional issues for study in this area include the extent of the mutual influence exerted by relationships and organizations. Do human relationships and environments influence one another in equal measure? Is it possible for two employees who are nested deep within a dysfunctional organizational system to construct and maintain a healthy relationship? Similarly, to what extent can a single healthy relationship transform the larger system? Our understanding of organizations and relationships would profit greatly from research addressing these questions and others that consider the complex and reciprocal influence exerted by both relationships and the environments in which they develop.

As the preceding discussion highlights, scholars have made great progress in the study of workplace relationships. In particular, there have been important strides in the examination of workplace relationships as communicative phenomena, and we encourage continued research in that vein. The ecological systems framework of our discussion highlights the dynamic and embedded nature of workplace relationships and their environments. We encourage researchers to devote their efforts to the study of workplace relationships and their environments as complex and dynamic entities.

NOTE

1. Workplace relationships can, and do, differ with respect to *informal* authority and status elements. Mentoring relationships, for example, can develop between partners with equivalent hierarchical authority, yet the mentor, by virtue of his or her role as "teacher" and "guide," possesses informal authority and status over the mentee or protégé. Relationships characterized by informal status differences (e.g., mentoring relationships) are subsumed by these two primary relationship types in our organizing system and are discussed as appropriate in those sections.

REFERENCES

Altman, I., & Taylor, D. A. (1973). *Social penetration: The development of interpersonal relationships.* New York: Holt, Rinehart & Winston.

Ashcraft, K. L. (2000). Empowering "professional" relationships: Organizational communication meets feminist practice. *Management Communication Quarterly, 13,* 347-392.

Ashforth, B. E., & Mael, F. A. (1998). The power of resistance: Sustaining valued identities. In R. M. Kramer & M. A. Neale (Eds.), *Power and influence in organizations* (pp. 89-119). Thousand Oaks, CA: Sage.

Ashkenas, R., Ulrich, D., Jick, T., & Kerr, S. (1995). *The boundaryless organization: Breaking the chains of organizational structure.* San Francisco: Jossey-Bass.

Austrin, T. (1994). Positioning resistance and the resisting position: Human resource management and the politics of appraisal and grievance hearings. In J. M. Jermier, D. Knights, & W. R. Nord (Eds.), *Resistance and power in organizations* (pp. 199-218). London: Routledge

Bandura, A., Barbaranelli, C., Caprara, G. V., & Pastorelli, C. (1996). Mechanisms of moral disengagement in the exercise of moral agency. *Journal of Personality and Social Psychology, 71*, 364-374.

Bateson, G. (1980). *Mind and nature.* New York: Bantam.

Baxter, L. (1988). A dialectical perspective on communication strategies in relationship development. In S. Duck (Ed.), *Handbook of personal relationships: Theory, research and interventions* (pp. 257-273). New York: John Wiley.

Bies, R. J. (1987). The predicament of injustice: The management of moral outrage. In L. L. Cummings & B. M. Staw (Eds.), *Research in organizational behavior* (Vol. 9, pp. 289-319). Greenwich, CT: JAI.

Bies, R. J., & Moag, J. S. (1986). Interactional justice: Communication criteria of fairness. In R. J. Lewicki, B. H. Sheppard, & M. H. Bazerman (Eds.), *Research on negotiation in organizations* (Vol. 1, pp. 43-55). Greenwich, CT: JAI.

Bies, R. J., & Tripp, T. M. (1995). The use and abuse of power: Justice as social control. In R. S. Cropanzano & K. M. Kacmar (Eds.), *Organizational politics, justice, and support: Managing the social climate of the workplace* (pp. 131-145). Westport, CT: Quorum.

Bies, R. J., & Tripp, T. M. (1998). Two faces of the powerless: Coping with tyranny in organizations. In R. M. Kramer & M. A. Neale (Eds.), *Power and influence in organizations* (pp. 203-219). Thousand Oaks, CA: Sage.

Bingham, S. G. (Ed.). (1994). *Conceptualizing sexual harassment as discursive practice.* Westport, CT: Praeger.

Bingham, S. G., & Burleson, B. R. (1989). Multiple effects of messages with multiple goals: Some perceived outcomes of responses to sexual harassment. *Human Communication Research, 16*, 184-216.

Boyd, N. G., & Taylor, R. R. (1998). A developmental approach to the examination of friendship in the leader-follower relationship. *Leadership Quarterly, 9*, 1-25.

Bridge, K., & Baxter, L. A. (1992). Blended relationships: Friends as work associates. *Western Journal of Communication, 56*, 200-225.

Bronfenbrenner, U. (1979). *The ecology of human development: Experiments by nature and design.* Cambridge, MA: Harvard University Press.

Brown, P., & Levinson, S. C. (1987). *Politeness: Some universals in language usage.* Cambridge: Cambridge University Press.

Burkhardt, M., & Brass, D. (1990). Changing patterns or patterns of change: The effects of a change in technology on social network structure and power. *Administrative Science Quarterly, 35*, 104-127.

Cahill, D. J., & Sias, P. M. (1997). The perceived social costs and importance of seeking emotional support in the workplace: Gender differences and similarities. *Communication Research Reports, 14*, 231-240.

Cameron, K. S., Freeman, S. J., & Mishra, A. K. (1993). Downsizing and redesigning organizations. In G. P. Huber & W. H. Glick (Eds.), *Organizational change and redesign: Ideas and insights for improving performance* (pp. 19-63). New York: Oxford University Press.

Carson, C. L., & Cupach, W. R. (2000). Facing corrections in the workplace: The influence of perceived face threat on the consequences of managerial reproaches. *Journal of Applied Communication Research, 28*, 215-234.

Clair, R. P. (1993). The use of framing devices to sequester organizational narratives: Hegemony and harassment. *Communication Monographs, 60*, 113-136.

Clair, R. P. (1998). *Organizing silence: A world of possibilities.* Albany: State University of New York Press.

Clegg, S. (1994). Power relations and the constitution of the resistant subject. In J. M. Jermier, D. Knights, & W. R. Nord (Eds.), *Resistance and power in organizations* (pp. 274-325). London: Routledge.

Cleveland, H. (1985). The twilight of hierarchy: Speculations on the global information society. *Public Administration Review, 45*, 185-195.

Collins, P. H. (1991). *Black feminist thought: Knowledge, consciousness, and the politics of empowerment.* New York: Routledge.

Contractor, N. S. & Grant, S. (1996). The emergence of shared interpretations in organizations: A self-organizing systems perspective. In J. H. Watt & C. A. VanLear (Eds.), *Dynamic patterns in communication processes* (pp. 215-230). Thousand Oaks, CA: Sage.

Cox, S. A. (1999). Group communication and employee turnover: How coworkers encourage peers to voluntarily exit. *Southern Communication Journal, 64,* 181-192.

Davidow, W. H., & Malone, M. S. (1992). *The virtual corporation: Structuring and revitalizing the corporation for the 21st century.* New York: HarperCollins.

Dienesch, R. M., & Liden, R. C. (1986). Leader-member exchange model of leadership: A critique and further development. *Academy of Management Review, 11,* 618-634.

DiTomaso, N. (1992). Sexuality in the workplace: Discrimination and harassment. In J. Hearn, D. L. Sheppard, P. Tancred-Sheriff, & G. Burrell (Eds.), *The sexuality of organization* (pp. 71-90). London: Sage.

Donaldson, T., & Dunfee, T. W. (1994). Toward a unified conception of business ethics: Integrative social contracts theory. *Academy of Management Review, 19,* 252-284.

Duck, S., & Pittman, G. (1994). Social and personal relationships. In. M. L. Knapp & G. R. Miller (Eds.), *Handbook of interpersonal communication* (2nd ed., pp. 676-695). Thousand Oaks, CA: Sage.

Einarsen, S., & Raknes, B. I. (1997). Harassment in the workplace and the victimization of men. *Violence and Victims, 12,* 247-263.

Eisenberg, E. M., & Goodall, H. L., Jr. (2001). *Organizational communication: Balancing creativity and constraint* (3rd ed.). Boston: Bedford/St. Martin's.

Ellison, N. B. (1999). Social impacts: New perspectives on telework. *Social Science Computer Review, 17,* 338-356.

Ely, R. J. (1995). The power in demography: Women's social constructions of gender identity at work. *Academy of Management Journal, 38,* 589-634.

Fairhurst, G. T. (1993). The leader-member exchange patterns of women leaders in industry: A discourse analysis. *Communication Monographs, 60,* 321-351.

Fairhurst, G. T. (2001). Dualisms in leadership research. In F. M. Jablin & L. L. Putnam (Eds.), *The new handbook of organizational communication: Advances in theory, research, and methods* (pp. 379-439). Thousand Oaks, CA: Sage.

Fairhurst, G. T., & Chandler, T. A. (1989). Social structure in leader-member interaction. *Communication Monographs, 56,* 215-239.

Fairhurst, G. T., Green, S. G., & Snavely, B. K. (1984). Face support in controlling poor performance. *Human Communication Research, 11,* 272-295

Ferguson, K. E. (1984). *The feminist case against bureaucracy.* Philadelphia: Temple University Press.

Fine, G. A. (1986). Friendships in the work place. In V. J. Derlega & B. A. Winstead (Eds.), *Friendship and social interaction* (pp. 185-206). New York: Springer-Verlag.

Folger, R., & Skarlicki, D. P. (1998). When tough times make tough bosses: Managerial distancing as a function of layoff blame. *Academy of Management Journal, 41,* 79-87.

Friedman, S. L., & Wachs, T. D. (Eds.). (1999). *Measuring environment across the life span: Emerging methods and concepts.* Washington, DC: American Psychological Association.

Fritz, J. H. (1997). Men's and women's organizational peer relationships: A comparison. *Journal of Business Communication, 34,* 27-46.

Fritz, J. H., & Dillard, J. P. (1994, November). *The importance of peer relationships in organizational socialization.* Paper presented at the annual meeting of the Speech Communication Association, New Orleans.

Fulk, J. (1993). Social construction of communication technology. *Academy of Management Journal, 36,* 921-950.

Fulk, J., Steinfield, C. W., Schmitz, J. A., & Power, J. G. (1987). A social information processing model of media use in organizations. *Communication Research, 14,* 529-552.

Giles, H., Coupland, J., & Coupland, N. (Eds.). (1991). *Contexts of accommodation: Developments in applied sociolinguistics.* Cambridge: Cambridge University Press.

Goffman, E. (1967). "On face-work." In E. Goffman, *Interaction ritual: Essays on face-to-face behavior* (pp. 5-45). New York: Pantheon.

Graen, G. B., & Scandura, T. (1987). Toward a psychology of dyadic organizing. In L. L. Cummings & B. M. Staw (Eds.), *Research in organizational behavior* (Vol. 9, pp. 175-208). Greenwich, CT: JAI.

Gutek, B. A. (1992). Sexuality in the workplace: Key issues in social research and organizational practice. In J. Hearn, D. L. Sheppard, P. Tancred-Sheriff, & G. Burrell (Eds.), *The sexuality of organization* (pp. 56-70). London: Sage.

Gutek, B. A., & Cohen, A. G. (1992). Sex ratios, sex role spillover, and sex at work: A comparison of men's and women's experiences. In A. J. Mills & P. Tancred (Eds.), *Gendering organizational analysis* (pp. 133-150). Newbury Park, CA: Sage.

Gutek, B. A., & Morasch, B. (1982). Sex ratios, sex-role spillover and sexual harassment of women at work. *Journal of Social Issues, 38*(4), 55-74.

Hearn, J., & Parkin, P. W. (1987). *"Sex" at "work": The power and paradox of organization sexuality.* New York: St. Martin's.

Hess, J. A. (2000). Maintaining nonvoluntary relationships with disliked partners: An investigation into the use of distancing behaviors. *Human Communication Research, 26,* 458-488.

Hesse, B., Sproull, L., Kiesler, S., & Walsh, J. (1993). Returns to science: Computer networks in oceanography. *Communications of the ACM, 36,* 90-101.

Hodgins, H. S., Liebeskind, E., & Schwartz, W. (1996). Getting out of hot water: Facework in social predicaments. *Journal of Personality and Social Psychology, 71,* 300-314.

Hornstein, H. A. (1996). *Brutal bosses and their prey: How to identify and overcome abuse in the workplace.* New York: Riverhead.

Jablin, F. M. (1979). Superior-subordinate communication: The state of the art. *Psychological Bulletin, 86,* 1201-1222.

Jablin, F. M. (1985). Task/work relationships: A life-span perspective. In M. L. Knapp & G. R. Miller (Eds.), *Handbook of interpersonal communication* (pp. 615-654). Beverly Hills, CA: Sage.

Jablin, F. M. (2001). Organizational entry, assimilation, and disengagement/exit. In F. M. Jablin & L. L. Putnam (Eds.), *The new handbook of organizational communication: Advances in theory, research, and methods* (pp. 732-818). Thousand Oaks, CA: Sage.

Jablin, F. M., & Krone, K. J. (1994). Task/work relationships: A life-span perspective. In M. L. Knapp & G. R. Miller (Eds.), *Handbook of interpersonal communication* (2nd ed., pp. 621-675). Thousand Oaks, CA: Sage.

Jablin, F. M., & Sias, P. M. (2001). Communication competence. In F. M. Jablin & L. L. Putnam (Eds.), *The new handbook of organizational communication: Advances in*

theory, research, and methods (pp. 819-864). Thousand Oaks, CA: Sage.

Jermier, J. M., Knights, D., & Nord, W. R. (1994). Resistance and power in organizations: Agency, subjectivity and the labour process. In J. M. Jermier, D. Knights, & W. R. Nord (Eds.), *Resistance and power in organizations* (pp. 1-24). London: Routledge.

Johnson, G. M., Staton, A. Q., & Jorgensen-Earp, C. R. (1995). An ecological perspective on the transition of new university freshmen. *Communication Education, 44,* 336-352.

Kahn, R. L. (2000). The effect of technological innovation on organizational structure: Two case studies of the effects of the introduction of a new technology on informal organizational structures. *Journal of Business and Technical Communication, 14,* 328-347.

Katz, D., & Kahn, R. L. (1978). *The social psychology of organizations* (2nd ed). New York: John Wiley.

Keashly, L., Trott, V., & MacLean, L. M. (1994). Abusive behavior in the workplace: A preliminary investigation. *Violence and Victims, 9,* 341-357.

Kirby, E. L. (2000). Should I do as you say, or do as you do? Mixed messages about work and family. *Electronic Journal of Communication, 10*(3-4).

Kirby, E. L., & Krone, K. J. (2002). "The policy exists, but you can't use it": Negotiating tensions in work-family policy. *Journal of Applied Communication Research, 30,* 50-77.

Knapp, M. L. (1978). *Social intercourse: From greeting to goodbye.* Boston: Allyn & Bacon.

Knights, D., & Vurdubakis, T. (1994). Foucault, power, resistance and all that. In J. M. Jermier, D. Knights, & W. R. Nord (Eds.), *Resistance and power in organizations* (pp. 167-198). London: Routledge.

Kram, K. E., & Isabella, L. A. (1985). Mentoring alternatives: The role of peer relationships in career development. *Academy of Management Journal, 28,* 110-132.

Kraut, R. (1987). Predicting the use of technology: The case of telework. In R. Kraut (Ed.), *Technology and the transformation of white-collar work* (pp. 113-133). Hillsdale, NJ: Lawrence Erlbaum.

Kreps, G. L. (Ed.). (1993). *Sexual harassment: Communication implications.* Cresskill, NJ: Hampton.

Krone, K. J. (1994). Structuring constraints on perceptions of upward influence and supervisory relationships. *Southern Communication Journal, 59,* 215-226.

Lee, J., & Jablin, F. M. (1995). Maintenance communication in superior-subordinate work relationships. *Human Communication Research, 22,* 220-257.

Lincoln, J. R., & Miller, J. (1979). Work and friendship ties in organizations: A comparative analysis of relational networks. *Administrative Science Quarterly, 24,* 181-199.

Louis, M. R., Posner, B. Z., & Powell, G. N. (1983). The availability and helpfulness of socialization practices. *Personnel Psychology, 36,* 857-866.

Loy, P. H., & Stewart, L. P. (1984). The extents and effects of sexual harassment of working women. *Sociological Focus, 17,* 31-43.

Magnusson, D. (1995). Individual development: A holistic, integrated model. In P. Moen, G. H. Elder, Jr., & K. Luscher (Eds.), *Examining lives in context: Perspectives on the ecology of human development* (pp. 19-60). Washington, DC: American Psychological Association.

Miles, R. E., & Creed, W. E. D. (1995). Organizational forms and managerial philosophies: A descriptive and analytical review. *Research in Organizational Behavior, 17,* 333-372.

Miller, V. D., & Jablin, F. M. (1991). Information seeking during organizational entry: Influence, tactics, and a model of the process. *Academy of Management Review, 16,* 92-120.

Moen, P., Elder, G. H., Jr., & Luscher, K. (Eds.). (1995). *Examining lives in context: Perspectives on the ecology of human development.* Washington, DC: American Psychological Association.

Morand, D. (1996). Dominance, deference, and egalitarianism in organizational interaction: A sociolinguistic analysis of power and politeness. *Organization Science, 7,* 544-556.

Mumby, D. K., & Putnam, L. L. (1992). The politics of emotion: A feminist reading of bureaucracy. *Academy of Management Review, 17,* 465-486.

Myers, S. A., Knox, R. L., Pawlowski, D. R., & Ropog, B. L. (1999). Perceived communication openness and functional communication skills among organizational peers. *Communication Reports, 12,* 71-83.

Nahapiet, J., & Ghoshal, S. (1998). Social capital, intellectual capital, and the organizational advantage. *Academy of Management Review, 23,* 242-266.

Nieva, V. F., & Gutek, B. A. (1981). *Women and work: A psychological perspective.* New York: Praeger.

Odden, C. M., & Sias, P. M. (1997). Peer communication relationships and psychological climate. *Communication Quarterly, 45,* 153-166.

Pelz, D. (1952). Influence: A key to effective leadership in the first-line supervisor. *Personnel, 29,* 209-217.

Rawlins, W. K. (1992). *Friendship matters: Communication, dialectics, and the life course.* New York: Aldine de Gruyter.

Ray, E. B. (1987). Supportive relationships and occupational stress in the workplace. In T. L. Albrecht & M. B. Adelman (Eds.), *Communicating social support* (pp. 172-191). Newbury Park, CA: Sage.

Rice, R., & Love, G. (1987). Electronic emotion: Socioemotional content in a computer-mediated communication network. *Communication Research, 14,* 85-108.

Romm, C. T. (1999). *Virtual politicking: Playing politics in electronically linked organizations.* Cresskill, NJ: Hampton.

Rousseau, D. M., & McLean-Parks, L. (1993). The contracts of individuals and organizations. In L. L. Cummings & B. M. Staw (Eds.), *Research in organizational behavior* (Vol. 15, pp. 1-43). Greenwich, CT: JAI.

Sheffey, S., & Tindale, R. S. (1992). Perceptions of sexual harassment in the workplace. *Journal of Applied Social Psychology, 22,* 1502-1520.

Sias, P. M. (1996). Constructing perceptions of differential treatment: An analysis of coworker discourse. *Communication Monographs, 63,* 171-187.

Sias, P. M. (2000, November). *From friends to coworkers: Narratives of workplace friendship deterioration.* Paper presented at the annual meeting of the National Communication Association, Seattle, WA.

Sias, P. M., & Cahill, D. J. (1998). From coworkers to friends: The development of peer friendships in the workplace. *Western Journal of Communication, 62,* 273-299.

Sias, P. M., & Jablin, F. M. (1995). Differential superior-subordinate relations, perceptions of fairness, and coworker communication. *Human Communication Research, 22,* 5-38.

Sias, P. M., Smith, G., & Avdeyeva, T. (in press). Sex and sex composition similarities and differences in workplace friendship development. *Communication Studies.*

Sigman, S. J. (1995). Order and continuity in human relationships: A social communication approach to defining "relationship." In W. Leeds-Hurwitz (Ed.), *Social approaches to communication* (pp. 188-200). New York: Guilford.

Sloan, D. K., & Krone, K. J. (2001, November). *Gendered abusive organizational communication: Thirty women define and describe their experience.* Paper presented at the annual meeting of the National Communication Association, Atlanta, GA.

Tancred-Sheriff, P. (1989). Gender, sexuality and the labour process. In J. Hearn, D. L. Sheppard, P. Tancred-Sheriff, & G. Burrell (Eds.), *The sexuality of organization* (pp. 45-55). London: Sage.

Tangri, S. S., Burt, M. R., & Johnson, L. B. (1982). Sexual harassment at work: Three explanatory models. *Journal of Social Issues, 38*(4), 33-54.

Taylor, B., & Conrad, C. (1992). Narratives of sexual harassment: Organizational dimensions. *Journal of Applied Communication Research, 20,* 401-418.

Taylor, J., & Van Every, E. (1993). *The vulnerable fortress: Bureaucratic organization and management in the information age.* Toronto: University of Toronto Press.

Tepper, B. J. (2000). Consequences of abusive supervision. *Academy of Management Journal, 43,* 178-190.

Thomas, L. T., & Ganster, D. C. (1995). Impact of family-supportive work variables on work-family conflict and strain: A control perspective. *Journal of Applied Psychology, 80,* 6-15.

Trempe, J., Rigny, A.-J., & Haccoun, R. R. (1985). Subordinate satisfaction with male and female managers: Role of perceived supervisory influence. *Journal of Applied Psychology, 70,* 44-47.

Vondracek, F. W., Lerner, R. M., & Schulenberg, J. E. (1986). *Career development: A life-span developmental approach.* Hillsdale, NJ: Lawrence Erlbaum.

Waldron, V. R. (1991). Achieving communication goals in superior-subordinate relationships: The multifunctionality of upward maintenance tactics. *Communication Monographs, 58,* 289-306.

Waldron, V. R. (1999). Communication practices of followers, members, and protégés: The case of upward influence tactics. In M. E. Roloff (Ed.), *Communication yearbook 22* (pp. 251-299). Thousand Oaks, CA: Sage.

Waldron, V. R. (2000). Relational experiences and emotion at work. In S. Fineman (Ed.), *Emotion in organizations* (2nd ed., pp. 640-682). London: Sage.

Waldron, V. R., & Krone, K. J. (1991). The experience and expression of emotion in the workplace: A study of a corrections organization. *Management Communication Quarterly, 4,* 287-309.

Wheatley, M. J. (1994). *Leadership and the new science: Learning about organization from an orderly universe.* San Francisco: Berrett-Koehler.

Wheatley, M. J. (2001). *Leadership and the new science: Discovering order in a chaotic world.* San Francisco: Berrett-Koehler.

Willemyns, M., Gallois, C., & Callan, V. (2000, June). *Employees' perceptions of managers' communication accommodation: A structural modeling approach.* Paper presented at the annual meeting of the International Communication Association, Acapulco.

Zorn, T. E. (1995). Bosses and buddies: Constructing and performing simultaneously hierarchical and close friendship relationships. In J. T. Wood & S. Duck (Eds.), *Understudied relationships: Off the beaten track* (pp. 122-147). Thousand Oaks, CA: Sage.

17

Interpersonal Processes in Romantic Relationships

ANITA L. VANGELISTI

Interpersonal communication is central to romantic relationships. The way two people interact when they first meet can either ignite or extinguish hopes of future romance (Davis, 1973). Couples' communication is associated with what partners think about each other (e.g., Ickes & Simpson, 1997; Sillars, Roberts, Dun, & Leonard, 2001), how they generally behave toward each other (Fitzpatrick, 1988), and how they feel about their relationship (e.g., Christensen, 1988; Noller, 1984). Patterns of interaction can even determine whether a relationship continues or ends (Gottman, 1994). In short, communication not only reflects romantic relationships, it defines them (Duck, 1994; Knapp, 1984).

My purpose in this chapter is to provide a selective review of the literature on interpersonal communication in romantic relationships.

The chapter is divided into three parts. The first section examines research and theory associated with the initiation of romantic relationships. In the second section, I review literature describing some of the interpersonal processes that typify ongoing romantic relationships, describing both individual characteristics (e.g., cognition and affect) and interpersonal patterns (e.g., couple types, behavioral sequences). Finally, I discuss studies focusing on relational dissolution and divorce.

It is important to acknowledge that the review of research and theory offered in this chapter is by no means comprehensive. A chapter of this length could not possibly do justice to a comprehensive review—the literature is simply too vast and too diverse. My goal here is to include many of the research findings that capture the spirit of what scholars know about interpersonal interaction in romantic relationships. Given the space constraints, I have had to make some difficult selections. I have had to omit some interesting studies as well as some topics that are relevant to romantic relationships. It is my hope that the reader will indulge these choices and use the ideas presented in this chapter as a stimulus for further study.

INITIATING ROMANTIC RELATIONSHIPS

The number of factors that can influence whether two people come together and form a long-term romantic relationship is daunting. Some say that individuals' selection of one mate over another happens largely by chance (Lykken & Tellegen, 1993). Others argue that attraction and relationship initiation are the result of biochemical reactions in the body (Fisher, 1992). Yet others suggest that mate selection involves a series of strategies employed by individuals who are attempting to maximize their reproductive value (Buss, 1994). Fortunately, the broad range of explanations offered for how and why people come together to form romantic relationships has not prevented researchers and theorists from systematically studying the phenomenon. Scholars have examined factors that affect the development of romantic relationships as well as variables that encourage people to initiate relationships. For instance, research suggests that the initiation of romantic relationships is constrained by both physical and social contexts. People are much more likely to start romantic relationships with individuals who are physically proximate than they are with those at a distance (Segal, 1974). Although the advent of e-mail and Internet chat rooms may facilitate the development of some long-distance relationships, long-term romantic relationships initiated over the Internet still are relatively few and far between (but see Parks & Roberts, 1998). In fact, studies have revealed

that people who spend a great deal of time on the Internet "chatting" with others tend to be lonely and socially isolated (Kraut et al., 1998).

Because most relationships are initiated through face-to-face interactions, the pool of potential partners available to an individual is typically limited by his or her social network (Parks & Eggert, 1991). People tend to interact with others who are similar to them in terms of variables such as age, socioeconomic status, and education. As a consequence, the group from which any given individual is likely to select a romantic partner is relatively homogeneous (Lykken, 2002).

Although the environmental constraints on relational initiation are stronger than many would like to admit, it is important to note that, within a relatively homogeneous pool of potential partners, individuals still make selections. The choices people make concerning relationship initiation may be influenced by any number of variables, ranging from their perceptions of the other person's social competence to how lonely they feel when they first meet a potential partner. Two of the most frequently studied issues associated with the initiation of romantic relationships are physical attraction and similarity.

Physical Attraction

Even though most people have been told not to "judge a book by its cover," physical attractiveness is one of the primary cues that an individual employs in deciding whether to initiate a relationship with another person (see, e.g., Walster, Aronson, Abrahams, & Rottman, 1966). People make decisions about approaching potential partners based, in large part, on how physically attractive they perceive those partners to be. After an individual has approached and talked to a potential partner, the way he or she evaluates the interaction also is affected by physical attractiveness. Indeed, Reis, Nezlek, and Wheeler (1980) found that physical attractiveness was associated with the degree to which interactions with others were perceived as pleasant.

Researchers and theorists suggest that part of the reason for the primacy of physical attractiveness in the initiation of romantic relationships is that people believe physical attractiveness is associated with positive qualities (for a meta-analysis, see Eagly, Ashmore, Makhijani, & Longo, 1991). In one of the first of many studies to suggest that "what is beautiful is good," Dion, Berscheid, and Walster (1972) found that both men and women judged physically attractive people as more likely than those who were physically unattractive to have a number of positive characteristics, including kindness, sexual warmth and responsiveness, poise, sociability, and sensitivity. Participants also thought those who were more physically attractive had better characters and would be more exciting dates than those who were unattractive. When asked about the futures of physically attractive and unattractive individuals, participants speculated that those who were attractive would be more likely to have happy marriages, to have social and professional success, to be competent in marriage, and to have more fulfilling lives. The bias that individuals appear to have for beauty provides at least one explanation for why people are drawn to those they see as physically attractive: In selecting physically attractive partners, they believe that they get partners with a number of other desirable characteristics as well.

It also is worth noting that although physical attractiveness plays a major role in the choices people make concerning their selection of potential partners, researchers have repeatedly found a gender difference with regard to the importance that men and women initially assign to physical attractiveness (but see Albada, Knapp, & Theune, 2002, for evidence that individuals' views of physical attractiveness can change over time). More specifically, men report stronger preferences for physically attractive mates than do women; women, by contrast, report stronger preferences than do men for partners who have good earning potential or other valued resources (Buss, 1989; Buss & Barnes, 1986; Sprecher, Sullivan, & Hatfield, 1994).

One of the most popular explanations provided for this gender difference is rooted in evolutionary psychology (Buss, 1994; Simpson & Kenrick, 1997). Scholars argue that, for example, men place greater importance on the physical attractiveness of their mates because they are seeking mates who are fertile and able to produce healthy offspring. Women, by contrast, place more importance on the earning potential of their partners because they are seeking mates who will be "good providers" for their children. This explanation is difficult to refute in part because the gender difference in question has been replicated across a number of cultures (Buss & Barnes, 1986). Even so, there are alternative explanations. For instance, it is possible the difference is due to the distinct ways in which men and women are socialized to talk and think about their choices in romantic partners. In support of this explanation, Sprecher (1989) found that differences in the importance that men and women assign to the physical attractiveness of potential partners were larger when self-report data were examined than when behavioral data were tested. When Sprecher asked men and women to report their preferences in potential mates, men were more likely to say that physical attractiveness affected their choice than were women, and women were more likely than men to report that their preference was based on the other's earning potential and expressiveness. However, when Sprecher examined the participants' behavior, she found that both men's and women's choices of partners were most influenced by the partners' physical attractiveness.

Similarity

In addition to focusing on the role of physical attractiveness in relationship initiation, scholars have studied the association between similarity and attraction. For instance, the literature on mate selection has yielded substantial evidence that people tend to choose spouses who are relatively similar to them in terms of race, religion, ethnicity, education, and age (see Surra, 1990). Further, studies examining the dynamics of ongoing relationships indicate that partners who have similar preferences with regard to role performance and leisure activities are more compatible than those who do not (e.g., Houts, Robins, & Huston, 1996).

Although researchers have explored attraction and partners' similarity with regard to a number of different variables, the association between attitudinal similarity and attraction has received the most attention. Most scholars suggest that the impetus for this line of research was a longitudinal investigation conducted by Newcomb (1961) in which he examined friendships that were formed between college housemates. Newcomb assessed the housemates' value similarity before they were acquainted and then later looked at the association between that variable and attraction. He found that value similarity was positively linked to the attraction that developed between housemates over the course of a semester.

To establish the association between attraction and attitude similarity more clearly, Byrne (1971) conceived what is now known as the "bogus stranger" experimental paradigm. This procedure involved the researchers' first measuring study participants' attitudes about a number of topics. The researchers then manipulated attitude similarity by presenting participants with what was supposed to be another set of attitudes toward the same topics. The participants typically were told that this second set of attitudes belonged to a stranger, who was portrayed as another participant. Finally, the participants were asked to report the extent to which they were attracted to the "bogus stranger." Byrne and his associates found that people reported greater attraction to strangers who were attitudinally similar to them than to

those who were dissimilar (e.g., Byrne & Clore, 1970; Byrne & Griffitt, 1966; Byrne & Nelson, 1965).

In spite of the evidence amassed by Byrne and his colleagues, a number of researchers have questioned the association between attitude similarity and attraction. For instance, Rosenbaum (1986) found evidence that the link between these two variables is not due to individuals' being attracted to similar others, but instead is based on individuals' feelings of repulsion for those who are dissimilar. Condon and Crano (1988) found that the association between attitude similarity and attraction is influenced by people's assumptions that others will evaluate them positively. Perhaps the most celebrated study on this issue within the field of communication is one conducted by Sunnafrank and Miller (1981). Following a modification of the bogus stranger manipulation, these researchers asked dyads to engage in conversation with each other. They selected conversational partners based on their similarity or dissimilarity on two controversial topics and told participants that they would meet and work together on a project involving those topics. Individuals who were in a no-interaction condition responded to Byrne's measure of attraction. Those in an initial-interaction condition talked to each other for 5 minutes and then responded to the same questionnaire. Sunnafrank and Miller found that the association between attitude similarity and attraction was eliminated when people were given the opportunity to interact (see also Sunnafrank, 1983, 1986).

Clearly, discussion concerning the nature of the link between attitude similarity and attraction is ongoing. Some scholars argue that the attitude similarity-attraction effect is "dead" (Bochner, 1991); others say that similarity is of "fundamental importance" to human relationships (Duck & Barnes, 1992). Some theorists note that difference and novelty are desirable features of relationships (Baxter & Montgomery, 1996); others suggest that familiarity and predictability are more attractive (Berger & Bradac, 1982). After several decades of research, there is little evidence that scholars will soon agree on the extent to which "birds of a feather flock together" and the conditions under which "opposites attract." Indeed, as Cappella and Palmer (1992) note, the zeal that scholars bring to this discussion and "the intensity and stridency of their comments are themselves testimony to the centrality of attitude similarity in the study of relationship formation" (p. 180).

Theoretical Approaches to Relationship Initiation

Although scholars still debate whether, and the various ways in which, similarity influences attraction, most agree that when individuals interact with similar others, their ability to make predictions (e.g., about how the other person will behave, how they should behave when they are around the other, and whether interactions with the other will be rewarding) is enhanced. Similarity, in other words, provides potential partners with information—and information is an important commodity for those who are interested in initiating romantic relationships.

The notion that people seek and exchange information when they initially interact is woven through many theories of relationship initiation. For instance, one of the most well-known theories of relationship development, Altman and Taylor's (1973) social penetration theory, conceives of information as a means for developing intimacy as well as a way to evaluate the rewards and costs that may be associated with a relationship. Altman and Taylor suggest that increases in relational breadth and depth are the result of individuals' sharing information about themselves with each other. When people first meet, they exchange information that is relatively impersonal and limit the number of different topics they discuss. As they come to know and trust

each other, partners share a greater number of topics (breadth) and disclose more intimate information to each other about those topics (depth). Indeed, research has revealed that partners who disclose more to each other report greater emotional involvement in their relationships (Rubin, Hill, Peplau, & Dunkel-Schetter, 1980) as well as greater relational satisfaction (Hendrick, 1981). Although, as Altman and Taylor suggest, disclosure is a vital component of relational development, it is important to note that the rate at which partners exchange intimate information varies over the course of their relationship. For instance, as partners come to know each other, their need to disclose information typically decreases (Derlega, Metts, Petronio, & Margulis, 1993). They begin to establish a balance between the disclosure of intimate information and privacy (Baxter & Montgomery, 1996; Petronio, 1991), and, for various reasons, they may even declare some topics off-limits for discussion (Baxter & Wilmot, 1985; Cloven & Roloff, 1994; Roloff & Ifert, 1998).

Drawing from social exchange theories (Burgess & Huston, 1979; Homans, 1961; Thibaut & Kelley, 1959), Altman and Taylor argue (1973) that people move further into a relationship as long as the perceived rewards associated with the relationship exceed the costs. If, for example, partners perceive their interactions to be more pleasing than not, they are likely to continue their association with each other. In addition to assessing how rewarding their interactions are, individuals consider what other alternative relationships might be available to them as well as how those alternatives compare to their current relationship. Rusbult's (1983, 1991) investment model suggests that partners' perception of their alternatives, their satisfaction, and the investments they make in their relationship operate together to influence how committed they are to continuing the relationship.

Rather than propose that partners' assessments of rewards and costs are the key factors in determining whether or not relationships will develop, Berger and Calabrese (1975) argue that "when strangers meet, their primary concern is one of uncertainty reduction or increasing predictability about the behavior of both themselves and others in the interaction" (p. 100). Uncertainty reduction theory suggests that, in order to reduce uncertainty during initial interactions, partners engage in information-seeking behaviors. When people initially encounter each other, they discuss relatively innocuous items—the weather, where they are from, what they do for a living (Berger, Gardner, Clatterbuck, & Schulman, 1976). Normally, they do not talk about highly charged personal matters such as their fears, anxieties, or fantasies. According to Berger and Calabrese, as the amount of verbal communication between partners increases, their uncertainty tends to decrease. It is after people come to know each other that they begin to exchange more intimate information, because their uncertainty has faded.

Both social penetration theory and uncertainty reduction theory suggest that as relationships develop, partners exchange different sorts of information. Miller and Steinberg (1975) note that individuals employ three types of information to make predictions about each other: cultural, sociological, and psychological. Cultural information typically provides a very general level of prediction: People anticipate how an individual will act based upon his or her culture. Sociological information emphasizes a person's group memberships. This type of information offers better predictability than cultural information, but it is still stereotypical. Finally, psychological information indicates how an individual differs from the groups to which he or she belongs. People know relatively few others at the psychological level, because to know someone at that level requires a great deal of communication. It is important to note that, over time, relationships can exist at different levels of prediction. Spouses who once knew

each other at the psychological level may grow apart and, as a consequence, may know each other only at the sociological level.

Although the types of information that individuals exchange when they initially meet provide an important perspective on what happens when relationships are first initiated, this obviously represents only part of the picture. In addition to seeking and providing information, people enact behaviors to make themselves attractive and likable to others. Indeed, Bell and Daly (1984) argue that individuals intentionally engage in behaviors to generate affinity in others. Using a four-step conceptual model, these researchers identified the strategies people typically use in actively initiating relationships. The various strategies clustered into seven general categories: focusing on commonalities (e.g., highlighting similarities, demonstrating equality), showing self-involvement (e.g., finding ways of regularly "running into" the other), involving the other (e.g., participating in activities the other person enjoys, including the other in activities), demonstrating caring and concern (e.g., listening, being altruistic), displaying politeness (e.g., letting the other have control over plans, acting interested), encouraging mutual trust (e.g., being honest, being reliable), and demonstrating control and visibility (e.g., being dynamic, looking good).

INTERPERSONAL PROCESSES IN ROMANTIC RELATIONSHIPS

Research on information-seeking and affinity-seeking behaviors clearly illustrates the centrality of interpersonal communication to the initiation of romantic relationships. When people initiate relationships, they have to communicate—whether to gather information about potential partners, to give information about themselves to partners, or to present themselves as attractive and likable. Obviously, these and other interpersonal behaviors do not cease once romantic relationships are established. The specific behaviors enacted by individual partners may change over time, and, certainly, the way people think about and respond to certain behaviors may change. As their relationships develop, partners also will begin to engage in patterns of interaction that they did not enact when they first met.

Research on the interpersonal processes that take place in the context of romantic relationships has focused on the behavior of individual partners as well as on the patterns of behavior enacted by romantic dyads. Individuals' communication patterns and the patterns of communication enacted by dyads are influenced by the cognitive and affective characteristics that individuals bring to their initial interactions. Further, because romantic relationships are dynamic and reflexive, the cognitive and affective characteristics that emerge from partners' interactions both influence and are influenced by their relationship.

Individual Characteristics of Relational Partners

Cognition

The ways people think about potential partners and relationships clearly influence whether and how they initiate relationships with others. Those who see relationships as risky and dangerous are likely to approach potential partners differently than those who view relationships as stable and rewarding. Similarly, once an individual is involved with a romantic partner, his or her thoughts about the partner and about the relationship are likely to affect relational outcomes. Research suggests that cognition in and about romantic relationships is associated with the ways people feel about their relationships, the ways they behave toward their partners, and even the ways their partners behave toward them (e.g., Sillars, Roberts, Leonard, & Dun, 2000).

The literature on cognition in close relationships is quite diverse in terms of focus, but three aspects of partners' cognition have received a great deal of attention from researchers and theorists in recent years: relational schemata, beliefs and standards, and attributions and accounts.

Relational schemata. People have mental representations that influence the ways they interpret information about their partners as well as the ways they behave in the context of their relationships. Planalp (1985) calls these mental representations *relational schemata* and describes them as "coherent frameworks of relational knowledge that are used to derive relational implications of messages and are modified in accord with ongoing experience with relationships" (p. 9).

Although scholars differ with regard to their opinions concerning the specific components of relational schemata, most agree that, among other things, relational schemata include knowledge structures about the *self*, the *other*, and the *relationship between self and other*. These representations differ from those traditionally discussed by psychologists (e.g., Markus, 1977) in that they are necessarily social. Whereas it is possible to have general views of the self, the other, or the relationship (e.g., "I like chocolate"; "He has gray hair"; "We've been married for 8 years"), relational schemata define what a person is like in relationship to others (e.g., "I'm a good listener"; "He is a caring person") (Andersen, Reznik, & Chen, 1997; Baldwin, 1992). Knowledge structures about the self, the other, and the relationship thus are interdependent: Each influences and is influenced by the other. Furthermore, each of these cognitive structures affects the way people experience and behave within their romantic relationships.

For instance, research on the way relational partners view themselves shows that self-representations affect partners' experiences within romantic relationships. Individuals tend to be drawn toward others who see them as they see themselves (Deutsch & Solomon,

1959). Swann, Hixon, and De La Ronde (1992) found that people with negative self-concepts were more committed to spouses who evaluated them negatively than to partners who evaluated them positively. Perhaps because they do not view themselves as strong or independent, people with low self-esteem also seem to be more swayed by their love experiences than do those with high self-esteem. Individuals with low self-esteem note that they have more intense experiences of love, report that their love experiences are less rational, and view their partners more positively than do people with high self-esteem (K. K. Dion & K. L. Dion, 1975; K. L. Dion & K. K. Dion, 1973, 1988). By contrast, those with high self-esteem tend to have more confidence that their own behavior (e.g., being friendly) will evoke affiliative behaviors from others (Baldwin & Keelan, 1999). Murray, Holmes, Griffin, Bellavia, and Rose (2001) further found that individuals with self-doubt underestimated the strength of their partners' love for them.

Studies on cognitive representations of potential partners similarly illustrate that activating particular expectations about a partner can influence social interaction. In a classic study, Snyder, Tanke, and Berscheid (1977) found that men who were told that a woman they were about to interact with for the first time was physically attractive rated the woman more favorably than did men who were told their interactional partner was unattractive. Further, when outside observers rated the women's conversational behavior, the researchers found that, indeed, the women behaved in more socially skillful ways. Snyder et al. concluded that the men's impressions of the women's physical attractiveness created a self-fulfilling prophecy—when the men expected women to behave in more positive ways, the women did so (see also Darley & Oleson, 1993).

In a similar vein, Andersen and Baum (1994) found that activating knowledge structures associated with a significant other can influence the way people evaluate strangers. These researchers asked study participants to describe a significant other whom they either liked or disliked. They also had each participant interact with a stranger who was portrayed as having the traits that the participant used to describe his or her significant other. The researchers found that individuals "transferred" the schemata of their significant others to the strangers—that is, participants evaluated the strangers based, in part, on the traits associated with their significant others.

Although studies focusing on representations of the self or the other provide interesting information about the way knowledge structures can influence people's relationships, they constitute a relatively small sector of the literature on relational schemata. Research on relational knowledge structures has been dominated, for the most part, by work emphasizing the ways partners represent their relationships with others. These investigations may be best exemplified by research and theory on adult attachment.

The literature on adult attachment is founded on the work of Bowlby (1969, 1973, 1980), who argued that individuals develop "internal working models" of relationships from the interactions they have as infants with caregivers. According to Bowlby, these models are composed of two distinct parts. One is a representation of the self, or a self-schema, that portrays the self as either worthy or unworthy of love and caring. The other is a representation of the caregiver that characterizes him or her as responsive and sensitive to the infant or as unresponsive and insensitive. Bowlby argues that the attachment relationships that individuals form as infants with their adult caregivers influence their behavior well past infancy and into adulthood.

Of course, in adulthood, attachments change. As people mature, they become less attached to their adult caregivers and, in many cases, become attached to romantic partners. Hazan and Shaver (1987) argue that the attachments people develop as infants are later embodied in their romantic relationships. Based on the three categories of attachment identified by Ainsworth, Blehar, Waters, and Wall (1978) to characterize infants' attachments to their caregivers, Hazan and Shaver posit three types of adult attachment. The first of these is *secure*. Individuals with a secure attachment style find it easy to get close to others, are comfortable depending on others, and tend not to be concerned about being abandoned or having someone become too emotionally close to them. The second type is *avoidant*. People who are avoidant tend to get nervous when others get too close to them and are uncomfortable trusting or depending on others. The third and final type of adult attachment described by Hazan and Shaver is *anxious-ambivalent*. Those who are anxious-ambivalent find that others are reluctant to get as intimate as they would like. They worry that their romantic partners do not really care about them, and they often want to become extremely close to their partners.

Bartholomew and Horowitz (1991) provide a slightly different conceptualization of adult attachment. Like Bowlby, they suggest that internal working models are made up of representations of the self and the other. Because, Bartholomew and Horowitz argue, both self and other can be evaluated in positive or negative fashions, combining these two dimensions yields four categories: one in which people have a positive view of themselves and a positive view of others (*secure*), one in which they have a positive view of self and a negative view of others (*dismissing*), one with a negative view of self and a positive view of others (*preoccupied*), and one with a negative view of self and a negative view of others (*fearful*). Although a great deal of research has been conducted based on these various categories, most researchers and theorists now argue that two or three dimensions (e.g., comfort with closeness, anxiety about being abandoned or unloved, comfort with depending on others)

best capture the essence of people's attachment styles (Collins & Read, 1990; Simpson, 1990).

Regardless of whether attachment is conceived of as a style or as dimensions along which individuals vary, a plethora of findings suggest that people who are secure tend to be involved in relationships that are more committed and satisfying than do individuals who are insecure (e.g., either anxious-ambivalent or avoidant). Those who are secure tend to be more trusting, have higher self-esteem, and have more positive beliefs about others. They experience more positive emotions and fewer negative emotions in the context of their relationships, and they appear to be more comfortable expressing their feelings to relational partners. In short, people who are secure tend to be better off—both as individuals and as relational partners—than those who are insecure. (For reviews, see Cassidy & Shaver, 1999; Feeney & Noller, 1996.)

The consistent associations between attachment and positive individual and relational outcomes raise important questions about whether these knowledge structures are subject to change. Is attachment stable or unstable? If an individual is insecurely attached as a child, is he or she doomed to a life of failed relationships?

Bowlby originally conceived of attachment as relatively stable. Indeed, much of the literature on social cognition emphasizes the stability of knowledge structures. People often seek out and attend to information that is consistent with their expectations (Rosenthal, 1993; Stangor & McMillan, 1992); they resist data that contradict their beliefs (Ross, Lepper, & Hubbard, 1975), and they bias their memories of events or circumstances to fit with their current perceptions and expectations (Ross, 1989). Consistent with the notion that there is a fair amount of stability in knowledge representations, studies on adult attachment have demonstrated that approximately 70% of people evaluate their own attachment style consistently over periods ranging from 1 week to

4 years (Baldwin & Fehr, 1995; Kirkpatrick & Hazan, 1994).

Although researchers and theorists have emphasized the stability of individuals' knowledge structures, most also acknowledge that these structures are dynamic and responsive to changes in the social environment. For instance, Davila, Karney, and Bradbury (1999) found that, on average, individuals' attachment representations changed in a predictable way over the early years of marriage. More specifically, spouses tended to become more secure—perhaps reflecting increased comfort with their relationship. These researchers also found significant changes in spouses' attachment based on both individual differences (e.g., psychological vulnerabilities) and interpersonal variables (e.g., relational satisfaction). Davila and her colleagues conclude that people's "past experiences, their current states of mind about relationships, and their experiences with partners all affect how secure they feel in relationships" (p. 798).

Clearly, the processes associated with change in relational knowledge representations are complex and multifaceted. Pietromonaco, Laurenceau, and Barrett (2002) suggest that a number of different cognitive processes may be associated with changes in people's knowledge representations, including temporary shifts in the accessibility of relationship knowledge, reorganization and reframing of relationship-relevant information, and incorporation of new knowledge into existing structures. Researchers have yet to explore what initiates processes such as these, how the processes unfold, and what sorts of effects they have on the quality of romantic relationships.

Beliefs and standards. In addition to including "internal working models" that provide partners with a basis for predicting the qualities individuals and relationships *will* have, most theorists suggest that relational knowledge structures include beliefs or standards about the qualities that individuals and relationships

should have (Baldwin, 1992; Baucom, Epstein, Sayers, & Sher, 1989; Surra & Bohman, 1991). Partners' relational beliefs and standards have been studied under a number of different labels, including *implicit theories of relationships* (Fletcher & Thomas, 1996), *relational standards* (Vangelisti & Daly, 1997), *unrealistic beliefs* (Epstein & Eidelson, 1981), and *ideal standards* (Fletcher, Simpson, Thomas, & Giles, 1999). Although the concepts associated with these labels all carry slightly different meanings, they all reflect criteria that provide people with a means for evaluating their relationships with others.

Relationship beliefs or standards are central to a number of well-known theories, including social exchange (Homans, 1961; Huston & Burgess, 1979), equity (Adams, 1965; Hatfield, Traupman, Sprecher, Utne, & Hay, 1985; Walster, Walster, & Berscheid, 1978), interdependence (Kelley & Thibaut, 1978; Thibaut & Kelley, 1959), and investment (Rusbult, 1980, 1983) theories. Scholars who employ these and other theories suggest that comparisons between individuals' beliefs or standards and their perceptions of their current relationships serve as a basis for the way individuals feel about their romantic partners (Beck, 1988; Duck, 1990; Lederer & Jackson, 1968). When individuals' relational standards or beliefs are met or upheld, they are relatively satisfied with their relationships; when their standards or beliefs are not fulfilled, they are likely to become dissatisfied or distressed.

Empirical research generally has confirmed the association between relational quality and the degree to which people report their standards or beliefs are fulfilled. For instance, studies examining commonly held relational standards have demonstrated that when individuals' standards were met, they tended to be relatively satisfied with their relationships; by contrast, when those standards were unfulfilled, they tended to be less satisfied (Vangelisti & Daly, 1997). The same association emerged when the standards individuals held for their relational partners were examined: There was a positive association between the fulfillment of people's standards for their partners and their relational satisfaction (Fletcher et al., 1999). Research also suggests that individuals are happier when they match their partners' ideal standards (Campbell, Simpson, Kashy, & Fletcher (2001).

Of course, some beliefs or standards are more difficult to meet than others. A number of researchers have examined beliefs about relationships that are "unrealistic." Because unrealistic relational beliefs involve extreme standards that are difficult, if not impossible, to meet (e.g., "Happy couples never fight"), partners who hold such beliefs are more likely to be disappointed with their relationships (Baucom & Epstein, 1990). Indeed, Bradbury and Fincham (1987) found a negative link between unrealistic romantic beliefs and marital satisfaction. Kurdek (1992) further reported that unrealistic beliefs were negatively associated with satisfaction in both heterosexual and homosexual couples.

People with unrealistic or extreme beliefs about relationships not only tend to be less relationally satisfied, they also tend to be less optimistic about their partners changing than those with more realistic expectations (Epstein & Eidelson, 1981). Furthermore, those who are dissatisfied tend to expect more negative behaviors and fewer positive behaviors from their partners during conflict episodes than do those who are satisfied (Vanzetti, Notarius, & NeeSmith, 1992). The negative views held by individuals who have unrealistic relationship beliefs and the disappointment they feel about their relationships may create a very undesirable relational context for partners: People who have unrealistic beliefs are more likely to be dissatisfied with their relationships; individuals who are dissatisfied, in turn, anticipate negative behaviors from their partners. Given the negative views these individuals have concerning their partners and their relationships, they are likely to become entrenched in their

disappointment—regardless of whether or not their partners try to change.

It is apparent that unfulfilled relational beliefs and standards are linked to the quality of romantic relationships, but the nature of the association appears to differ somewhat for women and men. For example, one study found that when asked to rate the importance of various relational standards, women and men rated the standards similarly, but women believed their standards were fulfilled less often than did men (Vangelisti & Daly, 1997). Fitzpatrick and Sollie (1999) further examined what they call "unrealistic gendered beliefs"— beliefs that focus on irreconcilable differences in men's and women's relational needs. These researchers found that women's unrealistic beliefs were associated with more alternatives, lower matches to ideal comparison levels, and lower commitment. By contrast, men's unrealistic gendered beliefs were not associated with either investment or commitment. Fitzpatrick and Sollie argue that the links between women's unrealistic beliefs and various aspects of relational investment may reflect the notion that women are supposed to be "relational experts." That is, because women see unfulfilled beliefs as having important implications for their romantic relationships, the association between women's unmet beliefs and their relational investment may be stronger than it is for men.

Attributions and accounts. Knowledge structures such as beliefs and standards serve as a framework for interpreting and evaluating relationships. These structures have been the focus of a great deal of theoretical and empirical work, but the processes that they influence are interesting subjects of study in their own right. Individuals engage in cognitive processes that enable them to explain relational events and behaviors. Research on attribution and accounts provides a glimpse of the interpretive processes that affect, and are affected by, romantic relationships.

For instance, the attributions that people provide for their partners' behaviors often reveal something about the way they regard their relationships. Studies suggest that individuals are particularly likely to seek out such explanations when something happens that is negative, unexpected, or out of the ordinary (Pyszczynski & Greenberg, 1981). People like their experiences to "make sense" (Heider, 1958). When romantic partners feel or behave in ways that are out of character, those who notice the discrepancies typically search for ways to explain them. Because their explanations may comment on the thoughts, feelings, or behavior of the other (e.g., "because she's tired," "because she's stingy," "because she's a neat person"), they reflect a certain relational context—one that may be satisfying, dissatisfying, affectionate, or hostile.

A large body of research on marital and romantic partners' attributions supports the notion that people's explanations for their partners' behaviors are linked to their relational satisfaction (e.g., Fincham, Beach, & Baucom, 1987; Fincham & Bradbury, 1989; Grigg, Fletcher, & Fitness, 1989; Orvis, Kelley, & Butler, 1976). Studies have repeatedly revealed that those who are dissatisfied with their relationships tend to opt for explanations that magnify the potential impact of their partners' negative behaviors and discount the influence of the partners' positive behaviors. Satisfied people, in contrast, select attributions that highlight their partners' positive behaviors and minimize their negative behaviors. In short, dissatisfied individuals tend to make relatively negative, "distress-maintaining" attributions for their partners' behaviors, whereas those who are satisfied make more positive, "relationship-enhancing" attributions (Holtzworth-Munroe & Jacobson, 1985).

Although the association between partners' attributions and the quality of their relationships is well established (Bradbury & Fincham, 1990; Seibold & Spitzberg, 1982), until recently, the nature of that association

has been less clear. Researchers and theorists have argued that the causal direction of the link between maladaptive attributions and relational distress is bidirectional, suggesting not only that attributions are influenced by relational satisfaction, but that relational satisfaction is affected by attributions (e.g., Fincham & Bradbury, 1989). Evidence from longitudinal studies now has confirmed that attributions made by partners are associated with the deterioration of marital relationships (Karney & Bradbury, 2000). Studies also show that negative, distress-maintaining attributions are associated with elevated rates of negative behaviors during problem-solving discussions (Bradbury, Beach, Fincham, & Nelson, 1996).

In line with the literature on attributions, research on accounts suggests that the explanations people provide for events associated with their romantic relationships are linked to relational quality. For example, Surra and her colleagues (e.g., Surra, Arizzi, & Asmussen, 1988; Surra, Batchelder, & Hughes, 1995) have studied people's accounts of "turning points" in courtship—times when relational partners perceive that the chance they will marry either increases or decreases (see also Baxter & Bullis, 1986; Lloyd & Cate, 1985). Using an interview procedure developed by Huston, Surra, Fitzgerald, and Cate (1981), Surra and her coresearchers asked their respondents to explain what happened at each perceived turning point. Their findings indicated that individuals' explanations for relational turning points were associated with relational satisfaction 4 years after marriage. Partners' satisfaction was positively linked to comments about spending time together and disclosure and negatively associated with references to alternative dating partners and attributions concerning one or both partners' social networks.

Research on accounts (see Harvey, Orbuch & Weber, 1992; Harvey, Weber, & Orbuch, 1990) also has focused on the storylike explanations people construct to deal with stressful life events, such as incest (Harvey, Orbuch, Chwalisz, & Garwood, 1991) and relationship dissolution (Sorenson, Russell, Harkness, & Harvey, 1993). These investigations have demonstrated that those who formulate accounts to explain the trauma they experience and then confide their accounts to close relationship partners are better off, both physically and psychologically, than those who do not. Whether accounts are elicited by events associated with individuals' romantic relationship or by other events, it appears that people benefit from sharing their explanations with others they are close to. The ability to talk about stressful events with romantic partners may not only reflect the quality of people's romantic relationships, it may affect the individuals' well-being (see Pennebaker, 1990).

In spite of the potential link between people's ability to express their explanations for traumatic events to others and their personal well-being, there are a number of reasons individuals may decide not to disclose the explanations they generate to their romantic partners. They may feel the information is irrelevant to their partners, that it is too personal to discuss, or that their partners will judge it negatively. Most of the literature on accounts and attributions has focused on explanations that individuals may opt not to disclose to others. Because these internal, cognitive explanations affect people's personal relationships, they are a very important area for emphasis in research. But distinguishing individuals' unspoken attributions and accounts from those they communicate also should yield interesting data about how individuals conceive of their romantic relationships. What types of explanations are people unwilling to discuss, and why? How are unspoken attributions modified when they emerge in conversations between romantic partners? What can spoken attributions and accounts tell us about partners' relationships that unspoken ones cannot?

Although scholars have noted that distinctions between expressed and unexpressed explanations are important (Antaki, 1987; Hilton, 1990), few have contrasted the two. In part as a consequence, we know relatively little about how the attributions and accounts people generate for themselves, to meet their own needs, differ from those they generate for the public eye. Baumeister and Newman (1994; see also Baumeister, 1991) underline the importance of this distinction when they discuss possible differences in the narratives people construct to interpret their experiences and those they devise to communicate with others. These researchers suggest that stories based on *interpretive* motives meet people's needs to make sense of their lives, whereas those constructed for *interpersonal* purposes focus on achieving particular effects on other persons. Because interpretive motives emphasize the needs of the individual rather than the impact of the individual on others, they should exert a less potent influence on the explanations people generate when they talk to relational partners than should interpersonal motives.

Affect

Even a cursory review of the literature on cognition in romantic relationships reveals that partners' affect is closely tied to what and how they think. Relational schemata are organized, in part, around individuals' affective orientation toward themselves and others. Beliefs and standards that people hold for their relationships evoke certain emotions when they are unmet. Attributions and accounts that individuals generate are influenced by the way people feel toward their relational partners. Clearly, affect and the expression of affect are central components of romantic relationships.

The literature on romantic partners' expressions of affect generally suggests that individuals in distressed relationships display more negative affect, less positive affect, and more reciprocity of negative affect than do those who are not distressed (Margolin & Wampold, 1981; Noller, 1984; Notarius & Johnson, 1982). In addition, although partners who are happy tend to engage in more positive behaviors than those who are unhappy (Cutrona, 1996; Weiss & Heyman, 1990), negative behaviors often are deemed the more sensitive barometer of marital satisfaction (Gottman & Levenson, 1986; Huston & Vangelisti, 1991). Studies demonstrate that partners' negative behaviors are more strongly linked to marital satisfaction than are their positive behaviors, particularly when couples are dissatisfied with their relationships (Barnett & Nietzel, 1979; Broderick & O'Leary, 1986; Jacobson, Waldron, & Moore, 1980; Wills, Weiss, & Patterson, 1974).

Longitudinal research further suggests that the association between the expression of negative affect and relational satisfaction holds up over time. Indeed, premarital assessments of negative affect and the intensity of couples' conflict predict satisfaction in the marriage later (Kelly, Huston, & Cate, 1985; Markman, 1981). Even when initial levels of satisfaction are controlled, the expression of negative affect predicts declines in relational satisfaction over time (Gottman & Krokoff, 1989; Levenson & Gottman, 1985).

Although studies have consistently established an association between negative affective behaviors and relational satisfaction, it is important to note that the link between these two variables may not be as straightforward as it first appears. Researchers and theorists who have focused their attention on romantic partners' expression of affect argue that the decline in relational satisfaction associated with negative behaviors is complicated by several issues.

First, some scholars have noted that the role of positive behaviors in romantic relationships has not yet been well defined (Bradbury, Fincham, & Beach, 2000). Social learning theory suggests that each partner's behavior

(whether positive and rewarding or negative and punishing) influences the attitude (satisfaction) of the other (Jacobson & Margolin, 1979). But the way in which this process occurs is still not clear. In spite of the stronger link generally found between negative behaviors and satisfaction, there is evidence that positive behaviors sometimes are more closely associated with satisfaction than are negative behaviors. For instance, Jacobson et al. (1980) used daily interaction records and demonstrated that day-to-day ratings of satisfaction for couples who were happy with their relationships were more closely linked to satisfaction than were negative behaviors. It may be that happy couples place a greater emphasis on the positive behaviors that occur in their relationships on a day-to-day basis than do unhappy couples. By contrast, it also is possible that there are certain conditions or circumstances in relationships when the expression of positive affect is particularly important. For example, Cutrona (1996) notes that positive supportive behaviors may contribute to relational quality when partners are under a great deal of stress. She suggests that under stressful circumstances, the expression of positive affect can prevent emotional withdrawal and isolation and that, as a consequence, it can help to alleviate damage to the relationship.

A second issue that affects the link between partners' negative behaviors and their satisfaction is gender. A number of studies suggest that there are important gender differences in the expression of affect and the influence of affective expressions on relational satisfaction. Research has shown that, on average, wives express more negativity as well as more positivity in their relationships than do husbands (Noller, 1984; Notarius & Johnson, 1982). Women tend to be more critical when they interact with their partners than do men (Hahlweg, Revenstorf, & Schindler, 1984). Further, wives who are distressed are more likely than distressed husbands to behave negatively toward their spouses (Gottman & Krokoff, 1989; Noller, 1985; Notarius, Benson, Sloane, Vanzetti, & Hornyak, 1989). Distressed wives also have a greater tendency than those who are not distressed to reciprocate negative behavior from their partners (Notarius & Pellegrini, 1987).

In addition to expressing more negativity toward their husbands, it appears that distressed wives have difficulty countering their husbands' negative behavior with positive behavior. Notarius and his colleagues (1989) found that distressed wives are less likely than distressed husbands to respond positively to negative messages. These wives, as a consequence, are less likely than others (distressed husbands, nondistressed husbands, and nondistressed wives) to break the cycle of negativity that characterizes the interactions of many dissatisfied couples.

Studies that have examined the behaviors of both partners suggest that there may be good reason for the greater negativity of distressed wives: Distressed wives are particularly likely to have unresponsive husbands. Because men experience greater physiological arousal during conflict than do women, Gottman and Levenson (1988) argue, men have a greater tendency than women to withdraw during conflict episodes. Inasmuch as this is the case, Gottman and Krokoff (1989) suggest that the increased negativity of wives may be due, in part, to a tendency among distressed husbands to suppress their negative behaviors during conflict. In other words, the ways in which distressed husbands and wives tend to respond to the negative feelings they experience during conflict may actually "feed" upon each other. Wives who are distressed may be particularly likely to express their negative feelings because their husbands are unresponsive. Distressed husbands may withdraw and become unresponsive as a consequence of their wives' increased negativity.

It is important to note that although wives (particularly those who are distressed) express more negativity in their relationships than do husbands, the negativity of wives does not necessarily affect couples' satisfaction as might be expected. Social learning theorists would predict that the greater negativity of wives would be experienced by husbands as punishing or costly and, as a consequence, would create declines in husbands' satisfaction. However, this does not appear to be the case. In fact, husbands' negativity seems to have more of an impact on spouses' satisfaction than does wives' negativity. Gottman and Krokoff (1989), for example, found that husbands' negativity, rather than wives' negativity, predicted declines in partners' relational satisfaction. Furthermore, wives appear to be more sensitive to their partners' negativity than do husbands. Huston and Vangelisti (1991) found that husbands' negativity predicted declines in wives' satisfaction, but wives' negativity did not similarly affect husbands' satisfaction.

A third issue that complicates the association between negative behaviors and satisfaction involves comparisons between the numbers of positive and negative behaviors that occur in partners' relationship. Gottman and Levenson (1992) argue that couples' satisfaction may be more strongly influenced by the ratio of positive to negative behaviors than it is by the absolute frequency of positive or negative behaviors. These researchers tested this argument by classifying couples into two groups: those that were regulated and those that were unregulated. Regulated couples were those in which both partners displayed more positivity than negativity when they spoke to each other. Unregulated couples, by contrast, were those in which both partners showed more negativity than positivity during interaction. Over a period of 4 years, Gottman and Levenson found that regulated couples were more satisfied, less likely to have considered divorce, less likely to have separated, and less likely to have divorced.

Interaction Patterns of Couples

Although research has demonstrated a fairly strong link between the positive and negative affect expressed by partners and their relational satisfaction, couples may differ in terms of the ways in which they enact and interpret affective behaviors. Some couples may maintain very satisfying relationships while engaging in a relatively high number of negative behaviors because they enact an even greater number of positive behaviors. Other couples who enact relatively few negative behaviors may be somewhat dissatisfied because the number of positive behaviors they engage in is so low. The patterns of interaction that couples engage in are important predictors of relational satisfaction and stability (e.g., Fitzpatrick, 1984; Gottman & Levenson, 1992; Heavey, Christensen, & Malamuth, 1995).

Scholars have studied the interaction patterns of couples in several different ways. Some have employed the amount of time couples spend together as a general indicator of their behavior and have examined the links between that time and relational quality. Others have used partners' behaviors and attitudes as a basis for grouping couples into categories or "types." Researchers also have analyzed specific behavioral sequences and have tested the associations between those sequences and partners' relational happiness. Finally, a number of researchers and clinicians have assessed partners' communication skills in terms of their potential influence on satisfaction.

Time Together

Most researchers would agree that evaluating the amount of time partners spend together is a rather crude way to measure couples' interaction patterns. It does not provide any information about the partners' beliefs, values, or specific behaviors. Assessing time together, however, does offer a potentially interesting (albeit indirect) indication of partners' attitudes and their behavioral intentions.

Couples who have maintained their relationships over a period of 50 years likely regard their partners and their relationships differently than do those who have been together for 2 or 3 years. Similarly, those who spend a great deal of time with each other on a daily basis probably have different attitudes toward each other than do those who spend very little time together.

Researchers have studied the amount of time couples spend together in both global and specific ways. Globally, they have examined the duration of couples' relationships in terms of its association with marital satisfaction. Specifically, they have focused on the amount of time couples spend engaged in various activities together on a day-to-day basis.

Global assessments. The duration of a relationship is regarded by many as a measure of relational stability. Partners who have been together for long periods of time are said to have more stable relationships than those who have been together for short periods or those who have ended their relationships. Although stability—conceived as the duration of a relationship—is an important variable, examining stability apart from variations in partners' satisfaction yields limited information about the quality of relationships. Relationships can be stable and happy or stable and unhappy. They can be stable with regard to duration, but quite volatile in terms of partners' feelings toward each other (Bradbury et al., 2000). Perhaps for these reasons, researchers often have examined the duration of relationships in terms of its association with partners' satisfaction.

Over time, marital satisfaction declines for many couples. The greatest decrease in satisfaction appears to take place during the first few years of marriage (Glenn, 1998). Theorists have long argued that this initial decline in satisfaction occurs as newlyweds' infatuation with each other wanes (Waller, 1938). Partners who might have been particularly careful to engage in positive, affectionate behaviors prior to marriage may begin to settle into more stable behavioral patterns after marriage (MacDermid, Huston, & McHale, 1990). Indeed, Huston, Robins, Atkinson, and McHale (1987) found that the frequency with which spouses engaged in affectional behaviors decreased significantly shortly after marriage. The frequency of partners' negative behaviors, by contrast, remained relatively stable. These findings suggest that the decline in marital satisfaction that occurs during the first few years of marriage may be due more to a decrease in positive behaviors than to an increase in negative ones.

Although research suggests that satisfaction declines continuously over the first few years of marriage, many textbooks that discuss this issue note that spouses' satisfaction tends to increase in the later years of marriage (typically after children leave home). This curvilinear pattern is regarded by many scholars with some skepticism. Researchers' questions about the U-shaped satisfaction curve stem from two issues: The first involves the explanation typically given for the drop and subsequent rise in the level of partners' happiness, and the second involves the nature of the data used to identify the pattern.

First, the explanation often provided for the initial decline in satisfaction is the arrival of children. Although there is evidence suggesting that couples who do not have children tend to be happier than those who do (Glenn & McLanahan, 1982; Ryder, 1973, Veroff, Douvan, & Kulka, 1981), the presence of children, per se, does not seem to cause marital dissatisfaction. Studies that have compared couples who have children during the initial years of marriage with those who do not have shown that both groups experience declines in marital satisfaction (McHale & Huston, 1985; White & Booth, 1985). Some research also has demonstrated that the presence of children delays the divorces of many couples who are unhappy with their marriages (White, Booth, &

Edwards, 1986). The results of studies such as these suggest that changes often attributed to the transition to parenthood instead may be associated with the duration of couples' relationships as well as systematic differences between couples who opt to have children and those who do not (Huston & Vangelisti, 1995).

The second reason many scholars regard the U-shaped satisfaction curve with caution is that much of the research supporting this pattern is based on either cross-sectional or retrospective data. The findings associated with cross-sectional data are subject to scrutiny because, as Glenn (1990) notes, they may reflect the effects of a number of factors, including "(a) duration of marriage, (b) the removal of many marriages from each marriage cohort through divorce as the cohort grows older, and (c) differences among different marriage cohorts" (p. 823). Further, Vaillant and Vaillant (1993) argue that the trajectories of partners' satisfaction differ depending on whether they are evaluated using retrospective reports or measurements of satisfaction at several points in time. In a longitudinal study, these researchers found that the curvilinear pattern appeared in partners' retrospective reports, but not in periodic measurements of their satisfaction. When looking back on their relationship, spouses may perceive that they experienced a decline and subsequent increase in their satisfaction. Those perceptions, however, do not necessarily match up with the feelings they report at various points in time over the course of their relationship. It may be that partners who stay together for long periods recognize that they experience ups and downs in their relationship, and they may take pride in having overcome difficulties. Indeed, Buehlman, Gottman, and Katz (1992) found that the most satisfied couples in their study told stories about having overcome difficulties together.

Specific assessments. In addition to examining the duration of relationships, a handful of scholars have looked at the amount of time partners spend together on a day-to-day basis. In general, the literature suggests that satisfied couples report spending more time together than do couples who are dissatisfied with their relationships (Kirchler, 1989). During courtship, partners who are more involved in their relationships tend to engage in more activities together (Surra, 1985). Studies have also revealed a positive association between marital happiness and the frequency of partners' interaction (Johnson, Amoloza, & Booth, 1992) as well as the amount of time partners spend talking to each other (Dickson-Markman & Markman, 1988).

It is interesting to note also that marital satisfaction has been positively linked to the number of pleasurable activities partners engage in together (Marini, 1976). It appears that people who are happy with their relationships not only spend more time together, they engage in activities that make their time together particularly rewarding.

Couple Types

Although the amount of time couples are willing to spend together provides some indication of the degree to which they are involved in their relationships, it offers only a very general picture of the interaction patterns that typify different couples. Fitzpatrick (1977, 1981) developed a typology for characterizing married couples that reflects variations in the patterns of behaviors and beliefs reported by partners. Her model, which is based on the work of Kantor and Lehr (1975), focuses on the associations between partners' ongoing patterns of interaction and marital satisfaction. Using the Relational Dimension Instrument (RDI), Fitzpatrick identified four different types of couples, which she labeled Traditional, Independent, Separate, and Mixed.

Couples who are *Traditional* have relatively conventional ideological values about marriage. They tend to be very interdependent, reporting

that they share time, space, and leisure activities together. These partners are not extremely assertive, but they do not avoid conflict. In *Independent* couples, both partners have relatively nonconventional values about relational and family life. Because Independents do not make assumptions about the roles men and women should assume in relationships, they have difficulty negotiating daily time schedules. These partners maintain separate physical spaces but demonstrate a great deal of interdependence in their marriages and tend to engage in, rather than avoid, conflict. *Separate* couples are ambivalent about their values concerning marriage and family life. They report having a conventional orientation toward marriage, but a nonconventional orientation toward individual freedom. These partners usually have less companionship and sharing than do the other couple types. They report being assertive, but they tend to avoid conflict. Finally, *Mixed* couples are those in which the two partners have different definitions of their relationship (e.g., the wife is an Independent and the husband is a Traditional).

Gottman (1993, 1994) later put forth a typology of couples that, as he noted, is similar in many ways to the one developed by Fitzpatrick. Gottman suggested that stable partnerships can include *validator* couples (those who display moderate negative affect, moderate positive affect, and a great deal of neutral interaction), *volatile* couples (those who express a great deal of negative affect, even more positive affect, and relatively little neutral interaction), and *avoider* couples (those who demonstrate little negative affect, little positive affect, and a great deal of neutral interaction).

Although typologies such as these cannot capture the full range of variation in couples' behaviors and attitudes, they do offer at least three advantages over models that categorize couples as either satisfied or dissatisfied (see Fitzpatrick, 1988). First, instead of placing partners at one of two extremes on a continuum of marital satisfaction, they include couples who are moderately satisfied or who disagree about the degree to which they are satisfied. Second, these typological approaches typically allow for increased variability because partners' scores on measures of marital quality often are skewed in a positive direction (Terman, 1938). Third, because the typologies include an assessment of characteristics other than partners' satisfaction, they can provide researchers with an indication of the criteria couples use to evaluate their relationships as satisfactory or unsatisfactory.

Behavioral Sequences

Rather than use assessments of partners' behavior as one of several means for grouping couples into categories, a number of researchers have examined couples' behaviors in their own right. Consistent with research that has focused on the individual behaviors of each partner, studies that have emphasized the behavioral patterns of couples generally suggest that couples who are dissatisfied engage in more negative behaviors and fewer positive behaviors than do those who are satisfied. For instance, distressed couples display more negative and fewer positive nonverbal cues than do nondistressed couples (Gottman, 1979; Noller, 1982). Those who are unhappy with their relationships tend to engage in fewer supportive behaviors than do those who are happy (Cutrona, 1996; Pasch & Bradbury, 1998). Couples who are distressed also report more frequent conflict, more time spent in conflict, and more conflict avoidance (Schaap, Buunk, & Kerkstra, 1988). Further, during conflict episodes, distressed couples engage in more criticizing, complaining, disagreeing, and sarcasm than do couples who are not distressed (Revenstorf, Vogel, Wegener, Hahlweg, & Schindler, 1980; Schaap et al., 1988; Ting-Toomey, 1983). The conflict of distressed couples also tends to be marked by expressions of contempt, criticism, defensiveness, and avoidance or "stonewalling" (Gottman, 1994). (For a review of literature on couples' conflict, see Canary, Cupach, & Messman, 1995.)

In addition to a general tendency to communicate increased negativity and decreased positivity, dissatisfied couples tend to exhibit two patterns of behavior that distinguish them from satisfied couples: negative affect reciprocity and demand/withdraw. These two behavioral sequences not only set dissatisfied couples apart from couples who are satisfied, but they predict declines in partners' satisfaction over time.

Negative affect reciprocity. Research has demonstrated that whereas both satisfied and dissatisfied partners reciprocate one another's positive behaviors, dissatisfied partners also reciprocate negative behaviors (Weiss & Heyman, 1990). Partners who are dissatisfied, in other words, respond to their spouses' negative behavior with more negative behavior. Gaelick, Bodenhausen, and Wyer (1985) offer one interesting explanation for why some couples may engage in more negative affect reciprocity than positive affect reciprocity. These researchers found that individuals tended to reciprocate the emotions they thought their partners were conveying. The study participants also perceived that their partners reciprocated their own affect. At first glance, these findings might seem to suggest that partners would be equally likely to reciprocate negative and positive affect. However, Gaelick et al. found that spouses had some difficulty decoding their partners' expressions of love. Because partners were able to decode expressions of hostility more accurately, they reciprocated hostility more frequently than they reciprocated love. Inasmuch as dissatisfied couples are more likely to express negative affect than positive affect, this effect is probably only intensified for couples who are unhappy with their marriages.

In some couples, the reciprocity of negative affect takes a form that appears to make it a particularly potent predictor of relational distress. Levenson and Gottman (1985) found that a decline in marital satisfaction over time was associated with more reciprocity of the husband's negative affect by the wife and less reciprocity of the wife's negative affect by the husband. The mismatch, or lack of symmetry, in the reciprocity of spouses' affect creates a situation where the affect of one partner (in this case, that of the husband) appears to exert more control over the course of the interaction than does the affect of the other (in this case, that of the wife). Of course, one partner's affect can have this sort of influence only if it is reciprocated. Given this, a number of researchers argue that the ability to avoid reciprocating negative affect—and thus to extricate oneself from negative sequences of communication—is an important skill for relationship partners (Escudero, Rogers, & Gutierrez, 1997; Gottman, Markman, & Notarius, 1977).

Demand/withdraw. The gender difference in negative affect reciprocity identified by Levenson and Gottman (1985) is closely related to the second communication pattern that distinguishes dissatisfied from satisfied couples. Typically labeled the demand/ withdraw pattern, this sequence of behaviors occurs during conflict when one partner communicates in "demanding" ways (e.g., attempts to discuss a problem or concern) while the other withdraws (e.g., attempts to avoid the conversation). Research has consistently demonstrated links between the demand/withdraw pattern and both marital dissatisfaction and divorce (e.g., Fogarty, 1976; Heavey et al., 1995; Noller, Feeney, Bonnell, & Callan, 1994; Peterson, 1979; Schaap et al., 1988). A number of studies examining the demand/withdraw pattern have found that wives more frequently engage in demanding

behavior than do husbands, whereas husbands tend to withdraw more often than do wives (Baucom, Notarius, Burnett, & Haefner, 1990; Christensen & Shenk, 1991; Gottman & Levenson, 1988). Several theorists have offered a social structural explanation for this particular finding (e.g., Christensen & Heavey, 1990; Heavey, Layne, & Christensen 1993; Jacobson, 1990; Klinetob & Smith, 1996). These scholars argue that because wives typically have less power in their marriages than do husbands, wives tend to be less satisfied with the state of affairs in their relationships. As a consequence, wives may be more likely than their husbands to desire changes in their marriages. Their desire for change may encourage wives to complain or demand. By contrast, because husbands have more relational power, they tend to desire relatively few changes in their relationships. Husbands may have little reason to engage in demanding behaviors and quite a few reasons to withdraw. For husbands, withdrawing may be a way to maintain the status quo and avoid their wives' demands for change.

Several researchers have tested the social structural explanation for the demand/ withdraw pattern. They found that when partners discussed a topic that was one about which husbands desired more change than wives, the tendency for wives to demand more frequently than husbands disappeared (Christensen & Heavey, 1990; Heavey et al., 1993). Further, one study suggested that a pattern of husband-demand/wife-withdraw occurred more often than wife-demand/ husband-withdraw when partners discussed an issue about which husbands desired more change than wives (Klinetob & Smith, 1996).

Although the social structural explanation has received some support, there also is evidence that the causal forces behind the demand/withdraw pattern may be more complex than originally thought. For instance, Caughlin and Vangelisti (1999) found that individuals' desire for change in their partners was positively associated with both husband-demand/wife-withdraw and wife-demand/husband-withdraw. Partners' desire for change, in other words, may be related to their engaging in both demanding and withdrawing communication. In addition, although wife-demand/husband-withdraw occurred more frequently than husband-demand/wife-withdraw, there was no difference between spouses' desire for change in their partners. Wives' greater tendency to engage in demanding behavior, thus, may not be explained entirely by their desire for change.

Communication Skills

Underlying much of the literature on communication in romantic relationships is an assumption that poor communication skills are the cause of many relational problems (Spitzberg, 1994). Burleson and Denton (1997) label this assumption the "skills-deficit model" of marital distress. The idea behind this model is that marital distress may be reduced, or even prevented, through the improvement of partners' communication skills. If, for example, partners could learn to express negative affect in different ways, or if they could remember to communicate more positive affect, the quality of their relationships might improve.

There is some evidence in the literature that poor communication skills can precede relational dissatisfaction (Markman, 1981; Markman, Duncan, Storaasli, & Howes, 1987). A number of studies, however, suggest that the association between couples' communication skills and relational satisfaction is anything but straightforward. For instance, a person may display high-level skills in one relational context (e.g., with coworkers) but not in another (e.g., with a spouse). Noller (1981) compared the skills of couples in terms of partners' ability to decode nonverbal cues under two conditions: In one, partners were instructed to decode the nonverbal communication of a

stranger; in the other, they were asked to decode the nonverbal cues of their spouses. Noller found that the difference in partners' nonverbal decoding skills under these two conditions was greatest for couples who were dissatisfied with their relationships. More specifically, partners in unhappy marriages were better able to decode the nonverbal communication of a stranger than that of their spouse. Dissatisfied partners were not at a deficit with regard to their decoding abilities—they were able to decode the nonverbal cues of the stranger. Rather, they seemed to be unable (or perhaps unwilling) to decode accurately the nonverbal behavior of their partner.

Burleson and Denton (1997) similarly found that communication skills (or the lack thereof) are not necessarily linked to relational satisfaction. They assessed several different communication skills (e.g., predictive accuracy, communication effectiveness) and examined the extent to which each was associated with marital happiness. They found that for satisfied couples, the presumed positive association between skills and satisfaction was validated. However, among distressed couples, satisfaction and communication were sometimes negatively correlated. Partners who are skillful communicators, in short, do not always express themselves in ways that are conducive to relational happiness. In fact, in some cases, the opposite may be true. Highly skilled communicators may opt to use their expertise to pursue antisocial (distress-maintaining) rather than prosocial (relationship-enhancing) goals. When this occurs, partners who are highly skilled may be particularly capable of saying or doing things to hurt each other or undermine their relationship.

RELATIONAL DISSOLUTION AND DIVORCE

Although popular media and political pundits argue that people often enter romantic relationships with the idea that they can end them with little difficulty, research suggests that relational dissolution is a very stressful, unpleasant process for most couples (Kitson & Morgan, 1990). Those who are divorced or separated tend to experience lower happiness and more symptoms of psychological distress than do those who are married (Kitson, 1992; Marks, 1996; Mastekaasa, 1997). They also have a greater tendency to be depressed and report lower levels of satisfaction with their life (Glenn & Weaver, 1988). People who are divorced are more likely to have health problems (Murphy, Glaser, & Grundy, 1997) and tend to be at greater risk of mortality than individuals who are married (Hemstrom, 1996).

The picture put forth in the literature of individuals who have experienced divorce is fairly bleak, but it is important to remember that this picture is one derived from between-group differences—typically, differences between those who have experienced the termination of long-term relationships and those who are involved in ongoing relationships. Variations also exist within the group of individuals who have dissolved their marital or romantic relationships. Indeed, a number of scholars have identified certain traits that are associated with divorce. Partners, in other words, bring individual characteristics with them into marriage (e.g., depression, neuroticism) that decrease the stability of their relationships and increase the chances that they will divorce (Christian, O'Leary, & Vivian, 1994; Davila, Bradbury, Cohan, & Tochluk, 1997; Karney & Bradbury, 1997). Using data from monozygotic and dizygotic twins, some scholars even argue that people have genetic predispositions toward certain behaviors or qualities that increase their risk of divorce (Jockin, McGue, & Lykken, 1996; Lykken, 2002). The overarching assumption behind much of this research is that individuals who are poorly adjusted are "selected out" of marriage. People who divorce are conceived of as relatively unfit to select partners, maintain

long-term romantic relationships, or deal with disruptions that occur in their relationships.

An alternative perspective is that divorce or relational dissolution as a stressor or crisis to which individuals adjust with varying levels of success. Although some who have adopted this perspective have characterized the termination of a relationship as a singular event, most now recognize that it is an event embedded in a system of other events and circumstances. Relational dissolution, in other words, can be seen as a chronic strain (Amato, 2000). It sets the stage for changes in partners' relationships, social networks, and economic well-being, and sometimes their parental status. These changes, in turn, create stressful conditions to which the partners must adjust over time.

Clearly, some individuals are better able to adjust to relational dissolution than others. Research suggests that a person's ability to cope with the termination of a relationship is affected by structural, social, and psychological resources. For instance, concrete, structural resources such as income and employment can influence well-being. If an individual's socioeconomic status is significantly diminished following a divorce, he or she is likely to have more difficulty adjusting to the separation (Amato, 1993; McLanahan & Booth, 1989; Weiss, 1984). Similarly, social resources such as network support can affect an individual's ability to adjust. Partners who have supportive social networks tend to experience less difficulty than do those without such networks (Gerstel, 1988).

Individuals' personal or psychological resources are particularly important contributors to postdivorce well-being. Part of the reason for this is that relational dissolution often depletes both structural and social resources. Divorcing partners (particularly women) can lose substantial income, and their social networks often are disrupted. As a consequence, individuals' ability to identify and recover their losses following the termination of a relationship can be critical. Those who are unable to do so may experience distress, not only because of their limited psychological resources, but also because those limited psychological resources put them at a disadvantage when it comes to accessing structural and social resources. Given this, it is not surprising that studies show that partners who feel guilty or preoccupied about their divorces generally appear to have more problems adjusting to their postdivorce state (Masheter, 1991; Walters-Champman, Price, & Serovich, 1995).

Harvey et al. (1990) underline the importance of psychological resources when they suggest that a critical factor in individuals' recovery from traumatic events such as relational dissolution is the ability to formulate accounts. Accounts provide individuals with a way of making sense of what happened in their relationships and give them a basis for talking with others about the termination of their relationships (Sorenson et al., 1993). The explanations people generate for why their relationships ended can offer them a way to save face concerning something that some might see as a major failure. For example, rather than portraying herself as unable to maintain a satisfactory relationship, a woman may depict herself as having made a decision that will improve the quality of her life. Indeed, research suggests that people's descriptions of relational termination often are biased in a self-serving manner. For example, Hill, Rubin, and Peplau (1976) found that people who had experienced the breakup of dating relationships tended to report that they wanted to end the relationships more than their partners did. In studying divorced couples, Gray and Silver (1990) found that former spouses had relatively positive perceptions of themselves and negative perceptions of their partners. Similarly, when Hopper and Drummond (1991) compared a conversation between two partners who were ending their relationship to later conversations between the partners and others in their social network, they found that the individuals reconstructed

their breakup conversation to portray themselves in a positive light.

In addition to helping people save face, accounts can reflect the way partners feel about their relationships ending. For instance, women who attempt to end physically abusive relationships may explain the dissolution as caused by unstable, external factors (e.g., the stress a partner has experienced on the job) or by stable, internal characteristics of their partners (e.g., the partner's immaturity or inability to control his temper). The accounts these women formulate to frame the termination of their abusive relationships may not only reflect how they feel about their partners, but also provide them with reasons to avoid going back to those relationships (Herbert, Silver, & Ellard, 1991).

Although existing research offers a fair amount of information about the factors that may influence partners' adjustment following relational dissolution or divorce, it does not provide a great deal of information about the dissolution process itself. Certainly, gathering data on the interpersonal processes that occur as relationships dissolve is no easy task. Partners who are in the midst of ending their relationships are unlikely to volunteer to bare their souls to researchers. In some cases, these individuals may not be aware that their relationships are in the process of coming apart. Nevertheless, scholars have formulated models that may be useful as research begins to explore the communication processes that are involved in dissolution.

Stage Models

Researchers and theorists have posited a number of different models to illustrate the various stages that partners go through as they dissolve their romantic relationships. Two models frequently cited by communication scholars are those proposed by Duck (1982) and by Knapp (1978). Duck's model suggests that partners move through four phases when their relationships come apart. The first is the *intrapsychic* phase. During this period, the partners evaluate each other's behavior and consider the extent to which that behavior provides a justification for ending the relationship. They also assess the positive aspects of alternative relationships and the costs of relationship dissolution. The *dyadic* phase is next. In this phase, the partners begin to discuss the problems they perceive. They talk about the costs associated with terminating the relationship as well as whether the relationship should be repaired. In the *social* phase, the partners begin to think about how they will present the dissolution of their relationship to their network of friends and family members. In doing so, they construct stories or accounts that help them (and others) make sense of the relationship. Finally, the *grave-dressing* phase is a period when the partners focus on ending the relationship. They reformulate the account of their breakup and start to disseminate that account to their social network. They also engage in behaviors that help them "get over" the relationship and each other.

Knapp's (1978) model is similar to Duck's, but it places slightly more emphasis on what takes place between partners and slightly less emphasis on the interface between partners and their social network. Knapp argues that the process of dissolution begins with what he calls the *differentiating* stage. When the partners start to disengage from each other, they begin to talk more about their differences. Joint possessions and joint activities become individualized. In some cases, communication during this stage is characterized by conflict, but the partners also may express the distinctions between them in ways that do not include overt disagreements. The next phase in Knapp's model is the *circumscribing* stage. During this period, communication between the partners becomes more restricted and controlled. The partners opt to talk about "safe" topics and begin to avoid issues that they

perceive as sensitive. They usually communicate less frequently; less information is exchanged, and the information that is exchanged is less intimate. In the *stagnating* stage, the partners' communication nearly comes to a halt. They often believe that communication is useless, and sometimes even avoid relatively superficial topics. They usually share the same physical environment, but emotionally they are quite distant. Next, in the *avoiding* stage, the partners do their best to avoid social contact. When they do communicate, they make it clear that they are not interested in each other or in the relationship. Interaction often is very direct (e.g., "I don't have time for you") because the partners have little, if any, concern about the impact of what they say. When the partners reach the *terminating* stage, their relationship finally ends. They may engage in a conversation in which they agree that they will no longer see each other, or they may avoid such an interaction and allow the relationship to fade away. If they do talk about the end of the relationship, their interaction is likely to be characterized by messages that emphasize the distance between them— whether psychological, physical, or both.

Both Knapp and Duck note that the models they describe should be interpreted with caution. By describing stages or phases that partners may experience, these theorists do not mean to imply that all couples experiencing relational dissolution will move toward that outcome in a direct, linear fashion. In fact, both Knapp and Duck argue that partners may move forward through the various stages of dissolution or backward from what appears to be a more advanced stage to one that is less advanced. They also note that some couples may skip stages altogether. The models, in short, are templates that researchers and laypersons alike can use to explore and explain some of the experiences individuals have when their relationships come apart.

DIRECTIONS FOR FUTURE STUDY

The preceding review offers only a glimpse of what has become a substantial scholarly literature (Reis, Collins, & Berscheid, 2000). In spite of the size and diversity of this literature, it is possible to identify a number of trends that have begun to influence what researchers study, as well as how they study it.

Identifying Patterns of Behavior

Research on behavioral sequences such as the demand/withdraw pattern (Christensen & Heavey, 1990) and the reciprocity of negative affect (Levenson & Gottman, 1985) has yielded important information about the influence of behavior on partners' relationships. Rather than isolating and identifying communication behaviors out of context, these and other similar studies have pinpointed behavioral patterns that affect the quality of partners' relationships over time (e.g., Heavey et al., 1995). Given the relatively sophisticated analytic strategies that have emerged in recent years (e.g., Kashy & Kenny, 2000; Kenny, 1996), as well as the increasing tendency of researchers to focus on couples as opposed to individual partners (Gottman & Notarius, 2000), it is likely that scholars will continue to identify behavioral sequences enacted by couples and explore the ways in which various patterns of behavior affect relational outcomes.

Focusing on Positive Behavior

Much of the literature on communication in romantic relationships has focused on partners' behavior during conflict or problem-solving episodes. Although there is evidence that negative behavior outweighs positive behavior in terms of its impact on relational quality (Barnett & Nietzel, 1979; Broderick & O'Leary, 1986; Gottman & Levenson, 1986; Huston & Vangelisti, 1991; Jacobson et al., 1980; Wills et al., 1974), researchers are beginning to explore the role of positive behavior—both in and out of the context of problem-solving discussions. The findings thus far suggest that the impact of positive behavior on relationships may be more complicated than theorists originally thought. Rather than a straightforward linear association between positive (rewarding) behavior and satisfaction, researchers are finding that the impacts of positive behaviors may emerge at certain times in relationships, and that they may appear only when positive behaviors are examined in concert with other behaviors. For instance, Gottman, Coan, Carrere, and Swanson (1998) looked at positive affect during conflict discussions early in marriage and found that expressions of positive affect in the early months of marriage predicted later marital satisfaction and divorce. Huston and Chorost (1994) examined the possible moderating effect of partners' expressions of affection on the longitudinal association between negative behavior and relational quality. They found that the link between negativity and the quality of couples' relationships was buffered by partners' expressions of affection for each other. Further research on the role of positive behaviors in romantic relationships is likely to reveal a very complex, multifaceted association between positive behaviors and relational outcomes.

Changing the Outcome Variable

Relational satisfaction has been the outcome variable of choice for most scholars studying interpersonal communication in romantic relationships. Both researchers and laypersons want to know what makes for a happy marriage. The underlying assumption made by many has been that if partners are happy, their relationship is likely to remain intact, and if they are unhappy, their relationship may come apart. In spite of the premium placed on relational happiness, scholars have begun to acknowledge that satisfaction—typically operationalized as partners' feelings about their relationship at a given point in time—is not the only way to conceptualize relational success. For instance, Glenn (1990) argues that a "marriage that is intact and satisfactory to both spouses is successful, while one that has ended in divorce or separation or is unsatisfactory to one or both spouses is a failure" (p. 821). Successful relationships, in short, may be conceived of as those that are both intact and satisfying. Because satisfaction is integral to relationship success, it certainly will continue to be a focus of interest for researchers. But variables other than satisfaction that are associated with intact relationships also have begun to move to the forefront. For example, researchers have begun to examine outcome variables such as commitment (Adams & Jones, 1997; Johnson, 1991; Rusbult, 1983), sacrifice (Van Lange et al., 1997; Whitton, Stanley, & Markman, 2002), trust (Rempel, Holmes, & Zanna, 1985; Rempel, Ross, & Holmes, 2001), and forgiveness (Enright, Freedman, & Rique, 1998; Fincham, 2000; McCullough, Worthington, & Rachal, 1997; Metts, 1994). They also have begun to reassess the structure of relational satisfaction, noting that positive and negative evaluations of relationships can be measured as separate, albeit related, variables (Fincham, Beach, & Kemp-Fincham, 1997).

Reexamining the Structure of Variables

Relational satisfaction is not the only variable that has come under scrutiny in recent years. The structure of other variables has been reassessed as well. For instance, researchers increasingly are conceiving of positive and negative affect as two separate dimensions rather than as a single, bipolar dimension (e.g., Cacioppo & Berntson, 1994). Similarly, instead of looking at partners' behavior on a unidimensional continuum ranging from positive to negative, scholars

have begun to examine positive and negative behavior separately (e.g., Huston & Vangelisti, 1991). Distinguishing positive and negative affect as well as positive and negative behavior is not simply a matter of developing more sophisticated measures; it represents an important theoretical issue. When positivity and negativity are assessed using unidimensional measures, couples who are rated as highly positive cannot also be evaluated as highly negative. Likewise, those who are assessed as low in positivity cannot also be rated as low in negativity. Similar concerns have been raised about other variables, such as commitment (Adams & Jones, 1997; Johnson, 1991) and love (Hendrick & Hendrick, 1986; Marston, Hecht, & Robers, 1987; Sternberg, 1986). Researchers examining these variables have argued that, for example, there are different forms of commitment and different types of love. Inasmuch as this is the case, using unidimensional measures to assess variables such as commitment or love may oversimplify constructs that are actually relatively complex, and may even offer a distorted view of couples' relationships.

Exploring the Role of Technology

In addition to reassessing the structure of many variables, researchers are beginning to examine the influence of technology on partners' relationships. The explosion of technological advances has made this a difficult issue to ignore: Computers, cell phones, and the Internet have infiltrated people's lives and, as a consequence, have touched their relationships. Much of the research that has been conducted in this area has focused on people's use of computer-mediated communication and the Internet. For example, researchers have examined the influence on intimacy of the restricted communication channels associated with computer-mediated communication (e.g., Walther, 1992) as well as the personality characteristics of those who spend a great deal of time on the Internet (Kraut et al., 1998). Although relatively few romantic relationships are initiated in on-line settings (Parks & Floyd, 1996), the nature of those relationships and the various ways in which partners negotiate those relationships are intriguing. Examining romantic relationships that are developed or maintained on-line may provide researchers with an interesting point of comparison for variables that have heretofore been studied in face-to-face settings. For instance, studies have established the importance of social networks on the development of romantic relationships (e.g., Eggert & Parks, 1987; Parks, Stan, & Eggert, 1983; Sprecher & Felmlee, 1992), but the Internet provides people with a context in which they can initiate relationships with little influence from network members. As Sprecher, Felmlee, Orbuch, and Willetts (2002) note, couples may experience greater difficulty in maintaining such relationships over time without network support. In addition to its obvious influence on relationships that are initiated online, the Internet may shape face-to-face romantic relationships indirectly by affecting partners' communication with their social networks. People who in the past have had little contact with family members may develop closer family relationships via the Internet. Those closer family ties, in turn, may influence their relationships with their partners. Individuals also may develop friendships and even sexual relationships on-line that affect their existing romantic relationships.

CONCLUDING COMMENTS

The research reviewed in this chapter underlines the notion that interpersonal communication is a defining feature of romantic relationships. People have to communicate when they initiate relationships. The ways in which they approach potential partners, the types of questions they ask, and the information they disclose all influence whether and how their relationships develop.

Communication also is central to partners' ongoing associations with each other. The cognitive and affective processes that partners bring to their relationships are reflected in their communication behavior. Further, the interactions in which individuals and couples engage provide important information about the quality of their relationships. Even when relationships come apart, the ways in which partners communicate shape the dissolution process.

Researchers and theorists who study romantic relationships are moving forward along several paths that are likely to highlight the centrality of communication to relational partners and relationships. They are examining patterns rather than isolated instances of behavior. They are expanding the scope of what they study, refining relevant variables, and exploring the impact of technological advances on romantic partners and romantic relationships. Surely, these are steps in the right direction.

REFERENCES

Adams, J. M., & Jones, W. H. (1997). The conceptualization of marital commitment. *Journal of Personality and Social Psychology, 72,* 1177-1196.

Adams, J. S. (1965). Inequity in social exchange. In L. Berkowitz (Ed.), *Advances in experimental social psychology* (Vol. 2, pp. 267-299). New York: Academic Press.

Ainsworth, M. D. S., Blehar, M. C., Waters, E., & Wall, S. (1978). *Patterns of attachment: A psychological study of the strange situation.* Hillsdale, NJ: Lawrence Erlbaum.

Albada, K. F., Knapp, M. L., & Theune, K. E. (2002). Interaction appearance theory: Changing perceptions of physical attractiveness through social interaction. *Communication Theory, 12,* 8-40.

Altman, I., & Taylor, D. A. (1973). *Social penetration: The development of interpersonal relationships.* New York: Holt, Rinehart & Winston.

Amato, P. R. (1993). Children's adjustment to divorce: Theories, hypotheses, and empirical support. *Journal of Marriage and the Family, 55*, 23-38.

Amato, P. R. (2000). The consequences of divorce for adults and children. *Journal of Marriage and the Family, 62*, 1269-1287.

Andersen, S. M., & Baum, A. (1994). Transference in interpersonal relations: Inferences and affect based on significant other representations. *Journal of Personality, 62*, 459-498.

Andersen, S. M., Reznik, I., & Chen, S. (1997). The self in relation to others: Motivational and cognitive underpinnings. In J. G. Snodgrass & R. L. Thompson (Eds.), *The self across psychology: Self-recognition, self-awareness, and the self-concept* (pp. 233-275). New York: Academy of Science.

Antaki, C. (1987). Performable and unperformable: A guide to accounts of relationships. In R. Burnett, P. McGhee, & D. D. Clarke (Eds.), *Accounting for relationships: Explanation, representation, and knowledge* (pp. 97-113). New York: Methuen.

Baldwin, M. W. (1992). Relational schemas and the processing of social information. *Psychology Bulletin, 112*, 461-484.

Baldwin, M. W., & Fehr, B. (1995). On the instability of attachment style ratings. *Personal Relationships, 2*, 247-261.

Baldwin, M. W., & Keelan, J. P. R. (1999). Interpersonal expectations as a function of self-esteem and sex. *Journal of Social and Personal Relationships, 16*, 822-833.

Barnett, L. R., & Nietzel, M. T. (1979). Relationship of instrumental and affectional behaviors and self-esteem to marital satisfaction in distressed and nondistressed couples. *Journal of Consulting and Clinical Psychology, 47*, 946-957.

Bartholomew, K., & Horowitz, L. M. (1991). Attachment styles among young adults: A test of a four-category model. *Journal of Personality and Social Psychology, 61*, 226-244.

Baucom, D. H., & Epstein, N. (1990). *Cognitive-behavioral marital therapy.* New York: Brunner/Mazel.

Baucom, D. H., Epstein, N., Sayers, S., & Sher, T. G. (1989). The role of cognitions in marital relationships: Definitional, methodological, and conceptual issues. *Journal of Consulting and Clinical Psychology, 57*, 31-38.

Baucom, D. H., Notarius, C. I., Burnett, C. K., & Haefner, P. (1990). Gender differences and sex-role identity in marriage. In F. D. Fincham & T. N. Bradbury (Eds.), *The*

psychology of marriage: Basic issues and applications (pp. 150-171). New York: Guilford.

Baumeister, R. F. (1991). *Meanings of life.* New York: Guilford.

Baumeister, R. F., & Newman, L. S. (1994). How stories make sense of personal experiences: Motives that shape autobiographical narratives. *Personality and Social Psychology Bulletin, 20*, 676-690.

Baxter, L. A., & Bullis, C. (1986). Turning points in developing romantic relationships. *Human Communication Research, 12*, 469-493.

Baxter, L. A., & Montgomery, B. M. (1996). *Relating: Dialogues and dialectics.* New York: Guilford.

Baxter, L. A., & Wilmot, W. W. (1985). Taboo topics in close relationships. *Journal of Social and Personal Relationships, 2*, 253-269.

Beck, A. T. (1988). *Love is never enough: How couples can overcome misunderstandings, resolve conflicts, and solve relationship problems through cognitive therapy.* New York: Harper & Row.

Bell, R. A., & Daly, J. A. (1984). The affinity-seeking function of communication. *Communication Monographs, 51*, 91-115.

Berger, C. R., & Bradac, J. J. (1982). *Language and social knowledge: Uncertainty in interpersonal relations.* London: Edward Arnold.

Berger, C. R., & Calabrese, R. J. (1975). Some explorations in initial interaction and beyond: Toward a developmental theory of interpersonal communication. *Human Communication Research, 1*, 99-112.

Berger, C. R., Gardner, R. R., Clatterbuck, G. W., & Schulman, L. S. (1976). Perceptions of information sequencing in relationship development. *Human Communication Research, 3*, 34-39.

Bochner, A. P. (1991). On the paradigm that would not die. In J. A. Anderson (Ed.), *Communication yearbook 14* (pp. 484-491). Newbury Park, CA: Sage.

Bowlby, J. (1969). *Attachment and loss: Vol. 1. Attachment.* New York: Basic Books.

Bowlby, J. (1973). *Attachment and loss: Vol. 2. Separation: Anxiety and anger.* New York: Basic Books.

Bowlby, J. (1980). *Attachment and loss: Vol. 3. Loss: Sadness and depression.* New York: Basic Books.

Bradbury, T. N., Beach, S. R. H., Fincham, F. D., & Nelson, G. M. (1996). Attributions and behavior in functional and dysfunctional marriages. *Journal of Consulting and Clinical Psychology, 64,* 569-576.

Bradbury, T. N., & Fincham, F. D. (1987). Affect and cognition in close relationships: Toward an integrative model. *Cognition and Emotion, 1,* 59-67.

Bradbury, T. N., & Fincham, F. D. (1990). Attributions in marriage: Review and critique. *Psychological Bulletin, 107,* 3-33.

Bradbury, T. N., Fincham, F. D., & Beach, S. R. H. (2000). Research on the nature and determinants of marital satisfaction: A decade in review. *Journal of Marriage and the Family, 62,* 964-980.

Broderick, J. E., & O'Leary, K. D. (1986). Contributions of affect, attitudes, and behavior to marital satisfaction. *Journal of Consulting and Clinical Psychology, 54,* 514-517.

Buehlman, K. T., Gottman, H. M., & Katz, L. F. (1992). How a couple views their past predicts their future: Predicting divorce from an oral history interview. *Journal of Family Psychology, 5,* 295-318.

Burgess, R. L., & Huston, T. L. (Eds.). (1979). *Social exchange in developing relationships.* New York: Academic Press.

Burleson, B. R., & Denton, W. H. (1997). The relationship between communication skill and marital satisfaction: Some moderating effects. *Journal of Marriage and the Family, 59,* 884-902.

Buss, D. M. (1989). Sex differences in human mate preferences: Evolutionary hypotheses tested in 37 cultures. *Behavioral and Brain Sciences, 12,* 1-49.

Buss, D. M. (1994). *The evolution of desire: Strategies of human mating.* New York: Basic Books.

Buss, D. M., & Barnes, M. (1986). Preferences in human mate selection. *Journal of Personality and Social Psychology, 50,* 559-570.

Byrne, D. (1971). *The attraction paradigm.* New York: Academic Press.

Byrne, D., & Clore, G. L. (1970). A reinforcement model of evaluative responses. *Personality, 1,* 103-128.

Byrne, D., & Griffitt, W. (1966). Similarity versus liking: A clarification. *Psychometric Science, 6,* 295-296.

Byrne, D., & Nelson, D. (1965). Attraction as a linear function of proportion of positive reinforcements. *Journal of Personality and Social Psychology, 1,* 659-663.

Cacioppo, J. T., & Berntson, G. C. (1994). Relationship between attitudes and evaluative space: A critical review, with emphasis on the separability of positive and negative substrates. *Psychological Bulletin, 115,* 401-423.

Campbell, L., Simpson, J. A., Kashy, D. A., & Fletcher, G. J. O. (2001). Ideal standards, the self, and flexibility of ideals in close relationships. *Personality and Social Psychology Bulletin, 27,* 447-462.

Canary, D. J., Cupach, W. R., & Messman, S. J. (1995). *Relationship conflict.* Thousand Oaks, CA: Sage.

Cappella, J. N., & Palmer, M T. (1992). The effect of partners' conversation on the association between attitude similarity and attraction. *Communication Monographs, 59,* 180-189.

Cassidy, J., & Shaver, P. R. (1999). *Handbook of attachment: Theory, research, and clinical applications.* New York: Guilford.

Caughlin, J. P., & Vangelisti, A. L. (1999). Desire for change in one's partner as a predictor of the demand/withdraw pattern of marital communication. *Communication Monographs, 66,* 66-89.

Christensen, A. (1988). Dysfunctional interaction patterns in couples. In P. Noller & M. A. Fitzpatrick (Eds.), *Perspectives on marital interaction* (pp. 31-52). Clevedon, Eng.: Multilingual Matters.

Christensen, A., & Heavey, C. L. (1990). Gender and social structure in the demand/withdraw pattern of marital conflict. *Journal of Personality and Social Psychology, 59,* 73-81.

Christensen, A., & Shenk, J. L. (1991). Communication, conflict, and psychological distance in nondistressed, clinic, and divorcing couples. *Journal of Consulting and Clinical Psychology, 59,* 458-463.

Christian, J. L., O'Leary, D., & Vivian, D. (1994). Depressive symptomatology in maritally discordant women and men: The role of individual and relationship variables. *Journal of Family Psychology, 8,* 32-42.

Cloven, D. H., & Roloff, M. E. (1994). A developmental model of decisions to withhold relational irritations in romantic relationships. *Personal Relationships, 1,* 143-164.

Collins, N. L., & Read, S. J. (1990). Adult attachment, working models, and relationship quality in dating couples. *Journal of Personality and Social Psychology, 58,* 644-663.

Condon, J. W., & Crano, W. D. (1988). Inferred evaluation and the relation between attitude similarity and interpersonal attraction. *Journal of Personality and Social Psychology, 54,* 789-797.

Cutrona, C. E. (1996). *Social support in couples.* Thousand Oaks, CA: Sage.

Darley, J. M., & Oleson, K. C. (1993). Introduction to research on interpersonal expectations. In P. D. Blanck (Ed.), *Interpersonal expectations: Theory, research, and applications* (pp. 45-63). New York: Cambridge University Press.

Davila, J., Bradbury, T. N., Cohan, C. L., & Tochluk, S. (1997). Marital functioning and depressive symptoms: Evidence for a stress generation model. *Journal of Personality and Social Psychology, 73,* 849-861.

Davila, J., Karney, B. R., & Bradbury, T. N. (1999). Attachment change processes in the early years of marriage. *Journal of Personality and Social Psychology, 76,* 783-802.

Davis, M. (1973). *Intimate relations.* New York: Free Press.

Derlega, V. J., Metts, S., Petronio, S., & Margulis, S. T. (1993). *Self-disclosure.* Newbury Park, CA: Sage.

Deutsch, M., & Solomon, L. (1959). Reactions to evaluations by others as influenced by self evaluations. *Sociometry, 22,* 93-112.

Dickson-Markman, F., & Markman, H. (1988). The effects of others on marriage. In P. Noller & M. A. Fitzpatrick (Eds.), *Perspectives on marital interaction* (pp. 294-322). Clevedon, Eng.: Multilingual Matters.

Dion, K. K., Berscheid, E., & Walster, E. (1972). What is beautiful is good. *Journal of Personality and Social Psychology, 24,* 285-290.

Dion, K. K., & Dion, K. L. (1975). Self-esteem and romantic love. *Journal of Personality, 43,* 39-57.

Dion, K. L., & Dion, K. K. (1973). Correlates of romantic love. *Journal of Consulting and Clinical Psychology, 41,* 51-56.

Dion, K. L., & Dion, K. K. (1988). Romantic love: Individual and cultural perspectives. In R. J. Sternberg & M. L. Barnes (Eds.), *The psychology of love* (pp. 100-118). New Haven, CT: Yale University Press.

Duck, S. (1982). A topography of relationship disengagement and dissolution. In S. Duck (Ed.), *Personal relationships 4: Dissolving personal relationships* (pp. 1-30). New York: Academic Press.

Duck, S. (1990). Relationships as unfinished business: Out of the frying pan and into the

1990's. *Journal of Social and Personal Relationships, 7,* 5-28.

Duck, S. (1994). *Meaningful relationships: Talking, sense, and relating.* Newbury Park, CA: Sage.

Duck, S., & Barnes, M. K. (1992). Disagreeing about agreement: Reconciling differences about similarity. *Communication Monographs, 59,* 199-208.

Eagly, A. H., Ashmore, R. D., Makhijani, M. G., & Longo, L. C. (1991). What is beautiful is good, but . . . : A meta-analytic review of research on the physical attractiveness stereotype. *Psychological Bulletin, 110,* 109-128.

Eggert, L. L., & Parks, M. R. (1987). Communication network involvement in adolescents' friendships and romantic relationships. In M. L. McLaughlin (Ed.), *Communication yearbook 10* (pp. 283-322). Newbury Park, CA: Sage.

Enright, R. D., Freedman, S., & Rique, J. (1998). The psychology of interpersonal forgiveness. In R. D. Enright & J. North (Eds.), *Exploring forgiveness* (pp. 46-62). Madison: University of Wisconsin Press.

Epstein, N., & Eidelson, R. J. (1981). Unrealistic beliefs of clinical couples: Their relationship to expectations, goals, and satisfaction. *American Journal of Family Therapy, 9,* 13-22.

Escudero, V., Rogers, L., & Gutierrez, E. (1997). Patterns of relational control and nonverbal affect in clinic and nonclinic samples. *Journal of Social and Personal Relationships, 14,* 5-29.

Feeney, J. A., & Noller, P. (1996). *Adult attachment.* Thousand Oaks, CA: Sage.

Fincham, F. D. (2000). The kiss of the porcupines: From attributing responsibility to forgiving. *Personal Relationships, 7,* 1-23.

Fincham, F. D., Beach, S. R. H., & Baucom, D. H. (1987). Attribution processes in distressed and nondistressed couples: 4. Self-partner attribution differences. *Journal of Personality and Social Psychology, 52,* 739-748.

Fincham, F. D., Beach, S. R. H., & Kemp-Fincham, S. I. (1997). Marital quality: A new theoretical perspective. In R. J. Sternberg & M. Hojjat (Eds.), *Satisfaction in close relationships* (pp. 275-304). New York: Guilford.

Fincham, F. D., & Bradbury, T. N. (1989). The impact of attributions in marriage: An individual difference analysis. *Journal of Social and Personal Relationships, 6,* 69-85.

Fisher, H. E. (1992). *The anatomy of love: The natural history of monogamy, adultery, and divorce.* New York: W. W. Norton.

Fitzpatrick, J., & Sollie, D. L. (1999). Unrealistic gendered and relationship-specific beliefs: Contributions to investments and commitment in dating relationships. *Journal of Social and Personal Relationships, 16,* 852-867.

Fitzpatrick, M. A. (1977). A typological approach to communication in relationships. In B. D. Ruben (Ed.), *Communication yearbook 1* (pp. 263-275). New Brunswick, NJ: Transaction.

Fitzpatrick, M. A. (1981). A typological approach to enduring relationships: Children as audience to parental relationships. *Journal of Comparative Family Studies, 12,* 81-94.

Fitzpatrick, M. A. (1984). A typological approach to marital interaction: Recent theory and research. In L. Berkowitz (Ed.), *Advances in experimental social psychology* (Vol. 18, pp. 1-47). Orlando, FL: Academic Press.

Fitzpatrick, M. A. (1988). *Between husbands and wives.* Newbury Park, CA: Sage.

Fletcher, G. J. O., Simpson, J. A., Thomas, G., & Giles, L. (1999). Ideals in intimate relationships. *Journal of Personality and Social Psychology, 76,* 72-89.

Fletcher, G. J. O., & Thomas, G. (1996). Close relationship lay theories: Their structure and function. In G. J. O. Fletcher & J. Fitness (Eds.), *Knowledge structures in close relationships: A social psychological approach* (pp. 3-24). Mahwah, NJ: Lawrence Erlbaum.

Fogarty, T. F. (1976). Marital crisis. In P. J. Guerin (Ed.), *Family therapy: Theory and practice* (pp. 325-334). New York: Gardner.

Gaelick, L., Bodenhausen, G., & Wyer, R. S. (1985). Emotional communication in close relationships. *Journal of Personality and Social Psychology, 49,* 1246-1265.

Gerstel, N. (1988). Divorce and kin ties: The importance of gender. *Journal of Marriage and the Family, 50,* 209-219.

Glenn, N. D. (1990). Quantitative research on marital quality in the 1980s: A critical review. *Journal of Marriage and the Family, 52,* 818-831.

Glenn, N. D. (1998). The course of marital success and failure in five American 10-year marriage cohorts. *Journal of Marriage and the Family, 60,* 569-576.

Glenn, N. D., & McLanahan, S. (1982). Children and marital happiness: A further specification of the relationship. *Journal of Marriage and the Family, 44,* 63-72.

Glenn, N. D., & Weaver, C. N. (1988). The changing relationship of marital status to reported happiness. *Journal of Marriage and the Family, 50,* 317-324.

Gottman, J. M. (1979). *Marital interaction: Experimental investigations.* New York: Academic Press.

Gottman, J. M. (1993). The roles of conflict engagement, escalation, and avoidance in marital interaction: A longitudinal view of five types of couples. *Journal of Consulting and Clinical Psychology, 61,* 6-15.

Gottman, J. M. (1994). *What predicts divorce? The relationship between marital processes and marital outcomes.* Hillsdale, NJ: Lawrence Erlbaum.

Gottman, J. M., Coan, J., Carrere, S., & Swanson, C. (1998). Predicting marital happiness and stability from newlywed interactions. *Journal of Marriage and the Family, 60,* 5-22.

Gottman, J. M., & Krokoff, L. J. (1989). Marital interaction and satisfaction: A longitudinal view. *Journal of Consulting and Clinical Psychology, 57,* 47-52.

Gottman, J. M., & Levenson, R. W. (1986). Assessing the role of emotion in marriage. *Behavioral Assessment, 8,* 31-48.

Gottman, J. M., & Levenson, R. W. (1988). The social psychophysiology of marriage. In P. Noller & M. A. Fitzpatrick (Eds.), *Perspectives on marital interaction* (pp. 182-200). Clevedon, Eng.: Multilingual Matters.

Gottman, J. M., & Levenson, R. W. (1992). Marital processes predictive of later dissolution: Behavior, physiology, and health. *Journal of Personality and Social Psychology, 63,* 221-233.

Gottman, J. M., Markman, H. J., & Notarius, C. I. (1977). The topography of marital conflict: A sequential analysis of verbal and nonverbal behavior. *Journal of Marriage and the Family, 39,* 461-477.

Gottman, J. M., & Notarius, C. I. (2000). Decade review: Observing marital interaction. *Journal of Marriage and the Family, 62,* 927-947.

Gray, J. D., & Silver, R. C. (1990). Opposite sides of the same coin: Former spouses' divergent perspectives in coping with their divorce. *Journal of Personality and Social Psychology, 59,* 1180-1191.

Grigg, F., Fletcher, G. J. O., & Fitness, J. (1989). Spontaneous attributions in happy and unhappy dating relationships. *Journal of Social and Personal Relationships, 6,* 61-68.

Hahlweg, K., Revenstorf, D., & Schindler, L. (1984). Effects of behavioral marital therapy on couples' communication and problem-solving skills. *Journal of Consulting and Clinical Psychology, 52,* 553-566.

Harvey, J. H., Orbuch, T. L., Chwalisz, K., & Garwood, G. (1991). Coping with sexual assault: The roles of account-making and confiding. *Journal of Traumatic Stress, 4,* 515-531.

Harvey, J. H., Orbuch, T. L., & Weber, A. L. (1992). Introduction: Convergence of the attribution and accounts concepts in the study of close relationships. In J. H. Harvey, T. L. Orbuch, & A. L. Weber (Eds.), *Attributions, accounts, and close relationships* (pp. 1-18). New York: Springer-Verlag.

Harvey, J. H., Weber, A. L., & Orbuch, T. L. (1990). *Interpersonal accounts: A social psychological perspective.* Oxford: Basil Blackwell.

Hatfield, E., Traupman, J., Sprecher, S., Utne, M., & Hay, J. (1985). Equity and intimate relations: Recent research. In W. Ickes (Ed.), *Compatible and incompatible relationships* (pp. 91-117). New York: Springer-Verlag.

Hazan, C., & Shaver, P. (1987). Romantic love conceptualized as an attachment process. *Journal of Personality and Social Psychology, 52,* 511-524.

Heavey, C. L., Christensen, A., & Malamuth, N. M. (1995). The longitudinal impact of demand and withdrawal during marital conflict. *Journal of Consulting and Clinical Psychology, 63,* 797-801.

Heavey, C. L., Layne, C., & Christensen, A. (1993). Gender and conflict structure in marital interaction: A replication and extension. *Journal of Consulting and Clinical Psychology, 61,* 16-27.

Heider, F. (1958). *The psychology of interpersonal relations.* New York: John Wiley.

Hemstrom, O. (1996). Is marriage dissolution linked to differences in mortality risks for men and women? *Journal of Marriage and the Family, 58,* 366-378.

Hendrick, C., & Hendrick, S. S. (1986). A theory and method of love. *Journal of Personality and Social Psychology, 50,* 392-402.

Hendrick, S. S. (1981). Self-disclosure and marital satisfaction. *Journal of Personality and Social Psychology, 40,* 1150-1159.

Herbert, T. B., Silver, R. C., & Ellard, J. H. (1991). Coping with an abusive relationship:

I. How and why do women stay? *Journal of Marriage and the Family, 53,* 311-325.

Hill, C. T., Rubin, Z., & Peplau, L. A. (1976). Breakups before marriage: The end of 103 affairs. *Journal of Social Issues, 32,* 147-168.

Hilton, D. J. (1990). Conversational processes and causal explanation. *Psychological Bulletin, 107,* 65-81.

Holtzworth-Munroe, A., & Jacobson, N. S. (1985). Causal attributions of married couples: When do they search for causes? What do they conclude when they do? *Journal of Personality and Social Psychology, 48,* 1398-1412.

Homans, G. C. (1961). *Social behavior: Its elementary forms.* New York: Harcourt Brace Jovanovich.

Hopper, R., & Drummond, K. (1991). Emergent goals at a relational turning point: The case of Gordon and Denise. *Journal of Language and Social Psychology, 9,* 39-65.

Houts, R. M., Robins, E., & Huston, T. L. (1996). Compatibility and the development of premarital relationships. *Journal of Marriage and the Family, 58,* 7-20.

Huston, T. L., & Burgess, R. L. (1979). Social exchange in developing relationships: An overview. In R. L. Burgess & T. L. Huston (Eds.), *Social exchange in developing relationships* (pp. 3-28). New York: Academic Press.

Huston, T. L., & Chorost, A. F. (1994). Behavioral buffers on the effect of negativity on marital satisfaction: A longitudinal study. *Personal Relationships, 1,* 223-239.

Huston, T. L., Robins, E., Atkinson, J., & McHale, S. M. (1987). Surveying the landscape of marital behavior: A behavioral self-report approach to studying marriage. *Applied Social Psychology Annual, 7,* 45-72.

Huston, T. L., Surra, C. A., Fitzgerald, N. M., & Cate, R. M. (1981). From courtship to marriage: Mate selection as an interpersonal process. In S. Duck & R. Gilmore (Eds.), *Personal relationships 2: Developing personal relationships* (pp. 53-88). New York: Academic Press.

Huston, T. L., & Vangelisti, A. L. (1991). Socioemotional behavior and satisfaction in marital relationships. *Journal of Personality and Social Psychology, 61,* 721-733.

Huston, T. L., & Vangelisti, A. L. (1995). How parenthood affects marriage. In M. A. Fitzpatrick & A. L. Vangelisti (Eds.),

Explaining family interactions (pp. 147-176). Thousand Oaks, CA: Sage.

Ickes, W., & Simpson, J. A. (1997). Managing empathic accuracy in close relationships. In W. Ickes (Ed.), *Empathic accuracy* (pp. 218-250). New York: Guilford.

Jacobson, N. S. (1990). Contributions from psychology to an understanding of marriage. In F. D. Fincham & T. N. Bradbury (Eds.), *The psychology of marriage: Basic issues and applications* (pp. 258-275). New York: Guilford.

Jacobson, N. S., & Margolin, G. (1979). *Marital therapy: Strategies based on social learning and behavior exchange principles*. New York: Brunner/Mazel.

Jacobson, N. S., Waldron, H., & Moore, D. (1980). Toward a behavioral profile of marital distress. *Journal of Consulting and Clinical Psychology, 48,* 696-703.

Jockin, V., McGue, M., & Lykken, D. T. (1996). Personality and divorce: A genetic analysis. *Journal of Personality and Social Psychology, 71,* 288-299.

Johnson, D. R., Amoloza, T. O., & Booth, A. (1992). Stability and developmental change in marital quality: A three-wave panel analysis. *Journal of Marriage and the Family, 54,* 582-594.

Johnson, M. P. (1991). Commitment to personal relationships. In W. H. Jones & D. Perlman (Eds.), *Advances in personal relationships* (Vol. 3, pp. 117-143). London: Jessica Kingsley.

Kantor, D., & Lehr, W. (1975). *Inside the family: Toward a theory of family process.* San Francisco: Jossey-Bass.

Karney, B. R., & Bradbury, T. N. (1997). Neuroticism, marital interaction, and the trajectory of marital satisfaction. *Journal of Personality and Social Psychology, 72,* 1075-1092.

Karney, B. R., & Bradbury, T. N. (2000). Attributions in marriage: State or trait? A growth curve analysis. *Journal of Personality and Social Psychology, 78,* 295-309.

Kashy, D. A., & Kenny, D. A. (2000). The analysis of data from dyads and groups. In H. T. Reis & C. M. Judd (Eds.), *Handbook of research methods in social psychology* (pp. 451-477). New York: Cambridge University Press.

Kelley, H. H., & Thibaut, J. W. (1978). *Interpersonal relations: A theory of interdependence.* New York: John Wiley.

Kelly, C., Huston, T. L., & Cate, R. M. (1985). Premarital relationship correlates of the erosion of satisfaction in marriage. *Journal of Social and Personal Relationships, 2,* 167-178.

Kenny, D. A. (1996). Models of nonindependence in dyadic research. *Journal of Social and Personal Relationships, 13,* 279-294.

Kirchler, E. (1989). Everyday life experiences at home: An interaction diary approach to assess marital relationships. *Journal of Family Psychology, 2,* 311-336.

Kirkpatrick, L., & Hazan, C. (1994). Attachment styles and close relationships: A four-year prospective study. *Personal Relationships, 1,* 123-142.

Kitson, G. C. (1992). *Portrait of divorce: Adjustment to marital breakdown.* New York: Guilford.

Kitson, G. C., & Morgan, L. A. (1990). The multiple consequences of divorce: A decade in review. *Journal of Marriage and the Family, 52,* 913-924.

Klinetob, N. A., & Smith, D. A. (1996). Demand-withdraw communication in marital interaction: Tests of interspousal contingency and gender role hypotheses. *Journal of Marriage and the Family, 58,* 945-958.

Knapp, M. L. (1978). *Social intercourse: From greeting to goodbye.* Boston: Allyn & Bacon.

Knapp, M. L. (1984). *Interpersonal communication and human relationships.* Boston: Allyn & Bacon.

Kraut, R., Patterson, M., Lundmark, V., Kiesler, S., Mukopadhyay, T., & Scherlis, W. (1998). Internet paradox: A social technology that reduces social involvement and psychological well-being? *American Psychologist, 53,* 1017-1031.

Kurdek, L. A. (1992). Assumptions versus standards: The validity of two relationship conditions in heterosexual and homosexual couples. *Journal of Family Psychology, 6,* 164-170.

Lederer, W., & Jackson, D. O. (1968). *The mirages of marriage.* New York: W. W. Norton.

Levenson, R. W., & Gottman, J. M. (1985). Physiological and affective predictors of change in relationship satisfaction. *Journal of Personality and Social Psychology, 49,* 85-94.

Lloyd, S. A., & Cate, R. M. (1985). Attributions associated with significant turning points in premarital relationship development and dissolution. *Journal of Social and Personal Relationships, 2,* 419-436.

Lykken, D. T. (2002). How relationships begin and end. In A. L. Vangelisti, H. T. Reis, & M. A. Fitzpatrick (Eds.), *Stability and change in relationships* (pp. 83-102). New York: Cambridge University Press.

Lykken, D. T., & Tellegen, A. (1993). Is human mating adventitious or the result of lawful choice? A twin study of mate selection. *Journal of Personality and Social Psychology, 65,* 56-68.

MacDermid, S. M., Huston, T. L., & McHale, S. M. (1990). Changes in marriage associated with the transition to parenthood: Individual differences as a function of sex-role attitudes and changes in division of labor. *Journal of Marriage and the Family, 52,* 475-486.

Margolin, G., & Wampold, B. (1981). Sequential analysis of conflict and accord in distressed and nondistressed marital partners. *Journal of Consulting and Clinical Psychology, 49,* 554-567.

Marini, M. (1976). Dimensions of marriage happiness: A research note. *Journal of Marriage and the Family, 38,* 443-447.

Markman, H. J. (1981). Prediction of marital distress: A five-year follow-up. *Journal of Consulting and Clinical Psychology, 49,* 760-762.

Markman, H. J., Duncan, S. W., Storaasli, R. D., & Howes, P. W. (1987). The prediction and prevention of marital distress: A longitudinal investigation. In K. Hahlweg & M. J. Goldstein (Eds.), *Understanding major mental disorder: The contribution of family interaction research* (pp. 266-289). New York: Family Process Press.

Marks, N. F. (1996). Flying solo at midline: Gender, marital status, and psychological well-being. *Journal of Marriage and the Family, 58,* 917-932.

Markus, H. (1977). Self-schemata and processing information about the self. *Journal of Personality and Social Psychology, 35,* 63-78.

Marston, P. J., Hecht, M. L., & Robers, T. (1987). "True love ways": The subjective experience and communication or romantic love. *Journal of Social and Personal Relationships, 4,* 387-407.

Masheter, C. (1991). Postdivorce relationships between ex-spouses: The roles of attachment and interpersonal conflict. *Journal of Marriage and the Family, 53,* 103-110.

Mastekaasa, A. (1997). Marital dissolution as a stressor: Some evidence on psychological, physical, and behavioral changes during the preseparation period. *Journal of Divorce and Remarriage, 26,* 155-183.

McCullough, M. E., Worthington, E. L., Jr., & Rachal, K. C. (1997). Interpersonal forgiving in close relationships. *Journal of Personality and Social Psychology, 73,* 321-336.

McHale, S. M., & Huston, T. L. (1985). The effect of the transition to parenthood on the marriage relationship: A longitudinal study. *Journal of Family Issues, 6,* 409-433.

McLanahan, S. S., & Booth, K. (1989). Mother-only families: Problems, prospects, and politics. *Journal of Marriage and the Family, 51,* 557-580.

Metts, S. (1994). Relational transgressions. In W. R. Cupach & B. H. Spitzberg (Eds.), *The dark side of interpersonal communication* (pp. 217-239). Hillsdale, NJ: Lawrence Erlbaum.

Miller, G. R., & Steinberg, M. (1975). *Between people: A new analysis of interpersonal communication.* Palo Alto, CA: Science Research Associates.

Murphy, M., Glaser, K., & Grundy, E. (1997). Marital status and long-term illness in Great Britain. *Journal of Marriage and the Family, 59,* 156-164.

Murray, S. L., Holmes, J. G., Griffin, D. W., Bellavia, G., & Rose, P. (2001). The mismeasure of love: How self-doubt contaminates relationship beliefs. *Personality and Social Psychology Bulletin, 27,* 423-436.

Newcomb, T. M. (1961). *The acquaintance process.* New York: Holt, Rinehart & Winston.

Noller, P. (1981). Gender and marital adjustment level differences in decoding messages from spouses and strangers. *Journal of Personality and Social Psychology, 41,* 272-278.

Noller, P. (1982). Channel consistency and inconsistency in the communications of married couples. *Journal of Personality and Social Psychology, 43,* 732-741.

Noller, P. (1984). *Nonverbal communication and marital interaction.* Oxford: Pergamon.

Noller, P. (1985). Negative communications in marriage. *Journal of Social and Personal Relationships, 2,* 289-301.

Noller, P., Feeney, J. A., Bonnell, D., & Callan, V. J. (1994). A longitudinal study of conflict in early marriage. *Journal of Social and Personal Relationships, 11,* 233-252.

Notarius, C. I., Benson, P. R., Sloane, D. Vanzetti, N., & Hornyak, L. M. (1989). Exploring the interface between perception and behavior: An analysis of marital interaction in distressed and nondistressed couples. *Behavioral Assessment, 11,* 39-64.

Notarius, C. I., & Johnson, J. S. (1982). Emotional expression in husbands and wives. *Journal of Marriage and the Family, 45,* 483-489.

Notarius, C. I., & Pellegrini, D. S. (1987). Differences between husbands and wives: Implications for understanding marital discord. In K. Hahlweg & M. J. Goldstein (Eds.), *Understanding major mental disorder: The contribution of family interaction research* (pp. 231-249). New York: Family Process Press.

Orvis, B. R., Kelley, H. H., & Butler, D. (1976). Attributional conflict in young couples. In J. H. Harvey, W. Ickes, & R. F. Kidd (Eds.), *New directions in attribution research* (Vol. 1, pp. 353-386). Hillsdale, NJ: Lawrence Erlbaum.

Parks, M. R., & Eggert, L. L. (1991). The role of social context in the dynamics of personal relationships. In W. H. Jones & D. Perlman (Eds.), *Advances in personal relationships* (Vol. 2, pp. 1-34). London: Jessica Kingsley.

Parks, M. R., & Floyd, K. (1996). Making friends in cyberspace. *Journal of Communication, 46*(1), 80-97.

Parks, M. R., & Roberts, L. D. (1998). "Making MOOsic": The development of personal relationships on line and a comparison to their off-line counterparts. *Journal of Social and Personal Relationships, 15,* 517-537.

Parks, M. R., Stan, C. M., & Eggert, L. L. (1983). Romantic involvement and social network involvement. *Social Psychology Quarterly, 46,* 116-131.

Pasch, L. A., & Bradbury, T. N. (1998). Social support, conflict, and the development of marital dysfunction. *Journal of Consulting and Clinical Psychology, 66,* 219-230.

Pennebaker, J. W. (1990). *Opening up: The healing power of confiding in others.* New York: William Morrow.

Peterson, D. R. (1979). Assessing interpersonal relationships by means of interaction records. *Behavioral Assessment, 1,* 221-236.

Petronio, S. (1991). Communication boundary management: A theoretical model of managing disclosure of private information between marital couples. *Communication Theory, 1,* 311-335.

Pietromonaco, P. R., Laurenceau, J. P., & Barrett, L. F. (2002). Change in relationship knowledge representations. In A. L. Vangelisti,

H. T. Reis, & M. A. Fitzpatrick (Eds.), *Stability and change in relationships* (pp. 5-34). New York: Cambridge University Press.

Planalp, S. (1985). Relational schemata: A test of alternative forms of relational knowledge as guides to communication. *Human Communication Research, 12,* 3-29.

Pyszczynski, T. A., & Greenberg, J. (1981). Role of disconfirmed expectancies on the instigation of attributional processing. *Journal of Personality and Social Psychology, 40,* 31-38.

Reis, H. T., Collins, W. A., & Berscheid, E. (2000). The relationship context of human behavior and development. *Psychological Bulletin, 126,* 844-872.

Reis, H. T., Nezlek, J., & Wheeler, L. (1980). Physical attractiveness in social interaction. *Journal of Personality and Social Psychology, 38,* 604-617.

Rempel, J. K., Holmes, J. G., & Zanna, M. P. (1985). Trust in close relationships. *Journal of Personality and Social Psychology, 49,* 95-112.

Rempel, J. K., Ross, M., & Holmes, J. G. (2001). Trust and communicated attributions in close relationships. *Journal of Personality and Social Psychology, 81,* 57-64.

Revenstorf, D., Vogel, B., Wegener, C., Hahlweg, K., & Schindler, L. (1980). Escalation phenomena in interaction sequences: An empirical comparison of distressed and nondistressed couples. *Behavior Analysis and Modification, 4,* 97-115.

Roloff, M. E., & Ifert, D. E. (1998). Antecedents and consequences of explicit agreements to declare a topic taboo in dating relationships. *Personal Relationships, 5,* 191-205.

Rosenbaum, M. E. (1986). The repulsion hypothesis: On the nondevelopment of relationships. *Journal of Personality and Social Psychology, 51,* 1156-1166.

Rosenthal, R. (1993). Interpersonal expectations: Some antecedents and some consequences. In P. D. Blanck (Ed.), *Interpersonal expectations: Theory, research, and applications* (pp. 3-24). New York: Cambridge University Press.

Ross, L., Lepper, M. R., & Hubbard, M. (1975). Perseverance in self-perception and social perception: Biased attribution processes in the debriefing paradigm. *Journal of Personality and Social Psychology, 32,* 880-892.

Ross, M. (1989). Relation of implicit theories to the construction of personal histories. *Psychological Review, 96,* 341-357.

Rubin, Z., Hill, C. T., Peplau, L. A., & Dunkel-Schetter, C. (1980). Self disclosure in dating couples: Sex roles and the ethic of openness. *Journal of Marriage and the Family, 42,* 305-317.

Rusbult, C. E. (1980). Commitment and satisfaction in romantic associations: A test of the investment model. *Journal of Experimental Social Psychology, 16,* 172-186.

Rusbult, C. E. (1983). A longitudinal test of the investment model: The development (and deterioration) of satisfaction and commitment in heterosexual involvements. *Journal of Personality and Social Psychology, 45,* 101-117.

Rusbult, C. E. (1991). Commentary on Johnson's "Commitment to personal relationships": What's interesting and what's new? In W. H. Jones & D. Perlman (Eds.), *Advances in personal relationships* (Vol. 3, pp. 151-169). London: Jessica Kingsley.

Ryder, R. G. (1973). Longitudinal data relating marriage satisfaction and having a child. *Journal of Marriage and the Family, 35,* 604-606.

Schaap, C., Buunk, B., & Kerkstra, A. (1988). Marital conflict resolution. In P. Noller & M. A. Fitzpatrick (Eds.), *Perspectives on marital interaction* (pp. 245-270). Clevedon, Eng.: Multilingual Matters.

Segal, M. W. (1974). Alphabet and attraction: An unobtrusive measure of the effect of propinquity in a field setting. *Journal of Personality and Social Psychology, 30,* 654-657.

Seibold, D. R., & Spitzberg, B. H. (1982). Attribution theory and research: Review and implications for communication. In B. Dervin & M. J. Voigt (Eds.), *Progress in communication sciences* (Vol. 3, pp. 85-125). Norwood, NJ: Ablex.

Sillars, A., Roberts, L. J., Dun, T., & Leonard, K. E. (2001). Stepping into the stream of thought: Cognition during marital conflict. In V. Manusov & J. H. Harvey (Eds.), *Attribution, communication behavior, and close relationships* (pp. 193-210). New York: Cambridge University Press.

Sillars, A., Roberts, L. J., Leonard, K. E., & Dun, T. (2000). Cognition during marital conflict: The relationship of thought and talk. *Journal of Social and Personal Relationships, 17,* 479-502.

Simpson, J. A. (1990). Influence of attachment styles on romantic relationships. *Journal of Personality and Social Psychology, 59,* 971-980.

Simpson, J. A., & Kenrick, D. T. (Eds.). (1997). *Evolutionary social psychology.* Mahwah, NJ: Lawrence Erlbaum.

Snyder, M., Tanke, E. D., & Berscheid, E. (1977). Social perception and interpersonal behavior: On the self-fulfilling nature of social stereotypes. *Journal of Personality and Social Psychology, 35,* 656-666.

Sorenson, K. A., Russell, S. M., Harkness, D. J., & Harvey, J. H. (1993). Account-making, confiding, and coping with the ending of a close relationship. *Journal of Social Behavior and Personality, 8,* 73-86.

Spitzberg, B. H. (1994). The dark side of (in)competence. In W. R. Cupach & B. H. Spitzberg (Eds.), *The dark side of interpersonal communication* (pp. 25-49). Hillsdale, NJ: Lawrence Erlbaum.

Sprecher, S. (1989). The importance to males and females of physical attractiveness, earning potential and expressiveness in initial attraction. *Sex Roles, 21,* 591-607.

Sprecher, S., & Felmlee, D. (1992). The influence of parents and friends on the quality and stability of romantic relationships: A three-wave longitudinal investigation. *Journal of Marriage and the Family, 54,* 888-900.

Sprecher, S., Felmlee, D., Orbuch, T. L., & Willetts, M. C. (2002). Social networks and change in personal relationships. In A. L. Vangelisti, H. T. Reis, & M. A. Fitzpatrick (Eds.), *Stability and change in relationships* (pp. 257-284). New York: Cambridge University Press.

Sprecher, S., Sullivan, Q., & Hatfield, E. (1994). Mate selection preferences: Gender differences examined in a national sample. *Journal of Personality and Social Psychology, 66,* 1074-1080.

Stangor, C., & McMillan, D. (1992). Memory for expectancy-congruent and expectancy-incongruent information: A review of the social and social developmental literatures. *Psychological Bulletin, 111,* 42-61.

Sternberg, R. J. (1986). A triangular theory of love. *Psychological Review, 93,* 119-135.

Sunnafrank, M. (1983). Attitude similarity and interpersonal attraction in communication processes: In pursuit of an ephemeral influence. *Communication Monographs, 50,* 273-284.

Sunnafrank, M. (1986). Communicative influences on perceived similarity and attraction: An expansion of the interpersonal goals perspective. *Western Journal of Speech Communication, 50,* 158-170.

Sunnafrank, M., & Miller, G. R. (1981). The role of initial conversations in determining attraction to similar and dissimilar strangers. *Human Communication Research, 8,* 16-25.

Surra, C. A. (1985). Courtship types: Variations in interdependence between partners and social networks. *Journal of Personality and Social Psychology, 49,* 357-375.

Surra, C. A. (1990). Research and theory on mate selection and premarital relationships in the 1980s. *Journal of Marriage and the Family, 52,* 844-865.

Surra, C. A., Arizzi, P., & Asmussen, L. A. (1988). The association between reasons for commitment and the development and outcome of marital relationships. *Journal of Social and Personal Relationships, 5,* 47-63.

Surra, C. A., Batchelder, M. L., & Hughes, D. K. (1995). Accounts and the demystification of courtship. In M. A. Fitzpatrick & A. L. Vangelisti (Eds.), *Explaining family interactions* (pp. 112-145). Thousand Oaks, CA: Sage.

Surra, C. A., & Bohman, T. (1991). The development of close relationships: A cognitive perspective. In G. J. O. Fletcher & F. D. Fincham (Eds.), *Cognition in close relationships* (pp. 281-305). Hillsdale, NJ: Lawrence Erlbaum.

Swann, W. B., Jr., Hixon, J. G., & De La Ronde, C. (1992). Embracing the bitter "truth": Negative self concepts and marital commitment. *Psychological Science, 3,* 118-121.

Terman, L. M. (1938). *Psychological factors in marital happiness.* New York: McGraw-Hill.

Thibaut, J. W., & Kelley, H. H. (1959). *The social psychology of groups.* New York: John Wiley.

Ting-Toomey, S. (1983). An analysis of verbal communication patterns in high and low marital adjustment groups. *Human Communication Research, 9,* 306-319.

Vaillant, C. O., & Vaillant, G. E. (1993). Is the U-curve of marital satisfaction an illusion? A 40-year study of marriage. *Journal of Marriage and the Family, 55,* 230-239.

Vangelisti, A. L., & Daly, J. A. (1997). Gender differences in standards for romantic relationships. *Personal Relationships, 4,* 203-219.

Van Lange, P. A. M., Rusbult, C. E., Drigotas, S. M., Arriaga, X. B., Witcher, B. S., & Cox, C. L. (1997). Willingness to sacrifice in close relationships. *Journal of Personality and Social Psychology, 72,* 1373-1395.

Vanzetti, N. A., Notarius, C. I., & NeeSmith, D. (1992). Specific and generalized expectancies in marital interaction. *Journal of Family Psychology, 6,* 171-183.

Veroff, J., Douvan, E., & Kulka, R. A. (1981). *Mental health in America: Patterns of help-seeking from 1957-1976.* New York: Basic Books.

Waller, W. (1938). *The family: A dynamic interpretation.* New York: Gordon.

Walster, E., Aronson, V., Abrahams, D., & Rottman, L. (1966). Importance of physical attractiveness in dating behavior. *Journal of Personality and Social Psychology, 4,* 508-516.

Walster, E., Walster, G. W., & Berscheid, E. (1978). *Equity: Theory and research.* Boston: Allyn & Bacon.

Walters-Champman, S. F., Price, S. J., & Serovich, J. M. (1995). The effects of guilt on divorce adjustment. *Journal of Divorce and Remarriage, 22,* 163-177.

Walther, J. B. (1992). Interpersonal effects in computer-mediated interaction: A relational perspective. *Communication Research, 19,* 52-90.

Weiss, R. L., & Heyman, R. E. (1990). Observation of marital interaction. In F. D. Fincham & T. N. Bradbury (Eds.), *The psychology of marriage: Basic issues and applications* (pp. 87-117). New York: Guilford.

Weiss, R. S. (1984). The impact of marital dissolution on income and consumption in single-parent households. *Journal of Marriage and the Family, 46,* 115-127.

White, L. K., & Booth, A. (1985). The transition to parenthood and marital quality. *Journal of Family Issues, 6,* 435-449.

White, L. K., Booth, A., & Edwards, J. N. (1986). Children and marital happiness: Why the negative correlation? *Journal of Family Issues, 7,* 131-147.

Whitton, S., Stanley, S., & Markman, H. J. (2002). Sacrifice in romantic relationships: An exploration of relevant research and theory. In A. L. Vangelisti, H. T. Reis, & M. A. Fitzpatrick (Eds.), *Stability and change in relationships* (pp. 156-181). New York: Cambridge University Press.

Wills, T. A., Weiss, R. L., & Patterson, G. R. (1974). A behavioral analysis of the determinants of marital satisfaction. *Journal of Consulting and Clinical Psychology, 42,* 802-811.

18

Interpersonal Communication and Health Care

TERESA L. THOMPSON
ROXANNE PARROTT

The social import of the context and the life-and-death nature of the phenomena under investigation may make the study of communication in health care the most interesting of interpersonal contexts. There is little other interpersonal research that can have the bottom-line impact of health communication. As the following review illustrates, interpersonal research in the health care context has impacts on diagnosis, adherence to treatment regimens, patient recovery and pain, and malpractice suits. Medical errors are frequently communication issues rather than just errors in judgment or negligence. These factors lead to some inherent interest in the topic of inter-

personal communication in health care, and we address them in this chapter. Our discussion begins with a focus on descriptive studies of communication and then moves to studies of the outcomes of communication. We examine such issues as communication skills and training, the coding of provider-patient interaction, nonverbal aspects of communication, disclosure issues, language, diversity, control, prevention, and theoretical perspectives. We present our review of interpersonal communication in health care with a recognition that health policies, laws and legal considerations, and organizational and cultural contexts influence the communication between health

AUTHORS' NOTE: Both authors contributed equally to this chapter.

care providers and patients, reflecting an ecological perspective on interaction in medical encounters (Street, in press).

Most of the research that we review herein has been conducted by social scientists and nurses. Increasingly, we find physicians and allied health professionals recognizing the relevance of communication issues to health care. We attempt to focus in this chapter on empirical examinations of communication issues, rather than on the "how-to-communicate" articles that are frequently found in the medical, nursing, and allied health literature. Although such articles are important for practitioners, they do not provide the knowledge claims appropriate for a review of the literature. Research on interpersonal communication in health care has expanded enormously in recent years, due to both the increasing numbers of publication outlets now available for such work and the increasing recognition of the relevance of the topic noted above. Given the large amount of research available, our review is representative rather than exhaustive.

A PRIMARY FOCUS ON DESCRIBING COMMUNICATION

Although the research that we review in this chapter does not break down neatly into clean categories, a rough distinction can be drawn between those studies that are more descriptive and those that look at communication as an independent variable that affects outcomes. Very little health research has looked at communication as a dependent variable, and most of the work that has done so has not been terribly illuminating. We discuss a few notable exceptions below. Although some of the studies that we discuss in the descriptive sections of this chapter also looked at the outcomes of communication, they did a particularly good job of delineating the interpersonal interaction that occurs in the health care context. We also review the outcomes of some of these studies, so that we need not go over this research again in the section on outcomes.

Descriptive Studies

Some of the most interesting studies of health communication have provided descriptions of various communicative processes observed in the medical context. Many, although not all, of these have been qualitative or discourse-analytic studies, and they have tended to take a very dyadic perspective. Some of this work has identified the functions of tag questions (Harres, 1998) and humor (Beck, 1997) in the medical consultation. Research has focused on different ways of "attending" (Bottorff & Morse, 1994), "transitioning" (Bottorff & Varcoe, 1995), providing support (Hinds & Moyer, 1997), communicating about dying (McGrath, Yates, Clinton, & Hart, 1999), and dealing with difficult patients (Juliana et al., 1997). Qualitative researchers have noted how the biopsychosocial model conflicts with patient-centered approaches to care (Bartz, 1999). Gilbert (1998) looked at relational themes in nurse-patient interaction, concluding that positive communication "is not necessarily precluded by the time constraints in contemporary nursing practice" (p. 5).

Other researchers have examined a wide range of issues. For example, Miller and Holditch-Davis (1992) studied parental versus nurse interaction with preterm infants, finding that these infants receive different kinds of stimulation from and react differently to the two types of caregivers; Street, Gold, and McDowell (1995) examined physician-prenatal patient discussions of quality-of-life issues; and Parrott (1994) studied physician-patient interactions about prescribed medications, identifying several concerns regarding such discussions.

Looking at communication as both an independent and a dependent variable, Levinson and Roter (1995) found that positive physician attitudes toward psychosocial aspects of care were associated with more statements of emotion, such as messages of empathy or reassurance, and fewer closed-ended questions. The patients of such physicians also participated in their own care more actively by expressing opinions and asking questions.

Much health communication research seems to be based on the simplistic assumption that health care providers are responsible for most communication problems (Thompson, 1984), although health care providers most often attribute communication problems to patients rather than to themselves (Levinson, Stiles, Inui, & Engle, 1993). Fortunately, simplistic assumptions of one-way communication are challenged in such work as that summarized by Sharf and Street (1997). Hirschmann's (1999) study tracing the pressures on a young intern as they affect communication also provides a more sophisticated conceptualization of relevant interactional concerns, as does LaBrecque's (1996) report on a day in the life of a physician. Similarly, Kemppainen, O'Brien, and Corpuz (1998) identify the communicative responses of AIDS patients toward their nurses. They found that participatory and angry behavioral responses were common. Other researchers have noted that communication problems are more common among breast cancer patients who are less optimistic about their disease and who have less assertive coping styles. Patient-reported communication problems are associated with increased anxiety, depression, anger, and confusion (Lerman et al., 1993).

Information Giving

Because of the importance of information exchange in health care interaction, many researchers have focused particularly on the adequacy with which such exchange occurs. Pointing out that, for many patients, shared information is a life-and-death issue (Holmes, 1996), researchers have determined that most support received by patients who are seriously ill is informational rather than social (Hinds & Moyer, 1997). Information exchange is particularly important during diagnosis, during the progression of a disease, and in regard to pain, sexual functioning, and financial issues (Blum & Blum, 1991). It has been argued that information provision is especially problematic in light of the large number of doctors seen by the typical patient (Smith, Nicol, Devereux, & Cornbleet, 1999). Various researchers have identified different information needs for patients with certain health problems (e.g., Frith, 1991). Some measuring instruments focus specifically on assessing the competence with which information exchange occurs (Boon & Stewart, 1998; Ravert, Williams, & Fosbinder, 1997), although some of this research has also been ethnographic (Lazcano-Ponce et al., 1999). Lazcano-Ponce et al. (1999) found that lack of information is a serious barrier for Mexican woman, causing them to avoid such preventive and early-detection screening methods as Pap smears. The failure of nurses to convey information about patients to doctors has also been associated with negative outcomes and medical malpractice (Sullivan, 1996).

Noting that some patients receive more information from physicians than do others, Street (1991a) examined patients' communicative styles and personal characteristics as determinants of the amount of information they receive from caregivers. His data indicate that (a) information regarding diagnosis and health matters is related to patients' anxiety, education, and question asking; (b) information relating to treatment is a function of patient question asking and expression of concerns; and (c) patients' assertiveness and expressiveness are influenced by physicians' use of partnership-building utterances. In a follow-up study, Street (1992b) found that physicians' characteristics also influence the amount of information exchanged, and that patients who express more negative affect receive more information. Summarizing a series of studies on doctor-patient communication, Waitzkin (1984) concludes that "physicians tend to underestimate patients' desire for information and to misperceive the process of information giving" (p. 2441).

Time Allocation

Some researchers who have attempted to describe various aspects of encounters between care providers and patients have focused specifically on the length of interactions, the amount of talk time contributed by the patient versus the provider, and the kinds of statements constituting these interactions. The data indicate that nurses report disappointment with the limited amount of time they have available to communicate with patients (Carlisle, 1996) and that physicians significantly overestimate the time they spend talking with patients, particularly about such issues as safety (Morrongiello, Hillier, & Bass, 1995). Roter, Hall, and Katz (1988) found that physician-patient interactions averaged about 16 minutes in length in the United States (5-6 minutes in Britain). Patients typically contributed about 40% of the dialogue, with physicians providing the other 60%. About half of patient talk was devoted to giving information, 20% to positive talk, and 67% to each of the categories of question asking, social conversation, and negative talk. These findings are consistent with those of Arntson, Droge, and Fassl (1978), who reported that doctors asked twice as many questions and gave twice as many commands as patients, and that patients typically did not ask for explanations.

This small amount of time devoted to question asking is important in light of the fact that increased patient question asking is associated with increased understanding of treatment regimens and better medical outcomes (Beisecker, 1990). Fisher (1983) found that

changes in treatment decisions occurred as a result of patient questions. The findings of Roter et al. (1988) noted above, however, are consistent with those of Korsch, Gozzi, and Francis (1968), who found that only 24% of the patients participating in their study asked the physician about their *main* concern. It is also consistent with research indicating that physicians discourage question asking (Weiss, 1986) even though patients desire information (McIntosh, 1974). Several more recent studies have documented methods that physicians can use to encourage patient question asking (e.g., Cegala, McClure, Marinelli, & Post, 2001).

In their meta-analysis mentioned above, Roter et al. (1988) also found that 38.5% of physician time was spent in information giving, followed by 22.5% of time spent in information seeking; another 15% of the time was positive talk, 10% was spent in partnership building, and 6% of the time was spent in social conversation. Partnership building included attempts to facilitate greater patient input and interpret and synthesize patients' talk.

The notion of allocation of time to communicative activities has also been addressed by researchers who have found that "lack of time" is the reason many care providers give for not communicating more with patients (MacLeod Clark, 1985), although there appears to be no relationship between the amount of time available and the quality of communication (MacLeod Clark, 1983).

Coding Provider-Patient Interaction

As interest in the study of interpersonal interaction in health care has grown, so has the number of measuring instruments. In a review of measuring instruments discussed in the research between 1986 and 1996, Boon and Stewart (1998) found 44 such tools, 21 of which were used in only one published study and 15 of which were never validated. Some of these instruments use real-time observation, others use rating scales (either with standardized patients or on video- or audio-taped interactions), and a few rely on self-report measures. Boon and Stewart note that most of these methods demonstrate acceptable reliability, but few have been directly compared with another instrument that assesses provider-patient interaction. They express concerns about validation of existing instruments and incorporation of some assessment of nonverbal communication.

Of most interest are the measuring instruments that involve the coding of provider-patient interactions. Commonly used coding systems include those developed by Greene, Adelman, Friedman, and Charon (1994); Inui, Carter, Kukull, and Haigh (1982); Stiles (1978); Kurtz and Silverman (1996); Callahan and Bertakis (1991); Roter (1995); Makoul (1995); Brown, Stewart, and Tessier (1995); Street (1991b, 1992a); and McNeilis (2001).

Some improvements have occurred since Boon and Stewart's (1998) analysis, although it is still true that few attempts have been made to include nonverbal communication in measuring instruments. A special issue of *Health Communication* published in 2001 provides a comparison of six different coding schemes that were applied to the same data set (Thompson, 2001). The coding schemes compared are those developed by Street, Stiles, Stewart, Roter, and McNeilis, mentioned above, as well as relational coding (von Friederichs-Fitzwater & Gilgun, 2001). This comparison indicates that the coding schemes vary in the breadth of the categories, their theoretical underpinnings, their foci, and even the conclusions drawn from them (Rimal, 2001). Whereas one coding scheme might lead to a conclusion that a particular provider-patient interaction was patient centered, another might conclude that the interaction was not. Clearly, the coding system selected by a particular researcher makes a difference.

In addition to the quantitative methods mentioned above, some researchers have advocated more qualitative approaches. These include Sharf's (1990) application of narrative theory and Waitzkin's (1990) multidimensional method incorporating both qualitative and quantitative measures. Ethnographic approaches can be seen in work such as that undertaken by du Pré (1998) and Beck (1997).

Communication Skills

Although the field of communication long ago moved from the notion of "communication skills" to the concept of "communicative competence," little research on communicative effectiveness within the nursing and medical professions has noted this shift (for exceptions, see Cegala, Coleman, & Turner, 1998; Cegala, McGee, & McNeilis, 1996; Gillotti, Thompson, & McNeilis, 2002; Kasch, Kasch, & Lisnek, 1998; McGee, 1997; Query & Kreps, 1996; Ravert et al., 1997). Thus we focus here on communication skills as they are commonly discussed in the literature. This area is the most frequent target of communication research within nursing and the allied health professions. Much of this writing includes lists of skills culled from introductory-level communication material rather than empirical examinations of skills and their outcomes. Behaviors such as responding and initiating skills (nonverbal communication, active listening, self-disclosure, questioning, and explaining) and interactional skills (counseling, influencing, and interviewing) are typically included in the lists that are generated (see, for instance, Ladyshewsky & Gotjamanos, 1997).

Much of this research has involved health care providers' self-assessments of their communication skills (Cegala et al., 1996, 1998; McLaughlin, 1999). It has shown that health care providers perceive communicating with patients about their difficulties to be a key skill (McLaughlin, 1999), and that care providers see their own skills as lacking, but not as sorely lacking as others' ratings of those skills, made by patients or through observational methods, would indicate (Dockrell, 1988). In many of the early studies, researchers asked care providers to rank communication skills in terms of importance to their work (Lubbers & Roy, 1990); these studies typically generated lists that were headed by "listening" as the most important skill.

Other researchers have sought input from patients on the perceived skills of their care providers. Bailey and Wilkinson (1998) found that patients see the following as important in effective care provider communication: listening; asking simple questions; being clear, articulate, and loud enough to be heard; and maintaining eye contact. They also found that some patients' main concerns remain hidden from care providers. Using their Medical Communication Competence Scale, Cegala et al. (1998) identified four main clusters of behaviors: information giving, information seeking, information verifying, and socioemotional communication. Patients participating in Fosbinder's (1994) research focused on four processes: translating (clarity in information transmission), getting to know you (humor, friendliness, personal sharing, and smiling), establishing trust (anticipating needs, being in charge and prompt, and following through), and going the extra mile (being a friend, delivering care above expectations).

Other researchers have used standardized patients to rate the communication skills of care providers (Colliver, Swartz, Robbs, & Cohen, 1999), sometimes combining this with peer assessment (Ladyshewsky & Gotjamanos, 1997), or have asked experts in particular fields to make such assessments (Gyllensten, Gard, Salford, & Ekdahl, 1999). Gyllensten et al. (1999) asked experienced physiotherapists to rate interactions; from these ratings, the researchers identified the following important skills: establishing contact and confidence, having a therapeutic role, being sensitive and intuitive, encountering, listening, and identifying patient resources.

Various methods for coding skills have been described in other research. These methods include Hardcastle's (1999) assessment instrument for psychiatric nurses, the Calgary-Cambridge Referenced Observation Guide (Kurtz & Silverman, 1996), the Interpersonal Competence Instrument for Nurses (Ravert et al., 1997), and the Prutting pragmatic protocol (Scherz, Edwards, & Kallail, 1995). Some researchers have used qualitative methods (Kotecki, 1997; Poggenpoel, 1997) or even questioned whether or not interpersonal skills lie within the realm of empirical inquiry (Jones, 1994) or should be taught (Peloquin, 1995). Kotecki (1997) determined that nursing students encountered problems relating to "saying the right things to patients." Kotecki describes a four-stage process through which the students went as they developed their interpersonal competencies: affirming the self, engaging the patient, experiencing communication breakdown, and refining the repertoire. Similarly, Poggenpoel (1997) identified five categories of nurses' responses to patients' communication, noting that the first four of these are not conducive to maintenance of the patient's health: reassuring, giving of advice, explaining, moralizing, and empathy. Reassurance, advice, explanations, and moralizing are typically communicated in a disconfirming way that does not acknowledge the patient's feelings and is counterproductive. Effective communication skills have also been associated with increased clinical competence (Colliver et al., 1999) and increased competence in bad news delivery (Gillotti et al., 2002); O'Brien (1992) has reported that more expert nurses are also more empathic.

The reasons that care providers do *not* utilize communication skills have also been discussed in the literature. Noting that interpersonal skills do not take place in isolation, some scholars have suggested that such organizational factors as lack of incentives and the desire of the administration to maintain power and control may contribute to a reluctance to develop skills (Gijbels, 1993), as may variables such as ward organization, remote management styles, and an emphasis on increased patient throughput (Naish, 1996). Gijbels (1993) also notes that using interpersonal skills may be anxiety provoking. Horsfall (1998) places the blame for ineffective skills on personal attributes of the care provider. Other research has indicated that different areas of health care require different skills (Tickle-Degnen, 1998).

As is evident from the above discussion, little research has focused on the communication skills of the patient in the medical encounter. Exceptions include the work of Cegala et al. (1996, 1998, 2001), Eaton and Tinsley (1999), McGee (1997), and McGee and Cegala (1998). McGee (1997) reports that patients who are trained in communication skills engage in significantly more information seeking and comprehension checking and recall more treatment information, and McGee and Cegala (1998) found that trained patients sought more information through the use of both direct and indirect questions and acquired more helpful information.

Training

It has now been well documented in the health literature that communication skills can be taught (Roter, Hall, & Kern, 1995). Many articles published in the medical literature are descriptions of training programs at various institutions (Parboosingh & Inhaber, 1999) or of the positive responses that such training programs have received (Rath et al., 1998). Still others report assessments of program directors' and medical educators' perceptions of the importance of communication skill training (Kurtz, Laidlaw, Makoul, & Schnabl, 1999), typically concluding that communication skills are perceived as important and that programs report that they include training in this area. Kurtz et al. (1999) summarize the major components of effective training programs, and Kurtz and Silverman (1996) describe the elements that should be included in such programs. Parle, Maguire, and Heaven

(1997) provide a conceptual model to be used as the basis of brief, problem-focused workshops for health professionals.

Effective communication skills training programs have been reported in the literature in regard to psychiatric nurses (Armstrong & Kelly, 1993), palliative care (Wilkinson, Roberts, & Aldridge, 1998), dental hygienists (Gleber, 1995), and cancer patients (Parle et al., 1997). Communication skills training programs have been reported to lead to better medical outcomes in patients, increasing speed of recovery and decreasing length of hospital stay (Abramson, 1997); increased life satisfaction in nursing home residents (Pilkington, 1993); improved caregiver consultation skills and patient satisfaction (Evans, Stanley, & Burrows, 1992); decreased communication difficulties and negative affect (Ripick, Ziol, & Lee, 1998); increased attention of physicians to patients' nonverbals (Foley, Nespoli, & Conde, 1997); improved staff retention, less use of leave, fewer patients' rights complaints, and fewer assaults on staff (Smoot & Gonzales, 1995); less stress for nurses (Hanlon, 1996); shifts toward a more patient-centered or psychosocial approach (R. C. Smith et al., 1995; Steyn, van der Merwe, Dick, Borcherds, & Wilding, 1997); gains in empathy (Gallagher, 1993); increased willingness to communicate and perceived competence of nurses in communicating with patients (Wong, Lau, & Mok, 1996); higher levels of psychosocial, family, and emotional involvement (Behen, 1996; Marvel, Doherty, & Weiner, 1998); and improved assertiveness (McDaniels, 1992). Jeffrey and Hicks (1997), however, found that a counseling skills module did not lead to improvements in the interpersonal skills of occupational therapy students.

Various instructional methods have been reported in the skills training literature. Ladyshewsky and Gotjamanos (1997), for instance, describe an experiential training program that includes self-directed student tutorals, dramatizations and theatrical improvisation with actors, videotape, and the use of standardized patients and peer assessment. Few researchers have undertaken comparative investigations of training approaches, although Eoaskoon, Sumawong, and Silpakit (1996) determined in a study of three training methods that interviewing of standardized patients with subsequent peer, tutor, and patient feedback was particularly effective. Within the past decade, the nursing literature has been replete with descriptions of CD-ROMs, videodiscs, and interactive computer-assisted instructional modules designed to teach interpersonal skills (see, for example, Walker & Ross, 1995). This approach is often described as the wave of the future in terms of communication skills training for nurses, although little research has empirically examined the effectiveness of these programs.

As in the case of the skills literature, all of the research mentioned above has focused on the training of care *providers*. Very little inquiry has examined training programs for patients operating within the health care context. Recently, however, Cegala et al. (2001) developed and tested a patient training program and found that trained patients demonstrated more effective and efficient information seeking, provided physicians with more detailed information about their medical conditions, and used more summarizing statements to verify information. Dyads containing a trained patient also showed more patient-centered communication than did other dyads.

Nonverbal Communication

Although it is not really possible to separate verbal from nonverbal communication in a meaningful way, given that the two forms are highly interdependent (for research that links verbal and nonverbal behaviors, see Caris-Verhallen, Kerkstra, & Bensing, 1999), some research has provided insight into aspects of nonverbal communication that are particularly relevant to the health care context. Work

in this area has focused on nonverbal dominance (Street & Buller, 1987) and relaxation (Smith & Larsen, 1984) of physicians, as well as the relationship between nonverbal behaviors and patient satisfaction (DiMatteo, Taranta, Friedman, & Prince, 1980). Rapport between doctors and patients is communicated nonverbally (Harrigan, Oxman, & Rosenthal, 1985), and research provides some evidence of nonverbal reciprocation or accommodation (Street & Buller, 1988). Some researchers have looked at factors influencing the perception of nonverbals (Sviden & Saljo, 1993), whereas others have examined such nonverbals as body gestures (Savage, 1997), eye contact (Davidhizar, 1992), and personal space issues (Scott, 1997). Reflecting an ecological model (Street, in press) in association with nonverbal communication between physicians and patients, one study that defined the subjective component of illness in terms of both personal and structural barriers to wellness—with illness beliefs constituting an example of the former and the organization and delivery of health care illustrating the latter—found that patients disclosed more in both realms when physicians used more facial reinforcers, such as head nods, and fewer negative facial behaviors, including indirect eye contact (Duggan & Parrott, 2001).

Much of the research concerning nonverbal communication in the health care context, however, has focused on cases in which the patient cannot speak and on the role of touch in the communicative process. This research has indicated the need for care provider attention to nonverbal behaviors in the assessment of patient anxiety (Sawada, Mendes, Galvao, & Trevizan, 1992) and pain (Hadjistavropoulos, McMurtry, & Craig, 1996). Both gender and physical attractiveness influence accuracy in the reading of nonverbal pain indicators, such that males and those who are more attractive are seen to be experiencing less pain (Hadjistavropoulos et al., 1996). Researchers have found rather low agreement between patients and care providers on the severity of symptom distress (Tanghe, Evers, & Paridaens, 1998) and on the communication needs of patients who cannot speak (Fitch, Remus, & Stade, 1998). Patients who are ventilator dependent (Coe, Chen, & Holliday, 1996), intubated (Fowler, 1997), or otherwise rendered nonvocal (Easton, 1988) experience severe communication difficulties leading to increased reliance on nonverbal communication, as do those who are unconscious or sedated (Elliott & Wright, 1999). Mallett (1990) has demonstrated that nurses are skilled communicators who take into account patients' levels of consciousness and adapt accordingly. Nurse perception of the responsiveness of a ventilator-dependent patient has been found to be positively associated with the amount of interaction with the patient (Hall, 1996). In addition to the difficulties of the silent patient and the cross-cultural meanings of silence (Davidhizar & Giger, 1994), researchers have also investigated the *value* of silence (King, 1995).

When researchers focus on care providers' communication with patients who cannot speak, the importance of touch is typically stressed (Verity, 1996). Relatively little expressive touch takes place between nurses and elderly patients (Oliver & Redfern, 1991). Patients experience touching by nurses as gentle, comforting, and important (Routasalo & Isola, 1996). Although patients touch nurses less frequently than the obverse, such touch is seen as easy and natural (Routasalo & Isola, 1996). Nurses use nonnecessary touch in connection with making statements or requests, waking a patient, encouraging, explaining, asking, comforting, teasing, telling off, hugging, and thanking (Routasalo, 1996; Routasalo & Lauri, 1996). Elderly patients who receive comforting touch from nurses feel more affection and immediacy (Moore & Gilbert, 1995). Touch is not related to patient prognosis, but caring touch is negatively related to a nurse's length of service (Adomat & Killingworth, 1994). Physicians use less task touch with anxious patients (Street & Buller, 1988), and those who are physically disabled or of low social status are touched less frequently (Watson, 1975). Some researchers, however, argue that nurses do not adequately understand the importance of touch (Carter & Sanderson, 1995) or when touch should not be used (Davidhizar & Giger, 1997). Gender differences have also been noted in reliance on silence, touch, and humor (Lane, 1989; Watson, 1975).

Language

Moving from a focus on nonverbal to verbal communication leads us to a discussion of language use. Although some of the research in this area looks at providers and patients who actually speak different languages (Munks, 1995), most is concerned with language issues in terms of reliance on medical terminology. This research bemoans the tendency of care providers to rely on jargonistic terms and acronyms (H. Spiers, 1998) because of the mystification, power differences, and lack of understanding produced by such reliance. Gelman (1980) contends that esoteric language becomes a double-edged sword that dominates and alienates, making vulnerable patients more vulnerable. Care providers report that they try to use everyday rather than medical language (Bourhis, Roth, & MacQueen, 1989), but empirical investigation does not support their claims (Scott & Weiner, 1984). Research has indicated that even terms such as *at risk, risk factors,* and *cancer* are not well understood by many patients (Roche et al., 1998). Although patient understanding of medical terms has improved somewhat over the years, that improvement has not been nearly as great as might be expected, and much misunderstanding of terminology still exists—even among physicians (Thompson & Pledger, 1993). Provider reliance on technical language is associated with decreased patient satisfaction, comprehension, and recall (Jackson, 1992). The use of medical jargon also increases care providers' tendency to perceive patients as the medical problems with which they have been labeled rather than as people (Baziak & Dentan, 1960).

Researchers have also addressed other issues involving language. Craig (1999) has raised concerns about the evaluative language used by care providers, and Waddie (1996) suggests that expressions of pain influence perceptions of pain. Barrett (1993) discusses "code terms" patients may use to which care providers should attend, such as "I'm managing," which frequently really indicates that the patient is not doing well at all.

Diversity

One area of study that has emerged only in recent years concerns diversity issues in health communication. The medical, nursing, and allied health literatures are replete with articles encouraging health care providers to be cognizant of cultural differences and the impacts of these differences on communicative processes (Hornberger, Itakura, & Wilson, 1997); many of these articles also offer guidance for health care providers about how they can increase their awareness and improve their communication with those who are culturally different from them. This work includes discussions of the role of interpreters in provider-patient interaction (Pakieser & McNamee, 1999) and articles that emphasize awareness of culturally specific nonverbals (Siantz, 1991) and potential illiteracy (Wright, 1996). Some researchers have tested the cross-cultural replicability of research findings on provider-patient interaction (Waitzkin, Cabrera, Arroyo de Cabrera, & Radlow, 1996). Others advocate that health care providers work to understand various cultural belief systems as they affect health care interactions (Herselman, 1996). Still other researchers have investigated the impact of nonnative physicians as message senders (Rubin, Healy, Gardiner, Zath, & Moore, 1997).

Also of interest is the relatively new emergence of research examining the role of disability in health care interaction. It has long been known that disabilities can have negative effects on interpersonal interaction (Braithwaite & Thompson, 2000). People with disabilities tend to visit health care providers more frequently than do the able-bodied, because their disabilities are likely to either be or cause health problems, and health care providers exhibit the same prejudices toward the disabled as do other people (Lys & Pernice, 1995). So it is somewhat surprising that this area has received relatively little investigation. Recently, however, researchers have undertaken examinations of communication with the visually impaired (Fry, 1994), the mentally challenged (Hahn, 1999), the hearing impaired (Ebert & Heckerling, 1995), the confused or demented (Ostuni & Mohl, 1995), and those with physical disabilities (Miller & Opie, 1994). Most of the literature in this area encourages care providers to adapt to the needs of their disabled patients, but provides little empirical examination of relevant issues. This would certainly seem to be an area ripe for future research.

Children

A small number of researchers have begun to address the special issues involved in communicating with children in the health care context (Endacott, 1998). They have suggested such techniques for care providers as asking children to draw to express their concerns (Teuscher, 1995), focusing on psychosocial concerns rather than on the etiology and biology of the illness (Whaley, 1999), and avoiding the figurative language that is frequently advocated in medical discussions of explaining illness to children (Whaley, 1994). More specifically, Wood's (1997) analysis of work in this area indicates that care providers who will be interacting with children need the following skills: knowledge about normal growth and development, avoidance of overestimating the child's level of understanding, awareness of context, careful listening and observation, avoidance of interference, empathy and respect for the child and his or her needs, and honesty to gain trust. For a more detailed review of this research, see Whaley (2000).

The Elderly

Another growing area of research in recent years has been that concerning health communication and the elderly (Moore & Proffitt, 1993; Oliver & Redfern, 1991), particularly because older adults and their families are especially susceptible to being treated in a routine, disease-focused manner (Kautzmann, 1993). Of particular concern to researchers has been the quality of interaction in nursing homes and other long-term care facilities. Caris-Verhallen, Kerkstra, and Bensing (1997) note an increasing reliance on observational studies in such contexts, but express concerns about the reliability and validity of the measuring instruments used in these studies. Their summary indicates that a great deal of inappropriate and poor communication takes place between nurses and elderly patients. Barriers that have been identified in the research include negative attitudes toward the elderly, patient visual and hearing impairment, patient stress and anxiety, and patient confusion (Moore & Proffitt, 1993). Shadden (1997), however, determined that the basic conversational skills of the normally aging are usually well preserved. In a recent study using Roter's Interaction Process Analysis system, Caris-Verhallen, Kerkstra, van der Heijden, and Bensing (1998) found increased levels of socioemotional interaction between nurses and elderly patients compared with the levels found in previous research.

Much of the research also focuses on the difficulties involved in communicating information to the elderly (for a summary of this research, see Halter, 1999), noting that the complexity of the medical problems of many elderly patients makes this task even more difficult than it is with younger patients. Majerovitz et al. (1997) report findings that support this conclusion; they note that care providers have particular difficulty in communicating with elderly patients about medications. Schommer (1994) found that older patients prefer to talk to their physicians rather than to their pharmacists about medications, although Smith, Cunningham, and Hale (1994) found that patients are more likely than physicians to initiate such discussion. Smith et al. also found that elderly patients would like more discussion of the side effects of medication, and that discussion of side effects does not discourage medication use (Smith, 1998).

Terminality

Communication in the health care setting becomes much more complicated when the patient is terminally ill, as health care providers are trained to cure patients. The avoidance that providers demonstrate when they are frustrated in their attempts to cure their patients is similar to the avoidance that the terminally ill experience from those who do not work in health care, but it is even more problematic because these patients continue to need care. Recent writings on this topic have focused on guidelines for care provider communication when the dying patient is a child (Huddleston & Alexander, 1999) and on the communicative needs of the terminally ill (Lefevre, 1992). Lefevre (1992) found wide variation between the perceived communicative competencies of trained hospice volunteers and the degree of anxiety and unease they felt when discussing death-related issues with the dying. In a qualitative study, McGrath et al. (1999) found that palliative care nurses reported much discomfort and inadequacy about communicating with the dying; these nurses articulated the following blocks to open communication: interference, denial, unrealistic optimism, resistance, collusion, and anger. The concerns expressed by care providers who have not received the special training of hospice workers and palliative care nurses are even stronger (Donaldson, 1999). In a review of the literature, McClement and Degner (1995) found that nurses identified as expert in the care of dying adults focus on the following behaviors: responding after death has occurred (creating a peaceful, dignified bedside scene for the family, supporting the realization that death has occurred, and maintaining a sense of calm and family involvement), responding to the family (in terms of information needs, allowing discussion of feelings, reducing the potential for future regret, and facilitating the transition from care to palliation), responding to anger by showing empathy and respect, responding to colleagues by providing emotional support and critical feedback, providing comfort care to reduce physical and psychological pain, and enhancing personal growth by demonstrating that the nurse has a defined, personal role in the care of the dying rather than expressing anxiety and lack of confidence. McClement and Degner also found that these nurses emphasized such behaviors as talking frankly with the terminal patient about the prognosis and his or her feelings, allowing the patient time to grieve, providing spiritual support, and avoiding nonverbal behaviors that signal despair. Wilkinson (1991) found that nurses use blocking behaviors more than 50% of the time during conversations with newly diagnosed, recurrent, and terminal cancer patients.

Training programs emphasize many of these needs (Coffman & Coffman, 1993). Noting that poor communication about illness probably causes more suffering than any other problem except unrelieved pain, Wist (1993) describes the positive results of a voluntary weekend training program for third-year medical students that uses improvisational role

plays with trained actors. Utilizing a similar simulated-patient method, Faulkner (1996) found small but significant improvements in communication skills, with a decrease in behaviors inhibiting disclosure. In particular, trained participants showed an increased reliance on open, directive questions, eliciting psychosocial concerns, and giving appropriate reassurance. Heaven and Maguire (1996) found significant improvement in psychological focus, blocking, identification of both emotional issues and the patient's biggest concern, and reliance on open questions immediately following training and at follow-up. They suggest that training programs should focus more than they have in the past on the handling of emotional concerns and on issues of self-efficacy.

Gender

Despite feminist criticisms of the paternalistic treatment women typically receive from doctors (e.g., Fisher, 1984) and concerns about women's health problems being ignored (e.g., Steingart, Packer, & Hamm, 1991), relatively little research has examined the impact of gender on provider-patient interaction. Gabbard-Alley (1995) concludes that "there is a lack of research using patient gender as a meaningful variable in health communication research" (p. 35). After reviewing the Commonwealth Fund's survey on women's health care, Kaplan et al. (1996) conclude that, compared with men, women visit more physicians and more different physicians, and women's ratings of physicians' interpersonal care are more favorable. Hall, Irish, Roter, Ehrlich, and Miller (1994b), however, conclude the opposite in regard to gender and satisfaction. They also found that female physicians were devalued, especially by male patients, and note that these "effects were not explained by patient and physician background characteristics or by measured communication during the visit" (p. 1216). In a study of family medicine physicians,

Wolfensberger (1997) found that female physicians tend to use an affiliative communicative style, whereas males are more likely to use a controlling style, and that patients had higher satisfaction with female physicians. Related research has found that female physicians are more empathic and less directive than male physicians. They also spend more time discussing lifestyle during patients' initial visits (Barnsley, Williams, Cockerill, & Tanner, 1999). Female physicians make more positive, partnership, and back-channel statements, and smile and nod more frequently than do male physicians (Hall, Irish, Roter, Ehrlich, & Miller, 1994a).

Research in this area has been most thoroughly summarized by Roter and Hall (1997), who conclude that there are gender differences in the verbal and nonverbal communicative styles of male and female physicians. Female physicians spend more time with patients, listen more attentively, and are less controlling and critical and more empathic than males. Female physicians also spend more time on preventive services and talk more. Both male and female physicians talk more to male than to female patients, although female physicians have more equal ratios of physician-to-patient talk than do males. Patients appear to tell their stories more fully to female physicians. The differences between male and female physicians are most marked during history taking.

Roter and Hall (1997) also summarize research on the impact of patient gender, noting that women ask more questions, receive less technical answers but more positive talk, express more tensions and ask for help, present fewer suggestions and opinions, and disagree less negatively than male patients. Roter and Hall note that patient gender effects are dwarfed by physician effects. Dunning and Lange (1993), who focused on dental students and their patients, found no gender differences. Interested readers should also see Roper's (1999) and Manss's (1994) discussions of the impact of gender on nurse-physician communication.

Control

Implicit in much of the research discussed above is the notion of control over the interaction. Control processes are seen as particularly important within the health care context because of the traditional paternalistic relationship between physicians and patients. Moving from a paternalistic to a consumeristic relationship necessitates a shift in numerous characteristics of the interaction (Ratzan, 1996). The paternalistic model is particularly inappropriate for chronic care and preventive health maintenance (Feldman, Ploof, & Cohen, 1999). Although some health care providers have attempted to move toward more shared control with patients, analyses of interactions indicate subtle ways in which providers' preferences tend to dominate (Gwyn & Elwyn, 1999). Observations of client-provider communication in a variety of contexts indicate the prevalence of provider dominance (e.g., Fisher, 1984; Kim, Odallo, Thuo, & Kols, 1999). Some research on interruption, however, shows that patients interrupt more frequently than do physicians, although patients interrupt with statements and physicians interrupt with questions (Irish & Hall, 1995). Similarly, Pepler and Lynch (1991) examined the behaviors of nurses in interactions with terminally ill patients and found more instances of nurses offering patients control or decision-making opportunities than any other behavior.

Several studies have applied relational coding to provider-patient interactions, although the results have not been completely consistent. O'Hair (1989) found that both physicians and patients attempted relational control maneuvers, although patients were not always successful. McNeilis and Thompson (1995) also found a substantial amount of provider dominance, but von Friederichs-Fitzwater, Callahan, Flynn, and Williams (1991) found frequent examples of neutralized symmetry rather than physician dominance. Cecil (1998) found that physicians showed more control submission and patients demonstrated greater control dominance. Cecil's results also showed more patient compliance with less physician control assertiveness and less patient control submission. Lack of physician control dominance is also associated with increased patient satisfaction (see also Cooper-Patrick et al., 1999). Other researchers have argued that "alliance building" influences patient decisions to participate in clinical trials (Ruckdeschel, Albrecht, Blanchard, & Hemmick, 1996). Patients interacting in an actively negotiated process of decision making also perceive greater feelings of control and power (Roberts, Krouse, & Michaud, 1995). That shared participation can be achieved is detailed in Smith-Dupre and Beck's (1996) analysis of how one physician self-discloses to downplay status differences and move toward a cooperative, shared relationship. Aronsson and Sätterlund-Larsson (1987) also found that physicians invited patient collaboration with open-ended "thinking-aloud" messages, although patients saw this indirectness as ambiguous. These researchers found little opportunity for patient participation after the initial extraction of information, however. Politeness norms led to vague and ambiguous talk as patients avoided challenging the physician and "lying" through omission. It has been suggested that patient noncompliance may be a way for patients to assert independence and control (Beisecker, 1990).

Individual and cultural factors influence patients' predispositions and opportunities to participate in health care interactions (Bennett, Smith, & Irwin, 1999; Brashers, Haas, & Neidig, 1999). Cooper-Patrick et al. (1999) found that patients whose races are different from those of their health care providers find that their visits are less participatory, even when age, gender, education, marital and health status, and length of relationship are controlled for. They also found that visits with female physicians are more participatory.

Patient coping style influences patient preference for participation; a monitoring style is associated with a preference for participation and detailed information and with increased patient question asking and dominance (Ong et al., 1999).

Disclosure and Truth-Telling Issues

The final decade of the 20th century witnessed a plethora of studies, in both the medical and the behavioral sciences, that addressed physician and patient disclosure issues. One explanation for this interest is that research revealed the positive effects of patient disclosure on patient outcomes. Weijts (1994) found that patients' expressions of concern about their symptoms actually reduce their concerns and that patient disclosure is positively related to patient satisfaction and to the reduction of high blood pressure in hypertensives. Other research has demonstrated that increases in psychosocial adaptation (e.g., attending school and participating in recreational activities) have been observed among heart transplant patients who disclose their feelings in concerns (Uzark et al., 1992). These results have undoubtedly contributed to interest in the phenomenon.

Legal pressures on health caregivers to satisfy the condition of informed consent have also provided impetus to the spate of research in this area. In the second edition of this *Handbook,* Thompson (1994) addressed the topic of disclosure in health communication tangentially as a subtopic within her discussion of "openness," for example. The contribution that communication scholars can make to an understanding of the barriers and facilitators to disclosure during medical interaction, however, together with medical professionals' enlarged role in this domain in association with informed consent issues, has contributed to a sustained focus on disclosure and truth-telling issues in health communication. Approximately half of the chapters in

Petronio's (2000) recent edited volume about privacy and disclosure, for example, are devoted to the topic of balancing disclosure and privacy with regard to health issues and contexts. Four chapters focus on the issue of how to balance private disclosures of HIV/AIDS in relationships, including in the health care context; another three chapters address efforts to balance private disclosures in formal health care settings.

The issues associated with disclosure during medical interaction involve both caregivers and patients. These include the patient's need to disclose sensitive information about personal practices in order to promote accurate diagnosis (Parrott, 1995) and to increase the appropriateness of the information exchanged (Parrott, Duncan, & Duggan, 2000). From the caregiver's side of the equation, it is the physician's professional responsibility to deliver bad news, ethical responsibility to discuss end-of-life (EOL) decisions, and legal responsibility to obtain informed consent. A number of patient characteristics affect caregivers' decisions to disclose to patients, including the patient's personality, anticipated reaction, age, literacy status, and sex (Mystakidou, 1996).

On the patient end of disclosure during medical interaction, patients may unintentionally fail to disclose information to health care providers about particular practices because those practices are simply part of their cultural upbringing. These acts of omission rather than commission can be illustrated by reference to such behaviors as the use of lead in folk medicine observed in some Hispanic, Arabic, South Asian, and Chinese communities and the use of lead-glazed pottery in many Mexican American households (Trotter, 1990). Beyond culture, other patient characteristics also predict how disclosive patients will be with caregivers. Women have been found to participate in medical interviews more actively than men, perhaps because "women in Western society have been given responsibility for the family's health" (Weijts, 1994, p. 261). Far

less attention has been given to the actual strategies patients use to disclose during medical interaction. An exception to the absence of empirical exploration in this arena is a study by du Pré and Beck (1997) in which they found that patients sometimes use "exaggerated self-disparagement to bid for a physician's forgiveness and reassurance" (p. 487). In this approach the patient claims disproportionate responsibility rather than disclaims responsibility, which may be a method of seeking reassurance or saving face (du Pré & Beck, 1997). Patients who are the oldest, have the least education, and have the most diminished cognitive capacity perceive involvement in decision making with physicians to be the least appropriate, according to a survey conducted by Hines, Moss, and Badzek (1997) with 142 randomly selected older dialysis patients. These patients nonetheless expect to be informed about their conditions and their treatment alternatives.

Informed Consent Issues

The legal boundaries of disclosure are the focus of study regarding informed consent. Smith (1993) asserts that the ethical dilemma during medical interaction lies in the reality that health care providers tend to express information in general and abstract terms, although their patients' experiences are specific and concrete. In one intervention designed to improve the informed consent practices of caregivers concerning prenatal testing, for example, Smith, Shaw, Slack, and Marteau (1995) used small group discussion focused around a video; the members of one group received individual feedback on their baseline behavior, whereas those in another group did not. Posttraining consultations with 26 midwives and 9 obstetricians revealed that, although training without feedback improved communication and some information giving, training with feedback on performance showed the greatest improvements. The researchers assessed communication by counting the number of open and closed questions used and by evaluating the explanations the participants gave for the technical terms they used; they also evaluated the participants' success in introducing fetal abnormality screening as a general topic, followed by efforts to gain a woman's self-disclosure about her attitude toward screening. An example of the more specific and concrete information provided after training is, "The results will be available in a week to 10 days," compared with a preintervention illustration, "If the test is abnormal we'll call you" (D. K. Smith et al., 1995, p. 321).

One variable predicting the likelihood that providers will disclose information to patients is physician uncertainty. Uncertainty may be based in physicians' lack of understanding of medical knowledge, including an inability to understand probability assessment, or the very real limitations of extant medical knowledge (Rizzo, 1993). For example, no well-controlled empirical studies have been conducted to assess the psychosocial impact of being a pediatric bone marrow donor (Weisz & Robbennolt, 1996), so, in the absence of knowledge, health care providers cannot disclose information to potential donors. Physicians may have difficulty in distinguishing between limitations in extant medical knowledge and limitations in their own understanding. As a result, they may feel uncertain due to the reality that the knowledge base in a specific area is uncertain, but they may attribute their uncertainty to limitations in their own understanding. In either case, physicians are unlikely to disclose their own uncertainty (Rizzo, 1993).

Patient advocates assert that the act of informing patients necessitates the assurance that access to all the information needed to make an informed decision has been guaranteed (Crockford, Holloway, & Walker, 1993). Thus disclosure begets informed decision making, which begets informed choice, which begets informed consent. However, several researchers have observed an unfortunate disjunction between what patients and nurses, compared with physicians, regard as important qualities of care with regard to informed consent issues. One study of 84 breast cancer patients, 64 doctors, and 140 nurses and nurse oncologists, for example, found that patients and nurses rated consistent information, involvement in preparation, and assistance to patients in coping with breast cancer treatment as far more important than doctors did (Schofield, Walkom, Ethics, & Sanson-Fisher, 1997). In another study, Hines, Badzek, and Moss (1997) interviewed 142 elderly hemodialysis patients to assess their informed consent status before dialysis and found that most were not informed, with patients' education level, cognitive capacity, and willingness to discuss medical contingencies being the strongest predictors of informed consent. The researchers note: "Obtaining written authorization from patients before treatment is now standard medical practice. However, the validity of the authorization depends on the nature of the doctor's disclosure, the level of patient understanding, and the assurance that the patient is allowed to make a truly voluntary choice" (p. 153). Lack of being adequately informed contributed to patients' thinking that they would eventually get better and be able to stop treatment, with only 65% knowing the cause of their own kidney failure and almost none understanding the risks of hemodialysis.

Some have argued that the meaning of *informed consent* should be enlarged to include not only information about procedures but public disclosure about practice profiles. Kluge (1999) asserts that open files promote an atmosphere of openness and mutual trust, and should include information about physicians' education, awards, and successful malpractice suits, as "patients have a moral right to seek out the physicians of their choice. However, patients cannot make an informed choice if they know nothing about a prospective physician beyond the fact that this person completed a medical degree" (p. 1321).

Providing a framework for understanding the relative merits of disclosure during medical interaction, Thomasma (1994) asserts that, although truth is important to human communication in general, truth telling has relative value, and truth is told in relationships because "it is a right, a utility, and a kindness" (p. 375). The different types of truth that Thomasma describes include (a) straightforward or direct truth, which answers interrogatory questions; (b) factual truth, which refers to objective realities; (c) personal truth, which requires a speaker to tell about an interior reality; and (d) interpretive truth, which represents a responder's effort to interpret the real reasons an individual makes an inquiry. These types of truth telling are reflected in health caregivers' informed consent disclosure practices. Deering (1999) argues that some valid reasons for physicians to disclose include educating clients, showing them that their experiences are not unusual, facilitating emotional catharsis, and expressing positive feelings to convey support. Situations in which Deering deems disclosure to be less appropriate include those times when a client asks whether the doctor thinks the client will respond well to a treatment. In this situation, Deering recommends more indirect responses, with equivocation illustrated through use of verbal strategies such as "Different things work for different patients."

The duration of the relationship between a medical provider and patient has been found to contribute to a provider's truth telling, affecting the realm of informed consent. According to Thomasma (1994):

> Over a longer period, the truth may be withheld for compassionate reasons more readily. Here, the patient and physician or nurse know one another. They are more likely to have shared some of their values. In this context, it is more justifiable to withhold the truth temporarily in favor of more important long-term values, which are known in the relationship. (pp. 378-379)

Length of relationship also affects patient disclosure, especially with regard to psychosocial issues beyond the experience of somatic symptoms. In one study of 308 adult patients, Robinson and Roter (1999) found that patients' disclosure of psychosocial problems to physicians was more likely to occur when the patients were more familiar with the physicians, as well as in response to physician inquiries.

To increase patients' disclosure, which may guide physicians' understanding about the appropriate content patients need to make informed decisions, Ashworth, Longmate, and Morrison (1992) encourage physicians to avoid asking standard lists of questions and instead attend to areas of mutual knowledge, giving emotional support to the patients' concerns. Additionally, some physicians have indicated that the inappropriateness of particular interaction settings has prevented them from fully informing some patients about issues regarding their health status (Fallowfield, 1997; Gostin, 1995; Mitsuya, 1997). The use of team treatment as well as the use of patients as models in teaching, and even the computerization of health information, may contribute to patients' reticence when it comes to disclosure of health information (Coleman & Shellow, 1995). Confidentiality in medicine has long been regarded as a priority and aim, but patients may not trust or understand the mechanisms in place to safeguard their private information (Parrott et al., 2000), and this can compromise the informed consent process. Perhaps most consistently, however, the topic of disclosure has been found to contribute to caregivers' disclosure practices, with end-of-life discussions proving to be particularly problematic.

End-of-Life Discussions

Terminality is one of the reasons physicians cite most often when explaining their decisions to withhold information from patients. Several studies in the medical literature provide evidence of the difficulty associated with physician disclosure about terminal illness. Patients have been found to prefer that EOL talks occur earlier and with greater honesty than doctors perceive their patients to want. Pfeifer et al. (1994) talked with 47 ambulatory patients (of whom 30% had been given a prognosis of less than 18 months by doctors; 30% of the interviewees were nonwhite, and 30% were over the age of 60) and 43 primary care doctors. They note: "Patients spoke clearly of their desire for honest discussions early in their medical course, a point of personally determined medical futility, and of a peaceful acceptance of eventual death" (p. 86). These results emphasize patients' desires to control the right to decide when to discontinue the use of medical systems as disease progresses, a right best protected through conversations about advance directives. In another study by Johnston, Pfeifer, and McNutt (1995) involving 329 outpatients, 282 resident physicians, and 272 practicing physicians, the findings revealed that the patients felt discussion about advance directives should occur earlier than did the physicians. Johnston et al. also found that the patients wanted to engage in these conversations at an earlier age, earlier in the natural history of disease, and earlier in their relationships, although most believed that it is the physician's responsibility to initiate these discussions. In order of priority, the participants said that the content of these conversations should consist of "description of life-sustaining treatments, the patient's health at the time of the discussion, the chance of surviving, the probability of full recovery, and the effects of life-sustaining treatment on the patient's family" (p. 1028).

Discussion of terminality causes physicians to confront "personal fear of illness and death" (Mystakidou, 1996, p. 198). Uncertainty also has been found to contribute to physicians' reluctance to discuss advance directives, with lack of knowledge emerging as a significant barrier to initiating these discussions (Morrison, Morrison, & Glickman, 1994). Certain patient characteristics, such as cultural background, present challenges to physicians' efforts to initiate such discussion as well. For example, Hepburn and Reed (1995) observe that among Native Americans—a group that comprises 535 tribes, 300 distinct languages, and 1.5 million people—a nonlinear pattern of organization, high values placed on strong autonomy and indirect communication, and suspicion of authority can create great barriers to physicians' obtaining advance directives before life-threatening events occur.

Although many physicians find disclosure difficult and challenging with regard to EOL decisions, training programs in communication associated with bad news delivery have been found to increase physician performance in this sensitive matter (Vaidya, Greenberg, Patel, Strauss, & Pollack, 1999). "Do not resuscitate" (DNR) decisions are the focus of Rusin's (1992) checklist for physicians' conversations with families of rehabilitation patients, which includes a preparation stage in which the physician is advised to assess his or her own level of comfort in discussing DNR in the particular case. Other items on the checklist include the need to assess the laws regarding advance directives and substituted judgment that apply in the case, to consider whether the patient is competent, and to find out whether the patient has a living will, other advance directive, or a legally authorized proxy. Rusin also emphasizes the importance of the physician's having a conversation with the proxy to determine the proxy's feelings as well as the level of the proxy's knowledge of the patient's wishes, understanding about the patient's medical situation, and awareness of what CPR involves and the outcome to be expected if it is administered.

Other research has supported the finding that patients' designated proxies often lack knowledge about the patients' advance directives and specific wishes, and that this impedes EOL decisions. Holley et al. (1999) conclude that withdrawal from dialysis is quite common but rarely discussed in advance care planning by dialysis patients. Patients with advance directives were more likely to have told their decision makers of their roles, but most had not discussed their wishes for specific interventions. In fact, Weiler, Eland, and Buckwalter (1996) found that one of three major factors contributing to failure to follow a living will is lack of information that it even exists. The other two most common contributors are family request that the living will be violated and the treating physician's refusal to honor the living will. In a survey of 2,697 nurses, Weiler et al. found that the medical record is the primary means to communicate about a living will, with some proposing that "it is a nursing responsibility to suggest to patients that they talk with family members or friends about what health care the patient wants if the patient is not able to participate in health care decisions" (p. 248)—a statement with which 72% of the nurses surveyed agreed.

One training model for improving graduate medical residents' communication skills in EOL discussions with patients emphasizes the provider's identifying his or her own personal feelings about death, role play, discussion of ethical and legal points, and the importance of working with patients and families (McCann et al., 1998). This approach reflects Steinmetz, Walsh, Gabel, and Williams's (1993) findings from their in-depth interviews of 28 family physicians; the physicians interviewed emphasized the importance of physicians' discussing dying patients in a support group, so that they can deal with their own professional and personal feelings as well as the needs of their patients and the patients' families. Ray (1996) discusses the importance of physicians' nonverbal communication during EOL discussions, offering a number of strategies that physicians can use to empower dying patients. These include watching how one stands, positioning one's head lower than the patient's head, being respectful and not too relaxed, putting away the pen, ending sentences on a positive point, avoiding too much touch, and recognizing the patient's and the patient's family's abilities and strengths.

Bad News Delivery

Terminality is one domain in which physician disclosure is difficult, but the realm of bad news delivery includes other sensitive subjects as well. In addition to EOL discussions, physicians report discomfort during disclosure when they have to talk with patients about serious health problems or about future health problems (Hines, Badzek, Leslie, & Glover, 1998). In a study with 84 breast cancer patients, 64 oncologists, and 140 oncology nurses who rated the importance of telling the patient a diagnosis as soon as it is certain, physicians ranked disclosure of this information as seventh among 12 goals, whereas patients ranked it as fourth and nurses ranked it first, tied with disclosure of information about the patient's legal and moral rights (Girgis, Sanson-Fisher, & Schofield, 1999). Variables that may contribute to the difficulty physicians have in breaking bad news have been found to include fear of hurting or upsetting the receiver and discomfort caused by being with those distressed by hearing bad news (Franks, 1997). Unstructured discussion produces more discomfort for providers than does structured talk (Hines et al., 1998). Caregivers' discomfort with conversations in these realms and their failure to disclose important information may contribute both to patients' failure to follow through with treatment or prevention recommendations and to patients' own hesitation to disclose personal information. One survey of 540 home health care nurses, for example, found that the more comfortable a nurse was in discussing serious illness, the more he or she communicated about patients' treatment preferences, leading to greater opportunities to learn patients' preferences (Hines et al., 1998).

Research that has considered the impact of prognosis of illness as a variable on physicians' disclosure suggests some differences between what physicians perceive they would ideally do versus what they may actually do. When presented with scenarios and asked how they would respond, physicians selected lying over equivocation or concealment only for child patients with acute illness (Robinson, Shepherd, & Heywood, 1998). This finding parallels the findings of other research in which physicians have asserted that they may withhold information in order to keep hope alive for the patient (Orona, Koenig, & Davis, 1994). Further support for this position is reflected in the fact that disclosure to cancer patients has been found to be controversial, both in the United States and in other nations. In one study of 228 Greek doctors randomly selected from records of the Greek Oncology Society, Mystakidou (1996) found that 11% disclosed the diagnosis of cancer to all patients, 78% communicated the diagnosis to some, and 11% communicated the diagnosis to none.

Patients' characteristics sometimes predict caregivers' disclosure patterns with regard to bad news delivery. In one study of seven U.S. cancer patients and their families followed over the course of 4 months, physicians' disclosure patterns revealed that different cultural expectations guided the physicians' practices. Two of the patients were of Chinese descent, three were Latino, and two were European American. The patients' family members sometimes worked with providers to keep the patients from "knowing too much" (Orona et al., 1994, p. 342). The reasons given for such

nondisclosure varied from explanations associated with the patient's well-being, such as that the disclosure would invite distress, to cultural norms, including that it is not polite, and may even be bad luck, to speak openly about death. In some instances, however, it is difficult to explain disclosure patterns directly as a result of patients' cultural expectations and preferences. Rather, research suggests that patients' cultural backgrounds present another source of discomfort for physicians. One study of 57 AIDS patients and their primary caregivers, for example, found that African American and Hispanic patients were less likely than non-Hispanic white patients to have communicated in depth with their physicians (Curtis, Patrick, Caldwell, Greenlee, & Collier, 1999). This finding did not relate to any expression of a desire for less communication on the part of the patients or their family members.

Like many of the studies discussed above concerning communication training, much of the literature regarding bad news delivery by health care providers describes programs designed to teach particular approaches, often without offering any evaluation of the efficacy of these methods. For example, Marrow (1996) encourages emergency department staff who must notify family members of a death to use nonverbal displays of comfort and compassion, such as a touch on the hand or arm, while being ready to disclose information about the legalities associated with the death, including organ transplantation. Green (1997) gives health care providers 12 tips on how to deliver tragic news with compassion; these include starting with an introduction that reveals that the news is unpleasant, speaking slowly and pausing after each sentence, using the patient's name (rather than referring to "the body"), offering a brief explanation of what happened, and encouraging questions. Franks (1997) also encourages providers to seek questions from those to whom they must deliver bad news; she suggests in addition that providers should make sure they take ample time for these conversations and that they are familiar with all the available information. R. M. Leash (1996), director of the Continuity of Care Department within Kaiser Permanente Medical Center's Medical Social Services Department, has facilitated notification of family members in more than 2,000 unanticipated deaths and has contributed to the development of guidelines for locating and notifying next of kin. These include specific advice about how to talk with family members—on the phone or in person—emphasizing the need to provide verbal support, and, when notifying someone to come to the hospital over the phone, encouraging them to bring someone along because they may be there for a while. Bowers (1999) offers the following regarding the delivery of bad news: "One of the most important things for the clinician to understand is what experts call the patient's and family's 'loss history'" (p. 3). Important things to know about a family's loss history include whether someone in the family has ever witnessed the sudden death of a loved one due to trauma; whether the family has ever experienced the lingering, painful death of a family member; and whether anyone in the family has personally experienced a life-altering illness, such as diabetes.

Sutton (1998) used the words of actor-simulators from more than 100 interviews in which health care professionals were trained to deliver bad news, so that the actors who played patients' relatives could reflect on feelings. Sutton found that doctors delivered information, whereas nurses provided sympathy:

> Too often the relative was asked if he understood, or was all right, but no space was left for the answer. Leaving space is important. Leaving space for the open expression of grief is most important. Discourse need not be framed verbally. Silence is a discourse. Weeping is a discourse. So what are the carers to say? One of the best said: "Go ahead and cry—it's O.K." The relative's grief was respected. Space was provided. (p. 625)

In the pediatric intensive care domain, Vaidya et al. (1999) utilized standardized patients in a one-day workshop to teach pediatric intensive care fellows how to communicate bad news to parents. Results demonstrated short-term improvement, with an increase in the accuracy of communication as well as displays of compassion and caring. Medical students trained to give bad news improved their humanistic skills in the delivery of bad news but showed no change from the old method for knowledge about bad news; the humanistic skills they displayed included introducing themselves to patients, using words the patients could understand, asking questions without acting judgmental, nonverbal cues of listening, and empathy displays (Vetto, Elder, Toffler, & Fields, 1999). Gillotti et al. (2002) have also reported a study of communicative competence in bad news delivery.

Health Promotion Issues

There is compelling evidence that members of the lay public depend on their primary caregivers as significant sources of health promotion. Although health campaigns have long been considered a health promotion strategy (Parrott, Egbert, Anderton, & Sefcovic, 2002), less emphasis has been given to the impact of face-to-face interactions with health caregivers on primary and secondary prevention. Pediatricians, almost by definition, maintain significant responsibilities in association with health promotion, with discussion about child safety constituting a significant component of well child exams. Other arenas of caregiving have less often been identified with health promotion. By the final decade of the 20th century, with the shift in emphasis in health care from acute care to chronic care and prevention, an emphasis on research concerning physicians' health promotion efforts was warranted. With regard to patients, for example, Price, Desmond, and Losh (1991) found in a survey of 382 patients that 70% believed doctors should counsel women about Pap smears and breast self-exams and should counsel smokers about smoking cessation. A little more than 40% believed family physicians should teach sex education to teens and discuss social support systems and home safety issues, and a little less than one-third believed it is appropriate for doctors to discuss financial problems or seat belt use. With regard to practitioners, Mullen and Holcomb (1990) surveyed 90 dental examiners, 262 registered dieticians, and 143 certified nurse midwives about their counseling practices for health promotion and disease prevention. They found that most counseling concerned high blood pressure and patients being overweight, followed by smoking, lack of exercise, and high-fat diets; seat belt use received the lowest score. These providers felt the most confident about their abilities to promote prevention with regard to patients being overweight, blood pressure, and smoking; their lowest self-efficacy scores for promotion were related to illicit drug use and isolation and loneliness.

Health care professionals are seen as preferred and credible sources of information for topics as varied as skin cancer (Parrott, Steiner, & Goldenhar, 1996), lead in tap water (Griffin & Dunwoody, 2000), and contraception and sexually transmitted diseases (Krishnan, 1996). With regard to secondary prevention, women have been found to be more likely to receive mammograms if physicians recommend that they do and the women perceive the physicians as being enthusiastic about promoting the screening test (Mickey, Luc Vezina, Worden, & Warner, 1997). As Rabinowitz, Beckman, Morse, and Naumburg (1994) observe, "Preventive health care has become a core function of primary care practice" (p. 20). The areas in which caregivers might provide health promotion counseling are vast, perhaps explaining the seeming reluctance on the part of some practitioners to discuss health promotion activities beyond the scope of a particular medical appointment. The time allocated to medical appointments is limited, and no research has yet focused on how physicians might place boundaries on discussions about prevention during appointments. Additionally, some caregivers may harbor appropriate concerns that their health promotion efforts could do more harm than good. This dilemma is illustrated by findings such as those in a study of patients' psychosocial adjustment following myocardial infarction, which revealed that when patients comprehend what the event means to their future, they are likely to consider the causes and experience subsequent feelings of guilt, with health caregivers "contributing to these feelings by 'interrogating' them about risk factors with an attitude of 'finger pointing,' making them feel they had done something wrong" (Malan, 1992, p. 62). Despite this dilemma, the recognition of the important role health caregivers may play in promoting changes in lifestyle has contributed to an increased focus on this issue over the past decade.

Patrick (1998) asserts, "Whether we are public health officers, occupational medicine specialists, managed care program administrators, primary care clinicians, or in any other role in which prevention must be accomplished, effective communication of information to—and from—those we serve is essential" (p. 46). With this emphasis have come some efforts to apply behavioral theory and research, including constructs from such models as the health belief model, to medical interaction and guidelines for health promotion. Arborelius (1996) recommends that the caregiver assess the patient's readiness to change, for example, and highlight the patient's health beliefs while encouraging the patient to reflect and decide on behavior. She further advises caregivers to present knowledge as neutral facts, not evaluations; to focus on actual behavior rather than information giving; and to discuss both the advantages and disadvantages of patients' experiences with lifestyle change efforts. The arena for caregivers' health promotion efforts is vast, but particular emphasis has been placed on efforts to address alcohol and tobacco use, given that these two legal drugs have wide-ranging impacts on health outcomes. Additionally, with the advent of HIV/AIDS, the medical interview has evolved to encompass questions regarding sexual history, and caregivers have increased their efforts to promote awareness about sexual practices and disease.

Alcohol Use

Questions about alcohol use are found on some medical history-taking forms. Patients may be asked whether they use alcohol and, if so, to describe their average weekly consumption rate. This provides one avenue for physicians to obtain general information about a patient's alcohol consumption, information that might be used as a springboard for discussion about health outcomes associated with alcohol use and strategies to reduce use. However, as Arborelius and Thakker (1995) found in interviews with 13 general practitioners, physicians often avoid initiating discussions about alcohol use with patients, especially discussions of excessive alcohol consumption, because of insufficient time and a fear of spoiling the relationship with a patient. Some practitioners have a condemning attitude toward excessive drinkers, asserting that "they just lie and deny" (p. 421). Other researchers affirm the difficulty associated with these discussions; Lamping (1995) states that "telling patients the diagnosis of addiction and motivating them to treatment is one of the greatest challenges physicians can face" (p. 460). Strategies to reduce the impediments to initiating these conversations emphasize, once more, the significance of uncertainty as a barrier to interaction in health care settings. Lamping notes that physicians' familiarity with "the modalities of available treatment and the prognosis with treatment" (p. 461) increases the success of such interactions.

The available evidence provides a compelling argument for both continued research into the effects and effectiveness of caregivers' health promotion efforts in the arena of alcohol use and the encouragement of such promotion efforts. In a longitudinal project that considered the responses of 395 alcoholics (from an original sample of 628; a 63% follow-up rate), Humphreys, Moos, and Cohen (1997) found that "individuals' motivation to change is shaped by the interactions they have with those who are trying to help them" (p. 237). In particular, outpatient treatment sessions attended in the first 3 years predicted a good outcome at 8 years; attendance at Alcoholics Anonymous meetings in the first 3 years was also a significant predictor. Inpatient treatment and attendance at religious services did not predict good outcomes. Interactions with caregivers in outpatient settings provide one avenue for promoting attendance at AA meetings. The range of available reinforcement strategies that caregivers may utilize in promoting lifestyle and behavior changes in association with alcohol consumption may be as broad as the spectrum of health communication activities, affording great opportunity and promise for future research in this area.

Tobacco Use

Early in the 1990s, Richards (1992) noted that "little attention has been paid to how the physician should approach the subject of smoking cessation" (p. 687). The personal, social, and financial effects of smoking reach beyond smokers, necessitating conversations about the effects of smoking on others aside from the smokers. Bellet (1994), for example, discusses strategies for caregivers who must talk with the smoking parents of a child with a reactive airway disease. He considers two approaches: a more paternalistic strategy in which the caregiver tells the parents that smoking makes their child wheeze, so they should stop, versus a more empathic strategy in which the caregiver tries to understand the parents, involving them in making decisions for the sake of their child's health. A direct comparison of the efficacy of these strategies remains for future study.

Richards (1992) draws a striking contrast between what caregivers tend to say to their patients about smoking and what they say about other conditions, asserting: "If the patient with a UTI came back in a few weeks with continued symptoms, the physician would not say, 'Gosh, I'm sorry but we tried an antibiotic and it didn't work. I guess you'll have to suffer until you get better on your own or get pyelonephritis, sepsis, and die'" (p. 687). Richards recommends that clinicians ask, "Do you use tobacco?" as part of taking vital signs on every visit. He even suggests that determining what brand of cigarettes a patient smokes can provide the health care professional with an idea about the motive behind the patient's smoking; for example, the brand Virginia Slims tends to be associated with a fashion image. Richards advances concrete approaches to negotiating smoking cessation, including asking a patient whether he or she has set a quit date or is willing to sign a contract to commit to becoming a nonsmoker. Richards also provides verbal strategies that health care professionals might use in response to patient blockers. For instance, when a patient says, "I've tried everything and I just can't stop smoking," the physician might ask, "What exactly have you tried? I'd like to write these down here in your chart" (p. 689).

Beyond primary care physicians, nurses have increased their health promotion activities as well. Nurses have been encouraged in recent years to assess patients' smoking status and readiness to quit at each medical visit (Gallagher & Holm, 1996). One program in New Zealand targeting dentists, hygienists, and therapists involved a training course to raise awareness of the importance of smoking-cessation counseling, contributing to caregivers'

increasingly active role in cessation efforts, including advising smokers to quit and assisting patients with quit strategies (Skegg, 1999). Dentists and dental hygienists may be particularly effective in promoting cessation efforts, because they can refer with authority to the effects of smoking on the appearance of a patient's teeth and gums. The effects and effectiveness of such strategies remain an unexplored dimension of patient care.

Sexuality Issues

Beyond alcohol and tobacco use, a third arena with impacts not limited to an individual's health or a single event or disease, HIV/AIDS, has contributed to increased emphasis on caregivers' efforts to communicate about sexuality issues. Research continues to show that patients lack understanding about the reproductive process and birth control, supporting recommendations that greater emphasis should be placed on improving practitioners' communication skills regarding sexuality issues (O'Connell, 1997). Improved communication may contribute to reductions in transmission of HIV and fewer unintended pregnancies (Schuster, Bell, Petersen, & Kanouse, 1996). In addition, discussions about sexuality should not be limited to efforts concerning the negative health outcomes associated with sexual practices. Interestingly, research has shown that for patients who have coronary artery disease, health care providers' reassurances regarding the patients' sexuality and encouragement to be sexually active can prevent depression and negative coping (Rankin, 1992).

OUTCOMES OF PROVIDER-PATIENT INTERACTION

The site of medical interaction has become a focal point for research and theorizing most prominently because of the outcomes associated with communication in medical settings. One trend that has been observed in health care settings where physicians communicate less than optimally is an increase in malpractice litigation. Data reveal that "although about 1% of hospitalized patients develop a significant injury related to negligence, less than 3% of them decide to sue their caregivers" (Cole, 1997, p. 649). In one review of malpractice depositions, 71% of claims were found to be related to doctor-patient communication (Beckman, Markakis, Suchman, & Frankel, 1994). Specific assertions were that the physician failed to understand a patient or family perspective (13%), that the physician abandoned the patient (32%), that the physician devalued the patient or family view (29%), and that the physician delivered information poorly (26%). In short, when patients feel ignored, they sue (Fielding, 1997), a finding that contributes to the addition of professional education courses on the topic of patient relations. Southern California Permanente Medical Group, for example, has implemented training intended to contribute both to a reduction in malpractice and to doctors feeling less irritated by patients' communication (Grandinetti, 1996). One summary of the physician behaviors that differentiate between patients who sue and those who do not has identified several specific physician actions associated with patient decisions not to sue. These include the physicians' use of more statements of orientation to educate patients about what to expect, more laughter and humor, more facilitation to solicit patients' opinions, and more efforts to check understanding and encourage patients to talk (Levinson, Roter, Mullooly, Dull, & Frankel, 1997). These same behaviors have been found to relate to numerous other outcomes in health care settings as well, long before they were ever related to decisions to pursue, or not pursue, legal settlements.

One of the most comprehensive presentations of the effects of communication in health care settings has been advanced by Kreps, O'Hair, and Clowers (1994), whose transformation model of communication and health identifies the outcomes as broadly fitting within three domains: cognitive, behavioral, and physiological. Although the majority of studies that include communication as a variable with regard to health outcomes address compliance and/or satisfaction, we organize our discussion here around Kreps et al.'s framework. Moreover, most of the research that examines the impact of communication on health outcomes evaluates patients, but we note those studies that examine the effects for communication on outcomes associated with caregivers.

Cognitive Outcomes

The cognitive outcomes identified in the transformation model of communication and health include understanding and knowledge, diagnostic information, a commitment to health, an adjustment of health beliefs, confidence, satisfaction and trust, self-efficacy, managed expectations, fears, and anxieties (Kreps et al., 1994). Lack of basic drug knowledge, for example, contributes to misuse of medication (Ryan & Jacques, 1997), illustrating the importance of patient understanding and knowledge. Diagnostic information contributes to patients' ability to cope with physical impairments, manage pain, and maintain greater self-sufficiency (Holman & Lorig, 1992). A commitment to health may intuitively seem to be a value underlying human existence. Some research, however, indicates that individuals from different cultural backgrounds or experiences in health care systems outside the United States may benefit from caregivers' discussions about the role patients play in their own personal health (Lantz, Dupuis, Reding, Krauska, & Lappe, 1994). Caregiver-patient conversations about these issues may contribute to changes in patients' health beliefs as a precursor to behavior affecting health, and they may build confidence in caregivers as well. Patients' confidence in the medical advice they receive has been found to be related to the patients' perceptions of their physicians' credibility, and physicians can enhance those perceptions through the cues they provide to patients in educational materials (Jackson, 1994).

By far, the greatest number of studies within the realm of cognitive outcomes have considered the effects of caregiver communication on patient satisfaction. The study of patient satisfaction over the past decade has at times reflected an assumed relationship between communication and satisfaction. Wellwood, Dennis, and Warlow (1995), for example, assert that "efforts to improve communication, discharge planning and follow-up, aimed at carers as well as the patients themselves, are likely to be rewarded with improved satisfaction with stroke services" (p. 519). Thus, although there has been no direct test of this relationship, the assumed positive relationship between good communication and patient satisfaction directs the allocation of resources and decision making in numerous health care organizations, even contributing to assessments of physicians' attending privileges. Danville-based Penn State Geisinger Health Plan, for example, served approximately 265,000 members in 1999 and measured patient satisfaction using a mail-in questionnaire. Physicians who were deemed to need improvement received coaching; they were given specific recommendations about what to focus on, and communication was highlighted in a two-day workshop "designed to improve communication skills" (Zablocki, 1999, p. 24).

Patient satisfaction is a multifaceted construct. Koehler, Fottler, and Swan's (1992) description of patient satisfaction, for example, encompasses evaluations of quality, access, and cost. Physician communication is believed to have the most direct impact on patient assessments of the quality of care, and patients' evaluations are often suggestive of the impact of communication on other cognitive outcomes, such as understanding and knowledge, diagnostic information, and health beliefs. Continuity of care has been found to be significantly related to satisfaction in a study of diabetics, with the first consultation contributing most importantly to building the relationship, the second meeting to discussion of treatment, and the third interaction to assessing psychosocial issues (van Dulmen, Verhaak, & Bilo, 1997). When physicians involve patients more in the discussion of psychosocial issues during medical interviews, offering greater emotional support to patients and including the patients' families, increased patient satisfaction has been observed (Marvel et al., 1998). Another physician behavior linked to patients' satisfaction is listening; Buck, Jacoby, Baker, Graham-Jones, and Chadwick (1996) found that epileptic patients rated such interpersonal skills as the most important factor affecting their satisfaction. Frankel (1995) notes that "among the most frequently cited findings in the literature on doctor-patient communication is the linkage between empathy and support, and patient satisfaction" (p. 167). Similar results have been found for nurses, with empathy and use of human touch (Perry, 1994) contributing to patient satisfaction.

In a review of the relationship between doctor-patient communication and satisfaction, Williams, Weinman, and Dale (1998) found consistent support for the positive impact on satisfaction of physicians' provision of general information, friendliness, courteous behavior, social conversation, encouragement, and empathic behavior, together with partnership building. Physician behaviors that they found to be inconsistently related to satisfaction include talk about a patient's history, anger or disagreement, and a negative tone. The caregiver verbal behaviors that Williams et al. found to be associated most consistently with patient satisfaction in general practice settings include information provision and seeking by both the doctor and/or the patient. Street,

Gold, and McDowell (1994) found that the issues that appear to influence patient satisfaction with regard to information seeking include physicians' questions about patients' perceptions of general health and such matters as pain or role limitations. Physicians may assume that patients will provide such information without the physicians' having to ask, but the social powers that physicians possess may contribute to patients' reticence to give or seek information (Lieberman, 1996), as we have noted above in our discussion of disclosure. Elderly patients have been found to be more satisfied when physician questions and support focus on topics raised by the patients, when physicians use questions worded in the negative (e.g., "No chest pain?"), and when physicians share laughter with patients (Greene et al., 1994).

Some scholars have noted the failure of most research to date to consider sex and gender as predictors of patients' views on satisfaction. Ellingson and Buzzanell (1999) found that women's narratives about breast cancer treatment revealed that respect, caring, and reassurance about the caregiver's expertise were prominent in predicting patients' satisfaction, suggesting once more how a positive impact on one cognitive outcome—in this case perceptions of credibility—may affect other evaluations as well. Physician satisfaction has also been linked to communication between doctors and patients; Koehler et al. (1992) found that physicians' negative affective response to their practice experience was related to the degree to which their actual experience failed to match their expectations. Several limitations have been identified in relation to patient satisfaction research, however, including the use of the Bales system for interaction analysis, which requires units to be categorized into 1 of 12 mutually exclusive categories (Williams et al., 1998). One verbal unit may function both to provide information and to give a suggestion (Bales, 1970), but the system's requirement that the verbal act be placed in only one of the two categories limits the conclusions that can be drawn.

The perception of self-efficacy is another cognitive outcome that has been emphasized in a growing number of studies focused on the importance of communication in health care. Women's knowledge about breast cancer symptoms, causes, and screening practices, for example, has a significant impact on women's confidence in their ability to perform breast self-exams (Carpenter & Colwell, 1995). Patients have also been found to be less affected by pain, anxiety, and depression when they have greater confidence in their ability to adapt to their health conditions (e.g., Beckman et al., 1994). Strategies used to increase the efficacy of physicians' communication with cancer patients have included the design and evaluation of pretreatment consultations by oncologists with patients an hour or two before the patients receive chemotherapy. Rutter, Iconomous, and Quine (1996) found that in a pretreatment program in which oncologists participated in a training workshop and provided patients with information booklets about the therapy they were to receive, patients reported less anxiety and depression (Rutter, Iconomous, & Quine, 1996). A reduction in patient anxiety has been observed in dental settings as well, where comforting messages have been found to lessen patients' treatment anxiety and indirectly increase positive perceptions of the providers' competence (Hamilton, Rouse, & Rouse, 1994). Physicians' perceptions of self-efficacy have also emerged as important in the practice setting, predicting the likelihood that caregivers will even broach prevention and health promotion topics with patients. Although physicians have been found to feel confident about their abilities to counsel with regard to healthy habits, they also report that they lack confidence that their patients will adopt the recommended practices (Hyman, Maibach, Flora, & Fortmann, 1992). This is a frequently cited concern within the realm of behavioral outcomes associated with communication in the health care setting.

Behavioral Outcomes

Behavioral outcomes found to be associated with communication include patients' compliance with treatment regimens, adoption of prevention/health promoting behaviors, communication competence, team/partnership building, relational quality, and assertiveness/motivation (Kreps et al., 1994). Although failure to comply with treatment recommendations has often been attributed to physicians' failure to communicate, a shift to valuing patient involvement in health care has begun to place responsibility on both patients and caregivers (Weijts, 1994). There is, in fact, some debate in the literature about the meaning attributed to the use of the word *compliance;* Perkins and Repper (1999) argue that compliance "is predicated on the assumption that the doctor is always right and the patient is wrong, unless they do what the doctor says. Such a perspective is entirely incompatible with the concept of choice: a person having access to the range of information they require in order to make their own decisions about their lives" (p. 127). They note that those who hold this view prefer to use the term *cooperation,* to emphasize both the alliance between caregiver and patient and the patient's decision making based on informed choice. Although most patient compliance is voluntary, the case of mental health reveals the tension associated with use of the term, as "the 1983 Mental Health Act has allowed forced treatment within psychiatric hospitals" (Perkins & Repper, 1999, p. 118). We have found that in the literature of the past several years, scholars have tended to use the terms *compliance, adherence,* and *cooperation* interchangeably. Thus, as our focus is on understanding to be gained from a review of this literature, we use these terms interchangeably as well.

Patient compliance has been identified as one outcome of patient satisfaction (Koehler et al., 1992), revealing how communication becomes indirectly related to behavioral health outcomes. To increase patient compliance with a medication regimen, caregivers have been advised to simplify the regimen and seek patient participation, leading the patient to become "a partner in the delivery of health care" (Strand, 1994, p. 53). Pharmacists are becoming increasingly involved with patient education in tandem with improving patient compliance, making it "imperative that they develop the necessary communication skills" (Fisher, 1992, p. 270). These skills have been consistently associated with simplifying medical routines, a finding maintained across more than a decade and varied contexts, including home health care, where complicated or tedious routines are less likely to be followed (Robinson, 1987).

Research has shown that some of the same variables that affect patient satisfaction also affect compliance; for example, empathy has consistently been found to be related "most strongly to adherence" (Frankel, 1995, p. 168). Among the patient characteristics that affect compliance is the patient's age; as Ryan and Jacques (1997) note, "Compliance with a drug regime is often a major problem among older people, particularly among those who live alone, are confused, have poor vision, impaired manual dexterity, or a failing memory" (p. 16). Elderly patients' adherence to medication regimens is affected by several factors, including the number of medications, their cost, the patient's insurance coverage, and the drug and dosage form, as well as communication with physicians, with the latter affording an opportunity to address the former issues (Balkrishnan, 1998) and again emphasizing the importance of a simplified regimen. Better communication of instructions and information associated with taking medications has been found to increase elderly patients' adherence to medication regimens

(Balkrishnan, 1998). However, if medications do not work, people stop taking them (Perkins & Repper, 1999), suggesting an area for physicians to pursue with patients in follow-up appointments regarding prescriptions.

Perhaps the most commonly used strategy to increase patient cooperation with provider-prescribed regimens is patient education (Landis, 1996). One model proposed by Robinson (1987) in the late 1980s represents a typical approach to patient education: The physician establishes a plan and specifies self-care behaviors to be performed, then helps the patient to develop competence and supports and reinforces the patient's successful self-care. Education is more likely to work if it is individualized. For example, if a caregiver relates a presentation to a patient's own medications and individual daily schedule, the patient will be more likely to follow the recommendations (Ryan & Jacques, 1997). Specific strategies that have been found to be effective in this regard include using patient information leaflets as reinforcement, assessing the readability of patient information leaflets being used, and considering both sensory and motor changes as they relate to a patient's cognitive function (Ryan & Jacques, 1997). Such an individualized approach contributes to informed choice, which has been defined in terms of a psychoeducational approach to educating patients through caregivers' communication of both the benefits of prescribed medication and the potential consequences of noncompliance (Perkins & Repper, 1999). As Lieberman (1996) observes, however, many psychosocial problems or barriers to understanding are not diagnosed during medical interaction; this is the first step in the cycle of noncompliance, with failure partially attributable to traditional approaches to medical interviewing.

Physiological Outcomes

The physiological outcomes found to be associated with communication in health care settings include disease prevention, recovery and recuperation processes, and maintenance of desired health, long-term survival, and quality of life (Kreps et al., 1994). Few studies have assessed physiological outcomes, both because longitudinal designs are costly to implement and because the effects of communication across time are indirect. Patients who do not cooperate with providers' prevention and detection recommendations, for example, will be less likely to prevent or detect disease, but the more direct link between communication and outcomes is compliance. Some outcomes' researchers label satisfaction and compliance as the short-term or "soft" outcomes associated with communication and call for research to examine communication's impact on such effects as the need for analgesics and length of stay in hospital after surgical operations—effects identified as long-term or "hard" outcomes (Rutter et al., 1996). Nurses' communication of empathy to patients has been found to relate directly to fewer relapse days after treatment for alcoholism (Olson, 1995); such findings are suggestive of the significant long-term effects of communication in health care settings.

Several studies have focused more specifically on immediate physiological/medical outcomes, however. Various aspects of communication have been linked to pain reduction (Bray, 1986; Doyle & Ware, 1977; Egbert, Battit, Welch, & Bartlett, 1964; Johnston, 1973; Krieger, 1975; McGrath & DeVeber, 1986; Tarasuk, Rhymes, & Leonard, 1965), postoperative complications (Boore, 1978; Hayward, 1975), length of hospital stays (Doyle & Ware, 1977; Egbert et al., 1964), postoperative vomiting (Dumas, Anderson, & Leonard, 1965), reliance on medication (Lemaitre & Finnegan, 1975), speed of recovery (Maguire, 1985), improved treatment results (Bass et al., 1986; Heszen-Klemens & Lapkinska, 1984; Starfield et al., 1981), blood pressure control (Orth, Stiles, Scherwitz, Hennrikus, & Valbonna, 1987), and blood sugar control (Kaplan, Greenfield, & Ware,

1989). Impacts have also been noted on such immediate indicators as heart rate (Garvin, Kennedy, Baker, & Polivka, 1992; Smith & Cantrell, 1988; Thomas et al., 1982) and blood pressure (Hellmann & Grimm, 1984).

Over the course of the past decade, a number of trends in health outcomes have been observed that may be partially attributable to communication. For example, glycemic control has improved in clinic settings where knowledgeable health care professionals provide frequent support to diabetic patients, communicating with them by telephone to give weekly advice (Edwards, 1999). As physicians and nurses increase their own understanding about patients and their individual situations, more opportunities to individualize treatment and prevention options will develop, leading to more informed understanding, decision making, consent, and choice.

THEORETICAL PERSPECTIVES

Perhaps the most significant development in the research on interpersonal communication in the health care context in the past 20 years has been the appearance of numerous attempts at theoretical offerings. Although we are still not close to a theory of health communication, scholars have taken steps in that direction. Most of this work has been published in communication or nursing journals, although some family practitioners have recently begun to pay attention to such concerns (e.g., Bartz, 1999). Many of these theories have very specific foci or scopes. These include theories or models from scholars such as Lambert et al. (1997), who discuss the "mangle of practice" and allow a focus on the patient rather than just the care provider; Frederikson (1993), who offers an integrative model for medical consultation; Reardon and Buck (1989), who discuss the role of communication, emotion, and cognition in patients' coping with cancer; Ellis, Miller, and Given (1989), who address communication and caregivers in home health care situations; Rouse (1989), who delineates

the role of emotional communication in dentistry; Williams, Giles, Coupland, Dalby, and Manasse (1990), who present a model of elderly social support and health; Ballard-Reisch (1990), who addresses participative decision making in the physician-patient relationship; Ratzan (1996), who presents a negotiation perspective for health decision making; Morse (1991), who examines the negotiation of commitment and involvement (see also her follow-up work on the comforting interaction; Morse, Havens, & Wilson, 1997); Cowley (1991), who presents grounded theoretical discussions of the symbolic awareness context; Heslin (1989), who presents a model of supportive nursing care; Squier (1990), who provides a model of empathic understanding as it affects adherence to treatment regimens; Babrow (1992; Hines, Babrow, Badzek, & Moss, 1997), who addresses problematic integration theory; and Nievaard (1987), who discusses communication climate and patient care.

Other theoretical perspectives are a bit broader, such as Kasch's (1986) discussion of nursing action as a process in social interaction. Kasch focuses on consensus as a process in negotiation that is determined, in part, by nurses' interpersonal competence. Pierloot (1983) contrasts four models of the doctor-patient relationship in an attempt to shed some light on the appropriateness of each to various contexts. Applying yet broader communication theories are Query and Kreps (1996), who present a relational model of health communication competence, and Lambert (1996) and J. A. Spiers (1998), who discuss applications of facework and politeness theory. Other scholars have applied communication accommodation theory (Street, 1991b; Watson & Gallois, 1998) or social exchange theory (Roter & Hall, 1991) to health care. Street (1991b) uses accommodation theory to integrate diverse and sometimes contradictory research findings, providing a strong dyadic perspective that looks at the interdependence of provider and patient communication. Similarly, the work of Cegala and colleagues (see also McNeilis, 2001) applies the Cegala and Waldron (1992) competence model to health care and also enables an understanding of this interdependence. Roter and Hall (1991) look at the reciprocity of behavior in health care. Perhaps most promising is Street's (in press) ecological model of health communication. All these offerings provide important foundations on which future health communication research and theory should build. They are also examples of how research or theory in a specific setting, such as health care, can help extend our understanding of communication in general.

CONCLUSION

As we have demonstrated in this review, researchers have generated a great deal of information about the interpersonal communication process as it operates within the health care context. Some of the most interesting research conducted to date has documented the interdependence of health care provider and patient communicative acts. It is apparent that how care providers communicate influences how patients communicate, and vice versa. Patient communicative acts, especially question asking, also influence treatment decisions. Such findings advance our understanding of health communication processes significantly beyond the early research, which focused almost exclusively on the care provider as the key player in medical interaction and the primary cause of communication difficulties (Thompson, 1984). Although there has been much improvement in the research, certainly much more is needed. Researchers should be encouraged to continue the movement toward studies that will provide a more dyadic, transactional understanding of interpersonal communication in health care.

Many of the communication problems found in past research continue to appear in more contemporary studies. For instance, research continually documents concerns about the amount of information patients receive compared with the amount of information they need, defining inadequacies and serious consequences. In this area, however, the research also indicates that patient communicative behaviors help determine the amount of information that patients receive. Language and control issues also continue to be a problem for patients in the medical context. And we know that differences among provider-patient coding schemes may lead to differing conclusions about health communication processes.

Many new research foci are apparent in the present review as well. Of particular note is the burgeoning research on diversity issues, informed consent concerns, end-of-life discussions, and health promotion as a factor in interpersonal interaction in health care. The positive effects of patient disclosure have been noted. Research on communication training programs is now documenting outcomes. Much more research has also been conducted in recent years on gender as it pertains to health communication. Several notable areas remain neglected, however. As we have noted above, communication and disability issues have yet to be investigated adequately in the medical context. And several of the outcomes of communication that Thompson (1994) identified as under-studied in the version of this review that appeared in the previous edition of this *Handbook* remain so. Outcomes such as the accuracy of diagnosis and altered health locus of control are important but have been the recipients of little investigation. Outcomes such as symptom resolution and functional status are still in need of a great deal of study, as are such long-term outcomes as costs and use of scarce resources.

Our primary goal in this chapter has been to provide information on which future researchers may build in their attempts to illuminate our understanding of communication in the health care context in particular and interpersonal communication processes in general. As researchers move to describe more adequately the dyadic communication that occurs during interactions between providers and patients and to uncover the outcomes of that communication, we have the opportunity to extend our understandings of interpersonal communication and the provision of health care—both processes of import.

REFERENCES

Abramson, H. (1997). *The effectiveness of communication skills training for older orthopedic patients*. Unpublished doctoral dissertation, University of Memphis.

Adomat, R., & Killingworth, A. (1994). Care of the critically ill patient: The impact of stress on the use of touch in intensive therapy units. *Journal of Advanced Nursing, 19,* 912-922.

Arborelius, E. (1996). Using doctor-patient communication to affect patients' lifestyles. Theoretical and practical implications. *Psychology and Health, 11,* 845-855.

Arborelius, E., & Thakker, K. D. (1995). Why is it so difficult for general practitioners to discuss alcohol with patients? *Family Practice, 12,* 419-422.

Armstrong, M. A., & Kelly, A. E. (1993). Enhancing staff nurses' interpersonal skills: Theory to practice. *Clinical Nurse Specialist, 7,* 313-317.

Arntson, P., Droge, D., & Fassl, H. E. (1978). Pediatrician-patient communication: A final report. In B. D. Ruben (Ed.), *Communication yearbook 2* (pp. 505-522). New Brunswick, NJ: Transaction.

Aronsson, K., & Sätterlund-Larsson, U. (1987). Politeness strategies and doctor-patient communication: On the social choreography of collaborative thinking. *Journal of Language and Social Psychology, 6,* 1-27.

Ashworth, P. D., Longmate, M. A., & Morrison, P. (1992). Patient participation: Its meaning and significance in the context of caring. *Journal of Advanced Nursing, 17,* 1430-1439.

Babrow, A. S. (1992). Communication and problematic integration: Understanding divergent probability and value, ambiguity, ambivalence, and impossibility. *Communication Theory, 2,* 95-130.

Bailey, K., & Wilkinson, S. (1998). Patients' views on nurses' communication skills: A pilot study. *International Journal of Palliative Nursing, 4,* 300-305.

Bales, R. F. (1970). *Personality and interpersonal behavior*. New York: Holt, Rinehart & Winston.

Balkrishnan, R. (1998). Predictors of medication adherence in the elderly. *Clinical Therapeutics, 20,* 764-771.

Ballard-Reisch, D. S. (1990). A model of participative decision making for physician-patient interaction. *Health Communication, 2,* 91-104.

Barnsley, J., Williams, A. P., Cockerill, R., & Tanner, J. (1999). Physician characteristics and the physician-patient relationship: Impact of sex, year of graduation, and specialty. *Canadian Family Physician, 13,* 935-942.

Barrett, D. (1993). Meaning on the streets. *Nursing Standard, 7*(23), 53.

Bartz, R. (1999). Beyond the biopsychosocial model: New approaches to doctor-patient interactions. *Journal of Family Practice, 48,* 601-607.

Bass, M. J., Buck, C., Turner, L., Dickie, G., Pratt, G., & Robinson, H. C. (1986). The physician's actions and the outcome of illness in family practice. *Journal of Family Practice, 23,* 43-47.

Baziak, A. T., & Dentan, R. K. (1960). The language of the hospital and its effects on the patient. *Etc., 17,* 261-268.

Beck, C. T. (1997). Humor in nursing practice: A phenomenological study. *International Journal of Nursing Studies, 34,* 346-352.

Beckman, H. B., Markakis, K. M., Suchman, A. L., & Frankel, R. M. (1994). The doctor-patient relationship and malpractice: Lessons from plaintiff depositions. *Archives of Internal Medicine, 154,* 1365-1370.

Behen, J. M. (1996). The relationship between medical residents' attitudes toward psychosocial issues in patient care and psychosocial interview skill level following communication training programs. *Dissertation Abstracts International, 56*(11-B), 6458.

Beisecker, A. E. (1990). Patient power in doctor-patient communication: What do we know? *Health Communication, 1,* 105-122.

Bellet, P. S. (1994). How should physicians approach the problems of their patients? *Pediatrics, 94,* 928-930.

Bennett, K., Smith, D. H., & Irwin, H. (1999). Preferences for participation in medical decisions in China. *Health Communication,* 11, 261-284.

Blum, D., & Blum, R. (1991). Patient-team communication. *Journal of Psychosocial Oncology,* 9(3), 81-88.

Boon, H., & Stewart, M. (1998). Patient-physician communication assessment instruments: 1986 to 1996 in review. *Patient Education and Counseling, 35,* 161-176.

Boore, J. (1978). *A prescription for recovery.* London: Royal College of Nursing.

Bottorff, J. L., & Morse, J. M. (1994). Identifying types of attending: Patterns of nurses' work. *Image: Journal of Nursing Scholarship, 26,* 53-60.

Bottorff, J. L., & Varcoe, C. (1995). Transitions in nurse-patient interactions: A qualitative ethology. *Qualitative Health Research,* 5, 315-331.

Bourhis, R. Y., Roth, S., & MacQueen, G. (1989). Communication in the hospital setting: A survey of medical and everyday language use amongst patients, nurses, and doctors. *Social Science and Medicine, 23,* 339-346.

Bowers, L. J. (1999). Back to basics . . . : "I've got some bad news." *Topics in Clinical Chiropractic, 6,* 1-8.

Braithwaite, D. O., & Thompson, T. L. (Eds.). (2000). *Handbook of communication and people with disabilities: Research and application.* Mahwah, NJ: Lawrence Erlbaum.

Brashers, D. E., Haas, S. M., & Neidig, J. L. (1999). The patient self-advocacy scale: Measuring patient involvement in health care decision-making interactions. *Health Communication, 11,* 97-121.

Bray, C. A. (1986). Postoperative pain: Altering the patient's experience through education. *AORN Journal, 43,* 672-683.

Brown, J. B., Stewart M. A., & Tessier, S. (1995). *Assessing communication between patients and doctors: A manual for scoring patient-centred communication of acute and complex illness.* London, ON: Centre for Studies in Family Medicine.

Buck, D., Jacoby, A., Baker, G. A., Graham-Jones, S., & Chadwick, D. W. (1996). Patients' experiences of and satisfaction with care for their epilepsy. *Epilepsia, 37,* 841-849.

Callahan, E. J., & Bertakis, K. D. (1991). Development and validation of the Davis Observation Code. *Family Medicine, 23,* 19-24.

Caris-Verhallen, W. M. C., Kerkstra, A., & Bensing, J. M. (1997). The role of communication in nursing care for elderly people: A review of the literature. *Journal of Advanced Nursing, 25,* 915-933.

Caris-Verhallen, W. M. C., Kerkstra, A., & Bensing, J. M. (1999). Nonverbal behaviour in nurse-elderly patient communication. *Journal of Advanced Nursing, 29,* 808-818.

Caris-Verhallen, W. M. C., Kerkstra, A., van der Heijden, P. G. M., & Bensing, J. M. (1998). Nurse-elderly patient communication in home care and institutional care: An explorative study. *International Journal of Nursing Studies, 35,* 95-108.

Carlisle, D. (1996). Careful talk saves lives . . . : Nurses say they do not have enough time to talk to patients. *Nursing Times, 92*(17), 16-17.

Carpenter, V., & Colwell, B. (1995). Cancer knowledge, self-efficacy, and cancer screening behaviors among Mexican-American women. *Journal of Cancer Education, 10,* 217-222.

Carter, A., & Sanderson, H. (1995). The use of touch in nursing practice. *Nursing Standard,* 9(16), 31-35.

Cecil, D. W. (1998). Relational control patterns in physician-patient clinical encounters: Continuing the conversation. *Health Communication,* 10, 125-149.

Cegala, D. J., Coleman, M. T., & Turner, J. W. (1998). The development and partial assessment of the medical communication competence scale. *Health Communication,* 10, 261-288.

Cegala, D. J., McClure, L., Marinelli, T. M., & Post, D. M. (2001). The effects of communication skills training on patients' participation during medical interviews. *Patient Education and Counseling, 41,* 209-222.

Cegala, D. J., McGee, D. S., & McNeilis, K. S. (1996). Components of patients' and doctors' perceptions of communication competence during a primary care medical interview. *Health Communication, 8,* 1-27.

Cegala, D. J., & Waldron, V. R. (1992). A study of the relationship between communicative performance and conversation participants' thoughts. *Communication Studies,* 43, 105-123.

Coe, M., Chen, J., & Holliday, C. (1996). What do you think? Question: What strategies are effective in communicating with ventilated and later-trached quadriplegic patients? *SCI Nursing, 13*(3), 82-83.

Coffman, S. L., & Coffman, V. T. (1993). Communication training for hospice volunteers. *Omega: Journal of Death and Dying,* 27, 155-163.

Cole, S. A. (1997). Reducing malpractice risk through more effective communication. *American Journal of Managed Care, 3,* 649-658.

Coleman, P. G., & Shellow, R. A. (1995). Privacy and autonomy in the physician-patient relationship. *Journal of Legal Medicine, 16,* 509-543.

Colliver, J. A., Swartz, M. H., Robbs, R., & Cohen, D. (1999). Relationship between clinical competence and interpersonal and communication skills in standardized-patient assessment. *Academic Medicine, 74,* 271-274.

Cooper-Patrick, L., Gallo, J. J., Gonzales, J. J., Vu, H. T., Powe, N. R., Nelson, C., & Ford, D. E. (1999). Race, gender, and partnership in the patient-physician relationship. *Journal of the American Medical Association, 282,* 583-589.

Cowley, S. (1991). A symbolic awareness context identified through a grounded theory study of health visiting. *Journal of Advanced Nursing, 16,* 648-656.

Craig, J. N. (1999). Clinicians set a dangerous precedent when they begin using a word like "queer." *American Journal of Orthopsychiatry, 69,* 267-269.

Crockford, E. A., Holloway, I. M., & Walker, J. M. (1993). Nurses' perceptions of patients' feelings about breast surgery. *Journal of Advanced Nursing, 18,* 1710-1718.

Curtis, J. R., Patrick, D. L., Caldwell, E., Greenlee, H., & Collier, A. C. (1999). The quality of patient-doctor communication about end-of-life care: A study of patients with advanced AIDS and their primary care clinicians. *AIDS, 13,* 1110-1131.

Davidhizar, R. (1992). Interpersonal communication: A review of eye contact. *Infection Control and Hospital Epidemiology, 13,* 222-225.

Davidhizar, R., & Giger, J. N. (1994). When your patient is silent. *Journal of Advanced Nursing, 20,* 703-706.

Davidhizar, R., & Giger, J. N. (1997). When touch is not the best approach. *Journal of Clinical Nursing, 6,* 203-206.

Deering, C. G. (1999). Self-disclosure with patients. *American Journal of Nursing, 99,* 34-39.

DiMatteo, M. R., Taranta, A., Friedman, H. S., & Prince, L. M. (1980). Predicting patient satisfaction from physicians' nonverbal communication skills. *Medical Care, 18,* 376-387.

Dockrell, S. (1988). An investigation of the use of verbal and nonverbal communication skills by final-year physiotherapy students. *Physiotherapy, 77,* 52-55.

Donaldson, D. (1999). Effective ways to communicate with the dying. *Caring, 18*(2), 18.

Doyle, B. J., & Ware, J. E., Jr. (1977). Physician conduct and other factors that affect consumer satisfaction with medical care. *Journal of Medical Education, 52,* 793-801.

Duggan, A. P., & Parrott, R. (2001). Physicians' nonverbal rapport-building behaviors and patients' talk about the subjective component of illness. *Human Communication Research, 27,* 299-311.

Dumas, R. G., Anderson, B. J., & Leonard, R. C. (1965). The importance of the expressive function in preoperative preparation. In J. K. Skipper & R. C. Leonard (Eds.), *Social interaction and patient care* (pp. 16-28). Philadelphia: J. B. Lippincott.

du Pré, A. (1998). *Humor and the healing arts: A multimethod analysis of humor use in health care.* Mahwah, NJ: Lawrence Erlbaum.

du Pré, A., & Beck, C. S. (1997). "How can I put this?": Exaggerated self-disparagement as alignment strategy during problematic disclosures by patients to doctors. *Qualitative Health Research, 7,* 487-503.

Dunning, D. G., & Lange, B. M. (1993). "Direction" in male and female dental students' interaction with patients: A confirmation of similarities. *Health Communication, 5,* 129-136.

Easton, J. (1988). Alternative communication for patients in intensive care. *Intensive Care Nursing, 4,* 47-55.

Eaton, L. G., & Tinsley, B. H. (1999). Maternal personality and health communication in the pediatric context. *Health Communication, 11,* 75-96.

Ebert, D. A., & Heckerling, P. S. (1995). Communication with deaf patients: Knowledge, beliefs, and practices of physicians. *Journal of the American Medical Association, 273,* 227-229.

Edwards, A. (1999). Insulin adjustment by a diabetes nurse educator improves glucose control in insulin-requiring diabetic patients: A randomized trial. *Canadian Medical Association Journal, 161,* 975-976.

Egbert, L. D., Battit, G. E., Welch, C. E., & Bartlett, M. K. (1964). Reduction of postoperative pain by encouragement and instruction of patients. *New England Journal of Medicine, 270,* 825-827.

Ellingson, L. L., & Buzzanell, P. M. (1999). Listening to women's narratives of breast cancer treatment: A feminist approach to patient satisfaction with physician-patient communication. *Health Communication, 11,* 153-183.

Elliott, R., & Wright, L. (1999). Verbal communication: What do critical care nurses say to their unconscious or sedated patients? *Journal of Advanced Nursing, 29,* 1412-1420.

Ellis, B. H., Miller, K. I., & Given, C. W. (1989). Caregivers in home health care situations: Measurement and relations among critical concepts. *Health Communication, 1,* 207-226.

Endacott, R. (1998). Needs of the critically ill child: A review of the literature and report of a modified Delphi study. *Intensive and Critical Care Nursing, 14,* 66-73.

Eoaskoon, W., Sumawong, V., & Silpakit, C. (1996). Evaluation of training medical students in patient-interviewing skills by three modes of learning. *Journal of the Medical Association of Thailand, 79,* 526-529.

Evans, B. J., Stanley, R. L., & Burrows, G. D. (1992). Communication skills training and patients' satisfaction. *Health Communication, 4,* 155-170.

Fallowfield, L. H. (1997). Truth sometimes hurts but deceit hurts more. *Annals of the New York Academy of Sciences, 809,* 525-536.

Faulkner, A. (1996). Dying and bereavement: Some educational issues. *Journal of Cancer Care, 5,* 123-125.

Feldman, H. M., Ploof, D., & Cohen, W. J. (1999). Physician-family partnerships: The adaptive practice model. *Journal of Developmental and Behavioral Pediatrics, 20,* 111-116.

Fielding, S. L. (1997). When patients feel ignored: Study findings about medial liability. *Academic Medicine, 72,* 6-7.

Fisher, R. C. (1992). Patient education and compliance: A pharmacist's perspective. *Patient Education and Counseling, 19,* 261-271.

Fisher, S. (1983). Doctor talk/patient talk: How treatment decisions are negotiated in doctor/patient communication. In S. Fisher & A. Todd (Eds.), *The social organization of doctor-patient communication* (pp. 135-157). Washington, DC: Center for Applied Linguistics.

Fisher, S. (1984). Doctor-patient communication: A social and micropolitical performance. *Sociology of Health and Illness, 6,* 1-29.

Fitch, M. I., Remus, S., & Stade, B. (1998). Communication needs of patients receiving mechanical ventilation: A pilot study. *CACCN, 9*(3), 16-23.

Foley, M. E., Nespoli, G., & Conde, E. (1997). Using standardized patients and standardized physicians to improve patient-care quality: Results of a pilot study. *Journal of Continuing Education in Nursing, 28,* 198-204.

Fosbinder, D. (1994). Patient perceptions of nursing care: An emerging theory of interpersonal competence. *Journal of Advanced Nursing, 20,* 1085-1092.

Fowler, S. B. (1997). Impaired verbal communication during short-term oral intubation. *Nursing Diagnosis, 8*(3), 93-98.

Frankel, R. M. (1995). Emotion and the physician-patient relationship. *Motivation and Emotion, 19,* 163-173.

Franks, A. (1997). Breaking bad news and the challenge of communication. *European Journal of Palliative Care, 4,* 61-65.

Frederikson, L. G. (1993). Development of an integrative model for medical consultation. *Health Communication, 5,* 225-237.

Frith, B. (1991). Giving information to radiotherapy patients. *Nursing Standard, 5*(34), 33-35.

Fry, A. (1994). Effective communication with people with visual disabilities. *Nursing Times, 90,* 42-43.

Gabbard-Alley, A. S. (1995). Health communication and gender: A review and critique. *Health Communication, 7,* 35-54.

Gallagher, C. A. (1993). *Empathy and assertiveness training in a nursing home environment.* Unpublished doctoral dissertation, Fordham University.

Gallagher, J., & Holm, L. (1996). Power of one: Nurses and tobacco control. *Seminars in Oncology Nursing, 12,* 270-275.

Garvin, B. J., Kennedy, C. W., Baker, C. F., & Polivka, B. J. (1992). Cardiovascular responses of CCU patients when communicating with nurses, physicians, and families. *Health Communication, 4,* 291-301.

Gelman, S. R. (1980). Esoterica: A zero sum game in the helping professions. *Social Casework, 61,* 48-53.

Gijbels, H. (1993). Interpersonal skills training in nurse education: Some theoretical and curricular considerations. *Nurse Education Today, 13,* 458-465.

Gilbert, D. A. (1998). Relational message themes in nurses' listening behavior during brief patient-nurse interactions. *Scholarly Inquiry for Nursing Practice, 12,* 5-21.

Gillotti, C., Thompson, T. L., & McNeilis, K. (2002). Communicative competence in the delivery of bad news. *Social Science and Medicine, 54,* 1011-1023.

Girgis, A., Sanson-Fisher, R. W., & Schofield, M. J. (1999). Is there consensus between breast cancer patients and providers on guidelines for breaking bad news? *Behavioral Medicine, 25,* 69-77.

Gleber, J. M. (1995). Interpersonal communications skills for dental hygiene students: A pilot training program. *Journal of Dental Hygiene, 69,* 19-30.

Gostin, L. O. (1995). Informed consent, cultural sensitivity, and respect for persons. *Journal of the American Medical Association, 274,* 844-845.

Grandinetti, D. (1996). Can't get no (patient) satisfaction? Try charm school. *Medical Economics, 73,* 134-142.

Green, D. B. (1997). How to deliver tragic news with compassion. *Nursing, 27,* 64.

Greene, M. G., Adelman, R. D, Friedman, E., & Charon, R. (1994). Older patient satisfaction with communication during an initial medical encounter. *Social Science and Medicine, 38,* 1279-1288.

Griffin, R. J., & Dunwoody, S. (2000). The relation of communication to risk judgment and preventive behavior related to lead in tap water. *Health Communication, 12,* 81-107.

Gwyn, R., & Elwyn, G. (1999). When is a shared decision not (quite) a shared decision? Negotiating preferences in a general practice encounter. *Social Science and Medicine, 49,* 437-447.

Gyllensten, A. L., Gard, G., Salford, E., & Ekdahl, C. (1999). Interaction between patient and physiotherapist. *Physiotherapy Research International, 4,* 89-109.

Hadjistavropoulos, T., McMurtry, B., & Craig, K. D. (1996). Beautiful faces in pain: Biases and accuracy in the perception of pain. *Psychology and Health, 11,* 411-420.

Hahn, J. E. (1999). Cueing in to patient language. *Reflections, 25,* 8-11.

Hall, D. S. (1996). Interactions between nurses and patients on ventilators. *American Journal of Critical Care, 5,* 293-297.

Hall, J. A., Irish, J. T., Roter, D. L., Ehrlich, C. M., & Miller, L. H. (1994a). Gender in medical encounters: An analysis of physician and patient communication in a primary care setting. *Health Psychology, 13,* 384-392.

Hall, J. A., Irish, J. T., Roter, D. L., Ehrlich, C. M., & Miller, L. H. (1994b). Satisfaction, gender, and communication in medical visits. *Medical Care, 32,* 1216-1231.

Halter, J. B. (1999). The challenge of communicating health information to elderly patients: A view from geriatric medicine. In D. C. Park & R. W. Morrell (Eds.), *Processing of medical information in aging patients: Cognitive and human factors perspective* (pp. 23-28). Mahwah, NJ: Lawrence Erlbaum.

Hamilton, M. A., Rouse, R. A., & Rouse, J. (1994). Dentist communication and patient utilization of dental services: Anxiety inhibition and competence enhancement effects. *Health Communication, 6,* 137-158.

Hanlon, J. M. (1996). Teaching effective communication skills. *Nursing Management, 27*(4), 48-49.

Hardcastle, M. (1999). Assessment of mental health nursing competence using level III academic marking criteria: The Eastbourne Assessment of Practice Scale. *Nurse Education Today, 19,* 89-92.

Harres, A. (1998). "But basically you're feeling well, are you?": Tag questions in medical consultations. *Health Communication, 10,* 111-123.

Harrigan, J. A., Oxman, T. E., & Rosenthal, R. (1985). Rapport expressed through nonverbal behavior. *Journal of Nonverbal Behavior, 9,* 95-110.

Hayward, J. (1975). *Information: A prescription against pain.* London: Royal College of Nursing.

Heaven, C. M., & Maguire, P. (1996). Training hospice nurses to elicit patient concerns. *Journal of Advanced Nursing, 23,* 280-286.

Hellmann, R., & Grimm, S. A. (1984). The influence of talking on diastolic blood pressure readings. *Research in Nursing and Health, 7,* 253-256.

Hepburn, K., & Reed, R. (1995). Ethical and clinical issues with Native-American elders: End-of-life decision making. *Clinics in Geriatric Medicine, 11,* 97-111.

Herselman, S. (1996). Some problems in health communication in a multicultural clinical setting: A South African experience. *Health Communication, 8,* 153-170.

Heslin, K. (1989). The supportive role of the staff nurse in the hospital palliative care situation. *Journal of Palliative Care, 5,* 20-26.

Heszen-Klemens, I., & Lapkinska, E. (1984). Doctor-patient interaction, patients' health behavior and effects of treatment. *Social Science and Medicine, 19,* 9-18.

Hinds, C., & Moyer, A. (1997). Support as experienced by patients with cancer during radiotherapy treatments. *Journal of Advanced Nursing, 26,* 371-379.

Hines, S. C., Babrow, A. S., Badzek, L. A., & Moss, A. H. (1997). Communication and problematic integration in end-of-life decisions: Dialysis decisions among the elderly. *Health Communication, 9,* 199-218.

Hines, S. C., Badzek, L. A., Leslie, N., & Glover, J. J. (1998). Managing uncertainty in conversations about treatment preferences: A study of home health care nurses. *Communication Research Reports, 15,* 331-339.

Hines, S. C., Badzek, L. A., & Moss, A. H. (1997). Informed consent among chronically ill elderly: Assessing its (in)adequacy and predictors. *Journal of Applied Communication Research, 25,* 151-169.

Hines, S. C., Moss, A. H., & Badzek, L. A. (1997). Being involved or just being informed: Communication preferences of seriously ill, older adults. *Communication Quarterly, 45,* 268-281.

Hirschmann, K. (1999). Blood, vomit, and communication: The days and nights of an intern on call. *Health Communication, 11,* 35-57.

Holley, J. L., Hines, S. C., Glover, J. J., Babrow, A. S., Badzek, L. A., & Moss, A. H. (1999). Failure of advance care planning to elicit patients' preferences for withdrawal from dialysis. *American Journal of Kidney Diseases, 33,* 688-693.

Holman, H., & Lorig, K. (1992). Perceived self-efficacy in self-management of chronic disease. In R. Schwarzer (Ed.), *Self-efficacy: Thought control of action* (pp. 305-323). Washington, DC: Hemisphere.

Holmes, B. C. (1996). Negotiation of meaning in physician-patient communication during cancer treatment. *Dissertation Abstracts International, 57*(6-B), 4069.

Hornberger, J., Itakura, H., & Wilson, S. R. (1997). Bridging language and cultural barriers between physicians and patients. *Public Health Reports, 112,* 410-417.

Horsfall, J. (1998). Structural impediments to effective communication. *Australian/New Zealand Journal of Mental Health Nursing, 7*(2), 74-80.

Huddleston, D., & Alexander, R. (1999). Communicating in end-of-life care. *Caring Magazine, 18*(2), 16-20.

Humphreys, K., Moos, R. H., & Cohen, C. (1997). Social and community resources and long-term recovery from treated and untreated alcoholism. *Journal of Studies on Alcohol, 58,* 231-238.

Hyman, D. J., Maibach, E. W., Flora, J. A., & Fortmann, S. P. (1992). Cholesterol treatment practices of primary care physicians. *Public Health Reports, 107,* 441-448.

Inui, T. S., Carter, W. B., Kukull, W. A., & Haigh, V. H. (1982). Outcome-based doctor-patient interaction analysis: I. Comparison of techniques. *Medical Care, 20,* 535-549.

Irish, J. T., & Hall, J. A. (1995). Interruptive patterns in medical visits: The effects of role, status, and gender. *Social Science and Medicine, 41,* 873-881.

Jackson, L. D. (1992). Information complexity and medical communication: The effects of technical language and amount of information in a medical message. *Health Communication, 4,* 197-210.

Jackson, L. D. (1994). Maximizing treatment adherence among back-pain patients: An experimental study of the effects of physician-related cues in written medical messages. *Health Communication, 6,* 173-191.

Jeffrey, B., & Hicks, C. (1997). The impact of counselling skills training on the interpersonal skills of undergraduate occupational therapy students. *British Journal of Occupational Therapy, 60,* 395-400.

Johnston, J. (1973). Effects of accurate expectations about sensations on the sensory and distress components of pain. *Journal of Personality and Social Psychology, 27,* 261-275.

Johnston, S. C., Pfeifer, M. P., & McNutt, R. (1995). The discussion about advance directives. *Archives of Internal Medicine, 155,* 1025-1030.

Jones, A. (1994). What interpersonal skills? *British Journal of Nursing, 3,* 992-995.

Juliana, C. A., Orehowsky, S., Smith-Regojo, P., Sikora, S. M., Smith, P. A, Stein, D. K., et al. (1997). Interventions used by staff nurses to manage "difficult" patients. *Holistic Nursing Practice, 11*(4), 1-26.

Kaplan, S. H., Greenfield, S., & Ware, J. E. (1989). Impact of the doctor-patient relationship on the outcomes of chronic disease. In M. Stewart & D. L. Roter (Eds.), *Communicating with medical patients* (pp. 228-245). Newbury Park, CA: Sage.

Kaplan, S. H., Sullivan, L. M., Spetter, D., Dukes, K. A., Khan, A., & Greenfield, S. (1996). Gender and patterns of physician-patient communication. In M. M. Falik & K. S. Collins (Eds.), *Women's health: The Commonwealth Fund Survey* (pp. 76-95). Baltimore: Johns Hopkins University Press.

Kasch, C. R. (1986). Toward a theory of nursing action: Skills and competency in nurse-patient interaction. *Nursing Research, 35,* 226-230.

Kasch, C. R., Kasch, J., & Lisnek, P. (1998). Women's talk and nurse-client encounters: Developing criteria for assessing interpersonal skill. *Scholarly Inquiry for Nursing Practice, 12,* 269-287.

Kautzmann, L. N. (1993). Linking patient and family stories to caregivers' use of clinical reasoning. *American Journal of Occupational Therapy, 47,* 169-173.

Kemppainen, J. K., O'Brien, L., & Corpuz, B. (1998). The behaviors of AIDS patients toward their nurses. *International Journal of Nursing Studies, 35,* 330-338.

Kim, Y. M., Odallo, D., Thuo, M., & Kols, A. (1999). Client participation and provider communication in family planning counseling: Transcript analysis in Kenya. *Health Communication, 11,* 1-19.

King, K. C. (1995). Using therapeutic silence in home healthcare nursing. *Home Healthcare Nurse, 13,* 65-68.

Kluge, E. W. (1999). Informed consent in a different key: Physicians' practice profiles and the patient's right to know. *Canadian Medical Association, 160,* 1321-1322.

Koehler, W. F., Fottler, M. D., & Swan, J. E. (1992). Physician-patient satisfaction: Equity in the health services encounter. *Medical Care Review, 49,* 455-484.

Korsch, B. M., Gozzi, E. K., & Francis, V. (1968). Gaps in doctor-patient communication: 1. Doctor-patient interaction and patient satisfaction. *Pediatrics, 42,* 855-871.

Kotecki, C. N. (1997). Learning a personal communication repertoire: How baccalaureate nursing students communicate with patients in a clinical setting. *Dissertation Abstracts International, 57*(10-B), 6178.

Kreps, G. L., O'Hair, D., & Clowers, M. (1994). The influences of human communication on health outcomes. *American Behavioral Scientist, 38,* 248-256.

Krieger, D. (1975). Therapeutic touch. *American Journal of Nursing, 75,* 784-787.

Krishnan, S. P. (1996). Health education at family planning clinics: Strategies for improving information about contraception and sexually transmitted diseases for low-income women. *Health Communication, 8,* 353-366.

Kurtz, S. M., Laidlaw, S. T., Makoul, G., & Schnabl, G. (1999). Medical education initiatives in communication skills. *Cancer Prevention and Control, 3,* 37-45.

Kurtz, S. M., & Silverman, J. D. (1996). The Calgary-Cambridge Referenced Observation Guides: An aid to defining the curriculum and organizing the teaching in communication training programmes. *Medical Education, 30,* 83-89.

LaBrecque, R. (1996). If you knew what I know: Do you really want to communicate better with doctors? Try standing in their shoes for a day. *Trustee, 49,* 16-20.

Ladyshewsky, R., & Gotjamanos, E. (1997). Communication skill development in health professional education: The use of standardised patients in combination with a peer assessment strategy. *Journal of Allied Health, 26,* 177-186.

Lambert, B. L. (1996). Face and politeness in pharmacist-physician interaction. *Social Science and Medicine, 43,* 1189-1198.

Lambert, B. L., Street, R. L., Jr., Cegala, D. J., Smith, D. H., Kurtz, S. M., & Schofield, T. (1997). Provider-patient communication, patient-centered care, and the mangle of practice. *Health Communication, 9,* 27-43.

Lamping, C. (1995). Telling the patient the diagnosis of alcoholism or drug addiction: An internist's perspective. *Maryland Medical Journal, 44,* 460-461.

Landis, N. T. (1996). Lessons from medicine and nursing for pharmacist-patient communication. *American Journal of Health-System Pharmacists, 53,* 1306-1314.

Lane, P. L. (1989). Nurse-client perceptions: The double standard of touch. *Issues in Mental Health Nursing, 10,* 1-13.

Lantz, P. M., Dupuis, L., Reding, D., Krauska, M., & Lappe, K. (1994). Peer discussions of cancer among Hispanic migrant workers. *Public Health Reports, 109,* 512-520.

Lazcano-Ponce, E. C., Castro, R., Allen, B., Najera, P., Ruiz, P. A. D., & Hernandez Avila, M. (1999). Barriers to early detection of cervical-uterine cancer in Mexico. *Journal of Women's Health, 8,* 399-408.

Leash, R. M. (1996). Death notification: Practical guidelines for health care professionals. *Critical Care Nursing Quarterly, 19*(1), 21-34.

Lefevre, C. J. (1992). *Communicative needs of the terminally ill elderly and the role of the hospice volunteer.* Unpublished doctoral dissertation, University of Oregon.

Lemaitre, G., & Finnegan, J. (1975). *The patient in surgery: A guide for nurses* (3rd ed.). Philadelphia: W. B. Saunders.

Lerman, C., Daly, M., Walsh, W. P., Resch, N., Seay, J., Barsevick, A., et al. (1993). Communication between patients with breast cancer and health care providers. *Cancer, 72,* 2612-2620.

Levinson, W., & Roter, D. L. (1995). Physicians' psychosocial beliefs correlate with their patient communication skills. *Journal of General Internal Medicine, 10,* 375-379.

Levinson, W., Roter, D. L., Mullooly, J. P., Dull, V. T., & Frankel, R. M. (1997). Physician-patient communication: The relationship with malpractice claims among primary care physicians and surgeons. *Journal of the American Medical Association, 19,* 553-559.

Levinson, W., Stiles, W. B., Inui, T. S., & Engle, R. (1993). Physician frustration in communicating with patients. *Medical Care, 31,* 285-295.

Lieberman, J. A. (1996). Compliance issues in primary care. *Journal of Clinical Psychiatry, 57,* 76-82.

Lubbers, C. A., & Roy, S. J. (1990). Communication skills for continuing education in nursing. *Journal of Continuing Education in Nursing, 21,* 109-112.

Lys, K., & Pernice, R. (1995). Perceptions of positive attitudes toward people with spinal cord injury. *International Journal of Rehabilitation Research, 18,* 35-43.

MacLeod Clark, J. (1983). Nurse patient communication in surgical wards. In J. Wilson-Barrett (Ed.), *Nursing research: Ten studies in patient care* (pp. 167-201). Chichester: John Wiley.

MacLeod Clark, J. (1985). Communication: Why it can go wrong. *Nursing, 2,* 1119-1120.

Maguire, P. (1985). Consequences of poor communication between nurses and patients. *Nursing, 2,* 1115-1118.

Majerovitz, S. D., Greene, M. G., Adelman, R. D., Brody, G. M., Leber, K., & Healy, S. W. (1997). Older patients' understanding of medical information in the emergency department. *Health Communication, 9,* 237-251.

Makoul, G. (1995). *SEGUE: A framework for teaching and evaluation communication in medical encounters.* San Francisco: American Educational Research Association, Division 1.

Mallett, J. (1990). Communication between nurses and post-anaesthetic patients. *Intensive Care Nursing, 6,* 45-53.

Malan, S. S. (1992). Psychosocial adjustment following MI: Current views and nursing implications. *Journal of Cardiovascular Nursing, 6,* 57-70.

Manss, V. (1994). Effective communication: Gender issues. *Nursing Management, 25*(6), 79-80.

Marrow, J. (1996). Telling relatives that a family member has died suddenly. *Postgraduate Medicine Journal, 72,* 413-418.

Marvel, M. K., Doherty, W. J., & Weiner, E. (1998). Medical interviewing by exemplary family physicians. *Journal of Family Practice, 47,* 343-348.

McCann, R., Chodosh, J., Frankel, R., Katz, P., Naumburg, E., Tulsky, A., & Hall, W. J. (1998). Advance care directives and end of life decisions: An educational module. *Gerontology and Geriatrics Education, 18,* 3-19.

McClement, S. E., & Degner, L. F. (1995). Expert nursing behaviors in care of the dying adult in the intensive care unit. *Heart and Lung, 24,* 408-419.

McDaniels, C. (1992). Enhancing nursing student communication: Experimental study. *Nurse Educator, 17*(2), 6.

McGee, D. S. (1997). In search of patient communication competence: A test of an intervention to improve communication in the primary-care medical interview. *Dissertation Abstracts International, 57*(7-A), 2739.

McGee, D. S., & Cegala, D. J. (1998). Patient communication skills training for improved communication competence in the primary care medical consultation. *Journal of Applied Communication Research, 26,* 412-430.

McGrath, P. A., & DeVeber, L. (1986). Helping children cope with painful procedures. *American Journal of Nursing, 86,* 1278-1279.

McGrath, P. A., Yates, P., Clinton, M., & Hart, G. (1999). "What should I say?": Qualitative findings on dilemmas in palliative care nursing. *Hospice Journal, 14,* 17-33.

McIntosh, J. (1974). Process of communication, information seeking and control associated with cancer: A selected review of the literature. *Social Science and Medicine, 8,* 167-187.

McLaughlin, C. (1999). An exploration of psychiatric nurses' and patients' opinions regarding in-patient care for suicidal patients. *Journal of Advanced Nursing, 29,* 1042-1051.

McNeilis, K. (2001). Analyzing communication competence in medical consultations. *Health Communication, 13,* 5-18.

McNeilis, K., & Thompson, T. L. (1995). The impact of relational control on patient compliance in dentist-patient interactions. In G. L. Kreps & D. O'Hair (Eds.), *Communication and health outcomes* (pp. 57-72). Cresskill, NJ: Hampton.

Mickey, R. M., Luc Vezina, J., Worden, J. K., & Warner, S. L. (1997). Breast screening behavior and interactions with health care providers among lower income women. *Medical Care, 35,* 1204-1211.

Miller, D. B., & Holditch-Davis, D. (1992). Interactions of parents and nurses with high-risk preterm infants. *Research in Nursing and Health, 15,* 187-197.

Miller, E. T., & Opie, N. D. (1994). Using triangulation to investigate the relationships between adults with physical disabilities and their primary care attendants. *Rehabilitation Nursing Research, 3,* 30-36.

Mitsuya, H. (1997). Telling the truth to cancer patients and patients with HIV-1 infection in Japan. *Annals of the New York Academy of Sciences, 809,* 279-289.

Moore, J. R., & Gilbert, D. A. (1995). Elderly residents: Perceptions of nurses' comforting touch. *Journal of Gerontological Nursing, 21,* 6-13.

Moore, L. W., & Proffitt, C. (1993). Communicating effectively with elderly surgical patients. *AORN Journal, 58,* 345, 347, 349-350.

Morrison, R. S., Morrison, E. W., & Glickman, D. F. (1994). Physician reluctance to discuss advance directives. *Archives of Internal Medicine, 154,* 2311-2318.

Morrongiello, B. A., Hillier, L., & Bass, M. (1995). "What I said" versus "what you heard": A comparison of physicians' and parents' reporting of anticipatory guidance on child safety issues. *Injury Prevention, 1,* 223-227.

Morse, J. M. (1991). Negotiating commitment and involvement in the nurse-patient relationship. *Journal of Advanced Nursing, 16,* 455-468.

Morse, J. M., Havens, G. A. D., & Wilson, S. (1997). The comforting interaction: Developing a model of the nurse-patient relationship. *Scholarly Inquiry for Nursing Practice, 11,* 321-343.

Mullen, P. D., & Holcomb, J. D. (1990). Selected predictors of health promotion counseling by three groups of allied health professionals. *American Journal of Preventive Medicine, 6,* 153-160.

Munks, J. J. (1995). On the scene. Diagnosis: Babel. *Emergency Medical Services, 24*(10), 54, 56, 70-71.

Mystakidou, K. (1996). Disclosure of diagnostic information to cancer patients in Greece. *Palliative Medicine, 10,* 195-200.

Naish, J. (1996). The route to effective nurse-patient communication. *Nursing Times, 92*(17), 27-30.

Nievaard, A. C. (1987). Communication climate and patient care: Causes and effects of nurses' attitudes to patients. *Social Science and Medicine, 24,* 777-784.

O'Brien, P. G. (1992). *The relationship of female nurses' expertise to empathic concern, perspective taking, cognitive complexity, and analytic interactive style.* Unpublished doctoral dissertation, Adelphi University.

O'Connell, M. L. (1997). Communication: The key to decreasing unintended pregnancy and sexually transmitted disease/HIV risk. *Journal of Perinatal Education, 6,* 35-41.

O'Hair, D. (1989). Dimensions of relational communication and control during physician-patient interactions. *Health Communication, 2,* 97-115.

Oliver, S., & Redfern, S. J. (1991). Interpersonal communication between nurses and elderly patients: Refinement of an observation schedule. *Journal of Advanced Nursing, 16,* 30-38.

Olson, J. K. (1995). Relationships between nurse-expressed empathy, patient-perceived empathy and patient distress. *Journal of Nursing Scholarship, 27,* 317-322.

Ong, L. M. L., Visser, M. R. M., Van Zuuren, F. J., Rietbroek, R. C., Lammes, F. B., & de Haes, J. C. J. M. (1999). Cancer patients' coping styles and doctor-patient communication. *Psycho-Oncology, 8,* 155-166.

Orona, C. J., Koenig, B. A., & Davis, A. J. (1994). Cultural aspects of nondisclosure. *Cambridge Quarterly of Healthcare Ethics, 3,* 338-346.

Orth, J. E., Stiles, W. B., Scherwitz, L., Hennrikus, B., & Valbonna, C. (1987). Patient exposition and provider explanation in routine interviews and hypertensive patients' blood pressure control. *Health Psychology, 6,* 29-42.

Ostuni, E., & Mohl, G. (1995). Communicating more effectively with the confused or demented patient. *General Dentistry, 43,* 264-266.

Pakieser, R. A., & McNamee, M. (1999). How to work with an interpreter. *Journal of Continuing Education in Nursing, 30*(2), 71-74.

Parboosingh, J., & Inhaber, S. (1999). A catalyst for change in communication skills: The Canadian Breast Cancer Initiative. *Cancer Prevention and Control, 3,* 19-24.

Parle, M., Maguire, P., & Heaven, C. (1997). The development of a training model to improve health professionals' skills, self-efficacy and outcome expectancies when communicating with cancer patients. *Social Science and Medicine, 44,* 231-240.

Parrott, R. (1994). Exploring family practitioners' and patients' information exchange about prescribed medications: Implications for practitioners' interviewing and patients' understanding. *Health Communication, 6,* 267-280.

Parrott, R. (1995). Topic-centered and person-centered "sensitive subjects": Managing barriers to disclosure about health. In L. K. Fuller & L. M. Shilling (Eds.), *Communicating about communicable diseases* (pp. 177-190). Amherst, MA: Human Resource Development Press.

Parrott, R., Duncan, V., & Duggan, A. (2000). Promoting patients' full and honest disclosure during conversations with health care providers. In S. Petronio (Ed.), *Balancing the secrets of private disclosures* (pp. 137-148). Mahwah, NJ: Lawrence Erlbaum.

Parrott, R., Egbert, N., Anderton, J., & Sefcovic, E. (2002). Enlarging the role of environment as a social influence construct in health campaigns. In J. P. Dillard & M. Pfau (Eds.), *The persuasion handbook: Developments in theory and practice* (pp. 633-660). Thousand Oaks, CA: Sage.

Parrott, R., Steiner, C., & Goldenhar, L. (1996). Georgia's harvesting health habits campaign: Formative evaluation. *Journal of Rural Health, 12,* 291-300.

Patrick, K. (1998). Prevention, public health, and interactive health communication. *American Journal of Preventive Medicine, 16,* 46-47.

Peloquin, S. M. (1995). Communication skills: Why not turn to a skills training model?

American Journal of Occupational Therapy, 49, 721-723.

Pepler, C. J., & Lynch, A. (1991). Relational messages of control in nurse-patient interactions with terminally ill patients with AIDS and cancer. *Journal of Palliative Care, 7,* 18-29.

Perkins, R. E., & Repper, J. M. (1999). Compliance or informed choice. *Journal of Mental Health, 8,* 117-130.

Perry, K. (1994). Increasing patient satisfaction: Simple ways to increase the effectiveness of interpersonal communication in the OPS/PACU. *Journal of Post Anesthesia Nursing, 9,* 153-156.

Petronio, S. (Ed.). (2000). *Balancing the secrets of private disclosures.* Mahwah, NJ: Lawrence Erlbaum.

Pfeifer, M. P., Sidorov, J. E., Smith, A. C., Boero, J. F., Evans, A. T., Settle, M. B., et al. (1994). The discussion of end-of-life medical care by primary care patients and physicians: A multicenter study using structured qualitative interviews. *Journal of General Internal Medicine, 9,* 82-88.

Pierloot, R. A. (1983). Different models in the approach to the doctor-patient relationship. *Psychotherapy and Psychosomatics, 39,* 213-224.

Pilkington, W. J. (1993). *Effects of a communication skill program on nursing home staff's attitudes and communication skills and residents' level of life satisfaction.* Unpublished doctoral dissertation, St. John's University, New York.

Poggenpoel, M. (1997). Nurses' responses to patients' communication. *Curatonis: South African Journal of Nursing, 20*(3), 26-32.

Price, J. H., Desmond, S. M., & Losh, D. P. (1991). Patients' expectations of the family physician in health promotion. *American Journal of Preventive Medicine, 7,* 33-39.

Query, J. L., & Kreps, G. L. (1996). Testing a relational model for health communication competence among caregivers for individuals with Alzheimer's disease. *Journal of Health Psychology, 1,* 335-351.

Rabinowitz, B., Beckman, H. B., Morse, D., & Naumburg, E. H. (1994). Discussing preventive services with patients: Can we make a difference? *Health Values, 18,* 20-26.

Rankin, S. H. (1992). Psychosocial adjustments of coronary artery disease patients and their spouses: Nursing implications. *Nursing Clinics of North America, 27,* 271-284.

Rath, D., Poldre, P., Fisher, B. J., Laidlaw, J. C., Cowan, D. H., & Bakker, D. (1998). Commitment of a cancer organization to a program for training in communication skills. *Journal of Cancer Education, 13,* 203-206.

Ratzan, S. (1996). Effective decision-making: A negotiation perspective for health psychology and health communication. *Journal of Health Psychology, 1,* 323-333.

Ravert, P., Williams, M., & Fosbinder, D. M. (1997). The Interpersonal Competence Instrument for nurses. *Western Journal of Nursing Research, 19,* 781-791.

Ray, M. C. (1996). Seven ways to empower dying patients. *American Journal of Nursing, 96,* 56-57.

Reardon, K. K., & Buck, R. (1989). Emotion, reason, and communication in coping with cancer. *Health Communication, 1,* 41-54.

Richards, J. W. (1992). Words as therapy: Smoking cessation. *Journal of Family Practice, 34,* 687-692.

Rimal, R. N. (2001). Analyzing the physician-patient interaction: An overview of six methods and future research directions. *Health Communication, 13,* 89-99.

Ripick, D. N., Ziol, E., & Lee, N. N. (1998). Longitudinal effects of communication training on caregivers of persons with Alzheimer's disease. *Clinical Gerontologist, 19*(2), 37-55.

Rizzo, J. A. (1993). Physician uncertainty and the art of persuasion. *Social Science and Medicine, 37,* 1451-1459.

Roberts, S. J., Krouse, H. J., & Michaud, P. (1995). Negotiated and nonnegotiated nurse-patient interactions: Enhancing perceptions of empowerment. *Clinical Nursing Research, 4,* 67-77.

Robinson, J. W., & Roter, D. L. (1999). Psychosocial problem disclosure by primary care patients. *Social Science and Medicine, 48,* 1353-1362.

Robinson, L. (1987). Patient compliance in occupational therapy home health programs: Sociocultural considerations. *Occupational Therapy in Health Care, 4,* 127-137.

Robinson, W. P., Shepherd, A., & Heywood, J. (1998). Truth, equivocation/concealment, and lies in job applications and doctor-patient communication. *Journal of Language and Social Psychology, 17,* 149-164.

Roche, R. A., Stovall, C. E., Suarez, L., Goldman, D. A., Wright, S. A., & Mendez, M. C. (1998). Language differences in interpretation of breast cancer health messages. *Journal of Cancer Education, 13,* 226-230.

Roper, T. A. (1999). Cooperative language in consultations by male and female doctors. *British Medical Journal, 318,* 1760-1761.

Roter, D. L. (1995). *The Roter method of interaction process analysis.* Baltimore: Johns Hopkins University, School of Hygiene and Public Health, Department of Health Policy and Management.

Roter, D. L., & Hall, J. A. (1991). Health education theory: An application to the process of patient-provider communication. *Health Education Research, 6,* 185-194.

Roter, D. L., & Hall, J. A. (1997). Gender differences in patient-physician communication. In S. J. Gallant, G. P. Keita, & R. Royak-Schaler (Eds.), *Health care for women: Psychological, social, and behavioral influences* (pp. 57-71). Washington, DC: American Psychological Association.

Roter, D. L., Hall, J. A., & Katz, N. R. (1988). Patient-physician communication: A descriptive summary of the literature. *Patient Education and Counseling, 12,* 99-119.

Roter, D. L., Hall, J. A., & Kern, D. E. (1995). Improving physician interviewing skills and reducing patients' emotional distress. *Archives of Internal Medicine, 155,* 1877-1884.

Rouse, R. A. (1989). A paradigm of intervention: Emotional communication in dentistry. *Health Communication, 1,* 239-252.

Routasalo, P. (1996). Non-necessary touch in the nursing care of elderly people. *Journal of Advanced Nursing, 23,* 904-911.

Routasalo, P., & Isola, A. (1996). The right to touch and be touched. *Nursing Ethics, 3,* 165-176.

Routasalo, P., & Lauri, S. (1996). Developing an instrument for the observation of touching. *Clinical Nurse Specialist, 10,* 293-299.

Rubin, D. L., Healy, P., Gardiner, T. G., Zath, R. C., & Moore, C. P. (1997). Nonnative physicians as message sources. *Health Communication, 9,* 351-358.

Ruckdeschel, J. C., Albrecht, T. L., Blanchard, C., & Hemmick, R. M. (1996). Communication, accrual to clinical trials, and the physician-patient relationship: Implications for training programs. *Journal of Cancer Education, 11,* 73-79.

Rusin, M. J. (1992). Communicating with families of rehabilitation patients about "do not resuscitate" decisions. *Archives of Physical Medicine and Rehabilitation, 73,* 922-925.

Rutter, D. R., Iconomous, G., & Quine, L. (1996). Doctor-patient communication and outcome in cancer patients: An intervention. *Psychology and Health, 12,* 57-71.

Ryan, A., & Jacques, I. (1997). Medication compliance in older people. *Elderly Care, 9,* 16-20.

Savage, J. (1997). Gestures of resistance: The nurse's body in contested space. *Nursing Inquiry, 4,* 237-245.

Sawada, N. O., Mendes, I. A. C., Galvao, C. M., & Trevizan, M. A. (1992). The importance of nonverbal communication during the preanesthesia period. *Clinical Nursing Research, 1,* 207-213.

Scherz, J. W., Edwards, H. T., & Kallail, K. J. (1995). Communicative effectiveness of doctor-patient interactions. *Health Communication, 7,* 163-177.

Schofield, M. J., Walkom, S., Ethics, M. A., & Sanson-Fisher, R. (1997). Patient-provider agreement on guidelines for preparation for breast cancer treatment. *Behavioral Medicine, 23,* 36-45.

Schommer, J. C. (1994). Effects of interrole congruence on pharmacist-patient communication. *Health Communication, 6,* 297-309.

Schuster, M. A., Bell, R. M., Petersen, L. P., & Kanouse, D. E. (1996). Communication between adolescents and physicians about sexual behavior and risk prevention. *Archives of Pediatrics and Adolescent Medicine, 150,* 906-913.

Scott, A. (1997). Psychometric evaluation of the Personal Space Boundary Questionnaire. *Journal of Theory Construction and Testing, 1*(2), 46-53.

Scott, N., & Weiner, M. F. (1984). "Patientspeak": An exercise in communication. *Journal of Medical Education, 59,* 890-893.

Shadden, B. B. (1997). Discourse behaviors in older adults. *Seminars in Speech and Language, 18,* 143-157, 193-194.

Sharf, B. F. (1990). Physician-patient communication as interpersonal rhetoric: A narrative approach. *Health Communication, 2,* 217-232.

Sharf, B. F., & Street, R. L., Jr. (1997). The patient as a central construct in health communication research. *Health Communication, 9,* 1-93.

Siantz, M. (1991). How can we become more aware of culturally specific body language and use this awareness therapeutically? *Journal of Psychosocial Nursing and Mental Health Services, 29*(11), 38-41.

Skegg, J. A. (1999). Dental programme for smoke-free promotion: Attitudes and activities of dentists, hygienists, and therapists at training and 1 year later. *New Zealand Dental Journal, 95,* 55-57.

Smith, B. J., & Cantrell, P. J. (1988). Distance in nurse-patient encounters. *Journal of Psychosocial Nursing and Mental Health Services, 26*(2), 22-26.

Smith, C. K., & Larsen, K. M. (1984). Sequential nonverbal behavior in the patient-physician interview. *Journal of Family Practice, 18,* 257-261.

Smith, D. H. (1993). Stories, values, and patient care decisions. In C. Conrad (Ed.), *The ethical nexus* (pp. 123-148). Norwood, NJ: Ablex.

Smith, D. H. (1998). Interviews with elderly patients about side effects. *Health Communication, 10,* 199-209.

Smith, D. H., Cunningham, K. G., & Hale, W. E. (1994). Communication about medicines: Perceptions of the ambulatory elderly. *Health Communication, 6,* 281-295.

Smith, D. K., Shaw, W., Slack, J., & Marteau, T. M. (1995). Training obstetricians and midwives to present screening tests: Evaluation of two brief interventions. *Prenatal Diagnosis, 15,* 317-324.

Smith, R. C., Mettler, J. A., Stoffelmayr, B. E., Lyles, J. S., Marshall, A. A., Van Egeren, L. F., et al. (1995). Improving residents' confidence in using psychosocial skills. *Journal of General Internal Medicine, 10,* 315-320.

Smith, S. D. M., Nicol, K. M., Devereux, J., & Cornbleet, M. A. (1999). Encounters with doctors: Quantity and quality. *Palliative Medicine, 13,* 217-223.

Smith-Dupre, A. A., & Beck, C. S. (1996). Enabling patients and physicians to pursue multiple goals in health care encounters: A case study. *Health Communication, 8,* 73-90.

Smoot, S. L., & Gonzales, J. L. (1995). Cost-effective communication skills training for state hospital employees. *Psychiatric Services, 46,* 819-822.

Spiers, H. (1998). Clarity begins at home. *Health Services Journal, 108*(5594), 28-30.

Spiers, J. A. (1998). The use of face work and politeness theory. *Qualitative Health Research, 8,* 25-47.

Squier, R. W. (1990). A model of empathic understanding and adherence to treatment regimens in practitioner-patient relationships. *Social Science and Medicine, 30,* 325-339.

Starfield, B., Wray, C., Hess, K., Gross, R., Birk, P. S., & D'Lugoff, B. C. (1981). The influence of patient-practitioner agreement on outcome of care. *American Journal of Public Health, 71,* 127-132.

Steingart, R. M., Packer, M., & Hamm, P. (1991). Sex differences in the management of coronary artery disease. *New England Journal of Medicine, 325,* 226-330.

Steinmetz, D., Walsh, M., Gabel, L. L., & Williams, T. (1993). Family physicians' involvement with dying patients and their families: Attitudes, difficulties, and strategies. *Archives of Family Medicine, 2,* 753-761.

Steyn, M., van der Merwe, M., Dick, J., Borcherds, R., & Wilding, R. J. C. (1997). Communication with TB patients: A neglected dimensions of effective treatment? *Curatonis: South African Journal of Nursing, 20,* 53-56.

Stiles, W. B. (1978). *Manual for a taxonomy of verbal response modes.* Chapel Hill: University of North Carolina, Chapel Hill Institute for Research in Social Science.

Strand, J. (1994). Strategies for improving patient compliance. *Physician Assistant, 19*(1), 48-53.

Street, R. L., Jr. (1991a). Information-giving in medical consultations: The influence of patients' communicative styles and personal characteristics. *Social Science and Medicine, 32,* 541-548.

Street, R. L., Jr. (1991b). Physicians' communication and parents' evaluations of pediatric consultations. *Medical Care, 29,* 1146-1152.

Street, R. L., Jr. (1992a). Analyzing communication in medical consultations. Do behavioral measures correspond to patients' perceptions? *Medical Care, 30,* 976-988.

Street, R. L., Jr. (1992b). Communicative styles and adaptations in physician-patient consultations. *Social Science and Medicine, 34,* 1155-1163.

Street, R. L., Jr. (in press). Communication in medical encounters: An ecological perspective. In T. L. Thompson, A. Dorsey, K. Miller, & R. Parrott (Eds.), *Handbook of health communication.* Mahwah, NJ: Lawrence Erlbaum.

Street, R. L., Jr., & Buller, D. B. (1987). Nonverbal response patterns in physician-patient interactions: A functional analysis. *Journal of Nonverbal Behavior, 11,* 234-253.

Street, R. L., Jr., & Buller, D. B. (1988). Patients' characteristics affecting physician-patient nonverbal communication. *Human Communication Research, 15,* 60-90.

Street, R. L., Jr., Gold, W. R., & McDowell, T. (1994). Using health status surveys in medical consultations. *Medical Care, 32,* 732-744.

Street, R. L., Jr., Gold, W. R., & McDowell, T. (1995). Discussing health-related quality of life in prenatal consultations. In G. H. Morris & R. J. Chenail (Eds.), *The talk of the clinic: Explorations in the analysis of medical and therapeutic discourse* (pp. 209-231). Mahwah, NJ: Lawrence Erlbaum.

Sullivan, G. H. (1996). When communication breaks down. *Medical Economics, 59*(4), 61-64.

Sutton, R. B. (1998). Supporting the bereaved relative; Reflections on the actor's experience. *Medical Education, 32,* 622-629.

Sviden, G., & Saljo, R. (1993). Perceiving patients and their nonverbal reactions. *American Journal of Occupational Therapy, 47,* 491-497.

Tanghe, A., Evers, G., & Paridaens, R. (1998). Nurses' assessments of symptom occurrence and symptom distress in chemotherapy patients. *European Journal of Oncology Nursing, 2,* 14-26.

Tarasuk, M. B., Rhymes, J. P., & Leonard, R. C. (1965). An experimental test of the importance of communication skills for effective nursing. In J. K. Skipper & R.C. Leonard (Eds.), *Social interaction and patient care* (pp. 110-120). Philadelphia: J. B. Lippincott.

Teuscher, G. W. (1995). Communication via the drawing board. *ASDC Journal of Dentistry for Children, 62,* 244, 297.

Thomas, S. A., Friedmann, E., Noctor, M., Sappington, E., Gross, H., & Lynch, J. J. (1982). Patients' cardiac responses to nursing interviews in a CCU. *Dimensions of Critical Care, 1,* 198-205.

Thomasma, D. C. (1994). Telling the truth to patients: A clinical ethics exploration. *Cambridge Quarterly of Healthcare Ethics, 3,* 375-382.

Thompson, C. L., & Pledger, L. M. (1993). Doctor-patient communication: Is patient knowledge of medical terminology improving? *Health Communication, 5,* 89-97.

Thompson, T. L. (1984). The invisible helping hand: The role of communication in the health and social service professions. *Communication Quarterly, 32,* 148-163.

Thompson, T. L. (1994). Interpersonal communication and health care. In M. L. Knapp & G. R. Miller (Eds.), *Handbook of interpersonal communication* (2nd ed., pp. 696-725). Thousand Oaks, CA: Sage.

Thompson, T. L. (Ed.). (2001). Coding provider-patient interaction [Special issue]. *Health Communication, 13*(1).

Tickle-Degnen, L. (1998). Working well with others: The prediction of students' clinical performance. *American Journal of Occupational Therapy, 52,* 133-142.

Trotter, R. T. (1990). The cultural parameters of lead poisoning: A medical anthropologist's view of intervention in environmental lead exposure. *Environmental Health Perspectives, 89,* 79-84.

Uzark, K. C., Sauer, S. N., Lawrence, K. S., Miller, J., Addonizio, L., & Crowley, D. C. (1992). The psychosocial impact of pediatric heart transplantation. *Journal of Heart and Lung Transplantation, 11,* 1160-1167.

Vaidya, V. U., Greenberg, L. W., Patel, K. M., Strauss, L. H., & Pollack, M. M. (1999). Teaching physicians how to break bad news. *Archives of Pediatric and Adolescent Medicine, 153,* 419-422.

van Dulmen, A. M., Verhaak, P. F. M., & Bilo, H. J. G. (1997). Shifts in doctor-patient communication during a series of outpatient consultations in non-insulin-dependent diabetes mellitus. *Patient Education and Counseling, 30,* 227-237.

Verity, S. (1996). Communicating with sedated ventilated patients in intensive care: Focusing on the use of touch. *Intensive and Critical Care Nursing, 12,* 354-358.

Vetto, J. T., Elder, N. C., Toffler, W. L., & Fields, S. A. (1999). Teaching medical students to give bad news. *Journal of Cancer Education, 14,* 14-17.

von Friederichs-Fitzwater, M. M., Callahan, E. J., Flynn, N., & Williams, J. (1991). Relational control in physician-patient interactions. *Health Communication, 3,* 17-36.

von Friederichs-Fitzwater, M. M., & Gilgun, J. (2001). Relational control in physician-patient encounters. *Health Communication, 13,* 75-87.

Waddie, N. A. (1996). Language and pain expression. *Journal of Advanced Nursing, 23,* 868-872.

Waitzkin, H. (1984). Doctor-patient communication. *Journal of the American Medical Association, 252,* 2441-2446.

Waitzkin, H. (1990). On studying the discourse of medical encounters. *Medical Care, 28,* 473-488.

Waitzkin, H., Cabrera, A., Arroyo de Cabrera, E., & Radlow, M. (1996). Patient-doctor communication in cross-national perspective. *Medical Care, 34,* 641-671.

Walker, D., & Ross, J. M. (1995). Therapeutic computing: Teaching therapeutic communications utilizing a videodisc. *Computers in Nursing, 13*(3), 103-108.

Watson, B., & Gallois, C. (1998). Nurturing communication by health professionals toward patients: A communication accommodation theory approach. *Health Communication, 10,* 343-355.

Watson, W. H. (1975). The meanings of touch: Geriatric nursing. *Journal of Communication, 25*(3), 104-112.

Weijts, W. (1994). Responsible health communication: Taking control of our lives. *American Behavioral Scientist, 38,* 257-270.

Weiler K., Eland, J., & Buckwalter, K.C. (1996). Iowa nurses' knowledge of living wills and perceptions of patient autonomy. *Journal of Professional Nursing, 12,* 245-252.

Weiss, S. J. (1986). Consensual norms regarding patient involvement. *Social Science and Medicine, 22,* 489-496.

Weisz, V., & Robbennolt, J. K. (1996). Risks and benefits of pediatric bone marrow donation: A critical need for research. *Behavioral Sciences and the Law, 14,* 375-391.

Wellwood, I., Dennis, M., & Warlow, C. (1995). Patients' and carers' satisfaction with acute stroke management. *Age and Ageing, 24,* 519-524.

Whaley, B. B. (1994). "Food is to me as gas is to cars??": Using figurative language to explain illness to children. *Health Communication, 6,* 193-204.

Whaley, B. B. (1999). Explaining illness to children: Advancing theory and research by determining message content. *Health Communication, 11,* 185-193.

Whaley, B. B. (2000). Explaining illness to children: Theory, strategies, and future inquiry. In B. B. Whaley (Ed.), *Explaining illness: Research, theory, and strategies* (pp. 195-208). Mahwah, NJ: Lawrence Erlbaum.

Wilkinson, S. (1991). Factors which influence how nurses communicate with cancer patients. *Journal of Advanced Nursing, 16,* 677-688.

Wilkinson, S., Roberts, A., & Aldridge, J. (1998). Nurse-patient communication in palliative care: An evaluation of a communication skills programme. *Palliative Medicine, 12,* 13-22.

Williams, A., Giles, H., Coupland, N., Dalby, M., & Manasse, H. (1990). The communicative contexts of elderly social support and health: A theoretical model. *Health Communication, 2,* 123-144.

Williams, S., Weinman, J., & Dale, J. (1998). Doctor-patient communication and patient satisfaction: A review. *Family Practice, 15,* 480-492.

Wist, E. (1993). Teaching communication with cancer patients and terminally ill patients to medical students. *Journal of Cancer Education, 8,* 119-122.

Wolfensberger, J. A. (1997). The impact of gender, gender attitudes, and communication on patient satisfaction during medical visits. *Dissertation Abstracts International, 58*(1-B), 123.

Wong, P., Lau, T., & Mok, E. (1996). Communication with cancer patients: Perception and practice. *Hong Kong Nursing Journal, 74,* 20-23.

Wood, I. (1997). Communicating with children in A&E: What skills does the nurse need? *Accident and Emergency Nursing, 5,* 137-141.

Wright, V. (1996). Illiteracy in patients and HCWs means safety concerns. *Healthcare Hazardous Materials Management, 4*(4), 8.

Zablocki, E. (1999, January). Engaging physicians in improving satisfaction requires communication. *Executive Solutions for Healthcare Management,* pp. 21-24.

19

Interpersonal Communication in Family Relationships

MARY ANNE FITZPATRICK
JOHN P. CAUGHLIN

There has been an enormous increase in the scholarly focus on family communication since the publication of the second edition of the *Handbook of Interpersonal Communication* (Knapp & Miller, 1994). This heightened interest is obvious from a number of visible changes in the field. The National Communication Association has recognized the Family Communication Division and has established the Bernard Brommel Award for outstanding scholarship on family communication. There is even a new publication outlet dedicated to the area, the *Journal of Family Communication* (Socha, 2001).

This increased interest is warranted because the family is where most of us learn to communicate and, even more important, where

most of us learn how to think about communication (Bruner, 1990). The family is a universal social form, usually a small kinship-structured group. Although many definitions of kinship suggest a biological reckoning (e.g., Wilson, 1975), it is the social definition of who is related to whom that is more critical (Reiss, 1971). Being kin to someone acknowledges a special tie of who stands in what relationship to whom, who owes what to whom, and how individuals of particular kin relationships are expected to pay their social debts. The kin group socializes the newborn to these obligations, and that socialization takes place through communication.

We present this review of family communication in three major sections. First, we discuss the three major classes of definitions of the family that guide the research enterprise. Second, we demonstrate the importance of communication in any theoretical or conceptual attempt to understand the family. Third, we selectively examine some of the research that has been conducted on family interaction. In the concluding section, we offer some suggestions for future research.

DEFINITIONS OF THE FAMILY

What is a family? Definitions of family are often thinly veiled political or ideological statements rather than scientifically neutral views. Activists argue that refusing to consider homosexual couples as "family," for example, severely limits the rights and duties these couples have with regard to one another. Following Wamboldt and Reiss (1989), we discuss below three classes of definitions of the family that can be excavated from the extant research on the family: family structure, task orientation, and transactional process.

Family Structure

The first group of definitions is based on family structure. Most of us use the term *family* in at least two ways: (a) when we mean partners and children (family of procreation) and (b) when we mean relatives by blood or marriage, such as parents and siblings, grandparents, aunts, uncles, and cousins (family of origin). Many singles and childless couples have families of origin even when they do not have families of procreation. A *family of origin,* then, is the extended family or any group of individuals who have established biological or sociolegal legitimacy by virtue of shared genetics, marriage, or adoption. A *family of procreation,* usually called a "nuclear family," is further restricted to those living in the same house. Family structure definitions presuppose clear criteria for membership in the family and hierarchies within the family based on sex and age.

Social changes such as high divorce rates, new birth technologies, and the rise in feminism are making definitions of the family based solely on structural characteristics less useful. A divorced family with a child who splits time between two households, each of which has a parent and stepparent, does not necessarily fit the same criteria for who is, and who is not, a member of the family. New fertility technologies (the use of donor eggs, surrogate mothers, and so forth) are challenging definitions of the family based on shared genetic heritage. The influence of feminism as a challenge to automatic male privilege is shaking the typical hierarchies in the family.

In spite of the obvious problems with structural definitions, most family research still uses "the household" as the working definition of the family. Much of the research that examines family interaction uses a family structure approach in that the families involved are sociolegal units and the members reside in the same household. It is much easier to determine who lives with whom than it is to assess the quality of family task performance or the subjective experience of group identity and affection.

Psychosocial Task Definitions

The second set of definitions focuses on whether certain tasks of family life are performed. Here a family is a psychosocial group, consisting of at least one adult member and one or more other persons, that works toward mutual need fulfillment, nurturance, and development. Task definitions are usually concerned with describing the functions of the family.

A good working task definition defines the family as the social unit that accepts responsibility for the socialization and nurturance of children (Lerner & Spanier, 1978). In this definition, although children are the essential ingredient, those adults who take responsibility for caring for the children are also included, whether there is one parent or two, whether the adults are/are not married to one another, and even whether the adults taking primary responsibility are/are not the biological parents of the children. One or more grandparents may even be the primary caretakers of the children. The structure of the family can vary in this definition, as its focus is on the fulfillment of the task of raising children.

A definition that focuses exclusively on the task of raising children ignores the variety of pathways through the family. In this model, the childless couple is usually considered a natural stage of the nuclear family at both ends of the cycle. But what about the couple who is childless throughout life, either through choice or because of infertility? Is it useful to distinguish between couples and families? And what about single households that include young adults, never-married men and women, the divorced, and the widowed? Singles do not constitute a family by either of the first two definitions.

Transactional Process Definitions

A final group of definitions of the family gives central importance to transactional processes. A family is defined as a group of intimates who generate a sense of home and group identity, complete with strong ties of loyalty and emotion, and an experience of a history and a future (Wamboldt & Reiss, 1989).

The definition of the family as a group of intimates requires an understanding of what constitutes intimacy. Two concepts central to the meaning of intimacy are interdependence and commitment. Interdependence involves the extent to which people influence one another's feelings, thoughts, or behaviors (Kelley, 1983). High interdependence does not necessarily mean that relationships will be free

of problems; in fact, some amount of conflict is a defining characteristic of interdependent relationships (Levinger & Huston, 1990).

According to Johnson (1999), commitment to relationships can involve at least three distinct experiences: personal, moral, and structural commitments. Personal commitment results from the satisfactions occasioned by being a member of a family. Moral commitments are the obligations one feels to one's family. Structural commitments include barriers to dissolving family relationships, such as a strong belief in the permanence of marriage (Levinger, 1976).

In addition to intimacy, a transactional process definition requires a sense of home and a group identity. These attributes of a family are captured by the concept that Reiss (1981) has called "family paradigms," or the worldviews that families hold affecting how they process information from the surrounding environment. Identity for one family may be tied to the members' concept of surviving in a complex or hostile world; another family's identity may revolve around religion, and yet another's around being fun-loving.

A transactional process definition of family also implies that the family members have mutual ties of loyalty and a sense of a joint history. These characteristics of families suggest that family experiences, both good and bad, are likely to be intense. Moreover, present experiences in the family are affected by previous family experiences (Hinde, 1979), including those from members' families of origin. (For a more elaborate description of family process definitions, see Noller & Fitzpatrick, 1993.)

Summary

The three classes of family definitions emphasize different aspects of the family. Family structure definitions include as family members those who have established biological or sociolegal legitimacy by virtue of shared genetics, marriage, or adoption. These definitions specify criteria for membership and particular hierarchies based on age and sex. A variety of societal changes make family structure definitions less viable.

Psychosocial task definitions define the family as a group that works toward mutual need fulfillment as well as the nurturance and development of the members. Although these definitions help us to focus on the goals of family life, the various stages and types of families have markedly different goals, making the definition less useful than it might be.

Transactional process approaches define the family as a group of intimates who generate a sense of home and group identity, have strong ties of loyalty and emotion, and experience a history and a future. Admittedly, this definition is complex and contains many abstract concepts that themselves need to be defined. Yet the transactional definition has two advantages over the other two approaches. First, the transactional definition of the family places a very strong emphasis on communication as the major vehicle in establishing levels of interdependence and commitment, forming ties of loyalty and identity, and transmitting a sense of family identity, history, and future. Second, this definition can encompass the many forms of modern family life because this approach allows families to define themselves rather than basing the definition of the family on sociolegal or genetic criteria.

A COMMUNICATION APPROACH

Historically, most theories applied to family communication originated outside communication departments. During the 1960s, the structural-functional, interactional, and developmental perspectives were predominant metatheoretical orientations (Nye & Berardo, 1981). During the 1980s, greater emphasis was placed on the conflict (Sprey, 1979), exchange (Nye, 1979), and systems theory (Broderick & Smith, 1979) perspectives.

During the late 1980s and the 1990s, feminist (Ferree, 1990) and ethnic theories (Vega, 1990) gained prominence. Since 1990, postmodernist theories of the family have become a strong influence (Doherty, 1999). Perhaps because of their origins outside the communication field, only one of these metatheoretical approaches, the interactionist approach, which defines the family as a "unit of interacting personalities" (Burgess & Locke, 1953), explicitly assigns a central role to communication. Bochner (1976) took up this theoretical framework in an early article on family communication (see also Yerby, Buerkel-Rothfuss, & Bochner, 1994).

In recent years there has been a trend among family scholars, regardless of discipline, to focus more on communication. The contributors to two major handbooks on family theory published in the 1990s argued that a communication perspective is one of the newest emerging paradigms for studying families (Boss, Doherty, LaRossa, Schumm, & Steinmetz, 1993; Sussman, Steinmetz, & Peterson, 1999). The earlier of these two influential handbooks contained a chapter on communication theory (Fitzpatrick & Ritchie, 1993) that was grouped with such emerging paradigms as feminist theory, ethnic and racial theories, discourse and ethnomethodological work, and biosocial perspectives on the family. In the chapter on biosocial perspectives, Whitchurch and Dickson (1999) provided an account of the theoretical heritage of family communication and identified a number of conceptual assumptions that underlie "a communication approach" (p. 693). Some of these assumptions (e.g., the family is an interacting system) overlap with common metatheoretical perspectives outside the communication discipline. Others, such as the assumption that family members constantly manage dialectical tensions (Baxter & Montgomery, 1996), have gained more prominence among communication scholars than among other family researchers.

It is important to recognize that a number of metatheoretical perspectives are pertinent to the study of family communication. Approaches that consider communication to be important only within one perspective, or even those that argue that there is *one* communication theory, are misdirected. It is also misleading to suggest that any small set of assumptions undergirds all family communication research.

Regardless of the metatheoretical orientation to the family, the concept of communication is necessary, albeit not always sufficient, in any attempt to explain, predict, and understand family outcomes. The linchpin of our rationale for the importance of communication in families is our modification of Hill's summary of the constructs that are used in all of the major theoretical treatments of family (Burr, Hill, Nye, & Reiss, 1979). This taxonomical effort lists the exogenous and endogenous factors of central concern to family theorists. In the following subsections, we discuss the major concepts of interest in analyses of the family, and we clarify the role of communication in improving our understanding of the family.

Exogenous Variables

Exogenous variables include the extreme exogenous factors affecting family structures and processes as well as the input variables that are more proximate to internal family processes. Extreme exogenous variables are those that deal with the social, political, and economic environment in which a kin group finds itself. Input variables include value orientations, social class, and access to resources and social networks (for reviews, see Menaghan & Parcel, 1990; Voydanoff, 1990). Historians who study both types of exogenous variables have shown us that nostalgia for a lost family tradition that never existed has prejudiced our understanding of the contemporary family (Coontz, 2000; Goode, 1963).

Without a historical framework, our understanding of current family difficulties such as incest and violence is severely hampered (Gordon, 1988). Providing a thorough historical perspective on families is beyond the scope of this chapter, but in Table 19.1 we present a summary of a number of myths about families that have not been supported by careful historical analyses (Coontz, 1992, 2000; Cooper, 1999; Hareven, 1980).

Despite the myths, family scholars generally agree that families have undergone substantial changes in the past few generations (Ganong & Coleman, 1999; Peterson & Steinmetz, 1999). There is, however, considerable controversy about the implications of these changes. According to one view, changes such as increased divorce rates since 1960 indicate a decline in the family that has potentially dire consequences, such as ineffective child rearing (Popenoe, 1993, 1999).

Functionalist scholars argue that the changes affecting American families are even more widespread than the increased divorce rates suggest. Families in the 20th century became situated in an increasingly bureaucratic environment (Parsons & Bales, 1955) that began fulfilling many of the historical functions of the family (for example, the education and socialization of children). Although it is not clear what happens when the family starts to lose some of its historical functions, some theorists argue that losing certain functions may hinder the family's ability to serve remaining functions, such as providing affectionate bonds (Lasch, 1977). When peers, and not parents, socialize adolescents, the emotional relationships between parents and adolescent children are probably significantly altered (Csikszentmihalyi, Rathunde, & Whalen, 1993). The emotional bonds between children and their parents may also be affected by nonparental care during infancy (Belsky, 1990).

The argument just noted is very controversial. Coontz (2000) argues that families historically have come in diverse forms and

Table 19.1   Seven Myths Not Supported by Historical Research on the American Family

Myth: Large extended family households were common in preindustrial America.
Fact: Although extended family households did exist, they represented a small proportion of households.

Myth: Migration associated with industrialization contributed to the decline of close family ties.
Fact: Because family members often followed each other to new locations, such migration actually helped keep extended family ties close in many instances.

Myth: Diversity in the forms of families is a new challenge in America.
Fact: There have been diverse family forms throughout all periods of American history.

Myth: Substance abuse is a greater challenge to American families now than ever before.
Fact: Alcohol and drug use was higher at the end of the 19th century than at the end of the 20th century.

Myth: The value placed on motherhood has declined in modern times.
Fact: Motherhood was not glorified as a career until the 19th century.

Myth: Stability and uniformity in family life-cycle transitions declined markedly in the 20th century compared to previous centuries.
Fact: In many ways, American families achieved unprecedented stability and uniformity in life-cycle transitions in the 20th century; for example, shorter life spans in earlier centuries contributed to comparatively short marriages.

Myth: In recent years, families have allowed children greater access to information about sex than ever before.
Fact: Open discussions about sex in front of children were common from the colonial period through the 18th century.

have served numerous functions. Although this suggests that the loss of some functions may not prevent families from serving other functions, Coontz asserts that this does not mean that all family forms are equally successful. In the 19th century, the children who were raised by full-time mothers in middle-class families were privileged in comparison with children in other families (whose mothers and children were needed for cheap domestic service and industrial labor).

Similarly, feminists argue that functionalist views privilege the experiences of men and fathers in families over those of women and mothers (e.g., Thorne, 1992). Three themes have especially mystified women's varied experiences of the family: ideologies of motherhood, the notion of the family as a domestic refuge,

and an emphasis on love and consensus as the sole basis of family relations. The feminist arguments for alternative conceptions of the family are compelling, although emotional and psychological factors have achieved preeminence in society's view of the family. Whereas feminist writers are correct in wanting women and mothers to have a voice in defining those emotional and psychological functions, the very demands for a female voice place increasing pressure on family members to communicate. If the major function of the modern family is emotional, greater demands are placed on all participants to engage in expressive communication.

A societal commitment to expressivity in families is potentially emotionally risky (Moscovici, 1967; Parks, 1982). For instance, in her line of research on hurtful messages, Vangelisti found that individuals often describe messages as most hurtful when they come from family members rather than somebody else (Vangelisti & Crumley, 1998). Moreover, whereas people are likely to distance themselves from others who hurt them, individuals often do not distance themselves from family members who convey hurtful messages, perhaps because they view their family members as irreplaceable (Vangelisti, 1994b, 2001; Vangelisti & Maguire, 2002). Also, an individual is more likely to observe, commit, or be a victim of violence within his or her own family than in any other setting (Gelles, 1974). The modern family is a place in which hatred and violence are felt, expressed, and learned as consistently as love.

A consideration of such exogenous variables strengthens our theoretical work on the family. Exogenous factors set the scope conditions for our conceptual efforts by reminding us of the historical and cultural limitations of our empirical generalizations. At the very least, these factors remind us of the range and diversity possible in family systems (van den Berghe, 1978). Environmental diversity dramatically affects the input variables, and through these the meaning and even the frequency of communicative exchanges are altered.

Additionally, exogenous variables can be directly and productively linked to internal family processes. There is growing evidence, for example, that exogenous factors interact with families through the mass media (Bryant & Bryant, 2001). Children exposed to television content frequently experience fear and other negative emotions that can affect the entire family (Cantor & Mares, 2001). Family members spending time together frequently do so with a television as a defining part of the context, allowing television (and the exogenous content that comes with it) to help shape themes of conversation, role expectations, and power relations (Alexander, 2001).

Endogenous Variables

Internal, performance, and output variables are the endogenous factors in theoretical approaches to the family. The specific variables covered by these factors are displayed in Figure 19.1. As we have argued, the exogenous variables can be used to predict kinship communication patterns. Communication—save in its most narrow definition of communication structure (i.e., who speaks to whom)—is overlooked in this taxonomy of major family variables. Although the centrality of communication in a variety of relational processes is one of the topoi for communication scholars, communication is assigned a peripheral role in traditional psychological and sociological studies of families and close relationships.

There are at least three senses in which communication can be conceptually related to these endogenous variables. First, communication can be construed as the underlying causal mechanism that translates the set of internal variables into the outcome variables. Second, communication can be seen as the intervening variable linking internal, performance, and output processes. Third, communication can be seen as constitutive in that it produces and reproduces the social structure of marriage and the family (R. D. McPhee, personal communication, May 1984). One's metatheoretical framework determines which of these three orientations toward communication in kin relationships one can most fruitfully adopt. Without an explication of the nature and function of communication, however, the specification of the relationships among the internal, performance, and output variables is incomplete.

Internal Variables

Internal family variables are frequently operationalized by a variety of verbal and nonverbal messages. The gestures, words, actions,

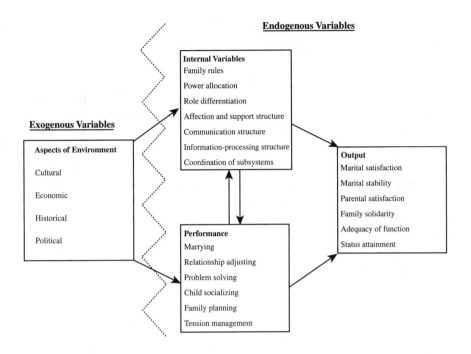

Figure 19.1 Exogenous Influences and Major Endogenous Variables Across All Theories of the Family

NOTE: This figure is essentially an analytic device isolating the central factors employed in theoretical approaches to the study of kin relationships. Theories that employ a constitutive approach would tend to see less of a conceptual differentiation between internal and performance factors (Poole, McPhee, & Seibold, 1982). For example, role differentiation would not exist separate and apart from its instantiation in the ongoing conflict or problem-solving activities of a couple or a family.

and silences, even the presence or absence, of a family member are representative of a number of different internal family concepts (Raush, Grief, & Nugent, 1979). Family rules are often defined through observation of the interaction that takes place among family members (Napier & Whitaker, 1978). Power allocation and role differentiation can be signaled by behaviors such as successful interruptions, talk-overs, and talk time (see, e.g., Folger, 1978; Millar & Rogers, 1976). The affection and support structure of a family are manifested by the occurrence or nonoccurrence of specific nonverbal affect cues (see, e.g., Lamb, 1976a) as well as language characteristics (Berger & Bradac, 1982). The communication structure is defined as who speaks

to whom and how often (Farace, Monge, & Russell, 1977; Waxler & Mishler, 1970). The information-processing structure is measured by how information is shared in a family (Reiss, 1981). Finally, coordination is defined as the meshing of interaction sequences among or between partners (Berscheid, 1983).

A close examination of these internal variables suggests that a more parsimonious structure is possible. Perhaps the basic dimensions internal to the family are affect and power or cohesion and adaptability (Olson, Sprenkle, & Russell, 1979). These are the major dimensions of interpersonal behavior according to a number of different perspectives (Bochner, Kaminski, & Fitzpatrick, 1977). Control subsumes the internal concepts of family rules, power allocations, role differentiation, communication and information-processing structures, and coordination, whereas affect subsumes the affection and support structures (Olson et al., 1983).

The use of verbal and nonverbal communication as operational definitions of internal family variables obscures important characteristics of these variables. Although the direct exchange of verbal and nonverbal messages is central to family processes, communication alone cannot explain all of the variance in family outcomes. The cognitive and affective perspectives represented by these internal family variables would be better operationalized through a consideration of the attitudes, values, and/or relational theories that individuals and families hold concerning family interaction (Fitzpatrick, 1988; Ritchie & Fitzpatrick, 1990). In other words, internal variables are best construed as the factors that account for the observed regularities in performance variables and not as performance variables per se.

Performance Variables

Performance variables are overt behavioral activities. For communication researchers, these activities are primarily verbal and nonverbal exchanges. The six performance variables isolated in Figure 19.1 are behavioral episodes that occur in families.

An explicit analytic separation of classes of internal and performance variables may help in the development of concepts and theories at the same level of abstraction, that is, the individual, dyadic, triadic, and so forth. Researchers can study performance variables at the individual level of social behavior by focusing on the communication style of a given individual (Norton, 1983). Researchers can also study these variables at the dyadic level by examining messages in sequence at the interact, double interact, or higher order. Many of the existing dyadic-level concepts are better considered as communication concepts

(for example, complementarity, reciprocity, dominance) because the linking between two individuals occurs behaviorally through the exchange of messages.

Although theories need not restrict themselves to concepts at the same order of abstraction, theories of communication in close relationships must explicitly deal with the issue of how these classes of concepts translate across various levels of analysis. Is it an individual's marital satisfaction that is explained by an interaction pattern between spouses, or is it some more abstract concept of satisfaction with the relationship for both people (and under what conditions)?

Output Variables

The very idea that central family processes should predict "outcomes" should give the reader pause. Studies of the modern family are based on powerful value assumptions, and these become very clear as we consider this set of ultimate dependent variables (see Figure 19.1). Our theories and research are aimed at predicting a set of value-laden goals. For example, although our research is very concerned with happiness for adults (marital and parental satisfaction), little attention is paid to happiness for children.

Here we need to struggle with a consideration of the "normalcy" of a family. If one takes a functional definition of families, normality could be defined in terms of the ability of the family to fulfill its functions. Transactional process definitions, however, require a way to deal with the complex variations in families, including those associated with ethnic, racial, and class differences (Walsh, 1992). Marxist and radical critiques of the family maintain that the family is an inherently dysfunctional and destructive social form that stymies the free formation of the individual's identity and exerts unnecessary controls on family members (Cooper, 1970). The very intensity of such critiques reminds us to scrutinize our values and to make those values clearer. As suggested by our review (which largely focuses on the set of outputs listed in Figure 19.1), we believe the common set of outcome variables is still important. We assume, for example, that people who marry genuinely do so with hopes that they will not become dissatisfied; thus studies of marital satisfaction are important—at least to that group of people. In our conclusion, we continue our discussion of suitable outcome variables for family research.

Most of the major family outcome variables isolated in Figure 19.1 are satisfaction and stability measures. Satisfaction concerns an individual's subjectively experienced contentment with either a marital or a parent-child relationship. Family solidarity is a stability dimension that objectively examines whether or not a given family is intact. Parents separate or divorce and children run away, and such events can be taken as measures of family instability.

The one output variable in Figure 19.1 that does not concern satisfaction or stability is *status attainment,* which refers to the achievement of a particular socioeconomic position for a family. Often, families are concerned about whether the children will attain a status equal to or better than that of the parents, particularly the fathers. Measuring status attainment involves comparing the occupational choices made by children with those of their fathers. Often the exposure to a model and the ability to talk with others about various occupations leads to children's awareness and eventual choices of specific jobs or careers (Woelfel & Haller, 1971).

The social-time dimension. Although not represented in Figure 19.1, another class of major factors is often treated in theories of the family. These factors are family development, family learning over time, intergenerational processes, economic life cycles and family performance, and family innovations. Each of these concepts adds the social-time dimension

to the model and recognizes the longitudinal nature of the family. Such concepts remind us that families follow repeated patterns of organization, disorganization, and change. Any comprehensive approach to the family must take into account the repeated continuities and discontinuities in family life (Vangelisti, 1993).

One of the difficulties in discussing the family in a developmental perspective is that much of the research conducted on the topic has used cross-sectional post hoc designs. Such designs provide a poor basis for detecting developmental trends (Baltes, 1968; Rollins, 1975) because there is potential for confusion between cohort effects and actual developmental changes (for a discussion of this point in regard to the aging couple, see Mares & Fitzpatrick, 1995).

Since the mid-1980s, there has been a tremendous increase in the number of longitudinal studies related to family communication. Even these studies, however, tend to have weaknesses that often limit their usefulness for any examination of development. Most of the longitudinal studies of marriage, for example, have begun with too few couples or have followed participants over too short a period to allow the researchers to gain a complete understanding of the developmental processes that lead many couples toward divorce (Huston, Caughlin, Houts, Smith, & George, 2001).

There has been some progress made in accounting for development in families. Whereas stage models in the past have focused on intact families and marked development according to the age of the oldest child (Duvall, 1971), more recent family development perspectives have attempted to include a wider range of developmental trajectories (Aldous, 1996).

Summary

Explicating the role of communication in predicting family outcome variables clarifies the ways different internal variables have led to different outcomes. A traditional orientation to male and female roles, for example, constrains the communication between marital partners, which leads to a high degree of satisfaction for some couples but not for others (Fitzpatrick, 1983).

In this section, we have delineated the major factors related to family processes and have argued that many family theories have underplayed or ignored the role of communication in predicting family outcomes. To rectify this omission, we have offered three ways to examine communication as the link among the internal, performance, and output variables. We have also proposed that a complete theory of family communication must take into account exogenous factors as they impinge on internal family processes. In the next section, we consider the empirical research on communication in the family.

OVERVIEW OF RESEARCH ON COMMUNICATION IN FAMILY RELATIONSHIPS

Four organizational principles guide this review. We adopt a systems theory metaphor (Galvin & Brommel, 2000), thus we split off subsystems in the family that have been examined apart from one another. In other words, we focus on dyads, triads, and so forth in organizing this section. Most of the empirical research has concentrated on dyads rather than on larger subsystem units.

Our second principle of organization concerns the issue of levels of analysis. The study of marital and family interaction cuts across many disciplines that approach the study of the family in varied ways. Part of the variation comes from the weights that researchers in different disciplines place on various levels of analysis. The endogenous and exogenous variables listed in Figure 19.1, for example, would be of differential interest to workers in various academic disciplines. One can conceptualize

these levels of analysis as the study of processes within individuals, interactions between individuals, properties of the component relationships themselves, the family group as a whole, and the influences of the broader community on the family (Fitzpatrick & Wamboldt, 1990). Given the enormous body of research on the family, we selectively concentrate here on studies concerned with the first two levels: processes within individuals and interactions between family members. We include these two levels because, at a minimum, a theory of communication must include how individual-level processes (e.g., cognitions, emotions) affect the encoding, exchanging, and decoding of messages between people.

Our third organizational principle limits discussion to research aimed at predicting at least one of the output variables listed in Figure 19.1. We try to give the reader a sense of the type and kind of empirical research that has been conducted on communication in kinship relations without any attempt to be comprehensive. Our fourth organizational principle takes the transactional definition seriously and incorporates different types of families, such as homosexual partners and cohabiting couples.

Family Dyads

In this subsection, we consider communication in marital (i.e., courting, established, and divorcing), homosexual, cohabiting, sibling, and mother-child dyads. Space limitations preclude a discussion of other family dyads (e.g., grandmother-grandchild); for a more comprehensive review, see Noller and Fitzpatrick (1993).

The Marital Pair: Courting

The voluminous research on initial attraction has been little help in explaining or predicting courtship progress or early marital processes (Huston & Levinger, 1978). One major explanation for this may be the over-identification of the concept of attraction with the concept of attitude (Berscheid, 1982). In ongoing relationships, individuals do not have the clear, bipolar, unambivalent responses to one another implied by the attitude construct. Treating attraction as an attitude skews research and theory on relationships into a stability framework, and an exclusively cognitive one at that (Berscheid, 1983; Graziano & Musser, 1982).

Surra and her colleagues have responded to the limits of the initial attraction research by focusing on individuals' commitment to marry during courtship (Surra, Batchelder, & Hughes, 1995; Surra & Hughes, 1997). This research indicates that "the processes by which individuals decide to wed are actually quite variable and multifaceted" (Surra et al., 1995, p. 113). Drawing on Johnson's (1999) marital commitment framework, Surra and Hughes (1997) argue that an individual considering marriage to a particular person weighs factors such as how much he or she wants to be with that person (e.g., attraction to the partner), how much he or she feels a moral obligation to that person (e.g., a promise to stay with that person), and how much he or she has structural reasons for committing (e.g., the extent to which the person fits into and is integrated into the individual's social network).

Processes within individuals. The early theoretical perspectives on how individuals select mates are stage or filter theories (Duck, 1976; Kerckhoff & Davis, 1962; Lewis, 1973; Murstein, 1967). Each implies that individuals progress toward long-term commitments by filtering various pieces of information concerning cognitive compatibility. The successful completion or passing through of a particular stage is accomplished through the (mutual) discovery of similarities and value consensus.

Such stage models have been critiqued for being too cognitive and for implying that there is one courtship script that most couples follow (Surra et al., 1995). One response to this criticism has been an increase in studies that focus on the variety of accounts that individuals have for courtship (Baxter & Bullis, 1986; Surra et al., 1995). Another interesting perspective on stage theories is that developed by Conville (1991), who grants priority to *how* partners move through transformations and representations of relationships rather than to questions of *what* stages are.

Interpersonal processes. Several scholars have proposed different typologies of courtship based on couples' accounts. Huston, Surra, Fitzgerald, and Cate (1981) developed one typology of courtship styles based on the time and rate trajectories of couples' reports of relational progress and commitment to the relationship (see Cate & Lloyd, 1992). They further discriminated these styles according to the frequency and character of the interaction within the couples as well as between the couples and others. Although we cannot fully describe the courtship styles here, one style is particularly striking: a couple type marked by less positive affect and less companionship than other couples. Intriguingly, couples of this type resemble married couples of the type called "Separates" identified in another theoretical perspective (Fitzpatrick, 1984). It appears that some couples begin marriage relatively disaffiliated and noncompanionate, yet holding traditional sex role ideologies (Huston et al., 1981).

Surra and her colleagues propose another distinction in courtship types: relationship-driven versus event-driven courtships (Surra et al., 1995; Surra & Hughes, 1997). Relationship-driven courtships are characterized by steadily increasing commitment to marry. Couples in such courtships cite fairly mundane reasons for their increases in commitment (e.g., spending more time together and communicating more with each other). In contrast, event-driven courtships involve many ups and downs in commitment and a variety of different courtship trajectories. Couples in these courtships often attribute such changes to external events or to interactions with or attributions about third parties (e.g., alternative partners).

Interaction during courtship is a significant predictor of early marriage outcomes. In a longitudinal study, Kelly, Huston, and Cate (1985) found that premarital conflict was inversely associated with wives' love and satisfaction 2 years later. Similarly, Markman (1979, 1981, 1984) found that dissatisfaction with the relationship after 1 year of marriage, 2.5 years of marriage, and 5 years of marriage was related to communication problems present before marriage. The more positively the partners rated their communication during a laboratory negotiation session before marriage, the more satisfied they were with their relationship at the later times. Additionally, Noller and Feeney's (1998) longitudinal research indicated that conflict before marriage was significantly related to husbands' dissatisfaction in the second year of marriage. Noller and Feeney also found that wives' premarital dissatisfaction predicted conflict in the second year of marriage. Based on their overall pattern of findings, these researchers conclude that "early satisfaction may be a stronger predictor of later communication than early communication is of later satisfaction" (p. 30).

The Marital Pair: Established

The two key output variables motivating most of the research on the marital pair are marital satisfaction and marital stability. Until recently, it was often assumed that dissatisfaction is the primary cause of divorce, and this has often led researchers to assume that the predictors of dissatisfaction and divorce are

the same (Huston, 2000). However, Karney and Bradbury's (1995) meta-analysis of longitudinal studies on marriage suggested that there is only a moderate association between marital dissatisfaction and eventual divorce. This led Karney and Bradbury to conclude that "decisions to divorce are affected by variables other than marital quality" (p. 21).

Processes within individuals. In the 1990s, probably the most frequently researched topic pertaining to adult romantic relationships was attachment styles (for a review, see Feeney, Noller, & Roberts, 2000). This perspective is based on Bowlby's (1972) theory about the need of an infant to establish an attachment bond with a primary caretaker. Because we address attachment theory more below in our discussion of parent-child communication, we do not examine it in depth here. It is important to note, however, that attachment styles may influence romantic partners' communication behaviors and their interpretations of each other's communication behaviors (Guerrero, 1996; Le Poire et al., 1997).

Married individuals' perceptions and evaluations of their relationship, and of the communication in their relationship, are important correlates of marital outcomes. Baucom, Epstein, Sayers, and Sher (1989) distinguished among several different types of marital cognitions that are important to spouses' interpretations of marital interaction. Two of these cognitions, attributions (i.e., individuals' causal explanations for marital behaviors) and standards (i.e., beliefs about what marital relationships ought to be like), have been the focus of considerable research related to marital communication.

Fincham, Bradbury, and their colleagues have conducted an extensive program of research on attributions in marriage (Bradbury, Beach, Fincham, & Nelson, 1996; Fincham, Harold, & Gano-Phillips, 2000; Karney & Bradbury, 2000). Spouses who rate their partners' negative behaviors as intentional, blameworthy, and selfishly motivated are more likely to behave negatively and less likely to behave positively toward their partners (Bradbury et al., 1996). Also, two longitudinal studies have shown that such maladaptive attributions are associated with declines in satisfaction and that dissatisfaction predicts increases in maladaptive attributions (Fincham et al., 2000; Karney & Bradbury, 2000).

Vangelisti and Daly (1997) examined the role of standards in close relationships, including marriage. Such standards reflect individuals' aspirations for relationships. A factor analysis suggested that the standards could be summarized in terms of seven dimensions: relational identity, integration, affective accessibility, trust, future orientation, role fulfillment, and flexibility. Consistent with the idea that standards are criteria for what relationships should be like, discrepancies between individuals' relationship standards and their perceptions of their current relationships are associated with marital dissatisfaction (Baucom, Epstein, Daiuto, et al., 1996; Baucom, Epstein, Rankin, & Burnett, 1996).

Another social cognitive factor that has received considerable attention is the notion of perspective taking. The inability to orient to the perspective of one's spouse has been cited by marital counselors as one of the most common causes of communication problems (Vangelisti, 1994a). Spouses who are comparatively skilled at perspective taking tend to have more communication skills, such as the ability to infer the intent of their marital partners' messages correctly (Denton, Burleson, & Sprenkle, 1995). However, a recent study of spouses' cognitions during conflict suggests that spouses rarely take their partners' perspectives during conflict and that attempts to do so often result in inaccurate inferences (Sillars, Roberts, Dun, & Leonard, 2001; Sillars, Roberts, Leonard, & Dun, 2000). Research in the coming years should attempt to rectify the

apparent importance of perspective taking with the evidence of its scarcity.

Interpersonal processes. Perhaps the most investigated question related to family communication concerns the connection between marital interaction and marital outcomes such as dissatisfaction and divorce. The most prevalent perspective on this issue is that "the way couples handle their disagreements is the best predictor of the long-term success of their relationships" (Notarius, Lashley, & Sullivan, 1997, p. 219). This view, which Huston et al. (2001) have labeled the *emergence of distress* model, focuses on destructive aspects of conflict, with the assumption that such behaviors "actively erode the positive factors that bring partners together and fuel relationship satisfaction" (Clements, Cordova, Markman, & Laurenceau, 1997, p. 343). Consistent with this view, the majority of studies that have sought to link observations of marital interaction to marital outcomes have asked participating couples to engage in some problem-solving task (Bradbury, Cohan, & Karney, 1998; Fincham, 1998).

Early work from the emergence of distress perspective was primarily cross-sectional, and it consistently found that happily and unhappily married couples can be distinguished by their rates of exchange of negative communication behaviors, such as criticizing, complaining, and sarcasm (Revenstorf, Vogel, Wegener, Hahlweg, & Schindler, 1980; Ting-Toomey, 1983). Also, happy and distressed couples differ in the sequence and patterning of their conflicts (Christensen, 1988). The pattern of communication in which one spouse demands or criticizes while the other withdraws is associated with concurrent marital dissatisfaction (Christensen & Heavey, 1990; Heavey, Christensen, & Malamuth, 1995; Noller, Feeney, Bonnell, & Callan, 1994).

Also, although all couples tend to reciprocate positive affect, unhappy couples are more likely than happy couples to reciprocate negative communication behaviors (Gottman, Markman, & Notarius, 1977). Such extreme patterning seems to occur even at the physiological level (Levenson & Gottman, 1983). As they communicate with one another, unhappily married spouses show a high degree of predictable physiological responses to one another's comments. Such physiological chaining of responses suggests one reason that couples report feelings of being trapped in a marriage.

In short, there is abundant evidence that seemingly destructive conflict patterns are associated with marital dissatisfaction. This perspective has been extended through a number of longitudinal studies that have demonstrated that negative conflict behaviors usually predict decreases in marital satisfaction over time (for a review, see Karney & Bradbury, 1995). Based on such findings, Gottman (1993; Gottman & Levenson, 1992) has proposed the *cascade model of marital dissolution*. Gottman's work suggests that there is a trajectory or cascade toward divorce, with couples who eventually divorce remaining unhappily married for some time, then seriously considering dissolution, then actually separating and divorcing. This cascade is predicted by a balance between positivity and negativity in couples' interactions. In this theory, Gottman isolates three stable types of marriages: volatile couples (highest in emotional expressivity), validating couples (at the middle level in emotional expressivity), and conflict-avoiding couples (lowest in emotional expressivity). Gottman (1994) acknowledges that these types are very similar to those isolated by Fitzpatrick (see discussion below).

Despite the impressive findings associated with the emergence of distress perspective, this view probably oversimplifies the connections between marital interaction and distress. First, even if seemingly destructive conflict behaviors predict decreases in marital satisfaction, this does not establish causality; in fact, the connection between changes in satisfaction and the emergence of negative behaviors is likely reciprocal (Noller & Feeney, 1998). Second, several studies have found examples of seemingly negative conflict patterns that are inversely associated with concurrent marital satisfaction but predict increases in satisfaction over time in marriage (Caughlin, 2002; Gottman & Krokoff, 1989; Heavey et al., 1995). Rather than suggesting a cascade toward divorce, such findings suggest that seemingly aversive conflict behaviors may be functional in some marriages. Third, the emergence of distress model fails to account for the evidence that the connection between dissatisfaction and divorce is moderate at best (Karney & Bradbury, 1995). The most dissatisfied couples are not necessarily the ones who get divorced; in fact, there is a significant minority of couples in stable marriages who are relatively unhappy throughout their marriages and whose marital interaction is characterized by comparatively frequent complaints and criticisms (Caughlin, Huston, & Houts, 2000; Huston et al., 2001). Such findings have led Bradbury, Rogge, and Lawrence (2001) to conclude that "conflict and marital problem-solving behavior can, at best, account for a relatively small proportion of the variability in eventual marital outcomes" (p. 72).

Given the evidence that the emergence of distress model cannot fully account for marital outcomes, other theoretical models of marital change must be explored. One, the *enduring dynamics model* (Huston et al., 2001), suggests that many of the processes in marriage tend to be relatively stable. This model is consistent with Karney and Bradbury's (1997) finding that neuroticism measured when couples were newlyweds was consistently related with the spouses' marital dissatisfaction over the next 4 years of marriage. Similarly, Caughlin et al. (2000) found that newlywed measures of trait anxiety were associated with marital dissatisfaction and with exchanges of negativity between spouses both early in marriage and 13 years later. Trait anxiety was not, however, associated with divorce. Such findings suggest that spouses' traits have a continuing influence on the interpersonal tenor of marriage. Thus some communication correlates of marital dissatisfaction probably endure (rather than instigate a cascade toward divorce).

A third model of marital change, the *disillusionment model,* suggests that the loss of positive feelings and behaviors leads some couples to divorce. In a 13-year longitudinal study that began when the participating couples were newlyweds, Huston et al. (2001) found that couples who divorced at least 2 years after their weddings were not particularly high in the negative behaviors typically associated with the emergent distress model. Instead, the trajectories of such couples were more consistent with disillusionment: Changes such as declines in affectionate behavior over the first 2 years of marriage foreshadowed divorce, even among couples who remained married for at least 5 years after the decreases in affectionate communication were observed. In contrast, couples who divorced before their second anniversaries seemed similar to the distressed couples described by Gottman (1994) in that their expressions of negativity far exceeded their expressions of affection. Similarly, in a 14-year longitudinal study, Gottman and Levenson (2000) found that expressions of negative affect predicted divorces in the first 7 years of marriage (but not divorces that occurred later), whereas the absence of positive affective expressions predicted divorce after 7 years of marriage (but not divorces that occurred earlier). Such findings suggest that there are multiple pathways to divorce and that there are multiple communication correlates of eventual relational dissolution.

Another trend in marital interaction research is the call for an increased focus on behaviors outside of conflict. Pasch and her associates developed a laboratory task designed to elicit social support (Pasch & Bradbury, 1998; Pasch, Bradbury, & Davila, 1997). One spouse was asked to "talk about something you would like to change about yourself" (Pasch et al., 1997, p. 366), and the other was told to respond however he or she wanted. The ways wives sought and provided social support predicted marital outcomes 2 years after these conversations, even after the researchers controlled for spouses' negative behaviors in a separate problem-solving discussion. Along similar lines, Stafford, Dainton, and Haas (2000) found both routine and strategic maintenance behaviors to be associated with marital satisfaction.

Not only are communication constructs outside of conflict important, but a full understanding of the link between communication and marital outcomes requires knowledge of the larger psychological and behavioral context of marriage. Burleson and Xu (2001), for example, found curvilinear associations between wives' marital satisfaction and discrepancies between experienced and expected social support from their husbands. These results suggest that the meaning of social support behaviors depend on spouses' perceptions that they may be over- or underbenefited. Other studies have suggested that frequently exchanging affectionate behaviors may buffer any deleterious effects of behaviors such as negativity (Huston & Chorost, 1994) and demand/withdraw (Caughlin & Huston, 2002).

Rogers and Farace (1975) have developed another alternative model of marital interaction. Rather than focusing on negative affect, this model is based on power. Coding schemes and theories define couples according to their usual patterns of control in conversations (Ericson & Rogers, 1973; Mark, 1971; Sluzki & Beavin, 1965). Three types of couples can be defined by the message exchange patterns: symmetrical, complementary, and parallel (Lederer & Jackson, 1968; Watzlawick, Beavin, & Jackson, 1967). Symmetrical couples have higher levels of role discrepancy; couples who manifest lower proportions of competitive symmetry have higher levels of satisfaction in their marriages (Rogers, 1972). Complementary couples in which the husband is dominant report higher levels of satisfaction and less role discrepancy than do complementary couples in which the wife is dominant (Courtright, Millar, & Rogers-Millar, 1979; Millar & Rogers, 1976). Parallel couples use a balance of these patterns across topics or situations. Because the research has been limited, both in the topics discussed and in interaction duration, it has been difficult to define parallel couples (see Noller & Fitzpatrick, 1993, pp. 136-140).

Fitzpatrick and her colleagues have conducted research using a major approach that links affect and power (Fitzpatrick, 1988; Noller & Fitzpatrick, 1993). This polythetic classification scheme (Fitzpatrick, 1976, 1983, 1984) is based on three conceptual dimensions: interdependence, communication, and ideology. Interdependence and communication are affect dimensions, measured through the self-reports of individuals. Control has been measured by gender role orientations, and the ideological beliefs and standards that couples hold on a variety of family issues have been salient in distinguishing among couples.

Based on these dimensions, individuals can be categorized in terms of one of three relationship definitions: Traditional, Independent, and Separate. Traditionals are very interdependent in their marriages, have conventional ideological values about marriage and family life, and report an expressive communication style with their spouses. Independents are moderately interdependent in their marriages, have nonconventional views about marriage and family life, and report a very expressive communication style with their mates. Separates are not very interdependent in their marriage, are ambivalent about their views on marriage and family life, and report very little expressivity in their marital communication. An active program of research has shown that the couple types can be discriminated on a number of self-report and behavioral dimensions (e.g., Fitzpatrick, 1988; Fitzpatrick, Fey, Segrin, & Schiff, 1993; Fitzpatrick & Ritchie, 1994; Fitzpatrick, Vangelisti, & Firman, 1994; Segrin & Fitzpatrick, 1992).

The Marital Pair: Divorcing

Nearly 50% of marriages end in permanent separation or divorce (Bradbury, Fincham, & Beach, 2000). Although scholars have noted that the divorce rate declined somewhat during the 1990s, divorces remained about half as plentiful as marriages in the 3 years leading up to December 2000 (National Center for Health Statistics, 2001). Most people marry, and marrying is associated with significant changes in the ways individuals view themselves, their partners, and their worlds. Consequently, the breakup (or potential breakup) of the marital relationship is a serious crisis (Bloom, White, & Asher, 1979). On most scales of stress and illness, the death of a spouse, divorce, and marital separation receive the highest stress scores (Holmes & Rahe, 1976).

Processes within individuals. Prior to 1960, most scholars were concerned with the identification of a broad range of demographic and personality correlates of marital happiness and stability (Burgess & Wallin, 1953; Terman, 1938). Longitudinal studies have shown that high levels of neuroticism in wives and low impulse control in husbands predict marital dissatisfaction and divorce (Kelly & Conley, 1987). Also, demographic characteristics such as fewer years of education, lower incomes, and shorter courtships distinguish couples who separate or divorce from those who do not (Kurdek, 1991).

Interpersonal processes. Divorce is not a single event but a series of legal, psychological, sexual, economic, and social events strung out over a period of time (Bohannan, 1970;

Wallerstein & Kelly, 1980). One of the difficulties of studying divorce is that the legal fact is a poor marker for an interpersonal process. This legal step can occur at any number of places along a psychological continuum of relational dissolution. The separation that precedes a divorce involves repeated distancing, partial reconciliation, new withdrawal, and eventual equilibrium for many couples (Weiss, 1975). This approach-avoidance conflict occurs because love erodes before attachment fades (Weiss, 1975). Attachment is a bonding process that gives rise to a feeling of ease when the partner is accessible (Bowlby, 1972). Attachment explains why many couples who are separating experience extreme distress, even if both partners desire to separate.

Like courtship, disengagement is now conceptualized as a process that does not follow the same trajectory for all couples (Graham, 1997). Research on what individuals actually say during relational disintegration is nonexistent, although Miller and Parks (1982) have developed a taxonomy of disengagement strategies. Disengagement processes are difficult to examine as they occur, but Graham (1997) has successfully examined variations in postdivorce relationships by adapting procedures originally developed for obtaining retrospective accounts of courtship (Huston et al., 1981).

What couples say to others during the dissolution process is critical. After separation, women rehash and ruminate on the causes of the relationship disintegration (Harvey, Weber, Yarkin, & Stewart, 1982). Women relate marital dissolution to interpersonal problems rather than to the structural factors that men mention (Hill, Rubin, & Peplau, 1976). Called "grave dressing" (Duck, 1982) or "accounts" (Harvey et al., 1982; Weiss, 1975), these statements are histories of a relationship that structure events in a narrative sequence to allocate blame for relationship failures. Similar to accounts of courtship (Surra et al., 1995), accounts of the divorce

process bring the social context into the study of relational development.

In considering marital dissolution, it is important to consider not only the stages through which a relationship passes but also patterned differences among individuals or couples. Kressel, Jaffee, Tuchman, Watson, and Deutsch (1980) isolated types of divorcing couples based on their differing approaches to divorce. Especially when children are involved, divorced couples continue in relationships with each other (Graham, 1997; Metts & Cupach, 1995). Ahrons (1994) describes these relationships as ranging from "Perfect Pals" to "Fiery Foes."

The Cohabiting Couple

Cohabitation is seen as a way to achieve closeness without sacrificing autonomy and independence (Newcomb, 1987). Most couples see cohabitation not as an alternative to marriage but as a prelude, because most plan to marry (Risman, Hill, Rubin, & Peplau, 1981). Cohabitation does, however, delay marriage (Newcomb & Bentler, 1980), and only 20-30% of cohabiting couples marry one another (Newcomb, 1987).

Processes within individuals. Compared with married couples, cohabitors overall report lower relational quality (Nock, 1995), but those cohabitors with plans to marry do not differ much from married couples (Brown & Booth, 1996). One large Australian study found no differences between married and cohabiting couples on expressiveness, sex practices, empathy, organization (planning, rules, and responsibilities), sex roles, the involvement of women in careers, or cultural activities (Sarantakos, 1984). Married couples did see their relationships as more stable and believed that they were more committed and helpful to their partners than were cohabiting couples. Finally, there was more conflict, even violent conflict, in cohabiting than in married couples.

Interpersonal processes. Does cohabiting help or hinder a subsequent marriage? Getting to know the foibles and idiosyncrasies of one's future partner potentially could prepare one for marriage. However, research has found lower levels of satisfaction and less satisfactory communication in marriages preceded by cohabitation (DeMaris & Leslie, 1984; Watson, 1983). Also, couples who cohabit before marriage are more likely to divorce than are couples who marry without cohabiting (Cunningham & Antill, 1995; Faust & McKibben, 1999). DeMaris and MacDonald (1993) found that the connection between premarital cohabitation and later divorce applied only to serial cohabitors—not to spouses who cohabited for the first time as a prelude to their first marriage.

The Homosexual Couple

Due to space limitations, we focus our attention here on homosexual dyads rather than larger family units (e.g., lesbians or gay men and their children). Patterson (2000) provides a more complete review.

Homosexual males, in particular, are stereotyped as promiscuous and not interested in establishing lasting relationships (Blumstein & Schwartz, 1983). Yet, even without the social support given to married couples (e.g., recognized marriages, joint income tax), significant numbers of homosexual men and women have established healthy, functioning relationships. Researchers have employed a number of different strategies to examine these relationships. Some have compared homosexual and heterosexual couples (e.g., Kurdek, 1998). Others have explored these relationships in depth and developed typologies of couples (e.g., McWhirter & Mattison, 1984). Still others have imported an idea from an established line of inquiry on heterosexual couples and use it with a homosexual sample (Fitzpatrick, Jandt, Myrick, & Edgar, 1993).

Processes within individuals. The most popular means of classifying homosexual couples has been according to sexual exclusivity or fidelity. Bell and Weinberg (1978) used this open-closed dichotomy to explain a number of individual differences. For instance, gay males in closed relationships reported a higher degree of self-acceptance, whereas those in open relationships were significantly more tense and depressed.

Reviews of studies comparing lesbian and gay couples to heterosexual couples report many similarities in terms of individuals' desires for and evaluations of their relationships (Peplau, Veniegas, & Campbell, 1996; Savin-Williams & Esterberg, 2000). Researchers have generally found no differences in terms of the desire to be in a committed relationship, attraction to partner, or satisfaction with the relationship. Peplau (2001), however, suggests that gay male couples likely differ from dyads with at least one woman because women's primary goal for sex is usually to express affection, whereas men's primary goal is often gratification.

Interpersonal processes. In a longitudinal study of relationship quality in homosexual couples, greater relationship quality was reported by lesbian couples, compared with homosexual male couples, and by couples who had lived together for more than 11 years (Kurdek, 1989). Reciprocal expressiveness and equality of power seem to be particularly important themes in lesbian relationships (Kurdek, 1998; Peplau & Cochran, 1981). However, Kurdek (2000) found striking similarities among lesbian, gay, and heterosexual couples in terms of the longitudinal predictors of satisfaction and commitment. Attractive features of relationships, such as receiving a desirable amount of affection and companionship, were associated with variability in commitment over time, regardless of couple composition.

Using the Relational Dimensions Instrument, Fitzpatrick, Jandt, et al. (1993) characterized a sample of lesbian and male homosexual couples as Traditional, Separate, Independent, and Mixed couples. Compared with a major random sample of heterosexual couples (Fitzpatrick & Indvik, 1982), there were significantly more male Separate couples, about the same proportion of Traditionals, and fewer Independents. For lesbian couples, there were significantly more Traditionals and fewer Separates and Independents. The sampling strategy may account for these results. The sample was drawn from Couples National Network, an organization formed to provide education and outreach to individuals involved in homosexual relationships. Indeed, Harry and Lovely (1979) found that individuals who were most integrated into the homosexual community were in relationships that were more "marriagelike." That is, they tended to live with their lovers, had monogamous arrangements, and had more emotional intimacy. In typology terms, such individuals are more likely to have traditional orientations toward relationships. Some of these individuals pair a traditional orientation with a close interdependent bond (i.e., Traditionals), and others pair that ideology with a less connected bond (i.e., Separates).

The Sibling Relationship

Sibling relationships are important throughout most people's lives. Most people spend a good portion of their childhoods living with siblings, and 80% of elderly individuals have living siblings (McKay & Caverly, 1995). Children's interactions with their siblings greatly influence their personal happiness when they are growing up (Bowerman & Dobash, 1974). Moreover, the affective tone of early sibling relationships predicts the quality of interaction between the siblings into adolescence (Dunn, Slomkowski, & Beardsall, 1994) and adulthood (Bank & Kahn, 1997).

Influenced by Freud (1949), much of the early literature on family interaction discussed sibling relationships in terms of negative affect (Bossard & Boll, 1950). Children show signs of hostility, anxiety, and competition at the birth of a younger sibling (Cameron, 1963). When they are young, siblings often compete in the family for the love, attention, and favor of one or both of the parents (Levy, 1937). During the beginning of the children's school years, however, increased positive behavior and decreased aggression may appear, particular if the siblings are separated in age by more than 4 years (Minnett, Vandell, & Santrock, 1983). Whatever the degree of hostility between siblings, it may be resolved by consistent parental affection, the development of an attachment bond between siblings, and the socialization of aggression (Tsukada, 1979).

Researchers have also reported on other positive aspects of the interaction between siblings. Siblings can aid each other in the development of social competence, which is important to children's establishing relationships with other children (Parke & O'Neil, 1997). They also offer one another companionship, security, and love (Duberman, 1973). Taken together, the research suggests that sibling relationships typically involve a mix of negative and positive elements; not surprisingly, many adults have ambivalent feelings toward their siblings (Treas & Lawton, 1999).

Processes within individuals. Extensive work has examined the effects of birth order in sibling relationships on personality development and achievement (Paulhus, Trapnell, & Chen, 1999; Toman, 1961). Such research describes characteristic personality traits associated with each place in the birth order. Even the eventual marital adjustment of an individual has been linked to his or her position in the family of origin (Toman, 1961).

Despite the intriguing findings pertaining to birth order, there is limited understanding as to why these differences exist. It is plausible that individual differences in tactics, aggression, sex role preferences, and interests in later-born children can be attributed to the processes of identification and modeling of older siblings. Alternatively, the conforming, achievement, and affiliative behaviors of first-born children may be attributed to the children's special relationship to the parents (Sutton-Smith & Rosenberg, 1970). This latter possibility would be consistent with the notion of differential treatment of siblings by parents (see the discussion of family triads below). It is important to note that some scholars have questioned the practical importance of birth-order effects (Schooler, 1972). Behavioral genetics researchers, for instance, argue that less than 2% of variation in the differences between siblings can be explained by birth-order position (Dunn & Plomin, 1990).

Interpersonal processes. Sibling status variables of age, birth order, birth interval, and sex do not fully account for sibling differences (Scarr & Grajek, 1982). Dunn (1983) argues that these constructs may be inadequate to account for sibling behavior because they reference complementary behaviors (A is older than B) in an attempt to predict reciprocal behaviors (A and B are mutually aggressive). Conceptual discriminations among peer, sibling, and parent-child interaction in terms of reciprocity and complementarity would help.

Although increased theoretical interest in the development and maintenance of peer relationships in children may not be directly applicable to the study of siblings (see, e.g., Hartup, 1978; La Gaipa, 1981), valuable lines of research could examine similarities and differences between peer and sibling interactions. Peer interactions are reciprocal interactions in that each partner can understand the reasoning and perspective of the other. Sibling relationships may be similar to the direct reciprocity of peer relationships because of their intensity, familiarity, and intimacy, as well as

siblings' recognition and sharing of interests. Examples of reciprocity of interaction between sibling pairs include siblings' frequent imitation of each other's actions, their demonstration of joy and excitement in coaction sequences, and their willingness to engage in prosocial and comforting actions.

Given the age differences between siblings, these relationships also have some similarities with the parent-child relationship (Dunn, 1983). Parent-child interactions are complementary interactions in that the behavior of each differs from but fits that of the other. Caregiving, teaching, and attachment in sibling relationships are inherently complementary. Unfortunately, few studies have actually examined the reciprocal or complementary structure of the interaction (see Dunn, 1983). Sibling studies generally report rates and/or frequencies; these are inadequate for summarizing social interaction over time.

Siblings adjust their communication behaviors to each other's developmental abilities (Shatz & Gelman, 1977). Even the 2- and 3-year-olds studied by Dunn and Kendrick (1982) made systematic adjustments when speaking to their 14-month-old siblings. Older siblings tended to clarify their speech for their conversational partner, but only those older siblings who had particularly warm relationships with the infants used expressive linguistic features. Conversational turns in these sibling interactions were shorter than those of the mother with the infant, and the infant did not respond to them as strongly. Both mother and infant attempted to maintain the attention of the other, whereas sibling-infant turns were primarily nonverbal sequences, such as alternate imitations of one another over a shorter span of time.

In comparing the interactions of 4- to 8-year-old children with parents and with siblings, Baskett and Johnson (1982) found that the interaction behavior of a target child was remarkably different with parents versus siblings. Interactions with the parent were more numerous and varied than were those with a sibling. Children talked, laughed, and touched the parents more and were more compliant with their wishes. Undesirable behaviors directed to parents seemed designed primarily to draw attention (e.g., whining). Only one prosocial behavior occurred more frequently in sibling interactions than in parent-child interactions: Siblings tended to play or work with one another more. In general, brothers and sisters used more physical aggression, yelling, hitting, and negative commands with one another than they did with parents. Regardless of the state of the relationships between the siblings, the siblings preferred interacting with a parent to interacting with a sibling.

Lamb (1978) found that preschool-age children both offered their toys and talked to their 18-month-old siblings. The toddlers watched and imitated the older children and took over the toys the older children abandoned. In a study of sibling dyads, Abramovitch, Corter, and Peplar (1980) found that both same- and mixed-sex dyads interacted a great deal. A sibling initiated or responded to the other member of the dyad once a minute. Regardless of the sex or age differences among the dyads, the older child in each pair initiated more (84%) of the antagonistic acts and most of the prosocial acts as well. In both same- and mixed sex dyads, younger children initiated most of the imitative behaviors. In same-sex dyads, older boys were more physically aggressive than older girls. Girls tended to initiate more prosocial acts and responded positively to the prosocial acts of a sister.

Peplar, Abramovitch, and Corter (1981) observed a subset of the same sibling pairs (mixed and same sex) 18 months later. The children's ages ranged from 3 years to 7 years, and the researchers categorized them according to the age spacing between siblings in a dyad: small age spacing (1 to 2 years) or large age spacing (2.5 to 4 years). The interaction patterns among the children were similar to those previously observed. Older children engaged in more cooperation, help, and praise. Although older children initiated interaction more often, the younger children maintained the interaction by reciprocating prosocial behavior, submitting to aggressive behavior, and imitating their siblings. As the children got older, they tended to increase the number of prosocial acts in their sibling contacts. Yet there also was an increase in mixed-sex antagonism and a decrease in mixed-sex imitation, perhaps indicating the beginning of sex typing.

Children as young as 4 years old serve as attachment figures for siblings. In one sample of young children, more than 52% were effective in caring for their younger siblings who were distressed when the mother left the room. Infants seem to use their siblings as attachment figures and as secure bases from which to explore (Stewart, 1983).

In middle childhood, sibling relationships often become more egalitarian. There is some disagreement as to whether this represents a decrease in dominance attempts by both siblings (Buhrmester, 1992) or an increase in the power exerted by young children on their older siblings (Vandell, Minnett, & Santrock, 1987).

Among preadolescents, Furman and Buhrmester (1985) found that affection, hostility, and rivalry are relatively independent dimensions of children's relationships with siblings. One study examined preadolescents' perceptions of their sibling relationships and the links between sibling relationships and parent-child relationships in 103 families. Sibling ratings of affection were highly correlated, but ratings of hostility and rivalry were not related. Children who spent the most time interacting with their fathers and who rated their relationships with their fathers as warm had the most positive and the least negative sibling relationships (Stocker & McHale, 1992).

Sibling relationships in adolescence and young adulthood continue to display a mix of conflict and rivalry (Raffaelli, 1992) and closeness (Floyd, 1995). Much of the research on sibling relationships in young adulthood has centered on two issues, factors accounting for variation in the quality of sibling relationships and the influence of sex differences on sibling dyads. Communication behaviors that are associated with satisfying sibling relationships among young adults include social support and self-disclosure (Avtgis, Martin, & Rocca, 2000; Martin, Anderson, & Mottet, 1997).

Generally, adult sister dyads are thought to be more affectionate than adult brother dyads (Myers & Knox, 1998), but Floyd (1996) argues that such sex differences may be due to a feminine definition of the behaviors that foster closeness. In a study of 80 adult brother dyads, participants were asked to describe times or situations that made them feel close. Many of the brothers cited behaviors that were in line with common notions of relational closeness (e.g., shared conversations). However, the most commonly cited events that brothers perceived to foster closeness involved companionship created by having shared interests or by engaging in joint activities.

More than peers or even other family members, siblings are accessible to one another during the entire length of the developmentally formative years. They share time, space, and personal history to a degree that is not common in peer relationships (Bank & Kahn, 1997). Siblings often provide each other with a sense of security later in life (McKay & Caverly, 1995). Indeed, at the ends of our lives, our living companions and our best friends often turn out to be our siblings (Bedford & Gold, 1989).

The Parent-Child Relationship

Two primary theoretical concerns of the research on parent-child relationships are the direction of influence between parents and children and developmental issues. Early work on the relationship between parents and children assumed that influence processes are unidirectional in a family. The assumption

underlying these *social mold* approaches was that children are passive partners in socialization, awaiting the molding of their parents (Hartup, 1978). With the realization that a child contributes to the marriage and the family, more child-centered theories emerged (Bell, 1968). Peterson and Rollins (1987) call these *mirror reverse* orientations because they stipulate that children's behavior may change or influence parents. Not only when they reach adolescence or adulthood, but also as infants, neonates, or even in utero, children can influence a broad variety of family processes, including communicative responses (Lerner & Spanier, 1978). The behavior of even the youngest child can stimulate, elicit, motivate, and reward the actions of parents. Currently, both the social mold and mirror reverse orientations have been supplanted by a perspective that views parents and children as simultaneously and mutually influencing one another. These *mutual influence* approaches (e.g., Barratt, 1995; Cappella, 1987) see each family member serving as a stimulus for the behavior of other family members. Most of the research on processes within individuals operates on a social mold framework, although we do see some development of the mirror reverse and mutual influence perspectives in studies of interpersonal processes.

Understanding parent-child relationships also requires an understanding of assumptions about child development. Often, rather than studying development directly, researchers choose to study children of a particular age group. Most commonly, the focus is on young children (e.g., Belsky, Woodworth, & Crnic, 1996) or adolescents (e.g., Bogenschneider, Wu, Raffaelli, & Tsay, 1998); researchers select these samples (at least implicitly) because of some developmentally relevant assumptions (Canary, Cupach, & Messman, 1995).

The use of message techniques should vary in subtlety as children develop cognitively (Applegate, Burleson, & Delia, 1992; Plumert & Nichols-Whitehead, 1996). Indeed, the ability of mothers or fathers to adjust their messages based on the developmental levels of their children is paramount. Also, in examining the effects of parental messages on children, researchers must consider both sex composition of the dyad (e.g., father-daughter) and developmental level of the child. Researchers need to examine not just parents and children but fathers and mothers, sons and daughters.

Processes within individuals. Research on individual social behaviors has generally focused on how parental messages influence the development of a variety of characteristics in children (Hess, 1981). Parental messages can be broadly characterized as support and control messages (Rollins & Thomas, 1979; Steinmetz, 1979). Behaviors that make a child feel comfortable in the presence of a parent are support messages. These include praising, approving, encouraging, physical displays of affection, giving help, and cooperating with the child.

Behaviors designed to gain compliance with the wishes of the parent are called control messages. Control messages include coercion, love withdrawal, and induction. Coercive messages focus on external reasons the child should comply with the parent. These messages involve physical punishment, the direct application of force, the deprivation of material objects or privileges, or the threat of any of these. Controlling strategies have been negatively associated with children's self-esteem, academic achievement, and creativity (Peterson & Rollins, 1987).

Love withdrawal uses a combination of internal and external forces for compliance. These techniques indicate disapproval of the child's behavior, with the implication that love will not be restored until the child does what the parent wishes. A parent manifests love withdrawal by ignoring the child, isolating the child, making explicit statements of rejection, or signaling coldness or disappointment

through nonverbal behaviors (Rollins & Thomas, 1979).

Induction messages focus on the internal reasons the child should comply with the parent. Induction involves explanations and reasons for compliance. A parent might, for example, point out the consequences of an act for the child or for others. Belsky et al. (1996) describe a parental strategy that is very similar to induction messages that they call "control plus guidance." These messages often include an implicit explanation for the controlling behavior (e.g., "Slow down so you don't fall"). There is indirect evidence that receiving such messages helps children to develop communication competence: Such messages are associated with less defiance and less escalation of negative affect by children (Belsky et al., 1996).

Another major program of research that examines differences in messages used by parents with children is that of the constructivists (e.g., Burleson, Delia, & Applegate, 1995). These theorists are particularly concerned with reflection-enhancing messages, which encourage children to see how communicative behaviors can serve as a means of adapting to the perspectives of others. Research in the constructivist tradition has shown that parents' use of reflection-enhancing messages is related to the development of communication competence in children.

Stafford and Bayer (1993) have written a comprehensive review of the effects of supportive and controlling parental messages on children's self-control, self-esteem, and communication competence. They note, for example, that the empirical research on love withdrawal has had mixed results, but that may be because the concept has been poorly operationalized.

Beyond considering the sex composition of the dyad and the developmental level of the child, it may be of great theoretical utility to link the input and performance variables that we have been discussing to the output variables shown in Figure 19.1. Certain compliance-gaining procedures may work equally well in socializing a child to the wishes of a parent yet have remarkably different effects on family solidarity. And as Stafford and Bayer (1993) point out, certain message styles may be effective at gaining compliance only in the short term.

Interpersonal processes. One historically important issue in research on parent-child interaction has concerned messages that contradict each other across various levels of meaning (Bateson, 1975). Such contradictions are taken to be related to a variety of dysfunctional outcomes for families. One type of inconsistent message is the *double bind,* in which messages from different channels (verbal, prosodic, kinesic, facial, and so forth) create a paradox by simultaneously asserting contradictory meanings (Abeles, 1976). Double binds were once thought to cause schizophrenia, but we now understand that there is a neurochemical basis to schizophrenia (Garmezy, 1974). Still, the onset of schizophrenia seems to require both a genetic predisposition and a disturbed family environment (Miklowitz, Goldstein, & Nuechterlein, 1995). (For a more extensive summary of the research concerning the double bind, see Fitzpatrick & Badzinski, 1994.)

Most of the research on parent-child interaction has focused on the mother-child dyad. Infants as young as 7 weeks and their mothers have been observed in "proto-conversations," or interactive sequences characterized by eye gazing, face-to-face orientation, patterns of turn taking, variations in vocal intonation, and obvious mutual pleasure (Stern, 1977). Researchers who have examined mother-infant interaction have developed elaborate models of dyadic interaction to explain these processes and have argued that these interactions facilitate cognitive and social development in the infant. Keller, Lohaus, Völker, Cappenberg, and Chasiotis (1999), for example, have

documented that mothers typically respond very quickly (in less than a second) to communicative signals (but not necessarily to other behaviors) from their infants. These researchers suggest that such quick responses help teach infants about causality.

Infants are predisposed to the development of primitive communication skills (Barratt, 1995). From early on, the behavior of an infant forms patterned, functional units that are easy to recognize. The first communication from a baby is a cry. As infants selectively attend to the world around them, they indicate a preference for human faces over other shapes and look at faces and try to talk to them rather than to bottles or breasts (Bell, 1974). Infants also have preferences for the human voice, and by the end of the first month can be quieted by soft, high-pitched talking (Kaplan & Kaplan, 1971).

Caregivers recognize these patterned units and assume that at least some of them provide indications of what is happening inside the infant (Richards, 1974). They respond to the differential cries of an infant and identify three types of cries: those caused by hunger, pain, and anger. Objectively, these cries differ in terms of pitch, pattern, and intonation (Wasz-Hockert, Lind, Vuorenkoski, Partenen, & Valarne, 1968; Wolff, 1971). The caregiver helps the infant not only to achieve appropriate levels of tension and arousal but also to organize the behavior to which the caregiver contingently responds (Sroufe, 1979). A baby's smiles, burps, and coos are responded to by an adult as turns in conversation. Caregivers use tag questions and other postcompleters to pass the conversational turn to a baby (Snow, 1972). Indeed, the greater the use of questions by the mother, the greater the mother's desire to interact reciprocally with her infant (Snow, 1977). Effective caregivers even fill in a turn for an inactive baby by acting as if the baby had responded in the appropriate sequence (Spieker, 1982).

These early interactions facilitate the learning of language. Reciprocity (sensitivity to the partner) and intersubjectivity (experience of two persons with shared knowledge of the world) set the stage for the onset of intentional communication. The infant begins to look at a desired object, gesture and vocalize toward it, and alternate glances between the desired object and the caregiver. The emergence at 9 months of this intentional signaling is a major stage in language development (Bates, 1979; Bates, Camaioni, & Volterra, 1975). By developing a stable group of conventional gestures, babies make the discovery that the objects they desire have names (Spieker, 1982). Primitive communication, followed by attachment between infants and caregivers, sets the stage not only for language learning but for most other facets of a child's development, such as social skills (Landry, Smith, Miller-Loncar, & Swank, 1998).

Caregivers adjust their speech when speaking to infants and children at early stages of language acquisition. Mothers adjust their speech to young infants to keep the interaction going and to engage the attention of the infants (Kaye, 1980; Snow, 1977). With an infant of 6 months or older, the mother adjusts her speech by using syntactically simpler utterances to make herself understood by the child. Many theorists believe that this adjustment helps both the child's understanding and the child's general linguistic capacity (Bellinger, 1980; but see Stafford & Bayer, 1993, pp. 81-84).

"Baby talk" differs from other talk in prosody, redundancy, and grammatical complexity (Wells & Robinson, 1982). The various features of baby talk serve distinct functions. The clarification function is served by the "comm register," which includes the attention-getting devices noted in "motherese" (Snow, 1977) and in the simplification of speech and its prosodic characteristics. The expressive function is served by the "aff register," which is primarily verbal and includes the use of pet names, the playful repetition of names, and the use of diminutives and endearments. Because babies are linguistically

incompetent and typically inspire affection, baby talk occurs in both comm and aff registers.

Clarification and expressive functions may be extended to adult conversations. In families or close relationships, those who are perceived as incompetent may periodically be addressed in the comm register and those who inspire affection may be addressed at certain times in the aff register. Young people who underestimate the communication abilities of elderly persons sometimes address them using "baby talk" (Harwood, Giles, & Ryan, 1995). Spouses and lovers sometimes address each other in the aff register (Bombar & Littig, 1996; Hopper, Knapp, & Scott, 1981).

The interaction we have been describing takes place during the first 6 months of an infant's life. These interaction patterns set the stage for the development of the attachment bond. Attachment is a tie that one person forms to another specific person, which binds them together in space and endures over time. Infants appear to become attached to the figures with whom they have the most interaction (Ainsworth, 1973; Ainsworth & Bell, 1969). Attachment is indicated by behaviors that promote proximity; these include signaling behaviors, such as crying, smiling, and vocalizing; orienting behaviors, such as looking, moving toward, or following the other; and active physical contact, such as clinging or embracing.

Attachment theory claims that during the first year of life children develop fairly stable attitudes about themselves and the world around them based on the responsiveness of their caregivers (Bowlby, 1980; but see Dunn, 1988). Children whose caregivers are responsive come to see themselves as worthy of love and others as trustworthy and dependable. Infants may be secure, avoidant, or anxious-ambivalent (Ainsworth, Blehar, Waters, & Wall, 1978). Secures are generally comfortable with closeness or intimacy and are not concerned with being abandoned; avoidants are generally uncomfortable with closeness; and anxious-ambivalents crave closeness but tend to be afraid of abandonment.

The attachment bond between a caregiver and an infant predisposes the infant to comply, at a later date, with the wishes of the caregiver. Matas, Arend, and Sroufe (1982) studied 24-month-old infants who had been categorized as securely or anxiously attached to their mothers at 18 months of age. Those who could employ their mothers as secure bases from which to explore and who positively greeted their mothers following a stressful separation experience displayed more skill in problem solving and were more cooperative than were the less securely attached toddlers. Infants appear to be initially inclined to be social and, somewhat later, ready to comply with the wishes of those persons who are most significant in their environment (Stayton, Hogan, & Ainsworth, 1982).

In our discussion, we have used the term *caregiver* when referring to attachment figures in general, but much of the research is specific to mothers. Early theories assumed the primacy of the mother-infant bond (Bowlby, 1972; Freud, 1949; Winnicott, 1964). In practical terms, the mother is often uniquely important in the child's life because she often interacts the most with the child (Yingling, 1995). However, the amount of actual mother-infant interaction is frequently overestimated, and simple time spent together is a poor predictor of the quality of an infant's relationship with anyone (Lamb, 1976a). Pleasurable interaction of even only a few hours' duration appears to be more conducive to the development of an attachment bond than more extensive hours with a less stimulating caregiver (Birnbaum, 1971; Lamb, 1976a). Additionally, more recent elaborations of attachment theory explicitly acknowledge that a child may have more than one attachment figure (Cassidy, 1999).

The ability of an infant to form attachments to more than one primary figure has clear survival value (Mead, 1942). Although infants may form attachments to both fathers and mothers, the nature of father-infant interaction usually differs from that of mother-infant interaction. Fathers engage in more play with infants, and mothers engage in more caregiving activities. Infants prefer the physical, nonintellectual, rough-and-tumble play initiated by fathers (Lamb, 1976b). American fathers do not seem to mind their role in child socializing, yet they still often reject child care (Slocum & Nye, 1976).

In a careful review of the existing literature, Belsky (1990) argues that inconsistent, unresponsive, and unsupportive care for children, particularly when it is tinged with negative affect, eventually fosters uncooperative and problematic behavior. Consistent with this view, Belsky et al. (1996) found that more than 20 hours a week of nonmaternal care during children's first year predicted behavioral problems when the children were 2 years old. There has been a firestorm of controversy on this issue, especially because the majority of mothers with preschool-age children are employed outside the home (Teachman, Polonko, & Scanzoni, 1999). There is also evidence that high-quality day care moderates any negative effects of nonmaternal care (e.g., Creps & Vernon-Feagans, 2000).

As suggested by this review so far, most research on the development of attachment has focused on parental behaviors as catalysts of secure bonds. Some scholars, however, have argued that the child's temperament is a crucial determinant of the attachment bond. Rosen and Burke (1999) provide support for this proposition with their findings from an examination of attachment bonds within 41 maritally intact families with two young children. Although both mothers and fathers were consistent in their behaviors with the children, there were many instances in which the siblings differed from each other in attachment styles. Also, individual children tended to have the same type of attachment bond with both parents. This constellation of findings suggests some role of temperament in the formation of attachment bonds.

Regardless of the specific etiology of attachment bonds, there is evidence for continuity of attachment style from infancy and into the school years (Main, Kaplan, & Cassidy, 1985), and this attachment style is associated with behavioral problems in school. Children with an insecure attachment when they were between 5 and 7 years old are more likely to be rated by their teachers as having behavioral problems 2 years later (Moss, Rousseau, Parent, St-Laurent, & Saintonge, 1998).

Although the primary focus here has been on parents' communication with young children, it is also important to note briefly that there is a large literature on parent-adolescent communication (for a review, see Noller, 1995). Negotiating closeness and control is central to parent-adolescent relationships, because adolescents generally seek increased autonomy. Adolescents who report communication problems with parents attribute those problems to the parents' attempts to control their behavior (Vangelisti, 1992). Also, adolescents who blame their parents for past communication problems are likely to be less satisfied with their relationships with their parents than are adolescents who blame other factors (Vangelisti, 1992). In highly salient situations, Comstock and Buller (1991) found that older adolescents willingly used competitive strategies with parents, but it was the parents' initial strategies that set the tone of the responses.

Although such research is sometimes interpreted as indicating that parent-adolescent relationships are rife with conflict, there is great variability in the extent to which adolescent development is associated with family conflict. In most instances, the amount of parent-child interaction decreases in adolescence (Larson & Richards, 1994), which may actually decrease the amount of overt conflict. Still, parents' communication with adolescents remains important. When mothers are responsive to their adolescents, the adolescents are less likely to orient their activities completely around peers and are consequently less likely to engage in deviant behaviors such as substance abuse (Bogenschneider et al., 1998). In contrast, adolescents are more likely to orient themselves toward peers if they view their parents' communication strategies as too controlling and restrictive (Fuligni & Eccles, 1993).

Family Triads and Beyond

Riskin and Faunce's (1972) observation that the least studied family unit is the family itself still holds today. Most of the research on the family to date has involved the examination of husband-wife or mother-child dyads. Still, as we summarize briefly below, some excellent research has considered triads or larger family units.

Processes Within Individuals

Family structure (e.g., stepfamily) is a social category that is potentially a cue for the formation of stereotypes. A stereotype is a special form of cognitive schema that oversimplifies and overgeneralizes. In exploring the degree to which family structure is stereotyped, Ganong, Coleman, and Mapes (1990) found that the nuclear family is the standard by which all other family forms are evaluated. Individuals believed to be from nuclear families are evaluated more positively than individuals from other family forms. Married adults are perceived more favorably than are nonmarried adults, and children whose parents are married to each other are perceived more favorably than are other children. We discuss some possible implications of these stereotypes below, in our recommendations for future research.

People have clear expectations about how family members and the family as a whole should communicate. To investigate these standards for family communication, Vangelisti, Crumley, and Baker (1999) asked individuals to write stories that described their families

Table 19.2   Influence Pathways in Triadic Family Interactions

1. P1's modification of P2's behavior on the child
2. P2's modification of P1's behavior on the child
3. P1-child relationship on P2-child interaction
4. P2-child relationship on P1-child interaction
5. P1's modification of child's behavior on P2-child interaction
6. P2's modification of child's behavior on P1-child interaction
7. P1-child relationship on P1-P2 relationship
8. P2-child relationship on P1-P2 relationship
9. P1-P2 relationship on the child

NOTE: P1 = first parent; P2 = second parent.

and then to rewrite the stories as they would be if their families were ideal. The differences between the stories tapped the individuals' standards for their families (e.g., care, togetherness, adaptability, and humor). Consistent with the research on standards for marital relationships (e.g., Baucom, Epstein, Rankin, & Burnett, 1996), discrepancies between family members' stories of their own families and the standards implied by their descriptions of an ideal family were associated with participants' dissatisfaction with their family relationships.

Interpersonal Processes

Howe and Reiss (1993) provide an excellent summary of the strengths and weaknesses of designs for studying families. They focus on two related observational methods for examining family process: simulation and experimentation. Howe and Reiss also provide an overview of many classic studies of family interaction and the decision processes through which researchers proceed in order to amplify, isolate, or contrast aspects of family process.

Studying the family group is a complicated enterprise. As summarized in Table 19.2, even with a family of only three people, there are at least nine different direct and indirect ways that the interaction can be modified (Parke, 1979). Each of these nine possibilities in a triad can be studied (and the possibilities increase with larger families). Each may be an

important piece of the puzzle of family process. A complete discussion of each of the triadic linkages is beyond the scope of the current chapter, but we discuss some of the primary research foci on triads and larger units below.

Baby makes three. One family process that has been studied extensively is the birth of the first child. From one dyad (husband-wife), the family now contains three dyads (husband-wife, father-child, mother-child) in addition to a triad (mother-father-child). Change from an existing pattern may induce stress, crisis, and even dysfunction, yet change is often a necessary condition for developmental growth.

Early research on the transition to parenthood focused on the negative impact of this transition on marital quality (LaRossa, 1977; LeMasters, 1957). The birth of the first child has even been called a "crisis" (LeMasters, 1957). Indeed, systematic research has confirmed that, on average, couples experience diminished satisfaction and increased conflict after the birth of their first child (Crohan, 1997).

Despite the traditionally gloomy forecast for marital partners during the transition to parenthood, three developments in the literature have moderated the negative picture. First, rather than focusing primarily on changes in satisfaction, scholars have begun to examine the complex shifts in identity, role behavior, and communication that occur with the transition to parenthood (Cowan & Cowan, 2000). Couples experience a variety of changes, and some of them may be positive. Many husbands, for example, increase their affectionate behaviors toward their wives (Huston & Vangelisti, 1995).

Second, retrospective and cross-sectional studies of the transition to parenthood have been supplemented by longitudinal studies (Huston & Vangelisti, 1995). Although numerous cross-sectional studies have found a negative association between marital satisfaction and the presence of children (Glenn & McLanahan, 1982), most of these studies have failed to account for the fact that marital satisfaction typically declines in the early years of marriage, regardless of parental status (Van Laningham, Johnson, & Amato, 2001). Longitudinal data reveal that the differences between parents and nonparents in satisfaction are smaller than often assumed (Huston & Vangelisti, 1995; MacDermid, Huston, & McHale, 1990).

Third, researchers have begun to examine variability among couples who become parents. A number of studies have pointed to individual characteristics as important predictors of whether spouses' marital union deteriorates after the birth of the first child. Wives with secure attachment styles tend to perceive more support from their husbands and tend to maintain more satisfying marriages than do new mothers with highly ambivalent attachment (Rholes, Simpson, Campbell, & Grinch, 2001). Spouses who are high in agreeableness and low in neuroticism tend to be relatively unlikely to experience declining satisfaction in the years following the birth of their first child (Belsky & Hsieh, 1998).

Spouses' expectations before the first birth are also important. Not surprisingly, when spouses' expectations about the changes they will experience as parents are positive yet unrealistic, their reports about marital satisfaction tend to decline over time (Belsky, Lang, & Huston, 1986). However, the connection between expectations and satisfaction is fairly complicated: Some wives actually report positive feelings when doing more child care and household labor than they had expected (Hackel & Ruble, 1992). Such seemingly counterintuitive findings may reflect the complex changes in behaviors and identities that come with parenthood. Even couples with relatively egalitarian relationships before they have children tend to become fairly traditional in terms of division of labor as parents (Huston & Vangelisti, 1995). Whereas this is dissatisfying for some wives, Johnson and Huston (1998) found that the more wives loved their husbands before they had children, the more the wives changed their preferences for child-care tasks to match their husbands' preferences. This suggests that some wives (especially those strongly attached to their husbands) may cope with unmet expectations by shifting their preferences and negotiating new identities rather than by becoming unhappy.

The communication between parents also predicts how successfully parents will move through the transition to parenthood. Stamp (1994) conducted an in-depth investigation of 10 couples' communication before and after the birth of their first child and found that the couples negotiated their new roles in a variety of ways. One particularly important distinction was that some spouses' behaviors facilitated their partners' role enactment, whereas others inhibited that enactment. Facilitation involves acting in ways that reinforce or aid the other spouse's parenting behavior (e.g., offering support or encouragement). Inhibiting occurs when one parent blocks or disrupts the other parent's role enactment. An example would be a case where one parent attempts to allow the child to be a bit fussy so as not to spoil the child while the other parent rushes in to express sympathy for the child. Belsky and Hsieh (1998) found that such episodes, which they label "unsupportive coparenting," were associated with declining marital satisfaction. Other communication behaviors that are associated with maintaining marital satisfaction across the transition to parenthood include fathers' caring for and playing with the child (Levy-Shiff, 1994) and few exchanges of negativity between the spouses (Shapiro, Gottman, & Carrere, 2000).

Influence of family interaction on children. A large body of research on family triads has examined the ninth path in Table 19.2, the influence of the relationship between the two parents on the child. A number of studies, for example, have documented a connection between marital conflict and dysfunctional outcomes for children, including externalizing problems such as bullying or being disobedient at school and internalizing problems such as depression or tension (Katz & Gottman, 1993; King, Radpour, Naylor, Segal, & Jouriles, 1995).

Since the early 1980s, Belsky and his colleagues in the Pennsylvania Infant and Family Development Project have been trying to examine direct and indirect effects in family process. In one study, Belsky, Youngblade, Rovine, and Volling (1991) found that husbands who are less in love with their wives and less maritally satisfied behave toward their children in a more negative and intrusive manner than do happily married husbands. Mothers seem less affected in their relationships with their children by the level of marital distress. In another study, Belsky et al. (1996) found that lack of love and high conflict between marital partners was associated with "troubled" families, one feature of which was children's behavioral problems. The researchers also found a number of other predictors of troubled families, including the husband's personality and the extent to which the husband's emotions at work influence his emotions at home. These findings are consistent with Belsky's (1984) family ecology model, suggesting that a focus even beyond the triad of a child and two parents is useful in explaining children's development.

Several lines of research have focused on the effects of entire family units on children. A major paradigm guiding research on the family as a unit has linked disturbed family communication processes to psychological and social deviance outcomes for offspring. The key question in this type of research is: What is the role of the family in the etiology, course, treatment, and prevention of psychopathological disorders (Jacob, 1987)? Such a perspective dates to at least the 1950s. Bateson's group at Palo Alto, Bowen and Wynne at the National Institute of Mental Health, Lidz and his associates at Yale, and Ackerman's research group at the Family Mental Health Clinic in New York independently concluded that observable, ongoing family interaction patterns could be directly linked to negative outcomes for children (Raush et al., 1979).

The purpose of this research is usually to discriminate functional from dysfunctional families on the basis of their interaction patterns. Whereas work in the early 1960s concentrated on the differences between normal and schizophrenic families (see the review by Jacob, 1975), research since then has branched out to include abusive and neglectful families (e.g., Burgess & Conger, 1978), families with an abnormally aggressive (e.g., Patterson, 1976) or delinquent child (e.g., Alexander, 1973), and families with an alcoholic (e.g., Steinglass, Bennett, Wolin, & Reiss, 1987) or depressed parent (e.g., Coyne, Kahn, & Gottlib, 1987). Overall, researchers have found that clinic-referred children and adolescents are likely to come from families in which positive, nurturant, and supportive behaviors occur at depressed rates and noxious, aversive, or negative interactions are relatively frequent (Conger, 1983).

Another line of research examining communication in entire family units is the scholarship on problem solving in families (e.g., Vuchinich, 1999; Vuchinich & Angelelli, 1995). Vuchinich (1999) describes a series of studies that used multiple methods to examine some of the complexities of family problem solving. In one study designed to overcome some of the limitations of typical laboratory-based observational studies, Vuchinich video-taped families while they had dinner with no researchers present.

In contrast to most laboratory studies of family conflict, which begin by assuming there is an objective conflict issue to discuss, Vuchinich's (1999) work suggests that family members often negotiate what counts as a problem and whether there should be a conflict about it. When families do engage in clearly observable conflict, they often do not engage in problem solving to end that conflict. There are four common ways that families stop engaging in overt conflict: submission, compromise, withdrawal, and standoff. Vuchinich has found that 60% of family conflicts end in standoffs: Family members simply stop discussing the issue with no apparent resolution. This suggests that most families, even functional ones, consider family conflict normal and part of ongoing family life.

Still, the way such problems are discussed in families does matter. Systems theorists suggest that one particularly dysfunctional way in which some families deal with problems is by forming intergenerational alliances; that is, a parent turns to a child rather than to his or her spouse for intimacy (e.g., Minuchin, 1974). Indeed, there is systematic evidence suggesting that such alliances are associated with dysfunctional outcomes for the child, including depression, low self-esteem, and anxiety (e.g., Jacobvitz & Bush, 1996). Such findings are often taken to imply that a strong coalition between mother and father is crucial to the raising of healthy children. However, Vuchinich and Angelelli (1995) found that strong mother-father coalitions were associated with poor problem solving in families, suggesting that some parents use their children as scapegoats for family problems. Thus Vuchinich's work suggests that any excessively strong coalition in a family can impede the

family's problem-solving capabilities and the children's well-being.

Family paradigms. A program of research comparing normal and disturbed families that is particularly relevant to communication scholars is that conducted by Reiss and his colleagues (Oliveri & Reiss, 1981a, 1981b; Reiss, 1981). Believing that theories of the family built around impulse, affect, or power have fared badly in explaining or predicting family behavior, Reiss (1981) developed a model that emphasizes the family's construction of reality, or family paradigms. Reiss asserts that families differ along three dimensions: (a) their experience of the world as ordered; (b) their belief in the world as open, accessible, or accommodating; and (c) their experience of novelty in the world.

This program of research is of special importance to communication researchers for three reasons. First, a family's construction of social reality is represented in the family members' interactions. The social construction of reality is indicated by the lexical speech, the nonlexical speech, and the nonverbal behavior of family members as it is organized into recurring patterns. Second, the model offers a rigorous communication explanation for how parental problems lead to deficiencies in offspring. Third, the family types elaborated by Reiss (1981) are consistent with those originally described by McLeod and Chaffee (1972) and later elaborated by Fitzpatrick and her colleagues (Fitzpatrick, 1990; Fitzpatrick & Ritchie, 1993, 1994). This family typology is based on two dimensions: conversation orientation (i.e., the extent to which the family encourages unrestrained interaction) and conformity orientation (i.e., the extent to which family members express a preference for homogeneous beliefs and values).

Koerner and Fitzpatrick (2002) argue that the conformity and conversation orientations tap into family schemata, or information-processing structures, driving family communication. Consistent with the notion that conversation and conformity orientations index family schemata, recent research has demonstrated that conversation and conformity orientations are associated with a wide variety of different family members' behaviors, including conflict resolution strategies (Koerner & Fitzpatrick, 1997), children's use of social withdrawal and social self-restraint (Fitzpatrick, Marshall, Leutwiler & Krcmar, 1996), and college students' commitment to engaging in family rituals (Baxter & Clark, 1996).

Genetic and environmental influences on sibling similarity. Since the late 1980s, Reiss, Hetherington, Plomin, and their associates have been conducting the Nonshared Environment in Adolescent Development (NEAD) project (Neiderhiser, Reiss, Hetherington, & Plomin, 1999; Reiss, 2000), which examines the ways in which behavioral genetic factors and family process factors combine to influence adolescents' development. Two key aspects of the project are that it includes questionnaire and observational data as well as different types of families that vary in the genetic relatedness of the siblings (e.g., identical twins, fraternal twins, full siblings from nondivorced families, full siblings in stepfamilies, half siblings, and stepsiblings who are not genetically related).

The studies from the NEAD project typically involve attempting to explain differences between siblings in terms of three factors: heritability, shared family environment, and "nonshared environment" (Reiss, Plomin, & Hetherington, 1991). *Shared environment* refers to the family circumstances that affect all children in the family equally, whereas *nonshared environment* refers to the unique circumstantial effects on particular children (e.g., due to the withdrawal of a depressed parent from one child but not others).

The findings from this project to date suggest that contributions of shared environment (e.g., the general level of conflict in the family) are often overestimated and that the effects of

genetic factors and nonshared environment are very important determinants of children's behaviors in families. However, three caveats to this general conclusion are necessary. First, some of the research from the NEAD project does suggest that shared environment can be crucial; for example, Bussell et al. (1999) found that similarities between mother-adolescent and sibling relationships were mostly accounted for by the shared environment. Second, Reiss (2000) and his associates are careful to note that a genetic link to particular family behaviors does not predetermine such behaviors. The extent to which (and whether) genetic factors manifest themselves in observable behaviors "depends on many factors" (Reiss, 2000, p. 51). Third, although the NEAD project has established the role of nonshared environment, little is known about the exact mechanisms by which siblings growing up in the same family have nonshared environments. A partial explanation may be found in the research on differential treatment of siblings, which demonstrates that differential maternal treatment is linked to more conflicted and hostile sibling relationships (Boer, Goedhart, & Treffers, 1992; Volling & Belsky, 1992). Interestingly, McGuire and Dunn (1994) found that perceptions of differential treatment of siblings may be partially explained by adjustments that mothers make as their children develop. Although mothers treat their children very similarly when the children are at the same ages, siblings (except for twins) are not the same ages at the same points in time. Thus similar treatment that accounts for children's development may be experienced as differential treatment. This finding also could be relevant to the aforementioned literature on birth-order effects.

CONCLUSION

We have had three goals in presenting this review. First, we have alerted the reader to a number of issues surrounding definitions of the family. We settled on a transaction definition because it allows us to study a broad range of families. It is important for researchers and theorists to think through their conceptual definition of the family at the beginning of a research project. The basic definition of the family sets the parameters and the constraints not only for the samples the researcher draws but also for the kinds of conclusions that he or she can make from the research.

Second, we have offered a taxonomy of variables that researchers need to consider when studying families, and we have argued that communication is central to understanding connections among these variables. A fundamental question for the study of communication in families is: In each of the subsystems of the family, how do the internal variables (see Figure 19.1) and performance variables interact and consequently lead to particular outputs? Throughout this review, we have seen that scholars in various traditions have approached pieces of this question. Some scholars have been concerned only with the performance variables, rarely linking these to major family outcomes. As Cappella (1991) has argued, extensive analyses of interaction sequences, although not without their descriptive charm, do not yield much information about potential connections among important concepts. Unfortunately, too much research on interactional differences has been unconnected to major family outcomes (but see Grych & Fincham, 1990). When links have been made, they have usually been made between performance and output variables, with little consideration of internal variables. Researchers, for example, often relate interaction patterns to levels of marital satisfaction. The proper domain of communication research is the study of messages, but these messages must be connected to the theoretically relevant internal and output family process concepts.

Third, we have reviewed the literature on various family dyads and triads in reference to both individual and interpersonal processes. In contrast to the manner in which we have built this review of the literature, newer programs of research are being built on *developmental family systems* perspectives. Here, we do not see the disconnected dyads in the family. Rather, theorists consider changes in life experiences, family processes, and individual adjustment. And researchers use multiple methods and multiple informants rather than rely on the perspectives of individual family members exclusively. Hetherington and her associates (1992), for example, conducted a longitudinal study to examine transformations in marital, parent-child, and sibling relationships and the effects these changes have on the adjustment of early adolescent children following the remarriage of a divorced mother.

Our review of the literature on family communication suggests directions for new research and theory. Although there has been progress in the past decade in terms of examining family dyads aside from husbands and wives, there is still a need to move beyond isolated dyads to the study of multiple dyads and triads. Also, communication scholars must take greater care to sample not only actors (family dyads or units) but also behaviors and contexts. One way of obtaining information about behaviors and contexts is through observational studies; the need for more well-designed laboratory studies of family interaction is apparent. Additionally, diary and beeper studies (Duck, Rutt, Hurst, & Strejc, 1991; Larson & Richards, 1994) have the potential to allow researchers to gain a better understanding of how family communication is shaped by context (see Huston, 2000).

Both observational and diary methods can help communication scholars augment data about frequencies of behaviors with information about pattern and sequence in family interaction. This focus on pattern and sequence should include both relatively microscopic analyses of sequence within a given conversation (e.g., Gottman, 1994; Sillars, 1980; Williamson, 1983) and more macroscopic examinations of co-occurring behaviors and sequences across days or longer periods.

Almeida, Wethington, and Chandler (1999), for example, found that both mothers and fathers were more likely to have tense interactions with their children if they had engaged in tense interactions with their spouses on the preceding day.

Even models of interaction that examine patterns of behaviors are incomplete without some consideration of cognitive or interpretive processes (Fitzpatrick & Ritchie, 1993). For example, parents who perceive conflict with their adolescent as temporally contingent on conflict with each other may have more favorable evaluations of their relationship with their adolescent than would parents who are unaware of the larger pattern.

Koerner and Fitzpatrick's (2002) theory of family communication is important because it links interactional and cognitive perspectives. This theory describes both the means by which family interaction influences family members' schemata about family relationships and the ways in which such schemata shape family interaction. A complete summary of this theory is beyond the scope of this chapter, but one key element of the theory is of particular interest here: It provides an explanation for how family members derive meaning—including shared meaning—from family interaction. Because family members' schemata are partially based on shared experiences, these schemata are partially shared, allowing for the creation of intersubjective meaning within the family. Such theoretical work highlights the inadequacy of some studies of family interaction: Coding interaction that occurs among family members without concern for the meanings that the individuals assign to the messages may lead us in the wrong direction.

Additionally, future family communication research needs to augment the focus on endogenous outputs such as satisfaction (see Figure 19.1) with greater attention to larger social issues that affect and are affected by families. Greater attention to such social outcomes will enhance the visibility of research on

family communication as well as the funding opportunities available for doing such research. There is now considerable evidence, for example, that marital interaction has a causal influence on physical health (Kiecolt-Glaser & Newton, 2001). Such effects are both indirect (e.g., by fostering depression in married individuals with dysfunctional marital interaction) and direct (e.g., by influencing the immune system). Family communication research can also play a greater role in helping family members to avoid or overcome problems with substance abuse (Bhattacharya, 2001; Le Poire, Hallett, & Erlandson, 2000).

Another important social outcome related to family communication is marital violence (for review, see Johnson & Ferraro, 2000). Fitzpatrick (2002) discusses ways in which family violence creates an intersection between family interaction and larger social concerns such as law enforcement. When police officers respond to domestic violence disputes, they are faced with a dilemma that can be described as a dialectical tension between enforcing the law and encouraging family solidarity and harmony. Research that will improve our understanding of family dynamics is crucial if we want to be able to help police officers (and perhaps courts) make informed decisions about how to proceed in such situations.

One solution is unlikely to be best in all cases, because there are different types of violence in marriages. In many instances, an individual's motivation for violence is to get his or her own way in a particular conflict. Johnson (1995) argues that such violence tends to be reciprocal between husbands and wives and tends to decline over time rather than escalate. Because such instances are not part of routinized violence, mandatory arrest policies may cause more family disruption than they prevent.

In contrast, Johnson (1995) notes that other marital violence is part of a pattern in which the husband uses violence and other tactics to control "his" wife. This type of violence, which Johnson labels "patriarchal terrorism," is almost always enacted at the expense of women, occurs frequently, and escalates over time. In such instances, the physical safety of the wife is in serious danger, and a police officer responding to such a situation ought to act accordingly. Although more research needs to be done to determine all the ways in which family communication scholars can help diminish marital violence, one role we certainly can play is in helping police officers to recognize the signs of patriarchal terrorism.

Since the second edition of the *Handbook of Interpersonal Communication* was published, scholars have paid increased attention to communication in different types of families. The rationale for this heightened focus hinges on the idea that some types of relationships have been "under-studied" in comparison with others (Wood & Duck, 1995). Ganong and Coleman (2000) have argued that the historical focus on nuclear families implies that such families are the benchmark for assessing families, implying a "deficit model" of other family forms. In response, many researchers have shifted their attention from comparisons of different family forms to asking questions about why some families within particular forms function better than others (Ganong & Coleman, 1994; Golish, in press). Such studies are reasonable given that there are some unique communication challenges encountered in various family configurations. Newly formed stepfamilies, for instance, must negotiate a balance between old family and new (Baxter, Braithwaite, & Nicholson, 1999; Braithwaite, Olson, Golish, Soukup, & Turman, 2001).

However, research that compares different forms of families is also necessary. Organizing communication research around specific forms of families highlights the family form and puts communication phenomena in the background, which could lead to a potentially harmful fragmentation of the field. There is tremendous diversity in family forms; even

family forms that are often thought of as being fairly specific (e.g., stepfamilies and single-parent families) have considerable variation in terms of custodial arrangements and sex of primary caretaker (Demo, Allen, & Fine, 2000). Although it is important for scholars to attend to such diversity, too much focus on family forms could prevent a general understanding of how communication functions across family forms.

Thus it is important for scholars to examine communication across different family forms. Such research need not imply that nonnuclear families are deficient; in fact, only comparative research can uncover ways in which communication functions similarly in various family forms (Caughlin, Golish, et al., 2000). Even when research uncovers differences among family forms, these differences need not imply the superior functioning of one type of family. Allen, Baucom, Burnett, Epstein, and Rankin-Esquer (2001), for example, found that remarried spouses, compared with spouses in their first marriages, were more likely to prefer greater autonomy in decision making, but the differences were not significantly associated with marital distress.

Such similarities across forms of families are congruent with Ahrons's (1994) argument that the functions of families remain the same even when the structures and sizes of families change. This view is consistent with arguments that the relationships and interaction among family members are more important to family well-being than is the family structure (Fitzpatrick & Vangelisti, 2001). Consider, for example, the well-documented (but generally small) association between parental divorce and relatively poor adjustment in children (Amato, 2001; Summers, Forehand, Armistead, & Tannenbaum, 1998). Although the average impact of divorce seems to be unfavorable, there is substantial variation in the effects of divorce (Amato, 2000), and family communication is an important factor determining divorce's ultimate effect on children. Children whose parents' marriage was high in conflict before the divorce seem to benefit from divorce (Amato, Loomis, & Booth, 1995; Booth & Amato, 2001; Jekielek, 1998), particularly when they are compared with children whose high-conflict parents do not divorce (Morrison & Coiro, 1999). Thus family communication, not the structure of the family per se, may be the primary predictor of the children's well-being. Such general conclusions about the connection between communication and family functioning can be made only if researchers conduct studies that include multiple family forms.

Innumerable pronouncements have been made about the modern family and its alleged demise. Yet the fact that families have survived myriad changes in values, social constraints, and structures suggests that families are flexible (Fitzpatrick & Vangelisti, 1995). Communication is a primary means through which families are able to adapt to such changes. Consequently, the study of communication in family relationships has become a major endeavor that will continue to influence interpersonal communication theory and research.

REFERENCES

Abeles, G. (1976). Researching the unsearchable: Experimentation on the double bind. In C. E. Sluzki & D. C. Ransom (Eds.), *Double bind: The foundation of the communication approach to the family* (pp. 113-150). New York: Grune & Stratton.

Abramovitch, R., Corter, C., & Peplar, D. J. (1980). Observations of mixed-sex sibling dyads. *Child Development, 51,* 1268-1271.

Ahrons, C. R. (1994). *The good divorce: Keeping your family together when your marriage comes apart.* New York: HarperCollins.

Ainsworth, M. D. S. (1973). The development of infant-mother attachment. In B. M. Caldwell & H. N. Riccinti (Eds.), *Review of child development research* (Vol. 3, pp. 1-94). Chicago: University of Chicago Press.

Ainsworth, M. D. S., & Bell, S. M. V. (1969). Some contemporary patterns of mother-infant interaction in the feeding situation. In J. A. Ambrose (Ed.), *Stimulation in early infancy* (pp. 133-163). London: Academic Press.

Ainsworth, M. D. S., Blehar, M. C., Waters, E., & Wall, S. (1978). *Patterns of attachment: A psychological study of the strange situation.* Hillsdale, NJ: Lawrence Erlbaum.

Aldous, J. (1996). *Family careers: Rethinking the developmental perspective.* Thousand Oaks, CA: Sage.

Alexander, A. (2001). The meaning of television in the American family. In J. Bryant & J. A. Bryant (Eds.), *Television and the American family* (2nd ed., pp. 273-287). Mahwah, NJ: Lawrence Erlbaum.

Alexander, J. F. (1973). Defensive and supportive communication in normal and deviant families. *Journal of Consulting and Clinical Psychology, 40,* 223-231.

Allen, E. S., Baucom, D. H., Burnett, C. K., Epstein, N., & Rankin-Esquer, L. A. (2001). Decision-making power, autonomy, and communication in remarried spouses compared with first-married spouses. *Family Relations, 50,* 326-344.

Almeida, D. M., Wethington, E., & Chandler, A. L. (1999). Daily transmission of tensions between marital dyads and parent-child dyads. *Journal of Marriage and the Family, 61,* 49-61.

Amato, P. R. (2000). The consequences of divorce for adults and children. *Journal of Marriage and the Family, 62,* 1269-1287.

Amato, P. R. (2001). Children of divorce in the 1990s: An update of the Amato and Keith (1991) meta-analysis. *Journal of Family Psychology, 15,* 355-370.

Amato, P. R., Loomis, L., & Booth, A. (1995). Parental divorce, marital conflict, and offspring well-being during early adulthood. *Social Forces, 73,* 895-915.

Applegate, J. L., Burleson, B. R., & Delia, J. G. (1992). Reflection-enhancing parenting as an antecedent to children's social-cognitive and communicative development. In I. E. Sigel, A. V. McGillicuddy-Delisi, & J. J. Goodnow (Eds.), *Parental belief systems: The psychological consequences for children* (Vol. 2, pp. 3-39). Hillsdale, NJ: Lawrence Erlbaum.

Avtgis, T. A., Martin, M. M., & Rocca, K. A. (2000). Social support and perceived understanding in the brother relationship. *Communication Research Reports, 17,* 407-414.

Baltes, P. B. (1968). Longitudinal and cross-sectional sequences in the study of age and generational effects. *Human Development, 11,* 145-171.

Bank, S. P., & Kahn, M. D. (1997). *The sibling bond.* New York: Basic Books.

Barratt, M. S. (1995). Communication in infancy. In M. A. Fitzpatrick & A. L. Vangelisti (Eds.), *Explaining family interactions* (pp. 5-33). Thousand Oaks, CA: Sage.

Baskett, L. M., & Johnson, S. M. (1982). The young child's interaction with parents versus sibling: A behavioral analysis. *Child Development, 53,* 643-650.

Bates, E. (1979). *The emergence of symbols.* New York: Academic Press.

Bates, E., Camaioni, L., & Volterra, V. (1975). The acquisition of performatives prior to speech. *Merrill-Palmer Quarterly, 21,* 205-226.

Bateson, M. C. (1975). Mother-infant exchanges: The epigenesis of conversational interaction. In D. Aaronson & R. Rieber (Eds.), Developmental psycholinguistics and communication disorders [Special issue]. *Annals of the New York Academy of Sciences, 263,* 101-113.

Baucom, D. H., Epstein, N., Daiuto, A. D., Carels, R. A., Rankin, L. A., & Burnett, C. K. (1996). Cognitions in marriage: The relationship between standards and attributions. *Journal of Family Psychology, 10,* 209-222.

Baucom, D. H., Epstein, N., Rankin, L. A., & Burnett, C. K. (1996). Assessing relationship standards: The inventory of specific relationship standards. *Journal of Family Psychology, 10,* 72-88.

Baucom, D. H., Epstein, N., Sayers, S., & Sher, T. G. (1989). The role of cognitions in marital relationships: Definitional, methodological, and conceptual issues. *Journal of Consulting and Clinical Psychology, 57,* 31-38.

Baxter, L. A., Braithwaite, D. O., & Nicholson, J. H. (1999). Turning points in the development of blended families. *Journal of Social and Personal Relationships, 16,* 291-313.

Baxter, L. A., & Bullis, C. (1986). Turning points in developing romantic relationships. *Human Communication Research, 12,* 469-493.

Baxter, L.A., & Clark, C.L. (1996). Perceptions of family communication patterns and the enactment of family rituals. *Western Journal of Communication, 60,* 254-268.

Baxter, L. A., & Montgomery, B. M. (1996). *Relating: Dialogues and dialectics.* New York: Guilford.

Bedford, V. H., & Gold, D. T. (Eds.). (1989). Siblings in later life: A neglected family relationship [Special issue]. *American Behavioral Scientist, 33*(1).

Bell, A. P., & Weinberg, M. (1978). *Homosexualities: A study of diversity among men and women.* New York: Simon & Schuster.

Bell, R. Q. (1968). A reinterpretation of the direction of effect in studies of socialization. *Psychological Review, 75,* 81-95.

Bell, R. Q. (1974). Contributions of human infants to caregivers and social interaction. In M. Lewis & L. A. Rosenblum (Eds.), *The effect of the infant on its caregivers* (pp. 1-20). New York: John Wiley.

Bellinger, D. (1980). Consistency in the pattern of change in mother's speech: Some discriminant analyses. *Journal of Child Language, 7,* 464-487.

Belsky, J. (1984). The determinants of parenting: A process model. *Child Development, 55,* 83-96.

Belsky, J. (1990). Parental and nonparental child care and children's socioemotional development: A decade in review. *Journal of Marriage and the Family, 52,* 885-903.

Belsky, J., & Hsieh, K. (1998). Patterns of marital change during the early childhood years: Parent personality, coparenting, and division-of-labor correlates. *Journal of Family Psychology, 12,* 511-528.

Belsky, J., Lang, M., & Huston, T. L. (1986). Sex typing and division of labor as determinants of marital change across the transition to parenthood. *Journal of Personality and Social Psychology, 50,* 517-522.

Belsky, J., Woodworth, S., & Crnic, K. (1996). Trouble in the second year: Three questions about family interaction. *Child Development, 67,* 556-578.

Belsky, J., Youngblade, L., Rovine, M., & Volling, B. (1991). Patterns of marital change and parent-child interaction. *Journal of Marriage and the Family, 53,* 885-899.

Berger, C. R., & Bradac, J. J. (1982). *Language and social knowledge: Uncertainty in interpersonal relations.* London: Edward Arnold.

Berscheid, E. (1982). Attraction and emotion in interpersonal relationships. In M. S. Clark & S. T. Fiske (Eds.), *Affect and cognition* (pp. 37-120). Hillsdale, NJ: Lawrence Erlbaum.

Berscheid, E. (1983). Emotions. In H. H. Kelley, E. Berscheid, A. Christensen, J. H. Harvey, T. L. Huston, G. Levinger, et al., *Close relationships* (pp. 110-168). New York: Freeman.

Bhattacharya, G. (2001). Parent-child communication in drug prevention among adolescents. In S. B. Kar & R. Alcalay (Eds.), *Health communication: A multicultural perspective* (pp. 193-209). Thousand Oaks, CA: Sage.

Birnbaum, J. A. (1971). *Life patterns, personality style and self-esteem in gifted family oriented and career committed women.* Unpublished doctoral dissertation, University of Michigan.

Bloom, B. L., White, S. W., & Asher, S. J. (1979). Marital disruption as a stressful event. In G. Levinger & O. C. Moles (Eds.), *Divorce and separation* (pp. 184-210). New York: Basic Books.

Blumstein, P., & Schwartz, P. (1983). *American couples.* New York: William Morrow.

Bochner, A. P. (1976). Conceptual frontiers in the study of families: An introduction to the literature. *Human Communication Research, 2,* 381-397.

Bochner, A. P., Kaminski, E. P., & Fitzpatrick, M. A. (1977). The conceptual domain of interpersonal communication behavior: A factor-analytic study. *Human Communication Research, 3,* 291-302.

Boer, F., Goedhart, A. W., & Treffers, P. D. A. (1992). Siblings and their parents. In F. Boer & J. Dunn (Eds.), *Children's sibling relationships: Developmental and clinical issues* (pp. 41-54). Hillsdale, NJ: Lawrence Erlbaum.

Bogenschneider, K., Wu, M., Raffaelli, M., & Tsay, J. (1998). Parent influences on adolescent peer orientation and substance use: The interface of parenting practices and values. *Child Development, 69,* 1672-1688.

Bohannan, P. (1970). The six stations of divorce. In P. Bohannan (Ed.), *Divorce and after* (pp. 29-55). New York: Doubleday.

Bombar, M. L., & Littig, L. W., Jr. (1996). Babytalk as a communication of intimate attachment: An initial study in adult romances and friendships. *Personal Relationships, 3,* 137-158.

Booth, A., & Amato, P. R. (2001). Parental predivorce relations and offspring postdivorce well-being. *Journal of Marriage and Family, 63,* 197-212.

Boss, P. G., Doherty, W. J., LaRossa, R., Schumm, W. R., & Steinmetz, S. K. (Eds.). (1993). *Sourcebook of family theories and methods: A contextual approach.* New York: Plenum.

Bossard, J. H. S., & Boll, E. S. (1950). *Ritual in family living.* Philadelphia: University of Pennsylvania Press.

Bowerman, C. E., & Dobash, R. M. (1974). Structural variations in intersibling affect. *Journal of Marriage and the Family, 36,* 48-54.

Bowlby, J. (1972). *Attachment and loss: Vol. 1. Attachment.* London: Hogarth.

Bowlby, J. (1980). *Attachment and loss: Vol. 3. Loss.* London: Hogarth.

Bradbury, T. N., Beach, S. R. H., Fincham, F. D., & Nelson, G. M. (1996). Attributions and behavior in functional and dysfunctional marriages. *Journal of Consulting and Clinical Psychology, 64,* 569-576.

Bradbury, T. N., Cohan, C. L., & Karney, B. R. (1998). Optimizing longitudinal research for understanding and preventing marital dysfunction. In T. N. Bradbury (Ed.), *The developmental course of marital dysfunction* (pp. 279-311). New York: Cambridge University Press.

Bradbury, T. N., Fincham, F. D., & Beach, S. R. H. (2000). Research on the nature and determinants of marital satisfaction: A decade of review. *Journal of Marriage and the Family, 62,* 964-980.

Bradbury, T. N., Rogge, R., & Lawrence, E. (2001). Reconsidering the role of conflict in marriage. In A. Booth, A. C. Crouter, & M. Clements (Eds.), *Couples in conflict* (pp. 59-81). Mahwah, NJ: Lawrence Erlbaum.

Braithwaite, D. O., Olson, L. N., Golish, T. D., Soukup, C., & Turman, T. (2001). "Becoming a family": Developmental processes represented in blended family discourse. *Journal of Applied Communication Research, 29,* 221-247.

Broderick, C., & Smith, J. (1979). The general systems approach to the family. In W. R. Burr, R. Hill, F. I. Nye, & I. L. Reiss (Eds.), *Contemporary theories about the family* (Vol. 2, pp. 112-129). New York: Free Press.

Brown, S. L., & Booth, A. (1996). Cohabitation versus marriage: A comparison of relationship quality. *Journal of Marriage and the Family, 58,* 668-678.

Bruner, J. (1990). *Acts of meaning.* Cambridge, MA: Harvard University Press.

Bryant, J., & Bryant, J. A. (Eds.). (2001). *Television and the American family* (2nd ed.). Mahwah, NJ: Lawrence Erlbaum.

Buhrmester, D. (1992). The developmental courses of sibling and peer relationships. In F. Boer & L. Dunn (Eds.), *Children's sibling relationships: Developmental and clinical issues* (pp. 19-40). Hillsdale, NJ: Lawrence Erlbaum.

Burgess, E. W., & Locke, H. (1953). *The family.* New York: American Book.

Burgess, E. W., & Wallin, P. (1953). *Engagement and marriage.* Philadelphia: J. B. Lippincott.

Burgess, R. L., & Conger, R. D. (1978). Family interaction in abusive, neglectful, and normal families. *Child Development, 49,* 1163-1173.

Burleson, B. R., Delia, J. G., & Applegate, J. L. (1995). In M. A. Fitzpatrick & A. L. Vangelisti (Eds.), *Explaining family interactions* (pp. 34-76). Thousand Oaks, CA: Sage.

Burleson, B. R., & Xu, Y. (2001, November). *Equity principles and the relationship of discrepancies between social support expectancies and experiences to marital adjustment: When spousal support becomes too much of a good thing.* Paper presented at the annual meeting of the National Communication Association, Atlanta, GA.

Burr, W. R., Hill, R., Nye, F. I., & Reiss, I. L. (Eds.). (1979). *Contemporary theories about the family* (Vols. 1-2). New York: Free Press.

Bussell, D. A., Neiderhiser, J. M., Pike, A., Plomin, R., Simmens, S., Howe, G. W., et al. (1999). Adolescents' relationships to siblings and mothers: A multivariate genetic analysis. *Developmental Psychology, 35,* 1248-1259.

Cameron, N. (1963). *Personality development and psychopathology: A dynamic approach.* Boston: Houghton Mifflin.

Canary, D. J., Cupach, W. R., & Messman, S. J. (1995). *Relationship conflict.* Thousand Oaks, CA: Sage.

Cantor, J., & Mares, M. (2001). Effects of television on child and family emotional well-being. In J. Bryant & J. A. Bryant (Eds.), *Television and the American family* (2nd ed., pp. 317-332). Mahwah, NJ: Lawrence Erlbaum.

Cappella, J. N. (1987). Interpersonal communication: Fundamental questions and issues. In C. R. Berger & S. H. Chaffee (Eds.), *Handbook of communication science* (pp. 184-238). Newbury Park, CA: Sage.

Cappella, J. N. (1991). The biological origins of automated patterns of human interaction. *Communication Theory, 1,* 4-35.

Cassidy, J. (1999). The nature of child's ties. In J. Cassidy & P. R. Shaver (Eds.), *Handbook of attachment: Theory, research, and clinical applications* (pp. 3-20). New York: Guilford.

Cate, R. M., & Lloyd, S. A. (1992). *Courtship.* Newbury Park, CA: Sage.

Caughlin, J. P. (2002). The demand/withdraw pattern of communication as a predictor of marital satisfaction over time: Unresolved issues and future directions. *Human Communication Research, 28,* 49-86.

Caughlin, J. P., Golish, T. D., Olson, L. N., Sargent, J. E., Cook, J. S., & Petronio, S. (2000). Family secrets in various family configurations: A communication boundary management perspective. *Communication Studies, 51,* 116-134.

Caughlin, J. P., & Huston, T. L. (2002). A contextual analysis of the association between demand/withdraw and marital satisfaction. *Personal Relationships, 9,* 95-119.

Caughlin, J. P., Huston, T. L., & Houts, R. M. (2000). How does personality matter in marriage? An examination of trait anxiety, interpersonal negativity, and marital satisfaction. *Journal of Personality and Social Psychology, 78,* 326-336.

Christensen, A. (1988). Dysfunctional interaction patterns in couples. In P. Noller & M. A. Fitzpatrick (Eds.), *Perspectives on marital interaction* (pp. 31-52). Clevedon, Eng.: Multilingual Matters.

Christensen, A., & Heavey, C. L. (1990). Gender, power and marital conflict. *Journal of Personality and Social Psychology, 59,* 73-85.

Clements, M. L., Cordova, A. D., Markman, H. J., & Laurenceau, J. (1997). The erosion of marital satisfaction over time and how to prevent it. In R. J. Sternberg & M. Hojjat (Eds.), *Satisfaction in close relationships* (pp. 335-355). New York: Guilford.

Comstock, J., & Buller, D. B. (1991). Conflict strategies adolescents use with their parents: Testing the cognitive communicator characteristics model. *Journal of Language and Social Psychology, 10,* 47-65.

Conger, R. D. (1983). Behavioral assessment for practitioners: Some reasons and recommendations. In E. E. Filsinger (Ed.), *Marriage and family assessment* (pp. 137-151). Beverly Hills, CA: Sage.

Conville, R. (1991). *Relational transitions: The evolution of personal relationships.* New York: Praeger.

Coontz, S. (1992). *The way we never were: American families and the nostalgia trap.* New York: Basic Books.

Coontz, S. (2000). Historical perspective on family studies. *Journal of Marriage and the Family, 62,* 283-297.

Cooper, D. (1970). *The death of a family.* New York: Pantheon.

Cooper, S. M. (1999). Historical analysis of the family. In M. B. Sussman, S. K. Steinmetz, & G. W. Peterson (Eds.), *Handbook of marriage and the family* (2nd ed., pp. 13-37). New York: Plenum.

Courtright, J. A., Millar, F. E., & Rogers-Millar, L. E. (1979). Domineeringness and dominance: Replication and extension. *Communication Monographs, 46,* 179-192.

Cowan, C., & Cowan, P. A. (2000). *When partners become parents: The big life change for couples.* Mahwah, NJ: Lawrence Erlbaum.

Coyne, J. C., Kahn, J., & Gottlib, I. H. (1987). Depression. In T. Jacob (Ed.), *Psychopathology and the family* (pp. 509-533). New York: Plenum.

Creps, C. L., & Vernon-Feagans, L. (2000). Infant daycare and otitis media: Multiple influences on children's later development. *Journal of Applied Developmental Psychology, 21,* 357-378.

Crohan, S. E. (1997). Marital quality and conflict across the transition to parenthood in African American and white couples. *Journal of Marriage and the Family, 58,* 933-944.

Csikszentmihalyi, M., Rathunde, K., & Whalen, S. (1993). *Talented teenagers: The roots of success and failure.* Cambridge: Cambridge University Press.

Cunningham, J. D., & Antill, J. K. (1995). Current trends in nonmarital cohabitation: In search of the POSSLQ. In J. T. Wood & S. Duck (Eds.), *Under-studied relationships: Off the beaten track* (pp. 148-172). Thousand Oaks, CA: Sage.

DeMaris, A., & Leslie, G. R. (1984). Cohabitation with the future spouse: Its influence upon marital satisfaction and communication. *Journal of Marriage and the Family, 46,* 77-84.

DeMaris, A., & MacDonald, W. (1993). Premarital cohabitation and marital instability: A test of the unconventionality hypothesis. *Journal of Marriage and the Family, 55,* 399-407.

Demo, D. H., Allen, K. R., & Fine, M. A. (Eds.). (2000). *Handbook of family diversity.* New York: Oxford University Press.

Denton, W. H., Burleson, B. R., & Sprenkle, D. H. (1995). Association of interpersonal cognitive complexity with communication skill in marriage: Moderating effects of marital distress. *Family Process, 35,* 101-111.

Doherty, W. J. (1999). Postmodernism and family theory. In M. B. Sussman, S. K. Steinmetz, & G. W. Peterson (Eds.), *Handbook of marriage and the family* (2nd ed., pp. 205-217). New York: Plenum.

Duberman, L. (1973). Step-kin relationships. *Journal of Marriage and the Family, 35,* 283-292.

Duck, S. (1976). Interpersonal communication in developing acquaintance. In G. R. Miller (Ed.), *Explorations in interpersonal communication* (pp. 127-148). Beverly Hills, CA: Sage.

Duck, S. (1982). A topography of relationship disengagement and dissolution. In S. Duck (Ed.), *Personal relationships 4: Dissolving personal relationships* (pp. 1-30). New York: Academic Press.

Duck, S., Rutt, D. J., Hurst, M. H., & Strejc, H. (1991). Some evidence truths about conversations in everyday relationships: All communications are not created equal. *Human Communication Research, 18,* 228-267.

Dunn, J. (1983). Sibling relationships in early childhood. *Child Development, 54,* 787-811.

Dunn, J. (1988). *The beginnings of social understanding.* Cambridge, MA: Harvard University Press.

Dunn, J., & Kendrick, C. (1982). The speech of two- and three-year-olds to infant siblings: "Baby talk" and the context of communication. *Journal of Child Language, 9,* 579-595.

Dunn, J., & Plomin, R. (1990). *Separate lives: Why siblings are so different.* New York: Basic Books.

Dunn, J., Slomkowski, C., & Beardsall, L. (1994). Sibling relationships from the preschool period through middle childhood and early adolescence. *Developmental Psychology, 30,* 315-324.

Duvall, E. (1971). *Family development.* Philadelphia: J. B. Lippincott.

Ericson, P. M., & Rogers, L. E. (1973). New procedures for analyzing relational communication. *Family Process, 12,* 245-257.

Farace, R. V., Monge, P. R., & Russell, H. M. (1977). *Communicating and organizing.* Reading, MA: Addison-Wesley.

Faust, K. A., & McKibben, J. N. (1999). Marital dissolution: Divorce, separation, annulment, and widowhood. In M. B. Sussman, S. K. Steinmetz, & G. W. Peterson (Eds.), *Handbook of marriage and the family* (2nd ed., pp. 475-499). New York: Plenum.

Feeney, J. A., Noller, P., & Roberts, N. (2000). Attachment and close relationships. In C. Hendrick & S. S. Hendrick (Eds.), *Close relationships: A sourcebook* (pp. 185-201). Thousand Oaks, CA: Sage.

Ferree, M. M. (1990). Beyond separate spheres: Feminism and family research. *Journal of Marriage and the Family, 52,* 866-884.

Fincham, F. D. (1998). Child development and marital relations. *Child Development, 69,* 543-574.

Fincham, F. D., Harold, G. T., & Gano-Phillips, S. (2000). The longitudinal association between attributions and marital satisfaction: Direction of effects and role of efficacy expectations. *Journal of Family Psychology, 14,* 267-285.

Fitzpatrick, F., & Wamboldt, F. (1990). Where is all said and done: Towards an integration of intrapersonal and interpersonal models of marital and family communication. *Communication Research, 17,* 421-431.

Fitzpatrick, M. A. (1976). *A typological approach to communication in relationships.* Unpublished doctoral dissertation, Temple University.

Fitzpatrick, M. A. (1983). Predicting couples' communication from couples' self-reports. In R. N. Bostrom (Ed.), *Communication yearbook 7* (pp. 49-82). Beverly Hills, CA: Sage.

Fitzpatrick, M. A. (1984). A typological approach to marital interaction: Recent theory and research. In L. Berkowitz (Ed.), *Advances in experimental social psychology* (Vol. 18, pp. 1-47). New York: Academic Press.

Fitzpatrick, M. A. (1988). *Between husbands and wives: Communication in marriage.* Newbury Park, CA: Sage.

Fitzpatrick, M. A. (1990). Aging, health and family communication. In H. Giles, N. Coupland, & J. M. Wiemann (Eds.), *Communication, health and aging* (pp. 213-228). Manchester, Eng.: Manchester University Press.

Fitzpatrick, M. A. (2002). Policing family violence. In H. Giles (Ed.), *Law enforcement, communication and community.* Amsterdam: John Benjamins.

Fitzpatrick, M. A., & Badzinski, D. M. (1994). All in the family: Interpersonal communication in kin relationships. In M. L. Knapp &

G. R. Miller (Eds.), *Handbook of interpersonal communication* (2nd ed., pp. 726-771). Thousand Oaks, CA: Sage.

Fitzpatrick, M. A., Fey, J., Segrin, C., & Schiff, J. (1993). Internal working models of relationships. *Journal of Language and Social Psychology, 12,* 103-131.

Fitzpatrick, M. A., & Indvik, J. (1982). The instrumental and expressive domains of marital communications. *Human Communication Research, 8,* 195-213.

Fitzpatrick, M. A., Jandt, F., Myrick, F. I., & Edgar, T. (1993). Gay and lesbian couple relationships. In R. J. Ringer (Ed.), *Queer words, queer images: Communication and the (re)construction of homosexuality.* New York: New York University Press.

Fitzpatrick, M. A., Marshall, L. J., Leutwiler, T. J., & Krcmar, M. (1996). The effect of family communication environments on children's social behavior during middle childhood. *Communication Research, 23,* 379-406.

Fitzpatrick, M. A., & Ritchie, L. D. (1993). Communication theory and the family. In P. G. Boss, W. J. Doherty, R. LaRossa, W. R. Schumm, & S. K. Steinmetz (Eds.), *Sourcebook of family theories and methods: A contextual approach* (pp. 565-585). New York: Plenum.

Fitzpatrick, M. A., & Ritchie, L. D. (1994). Communication schemata within the family: Multiple perspectives on family interaction. *Human Communication Research, 20,* 275-301.

Fitzpatrick, M. A., & Vangelisti, A. L. (Eds.). (1995). *Explaining family interactions.* Thousand Oaks, CA: Sage.

Fitzpatrick, M. A., & Vangelisti, A. L. (2001). Communication, relationships, and health. In W. P. Robinson & H. Giles (Eds.), *The new handbook of language and social psychology* (2nd ed., pp. 505-530). New York: John Wiley.

Fitzpatrick, M. A., Vangelisti, A. L., & Firman, S. (1994). Marital interaction and change during pregnancy: A typological approach. *Personal Relationships, 1,* 101-122.

Floyd, K. (1995). Gender and closeness among friends and siblings. *Journal of Psychology, 129,* 193-202.

Floyd, K. (1996). Brotherly love I: The experience of closeness in the fraternal dyad. *Personal Relationships, 3,* 369-385.

Folger, J. (1978). *The communicative indicants of power, dominance and submission.*

Unpublished doctoral dissertation, University of Wisconsin–Madison.

Freud, S. (1949). *An outline of psychoanalysis.* New York: W. W. Norton.

Fuligni, A. J., & Eccles, J. S. (1993). Perceived parent-child relationships and early adolescents' orientation toward peers. *Developmental Psychology, 29,* 622-632.

Furman, W., & Buhrmester, D. (1985). Children's perceptions of the qualities of sibling relationships. *Child Development, 56,* 448-461.

Galvin, K. M., & Brommel, B. J. (2000). *Family communication: Cohesion and change* (5th ed.). New York: Longman.

Ganong, L. H., & Coleman, M. (1994). *Remarried family relationships.* Thousand Oaks, CA: Sage.

Ganong, L. H., & Coleman, M. (1999). *Changing families, changing responsibilities: Family obligations following divorce and remarriage.* Mahwah, NJ: Lawrence Erlbaum.

Ganong, L. H., & Coleman, M. (2000). Remarried families. In C. Hendrick & S. S. Hendrick (Eds.), *Close relationships: A sourcebook* (pp. 155-168). Thousand Oaks, CA: Sage.

Ganong, L. H., Coleman, M., & Mapes, D. (1990). A meta-analytic review of family structure stereotypes. *Journal of Marriage and the Family, 52,* 287-297.

Garmezy, N. (1974). Children at risk: The search for antecedents of schizophrenia. *Schizophrenia Bulletin, 1,* 14-90.

Gelles, R. J. (1974). *The violent home: A study of physical aggression between husbands and wives.* Beverly Hills, CA: Sage.

Glenn, N., & McLanahan, S. (1982). Children and marital happiness. *Journal of Marriage and the Family, 44,* 63-72.

Golish, T. D. (in press). Stepfamily communication strengths: Understanding the ties that bind. *Communication Research.*

Goode, W. J. (1963). *World revolution and family patterns.* New York: Free Press.

Gordon, L. (1988). *Heroes of their own lives: The politics and history of family violence.* New York: Viking.

Gottman, J. M. (1993). A theory of marital dissolution and stability. *Journal of Family Psychology, 7,* 57-75.

Gottman, J. M. (1994). *What predicts divorce? The relationship between marital processes and marital outcomes.* Hillsdale, NJ: Lawrence Erlbaum.

Gottman, J. M., & Krokoff, L. J. (1989). Marital interaction and satisfaction: A longitudinal view. *Journal of Consulting and Clinical Psychology, 57,* 47-52.

Gottman, J. M., & Levenson, R. W. (1992). Marital processes predictive of later dissolution: Behavior, physiology, and health. *Journal of Personality and Social Psychology, 63,* 221-233.

Gottman, J. M., & Levenson, R. W. (2000). The timing of divorce: Predicting when a couple will divorce over a 14-year period. *Journal of Marriage and the Family, 62,* 737-745.

Gottman, J. M., Markman, H. J., & Notarius, C. I. (1977). The topography of marital conflict: A sequential analysis of verbal and nonverbal behavior. *Journal of Marriage and the Family, 39,* 461-477.

Graham, E. E. (1997). Turning points and commitment in post-divorce relationships. *Communication Monographs, 64,* 350-368.

Graziano, W. G., & Musser, L. M. (1982). The joining and the parting of the ways. In S. Duck (Ed.), *Personal relationships. 4: Dissolving personal relationships* (pp. 75-106). New York: Academic Press.

Grych, J. H., & Fincham, F. D. (1990). Marital conflict and children's adjustment: A cognitive-contextual framework. *Psychological Bulletin, 108,* 267-290.

Guerrero, L. K. (1996). Attachment-style differences in intimacy and involvement: A test of the four-category model. *Communication Monographs, 63,* 269-292.

Hackel, L. S., & Ruble, D. N. (1992). Changes in the marital relationship after the first baby is born: Predicting the impact of expectancy disconfirmation. *Journal of Personality and Social Psychology, 62,* 944-957.

Hareven, T. K. (1980, April). *American families in transition: Historical perspectives in change.* Paper presented at the White House Conference on Families, Research Forum on Family Issues, Washington, DC.

Harry, J., & Lovely, R. (1979). Gay marriages and communities of sexual orientation. *Alternative Lifestyles, 2,* 177-200.

Hartup, W. W. (1978). Perspectives on child and family interaction: Past, present and future. In R. M. Lerner & G. B. Spanier (Eds.), *Child influences on marital and family interaction: A life-span perspective* (pp. 23-46). New York: Academic Press.

Harvey, J. H., Weber, A. L., Yarkin, K. L., & Stewart, B. E. (1982). An attributional approach to relationship breakdown and dissolution. In S. Duck (Ed.), *Personal relationships 4: Dissolving personal relationships* (pp. 107-126). New York: Academic Press.

Harwood, J., Giles, H., & Ryan, E. B. (1995). Aging, communication, and intergroup theory: Social identity and intergenerational communication. In J. F. Nussbaum & J. Coupland (Eds.), *Handbook of communication and aging research* (pp. 133-159). Mahwah, NJ: Lawrence Erlbaum.

Heavey, C. L., Christensen, A., & Malamuth, N. M. (1995). The longitudinal impact of demand and withdrawal during marital conflict. *Journal of Consulting and Clinical Psychology, 63,* 797-801.

Hess, R. D. (1981). Approaches to the measurement and interpretation of parent-child interaction. In R. W. Henderson (Ed.), *Parent-child interaction: Theory, research, and prospects* (pp. 207-234). New York: Academic Press.

Hetherington, M., Clingempeel, W. G., Anderson, E. R., Deal, J., Hagan, M., Hollier, E., & Lindner, M. (1992). Coping with marital transitions: A family systems perspective. *Monographs of the Society for Research in Child Development, 57*(2-3, Serial No. 227).

Hill, C. T., Rubin, Z., & Peplau, L. A. (1976). Breakups before marriage: The end of 103 affairs. *Journal of Social Issues, 32*(1), 147-168.

Hinde, R. A. (1979). *Towards understanding relationships.* New York: Academic Press.

Holmes, T. H., & Rahe, R. H. (1976). The social readjustment rating scale. *Journal of Psychosomatic Research, 11,* 213-218.

Hopper, R., Knapp, M. L., & Scott, L. (1981). Couples' personal idioms: Exploring intimate talk. *Journal of Communication, 31*(1), 23-33.

Howe, G., & Reiss, D. (1993). Simulation and experimentation in family research. In P. G. Boss, W. J. Doherty, R. LaRossa, W. R. Schumm, & S. K. Steinmetz (Eds.), *Sourcebook of family theory and methods: A contextual approach* (pp. 303-324). New York: Plenum.

Huston, T. L. (2000). The social ecology of marriage and other intimate unions. *Journal of Marriage and the Family, 62,* 298-320.

Huston, T. L., Caughlin, J. P., Houts, R. M., Smith, S., & George, L. J. (2001). The connubial crucible: Newlywed years as predictors of marital delight, distress, and divorce. *Journal*

of Personality and Social Psychology, 80, 237-252.

Huston, T. L., & Chorost, A. (1994). Behavioral buffers on the effect of negativity on marital satisfaction: A longitudinal study. *Personal Relationships, 1,* 223-239.

Huston, T. L., & Levinger, G. (1978). Interpersonal attraction and relationships. *Annual Review of Psychology, 29,* 115-156.

Huston, T. L., Surra, C. A., Fitzgerald, N. M., & Cate, R. M. (1981). From courtship to marriage: Mate selection as an interpersonal process. In S. Duck & R. Gilmour (Eds.), *Personal relationships 2: Developing personal relationships* (pp. 53-88). London: Academic Press.

Huston, T. L., & Vangelisti, A. L. (1995). How parenthood affects marriage. In M. A. Fitzpatrick & A. L. Vangelisti (Eds.), *Explaining family interactions* (pp. 147-176). Thousand Oaks, CA: Sage.

Jacob, T. (1975). Family interaction in disturbed and normal families: A methodological and substantive review. *Psychological Bulletin, 82,* 33-65.

Jacob, T. (1987). *Family interaction and psychopathology.* New York: Plenum.

Jacobvitz, D. B., & Bush, N. F. (1996). Reconstructions of family relationships: Parent-child alliances, personal distress, and self-esteem. *Developmental Psychology, 32,* 732-743.

Jekielek, S. (1998). Parental conflict, marital disruption and children's emotional well-being. *Social Forces, 76,* 905-936.

Johnson, E. M., & Huston, T. L. (1998). The perils of love, or why wives adapt to husbands during the transition to parenthood. *Journal of Marriage and the Family, 60,* 195-204.

Johnson, M. P. (1995). Patriarchal terrorism and common couple violence: Two forms of violence against women. *Journal of Marriage and the Family, 57,* 283-294.

Johnson, M. P. (1999). Personal, moral, and structural commitment to relationships: Experiences of choice and constraint. In J. M. Adams & W. H. Jones (Eds.), *Handbook of interpersonal commitment and relationship stability* (pp. 73-87). New York: Plenum.

Johnson, M. P., & Ferraro, K. J. (2000). Research on domestic violence in the 1990s: Making distinctions. *Journal of Marriage and the Family, 62,* 948-963.

Kaplan, E., & Kaplan, G. (1971). The pre-linguistic child. In J. Elliot (Ed.), *Human development and cognitive processes* (pp. 358-380). New York: Holt, Rinehart & Winston.

Karney, B. R., & Bradbury, T. N. (1995). The longitudinal course of marital quality and stability: A review of theory, method, and research. *Psychological Bulletin, 118*, 3-34.

Karney, B. R., & Bradbury, T. N. (1997). Neuroticism, marital interaction, and the trajectory of marital satisfaction. *Journal of Personality and Social Psychology, 72*, 1075-1092.

Karney, B. R., & Bradbury, T. N. (2000). Attributions in marriage: State or trait? A growth curve analysis. *Journal of Personality and Social Psychology, 78*, 295-309.

Katz, L. F., & Gottman, J. M. (1993). Patterns of marital conflict predict children's internalizing and externalizing behaviors. *Developmental Psychology, 29*, 940-950.

Kaye, K. (1980). Why we don't talk "baby talk" to babies. *Journal of Child Language, 7*, 489-508.

Keller, H., Lohaus, A., Völker, S, Cappenberg, M., & Chasiotis, A. (1999). Temporal contingency as an independent component of parenting behavior. *Child Development, 70*, 474-485.

Kelley, H. H. (1983). Love and commitment. In H. H. Kelley, E. Berscheid, A. Christensen, J. H. Harvey, T. L. Huston, G. Levinger, et al., *Close relationships* (pp. 265-314). New York: Freeman.

Kelly, C., Huston, T. L., & Cate, R. M. (1985). Premarital relationship correlates of the erosion of satisfaction in marriage. *Journal of Social and Personal Relationships, 2*, 167-178.

Kelly, L. E., & Conley, J. J. (1987). Personality and compatibility: A prospective analysis of marital stability and marital satisfaction. *Journal of Personality and Social Psychology, 52*, 27-40.

Kerckhoff, A. C., & Davis, K. E. (1962). Value consensus and need complementarity in mate selection. *American Sociological Review, 27*, 295-303.

Kiecolt-Glaser, J. K., & Newton, T. L. (2001). Marriage and health: His and hers. *Psychological Bulletin, 127*, 472-503.

King, C. A., Radpour, L., Naylor, M. W., Segal, H. G., & Jouriles, E. N. (1995). Parents' marital functioning and adolescent psychopathology. *Journal of Consulting and Clinical Psychology, 63*, 749-753.

Knapp, M. L., & Miller, G. R. (Eds.). (1994). *Handbook of interpersonal communication* (2nd ed.). Thousand Oaks, CA: Sage.

Koerner, A. F., & Fitzpatrick, M. A. (1997). Family type and conflict: The impact of conversation orientation and conformity orientation on conflict in the family. *Communication Studies, 48*, 59-78.

Koerner, A. F., & Fitzpatrick, M. A. (2002). Toward a theory of family communication. *Communication Theory, 12*, 70-91.

Kressel, K., Jaffee, N., Tuchman, B., Watson, C., & Deutsch, M. (1980). A typology of divorcing couples: Implications for mediation and the divorce process. *Family Process, 19*, 101-116.

Kurdek, L. A. (1989). Relationship quality of newly married husbands and wives: Marital history, stepchildren and individual difference predictors. *Journal of Marriage and the Family, 51*, 1053-1064.

Kurdek, L. A. (1991). Marital stability and changes in marital quality in newlywed couples: A test of the contextual model. *Journal of Social and Personal Relationships, 8*, 27-48.

Kurdek, L. A. (1998). Relationship outcomes and their predictors: Longitudinal evidence from heterosexual married, gay cohabiting, and lesbian cohabiting couples. *Journal of Marriage and the Family, 60*, 553-568.

Kurdek, L. A. (2000). Attractions and constraints as determinants of relationship commitment: Longitudinal evidence from gay, lesbian, and heterosexual couples. *Personal Relationships, 7*, 245-262.

La Gaipa, J. J. (1981). Children's friendships. In S. Duck & R. Gilmour (Eds.), *Personal relationships 2: Developing personal relationships* (pp. 67-70). New York: Academic Press.

Lamb, M. E. (1976a). Proximity seeking attachment behaviors: A critical review of the literature. *Genetic Psychology Monographs, 93*, 63-89.

Lamb, M. E. (Ed.). (1976b). *The role of the father in child development*. New York: John Wiley.

Lamb, M. E. (1978). The development of sibling relationships in infancy: A short-term longitudinal study. *Child Development, 49*, 1189-1196.

Landry, S. H., Smith, K. E., Miller-Loncar, C. L., & Swank, P. R. (1998). The relation of change in maternal interactive styles to the developing social competence of full-term and preterm children. *Child Development, 69*, 105-123.

LaRossa, R. (1977). *Conflict and power in marriage: Expecting the first child.* Beverly Hills, CA: Sage.

Larson, R., & Richards, M. H. (1994). *Divergent realities: The emotional lives of mothers, fathers, and adolescents.* New York: Basic Books.

Lasch, C. (1977). *Haven in a heartless world.* New York: Basic Books.

Lederer, W. J., & Jackson, D. D. (1968). *The mirages of marriage.* New York: W. W. Norton.

LeMasters, E. E. (1957). Parenthood as crisis. *Marriage and Family Living, 19,* 352-355.

Le Poire, B. A., Hallett, J. S., & Erlandson, K. T. (2000). An initial test of inconsistent nurturing as control theory: How partners of drug abusers assist their partners' sobriety. *Human Communication Research, 26,* 432-457.

Le Poire, B. A., Haynes, J., Driscoll, J., Driver, B. N., Wheelis, T. F., Hyde, M. K., et al. (1997). Attachment as a function of parental and partner approach-avoidance tendencies. *Human Communication Research, 23,* 413-441.

Lerner, R. M., & Spanier, G. B. (Eds.). (1978). *Child influences on marital interaction: A life-span perspective.* New York: Academic Press.

Levenson, R. W., & Gottman, J. M. (1983). Marital interaction: Physiological linkage and affective exchange. *Journal of Personality and Social Psychology, 45,* 587-597.

Levinger, G. (1976). A social psychological perspective on marital dissolution. *Journal of Social Issues, 32*(1), 21-47.

Levinger, G., & Huston, T. L. (1990). The social psychology of marriage. In F. D. Fincham & T. N. Bradbury (Eds.), *The psychology of marriage: Basic issues and applications* (pp. 19-58). New York: Guilford.

Levy, D. M. (1937). Studies in sibling rivalry. *American Orthopsychiatric Association Research Monographs, 2.*

Levy-Shiff, R. (1994). Individual and contextual correlates of marital change across the transition to parenthood. *Developmental Psychology, 30,* 591-601.

Lewis, R. A. (1973). A longitudinal test of a developmental framework for premarital dyadic formation. *Journal of Marriage and the Family, 35,* 16-25.

MacDermid, S. M., Huston, T. L., & McHale, S. M. (1990). Changes in marriage associated with the transition to parenthood: Individual differences as a function of sex-role attitudes

and changes in the division of household labor. *Journal of Marriage and the Family, 52,* 475-486.

Main, M., Kaplan, N., & Cassidy, J. (1985). Security in infancy, childhood, and adulthood: A move to the level of representation. *Monographs of the Society for Research in Child Development, 1-2*(Serial No. 209).

Mares, L., & Fitzpatrick, M. A. (1995). Communication and the aging couple. In J. F. Nussbaum & N. Coupland (Eds.), *Handbook of communication and aging research* (pp. 185-205). Mahwah, NJ: Lawrence Erlbaum.

Mark, R. A. (1971). Coding communication at the relationship level. *Journal of Communication, 21,* 221-232.

Markman, H. J. (1979). Application of a behavioral model of marriage in predicting relationship satisfaction of couples planning marriage. *Journal of Consulting and Clinical Psychology, 47,* 747-750.

Markman, H. J. (1981). Prediction of marital distress: A five year follow-up. *Journal of Consulting and Clinical Psychology, 49,* 760-762.

Markman, H. J. (1984). The longitudinal study of couples' interactions: Implications for understanding and predicting the development of marital distress. In K. Hahlweg & N. S. Jacobson (Eds.), *Marital interaction: Analysis and modification* (pp. 253-281). New York: Guilford.

Martin, M. M., Anderson, C. M., & Mottet, T. P. (1997). The relationship between perceived understanding and self-disclosure in the sibling relationship. *Communication Research Reports, 14,* 331-338.

Matas, L., Arend, R. A., & Sroufe, A. (1982). Continuity of adaptation in the second year. In J. Belsky (Ed.), *In the beginning: Readings on infancy* (pp. 144-156). New York: Columbia University Press.

McGuire, S., & Dunn, J. (1994). Nonshared environment in middle childhood. In J. C. DeFries, R. Plomin, & D. W. Fulker (Eds.), *Nature and nurture during middle childhood* (pp. 201-213). Cambridge, MA: Blackwell.

McKay, V. C., & Caverly, R. S. (1995). Relationships in later life: The nature of inter- and intragenerational ties among grandparents, grandchildren, and adult siblings. In

J. F. Nussbaum & N. Coupland (Eds.), *Handbook of communication and aging research* (pp. 207-225). Mahwah, NJ: Lawrence Erlbaum.

McLeod, J. M., & Chaffee, S. H. (1972). The construction of social reality. In J. T. Tedeschi (Ed.), *The social influence process* (pp. 50-99). Chicago: Aldine.

McWhirter, D., & Mattison, A. M. (1984). *The male couple: How relationships develop.* Englewood Cliffs, NJ: Prentice Hall.

Mead, M. (1942). *And keep your powder dry: An anthropologist looks at America.* New York: William Morrow.

Menaghan, E. G., & Parcel, T. L. (1990). Parental employment and family life: Research in the 1980s. *Journal of Marriage and the Family, 52,* 1079-1098.

Metts, S., & Cupach, W. R. (1995). Postdivorce relations. In M. A. Fitzpatrick & A. L. Vangelisti (Eds.), *Explaining family interactions* (pp. 232-251). Thousand Oaks, CA: Sage.

Miklowitz, D. J., Goldstein, M. J., & Nuechterlein, K. H. (1995). Verbal interactions in the families of schizophrenic and bipolar affective patients. *Journal of Abnormal Psychology, 104,* 268-276.

Millar, F. E., & Rogers, E. (1976). A relational approach to interpersonal communication. In G. R. Miller (Ed.), *Explorations in interpersonal communication* (pp. 87-104). Beverly Hills, CA: Sage.

Miller, G. R., & Parks, M. R. (1982). Communication in dissolving relationships. In S. Duck (Ed.), *Personal relationships 4: Dissolving personal relationships* (pp. 127-154). New York: Academic Press.

Minnett, A. M., Vandell, D. L., & Santrock, J. W. (1983). The effects of sibling status on sibling interaction: Influence of birth order, age spacing, sex of child, and sex of sibling. *Child Development, 54,* 1064-1072.

Minuchin, S. (1974). *Families and family therapy.* Cambridge, MA: Harvard University Press.

Morrison, D. R., & Coiro, M. J. (1999). Parental conflict and marital disruption: Do children benefit when high-conflict marriages are dissolved? *Journal of Marriage and the Family, 61,* 626-637.

Moscovici, S. (1967). Communication processes and the properties of language. In L. Berkowitz (Ed.), *Advances in experimental social psychology* (Vol. 3, pp. 225-270). New York: Academic Press.

Moss, E., Rousseau, D., Parent, S., St-Laurent, D., & Saintonge, J. (1998). Correlates of attachment at school age: Maternal reported stress, mother-child interaction, and behavior problems. *Child Development, 69,* 1390-1405.

Murstein, B. I. (1967). Empirical tests of role, complementary needs and homogamy theories of mate choice. *Journal of Marriage and the Family, 29,* 689-696.

Myers, S. A., & Knox, R. L. (1998). Perceived sibling use of functional communication skills. *Communication Research Reports, 15,* 397-405.

Napier, A., & Whitaker, C. (1978). *The family crucible.* New York: Harper & Row.

National Center for Health Statistics. (2001). Births, marriages, divorces, and deaths: Provisional data for January-December 2000. *National Vital Statistics Reports, 49*(6). Retrieved April 17, 2002, from http://www.cdc.gov/nchs/data/nvsr49_06.pdf

Neiderhiser, J. M., Reiss, D., Hetherington, E. M., & Plomin, R. (1999). Relationships between parenting and adolescent adjustment over time: Genetic and environmental contributions. *Developmental Psychology, 35,* 680-692.

Newcomb, M. D. (1987). Cohabitation and marriage: A quest for independence and relatedness. In S. Oskamp (Ed.), *Family processes and problems: Social psychological aspects* (pp. 128-156). Newbury Park, CA: Sage.

Newcomb, M. D., & Bentler, P. M. (1980). Cohabitation before marriage: A comparison of couples who did and did not cohabit before marriage. *Alternative Lifestyles, 3,* 65-85.

Nock, S. L. (1995). A comparison of marriages and cohabiting relationships. *Journal of Family Issues, 16,* 53-76.

Noller, P. (1995). Parent-adolescent relationships. In M. A. Fitzpatrick & A. L. Vangelisti (Eds.), *Explaining family interaction* (pp. 77-111). Thousand Oaks, CA: Sage.

Noller, P., & Feeney, J. A. (1998). Communication in early marriage: Responses to conflict, nonverbal accuracy, and conversational patterns. In T. N. Bradbury (Ed.), *The developmental course of marital dysfunction* (pp. 11-43). Cambridge: Cambridge University Press.

Noller, P., Feeney, J. A., Bonnell, D., & Callan, V. J. (1994). A longitudinal study of conflict in early marriage. *Journal of Social and Personal Relationships, 11,* 233-252.

Noller, P., & Fitzpatrick, M. A. (1993). *Communication in family relationships.* Englewood Cliffs, NJ: Prentice Hall.

Norton, R. (1983). *Communication style: Theory, applications, and measures.* Beverly Hills, CA: Sage.

Notarius, C. I., Lashley, S. L., & Sullivan, D. J. (1997). Angry at your partner? Think again. In R. J. Sternberg & M. Hojjat (Eds.), *Satisfaction in close relationships* (pp. 219-248). New York: Guilford.

Nye, F. I. (1979). Choice, exchange, and the family. In W. R. Burr, R. Hill, F. I. Nye, & I. L. Reiss (Eds.), *Contemporary theories about the family* (Vol. 2, pp. 1-41). New York: Free Press.

Nye, F. I., & Berardo, F. M. (1981). Introduction. In F. I. Nye & F. M. Berardo (Eds.), *Emerging conceptual frameworks in family analysis* (pp. 1-9). New York: Praeger.

Oliveri, M. E., & Reiss, D. (1981a). The structure of families' ties to their kin: The shaping role of social constructions. *Journal of Marriage and the Family, 43,* 391-407.

Oliveri, M. E., & Reiss, D. (1981b). A theory-based empirical classification of family problem-solving behavior. *Family Process, 20,* 409-418.

Olson, D. H. L., McCubbin, H. I., Barnes, H., Larsen, A., Muxen, M., & Wilson, M. (1983). *Families: What makes them work.* Beverly Hills, CA: Sage.

Olson, D. H. L., Sprenkle, D. H., & Russell, C. S. (1979). Circumplex model of marital and family system: Cohesion and adaptability dimensions, family types, and clinical applications. *Family Process, 18,* 3-28.

Parke, R. D. (1979). Perspectives on father-infant interaction. In J. D. Osofsky (Ed.), *Handbook of infant development* (pp. 549-590). New York: John Wiley.

Parke, R. D., & O'Neil, R. (1997). The influence of significant others on learning about relationships. In S. Duck (Ed.), *Handbook of personal relationships: Theory, research and interventions* (2nd ed., pp. 29-59). New York: John Wiley.

Parks, M. (1982). Ideology in interpersonal communication: Off the couch and into the world. In M. Burgoon (Ed.), *Communication yearbook 5* (pp. 79-108). New Brunswick, NJ: Transaction.

Parsons, T., & Bales, R. F. (1955). *Family socialization and interaction process.* New York: Free Press.

Pasch, L. A., & Bradbury, T. N. (1998). Social support, conflict, and the development of marital dysfunction. *Journal of Consulting and Clinical Psychology, 66,* 219-230.

Pasch, L. A., Bradbury, T. N., & Davila, J. (1997). Gender, negative affectivity, and observed social support behavior in marital interaction. *Personal Relationships, 4,* 361-378.

Patterson, C. (2000). Family relationships of lesbians and gay men. *Journal of Marriage and the Family, 62,* 1052-1069.

Patterson, G. R. (1976). The aggressive child: Victim and architect of a coercive system. In E. J. Marsh, L. A. Hammerlynck, & L. C. Handy (Eds.), *Behavior modification and families* (pp. 267-316). New York: Brunner/Mazel.

Paulhus, D. L, Trapnell, P. D., & Chen, D. (1999). Birth order effects on personality and achievement within families. *Psychological Science, 10,* 482-488.

Peplar, D., Abramovitch, R., & Corter, C. (1981). Sibling interaction in the home: A longitudinal study. *Child Development, 52,* 1344-1347.

Peplau, L. A. (2001). Rethinking women's sexual orientation: An interdisciplinary, relationship-focused approach. *Personal Relationships, 8,* 1-19.

Peplau, L. A., & Cochran, S. D. (1981). Value orientations in the intimate relationships of gay men. *Journal of Homosexuality, 6*(3), 1-9.

Peplau, L. A., Veniegas, R. C., & Campbell, S. M. (1996). Gay and lesbian relationships. In R. C. Savin-Williams & K. M. Cohen (Eds.), *The lives of lesbians, gays, and bisexuals: Children to adults* (pp. 250-273). Fort Worth, TX: Harcourt Brace.

Peterson, G. W., & Rollins, B. C. (1987). Parent-child socialization. In M. B. Sussman & S. K. Steinmetz (Eds.), *Handbook of marriage and the family* (pp. 471-506). New York: Plenum.

Peterson, G. W., & Steinmetz, S. K. (1999). Introduction: Perspectives on families as we approach the twenty-first century—challenges for future handbook authors. In M. B. Sussman, S. K. Steinmetz, & G. W. Peterson (Eds.), *Handbook of marriage and the family* (2nd ed., pp. 1-12). New York: Plenum.

Plumert, J. M., & Nichols-Whitehead, P. (1996). Parental scaffolding of young children's spatial communication. *Developmental Psychology, 32,* 523-532.

Poole, M. S., McPhee, R. D., & Seibold, D. R. (1982). A comparison of normative and interactional explanations of group decision-making: Social decision schemes versus valence distributions. *Communication Monographs, 49,* 1-19.

Popenoe, D. (1993). American family decline, 1960-1990: A review and appraisal. *Journal of Marriage and the Family, 55,* 527-555.

Popenoe, D. (1999). *Life without father: Compelling evidence that fatherhood and marriage are indispensable for the good of children and society.* Cambridge, MA: Harvard University Press.

Raffaelli, M. (1992). Sibling conflict in early adolescence. *Journal of Marriage and the Family, 54,* 652-663.

Raush, H. L., Grief, A. C., & Nugent, J. (1979). Communication in couples and families. In W. Burr, R. Hill, F. I. Nye, & I. L. Reiss (Eds.), *Contemporary theories about the family* (Vol. 1, pp. 468-492). New York: Free Press.

Reiss, D. (1981). *The family's construction of reality.* Cambridge, MA: Harvard University Press.

Reiss, D. (with Neiderhiser, J. M., Hetherington, E. M., & Plomin R.). (2000). *The relationship code: Deciphering genetic and social influences on adolescent development.* Cambridge, MA: Harvard University Press.

Reiss, D., Plomin, R., & Hetherington, M. (1991). Genetics and psychiatry: An unheralded window on the environment. *American Journal of Psychiatry, 148,* 283-291.

Reiss, I. L. (1971). *The family system in America.* New York: Holt, Rinehart & Winston.

Revenstorf, D., Vogel, B., Wegener, C., Hahlweg, K., & Schindler, L. (1980). Escalation phenomena in interaction sequences: An empirical comparison of distressed and nondistressed couples. *Behavior Analysis and Modification, 2,* 97-116.

Rholes, W. S., Simpson, J. A., Campbell, L., & Grinch, J. (2001). Adult attachment and the transition to parenthood. *Journal of Personality and Social Psychology, 81,* 421-435.

Richards, M. P. M. (1974). The development of psychological communication in the first year of life. In K. J. Connolly & J. S. Bruner (Eds.), *The growth of competence* (pp. 119-134). New York: Academic Press.

Riskin, J., & Faunce, E. E. (1972). An evaluation review of family interaction research. *Family Process, 11,* 365-455.

Risman, B. J., Hill, C. T., Rubin, Z., & Peplau, L. A. (1981). Living together in college: Implications for courtship. *Journal of Marriage and the Family, 43,* 77-83.

Ritchie, L. D., & Fitzpatrick, M. A. (1990). Family communication patterns: Measuring intrapersonal perceptions of interpersonal relationships. *Communication Research, 17,* 523-544.

Rogers, L. E. (1972). *Dyadic systems and transactional communication in a family context.* Unpublished doctoral dissertation, Michigan State University.

Rogers, L. E., & Farace, V. (1975). Analysis of relational communication in dyads. *Human Communication Research, 1,* 229-239.

Rollins, B. C. (1975). Response to Miller about cross-sectional family life cycle research. *Journal of Marriage and the Family, 37,* 259-260.

Rollins, B. C., & Thomas, D. L. (1979). Parental support, power, and control techniques in the socialization of children. In W. R. Burr, R. Hill, F. I. Nye, & I. L. Reiss (Eds.), *Contemporary theories about the family* (Vol. 1, pp. 317-364). New York: Free Press.

Rosen, K. S., & Burke, P. B. (1999). Multiple attachment relationships within families: Mothers and fathers with two young children. *Developmental Psychology, 35,* 436-444.

Sarantakos, S. (1984). *Living together in Australia.* Melbourne: Longman Cheshire.

Savin-Williams, R. C., & Esterberg, K. G. (2000). Lesbian, gay, and bisexual families. In D. H. Demo, K. R. Allen, & M. A. Fine (Eds.), *Handbook of family diversity* (pp. 197-215). New York: Oxford University Press.

Scarr, S., & Grajek, S. (1982). Similarities and differences among siblings. In M. E. Lamb & B. Sutton-Smith (Eds.), *Sibling relationships: Their nature and significance across the lifespan* (pp. 357-382). Hillsdale, NJ: Lawrence Erlbaum.

Schooler, C. (1972). Birth order effects: Not here, not now. *Psychological Bulletin, 78,* 161-175.

Segrin, C., & Fitzpatrick, M. A. (1992). Depression and verbal aggression in various types of marriages. *Communication Studies, 43,* 79-91.

Shapiro, A. F., Gottman, J. M., & Carrere, S. (2000). The baby and the marriage: Identifying factors that buffer against the decline in marital satisfaction after the first baby arrives. *Journal of Family Psychology, 14,* 59-70.

Shatz, H., & Gelman, R. (1977). Beyond syntax: The influence of conversational constraints on speech modifications. In C. E. Snow & C. A. Ferguson (Eds.), *Talking to children: Language input and acquisition* (pp. 189-198). Cambridge: Cambridge University Press.

Sillars, A. (1980). *Communication and attributions in interpersonal conflict.* Unpublished doctoral dissertation, University of Wisconsin–Madison.

Sillars, A., Roberts, L. J., Dun, T., & Leonard, K. E. (2001). Stepping into the stream of thought: Cognition during marital conflict. In V. Manusov & J. H. Harvey (Eds.), *Attribution, communication behavior, and close relationships* (pp. 193-210). New York: Cambridge University Press.

Sillars, A., Roberts, L. J., Leonard, K. E., & Dun, T. (2000). Cognition during marital conflict: The relationship of thought and talk. *Journal of Social and Personal Relationships, 17,* 479-502.

Slocum, W. L., & Nye, F. I. (1976). Provider and housekeeper roles. In F. I. Nye (Ed.), *Role structure and analysis of the family* (pp. 81-100). Beverly Hills, CA: Sage.

Sluzki, C. E., & Beavin, J. (1965). Simetra y complementaridad: Una definición operacional y una tipologia de parejas. *Acta Psiquiatrica y Psicologica de America Latina, 11,* 321-330.

Snow, C. E. (1972). Mothers' speech to children learning language. *Child Development, 43,* 549-565.

Snow, C. E. (1977). Mother's speech research: From input to interaction. In C. E. Snow & C. A. Ferguson (Eds.), *Talking to children: Language input and acquisition* (pp. 31-50). Cambridge: Cambridge University Press.

Socha, T. J. (2001). Home, family, and communication: The horizon through a wide lens. *Journal of Family Communication, 1,* 1-7.

Spieker, S. (1982). Early communication and language development. In J. Belsky (Ed.), *In the beginning: Readings on infancy* (pp. 121-132). New York: Columbia University Press.

Sprey, J. (1979). Conflict theory and the study of marriage and the family. In W. R. Burr, R. Hill, F. I. Nye, & I. L. Reiss (Eds.), *Contemporary theories about the family* (Vol. 2, pp. 130-159). New York: Free Press.

Sroufe, L. A. (1979). Socioemotional development. In J. D. Osofsky (Ed.), *Handbook of infant development* (pp. 462-516). New York: John Wiley.

Stafford, L., & Bayer, C. L. (1993). *Interaction between parents and children.* Newbury Park, CA: Sage.

Stafford, L., Dainton, M., & Haas, S. (2000). Measuring routine and strategic relational maintenance: Scale revision, sex versus gender roles, and the prediction of relational characteristics. *Communication Monographs, 67,* 306-323.

Stamp, G. H. (1994). The appropriation of the parental role through communication during the transition to parenthood. *Communication Monographs, 61,* 89-112.

Stayton, D., Hogan, R., & Ainsworth, M. D. S. (1982). Infant obedience and maternal behavior. In J. Belsky (Ed.), *In the beginning: Readings on infancy* (pp. 194-203). New York: Columbia University Press.

Steinglass, P., Bennett, L. A., Wolin, S. J., & Reiss, D. (1987). *The alcoholic family.* New York: Basic Books.

Steinmetz, S. K. (1979). Disciplinary techniques and their relationship to aggressiveness, dependency, and conscience. In W. R. Burr, R. Hill, F. I. Nye, & I. L. Reiss (Eds.), *Contemporary theories about the family* (Vol. 2, pp. 405-438). New York: Free Press.

Stern, D. (1977). *The first relationship: Infant and mother.* London: Fontana.

Stewart, R. B. (1983). Sibling attachment relationships: Child-infant interactions in the strange situation. *Developmental Psychology, 19,* 192-199.

Stocker, C. M., & McHale, S. M. (1992). The nature and family correlates of preadolescents' perceptions of their sibling relationships. *Journal of Social and Personal Relationships, 9,* 179-195.

Summers, P., Forehand, R., Armistead, L., & Tannenbaum, L. (1998). Parental divorce during early adolescence in Caucasian families: The role of family process variables in predicting the long-term consequences for early adult psychosocial adjustment. *Journal of Consulting and Clinical Psychology, 66,* 327-336.

Surra, C. A., Batchelder, M. L., & Hughes, D. K. (1995). Accounts and the demystification of courtship. In M. A. Fitzpatrick & A. L. Vangelisti (Eds.), *Explaining family interactions* (pp. 112-141). Thousand Oaks, CA: Sage.

Surra, C. A., & Hughes, D. K. (1997). Commitment processes in accounts of the development of premarital relationships. *Journal of Marriage and the Family, 59,* 5-21.

Sussman, M. B., Steinmetz, S. K., & Peterson, G. W. (Eds.). (1999). *Handbook of marriage and the family* (2nd ed.). New York: Plenum.

Sutton-Smith, B., & Rosenberg, B. G. (1970). *The sibling.* New York: Holt, Rinehart & Winston.

Teachman, J. D., Polonko, K. A., & Scanzoni, J. (1999). Demography and families. In M. B. Sussman, S. K. Steinmetz, & G. W. Peterson (Eds.), *Handbook of marriage and the family* (2nd ed., pp. 39-76). New York: Plenum.

Terman, L. M. (1938). *Psychological factors in marital happiness.* New York: McGraw-Hill.

Thorne, B. (1992). Feminism and the family: Two decades of thought. In B. Thorne & M. Yalom (Eds.), *Rethinking the family: Some feminist questions* (Rev. ed., pp. 3-30). Boston: Northeastern University Press.

Ting-Toomey, S. (1983). An analysis of verbal communication patterns in high and low marital adjustment groups. *Human Communication Research, 9,* 306-319.

Toman, W. (1961). *Family constellation.* New York: Springer.

Treas, J., & Lawton, L. (1999). Family relations in adulthood. In M. B. Sussman, S. K. Steinmetz, & G. W. Peterson (Eds.), *Handbook of marriage and the family* (2nd ed., pp. 425-438). New York: Plenum.

Tsukada, G. K. (1979). Sibling interaction: A review of the literature. *Smith College Studies in Social Work, 3,* 229-247.

Vandell, D. L., Minnett, A. M., & Santrock, J. W. (1987). Age differences in sibling relationships during middle childhood. *Journal of Applied Developmental Psychology, 8,* 247-257.

van den Berghe, P. L. (1978). *Human family systems: An evolutionary view.* New York: Elsevier.

Vangelisti, A. L. (1992). Older adolescents' perceptions of communication problems with their parents. *Journal of Adolescent Research, 7,* 382-402.

Vangelisti, A. L. (1993). Communication in the family: The influence of time, relational prototypes and irrationality. *Communication Monographs, 60,* 42-54.

Vangelisti, A. L. (1994a). Couples' communication problems: The counselor's perspective. *Journal of Applied Communication Research, 22,* 106-126.

Vangelisti, A. L. (1994b). Messages that hurt. In W. R. Cupach & B. H. Spitzberg (Eds.), *The dark side of interpersonal communication* (pp. 53-82). Hillsdale, NJ: Lawrence Erlbaum.

Vangelisti, A. L. (2001). Making sense of hurtful interactions in close relationships: When hurt feelings create distance. In V. Manusov & J. H. Harvey (Eds.), *Attribution, communication behavior, and close relationships* (pp. 38-58). New York: Cambridge University Press.

Vangelisti, A. L., & Crumley, L. P. (1998). Reactions to messages that hurt: The influence of relational contexts. *Communication Monographs, 65,* 173-196.

Vangelisti, A. L., Crumley, L. P., & Baker, J. L. (1999). Family portraits: Stories as standards for family relationships. *Journal of Social and Personal Relationships, 16,* 335-368.

Vangelisti, A. L., & Daly, J. A. (1997). Gender differences in standards for romantic relationships. *Personal Relationships, 4,* 203-219.

Vangelisti, A. L., & Maguire, K. (2002). Hurtful messages in family relationships: When the pain lingers. In J. H. Harvey & A. Wenzel (Eds.), *A clinician's guide to maintaining and enhancing close relationships* (pp. 43-62). Mahwah, NJ: Lawrence Erlbaum.

Van Laningham, J., Johnson, D. R., & Amato, P. R. (2001). Marital happiness, marital duration, and the U-shaped curve: Evidence from a five-wave panel study. *Social Forces, 79,* 1313-1341.

Vega, W. A. (1990). Hispanic families in the 1980s: A decade of research. *Journal of Marriage and the Family, 52,* 1015-1024.

Volling, B., & Belsky, J. (1992). The contributions of mother-child and father-child relationships to the quality of sibling interaction: A longitudinal study. *Child Development, 63,* 1209-1222.

Voydanoff, P. (1990). Economic distress and family relations: A review of the eighties. *Journal of Marriage and the Family, 52,* 1099-1116.

Vuchinich, S. (1999). *Problem solving in families: Research and practice.* Thousand Oaks, CA: Sage.

Vuchinich, S., & Angelelli, J. (1995). Family interaction during problem solving. In M. A. Fitzpatrick & A. L. Vangelisti (Eds.), *Explaining family interactions* (pp. 177-205). Thousand Oaks, CA: Sage.

Wallerstein, J. S., & Kelly, J. B. (1980). *Surviving the breakup.* New York: Basic Books.

Walsh, F. (Ed.). (1992). *Normal family processes.* New York: Guilford.

Wamboldt, F., & Reiss, D. (1989). Task performance and the social construction of meaning: Juxtaposing normality with contemporary family research. In D. Offer & M. Sabshin (Eds.), *Normality: Context and theory* (pp. 2-40). New York: Basic Books.

Wasz-Hockert, O., Lind, J., Vuorenkoski, J., Partenen, T., & Valarne, E. (1968). The infant cry: A spectrographic and auditory analysis. *Clinics in Developmental Medicine, 29.*

Watson, R. E. L. (1983). Premarital cohabitation vs. traditional courtship: Their effects on subsequent marital adjustment. *Family Relations, 32,* 139-147.

Watzlawick, P., Beavin, J. H., & Jackson, D. D. (1967). *Pragmatics of human communication: A study of interaction patterns, pathologies, and paradoxes.* New York: W. W. Norton.

Waxler, N. E., & Mishler, E. G. (1970). Sequential patterning in family interaction: A methodological note. *Family Process, 9,* 211-220.

Weiss, R. S. (1975). *Marital separation.* New York: Basic Books.

Wells, C. G., & Robinson, W. P. (1982). The role of adult speech in language development. In C. Fraser & K. R. Scherer (Eds.), *Advances in the social psychology of language* (pp. 11-77). Cambridge: Cambridge University Press.

Whitchurch, G. G., & Dickson, F. C. (1999). Family communication. In M. B. Sussman, S. K. Steinmetz, & G. W. Peterson (Eds.), *Handbook of marriage and the family* (2nd ed., pp. 687-704). New York: Plenum.

Williamson, R. (1983). *Relational control and communication in marital types.* Unpublished doctoral dissertation, University of Wisconsin–Madison.

Wilson, E. O. (1975). *Sociobiology: The new synthesis.* Cambridge, MA: Harvard University Press.

Winnicott, D. W. (1964). *The child, the family and the outside world.* London: Penguin.

Woelfel, J., & Haller, A. O. (1971). Significant others, the self reflective act and the attitude formation process. *American Sociological Review, 36,* 74-87.

Wolff, P. H. (1971). Mother-infant relations at birth. In J. G. Howels (Ed.), *Modern perspectives in international child psychiatry* (pp. 80-97). New York: Brunner/Mazel.

Wood, J. T., & Duck, S. (Eds.). (1995). *Understudied relationships: Off the beaten track.* Thousand Oaks, CA: Sage.

Yerby, J., Buerkel-Rothfuss, N. L., & Bochner, A. P. (1994). *Understanding family communication.* Scottsdale, AZ: Gorsuch Scarisbrick.

Yingling, J. (1995). The first relationship: Infant-parent communication. In T. J. Socha & G. H. Stamp (Eds.), *Parents, children, and communication: Frontiers of theory and research* (pp. 23-41). Mahwah, NJ: Lawrence Erlbaum.

Author Index

Baker, E. L., 572
Baker, G. A., 705
Baker, J. L., 753
Baker, T., 407
Bakhtin, M. M., 79, 324
Bakker, D., 686
Baldwin, M., 460, 501
Baldwin, M. W., 155, 352, 584, 649, 650, 652
Bales, R. F., 4, 706, 730
Balkrishnan, R., 707, 708
Ball, L. J., 532
Ballard-Reisch, D. S., 709
Baltes, P. B., 735
Banas, J., 273
Bandalos, D. L., 50
Bandura, A., 544, 625
Bank, S. P., 745, 748
Banks, A., 83, 90
Banks, S. P., 83, 90
Banse, R., 255
Barash, M., 325
Barbara, A. M., 357
Barbaranelli, C., 625
Barbarin, O. A., 411
Barbato, C. A., 584, 585, 586, 589
Barbee, A. P., 143, 349, 375, 382, 384, 386,
    393, 394, 404, 405, 406, 408, 409, 410
Barbour, A., 581
Barclay, A. M., 254
Bargh, J. A., 191, 199
Barker, R G., 189
Barmezy, N., 750
Barndollar, K., 191, 192, 199
Barnes, H., 734
Barnes, M., 645
Barnes, M. K., 646
Barnes, R. D., 149
Barnett, L. R., 656, 667
Barnicott, E., 431, 435
Barnlund, D. C., 6
Barnsley, J., 692
Bar-On, R., 145
Baron, R. A., 149, 478
Barr, P. K., 510
Barraclough, R., 445
Barratt, M. S., 748, 750
Barrera, M., Jr., 380, 381, 382, 405
Barrett, D., 689
Barrett, D. W., 428
Barrett, K. C., 253, 257
Barrett, L. F., 138, 142, 652
Barrick, M. R., 136, 145, 151
Barsevick, A., 682
Barthes, R., 79
Bartholomew, K., 154, 155, 270, 357, 651
Bartlett, F. C., 104
Bartlett, M. K., 708
Bartz, R., 681, 709
Basden-Murphy, L., 382

Basham, R. B., 588
Basil, M. D., 455
Baskett, L. M., 746
Bass, M., 683
Bass, M. J., 708
Bassett, D. M., 566
Bassett, R., 457
Bassett, R. E., 573
Batchelder, M. L., 654, 737, 743
Bates, E., 751
Bateson, G., 5, 13, 271, 311, 314, 315, 615, 750
Batson, C. D., 384, 455
Battaglia, D. M., 435
Batten, P. G., 146
Battit, G. E., 708
Battmann, W., 198
Baucom, D. H., 151, 652, 653, 654, 662,
    739, 754, 761
Bauer, C., 534
Baukus, R. A., 150
Baum, A., 650
Baum, K. L., 273
Baumann, U., 402
Bauman, R., 323, 324
Baumeister, R. F., 136, 149, 345, 478, 481,
    483, 486, 570, 655
Baumrind, D., 158
Bavelas, J. B., 108, 109, 110, 112, 113, 116,
    117, 118, 120, 123, 125, 215, 244, 247,
    248, 346, 347, 535
Baxandall, M., 325
Baxter, J. S., 149
Baxter, L. A., 7, 28, 35, 81, 270, 358, 362, 431,
    432, 435, 441, 487, 516, 554, 555, 570,
    584, 585, 589, 620, 621, 623, 646, 647,
    654, 729, 737, 761
Bayer, C. L., 150, 749, 750, 751
Baym, N. K., 530, 531
Baziak, A. T., 689
Beach, S. R. H., 147, 567, 654, 656, 658,
    668, 738, 739, 742
Beard, J. F., 149
Beardsall, L., 745
Beatty, M. J., 8, 134, 150, 433
Beavin, J. H., 5, 6, 243, 741
Beavin Bavelas, J., 110
Bechman, H. B., 701, 704
Beck, A. T., 156, 652
Beck, C. S., 693, 694
Beck, C. T., 681, 684
Becker, J. A., 441
Becker-Stoll, F., 357
Beckett, L. A., 571
Beckman, H. B., 41, 706
Bedell, B. T., 343, 345
Bedell, J. R., 574
Bedford, V. H., 748
Beebe, B., 277
Begin, J., 499

Subject Index

About the Editors

Mark L. Knapp (Ph.D., Penn State University, 1966) is the Jesse H. Jones Centennial Professor in Communication and Distinguished Teaching Professor at the University of Texas at Austin. His publications include *Nonverbal Communication in Human Interaction* (with J. A. Hall) and *Interpersonal Communication and Human Relationships* (with A. L. Vangelisti). He is past President of the International Communication Association and the National Communication Association, a Fellow of the International Communication Association, and a Distinguished Scholar in the National Communication Association. He has served as editor of *Human Communication Research,* and he developed and edited the Sage Series in Interpersonal Communication.

John A. Daly (Ph.D., Purdue University, 1977) is the Liddell Professor of Communication, TCB Professor of Management, and University Distinguished Teaching Professor at the University of Texas at Austin. He has served as President of the National Communication Association and on the Board of Directors of the International Communication Association and the International Customer Service Association. He is the author of more than 100 scholarly articles and book chapters, and he has served as editor of the journal *Communication Education* and as coeditor of the journal *Written Communication.*

About the Contributors

Kelly Fudge Albada (Ph.D., University of Texas at Austin, 1997) is Assistant Professor in the Department of Communication at North Carolina State University. Her research interests include the influence of media in close relationships, with a focus on healthy and/or risky behaviors.

Jason W. Anderson (M.S., Illinois State University, 1997) is a dissertator in the Department of Communication Arts at the University of Wisconsin–Madison. His research interests focus on the roles of emotion and commitment within the influence process.

Janet Beavin Bavelas (Ph.D., Stanford, 1970) is Professor of Psychology, University of Victoria, in Victoria, British Columbia, Canada. Her books include *Pragmatics of Human Communication: A Study of Interactional Patterns, Pathologies, and Paradoxes* (with P. Watzlawick and D. D. Jackson, 1967) and *Equivocal Communication* (with A. Black, N. Chovil, and J. Mullett, 1990). Her research is primarily on face-to-face dialogue, most recently on the features that make it a unique form of language use, such as the availability of hand and facial gestures and the influence of an addressee. She is a Fellow of the International Communication Association, the Canadian Psychological Association, and the Royal Society of Canada (which includes all academic disciplines).

Charles R. Berger (Ph.D., Michigan State University) is Professor in the Department of Communication, University of California, Davis. He is a former editor of *Human Communication Research* and former coeditor of *Communication Research*. He is a past President and Fellow of the International Communication Association. His most recent book is titled *Planning Strategic Interaction: Attaining Goals Through Communicative Action* (1997). His research interests include the role cognitive processes play in social interaction and the ways in which individuals process risk messages.

Arthur P. Bochner (Ph.D., Bowling Green State University, 1971) is Professor of Communication and Codirector of the Institute for Interpretive Human Studies at the University of South Florida. He is coeditor (with Carolyn Ellis) of the book series Ethnographic Alternatives. His most recent book (coedited with Carolyn Ellis) is *Ethnographically Speaking: Autoethnography, Literature, and Aesthetics* (2002). He is the author of more than 50 articles and book chapters on personal relationships, narrative, and research methodology. His current research focuses on ethnographic and qualitative studies of memory, narrative, and aging.

Judee K. Burgoon is Professor of Communication, Professor of Family Studies and Human Development, and Director of

Human Communication Research for the Center for the Management of Information at the University of Arizona. She has authored or coauthored seven books and monographs and nearly 200 articles, chapters, and reviews related to nonverbal and relational communication, interpersonal relationship management, dyadic interaction patterns, deception, computer-mediated communication, research methods, and public opinion toward the media. Her research has been supported by extramural grants from the Department of Defense, the National Institutes of Mental Health, and Gannett Foundation, among others. A recipient of the National Communication Association's Distinguished Scholar Award, the Golden Anniversary Monographs Award, the Charles H. Woolbert Research Award for Scholarship of Lasting Impact, and the International Communication Association's B. Aubrey Fisher Mentorship award, she is an ICA Fellow and elected member of the Society for Experimental Social Psychology.

Brant R. Burleson (Ph.D., University of Illinois, Urbana-Champaign, 1982) is Professor in the Department of Communication at Purdue University. His research, which has been featured in numerous journals and edited volumes, centers on communication skill acquisition and development, the role of emotion in communication and relationships, the effects of communication skills on relationship outcomes, and supportive forms of communication such as comforting. He has served as editor for *Communication Yearbook* and is coeditor of *Communication of Social Support: Messages, Interactions, Relationships, and Community* (1994). Among the awards he has received are the Berscheid-Hatfield Award for Distinguished Mid-Career Achievement, from the International Network on Personal Relationships, and the National Communication Association's Brommel

Award for Outstanding Scholarship in Family Communication.

Daniel J. Canary (Ph.D., University of Southern California, 1983) is Professor in the Hugh Downs School of Human Communication at Arizona State University. His research focuses on conflict management, relational maintenance, conversational argument, interpersonal goals, and sex differences in communication. He serves on several editorial boards and is editor of the *Western Journal of Communication*. He enjoys traveling, golfing, and writing songs.

John P. Caughlin (Ph.D., University of Texas at Austin, 1997) is Assistant Professor of Speech Communication at the University of Illinois at Urbana-Champaign. His research examines conflict and privacy in families and other close relationships. His recent work has appeared in such journals as *Communication Monographs, Human Communication Research, Journal of Personality and Social Psychology,* and *Journal of Social and Personal Relationships*.

William R. Cupach (Ph.D., University of Southern California, 1981) is Professor in the Department of Communication at Illinois State University. His research pertains to problematic interactions in interpersonal relationships, including such contexts as embarrassing predicaments, relational transgressions, and conflict. With Brian Spitzberg, he is coeditor and contributor to *The Dark Side of Interpersonal Communication* and *The Dark Side of Close Relationships* and coauthor of *Interpersonal Communication Competence* and *Handbook of Interpersonal Competence Research*. He has served as associate editor for the *Journal of Social and Personal Relationships* and currently sits on the editorial boards of several scholarly journals.

James Price Dillard (Ph.D., Michigan State University, 1983) is Professor of Communication Arts and Director of the Center for Communication Research at the University of Wisconsin–Madison. His research interests revolve around the study of influence and persuasion, with a special emphasis on the role of emotion in persuasion. He is the editor of *Seeking Compliance: The Production of Interpersonal Influence Messages* (1990) and coeditor (with Michael Pfau) of *The Persuasion Handbook: Developments in Theory and Practice* (2002). In recognition of his research achievements, he received the Vilas Associate Award from the University of Wisconsin–Madison in 1994 and the John E. Hunter Award for Meta-Analysis in 1995.

Mary Anne Fitzpatrick (Ph.D., Temple University, 1976) is the WARF Kellett Professor of Communication and Deputy Dean of the College of Letters and Science at the University of Wisconsin–Madison. Her publications include *Between Husbands and Wives: Communication in Marriage, Communication Theory and AIDS,* and *Explaining Family Interaction.* She is a Fellow and past President of the International Communication Association and a recipient of the 2001 ICA Career Productivity Award.

Gregory D. Hoobler is a doctoral student in the Department of Communication and University Distinguished Fellow at Michigan State University; he received his M.A. degree from San Diego State University. He has taught and published in the areas of international conflict negotiation, nonverbal communication, intercultural communication, public speaking, and conflict and persuasion. His current research interests focus primarily on the investigation of the interactive process of international conflict diplomacy and negotiation, including third-party intervention efforts.

Fredric M. Jablin (Ph.D., Purdue University) is the E. Claiborne Robins Chaired Professor of Leadership Studies in the Jepson School of Leadership Studies at the University of Richmond. His research, which has been published in a wide variety of communication, psychology, personnel, and management journals and scholarly books, has examined various facets of leader-member communication in organizations, group problem solving, communication competence, and communication processes associated with organizational entry, assimilation, and exit. He is coeditor of *The New Handbook of Organizational Communication: Advances in Theory, Research, and Methods* (2001). He has been a member of the editorial boards of more than a dozen different journals and has received numerous awards for his research and teaching.

Christine Kenwood (M.A., University of Victoria, 2001) is a doctoral student in psychology at the University of Victoria. She has published "Using Face-to-Face Dialogue as a Standard for Other Communication Systems" in the *Canadian Journal of Communication* (with J. B. Bavelas, S. Hutchinson, and D. H. Matheson, 1997) as well as "Social Constructionism: Implications for Psychotherapeutic Practice" in *Social Constructionist Psychology: A Critical Analysis of Theory and Practice* (edited by D. J. Nightingale and J. Cromby, 1999). She is currently working on topics as diverse as hand gestures, sexual assault, and public sector performance measurement.

Leanne K. Knobloch (Ph.D., University of Wisconsin–Madison, 2001) is Assistant Professor in the Department of Speech Communication at the University of Illinois. Her research focuses on processes of interpersonal relating, particularly the ways in which people negotiate their close relationships.

Kathleen J. Krone (Ph.D., University of Texas at Austin) is Associate Professor of Communication Studies at the University of Nebraska at Lincoln. Her research and teaching interests are in the area of organizational communication, with special emphasis on emotion, conflict/negotiation, and gender. Her current research projects include studies of how managers frame intercultural conflicts in Sino-American joint ventures and turning points in community consensus building. Her research has been published in *Management Communication Quarterly, Journal of Applied Communication Research,* and *Emotion in Organizations* (second edition, edited by S. Fineman). She is a past chair of the Organizational Communication Division of the National Communication Association.

Erina L. MacGeorge (Ph.D., University of Illinois, Urbana-Champaign, 1999) is Visiting Assistant Professor in the Department of Communication at Purdue University. Her dissertation received the Miller Outstanding Dissertation Award from the National Communication Association, as well as the Outstanding Dissertation Award from the Interpersonal Communication Division of the International Communication Association. Her research, which has been published in both *Communication Monographs* and *Human Communication Research,* focuses on communication processes in social support, particularly the properties of effective forms of advice, the effects of attribution processes on the formation of supportive goals, and gender differences in the production and reception of supportive messages.

Robert D. McPhee (Ph.D., Michigan State University, 1978) is Professor in the Hugh Downs School of Human Communication at Arizona State University. Specializing in communication theory and methods and in organizational communication, he has served as Chair of the Organizational Communication Division of the National Communication Association, as associate editor of *Human Communication Research,* and as book review editor of *Communication Theory.* Among his specific research interests are organizational hierarchies and structuration theory.

Sandra Metts (Ph.D., University of Iowa) is Professor in the Department of Communication, Illinois State University. Her research interests include emotion in close relationships, especially forgiveness, sexual communication, relationship dissolution, and facework. Her books include *Facework* (with W. R. Cupach, 1994) and *Self-Disclosure* (with V. J. Derlega, S. Petronio, and S. T. Margulis, 1993). She is a past President of the Central States Communication Association, former editor of *Communication Reports,* former associate editor of *Personal Relationships,* and currently associate editor of the *Journal of Social and Personal Relationships.*

Gerald R. Miller was Chair of the Department of Communication and University Distinguished Professor of Communication at Michigan State University. He was the author of nearly 150 articles on interpersonal communication and related areas. He was a past President of the International Communication Association and the founding editor of *Human Communication Research.* He was a Fellow of the International Communication Association and the American Psychological Association as well as a Distinguished Scholar of the Speech Communication Association. He succumbed to cancer in 1993.

Malcolm R. Parks (Ph.D., Michigan State University, 1976) is Associate Vice Provost for Research and Associate Professor of Speech Communication at the University of

Washington. He is interested in the analysis of complex communication systems, interpersonal communication, and communication theory. His work falls into three main areas: organizational analysis, Internet studies, and the dynamics of close relationships. His research has been published in *Human Communication Research, Communication Monographs, Communication Theory, Journal of Computer-Mediated Communication, Journal of Social and Personal Relationships*, and *Social Psychology Quarterly*, as well as a variety of other journals and edited volumes across the social sciences. He is the recipient of the Hammer Award from the Office of the Vice President for innovation in federal government and the Woolbert Award from the National Communication Association for his research. In addition to his continuing research on computer-mediated communication, he pursues policy interests in human subjects research management and intellectual property management.

Roxanne Parrott, Ph.D., is Professor in the Department of Communication Arts & Sciences and Director of the Health Communication Program at Pennsylvania State University. She examines strategies for communicating health information to the lay public. Her funded research has focused on cancer communications and human genetic research, emphasizing social influence theories and community-based models in health message design and evaluation. In 1999, she was corecipient of a Linkages Award from the National Association of County and City Health Officials and the Association of State and Territorial Health Officials in recognition of her work in developing an innovative national model of collaboration between public health agencies and institutions of higher learning. She is coeditor of *Designing Health Messages: Approaches from Communication Theory and Public Health Practice* and

Evaluating Women's Health Messages: A Resource Book.

Bruce Phillips (M.A., University of Victoria, 2000) is a doctoral student in psychology at the University of Victoria and a usability engineer at the Microsoft Corporation. His master's thesis was published in *Mediation Quarterly* as "What You're Saying Is: Reformulating Dispute Narratives Through Active Listening," and he is also the coauthor of forthcoming works on hand gestures and analysis of newspaper coverage of a major crime. His doctoral dissertation is an experimental comparison of computer-mediated communication with face-to-face dialogue; one of these experiments was the top paper in the Language and Social Interaction Division at the 2000 International Communication Association conference.

Sally Planalp (Ph.D., University of Wisconsin) is Professor in the Department of Communication at the University of Utah and Adjunct Professor in the Department of Management Communication at the University of Waikato, Hamilton, New Zealand. She is the author of *Communicating Emotion: Social, Moral, and Cultural Processes* (1999), for which she won the book award of the Interpersonal Division of the National Communication Association. Her current research interests center on the role of emotion in interpersonal communication processes, especially in close relationships; her earlier work concerned interaction analysis, social cognition, and discourse processing.

Marshall Scott Poole (Ph.D., University of Wisconsin–Madison) is Professor of Speech-Communication and Information and Operations Management at Texas A&M University. He has conducted research and published extensively on the topics of group and organizational communication, computer-mediated communication systems, conflict management, and organizational innovation. He has coauthored or coedited seven books, including *Communication and Group Decision-Making*, *Research on the Management of Innovation*, and *Organizational Change and Innovation Processes: Theory and Methods for Research*. He has also published in a number of journals, including *Human Communication Research*, *Communication Research*, *Academy of Management Journal*, *Management Science*, *MIS Quarterly*, and *Communication Monographs*. He is currently a senior editor of *Organization Science*.

Michael E. Roloff (Ph.D., Michigan State University, 1975) is Professor of Communication Studies at Northwestern University. His research interests include bargaining and negotiation, and conflict management. He is the author of *Interpersonal Communication: The Social Exchange Approach* and coeditor of *Persuasion: New Directions in Theory and Research*, *Interpersonal Processes: New Directions in Communication Research*, *Social Cognition and Communication*, and *Communication and Negotiation*. His work has been published in such journals as *Communication Monographs*, *Communication Research*, and *Human Communication Research*. He is senior associate editor of the *International Journal of Conflict Management*, and he has served as editor of the *Communication Yearbook* and as coeditor of *Communication Research*.

Patricia M. Sias is Associate Professor of Communication in the Edward R. Murrow School of Communication at Washington State University. Her research centers primarily on workplace relationships. In particular, her work focuses on the development of peer relationships and workplace friendships and the ways such relationships influence and are influenced by the environments in which they develop. She has published articles in a variety of academic journals, including *Communication Monographs*, *Human Communication Research*, *Communication Research*, *Western Journal of Communication*, *Communication Quarterly*, and *Journal of Applied Communication Research*. In 1993, she received the W. Charles Redding Award for the Outstanding Dissertation in Organizational Communication.

Kari P. Soule (Ph.D., Northwestern University, 2001) has published in the *Journal of Social and Personal Relationships* and has a chapter in the *Handbook of Communication and People With Disabilities: Research and Application* (edited by D. O. Braithwaite and T. L. Thompson). She has also served as assistant editor of *Communication Research*. Her research interests include persuasion, conflict, and communication among people with and without disabilities.

Brian H. Spitzberg (Ph.D., University of Southern California, 1981) is Professor in the School of Communication at San Diego State University. With William Cupach, he is coeditor and contributor to *The Dark Side of Interpersonal Communication* and *The Dark Side of Close Relationships* and coauthor of *Interpersonal Communication Competence* and *Handbook of Interpersonal Competence Research*. He is also author or coauthor of numerous scholarly publications on communication competence, communication assessment, conflict management, jealousy, and stalking. He currently serves on several editorial boards and as a member of the San Diego Stalking Strike Force and Association of Threat Assessment Professionals.

Jürgen Streeck (Ph.D. in linguistics, Free University Berlin) is Associate Professor of Communication Studies and Germanic Studies at the University of Texas at Austin.

He has taught at the Free University Berlin, the University of Odense (Denmark), the University of Vienna, and the University of Utrecht (Netherlands). His research is concerned with the microanalysis of uses and coordinations of language, embodied communication resources (especially gesture), and artifacts in everyday face-to-face communication, especially in the workplace, as well as studies of intercultural communication. He has conducted fieldwork among African Americans and in Luzon (Philippines), and he has directed graduate student research on multimodal communication within creative processes, notably in the design professions. His work has appeared in such journals as *Discourse Processes, Journal of Pragmatics, Communication Monographs, Journal of Communication, Research on Language and Social Interaction,* and *Zeitschrift für Sprachwissenschaft.* He is currently working on a book on gesture.

Teresa L. Thompson, Ph.D., is Professor in the Department of Communication at the University of Dayton. She is the founding and current editor of the journal *Health Communication* and has published six books and more than 40 articles on various aspects of health communication. Her work focuses on health care provider-patient interaction and communication and disability issues.

Anita L. Vangelisti (Ph.D., University of Texas) is interested in interpersonal communication among family members and between romantic partners. Her work has been published in journals such as *Communication Monographs, Human Communication Research, Journal of Personality and Social Psychology, Personal Relationships, Family Relations, Journal of Adolescent Research,* and *Journal of Social and Personal Relationships.* She is coeditor of three books and coauthor of one, and she is currently working on two more volumes. She has been associate editor of *Personal Relationships* and editor of the *ISSPR Bulletin,* and has served on the editorial boards of numerous scholarly journals.

Joseph B. Walther (Ph.D., University of Arizona, 1990) is Associate Professor of Communication at Cornell University. He has previously taught at Rensselaer Polytechnic Institute, Northwestern University, and the Universities of Manchester (England), Kansas, and Oklahoma, in communication and psychology. His research concerns the use of new communication technologies in interpersonal, group, organizational, and educational settings. He has held offices in the Academy of Management and in the International Communication Association's Communication and Technology Division. He is founding editor of the *Journal of Online Behavior,* and he also serves on the editorial boards of several international journals.